Proceedings of the
Eighth International Conference
of Ethiopian Studies

Volume 1

Proceedings of the Eighth International Conference of Ethiopian Studies

University of Addis Ababa, 1984

Edited by
Dr Taddese Beyene

Volume 1

isbn — Volume 1: 1 85450 000 7

Institute of Ethiopian Studies, Addis Ababa
1988

Sponsors: Frobenius Insitut an der Wolfgang Goethe-Universitat,
Frankfurt am Main

© Dr Taddese Beyene, Institute of Ethiopian Studies, Addis
Ababa, Ethiopia, 1987 and 1988.

First volume published in August, 1988 by The Institute of Ethiopian Studies, Addis Ababa,
with the sponsorship of the Frobenius Institut, Frankfurt. Simultaneously published in the UK
by ELM Publications, Huntingdon, Autumn, 1988.

isbn Volume 1 - 1 85450 000 7
     Volume 2 - 1 85450 005 8

Typesetting and pre-press preparation by ELM Publications, Seaton House, Kings Ripton,
Huntingdon, England; printing and binding by Woolnough Bookbinding of Irthlingborough,
Northamptonshire, England.

Table of Contents

History Since 1800

Contemporary Issues

Linguistics and Literature

Anthropology

PREFACE

The Eighth International Conference of Ethiopian Studies was held in Addis Ababa between November 26-30, 1984. It was a conference marked by the highest level of attendance in the series. Understandably, in view of its venue the number of Ethiopian participants was also remarkably high. To accommodate such a breadth of participation, the conference was organized in six panels — Pre-history and Archaeology, History to 1800, History since 1800, Linguistics and Literature, Anthropology, and Contemporary Issues. Papers of general relevance and interdisciplinary character were discussed in plenary and joint sessions.

The unprecedented level of the participation has had its effect on the publication of the Proceedings as well. A total of two hundred and seventeen papers were presented at the Conference. To publish all these papers in one volume has been found to be an impossible task, the editorial committee has therefore decided to bring out the Proceedings in two volumes. The basis for division that has been deemed most sensible is the alphabetical one. Effort is made to include about half the papers of each panel in the first volume. The only deviation from the alphabetical order has been the inclusion of opening and closing addresses as well as plenary papers in the first volume.

The editorial committee, consisting of the chairmen of the six panels and the Director of the Institute of Ethiopian Studies, have reviewed all the papers and rejected a few for lack of depth and originality. Others were also rejected because their authors were unwilling to reduce them to a reasonable length of between twenty-five and thirty pages. One or two papers have been left out on the authors' requests. The Committee has not tried to standardise the bibliographic and transliteration styles of the different papers.

The Institute of Ethiopian Studies of Addis Ababa University would like to express its gratitude to the Workers' Party of Ethiopia, the Municipality of Addis Ababa, the Ethiopian Tourism Organization, Ethiopian Airlines, Shell (Ethiopia), the office of the President of Addis Ababa University, the Ford Foundation and the Swedish Agency for Research Cooperation (SAREC) for making the Eighth International Conference of Ethiopian Studies a very successful meeting for as many Ethiopicists as possible.

Thanks are also due to the Ford Foundation, SAREC and the Addis Ababa University for the financial contributions which have made possible the Publication of the Proceedings of the Eighth International Conference of Ethiopian Studies.

Taddese Beyene
Director
Institute of Ethiopian Studies, and
Chief Editor.

OPENING ADDRESS

Comrade Fikre Sellassie Wogderesse
Member of the Political Bureau of the Workers' Party of Ethiopia
and Deputy Chairman of the Council of Ministers

Distinguished Participants
of the Conference,
Distinguished Guests,
Comrades,

On behalf of the Government and People of Socialist Ethiopia and on my own behalf, I have the pleasure to welcome you all, participants in the Eighth International Conference of Ethiopian Studies, to Addis Ababa.

From time immemorial, Ethiopia has been a subject of inexhaustible enquiry for scholars of many foreign lands. The strategic geographical location of the country, straddling as it does the ancient avenues of trade and civilization between Africa, the Middle East, and the Mediterranean world, had enabled it to become part and parcel of decisive regional historical processes whose influence in many cases has been of worldwide significance. Consequently, Ethiopia has had close and fruitful relations with the civilizations that at different times in history flourished in North East Africa, in the Middle East, in Western Asia and in the Mediterranean world. This relationship has, in turn, exerted a most extensive historical and cultural influence on the internal developments and historical processes within Ethiopia.

Ethiopia has also been found to be a major source of material evidence for the study of such sciences as palaeontology and archaeology, both of which have achieved a high degree of scientific rigour in our times. Sites found in different parts of the country, and particularly those in the Eastern lowlands, have provided impressive data which have already won international standing as vital sources for the study of the origin of Man. Ten years ago, it was here that the oldest and most complete remains of a hominid ancestor of man was discovered. In other respects, too, Ethiopia has considerable possibilities for the study of early human history, as it provides one of the earliest instances of the domestication process and, thus, of the transition of Man's life from that based on hunting and the gathering of fruit to one of agriculture and sedentarization.

We understand that over the next few days, your Conference will discuss in detail papers dealing with these and other related topics. The pursuit of science and knowledge ought to be conducted without the inhibitions of frontiers or regions. This is as it should be. We believe that this Conference will provide one such forum where these principles of the pursuit of knowledge will be fully applied. And I would like to state here that we, on our part, will not stint any effort in doing everything possible to assure the success and fruitful outcome of all such endeavours.

Currently, we are in the final stages of drafting rules and regulations whereby foreign research institutions will cooperate with their national counterparts in the conduct of every field of research, and particularly those of palaeontology and archaeology.

The establishment and expansion of the organizations, laboratories and educational institutions necessary for this task will not only increase our research capacity, but will also strengthen the cooperation between Ethiopian scholars and scholars from abroad.

Furthermore, I would like to seize this opportunity to express my Government's appreciation to this assembly of eminent scholars for doing so much in the field of research in Ethiopian studies and for publishing significant works. The publication of the research materials and their dissemination through journals, periodicals, books and other means have made a tremendous contribution towards making the Ethiopian State a well known entity the world over. I hope to see the continuation of that tradition.

Ethiopian studies, while concentrating, in the main, on Ethiopia, should also examine the cultural, educational, scientific and technological relationships with other States and in particular with those of Africa. Knowledge knows no frontiers and as such it should be examined in a sub-regional, regional and global context.

Participants of the Conference,
Invited Guests,
Comrades,

I would now like to raise certain pertinent points that have been important characteristics of our Nation's history.

Ethiopia has, throughout its long history, grown and developed as the home of a mosaic of nationalities, a variety of languages and diverse cultural manifestations. It is a home for mankind's cultural heritage as defined and accepted by UNESCO. It has also enriched a number of world famous museums in Europe and elsewhere, wherein Ethiopia's cultural relics are still to be found. Ethiopia, therefore, will continue to support and struggle for the realization of this decision of UNESCO and the restitution of cultural relics to their country of origin.

The cultural and historical heritage has given rise to certain fundamental characteristics of present day Ethiopia. On the one hand, it accounts for the Nation's rich and complex diversity in languages, culture and other aspects of social life while, on the other hand, the different nationalities of Ethiopia have come, in the course of the long and tortuous historical process, to share and develop a common bond of history. And it is on this commonly shared historical bond that the unity of the Nation is founded. The struggle of the Ethiopian people to defend their independence, sovereignty and territorial integrity against all kinds of invaders from the Ottoman Turks down the line to the fascist colonial forces and expansionists, over the past centuries to the present, has gone to further reinforce the foundations of their unity.

Different scholars at different points in time have carried out profound studies of one or other aspect of Ethiopia's long and checkered history; and the body of knowledge thus accumulated is of inestimable value. But we cannot claim that any satisfactory overall study has yet emerged as regards the general dialectics governing the historical experience of the Ethiopian people. This, we believe, is a task to which the scholars of this and the succeeding generations should seriously address themselves.

The other point I wish to raise here, has to do with the long history of feudalism in our country. As you all know, feudalism not only has a long and established history in Ethiopia but, with only minor capitalistic accretions, survived in all its essential aspects right up to the eve of our Revolution. Indeed it was this heavy burden of feudalism which, weighing as it did so oppressively on the life of the people and the development of the country, became the direct cause of the revolution.

The particular historical conditions that accompanied the development of feudalism in Ethiopia made it inevitable that it should be encumbered by extremely backward economic, political and social characteristics. This tendency was further exacerbated by the coincidence of the country's isolation from the outside world, and the severing of its trade and cultural links at the very time when feudalism was taking root in society. The dynamic urban centers of trade and the crafts that elsewhere played such a focal role in the weakening of feudalism and the transition to more advanced levels of development could not, therefore, flourish here.

In addition, the continuous civil wars and the almost uninterrupted political disorders of feudal Ethiopia did not in any way encourage economic and social development. These wars, which arose out of the rivalry of the different regional warlords for political and commercial supremacy, can be said to be almost permanent features of the long history of feudalism in the country. At times conducted along regional or tribal lines, and at others camouflaged as religious conflicts, these wars were largely responsible for the stagnation of economic and social development. In particular, the ravages wrought on the peasantry by the hordes of feudal armies constantly on the march, exposed the former to regular waves of plunder and famine. It is worth bearing in mind that it was despite this cruel burden and in conditions of extreme feudal backwardness that the Ethiopian people rose to successfully withstand the onslaughts of colonialism.

Ethiopia is currently engaged in the immense task of nation-building in a new revolutionary era, which had its deep roots in the foundations of the history of the people. The Revolution is a natural historical process that developed from the incompatible contradictions inherent in the old society. I am glad to state that we have now established the Workers' Party of Ethiopia, the Programme and the Ten Year Economic Plan of which have been adopted by its First Congress. The creation of the vanguard party of Ethiopia is a great historical achievement in which equality, justice and freedom will be guaranteed on Socialist lines. The task that remains for completion will be the birth of a People's Democratic Republic of Ethiopia — a final act of the will of the people in their march for political victory.

Distinguished participants of
the Conference,
Distinguished Guests,
Comrades,

I have full confidence that the discussions you will be holding over the next few days in different branches of knowledge will be inspired by the genuine pursuit of truth. You will also have the opportunity, if only briefly, of acquainting yourselves at first hand with the progress that Revolutionary Ethiopia has made in the last decade. As scholars in different fields of Ethiopian studies, I have no doubt that you will grasp the full stature and significance of the revolutionary transformations that have taken place here.

Finally I would like to take this opportunity to reaffirm that we will do everything in our capacity to make this conference a success.

I wish you all the best.

Thank you.

THE NEW ETHIOPIA:

MAJOR DEFINING CHARACTERISTICS

Comrade Tesfaye Shewaye

Mr. Chairman,
Distinguished Participants in the Eighth
International Conference of Ethiopian Studies:

The Ethiopian popular revolution of 1974 has brought about fundamental changes in the economic, social and political life of our people. As a result, one can justifiably call the Ethiopia of post-1974 the New Ethiopia, and identify the following major defining characteristics:

1. Revolutionary Leadership

Pre-1974 Ethiopia was a country ruled by one of the most obsolete monarchic institutions. The head of this institution, the emperor, claimed descent from the mythical fable of the union of the Queen of Sheba and King Solomon. Article 2 of the defunct Constitution reads as follows:

> The Imperial dignity shall remain perpetually attached to the line of Haile Sellassie I, descendant of King Sahle Sellassie, whose line descends without interruption from the dynasty of Menelik I, son of the Queen of Ethiopia, the Queen of Sheba, and King Solomon of Jerusalem.

This constitutional claim was strongly supported and reinforced by religious teachings, which considered the emperor to be Elect of God. The imperial constitution of 1955, too, was trying to emphasise the same when in Article 4 it stated:

> By virtue of His Imperial Blood, as well as by the anointing which He has received, the person of the Emperor is sacred, His dignity is inviolable and His power indisputable. He is, consequently, entitled to all the honours due to Him in accordance with tradition and the present Constitution.

Under such cover of mystical embellishments and legal garb, pre-1974 Ethiopia was ruled in a manner alien to the practices of the twentieth century. No political party was allowed to function in the country. The emperor, surrounded by personages with insatiable greed for wealth, was the sole arbiter of political activities. Even though parliamentary democracy was allowed in theory, in practice, it proved to be nothing more than a make-believe. On paper, the 1955 Constitution guaranteed some rights to the people. In practice again, the Constitution was intentionally ignored by those in power. The state machinery in all its capacities served the personal whims of the emperor and his close associates while the broad masses languished in utter darkness.

Moreover, the person of the emperor and the state were made to appear as one and the same to such an extent that it was thought that on the death of Haile Sellassie Ethiopia would 'cease' to exist. In fact many had liked not to think of the question "after Haile Sellassie, who?". In other words, they wished the impossible — eternal life for the emperor and his regime.

But the bitter struggle that the broad masses waged for years against the feudal regime gained momentum in February 1974 and began serving it repeated and serious blows. These blows effected the final abolition of the doddering feudal order in September 1974.

In the absence of a political party or an organized leading force, the old order seemed to be confident of curbing the uprising of the masses. However, because of the founding of the Co-ordinating Committee of the Armed Forces, the Police and Territorial Army, the confidence and wish of the reactionary regime of curbing the Ethiopian revolution was shattered. The Co-ordinating Committee was formed by democratically elected representatives of the various units of the military. Thus, one already begins to see a democratic practice in the formation of this Committee, the committee which upon the overthrow of the monarchy took power under the name of Provisional Military Administrative Council.

The Provisional Military Administrative Council gave the question of leadership first priority, and worked steadfastly towards its proper solution. In so doing, it established the Provisional Office for Mass Organizational Affairs, whose primary task was organizing the broad masses so that they could exercise their democratic rights.

Ironical as it may seem, the Provisional Military Administrative Council also gave every support — be it material or moral — to 'underground' political organizations to strengthen themselves and to push the revolution a step forward. It also facilitated the formation of the Common Front of Marxist-Leninist Organizations that was intended to form the ruling Party of the New Ethiopia. However, as events showed later, the formation of the Party was not and could not be realized through such an approach. This was mainly because of the fact that ideological unity and commitment to the popular revolution that was basic to the establishment of the ruling Party was lacking in most of the Political Organizations. Worse still, some of the member Organizations of the Front exposed their true nature when they attempted to undermine the popular revolution. The move taken by the MEISON group in 1976-77 to break away from the Front can be cited as an example.

Even after the MEISON treason, the attempt of the remaining member organizations of the Front to form a party faced a number of problems. As a result, the process of party formation had to follow an entirely new approach. This new approach was to empower Comrade Mengistu Hailemariam to select individuals on the basis of their ideological strength and revolutionary contribution. This power was vested in him by the three remaining political Organizations that had formed the Front. Consequently, the Commission to Organize the Party of the Working People of Ethiopia (COPWE) was established by Proclamation No.212, 1980. And the broad objectives of the Commission were (a) to disseminate the science of Marxism-Leninism among the broad masses of Ethiopia; and (b) to organize the Workers' Party of Ethiopia. After four years of concerted effort and struggle to implement these objectives, the Commission succeeded in founding the long-awaited Workers' Party of Ethiopia (WPE) in September of 1984. This occasion is indeed a landmark in the history of Ethiopia because, in the first place, we have succeeded in forming a Party only ten years after the overthrow of the monarchy, the monarchy which had obstructed Party work for years. Secondly, we succeeded not only in forming a Party but a working class Party, the Workers' Party of Ethiopia, whose guiding principle is Marxism-Leninism. Revolutionary Party leadership is thus one of the defining characteristics of the New Ethiopia.

2. Ownership of the Means of Production

The second major defining characteristic of the New Ethiopia is the change of ownership of the means of production from a handful of individuals to the broad masses. As Ethiopia was and still is one of the developing countries, one of the major means of production is farmland. The other means of production include industrial establishments of various kinds and sizes. These again were owned by a handful of Ethiopian or foreign nationals and companies.

The oppression and exploitation of the workers employed in such private firms in pre-1974 Ethiopia was indeed very severe. In the first place, the rate of pay was extremely low as there was no regulation for minimum wage. Secondly, there was no job security for the majority of the workers. Every employer hired and fired workers at will. Even though there existed the Confederation of Ethiopian Labor Unions, it was entangled by the legal webs of the regime and was made absolutely ineffective. Pension, insurance, health care and maternity leaves were unknown to workers in many of the business establishments.

The Ethiopian workers, however small in size, did not accept such exploitative conditions quietly. They had undertaken a series of determined struggles, that cost many lives, to have their rights respected. Strike actions of various degrees and intensity had been taken at various times. In fact, even the establishment of the Confederation of Ethiopian Labour Unions was the outcome of the struggle waged by the working class and not an 'imperial gift'.

The continued struggle of the Ethiopian workers against exploitation and oppression gained the upper hand with the outbreak of the popular revolution of 1974. The first major step taken in the area of economic change was, therefore, the nationalization of industrial, financial and transportation enterprises as early as December 1975, less than four months after the overthrow of the monarchy.

Somewhat the same kind of former bleak condition of the workers can be stated about the Ethiopian peasantry. Most of the arable land was in the hands of the royal family, the Church and a small number of individuals. The big majority of the farmers were tenants, who were required to give as high as 75% of their farm produce. In addition to the handing over of such a big share to the landowner, the farmer was required to give other auxiliary services that left him little or no time to spend on agricultural activities. Moreover, the farmer had no guarantee for being continually employed on the land. He was at the mercy of the landlord, who could evict him anytime he liked. As a result of all these factors, the farmer was often exposed not only to meagre and depressing existence, but also to severe famine.

Just like the Ethiopian worker, the Ethiopian peasantry did not accept such a life peacefully. On one pretext or another, there were sporadic unrests of the peasantry in different parts of the country. The struggle of the Ethiopian farmers against their landlords was also supported and strongly voiced by high school and university students. "Land to the Tiller" had been the forefront slogan of the student movement. Through demonstrations, speeches, poems, etc., the students exposed the cruel face of the feudal regime, risking not only their educational career, but also their lives.

The translation of the slogan "Land to the Tiller" into reality was thus one of the primary objectives of the popular revolution of 1974. Immediately after taking power, the Provisional Military Administrative Council saw to it that this slogan was implemented. And in March 1975, a "Proclamation to Provide for the Public Ownership of Rural Lands" was issued. Through this Proclamation the broad masses of Ethiopia were liberated from age-old feudal oppression and injustice. Article four of the Proclamation clearly stated the essence of the new system of land possession in the following words:

Without differentiation of the sexes, any person who is willing to personally cultivate land shall be allotted rural land sufficient for his maintenance and that of his family.

Any person who has been a landowner and is willing to personally cultivate land shall likewise be allotted land.

As a further safeguard against a possible seizure of land through purchase and other related acts, article five of the Proclamation states "no person may sell, exchange, succession, mortgage, antichresis, lease or otherwise transfer his holding to another; upon the death of the holder the wife or husband or minor children of the deceased or where these are not present, any child of the deceased who has attained majority, shall have the right to use the land".

In a country where "a person's right, honour, status and standard of living is determined by his relation to his land", it is not difficult to assess how the promulgation of this Proclamation was to transform radically the structure of Ethiopian society. Thanks to this Proclamation and its practical implementation, the broad masses have emancipated themselves from ruthless oppression, exploitation and degradation.

The Proclamation on Rural Land Ownership was not confined to implementing the slogan "Land to the Tiller". It also stamped out protracted litigations regarding land tenure disputes that had been the preoccupation of not a few people. Thus, Article 28 of the Proclamation stated that "all cases involving rural lands pending in the ordinary courts on the effective date of this Proclamation are hereby annulled".

The implementation of the Proclamation on rural land ownership had met, as could be expected, resistance from former landlords. In various parts of the country many attempts have been made to stop the process of implementing the Proclamation. However, because of the determined struggle of the peasantry, the army and other revolutionaries, the armed oppositions of the reactionaries were crushed. Today peasants, organized at various levels, have their own defence forces and are safeguarding their gains effectively. The feudal agrarian relations are thus crushed, never to surface again.

The emancipation of the masses is not limited to people in the rural areas. In feudocapitalist Ethiopia, urban dwellers were also subjected to severe forms of exploitation through exorbitant house rents and urban land sales. Unreasonable increase of house rents, and ever soaring prices of urban land had made worse the life of urban dwellers. There was, therefore, an intensified struggle to change this condition of the urban sector. Consequently, in July 1975 a "Proclamation to Provide for Government Ownership of Urban Lands and Extra Urban Houses" was issued. This Proclamation benefited the urban dwellers in many respects. The reduction of house rent by as much as 50% (Article 20), and the right to a free possession of urban land up to 500 square metres for building a dwelling house can be cited among the major benefits.

3. Mass Organizations

In pre-1974 Ethiopia, the right to organize was very limited. In fact, it was the workers' two or three organizations such as unions and the teachers' associations that had legal recognition of some kind. Even these organizations were controlled by the government through the issuance of various restrictive directives and underhanded manipulations.

Since the outbreak of the revolution, however, the Ethiopian people have been organized along different aspects. The workers are re-organized into the All-Ethiopia Trade Unions, with the following new and dynamic objectives:

To enable workers to play their vanguard role as the advanced class in the struggle to translate into action the National Democratic Revolution Programme and to build the new people's democratic Ethiopia;

To make every effort to protect the rights and interests of workers under the laws issued from time to time and to fulfil, stage by stage, their social needs;

To enable workers to discharge their historical responsibilities in building the national economy by handling with care the instruments of production and their produce, and by enhancing the production and proper distribution of goods and services;

To enable workers to ally with the forces of democracy and peace, in accordance with the principles of proletarian internationalism, and to contribute their due share in the struggle to achieve peace, the welfare and equality of man, the liberation of peoples and collective advancement. (Proclamation No.222/1982)

The peasants are also organized into the All-Ethiopia Peasant Association for the fulfilment of responsibilities such as:

To agitate, educate, coordinate the peasantry and render the necessary assistance thereto with a view to expanding and strengthening agricultural producers' cooperatives which are the bases for socialist construction in rural areas;

To agitate, educate and coordinate the peasantry, with a view to liberating it from backwardness, by establishing and strengthening agricultural service cooperatives, increasing production and expanding social services;

To coordinate the peasantry with a view to liberating it from archaic mode of production and backward practices and cultures by advancing its ideological outlook and developing its initiative and thereby enhance productivity;

To make the necessary participation in the effort to enable the peasantry to gain rapid progress in education, health, transport and similar social services. (Proclamation No.223/1982)

The country's youth and women, too, are organized into the Revolutionary Ethiopia's Youth Association and Revolutionary Ethiopia's Women Association respectively. Among the tasks expected of the Youth Association are:

To conduct the appropriate agitational work among the broad masses in general and the youth in particular with a view to implementing the programme designed to liberate the people from illiteracy, to achieving the participation of the literate in teaching and the illiterate in learning;

To politicize and agitate the youth to embrace the constructive cultures, customs and practices of the society, to condemn reactionary and backward cultures and to fight against imperialist cultural influences and the bourgeois ideology;

To identify the basic needs of the youth, submit constructive recommendations to satisfy such needs; in cooperation with the appropriate government offices and mass organizations, make efforts to implement such recommendations;

To make the necessary efforts with a view to making the youth realize that the struggle of the youth of Revolutionary Ethiopia is part of the world anti-imperialist struggle, to ensuring that their outlook, dispositions and actions with respect to struggles for peace, equality, freedom, justice, democracy and social development are guided by the principles of proletarian internationalism and to enabling them to contribute their share to the world democratic youth movement. (Proclamation No.187/1980)

The Women Association has, among others, the following duties:

To politicize and agitate women to make the contributions expected of them in building the economy of Socialist Ethiopia;

To make every effort to ensure that women are afforded the skills and the opportunity which enable them to be productive citizens and that, to this end, appropriate working conditions are created for them;

To make every effort to eradicate cultures, customs and practices which deny women of their human rights; participate in the effort to eliminate prostitution and unemployment;

To participate in the world democratic movement of women; cooperate with women's associations which struggle for peace, equality, freedom, democracy, social progress, the rights of women and the welfare of children. (Proclamation No.188/1980)

The urban dwellers are organized into the Urban Dwellers' Associations with the aim of implementing the following tasks:

To enable the broad masses of urban dwellers to administer themselves;

To create the necessary conditions for moulding the ideology of the broad masses of urban dwellers with the philosophy of Marxism-Leninism with a view to liquidating feudalism, imperialism and bureaucratic capitalism and their influences and thereby, to achieving the objectives of the National Democratic Revolution Programme and intensifying the building of Socialism;

To educate the masses to condemn and stamp out acts and conducts which are social vices; to cooperate in the implementation of social defence programmes organized by the appropriate government offices;

To establish people's shops and other people's services, to encourage the establishment of, and give the necessary assistance to cottage industries and other cooperatives by coordinating dwellers. (Proclamation No.206/1981)

Professional associations of teachers, writers, journalists, artists, musicians, etc. are also formed. The responsibilities of these associations include developing a sense of professionalism among their respective members and also enhancing their contribution to the well being of society.

Generally speaking, we can confidently state that in today's Ethiopia it is close to impossible to find persons who are not members of one organization or another. For most of you here who are familiar with the situation of pre-1974 Ethiopia, it may be a surprise to hear that today all our urban houses are numbered, and most administrative and legal affairs are undertaken at various levels of mass organizations by democratically elected members. The broad masses are actively and effectively exercising their democratic rights of self-administration and self-management. And above all else, they are confidently building the New Ethiopia.

4. Development Direction

The change in development direction is the fourth characteristic of the New Ethiopia. Prior to the upsurge of the popular revolution the development scheme was so unbalanced that it was criticised for a number of reasons. For one thing, it concentrated around two or three regions. The provinces of Shoa, Eritrea and Hararge were very often cited as the favoured regions. But even here, it was only a limited number of towns, rather than the regions as a whole, that were beneficiaries of some development projects. Secondly, there were very marked differences in the availability of institutions of health, education and the like. Thirdly, job assignments to places other than the ones cited above were considered as punishments. As a result, such provinces were left with no sign of development while the two or three places enjoyed, compared to the Ethiopian situation in general, the fruits of modern life.

Since the advent of the revolution, however, determined efforts have been made to establish a balanced scheme of development. And in line with this, many roads reaching remote areas have been opened; schools, hospitals and health centres have been built. The Water Development Institute of Gamo Gofa, the Farmers' Training Institute of Bale, the Institute for Training Cooperative Workers of Arsi, the Teacher Training Institutes of Wollo and Wollega, the Textile Mill of Kombolcha can be prominent examples.

Today, water and electricity supplies are also being provided to a number of provincial towns. Through the formation of cooperatives, farmers are also contributing their share to rural development. They are opening schools and clinics and are also buying generators for the supply of electricity and pipe water. To better coordinate their efforts, they have begun to change their manner of settlement from scattered to collective village settlement.

The constructing of roads and the establishment of institutions and various development projects have become very instrumental in opening employment opportunities for many of those living in remote areas. All said, definite and encouraging beginnings that are changing the face of rural Ethiopia are clearly observable. These and the other beginnings that will result in building the New Ethiopia are being systematized by the Ten-Year-Development Guideline issued last September.

5. Cultural Values

The fifth major defining characteristic of the New Ethiopia is the growth of new cultural values. In pre-1974 Ethiopia the cultural values associated with nationality, language, sex, health practices and work activities were reactionary and of very negative nature. Different nationalities were encouraged to look down upon one another. The languages of some were favoured to the neglect of the others. Women were given low status in the society. Backward health practices, such as those administered by sorceresses and magicians were widespread. As for the attitudes towards labour that had prevailed in pre-1974 Ethiopia, no explanations seem to be necessary. Work, especially manual labour, was high despised. In particular, jobs in the areas of woodworking, tanning and blacksmithing were considered to be very low, to the extent that those who were engaged in them were highly segregated.

Today, however, clear marks of change are taking place. Insults related to nationalities or languages have become things of the past. Women have begun to exercise their rights of equality. Health practices are also gradually changing. Especially with regard to sorcery, encouraging steps are being taken by the people in exposing individuals who are practising the same. Positive attitudes towards manual work are also developing. In fact, since the establishment of cooperatives in various handicrafts, the status of the workers in these areas has been greatly enhanced. With the strengthening of such cooperatives and their gradual transformation into small scale industries, we hope that the society of the New Ethiopia will foster even greater positive socialist attitudes towards any kind of useful work.

6. Ideology

Ideologically, the Ethiopia of pre-1974 was essentially feudo-bourgeois. Mysticism and related religious sentiments surrounded the monarchy. Whatever happened was interpreted to be the will or the work of God. The struggle to overcome the problems of this world was considered to be futile and people were preached at to prepare for the life "in the next world".

Coupled with this, bourgeois sentiments of selfishness and greed were also taken as virtues. These, however, are values that accrue of necessity from the prevailing economic relations. At the time, these values were regarded by the beneficiaries of the system as eternal and cardinal.

Since the early days of the Revolution, a series of measures have been taken against these and related values. The underlying principle of the slogan "Ethiopia Tikdem" can be taken as an illustration of this. And with the political and economic measures taken by the revolution, the breeding ground for the exploitative values has been disinfected. Today, scientific attitudes, on the basis of the teachings of Marxism-Leninism, are being developed. Cooperation, group-work, mutual respect and the drive to learn and work for the common good are elements that are being nurtured by many of the people.

The struggle for the further development of the ideological strength of the people is enhanced through the instrumentality of various organizations. Through the mass media — the newspapers, the radio and TV services — the broad masses are assisted to learn the essence of scientific socialism. Through film shows, plays and musical programmes the people are provided with opportunities to raise their cultural levels. Through the discussion forms formed at work places, the broad masses raise their level of consciousness. Such endeavours on the part of the people are assisted by the political education programmes undertaken by cadres. The contribution of the availability of Marxist-Leninist literature in Ethiopian languages too, cannot be underestimated.

The raising of the political consciousness of the masses is effected also through educational activities. Fundamental changes are made in the contents of subjects that are taught at various levels of the educational system. But what is more significant is the campaign being undertaken to eradicate illiteracy. Thanks to the concerted efforts of all Ethiopians, the illiteracy rate of Ethiopia has today fallen from 93%. Consequently, if we try to rephrase Lenin's statement which says "An illiterate person stands outside politics" to read "A literate person stands in politics", we can guess how many of those Ethiopians who were "outside politics" in pre-1974 Ethiopia are "inside politics" in the New Ethiopia.

Mr. Chairman

More could be added to the list of "major defining characteristics" of the New Ethiopia, as the fundamental changes brought about by the popular revolution are many and varied. However, this should not imply goals set by the Revolution have been achieved. In fact, in the field of economic development the achievements have not been as high as desired because, in the first place the economic base inherited from the defunct regime was extremely low. Secondly, in the course of The Revolution, development efforts have been hampered by wars and natural calamities. Thirdly, by its very nature, economic and social transformation requires a long time. Therefore, the outcomes of the defining characteristics noted above lay only the necessary foundations for the building of the New Ethiopia through the conscious and active participation of the masses.

Through the guidance of the Workers' party of Ethiopia, we are confident of attaining the goals set by the Revolution and of building The New Ethiopia where justice, equality, peace, friendship and prosperity will prevail. And the systematic and in depth studies of efforts towards this goal should be taken by all us here as an academic challenge.

RESEARCH TRENDS IN ETHIOPIAN STUDIES

AT ADDIS ABABA UNIVERSITY

OVER THE LAST TWENTY-FIVE YEARS

Merid Wolde Aregay

Mr. Chairman,
Distinguished Participants,
Ladies and Gentlemen.

The time at my disposal is too limited to enable me to review extensively the policies of research and the results that have been achieved in the last twenty-five years and I shall try to limit myself to general developments in research in Ethiopian Studies.

Such a review may not have anything to tell scholars from Addis Ababa University itself or from institutions outside Ethiopia which have had close contact with it. I feel, however, that other scholars may benefit to some extent from this review. Many outstanding, though local, contributions concern Ethiopian historical and social issues. Although few of these have been published and, therefore, have not reached universities in Europe, the Americas or, of course, other African countries.

The contributions by students and staff of Addis Ababa University are all the more remarkable since, in the establishment of the University, priority was given to the training of students at the undergraduate level only. In its early years the University was hardly different from undergraduate colleges in North America, especially as the great majority of the officials and lecturers of the University were recruited from Canadian and American institutions.

Very soon in the history of Addis Ababa University it became obvious that undergraduates saturated with English literature, classical and scholastic philosophy, Greek and Roman history were ill-prepared to satisfy the manpower needs of the country. The policy for devising a Social Sciences curricula steeped in liberal arts was that courses of specialization would be obtained abroad by those students who graduated successfully. But the number of scholarships made available to these graduates were quite limited, and of those sent for their M.A. degrees, few wanted to return before obtaining their doctorates. The result of this was that the B.A. programme of the University had to be overhauled.

Specialization courses began to be offered in place of the general liberal arts courses. New departments were opened to make this possible. General courses, now trimmed down to those which would satisfy the language and other background requirements for the specialized courses, were offered only in the first year. The remaining three years were devoted to specialized training. This had a dramatic effect on the staff requirements of the new departments.

Instead of lecturers with limited specializations, others with better training and more experience began to fill the different departments. In order to make the courses relevant to Ethiopian situations and problems, the staff research interests and outputs increased. Students, especially as they came from the different provinces and various strata of Ethiopian societies, became potential source materials. They came to be required to produce serious term papers and original research theses in partial requirement for graduation. As more and more properly qualified lecturers, expatriate as well as national, joined the various departments, the research quality and input continued to improve tremendously. By the end of 1970 these essays, produced for the different departments of the then Faculties of Arts, Education and Law, as well as for the School of Social Work, became notable not only for the originality of their materials, but also for their depth of analysis in terms of relevance to Ethiopian issues and developments. Already in this early history of the departments and the courses of specialization which they offered, many of the B.A. theses were considered to be on a par, if not better, than M.A. theses written for American and European universities.

It will not be necessary for me to take your time by describing the research output of the staff. Many of the lecturers who taught in the different departments of the Faculty of Arts and the Law School are present in this hall today. Of those who, for some reason or another, have not been able to come to this Eighth Conference of Ethiopian Studies, many are well known to you. The results of their researches have been published in the form of books, monographs and articles.

The increasing research output of staff and students, the need to systematize the funding and direction of research, the need to help prevent duplication, as well as the need to provide adequate information centres, led to the establishment of the different Institutes. The Institute of Ethiopian Studies was followed by the Institute of Development Research and the Institute of Education Research. The now well known publications, *The Journal of Ethiopian Law*, *The Journal of Ethiopian Studies*, *The Ethiopian Journal of Development Research* and *The Journal of Education* were started. The Law School and the Institute of Ethiopian Studies separately, as well as jointly, sponsored the publication of several specialized works on Ethiopian law and land tenure. *The Register of Current Research*, published by the Institute of Ethiopian Studies, enabled established, as well as aspiring, Ethiopicists to follow global research trends and developments on Ethiopian themes and, above all, to avoid unnecessary and irritating duplications.

As indicated earlier, however, only a fraction of the research output of staff and students of Addis Ababa University has so far been published. Like the B.A. theses of the students, most of the seminar and research papers of staff, as well as their teaching manuals, remain still at mimeographed stages. The valuable baseline surveys conducted through the Institute of Development Research by the economists, geographers and sociologists of the Faculty of Arts are still mostly unpublished.

Much of the research done by staff and students until the outbreak of the Revolution in 1974 was concerned with social, economic and political issues. There can be no doubt that the research interests and output of staff and students contributed to the heightening of the social consciousness of the researchers themselves and of the rest of the University community. For this reason the monarchical regime of the time not only failed to make use of the research findings of staff and students, but held suspect all those who were trying, through research, writing and teaching, to understand the nature and working of the regime and its different institutions.

For the two years between 1974 and 1976, the University was closed in connection with the implementation of the programmes of the Development through Cooperation Campaign. From the two years experience in rural Ethiopia, experience in spreading literacy and implementing the proclamation which nationalized rural land, the majority of staff and students returned to the University with a first hand and better knowledge of their country and people. During those two years, however, a large number of the expatriate staff had returned to their various countries. A situation emerged in which the University's enrolment increased considerably, while the number of staff members decreased drastically. The staff situation was further aggravated, partly because the Revolutionary government had, so to speak, borrowed quite a number of experienced Ethiopian lecturers, and partly because the intensification of the class struggle in the country had forced some others to leave the country.

The Revolutionary government's need for well trained manpower and the University's desire to improve the situation created by the shortage of staff led to the beginning of post-graduate programmes in the 1978/79 academic year. It should be noted however, that the the University was in a much better situation in the years before the outbreak of the 1974 Revolution to begin instituting post-graduate programmes. If I remember correctly, as early as 1970 or 1971 some departments of the Faculty of Arts, especially the Departments of History and Ethiopian Languages, had made urgent recommendations to that effect. The University Faculty Council had, however, failed to consider these recommendations.

Post-graduate programmes are now offered in history, geography, economics, the Teaching of English as a Foreign Language literature, and linguistics. Each programme is of two years duration, but the rigour of the course and thesis requirements is such that very few students finish their studies within the two-year period. There is a five year limit for completing the programme and not a few number of students have failed to finish their studies within this five year limit. Originality is the basic criteria for all the M.A. theses. Each student defends his thesis before a panel of at least four examiners, one of whom has to be an external examiner. Each student is expected to acquire a knowledge of the foreign languages necessary for his research. In the history programme a knowledge of two European languages, in addition to English, is necessary. As it is mandatory that the thesis be not based on already published materials, the history M.A. candidate is forced to rely on oral information for which he also needs to have the necessary command of at least two or more Ethiopian languages.

Clearly therefore, the University, out of its desire to maintain an international academic standard, has stiffened its requirements. Quite a number of the external examiners have stated that the M.A. theses presented here compare with the standard of good Ph.D. theses presented to European and North American universities. It is, however, regrettable that theses of such originality and high quality of presentation are not published wholly or partially. It is true that several copies (thanks to the generosity of the Swedish Agency for Research Cooperation) are made of each thesis, to be deposited in the various libraries of the University. Still something remains to be done so that the results and conclusions of such intensive research are made available to Ethiopicists outside the country.

The School of Graduate Studies envisages that M.A. programmes in sociology, psychology and educational administration will begin shortly. Arrangements have already been made for the Institute of Language Studies to begin a Ph.D. programme in Literature and TEFL in co-operation with the School of Oriental and African Studies and the Institute of Education at London University. The British government has shown interest in this arrangement and it is hoped that it will make three to four scholarships available every year so that students can do part of their researches in England. Each student will be advised and supervised by two professors, one from Addis Ababa University and one from the relevant institution of London University. Discussions are also underway between the School of Graduate Studies and the Swedish Agency for Research Cooperation to begin a post-graduate programme in ethnography and museology. The programme, it is anticipated, will be run jointly by the Institute of Ethiopian Studies and an institute of Stockholm University.

Another significant development which followed the 1974 Revolution was the preparation of teaching materials. Even before this time the inadequacies of the textbooks for the various courses in the Social Sciences had become apparent. Most of the textbooks were prepared for European and American students and had limited relevance for Ethiopian readers. In spite of the staff shortage, significant achievements have been made in the preparation of textbooks and reading materials. Practically all departments are involved in this task. The Departments of History, Geography, Sociology and others have now relevant textbooks for a number of the courses they offer. Most departments hold annual seminars in which staff members read papers on issues of interest to their students, as well as to experts in their areas. The seminars of the Departments of Geography, History and Economics have become regular events. The Department of Geography is making preparations towards the publication of a journal.

Great success is also being scored by the Institute of Language Studies. Textbooks for the general courses in English language, linguistics, African literature, theatre arts, etc., written by staff members are already in use. An Amharic-English dictionary is in press. An Oromo-English dictionary is near completion. The second volume of the *Journal of the Institute of Language Studies* is also being prepared for publication. The work being done in the area of scientific and technical terminology is very promising. Under the chairmanship of staff members of the Institute of Language Studies, several panels have been set up so far and have translated over 16,000 scientific and technical terms into Amharic.

The Law School has continued the publication of its well-known *Journal of Ethiopian Law*. Supplements to the volume of *Consolidated Law of Ethiopia* are in preparation for press. Publication of its equally famous *African Law Digest* will resume soon.

Another body of the University that has been prolific in its research output is the Institute of Development Research. Because of its generous encouragement its own staff members, together with members of the Departments of Geography, Economics, Sociology and Psychology, have produced numerous monographs on rural and urban cooperatives, marketing and the adoption of appropriate technology. Its Documentation Centre has now emerged as an excellent library on development literature.

Research in all these areas has been made possible by University funding through the Research and Publications Office. This office has succeeded in disseminating the results of some of the research activities among the country's universities, colleges and interested government institutions. One thing that remains to be done, however, is to make available all these achievements to scholars and other readers outside Ethiopia.

EARLY STONE AGE CULTURES IN ETHIOPIA

Alemseged Abbay

INTRODUCTION

> In each great region of the world the living mammals are closely related to the extinct species of the same region. It is therefore probable that Africa was formerly inhabited by extinct apes closely allied to the gorilla and chimpanzee; and as these two species are now man's nearest allies, it is some what more probable that our early progenitors lived on the African continent than elsewhere (Darwin, 1871).

This type of suggestion was made at a time when there was very little tangible fossil evidence. What gave him a clue was the present day distribution of the primates. Since the discovery of the Taung fossil in 1924, numerous other fossils have been collected in different parts of Africa, all of which are contributing factors to prove the prophesy of Darwin acceptable. Africa which at one time was regarded as a continent which did not contribute much to world civilization now can be seen as the cradle of mankind.

Besides the fact that man emerged and evolved in Africa, it is also in this part of the world that the first major technological breakthrough in human history took place. Our ancestors began to make stone tools. The earliest tools, the Oldowan, have been found only in Africa. This technological achievement is the most decisive one in our history since it divorced our ancestors from the rest of the animal kingdom and made man — man.

The pioneer discoveries of the remains of our ancestors were made in southern Africa. However, since the late 1950's attention has been diverted towards the east. Numerous tools have been discovered in the eastern part of Africa which enable one to trace the technological evolution of human culture. Within this part of Africa, Ethiopia has emerged as the prominent hunting ground for pre-historians of the world. It is in Ethiopia that the earliest known ancestors of man as well as the oldest tools have been discovered.

OMO

Following the discovery of Lake Rudolf, the first European explorers, S. Teleki and L. Ritter, visited the Omo Valley in 1888. In 1933, C. Arambourg of the *Mission Scientific de L'Omo* made the first geological and palaeontological reconnaissance. Further reconnaissance in the region was made in 1959 by C. Howell who recognized the geological deposits and their fauna (Heinzein, in Coppens *et al.*). In 1966 an interdisciplinary mission, the International Omo Research Expedition, was formed and in 1967 a Kenyan team under R. Leakey, a French contingent under Y. Coppens and an American team led by C. Howell undertook long term research in the area.

The Omo region preserves a very thick and continuous fossiliferous record of Plio-Pleistocene sedimentalogy. It is almost one km. thick and the sediments outcrop over an area of some 200 km.^{2} (Howell, 1976). The fossiliferous Omo region has been divided into a number of geological formations. The most important of these is the Shungura Formations.

This sequence of deposits is subdivided into a number of members from the Rasal Member at the bottom to Member L at the top. These members are interstratified with volcanic tuffs which provide very important marker horizons for correlation. They also provide a unique chronological sequence based on Potassium-argon age determinations and the palaeo-magnetic reversal chronology.

The Shungura Formation like most of the Omo region is predominantly fluvial, deltaic and flood plain sediment with some lacustrine beds (Howell, in Isaac & McCown 1976; Merrick, in Isaac & McCown 1976).

The most important Member which has yielded artefacts in the Shungura Formation is Member F. The K/Ar dating technique has given an age of 2.04±0.10 for Tuff F which is at the base of Member F (Merrick et al.,1973).

In the site Ft Ji 1, as many as 270 artefacts were collected. The artefacts seem to be in a secondarily derived context because their physical condition varies from fresh to heavily abraded. They were also found in gravel lenses of the channel fill. The fossils that are associated with the artefacts also vary from unrolled to heavily abraded indicating fluvial transportation (Merrick, 1973; 1976).

In site Ft Ji 2 224 artefacts were collected *in situ*. These artefacts were in primary context since they are in fresh condition and the sediments in which they are found contain no large cobbles or coarse gravels – a clear indication of minimal transportation.

The artefacts from both sites are small and shattered pebbles mostly of quartz. In contrast with Olduvai and Lake Rudolf they do not contain any large core tools, i.e. choppers, manuports, etc. They are as small as 16 mm. to 13.4. Some of those from Ft Ji 2 show traces of edge damage probably as a result of utilization. The artefacts in Ft Ji 2 which are fresh occur in vertical and horizontal orientation. Whereas small fragments of quartz were discovered, no quartz lumps and their shattered fragments have been collected. Therefore, quartz is exotic and consequently must have been brought in. Hence, there appears no doubt this collection is due to hominid activity. Merrick (1973) calls it a "hominid occupation". But this is a very general interpretation. This site can not be a workshop due to the fact that the artefacts are not found in association with their cores and other waste pieces of manufacture. The paucity of both bone fragments and artefacts may probably suggest a transitory camp.

Pollen analysis shows that 2-3 m.y.a the Lower Omo region was one of bush and wooded savannah with riverine and montane forest in adjacent highlands. Many non-hominid fossils were also collected from the Omo. They include invertebrates such as fish, reptiles and crocodiles, and 50,000 mammalian fossil specimens. Nine out of the twelve Members yielded hominid fossils – the two forms of *Australopithecus* as well as *Homo habilis*. They all fall within 2.9-1.0 m.y.a according to the K/Ar as well as palaeomagnetic reversal determinations (Howell, 1976).

HADAR

Hadar is located in the Afar Depression of the northern extension of the East African Rift System. Here the Rift System is intersected by the Red Sea and Gulf of Aden Rifts. Three of these Systems participated in the formation of the Afar Depression since the Miocene (Johanson et al., 1978).

In the 1960's M. Taieb recognized the geological and palaeoanthropological significance of Hadar within the funnel shaped Afar Depression. Johanson, Coppens, Kalb and Taieb made surveys in the region in 1971 and in 1972 and the next year they formed the International Afar Research Expedition. Since then a large amount of material was collected from the region in four field seasons, 1973-1976/7.

The Plio-Pleistocene deposits of Hadar are about 280 meters thick and extend over 65 km³ (Harris, 1984). The exposure of this sequence is made possible by the dissection of the Awash River. It contains four stratigraphic Members intercalated by volcanic tuffs which serve as marker horizons. The four members are the Basal, Sidi Hakoma tuffs, the Denen Dora basalt and the Kada Hadar tuff (Johanson et al., 1978). These Members are fluvial, deltaic and lacustrine sediments.

In the site of Kada Hadar 2-3-4, artefacts were found dispersed and in secondarily derived contexts. Those artefacts seem to have been transported by high energy streams since the stream channel deposits contain very thick conglomerates and large cobble-sized clasts. Furthermore, the stone artefacts have an abraded physical condition which suggests significant transportation (Harris, 1984).

In the West Gona Site, however, the stone artefacts were discovered *in situ* and in primary context. This is manifested in the low energy nature of the deposition i.e. there are not any very thick conglomerates and large cobbles but fine sand silt. Besides, size sorting is absent in the archaeological accumulations. The absence of abrasion and the fresh condition of the stone artefacts suggest the site is minimally disturbed (Harris, 1984).

Hadar is not rich in stone artefacts, at least from the work there has so far been accomplished. In Kada Hadar, 16 artefacts were collected. They included unifacially and bifacially falked cobbles (chopper-cores including polyhedrons and wholeflakes). The raw material for these was trachyte and basalt. In West Gona also flaked cobbles as well as whole and fragmentary broken flakes were discovered. The flaked cobbles were small in size (100 mm) and have several flake scars as evidence of flake reduction sequences. These artefacts do not show any signs of utilization and they have still fresh and sharp edges and are cores from which the accompanying flakes were derived; in such circumstances the term "chopper" is reserved, therefore. The fact that they are artefacts is beyond all doubts since they show typical striking platforms and pronounced bulbs of percussion. The artefacts belong within the Oldowan Industrial Complex and are similar to those from Olduvai, Koobi Fora and Lake Turkana.

The West Gona artefacts were discovered in direct association with bone fragments. Harris seems to have no doubt about the hominid origin of this assemblage, but the possibility of carnivores as an added agency for bone modification can not be completely dismissed. Even if both the stone artefacts and the bones were the work of hominids, it still remains to identify what sort of a site it was: a home base; a butchery site; a workshop or a transitory camp.

The stone artefacts from Hadar are as yet the oldest dated specimens. The fission track has given 2.7±0.2 million years for the tuff immediately under which the artefacts occur. Because the Gona sequence did not have continuous stratigraphic links with the sequences in the Hadar basin, the geologists Walter and Tiercelin matched the sediments between the Gona and Hadar catchments. They wanted to establish a sequential relationship between the tools and flood plain stratigraphically to the Gona site with Hadar volcanic marker sediments (Johanson and Edey, 1982).

Numerous fossils, both hominid as well as non-hominid, were discovered at Hadar. As many as 240 hominid specimens representing 35 individuals were collected. The most relevant to this paper is the discovery of hominid fossils at site 333. Here fossils of 13 individuals: men, women, and at least four children, were collected. Johanson suggests more than 13 individuals may have been fossilized at Locality 333 (Johanson and Edey, 1982). The "Hadar Family" which is about 3m. yrs. old, shows that there was social group life. It also implies food sharing. In order to share there must have been an adequate amount of food which could, so far as meat is concerned, have been available mainly by butchering large animal carcases. The hunting of large animals must have required efficient and relatively speaking advanced tools and it is with these tools that much of the meat was consumed. Thus it is very likely that as early as this, i.e. 3.0 m.y.a., there must have existed the idea of tool making. There is no direct and tangible evidence for this, but it seems logical. At least, it could be corroborative evidence to the already existing date of the artefacts. It is also possible to speculate that there was indeed, relatively speaking, a sophisticated social organization which may have been facilitated by a complicated system of sounds and gestures and possibly also some basic forms of language.

MIDDLE AWASH

The Middle Awash region is located in the center of the Awash and close to the bank of the river in Ethiopia. The sequences consist of thick fluvial, deltaic sediments and lacustrine beds intercalated with volcanic tuffaceous horizons extending back as much as 6 million B.P. (Harris, 1984). The pioneer research activities in this region were undertaken by M. Taieb and J. Kalb's Rift Valley Research Mission in Ethiopia between 1975-78. Survey of the west side was continued in 1981 by an expedition from the University of California (Clark et al., 1984).

Kalb et al have reported that they have found Oldowan assemblages ". . . in apparent primary association with the remains of a single large- or medium-sized mammal, suggesting butchery-sites . . ." (Kalb et al., 1982). With regard to the interpretation no reason is given to dismiss the possibility that this association could also be due to either fluvial or carnivore action or both. Besides, even if the hominids were solely responsible for the association of the arte-facts and bones, the site may not necessarily have been only a butchery site. It could alterna-tively have been either a living area or a transitory camp site or even primarily a workshop.

The second point worth mentioning is that in the area where Kalb *et al.* worked, Clark *et al.* made close search and could not locate any *in situ* artefacts. They only came across heavily patinated choppers and flakes lying on the gravels of some slopes (Clark *et al.*, 1984).

At Bod-A3, in the Middle Bodo Beds, a number of stone artefacts were discovered. They include flake scrapers, modified and utilized flakes and cobbles including hammerstones. The vast majority of the assemblage consists of cores, unmodified flakes and debitage. Along with the artefacts, faunal remains, mainly long bone fragments showing longitudinal and spiral fracture, but no cut marks, were also collected. All these were deposited in a low-energy environment in a minimally disturbed context as manifested by the fresh condition, lack of size sorting, lack of preferred orientation and sedimentary matrix of the specimens (Clark *et al.*, 1984).

Kalb *et al.* further say that they collected numerous Acheulean tools in direct association with faunal remains. They have considered these sites also to be butchery sites (Kalb *et al.*, 1982).

In test excavations made by Clark *et al.* in 1981 in the Middle Pleistocene (Upper Bodo Beds) sediments, one type of site yielded hand axes and cleavers together with flakes, while other sites produced assemblages of core/choppers with flakes which resemble those of the Developed Oldowan-type artefacts and were those commonly associated with broken bone accumulations and one test excavated site which revealed a partial hippo skeleton may perhaps be a minimally distorted butchery site (Clark *et al.*, 1984). However, most of the artefact/bone associations were found in fluvial contexts. Channel sands and gravels represent fortuitous secondary accumulations.

The hominid fossils so far discovered by Tim White come from Pliocene Beds and show similar anatomy to that of *Australopithecus afaresis*. The date for the tuff associated with these fossils is 3.9-4.0 m.y. on Potassium-Argon dating method which is corroborated by a fission track age of 4.0±0.2 m.y.

MELKA-KUNTURE

Melka-Kunture is on the bank of Upper Awash on the Ethiopian plateau before the descent to the Rift. It is therefore, a series of sites with deposits of pebbles, sand and clays. These deposits are intercalated with volcanic tuffs which serve as marker horizons and offering chances for dating purposes. The French team, which had been undertaking research annually, gives 1.7 m.y. for their earliest site. But J. D. Clark does not think that there is any site in Melka-Kunture that goes beyond 1.5 m.y. (1983, personal communication).

The sites of Gombore 1B, Garba IV and Gombore 1 have predominantly choppers and polyhedrons, and on morphological and technological grounds they are said to be comparable with the Oldowan and Developed Oldowan of M. Leakey's Olduval (Chavaillon, 1976). These sites are particularly located just on the bank of the river unlike the other sites such as Garba XII, Garba I, Garba III which are located, relatively speaking, a bit further from the Awash in more or less deeply embedded channels. The latter sites have a lot of cleavers and handaxes and therefore, they are classified within the Acheulean (Chavaillon, 1976; Chavaillon *et al.*, 1979).

From this the French prehistorians conclude that the Acheulean hominids were less dependent on the close proximity of their sources of raw materials than the Oldowan hominids, i.e. on the pebble beaches from which they extracted basalt for their tools. This conclusion is made on the basis of the proximity of the Oldowan sites to the river. This seems to me unacceptable because the distance that exists between the Acheulean sites and the river is not considerable enough to lead to this conclusion. The distance of those Acheulean sites from the river is only tens of meters or about a hundred meters. If the Oldowan hominids could not live about a hundred meters away from the river then it is surprising that they were so incapable and weak, and yet they managed to survive *vis-a-vis* the predators. To say that the Acheuleans were less dependent on river is also tantamount to say that they could store water in their site which, ostensibly, is too much to swallow.

The Oldowan sites have large stones, 40-50 cms. in diameter and 50 kgs. in weight. Normally this stone is surrounded by remains of bones, teeth and horns. This occurrence ". . . is usually associated with an exceptional concentration of tools and manuports. Often too, when the density of remains is very high it is possible to observe nearby a striking bare area, with no remains at all". In Garba IV alone this occurs six times (Chavaillon *et al.*, 1979). The French call this an "occupation floor" which includes various activities such as butchery and flaking. The extraordinary abundance of bones and tools just on the bank of the Awash river makes one suspect the primary context of the materials. Even if the archaeological remains are in primary context there is the problem of identifying the purpose of every site. According to Brain (1982) and Isaac (1971; 1983) a butchery site is not one that has tools in abundance but one that has abundant bones and fewer tools.

The Acheulean sites are believed to be places where specialized activities took place such as knapping and meat-slicing areas as in Garba I and II. The discovery of small side-scrapers retouched flakes, very small bone fragments has made the scientists believe that it was a meat-slicing area. This is possible but the evidence is not enough for such bold statements.

From the faunal evidence (hippo, equidae, antelopes, suidae) and the pollen analysis made by Bonnefille, Gombore I was occupied during a wet period (Chavaillon, 1976; Chavaillon *et al.*, 1979). No fossils of predatory animals were discovered in this site. All these data pieced together suggested to the French prehistorians that the hominids were hunters. On Garba IV, Gombore II and Garba 1, again on the basis of palaeontological and pollen evidence similar conclusion is reached. Obviously, this argument does not seem sound. For carnivores or predators to be responsible for the accumulation of the bones, there does not necessarily have to be their fossils in the sites. The hominids could also have been scavenging.

The Acheulean sites have more diversified game composition due to, according to the French team, the relative independence of the hominids, i.e. they did not necessarily have to remain near the rivers. If they were, indeed hunters, then this makes sense.

The Oldowan Industry (1.7-1.3 m.y.a.), characterized by the existence of considerable number of manuports and choppers, was represented in Gombore I and Garba IV. From the Oldowan of Gombore 1B onwards we see evolution and progress in the technology. The discoidal choppers and retouched flakes increase in number. More elaborate debitage such as flakes and the increased use of obsidian are common. Bones are more finely broken and have signs of having been utilized. These features are seen in Garba IV and Gombore 1y. Early forms of Acheulean have choppers that have more acute angles, handaxes and cleavers of early form, and standard scrapers. In Melka Kunture these appear around 1 m.y.a. in Garba XII. Handaxes, cleavers and end scrapers increase in the Middle Acheulean site of Gombore II. In Gombore I, handaxes and cleavers outnumber others and there are signs of the use of fire. This is classified within the Late Acheulean. The appearance of the Levallois technique and the sudden decrease in the number of cleavers and the increase of the small bifacial pieces in Garba III made the scientists classify it within the Final Acheulean (Chavaillon *et al.*, 1979).

Therefore the most interesting aspect of Melka Kunture is the gradual evolution of technology and the culture change from the Oldowan up to the Middle Stone Age.

GADEB

The site of Gadeb is located near the base of the Bale mountains. These fluvio-lacustrine deposits are located 2,300 meters on the plains of Gadeb (Williams *et al.*, 1979).

Excavations were made in different parts and among others: Gadeb 2B by Hiro Kurashina, Gadeb 2C by Steven Brandt, Gadeb 8A by J. D. Clark and S. Brandt, Gadeb 8B by H. Kurashina and A. Galloway, and other sites as well (J. D. Clark and H. Kurashina, 1979 b).

The 8E excavation alone yielded 20,276 artefacts and small quantity of fauna. Most of the bones are unidentified except for a nearly complete zebra mandible and a hippo tooth. The excavators conclude that due to the fact that bone was not being accumulated it would appear that butchery was not a major activity (Clark and Kurashina, 1979 b).

Some of the welded tuff appears to show alteration by fire. This may probably be an earlier evidence for the use of fire. In the same site there is a concentration of artefacts closely associated with bones of hippo. The discovery of bones and artefacts has made Clark and Kurashina call it a butchery site.

It looks as if hominids started to penetrate the plateau from the Rift Valley when they achieved the Acheulean Industrial Complex. The K/Ar dates and the palaeomagnetic reversal evidence show that the Earlier Stone Age occupation of the plateau dates, to 1.5-0.7 m.y.a. (Clark and Kurashina, 1979 a). It is interesting to note that the other site on the plateau, Melka Kunture, was occupied at about the same time.

CONCLUSION

It is apparently clear that most conclusions and theories in the prehistoric research become outdated and obsolete, some very fast and others slowly. So it is imperative that in future works more caution in interpretation be made.

It is quite possible that if artefacts are found with the bones of a large animal the place may be a butchery site. It is again possible that if a cluster of artefacts are discovered in association with broken bones from many different animals the floor may be a living place. However, the simple association of bones and artefacts is not necessarily and always due to the hominid agency. Such features could be the result of hydraulic jumbles, smaller bones being sorted out. Also, it is not impossible that after the hominids left the artefacts carnivores may have brought the fragments of bones. Carcasses are available on the margin of rivers and lakes or on a bend of a river where they are washed up or where prey animals coming for water are killed by predators. In such areas hominids could make artefacts for temporary use and discard them. So the possibility has to be considered that such assemblages may be neither a butcher site, a living floor nor a workshop.

The association of tools with fossils of medium to large animals is believed to show scavenging and the association with medium to small suggesting hunting. These by themselves can not, indeed, be considered as evidences but possible clues that need more reliable corroborative evidence.

The proportion of artefacts and bones *vis-a-vis* one another gives some idea about the type of the site. Normally a home-base camp has both an increasing number of artefacts and a large bone density. The discovery of abundant bones with some tools may suggest a 'kill' or butchery site and workshop sites are usually identified with a lot of artefacts and some bones. Besides, stone knapping and bone breaking could be identified by using experimental archaeology, i.e. looking for overlapping conjoining pieces. Normally if knapping and bone breaking activity existed in the past one encounters a central cluster and a periphery of diminishing densities. The contrary is true in the case of living floors where there is refuse forming activity, i.e. the densest accumulation of large items is on the periphery (Kroll and Isaac, In press; Isaac, 1983).

All these issues have to be considered and accumulations of archaeological materials do not have to be judged at their face value. Meticulous interpretation is something which can not be dispensed with.

BIBLIOGRAPHY

Brain, C. K.   *The Hunters or the Hunted?* Chicago: The University of Chicago Press, 1981.

Chavaillon, J.   *L'Ethiopie Avant L'Histoire*. CNRS, 1976.

Chavaillon, J, Chavaillon, N.,   "From the Oldowan to the Middle Stone Age at Melka-Kunture
Hours,F., Piperno,M.   (Ethiopia). Understanding Cultural Changes", *Quaternaria*. Vol. XXI, Roma, 1979.

Clark, J. D. and Kurashina, H.	"New Plio-Pleistocene Archaeological Occurrences from the Plain of Gadeb, Upper Webi Shebeli Basin, Ethiopia, and a Statistical Comparison of the Gadeb Sites with other Early Stone Age Assemblages", *Union International Des Sciences Prehistoriques et Prehistoriques*, IXe Congres, Nice 13-18 September, 1976.
—————————————	(a) "An Analysis of Earlier Stone Age Bifaces from Gadeb (Locality 8E), Northern Bale Highlands, Ethiopia", *South African Archaeological Bulletin*, Vol.34, 1979.
—————————————	(b) "Hominid Occupation of East-Central Highlands of Ethiopia in the Plio-Pleistocene", *Nature*, Vol.282, No. 5734, 1979.
Clark, J. D., Asfaw, B., Assefa,G., Harris, J., Kurashina,H., Walter,R., White, T., and Williams, M.	"Palaeoanthropological Discoveries in the Middle Awash Valley, Ethiopia". *Nature*, Vol.307, No.5950. 1984.
Coppens,Y., Howell, G., Isaac, G. and Leakey, R. eds.	*Earliest Man and Environments in the Lake Rudolf Basin*. Chicago: University of Chicago Press, 1976.
Darwin, C.	*The Descent of Man in Relation to Sex*. New York: D. Appleton and Company, 1897.
Harris, J.	"Cultural Beginnings: Plio-Pleistocene Archaeological Occurrences from the Afar Rift, Ethiopia", *African Archaeological Review*, 1984. New York: Cambridge University Press.
Isaac, G.	"The Diet of Early Man: Aspects of Archaeological Evidence from Lower and Middle Pleistocene Sites in Africa", *World Archaeology,* Vol. No.3., Derek Rae ed., London: Routledge and Kegan Paul, February, 1972.
—————————————	"Archaeological Tests of Alternative Models of Early Hominid Behaviour: Excavation and experiments", *The Emergence of Man*. London: The Royal Society and the British Academy, 1971.
—————————————	"Early Stages in the Evolution of Human Behaviour: The adaptive significance of stone tools". April, 1983. Mimeographed.
Isaac, G. and McCown E. eds.	*Human Origins*. Menlo Park: W. A. Benjamin, 1976.
Johanson, D. and Edey, M.	*Lucy: The Beginning of Mankind*. New York: Warner Communication Company, 1982.
Johanson, D., Taieb, M., Gray, B. and Coppens, Y.	"Geological Framework of the Pliocene Hadar Formation (Afar, Ethiopia) with Notes on Palaeontology Including Hominids", W. W. Bishop ed. *Geological Background to Fossil Man*. Edinburgh: Scottish Academic Press, 1978.

Kalb, J., Jolly, C., Mebrate, A., Tebedge, S., Smart, C., Oswald, E., Cramer, D., Whitehead, P., Wood, C., Conroy,G., Adefris, T., Sperling, L., and Kana, B. — "Fossil Mammals Artefacts from the Middle Awash Valley, Ethiopia", *Nature*, Vol.298, No.5869, 1982.

Kroll, E. and Isaac, G. — "Configuration of Artefacts and Bones at Early Pleistocene Sites in East Africa". Paper prepared for the publication in *Intrasite Spatial Analysis in Archaeology*.

Merrick, S., Heinzelin, J. De., Haesaerts, P., and Howell, C. — "Archaeological Occurrences of Early Pleistocene Age from the Shungura Formation Lower Omo Valley, Ethiopia", *Nature*, Vol.242, No.5400, 1973.

Williams, M., Williams, F., Casse, F., Curtis, G., and Adamson, D. — "Plio-Pleistocene Environments at Gadeb Prehistoric Site, Ethiopia", *Nature*, Vol.282, 1979.

LES MONUMENTS GONDARIENS
DES XVIIe ET XVIIIe SIECLES

Une vue d'ensemble

Francis Anfray

La région du lac Tana possède un riche patrimoine de documents et de monuments histo-riques.Des oeuvres de peinture, de sculpture, d'orfévrerie, de littérature, d'histoire et de poésie y ont été exécutées en grand nombre au cours des siècles, — et des ouvrages d'architecture.

Les dix-septième et dix-huitième siècles y ont laissé des monuments d'un caractère parti-culier. Plusieurs dressent haut encore des murs que leur qualité de maçonnerie a préservé de la destruction totale. Certains sont en ruine. D'autres ont été restaurés. Tous témoignent de temps et d'évènements dont les annales ont aussi conservé la mémoire. Ces restes d'établissements aux installations diverses appartiennent, pour la plupart, à une époque qui s'étend sur un siècle et demi — du règne de Susenyos à celui de Iyoas qui finit en 1769.

Ces monuments sont appelés "gondariens", de manière conventionnelle, parce que le type architectural qu'ils représentent connut à Gondar un essor exceptionnel.[1] Durant une grande partie des dix-septième et dix-huitième siècles ce site fut dans le pays un centre politique, eco-nomique et religieux de première importance, et la résidence favorite des rois. On sait que ce type architectural était pleinement formé lorsque le roi Fasiladas s'établit à Gondar environ 1636 et y fit entreprendre la construction du château qui conserve aujourd'hui son nom.

Sites et monuments gondariens donc, puisque l'usage veut qu'on appelle ainsi un style par-ticulier d'architecture qui pourrait aussi bien (sinon mieux) être désigné par le nom du père de Fasiladas, car selon toute apparence, il fut créé sous le règne de Susenyos (1607-1632) en des sites comme Gorgora, Gannata-Iyasus et Danqaz.

Les caractéristiques majeures du style gondarien en architecture

Elles apparaissent en des édifices de cinq catégories, principalement: châteaux, ponts, églises catholiques, résidences des jésuites, églises orthodoxes.

Tous ces édifices sont en maçonnerie de pierre que lie un mortier de chaux. Souvent un enduit crépit les murs.

Les bâtiments ont un plan rectangulaire ou carré, ou bien circulaire (églises orthodoxes fréquemment entourées d'arcades).

Certains de ces bâtiments comportent un ou même deux étages auxquels accéder par des escaliers intérieurs et extérieurs. A l'extérieur, dans plusieurs cas, ces escaliers forment angle droit avec l'édifice.

Les couvertures sont (étaient) en voûte ou en terrasses. Les voûtes ont une forme surbaissée comme à Bahar-Dar-Gyorgis ou en plein cintre (château de Iyasu à Gondar).

Des tourelles rondes, coniques, à coupoles, s'élèvent aux angles de quelques édifices, et aussi, à intervalles réguliers, sur les murs d'enceintes. On voit aussi des tours carrées. Des façades comportaient des balcons de bois.

Portes et fenêtres sont surmontées de linteaux ou de voussures. Il advient que des arcs de décharge se dessinent sur les linteaux.

Deux installations ont un intérêt notable: des cheminées aménagées dans la structure même des bâtiments domestiques, avec un conduit vertical dans le mur; de grandes citernes maçonnées (avec enduit d'étanchéité) dans l'enclos, à proximité de ces bâtiments.

Des éléments décoratifs et symboliques ornaient cette architecture, parcimonieusement: des merlons couronnaient les murs de certains édifices et, s'ajoutant au caractère massif de ceux-ci, leur donnaient un aspect de forteresse[2] ; des pierres moulurées de couleur cinabarine (pas toujours) étaient placées symétriquement sous les extrémités des arcs de voussure des ouvertures en vue de produire un effet esthétique; des pierres sculptées de bas-reliefs représentant des figures humaines ou animales, des motifs géométriques, la croix, animaient les façades de certains édifices.

Ce type d'architecture apparaît au dix-septième siècle; c'est ce qu'il semble possible d'affirmer, encore que cette question de l'origine soit objet de débat (elle est évoquée en conclusion). Ainsi qu'il a été dit, la tradition s'en maintint jusqu'au règne de Iyoas. Quelques édifices, peu nombreux, furent encore construits en style gondarien postérieurement: par exemple, l'église Debra-Berhan-Sellassie à Gondar rebâtie dans le premier tiers du XIXe siècle. D'autres monuments que l'érosion du temps ou l'action des hommes détériorèrent furent restaurés partiellement. L'ensemble appartient aux règnes de Susenyos, Fasiladas, Yohannes, Iyasu (Adyam-Sagad), Tekla-Haymanot, Tewoflos, Yostos, Dawit, Bakaffa et Mentewab, Iyasu (Berhan-Sagad), Iyoas. Une interrogation cependant: quels monuments attribuer aux règnes de Tewoflos et Yostos (une période de huit ans)?

La carte des sites gondariens hors de Gondar

L'objet de cette note est de présenter, accompagnée d'une brève description, une localisation géographique des sites qui se trouvent en dehors de la cité de Gondar. Les sites et monuments de la vieille capitale ont fait l'objet d'un recensement à peu près complet: descriptions, dessins et photographies figurent dans plusieurs ouvrages, notamment celui de Monti Della Corte. Il convient cependant de préciser qu'aucune étude archéologique détaillée n'a été produite des édifices anciens de la cité.

Cette note se compose de renseignements recueillis par la Mission française d'archéologie lors de reconnaissances entreprises dans le cadre des activités du Centre du patrimoine (Ministère de la Culture d'Ethiopie) touchant le domaine de l'inventaire et celui de la conservation des monuments historiques.

Au nombre de quarante-neuf les sites gondariens ici cartographiés se rencontrent dans une vaste région en forme de croissant dont l'une des pointes est, au nord, le site de May-Gwagwa près d'Adwa dans le Tigray et l'autre, au sud, à Tchaga près de Debra-Libanos dans le Shoa. Leur concentration est forte autour de Gondar, sur la rive est du lac et dans les îles.

La liste n'est pas complète. Y manquent, qui n'ont pas été visités par la mission de recherches, les monuments des îles de Galila-Yasus, Birgidda-Maryam, Giyorgis, et celui de Mandaba au nord du lac Tana. L'île de Dek conserve aussi probablement des vestiges gondariens.[3] Ont été signalées les églises de Waybela-Maryam et de Wahni-Giyorgis au nord-est de Addis-Zaman; la possibilité d'aller les voir ne s'est pas trouvée. Puis il y a les sites dont les collines gardent encore le secret.

Les sources relatives aux circonstances qui favorisèrent le choix de ces sites et déterminèrent la construction de ces monuments sont connues, tout au moins en ce qui concerne les faits dans leur généralité. Quant au détail les précisions font souvent défaut, et combien difficile est, en face de plusieurs monuments, l'établissement d'une chronologie exacte.

Les annales des rois constituent ces sources ainsi que les récits (ouvrages et lettres) des jésuites espagnols ou portugais qui séjournèrent en Ethiopie au temps de Susenyos surtout et qui se nommèrent Pedro Paez (Pero Pais)[4], Affonso Mendez, Emmanuel de Almeida, Emmanuel Barradas, Jeronimo Lobo, Gaspar Paez, Balthazar Tellez, auxquels il y a lieu d'ajouter les noms, parmi d'autres, des voyageurs Charles Poncet et James Bruce qui eux aussi furent les hôtes du pays gondarien, le premier en 1699-1700, le second de 1769 à 1771.

Entre 1640 et 1645, Emmanuel d'Almeida établit une carte des régions d'Ethiopie et des principaux sites dont il avait connaissance. Une copie de 1662 est reproduite en fac-similé dans le premier volume (entre les pages 302 et 303) de *Rerum Aethiopicarum Scriptores Occidentales* de Camillo Beccari (1969).

La carte archéologique des sites ici présentée a été dessinée par Yves Baudouin — auteur également des dessins et des photographies.

1. MAY-GWAGWA

Nom du site qui fut aussi appelé FREMONA, et qui est localement désigné par le toponyme Endiet-Nebersh (cf. *la Guida dell'Africa orientale*, p.243).

Sur une colline, dans le Tigray, à environ six kilomètres au nord-ouest d'Adwa, une église ordinaire est dédiée à Giyorgis. Des ruines, peu importantes, y subsistent de l'ancien établissement jésuite. Restes du mur d'enceinte en maçonnerie gondarienne. Ce mur comportait de petites tours espacées.

La station fut fondée par le jésuite espagnol Andre d'Oviedo en 1557; il mourut à Fremona en 1580. Maigoga, Maegoga, Maigwagwa (nom d'une rivière qui coule au pied de la colline), telles sont les appellations que dans leurs récits les Portugais donnent au site. Affonso Mendez et Jeronimo Lobo y arrivèrent en 1625. Emmanuel d'Almeida les avait précédé en 1624. On trouve dans leurs ouvrages plusieurs indications sur le lieu. Emmanuel d'Almeida, *Historia Aethiopiae* (C. Beccari, 1969, vol.VI, p.378, 379, 502), Lobo, *Itinerarie* (Hakluyt Society, 1984, p.182 et 183), Mendez, *Expedition Aethiopica* (C. Beccari, VIII, p.199). Luigi de Azevedo, dans une lettre en date du 8 juillet 1619 parle de "la nostra chiesa vecchia di legno e paglia" et d'un projet de nouvelle construction (C. Beccari, I, p.128). En 1627, fut bâtie à Fremona une église de pierre et de chaux. (Almeida, in C. Beccari, vol.VI, p.378: "huma fermosa igreia de pedra e cal").

Il y avait également une citerne. E. Barradas in C. Beccari, VIII, p.482, et IV, p.198: "E basta saber que em toda Ethiopia nunca ouve cisterna alguma pera recolher agoa, quanto mais pera vinho, nem o nome de cisterna sabiao até agora, que em nossos tempos se fez a primeira em Fremona, cavada em huma rocha dentro de huma fortaleza de pedra e barro que alli temos pera huma necessidade".

Une description du site de Fremona au début du vingtième siècle dans l'ouvrage de la Deutsche Aksum-Expedition, tome III, p.64-66.

2. AXOUM

L'église Maryam-Tsyon a été construite vers 1655 sous le règne de Fasiladas (et l'objet de quelques travaux sous celui de Iyasu, Berhan-Sagad). Elle a été restaurée plusieurs fois, notamment au début de ce siècle par le génie militaire italien. Une photographie dans le livre de Jacques Faitlovitch (*Quer durch Abessinien*, Berlin, 1910, p.35), prise en 1908, montre l'église en reconstruction partielle. Puis, en 1972, par un groupe d'architectes sous la direction de S. Angelini. L'opération était placée sous le patronage d'un Comité des monuments historiques en liaison avec l'Administration éthiopienne des antiquités.

Cette église du dix-septième siècle fut bâtie sur les vestiges d'édifices ruinés d'époques anciennes. Le soubassement remonte à l'âge axoumite. Une certaine continuité semble s'être maintenue sur le site depuis l'antiquité. Des destructions eurent lieu notamment au XVIe siècle et au début du XVIIe siècle (en 1611).

Le *Liber Axumae* conserve une tradition historique. F. Alvarez, à Axoum en 1520, décrit l'église.

C. Beccari, XI. Lettre de Luis de Azevedo, 22 juillet 1907, p.107. P. Paez (14 septembre 1612, p.260, 291). Vol. IV, p.227 (E. Barradas). Vol. V, p.136, 155, 168, 392 (E. d'Almeida).

Deutsche Aksum-Expedition, 1913, II, p.136-140.

U. Monneret de Villard. *Aksum*. 1938.

3. DAKWA-KIDANE-MEHRET

Au nord-est de Gondar, à quelque distance de la grand-route en direction de l'Est, une église préserve des vestiges d'un édifice en style gondarien. Il remonterait au temps du roi Adyam Segad-Iyasu (1682-1706).

4. GORENKO-MARYAM (Pl.I)

Église rectangulaire (22m 40 x 18m 70) dans le district de Wogera, canton de Amba-Giyorgis (Maryam-Debber), à 54 kilomètres au nord-nord-est de Gondar. La tradition locale en attribue la construction au roi Adyam Sagad Iyasu.

Monument en assez bon état de conservation; rebâti naguère dans sa partie ouest. La façade du sanctuaire (*maqdas*) est ornée de pierres sculptées (fraîchement peintes) qui représentent des motifs géométriques en rosette.

5. BAMBULO (Pl.IIa)

Dans le district de Gondar-Zuriya, canton de Tekel-Dingay, à sept kilomètres au nord de Gondar, un pont sur la rivière Magach, en partie détruit, conserve trois arches, celle du milieu est brisée. Il mesure 29m 10 en longueur et 4m 10 en largeur.

6. DEFECHE-KIDANE-MEHRET (Pl.IIb)

Sur les hauteurs qui dominent la rivière Angareb à l'est de la cité et de la vallée, district de Gondar-Zuria, canton de Tedda, se dressent les murs d'une église ronde à galerie extérieure de 27 piliers.

Selon la tradition locale, cette église fut construite au temps de Bakaffa (1721-1730), et détruite par les Derviches lors du sac de la région en 1888. (Aujourd'hui en cours de reconstruction).

7. DEFECHE (Pl.III)

Pont sur la rivière Angareb dans le district de Gondar-Zuria, au pied de la haute colline de Debra-Berhan-Sellassie. Il est long de 28m et large de 4m. Il possède quatre arches. Son état de conservation est satisfaisant.

8. KORATA (Pl.IVa)

Pont sur la rivière Qaha au sud de Gondar, district de Gondar-Zuriya. Ruiné. Une seule arche subsiste au bord de la rivière. Elle mesure 4m 10 sur 2m. Sa hauteur est de 1m 80.

9. LIDETA-MARYAM (Pl.IVb)

Église ronde avec une galerie extérieure de piliers et d'arcatures, près de la rivière Qaha. Elle est en partie détruite (grossièrement réparée). Mur d'enceinte à petites tours coniques.

10. GOBATIT (Pl.IVc)

Pont de quatre arches sur la rivière Angareb au sud de Gondar. Il est long de 35m 50 et large de 4m 15. La plus grande arche mesure 8m 80 de pilier à pilier; est haute de 5m 80.

11. ARWAGHE-MARYAM (Pl.V)

Église ronde sur le haut plateau du canton de Tedda, à l'est de Uzaba. Elle est en grande partie détruite. Le sanctuaire (*maqdas*) a été reconstruit récemment de manière hâtive. Sur le mur de la galerie extérieure de l'église, on observe des motifs décoratifs, en creux, semblables à ceux qui ornent intérieurement la première salle, en haut de l'escalier, du château de Fasil à Gondar.

Un porche monumental (*dedjeselam*) est dans un état de conservation exceptionnel. Le mur d'enceinte est rectangulaire, irrégulièrement.

Selon la tradition recueillie localement, l'église aurait été construite par Woizero Wellette-Hawaryat, soeur du roi Yohannes.

12. DEWADO-MARYAM

Église ronde à trente-cinq kilomètres, par la route, à l'est de Azazo, dans le district de Chilga. En partie détruite. Elle aurait été construite par Welette-Rufael, petite-fille du roi Sagad Iyasu.

Description, photographies et plan dans *Rassegna di Studi Etiopici*, 1981, vol.XXVIII, p.6 et 7.

13. AZEZO-TEKLE-HAYMANOT (Pl.VIa)

Au sud de Gondar, à l'est de la grand-route, non loin du village de Azezo, sur une colline, sont conservés quelques vestiges architecturaux d'une église construite au temps de Susenyos (selon une tradition incertaine): un mur d'enceinte rectangulaire et une tour carrée à merlons sur le côté nord du mur d'enceinte; un escalier à angle droit, extérieur à la tour, donne accès à l'étage de cette tour. Une autre tour carrée, haute de six mètres, s'observe sur le mur d'enceinte, à l'ouest. (Au milieu de l'enclos est une église de construction récente.)

"Un pittoresco palazetto con 4 torri", dit la Guida, (p.359), existait jadis au côté nord de l'église. Il n'en subsiste presque rien aujourd'hui.

A environ quatre cents mètres au nord-ouest de l'église de Tekla-Haymanot, en contrebas de la colline, existent encore une tour conique partiellement détruite et les restes d'un mur. En ce site l'amas de ruines est important.

C'est vraisemblablement dans ce secteur (appelé Atie-Wogen), que fut construit au temps de Susenyos le palais de Gannata-Iyasus sommairement décrit par Jeronimo Lobo (p.249 de *l'Itinerario*, Hakluyt Society, 1984). Description plus étendue par Emmanuel d'Almeida (dans Beccari VI, p.387-390), selon qui ce fut à Azazo "Ganeta-Jesus" que Manoel Magro découvrit en 1624 le moyen de confectionner cette fameuse chaux si souvent utilisée par la suite dans les constructions gondariennes. "Metua no fogo, cozeuse, sayo chunambo ou cal excellente". Elevé près de l'église, le palais est ainsi décrit par Almeida, p.390: "huns fermosos paços de pedra e cal, de dous sobrados, com seu terrado, duas salas, e coatro camaras nos baixos e outras tantas nos altos, afora dous como cubellos ou baluartes em dous cantos com que ficarao seguros e com alguma semelhança de fortaleza. Fezse esta obra em tres ou quatro annos gastandosse tanto tempo por falta de offices; logo mandou faser a roda da igreia huma cerqua de muro e baluartes, com que ficou huma boa fortaleza pera a terra, e despois acrecentou dentro no jardim, que aly como disse tinha plantado, hum tamque muito largo e comprido cavado na terra e fazendolhe em quem quadro paredas de pedra e cal acafeladas, pera que a agua se nao summisse".

Sur l'initiative de Pero Paez, une église avait été construite antérieurement à Azazo. (Almeida dans Beccari VI, p.357, 387).

14. FANTER (Pl.VIb)

Pont sur la rivière Magach, au sud de Gondar, dans le canton de Tedda. Il comporte cinq arches. Sa longueur est de 44m 70; sa largeur de 4m 20. Orientation: NE-SO.

Une photographie dans Sigfrid Siwerz. *En färd till Abessinien*. Stockholm, 1926, p.250.

15. EGZIABHER-AB (Pl.VIc)

Église ronde de belles dimensions au sommet d'une colline (est de la route) dans le canton de Tedda. Une grande partie est détruite. Un mur d'enceinte haut de quatre mètres que domine une tour carrée, haute de six mètres.

Deux tourelles à coupoles s'élèvent sur le mur d'enceinte. (Il n'a pas été possible d'obtenir de renseignements sur l'histoire de ce site.)

Ce site du canton de Tedda, à environ soixante-dix kilomètres (par la route) de Gondar et quatre heures de marche à partir de la bourgade de Deguma, conserve les restes importants d'un château et d'une église, sur une hauteur (alt. 2750m), au bord d'une vallée profondément et abruptement entaillée — Ghedam Giyorgis.

De par sa difficulté d'accès le site a reçu peu de visiteurs. Il paraît intéressant de reproduire quelques lignes de la description que firent de ses monuments Combes et Tamisier qui passèrent par Dankaz en 1835 (le 7 et le 8 août): "Ce castel abandonné depuis que la cour se transporta à Gondar, est environné et surmonté d'arbres qui semblent vouloir le dérober à la vue et qui lui donnent l'aspect d'un ermitage pittoresque. — L'édifice, précédé par une immense cour, était autrefois entouré d'une muraille élevée; mais aujourd'hui cette enceinte est entièrement détruite; un seul montant de la principale porte d'entrée est resté debout comme pour annoncer la place qu'elle occupait . . . Le rez-de-chaussée était couvert de terre et de bois de charpente tombés de la toiture et des murs. On remarquait, à hauteur d'homme, de larges pierres de taille où l'on avait représenté, d'une manière assez grossière, des éléphants et des chevaux montés par des cavaliers armés d'une lance au bout de laquelle flottait un étendard. Nous observâmes aussi quelques vestiges d'inscriptions en langue éthiopienne effacées par les pluies; tous les appartements paraissaient avoir été peints avec soin; . . . Au dessous du rez-de-chaussée, on avait creusé une immense citerne soutenue par douze arceaux, et, malgré l'humidité de ce lieu souterrain, le ciment était encore parfaitement conservé; un escalier encombré de débris conduisait dans ce caveau où nous ne parvînmes qu'avec beaucoup de peine. En dehors et tout près de la porte d'entrée, on voit encore une auge énorme qui servait, d'après le rapport du cicerone, à abreuver les chevaux favoris du maître du château . . . Cet édifice avait un premier étage dominé par une terrasse: les quatre angles sont surmontés de flèches coniques . . . On avait bâti, à côté du château, une grande chapelle dont on voit encore les ruines . . . La voûte composée de pierres sculptées et artistement taillées, aurait mieux résisté aux atteintes du temps . . . Ces édifices avaient été construits en 1625 par les soins d'Alphonse Mendez . . . Les missionnaires . . . . bâtirent à Dancaz un palais, une chapelle, et un vaste collège destiné à recevoir soixante jeunes Abyssins qui devaient y faire leurs études de théologie romaine sous la surveillance du patriarche Mendez. Les ruines du séminaire ont entièrement disparu". (*Voyage en Abyssinie. 1835-1837*. Paris, 1839, tome II, p.29, sq.).

Les vestiges de Danqaz sont à peu près dans l'état que décrivent Combes et Tamisier. Les arbres ne sont plus qu'en petit nombre. Des pans de murs se sont écroulés. On ne voit plus les tourelles d'angle, et non plus les pierres sculptées et les inscriptions qui sans doute se trouvent dans les amoncellements de gravats.[5] En revanche, les traces de peinture décorative se discernent bien sur l'enduit des murs à l'intérieur de l'édifice: des rosettes aux couleurs éteintes (brun, orange et bleu).

Ces rosettes ne sont pas sans rappeler les motifs sculptés de Maryam-Ghemb et de Gorenko-Maryam. Une paroi murale au sud du château, à l'extérieur, offre encore les traces d'un dessin au trait rouge — figurant deux chiens. Les salles ont des fenêtres à voussure et des sortes d'étagères aménagées dans les murs (comme à Debsan), ainsi que des cheminées et des gouttières.

Au sud-ouest du château, souterraine, la citerne est un monument étonnant par ses dimensions et son état de conservation. Quatorze mètres de longueur, cinq mètres cinquante de largeur et huit mètres trente de profondeur. Un escalier en équerre permet d'y descendre. Sa couverture est presque intacte. (Une autre grande citerne est celle du château de Fasil à Gondar: 7 mètres de profondeur, 10m 70 de longueur, 4m 50 de largeur, avec également un escalier en équerre.) Emmanuel Barradas fait état de cette citerne de Danqaz "muito grande e fermoza abobadada com arcos, e a encheo de agoa". (C. Beccari, IV, p.198.)

Les ruines de l'église sont à environ trois cents mètres au sud du château. Son plan en croix latine indique qu'il s'agit d'une église catholique. Elle est longue de vingt-sept mètres. Au transept les grands arcs sont encore en place. La voûte est tombée; il en subsiste une partie à l'ouest où l'on peut remarquer qu'elle était faite de caissons sculptés. Sur le mur du fond de la branche nord-ouest du transept figure, maçonné en relief, un faux baldaquin surmonté d'une croix qui a été martelée. Sa hauteur est de cinq mètres.

Une pierre grise (une sorte de basalte) a été utilisée pour la construction de l'église. Il n'y a pas de crépi (alors qu'on l'observe partout sur les murs du château), ni ces pierres violâtres qui se remarquent en d'autres monuments gondariens — parfois appelées "pierres de Danqaz". Certains détails rappellent des caractéristiques notées à Debsan où également le crépi a presque entièrement disparu: les arcs de décharge sur les ouvertures notamment.

Cette église fut une fondation de Affonso Mendez. Sa construction eut lieu en 1628. (C. Beccari. VII, 3 et VIII, 228). Danqaz est décrit par E. Barradas (C. Beccari, IV, 9) et par E. d'Almeida (C. Beccari, VI, p.382; XII, p.258).[6]

17. LWA-MARYAM

Ruine d'une église ronde sur une éminence à environ 2km 5 à l'ouest de Menzoro-Tekla-Haymanot, dans le district de Gondar-Zuriya, canton de Tedda.

Le côté du *maqdas* mesure six mètres. Il n'y a plus de toit. L'église est aussi appelée Addi-Alem.

18. MENZORO-TEKLA-HAYMANOT

Une tour carrée près d'une église récemment reconstruite au sommet d'une colline, dans le district de Gondar-Zuria, canton de Tedda, à environ un kilomètre à l'ouest de la grand-route.

Fr. Anfray. Vestiges gondariens. *Rassegna di studi etiopici*. 1981, XXVIII, p.7 et 8. Photographies 4 et 5.

19. MEROW

Ruine d'une église ronde, au sommet d'une colline élevée, dans le district de Gondar-Zuriya, le canton de Dembea (Kuolla-Debba). L'église est appelée Abba-Qiros. Elle n'a plus de toit. La destruction serait due aux Derviches. Selon la tradition locale, l'église aurait été bâtie au temps de Fasiladas.

20. BARIE-GEMB

Sur une colline, à l'est de la grand-route, dans le district de Gondar-Zuriya, canton de Tedda, au sud, une église de plan carré avec une haute coupole centrale est dédiée à Qeddus-Mikael. Une tradition situe au XVIe siècle sa fondation.

G. Annequin a fait une étude de cette construction. *Annales d'Ethiopie*, 1965, VI, p.17-22. Pl. XVI, XVII et XVIII.

Il est vraisemblable que ce monument est une reconstruction du XVIIe ou du XVIIIe siècle. (L'église de Waybela-Maryam aurait un dôme semblable.)

21. GOHEL-GIYORGIS

Petite église très ruinée, à l'ouest de la route de Delghi, sur une colline, dans le district de Gondar-Zuriya, canton de Dembea, à 66 kilomètres par la route au sud-ouest de Gondar — non loin de Alwa-Maryam.

Ne se dresse plus au milieu de l'éboulis qu'une partie du sanctuaire carré (*maqdas*) qui était divisé en deux parties par un mur à arcatures — comme dans la vieille église de Metraha.

22. MARYAM-GEMB

Au nord du lac Tana, sur les hauteurs de la péninsule, district de Gondar-Zuriya, canton de Dembea, s'élève un vaste pan de mur aux sculptures remarquables. Une bonne photographie de ce mur aux motifs géométriques figure dans le livre de J. Leroy (*Ethiopie. Archéologie et Culture*. 1973. p.224 et 234). Au voisinage de ce haut mur subsistent des ruines d'autres constructions où s'observe dans la maçonnerie une analogie avec l'édifice de Debsan au pays d'Emfraz (Fr. Anfray. Vestiges gondariens. *Rassegna di Studi Etiopici*. XXVIII. 1981, p.9, phot. 7).

La ruine principale est ce qui reste de l'église construite en 1627 sous la direction du frère jésuite Joao Martinez. Ce fut la dernière en date des constructions qui furent élevées à Gorgora. En fait, ce toponyme s'applique à deux sites: l'ancien Gorgora ou Ombabaqua et le nouveau Gorgora ou Cundamba (C. Beccari. VII. p.537). Selon A. Mendez: "Earum prima fuit templi et residentiae in Gorgorrae peninsula architectio, quae dicta est Nova Gorgorra ad distinctionem veteris, ab ea ad duo vel tria milliaria disiunctae". (C. Beccari, VIII, p.189). Ce sont les numéros 26 et 27 de la carte de E. d'Almeida.

La première construction importante fut d'abord, au vieux Gorgora, une maison haute édifiée en 1614 par P. Paez (Mendez dans Beccari, VIII, p.189 et Almeida, VI, p.293-294). Cette bâtisse édifiée pour l'empereur fut appelée Babet Laybet", c'est-à-dire "domum supra domum" selon Mendez (Beccari, VIII, p.105), "em cima de casa, casa" selon Almeida (Beccari, VI, p.294). Il semble que le vieux Gorgora s'identifiait aussi avec la région ou le site de Deqana (Beccari, XI, p.402. Une lettre de Paez en date de juin 1618 indique Gorgora-Deqana).

D'autres édifices par la suite furent bâtis à Gorgora: palais ("huns paços fermosos de pedra branca muyto bem lavrada, com seus aposentos e salas", Paez dans Beccari, II, p.194, avec la description) et églises, notamment une de 1618 à 1620, sous la direction de Paez, aux frais du Ras Seela-Krestos, frère de l'empereur Seltan Sagad (Susenyos). Église "de pedra muito branca e fermosa, lavrada muito bem; arco capela mor, na frontaria seis colunas ionicas, sura torrinha de sinos, seu terrado com parapeito, donde se descubria o mar e as grandes campinas de Dambea" (Almeida dans Beccari, II, pp.194, 296-297, 496; XI, pp.406-407, 414-417. Aloysius de Azevedo, XI, p.417).

Cette église de Paez fut construite sans mortier de chaux (Almeida dans Beccari, VI, p.345). En revanche, le mortier de chaux fut utilisé dans la construction, en 1627, au nouveau Gorgora, de l'église édifiée par Joao Martinez dont Almeida dit qu'il est "em Gorgorra occupado ne fabrica da Igreia nova" (dans Beccari, XII, p.258); il donne de cette église une brève description: "com ous arcos e paineis, . . . os de capella com suas rosas muito bem feitas" (dans Beccari, XII, p.268). Il est probable que le "maître d'oeuvre" (Beccari, VII, p.7. Ainsi l'appelle Almeida) Joao Martinez s'inspira largement du monument de son prédécesseur, surtout si l'on se reporte à la description de Paez lui-même (Beccari, II, pp.496-497) où l'on voit que sa construction comportait déjà "parte bem ornadas per fora com rosas e molduras na mesma pedra". — De cette église de Paez il est dit qu'elle était "blanca y bermeja . . . y luego vido de espacio los ornamentos y imagines de la iglesia, que comforme a nuestre probeza esteva bien ornada" (Paez dans Beccari, XI, p.403). Azevedo (dans Beccari, XI, p.414) note: "Comesouse logo a juntar pedra parte branca e parte vermelha a modo de jaspe"; il donne d'autres détails et les dimensions.

D'après Almeida (Beccari, VI, p.494), le nouveau Gorgora fut fondé en 1626.

A. Kammerer, il y a quarante ans, avait déjà relevé que l'église dont il subsiste de vastes pans de murs datait de 1627 (L'éphémère triomphe du catholicisme en Abyssinie. 1622-1632 — *Revue d'Histoire diplomatique*. Septembre-décembre 1946, p.24).

Des photographies des ruines de Gorgora, prises il y a près de cinquante ans, se trouvent dans l'article de A. A. Monti Della Corte. La Chiesa portoghese di Gorgora sul Tana. *Gli Annali dell'Africa italiano*. Anno I, numéro 2. Agosto 1938. XVI. Roma, pp.631-639. Avec un dessin de Elio Zacchia.

23. DEBSAN

Au sommet d'une colline, dans le district de Gondar-Zuriya, canton d'Emfraz, à trois kilomètres environ à l'est de la grand-route se trouvent les vestiges d'une église catholique et de la résidence (démolie) du patriarche Affonso Mendez. Une citerne rectangulaire est à proximité de l'église.

Fr. Anfray. Vestiges gondariens. *Rassegna di Studi etiopici*. 1981. XXVIII, pp.9-11. Photographies 6, 7, 8, 9. Plan C.

24. WAHNI-AMBA

Mont aux parois abruptes au nord-nord-est de Addis-Zaman, district de Libo, canton de Kamkam. Il faut cinq heures de marche dans les hautes collines à partir de Addis-Zaman pour atteindre ce rocher escarpé qui fut lieu de relégation au temps des rois gondariens.

Des vestiges de constructions y subsistent. Des poteries. Cf. Barbara Toy, *In search of Sheba*. 1961. Photographies entre les pages 228 et 229.

25. TEKARA (Pl.Xa et XI)

Pont sur la rivière Garno dans le district de Gondar-Zuriya, canton de Emfraz (Koga), à l'est de la grand-route, au sud de Koga, sur le chemin qui mène au château de Guzara.

Ce pont est fait d'une seule arche de 7 mètres, haute de 5m 70. Orienté nord-sud, il est long de 11 mètres.

Paez (Beccari, III, p.326) dans son *Histoire de l'Ethiopie* parle d'une "terra Tacara" où résidait l'impératrice Malac Mogoça.

26. GUZARA (Pl.Xb — une cheminée)

Ruine importante d'un château sur une haute colline dans le district de Gondar-Zuria, canton de Emfraz. Il mesure 18 mètres en longeur, 12 mètres en largeur. (Une cheminée est aménagée dans le mur d'une salle.)

Description et étude, avec plan et photographies, dans l'article de G. Annequin. *Annales d'Ethiopie*. 1965. Tome VI, pp.22-25.

Non loin de cet édifice, sur une éminence au nord-est, se distinguent les vestiges très ruinés d'un établissement de l'époque gondarienne.

Il est devenu habituel d'attribuer la construction de cet édifice au roi Sartsa-Dengel, vers 1570 (cf. Monti Della Corte. *I Castelli di Gondar*. 1938, pp.105-108). Pourtant rien ne permet d'affirmer que ce château, avec ses particularités gondariennes, est bien celui qui bâtit Sartsa-Dengel. Il est très probable que ce château de Guzara fut construit sous le règne de Susenyos ou de Fasiladas.

Le nom de Guzara n'apparaît pas dans les écrits des Portugais. Il s'agit vraisemblablement du site de Coga ou Gubae nouveau (Gubai novo) des jésuites (P. Paez dans Beccari, II, p.203, et III, pp.136-137) au pays de Emfraz. Cf. I. Guidi, *Scriptores Aethiopici*, Chronique de Yohannes, p.18: "Enferaz, où est une tour ou une enceinte qui l'environne". Charles Poncet décrit: "Le palais de l'empereur est situé sur une éminence qui commande toute la ville". (*Voyage d'Ethiopie*. 1713, p.114).

27. METRAHA

C'est une île au nord-est du lac Tana relevant de l'administration du district de Gondar-Zuria, canton de Emfraz. Une demi-heure de tankwa permet de l'atteindre. L'île est quasi-déserte. Un ermite est son seul occupant humain. Une végétation épaisse cache les ruines d'une église ronde qui, selon la tradition, aurait été bâtie au temps du roi Alaf-Sagad-Yohannes (1667-1682), et détruite par les Derviches. Une partie du sanctuaire (*maqdas*) est conservée. Il était divisé en deux parties par un mur à arcatures.

Très délabré, un mausolée près de l'église contient la tombe de Iyasu I, mort en 1706. A Metraha furent ensevelis également Yostos, frère aîné de Yohannes, Yohannes-Alaf-Sagad mort en 1682, et Sabla-Wangel (Alaf-Mogesa), mère de Iyasu. (I. Guidi. *Scriptores Aethiopici*, pp.59, 150). Les sépultures sont sans identité. Partout des ossements éparpillés.

28. SAY-DEBBER

Ruine d'une église ronde au sommet d'une colline sur la rive occidentale du lac Tana, à 181 kilomètres au sud-ouest de Gondar, dans le district de Chilga et le canton de Alefa.

La tradition locale affirme que cette église de type gondarien (actuellement en cours de réfection) fut construite par Woyzero Maryam-Tsena, fille du Dedjaz Adwa.

29. NARGA-SELLASSIE

Église ronde construite, selon la tradition, aux frais de la reine Mentewab, sur la presqu'île de Narga qui aujourd'hui relève de l'administration de Bahr-Dar dans le Godjam. Cette église fut consacrée par le métropolite Yohannes (Ignazio Guidi. *Storia della letterature etiopica*. 1932, p.91).

Vingt-quatre piliers constituent la galerie extérieure. Des tours à coupoles sont élevées sur le mur d'enceinte.

30. WEMBERGHE (Pl.XII)

Pont au sud de Addis-Zamen sur la rivière Reb, dans le district de Libo, canton de Kamkam.

Il est brisé. Quatre arches subsistent. Sa longueur est de 34 mètres et sa largeur de 5 mètres. Orientation sud-est/nord-est.

Une description dans le livre de Maurizio Rava: *Al Lago Tsana*. Roma, 1913, p.93. "Senza parapetti, largo m.5.40, e lungo m.35; ha 5 archi disuguali di m.5.40, 4.87, 4.90, 4.86 del luce; dal letto asciutto e alto m.5.10. E ancora in buono stato, ma indubbia traccie indicano che presto cadrà se non si ripara". C'est en 1908 que M. Rava vit ce pont.

Une photographie dans Giotto Dainelli. *La Regione del Lago Tana*. 1939, tav.CXIX.

31. TCHEKLA-MENZO

Petite île au nord de Tana-Qirqos où sont les ruines d'une construction (château?) que la tradition attribue au roi Adyam-Sagad-Iyasu (1682-1706).

32. TANA-QIRQOS

Sur la péninsule de la rive est du lac, une église restaurée par les soins du ras Gugsa (premier quart du XIXe siècle), conserve quelques éléments d'architecture à dater du règne de Bakaffa.

33. ARINGO (Pl.XIIIa)

Important site archéologique au nord-ouest de Debra-Tabor, près des collines de Tayru-Giyorgis. (Alt. 2515m).

Un mur d'enceinte circulaire aux tourelles coniques enclôt un vaste espace. Dans la partie sud de l'enclos une construction singulière, de plan rectangulaire, divisée en trois parties, est appelée Af-Mekurabia. Elle mesure 9m 30 en longueur et 2m 35 en largeur. La couverture est détruite. Les murs, épais, montrent une grande solidité. Il est difficile de déterminer quel fut l'usage de cette construction d'un caractère unique dans l'architecture gondarienne. L'enduit sur les murs est comme glacé. On pense à un silo.

Les rivières Senkula, à l'ouest, et Atsié-Weha, à l'est, bordent le site qui s'étend sur un plateau.

Aringo n'apparaît pas dans les écrits des jésuites. A moins qu'au début du XVIIe siècle, au temps de Susenyos, le site n'ait été connu sous un autre nom; par exemple, les jésuites avaient une résidence à Atqhana dans le Begameder qu'il est malaisé de localiser, Beccari (Mendez) XII, p.282. Atqhana est peut-être l'ancien site de Aringo — simple hypothèse.

Aringo se manifeste historiquement au temps de Fasiladas qui y présida un synode dans la vingt-deuxième année de son règne. Plus tard, en ce même lieu, il y aurait brûlé les livres des jésuites. (Wallis Budge, *A History of Ethiopia*, p.398). Aringo fut la résidence temporaire des rois Yohannes, Iyasu I, Takla-Haymanot, Tewoflos et Bakaffa.

Cf. I. Guidi, *Scriptores Aethiopici*, Paris, 1903, p.9 (Yohannes). Ch. J. Poncet, *Voyage d'Ethiopie*, 1713:" Le palais d'Arringon n'est pas moins magnifique que celui de Gondar", p.97

34. REMA-MEDHANE-ALEM

Petite île non loin de Tana-Qirqos. Sur cette île, une église conserve un certain nombre d'objets d'intérêt historique et artistique parmi quoi des pierres sculptées dont les motifs ne sont pas totalement sans ressemblance avec quelques sculptures entreposées au château de Fasil à Gondar, et trouvées dans les environs. Ces pierres de Rema sont-elles les vestiges d'un ancien édifice gondarien (détruit) sur l'île ou bien y ont-elles été apportées?

Cf. Beccari, II, p.279.

Une église fut construite à Rema par le roi Yeshaq (1414-1429). Sarsa-Dengel fut inhumé sur cette île. (E. Pereira, *Chronica de Susenyos, rei de Ethiopia*, 1900, p.443).

35. KEBRAN-GABRIEL

Au sommet de l'île de Kebran, à l'ouest de Bahr-Dar, l'église de Gabriel — ronde, ceinte d'une galerie de douze piliers — fut bâtie en 1687 (début de la construction) sur ordre du roi Iyasu. (I. Guidi, *Scriptores Aethiopici*, 1903, p.109.)

36. BAHR-DAR-GIYORGIS (Pl.XIIIb)

Dans la ville de Bahr-Dar, près de l'église de Giyorgis, une haute construction carrée (hauteur: 8 mètres) n'est pas sans similitude avec celle de Menzoro-Tekla-Haymanot. Une particularité remarquable: sa couverture voûtée; rares sont les édifices gondariens qui aient conservé leur couverture d'origine. (Cf. Fr. Anfray, Vestiges gondariens, *Rassegna di Studi Etiopici*, 1981, pp.11 et 12. Photos 10 et 11. J. Duchesne-Fournet, *Mission en Ethiopie*, 1909, p.117.)

37. BAHR-DAR-MIKAEL

Une église ordinaire au sud de la ville, près du rivage. A côté, on voit un pan de mur gondarien avec merlons, vestiges d'anciennes constructions du temps de Adyam-Sagad-Iyasu, selon une tradition locale. Cf. Fr. Anfray, *Rassegna di Studi Etiopici*, 1981, vol. XXVIII, photo no.12.

38. TIS-ABBAY

Pont sur le Nil à trente kilomètres à l'est de Bahr-Dar. Il est fait de huit arches. Sa forme dessine une courbure. Sa longueur totale est de 64 mètres (36 mètres pour la première section et 28 mètres pour la seconde).

La tradition en attribue la construction au roi Fasiladas, comme il en va pour plusieurs autres monuments. Au dire de Jeronimo Lobo (*Itinerario*, p.234, Hakluyt Society, 1984), il fut construit au temps de Susenyos, avec l'aide d'ouvriers indiens: "the first permanent one that the Nile saw over it". D'après Almeida, la construction eut lieu en 1626 (Cf. C. F. Beckhingham and G. W. B. Huntingford, *Some records of Ethiopia*, 1954, pp.26 et 27; et C. Beccari, VII, p.231). Le site du pont était appelé Alata: "ad Alata . . . a fabro coementario, quem nobiscum ab india . . . Sub unicum arcum fuit". (Mendez dans Beccari, VIII, p.32). Les chutes sont en amont; Tis-Isat est le nom qui leur est donné.

Avec ses huit arches aujourd'hui, le pont de Tis-Abbay n'est pas identique à celui que décrit Lobo. On pourrait même se demander s'il s'agit du même emplacement. Lobo signale "a place where the rock, arching on both sides toward the middle, brings the two edges at the top so close together that, because the distance is so short from one side to the other, some of the boldest people dare to cross the great Nile here in one jump" (p.233). Il est probable que le pont de Susenyos fut bien bâti à cet endroit, puis postérieurement détruit, ensuite à une époque indéterminée rebâti avec plus de hauteur et de longueur.

Achille Raffray (*Abyssinie*, Paris, 1876, pp.252-253) présente un dessin de ce pont. Il comporte six arches (description p.298 et 299). On y voit une échauguette.

Maurizio Rava décrit ce pont dans son ouvrage *Al Lago Tsana*, 1913, p.134 et suivantes. En page 136, il note: "Il ponte ha un'arcata grande, quattro arcate minori e tre piccoli archetti". Donc huit arches. D'où il faut conclure que si le dessin de Raffray est exact, le pont de Tis-Abbay a été partiellement reconstruit entre 1874 et 1908, date de la visite de Rava.

Dans le livre de R. E. Cheesman, *Lake Tana and the Blue Nile*, 1936, p.226, une photo du pont de Tis-Abbay.

Le pont d'aujourd'hui a été largement restauré il y a une dizaine d'années par les soins de l'administration éthiopienne du patrimoine culturel.

39. YIBABA

Dans le district de Bahr-Dar et le canton de Adiet, au site de Yibaba, un mur circulaire enferme un vaste espace de vestiges archéologiques. Le mur comporte tours et porches.

Cf. Fr. Anfray, Vestiges gondariens, *Rassegna di Studi Etiopici*, 1981, vol.XXVIII, pp.12-14. Photos 13, 14, 15. Plan E.

Ce site est souvent mentionné dans les chroniques anciennes à partir du roi Yohannes. Cf. Ignazio Guidi, *Scriptores Aethiopici*, 1903, p.12 et suivantes.

Cf. C. Annaratone, *In Abyssinia*, 1914, p.252. Photo 94.

40. GEMB-MARYAM

Au sommet d'une colline dans le district de Bahr-Dar, canton de Metcha, s'élèvent les murs en grande partie conservés d'une ancienne église catholique. Cf. Fr. Anfray, Vestiges gondariens, *Rassegna di Studi Etiopici*, Vol. XXVIII. 1 & 81, pp.15-17. Photos 19, 20, 21, 22. Plan G.

Il semble bien que ce site soit à identifier avec celui de Serka des jésuites portugais. Si l'identification est correcte, l'église fut construite en 1625 (Almeida dans Beccari, VI, p.427), et dédiée à "Virgem Maria Senhora".

41. GEMB-GIYORGIS

A cinq cents mètres environ de Gemb-Maryam, sur une autre colline, d'importantes ruines sont vraisemblablement celles d'une ancienne résidence jésuite (Serka).

Cf. Almeida dans Beccari, VI, p.427 et VII, p.565. (Seela-Krestos). Fr. Anfray, Vestiges gondariens, *Rassegna di Studi Etiopici*, XXVIII, 1981, pp.14-15; photos 16, 17, 18, plan F.

42. SABARA-DILDIY (Pl.XIVa, b, c, d)

Pont sur le Nil dans le Godjam, district de Mota, canton de Hulet-Yidju-Ennessie.

Il est porté sur la carte d'Antoine d'Abbadie, *Géodésie d'Ethiopie*, 1873. 2e partie.

Ce pont est brisé dans sa partie médiane (et grossièrement réparé avec des branches et des trons d'arbres). Il est courbe et comporte dix arches. Sa longueur est de 63 mètres; sa largeur de 3m 50 et sa hauteur au milieu, sur l'eau du fleuve, de 12m 60.

Il a été restauré au temps de Menelik, environ 1906, ainsi que l'indique une inscription sur la porte bastionnée construite à l'entrée du pont au sud-ouest. (Nombreux aujourd'hui sont les gens qui utilisent ce pont, – notamment les pélerins de Lalibela.)

Dans le livre de Sigfrid Siwerz, *En färd till Abessinien*, Stockholm, 1926, pp.226-227, deux photos du pont — qui apparaît en bon état, conséquence vraisemblablement de la restauration du temps de Menelik; depuis lors, il a été de nouveau brisé.

43. QOLELA-KIDANE-MEHRET (Pl.XV)

C'est aujourd'hui une église ronde du nom de Yewezazert-Kidane-Mehret. De caractère traditionnel, elle ne semble pas d'une grande ancienneté, dans sa reconstruction tout au moins. (Elle était fermée lors de la visite.)

Près de cette église s'élève un haut édifice carré de maçonnerie gondarienne, avec un escalier extérieur sur le côté ouest. Cet édifice est assez semblable à celui de Bahr-Dar-Giyorgis. (Il abrite une cloche dans sa partie haute.)[7]

Il n'est guère douteux qu'il s'agisse de l'ancien site de Qolela (résidence jésuite où, en 1626, fut bâtie une église dans le fief du Ras Seela-Krestos).

Emmanuel d'Almeida dans C. Beccari, VI, p.500. Numéro 43 sur la carte de Emmanuel d'Almeida (Beccari, I).

44. GEMB-KIDANE-MEHRET

Dans le district de Bahr-Dar, canton de Adiet, au sud de la route, au sommet d'une colline, un haut pan de mur s'élève au milieu de ruines. Il témoigne d'une grande construction. Restes d'un château bâti pour le ras Seela-Krestos, frère de Susenyos?

45. ABBA-GIS-FASIL

Dans le district de Fenote-Selam, canton de Sakala, au sud de Bahr-Dar dans le Godjam, sur un piton rocheux s'érigent les hauts murs d'une ancienne construction de type gondarien. Ce site est aussi appelé Akesken-Maryam et Atchano (noms de villages voisins). Cf. Fr. Anfray, Notes archéologiques, *Annales d'Ethiopie*, 1970, VIII, pp.32 et 34, pl.III et IV.

N'y a-t-il pas un rapprochement à faire entre ce site et l'établissement des jésuites appelé Ligenegus ou Gabreramo. (Beccari, VI, pp.493 et 533; VII, p.519) au Damot? Le numéro 41 de la carte de Emmanuel d'Almeida.

46. MERTULA-MARYAM (Pl.XVI)

Dans le Godjam, district de Mota, canton de Ennebse-Sarmeder, au sommet d'une colline se dressent les hauts murs (en partie écroulés) de ce qui fut une église rectangulaire, à trois nefs, de maçonnerie gondarienne. La toiture a disparu. Subsistent, aux encadrements des ouvertures notamment, de nombreuses pierres ornées de motifs géométriques (pour la plupart) finement sculptés. Ces motifs ne sont pas identiques à ceux qu'on voit dans la région de Gondar. Quelques-unes de ces sculptures représentent des figures humaines et aussi des ornements floraux.

Ce sont les restes — importants — d'une église reconstruite au temps de Susenyos (1628) par le jésuite romain Bruno Bruni sur les ruines et avec les matériaux de celle qui avait été élevée, à la fin du XVe siècle par les soins de la reine Heleni, veuve de Baeda-Maryam, avec l'aide d'artisans égyptiens si l'on en croit Emmanuel d'Almeida: "mandou vir os offiçiaes do Egypto . . . . que eras primos em sua arte" (Dans Beccari, V, p.250). Cette église ancienne fut détruite par les bandes de l'imam Ahmad et par les Oromo. Elle était quadrangulaire "mas ornada e dotada com larguesa". Almeida vit dans les ruines des "pedras muito grandes" ainsi que des "rozas varias" (p.251). Le site de Mertula-Maryam est le plus souvent appelé Nebesse par les jésuites. C'est le numéro 35 de la carte de Emmanuel d'Almeida (Beccari, I, p.306). Elle n'était pas totalement achevée au départ des jésuites en 1633.

C. Beccari, VI, p.484; VII, p.437; XII, pp.258, 460-461; VIII, p.192. Une citerne y aurait été aménagée. Beccari, IV, p.198.

Deux autres églises ont été construites par la suite dans l'enclos sacré, près des ruines. Des fouilles révèleraient sans doute des vestiges d'une époque antérieure à celle de la reine Heleni. Le donnent à penser quelques pierres sculptées (rinceau) déterrées à l'occasion de terrassements.

Au sujet de Mertula-Maryam, cf. Ch. T. Beke, Description of the Ruins of the Church of Martula-Maryam, *Archaeologia*, vol. XXXII, 1847. Beke visita le site en 1842 et grava son nom sur une pierre du monument.

C. Annarotone. *In Abissinia*, 1914, p.184. E. Cerulli, Arte Italiana nelle sculture di Martula-Maryam, dans *Africa Italiana*, 1933, vol. V, no.1-2, pp.107-112.

47. DEBRA-WORQ

Dans cette localité, au sommet d'une colline, près d'une église qui n'est pas ancienne, une tour carrée de maçonnerie gondarienne.

Combes et Tamisier; *Voyage en Abyssinie*, 1839, III, p.274.

M. de Coppet, *Chronique du règne de Menelik II par Guebre Sellassie*, p.563.

48. WONGHE (Pl.XVIIa)

Pont de quatre arches sur la rivière Birr, à douze kilomètres de Fenote-Selam (est), au sud de la grand-route d'où il est visible. District de Kola-Dega-Damot.

Longueur (préservée): 34m 30. Largeur: 4m 10. Il comporte des parapets sur toute sa longueur. Il est en partie ruiné, notamment à l'extrémité sud-ouest.

Un point requiert quelque attention. L'italien Augusto Salimbeni — assisté par le maître maçon Giuseppe Andreoni — construisit du 15 décembre 1884 au 26 mars 1885 un pont sur la rivière Temcià (Temsha) "che si versa nell Birr". Cette construction fut entreprise à la demande du roi Tekla-Haymanot. Le roi du Godjam voulait un pont "ricordando quelle costruito in altri secoli dai Lusitani", rapporte Salimbeni (*Tre anni di lavoro nel Gojjiam*, 1886, Boll. Soc. Geogr. Ital., II, vol. XI). Voir également, dans le bulletin de la société italienne: "Il Conte A. Salimbeni ed il suo ponte sul Temcià" où figure un dessin du pont, d'après lequel le pont est à trois arches (une arche médiane de 8m 50 de corde encadrée de deux petites arches symétriques). Il mesure 38 mètres en longueur et 4 mètres en largeur.

Ce pont présente donc à peu près les mêmes dimensions que le pont de Wonghe. Salimbeni parle de la rivière Temcià "qui se jette dans le Birr". On est dans les mêmes parages. On pourrait se demander s'il n'y a pas confusion de noms et si le pont de Wonghe ne serait pas l'oeuvre de Salimbeni. Il est curieux que dans sa relation l'italien ne fasse pas état du pont ancien. Une allusion semble cependant s'y déceler quand il parle, au singulier, de "quello costruito in altri secoli dai Lusitani". Surtout entre les deux ponts il y a d'importantes différences: le pont de Salimbeni possède trois arches, celui de Wonghe, quatre. Et les profils n'ont guère de rapport.

Une enquête locale permettra de résoudre assez facilement cette question.

Giuseppe Andreoni aurait par la suite construit un autre pont — d'une seule arche de quatorze mètres — sur la rivière Ghedev dans le Damot (*Tre Anni*, p.291).

49. TCHAGA (Pl.XVIIb)

Pont sur la rivière Gour, non loin de Debra-Libanos dans le Shoa, district de Selale, canton de Djarso. Il comporte trois arches.

Sa longueur est de 37 mètres, sa largeur de 3m 35, sa hauteur, au milieu de 10 mètres.

Comme pour le précédent, ce pont de Tchaga suscite une interrogation. Selon la tradition locale, rapportée par des habitants du voisinage, il aurait été construit sur ordre du ras Darghè, fils du roi Sahle-Sellassie et oncle de Menelik, dans les dernières années du dix-neuvième siècle. (Le ras Darghè résidait souvent à Fitché dont il gouvernait le pays; il mourut en 1900).

Ce pont dans sa structure et sa maçonnerie offre une similitude tellement étroite avec les autres ponts gondariens qu'il faut peut-être comprendre qu'au temps de Menelik il a fait l'objet d'une restauration — comme au début du vingtième siècle il en a été pour Sabara-Dildiy dans le Godjam.

Quelques remarques

L'étude détaillée et approfondie de ces sites reste à faire. Certains furent des établissements importants par leur superficie, par le nombre et la qualité de leurs monuments, pendant des périodes plus ou moins longues: ainsi Gorgora, Ganata-Iyasus (Azazo), Danqaz, Emfraz (Guzara), Aringo, Yibaba. Des fouilles archéologiques apporteront des éclaircissements sur l'histoire de ces sites, en révèleront de nouveaux aspects. On découvrira de nombreux éléments qui documenteront le dossier de l'économie domestique aux XVIIe et XVIIIe siècles. Un type spécial de poterie fut alors fabriqué dont on possède quelques vestiges — notamment des vases de bonne facture à couverte orange.

Ces études, qui devront s'accompagner du relevé des monuments, favoriseront graduellement l'établissement d'une chronologie. Elles permettront de déterminer avec précision les facteurs qui furent aux origines de l'architecture gondarienne.

A cet égard, si l'on considère la formule mise en oeuvre (programme, mode de construction, appareil), il apparaît que cette architecture n'est pas la simple imitation d'un style dont on trouverait le modèle au Portugal, en Inde ou en quelque autre contrée. Pour dire les choses en quelques mots, cette formule a été en partie élaborée localement; elle emploie divers éléments structurels de provenance extérieure[8] (l'Inde des comptoirs portugais notamment); elle les combine de telle manière que voit le jour une forme particulière d'édifice.

La période de formation fut de brève durée. Le site de Gorgora, au nord du lac Tana, en fut le cadre géographique (Ombabaqua ou le vieux Gorgora). Plusieurs indications montrent que l'architecture gondarienne prit son essor dans les années vingt du dix-septième siècle, principalement lorsque fut trouvé le moyen de faire ce mortier de chaux qui assurât solidité et durée aux édifices ("prometem longa duraçao de tempo" comme dit Barradas, dans Beccari, IV, p.272). Ce fait d'ordre technique se produisit en 1624 à Azazo, d'après les témoignages d'Emmanuel d'Almeida et d'Affonso Mendez qui, avec Emmanuel Barradas, attribuent à Manoel Magro le mérite de la découverte.

Manoel Magro était un prêtre, d'origine indienne vraisemblablement, secrétaire (capellao) de Mendez. (Beccari, V, p.76; VI, p.390; VIII, pp.32 et 111; XII, pp.449, 443, 583.)

Almeida (Beccari, V, p.76) rapporte: "hum homen da India curioso descubriu huma costa de pedra meuda, leve e como carcomida, de quel no Guzarate pela parte de Baroche tinha visto fazer cal ou chunambo como lhe chamao na India e ca a chamo Nura". Et encore (Beccari, VI, p.390): "Veo com nosco da India . . . Manoel Magro: no anno de 1624 tinha visto em algumas terras de Cambaya, certa laya de pedra de que ali fazio chunambo, e notando bem em varias partes de Ethiopia achou outra semelhante: meteua no fogo, cozeuse, sayo chunambo ou cal excellente". Il ajoute ces détails: "deu Manoel Magro ao Emperador o alvitre, nostroulhe a pedra e o modo como se cozia e fazia cal; estimouo grandemente e deulhe boas alviçaras, e logo, acabado o inverno, no fin do ano de 1624 começou em Ganeta Jesus iunto a igrea huns fermosos paços de pedra e cal, de dous sobrados, com seu terrado, duas salas, e coatro camaras nos baixos e outras tantas nos altos, afora dous como cubellos ou baluartes em dous cantos com que ficarao seguros e com alguma semalhança de fortaleza". — Et page 575: "Manoel Magro, homem da India".

Negativement, Paez qui mourut en 1622 écrivait: "As igreias que nostos tempos edifiçao, todas sao de pedra e barro, que nemhuma cal entra nellas" (Dans C. Beccari, II, p.493) ou encore (p.203): "Nem os muros eram de argamasa, que chunambo nam tinham".

Après 1624, tous les monuments (châteaux, églises, ponts, plusieurs demeures) seront faits "de pedra e cal" selon l'expression maintes fois employée dans les écrits des jésuites.

Des artisans indiens, venus à la suite des jésuites, s'installèrent dans le pays.[9] Emmanuel d'Almeida et Jeronimo Lobo à plusieurs reprises font état des activités de ces artisans. Un ambassadeur yéménite, à Gondar en 1648, note que le constructeur du château de Fasiladas est un indien. Ces faits ne signifient nullement que les Ethiopiens ne possédaient aucune tradition architecturale et que dans certaines régions, antérieurement au dix-septième siècle, ils n'utilisèrent pas un mortier de chaux dans leurs constructions. Merid Wolde-Aregay a rappelé avec raison que les Ethiopiens n'attendirent pas les jésuites et leurs auxilliaires indiens (ou autres) pour bâtir – aux quinzième et seizième siècles notamment – des édifices qui firent l'admiration des visiteurs.[10] Il discute aussi la question de la chaux et signale qu'il existe dans des textes éthiopiens de date ancienne des mots comme *genfal* et *nora* pour désigner ce produit – mots qui ne sauraient revendiquer une origine indienne, et dont l'existence signale en effet qu'un certain type de chaux était connu. Il mentionne un passage d'Emmanuel Barradas selon lequel une église ronde à Asmara, antérieure au dix-septième siècle, où se remarquent: "alguns arcos pequenos, mas muy bem feitos e acabados todas de tijolos e cal". (dans Beccari, IV, p.269). On peut ajouter à ces observations judicieuses que dans le Tigray d'antiques monuments de la période post-axoumite montrent l'emploi d'un mortier de chaux dans la maçonnerie: l'édifice ruiné de Agoula-Tcherqos à 270 kilomètres au sud d'Asmara, près de la grand-route, et non loin, le monument de Nazret. (Fr. Anfray, *Notes archéologiques*, 1970. Vol. VIII, pp.37, 39 et 40.)

Il n'en demeure pas moins qu'au dix-septième siècle, avant la troisième décennie, l'usage de la chaux n'est pas attesté dans l'architecture des régions occidentales (Begamder et Godjam).

On considère habituellement que deux édifices sont les prototypes de l'architecture gondarienne: l'église de Barie-Gemb et le château de Guzara. Ils dateraient du seizième siècle l'un et l'autre. Ces deux constructions présentent toutes les caractéristiques gondariennes – singulièrement le château de Guzara. La chronique de Sartsa-Dengel rapporte que ce roi, en 1572, "établit sa résidence à Dobit". Dobit (aujourd'hui) est le nom d'une rivière au sud de la colline de Guzara. L'édifice de Guzara serait celui que Sartsa-Dengel fit construire. Mais l'indication de la chronique n'est pas explicite quant à la structure de l'édifice ("belle construction et d'un extérieur admirable"). Nulle autre description n'est fournie. Il faut au contraire conjecturer que le château de Guzara, campé en solitaire hautain, sur une colline du pays d'Emfraz, ne s'identifie pas avec la résidence royale de Sartsa-Dengel. Il s'agit selon toute vraisemblance d'une construction d'époque ultérieure. Et ainsi en va-t-il très probablement pour l'église de Barie-Gemb.

Si, comme il existe des raisons fortes de l'admettre, l'emploi d'un mortier de chaux (de type spécifique) dans les édifices gondariens a débuté environ 1624, peut-on sans incohérence soutenir la thèse de l'antériorité chronologique de ces monuments dans lesquels ce mortier est pleinement utilisé? D'autre part, est-il concevable que ces édifices de structure gondarienne évidente (toutes les caractéristiques "gondariennes" s'y discernent) aient été bâtis plus de quarante ans avant les monuments de Gorgora et de Gannata-Iyasus qui par leur nouveauté suscitèrent l'admiration des contemporains, ainsi que le rapportent les écrits d'époque? Et comment Pedo Paez qui se déplaça dans la région, ainsi que Merid Wolde-Aregay le relève, ne les aurait-il pas vus (en 1604, à Ondegue au sud du lac, il observait "humas casas muyto altas", Beccari, III, p.238)? Le château de Guzara, s'il n'est pas un ouvrage du temps de Susenyos dont on sait cependant qu'il se rendait à Emfraz, a pu être construit sous le règne de Fasiladas ou sous celui d'un de ses successeurs immédiats. Yohannes et Iyasu Adyam Sagad faisaient des séjours à Emfraz (I. Guidi, *Scriptores Aethiopici*, 1903. pp.13, 15, 16, 60, 62, 66, 99, 117, 126, 153, 157, 172). Ces rois furent des bâtisseurs. On remarquera que dans les textes figurent très peu d'indications sur les édifices que pourtant ils firent élever à Gondar, Aringo, Yebaba, Tchekla-Manzo et ailleurs.

Il semble bien qu'à Gorgora, en 1614, furent créés les rudiments du style gondarien, avec l'édifice de deux étages (Babet-Laybet) construits d'après les indications de Paez. Dans les années suivantes d'autres bâtiments y furent élevés. Les descriptions de Paez, Almeida, Azevedo[11], notamment, révèlent que ces édifices dans leur structure possédaient plusieurs des éléments constitutifs de l'architecture gondarienne. Il y a lieu de présumer que les maçons éthiopiens qui sans nul doute participèrent largement à l'oeuvre de construction introduisirent dans les édifices une part de leurs traditions propres dont on peut penser que Paez lui-même (ses remarques au sujet de Ondegue) ne dédaigna pas de s'inspirer.

NOTES

1. Il convient de noter que l'architecture "gondarienne" ne remplaça pas l'architecture traditionnelle. A la même époque les types traditionnels (séculaires) de construction continuèrent d'être élevés. Constructions domestiques et églises rondes couvertes de chaume.

2. Ce que, dans leurs écrits, les Portugais constatent – et il semble d'ailleurs que le côté défensif n'ait pas été négligé. Cf. Almeida dans Beccari, VI, p.497: "nossas igreias e residencias era fortalezas".

3. Cf. Dainelli G., *La Regione del Lago Tana*, 1939. Tav.CXIV. Et R. E. Cheesman, *Lake Tana and the Blue Nile*, 1936, p.133 (Kota-Maryam).

4. Ce nom apparaît dans une chronique éthiopienne de l'époque. Cf. E. Pereira, *Chronica de Susenyos, re de Ethiopia*, 1900, p.199. "Frange, mestre de construçao; cujo nome era Padri Pay", dans la traduction de Pereira.

5. Mendez parle d'inscriptions à Danqaz, dans Beccari, XII, p.381: "Aparelhouse huma grande e fermosa pedra com letras emtalhadas em amara e portugues e muito bem pintadas".

6. Cf. J. Perruchon, Notes pour l'histoire d'Ethiopie, *Revue sémitique*, 1896, pp.77 et 184 (Chronique éthiopienne).

7. Les jésuites firent construire des clochers. Cf. E. d'Almeida, dans Beccari, VI, p.388, (torre de sinos), et Azevedo, dans Beccari, XI, p.417: "torrinha pera os sinos".

8. Des indications à ce sujet dans les écrits de Paez (Beccari, II, p.457), Almeida (Beccari, VI, p.293), Mendez (Beccari, VIII, p.105).

9. R. Pankhurst, The History of Ethiopia's Relations with India prior to the Nineteenth Century, *IV Congresso Internazionale di Studi Etiopici*, Roma 1974, pp.205-311.
    Three urban precursors of Gondar: Emfraz, Gorgora and Danqaz, *Proceedings of the Fifth International Conference on Ethiopian Studies*, Chicago 1978, pp.415-429.
    History of Ethiopian Towns, Viesbaden 1982, p.94 et suivantes.

10. Merid Wolde Aregay, Society and Technology in Ethiopia 1500-1800, *Journal of Ethiopian Studies*, Vol. XVII, 1984, pp.134-137 spécialement.

11. Beccari, XI, p.417.

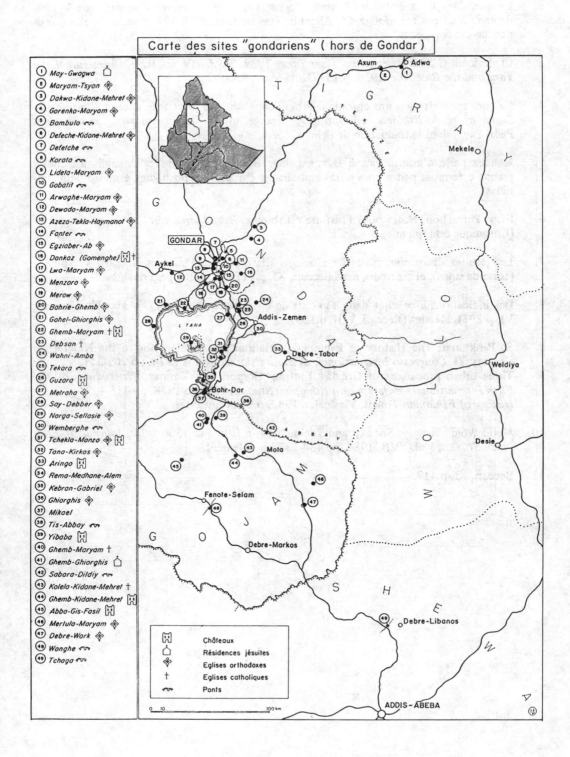

Carte des sites "gondariens" (hors de Gondar)

①	May-Gwagwa
②	Maryam-Tsyon
③	Dakwa-Kidane-Mehret
④	Gorenko-Maryam
⑤	Bambulo
⑥	Defeche-Kidane-Mehret
⑦	Defetche
⑧	Korata
⑨	Lideta-Maryam
⑩	Gobatit
⑪	Arwaghe-Maryam
⑫	Dewado-Maryam
⑬	Azezo-Tekla-Haymanot
⑭	Fanter
⑮	Egziaber-Ab
⑯	Dankoz (Gomenghe)
⑰	Lwa-Maryam
⑱	Menzoro
⑲	Merow
⑳	Bahrie-Ghemb
㉑	Gohel-Ghiorghis
㉒	Ghemb-Maryam
㉓	Debson
㉔	Wahni-Amba
㉕	Tekara
㉖	Guzara
㉗	Metraha
㉘	Say-Debber
㉙	Narga-Sellasie
㉚	Wemberghe
㉛	Tchekla-Manzo
㉜	Tana-Kirkos
㉝	Aringo
㉞	Rema-Medhane-Alem
㉟	Kebran-Gabriel
㊱	Ghiorghis
㊲	Mikael
㊳	Tis-Abbay
㊴	Yibaba
㊵	Ghemb-Maryam
㊶	Ghemb-Ghiorghis
㊷	Sabara-Dildiy
㊸	Kolela-Kidane-Mehret
㊹	Ghemb-Kidane-Mehret
㊺	Abba-Gis-Fasil
㊻	Mertula-Maryam
㊼	Debre-Work
㊽	Wonghe
㊾	Tchaga

Légende:
- 🏰 Châteaux
- ⛪ Résidences jésuites
- ✣ Eglises orthodoxes
- † Eglises catholiques
- ⌒ Ponts

0   10   100 km

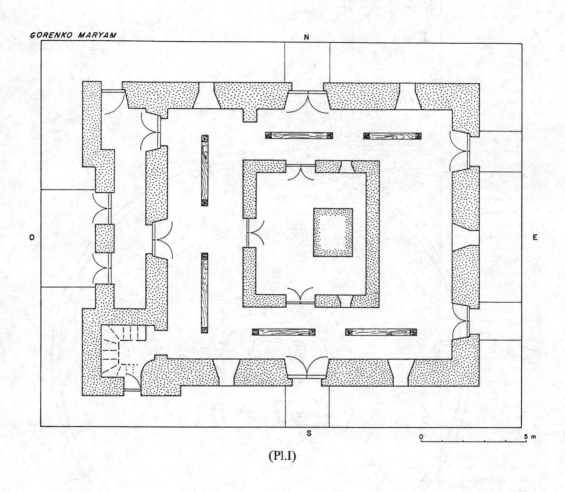

GORENKO MARYAM

(Pl.I)

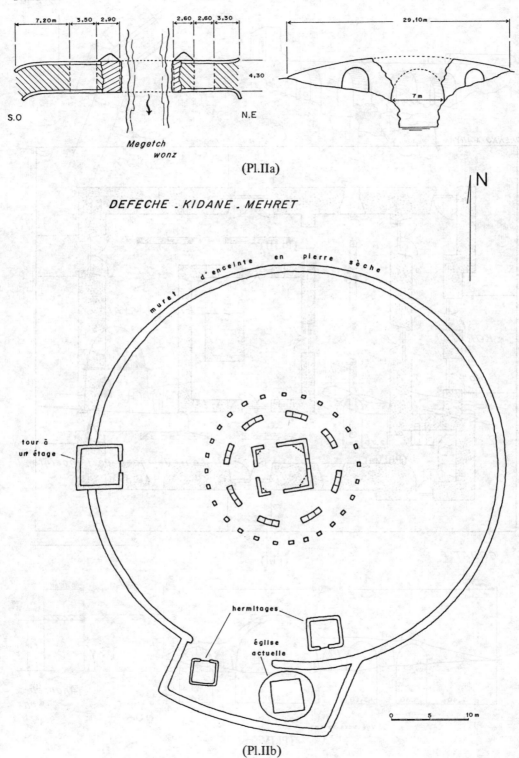

BAMBULO

7,20m 3,50 2,90   2,60 2,60 3,30

4,30

S.O   N.E

Megetch
wonz

(Pl.IIa)

29,10m

7 m

N

DEFECHE - KIDANE - MEHRET

muret d'enceinte en pierre sèche

tour à
un étage

hermitages

église
actuelle

0   5   10 m

(Pl.IIb)

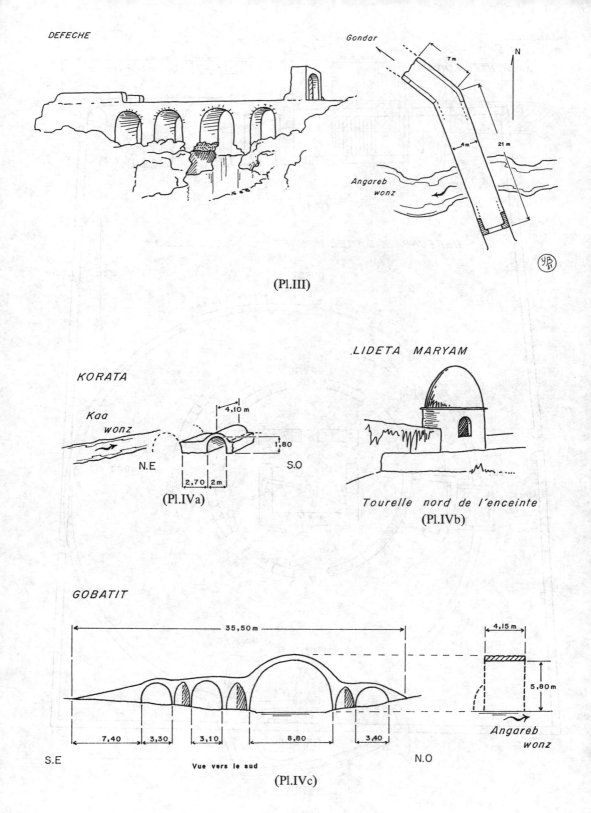

DEFECHE

Gondar

Angareb
wonz

(Pl.III)

KORATA

Kaa
wonz

N.E

4,10 m

1,80

2,70 2m

S.O

(Pl.IVa)

.LIDETA MARYAM

Tourelle nord de l'enceinte
(Pl.IVb)

GOBATIT

35,50 m

4,15 m

5,80 m

Angareb
wonz

7,40   3,30   3,10   8,80   3,40

S.E

Vue vers le sud

N.O

(Pl.IVc)

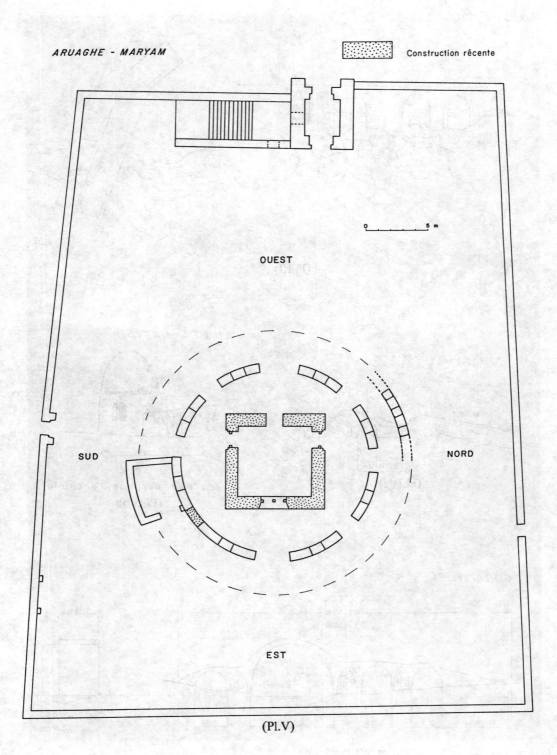

ARUAGHE - MARYAM

Construction récente

0   5 m

OUEST

SUD

NORD

EST

(Pl.V)

30

(Pl.Vb)

(Pl.Vc)

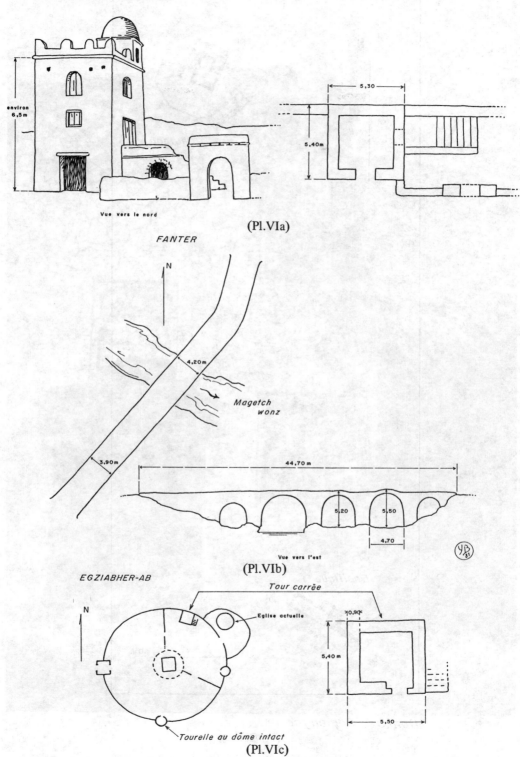

AZEZO - TEKLA - HAYMANOT

environ
6,5 m

5,30

5,40m

Vue vers le nord

(Pl.VIa)

FANTER

N

4,20 m

Magetch
wonz

3,90 m

44,70 m

5,20   5,50

4,70

Vue vers l'est

(Pl.VIb)

EGZIABHER-AB

Tour carrée

N

Eglise actuelle

0,90

5,40 m

5,50

Tourelle au dôme intact

(Pl.VIc)

33

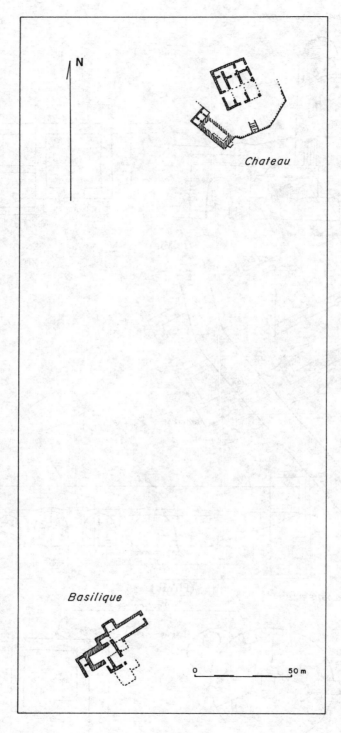

Chateau

Basilique

0   50 m

Dankaz Gomenghe

(Pl. VII)

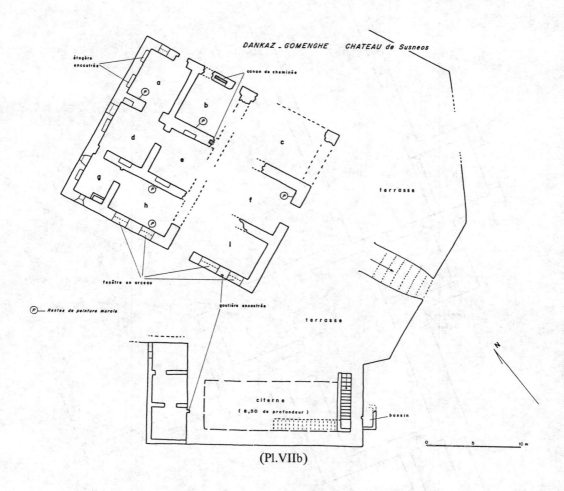

DANKAZ _ GOMENGHE   CHATEAU de Susneos

étagère encastrée

canon de cheminée

a

b

d

e

c

terrasse

g

h

f

i

fenêtre en arceau

goutière encastrée

terrasse

Ⓟ Restes de peinture murale

citerne
(8,30 de profondeur)

bassin

N

0   5   10 m

(Pl.VIIb)

Basilique de DANKAZ GOMENGHE

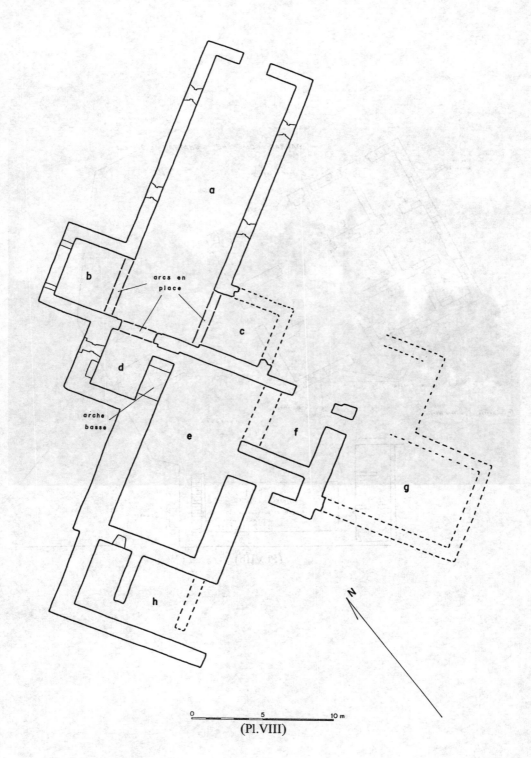

(Pl.VIII)

36

(Pl.IX)

TEKARA

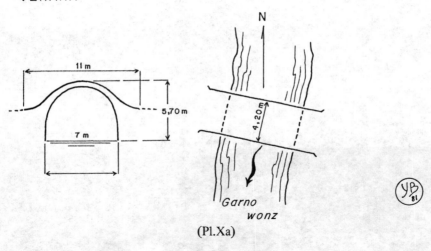

11 m

5,70 m

7 m

N

4,20 m

Garno wonz

(Pl.Xa)

GUZARA

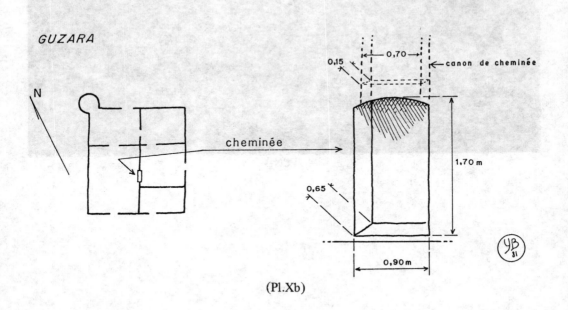

N

cheminée

0,15

0,70

canon de cheminée

1,70 m

0,65

0,90 m

(Pl.Xb)

(Pl.XI)

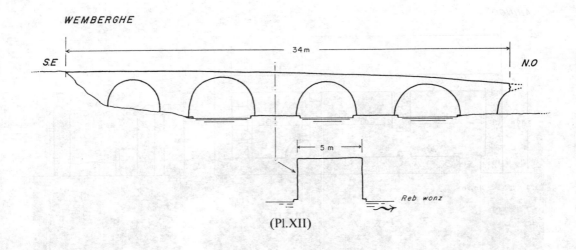

WEMBERGHE

S.E

N.O

34 m

5 m

Reb wonz

(Pl. XII)

(Pl. XIIb)

40

ARINGO

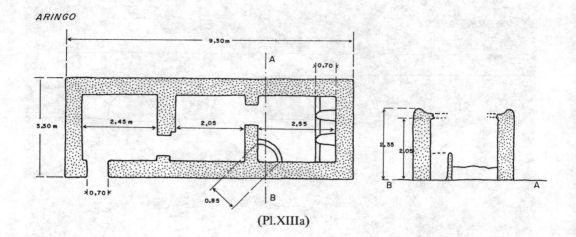

(Pl.XIIIa)

GHIORGHIS (Bahr - Dar)

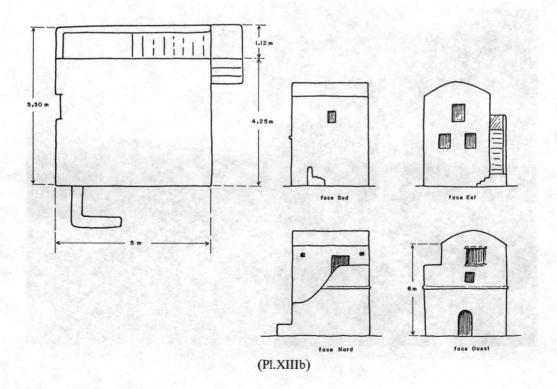

face Sud

face Est

face Nord

face Ouest

(Pl.XIIIb)

41

(Pl.XIVa)

(Pl.XIVb)

(Pl.XIVc)

SABARA - DILDIY

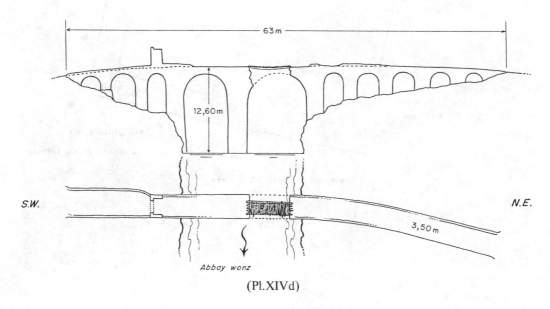

(Pl.XIVd)

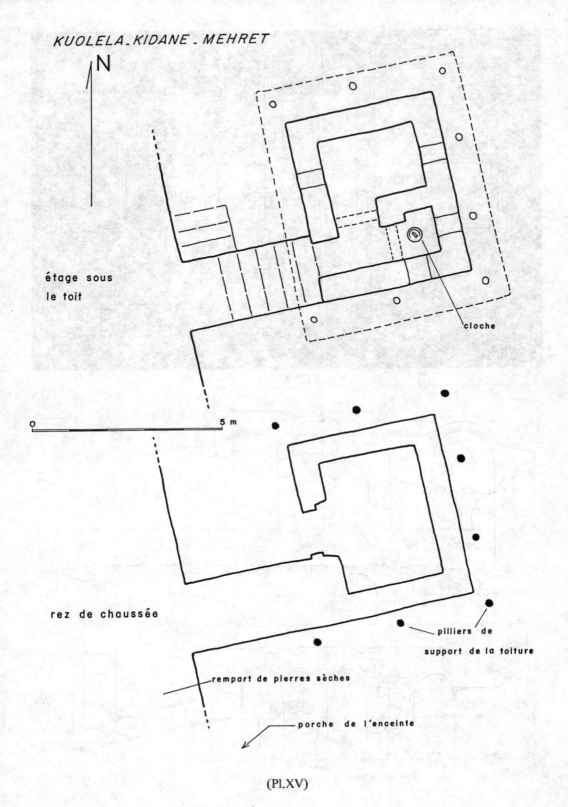

KUOLELA-KIDANE-MEHRET

N

étage sous
le toit

cloche

0   5 m

rez de chaussée

pilliers de
support de la toiture

rempart de pierres sèches

porche de l'enceinte

(Pl.XV)

44

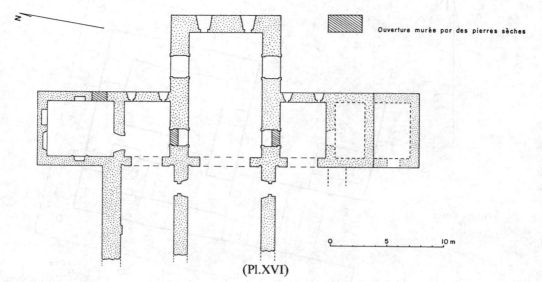

Ouverture murée par des pierres sèches

(Pl.XVI)

WONGHE

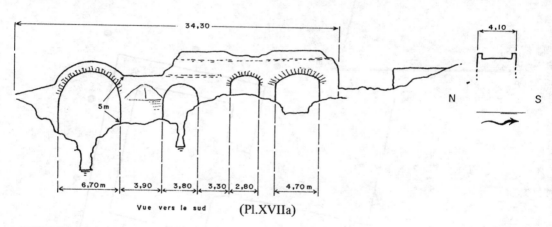

34,30

4,10

N   S

5m

6,70 m | 3,90 | 3,80 | 3,30 | 2,80 | 4,70 m

Vue vers le sud   (Pl.XVIIa)

TCHAGA

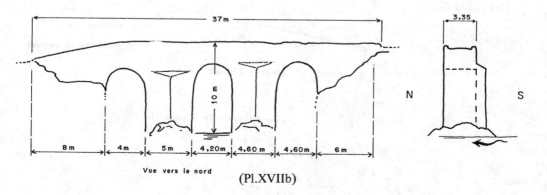

37 m

3,35

N   S

8 m | 4 m | 5 m | 4,20 m | 4,60 m | 4,60 m | 6 m

Vue vers le nord   (Pl.XVIIb)

LE GISEMENT PALEOLITHIQUE DE MELKA–KUNTURE

EVOLUTION et CULTURE

Jean Chavaillon

Melka-Kunturé est un gisement de vallée situé à 50 km. des sources de l'Awash, à 2000 m. sur les Hauts Plateaux éthiopiens. C'est un site exceptionnel en ce sens que l'on trouve dans le même milieu des vestiges d'une occupation continue depuis une période antérieure à 1.6 M.A. jusqu'à l'ère chrétienne. Plus d'une trentaine de couches archéologiques, tous sols d'habitat ont été fouillés. Certains niveaux d'occupation ont livré plus de 14.000 artefacts et les fouilles couvrent parfois 250 m² ce qui permet de se faire une opinion raisonnable sur le matériel technique et sur le mode de vie des occupants. Il s'intègre dans le système de fractures de la Rift Valley. On y trouve principalement de cailloutis, des sables et des argiles ainsi que les produits de l'altération des roches volcaniques qui cernent le site. Les sédiments ont été fréquemment détruits par l'action des phénomènes d'erosion; puis il y eu de nombreux dépôts fluviatiles emboîtés dans les formations antérieures. Enfin des cinérites (Tuff ou cendres volcaniques) viennent rompre heureusement les séries fluviatiles; elles sont d'excellents niveaux repères, d'un gisement à l'autre mais permettent également d'obtenir des datations absolues par la méthode du K/Ar.

On trouve à Melka-Kunturé le témoignage des grandes civilisations d'Afrique orientale: Oldowayen, Acheuléen, Middle Stone Age et Late Stone Age. Dans le cadre d'une équipe multidisciplinaire, J. Chavaillon a demandé à des géologues, paléontologues et préhistoriens de collaborer à une action commune. Les fouilles de Gomboré IB, Garba XII et Garba I ont été effectuées par J. et N. Chavaillon, celle de Gomboré I par J. L. Boisaubert, de Garba IV par G. et M. Piperno, de Gomboré II et de Simbirro par Cl. Brahimi et O. Oussedik, enfin celles de Garba III par Fr. Hours.

Plusieurs sites recèlent des sols d'occupation oldowayens (pré-acheuléen). Une chronologie a pu être établie de 1.7 à 1.3 M.A. Onze niveaux ont été prospectés. Parmi les sols oldowayens (1.7 – 1.6 M.A.) ceux de Gomboré IB sont les plus anciens avec de nombreux galets aménagés. N. Chavaillon découvrit, mêlé aux outils, l'humérus d'un Homo erectus archaïque. Le site de Garba IV, Oldowayan évolué (1.4 – 1.3 M.A.) est encore plus riche en pièces lithiques et vestiges de faune. M. Piperno découvrit dans un niveau de base daté de 1.5 M.A, la demi-mandibule d'un jeune enfant de l'espèce Homo erectus. Garba XII (1.0 – 0.8 M.A.) est un site de transition entre l'Oldowayen et l'Acheuléen moyen, renferme des bifaces et hachereaux en assez grand nombre; Cl. Brahimi découvrit un fragment de crâne d'Homo erectus. A Garba I, Acheuléen récent, les bifaces, hachereaux et bolas sont très nombreux. Par contre le site Acheuléen final de Garba III est intermédiaire entre cette civilisation et celle du Middle Stone Age. Fr. Hours y récolta quelques fragments craniens d'un Homo sapiens archaïque.

Actuellement le site de Melka-Kunturé est un plateau entaillé par la vallée de l'Awash et occupé par une savane à Acacias, rompue par les champs cultivés. Les nombreux petits affluents de l'Awash s'encaissent dans les sédiments déposés antérieurement par la rivière, dans les cendres volcaniques et dans les coulées de lave.

EMPLACEMENT SÉLECTIF DES CAMPEMENTS PALÉOLITHIQUES

Lorsqu'il s'agit d'une même localité il est instructif de connaître les emplacements choisis par les Hominidés quel que soit l'espace de temps qui sépare deux campements différents: quelques générations ou plusieurs dizaines de milliers d'années. On s'aperçoit alors que curieusement la haute vallée de l'Awash a été abondamment occupée et tout particulièrement le secteur proche des chutes et du gué actuels de Melka-Kunturé. En fait la plupart des campements étaient établis à proximité de la rivière, installés sur les rives mêmes ou bien à quelque distance. En tenant compte de la position topographique, de la nature pétrographique du substratum, des relations entre camps et sources de matière première nécessaires pour la préparation des outils ou l'aménagement de l'habitat, on peut envisager l'évolution suivante:

A l'Oldowayen (1.7 M.A) les campements sont situés sur les rives du fleuve; le substratum est argilo-sableux ou argileux et les vestiges d'occupation ont été le plus souvent recouverts de nappes d'argiles, épaisses de plusieurs mètres. Les galets façonnés et les cailloux proviennent vraisemblablement d'un lieu très proche du campement et faisaient partie d'anciens sédiments déposés par la rivière. On peut les considérer comme ayant été en majeure partie apportés et même regroupés, déplacés par l'homme; on retrouve des caractères identiques à Olduvai. Dans ce dernier site les Oldowayens ne s'installaient que sur des berges argileuses. On peut penser que les rives pouvaient être couvertes ou non d'herbes. L'homme avait donc à sa disposition immédiate, l'eau, les galets de la plage voisine et le gibier qui venait boire.

A l'Oldowayen évolué (Garba IV, Gomboré Iγ 1.4 – 1.2 M.A.) on retrouve les mêmes dispositions. Si le soubassement est encore argileux, il peut être aussi sableux. Les galets proviennent toujours d'une plage voisine voire même de celle sur laquelle les hommes étaient installés: ils n'avaient alors qu'à rassembler les galets selon leurs besoins.

A l'Acheuléen ancien (Garba XII J, 1.0 M.A.), il semble y avoir un compromis entre les types d'établissements des Oldowayens et ceux des Acheuléens: même substratum argilo-sableux, même proximité d'une plage de galets que dans les gisements oldowayens mais l'occupation n'a plus lieu sur la rive principale de l'Awash: c'est un petit talweg assez étroit, proche toutefois de la rivière qui accueille la population acheuléenne de Garba XII. A l'Acheuléen moyen, supérieur et final (900.000 à 200.000 ans), la plupart des campements sont installés sur du sable et le plus souvent dans le talweg étroit de petits affluents, pouvant ne pas dépasser 6 à 8m. de largeur. Le campement de Gomboré II était établi sur une plage sableuse et surtout caillouteuse; les acheuléens n'avaient qu'à se baisser pour ramasser les galets. Dans tous les gisements oldowayens et acheuléens, les habitants ont utilisé les galets de la plage, mais dès 840.000 ans (Gomboré II) on s'aperçoit qu'ils ont aussi exploité de véritables carrières où ils devaient préparer les grands bifaces et les hachereaux. On retrouve des observations identiques au Kenya et en Tanzanie.

Le site acheuléen final de Garba III présente de caractères différents de ceux des sites acheuléens antérieurs: il est toujours installé dans le talweg d'un petit ravin, mais le sol était argileux, rougeâtre constitué par des alluvions déposées non plus seulement par l'Awash mais aussi par le ravinement dû aux pluies dont les eaux étaient collectées, entre autres, par ce petit affluent. Les sites du Middle Stone Age qui succèdent à ceux de l'Achuléen final, sont de plus en plus éloignés de rives du fleuve et reposent sur un substratum de sédiments variés: limons, alluvions, cendres volcaniques, bancs rocheux, etc. Le soubassement paraît davantage lié à l'amélioration des conditions d'habitat: par exemple le choix d'une terrasse fluviatile découpée par l'érosion, mais légèrement surélevé, à l'abri des crues. La proximité d'un point d'eau était toujours une nécessité absolue mais les relations entre sources de matière première et habitat évoluent et deviennent moins contraignantes. En résumé, à l'Oldowayen et à l'Acheuléen ancien, le choix d'un campement dépendait de la présence proche d'une nappe de galets de rivière (basalte, parfois obsidienne). A l'Acheuléen moyen et supérieur, certains outils proviennent de roches extraites de "carrières" de basalte et de "tuff" (cinérites) les galets de rivière étant plutôt destinés au matériel grossier. Quant à l'obsidienne elle s'impose pour la préparation de petits outils. Dès l'Acheuléen final la miniaturisation de pièces est déjà fréquente mais elle se généralisera au Middle Stone Age et atteindra, comme un peu partout dans le monde, son optimum au Late Stone Age. Mais du fait de la réduction considérable de la dimension des outils les sources de matière première ne commandaient plus la fixation d'un camp à proximité immédiate d'une plage des galets. Peut-être les hommes effectuaient-ils déjà, comme cela se passa au Late Stone Age, 6 à 7 km. pour atteindre une exploitation d'obsidienne.

Les habitats du Late Stone Age (équivalent du Néolithique) reposent sur un substratum fait de sédiments argileux en relation avec des accumulations de petits galets et graviers, dépôts de nappes ruisselées. Souvent aussi les industries du Late Stone Age couronnent les collines, parfois éloignées de tout point d'eau, car à cette époque, le transport et la conservation de l'eau pouvaient se faire à l'aide d'outres en peaux ou de cruches en poterie. L'homme s'était libéré des contraintes liées aux sources de matière première et aux points d'eau et, plus tard grâce à l'agriculture et à l'élevage, les contraintes liées à la cueillette et à la chasse disparaîtront progressivement.

AIRES D'ACTIVITÉ PRIVILÉGIÉES

Lorsqu'on a la chance de découvrir un ancien campement enfoui depuis des centaines de millénaires l'un des buts est d'en rechercher l'organisation et d'apporter une ou plusieurs interprétations cohérentes. Tous les campements de Melka-Kunturé témoignent de la structuration de l'espace d'occupation, plus ou moins perturbé par des séjours successifs, par le passage des animaux ou lors de l'ensevelissement sous les sédiments fluviatiles charriés par le cours d'eau en crue.

Paradoxalement ce sont les sites les plus anciens de Melka-Kunturé qui offrent au préhistorien le plus d'informations; mêmes remarques pour le site d'Olduvai en Tanzanie. Les conditions d'ensevelissement et de conservation liées parfois au climat en sont sans doute la cause.

L'organisation de l'espace fait apparaître deux types de secteurs opposés: les uns se caractérisent par l'accumulation d'objets et de cailloux, les autres peuvent être en partie ou totalement dépourvus de pièces et de galets.

Dans un campement où les objets et les galets sont jointifs et parfois se chevauchent, les espaces vides qu'ils aient 1, 2 ou 10 m^2 ont une signification précise. Nous connaissons à Melka-Kunturé deux aires principales quasiment dépourvues d'artefacts: l'aire de Gomboré IB (1.7 M.A.) et celle de Garba XII J (1.0 M.A.).

Ces deux zones sont entourées d'une nappe ou d'un bourrelet formé de cailloux et d'outils. Dans les deux habitats, les pierres de calage de piquets, soit nettement réunies et encore à leur place à Garba, soit légèrement déplacées à Gomboré, peuvent être interprétés comme étant en relation avec des branches ou des piquets formant un abri avec toit ou consolidant un enclos buissonneux. L'abri de Garba XII, Acheuléen ancien est sans conteste mieux marqué mais 600.000 ans se sont passés depuis la construction de celui de Gomboré I lui-même légèrement plus récent que le cercle de pierres d'Olduvai.

La limite de ces abris est matérialisée par un tracé continu, assemblage de nappes de pierres et d'outils, situé à l'extérieur d'une haie buissonnante ou du "mur" en branches d'une hutte. Les abris de ce type devaient être bâtis dans les camps de base pour abriter l'homme et sa famille pendant la nuit voire parfois dans la journée: enclos fermé au milieu du campement qui par ailleurs ne devait pas avoir de limites nettes, de limites défensives.

A Olduvai, dans le Bed I, vers 1.8 M.A. Louis et Mary LEAKEY avaient remarqué la présence d'un petit talus de pierres formant un cercle; quelques pièces étaient à l'intérieur. L'interprétation qui en fut donnée était celle d'une hutte, recouverte de paille et de branchages, la base étant calée par des pierres formant bourrelet. A Melka-Kunturé les pierres qui entourent non plus le cercle mais l'ovale ne constituent pas un talus. On peut penser que l'espace vide dessiné par les artefacts et manuports jointifs était lié ici à la présence d'une sorte de haie ou d'une paroi de branchages sans qu'il y ait eu pour autant de toit. Cependant, la réunion de 4 à 5 pierres de taille supérieure à la moyenne, leur disposition circulaire laissant un très petit espace vide entre elles, ressemble fort à l'emplacement d'un piquet ou d'une branche, enfoncé dans le sol ou simplement posé. Dans le site de Garba I, Acheuléen supérieur (0.4 M.A.) on a même pu observer l'emplacement de trous de piquets, la branche ayant pénétré dans le sable de la plage qui à cette époque était meuble.

La fabrication d'outils, l'installation de camps provisoires et sommaires, puis de camps de base vastes et longuement occupés, enfin l'édification de huttes ou d'abris à l'intérieur du campement ont été les toutes premières acquisitions d'Homo habilis et d'Homo erectus. Curieusement l'abri construit apparaît très tôt dans la hiérarchie des acquisitions économiques. Il faut se rappeler que la construction d'abris n'est pas le propre de l'homme et que les Primates, entre autres le chimpanzé, bâtissent dans les arbres des sortes de nids de branchages. Avant l'installation des premiers campements l'homme devait passer une partie de son existence dans les arbres pour se préserver des prédateurs. La construction d'un abri "terrestre" est incontestablement l'affirmation de structures de groupes et le témoignage de l'organisation du territoire avec ses zones de chasse, de cueillette, ses aires d'activité matérielles ou de repos.

Dans les sites de l'Oldowayen mais aussi de l'Acheuléen ancien, certaines aires d'activité se distinguent nettement par leur organisation: ce sont de grosses pierres, d'un diamètre parfois supérieur à 50 cm, d'un poids pouvant dépasser 50 kg et qui se trouvent groupées au nombre de 3 ou 4 dans un secteur particulièrement dense en objets lithiques et en vestiges de faune. A proximité immédiate de ces pierres, une petite surface de 1 à 2 mètres carrés, sans objets, contraste vivement avec l'accumulation voisine. Dans le site de Garba IV, 1.4 M.A., on a pu repérer six aires présentant ces caractéristiques. L'une d'elles est vraisemblablement liée à des activités de dépeçage ou de découpage de la viande: la présence de gros ossements d'hippopotames, d'éléphants ou de bovidés justifie l'emploi d'enclume ou de billot. Dans le site acheuléen de Garba XII J (1.0 M.A.) on a pu observer, autour de gros blocs portant des marques de chocs, de nombreux percuteurs, des choppers ou tranchoirs: ce devait être une aire servant au concassage d'ossements, de branches ou liée à d'autres activités économiques.

La présence de zones vides, associées ou non à de grosses pierres est fréquente dans les gisements de Melka-Kunturé. Certes les sols de ces périodes anciennes se répartissent en secteurs dont certains sont pauvres en artefacts ou totalement dépourvus de pièces ou manuports. Mais les limites de ces espaces vides sont floues et imprécises, évoquant plutôt un secteur sans activités précises. Par contre lorsqu'il y a une limite nette à ces zones dénudées on est en droit de s'interroger sur les raisons de la limite. Première hypothèse: il s'agirait de la présence naturelle de buissons, les pièces butant contre l'accumulation végétale. Deuxième hypothèse: la zone dénudée serait un lieu de repos ou d'occupation par l'homme, recouvert de peaux ou d'un tapis végétal (on a retrouvé des empreintes de végétaux sur des galets proches des zones vides de Garba XII J). Troisième hypothèse: la superficie mise à part, il existe certaines similitudes entre les grands abris et les petites surfaces; on peut alors être tenté d'y voir l'indication de micro-abris en branchages, édifiés pour préserver un être vivant ou une réserve de viande, sorte de garde manger contre les prédateurs. Le fait que les objets ne sont pas uniformément répartis sur toute la surface d'un site suppose la présence et l'action consciente de ses habitants. Les espaces vides peuvent résulter de causes différentes selon les époques.

EVOLUTION DE L'ÉQUIPEMENT TECHNIQUE

Dans un gisement préhistorique l'industrie lithique occupe une place prédominante, disproportionnée avec ce que fut la réalité, car elle demeure souvent l'unique témoignage d'une occupation humaine. L'équipement technique est en fait ce que les occupants des divers sites ont apporté ou fabriqué.

Nous avons conservé le mot anglo-saxon de *manuport* pour désigner tout caillou déplacé, apporté afin d'aménager un abri ou une aire d'activité. Ils sont particulièrement nombreux dans les sites de l'Oldowayen et de l'Acheuléen ancien. Ils diminuent en nombre dans les habitats de l'Acheuléen supérieur. Si certains gisements de l'Acheuléen final et du Middle Stone Age en sont encore bien fournis, d'autres en sont dépourvus. De même la proportion du *matériel de percussion* nous amène à des observations identiques. Les galets brisés, les percuteurs provisoires, galets marqués de quelques chocs — écaillures ou écrasements — enfin les vrais percuteurs qu'ils soient actifs, passifs, manuels ou posés (enclumes) sont très abondants à l'Oldowayen et à l'Acheuléen ancien: ils représentent 50% des artefacts dans les sites oldowayens, mais se raréfient jusqu'à atteindre 15 à 10% à l'Acheuléen supérieur. En fait il y a même accroissement des percuteurs vrais au détriment des galets qui ne portent que quelques marques de chocs.

Ce qu'on nomme *débitage* est l'opération qui aboutit à l'obtention d'éclats, de lames ou de lamelles à partir d'un noyau de matière première, le nucleus. Le nombre des éclats et leurs caractéristiques évoluent avec le temps. Les éclats de préparation primaire qui gardent des zones de cortex témoins de la surface naturelle du caillou, sont plus abondants à l'Oldowayen qu'à l'Acheuléen final. Le talon de l'éclat lorsqu'il n'est pas cortical peut être lisse ou écrasé pas des chocs antérieurs au détachement. Il peut aussi avoir été préparé, dès les périodes les plus anciennes: un, deux ou plusieurs coups ont alors enlevé de petits éclats et le talon est "dièdre"

(2 facettes et une arête) ou "facetté" (plusieurs petites facettes). Toutefois ce dernier cas est rare mais est présent à l'Acheuléen final et au M.S.A. On peut y voir alors une relation avec le débitage Levallois, bien que cette technique soit peu développée et de plus très tardive à Melka-Kunturé. Sans présenter ici l'inventaire de l'outillage lithique, plusieurs lignes évolutives se dégagent.

1. *Les choppers et les bifaces:* Le nom de chopper désigne un tranchoir aménagé par une taille unifaciale ou bifaciale; certains préhistoriens nomment ce dernier chopping-tool. Les pièces sont de forme très variées. Le tranchant peut être réduit à un biseau étroit ou bien occuper presque toute la périphérie du galet. Les choppers peuvent être très grands et lourds ou bien être petits et légers; ils servaient probablement à des usages différents. La multiplicité des types, la belle qualité de leur préparation sont particulièrement nettes aux périodes les plus anciennes. On assiste à plusieurs évolutions parallèles ou successives dont la charnière se situe à l'Acheuléen ancien (Garba XII) ou à l'Acheuléen final (Garba III). Tout d'abord l'angle du tranchant formé par la rencontre des deux faces du chopper était en moyenne compris entre 85° et 95° à l'Oldowayen. Il tend à se réduire à 70°, même à 60° pendant l'Acheuléen, rendant ainsi plus efficace la partie active de l'outil. En fait il est vraisemblable que les nouvelles techniques appliquées à la taille du biface aient modifié celles de la préparation des choppers. Puis à l'Acheuléen supérieur l'efficacité des choppers se réduit considérablement. On assiste à la dégénérescence d'outils qui ne sont plus utilisés qu'à des tâches grossiers, le biface supplantant le chopper. Enfin à l'Acheuléen final ces outils sont de moins en moins nombreux.

Il est vraisemblable qu'en divers points de l'Afrique orientale et aussi de l'Afrique en général et de l'Eurasie, le biface ait pour origine le chopper à tranchant périphérique dont il possède de nombreux caractères, parmi lesquels la taille bifaciale plus ou moins totale. Cependant le biface se distingue du chopper et du chopping-tool par une symétrie axiale, par un meilleur équilibre de l'outil, par le dégagement d'une extrémité plus ou moins arrondie ou pointue. Le biface pouvait selon son profil, son poids et sa préparation servir de couteau, de pointe ou de pic. Plus tard le façonnage des bifaces ne se fera plus à partie de blocs ou de galets mais sur de gros éclats. A l'Acheuléen supérieur et surtout final ainsi qu'au Middle Stone Age, la miniaturisation affectera aussi les bifaces: on verra apparaître de petites pièces bifaces, sortes de pointes, de 5 à 6 cm de long. Toutes ces transformations évolutives indiquent, à partir de relais technologiques successifs, une continuité de l'occupation humaine et de l'organisation sociale.

2. *Pièces sur galets et pièces sur éclats:* Le support de l'outil, ses dimensions, la matière première utilisée varient avec le temps et les caractéres des gisements. Ainsi certaines pièces nommées "encoches" ou bien "outils denticulés" devaient servir principalement à gratter. On les connaît dès l'Oldowayen de Gomboré. Elles étaient alors taillées sur de grand galets plats ayant une face lisse, ou bien sur des éclats de dimensions variées; le basalte était alors la roche préférée. A l'Oldowayen évolué (Garba IV) les pièces sur éclats dominent. A l'Acheuléen supérieur (Garba I) les pièces à encoches et à denticulations sont presque toutes taillées sur éclats. De plus il y a réduction de la dimension des éclats, donc miniaturisation; enfin la roche la plus souvent utilisée est l'obsidienne. De même les gros rabots et les grattoirs sur galets de l'Oldowayen disparaissent peu à peu à l'Acheuléen. Ils céderont la place — mais il faudra près de 800.000 ans pour cela — aux grattoirs sur éclats, petits, plus maniables, plus efficaces.

3. *Les boules à facettes et les bolas.* Dès l'Oldowayen on connaît des boules à facettes de forme plus ou moins sphérique préparées sur blocs anguleux ou sur galets et nommées polyèdres. Ces objets, nucléus à l'origine, ont pu servir de percuteurs, de broyeurs ou d'armes de jet. On trouve certes des polyèdres sphériques à l'Oldowayen, de dimensions et de poids variés; certains sont en obsidienne, roche vitreuse et fragile: ces objets là étaient plutôt des nucléus, fournisseurs d'éclats que des percuteurs. Dans le site acheuléen supérieur de Garba I on trouve des polyèdres en basalte, en "tuff", bien sphériques, d'un volume voisin de celui d'une boule de pétanque. Dans ce gisement on décèle toute une évolution depuis les pièces grossièrement aménagées, les boules à facettes, jusqu'aux bolas dont le piquetage des faces et des arêtes accentue l'émoussé et

permet d'obtenir une sphéricité quasi totale. Quant à l'emploi des bolas il devait être multiple: usage à la chasse, les bolas placées dans un filet de peau ou de lianes, pouvaient être jetées dans les pattes des chevaux ou des antilopes; au campement elles devenaient des percuteurs ou broyeurs.

LA VIE ÉCONOMIQUE

Les principales activités de l'homme paléolithique étaient la cueillette et la chasse. La présence d'ossements, de dents ou de cornes d'animaux à la surface du sol d'habitat est très importante pour la compréhension de la vie domestique mais aussi pour la composition faunique du milieu naturel. De plus c'est avec la détermination des pollens l'un des moyens les plus sûrs de se faire une idée du climat: la faune dominante des périodes sèches (antilopes, chevaux) s'opposant à celle des périodes humides (hippotame). Le fait de trouver certaines parties anatomiques plutôt que d'autres nous renseigne sur plusieurs points: les fragments de membres, de côtes, de bassins indiquent l'apport dans le campement de quartiers de viande. La fracturation longitudinale des os est par exemple en rapport avec la recherche de la moelle. Plus on s'élève dans l'échelle des temps ainsi que dans la progression de l'humanité, plus on observe une fracturation croissante des ossements. Il y a certes des exceptions mais il est exact que l'on trouve davantage de petites esquilles d'os dans les habitats de la fin de l'Acheuléen que dans ceux de l'Oldowayen.

A Garba IV, habitat oldowayen, on a découvert environ 120 cornes d'antilopes alors que les ossements des membres de ces animaux sont moins nombreux. Les canines et incisives d'hippopotame souvent taillées ou appointées pouvaient servir d'outils, employées par exemple comme pics. Par contre les cornes pouvaient jouer un rôle dans l'installation du campement.

Le feu domestique est une preuve d'évolution technologique mais aussi sociale. Les plus anciennes traces de la présence du feu datent d'environ 1.6 M.A.: c'est à Chesowanza, au Kenya, mais l'argile brulée que l'on a retrouvée indique-t-elle un foyer volontairement allumé ou bien est-elle simplement le témoignage d'un feu de brousse? A Melka-Kunturé ce n'est que vers 400.000 ans que l'on peut déceler des traces de foyer: ce sont des pierres brûlées. Dans le même habitat il y avait de très nombreux fragments d'ocre rouge qui nécessitent l'utilisation du feu et qui ont pu être utilisées à des fins esthétiques ou techniques. Dans le même gisement on avait noté l'emplacement d'une vaste cuvette, régulière, peu profonde, qui peut être artificielle. Alors que dans le site acheuléen final de Garba III, les cuvettes plus ou moins rectangulaires, sont plus petites, profondes et manifestement creusées. Rien ne prouve l'existence de fosses liées à des foyers mais rien ne s'y oppose non plus.

LES CHANGEMENTS DE CIVILISATIONS

En suivant à Melka-Kunturé les différentes lignes technologiques ou sociales on prend conscience d'une évolution continue bien qu'irrégulière. Or les stades de changements ne sont pas nécessairement contemporains: à une réelle avance technologique s'oppose un retard du mode de vie. Par example à Garba XII les caractères techniques des outils sont déjà ceux de l'Acheuléen alors que l'aménagement du sol reste celui des Oldowayens. On a cependant le sentiment qu'il s'agit de populations appartenant à la même ethnie et assimilant progressivement les découvertes réalisées soit au contact d'autres populations soit du fait des progrès techniques s'effectuant au sein même du groupe. Cette évolution par saccades et non synchrone est caractéristique de Melka-Kunturé.

D'ailleurs le traditionnel couple: Oldowayen/Homo habilis, Acheuléen/Homo erectus, Paléolithique moyen-supérieur/Homo sapiens, est quelque peu modifié. En effet à 1.7 M.A. un Homo erectus est associé à des outils oldowayens; de même un Homo sapiens est contemporain de l'Acheuléen final. Il n'y a pas en fait de grandes coupures à Melka-Kunturé mais tout ne change pas en même temps: les espèces humaines, la technologie, la vie économique. On observe plutôt des transformations progressives qui évoquent une évolution en mosaïque. A ce schéma pourrait se rattacher quelques gisements d'Afrique du Nord et particulièrement du Maroc (Sidi-Abderhaman).

Il y a d'autres conceptions des changements de civilisation: par exemple le cas d'Olduvai Gorge, en Tanzanie. Pour M. Leakey, dès 1.4 M.A., date de l'apparition des premiers bifaces, on assisterait à une occupation alternée sur les rives du lac d'Olduvai: tantôt c'est une industrie à bifaces, avec H. erectus, donc acheuléenne; tantôt on trouve une industrie à dominance de galets aménagés, associée à quelques bifaces et parfois à Australopithecus robustus, donc oldowayenne (Developed Oldowan). Cette dualité est basée principalement sur un caractère typologique. Pour M. Leakey s'il y a plus de 40% de bifaces on est en présence d'un campement acheuléen; si le chiffre est inférieur c'est l'industrie du Developed Oldowan. Les fouilles effectuées à Melka-Kunturé ont bien montré le danger d'utiliser des pourcentages aussi rigoureux; dans un même gisement les proportions de certaines pièces parmi lesquelles les bifaces varient considérablement d'un secteur à l'autre. Si la méthode est criticable, les fouilles effectuées par M. Leakey sont de très belle qualité. Il est fort possible que les problèmes humains et sociaux aient été différents à Olduvai et à Melka-Kunturé.

Ces exemples montrent suffisamment la difficulté que l'on éprouve à définir une culture. Je ne pense pas que le biface soit suffisant pour caractériser l'Acheuléen, pas plus qu'une certaine proportion de ce type d'object. D'autres critères permettront un jour de nuancer nos affirmations. Je crois toutefois que le fait de tenir compte de plusieurs données, géologiques (substratum, topographie des lieux), technologiques (type de pièces, façonnage), économiques (organisation du campement) est plus sûr et permet d'approcher une vérité que l'on croit saisir mais qui s'échappe et se modifie au fil de chaque nouvelle découverte.

REMERCIEMENTS

Je tiens à remercier en premier lieu le Ministère de la Culture d'Addis-Abeba qui de 1965 à 1982 m'a permis de diriger les fouilles de Melka-Kunturé. Je remercie également la Sous Direction des Sciences Sociales et Humaines du Ministère des Relations Extérieures de la République Française et les formations du Centre National de la Recherche Scientifique dont l'aide et les moyens matériels m'ont été indispensables pour mener à bien ces recherches archéologiques.

BIBLIOGRAPHIE SOMMAIRE

Bonnefille, R. (1972)   Associations polliniques actuelles et quaternaires en Ethiopie. Thèse de Doctorat es-Sciences. Paris.

Chavaillon, J. (1979)   Stratigraphie du site archéologique de Melka-Kunturé. *Bull. Soc. Géol. Fr.*, 7° série, XXI, n° 3, p.227-232.

Chavaillon, J., Brahimi, Cl.,   Première découverte d'Hominidés dans l'un des sites acheuléens
Coppens, Y. (1974)   de Melka-Kunturé. *C. R. Acad. Sc.*, série D, 273, p.623-625.

Chavaillon, J. et N. (1976)   Le Paléolithique ancien en Ethiopie: caractères techniques de l'Oldowayen de Gomboré I à Melka-Kunturé. Colloque V du IX° Congrès UISPP Nice, p.43-69.

——————————   (1980) Evolution de l'Acheuléen à Melka-Kunturé, *Anthropologie*, ed. Jelinek, Brno, XVIII — 2:3 p.153-159.

——————————   (1982) Les habitats paléolithiques de Melka-Kunturé, *Abbay* n° 11, ed. CNRS, Paris, p. 23-46.

Chavaillon, J., Chavaillon, N., Coppens, Y., Senut, B. (1977)	Présence d'Hominidé dans le site oldowayen de Gomboré I à Melka-Kunturé. *C. R. Acad. Sc.*, série D, 285, p. 961-963.
Chavaillon, J., Chavaillon, N., Hours, Fr., Piperno, M. (1979)	From the Oldowan to Middle Stone Age at Melka-Kunture (Ethiopia); Understanding cultural Changes. *Quaternaria* XXI, Roma, p. 87-114, Biblio.
Clark, J. D. and Kurashina, H. (1976)	New Plio-Pleistocene Archeological Occurrences from the plain of Gadeb, Upper Webi Shebelle basin. Colloque V du IX° Congrès UISPP Nice,P. 158-216.
Cressier, P. (1980)	Magnétostratigraphie du gisement pleistocène de Melka-Kunturé. Datation des niveaux oldowayens et acheuléens. Thèse 8 Nov. 1980, Univers. Louis Pasteur, Strasbourg.
Geraads, D. (1979)	La faune des gisements de Melka-Kunturé: artiodactyles primates. *Abbay* n° 10, ed. CNRS, Paris, p. 21-50.
Leakey, M. D. (1971)	*Olduvai Gorge: excavation in the Bed I-II: 1960-1963.* Cambridge University Press, 306p.
Sabatier, M. (1979)	Les rongeurs des sites à Hominidés de Hadar et de Melka-Kunturé, Thèse Acad. Montpellier Sept. 1979.
Piperno, M., Bulgarelli-Piperno, G. (1974-5)	First Approach to the ecological and cultural significance of the Early Paleolithic Occupation site of Garba IV at Melka-Kunturé (Ethiopia). *Quaternaria*, 18, Roma, p. 347-382.
Taieb, M. (1974)	Evolution quaternaire du basin de l'Awash. Thèse Doctorat es-Sciences, 2 vol.
Wesphal, M., Chavaillon, J., Jaeger, J. J. (1979)	Magnétostratigraphie des dépôts pleistocènes de Melka-Kunturé: premières données. *Bull. soc. Géol. Fr.*, 7° série, XXI, n° 3, p.237-241.

A REVIEW OF THE ARCHAEOLOGICAL

EVIDENCE FOR THE ORIGINS OF FOOD

PRODUCTION IN ETHIOPIA

John Desmond Clark
Department of Anthropology
University of California

Ethiopia's rich and ancient civilization is founded upon its agriculture that supported the towns and cities in which its past history is best reflected. This agricultural record is preserved in many different ways — in plant and animal genetics, in historical linguistics, in the written word, in the present-day ethnic diversity and in the buried remains of past populations. It is the special task of the archaeologist to give substance and precision to these many facets of the record and in particular to provide a reliable time scale in which we can have confidence and without which the prehistoric record of socio-economic change is at best vague and insubstantial and at worst downright misleading. This paper is, therefore, a review of the archaeological evidence and a presentation of some of the ways archaeologists seek to interpret the record and give it substance.

Geography and ecology are two of the most influential phenomena that are reflected in all human behavioural systems. Ethiopia is distinguished ecologically by having two main eco-systems, that of the cool, temperate high plateaux between c.2100-4000 m, and that of the lowlands to the west and east, in particular that part of the Great Rift Valley known as the Afar Rift. The Ethiopian Plateau experiences two rainy seasons a year and has been intensively cultivated by mixed farmers for a very long time. In the northern parklands and grass savanna the emphasis is on cereals — tef, barley, wheat and finger-millet together with pulses and legumes. In the southern part and on the South-East Plateau, much of which is a mosaic of forest and grassland, the staple for many peoples is the *enset* together with root crops and, in the lower and drier parts, sorghum. In the more arid lowlands sorghum, bullrush-millet and finger-millet are the main crops where rainfall is sufficient. The emphasis on animal husbandry has from antiquity been on cattle, formerly humpless African breeds but now on zebu, in both the plateaux and the Rift. Small stock, ovicaprids, are ubiquitous as also is the domestic donkey for transport. Camels become important only in those areas that are sufficiently hot and arid that cattle can no longer be kept on the sclerophytic thorn scrub below 800 m. This is the home of nomadic pastoralists who have been in the Rift since the beginning of the 2nd millennium B.C. (Clark 1976). The emphasis here is on mobility and the basic pattern of movements has probably always been between lowlands and plateau, a system fostered by traditional exchange relationships and dictated by the seasonal availability of grazing.

There is much else also that distinguishes the peoples of the highlands from those in the lowlands — differences of race, religion, language and cultural adaptation. These differences are documented for as far back as the 1st millennium B.C. and they have been induced partly by the geographic isolation of the populations of the high plateaux from peoples occupying other parts of North-East and East Africa. At other times in the past, catastrophic factors such as drought, famine, disease and cultural events have resulted in permanent movements by peoples from the lowlands settling on the plateaux, and migrations into the drier parts of the Horn, into the hot and humid plains of the Sudan and southwards into East Africa. Such movements can be verified in the surrounding regions for as far back as the 3rd millennium B.C. (Barthelme 1984: Ambrose 1984).

The peoples of the plateaux at some time in the past domesticated wild species of grasses and other plants that are specifically Ethiopian cultigens and, though today many of the plants that are grown originated elsewhere (wheat and barley for example), the clue to the events that resulted in the emergence of a fully developed food-producing economy in Ethiopia must lie in those domesticated species that are peculiar to the country — *tef (Eragrostis tef), nug (Guizotia abyssinica), enset (Ensete ventricosum), gesho (Rahmnus prinoides), chat (Catha edulis), buna (Coffea arabica),* and probably *dagusa (Eleusine corocana).* We know appreciably more about the behaviour of early hominids in Ethiopia than we do about the origins of its traditional agricultural systems. The archaeological evidence is minimal — a few small excavations. The same is the case for the skeletal remains of the populations that were responsible for these culture residues. We have much more evidence of Plio-Pleistocene hominids than we have of our own kind, Modern Man. Historical data are sporadic and ambiguous and mostly too late to be of much use except to confirm the antiquity of Ethiopian agriculture. Some have tried to construct a chronology from historical linguistics but without the archaeological data to give it verisimilitude it would be unwise to place too much reliance on it time-wise (Ehret 1979). We have little more data today than we had when I wrote on the same subject of Ethiopian agricultural origins in 1976, eight years ago. Mostly this is due to events outside the control of the archaeologists themselves so that the new evidence that can be reported is small. In particular it is regrettable that no new work has been possible in the northern parts of the country which can be seen as one, if not *the* nuclear region where plant and animal domestication was first established in Ethiopia (Harlan 1969; 1971). We do have a little more information from the lowlands (Brandt 1980) but of especial importance is the new work being done in the central and eastern Sudan (Haaland 1981: Fattovich *et al.* 1984), in northern and central Kenya (Barthelme *op. cit*: Ambrose *op. cit*: Phillipson 1977: 71-85), and in Somalia (Brandt & Brook 1984). The appearance of livestock and in one instance a reported plant domesticate is of great importance for trying to identify the causes and processes whereby the hunter/gatherer populations of the high plateau developed their uniquely Ethiopian economic systems of arable farming and stock-raising.

Various hypotheses have been put forward, often on the slenderest evidence, to explain this 'economic revolution'. The Hamitic hypothesis (Seligman 1957: 85-139) explained it as the result of the migration into the highlands of agricultural peoples with cattle and small stock from their homeland in the Near East. They are credited with bringing barley, wheat and domesticating sorghum in their new homeland. Another model first put forward by Murdock (1959: 170-187) sees the knowledge of plant cultivation having been introduced to Cushitic speakers in western Ethiopia by East Sudanic speaking 'Pre-Nilotes'. Local wild plants in common use on the plateau were brought under cultivation so that two main economies were developed, one in the north based on the cultivation of *tef*, finger-millet and other plants used in intercropping and a second centre in the south based on *enset* and root crops. A third series of hypotheses sees the initiative coming first from the movements of pastoral cattle peoples along the Sudanese Nile and in the clay plains to the east in the late 3rd or at the beginning of the 2nd millennium B.C. who migrated up onto the plateau and down the coastal plains and the Rift Valley (Clark 1976: 79-82). These pastoralists are identified as being related to the C-Group people of Nubia and, either as a result of direct or stimulus diffusion, were the cause inducing some of the indigenous Cushitic-speaking, specialised foragers to start cultivating some of their staple food plants. In the arid lowlands the pastoralists remained nomadic or at best cultivated small plots of sorghum. The agricultural implements are seen as those of the Sudan — the hoe and the digging-stick, the sickle and threshing sticks and the winnowing basket; all based on a long fallow system of swidden cultivation (Simoons 1958). More intensive methods of agriculture are seen usually as originating with the Pre-Axumite immigrants from South Arabia, bringing wheat, barley and the plough around the middle of the 1st millennium B.C. (Kobishchanov, Y. M. 1979: 128-129). As in West Africa agricultural systems in Ethiopia can be seen as the outcome of a complex series of interacting phenomena some natural, some cultural that helped to shape the ways in which the hunter/gatherers of the plateaux and Rift chose to adapt to the climatic, environmental and cultural changes taking place during the middle to later Holocene.

Such is the perversity of humankind that significant behavioural changes do not usually come about voluntarily until sufficient pressure of one kind or another makes it more advantageous for the whole system to readjust. Such pressures were surely of many kinds. Some of the more important can be seen as climatic and environmental, either in the form of episodes of increased rainfall, or of desiccation and famine. Or again as demographic, such as results from elimination of the famine months, or a greater degree of sedentariness due to improved resource procurement and storage. Demographic pressure from immigration of new ethnic peoples can result in competition for local resources so that more intensive manipulation of those resources becomes necessary. Other pressures may be socio-cultural such as are brought about by either external or internal factors that favour change. For example improved storage facilities for essential foods and a system of regular exchange of commodities make possible the advantages that come from the accumulation of resources and so wealth by individuals and clans, thereby develops a hierarchically structured society and possibly the change in status of one or other social group, for example women and girls on account of their importance as a labour force for crop raising. Such changed status may necessitate new kinds of dwellings and other structures and of course new patterns of settlement. Times of plenty are times of equilibrium within the system, when there is leisure to experiment with new ways of doing things, but more generally it is only in times of adversity that new improved strategies are put into effect in order to maintain the population at the level it had reached during the previous time of equilibrium.

The early Holocene from c. 12000 to 7500 years ago was a time of increased rainfall and humidity in the tropics; the Sahara was green and the equatorial forests began to expand from the limited refuges to which they had retreated during the maximum of the Last Glaciation. At this time water resources generally became more abundant in streams and lakes and savanna vegetation zones were able to expand into the desert which became highly favourable for the herbivores as well as for the human populations that depended on them. This was a time also when the fresh water food sources – molluscs, fish, crocodile and hippopotamus, as well as water plants – made it possible for the level of mobility to be reduced, larger, waterside settlements could be occupied seasonally for longer periods. Economically the human populations at this time were specialised hunting/fishing/gathering peoples making regular use of the products of several different habitats according to a regular system of transhumance. Such a system is well seen on the upper Nile in the central and northern Sudan, in the easter and central Sahara, in northern Kenya and the central African lakes region. In Ethiopia, it is known archaeologically from the Lake Besaka area, at Matahara, where a long lived blade tradition "the Besaka Industry" existed from c. 23000 to 5000 B.P. The economy of the first three Phases was based on hunting and fishing and presumably collecting (Clark and Williams 1978: Brandt 1980, 1984). The human population with the 3rd Phase showed marked alveolar prognathism but whether this derived from diet and the ways food was processed or whether it indicates that the southern Afar was at this time occupied by a negroid people remains to be shown. There is reason to think that the Ethiopian lakes region south of Besaka supported a similar Later Stone Age economy and technology, and the earliest date for this Ethiopian blade tradition in the Zwai-Shala basin is more than 27,000 B.P. (Street 1980). No comparable evidence is available from any other part of the country but one might speculate that the Lake Tana basin was occupied by similar hunting/fishing/collecting groups of which the Wayto, formerly hippopotamus hunters living in large settlements along the south shore of the lake, are the sole survivors (Gamst 1979: Clark 1985). Possibly also the Tegu hunters and fishers of the lower Omo valley (D. Turton: Per. Com), and the Elmolo of Lake Turkana (Dyson & Fuchs 1937) are also isolated survivals of a one time much more widely distributed way of life. From about 7000 years ago the climatic trend has been one of increasing desiccation. In the mid Holocene between 4000-3000 years ago the specialised foragers in the Nile Valley in the central Sudan and the clay plains to the east acquired livestock; sheep/goats to begin with and later cattle, though there is no evidence, contrary to some statements, that they also cultivated (Krzyzaniak 1978). So by 3000 BC groups practising several different patterns of economic adjustment can be identified – hunters and fishers close to the river and lakes, herders and hunters and fishers using both river and plains and making variable use of wild plants in particular the cereal grasses that grew there in such abundance (Clark 1984). In the Lake Turkana basin both ovicaprids and cattle are known to be present at sites in the north-east side of the lake by the middle to end of the 3rd millennium BC (Barthelme 1984), but at Ele Bor, in the Chalbi desert further to the east, though the industry was similar most of the meat was derived from wild animals

(Phillipson 1985: 143). At this time in north-east Africa as also in much more recent times economic behaviour has been highly adaptable to allow for considerable fluidity so that the degree to which a group made use of the products of the hunt, of the water and of wild plant resources was in direct relationship to the ecological and cultural circumstances of the time.

There is good evidence for several periods of severe desiccation resulting, it may be inferred, in equally severe drought and famine. Evidence for similar arid episodes is recorded in detail from north, west and east Africa (Talbot 1980: Servant & Servant-Vildary 1980). Lake Abbé in the Afar shows periods of aridity between 5800-5000 B.C., between 2000-1000 B.C., and 1000-1400 A.D., with the final desiccation beginning 100-200 years ago (Gasse *et al.* 1980). In the Zwai-Shala basin the early Holocene wet phase 12,000-5000 B.P. was interrupted by several periods of drought when the lakes fell between 11,000-10,000 B.P., 8500-6500 B.P. and 6200-5800 BP. About 5000 BP there was a major recession of the lakes in the basin and since then dry conditions have prevailed, though a short lived high stand is recorded c. 2510 B.P. (Gillespie *et al.* 1983). For examples of the effects of such droughts one need look no further than those that have affected the Sahel since the 1970s. One of these outcomes is mass migration, where this is possible, and the movements of the Oromo and Somali peoples are examples of this (Clark 1976: 74-75). That drought and famine must bring about drastic readjustments to the lives of those who suffer them there is no doubt. What is less visible are the effects of aridity on human populations in the prehistoric past, since the evidence is mostly indirect, and drought is but one phenomenon that can cause economic change. In some instances there does seem to be a significant correlation, in others it is less easy to see and other, perhaps internal cultural factors, should be looked for.

General interaction and contacts for prehistoric Ethiopians came in the main from four directions. In the north and east a two way move into the Ethiopian highlands and down into the plains of the Sudan and the Red Sea coast. In the west the movements and contacts are more likely to have been onto not away from the highlands, though pressure from the Cushites on the plateau in historic times has forced some 'Pre-Nilotes' into the lowlands (Simoons 1960). In the south the movements are again those of emigration rather than immigration; those of southern Cushites and later early Nilotes moving south to Uganda, western Kenya and central Tanzania (Ehret 1974). So on the one hand we need to look at the evidence, such as it is, in the light of possible autochthonous processes leading to economic change as well as to those that derive from external processes of interaction and exchange.

ARCHAEOLOGICAL DATA

In the northern Ethiopian centre of cereal cultivation there are a meagre four excavated and four or five surface sites that throw light on the beginnings of domestication there. The first of these is Gobedra rockshelter close to Axum in the Tigre Province (Phillipson 1977). This site has a cultural sequence going back to at least 5000 B.C. The industry is a Later Stone AGe one using pottery and manufacturing small blades of chert that were worked into microliths and scrapers, some of the latter resembling those used for cleaning hides by the Fuga today (Gallagher 1977: Clark & Kurashina 1981). Possible *Bos* remains come from a level dated to c.1000 B.C. In the deposits dated between 1000-5000 B.C. was found a small quantity of very fresh looking, uncarbonised finger-millet grains and a camel tooth; a date in the 3rd millennium B.C. is considered by Phillipson the most likely age of the level from which these finds came. Unless there existed an as yet unrecognized race of wild camels in the Horn this animal is more likely to have reached the Horn first from south Arabia in the 1st millennium B.S., but most probably later as all historical references to the camel are late (Kobischanov 1979: 131-2). It is unknown in the rock art until the late and last styles. Though the excavator of Gobedra does not report any observable disturbance of the terrace outside the shelter where these finds were made, such would not be unexpected at a site within such close proximity to a major Axumite palace complex. Until the grains themselves are dated it must be considered that the occurrence of domestic finger-millet in the 3rd millennium B.C. at Axum remains unproven.

The second site is another shelter situated at Quiha, near Macalle in south west Eritrea. The site was excavated by Colonel Moysey in 1941. No notes on the excavation exist but the collection is preserved in the National Museum, Nairobi (Clark 1954: 324). The finds come from four levels and there does not appear to be any significant difference between those from Levels 2-4 which are the artefacts and fauna that concern us here. The industry is a ceramic Later Stone Age one using obsidian for the manufacture of the stone artefacts. Since there is no known local source for this rock it is likely to have been brought in from one of the lowland sources in the east or from the north. Artefacts comprise backed bladelets and lunates, splintered pieces (outils écaillés), short convex scrapers and longish, larger blades with marginal retouch not unlike those of the East African Elmenteita Industry. The potsherds come from round based pots and deep bowls in a red-brown, mostly unburnished ware, and a finer, thinner red ware often with a red slip and burnished. Decoration may be applied to the tops of the rims, and forms bands round the neck and shoulder. Sometimes the decoration covers the whole body of the pot, as for example a matt or scraped pattern or a design of incised continuous chevrons. Undecorated pots are present as also are one or two sherds having a red or black burnish to the rim inside and out. There is also one pierced lug handle, and a short cylinder of fired clay slightly flared at one end that is possibly an ear or nose plug. There is little doubt that the pottery shows similarities to that from the group of sites reported by Arkell close to Agordat (Arkell 1954) and also to the pottery tradition named after the Atbai in the eastern Sudan discussed below. What is of particular interest at Quiha is the fauna which was examined recently by Fiona Marshall. Zebra is represented by two molar teeth, domestic donkey is less certainly identified on the basis of two other cheek teeth, cattle are certainly identified from a premolar, two molar teeth and probably on six further specimens. I am much indebted to Joseph Michels of Pennsylvania State University for an obsidian hydration date for a sample from Level 3. The Quiha specimen belongs to a compositionally distinctive obsidian group present also in small quantities at Axum and known as 'Axum D'. The geological origin is as yet unknown. Quiha lies within the Axumite trade area and it is not without interest that Quiha and Macalle lie at the end of an important salt caravan route from the Danakil and the Red Sea coast, (O'Mahoney 1970). The date obtained is 71 ± 107 years B.P. This is younger than was expected in view of the pottery traits in common with those of Agordat and the Eastern Sudan sites. If confirmed it is an indication of the continuity of this tradition in northern Ethiopia until comparatively late times as well as showing that stone was still the common material in use in rural areas for cutting/scraping artefacts at the beginning of the present era at a time when iron begins to be used at Axum.

The four sites in the vicinity of Agordat, in the Baraka valley, have been known since 1942 when they were visited briefly by the late A. J. Arkell. They have never been reexamined so that Arkell's report is the sole record of the settlements and their contents (Arkell 1954). The four sites are low settlement mounds adjacent to granite hills and ridges all within a ten mile radius of Agordat. If this is any indication of demographic density on the northern part of the plateau at the time these settlements were occupied, it would seem this must have been a region well populated by subsistence farmers. Moreover these were not ephemeral settlements but were occupied for a sufficient time to allow some 0.75 m. of occupation debris to accumulate. Today the region is one of treeless shrub and open grassland but the original pre-agricultural vegetation of the Axum region has been shown by Butzer (1981: 476) to have been one of open, mainly deciduous woodland on well drained ground, more scrubby on steep, rocky slopes and with evergreen elements such as cedar, olive, fig and palms near streams and springs. The poorly drained, black cracking soils in the valleys would probably have remained as open grassland. This is exactly the kind of soil on which *tef* grows best for it is a crop that is very hardy and tolerant of temperature and aridity provided the moisture content of the soil is good during the initial growing period (Brown & Cocheme 1969: 302-310).

The cultural remains from these four Agordat sites are similar, so that Arkell considered them to have been occupied contemporaneously and to belong to a single cultural tradition. What is not known due to lack of excavation and any stratigraphic control is whether there are any developmental trends from beginning to end of the occupation. The Agordat area is strategically situated for peoples and their animals to move in either direction via the Baraka Valley into the lowlands and to the Red Sea coast.

The stone equipment comprises much flaked, ground and polished stone; spherical and disc maceheads, pecked and polished axes, some lugged and some with splayed cutting edges. The lugged forms Arkell suggests may have been copies of the bronze lugged axe of Dynastic Egypt. Flattened stone cylinders with incised grooves may have been used to squeeze out the seeds from cotton fibre; palettes and stone dishes, lower and upper grindstones, and a lot of obsidian flaking debitage and microliths are other characteristic stone artefacts. Additional objects of stone include a headless carving of an animal, probably a domestic *Bos*, stone bracelet fragments, stone beads, ear and nose plugs and fragments of imported amazonite and malachite. A copper finger ring, bracelet and two fragmentary toilet knives all found together in an erosion gully, as also an eyed bead of blue glass could, but need not necessarily belong to a later occupation.

The pottery comprises narrow-mouthed globular pots and deep bowls of different forms. The ware is red to red-brown, and there is also a thin red ware with a burnished red or black slip on the neck and both sides of the rim. Pots and bowls may be undecorated and have thick, everted or inturned rims. Decoration is both scraped and comb-impressed, cross-hatched or horizontal line incisions, panels of incised and impressed cuneiform decoration to produce false relief chevrons, and lines of finger-nail impression. Decoration occurs on the top of the rim, and on the short neck and shoulder or it may cover the whole pot. Perhaps the most characteristic decoration is formed by the application of impressed balls or knobs of clay to form panels often applied over a scraped or washed background. Lugs and spouts are also a feature of this pottery. Another feature of the Agordat ceramics are the small flat and sometimes tri-lobate-based vessels that Arkell refers to as 'pot stands'. An alternative explanation of their use is as incense burners; incense occurred prolifically in Punt and does still today in the less accessible parts of the northern escarpment.

Arkell saw similarities with the pottery of the C-Group sites in Nubia and at Kerma and considered these Agordat sites to belong in time, probably to that of the 2nd Intermediate Period and the beginning of the New Kingdom in Egypt. If the stone lugged form is a copy of the Egyptian lugged axe of bronze this also suggests a 2nd millennium date for Agordat since these Egyptian axes were made from the end of the 17th to the end of the 18th Dynasties.

The Agordat sites remained in a vacuum as it were, undated and with no very clear relationship with any other ceramic tradition until 1980 when the Italian Mission to Kasala Province led by Rudolfo Fattovich and the joint University of Khartoum/Southern Methodist University Butana Project led by A. E. Marks and A. Mohamad-Ali began work in the eastern Sudan previously an almost unknown region archaeologically. To them we owe knowledge of what they have termed the "Atbai Tradition" found in particular in that area between the Atbara and Gash rivers in the flat clay plains of the southern Atbai (Fattovich, Marks and Mohamed-Ali 1984). Here, out of a base in a ceramic tradition similar to that of "Early Khartoum" there developed the "Atbai Tradition" between 5000 B.C. and 500 A.D. which has been subdivided into several consecutive Phases and several contemporaneous facies or Groups.

The vessel forms of the red and brown wares and the decorative techniques — scraping, combing and incision as well as the motifs that are found on the top of the rim, as bands on the rim and neck, applied knob decoration, and a thin red slip ware with red and black burnished rim and neck — are all characteristic, as we have seen, of the ceramics of Agordat. More particularly the similarities lie with the Kassala Phase between c. 3500-500 B.C., and more specifically with the Jebel Mokram Group in the later half of the Phase occupying the steppe lying between the Atbara and the Gash valleys between about 2000-1700 B.C. In the 3rd millennium the Kassala Phase ceramics here spread widely and are found in the Nile Valley, in the northern Butana at Shaquaddud and as far north as the 3rd Cataract. They occur also to the north-east at Erkowit in the Red Sea Hills where this pottery is dated to 2500 B.C. (Callow & Wahida 1981). To the south in Ethiopia it extends certainly as far as Quiha. The flaked, ground and polished stone equipment also appears to be similar. There is reason to believe, therefore, that the Agordat sites probably date to the earlier part of the 2nd millennium B.C. though the date from

Quiha suggests that this regional tradition continued up to the beginning of the 1st millennium B.C.

It might also be inferred that the nature of the settlements and the economy may well have been similar. During the earlier part of the Kassala Phase in the Sudan settlements were all extensive (45,000m² - 120,000m²) in area with an accumulated depth of c. 2.0m. These settlements occur both in the river valleys and on the steppe. The economy during this Phase was based mostly on the hunting of small wild bovids and fish, together with a low % of domestic animals. During the later Jebel Mokram facies in the 2nd millennium B.C. the sites are now comparatively small, some 10,000m² and have little depth. The excavators believe these represent short term temporary camps. All the faunal remains are those of domestic cattle, and domestic sorghum has been identified from hearths, though the details remain to be published. If confirmed this would be the earliest firm evidence for domestic sorghum known so far. It is suggested (Fattovich *et al.* 1984: 182) that the economy was one of mixed herding and cultivating. Such may also have been the pattern on the Ethiopian high plateau at this time. Fattovich, Marks & Mohamed-Ali see the late Phase Jebel Mokram facies in the Atbai as representing perhaps one half of a transhumant pattern such as is practised by the Beja and Beni Amer today (Shack 1974: 75-76). If this interpretation is confirmed it may very well be that the other half of the pattern is represented by settlements such as those at Agordat, Quiha and other sites on the plateau.

To return to the material culture at the Agordat sites. The lugged axes, disc maceheads, palettes and possibly also the copper objects and the glass bead suggest the existence of some kind of exchange system and it is not impossible that this is a direct outcome of Dynastic Egyptian seagoing voyages down the Red Sea to Punt. Kitchen (1971) has made out a very convincing case for the country of Punt's lying inland in an arc between the latitudes of Port Sudan and Suakin. He further suggests that winds and currents would have made it possible, indeed necessary, to remain for two to three months in Punt which lay in the plains and the border country of northern Ethiopia. This would include some or all of the country in which the Atbai tradition has been found. Contacts with Punt, if they are somewhat ambiguous for Old Kingdom times, are certainly authenticated during the Middle Kingdom and again in the detailed account of Hatshepsut's expedition in New Kingdom times around 1470 B.C. (*Op. cit.*: 192). The Baraka valley and the lower divide between the Red Sea Hills and the Eritrean highlands could have formed a relatively easy access to Punt if such this region proves to be. In exchange for the exports some of the imports mentions in the Deir-el-Bahari texts may well have found their way to the settlements on the northern parts of the Ethiopian plateau. It remains for future archaeological investigations in this region to confirm or refute this suggestion.

No early plant remains, except possibly the finger-millet from Gobedra, have yet been found on the Ethiopian Plateau other than the wheat and chick-pea and unidentified legumes from Lalibela Cave north of Bahr Dar, which are late and date only to the 14th century A.D. (Dombrowski 1970). Both wheat and chick-pea are cultigens of the Middle East complex of domesticated plants so, in spite of the diversity of wheat forms found in Ethiopia, this cereal is generally considered to be exotic. It is not impossible, however, as I have previously suggested (Clark 1985) that both barley and wheat, since they are thought to have been growing in north Africa at the time of the maximum of the last Glacial 18,000-20,000 years ago (Harlan & Zohary 1966), might have migrated down the Red Sea Hills and reached the Ethiopian highlands before the end of the Pleistocene. Alternatively both grains might have been introduced to Cushitic Agau via the Egyptian expeditions to Punt and the Deir-el-Bahari texts speak of a banquet at which Puntites were served Egyptian food and drink. Moreover the probable true age of the barley grains from the Wadi Kubbanya west of Aswan is thought to be c. 3000 B.C. (Wendorf *et al.* 1984) showing that barley may have been present in Upper Egypt at the latitude of the Tropic at this early time. Further hypotheses are that wheat and barley, which in Meroitic times were still only grown in small river-side patches on the Nile, may not have reached Ethiopia before the coming of the Himyarite immigrants who brought also the plough (Clark 1976: 78).

Remains in prehistoric contexts of *tef, nug, gesho*, sorghum and perhaps finger-millet, together with wheat and barley, still, therefore, await discovery in Ethiopia. Now however the discoveries of the Expeditions to the eastern Sudan make it possible to suggest that the specifically Ethiopian plants may have been domesticated on the northern plateau some time in the earlier part of the 2nd or possibly towards the end of the 3rd millennium B.C., prior to the time when wheat and barley began to be cultivated by the early Cushites. It appears more likely if there were not already wild immigrant forms present via the Red Sea Hills, that the last two cereals began to be grown in Ethiopia only after *tef* and finger-millet had been domesticated and grown for some time. Sorghum is a lowland, drought resistant crop that does not do well in the highlands, *tef* and finger-millet on the other hand are highly temperature tolerant plants and the most favoured locality for growing *tef*, as previously stated, is on the black clay soils of the plateau.

Also it is just possible that in the narrow necked jars at the Agordat sites and that have been described as 'beer pots' there is an indication that beer was brewed, in which case the use of *gesho* bark (a substitute for hops) may also have a similar high antiquity. Nothing is known as to when *nug* was first used but vegetable oils are likely to have been used at least by the end of the Pleistocene and it is possible that the flattened cylindrical stones with incised grooves found at the Agordat sites and which resemble the *tet* stones used traditionally in the preparation of cotton and the extraction of seeds could have featured in a process of early oil extraction (Dombrowski 1970: 24).

Turning now to the *enset*-growing regions of the southern parts of the Ethiopian and the South-East Plateaux it is again not possible to say anything about the history and development of the intensive agricultural system that is usually associated with this plant (Smeds 1955). Simoons (1965) and Brandt (1984: 185-190) have speculated that this could have been a very ancient staple used by hunter/gatherers as far back as the late Pleistocene. I would agree with this view and have suggested (Clark 1978: 85) that an early '*enset* culture' may underlie that of the East African 'banana cultures'. *Enset* is still used today as a famine food by the Kipsigis and other Nilotic peoples in western Kenya (Huntingford 1953: 59; Ambrose 1984: 24). Brandt (1984:189) considers that *enset* cultivation may have archaeological visibility unlike most tuberous and root plants that leave no trace. He suggests that genetic changes may be observable in the seeds which are extremely hard and could survive for long periods. Also that the remains of the pits to store and ferment the processed *enset*, the use of stone footings to dwellings and other structures, terracing of hillsides and settlement patterns may provide in excavations the kind of evidence needed to identify an '*enset* culture'. Brandt also points out there is considerable variation in the way *enset* is used by the peoples of South-Western Ethiopia, ranging from small settlements based on shifting cultivation methods and simple ways of preparing and cooking the pseudostem, to an intensive monoculture growing *enset* in dense-manured plantations that support a complex socio-economic and ritual system centered on the plant. In this system domestic stock are important on account of the manure required for the growing plants. Together with the *enset*, root crops such as the coco-yam, the Galla potato, *Afromomum*, yams (*Dioscorea* sp.), the Cow-pea, *nug* and sesame oil are important. Cow-pea incidentally is known from a Late Stone Age context near Dire Dawa. There are important plants in the highlands where also small quantities of *tef*, finger-millet and sorghum are grown. This is a region where archaeological survey and excavation are both possible and can be expected to reveal something of the developmental stages of *enset* cultivation. Such a study is long overdue.

The last region with which this paper will deal is the Rift Valley, in particular that part from the northern boundary of the country in Eritrea to the region of the Ethiopian lakes. These hot and arid lowlands and the immediately adjacent parts of the plateaux with their escarpments have produced evidence of cattle pastoralists and keepers of fat-tailed sheep. I have previously listed the evidence of the rock-art from as far north as Keren to the Chercher mountains and the south side of the Harar plateau (Clark 1976: 75-77) Several different styles of painting and engraving are represented and are thought to cover a long period of time, though there is as yet no direct means of dating this art. Subject matter and inferred associations are all that can be used at present. All this art reflects the pastoral way of life. In the earlier stages the animals depicted are cattle of long-horned humpless African breeds and there are similarities in the techniques employed by the artists that suggest a relationship with the early 2nd and late 3rd millennium B.C. art of Nubia and the eastern Sahara. Bulls and cows are shown, the latter often with calves and with the udders clearly drawn suggesting that milk formed an important part of the pastoral diet. On the South-East Plateau escarpment fat-tailed sheep are sometimes shown herded with cattle. Sheep are not indigenous to Africa and derive from South West Asia. It is thought that the fat-tailed variety were domesticated in Arabia sometime between the middle of the 2nd millennium B.C. and the 1st millennium A.D.; not very helpful for our purpose, however. It could be argued that they entered Ethiopia no earlier than the time of the Himyaritic migrations but since these paintings are all in the earlier styles an earlier introduction is preferred. The presence of sea shell ornaments with burials of hunting/fishing peoples in the Lake Besaka basin some 5000 years old and some 500 kms from the coast are an indication that some form of contact between the interior and the coast already existed at this early time (Clark & Williams 1978).

That these prehistoric pastoralists were also hunters is shown not only by the bone food waste from the excavations but in the depiction in the rock-art of elephant, giraffe, lions, antelope and possibly dogs. The humans are shown semi-naturalistically and schematically as a capital 'H' figure. They are probably all male and carry sticks or simple pointed wooden spears. Some enigmatic hatched geometric motifs could be representations of mats. Only in the later styles found in the highlands of Eritrea and eastern Tigre are there more elaborate scenes showing warriors with metal headed spears and round shields, musicians, milking and ploughing scenes. Rarely, a Pre-Axumite inscription is associated, and it would seem that these paintings are probably no earlier than the mid-1st millennium B.C.

Representations of humped cattle and camels that are seen only in the latest styles may date from Axumite up to recent times. These are stylised depictions of single animals and they have the appearance of being casual paintings or pecked engravings lacking in the symbolism and ritual that is clearly a significant element in the earlier styles.

Two archaeological excavations throw some light on the time when domestic cattle may have been introduced to the Rift. At the double rock shelter site of Laga Oda in the Chercher escarpment, there are several different painting styles that suggest the site was used over a long period of time. An excavation in the lower shelter showed that it had been sporadically occupied over the past 15,000 years. The commonest tool was a backed bladelet or microlith that was mounted to form the cutting parts of composite tools and weapons. In the level dated to 1500 B.C. we found phalanges of domestic *Bos*. Camel remains occur only in the uppermost levels dating between 1300-1600 A.D. Low-power microscopic examination of the working edges of the microliths showed that a large proportion preserved evidence of micro-chipping and a high gloss known as sickle sheen. This gloss is the result of cutting plants, such as reeds and grass stems, that have a high silica content. Some of these microliths also preserved evidence of the mastic with which they had been mounted in the haft showing that they had been set obliquely in a handle in a manner commonly used in north Africa and the Middle East. The greatest concentration of these tools showing silica gloss occurred in the 2nd millennium levels. Of course there is no means of knowing whether the plants being processed were domesticated or not, but it is by no means impossible that some were cultivated species. Associated cultural remains include ostrich egg-shell beads, pottery and ochre. While the presence of ceramics is no evidence of food production at this late time it lends support to the view that some cultivation was being practised. The most likely grain in a low rainfall region such as the Rift is sorghum but it would not be unlikely that *tef*, whether wild or domestic, was being harvested on the escarpment of the South-East plateau at this time. Until, however, such time as carbonised remains of actual grains or impressions in pottery are recovered further speculation would serve no useful purpose.

The latest occupation at Lake Besaka is associated with a low level of the lake and is dated by charcoal to c.1,500 B.C. The stone artefact assemblage is significantly different from the earlier stages of the 'Besaka Industry'. Scraper forms now predominate over microliths, which are small, well made lunates. With these are grindstone fragments, a pestle and, from an adjacent locality but a contemporary level, a small stone bowl of lava. Both decorated and undecorated ceramics are present. These are mostly unburnished but a few sherds show a burnished exterior red slip. Vessel form is difficult to determine but one partially reconstructed pot shows a carinated profile and a pointed base. Rims suggest a number of bowl forms of varying diameter. Decorative techniques and motifs are diagonal comb, linear cord and finger nail impressions and stamping. One sherd shows incised decoration on the top of the rim. Others exhibit stamping over the whole surface of the pot and a red slip or wash. Though not the same, this pottery is reminiscent of that found with the Agordat sites. Faunal remains are all of land mammals and fish are no longer present. Domestic cattle have been provisionally identified on the basis of several teeth.

These changes in the material culture have been tentatively interpreted as showing the replacement of the hunting/fishing/collecting economy by one of stock-raising and hunting. The scrapers are seen as possible indicators of hide dressing (Haaland 1980). Much further north on the Gulf of Aden coast at Karin Heganeh in Somalia a Later Stone Age industry has been found by Steven Brandt in a rock-shelter with early style paintings of pied cattle; a date of c.2000 years B.P. (S. Brandt: Per. Com.) was obtained for a sample of charcoal from the excavated cultural deposit though its relationship to the paintings is difficult to determine.

Though all this is still slender evidence it does indicate that cattle pastoralists were present in the Rift and escarpments of Ethiopia by at least 1500 B.C., an age consistent with the evidence from the eastern Sudan.

CONCLUSION

In conclusion, therefore, the available archaeological evidence points to the earliest indigenous crop cultivation as having taken place by the beginning of the 2nd, possibly during the 3rd, millennium B.C. At the same time, though it needs to be borne in mind that domestication of livestock could have been quite independent of cultivation, cattle and probably small stock were acquired by both highland and lowland populations. The latter are more likely to have been nomadic, milk-using pastoralists who migrated considerable distances between the Rift and plateau with the seasons as such people do today. Highland people in the North may similarly have practised seasonal transhumance between their permanent settlements on the plateau and the Sudanese lowland steppe seeking grazing for their livestock. The move to the plains might be seen as involving mostly the male part of the population, while the women, girls and elderly remained in the villages to tend the crops. Cultivation would have been a system of long fallow and shifting swidden agriculture. A long distance exchange system via Punt may have given knowledge of and access to the products of Dynastic Egypt. It may similarly have been a source of diffusion of wheat, barley and possibly the plough to Ethiopia. Later innovations introduced from South Arabia in the 1st millennium B.C. would have included more general use of metal, bronze and later iron, for tools and weapons, a more intensive agricultural system, certainly including irrigated terracing and plough cultivation, and a pattern of urban markets and religious centres each supported by a number of satellite villages.

When archaeological research can be actively pursued again the following considerations need to be borne in mind:-

1. Normally, if the presence of one domesticated plant can be established, then others can also be expected to occur and a system of intercropping should be looked for, though this need not have happened all at one time.
2. Domestic plants and animals may *at first* have been only a minor constituent of the food supply most of which would have continued to have been supplied by wild resources as was the case on the Nile and in the eastern Sudan.
3. No significant change in settlement patterning, location and technology can be expected, therefore, in the initial stages of an early food-producing economy.
4. As soon as domestic plants and animals dominate the economy, however, settlement forms may be expected to undergo considerable modification, location will be different, and significant changes in the technology will occur. Effective crop production requires

new kinds of equipment for breaking new ground, manuring, cultivating, reaping and threshing as well as for food preparation. This last is probably best seen in the new ceramic forms that make their appearance. Social organization will also undergo considerable modification and an hierarchical system can be expected; this should be readily visible archaeologically. Short and long distance trade networks can also be expected, for example in salt, obsidian, metal ores and metal artefacts and exotic prestige articles coming with long distance trade; these networks should also be visibly traceable.

Causes of change are less easy to identify, but natural and earth scientists are refining considerably the record of post-Pleistocene climatic fluctuations with the result that archaeologists will be able to show more precisely the extent to which climatic episodes may correlate with cultural changes. One of the most successful ways used by African peoples to adapt to change is temporary readjustment of a fluid socio-economic system. For example, in times of adversity populations of mixed farmers may become nomadic stock herders, or alternatively, pastoralists if they have lost their stock may become temporary cultivators, but only until such time as they can resume their traditional way of life.

A feature of traditional, shifting agriculture in Africa is the persistent use of wild resources, both plant and animal, and in times of famine wild plant resources in particular become of major importance. Finally, it should not be forgotten that there is ample evidence for the simultaneous presence of more than one very different way of life. Hunter/gatherers continue to exist, either in a position of inferior status with food-producers, or more successfully in symbiotic relationship with them by means of a system of mutually respected social obligations and exchange. Similarly, cultivators and pastoralists co-exist successfully. Such patterns should be looked for since they would be traceable in the archaeological record.

These then are some of the situations and patterns that the archaeologist needs to be aware of and that need to be identified in any future research into the origins of food production in Ethiopia, for, to quote Louis Pasteur, "in the fields of observation chance favours only the mind that is prepared". When renewed this will be a highly rewarding field of research, for, whereas the discoveries of the early hominid fossils belong to the whole world of humanity, this later period of research is of especial interest to all Ethiopians as it lies at the very root of Ethiopian culture.

ACKNOWLEDGEMENTS

Grateful thanks are recorded here to the Ministry of Culture and Sport of the Military Government of Ethiopia for making possibly my own fieldwork in Ethiopia; to Steven Brandt, Martin Williams and Donald Adamson for their valued collaboration in the field; to Steven Brandt also for information on his sites in Somalia; to the National Museum, Nairobi, for providing an obsidian sample from Quiha and to Joseph Michels for the hydration analysis date; to Rudolfo Fattovich for much useful discussion. Also to Judith Ogden for the Map and to Suzanne Sundholm and to my wife for typing the text, my grateful thanks.

BIBLIOGRAPHY

Ambrose, S. H. (1984)

(a) *Holocene environments and human adaptations in the central Rift Valley, Kenya*. Doctoral dissertation, Dept. of Anthropology, University of California, Berkeley.

————————

(b) "The introduction of pastoral adaptations to the Highlands of East Africa" *In* J. D. Clark and S. A. Brandt (*eds.*) *From Hunters to Farmers*, Univ. of California Press, Berkeley: 212-39.

Arkell, A. J. (1954)

"Four occupation sites at Agordat", *Kush* 11: 33-62.

Barthelme, J. W. (1984) "Early evidence for animal domestication in eastern Africa" *In* J. D. Clark and S. A. Brandt (*eds.*). *From Hunters to Farmers*, Univ. of California Press, Berkeley:200-205.

Brandt, S. A. (1980) "Investigation of Late Stone Age occurrences at Lake Besaka, Ethiopia" *In Proc. Eighth Pan-African Cong. on Prehist. and Quat. Studies, 1977*, Nairobi: 239-243.

——————— (1984) "New perspectives on the origins of food production in Ethiopia" *In* J. D. Clark and S. A. Brandt (*eds.*), *From Hunters to Farmers*, Univ. of California Press, Berkeley: 173-190.

Brandt, S. A. and G. A. Brook (1984) "Archaeological and Palaeoenvironmental research in northern Somalia", *Current Anthropology* 25 (1): 119-120.

Brown, L. H. and Cocheme, J. (1969) *A study of the agroclimatology of the Highlands of eastern Africa*, F.A.O., Rome.

Butzer, K. W. (1981) "Rise and fall of Axum, Ethiopia: A geo-archeological interpretation", *American Antiquity*, 46 (3): 471-495.

Callow, P and G. Wahida (1981) "Fieldwork in northern and eastern Sudan, 1977-1981", *Nyame Akuma*, 18: 34-36.

Clark, J. D. (1954) *The prehistoric cultures of the Horn of Africa*, Cambridge University Press, Cambridge.

——————— (1976) "The domestication process in sub-Saharan Africa with special reference to Ethiopia" *U.I.S.P.P., IXe Congrès (Nice, 1976)*, Colloque XX *Origine de l'élevage et de la domestication Prétirage:* 56-115.

——————— (1984) "Prehistoric cultural continuity and economic change in the central Sudan in the early Holocene" *In* J. D. Clark and S. A. Brandt (*eds.*) *From Hunters to Farmers*, Univ. of California Press, Berkeley: 113-126.

——————— (1985) (a) "The domestication process in northeastern Africa: ecological change and adaptive strategies in riverine, desert and high plateau eco-systems" *In* L. Krzyzaniak and M. Kobusiewicz (*eds.*), *Origin and early development of food producing cultures in northeastern Africa*. Polish Acad. Sci. Warsaw.

(b) "Speculations on the origins of cereal cultivation in northeast Africa". *Volume in honour of Professor M. Puglisi*, I. Caneva *et al.* (*eds.*) Universita di Roma, Instituto di Paletnologia.

Clark, J. D. and Kurashina, H. (1981) "A study of the work of a modern tanner in Ethiopia and its relevance for archaeological interpretation" *In* R. A. Gould and M. B. Schiffer (*eds.*), *Modern material culture: The archaeology of us*. Academic Press, New York:303-321.

Clark, J. D. and Williams, M. A. J. (1978) "Recent archaeological research in southeastern Ethiopia (1974-1975): Some preliminary results", *Annales d'Ethiopie*, 11: 19-44.

Dombrowski, J. (1970)   "Preliminary report on excavations in Lalibela and Natchabiet caves, Begemeder", *Annales d'Ethiopie* 8: 21-29.

Dyson, W. S. and Fuchs, V. E. (1937)   "The Elmolo", *Journ. Roy. Anthrop. Inst.* 67: 327-338.

Ehret, G. (1979)   "On the antiquity of agriculture in Ethiopia", *Journ. of Afr. History*, 20: 161-177.

Fattovich, R., Marks, A. E. and Mohammed-Ali, A. (1984)   "The archaeology of the eastern Sahel, Sudan: Preliminary results". *The African Archaeological Review*, 2: 173-188.

Gallagher, J. P.   "Contemporary stone tools in Ethiopia: Implications for archaeology", *Journal of Field Archaeology*, 4: 407-414.

Gamst, F. C. (1979)   "Wayto ways: Change from hunting to peasant life", *In* R. L. Hess (*ed.*). *Proc. 5th Int. Conf. on Ethiopian studies*, Chicago: 233-238.

Gasse, F., Rognon, P., and Street, F. A. (1980)   "Quaternary history of the Afar and Ethiopian Rift lakes" *In* M. A. J. Williams and H. Faure (*eds.*), *The Sahara and the Nile*, Balkema, Rotterdam: 361-400.

Gillespie, R., Street-Perrot and Switsur, R. (1983)   "Post-Glacial arid episodes in Ethiopia have implications for climatic prediction", *Nature*, 306: 680-683.

Haaland, R. (1980)   "Lithic tools as possible indicators of early domestication" *In* R. E. Leakey and B. A. Ogot (*eds.*), *Proc. 8th Pan-African Congress on Prehistory and Quaternary Studies, Nairobi, 1977*, Nairobi: 263-264.

Harlan, J. R. (1969)   "Ethiopia: A center of diversity", *Economic Botany*, 23: 309-314.

————————— (1971)   "Agricultural origins: Centers or non-centers", *Science*, 174: 468-474.

Harlan, J. R. and Zohary, D. (1966)   "Distribution of wild wheats and barley", *Science*, 153: 1074-1080.

Huntingford, G. W. B. (1953)   *The southern Nilo-Hamites*, Ethnographic Survey of Africa, Int. African Inst., London.

Kitchen, K. A. (1971)   "Punt and how to get there", *Orientalia*, 40 (NS [2]), Pontificium Institutum Biblicum, Rome: 184-207.

Kobishchanov, Y. M. (1979)   *Axum*. English translation, Pennsylvania State Univ. Press, University Park.

Krzyzaniak, L. (1978)   "New light on the early stages of food production in the central Sudan", *Journ. Afr. History*, 19 (159-172).

Murdock, G. P. (1959)	*Africa: Its people and their culture history*, McGraw Hill, New York.
O'Mahoney, K. (1970)	"The salt trail", *Journ. of Ethiopian studies*, 8(2): 147-154.
Phillipson, D. W. (1977)	(a) *The later prehistory of eastern and southern Africa*, Heinemann, London.
————————	(b) "The excavation of Gobedra Rock Shelter, Axum: An early occurrence of cultivated finger-millet in northern Ethiopia", *Azania*, 12: 53-82.
———————— (1985)	*African archaeology*, C.U.P., Cambridge.
Seligman, C. G. (1957)	*Races of Africa*, O.U.P., Oxford.
Servant, M. and Servant-Vildary, S. (1980)	"L'environnement quaternaire du bassin du Tchad", *In* M. A. J. Williams and H. Faure (*eds.*), *The Sahara and the Nile*, Balkema, Rotterdam: 133-162.
Shack, W. A. (1974)	*The central Ethiopians – Amhara, Tigrina and related peoples*, Ethnographic Survey of Africa, Int. Afr. Inst., London.
Simoons, F. (1958)	"The agricultural implements and cutting tools of Begemder and Semyen, Ethiopia", *Southwestern Journ. of Anthrop.* 14: 386-406.
Simoons, F. D. (1965)	"Some questions on the economic prehistory of Ethiopia", *Journ. Afr. Hist.*, 6: 1-13.
Smeds, H. (1955)	"The Ensete planting culture of eastern Sidamo, Ethiopia", *Acta Geographica*, 13(4): 3-39, Helsingfors.
Street, F. A. (1980)	"Chronology of late Pleistocene and Holocene lake-level fluctuations, Ziway-Shala Basin, Ethiopia" *In* R. E. Leakey and B. A. Ogot (*eds.*), *Proc. 8th Pan-Afr. Cong. on Prehist. and Quat. Studies, Nairobi, 1977*, Nairobi: 143-146.
Talbot, M. R. (1980)	"Environmental responses to climatic change in the west African Sahel over the past 20,000 years" *In* M. A. J. Williams and H. Faure (*eds.*), *The Sahara and the Nile*, Balkema, Rotterdam: 37-62.
Wendorf, F., Schild, R., Close, A. E., Donahue, D. J., Jull, A. J. T., Zabel, T. H., Wieckowska, H., Kobusiewicz, M., Issawi, B. and Hadidi, N. el., (1984)	"New radiocarbon dates on the cereals from Wadi Kubbaniya", *Science*, 225: 645-646.

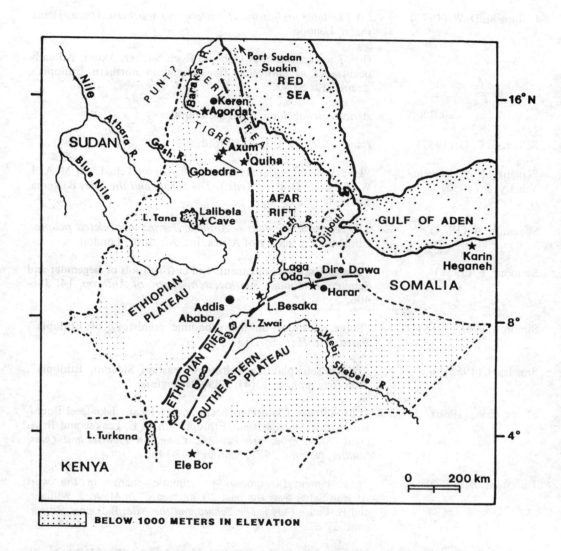

PLACES AND SITES IN ETHIOPIA REFERRED TO IN THE TEXT

BELOW 1000 METERS IN ELEVATION

0   200 km

REFLECTIONS ON THE ORIGINS OF THE

ETHIOPIAN CIVILIZATION

Ephraim Isaac   Cain Felder
Princeton University   Howard Divinity School

One of the most enigmatic inquiries in Ethiopian history concerns the question of Ethiopian-South Arabian relations, its nature and extent.

Several centuries ago, the Greek grammarian Stephanus of Byzantium (6th cent.) asserted *"Abasenoi ethnos Arabias . . . "*, further suggesting that the Ethiopians, together with the Sabaeans and the Hadramawti, form three Arabian tribes[1]. But Stephanus was neither a historian nor a geographer; he was simply a linguistic compiler who brought material together from diverse sources.

Among modern historians, Ludolphus Hiob first posited the hypothesis that the founders of Ethiopian culture were foreign immigrants: *"indigenae enim non sunt sed venerunt ex ea Arabiae parte que felix vocatur . . ."*[2].

But it was not until the late nineteenth century, however, that the South Arabian origin of the Ethiopian civilization hypothesis got a seemingly firm foundation from the discovery and decipherment of Sabaean inscriptions. Since then, the subsequent study of Semitic languages and civilizations and research in ancient history both appeared to give it strong credence. In particular, the works of Halevy, Muller, Bent, Glazer, Conti Rossini, Littman, *et al.* in Northern Ethiopia and Southern Arabia respectively during the nineteenth and early twentieth centuries confirmed an indisputable Ethiopian-South Arabian tie.

The first detailed European reconstruction of South Arabian and early Ethiopian histories by E. Glaser and Conti Rossini respectively appeared to be definitive of South Arabian influence on Ethiopian culture[3]. Both of these scholars attached special significance to the name *hbst* which appeared in a number of Sabaean texts. The obvious similarity between *hbst* and the Arabic *al-habasa* (Abyssinia) was believed to be explicit proof of the Sabaean origins of Ethiopian civilization. In particular, the well-known Italian Ethiopist Conti Rossini worked this view into his historical doctrine. As one critic interprets the theory which came to be taken for granted, "By a process of conquest of absorption (the habashat) merged with the local native Hamitic population and became 'Africanized'. From this arose the proto-Ethiopian civilization and the proto-Ethiopic texts of Ethiopia"[4]. It thus came to be widely accepted that *hbst* referred to a South Arabian tribe, which some time before the fifth pre-Christian century crossed the Red Sea and settled in northern Ethiopia.

Since the days of Conti Rossini, little, if any, scholarly doubt has been expressed concerning what came to be accepted as a fact of South Arabian origin and/or influence on Ethiopian culture. Instead the new theory of large population movement from South Arabia to Ethiopia was accepted by historians as a matter of fact and promoted vigorously. Only recently have serious historians of Ethiopia began to question the old theory, particularly, the view that a large migration had taken place from South Arabia into Ethiopia. But even those, like Irvine and Schneider, who doubt the total veracity of the old theory do not, however, question, as we do here, the concept of the so-called South Arabic cultural influence in Ethiopia.[5]

Taken in the context of post-eighteenth century historiography, the cultural and racialistic overtones of this theory cannot be minimized or ignored. As with ancient Egypt, Benin, or Zimbabwe, a clear attempt was made to "Caucasianize" a major African civilization[6]. Ethiopian civilization has been attributed to a core group of superior Semitic colonists. Even those who later came to have a lingering doubt about a large population movement from South Arabia to Ethiopia would not think of questioning the superior nature of the non-African founders of the Ethiopian civilization. One author writes explicitly:

"numerically the South Arabian leaven was not significant, but its *superior quality* (emphasis mine) revolutionized life in the Abyssinian highlands and infused into the predominantly Cushite element that peculiarly Semitic ingredient which has throughout the ages given Ethiopian civilization its special character."

Based on linguistic, epigraphic, and literary evidences, there is little doubt that there was a strong tie between Ethiopia and South Arabia during the first millennium BCE and in early Christian times. It is also clear that the two shores of the southern end of the Red Sea share a veritable linguistic, literary, religious and historical tradition, attested in ancient historical and geographic writings, as well as in modern archaeological discoveries.

Nonetheless, there is an essential difference between historical and cultural ties and the concept of cultural domination directly or indirectly. In the case of Ethiopian-South Arabian relations, the former is a demonstrable fact, the latter, however, an unproven hypothesis containing erroneous historical, linguistic, and archaeological assumptions — that no Semitic language is indigenous to Ethiopia, that Proto-Ethiopic inscriptions were brought to Ethiopia from South Arabia, and that no indigenous high culture developed in Africa (a Hegelian Euro-centric philosophical perspective of history).

We are of course not yet at the stage when we can conclusively demonstrate scientifically the historical roots of Ethiopian culture. Nonetheless, we are in a position to question the bases of the old hypothesis about its South Arabian origins. The objective of this paper is not to analyze and describe ancient Ethiopian cultural ties with Egypt and Nubia in the distant antiquity. But, it must be said before we proceed that, above and beyond our present criticism of the old theories with which we are concerned here, that, in general, research into Ethiopian history has overlooked these ties, and that a closer look at Ethiopian culture and history in the context of the Nile civilizations should in the future be required by students studying the roots of Ethiopian civilization.

Firstly, it can no longer be taken for granted that Semitic languages necessarily originate in the Near East. Various attempts at placing the ultimate origin of the Semitic languages in the Fertile Crescent or in Arabia have not altogether proven successful. Contrary to some older assumptions, it cannot be shown that "Semitic" is a major language family like Indo-European; rather, it is more or less like "Slavic" or "Germanic", a smaller subdivision of a major family of languages. The debate on the origin of "Semitic" continues. Meanwhile, however, many serious scholars accept the view that it is a branch of a major language family called Hamito-Semitic or Afro-Asiatic. It is now further thought by some that Proto-Hamito-Semitic originates in Africa rather than in the Near East. The well-known Russian Assyriologist, Diakonoff, for instance, proposes Proto-Hamito-Semitic to be a language spoken in the eastern Sahara somewhere around present day Chad, about six thousand years ago[7]. However, he does not question the fact that Proto-Semitic developed in the Near East after it branched off of Proto-Hamito-Semitic, or that the original Semitic language(s) of Ethiopia come from there. On the other hand, Murtonen has gone as far as proposing the Horn of Africa in which Ethiopia is centrally embedded as the original home of Proto-Semitic[8].

It is hence not impossible that some form of Semitic languages are indigenous to Ethiopia. Nonetheless, it is not our task here to demonstrate the veracity of such a theory, nor to argue for or against one or another theory concerning the origin of Semitic languages. It is enough to point out that the premise of a South Arabian origin of Ethiopian Semitic language(s) is undermined by the facts that there remain lingering problems as to the origin of Semitic languages and that no scholar has yet fully demonstrated scientifically the origin of Ethiopian Semitic languages (or how exactly the first Semitic language(s) arrived in Ethiopia from South Arabia, if they did so).

Secondly, there is a historical problem with the chronology proposed for the migration of South Arabian tribes to Ethiopia. If tribes have migrated to Ethiopia so recently during the first millennium BCE, one would naturally expect the peoples of the Ethiopian side of the Red Sea to speak the linguistic dialect of the dominating colonists of South Arabia at least up to the third century. However, at least one visitor to this area, the author of the *Periplus of the Eryth-*

raean Sea, does not seem to be aware of any one single language that was spoken in common on the two shores of the Red Sea[9]. Furthermore, scholars believe that *hbst* is the name of (one of) the principal South Arabian tribe(s) which migrated to Ethiopia. But A. J. Drewes has pointed out that this name, found in Sabaean inscriptions in South Arabia, does not appear in the Ethiopian ones at least until Esana's time about 350[10]. It is equally significant that none of the inscriptions on either side had any information about any extensive migrations from South Arabia to Ethiopia.

Clearly, the identification of the *hbst* as the South Arabian precursors of the Ethiopian civilization is at best a guess. At least one scholar has recently suggested that *hbst* refers not to a South Arabian tribe, but to a region around Axum. Using Albert Jamme's more recent contributions to the study of Sabaean inscriptions in South Arabia, A. K. Irvine has cogently argued in his *The Identity of Habashat*, that the term *hbst* is the nomenclature of a geographical region, not of a tribe[11]. He argues that *hbst* is grammatically not a form of a tribe's name, apart from the fact that there is so far no mention of such a tribe in the inscriptions. He concludes, "There is little or no reason to suppose that any case of Habasat or Habasa refers to a South Arabian tribe or district . . . Whenever Habasat occurs in a context which permits identification, it is reasonable to suppose that it refers to Abyssinia . . . It would not therefore be legitimate to accord the Habasat with certainty the honour of having laid the foundations of a civilization which is at least eight centuries older than their first apparent mention in the country"[12]. Irvine's suggested identification of *hbst* with the Axumite region is far from certain. In particular, his theory fails to explain the reasons why the name *hbst* is absent from the earliest Ethiopian inscriptions, as opposed to the South Arabian ones. Nevertheless, Irvine is doubtless correct in challenging the unsubstantiated theories of earlier scholars.

We shall here allude in passing to the presence of the title *mkrrb* in Ethiopia in the post-fifth century BCE inscriptions. Some have suggested that this word, believed to be the pre-fifth century BCE title of the king of Saba in South Arabia, indicates South Arabian origin of early Ethiopian state and royal tradition[13]. This is a meaningless assertion based simply on a secondary inference rather than on tangible evidence. It neither warrants a conclusion that the Ethiopian political state is of South Arabian origin nor that the title was a necessary loan from outside. At best it indicates that the early Ethiopians and South Arabians shared a common or similar political structure, perhaps originating from a single earlier civilization on both banks of the Red Sea.

Thirdly, examining the inscriptions more closely, we find certain revealing facts. In most cases, the earliest Sabaean inscriptions found in Northern Ethiopia (before c. 400 BCE) cannot be distinguished from those found in South Arabia, both in style and content. They are monumental and elegant in character and resemble the standard South Arabic inscriptions in their form of dedications. Yet, the inscriptions of Ethiopia are no mere imitations of the South Arabian ones; they manifest a certain degree of independence and initiative. Compare, for instance, examples (a) and (b), two Melazo inscriptions below described by A. J. Drewes (*Annales d'Ethiopie*, III [1959], pp.84-99):

(a) T. 3 = J.E., 100 (p.89f.)

1. . . .]/grbyn [hn	Two GRBites
2. ḏ mryb / hqny/'	of MRYB dedicated
3. lmqh / mhrt / yd	to 'LMQH the work of their hands
4. hmy / bn ḫ /w'rn	for W'RN

The expression *hqny* in line 2 is standard form in South Arabian dedicatory inscriptions. [2] 'LMQH is believed to be the Sabaean national lunar deity. [3] On the other hand, another inscription reads:

(b) T. 7 = J.E., 111 (p.92f.)

1. ylbb	YLBB
2. grbyn	the GRBite
3. hqnyl 'lmqh	dedicated to 'LMQH

As in the previous text, this is also a GRBite offertory inscription to 'LMQH. However, rather than the dedication *hqny* found in line 2 of our first sample, we find here the formula *hqny l-*. This formula has not yet been attested in South Arabia, but appears in numerous Ethiopian texts. Moreover, it appears to be related to the Ethiopic expression *'aqnaya l-*.

Drewes explains the differences between the two examples above by positing two types of inscriptions during the middle of the first millennium BCE. The first belongs to a group of inscriptions which is the product of South Arabian colonists. The language of these inscriptions "appears to be an authentic form of Sabaean, despite certain traits which distinguish it from the Sabaean found in South Arabia". The second belongs to another group of inscriptions which manifest "certain peculiarities that can be explained by the supposition that the inscriptions of this group are not derived from South Arabian colonies in Ethiopia, but from Ethiopians".

Drewes's division of the inscriptions into two groups is indeed an enlightening one. Nonetheless, it is not clear on what grounds he claims the first type to be of direct South Arabian provenance. In fact, we find in Text A.I., the word *bn ḥ* in line 4. This term has not so far been found in any South Arabian inscription. Drewes offers no explanation for the existence of such "distinguishing traits" in the writing of what he calls Sabaean colonists.

Other examples also show *no necessary* South Arabian influence on Ethiopian epigraphy. See, for instance the Enda Cerqos inscription described by R. Schneider (*Ibid*, IV [1961], pp.61-65):

J.E., 1384 (p. 63f.)

1. ... .mn/mlkn/sr'n/yg' ḏ yn/mkrb/d'mt/wsb'/bn/rb ...
2. ... .h/mlkn/hyww/whhdsw/m ḏ qnt/'wsn/bytmw/ywm[/ ...

Various scholars have translated this inscription in different ways. Schneider gives: 1. . . . . MN MLKN SR'N, (of the tribe of) YG' Ḏ, mkrb of D'MT and of SB', . . . 2. . . . . H MLKN restored and renovated the chapel of idols of their house, when . . . T. Tamrat (*Church and State* . . . , pp. 9ff.) suggests for the first line: "King of Sr'n, (and) Ygzyan, Mkrb of D'mt and SB". A. J. Drewes (*Inscriptions de l'Ethiopie Antique*, p.97) offers a third possible rendition for the opening of the first line: "the just king YG' Ḏ ite".

As with the previous examples this inscription diverges from standard South Arabian ones in two aspects. First, instead of the South Arabian t, we find s as in other Ethiopian inscriptions (cf. Drewes, *Ibid*.). As Schneider rightly suggests this appears to be the case in the word *'wsn* of line 2, for that word is almost certainly a variant of the South Arabian *'wtn*, an idol of stone or wood. Second, as Schneider shows, in the word *lytmw*, the standard South Arabian *hmw* has been replaced by the third person plural suffix *-mw*.

During the succeeding centuries from c. 400 BCE to late first century BCE, Ethiopian inscriptions reflect even more independence in epigraphic execution, despite what F. Anfray calls the continuing South Arabian influence upon them (*AE*, VII [1967], p.50). As a result of internal evolution, changes in style and syntactical structure begin to take place. The writing becomes less geometrical, and the monumental form of inscriptions begins to disappear by the end of the fourth century BCE. Many of the inscriptions which Drewes describes under the title "Petites Inscriptions" (Chapter II, *Inscriptions de l'Ethiopie Antique*, pp.71ff.) belong to this period. A couple of examples will suffice:

Drewes 43 (p.19) Feqya

| Symbole / sqm / bn /b'l | symbol/SQM son of B'L |
| hqny / l d̲ t/ hmn | dedicated to D̲ T HMN |

It was noted above that the inscriptions of Melazo contain variant dedicatory formulae. As Drewes rightly points out the one dedicatory formula found at Feyqa is *hqny l*, not *hqny* as in as in the South Arabian formulae. Moreover, the name of the deity, "D̲ T HMN", in this and other inscriptions varies from the standard South Arabian manner of writing that name, "D̲ T HMYN".

Drewes 58 (p. 23) Zeban Motoro

| symbole / 'n°n /bn /whbm | symbol / 'N'N son of WHBM |
| lyhw / 'wb | live 'WB |

Drewes 61 = Franchini 32 (p. 24) La'lay Addi

| symbole / lthw / d̲ | symbol / live D[T] |
| h | H[MN] |

"*Lyhw* so-and-so" and "*lthw* so-and-so" appear in numerous Ethiopian texts. But, neither verbal form is found in South Arabian inscriptions. The names (e.g. *'wb*, not attested elsewhere) following the invocation "live" are thought to be those of divinities.

Numerous other inscriptions may be adduced to show Ethiopian independent epigraphic development of indigenous authorship. The cultural ties between Ethiopia and South Arabia should not be used as precedent to show a one-way flow of influence. The Ethiopians neither copied nor imitated the South Arabians but freely produced these proto-Ethiopic texts, the major body of Sabaean epigraphic literature.

We must underline here again that there can be no doubt about the significant contact and interaction between the South Arabians and the Ethiopians by the fifth pre-Christian century. But facts such as that the monumental script appears in Ethiopian inscriptions only later (in the fifth and fourth centuries BCE?) are at this stage of our knowledge of Ethiopian inscriptions not adequate proof of the South Arabian ethnic origin of the Ethiopian people or of Ethiopian civilization let alone of a dominance and expansion. At most what they show is a common cultural heritage.

Fourthly, scholars had conjectured at different times since the seventeenth century the origin of the Ethiopic alphabet to be Samaritan (Ludolphus, Silvestre), Syriac (Kopp), or Sabaean (Glazer, Hommel, Conti Rossini). But we now know that Ethiopic is a cursive form of monumental Sabaean, hence, the immediate southern branch of Sinaitic or the first known alphabet from which also comes the Phoenician (Canaanite/Hebrew) script.

Some scholars trace the origin of writing to the ancient Near East, in general, and to Mesopotamia, in particular, where they believe the first system of writing was invented by the Sumerians about 3500 BCE. Others, however, consider Egypt the home of the first system of writing dating back to the end of the pre-dynastic times, or roughly about the same time as in Mesopotamia. Not only did the Egyptians develop a systematic pictographic and ideogrammic form of writing but also a whole series of unilateral symbols, in fact a system of an entire proto-alphabet of 24 characters, which some scholars believe might have inspired the invention of the ingenious device of symbols of sounds which we call the alphabet.

By whom and when the alphabetic system was invented is still a matter of conjecture, but the earliest known examples of it, the Proto-Sinaitic, have so far come from about twenty-five inscriptions in the Sinai Peninsula, discovered in 1906 in Egyptian turquoise mines by the English archaeologist Flinders Petrie. Proto-Sinaitic, a linear consonantal script alphabet that developed from hieroglyphs or pictographic writing on the acrophonic principle, evolved into

Sinaitic during the second half of the second millennium BCE[14]. Sabaean (which can rightly be called Proto-Ethiopic), like Phoenician/Hebrew, derived from Sinaitic, and is one of the oldest alphabetic forms of writing. It has preserved many of the original forms and shapes of the Sinaitic (or Proto-Sinaitic).

A monograph incised on a sherd in South Arabia has been dated to the 8th century BCE by the radiocarbon method, and some earlier inscriptions have been dated to the end of the second or early first millennium BCE on paleographic grounds. But when and how Sinaitic first reached the southern end of the Red Sea (Ethiopia or Yemen?) is still unknown; it could not have been much before the beginning of the first millennium BCE.

The fact that the earliest Sabaean inscriptions so far found in Ethiopia are not dated much before the fifth century BCE does not warrant a conclusion that the alphabet came to Ethiopia through South Arabia. Such a conclusion awaits an exhaustive survey and definitive study of ancient inscriptions in Ethiopia. We should note, however, that only in Ethiopia significantly did the Sinaitic-Sabaean script become fully exploited and developed. Not only did the Ethiopians quite early modify the script from the graphic monumental into a less symmetrical style, but also over the centuries they developed a new order of the letters, completely different from Phœnician. Moreover, they became the first to innovate and vocalize the script of a Semitic language, change and standardize the direction of its writing, and use it in manuscripts and literature. It is equally significant that the South Arabians, on the contrary, never developed Sabaean much beyond its earliest form, nor were able to adapt it to literature as the Ethiopians did. (It was not until after the rise of Islam that they produced local manuscripts in borrowed Arabic script.) The manner in which the Ethiopians used Sabaean, with freedom and originality, hardly betrays the behavior of simple borrowers.

Fifthly, historians have used ancient literary references to the Sabaeans, in particular the Biblical story of the Queen of Sheba, as proof for the precedence of South Arabia over Ethiopia. The origin of the people whom we call Sabaeans is shrouded in mystery. The earliest known literary source that mentions them is believed to be Gen. 10:7 (cf. I Chr. 1:9) where we find Sheba and Seba listed as descendants of Ham through Kush. In this and other Biblical sources, Sheba is associated with Egypt and Nubia (cf. also Is 43:3) and hence, as one scholar says, "it is probable that Seba was located in Africa"[15]. On the other hand in Gen. 10:28 (cf. I Chr. 1:22) Sheba is listed among the sons of Shem. According to another source in Gen.25:3 (I Chr. 1:32), Sheba is a descendant of Abraham and of a Keturah. In these latter respects the Sabaeans would be regarded as a group related to the peoples of the Fertile Crescent and Arabia. At any rate, "the genealogical references indicate that the Israelites thought that the Sabaeans were related to the peoples of the Fertile Crescent — including themselves — on the one hand, and to the peoples of Africa on the other"[16].

When the Deuteronomic redactor, who functioned some time between 620 and 610 BCE in Judea, decided to insert the short story about the Queen of Sheba (I Kings 10:1 - 10,13) into his larger narrative of I Kings,[17] little did he know that he was initiating a controversy of no small historical significance. The Queen of Sheba story is actually incidental to the redactor; a tradition about her is merely pressed into service in I Kings 10 in order to aid the writer's own theological design. His primary purpose in using the story about the Queen of Sheba is to dramatize his consistent theological claim that the God of Israel rewards those who obey the Deuteronomic laws (I Kings 3:12). In this respect, he focuses upon the wisdom and glory of Solomon as loyal and obedient leader of the people of God.

Yet, despite this intended focus for the earliest biblical account about the Queen of Sheba, a wide variety of interpretations have been spawned by certain problematic features of the I Kings 10:1 - 10,13 story.

The text of I Kings 10:1 - 10,13, essentially repeated nearly 300 years later by the author of II Chronicles 9:1-12, indicates that the Queen who visited Solomon in Jerusalem hailed from a place called Sheba; she is called *malchat sb'* (LXX: *Basilissa Saba*). A major problem caused by such a designation is the paucity of biblical evidence which would help one identify more precisely the geographical location of this land of Sheba and the ethnic identity of the Queen. Do we have here a reference to a Kushite/Ethiopian Queen of ancient Africa or is this a Queen of Arabia? For centuries Ethiopians have insisted on the former and have named her Makeda. Some modern scholars have insisted on the latter[18]. In accordance with the various claims, the story of the Queen of Sheba has undergone extensive Arabian, Ethiopian, Jewish and other elaborations and has become the subject of one of the most ubiquitous and fertile cycles of legends in the Middle East[19].

Before turning to some of these expansions and re-interpretations of the original Old Testament story about the Queen of Sheba, a word needs to be said about the rationale for considering this topic important within the context of Ethiopian history. Modern western scholarship generally insists that the Sheba mentioned in I Kings 10:1 is to be located in Arabia[20]. The implication is that the Queen of Sheba was in no sense an African. In order to dispel this possible implication, we wish to argue three points. First, the biblical evidence is noticeably silent or confusing regarding the location of Sheba and the racial identity of the Queen. Secondly, the non-biblical evidence which would place Sheba in Arabia is drawn from cuneiform (Assyrian) inscriptions which are in a number of respects problematic in themselves. Thirdly, to place the Queen of Sheba in the southern part of the Arabian peninsula still leaves open the question of her ethnic identity, given the close relations between Cush and ancient Sheba — wherever it was. The curious persistent testimonies of Josephus, Origen, Jerome and the Ethiopians themselves, who all considered the Queen of Sheba to be an Ethiopian may throw light upon the third point. The basis of their belief may offer for us an opportunity to discern a certain historical basis beneath the legend of the Queen of Sheba.

What, then, are the more significant biblical passages which appear to be of some assistance in identifying the geographical location of ancient Sheba? Our attention is first directed to the famous Table of Nations in Genesis 10. Here set forth as part of the descendants of Noah are three references to Sheba. At a glance, Genesis 10 seems to be a single listing of the descendants of Noah; but on close inspection, with the aid of the source, form, and redaction critics, it becomes clear that, in Genesis 10, we have an older so-called (J) list synthesized by a priest redactor who has his own separate list (P)[21]. The conflation of these two lists may account for the fact that a son of Cush, son of Ham, is named Seba (Sb') and a grandson of Cush is named Sheba (Sba') on the one hand, whereas in Gen. 10:28, Sheba (Sb') is also mentioned as a descendant of Shem. Assuming that the Queen of Sheba would be associated with one of these persons is of little consequence, when it is virtually impossible to determine which is the correct person.

In the Genesis 10 Table of Nations, it will be recalled, Seba and Sheba are both descendants of Ham. The term Sb' with the initial samech has been identified as an Old South Arabic equivalent of Sb'[22]. If this is the case, we have in Genesis 10 the curious fact that two persons named Sheba are listed as descendants of Cush, while only one person by the name of Sheba is listed as a descendant of Shem. A further anomaly is encountered as one turns to Deutero-Isaiah. In Isaiah 43:3, God stands prepared to offer the richest and furthest countries among which are Egypt, Ethiopia, and Seba (Masoretic: Misrayim, Cush, Sb'). Here as in Isaiah 45:14, we find Seba spelled with the initial samech and yet distinguished from Cush. No doubt, this may be explained as an attestation of the fact that part of Gen. 10 and Deutero-Isaiah as a whole are products of the exilic period and the initial samech may represent a South Arabian intrusion[23].

Any conclusions to be safely drawn from this evidence must be modest. The Table of Nations presents not so much an objective historical account of genealogies as a theologically motivated collection. The names are listed to some extent without regard for consistency of detail which would be of interest to the student of geography and ethnography. Despite this, we may further infer that in the midst of the Babylonian exile, Deutero-Isaiah's image of the most remote nations does help us to see that wherever Sheba was, it was not the same place as Cush (Meroitic Ethiopia) or Egypt. Yet, Genesis 10 has informed us that two of Cush's descendants were called Sheba. This fact may serve to show how very close ancient Sheba was to the land of the Cushites. Thus, Sheba was either somewhere else in Africa or quite near the African coast.

Having drawn attention to the sense in which general biblical references to Sheba are somewhat limited, we must further now examine the larger context of I Kings 10 in order to discover other clues about the land of Sheba. One need not look beyond I Kings 10:15. Here, following the Queen of Sheba story, the Deuteronomic redactor resumes his narrative. In 10:14 the reader is told about the 666 talents of gold which Solomon received in one year. Then in v.15 the reader is told that this wealth was augmented by that which was brought by all the kings of Arabia[24].

This expression, "all the kings of Arabia" (kol-malchai h'ereb) is also found in Jeremiah 25:24 as a description of one of the groups which is to drink the cup of death[25]. Since Jeremiah's oracles are part of the Zeitgeist for understanding the Deuteronomic Reforms of Josiah (621 BCE) and their aftermath, the use of the phrase, "all the kings of Arabia", appears not to be coincidental. Indeed, Jeremiah and the editor responsible for I Kings 10:15 in their use of this phrase may be informing us rather intentionally that in the land which they understood to be Arabia, kings ruled — not queens.

Just as Sheba has been shown not to be in the land of Cush, the use of the phrase, "all the kings of Arabia", by Jeremiah and the first editor of I Kings may demonstrate that Sheba was not considered to be part of Arabia. The most frequently cited non-biblical evidence appealed to by scholars are the cuneiform inscriptions of Tiglath-Pileser II (744-727 BCE) and Sargon II (721-705 BCE)[26]. While these inscriptions do attest to the fact that there were queens in North Arabia in the eighth century[27], they tell us nothing about the tenth century reign of Solomon (962-922 BCE), nor do they tell us anything about queens in Arabia during the time in which I Kings 10:1 - 10,13 was written. Moreover, we have the testimony of Jeremiah and the redactor of I Kings 10, who explicitly distinguish between the Queen of Sheba and "all the kings of Arabia". Therefore, it seems reasonable to conclude that, whatever had been the case a century earlier, at the time of the I Kings redactor and Jeremiah Sheba was not considered part of Arabia, for Arabia at that time may not have had any queens.

As far as we know no inscriptions from South Arabia indicate that there ever was a queen ruler of the Sabaeans[28]. We apparently have mukarribs (priest-kings) before about the fifth century BCE. Besides that all that we possess would be silence and conjecture regarding South Arabia of the Solomonic reign. Regrettably, the situation is scarcely better with Cushite history. The period between the eleventh and eighth centuries is shrouded in obscurity with regard to Egyptian-Cushite relations[29]. If, then, we have no biblical or non-biblical hard data by which the story of the Queen of Sheba can emerge from the realm of legend into the full light of history, why have Josephus, a number of the Church Fathers and the Ethiopians themselves maintained that the Queen of Sheba was an African woman? Josephus calls her "the Queen of Egypt and Ethiopia" as he amplifies considerably the text of I Kings 10:1 - 10,13[30]. The most striking feature of the Josephus rendition of the Queen of Sheba story is that it is faithful to the text of I Kings 10:1 - 13, even though it provides much more detail. The immediate issue which this fact might raise is the nature of Josephus's source. Does he have a specific source or two in much the same manner as the first redactor of the I Kings 10 story, or is Josephus's report otherwise motivated? Quite possibly, an answer to this question may help explain why some early Christian writers thought the Queen of Sheba to be an African.

As a point of departure, let us postulate the thesis that Josephus, who claims to be writing from "his own books", does in fact have a version of the Acts of Solomon mentioned as a source for the original story in I Kings 11:41[31]. There are a number of factors which catapult such a thesis into the realm of possibility. First, the most significant discrepancy between Josephus's account and that of I Kings 10 and II Chronicles 9 is that Josephus never refers to the royal visitor as the Queen of Sheba. Rather, Josephus insists that "his own books" inform him that after Pharaoh, the father-in-law of Solomon, no other king of Egypt was called Pharaoh. Clearly, Josephus has ignored the Old Testament record on this point, in favor of "his own books"[32]. The crucial issue is not that the Old Testament disputes Josephus's source and therefore Josephus is simply wrong. Rather, the central issue is this: Why would Josephus prefer his own source, when he was probably aware of Old Testament citations which contradicted his source? One explanation would be that one of "his own books" was treasured precisely because it was a copy of the very ancient Acts of Solomon, a document which may not have used the term Sheba at all.

A second factor is that, while Josephus twice describes Solomon's visitor as the Queen of Egypt and Ethiopia, his final designation for her is simply the Queen of Ethiopia. Josephus may not only be aware of the 25th Egyptian Dynasty established by an Ethiopian, which ruled Egypt for about 70 years, but his source may antedate this period, going back to the time in which Egypt exercised an hegemony over Ethiopia.

A third and most persuasive factor is that Josephus's story may be an indication that, within segments of first century Jewish communities, there was an awareness of a larger story which focused on the Queen more than on Solomon. As one author says, "the way in which [Josephus] tells the story no doubt reflected the state of contemporary interpretation . . ."[33]. If this be true, then for some first century Jews, the Queen of Sheba was an African.

If there is any merit in our thesis that Josephus may have had an ancient source which knew of a Queen of Egypt and Ethiopia instead of a Queen of Sheba, the suspicion of quite a few theologians would be confirmed, if we briefly consider the pertinent New Testament passages. Matthew 12:42 and Luke 11:31 make mention of a *basilissa notou* (Queen of the South) who has an eschatological function. This image preserved in the Q source of the Synoptics immediately called to mind, for some, the Queen of Sheba as a person who knew how to respond to God's initiative among his people. Inasmuch as Luke in Acts 8:26 - 40, also provides a story about another queen and specifically refers to her as Candace, Queen of the Ethiopians, it was inevitable that not a few would identify the Queen of the South with the Queen of the Ethiopians. It is clear that there was, of course, no relation between the two, even though Alvarez confuses the two[34]. Certainly, any careful student of biblical history would have to discriminate between the vastly different periods of time in which the Queen of Sheba, i.e. Queen of the South, and the one-eyed Queen Candace were alive[35]. This fact aside, insisting that there is no relation between the two queens may be overstating the case. If both queens were of African lineage and related to Ethiopia, there certainly would be a relationship here and a most significant one at that.

Unfortunately no definitive conclusion can be drawn which would establish the certainty of the African descent of the Queen of the South. What can be certainly established is that early Christian scholars like Origen and Jerome, much like the historian Josephus, believed her to be of African ancestry and built some of their exegetical opinion upon the idea about which they never expressed any doubt[36]. Any assertion that the Queen of Sheba was South Arabian instead of Ethiopian must therefore begin from a defensible criticism of some of the most notable historians and biblical scholars of two thousand years ago.

The ambivalent picture of the location of the tribes of Sheba that we get in the Bible is ironically similar to that which we find about the people called "Ethiopians" in some classical literature. The term Ethiopians is used throughout Classical literature to refer in a general way to Black people who inhabited Africa South of Egypt; occasionally the expression is used to refer to specific African peoples like the Nubians or the Cushites. Nevertheless, in some Greek textual sources the expression refers to a people who inhabited the two shores of the Red Sea.

By the beginning of the 2nd century BCE, when Strabo lived, the Sabaeans had come to be known as a distinct Arabian people; and Strabo identifies them as such without questioning. In this regard, Strabo (Book 15:4:2)[37] quotes Eratosthenes (276-194 BCE) saying that the extreme southern corner of Arabia, facing Ethiopia, is inhabited by four Arabian peoples: the Minaeans on the Red Sea, whose capital town is Qarna; the Sabaeans, whose capital is Mariaba; the Qatabanians near the Straits of Bab-el-Mandab, whose capital is Tamna; and the Hadramawti (Chatramotitae), whose capital is Sabota. He also gives a description of their trade of myrrh (Hadramuti) and frankincense (Qataban). Additionally Strabo quotes Agatharchides (c. 120 BCE) who speaks of the Sabaeans in South Arabia.

On the other hand, Strabo comments extensively and revealingly on a subject which seemed to fascinate him, the location of the people called Ethiopians. In Book I, he opens the discussion of the subject saying "It is incredible that [Homer] mentioned Ethiopia . . . and the fact that the Ethiopians are 'sundered in twain' but did not know what was well-known . . ."[38]. What is the meaning of "the Ethiopians sundered in twain"? The cynic philosopher Crates (c. 325 BCE) had interpreted the phrase from Homer saying that "the Ethiopians stretch along both shores of Oceanus from the rising to the setting of the sun" (I:2:24). In agreement with Aristarches (c. 320 BCE), Strabo rejects the hypothesis of Crates. Nonetheless, Aristarches's own hypothesis that the meaning of the Ethiopians "sundered in twain" may mean the division of Ethiopia by a river into east and west like Egypt by the Nile is also rejected by Strabo.

Strabo in this way examines the various interpretations of Homer, including those of Aeschylus (525-456 BCE), Euripides (480-406 BCE), Ephorus (4th cent. BCE), and then proceeds to investigate various possible ways in which Ethiopia may be said to be "sundered in twain" (I, 2:25 - 28). He finally draws his own conclusions based on various points made by his forerunners, more importantly , from those who made coasting-voyages on the ocean along the shores of Libya and in the Red Sea. From such a basis Strabo concludes that Oceanus must be understood in a more general sense: "a body of water that extends along the entire southern belt" and Ethiopians, "the people along the same extent".

Ethiopia, according to Strabo, stretches from the south of Egypt all the way to Asia from east to west. "Sundered in twain" means nothing but divided into two by the Red Sea. So Strabo argues over and over again, saying "I contend in the case of the Ethiopians that 'sundered in twain' [means] . . . [they] extend along the whole sea-board of Oceanus . . . For the Ethiopians that are spoken of in this sense are 'sundered in twain' naturally by the Arabian gulf [the Red Sea] . . . as by a river [like Egypt by the Nile]" (I, 2:28). He goes on to say that the Arabian gulf is a natural boundary of division in the manner the other geographers divide Africa from Asia.

Furthermore, Strabo still goes on to say that probably rightly "Homer divides the Ethiopians into two groups . . . not because he knew that the Indians were physically similar to the Ethiopians (for Homer probably did not know of the Indians at all . . .), but rather on the basis of the division of which I have spoken above (II 3.8) that in the Ethiopians that border on Egypt are themselves, also, divided into two groups; for some of them live in Asia, others in Libya [Africa] though they differ in no respect from each other [!] " (II:3:8).

The question of a people which straddle the Red Sea is examined by Strabo with profound interest. The picture which he draws of the Ethiopians who inhabit both Africa and Asia calls to mind the Biblical genealogies of the two Shebas. It is indeed interesting to note that two such diverging witnesses draw an almost identical picture of the location of the Sabaeans and the Ethiopians respectively.

In conclusion, serious methodological questions must be raised concerning theories which seek to reconstruct the origins of the Ethiopian civilization from South Arabia. In general any idea of cultural influence should not be taken at face value, in particular, since such a concept often tends to be a complicated, if not a simplistic, one.

In every case where cultural influence is discussed the complex issues often do not warrant an easy solution. Thus in the present case, it is possible to reverse the argument and demonstrate Ethiopian influence on the South Arabians. Gus van Beek (JAOS, 1967), while not questioning the old hypothesis of a South Arabian origin of Ethiopia, has nonetheless argued that certain South Arabian pre-Christian pottery, perhaps as early as about 8th BCE, shows Ethiopian influence. Moreover, there is hardly any period in Ethiopian history during which time it can be demonstrated that South Arabia directly governed Ethiopia or dominated it politically and militarily. In other words, no single evidence for direct South Arabian rule in Ethiopia has been demonstrated, despite Conti Rossini's conjectures. On the other hand, it can be shown that South Arabia was under actual Ethiopian domination several times during its history, in particular, from about 335 to 370 and from about 525 to 575 of this era. During the first period, it is thought by some that Christianity was introduced from Ethiopia to South Arabia, apparently through the active missionary work of Tewoflos; even though Haenchen gives an earlier date for the Christianization of South Arabia[39]. During the second period, Abraha extended Christian missionary religious activity in South Arabia and used it as a launching region for the Christianization of the Arabian peninsula. During this latter period, the northern sluice of the great dam of Marib was constructed with protruding headers beyond the wall face. Gus van Beek has rightly argued that "This technique has no construction antecedents in South Arabian architecture. In Ethiopian architecture, on the other hand, the ends of wooden joists frequently protruded beyond the face of the building . . . and often done also in stone. In view of the fact that Ethiopians dominated Sabaeans throughout much of this period, it seems likely that they are also responsible for such architectural forms . . . this technique should probably be interpreted as cultural influence coming from Ethiopia to South Arabia".

Were one to attempt a demonstration of an Ethiopian origin of South Arabian culture, there is no reason why such examples, expanded and exaggerated like the former hypothesis about Ethiopian origins, cannot be used to show the opposite. For our part, however, we wish to pass no such judgment at this stage of international scholarship on the subject. For the time being, however, we would prefer to view, at least hypothetically, South Arabia as a common cultural sphere with Ethiopia from prehistoric times, and nothing more.

NOTES

1. Thomae de Pinedo, *De Urbibus*, 1678. Cf. Thomae de Pinedo, *Stephanus of Byzantinus cum Annotationibus*, Lipsiae, 1825, IV:5: "Populi Arabiae sunt Abaseni . . . "

2. Ludolphus Hiob, *Historia Aethiopica*, Frankfurt, 1691, Book I, chap.1.

3. E. Glaser, *Abessinier in Arabien und Afrika*, C. Conti Rossini, "Sugli Habasat", *Rendiconti, Regia Academi dei Lincei*, ser. 5, XV (1906), 39-59; "Expeditions et possessions des Habasat en Arabie, *Journal Asiatique*, ser. XVIII (1921) pp.5ff.; also see his *Storia d'Etiopia* (Bergamo, 1928).

4. K. Irvine, "On the identity of the Habashat in the South Arabian Inscriptions", *Journal of Semitic Studies*, X, p.181.

5. Cf. C. A. Diop, *The African Origin of Civilization*, New York: Lawrence Hill and Company, 1974. Concerning the various theories about the origin of Zimbabwe see G. Caton-Thompson, *Zimbabwe Culture*, Oxford, 1931.

6. E. Ullendorff, *The Ethiopians, Ethiopians, 2nd ed.* Oxford Univ. Press, 1965, p.51.

7. Diakonoff, *Hamito-Semitic* (Someone has stolen my copy, I have to find another soon!)

8. A. Murtonen, *Early Semitic*, E. J. Brill, 1967.

9. See *The Periplus of the Erythraean Sea*, trans. and edit. by G. W. B. Huntingford, The Hakluyt Society, London, 1980. (Concerning earlier editions and translations of this work, it is good to consult the introduction to this book.)

10. E. Littmann, *Deutsche Aksum Expedition*, Berlin, 1913, IV, pp.4-17.

11. A. K. Irvine, "On the Identity of the Habashat . . . ", p.178-196.

12. *Ibid.*, p.182.

13. Cf. Tadesse Tamrat, *Church and State*, Oxford Univ. Press, 1972, p.9. According to J. Ryckmans the title *mkrrb* designates "Pretre-Prince" ("Prince-Priest") and Prince-Sacrificateur" ("Prince-Sacrificer"). *L'institution monarchique en Arabie meridionale avant L'Islam*, Louvain, 1951, pp.51-53.

14. W. F. Albright, *The Proto-Sinaitic Inscriptions and Their Decipherment*, Harvard Theological Studies XXII, Harvard Univ. Press, 1969. Cf. also T. O. Lambdin, "Alphabet" in *Interpreter's Dictionary of the Bible* (Abingdon Press, 1964).

15. Gus W. Van Beek, "Sheba, Queen of", *Interpreter's Dictionary of the Bible*, pp.144f.

16. *Ibid.*, p.145.

17. Otto Eissfeldt, *The Old Testament: An Introduction* (New York: Harper & Row, 1965), pp.287-290. Norman H. Snaith, *Interpreter's Bible*, Vol.3., pp.10-11.

18. Snaith, *Interpreter's Bible*, Vol.3, p.96. Edward Ullendorff, *Ethiopia and the Bible*, London: Oxford University Press, 1968, p.142. Cf. also Irfan Shahid on Kebra Nagast.

19. Ullendorff, *Ethiopia and the Bible*, p.132.

20. *Ibid.*, p.134. Also cf. *Oxford Annotated Bible* (RSV), Wm. Stinespring, I Kings 10 note; Victor Gold, Isaiah 60:6 not. Also Snaith, *Interpreter's Bible, loc. cit.*; and D. Harvey, *Interpreter's Dictionary of the Bible*, Vol.4, p.311.

21. Eissfeldt, p.184. Also Bernhard W. Anderson, *Understanding the Old Testament*, Englewood Cliffs, N. J.: Prentice-Hall, 1975, 3rd ed., pp.423-424.

22 D. Harvey, *IDB, loc. cit.*

23. Cf. Isaiah 60:6 misba = from Sheba.

24. Cf. II Chronicles 9:14.

25. Jer. 25:24 points the Hebrew term for Arabia (without the article).

26. Harvey, *Interpreter's Dictionary of the Bible, loc. cit.* and Pritchard, *Ancient Near Eastern Texts,* Vol.I, pp.285f.

27. James B. Pritchard, *Ancient Near Eastern Texts*, Vol.I, Princeton University Press, paperback edition, 1973, pp.193-201.

28. Cf. also Ullendorff, *Ethiopia and the Bible*, p.134.

29. Frank M. Snowden Jr., *Blacks in Antiquity*, Harvard University Press, 1970, p.113.

30. Flavius Josephus, *Complete Works*, Grand Rapids: Kregel Publications, 1960; 12th printing 1974, p.180: *Antiquities*, Book 8, Ch. VI, 3, 5.

31. See *Intepreter's Bible*, I Kings, Introduction.

32. Josephus, translator's note cites II Kings 23:29, Jer. 44:30 plus general usage of term Pharaoh by other prophets, p.180n. Also Snowden, p.334, calls attention to the note in the Loeb edition of *Antiquites Judaicae* which on pp.660-661 states that Josephus was probably acquainted with some native Egyptian or Ethiopian tradition which connected the Queen of the Arabian Kingdom with Egypt and Ethiopia.

33. Ullendorff, *Ethiopia and the Bible*, p.135. Cf. H. Danby, *Mishnah* and E. Lohse.

34. It is interesting to note, however, that the two may be queens of Ethiopia.

35. Ernst Haenchen, *Acts of the Apostles*, p.310.

36. Origen, *Commentarius in Canticum Canticorum*, 2: 367-370; Jerome, *De Actibus Aposto-lorum*, 1:673-370. Cf. also F. M. Snowden, *Blacks in Antiquity*, Harvard Univ. Press, 1970, pp.202-204.

37. All quotations from Strabo are from the Loeb Classical Edition, *The Geography of Strabo*, ed. and trans. by H. L. Jones (Based in part upon the unfinished version of J. R. S. Sterrett), Harvard Univ. Press, 1949.

38. This reference is to Homer's "the Ethiopians that are sundered in twain . . ." — *aithiopas toi dichtha dedaistai . . .* " in Od. 1:23.

39. See Gregory of Nyssa, *Contra Eunomium* 1 (Pat. Graec. 45:264) and F. Cabrol and H. Leclerq, *Dictionnaire d'archeologie chretienne et de liturgie*, V (1), Paris, 1922, pp.590-592. Philostargius calls Theophilus Indian (Historia ecclesiastica 2:6; Pat. Graec. 65:469); but the word Indians was widely applied to Ethiopia in his time.

REMARKS ON THE LATE PREHISTORY

AND EARLY HISTORY OF NORTHERN ETHIOPIA

Rodolfo Fattovich

The purpose of this paper is to outline the cultural-historic sequence of Northern Ethiopia in the late prehistoric and early historic times up to the rise of Aksum on the basis of the available archaeological evidence. The region under examination includes the northwestern highland and associated lowlands of Ethiopia from the Red Sea and the Sudanese alluvial plains to the Afar Depression, the Rift Valley and the Abbay Valley (see Mesfin W. Mariam, 1972). I am aware that the actual evidence from this region is very scanty. In my opinion, however, we have enough data to reconstruct the major cultural developments in this area and to generate some hypotheses on the formation of complex societies in Tigrai and Eritrea.

1. The earliest stages of Northern Ethiopia being populated (8th - 3rd mill. BC) are indicated by two main lithic complexes respectively characterized by 'macrolithic' and microlithic tools.

The macrolithic industries are characterized by retouched tools, more than 5cm in size, on coarse flakes and blades of flint and other stones. Irregular or discoidal scrapers in particular are frequent (see Franchini, 1953). They have been recorded on the highland of the Tigrai and Western Eritrea (Puglisi, 1941, 1946; Clark, 1972; Franchini, 1971; Phillipson, 1977b). Some specimens have also been collected near Agordat in the Baraka Valley (Fattovich, 1979). Such industries appeared likely in the 8th mill. BC, but they survived up to the historical times (Phillipson, 1977b; Fattovich, 1977a). Coarse discoidal scrapers in fact have been found in pre-Aksumite and post-Aksumite assemblages at Sequalu and Yeha (Anfray, 1973c; Fattovich, 1972b).

The microlithic industries are characterized by different kinds of scrapers, crescents and backed bladelets. They have been recorded in Eritrea, Tigrai, Wollo, Begemeder and Gojjam (D'Errico, 1937; Blanc, 1955; Teti, 1960; Anfray, 1965b; Franchini, 1971; Clark, 1972; Dombrowski, 1970, 1972; Phillipson, 1977b). They are comparable to the L.S.A. industries of Eastern and Southern Africa; most of them might be ascribed to the Wilton Technocomplex (see Phillipson, 1977a). The assemblage from Dahlac Kebir in particular recalls the Somalian Wilton (Phillipson, 1978a). Their age is uncertain. The evidence from Gobedra, near Aksum, indicates a dating back to c.7000 - 3000 BC (Phillipson, 1977b). Yet, obsidian microliths are frequent in the pre-Aksumite and Aksumite sites (Fattovich, 1977a) and microlithic steep scrapers are still made in some regions of Central Ethiopia (see Gallagher, 1972, 1974, 1976, 1977; Clark, 1981). The origins of these industries are obscure. It is possible anyway that they spread into Northern Ethiopia from the Horn and/or East Africa (Phillipson, 1977a, 1978a).

2. We have no sure information about the beginning of food production in Northern Ethiopia (Phillipson, 1978b; Brandt, 1984). Ehret (1979) suggested, basing his assumption on linguistic grounds, that it might have started in the 7th mill. BC, but his arguments cannot be indisputably accepted. There is also no evidence supporting Vavilov's assumption (1951) that Ethiopia was an independant center of plant domestication. On the contrary, it seems that the domestication of plants and animals occurred on the highland due to outside stimuli from the North (Clark, 1962a, b, 1967, 1970, 1976a, b, 1980; De Wet, 1977).

So far the earliest possible evidence of the domestication of plants and animals in Northern Ethiopia has been discovered at Gobedra (Tigrai), in the stratum IIb provisionally dated back to 4000 - 2000 BC (Phillipson, 1977b). It consists of a few finger millet seeds and a camel's tooth. Such materials, however, might be intrusive (Brandt p.c.). In the same stratum some undecorated potsherds were also collected, comparable to the Butana Group ware of the Southern Atbai in Sudan (see Shiner, 1971; Fattovich, Marks, Ali, 1984). The lithic industry on the other hand was the same as that of the lower strata, suggesting that there was no break in the cultural sequence of the site.

We can tentatively date some sherds and artefacts from Sirba in the Abbay Valley to the same period (Spratling, 1970). They recall the Khartoum Neolithic material and might indicate contacts with the Central Sudan. Such contacts might be also supported by some *teff* and finger millet impressions on potsherds from Kadeo near Khartoum (Krzyżaniak, 1978; Klichowska, 1978).

The domestication of cattle was probably introduced in Northern Ethiopia between 4000 and 1000 BC. Cattle were already being bred along the northern Ethiopian-Sudanese borderland in the 4th - 3rd millennium BC (Fattovich, Marks, Ali, 1984) and probably occurred in the Rift Valley in the 2nd millennium BC (Clark, Williams, 1978).

In the early 2nd millennium BC nomadic or seminomadic herders inhabited the middle of the Baraka valley, as we can infer from the evidence collected at Kokan, Ntanei, Shabeit and Dandaneit near Agordat (Arkell, 1954). These sites were originally ascribed to the Nubian C Group, but the recent field work in the Gash Delta (see Fattovich, 1981, 1984b; Fattovich, Piperno, 1982) has demonstrated that they represent a regional variant of the Atbai Ceramic Tradition of Eastern Sudan. They can be ascribed, therefore, to an indigenous people of the western lowlands of Eritrea. The artefacts from these sites include pots with decorations like those of the C Group and those of Kerma from the middle Nile, axes and earrings reproducing Egyptian prototypes of the 17th-18th Dynasty, and obsidian microliths (mainly crescents). Such material indicates that there were contacts with Nubia, perhaps Egypt and the Ethiopian highlands. Some copper artefacts from Kokan in turn might suggest that metal objects were imported or possibly manufactured by the Agordat people. According to Clark (1962b, 1967) this people introduced wheat and barley into Ethiopia. This hypothesis, though not yet confirmed, might be supported by the discovery of barley in a level bearing pottery comparable to the Kerma and Agordat one at Mahal Teglinos in the Gash delta (Costantini *et al.*, 1982).

Some 'Neolithic' grinding stones have also been recorded at Barentu, but this evidence is too scanty to be significant (D'Errico, 1935).

Cattle breeders certainly moved along the edges of the highland in Eritrea and Eastern Tigrai in the 2nd millennium BC, as we can infer from the numerous rock drawings discovered in these regions (Graziosi, 1964b; Červiček, 1976a, b; Clark, 1976a; Fattovich, 1977a; Joussaume, 1981).

The rock paintings depict mainly cattle, anthropomorphic figures and symbols. The cattle are represented in the Ethiopian-Arabian, seminaturalistic and naturalistic styles. The animals are longhorned and shorthorned humpless bovines. The anthropomorphic figures are represented in the 'Bushman' and 'Iberian' styles. The 'Bushman' figures — with false tails(?), spears, round shields, swords and perhaps musical instruments — are associated only with the longhorned bovines. The schematic 'Iberian' figures are associated only with the shorthorned bovines. A scene of milking and a scene of ploughing in particular have been recorded respectively at Zeban Ona Libanos (Mai Aini) and at Amba Focada (Senafé), but they might go back to the late 1st millennium BC (Dainelli, Marinelli, 1912; Mordini, 1941; Graziosi, 1941, 1963, 1964a, b; Franchini, 1951, 1952, 1961, 1964; Ricci, 1953, 1955-1958, 1959; Vigliardi Micheli, 1957; Leclant, Miquel, 1959).

The prehistoric rock engravings represent longhorned humpless cattle in Ethiopian-Arabian style, except for one figure in naturalistic style (Franchini, 1963, 1980; Tesfaye, 1979).

This evidence indicates that longhorned bovines were bred in the northern Tigraen plateau, from Agamè to the coastal plains on the Sudanese border. The shorthorned bovines, on the contrary, seem to occur only in the upper Mareb-Gash valley and near Karora close to the Red Sea. At the same time this would suggest that during the 2nd millennium BC peoples from different regions moved to Northern Ethiopia. The Ethiopian-Arabian figures may indicate movements from the Horn (Červiček, 1971, 1978-1979), while those with a naturalistic and seminaturalistic style might suggest movements from the Sahara (Bailloud, 1959; Clark, 1976a).

The notion of movements from the north, on the other hand, might also be supported by some big tumuli recorded at Ham (Senafé) and near Dabra Damo, which recall the C Group tumuli of Nubia (Anfray, 1965a; Mordini, 1945).

3.   The cultural picture of Northern Ethiopia at the beginning of the 1st millennium BC is quite complex. It seems that peoples with different traditions inhabited the Red Sea coast, Central Eritrea, Western Tigrai and Begemeder. Some of them, moreover, were probably in contact with the populations of the Arabian Peninsula.

Two protohistorical levels have been brought to light at Adulis, on the Red Sea coast (Paribeni, 1907). The upper level was characterized by black or red ware, decorated with geometric and anthropomorphic patterns. The lower level was characterized by coarse yellow or reddish ware. At the bottom, traces of copper slag were also found. In both levels obsidian microlithic blades and points were collected.

Another cultural unit (Ona Culture) has been identified near Asmara in Hamasien (Tringali, 1965, 1967, 1969, 1973-77, 1980-81). This is characterized by polished red and black topped ware, decorated with geometrical rim bands recalling that of Kerma in Nubia, hammerstones, big scrapers, small polished axes and big stone crescents representing, perhaps, bull-heads.

Some rock sculptures at Daarò Caulòs (Asmara) might be ascribed to the same cultural context. They represent anthropomorphic figures with round heads, long hair, big hands and feet, a false tail or phallus (Conti Rossini, 1928; Consociazione Turistica Italiana, 1938: 209-210; Fattovich, 1983). These figures can be compared with Arabian rock drawings dating back to 3000 - 500 BC, and suggest possible contacts with the Arabian Peninsula (Fattovich, 1983).

This influence, in turn, might be supported by numerous stone cairns with stelae scattered throughout Eritrea (Trucca 1980).

Very schematic rock engravings of cattle, bull-heads and symbols have been recorded in Hamasien (Eritrea) and Agamè (Tigrai) (Mordini, 1947; Conti Rossini, 1948; Ricci, 1953; Franchini, 1963; Červiček, 1976a, b). Their age is uncertain, but a dating to the middle/late 1st millennium BC is suspected (Červiček, 1976b; Mordini, 1947). They might be connected to the Ona Culture, as the areas of diffusion of both kinds of evidence virtually overlap.

Burials of uncertain age, usually with the remains of the inhumed in a huddled position, have also been recorded at Debaroa, Addi Ugri, Medrì Zien and Keren (Gaudio, 1953; Conti Rossini, 1900, 1928). Only at Medrì Zien the skeleton was found in a sitting position on some animal remains.

At Gobedra, in Western Tigrai, some protohistorical remains have been discovered in stratum IIa and dated to 856 ± 53 BC (Phillipson, 1977b). They include undecorated and decorated pottery, microlithic tools, wild bovines, antelopes, perhaps domestic cattle and iron slags. The pottery and the lithic industry bear the same features as those in stratum IIb. The pottery in particular reveals an affinity with the ware of the Butana and Jebel Mokram Groups in Southern Atbai (see Fattovich, Marks, Ali, 1984). The occurrence of iron slags, in turn, might indicate possible contacts with Southern Arabia, where the iron tools could be ascribed to the 11th - 10th century BC (van Beek, 1969).

Finally, some remains dating back to the late 1st millennium BC have been found at the Lalibela and Natchabiet caves near Lake Tana (Dombrowski, 1970, 1972). They represent one cultural unit characterized by red burnished channelled ware, red orange brushed ware, microlithic tools, grinding and polishing stones. The vegetal remains include barley, chickpeas, horsebeans(?), peas(?), vetch and unidentified legumes. The faunal remains include both wild and domestic animals (cattle, sheep, goats). The occurrence of channelled ware like that of the Jebel Mokram Group in Southern Atbai might suggest contacts with the Sudanese lowlands.

4.   In the middle 1st millennium BC the earliest complex societies appeared in Tigrai and Eritrea. According to Schneider (1976b), chiefdoms were already in existence at the beginning of the 1st millennium BC, but this hypothesis has not yet been supported by any substantial evidence.

This stage of the cultural history of Northern Ethiopia, immediately preceding the rise of Aksum, is named the 'Pre-Aksumite Period' and the archeological remains ascribable to it represent the 'Pre-Aksumite Culture' (Anfray, 1964, 1967, 1968; Fattovich, 1977a, b; De Contenson, 1981).

Pre-Aksumite sites have been recorded in many localities of Eritrea and Tigrai (see Godet, 1977, 1980-2; Michels, 1975). Some traces have also been found at Tana Qirqos Island in Begemeder, but their meaning is uncertain (Cheesman, 1968). The pre-Aksumite cultural area seems to stretch from the Rore region in Eritrea to Enderta in Tigrai (Fattovich, 1977a). Most sites are located in the regions of Akkele Guzay (Eritrea), Agamè, Adwa and Aksum (Tigrai). They are scattered throughout the *woina dega* environmental zone, at an altitude of 1800-2500m.

The settlements include towns, ceremonial centers, villages and/or camps. Towns have been discovered at Matara and Yeha. They occupy areas of approx. 40,000 m^2 (Matara) and approx. 75,000 m^2 (Yeha) (Anfray, Annequin, 1965; Anfray, 1970a, 1973a; Fattovich, 1972a, b). Another town was probably located at Kaskasè, but this site has not yet been extensively explored (Dainelli, Marinelli, 1912; Krencker, 1913). Ceremonial centers have been identified at Enzelal(?), Der'a, Li'ali'o, Zeban Kutur, Addi Grameten, Grat Mahdere, Fykia, Hawlti and Melazo. They are mostly located at the opening of valleys sinking towards the lowlands (Sapeto, 1941; Conti Rossini, 1947; Ricci, 1955-58, 1960; Davico, 1946; Duncanson, 1947; Franchini, 1961; Anfray, 1965a; De Contenson, 1963b; Leclant, 1959). Small villages or camps have been recorded at Ona Hachel (Eritrea), Sefra Abun and Sefra Turkui (Tigrai) (Anfray, 1970b, 1973c).

On the basis of the pottery evidence we can recognize two main regions in the pre-Aksumite cultural area (Fattovich, 1976a, b, 1980). They correspond respectively to the regions of Aksum and Adwa to the West and Agamè and Akkele Guzay to the East.

The pre-Aksumite remains include buildings, graves, inscriptions, sculptures, incense altars, bronze seals, bronze and iron tools and weapons, pottery, and microlithic tools (Fattovich, 1977b; De Contenson, 1981).

Anfray (1967, 1968) has distinguished two main developmental stages of the Pre-Aksumite Culture: i. the *Ethiopian-Sabean Period* (c.500-300 BC), characterized by a notable South Arabian influence; ii. the *Intermediary Period* (c.300 BC - AD 100), characterized by the development of a fully autochthonous culture evolving toward the Aksumite cultural pattern.

In my opinion three phases can be recognized on strictly archaeological grounds (Fattovich, 1977a, b, 1980).

The Pre-Aksumite 1 Phase is documented by the lower strata at Matara (VIII - V) and Yeha (II) and by the surface collections at Matara, Sefra Turkui and Sefra Abun. No architectural remains can be safely ascribed to this phase. The collected evidence suggests that there was a cultural diversity between Central Eritrea and Western Tigrai. In any case, contacts between these regions may be indicated by the occurrence of red polished ware at Matara and Yeha and orange ware at Yeha and Kaskase. At Matara and Yeha, moreover, some potsherds comparable to South Arabian specimens have been collected. Orange unburnished ware identical to that from Yeha has been found in Late Butana and Late Jebel Mokram sites at Shurab el Gash some 40km to the south of Kassala (Fattovich, 1984b, c).

The Pre-Aksumite 2 Phase is documented in most sites of this culture. This corresponds to the Ethiopian-Sabean Period suggested by Anfray. This phase was characterized by the development of towns with large public monuments and stone buildings, the use of writing, the manufacture of bronze objects and the making of statues. We know, moreover, from the inscriptions that an early state appeared at this time (Drewes, 1962; Schneider, 1976). It seems that in this phase the pre-Aksumite cultural area was quite homogeneous (Fattovich, 1980). During this phase, Northern Ethiopia was affected by a strong South Arabian influence, which suggested to some scholars a political dependency on the kingdom of Saba (von Wissmann, 1975). Evidence of contacts with the Sudanese lowlands and the Nile valley on the other hand is scanty (Fattovich, 1982). Some Meroitic objects found at Matara, Yeha and Hawlti however suggest some occasional relationships between the two kingdoms (see Anfray, 1973a; Leclant, 1965; De Contenson, 1962, 1963; Pirenne, 1967).

The Pre-Aksumite 3 Phase is documented at Yeha, Hawlti and Melazo. The small temples at

Hawlti and Melazo can most likely be dated to it. The clay figures from Hawlti in particular indicate that humpless cattle were still bred and the plough was in use. These also include models of conical and rectangular huts (De Contenson, 1963). The South Arabian elements are practically non existent. A Meroitic influence is perhaps recognizable in the monuments at Hawlti and Melazo, as well as in some beakers from Hawlti (Fattovich, 1982). Contacts with the populations of the lowlands might be indicated by an affinity with the pottery of the Hagiz Group in the Gash delta and that of the late pre-Aksumite period of the Tigrai (Fattovich, 1984c).

At the present stage of the research we can tentatively date the first phase to before the 5th century BC, the second phase to the 5th - 3rd century BC, and third phase to the 2nd/1st century BC - 1st/2nd century AD (Fattovich, 1977a, b, 1980; Michels, 1975). The monumental inscriptions in particular can be dated back to the 5th - 3rd century BC, in conformity with the dating of the South Arabian epigraphical evidence suggested by Pirenne (1955, 1956) and confirmed by Garbini (1973).

The origins of the pre-Aksumite culture are still under discussion. Bent (1893), Conti Rossini (1906, 1928), von Wissmann (1975), Ricci (1984) suggested that some South Arabian tribes, namely the Sabeans, colonized Northern Ethiopia and imposed their culture on the indigenous population. Drewes (1956, 1959, 1962), Anfray (1967, 1968) and Schneider (1976b) have emphasized an acculturative process developed through political and commercial links with the kingdom of Saba. The available archaeological evidence seems to support this hypothesis. In fact, few South Arabian features, most ascribable to the élite of the population, can be recognized in this culture (Fattovich, 1977b). The pottery and other aspects of it can be linked, on the contrary, with African traditions (Fattovich, 1975, 1977b, 1978a, 1980).

This evidence also suggests contacts with different regions of South Arabia: Saba, Hadramawt, Aden, and possibly Main and Qataban. It seems that initially there were contacts with the regions of Aden and possibly Hadramawt, while relationships with the kingdom of Saba commenced only in the second phase. At the same time it seems that Western Tigrai was originally more directly connected to South Arabia than to Central Eritrea (Fattovich, 1977b, 1980). This statement however is confirmed by the epigraphical evidence, insofar as the oldest South Arabian inscriptions have been discovered in Tigrai with the exception of a rock inscription at Zeban Mororo in Eritrea (Pirenne, 1956; Drewes, 1959; Schneider, 1973, 1976a).

5. The emergence of Aksum (c. AD 100/200-400) is still obscure from both an historical and an archaeological point of view (Fattovich, 1977a; Kobishchanov, 1978, 1979, 1981).

According to the historical record, Aksum was already in existence in the 1st or 2nd century AD (Conti Rossini, 1928; De Contenson, 1960; Pirenne, 1961; Mathew, 1973). At this time, however, Northern Ethiopia was probably divided into small kingdoms and Aksum was just one of these (Cerulli, 1960; Drewes, 1962; Huntingford, 1974; Mazzarino, 1974). In any case the kingdom of Aksum was already included in the commercial network connecting the Roman Empire to India, as we can infer from the *Periplus of the Erythrean Sea* (Schoff, 1912; Huntingford, 1980) and some coins and figurines of the Indian types found at Debra Damo and Hawlti (Mordini, 1960; De Contenson, 1963b). Iron, textiles and vessels in particular were imported from Roman Egypt, while ivory, tortoise shells and skins were exported to Rome. In these centuries humped cattle were introduced into the country, as we can infer from a small figurine of bovine, going back to the 2nd century AD, discovered at Zeban Kutur (Ricci, 1955-58; Drewes, 1962; Drewes, Schneider, 1976), as it was suggested by Clark (1976a) and Fattovich (1977a). The true kingdom rose up in the 3rd century AD when the whole country was unified and military expeditions were sent to South Arabia and the Nile Valley (Conti Rossini, 1928; Doresse, 1957; Kirwan, 1960; Mazzarino, 1974; Robin, 1984). In this century coins were also forged (Anzani, 1926, 1941; Conti Rossini, 1927; Anfray, 1968b; Munro-Hay, 1981-1982). In the 4th century Christianity was introduced into the kingdom.

So far, the archaeological evidence going back to the Early Aksumite Period is scarce. It includes remains of buildings, tombs, stelae, thrones, pottery, coins, lithic tools and further minor findings (glasses, ornaments, etc.) (Anfray, 1967, 1968a, 1981; Fattovich, 1977a). We can also date some Greek and Ethiopian inscriptions recording the names of some proto-

Aksumite and early Aksumite kings to this phase (Conti Rossini, 1928; Drewes, 1962; Drewes, Schneider, 1976).

The cultural historic phase is presently documented by the more ancient Aksumite monuments at Adulis, Matara and Aksum, and perhaps by a cemetery at Salaclacà near Aksum (Paribeni, 1907; Anfray, 1963c; Anfray, Annequin, 1965; Puglisi, 1941; De Contenson, 1959, 1963a; Chittick, 1974, 1976; Butzer, 1981; Cossàr, 1945). Some evidence was also recorded between Aksum and Yeha by Michels (1975), but it has never been adequately published. A settlement and a cemetery possibly going back to this early period was recorded on top of the Bieta Ghiorghis hill to the West of Aksum (Ricci, 1974). This may correspond to one of the first capitals of the kingdom quoted in the *Liber Aksumae* (see Monneret de Villard, 1938). Some potsherds like those of the late pre-Aksumite/early Aksumite period from Matara were, moreover, collected near Keren and in the Hagher Abai (Fattovich, 1979). They would suggest that the early Aksumite culture spread into Northern Eritrea along the tracks to Aqiq and Suakin (Fattovich, 1984a).

It seems that during this phase, towns surrounded by small settlements of farmers sprang up along the caravan track from Aksum to Adulis (Michels, 1975). The only certain evidence of early Aksumite urban settlements, going back to the 3rd century AD, was however discovered at Aksum, Matara and Adulis (Anfray, 1972, 1974; De Contenson, 1976). A ceremonial and burial area, however, already existed at Aksum in the 1st/2nd century AD (Chittick, 1974, 1976; Butzer, 1981).

The origins of the Aksumite Culture are obscure. In fact, since the earliest stage it displays many distinct features from the pre-Aksumite culture (Anfray, 1968a, 1981; Fattovich, 1977a). The most striking feature is represented by the stelae recorded at Aksum, Henzat, Anza and Matara (Krencker, 1913; Conti Rossini, 1928, 1942; Mordini, 1945; Ricci, 1974). They include rough stelae, coarsely shaped stelae and round topped stelae with smoothed sides, sometimes decorated with the South Arabian symbols of the crescent moon and the sun disc. They are usually attributed to a general Semitic tradition (Kammerer, 1929; Anfray, 1972). The round topped stelae in particular could be compared to Anatolian specimens of the 1st millennium BC (see Pecorella, 1978). The most recent discoveries (winter 1985) of a stelae field possibly dating back to the late 2nd millennium BC, with the prototypes of the Aksumite monuments at Kassala, by the Italian Archaeological Mission in Sudan (Kassala of the Istituto Universitario Orientale, Naples, could suggest, on the contrary, an African origin for these monuments).

Nonetheless, there are some elements that suggest a continuity with the Pre-Aksumite Culture and some influences possibly of South Arabian, Meroitic and Greek-Roman origin (Fattovich, 1977a; Anfray, 1981).

The continuity between the pre-Aksumite and Aksumite cultures is indicated by certain architectural elements, pottery and writing. The podiums of Aksumite buildings might derive from prototypes visible in the 'palace' and the temple at Yeha. The 'monkey's heads' technique has already been documented by some remains of wooden frame in the 'palace' at Yeha and by a model of a hut from Hawlti. The tombs with shafts are exactly like those at Yeha and Matara (Fattovich, 1977a; Plant, 1978). The pottery shares certain kinds of fabrics, surface finishing, forms and decorations with its immediate antecedent. The orange ware and the coarse red and black ware, typical of the early Aksumite period, in particular derive directly from the pre-Aksumite ware of the same colour (Fattovich, 1980). The writing of the earliest Aksumite inscriptions indisputably derives from that of South Arabia of the previous period (Drewes, Schneider, 1976). The crescent moon and the sun disc finally appear on monuments of both cultures.

A later South Arabian influence might be indicated by the indented plan of the Aksumite buildings. It is absent in pre-Aksumite architecture, although it has been documented in Southern Arabia in the 1st millennium BC (see Grohman, 1963; Doe 1971, 1983).

A Meroitic influence could be indicated by the *tiara* of the early Aksumite kings and by their custom of taking a new name when rising to the throne (Conti Rossini, 1928). Contacts with Meroe, on the other hand, might be confirmed by two bronze carved Meroitic cups from Addi Galamo, dating back to AD 100/200 (Doresse, 1960; Caquot, Drewes, 1955; Leclant,

1961-1962). Moreover, a Meroitic origin might be suggested for the lion-head spout found at Aksum, the carved lioness at Gobedra and the grape or oil press at Ashafi near Aksum (see Krencker, 1913). This latter is particularly comparable to Nubian specimens of the 3rd/4th century AD (see Adams, 1966).

A Greek-Roman influence can be recognized in the use of Greek on some inscriptions and in the coinage, which was probably minted to replace the imported Roman coins originally used in the kingdom as we can also gather from specimens collected in Northern Ethiopia (Conti Rossini, 1927, 1928). According to Anfray (1974), the Aksumite 'palaces' might derive from the Roman *villae* of Northern Syria. In my opinion the palace-complex of Ta'aka Maryam (Aksum) particularly recalls the palace of Diocletianus at Spalato (see Ducati, 1952). The use of bricks might have also been introduced into Ethiopia from the Roman world (Angelis d'Ossat, 1937). Finally the pots with squat globular body and cylindrical or truncated conical necks, typical of the region of Aksum, are reminiscent of pots of the Roman age from Haraga in Egypt (see Petrie, 1914).

Insubstantial evidence *might* also indicate a specific North Syrian influence. The pointed crowns of the Aksumite kings and the thrones at Aksum in fact recall the crown of Anthiocus I of Commagenes and the thrones in front of his tomb at Nimrud Dagh (see Humann, Puchstein, 1890).

This evidence would therefore suggest that the emergence of the Aksumite culture was a complex process involving many different factors. The core was most likely represented by local traditions, including the pre-Aksumite one which was not necessarily the main cultural antecedent. This core was in turn affected by external influences with different origins. The result was a new culture which represented the basis of the successive Ethiopian civilizations.

6. The picture we are able to infer from the reviewed evidence is still very fragmentary. This is mainly due to the lack of consistent data for the more ancient periods and uncertainty regarding the chronological framework. Any conclusion must therefore be regarded as largely speculative. Nevertheless, it becomes evident that the cultural history of Northern Ethiopia in late prehistorical and early historical times was very complex. It was probably characterized by the reciprocal interaction of local traditions which had been affected by external influences, therefore progressively changing their cultural patterns.

In particular, it seems that the cultural history of Tigrai and Eritrea was different up to the 1st millennium BC. In Tigrai we can recognize a cultural continuity from the 7th millennium BC to the early 1st millennium AD. It is indicated by the persistence up to the pre-Aksumite and early Aksumite times of the same basic macrolithic and microlithic industries and the occurrence by the 5th millennium BC of the same kind of pottery (orange ware). In Eritrea, on the other hand, different cultural components intermingled during the 2nd and early 1st millennium BC, probably generating a more composite culture. These most likely originated in the Nilo-Saharan area, the Horn and later the Arabian Peninsula.

These two regions were included in one cultural context by the 5th century BC with the rise of an early state in pre-Aksumite times. They were finally unified in the early 1st millennium AD, when Aksum dominated the country.

The emergence of the pre-Aksumite and Aksumite states in turn was probably caused by the progressive inclusion of Northern Ethiopia in the complex network of long distance trade which gradually involved the peoples of Northeastern Africa, from Egypt to Somalia, and Southern Arabia (see Fattovich, 1978b).

At present, we can recognise three main stages in this process on the basis of the archaeological and historical evidence.

In the late 3rd-early 2nd millennium BC only the western lowlands of Eritrea and the adjacent plains of the Baraka and Gash deltas in Eastern Sudan had more or less regular exchanges with the Middle Nile Valley and possibly Egypt (see Fattovich, Marks, Ali, 1984; Fattovich, 1984b). In fact this region was rich in resources (gold, spices, ivory, precious skins, ebony?) particularly prized by the ancient Egyptians. It is also possible that the land of Punt was located in this area (Kitchen, 1971, 1982; Fattovich 1984d). Chiefdoms might therefore have developed along the fringes of the highland in the middle 2nd millennium BC (see Fattovich, 1978b, 1984a). The occurrence of obsidian microlithic tools at Agordat, Kassala, as well as in other localities of the Red Sea coast to the South of Port Sudan, might also suggest contacts between the Northern Ethiopian and Eastern Sudanese peoples in this early period (see Callow, Wahida, 1981). The discovery of pottery comparable to that of Butana in the Sudanese lowlands at Gobedra IIb might in turn indicate contacts with peoples inhabiting the Atbara and Gash alluvial plains.

At the end of the 2nd millennium BC a sudden desiccation of the whole of Northeastern Africa (see Butzer, 1976) probably brought about an interruption in exchanges with the Nile Valley, as is suggested mainly by the Egyptian sources. In the meantime, the use of the camel most likely allowed the development of South Arabian trade along the Western Arabian Peninsula and the rise of the first South Arabian kingdoms (see Doe, 1971). The need at that time to control the African resources of Northwestern Ethiopian lowlands compelled the Arabian peoples to include Northern Ethiopia in their exchange network. At the very beginning, at least, it is possible that there were direct contacts between the peoples of Central Eritrea and Northern Arabia. They are suggested by the archaeological evidence at Daarò Caulòs as well as linguistic evidence (see Garbini, 1972). Such contacts possibly occurred along the traditional route which connected Hamasien to Aqiq, or Suakin along the Baraka and Anseba valleys, and crossed the Red Sea to Jedda, continuing along the West Arabian mountains to the Mediterranean Sea.

Contacts with South Arabian peoples started in the middle 1st millennium BC. They probably came about due to the need to obtain African ivory which was in increasing demand by the Greek world in the 6th/5th century BC. We can state with certainty that Greek traders were in contact with the Southern Arabians at this time (see Pirenne, 1955). The sherds collected in the lower strata at Yeha recall specimens from Hadramawt and Aden, suggesting that initially they moved directly to Western Tigrai, given the strategical position of this region, to exploit the resources of the lowlands. The discovery of early pre-Aksumite-like potsherds at Shurab al Gash near Kassala confirms that the two regions were in contact in this period.

At the same time, African products were probably also in demand by the Achemenids. In the Suez stela, Darius states that travels to Punt have started again. In the inscription at Naqš-i-Rustem (486-485 BC) he claims that payment was made by the Paul(n)tiyā the inhabitants of Punt (see Monneret de Villard, 1938b). Moreover, three 'Ethiopians' offering a pot, and ivory tusk and an okapi are represented on the reliefs of the Apadana in Persepolis (Leroy, 1963). An Achemenid influence can also be recognized in the technique of the reliefs on the so-called 'throne' found at Hawlti (De Contenson, 1962, 1981).

By the late 5th century BC, there were direct contacts with the kingdom of Saba. The result of such contacts was the emergence of an early state in Western Tigrai. Its process of formation is obscure. Two hypotheses can be advanced, drawing on the archaeological and epigraphical evidence. The first one is that autochthonous chiefs wanted to control trade activity, as often happened in other African countries. The second one is that South Arabian traders, after settling in Ethiopia and intermarrying with the natives, obtained political power and became the ruling class as the Islamic traders in Wollega did in the 18th-19th century AD (see Triulzi, 1981).

By the 3rd century BC links with South Arabians are less evident in the archaeological record, perhaps due to the decline of the Sabena kingdom. It is possible that in this period there were some contacts with Meroe, which was expanding to the east and south, subjecting the peoples of the Butana and Taka (Gash Delta) (see Budge, 1966). The scarce evidence we have seems to suggest that in late pre-Aksumite times the peoples living in the lowlands between the Gash and Atbara rivers were included in the area of Ethiopian influence.

Finally, the increase of Roman trade along the Red Sea and Indian Ocean routes in the early 1st millennium AD gave a new impulse to the cultural and political development of Northern Ethiopia. This country was in fact the major source of African ivory, which came from Kueneion (Sennar?) in the Sudanese lowlands. The archaeological evidence (see Fattovich, 1979, 1984a) indicates that the northern route to Aqiq and perhaps Suakin was still used. It is also possible that some North Syrian elements penetrated into the country along this path. At any rate, the archaeological and historical record confirms that in these centuries Adulis became the main harbour of the region, connecting the hinterland to the sea by a shorter path.

The emergence of this exchange network, via Adulis, opened Northern Ethiopia to more direct influences from the Mediterranean world. At the same time it allowed the rise of Aksum which represented the continental gateway for the commercial routes from the Abyssinian plateau and the Sudanese lowlands (Butzer, 1981). The kingdoms arose on the pre-Aksumite social and cultural foundation, but it immediately revealed a differnt pattern reflecting indigenous traditions that were not yet evident in the previous period. The dynamics of state formation was characterized at this time by the progressive amalgamation of the single principalities of Northern Ethiopia into one kingdom (Kobischanov, 1978) which may have subsequently entered into hostilities against Meroe (Fattovich, 1982). At the end the kingdom of Aksum obtained a monopoly over the trade routes to the hinterland of Central Africa, a monopoly that it maintained until the 10th century AD.

REFERENCES

Adams, W. Y., 1966   *The vintage of Nubia*, Kush, 14: 262-283.

Anfray, F., 1963   La première campagne de fouilles à Maṭarā, près de Sénafé (Nov. 1959 - Jan. 1960), *Annales d'Ethiopie*, 5: 87-112.

——————— 1964   Notre connaissance du passé éthiopienne d'après les travaux archéologiques recentes, *Journal of Semitic Studies*, 9 (1): 247-249.

——————— 1965a   Chronique archéologique (1960-1964), *Annales d'Ethiopie*, 6: 3-26.

——————— 1965b   Le Musée Archéologique d'Asmara, *Rassegna di Studi Etiopici*, 21: 5-15.

——————— 1967   Maṭarā, *Annales d'Ethiopie*, 7: 33-53.

——————— 1968a   Aspects de l'Archéologie éthiopienne, *Journal of African History*, 9: 345-366.

——————— 1968b   *Les rois d'Axoum d'après la numismatique*, 6: 1-5.

——————— 1970a   Maṭarā, *Travaux de la R.C.P*, 230, 1: 53-60.

——————— 1970b   Notes Archéologiques, *Annales d'Ethiopie*, 8: 31-42.

——————— 1972   L'archéologie d'Axoum en 1972, *Paideuma*, 18: 60-78.

——————— 1973a   Yeha, bercau d'une civilisation, *Archéologia*, 64: 34-44.

——————— 1973b   Nouveaux sites antiques, *Journal of Ethiopian Studies*, 11: 13-20.

——————— 1974   Deux villes axoumites: Adulis et Maṭarā, *Atti IV Congresso di Studi Etiopici – Roma 1972*, pp.745-765, Roma: Accademia Nazionale dei Lincei.

———————— 1981   The civilization of Aksum from the first to the seventh century, *General History of Africa*, II. Ancient Civilizations of Africa (G. Mokhtar, ed.), pp.362-378, Berkeley: UNESCO/University of California Press.

Anfray, F., and G. Annequin 1965   Maṭarā, deuxième, troisième et quatrième campagnes de fouilles, *Annales d'Ethiopie*, 6: 49-86.

Angelis d'Ossat, G. de, 1937   Su un particolare sistema costruttivo aksumita, *Palladio*, 5: 1-12.

Anzani, A., 1926   Studi di numismatica aksumita, *Rivista Italiana di Numismatica*, 39: 5-96.

———————— 1941   Monete e storia d'Etiopia, *Rivista Italiana di Numismatica*, 43: 49-73, 81-99, 113-129.

Arkell, A. J., 1954   Four Occupation Sites at Agordat, *Kush*, 2: 33-62.

Bailloud, G., 1959   La préhistoire de l'Ethiopie, *Cahiers de l'Afrique et de l'Asie*, 5: 15-43.

Beek, G. van, 1969   *Hajar Bin Humeid*, Baltimore: The John Hopkins Press.

Bent, T., 1893   *The Sacred City of the Ethiopians*, London, Loghans, Green and Co.

Blanc, A. C., 1955   L'industrie sur obsidienne des Iles Dahlac, *Actes IIe Congrés Panafricaine de Préhistoire - Alger*, 1952, Paris.

Brandt, S., 1984   New Perspectives on the Origins of Food Production in Ethiopia, in *From Hunters to Farmers: The Causes and Consequences of Food Production in Africa* (J. D. Clark, S. Brandt, eds.), p.173-190, Berkeley: University of California Press.

Budge, E. A. W., 1966   *A History of Ethiopia: Nubia and Abyssinia*, Oosterhout N. B.: Anthropological Publications.

Butzer, K., 1976   *Early Hydraulic Civilization in Egypt*, Chicago: The University of Chicago Press.

———————— 1981   Rise and Fall of Axum, Ethiopia: a Geo-Archaeological Interpretation, *American Antiquity*, 46: 471-495.

Callow, P. and G. Wahida 1981   Fieldwork in Northern and Eastern Sudan 1977-80, *Nyame Akuma*, 18: 34-36.

Caquot, A. and A. J. Drewes 1955   Les monuments recueillis à Magallé (Tigré), *Annales d'Ethiopie*, 1: 17-41.

Cerulli, E., 1960   Punti di vista sulla storia dell'Etiopia, *Atti I Convegno Internazionale di Studi Etiopici - Roma 1959*, pp.5-27, Roma: Accademia Nazionale dei Lincei.

Červiček, P., 1971   Rock Paintings of Laga Oda (Ethiopia), *Paideuma*, 17: 126-136.

—————— 1976a   *Catalogue of the Rock Art Collection of the Frobenius Institute*, Wiesbaden: Franz Steiner Verlag GMBH.

—————— 1976b   Rock Engravings from the Hamasén Region, Eritrea, *Paideuma*, 22: 237-256.

—————— 1978-79   Some African Affinities of Arabian Rock Art, *Rassegna di Studi Etiopici*, 27: 5-12.

Cheesman, R. E., 1968   *Lake Tana and the Blue Nile*, London: Frank Kass.

Chittick, H. N., 1974   Excavations at Aksum: a Preliminary Report, *Azania*, 9: 159-205.

—————— 1976   Radiocarbon dates from Aksum, *Azania*, 11: 179-181.

Clark, J. D., 1962a   Africa South of the Sahara in *Courses toward Urban Life*, (R. J. Braidwood and G. R. Willey, eds.), pp.1-34, Edinburgh: University Press.

—————— 1962b   The spread of food production in sub-Saharan Africa, *Journal of African History*, 3: 211-228.

—————— 1967   The problem of Neolithic culture in sub-Saharan Africa in *Background to Evolution in Africa*, (W. W. Bishop and J. D. Clark, eds.), pp.601-627, Chicago: The Chicago University Press.

—————— 1970   *The Prehistory of Africa*, London: Thames and Hudson.

—————— 1972   *The Prehistoric Cultures of the Horn of Africa*, New York: Octagon Press.

—————— 1976a   The Domestication Process in Sub-Saharan Africa with special reference to Ethiopia, in *Origine de l'élevage et de la domestication* (E. Higgs, ed.), pp.56-115, Nice: IXe Congrés UISSP, colloque XX, prétirage.

—————— 1976b   Prehistoric Populations and Pressures Favoring Plant Domestication in Africa, in *Origins of African Plant Domestication* (J. R. Harlan, J. M. J. de Wet and A. B. Stemler, eds.), pp.68-105, The Hague: Mouton Publishers.

—————— 1980   The origins of domestication in Ethiopia, *Proceedings of the 8th Panafrican Congress of Prehistory and Quaternary Studies - Nairobi 1977* (R. E. Leakey and B. A. Ogot, eds.), pp.268-270, Nairobi: The International Louis Leakey Memorial Institute for African Prehistory.

—————— 1981   Ethno-Archaeology in Ethiopia and its Relevance for Archaeological Interpretation, in *Préhistoire Africaine* (C. Roubet, H. J. Hugot and G. Souville, eds.), pp.69-79, Paris: Editions A.D.P.F.

Clark, J. D., and M. A. J. Williams, 1978	Recent archaeological research in Southeastern Ethiopia (1974-1975): some preliminary results, *Annales d'Ethiopie*, 11: 19-44.
Consociazione Turistica Italiana, 1938	*Guida dell'Africa Orientale Italiana*, Milan.
Conti Rossini, C., 1900	Ricerche e studi sull'Etiopia, *Bollettino della Società Geografica Italiana*, serie IV, 1: 104-120.
——————— 1906	Sugli Ḥabašāt, in *Rendiconti della Reale Accademia dei Lincei*, 15: 39-59.
——————— 1927	Monete Aksumite, in *Africa Italiana*, 1: 171-211.
——————— 1928	*Storia d'Etiopia*, Bergamo: Istituto Italiano d'Arti Grafiche.
——————— 1942	Un'iscrizione su obelisco di Anza, *Rassegna di Studi Etiopici*, 2: 21-28.
——————— 1947	Iehà, Tsehùf Emnì e Derà, *Rassegna di Studi Etiopici*, 6: 12-22.
——————— 1948	Incisioni rupestri a Mumāt Ĕzùm, *Rassegna di Studi Etiopici*, 7: 113.
Cossàr, B., 1945	Necropoli precristiana di Selaclacà, *Studi Etiopici* (C. Conti Rossini, ed.), pp.7-16, Roma: Istituto per l'Oriente.
Costantini, L., Fattovich, R., Pardini, E., and M. Piperno, 1982	Preliminary report of archaeological investigations at the site of Mahal Teglinos (Kassala), November 1981, *Nyame Akuma*, 21: 30-33.
Dainelli, G., and O. Marinelli, 1912	*Risultati di un viaggio scientifico nella Colonia Eritrea*, Firenze: Galletti e Cocci.
Davico, A., 1946	*Ritrovamenti sudarabici nella zona di Cascasé*, 5: 1-6.
De Contenson, H., 1959	Les fouilles d'Axoum en 1957. Rapport préliminaire, *Annales d'Ethiopie*, 3: 25-34.
——————— 1960	Les premiers rois d'Axoum, *Journal Asiatique*, 248: 75-95.
——————— 1962	Les monuments d'art sud-arabe découverts sur le site de Haoulti (Ethiopie) en 1959, *Syria*, 39: 64-87.
——————— 1963b	Les fouilles à Axoum en 1959. Rapport préliminaire, *Annales d'Ethiopie*, 5: 41-52.
——————— 1963d	Les fouilles à Haoulti en 1958. Rapport préliminaire, *Annales d'Ethiopie*, 5: 3-16.
——————— 1976	A propos d'une révision de la chronologie axoumite, *L'Anthropologie*, 80: 520-521.
——————— 1981	Pre-Aksumite Culture, in *General History of Africa*, II. Ancient

Civilizations of Africa, (G. Mokhtar, ed.), pp.341-361, Berkeley: UNESCO/University of California Press.

D'Errico, L., 1935   Cenni sulla preistoria etiopica, in *Le opere per l'organizzazione civile in A.O.I.*, pp.189-194, Addis Ababa: Ministero delle Colonie.

————— 1937   Una stazione litica nell'Amara, *L'Africa Italiana*, 55: 40-41.

De Wet, J. M. J., 1977   Domestication of African Cereals, *African Economic History*, 3, 15-32.

Doe, B., 1971   *Southern Arabia*, London: Thames and Hudson.

————— 1983   *Monuments of South Arabia*, Cambridge: The Oleander Press.

Dombrowski, J. C., 1970   Preliminary Report on Excavations in Lalibela and Natchabiet Caves, Begemeder, *Annales d'Ethiopie*, 8: 21-29.

————— 1972   *Excavations in Ethiopia; Lalibela and Natchabiet Caves, Begemeder Province*, Boston University Graduate School Ph.D. Dissertation, Ann Arbor: University Microfilms Company.

Doresse, J., 1957   L'Ethiopie et l'Arabie Meridionale aux IIIe et IVe siècle A.D., *Kush*, 5: 49-58.

————— 1960   La découverte d'Asbi-Dera. Nouveaux documents sur les rapports entre l'Egypte et l'Ethiopie à l'époque axoumite, *Atti del Convegno Internazionale di Studi Etiopici — Roma 1959*, pp.413-434, Roma: Accademia Nazionale dei Lincei.

Drewes, A. J., 1956   Nouvelles Inscriptions de l'Ethiopie, *Bibliotheca Orientalis*, 13: 179-182.

————— 1959   Les inscriptions de Melazo, *Annales d'Ethiopie*, 3: 83-99.

————— 1962   *Inscriptions de l'Ethiopie Antique*, Leiden: E. J. Brill.

Drewes, A. J. and R. Schneider, 1976   Origine et development de l'ecriture éthiopienne jusqu'à l'époque des inscriptions royales d'Axoum, *Annales d'Ethiopie*, 10: 95-107.

Ducati, P., 1952   *L'arte classica*, Torino: U.T.E.T.

Duncanson, D. J., 1947   Girameten: a new archaeological site in Eritrea, *Antiquity*, 21: 158-163.

Ehret, C., 1979   On the antiquity of agriculture in Ethiopia, *Journal of African History*, 20: 161-167.

Fattovich, R., 1972a   Sondaggi stratigrafici: Yeha 1971, *Annales d'Ethiopie*, 9: 65-84.

————— 1972b   Yeha 1972: sondaggi stratigrafici, *Travaux de la R.C.P.*, 230, 3: 65-75.

——————— 1975   The contribution of the Nile Valley's cultures to the rising of the Ethiopian civilization: elements for an hypothesis of work, *Meroitic Newsletter*, 16: 2-8.

——————— 1976a   Osservazioni generali sulla ceramica preaksumita di Yeha (Etiopia), *Africa* (Rivista dell'Istituto Italo-Africano), 31: 587-595.

——————— 1976b   La ceramica preaksumita di Yeha: elementi di comparazione, *Documents Historie Civilisation Ethiopienne*, R.C.P. 230, CNRS, 7: 31-39.

——————— 1977a   Some data for the study of the cultural history in ancient Northern Ethiopia, *Nyame Akuma*, 10: 6-18.

——————— 1977b   Pre-Aksumite Civilization of Ethiopia: a Provisional Review, *Proceedings of the Seminar for Arabian Studies*, 7: 73-78.

——————— 1978a   Traces of a possible African component in the pre-Aksumite Culture of Northern Ethiopia, *Abbay*, 9: 25-30.

——————— 1978b   L'Etiopia e i regni sudarabici, *Archeologia* (Autori Vari), p.349-359, Milano: Mondadori.

——————— 1979   Alcuni siti inediti dell'Eritrea settentrionale, *Abbay*, CNRS, 10: 77-86.

——————— 1980   Materiali per lo studio della ceramica pre-Aksumita etiopica, *Supplemento 25, Annali dell'Istituto Universitario Orientale di Napoli*, 40 (4).

——————— 1981   Ricerche archeologiche nel delta del Gash, provincia di Kassala (Sudan), *Africa* (Rivista dell'Istituto Italo-Africano), 36: 315-327.

——————— 1982   The problem of Sudanese-Ethiopian contacts in antiquity: *status quaestionis* and current trends of research, in *Nubian Studies* (J. M. Plumley, ed.), pp.76-86, Warminster: Arris & Phillips Ltd.

——————— 1983   I 'rilievi' rupestri di Daarò Caulòs presso Asmara (Etiopia), *Annali dell'Istituto Universitario Orientale di Napoli*, 43: 241-247.

——————— 1984a   Data for the history of the ancient peopling of the Northern Ethiopian-Sudanese borderland, *Proceedings of the 7th International Conference of Ethiopian Studies* (S. Rubenson, ed.), pp.177-186, Uppsala: Scandinavian Institute for African Studies.

——————— 1984b   The Late Prehistory of the Gash Delta, Sudan, in *The Late Prehistory of the Nile Basin and the Sahara* (L. Krzyżaniak, ed.), *in press*, Warsaw: Polska Akademia Nauk.

—————————— 1984c   The Gash Delta between 1000 BC and AD 1000, *Proceedings of the 5th International Conference for Meroitic Studies – Rome 1984* (S. Wenig, ed.), Berlin: Akademie-Verlag, *in press*.

—————————— 1984d   In search of Punt, *Ligabue Magazine*, 5, 104-109.

Fattovich, R., Marks, A. E., and A. M. Ali, 1984   The Archaeology of the Eastern Sahel, Sudan; Preliminary Results, *The African Archaeological Review*, 2: 177-188.

Fattovich, R. and M. Piperno, 1982   Archaeological Researches in the Gash Delta, Kassala Province (1980-1981 Field Seasons), *Proceedings of the 5th International Conference of Nubian Studies – Heidelberg 1982* (D. W. Krause, ed.), *in press*.

Franchini, V., 1951   Pitture rupestri a Sollum Ba'atti, *Rassegna di Studi Etiopici*, 10: 121-123.

—————————— 1952   Pitture rupestri nel Ba'atti Sollum nel Deghiem, *Rassegna di Studi Etiopici*, 11: 42-48.

—————————— 1953   Stazioni litiche in Eritrea, *Bollettino (Asmara)*, 1: 25-30.

—————————— 1961   Pitture rupestri e antichi resti archittetonici dell'Acchelè Guzài, *Rassegna di Studi Etiopici*, 17: 5-10.

—————————— 1963   I graffiti rupestri di Edit, *Bollettino (Asmara)*, 3: 9-12.

—————————— 1964   Nuovi ritrovamenti di pitture rupestri e graffiti rupestri in Eritrea, *Rassegna di Studi Etiopici*, 20: 97-102.

—————————— 1971   La stazione rupestre di Mehrad Tiél, *Journal of Ethiopian Studies*, 9: 27-34.

—————————— 1980   Note su alcune stazioni d'arte rupestre in Eritrea, *Quaderni di Studi Etiopici*, 9: 27-34.

Gallagher, J. P., 1972   A preliminary report on archaeological research near Lake Zuai, *Annales d'Ethiopie*, 9: 13-18.

—————————— 1974   The Preparation of Hides with Stone Tools in South Central Ethiopia, *Journal of Ethiopian Studies*, 12: 177-182.

—————————— 1976   Ethno-Archaeology in South Central Ethiopia, *Proceedings of the Panafrican Congress of Prehistory and Quaternary Studies, VIIth Session, Addis Ababa 1971*, (B. Abebe, J. Chavaillon, J. E. G. Sutton, eds.), p.325-328, Addis Ababa: Provisional Military Government of Socialist Ethiopia, Ministry of Culture.

—————————— 1977   Contemporary Stone Tools in Ethiopia: Implications for Archaeology, *Journal of Field Archaeology*, 4: 407-414.

Garbini, G., 1972   *Le Lingue Semitiche*, Napoli: Istituto Universitario Orientale.

———————— 1973   Un nuovo documento per la storia dell'antico Yemen, *Oriens Antiquus*, 12: 143-163.

Gaudio, A., 1953   Quattro ritrovamenti archeologici e paleografici in Eritrea, *Bollettino (Asmara)*, 1: 44-49.

Godet, E., 1977   Répertoire de sites pré-axoumites et axoumites du Tigré (Ethiopie), *Abbay*, CNRS, 8: 19-58.

———————— 1980-82 Répertoire des sites pré-axoumites et axoumites d'Ethiopie du Nord, IIème partie: Erythrée, *Abbay*, CNRS, 11: 73-114.

Graziosi, P., 1941   Le pitture rupestri dell'Amba Focada (Eritrea), *Rassegna di Studi Etiopici*, 1: 61-70.

———————— 1963   Brevi osservazioni sulle pitture rupestri dell'Acchele Guzay, *Bollettino (Asmara)*, 3: 13-17.

———————— 1964a   Figure schematiche nell'Acchele Guzay, *Rivista di Scienze Preistoriche*, 19: 265-275.

———————— 1964b   New Discoveries of Rock Paintings in Ethiopia, *Antiquity*, 138: 91-99, 187-190.

Grohmann, A., 1963   *Arabien*, München: C. H. Beck'sche Verlags Buchhandlung.

Humann, K. and O. Puchstein, 1890   *Reisen in Kleinasien und Nordsyrien, Atlas*, Berlin: Dietrich Reimer.

Huntingford, G. W. B., 1974   Three notes on early Ethiopian Geography, *Folia Orientalia*, 15: 197-204.

———————— 1980   *The Periplus of the Erythrean Sea*, London: Hakluyt Society.

Joussaume, R., 1981   L'art rupestre de l'Ethiopie, in *Préhistoire Africaine* (C. Roubet, H.-J. Hugot, G. Souville, eds.), pp.159-175, Paris: Editions A.D.P.F.

Kammerer, A., 1929   *Le Mer Rouge, L'Abyssinie et l'Arabie depuis l'Antiquité*, Cairo: Institut Français d'Archéologie Orientale.

Kirwan, L. P., 1960   The decline and fall of Meroe, *Kush*, 8, 163-173.

Kitchen, K. A., 1971   Punt and how to get there, *Orientalia*, 40: 184-207.

———————— 1982   Punt, *Lexikon der Ägyptologie*, 32 (IV, 8): 1198-1201, Wiesbaden.

Klichowska, M., 1978   Preliminary results of palaeoethnobotanical studies on plant impressions on potsherds from the Neolithic settlements at Kadero, *Nyame Akuma*, 12: 42-48.

Kobishchanov, I. M., 1978   Axum in *The Early State* (H. J. M. Claessen, P. Skalnik, eds.), pp.151-167, The Hague: Mouton Publishers.

———————— 1979   *Axum*, Philadelphia: Pennsylvania State University Press.

———————— 1981   Axum: political system, economics and culture, first to fourth century, *General History of Africa*, II. Ancient Civilizations of Africa (G. Mokhtar, ed.), pp.381-399, Berkeley: UNESCO/University of California Press.

Krencker, D., 1913   *Deutsche Aksum-Expedition*, Berlin: Georg Reimer Verlag.

Krzyżaniak, L., 1978   New Light on Early Food-Production in the Central Sudan, *Journal of African History*, 19: 159-172.

Leclant, J., 1959   Haoulti-Melazo (1955-1956), *Annales d'Ethiopie*, 3: 43-57.

———————— 1961-1962   Le Musée d'Antiquités d'Addis Ababa, *Bulletin de la Société d'Archéologie Copte*, 16: 283-304.

———————— 1965   Note sur l'amulete en cornaline J.E. 2832, *Annales d'Ethiopie*, 6: 87-88.

Leclant, J. and A. Miquel, 1959   Reconnaissance dans l'Agamé: Goulo-Makéda et Sabéa (Octobre 1955 et Avril 1956), *Annales d'Ethiopie*, 3: 107-114.

Leroy, J., 1963   Les 'Ethiopiens' de Persépolis, *Annales d'Ethiopie*, 5: 293-295.

Mathew, G., 1975   The dating and the significance of the *Periplus of the Erythrean Sea, East Africa and the Orient* (N. H. Chittick, R. I. Rotberg, eds.), pp.147-163, New York: Africana Publishing Company.

Mazzarino, S., 1974   Gli Aksumiti nella tradizione classica, *Atti IV Congresso Internazionale di Studi Etiopici - Roma 1972*, pp.75-84, Roma: Accademia Nazionale dei Lincei.

Mesfin W. Mariam, 1972   *An Introductory Geography of Ethiopia*, Addis Ababa: Berhanena Selam H.S.I. Printing Press.

Michels, J. W., 1975   Archaeological Survey of the Aksumite Kingdom, Tigre Province, Ethiopia, paper presented to the 'African Archaeological Meetings' - Boston 1975.

Monneret de Villard, U., 1938a   *Aksum. Ricerche di Topografia generale* (Analecta Orientalia 16), Roma: Pontificium Institutum Biblicum.

———————— 1938b   Note sulle influenza asiatiche nell'Africa Orientale, *Rivista degli Studie Orientali*, 17: 309-349.

Mordini, A., 1941   Un riparo sotto roccia con pitture rupestri nell'Amba Focada (Agamè), *Rassegna di Studi Etiopici*, 1: 54-60.

———————— 1945   Informazioni preliminari sui risultati delle mie ricerche in Etiopia dal 1939 al 1944, *Rassegna di Studi Etiopici*, 4: 145-154.

——————— 1947   Le incisioni rupestri di Gazien (Medrì Senafè) nell'Endertà (Etiopia), *Rivista di Scienze Preistoriche*, 2: 321-323.

——————— 1960   Gli aurei kushāna del convento di Dabra Damo, *Atti I Convegno di Studi Etiopici - Roma 1959*, pp.249-259, Roma: Accademia Nazionale dei Lincei.

Munro-Hay, S. C., 1981-1982   A Tyranny of Sources: the History of Aksum from its coinage, *Northeast African Studies*, 3: 1-16.

Paribeni, R., 1907   Ricerche sul luogo dell'antica Adulis, *Monumenti Antichi*, 437-572.

Pecorella, P. E., 1978   L'Anatolia tra IIIe I millennio a. Cr., *Archeologia* (Autori Vari), pp.421-450, Milano: Mondadori.

Petrie, W. Flinders, 1914   *Tarkhan II*, London: British School of Egyptian Archaeology.

Phillipson, D. W., 1977a   *The Later Prehistory of Eastern and Southern Africa*, London: Heinemann.

——————— 1977b   The Excavation of Gobedra Rock-shelter, Axum, *Azania*, 12: 53-82.

——————— 1978a   The Later Stone Age in sub-Saharan Africa, *The Cambridge History of Africa*, I: From the Earliest Times to c. 500 BC (J. D. Clark, ed.), pp.410-477, Cambridge: Cambridge University Press.

——————— 1978b   Early Food Production in sub-Saharan Africa, *The Cambridge History of Africa*, I: From the Earliest Times to c. 500 BC (J. D. Clark, ed.), pp.770-829, Cambridge: Cambridge University Press.

Pirenne, J., 1955   *La Gréce et Saba*, Paris: Impt. Nationale.

——————— 1956   *Paléographie des Inscriptions Sub-Arabes*, Brussels: Académie Royale Flammande de Belgique.

——————— 1961   Un probléme-clef pour la chronologie de l'Orient: la date du "Periple de la Mer Erythrée", *Journal Asiatique*, 249: 441-459.

——————— 1967   Haoulti et ses monuments, nouvelle interpretation, *Annales d'Ethiopie*, 7: 125-133.

Plant, R., 1978   A Hypothesis on the Origins of Ethiopian Architecture, *Abbay*, CNRS, 9: 21-24.

Puglisi, S. M., 1941   Primi risultati delle indagini compiute dalla Missione Archeologica di Aksum, *Africa Italiana*, 8: 95-153.

——————— 1946   Industria litica di Aksum nel Tigrai Occidentale, *Rivista di Scienze Preistoriche*, 1: 284-290.

Ricci, L., 1953   Ritrovamenti archeologici in Eritrea, *Rassegna di Studi Etiopici*, 12: 5-28.

———————— 1955-1958   Ritrovamenti archeologici in Eritrea, II, *Rassegna di Studi Etiopici*, 14: 48-68.

———————— 1959   Iscrizioni rupestri dell'Eritrea, I, *Rassegna di Studi Etiopici*, 15: 59-95.

———————— 1960   Notizie archeologiche, *Rassegna di Studi Etiopici*, 16: 120-123.

———————— 1974   Scavi archeologici in Etiopia, *Africa* (Rivista dell'Istituto Italo-Africano), 29: 435-441.

———————— 1984   L'Expansion de l'Arabie Meridionale, *L'Arabie du Sud, Histoire et Civilisation*, I: Le Peuple Yemenite et ses racines, (S. Chellod, ed.), pp.249-257, Paris: Maisonneuve et Larose.

Robin, C., 1984   Les Abyssins en Arabie Meridionale (IIe - IVe S), VIIIth International Conference of Ethiopian Studies, Addis Ababa 1984.

Sapeto, G., 1941   *Viaggio ai Mensa, ai Bogos ed agli Habab*, Milano: Istituto per gli Studi di Politica Internazionale.

Schneider, R., 1973   Deux inscriptions sudarabiques du Tigrè, *Bibliotheca Orientalis*, 5/6: 385-387.

———————— 1976a   Documents epigraphiques de l'Ethiopie, V., *Annales d'Ethiopie*, 10: 81-93.

———————— 1976b   Les debuts de l'histoire éthiopienne, *Documents pour servir a l'Histoire de la Civilisation Ethiopienne*, 7: 47-54.

Schoff, W. H., 1912   *The Periplus of the Erythrean Sea*, New York: Longmans, Green and Co.

Shiner, J., 1971   *The Prehistory and Archaeology of Northern Sudan*, Report to the National Science Foundation, Dallas.

Spratling, M. G., 1970   Interim Report on the Archaeological Finds (Blue Nile Expedition 1968), *The Geographical Journal*, 136: 59-60.

Tesfaye, G., 1979   Découverte des gravures préhistoriques dans la valée du Gunda Gundie (Agame, Tigray), *Abbay*, CNRS, 10: 75.

Teti, A., 1960   Industrie litiche delle Isole Dahlac, Testi di Laurea, Università di Roma, AA 1959-60, Roma.

Tringali, G., 1965   Cenni sulle 'ona di Asmara e dintorni, *Annales d'Ethiopie*, 6: 143-152.

———————— 1967   Necropoli di Curbacaiehat (Asmara), *Journal of Ethiopian Studies*, 5 (1): 109.

——————— 1969   Varietà di asce litiche in ouna dell'altiplano eritreo, *Journal of Ethiopian Studies*, 7 (1): 119-120.

——————— 1973-1979   Necropoli di Cascasé e oggetti sudarabici (?) della regione di Asmara (Eritrea), *Rassegna di Studi Etiopici*, 26: 47-66.

——————— 1980-1981   Note su ritrovamenti archeologici in Eritrea, *Rassegna di Studi Etiopici*, 28: 99-113.

Triulzi, A., 1981   *Salt, Gold and Legitimacy*, Napoli: Istituto Universitario Orientale.

Trucca, B., 1980   Il culti delle pietre ritte (ansab) in terra etiopica, *Quaderni di Studi Etiopici*, 1: 66-76.

Vavilov, N. I., 1951   The Origin, Variation, Immunity and Breeding of Cultivated Plants, *Chronica Botanica*, 13.

Vigliardi, Micheli A., 1957   Le pitture rupestri di Carora, *Rivista di Scienze Preistoriche*, 11: 193-210.

Wissmann, H. von, 1975   *Über die Frühe Geschichte Arabiens und das Enstehen des Sabaerriches – Die Geschichte von Saba', I.*, Wien: Akademie Verlag.

IS NÄWA BÄG'U AN ETHIOPIAN CROSS?*

Ewa Balicka-Witakowska

When Mrs. Diana Spencer visited the Ethiopian monastery of Tädbabä Maryam in Sayint[1], in search of icons attributed to St. Luke[2], an unusual cross was drawn from the 'əka bet and shown to her. According to local tradition it belonged to John the Baptist, who used it when he baptized Jesus. This is why the cross is called *Näwa Bäg'u* (ፈ፞ꝑ ብግዑ), i.e. "Behold the Lamb" (cf. John 1, 29). The cross is believed to have the miraculous power of healing blindness.[3]

The traditional attribution transmitted by the monks of the monastery is based undoubtedly on a legend connected with emperor Ləbnä Dəngəl. This legend tells of the coming of a fragment of Christ's Cross from Egypt to Ethiopia, together with other valuable relics, among them the cross of John the Baptist.[4]

It is generally said in Ethiopia that the piece of the Holy Cross is in the possession of Ǝgzi'abḥer Ab church on Amba Gəšen.[5] Tädbabä Maryam possesses, however, besides *Näwa Bäg'u*, the hair of St. Anne and the bones of St. George[6], both mentioned in the narration on Ləbnä Dəngəl.

Näwa Bäg'u is a processional cross, today without its staff[7] (Pl.I), which measures 20 x 16cm and is made of chased silver or silver-dipped bronze.[8] The frame is in the form of an elongated quatrefoil decorated with three small Greek crosses and with an ornament in the form of drops and trefoils, and embraces the flared arms of the central cross. It has the form of a flat box with a cover. Inside, there is a bronze figure of the Crucified Christ in high relief. The silver or silver-plated cover is decorated with engravings: on the outside a sitting angel above which there is the inscription *Mika'el* (Pl.II); on the inside a standing angel with the inscription *Gabrə'el* (Pl.III). On the reverse side of the cross there is a third engraving of a six-winged figure, with his head in the form of a romb, labelled *Suraf'el* (Pl.IV). The angels have gilded halos; their wings and clothes are gilded, too, but only every other section or fold – the remaining folds or sections being silver-plated. On the front of the shaft there is a sculpture of the head of a ram with long horns, in silver or silver-plated (Pl.V).[9] The reverse side of the shaft is decorated with an incised cross.

Among the processional and hand crosses known today from Ethiopia[10] *Näwa Bäg'u* is totally unique, especially in respect to its form and the three-dimensional figure of Christ placed in its interior. Among questions which could be asked concerning this unusual object, there are many which still cannot be answered thus far.[11] Here we would like only to try to establish whether the cross is a product of Ethiopian art or of foreign provenance.

* * * * * *

To judge from the repertory of crosses from Ethiopia, bronze[12], as well as copper, was the material preferred for cross making up to the 15th century. Crosses of pure silver are very rare before the 17th century.[13] Gilding was a technique applied quite frequently, especially for bronze crosses, but only from the 17th century.[14] Earlier examples of crosses made with goldsmith techniques are rare and most probably imports.[15]

Among Ethiopian crosses, the framed ones belong to the group of works now regarded as the earliest. They are dated, in some cases, to the Zague epoch but most often to the 14th and 15th centuries. Besides the oval, double oval and pear-shaped frames, the form of the quatrefoil frame, more or less elongated, also occurs (Pl.VI). Their superior and side finials are usually decorated with small Greek crosses. Often they are accompanied by woven bands, looped zigzags, cables or circles.[16] These, however, do not occur in *Näwa Bäg'u*. It does not have the two rings on both sides of the shaft, through which a piece of material – symbolizing Christ's garments according to tradition – was often drawn. On our cross, this function was possibly filled by the long horns of the ram's head.

Such a sculpture, although placed differently, can also be found on the bronze cross of the monastery of Abräntant, Waldəbba (Pl.VII)[17], which belongs to the class of short armed crosses emerging in the 15th century. The ends of their arms are usually decorated with a cable band and ribbon loops forming circles surmounted by a pattée cross.[18] The cross of Abräntant is distinguished from the rest of the group by unusual encrustation of blue glass.

The authors who wrote on *Näwa Bäg'u* and the cross of Abräntant are not sure if the heads of the rams belonged originally to the respective crosses. Since the shaft is a part which is most often changed and repaired, it cannot be excluded that the head could have been added later. In any case, we can suppose that its function on *Näwa Bäg'u* was not only that of decoration. Putting together the head of the ram and the Crucifixion is not accidental. The ram, the animal God caused to be placed in a thorny bush so that Abraham might sacrifice it in place of his son, was conceived as the symbol of Christ crowned in thorns and sacrificed for mankind. This idea was not unknown in Ethiopia. In early churches, e.g. Gännätä Maryam, Lasta, or Qorqor Maryam, Gär'alta, the sacrifice of Abraham is a part of the iconographic programme of the wall paintings as a symbolic scene instead of the Crucifixion.[19] One of the liturgical texts for the Festival of the Cross, *Mäsqäl*, reads: "They saw a ram caught by its horns in a thicket. The shrub, that is the Tree of Forgiveness — the Cross; since the Cross won — Death was defeated. The power of His Cross explains it".[20]

* * * * * *

One of the characteristics which distinguishes *Näwa Bäg'u* from other crosses is its central part, which is a cruciform box closed with a cover of the same form. It imparts to the work a character of a reliquary, inside which there is a representation of the Crucified Christ, instead of a relic. This is a type which, as A. Frolow remarks in his detailed study on the reliquaries of the True Cross, reflects para-dogmatic beliefs.[21]

The use of a cover, which screens the inside of a reliquary, expresses the idea that the presence of God — since it is He who inhabits it — should be kept secret. It is also a practical application of the rule according to which the liturgical implement revealing the secrets of God's Wisdom should not be displayed for the laity.[22]

Among the cross reliquaries which are known today, there is none like *Näwa Bäg'u*. However, pectoral Byzantine and Oriental crosses meant for containing particles of the True Cross could be regarded as the actualization of the ideas mentioned above. These are, for instance: the cross in the treasury of the Cathedral of Monza (Pl.VIII), the cross in the Benaki Museum (Pl.IX) or the crosses in the Działyński collection in Gołuchów, Poland, and in the Dumbarton Oaks collection.[23] All of them open. Inside, each contain a movable cruciform plate decorated in different ways, which has a cavity for the relic of the Wood of the Holy Cross. The Crucifixion is represented on the obverse of the outer part of the reliquaries. It is fully visible, since what should be concealed in these cases are the relics.[24]

Reliquaries of different types, including *staurothecas*, must have been known in Ethiopia at least since the coming to the country of the fragment of the Holy Cross and other relics. Besides the story mentioned above, connected with Ləbnä Dəngəl, the Ethiopian tradition ascribes the same events to two other emperors: David and Zär'a Ya'qob.[25] There is a narration on the latter contained in *Maṣḥafa Ṭefut*[26], where it is said that in the church on Amba Gəšen a gold casket containing a fragment of the Holy Cross was put into a gold cross and placed on a golden pedestal. The text ascribes the work to Francs, i.e. European artists.[27] An almost identical relation can be found among the historical notes of the MS. British Museum Or 481.[28] Although both texts are of a rather late date[29], it is very probable that they are based on authentic documents relative to Ǝgzi'abḥer Ab church and the cult of the Holy Cross which developed there.[30]

We can surmise that the cross described in the texts mentioned did exist, and was the work of foreign artists just as the stories say it was. In the monastery of Daga Ǝstifanos, a bronze processional cross is preserved (Pl.X). Both front and back are inlaid with gold and glass. On the central part, screening the cavity for relics, there are figures in high relief of the Crucified Christ and *Maiestas Domini*.[31] There is also an inscription: "This cross has been given by the king Zär'a Ya'qob to [the monastery] Däbrä Nəgwädgwad for the eternal life of his soul".

Of course, we cannot be sure if this is the cross described in *Maṣḥāfa Ṭefut*. This is an alluring hypothesis, however, and some facts make it even very probable. Firstly: the cross is decorated with the Crucifixion in high relief, which is a highly unusual phenomenon in Ethiopia, the only known analogy being *Näwa Bäg'u*. Secondly: in the description of the reliquary in *Maṣḥāfa Ṭefut* the word *qämaṭər* is used, which can be translated as 'open-work' or 'filigree'[32], but it can also designate a box of any form made in such a metalwork or goldsmith technique which was unknown to the Ethiopians.[33] Doubtless, the cross of Daga Əstifanos represents such an alien technique (open-work and, especially, encrustation). Few examples of encrustated crosses are known from Ethiopia, moreover they are thought to be imports, e.g. another cross in the Abräntant monastery (Pl.XI), which is even named Jerusalemian or Egyptian. What is most important, however, is that the cross from Daga Əstifanos, according to the donor's inscription, was intended for Däbrä Nəgwädgwad. From the chronicle of Zär'a Ya'qob it is known that he founded a church by that name in Amhara[34], but on the other hand, according to *Maṣḥāfa Ṭefut*, Däbrä Nəgwädgwad was the original name of Amba Gešen.[35]

* * * * * *

Let us turn back to *Näwa Bäg'u*. Here also, as is the case with most similar reliquaries, the cover has a double function — it protects what is inside and gives an additional area for decoration, increasing the possibilities for developing the iconographical programme of the object. The artist engraved an angel on each side of the cover and enclosed a third figure on the reverse side. What is amazing about the engravings is their unusual elaborateness and precision of work. It is not just lines that give the outline of the figures. The lines are supplemented with punctures, which bring out the design very clearly. The figures, in correct proportions, have been skillfully composed within the fields of the cross. Most of the details have been made with high accuracy, e.g. strands of hair, the toes, the short and long features of the wings, as well as varying structures of the folds of the garments. The garments of the angel on the outside of the cover bring out his sitting position; those of the angel on the inside allow us to discern his undergarments extending below his cloak, the fold of which form an ornamental volute. Both angels have regular facial features and characteristic short, boyish haircut. Gabriel and a six-winged figure are presented frontally, but Michael in three-quarter profile. The latter sits resting his head on his hands, with his elbows resting on his knees — the position resembling Joseph in the Byzantine Nativity scenes.

In the Ethiopian processional crosses engraving was the most often used technique. Besides many examples of engravings of a rather schematic character as, for instance, the crosses IES No.4651 or No.4428 (Pls.XII, XX), there are some other crosses showing that the artist tried to follow the styles of the miniature painting he knew, e.g. the cross IES No.3970[36], or that of Wäqət monastery, Tämben (Pl.XIII), which are comparable to the miniatures of three manuscripts: the Gospels *Senodos* and *Ta'ämra Märyäm* of Amba Gəšen and *Läḥa Märyäm* of Betäləhem church near Däbrä Tabor[37]; the crosses IES No.4142 (Pl.XIV) and No.4486[38] are comparable to miniatures of the so-called Gunda Gunde school.[39] From the 18th century, the figures on almost all crosses are modelled on the painting style called the second Gondarene (Pl.XV).

The engravings of *Näwa Bäg'u* have nothing in common, however, with any of the groups mentioned. On account of the elaborateness of the detailed workmanship, they display similarity to two silver crosses of the Lalibäla type, usually dated to the 14th-15th centuries — one from Maryam Dəngəlat church, Tigre (Pl.XVI) and the second of unknown origin[40] (Pl.XVII). In both cases, the engravings represent the Crucified Christ. His somewhat elongated but well proportioned body is shown with many carefully drawn anatomical details. The same carefulness is seen in the drawing of the folds of the *perizonium*. Moreover, on the second cross, the figure of Christ is brought out from the background by contrasting the bright smooth surface of his body against the dark, punched background. The same contrast was brought out on the frame between the vegetal forms and their background. Another interesting detail of this cross is the lamb engraved on the upper part of the shaft. It is presented in full, with its head surrounded by a halo. It stands on a stylized branch — a symbol of the shrub of Abraham's sacrifice.

Both silver crosses are decorated with zigzags on the tops of the frames and at their feet with small wings, which are the result of a far-advanced stylization of fish or dolphins. J. Doresse showed that those ornaments belong to the usual repertory of Coptic art.[41] Also very Coptic in character are interlace and vegetal ornaments engraved on the frames of the crosses. All these elements suggest that both crosses could have been produced in Egypt. The most significant, however, is the inscription IC XC over the Christ, which does not occur on objects of Ethiopian provenance.

* * * * * *

The elaborate engravings of *Näwa Bäg'u* contrast with the figure of Christ, which is made rather rudely (Pl.XVIII). His long and thin arms have very large hands. His feet are also large. His chest is a bulged, unmodelled triangle. His long hair falling on his arms reminds one of a kerchief. The facial features have not been sculptured, but only marked with strokes. The knees, however, have been clearly modelled, as well as the *perizonium* with the belt and folds accentuated by quite deep cuts.

This representation of the Crucified Christ belongs to the early Christian type *Christus triumphans*. His body outstretched on the cross follows the shape of the cross. His eyes are open, the head is kept upright, the whole figure seems to stand in front of the cross, rather than be fastened to it. This impression is strengthened by the fact that no traces of the nails can be seen on his hands and feet. An obvious archaization is made by depicting Christ directly on a liturgical cross without the historical one. Such a type of image occurred sometimes on early pectoral crosses[42] often of Coptic provenance.[43]

The representation of the Crucified Christ on Ethiopian processional crosses is not rare. In fact, these are the objects which have preserved the oldest known examples of this scene from Ethiopia.[44] The living *Christus victor* is represented on them as on *Näwa Bäg'u*. These are, however, the only similarities between *Näwa Bäg'u* and these crosses. The bronze cross IES No.4104 (Pl.XIX)[45] depicts a young or rather childlike Christ, clothed in a *colobium*, with feet and hands nailed to the cross. Christ on the cross IES No.4651 (Pl.XX)[46] also wears a *colobium*. Another type of Jesus, with his head slightly turned to the right but with open eyes, with his feet and hands nailed and clothed in a long *perizonium* with a belt, is shown by two silver crosses mentioned before.[47] Christ in a *perizonium*, already dead, with his head surrounded by a cruciform halo, can be seen on the bronze cross IES No.3988 (Pl.XXI).[48]

The most conspicuous difference between the *Näwa Bäg'u* Crucifixion and those on the crosses described above, is the using of high relief in the former and engraving in the latter cases. Apart from the cross of Zära Ya'qob, which was almost surely an import, we do not know either high relief or sculpture in the round Crucifixion from Ethiopia.[49] This is most probably because the religious art of Ethiopia accepted neither sculpture, nor images of any similarity to sculpture. We find this rule formulated in the official publication of the Ethiopian Church edited in 1970, where in the section on the sacramentals we read: " The Cross is one of the most important of the Ethiopian Church emblems, which symbolizes the redemption through the death of Jesus Christ. In every church there are many crosses of wood and silver, some small and some large, bearing the picture of the Crucifixion. The Crucifix is unknown, since graven images are not allowed".[50]

* * * * * *

Another question concerning the images on *Näwa Bäg'u* is whether the artist just put together some popular motifs without a deeper meaning, or whether he planned to express a definite idea through the juxtaposition of specifically chosen motifs. As was already pointed out above, the ram's head, whether original or added later, combined with the figure of Christ on the cross, should accentuate the sacrificial character of His death. The appearance of a cherub or, according to the inscription, of a seraph[51] on the reverse of the Crucifixion is well grounded too. The creature presented here according to the text of the Apocalypse (4, 6-11), i.e. with one head and six wings, indicates that the Cross should be regarded as the visible throne of Christ's invisible kingdom.

It is not clear, however, what rôle is played by the angels on the cover. They are deprived of all attributes and it is only the inscription which tells that they are Michael and Gabriel. Were it not for the inscriptions, we could surmise that they are any two angels, for instance those nameless angels which often accompany the scene of the Crucifixion. They were usually shown either with a gesture of acclamation, as adoring Christ or moaning over him. If we take a closer look at the angels on Näwa Bäg'u, we see that they fit very well in the latter category. The angel on the outside of the cover supports his cheek with his hand, which is the typical gesture of grief, the other stands with lowered clasped hands — this is a gesture of grief, too. However, the angels are called Michael and Gabriel and it can hardly be surprising, since both archangels hold a prominent position in the theology and devotion of the Ethiopian Church. In Ethiopian art they are the most often represented angels, usually on both sides of Mary with Child, with swords and processional crosses in their hands. If the inscriptions were added later, as we suppose, the man who wrote them had probably such a scene before his eyes. It cannot be excluded that the introduction of the archangels to the iconographical programme of Näwa Bäg'u was due to a preconceived idea, organizing all the pictorial elements of the cross. It could be understood as follows: one of the most important functions of Michael, who among the seven archangels stands closest to God, is to intercede for sinners. He is also the herald at the general resurrection. Gabriel is the messenger of good news. The rôle of cherubs and seraphs is to praise and glorify God and witness by their presence to the eternal sovereignty of Him, who has died on the cross. The victory over Death announced by Gabriel has been accomplished. In the presence of Christus triumphans, venerated by the celestial powers, sinners are introduced by Michael, who intercedes for them with the victorious.

* * * * * *

As we can see from the above analysis of Näwa Bäg'u, there are very little grounds for regarding the cross as an object of Ethiopian art. The most important argument for this attribution, based on the presence of the Ethiopian inscriptions, is easy to abolish. It is known that the providing of such inscriptions to foreign works of art in Ethiopia was a widespread practice, especially when their iconography was different from that known in the country.[52] It seems that this was the case of Näwa Bäg'u, since Michael and Gabriel are represented here without their attributes usual in Ethiopian art.

Let us list other indications of non-Ethiopian origin with Näwa Bäg'u. According to a tradition preserved in Tädbabä Maryam monastery, the cross comes from Palestine. Also the Palestinian or Egyptian origin of the cross is indicated by the story connected with Ləbnä Dəngəl.[53]

The technique of bronze gilding became widespread in Ethiopia only from the 17th century and applied first of all to the Gondarene crosses — Näwa Bäg'u definitely does not belong to this type. The Ethiopian provenance of all older crosses to which the gilding technique was applied is dubious.

The unusual decoration by the ram's head occurs elsewhere only on the cross of Abräntant which is probably an import, judging by its unusual material and technique.

The reliquaries for the preservation of the relics brought to Ethiopia were either of foreign provenance themselves or produced in Ethiopia by foreigners — as we are told by Mashafa Tefut.

The type of cross which could be opened as a kind of little shrine does not occur in Ethiopia except in Näwa Bäg'u'

The engraving technique on Näwa Bäg'u. is rather complicated and without parallel on other Ethiopian crosses. The figures are drawn with skill and presented with details to which

Ethiopian artists did not pay much attention. The most similarities to our cross in this respect are displayed by the engravings of two silver crosses which most probably were produced in Egypt.

The figure of Christ in high relief has no parallel in Ethiopian art, which is only natural if we consider the rules of the Ethiopian Church in this respect.

Some arguments drawn above also give suggestions as to where the *Näwa Bäg'u* cross could come from. It could either be from Palestine or Egypt, in both cases regions with which Ethiopia had had close religious contact. If we try to compare *Näwa Bäg'u* with similar Palestinian objects, we shall have difficulties, since it is not easy to find a similar cross absolutely known as a Palestinian work.[54] The Coptic crosses, however, are relatively numerous. At least three among them display traits reminiscent of *Näwa Bäg'u*: two processional crosses kept in the Benaki Museum, inv. nos. 11421 and 11422 (Pl.XXII)[55] and the cross from the former collection of Königliches Museum in Berlin (Pl.XXIII).[56] All of them have the same form as *Näwa Bäg'u* — a central cross with flared finials surrounded by a quatrefoil frame. Its decoration — each of the arms of the quatrefoil surmounted by a simple pattée cross, is also common. Moreover, the cross of the Benaki Museum, no.11422, is similar to *Näwa Bäg'u* in its drop-shaped ornament.

If we accept the Coptic provenance of *Näwa Bäg'u*, we still have to explain the problem of Christ's figure in high relief, since the Coptic Church is also regarded as having reservations as to sculpture in the round and sculptured crucifixes.[57] It seems, however, that if this form of art was totally discarded in Ethiopia, in Egypt it was partly tolerated.[58] The Crucifixion with a three-dimensional figure of Christ does occur on several Coptic liturgical implements, e.g. on the bronze censors: from Amba Shenuti monastery (today in the Coptic Museum in Cairo) (Pl.XXIV); in the collection of Prince Johan Georg of Saxony, from Akhmin (today in the Louvre); from Mar Musa el Habashi (today in the British Museum)[59]; on the pectoral crosses: in the Dumbarton Oaks collection and in the Coptic Museum in Cairo (Pl.XXV)[60]; in the British Museum[61]; two in the Berlin Museum (von Gans collection)[62]; on the cover of a copper bowl in the Coptic Museum in Cairo; on the upper part of the central bronze cross decorating a large tomb door in that museum (Pl.XXVI).[63]

The two last examples, as well as many other Coptic bronze objects, come from Fayum, which seems to have been eminent in the production of large scale metal articles, particularly in copper and bronze.[64] Perhaps, but this is only a tentative hypothesis, it was in one of the Fayum workshops that our cross, together with the figure of Christ, was made. As to the engravings, the technique of incising and gilding make us think of a greater artistic center, possibly Alexandria itself.

NOTES

*   I received the photographs of *Näwa Bäg'u* cross from Mrs. Diana Spencer and I wish to thank her for her help and permission to reproduce them.

1.   The monastery was an important religious center. During the reign of Lalibela its abbot, entitled patriarch, was also governor of the north-west provinces of Ethiopia, cf. Sergew Hable Sellasie, *Ancient and Medieval Ethiopian History to 1270*, Addis Ababa, 1972, p.268. The emperor Gälawdewos gave special privileges to the monastery, cf. W. E. Conzelman, *Chronique de Galâwdêwos (Claudius) roi d'Éthiopie*, Paris, 1895, pp.150-153, 156, 163. The emperor was buried in the monastery, as were some of his successors. Tädbabä Maryam was also an important center of church education.

2.   D. Spencer, "In Search of St. Luke: Icons in Ethiopia", *Journal of Ethiopian Studies*, X, 2, 1972, pp.67-95.

3.   *Ibid.*, p.73.

4. J. Perruchon, "Légendes relatives à David II (Lebna Dengel) roi d'Éthiopie", *Revue Semitique*, 6, 1989, p.166. This story is also known in other versions, but the cross of John the Baptist is mentioned only in that connected with the emperor Ləbnä Dəngəl.

5. A. Caquot, "Aperçu préliminaire sur le Maṣḥāfa Ṭēfut de Geshen Amba", *Annales d'Éthiopie*, 1, 1955, p.102n; Aymaro Wondmagegnehu and Joachim Motovu (eds), *The Ethiopian Orthodox Church*, Addis Ababa, 1970, p.70.

6. Spencer, *op. cit.*, p.77.

7. According to what was observed by D. Spencer, the cross is no longer used in services but is always kept in the church treasury.

8. The cross is regarded as having great holiness and, as D. Spencer has experienced, it is impossible to take it one's hands. She got permission to photograph it only during her second visit to the monastery. From a distance she could not, however, observe exactly what techniques were used in the production of the cross.

9. Cf. note 8.

10. *Koptische Kunst. Christentum am Nil*, Villa Hügel, Essen, 1963, nos.492-518; E. Moore, *Ethiopian Processional Crosses*, Addis Ababa, 1971; *Religiöse Kunst. Äthiopiens. Katalog der Ausstellung im Forum für Kulturaustausch des Instituts für Auslandsbeziehungen*, Stuttgart, 1973, nos.38-61; Murad Kamil, "Die äthiopische Prozessions – und Anhängekreuze", *Ethnologische Zeitschrift*, 1, 1975, pp.69-108; W. Korabiewicz, *La croix copte et son évolution*, Varsovie, 1976; C. Fabo Perczel, "Ethiopian Crosses at the Portland Art Museum", *African Arts*, 14, 1981, pp.52-55; see also a few previously unpublished objects in St. Chojnacki, *Major Themes in Ethiopian Painting*, Wiesbaden, 1983, figs. 45ab, 80ab, 158ab.

11. One of the most important tasks would be to find out the age of *Näwa Bäg'u*, because so far no dating attempt has been made. It is, however, a very difficult problem to solve. Firstly, no scholar can see it closely in order to get knowledge on the techniques used. No paleographer has uttered an opinion on the inscriptions. A comparison with other Ethiopian crosses is of no use, since *Näwa Bäg'u* is unique in its class. A similarity of *Näwa Bäg'u* to some Coptic crosses does not tell us anything about the time of its production, since we do not know how old the Coptic crosses are either. An indication seems to be only the iconography of Christ. His long hair falling on the arms and the *perizonium* are similar to the type which occurs in the Middle-Byzantine period. On the other hand, the living *Christus triumphans* is seldom met after the 15th century, even in peripheral art.

12. It is most often a melt of copper and tin, sometimes of lead and zinc, Moore, *op. cit.*, p.4.

13. The examples known today are: the cross from Maryam Dəngəlat church dated to the 14th century and similar cross of unknown origin, cf. Pls.XVI, XVII; the cross of the Institute of Ethiopian Studies (further IES) no.4484, dated to the 15th century, cf. Moore, *op. cit.*, Pl.XXIII; the cross IES no.4142, dated to the 15th-16th century, cf. *Religiöse Kunst. . . op. cit.*, p.193; the cross from Maryam church in Sawne, cf. Gigar Tesfaye, "Reconnaissance de trois églises antérieurs a 1314", *Journal of Ethiopian Studies*, XIII, 2, 1975, pl.Ic.

14. E.g. the cross of Narga Səllase, cf. *Koptische Kunst. . .*, no.503; the cross IES no.4433 from the 18th century, cf. Moore, *op. cit.*, figs.48-49; the cross IES no.4670 from the period 1682-1706, *ibid.*, fig.36. Some others are made in gilded brass, e.g. the cross IES

no.4195 from the beginning of the 17th century, *ibid.*, figs.39-40; the cross IES no.4193 from the period 1730-1755, *ibid.*, fig.47.

15. The cross IES no.4142 mentioned in note 13 is decorated with small concave discs of gold fastened with silver pins. Only a few of these remain; the cross IES no.3970, dated to the 15th century, is made in gilded bronze, cf. Moore, *op. cit.*, fig.19; the cross from Daga Ǝsṭifanos monastery, dated to 1434-1468, has openwork encrusted with glass and gold, cf. Pl.X; the cross from Abräntant monastery in Waldǝbba dated to the 14th-15th century cf. Pl.XI, for its detailed description see Girma Elias, "The Monastery of Abrentant in Waldibba", *Abbay* 8, 1977, p.118; C. Lepage, "Recherches sur l'art chrétien d'Éthiopie du Xe au XV^{e}s. Résultats et Perspectives", *Document pour servir à l'histoire des civilisations éthiopiennes*, 4, 1974, p.46, mentions two crosses inlaid with gold and gilded in Mika'el church on Amba Dära.

16. Cf. Moore, *op. cit.*, figs.7-14. The most similar in form to *Näwa Bäg'u* is the cross IES no.3988, cf. Pl.XXI. Here, however, the whole of the quatrefoil is filled with woven bands and the cross which is in its center is very small.

17. This cross was first published by Girma Elias, *op. cit.*, p.118, who also mentions another cross with a ram's head without any statement on the place of its preservation. It should be a cross connected with the emperor Ṭäṭṭodǝm (Ṭänṭäwǝdǝm) – Zague dynasty.

18. Cf. Moore, *op. cit.*, pp.29-31, figs.20-21.

19. Cf. C. Lepage, "Peintures murales de Ganata Maryam, (rapport préliminaire)", *Documents pour servir . . .*, 6, 1975, fig.6. The painting from Qorqor Maryam is not published.

20. B. Velat, *Études sur le Me'eräf commun de l'office divin éthiopien*, Patrologia Orientalis XXXIII, Paris, 1966, p.258, text p.60.

21. A. Frolow, *Les reliquaires de la vraie croix*, Paris, 1965, p.11.

22. *Ibid.*, p.31.

23. For a detailed description of the crosses cf. A. Frolow, *La relique de la vraie croix. Recherches sur le développement d'un culte*, Paris, 1961, pp.246-248; M. C. Ross, *Catalogue of the Byzantine and Early Mediaeval Antiquities in the Dumbarton Oaks Collection*, Washington, 1965, t.II, no.98, pl.LIII.

24. On the cross of Monza, the Crucifixion is engraved on the obverse of the cruciform plate, which is fitted into the interior of the cross. It can be seen, however, since the cover is made of a piece of rock crystal.

25. In Caquot, *op. cit.*, pp.91n and Taddesse Tamrat, *Church and State in Ethiopia 1270-1527*, Oxford, 1972, p.267, all texts transmitting this tradition are quoted.

26. Caquot, *op. cit.*, pp.101-107.

27. *Ibid.*, p.104. In the story, the reliquary is described three times, each time a little differently. One of the versions says that the golden cross containing the relic was placed, not on a pedestal, but in a golden box, which in its turn was put in a wooden box inlaid with gold. Another version says it was placed in a silver case, which was put into a bronze one and this, in its turn, into an iron coffer. From this unclear record it can be understood that the relics closed in a golden cross reliquary were displayed during services on a pedes-

tal near the altar (cf. *ibid.*, p.103) to be later put away into the treasury closed in a whole set of boxes.

28. Folios 208v-209r.

29. *Maṣḥāfa Ṭefut* — 'the Book of Ethiopian Genealogies' exists in only one manuscript (Taddesse Tamrat, *op. cit.*, p.267, note 2, suggests the existence of a copy of this document in the Institute of Archaeology in Addis Ababa), kept in Ǝgzi'abḥer Ab church on Amba Gəšen. It is read publicly once a year on the feast of the Invention of the Holy Cross (Mäggabit 10th) According to informants, neither close examination nor copying is allowed. It should contain the text of the Gospels, Senodos and a series of historical documents concerning the history of the Ethiopian church, cf. Caquot, *op. cit.*, p.90. It cannot be excluded, however, that just this book was shown to D. Spencer, cf. her "Trip to Wag and Northern Wällo", *Journal of Ethiopian Studies*, V, 1, 1967, p.103. She saw a manuscript with many miniatures, which usually accompany the Gospel text. The book was called by the priests "Zär'a Ya'qob's prayer-book". D. Spencer was allowed to photograph the miniatures, but not the unilluminated beginning of the manuscript (historical notes?). To judge on the basis of the miniatures, the manuscript should be dated to the second half of the 15th century. As to the historical text relating the arrival of relics to Ethiopia, A. Caquot thinks that it is one of the pseudo-historical compilations widespread in Ethiopia at the end of the 18th century. The manuscript, British Museum Or.481, was written most probably for the emperor Fasilides (both the writing and the miniatures corroborate this dating). The historical note is most probably from the 18th century, too.

30. Caquot, *op. cit.*, p.96; Taddesse Tamrat, *op. cit.*, p.268, associates the arrival of the relics with the mission of Pietro Rombulo.

31. The photography of the cross was published for the first time in *Koptische Kunst. . .*, Kat. No.492, after by E. Hammerschmidt, *Äthiopische Handschriften von Ṭānāsee*, 1, Wiesbaden, 1973, Abb.12, and in Murad, *op. cit.*, Abb.13. In all cases only the reverse with *the Maiestas Domini* scene is seen.

32. Caquot, *op. cit.*, p.104.

33. In Amharic ቀማጥር , *qämaṭər* — I. Guidi, *Vocabolario amarico-italiano*, Roma, 1901, p.252 — 'filigrane?'; after Säwasaw of Moncullo — 'voglio, crivello'; E. Gankin, *Amharsko-russkij slovar*, Moskva, 1969, p.286 — 'proséivanie'; A. d'Abbadie, *Dictionnaire de la langue amariñña*, Paris, 1868, p.262 — 'filigran'; in Arabic, قمطر *qimaṭr, qamāṭir* — E. W. Lane, *Arabic-English Lexicon*, London, 1885, p.2565 — a repository for books or writings made of reeds woven together; in Greek *kamptra*, 'case', *kámpsa*, 'basket', H. G. Liddell, R. Scott, *A Greek-English Lexicon*, Oxford, 1968, p.873.

34. J. Perruchon, *Les chroniques de Zar'a Ya'qob et de Ba'eda Māryām*, Paris, 1893, p.52.

35. Caquot, *op. cit.*, p.95.

36. Moore, *op. cit.*, fig.13.

37. Spencer, *Trip to Wag . . .*, *op. cit.*, p.105, 107; E. Heldaman, *Miniatures of the Gospels of Princess Zir Gānēlā, An Ethiopic Manuscript dated A.D.1400/1*, Saint Louis, Missouri, 1972, figs.143-150; O. Jäger, *Äthiopische Miniaturen*, Berlin, 1957, Abb.3, 3, 9, 12, 15.

38. Moore, *op. cit.*, fig.28.

39. Its description cf. C. Lepage, "Esquisse d'une histoire de l'ancienne peinture éthiopienne du Xe au XVe siècle", *Abbay* 8, 1977, pp.74n.

40. A photograph without any information has been published by J. Leroy, *Éthiopie. Archéologie et Culture*, Paris, 1973, fig.91.

41. J. Doresse, "Nouvelles recherches sur les relations entre l'Egypte Copte et l'Éthiopie: XIIe - XIIIe siècle", *Comptes Rendues de l'Accadémie des Inscriptions et Belles-Lettres*, juillet-octobre 1970, pp.560-561.

42. A rich repertory of crosses of the type in: M. von Bárány-Oberschall, "Byzantinische Pektoalkreuze aus Ungarischen Funden", Wandlungen Christlicher Kunst im Mittelalter, *Forschungen zur Kunstgeschichte und Christlichen Archäologie II*, Baden-Baden, 1953, pp.207-251.

43. E.g. the gold pectoral cross from Alexandria, today in the British Museum, cf. O. M. Dalton, *Catalogue of Early Christian Antiquities. . . of the British Museum*, London, 1901, no.286, pl.V. On other crosses of Egyptian provenance cf. E. S. King, "The Date and Provenance of a Bronze Reliquary Cross in the Museo Cristiano", *Atti della Pontificia Accademia Romana di Archeologia, Memorie,* vol.II, Roma, 1928, p.201 et note 62.

44. The earliest known Crucifixion scenes in wall-paintings today date from the 17th century, on icons from the 16th century. The earliest Crucifixion scenes in the manuscripts from the 13th and 14th centuries represent the type of so-called *crux nuda*; the earliest known miniature with Christ on the cross, in the Kəbran Gospels, comes from ca.1412.

45. Moore, *op. cit.*, pp.17-18, dates the cross to the 12th-13th century. This early dating is based on the iconography of the image of Christ and on the archaic form of the inscription.

46. *Ibid.*, p.18. The author thinks that the cross comes from the 13th-14th century, but in this case the dating is a very difficult task, since the cross was never quite finished.

47. C. Lepage, "Les croix éthiopiennes", *Les dossiers de l'archéologie*, 8, 1975, p.76, writes that the crosses would not be post-14th century.

48. Moore, *op. cit.*, p.21, dates the cross to the 13th-14th century. It would then be the earliest representation of Christ dead on the cross known from Ethiopia. In the manuscripts this type appears in the 15th century: the Gospels of Gunda Gunde (nos.162 and 180, according to the list of the manuscripts from this monastery by R. Schneider) and *Lāḥa Māryām* from Betäləḥem church near Däbrä Tabor.

49. The crucifix from Əgzi'abḥer Ab church on Amba Gəšen is new, cf. Spencer, "Trip to Wag . . .", p.102, as well as the wooden hand cross with the figure of Christ in low relief in the collection of W. von Armin, cf. Korabiewicz, *op. cit.*, il.24. The few crucifixes known in Ethiopia were often gifts from Europeans, as for instance that which Iyassu I received from the French consul, cf. *The Red Sea and Adjacent Countries at the Close of the Seventh Century as described by Joseph Pitts, William Daniel and Charles Jacques Poncet*, W. Foster (ed.), London, 1949, p.139.

50. *The Ethiopian Orthodox Church . . . , op. cit.*, p.70.

51. It seems that it is a cherub, rather than a seraph, which is represented here. The inscription, which gives the name of the figure, was probably added later, as in the case of the

angels. The seraphim, as opposed to the cherubim, were often represented with eyes strewn over their wings, but differentiation of both kinds in the iconography was not always clear. The images of seraphim and cherubim occur very seldom in Ethiopian art. For the early period one can mention the miniature of the Nativity in Zir Ganela Gospels, where a creature with a romboid head, two pairs of wings, a kind of base instead of the legs and the pair of hands holding the processional crosses, is called cherub, cf. Heldman, *op. cit.*, fig.13, or the miniature from the manuscript published by C. Lepage, " Révélation d'un manuscrit particulièrement fascinat de l'Éthiopie au 15ᵉ siècle", *Connaissance des Arts*, 274, 1974, p.96, where the cherubs or the seraphs are represented as angels standing on small wheels.

52. E.g. the triptych with Pantokrator from Mädhane 'Aläm church in Tädbabä Maryam; the triptych from Yämmadu Maryam called *šə'əl gəbṣāwi* cf. Spencer, " In Search . . .", pp.77, 80; the Limoges triptych from Maryam Dəngəlat church, cf. *Rock-Hewn churches of Eastern Tigray. An Account of the Oxford University Expedition to Ethiopia 1974*, Oxford, 1975, the plate facing p.8; the icon from Däbrä Šahəl in Šəre; the triptych from Wafa Iyasus church, Goğğam, cf. Chojnacki, *op. cit.*, figs.158, 192. Ch. Poncet writes that when he gave the emperor the miniatures of the saints he had brought from Europe, the names of the saints in Ethiopic were inscribed on them, cf. *Red Sea . . .*, p.139.

53. C. Lepage points out that most of the really old crosses treated as relics are considered, by the tradition of the churches where they are preserved, to have been brought by their founders from Jerusalem or Egypt, cf. " Recherches . . .", p.46.

54. A. Grabar, " La précieuse croix de la Lavra Saint Athanase au Mont-Athos", *Cahiers archéologiques*, XIX, 1969, p.112 note 23.

55. According to a letter from Lascarina Bouras, the keeper of the Byzantine collection in Benaki Museum, to whom we would like to express here our thanks. The photography of the cross no.11422 was first published in W. Korabiewicz, *Śladami amuletu*, Warszawa, 1974, il.162.

56. O. Wulff, *Altchristliche und mittelalterliche byzantinische und italienische Bildwerke*, Teil I, Berlin, 1909, Pl.XLIV, Nr.963.

57. J. D. Cooney, " Problems of Coptic Art in Coptic Egypt", *Papers read at a symposium held under the joint auspices of the New York University and the Brooklyn Museum*, New York, 1944, p.39; A. A. King, *The Rites of Eastern Christendom*, Roma, 1947, t.I, pp.383-384.

58. See e.g. E. L. Butcher, *The Story of the Church of Egypt*, London, 1897, vol.I, p.409, where a description of the church of St. Mena in the Mareotis decorated with statues by Al-Bukri is quoted.

59. *Koptische Kunst . . .*, no.203; Johann Georg Herzog zu Sachsen, *Striefzuge durch Kirchen und Klöster Aegyptens*, Leipzig-Berlin, 1914, pp.72-73, Pl.108; Dalton, *op. cit.*, no.540. Their Egyptian provenance was discussed by G. de Jerphanion, " Un nouvel encensoir syrien et la série des objets similaires", *Mélanges Syriens offerts à René Dussaud*, Paris, 1939, t.I, p.311.

60. Ross, *op. cit.*, vol.II, no.15, pp.21-22, pl.XXIII; J. Werner, " Zwei byzantinische Pektoral-kreuze aus Ägypten", *Seminarium Kondakovianum*, VIII, 1936, pp.183-186.

61. Dalton, *op. cit.*, no.286, pl.V.

62.   King, *The Date and Provenance* . . . , tav.XXX, fig.19.

63.   Both objects are described in M. H. Simaika Pacha, *Guide Sommaire du Musée Copte et des principales églises du Caire*, Le Caire, 1937, p.43.

64.   Habib Raouf, *The Coptic Museum. A General Guide*, Cairo, 1967, pp.72-73.

LIST OF PLATES

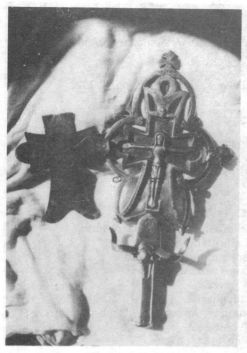

(Pl. I)

(Pl.II)

(Pl. III)

(Pl. IV)

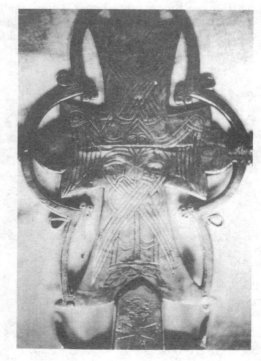

117

(Pl. V)

(Pl. VII)

(Pl. VI)

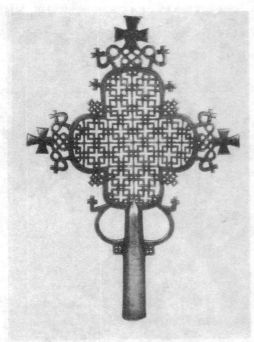

(Pl. VIII)

(Pl. IX)

(Pl. X)

(Pl. XI)

(Pl. XII)

(Pl. XIV)

(Pl. XIII)

(Pl. XV)

(Pl. XVI)

(Pl. XVII)

(Pl. XVIII)

(Pl. XIX

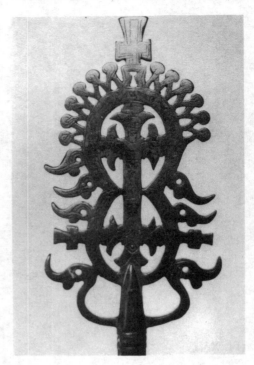

(Pl. XX)

(Pl. XXI)

(Pl. XXII)

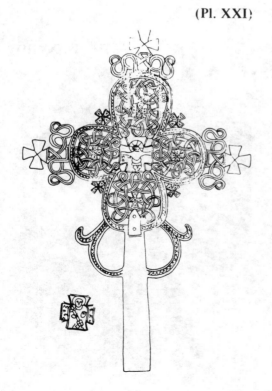

(Pl. XXIII)

(Pl. XXIV)

(Pl. XXV)

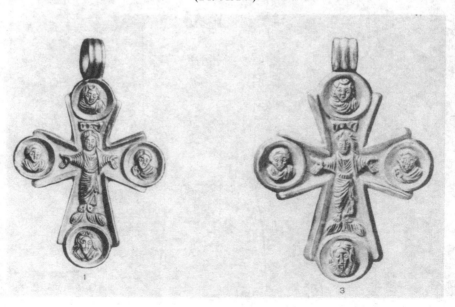

123

(Pl. XXVI)

THE RUINS OF MERTOLA-MARYAM

Stephen Bell

Within the compound of the hill-top church of Mertola-Maryam, a village 2,600 metres above sea level in the district of Enabsie (or Nabesse) and some 110 kilometres North-East of Dabra Marqos, the roofless remains of an imposing structure in stone have survived for three and a half centuries.

In its heyday in the early sixteenth century, Mertola-Maryam was famous for the magnificence of its church, but is now little known. Its obscurity today is no doubt more the result of the remoteness of this district, which adjoins the Abai valley at the easternmost extremity of the Gojam plateau and is yet to be served by an all-weather road, than of the lack of potential interest to the archaeologist or the historian. Few travellers, Ethiopian and foreign, to this region have left descriptions of this site.

The ruin is all that remains of the eastern half of a rectangular church with two transepts. Its ornate style suggests a derivation from the architectural forms of Renaissance Spain and Portugal[1] and it can be dated with certainty to the last few years of the reign of Susneyos (1607-1632). But of equal interest to these standing remains is an earlier church, completed over a century before, which stood upon the same foundations and of which, it would appear, nothing has survived above ground.[2]

Our knowledge of the history of this building and its precursor is dependent upon Portuguese sources, and in particular upon the *Historia geral de Ethiopia a Alta ou Prete Joam* of Manoel d'Almeida, a Jesuit missionary who reached Ethiopia in 1622, shortly after the conversion of Susneyos to Catholicism, and who stayed until the expulsion of the Order from the country twelve years later. He started writing his unpublished history while still in Ethiopia, completing it later in India.[3] We may assume that for much of his references to the earlier building at Mertola-Maryam, which concern events a century before his arrival in Ethiopia and therefore out of living memory, he had access to oral and written sources no longer available to us.

*   *   *

The earlier church, completed around 1510, enjoyed renown throughout the land for its splendour and the wealth of its treasure, but fell victim within twenty years to the depradations of the Moslem forces of Ahmed Gragn. It was founded by Empress Illeni when she was Regent during the minority of her step-grandson, Lebna Dengel. The widow of Zera Yaqob and Ba'eda Maryam, she was left with great wealth and became a generous benefactor of churches.

According to Almeida, the church was built by craftsmen imported from Egypt. It was square in plan, in contrast to the traditionally round churches of this and other southern regions of the highlands. Between the inner sanctum, which he refers to as the chapel, and the outer walls was "a space of about twenty spans serving as the body of the church, or cloister".[4] The floor of the chapel was "a platform raised eight or nine spans above the cloisters, so that from them twelve or fifteen steps led up to the chapel".

Almeida visited Mertola-Maryam before its reconstruction, when enough of the ruins of Illeni's church was extant for him to observe:

> In the sides that were standing, and in many very big pieces of stone that were lying on the ground, broad and smooth, could be seen as many varied and different roses as there were stones, each of them so perfectly done in fine tracery that they looked as if they could not be bettered, I do not say in gold or silver with a burin, but even in wax or painted with brush and pen. This is what I saw; what I heard is that many were covered over with silver and gold . . . It is certain that the church was built not only at great expense, but was adorned and endowed with liberality. It was endowed with the

entire district of Nebesse which is large and productive, and so the monks, clergy and beneficed clergy or canons, Debteras they call them, were very numerous and all had fat prebends.

The ornaments were very rich. There were some chalices and patens of gold of great weight, and two altar stones of solid gold, one of which weighed 800 oqueas, the other 500. I am a witness of this, for they were saved from the Moors and Gallas and came into the hands of the Emperor Seltan Cegued (Susneyos).

Corroboration of the wealth of Mertola-Maryam is provided by Francisco Alvares, another Portuguese source but of a century earlier, before the church was destroyed by Gragn. The chaplain to the Portuguese Embassy of 1520-26 did not himself visit the church which, he informs us, was consecrated by the Abuna (Marqos). He learnt of it from Pero da Covilham, a compatriot and nobleman who had reached Ethiopia in 1494, while under royal instructions from Joao of Portugal to locate the kingdom of "Prester John". He had not been permitted to leave the country, and was contentedly settled in the country of his adoption, with a family and lands of his own, enjoying also much influence at court. As Alvares records:

I heard Pero da Covilham say that he had gone by order of Queen Elena (Illeni) to show how an altar should be made in a church which she had ordered to be built in this kingdom (Goyame, or Gojam), where they buried her, and they made this altar of wood, and crammed it full of solid gold, and also that the altar stone was of solid gold ... I always heard say while we were in the neighbourhood of this kingdom that there was a big guard at the church, who guarded it on account of the great amount of gold that was in it.[5]

We may assume that Covilham's altar comprised in part the two heavy gold stones seen by Almeida in the safekeeping of Susneyos over a century later.

Inevitably the allure of a celebrated religious house beckoned a powerful invader bent on the ruthless and wholesale eradication of Christianity in Ethiopia, the destruction of its churches and the plunder of their treasure. It is not possible to establish with certainty the year in which Gragn reached Mertola-Maryam, first looting the building, according to Almeida, then putting it to the torch. From Almeida's assertion that this took place within twenty years of its completion, we may assume that it was no later than 1530, an early phase in Gragn's campaigns that finally ended with his defeat and death on the battlefield in 1542.

In later years (Almeida is imprecise) "some lords" restored the blackened and empty shell left by Gragn, though not to its former splendour. Their work was undone by the Gallas, presumably during their encroachments into the highlands in the 1560's and, for the second time in its short existence, the church was sacked.

It fell to Susneyos to order the complete reconstruction of the church, the remains of which were seen by the author during a visit to eastern Gojam in 1967. The conversion of the Emperor to Catholicism marked the zenith of Jesuit influence in Ethiopia, and in 1627 the Order was permitted to establish a residency at Mertola-Maryam, one of at least four others in Gojam.[6] It is likely that Susneyos felt a special fondness for this place; Balthezar Tellez provides a more detailed explanation of the Emperor's motives than does Almeida.[7]

As the emperor was the great grandson of the Emperor David (Lebna Dengel), whom that empress (Illeni) brought up as her son (and governed the empire for him), he desired much to restore that church, and with it to perpetuate the memory of that empress.

Perhaps Mertola-Maryam had another fond association for Susneyos, for it was here that he had been offered the crown in 1604.[8]

Almeida's reference to the construction of the new church is brief:

Now a Roman Father of ours is working with the help of the Emperor Seltan Cegued to resurrect from the ashes of this phoenix another improved, and as we hope, more enduring one, for it is of stone and lime, in honour of God and Our Lady the Virgin, whose church it was. It was called Mertola Mariam, meaning Mary's lodging.

Tellez, writing several years after the expulsion of the Jesuits, is more informative than Almeida's contemporary account. The "Roman Father" was Bruno Bruni, an Italian whose missionary endeavours are recounted in an appendix to Tellez's work, and from which we are given a hint of the plan of the new church:

He was chosen to establish a residency within the kingdom of Godjam, in the district of Enabesie, where the Emperor Sultan Segued desired to re-erect the famous church which had been founded in that place by the Empress Helena ... The father laboured much in the rebuilding of this material temple, and left it almost finished of stone and mortar, with three naves, three chapels, a sacristy, enclosure walls, and with good houses.

The death of Susneyos, shortly after his decree of June 1632 restoring the national faith, drastically altered the fortunes of the Jesuit mission in Ethiopia. Upon gaining the throne, one of the first acts of Fasil, his anti-Catholic son, was to close the Jesuit centres. This was followed by the expulsion, in 1634, of the missionaries from the country altogether. By 1633, when the Jesuits were ejected from their residencies in Gojam, the walls of Bruni's church had been raised to their full height, and spanned by the first rafters of the roof. In its unfinished state, his creation is an apposite monument to an abruptly terminated period of Ethiopian history and a brief, at times close, but ultimately disastrous relationship with Portugal and Counter-Reformation Europe.

*   *   *

Over two centuries passed before another foreigner appeared at Mertola-Maryam. C. T. Beke, the English traveller, came across the ruins in the course of a journey through Gojam in 1842. Unaware of their existence until he reached the district, he found intact the eastern portion of the church, which he estimated to be half of its original length. The remains comprised the entire inner chapel, much of the length of the two naves on either side, the two small side chapels and the chambers of both transepts. The remainder of the structure, westwards, had been demolished in recent years to furnish stone for the round church within its shadow a few yards away. His description of the site, presented in London as a paper for the Society of Antiquaries[9], contains many useful observations, and is illustrated with detailed sketches. Quoting fully from Tellez, he asserts its Jesuit origins and attributes it in particular to Bruno Bruni. His drawing of the ground plan contains several inaccuracies.

A further eighty or so years appears to have elapsed until the next visit by a foreigner is recorded. M. de Coppet, the French Minister in Addis Ababa in the early 1920's, admired the well-preserved remains and their delicate carvings. He believed the building to be a product of the Italian Renaissance, erected under the sponsorship of "l'impératrice Eleni (Hélène)" at the end of the fifteenth century, and that it had survived the Moslem invasions of the mid-sixteenth century, because Gragn was too occupied elsewhere during the years of his campaigning in Ethiopia to destroy this particular church.[10]

The misconception that these ruins survive from Illeni's earlier church gained wider currency over later years.[11] Given the evidence of Portuguese sources it is clear that, substantially if not perhaps entirely, they must belong to a later date, and to the "almost finished" church recorded by Tellez. Its incomplete state is tellingly evident from the holes for scaffolding, evenly positioned within the length of its walls and remaining unfilled. The symmetry and homogeneity of style suggest that the walls, above ground at least, belong to one integral design.

In 1967, the author found the church to be much as Beke had described it, but in the intervening century and a quarter the western wall of the inner chapel (an ashlar screen pierced by a central Norman doorway and two small latticed windows) and what remained in 1842 of the southern nave had since vanished. There has been no further demolition since 1967, and surviving today is a substantial and finely proportioned structure with intricate carved stonework. Though as alien to Ethiopian tradition as the religion that spawned it, it is nevertheless as much a part of her rich heritage of architecture as the monuments of Axum, Lalibela and Gonder. This ruin is now targeted for preservation by the Ministry of Culture in Addis Ababa. Plans for a prefabricated protective canopy were shown to the author by Solomon Worede Kal, an official of the department of the Ministry concerned with the preservation and restoration of historical monuments in Ethiopia. We must be grateful that Mertola-Maryam will remain for future generations to admire.[12]

NOTES

1. There are notable similarities between the church at Mertola-Maryam and the palace at Gorgora, constructed for Susneyos under the supervision of the Jesuit missionary, Pero Paez, and completed around 1621. There are numerous descriptions of this ruin; see for instance: R. E. Cheesman's *Lake Tana and the Blue Nile: an Abyssinian Quest* (London, 1936), pp.206-9.

2. See, however, Note 11 below.

3. This manuscript (Add: 9861) is in the possession of the British Library in London, extracts from which were published for the Hakluyt Society: *Some Records of Ethiopia, 1593-1646*, trans. and ed., C. F. Beckingham and G. W. B. Huntingford (London, 1954). The School of Oriental and African Studies, University of London, holds a later copy of the manuscript, with minor amendments. Much of the similarly titled work of Balthezar Tellez, published in Coimbra in 1660, is closely based upon Almeida's manuscript.

4. These quotations are taken from *Some Records of Ethiopia, 1593-1646* (see Note 3, above), pp.103-7.

5. Francisco Alvares: *The Prester John of the Indies*, translation by Lord Stanley of Alderley for the Hakluyt Society, with revisions by C. F. Beckingham and G. W. B. Huntingford (London, 1961), p.459.

6. Ligenegus and Collela are marked as residencies on the map attached to Almeida's manuscript. The map published with Balthezar Tellez's *History* of 1660 marks Adaxa (Hadasha) and Nanina as two more.

7. See Note 3, above. This and other extracts from Tellez are of translations provided by C. T. Beke (Note 9, below).

8. As recounted in the Chronicle of the reign of Susneyos: *Chronica de Susenyos, Rei de Ethiopia*, with Portuguese translation and commentary by F. M. Esteves Pereira (Lisbon, 1892 and 1900), Volume 2, p.46. Here is the only reference to Mertola-Maryam from Ethiopic sources of the sixteenth and seventeenth centuries that I have found.

9. *Archaeologia*, Volume XXXII, 1847 (published by the Society of Antiquaries, London), pp.38-57.

10. M. de Coppet, D'Addis Abéba à Asmara, La Géographie (*Bulletin de la Société de Géographie*, Paris), Volume 40 (1923), pp.426-7.

11. S. Chojnacki's study of the scant remains of a late fifteenth or early sixteenth century stone building at Day Giyorgis (*Journal of Ethiopian Studies*, Volume VII, No.2 [July 1969], pp.43-8), cites F. W. Heinze, who visited Mertola-Maryam around 1930 and declared it to be "an important monument of Coptic art which survived the Moslem destructions", and E. Cerulli, who did not visit the site but examined photographs and concurred with de Coppet's fifteenth century date, the sculpture and carved stonework suggesting however an Italian influence. Chojnacki moreover detects similarities in a "rope" pattern of decorative carving which he noticed both at Day Giyorgis and in photographs of what he refers to as the South-East porch of Mertola-Maryam (which would appear to be the window overlooking the east end of the inner chapel, erroneously represented as a niche in the wall on Beke's plan). The author, who visited Mertola-Maryam before the appearance of Chojnacki's article, was unable to carry out more than a cursory examination of the ruins and, failing to notice this particular detail of ornamentation at the time, cannot comment on its significance other than to suggest that some of the carved stonework from Illeni's church may have been incorporated into Bruni's later building. A study of the site, more detailed than the author himself was able to undertake, would be necessary to discern what, if anything, of Illeni's church has survived the turbulence of the sixteenth century and Bruni's reconstruction.

12. The author is indebted to the priests and villagers of Mertola-Maryam for their friendly cooperation at the time of his visit. He is also grateful to John Fynn who accompanied him on this trip and who has allowed him unhindered use of photographs taken on that occasion.

WHO WROTE

"THE HISTORY OF KING SARSA DENGEL" -

WAS IT THE MONK BAHREY?

S. B. Chernetsov
Academy of Sciences of the USSR
Africa Institute

The History of King Sarsa Dengel,[1] which was written piecemeal — chapter by chapter — between 1579 and 1592, is among the works of official royal historiography whose tradition lasted without major interruptions from the 14th century to the 20th. In scholarly literature these works are usually referred to as the "royal chronicles", a term that does not seem to me to be quite adequate. As a matter of fact, the majority of the writings in question (at least up to the middle of the 17th century) are not chronicles at all. *The Chronicle of King Amada Seyon* (14th century),[2] for example, may better be called a military tale; *The Chronicle of King Zar'a Yaeqob* (15th century),[3] a narrative dealing with the creation of the state of Ethiopia; and *The Chronicle of King Claudius* (16th century),[4] a laudatory oration. *The History of King Sarsa Dengel* and *The History of King Socinnius*,[5] extensive historiographic works which date from the late 16th and early 17th centuries, may well be considered the high-point of official Ethiopian historiography. Because their authors were not limited in terms of space, they could amply demonstrate their literary talents. As a result, the historiographic writings dealing with the reigns of Sarsa Dengel and Socinnius are among the best works not only of Ethiopian but world medieval literature. On the whole, however, all official historiographical works have only one feature in common, namely, that the invariable central character of the narrative is the king. As for the literary form, we have here a rich diversity uncommon for the Middle Ages. If these works are to be grouped under the single genre of "royal chronicles", it must be admitted that the genre itself was in constant state of development and change.

The authors of the works in question are known to us only beginning with *The History of King Socinnius*, which was begun by abba Meherka Dengel[6] and completed by Azaj Takla Sellasé, who is better known by his Galla nickname tino — "Tiny".[7] There is an earlier work, however, whose author is also known. This is *The History of the Galla*,[8] written by the monk Bahrey. But *The History of the Galla*, stands apart not only from the works of Ethiopian historiography, but also from all of medieval Ethiopian literature, something that Bahrey must have been aware of. Seeking literary precedents for his work, he begins it thus: "I began to write the history of Galla to show the number of their tribes, and their murderous deeds, and their bestial customs. And if someone were to ask me, 'Why do you write the history of the wicked as though you were writing the history of the good?' I should answer him and say, 'Seek in the books, and you will find the history of Mohammed and of the Moslem kings, who are our enemies, has been written . . .' ". And then Bahrey alludes to the *History* of al-Makin.[9] But the laconic and matter-of-fact style of the narrative, the original and very elastic structure of *The History of the Galla*, and its clear-cut political idea are reminiscent not so much of the *History* of al-Makin as of a report to the monarch written by a proficient and knowledgeable secretary well-versed in court politics.

The History of the Galla contains a concise and thorough review of the structure and interrelationship of Galla tribes, as well as an account of their conquests and wars with the Ethiopians. Bahrey's analysis of Galla victories and Ethiopian defeats leads him to compare the two societies. As a result, he produces an interesting and in its own way very precise picture of Ethiopian feudal society and its class structure. The whole is set forth with considerable skill and is marked by an objectivity quite rare for a work of medieval literature. What we have here, then, is an interesting example of how a unique set of historical circumstances — in this case, the invasion of the Ethiopians by Galla tribes — can give rise to unusual literary works that fall outside of the generic system of the time.

If one were to attempt to place *The History of the Galla* in Ethiopian literature, one would have to call it the predecessor of the "literature of the chancellery" — a genre that was consolidated much later, during the so-called Gondarine period (1636-1855). The genre was strongly influenced both by oral rhetorics, the so-called culture of "verbal eloquence", and by the literary tradition,[10] and it is difficult to say which influence predominated. It should be noted in this regard that the King's secretary (the sehafe-te'ezaz — the "scribe of orders") was usually not only the royal chancellor, but the royal historiographer as well. And *The History of the Galla*, despite its matter-of-fact style, has many features in common with the literary works of its time. The utmost brevity of his work notwithstanding, Bahrey's literary devices are numerous and diverse. They deserve special consideration.

Bahrey twice uses the device of a dispute with an imaginary opponent, whom he proceeds to refute: once at the very beginning of his *History* and again in the second chapter: "There are those who say that they [Dawe Galla] arose from others and cite as evidence their war against Boran. But this information is incorrect, it is not true. The learned say . . .".[11] No less interesting is the device wherein two lines of evidence — one divine, the other "earthly" — are offered to explain the single event: "The learned conduct many studies and they say: 'How is it that the Galla defeat us when we are more numerous and are better armed?' Some say: 'God allowed it because of our sins'. And others say: 'It is because our people are divided into ten classes, nine of which don't go to battle, their fear knowing no shame. It is only the tenth class that fight and wages war as best it can. And though we are numerous, there are few capable to fight and many who don't fight at all . . .'. Know this, oh learned ones — you, whose words are true among disputants, be they first or last!"[12]

It should be said that the literary devices in question are not at all characteristic of Ethiopian historiography in general and can be found only in one other work besides *The History of the Galla*, namely in *The History of King Sarsa Dengel*.[13] Nor does the stylistic similarity between these two works end there. For example, paired epithets used by Bahray with respect to the King[14] are characteristic of the style of *The History of King Sarsa Dengel* as well.[15] Also common to both works is the idea that, despite the vicissitudes of life, King Sarsa Dengel — and he alone — is destined to know power and victory:

Were Birmajje in Dambea, the same fate would have befallen them that befell Robale. But in order that everyone be victorious in his turn, God directed our King to Damot. And he found victory where he was, and the nobles found defeat where he was not. (*The History of the Galla*).[16]

It is wonderous and amazing: yesterday these were decorated, today others receive decorations. Such are the vicissitudes of this world: one day is given to one, the next to another! But when the right and proper day comes, [everything] returns to this victorious King. (*The History of King Sarsa Dengel*).[17]

We see a similar attitude in both works towards the prophetic gift of priests. But if Bahrey, in speaking of his own prophesy, finds it necessary to substantiate it ("And it came to pass in accordance with his words, for the spirit of prophesy does not forsake priests"), in *The History of King Sarsa Dengel* the fulfilled prophesy of an abbot is left unexplained: "One of the sailors fired a cannon and killed the abbot of one of the Tigre monasteries. And his killing was the fulfillment of the words he had spoken: 'I must sacrifice my blood to God as Our Lord had said: "The son of man must be delivered into the hands of sinful men, and he will be crucified and killed" (Luke 24,7). And thus this monk was killed according to his own prophecy."[19]

Though *The History of the Galla* was obviously written for the same court circles as *The History of King Sarsa Dengel*, it is not a 'royal chronicle' and therefore lacks the official, ceremonial character of the latter. Perhaps that is why Bahrey not only mentions himself by name but provides the reader with much interesting information about himself. We learn, for example, that he is one of those who "took their vows in early youth, enticed by monks during their education",[20] and that Dawe Galla warriors "left his county Gomo in ruins and seized all his belongings".[21] No such information can be gleaned from *The History of King Sarsa Dengel*, except for the fact that its author, by medieval standards, was probably quite old: "If in our corporal life we should witness what God will perform by the hands of this King — his deeds and victories, as He had performed before — we shall describe it. And if the fate of every man befalls us and we join ranks with those who are dead, let not the living neglect the description of God's miracles wrought by the hand of the Christian King".[22] A similar plea to continue his work can be found in Bahrey's *History*: "And when this book was written, it was the seventh year since the nomination of Mul'ata, the sons of Bifole; the circumcision and nomination of the sons of Mesle should follow. And of the events of their lives, of the battles and struggle, I shall write later, if I am alive. And if I should die, others will finish my story and the story of the future Luba. This [I will say] : 'Blessed is he who has dies, for he knows peace".[23]

The similarity between *The History of the Galla* and *The History of King Sarsa Dengel* is no accident. Two alternate explanations suggest themselves: either Bahrey deliberately and consistently imitated *The History of King Sarsa Dengel* (the reverse is out of the question), or both works belong to the same author, that is, the monk Bahrey. Let us consider the first possibility. It is generally regarded that medieval historiography knows nothing of stylized imitation. The imitation that does exist "is of entirely different, mechanical nature. It borrows individual ready elements or form, but does not develop or expand the original in a creative way. This kind of imitation is not stylization".[24] But in Bahrey's work there is no trace of the "ready elements or form" of *The History of King Sarsa Dengel*. Both in form and content Bahrey created an original work, though the literary *methods* he used are those of *The History of King Sarsa Dengel*. What we have here, then, is either two works by a single writer, or, despite all theory, a case of stylistic imitation. Is it possible however, that Bahrey not only produced a stylized imitation of the work of another writer (who, though unknown to us, must have been very well known in his own day), but that he then went on to sign that work? That, it seems to me, is highly doubtful. Besides, in medieval literature, only works sanctified by time and tradition were considered worthy of imitation, whereas *The History of the Galla*, according to E. Knutsson's calculation, was written circa 1593 — only one year after the completion of *The History of King Sarsa Dengel*.

The History of King Sarsa Dengel and *The History of the Galla* are works not only literary in form, but historical in content. It is instructive to compare the two with regard to the latter aspect. One should bear in mind, however, the peculiarities of each. Though *The History of the Galla* is fifteen times less voluminous than *The History of King Sarsa Dengel*, it deals with a much lengthier chronological period — from 1523 to 1593. The latter work, on the other hand, is not only limited to the reign of Sarsa Dengel (1563-81, 1585-92), but focuses attention on the person of the monarch, mentioning other figures only insofar as they were involved with him. Thus, King Sarsa Dengel is mentioned in *The History of the Galla* six times in connection with historical events,[26] five of which are described (usually at much greater length) in *The History of King Sarsa Dengel*.[27]

The History of the Galla	*The History of King Sarsa Dengel*
Chap. 12: "His Majesty fought them in Zway and killed many of them . . . " (p.226)	Chap. 5, p.45-46
Chap. 12: "And five years later His Majesty fought Robale . . . " (p.226)	Chap. 6, p.53
Chap. 13: "And it happened where our King was not . . . " (p.227)	Chap. 8, p.84-85

Chap. 15: "And when he was on his way, news reached him that the Galla had attacked the land of Gojjam . . . " (p.228)

Chap. 8, p.118-119

Chap. 16: "And he went to Waj to wage war against the Galla called Dawe . . . " (p.228-229)

Chap. 9, p.127-128

Thus, we can say that the data of the *History of the Galla* are quite in conformity with the data of *The History of King Sarsa Dengel*.

These are the results of both literary and historic analysis of the two writings. A certain similarity of language is manifest in both *The History of the Galla* and *The History of King Sarsa Dengel* as well. But the utmost brevity and a very peculiar composition of *The History of the Galla* leave no hope for the trustworthy results of linguistic analysis. Nevertheless, all the considerations stated above permit, I hope, to propose an assumption that monk Bahrey is the author of *The History of King Sarsa Dengel*. It is impossible of course to insist on it with full safety, but some additional evidence can be found on the pages of a fragment of *The Shorter Chronicle* published by Carlo Conti Rossini, where the confessor of King Sarsa Dengel named Bahrey is mentioned. The fact that royal confessors happened to be royal historiographers as well is known from *The Chronicle of King Ba'eda Maryam* (15th century) already. And if Bahrey, the author of *The History of the Galla* is identical to Bahrey, the confessor of Sarsa Dengel, our assumption becomes more probable.

NOTES

1. *Historia regis Sarsa Dengel* (Malak Sagad), edidit C. Conti Rossini — Corpus Scriptorum Christianorum Orientalium, Scriptores Aethiopici, series altera, t. III, Parisiis, 1907.

2. J. Perruchon. "Histoire des guerres d'Amda Seyon, roi d'Ethiopie", *Journal Asiatique*, ser.8, t. XIV, 1889, pp.271-363, 381-493.

3. J. Perruchon. *Les chroniques de Zar'a Ya'eqob et de Ba'eda Maryam*. Paris, 1893.

4. W. E. Conzelman. *La chronique de Galawdewos, roi d'Ethiopie*. Paris, 1895.

5. F. M. E. Pereira. *Chronica de Susenyos, rei de Ethiopia*, t. I, Lisboa, 1892.

6. *Ibid*, p.70.

7. *Ibid*, p.208.

8. *Historia gentis Galla*, edidit Ignatius Guidi — Corpus Scriptorum Christianorum Orientalium, Scriptores Aethiopici, series altera, t. III, Parisiis, 1907, pp.221-231.

9. *Ibid*, p.223.

10. The evidence for it may be found in such a writing as the "epistle charters" which are sometimes cited at length by Ethiopian historiographers. It is as a rule just very laconic orders and messages to be retold orally, because only a few of the addressees were literate. Here the "characters" itself played probably just a ceremonial role. But there were other cases when the text of the epistles was not only verbose, but written with elegance and literary taste. Such an epistle we can find in the 29th chapter of *The History of King Socinnius*, where is cited the royal answer to the insulting message of the rebellious regiment called Qurban: "The epistle of yours isn't good, and there are no words that are

134

beautiful and adorning. And when had I said to you: 'Make me king'? It doesn't become to you to say this way: 'We shall never make you king; we would better make king a daughter of King Malak Sagad, and if not, then one of the Israel who are on the amba.' Have I asked the grace of the kingdom from you and not from God, the Lord of the skies and the earth and the Judge of all creatures, Who make disgraced and glorious, poor and rich? You are human beings, like myself, and you have no power to take from me or to give me the kingdom. And what are you saying: 'Choose and wait for us at the place of death and battle, don't be afraid and don't flee as your usual custom is'? Whether since God had made me king and up to now was I afraid in Wagda or in Chachaho? My fear and my valour is known for those who have heart. And what have you written: 'There is no army we hadn't defeated and there is no spear we hadn't dispersed since the former reign of King Malak Sagad and up to now. What mighty and what man had defeated Fasil and Ase, Mohammed and Isaak, except only Daharagot and Barnabas'? Whether didn't they all pass away, those who had mounted horses? Some of them had ended their day at an advanced age and they are no good for battle, and others had perished and been buried. Do you frighten me with dead bones or do you scare me with earth? I am not afraid of all you frighten me and I don't tremble before you, but I do believe in Our Lord, Who exalts the humble and disgrace and haughty. And you are writing: 'Choose the place of death and battle'. Whether it's me who choose? It is God Who choose where He wills and wants the place of death for those who will die and the place of life for those who will live!"

The fact that the high-flown style was considered *conditio sine qua non* of such epistles is evident from the words of a dignitary who was at that time with Qurban: "And Azaj Maeqabo who had taken no part when they had been sending their haughty message to King Seltan Sagad shivered with much anger and said: 'Why didn't you consult with me when you were sending your epistle, unbecoming to pronounce? And here is defeated your epistle with his epistle, and we shall be defeated like this. You say he is a brigand, but look how he has adorned his epistle with the decoration of words and the beauty of speech!" (F. M. E. Pereira, *Chronica de Susenyos*, p.57-58).

11. *Historia gentis Galla*, p.224.

12. *Ibid*, p.229-230.

13. The dispute with an imaginary opponent is found in *The History of King Sarsa Dengel* 6 times (pp.19, 26, 82, 103, 108 and 111), and two reasons for the same event — twice (pp.8 and 8-9).

14. Bahrey calls the king "mighty in deeds and wise in council" (p.227).

15. Compare the royal epithets in *The History of King Sarsa Dengel*: "mighty in deeds and wise in council" (p.4), "great in council and full of wisdom" (p.48), "clement and merciful" (p.76), "mighty and victorious" (p.82, "merciful and soft-hearted towards poor and miserable" (p.84).

16. *Historia gentis Galla*, p.227.

17. *Historia regis Sarsa Dengel*, p.75.

18. *Historia gentis Galla*, p.224.

19. *Historia regis Sarsa Dengel*, p.131.

20. *Historia gentis Galla*, p.229.

21. *Ibid*, p.224.

22. *Historia regis Sarsa Dengel*, p.80-81.

23. *Historia gentis Galla*, p.229.

24. D. S. Likhachev. *The poetics of Ancient Russian literature*. 3rd edition, Moscow, 1979, p.185 (in Russian).

25. E. K. Knutsson. *Authority and change: A study of the Kallu institution among the Macha Galla of Ethiopia*. Goteborg, 1967, p.158.

26. Out of this connection he is mentioned only in the end of the *History*: "Nobody met such a foe like ours, so energetic in evil deeds, but nobody also met such a sovereign and such a king like ours, so energetic in good deeds" (p.231).

27. The seventh event ("And when His Majesty had returned and found the country saved by the labours of Walda Krestos and his valour, he made him the chief of the royal house and put him over the whole kingdom" − p.229) isn't mentioned in *The History of King Sarsa Dengel*, may be because it deals more with Walda Krestos, than with the king himself.

28. C. Conti Rossini. *Due scarci inediti di Cronica Etiopica* − Rendiconti della Reale Accademia dei Lincei, Roma, 1893, p.18.

LES AFFLUENTS DE LA RIVE DROITE DU NIL

DANS LA GÉOGRAPHIE ANTIQUE

Jehan Desanges

Parler d'affluents de la rive droite du Nil dans la géographie antique est certes légitime, car un certain nombre d'auteurs anciens ont eu conscience que des fleuves importants venus de l'Est se jetaient dans le Nil. Toutefois la représentation qu'ils se faisaient de leur articulation avec le Nil est toujours restée incertaine. On le comprendra en écoutant le témoignage d'Eratosthène, rapporté par Strabon:[1]

> "Deux fleuves se jettent dans le Nil. Ils viennent tous deux de certains lacs situés à l'Est et enserrent une île de grande dimension du nom de Méroë. L'un d'eux s'appelle Astaboras: c'est celui qui coule le long du côté orien- tal de celle-ci; l'autre est l'Astapous; mais d'autres auteurs le nomment Astasobas et disent que l'Astapous est un autre fleuve qui coule à partir de lacs situés au Sud, et qu'il s'agit du cours principal à peu près rectiligne du Nil; ce seraient les pluies d'été qui causeraient la crue de ce dernier. En amont du confluent de l'Astaboras et du Nil, à 700 stades, il y a la ville homonyme de l'île, Méroë."

Ainsi Eratosthène, qui vécut à Alexandrie dans la seconde moitié du IIIe siècle avant notre ère, admet l'existence de deux fleuves venant de l'Est. Il nous indique au passage que l'identité de l'un d'eux est mal fixée et qu'on peut le confondre avec le "corps du Nil" pour reprendre lit- téralement son expression (τὸ κατ' εὐθεῖαν σῶμα τοῦ Νείλου). Il reconnaît que les érudits se partagent à ce sujet, et il ne se prononce pas. Mais il manque lui-même de cohérence en affir- mant, d'une part, que les deux fleuves venus de l'Est enserrent l'île de Méroë et en plaçant, d'autre part, le confluent de l'Astaboras et du Nil au Nord de l'île de Méroë, ce qui implique soit qu'il existe trois fleuves en bordure de l'île, le Nil, l'Astaboras et l'Astapous, soit que l'Astapous se confond avec le Nil en délimitant à l'occident la soi-disant île de Méroë.[2]

Ce flottement provient de ce que les Anciens ont toujours hésité dans le choix du cours principal dans un système fluvial[3], un choix d'ailleurs difficile. Ils appelaient, comme on le sait, "île de Méroë" la vaste superficie que délimitent le Nil, de Khartoum au confluent de l'Atbara, l'Atbara lui-même, dont le nom rappelle encore l'hydronyme antique Astaboras, et enfin le Nil Bleu. Comme le haut cours de l'Atbara n'est guère éloigné du haut cours de certains affluents de la rive droite du Nil Bleu, il n'était pas absurde de parler d'une île de Méroë. Mais le segment du Nil entre Khartoum et l'Atbara pouvait dans l'Antiquité être attribué soit au fleuve que nous appelons aujourd'hui Nil Blanc et qui est aussi pour nous tout simplement le Nil, soit à celui que nous appelons Nil Bleu.

De là viennent les divergences dans l'emploi des hydronymes Astapous et Astasobas, de là le fait que l'"île" pouvait paraître entourée tantôt par deux et tantôt par trois fleuves[4], de là en- fin sans doute l'erreur de Ptolémée[5], inventant depuis Alexandrie au IIe siècle de notre ère un confluent de l'Astapous (qui pour lui est le Nil Bleu) et de l'Astaboras (l'Atbara) ce qui lui per- mettait d'imposer la représentation cartographique d'une île parfaite, délimitée par trois con- fluents. L'anomalie constituée par un affluent se jettant successivement dans deux fleuves aurait dû l'arrêter, mais dans une certaine mesure on peut comprendre son erreur: quand les Anciens parlaient du confluent des fleuves que nous appelons le Nil et l'Atbara, ils disaient parfois que l'Astaboras se jetait dans le Nil, et parfois qu'il se jetait dans l'Astapous, puisque nous savons par Eratosthène qu'Astapous était pour certains le nom du Nil. Quant à l'Astasobas, il désignait pour les uns le Nil Bleu[6] que les autres appelaient Astapous. Bien que nous n'en ayons pas la preuve, il ne nous semble pas impossible que ces derniers aient réservé dès lors le nom d'Asta- sobas au troisième grand affluent de la rive droite du Nil, le Sobat. A. Dillmann[7] était d'avis que ce nom signifie "le fleuve Soba". En tout cas, on a reconnu depuis longtemps que la base *Ast^a/i* signifie 'eau', 'onde', 'flot' dans de nombreuses langues parlées sur le Nil depuis les temps les plus reculés.[8]

Il convenait donc d'insister en préliminaire sur ces graves confusions qui se sont perpétuées durant toute l'Antiquité, bien que la célèbre expédition des éclaireurs de Néron[9] les ait sans doute conduits jusqu'aux marécages du Bahr el-Ghazal (le Sudd). Cela posé, les Anciens n'en ont pas moins collecté un certain nombre de renseignements sur le cours de l'Atbara et sur celui du Nil Bleu, ainsi que sur les riverains de ces fleuves.

Attachons-nous d'abord à l'Astaboras, l'actuel Atbara: selon Strabon[10], qui semble ici suivre Artémidore[11], si une partie du cours de ce fleuve, qui serait issu d'un lac, est tributaire du Nil, l'autre se jette dans la mer Rouge dans la région de Ptolémaïs, mais en deçà de ce comptoir, à ce qu'il nous paraît. Agatharchide avait déjà décrit la région, mais sans évoquer une soi-disant embouchure de l'Astaboras, dont on ne trouve en tout cas trace ni dans la version de Diodore[12], ni dans celle de Photius.[13] Il semble que l'on soit en droit de penser ici à la rivière Baraka, dont le lit aboutit sur la mer Rouge dans la région de Tokar et dont les origines ne sont pas situées loin du haut cours du Gash, c'est-à-dire du système de l'Atbara, avec lequel une tradition a pu la mettre en communication.

Que savait-on des populations riveraines de l'Atbara? Nous écarterons comme essentiellement romanesque le témoignage d'Héliodore dans ses *Ethiopiques*[14], à dater du IIIe ou du IVe siècle de notre ère, selon lequel les habitants de Méroë traversaient à l'occasion l'Astaborras par un pont de bateau (ζεῦγμα) ou au moyen de barques de roseau fort rapides. Plutôt que vers un romancier, nous nous tournerons vers un ethnographe comme Agatharchide[15], qui a puisé dans les archives de Ptolémée II. Cet auteur décrit les riverains de l'Atbara[16] comme des Rhizophages ou "mangeurs de racines" et des Héléens ou "habitants des marais" la version de Photius précise qu'ils sont peu nombreux. Ayant réduit en une pâte lisse et compacte les racines des roseaux cueillis dans les marécages voisins du fleuve, ils la font cuire au soleil et s'en nourrissent. Leur pays est infesté de lions qui viennent fuir la chaleur au bord de ces marais et se repaître de petit gibier. Ils dévoreraient assurément les Ethiopiens rhizophages qui ignorent l'usage des armes, si, à l'époque de la canicule, c'est-à-dire à la saison des pluies, une nuée de moustiques[17] ne mettaient en fuite les fauves qui ne supportent pas leur vrombissement. Strabon[18], qui fait des Rhizophages et des Héléens les riverains non seulement de l'Astaboras, mais aussi de l'Astapous et de l'Astasobas, résume les mêmes données, ainsi qu'Elien[19] qui, tout en attribuant aux Rhizophages les seules rives de l'Astabora, les qualifie d'Indiens, sans doute parce qu'ils sont relativement proches de la mer Rouge considérée comme un appendice de l'océan Indien. Nous ne saurions dire si ce sont les Rhizophages que Flavius Josèphe[20] désigne sous le nom d'Astabaroi, en usage chez les Grecs selon lui. En tout cas l'ethnique est forgé sur le nom du fleuve. C'était le nom grec des Sabathenoi, à en croire notre auteur. L'assimilation des deux noms est peut-être à rapprocher du fait que Flavius Josèphe[21] tenait Saba pour l'ancien nom de Méroë.

Venons-en au Nil Bleu, appelé dans l'Antiquité tantôt Astapous, tantôt Astasobas. Pour Ptolémée[22], qui l'identifie à l'Astapous bien distinct du Nil, sa source est le lac Koloë qu'il situe sur un méridien de deux degrés plus oriental que celui d'Adoulis, mais à près de douze degrés plus au sud et non loin de la terre de la myrrhe[23], riveraine du golfe d'Aden. En fait, il ne peut s'agir que du lac Tana, dont le Nil Bleu (Abbai) tire origine. Mais Julius Honorius[24] prétend que le lac Foloë (à corriger en Coloë) est situé sur le cours du Nil, alors qu'il fait naître l'Astapus d'un mont Panchaeus, que la recension B de sa *Cosmographie* place à 250 milles (quelque 370 km) de la source de l'Astroboris (l'Atbara). Il faut sans doute identifier ce mont Panchaeus[25] avec un massif montagneux proche du lac Tana. Enfin, c'est très probablement aussi le Nil Bleu que Cosmas Indicopleustès[26], au VIe siècle de notre ère, désigne simplement sous le nom de Nil, en prétendant que la source de ce fleuve se trouve dans le pays de Sasou, riche en mines d'or. En effet, le pays de Sasou est en relation de commerce avec Axoum, par l'intermédiaire de la province axoumite d'Agau. Sa localisation n'est pas assurée de façon précise, mais Y. M. Kobiščanov[27] l'a situé avec vraisemblance au sud du lac Tana.

Certains auteurs ont imaginé un Nil encore plus oriental que l'Astapous ou Nil Bleu. Ils n'ont pas hésité à le faire déboucher dans le golfe d'Aden. Pomponius Méla[28] mentionne, après une Bérénice qui doit être celle du Bab el-Mandeb, un cours d'eau artificiel qui puise ses eaux dans le lit du Nil au moyen d'un canal d'adduction.[29] Strabon[30], d'après Artémidore, signale dans le pays de l'encens (libanôtophore), à l'intérieur des terres, une vallée fluviale nommée Nil. Apparemment il s'agirait d'un petit Nil somalien.[31] Le *Périple de la mer Erythrée*[32] cite, entre Mosyllon (Bandar Kasim?) et le promontoire Elephas (Ras Filak), le "Nil dit de Ptolémée", appelé sans doute ainsi parce qu'il n'a pu être reconnu par les Grecs que sous le règne d'un Ptolémée. Peut-être faut-il rapprocher de cette indication le texte de Méla que nous avons déjà allégué. Un canal d'adduction censé communiquer avec quelque ramification du Nil a pu être creusé sur l'ordre d'un officier lagide en un point de la côte des Somalis, mais ce n'est là qu'une hypothèse fragile. Enfin, Orose[33], renouant avec la vieille tradition qui fait sortir le Nil de l'Océan, prétend que le Nil semble issu du littoral au lieu-dit "comptoir Mossylon".

Quels sont dans l'Antiquité les riverains du Nil Bleu dont la mémoire est parvenue jusqu'à nous? Quelques tribus dont nous ne connaissons guère que le nom: les Menismini, par exemple, dont un passage corrompu de Pline l'Ancien[34] fait des nomades situés en bordure du cours septentrional du fleuve Astragum, qu'il faut corriger certainement en Astapum. Ils vivent du lait des femelles de cynocéphales. Il est vrai que, dans un autre passage[35], Pline distingue les Medimni (*sic*) de Nomades se nourrissant du lait des cynocéphales; au surplus, il les situe — certainement à tort — sur la rive africaine, c'est-à-dire occidentale, du Nil. Pour sa part, Diodore[36] mentionne des Molgii sur le territoire desquels plusieurs sources contribuent à former le Nil. Ils sont dans une position assez orientale, puisqu'ils sont issus des Troglodytes selon cet auteur. On serait tenté de les rapprocher des Cynamolgi[37] d'Agatharchide, mentionnés par Strabon[38], dans l'intérieur des terres à partir de la région du Bab el-Mandeb. Comme on le voit, aucune localisation tant soit peu précise n'est dans ce cas possible. Mais il conviendrait d'évoquer encore, entre le Nil Bleu et l'Atbara, des Struthophages ou "mangeurs d'autruche", si du moins on veut bien admettre une indication de l'Anonyme d'Hudson[39], auteur d'une description du cours du Nil tardive et assez méconnue, dont nous allons reparler: en effet celui-ci situe ces chasseurs entre l'Astapous et l'Astaboras. C'est déjà sans doute dans la même aire que les avait placés Ptolémie[40], qui s'exprime à ce sujet moins clairement. Sur les Struthophages, les secrets de leur chasse et leurs luttes contre les Ethiopiens "camus", contre lesquels ils utilisaient des cornes d'antilope, nous sommes par ailleurs quelque peu renseignés depuis Agatharchide.[41]

Enfin, non loin du haut cours du Nil Bleu (Abbaï), au Sud du lac Tana, nous avons déjà mentionné le pays de Sasou, dont les habitants, selon Cosmas Indicopleustès[42], ne parlaient pas la même langue que les Axoumites; ils commerçaient donc avec eux "à la muette", en échangeant de l'or contre des boeufs, des blocs de sel et du fer. L'hivernage chez eux, marqué par de très grosses pluies, durait trois mois, de juin/juillet à août/septembre.

Il nous reste à revenir plus longuement sur la description du Nil d'époque tardive qui fut publiée par J. Hudson[43] en 1712 d'après un manuscrit que l'on suppose provenir de la bibliothèque Bodléienne (Oxford). Ce texte propose une vision très schématique du cours du Nil: huit fleuves descendent des mont de la Lune (réminiscence de la *Géographie* de Ptolémée?), quatre à l'ouest et quatre à l'est.[44] Tous ceux de l'ouest se jettent dans le lac des Cataractes, tous ceux de l'est dans le lac des Crocodiles. Chacun donne ensuite issue à deux fleuves seulement et chaque paire de fleuves se fond en un seul fleuve; puis les deux fleuves qui subsistent se réunissent à leur tour pour former "le grand fleuve", lequel reçoit alors l'Astapous (notre Nil Bleu) en provenance du lac Kolé ou Koléê (le lac Tana). L'Astapous reçoit de son côté l'Astaboras (l'Atbara) qui coule le long de la terre des Axoumites. Leur confluent est d'ailleurs encore situé sur cette terre. Ensuite, la description devient particulièrement fantaisiste: le Nil se sépare d'un fleuve réunissant les eaux de l'Astapous et de l'Astaboras. Alors qu'en coulant vers l'ouest, le Nil en vient à recevoir les eaux du fleuve Gabakhi[45], le fleuve formé des eaux de l'Astapous et de l'Astaboras contourne à l'est l'île de Meroë, avant de se mêler derechef au Nil.

La complication peu réaliste de cette description fondée sur mainte confusion pourrait nous inciter à abandonner ce texte à l'oubli presque total d'où J. Hudson et C. Müller n'ont guère réussi à le tirer. Toutefois il convient de remarquer qu'il présente une assez grande richesse en hydronymes, toponymes et ethniques dont notre bref résumé ne saurait donner une idée. Or un certain nombre d'entre eux se retrouvent sous des formes à peine différentes dans l'inscription que Cosmas Indicopleustès[46] copia à Adoulis sur le trône d'un roi axoumite inconnu (*Monumentum Adulitanum*). On pourrait dès lors admettre que l'Anonyme d'Hudson a connu la *Topographie chrétienne* et utilisé habilement le matériel toponymique et ethnonymique qu'il trouvait dans la transcription de l'inscription, en changeant quelque peu l'orthographe et en transformant tel nom de peuplade en nom de ville[47] et tel autre en hydronyme.[48] Il faut avouer que l'emprunt est loin d'être évident. De plus, il faut être très attentif au fait que l'Anonyme d'Hudson signale une ville de Χάζα. Or les Χαοα sont attestés comme un peuple soumis par Ezana dans l'inscription grecque d'Axoum publiée en 1970 par MM. F. Anfray, A. Caquot et P. Nautin.[49] Doit-on considérer ce rapprochement comme une pure coïncidence, ou doit-on admettre que la ville de Χάζα de l'Anonyme provient du nom de peuplade Γάζη signalée par Cosmas?[50] En tout cas, les hydronymes, toponymes et ethniques mentionnés par notre Anonyme paraissent bien réels, qu'ils aient été ou non empruntés de façon livresque et malgré leur insertion dans un tableau d'ensemble des plus suspects. Il ne fait pas de doute qu'ils sont à localiser en grande partie dans l'aire d'expansion des souverains axoumites. Il est donc, à notre avis, très vraisemblable que certains d'entre ceux qui n'ont pu encore faire l'objet d'un rapprochement seront éclairés grâce aux données actuelles et surtout futures de l'épigraphie du royaume d'Axoum.

NOTES

1. Strabon, XVII, 1, 2 (C 786).

2. C'est au second terme de l'alternative que se rallie apparemment Méla, I, 50. Curieusement, Pline l'Ancien, V, 53, qui imagine qu'autour de l'île de Méroë l' *Astapus* se divise en deux bras, réserve le nom d'*Astabores* à celui de gauche en descendant le cours général du fleuve, situant en somme l'Atbara à l'ouest de l'île, alors qu'il appelle le bras de droite (c'est-à-dire le bras oriental) *Astosapes*. Il est copié par Solin, 32, 5-7, éd. Th. Mommsen, pp.138-139, copié lui-même par l'Anonyme, auteur d'un *De situ orbis*, éd. M. Manitius, Stuttgart, 1884, pp.65-66 (*Astapes* au lieu d'*Astosapes*). Photius, *Bibl.*, 250, 50, éd. R. Henry, VII, Paris, 1974, p.164, dit, en résumant sa lecture du récit d'Agatharchide sur la mer Rouge, que l'Astabaras coule à travers l'Ethiopie et la Libye. Traditionnellement, c'est le Nil qui limite ces deux ensembles. Agatharchide situait donc apparemment l'Astabaras à l'ouest du système fluvial nilotique. Cette erreur n'est donc pas limitée aux auteurs latins, comme semble le croire B. Postl., *Die Bedeutung des Nil in der römischen Literatur*, Vienne, 1970, p.100.

3. L'*Ampsaga* (oued el-Kebir du Constantinois) était censée prendre sa source en deux endroits différents d'après des témoignages épigraphiques, cf. Pline l'Ancien, *Histoire Naturelle, Livre V, 1-46, L'Afrique du Nord*, éd. J. Desanges, Paris (Les Belles Lettres), 1980, p.175. Même flottement pour le *Bagrada* (Medjerda), cf. *ibid.*, pp.216-217.

4. Plus encore, sans doute d'après l'exposé confus de Vitruve, VIII, 2, 6, éd. L. Callebat, Paris (Les Belles Lettres), 1973, p.10; cf. le commentaire de l'éditeur, *ibid.*, p.81. L. Callebat, p.83, pense que l'*Astasobas* (*Astansobas* chez Vitruve) a parfois désigné dans l'Antiquité, non le Nil Bleu, mais son affluent, le Rahad.

5. Ptolémée, IV, 7, 7, éd. C. Müller, p.775. Strabon, XVII, 2, 2, (C 821 *in fine*) est aberrant.

6. Il semble que ce soit le cas dans Héliodore, *Eth.*, X, 5, 1 (Asasobas), bien que le cadre fluvial de l'île de Méroë soit esquissé de façon très confuse.

7. A. Dillmann, *Über die Anfänge des axumitischen Reiches*, Abhandl. d. königl. Akad. d. Wissens., Berlin, 1878, pp.184 et 225.

8. Cf. G. A. Wainwright, *The Position of Ast-Raset*, dans *J. E. A.*, XXXII, 1947, pp.59-60; J. Yoyotte, *Le toponyme Napata comme témoin linguistique* dans *G. L. E. C. S.*, VII, 1954-1957, pp.106-108; B. G. Trigger, *Meroitic and Eastern Sudanic: a linguistic Relationship?*, dans *Kush*, XII, 1964, p.191. Une étude très complète de G. Roquet sera publiée. Elle montre que la base *ast^a/i- a connu deux développements phonétiques essentiels: *ass^a/i- et *att^a/i-.

9. Sénèque, *Q. N.*, VI, 8, 3-4; Pline l'Ancien, VI, 181; 184-186; XII, 19; Cassius Dio, LXIII, 8, 1. Ces textes ne mentionnent aucun affluent du Nil.

10. Strabon, XVI, 4, 8 (C 770).

11. Effectivement, selon un fragment (no. 90) d'Artémidore (cf. E. Stiehle, *Der Geograph Artemidoros von Ephesos*, dans *Philologus*, XI, 1856, p.221), conservé dans le *codex Graec. Monacensis* 287, une des branches de l'Astaboras se dirige vers la mer Erythrée (océan Indien ou, à la rigueur, mer Rouge). Ce fragment présente d'ailleurs les affluents du Nil d'une façon particulièrement confuse. Artémidore ne reconnaît explicitement qu'un grand affluent du Nil venant de l'Est et des montagnes d'Arabie et le laisse dans l'anonymat. L'Astaboras, cité en premier, viendrait du Sud. Comme le géographe mentionne encore en troisième lieu l'Astosobas sans en préciser sa position, il est facile de conclure que le fleuve anonyme doit être l'Astapous qu'Artémidore aurait peut-être confondu avec le Nil Bleu. L'Astosobas serait-il alors le Sobat? Le fragment 90 a été récemment étudié avec acribie par P. Pédech, *Sur un fragment du géographe Artémidore*, dans *Le Monde grec. Hommages à Claire Préaux*, Bruxelles, 1975, pp.318-324.

12. Diodore, III, 41, parle seulement, en traitant du littoral au delà de Ptolémaïs, de fleuves qui ont leur source dans les monts Psébées. Selon D. Woelk, *Agatharchides von Knidos, Über das Rote Meer, Übersetzung und Kommentar*, Bamberg, 1966, p.205, il s'agirait de monts des confins érythréo-soudanais. Mais on connaît un lac Psebo que Strabon, XVII, 2, 3 (C 822), situe "au-dessus de Méroë", et que l'érudition moderne assimile volontiers au lac Tana, qui s'appelait en tout cas *Coloe* dans l'Antiquité.

13. Photius, 250, 84, éd. R. Henry, VII, p.171, parle aussi des cours d'eau issus des monts Psébées.

14. X, 4, 6.

15. Diodore, III, 23; Photius, 250, 50, pp.164-165.

16. Diodore, *loc. cit.*, appelle Asa le fleuve que Photius, *loc. cit.*, nomme Astabaras, cf. *supra* (8). Héliodore, *Eth.*, X, 5, 1, écrit Asasobas et non Astasobas.

17. Ce pays des moustiques correspondrait, selon D. Woelk, *op. cit.*, p.142-144, aux marais du Mareb en amont du Gash. Mais il y a également des mares dans le lit de l'Atbara, cf. R. Lepsius, *Briefe aus Aegypten, Aethiopien und der Halbinsel des Sinai*, Berlin, 1852, p.140; S. M. Baker, *The Nile Tributaries of Abyssinia*, Londres, 1867, p.31.

18. Strabon, XVI, 4, 9 (C 771).

19. Elien, *N. A.*, XVII, 40.

20. Flavius Josèphe, *Ant.*, I, 6, 2.

21. *Id., ibid.*, II, 10, 2.

22. Ptol., IV, 7, 7, p.775.

23. *Id.*, IV, 7, 10, p.782.

24. Julius Honorius, *Cosm.*, 45, dans A. Riese, *Geographi Latini minores*, Heilbronn, 1878, p.48. Même référence pour la recension B.

25. On hésite à rapprocher de cet oronyme les Panchai de Méla, III, 81, voisins de la mer Rouge, qui sont des Ophiophages comme les Candai de Pline l'Ancien, VI, 169, situés dans le même contexte. Pline, prétend qu'il n'y a pas de région plus fertile que la leur (*eorum*), peut-être par confusion avec les Panchaei de l'île Panchea de Diodore, V, 42-46 (extrême fertilité: 43, richesse en or, si l'on préfère pour le texte de Pline la correction de Detlefsen, *auro*: 46); cf. H. Braunert, *Die heilige Insel des Euhemeros in der Diodor-Überlieferung*, dans *Rh. Mus.*, CVIII, 1965, pp.255-268. On pourrait suggérer de rapprocher le mont Panchaeus des Pechinoi de Ptol., IV, 7, 10, p.782, voisins orientaux des Struthophages, entre l'Astapous et le mont Garbaton. On doit seulement admettre une métathèse, banale chez Ptolémée.

26. Cosmas Indicopleustès, *Top. Chr.*, II, 51-53, éd. W. Wolska-Conus, Paris, 1968, I, pp.360-363 (= Sources chrétiennes, 141).

27. J. M. Kobiščanov, *Zolotonosnaja strana Sasu* ("Sasou, pays aurifère"), dans *Palestinskij Sbornik*, 11 (74), pp.94-112; *Id., Axum*, Univ. Park et Londres, 1979, p.186.

28. Méla, III, 80.

29. Je m'inspire de la traduction d'A. Silberman, à paraître dans la Collection des Universités de France (Les Belles Lettres).

30. Strabon, XVI, 4, 14 (C 774); cf. *supra* (11)?

31. On remarquera que l'Anonyme d'Hudson, *in fine* (cf. Ptol., éd. C. Müller, p.777, col.a *infra*), fait provenir le Nil pour partie des monts de la Lune et pour partie de la Cinnamômophore ou Côte de la cannelle (extrémité orientale de la côte des Somalis).

32. *Périple de la mer Erythrée*, 11, éd. H. Frisk, Göteborg, 1927, p.4.

33. Orose, *Adu. Pag.*, I, 2, 28, cf. le commentaire de Y. Janvier, *La géographie d'Orose*, Paris, 1982, pp.211-212.

34. Pline l'Ancien, VII, 31.

35. *Id.*, VI, 190.

36. Diodore, I,37, 8.

37. Diodore, III, 31 et Photius, 250, 60, p.170.

38. Strabon, XVI, 4, 10 (C 771).

39. Cf. *supra* (31).

40. Ptol., IV, 7, 10, p.782.

41. Diodore III, 28 et Photius, 250, 57, p.168; Strabon, par l'intermédiaire d'Artémidore, XVI, 4, 11 (C 772).

42. Cf. *supra* (26).

43. J. Hudson, *Geographiae veteris scriptores Graeci minores*, IV, Oxford, 1712, pp.38-39.

44. Sur la pluralité des sources du Nil, cf. déjà Diodore, I, 37, 8.

45. On doit rapprocher de cet hydronyme les Gapachi de Ptol., IV, 7, 10, p.784, établis, semble-t-il, au sud de l'île de Méroë. Le fleuve Gabakhi de l'Anonyme provient du lac Psébolè, c'est-à-dire le lac Psébo que Strabon, XVII, 2, 4 (C 822) situe "au-dessus de Méroë". L'Anonyme a assurément tort de prétendre que c'est en infléchissant son cours vers l'ouest que le Nil peut recevoir les eaux d'un émissaire du Psébo.

46. Cosmas Indicopleustès, *Top. chr.*, II, 60-63 (surtout 60), pp.372-379.

47. Μετίνε, nom de peuplade habitant des montagnes abruptes: Cosmas, II, 60 *in fine*, et Μέτω (accusatif ou plutôt forme indéclinée), ville: Anonyme, dans Ptol., éd. C. Müller, p.776, col.b.

48. Γαβαλά, peuplade qui occupe une montagne caractérisée par ses sources chaudes: Cosmas, II, 60, et Γανβάλας, le quatrième des fleuves orientaux situés aux origines du Nil.

49. F. Anfray, A. Caquot et P. Nautin, *Une nouvelle inscription grecque d'Ezana, roi d'Axoum*, dans *Journal des Savants*, 1970, p.265, ligne 24, traduction p.266, commentaire, p.268. On trouve ḥasā dans *D. A. E.*, 11, ligne 9.

50. Anonyme, dans Ptol., éd. C. Müller, p.777, col.A; Cosmas, II, 60, *initio*.

ANONYME D'HUDSON
(Traduction J. Desanges)

Voici l'origine des sources du Nil. A partir de la grande montagne de la Lune coulent huit fleuves, quatre de la partie occidentale de la montagne et, de même, quatre de la partie orientale. Du côté du couchant, le premier est celui qu'on appelle Kherbalas, le second celui qu'on appelle Khemset. Ces deux-là se réunissent près de la ville de Métin (*ou Métis?*), ensuite ils n'ont plus qu'un seul cours. Le troisième est le Khiagonas, le quatrième le Ganbalas. Ces quatre fleuves se jettent dans un lac appelé lac des Cataractes. Quant aux quatre fleuves du côté du levant, ils sont disposés comme suit: le premier qui est auprès de la terre des Pygmées n'a pas de nom et le second de la même façon n'a pas de nom. Tous deux se réunissent et ensuite n'ont plus qu'un seul cours. Et le troisième est semblablement anonyme. Le quatrième, à l'extrémité orientale, s'appelle Kharalas. Ces quatre fleuves se jettent dans un lac appelé lac des Crocodiles. Puis le lac des Cataractes donne issue aux cours de deux fleuves qui s'unissent près des villes de Singon et d'Aba. Donc ces deux-là et les deux autres qui se sont réunis près de la ville de Khaza deviennent un seul fleuve près de la terre des Eléphantophages, et on l'appelle le Grand fleuve. Au milieu de ces fleuves se trouvent la Kinnamômophore (*Terre de la Cannelle*) et les Pygmées. Dans son cours, le Grand fleuve parvient jusque chez les Khampésides. A ce Grand fleuve s'unit le fleuve qui coule à partir du lac Kolé ou Koléê, appelé Astapous. A cet Astapous s'unit le fleuve appelé Astaboras, grand lui aussi au long de la terre des Axoumites avant qu'il ne s'unisse au Grand fleuve. A l'intérieur de l'Astaboras et de l'Astapous sont établis les Struthophages. Ensuite l'Astapous et l'Astaboras, réunis au long de l'Auxoumitis (*pays d'Axoum*), ne font plus qu'un seul avec le Grand fleuve chez les dénommés Macrobii. Ensuite ils se divisent en deux, et le Grand fleuve, coulant vers le couchant, se trouve accueillir dans son propre courant un autre fleuve qui coule depuis le lac Psébolê et s'appelle Gabakhi.

Mais l'Astapous et l'Astaboras, coulant en un seul fleuve en direction du couchant, se mêlent ensuite au Grand fleuve, entourant au milieu une grande île nommée Méroë, égale à peu près au Péloponnèse. De là, roulant un seul cours, le Nil se jette avec des méandres dans la Grande mer, celle du Phare, par sept bouches.

Le Nil, partant des monts Lunaires et de la terre Kinnamômophore (*Terre de la Cannelle*) qui sont aux extrémités de l'Ethiopie, traverse en ligne droite toute l'Egypte. Après avoir infléchi sa direction et commencé cet infléchissement à partir de la Petite cataracte au-dessus de Syène et de la ville d'Eléphantine, il doit accueillir en lui deux fleuves venus d'orient qui entourent une île grande et célèbre, Méroë. De ces deux fleuves, l'un s'appelle Astaboras, l'autre Astapous. Méroë a 3000 stades de long, 1000 de large. Elle est décrite par Héliodore de Trikka dans le livre X des *Ethiopiques* en ces termes: " Méroë, qui est la capitale . . ." (Héliodore, *Eth.*, X, 5, 1-2).

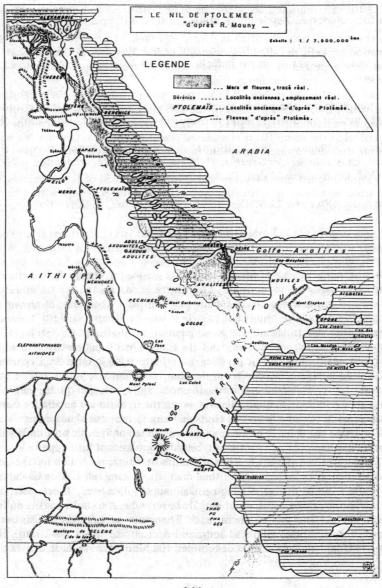

ETHIOPIAN ATTITUDES TOWARDS EUROPEANS UNTIL 1750

Franz Amadeus Dombrowski

No nation can close its doors to aliens and foreign influence completely. Cultural exchange is part of life. No wonder that, since Antiquity, Ethiopia has been a point of interest for foreigners from all walks of life, coming as adventurers, travellers, traders, missionaries, craftsmen and labourers.

However, throughout the centuries their reception has varied considerably, depending *inter alia*, on the roles individuals or groups of them played in Ethiopia, their professions and the reputation of their countries of origin among Ethiopians and their officials.

The purpose of this paper is, therefore, to follow up some of the documented statements and main lines in Ethiopian attitudes towards aliens and to take a brief look at Ethiopian history, searching for variations and consistencies in said attitudes and major events which caused them.[1]

Foreigners were generally classified as *Afrang* (= Franks[2]), i.e. West- and Central-Europeans (for simplification henceforth called 'Europeans'), and as *Non-Afrang*, i.e. all others. Since these Europeans, as they appeared on the Ethiopian scene were considered a rather coherent group, we felt induced to turn our attention to them.

One of the indicators of the role of foreigners from Europe and their significance can be the extent to which they are mentioned in the various *Tārika nagaśtāt*[3] that provide an overview of all Neguśa nagaśt until Bakāffā (1721-30) and must, by necessity, confine themselves to presentations of what the compilers considered the most important events. We will begin with the materials on attitudes towards Europeans until approximately 1750.

1) "Zar'a Yā'qob reigned for 34 years and 2 months [1434-68]. During his reign a controversy arose pertaining to faith, and Abbā Giyorgis had a debate with a European, until he had refuted (him)."[4]

2) "In the same year [1541], Europeans came, who had left (the others) from Portugal. Their commander was Dangeśtobu . . . The Europeans departed from Dabarwā. With them was Etēgē Sabla Wangēl. Through prudence and advice she encouraged them; she also provided them with victuals and equipment. They encountered Grāñ in the land of Anaḍā and fought a battle there on the 29th of Maggābit [25 March 1542]. Somebody struck him there with a rifle; Grāñ, however, did not die. During Keramt he sojourned in Zābl. The Etēgē Sabla Wangēl on the other hand spent Keramt together with the Europeans in Aflā. In the 2nd year of his (Galāwdēwos') reign [from 29 August 1542 on] on the 3rd of Maskaram [31 August 1542] they (Grāñ and the Europeans) fought a battle in which the commander (i.e. Dangeśtobu) fell. In the month of Ṭeqemt King Aṣnāf Sagad came and met his mother and the surviving Europeans in the land of Semēn . . .On the 16th of Yakkātit [10 February 1543] Grāñ raised himself arrogantly and confident in his cannon, rifles and Turks. He spoke: 'So many years I have pursued them, will they be able to stand before my face?' King Aṣnāf Sagad trusted in God and hoped that our Lady Mary would hear his pleas. Soldiers of the King, however, who went ahead of him killed him (Grāñ) before he could reach the King."[5] . . ." And it was an Afrang who had killed him and cut one of his ears off, and before he (Grāñ) reached the cliffs of Zantarā, he died by the will of God in the third hour of a Wednesday. After that man (the Afrang) an Ethiopian came and cut his (Grāñ's) throat and went to the King proclaiming 'I killed him'. Thereupon, the King gave him all the jewels (that Grāñ had worn). However, when he (the King) could not find one of his ears, he enquired, 'Where is his ear?' Then that Afrang brought his ear and he (the King) made the Ethiopian who had lied hand over all the jewels (of Grāñ). Thereafter, he ordered all Ethiopians should honour him and rise before him regardless, whether they met him in the camp, the market or at any other place."[6]

3. "Two years after Grāñ's death, he (Galāwdēwos) killed 'Abbās. The Europeans he allotted, in accordance with their agreement and alliance, many areas, as soon as they arrived from Rome. Regarding their faith severe strife and many disputes were roused. They fought and quarrelled with the Liqāwent, the disciples of Abbā Zekrē, and all the monks. The heart of the King, however, did not take love of the faith of the Europeans, (although) he appointed Endernos to be Patriarch. However, he feared that Ethiopia's people would bring unrest over his country like that (which had occurred) during the era of Grāñ and, thus, he declared himself firmly for the Alexandrian faith, causing the Europeans to be very disheartened."[7]

"Because of the alliance which had brought them out of their country, he allotted the Europeans many villages and, because a solemn oath had existed between Aṣnāf Sagad and the King of the Europeans, he ordered that he (the latter) be given one third of Ethiopia."[8]

4. "At that time the King (Susenyos [1607-32]) turned away from the Alexandrian faith. He preferred the faith of the Europeans and secretly associated with them. In the 12th year [from 8 September 1618 on] he stayed in Danqaz, spent Keramt there, and established a residence. The Europeans built two palaces, one in Danqaz, the other in Gwargorā."[9]

5. "In the 14th year, the Neguś went to the Land of Angot to attack Yonā'ēl who had been Daǧāzmāč of Bagēmeder. Like Yolyos he had rebelled because of the Europeans."[10]

6. "And there was established a place in his (Susenyos') country so that they (the Europeans) could come in and have preference and none would be prevented from entry. At that time came Safonsu."[11]

7. "In the 23rd year [from 8 September 1629 on] he (Susenyos) did not leave his residence. At that time Lāstā rebelled, because the Europeans exerted immense influence in all parts of Ethiopia. In the 24th year [from 9 September 1630 on] the King went to Lāstā in order to attack it. However, the King's soldiers were vanquished and then he himself was defeated. In the 25th year [from 9 September 1631 on] the King fought in Waynā Dagā against a rebel and defeated him. He also killed Bikono and Retu'ā Amlāk."[12]

"His son Fāsiladas appealed to him: 'Oh King, our Lord, alas! Everywhere there is rebellion and division because of this question of the Europeans, whom we have not seen[13], with whom we do not intend to speak and whose books are not those of our fathers. Certainly we fear you and stand in awe of your face, but we are with you (only) by mouth and not the heart. But if you undertake a pledge to God to restore the Alexandrian faith, then you will gain victory over your foes.' The King replied, 'Yes!' "[14]

"Then he reverted to the original Alexandrian faith . . . Thereafter his son Fāsiladas [1632-67] ruled . . ."[15] "That year an Abun arrived whose name was Rezeq. The Frank Afonsu returned to his country . . ."[16] "In the first year of his reign [from 8 September 1632 on] . . . he consolidated the Alexandrian faith and banned Rās Se'ela Krestos to Šawāda"[17] ["where he was hung on a cedar and died"[18]].

8. "In the 2nd year [from 8 September 1668] a church council was held in Gondar. He (Yoḥannes [1667-82]) expelled the Europeans and sent (them) from Ethiopia back to Romyā . . . In the 3rd year he separated the Muslims and isolated them so that they would have no contact with the Christians and let them be brought out of the settlement to have them live on the banks of the Qāḥā, i.e. in Aborā."[19]

9. "On the 27th of Yakkātit [4 March 1716] a Synod was held in Ašawā to discuss the matter of the three Europeans that Yoṣtos [1711-16] had let come for council and advice

146

and who had been established in Ayānā Egzi'e. The whole world was in strife because of them. King Dāwit ordered them to be brought out of the land of Ayānā Egzi'e and to be produced before the Synod in Aṣawā. Abbā Mazmurē and Edug Tasfā examined their faith in Arabic. Those Europeans declared, 'We are followers of Leo, and Kēlqēyon (Chalcedon) is our church council.' They were condemned to death. Liqē Keflē stood in the centre of the Synod, he proclaimed the judgement and they were stoned below the town limits. The names of these Europeans were Sāmu'ēl, Dāwit and Mikā'ēl. The King spared Abbā Gorgoryos, the interpreter of their language, from the death penalty and sentenced him to jail, because he had said 'I did not participate in the faith and Communion of the Europeans, King Yoṣtos had ordered me to safeguard their property and interpret their language."[20]

10. "On the 11th of Yakkātit [17 February 1728] died Wayzaro Walatta Negeśt, a daughter of Haḍē Fāsil and the wife of the European Fāsil."[21]

As these passages show, the Chroniclers gave coverage to the arrival, sojourn, and departure of the Portuguese predominantly throughout the 16th to the 18th centuries. They have tried to present a fairly realistic picture. On the one hand, they pointed out the Portuguese merits in the defeat of Aḥmad Grāñ, who threatened to conquer all of Ethiopia. This is especially apparent in the passage telling how an Ethiopian was rebuffed for taking credit for the slaying of Grāñ which had been achieved by one of the foreigners. On the other hand, they tell quite openly the reasons for the expulsion of these aliens, the main cause being their attempts to convert Ethiopians from the Alexandrian to the Catholic faith.

In many ways the experiences with foreigners from Portugal have left deep imprints on the attitudes of Ethiopians towards Europeans in general and strengthened their desire for religious and political self-determination and independence. Certainly, as the first cited passage, narrating that Abbā Giyorgis (Walda Ḥezba Ṣeyon) of Saglā had a religious dispute with an unknown European, an episode which probably occurred during the reign of Yeshaq (1414-29) and not of Zar'a Yā'qob (1434-68)[22], demonstrates, Ethiopians had had experiences with individual Europeans who had come to their country for a long time. Now, the opening of navigation to India around the Cape through Vasco de Gama in 1499 paved the way for vessels to reach Ethiopia directly, bypassing the traditional overland routes via Egypt. For the first time larger groups of Europeans could reach the country.

Faced by a 'sea' of Islam, raked by the Sultanate of Adal, Ethiopia turned to Portugal which through the firepower of its cannon and galleons was able to control the Indian Ocean, the Emperors appealing for the aid of their fellow Christian brethren in the struggle against Islam. For the examination of Ethiopian attitudes towards aliens, it must be stressed that the initiative came from Ethiopians who, at that time, knew of no bias nor fostered any particular antipathies *vis à vis* Europeans, but rather considered them as Christians to be their natural allies. The first significant Ethiopian attempt to reach an agreement with the Portuguese was the legation sent by the Etēgē Elēni, the mother of Lebna Dengel (1508-40), to King Manuel I of Portugal (1495-1521) which was led by Matthew, an Armenian[23], who arrived in Lisbon in 1513. The Etēgē proposed the conclusion of an anti-Muslim alliance to be sealed through a marriage arranged between both dynasties and the dispatch of a Portuguese fleet to the Red Sea. Portugal was interested in the proposal and sent a mission under the leadership of Dom Edoardo Galvam, who died on the way and was replaced by Dom Rodrigo de Lima. A member of the mission was Father Francisco Alvarez who had been appointed by Pope Leo X and whose presence reveals one of the essential problems that arose out of Ethiopian-European contacts, i.e. the idea of leading Europeans that Ethiopia had to become an 'officially Christian' nation, that she should be converted to Catholicism.[24] The combination of religion and business, i.e. of "Priests and Politicians"[25], should call for Ethiopian tolerance of missionary activity. However, it produced no concrete results because of Lebna Dengel's reluctance to grant major concessions to the Portuguese. The Emperor was chiefly interested in gaining access to European technology, in particular, weapons and methods of warfare. He was not prepared, as the letters which the delegation took back to Europe show, to grant more than permission to establish Portuguese control over a number of Red Sea ports and adjacent coastline and to allow missionary activity merely in these protracted areas.

Certainly, there were several reasons for Lebna Dengel's reservations:

1) He had not been the instigator of the plan for an alliance, but his mother, while he was still inexperienced so that she could embark on such a venture.

2) He had defeated the Muslim Emir Maḥfūẓ of Adal quite handily in 1516. So he thought that he could cope with the Muslim threat alone.[26]

3) The delegate of the Pope, Father Alvarez had debated with and caused unrest among members of the clergy already deeply divided on questions of faith.[27] He had conducted mass several times following the Roman Catholic rite and even induced the Emperor to attend.

However, more important and relevant to our topic is, that Lebna Dengel, like his successors, was a proud man who wished and intended to maintain the country's independence, considering the Europeans merely as tools to his avail for the development of his own power and of his country. Nonetheless, despite his sentiments, Lebna Dengel's relations with Europeans were, at least outwardly, of a cordial nature. This is confirmed by the fact that Lebna Dengel sent to Europe a golden crown for King João of Portugal, a golden cross for Pope Clement VII, and other precious gifts, as well as several Ethiopians including the famous legate Ṣeggā Za'āb.

It is against this background, that the passage about Dangeśtobu, i.e. Dom Cristovão da Gama, in the *Tārika nagaśtāt* must be seen. The story of the heroic feats of the 400 Portuguese has been told many times and the substance of the version presented above is corroborated in the more detailed Portuguese accounts[28] and need not be retold in this context. However, important for our topic is that once again the initiative went out from the Ethiopian side. The attitudes of the Ethiopians towards the Portuguese have been lent most vivid expression in the letter of the Emperor that Bāḥr nagāś Yeshaq conveyed to the commander of the Portuguese fleet, Dom Estevão da Gama, when his ships had cast anchor before Massawa:

> The Emperor "asked him that he might see how for fourteen years his lands had been ruled by the Moors and how most of his subjects were being held in captivity; and since he, the King (of Portugal), his brother, was accustomed to helping those who were in need . . . he should kindly accede to sending him help, as his (the Emperor's) lands belonged to His Majesty (the King of Portugal), and he possessed them in his name."[29]

Even after this offer of vassalage by Lebna Dengel in his distress, and after Grāñ's defeat, the Emperor's positive attitude continued, as is demonstrated by the passage concerning the allotment of land to Europeans through Lebna Dengel's son Galāwdēwos (1540-59) confirmed by the report of Castanhoso[30] who states that:

> "The Prester (John) stayed in his residence in the town and he let us Portuguese be settled in a quarter of the town, that was located a distance of two shots of a flintlock away, and some villages he assigned for our support. They brought us wheat and barley for the horses and mules, as well as honey, butter, meat, and everything in abundance."

However, passage No.2 (above) shows in its latter section that in the middle of the 16th century the first serious attempt was made by Jesuits to meddle with the internal affairs of the country. Emperor Galāwdēwos had to hold on to the Alexandrian faith and ward off attempts to romanise Ethiopia. In the context of the wars against Grāñ, Lebna Dengel had sent a certain João Bermudez to Portugal to seek aid. On his arrival, Bermudez claimed the Emperor had appointed him to the office of Patriarch, pledged to submit himself to Catholicism, and that he had promised half or a third of the country to the Europeans. By his own account, Bermudez was received by Pope Paul III (1534-49) and King João III of Portugal. His role is disputed, however, as is demonstrated by the fact that Pope Paul sent Galāwdēwos a letter in which he declared that he would send a papal legate to effect the deposition of Bermudez.[31]

At any rate, Bermudez' influence at the court must have been so powerful that in November 1543 he dared to demand the fulfilment of Lebna Dengel's alleged undertakings. This was the context of the debates between the Abbās Zekrē and Pāwlos and a European in 1545.[32] The layman Bermudez, a trained barber, naturally provoked a generally poor impression, showing that he was largely ignorant of church matters. Concerning the territorial concessions, the indigenous clergy was able to argue effectively that these were not appropriate, since the help had come from one Christian nation to another. The conversion to Catholicism, they claimed, was not possible, because the Ethiopian faith was monophysite.[33] To support his decision Galāwdēwos claimed that he could hold contact with his father only sporadically, so that he did not know whether Bermudez had been appointed Patriarch or was merely pretending to have been so.

The episode with Bermudez contributed considerably to the formation of Ethiopian attitudes towards Europeans. For the first time, as far as has become known, Ethiopians were confronted with a European who demanded substantial renunciation of Ethiopian religious, political, and territorial independence. However, the growth of antipathy and estrangement was strengthened in many ways through the continuation of the attempts to romanise Ethiopia.

The Jesuits were not prepared to accept Galāwdēwos' firm stand, nor was the Pope. The leader of the Society of Jesus, Ignatius of Loyola, had meticulous preparations made to change the "heart" of the Emperor and the Ethiopians. A centre for their efforts became the special school San Stefano dei Mori where missionaries to be sent to Ethiopia were taught the Ethiopian languages, customs, theology and other matters relevant to faith. Through a papal bull in 1554, Nuñez Barreto was appointed to be "Patriarch" of Ethiopia. In order to prepare for a suitable reception, the Jesuit Gonçalo Rodriguez was sent ahead. In Ethiopia he received nothing more than Galāwdēwos' confirmation that he was prepared to receive Barreto. Barreto, however, never reached Ethiopia but rather decided to send André de Oviedo, after he had failed to persuade the Portuguese governor of Goa to provide him with six hundred men, so that he might coerce, if necessary, Galāwdēwos to embrace Catholicism. De Oviedo, accompanied by five other Jesuits[34], came to Ethiopia where he was appointed Bishop and allowed to take care of the Portuguese Catholics and of a few Ethiopian Catholics consisting mostly of wives and slaves of the Portuguese. Very much like Bermudez, Oviedo did as much as he could to stir Ethiopian antipathies. He debated with the Emperor and Abuna Yosab, who upon the wish of the Emperor had come from Alexandria in 1548. The Emperor convoked a Synod which decided against the Jesuits, prompting Oviedo to leave the country in 1558 and bringing Galāwdēwos to reaffirm his abidance by the Alexandrian faith in the famous "Confessio Claudii".[35] The actual appointment of Oviedo to the position of Patriarch did not occur until 20th December 1562, after Barreto had died. The choice of words ወሠሞ ለእንድርኖስ በትረ ያርክ *wa-śemo la-endernos batra-yark*[36] = "and he appointed Endernos (André de Oviedo) to be Patriarch" in the *Tārika nagaśtāt* is significant for the attitude of Galāwdēwos and the Chroniclers concerning the Jesuits.

The employment of the loanword Patriarch signifies the limits of de Oviedo's power from the outset. The proper Ethiopian word for Patriarch, referring to the Patriarchs of Alexandria is ሊቀ ጳጳሳት *Liqa pāppāsāt*, chief Metropolitan. Through the appointment of Barreto to the position of Patriarch, the Pope had tried to put him on a par with the Patriarch of Alexandria. The title Patriarch was bestowed as an honour *inter alios* on the Bishops of Venice (1451), Lisbon (1716), the Bishop of Goa and West India which had been founded in 1540 and on the leaders of churches united with Rome.[37] The Patriarchs of such Churches were supposed to become intermediaries between the Pope and the Metropolitans and other church officials in their area.[38]

What the Ethiopians made out of this title is notable for their opinion of the alien as a minor figure. Like several other titles that were introduced by foreigners, the Ethiopians scaled its importance down to a considerable extent.[39] "Patriarch" became the title of the Abbot of Tadbāba Māryām which had been consecrated by Abuna Yoḥannes I in 1552 and was founded by Galāwdēwos.[40]

In fact, in the latter years of his reign, many of the clergy became dissatisfied with Galāwdēwos' tolerant attitude towards the Europeans. They felt especially uncomfortable with his permission to the Jesuits to continue staying in the country and to engage in evangelic work.

The majority of the people were distressed when the news of the Emperor's death at the hands of Nur in 1559 spread in the country. The sentiments of some that are expressed in his elegy[41] may stand out as typical:

> "Why do my eyes become no clouds
> and burst into tears like the rain that drops,
> so that I can lament over our Lord Galāwdēwos
> and shed tears because of him . . .
>
> Come back! Galāwdēwos, Lord of Peace!
> bring us, Your people, the mercy of reconciliation,
> leave the place of your peace,
> so that the Muslims cannot steal our land,
> and the Romans are not able to seize our country."

So Galāwdēwos was seen as protector and guardian of the Alexandrian faith and the integrity of the country from Muslims and Europeans, especially the representatives of the Roman Catholic Church. Certain elements in the clergy were still feeling, however, that Galāwdēwos had been too lenient in his policies towards the *Afranǧ*. They saw his death in battle at the hands of Nur as God's recompensating restitution of justice for both the Emperor and the land.

This is seemingly confirmed by a passage in the *Tārika nagaśtāt*[42], whose interpretations and implications have not been, so far, properly understood, but that was assumed to be a relation of the Emperor's piety and the monks' prophetic powers.

> "Thereafter, in the 19th year [from 29 August 1558 on] a Muslim named Nur came from Adal. As soon as the King heard of his arrival he assembled his army and went into battle. When they stood face to face, monks of Abbā Yoḥannes of Dabra Libānos[43] and of Abbā Maqāres[44] and many other monks came to the King and spoke . . . 'Choose between worldly and heavenly realm. If you refrain [from going to battle] today, you will survive[45], if, however, you do not refrain, you will die and enter into the heavenly realm.' The King answered them: 'It is better for me for the sake of the heavenly realm to die (now)'. On the next day [23 March 1559] he marched into battle, in the nineteenth year of his reign, and thus he became a martyr."

If one considers the background to the monks' appearance before the Emperor, it is feasible to conclude that they did not only wish to warn him, but had in mind to test his faith.

In this awkward situation, the Portuguese did still more to rouse Ethiopian antipathy by involving themselves in the struggle for succession after Galāwdēwos' death to exploit the rivalries among the nobility, in order to enhance their power and influence in the country. Regarding the new Emperor Minās (1559-63), his chronicle states that: "The Portuguese soldiers did not hide their contempt for the 'Infante' who became a Muslim when he could have won fame and glory through martyrdom!"[46] From the outset the Portuguese associated themselves with the anti-Minas faction which included Galāwdēwos' and Minās' mother, Etēgē Sabla Wangēl, Bāḥr nagāś Yesḥaq, and the sons of Minās' elder brother Yā'qob, who were considered by many Mak^wānnent to be the rightful heirs to the throne.[47] Consequently, Minās pursued a policy to render his opponents innocuous, starting with the deposition of Etēgē Sabla Wangēl, his mother, and her replacement through his wife, Ṣellus Ḥāyla.

The missionary activities of the Jesuits were prohibited, and they were banned to Fremona (Maygoggā). The power of the old Mak^wānnent was reduced; they were demoted or even discharged. This especially angered Bāḥr nagāś Yesḥaq, the most powerful nobleman in the land, who entered into open rebellion and appointed Tazqāra Qāl, the son of Yā'qob, to be (a pseudo-) Neguśa nagaśt. The latter concluded an alliance with the "Patriarch" de Oviedo who coaxed other Portuguese to join by promising reinforcements from Goa. However, such Portuguese assistance from Goa never arrived, and it was only a matter of time before the Emperor would attempt to quell the rebellion. For the first time, an Ethiopian Emperor would take up arms against his former allies, Europeans. The anti-Minās faction lost both battles against the Emperor in Adyābo and Wagarā in 1561. Most of the Portuguese, including de Oviedo, were led away into captivity. Meanwhile Yesḥaq, who had escaped, formed an alliance with the Turk Özdemir Pasha or Zemur Bāśā[48], this time using as a puppet or pseudo-Emperor one of Tazqāra's younger brothers. In due course, Yesḥaq was able to free Oviedo and many of the other Portuguese in the Emperor's camp. He ordered them to settle in Fremona, and secretly he encouraged de Oviedo to continue seeking support from Goa, promising him that he would convert to Catholicism. Not only were the Portuguese now allied against the Emperor and the Ethiopian Church, they were now indirectly associated with the Muslims. This could not but cause doubts in the idea still prevalent under Lebna Dengel and Galāwdēwos that Christian brethren and countries were natural allies against the onslaught of Islam.

With Minās' victory on the 20th of April 1562, the chance of the Portuguese to play a successful role in Ethiopia was doomed for some time to come. The soldiers lost their privileges and the Jesuits were merely allowed to grow old in confinement at Fremona. Within 20 years the Portuguese had worn out the welcome they had been accorded formerly. They had become undesirable aliens and were removed from the scene. Typical is that they are no longer mentioned in the *Tārika nagaśtāt* until Susenyos (1608-32) came to rule.

Emperor Sarṣa Dengel (1563-97), although in his latter years he resumed some of the contacts with Europe[49] and returned to the Portuguese some of the privileges they had enjoyed under Galāwdēwos[50], maintained Minās' policy of isolation.

However, Sarṣa Dengel's death left a deep cleft, and a struggle for the throne ensued between Yā'qob, Za-Dengel and Susenyos. This gave the missionaries another chance to meddle with internal Ethiopian affairs and to extract new privileges for their support in the rivalries and strife. Inspired by the role played by de Oviedo, the contenders considered the Europeans as pawns on their assumed road to kingship.

The matter was complicated by the activities of the Mak^wānnent Rās Aṭanāsyos of Bagēmeder and Dağāzmāč (later Rās) Za-Śellāsē, and his Qurbān regiment, who attempted to appoint and depose the Neguśa nagaśt as they saw fit. So Yā'qob, appointed by the two Kingmakers as a seven year old in 1597 to serve as a pseudo-Neguś under them, was the first attempting to gain his independence with the help of Europeans. He allowed them to establish schools and to engage in missionary work, to cross, thus, the policy of his mentors who strove to sever all ties with Europe[51], while he adopted the pro-European position of his opponents Za-Dengel and Susenyos. When in the 7th year of his reign (1603) Yā'qob had been ousted from power by Aṭanāsyos and Za-Śellāsē and banned to exile in Enarya, Za-Dengel was made Neguś.[52]

In the same year, Father Paez established himself in Ethiopia.

Za-Dengel, however, did even more to anger Rās Za-Śellāsē and Rās Aṭanāsyos by initiating a tax-reform to fix the taxes according to the productivity of the land and not the will of the rās.[53] Moreover, Za-Dengel increased again Ethiopia's contacts with Europe by letters to Pope Clement VIII (1592-1605) and the ruler of Spain and Portugal, King Philip III (1598-1621). He offered to subject himself to the Holy See and requested that missionaries be sent to Ethiopia. In the manner of Etēgē Elēni, he proposed to King Philip a close alliance of their royal houses through marriage and a combined effort against the Turks at Massawa, hoping that the European powers would help him to defeat his internal foes in Ethiopia.[54]

In fact, the missionaries from Europe were well received at first and theological disputes with the native clergy ensued. Through the acceptance of 200 rifles and the support of the missionaries Za-Dengel expected to be in a position to counter his opponents, the Abun, the Ečagē, and other high officials of the Ethiopian Church and, thus, expand his power.[55] However, Za-Dengel did not succeed in obtaining support from the peasantry to check and possibly obstruct their rās, as he had intended through his tax-reform. Yet, on account of his tolerance of the Europeans, he caused revolt. The peasant reaction was far more immediate and effective than it had been a century ago. Everywhere the commonfolk flocked around a warañña[56], who posed as a "false Messiah" in Ambā Sanāyt. While Za-Dengel could still defeat this rebel, he was unable to deal with the coalition between Za-Śellāsē and the Church. For Abuna Pēṭros had excommunicated the Emperor after the news had spread that he and Dağāzmāč Lā'eka Māryām had secretly become Catholics.[57] Za-Dengel was subsequently killed in the battle of Barča on the 7th of Ṭeqemt (= 15 October 1604). As Emperor the two kingmakers decided to proclaim Yā'qob who had apparently now won the support of Orthodoxy and of Abuna Pēṭros.[58] So Yā'qob returned to the throne.

This provided Za-Dengel's cousin, Susenyos, with an opportunity to form a coalition between elements that were pro-European and the Gāllā groups that had protected him all the time. Consequently, both sides met on the battlefield near Dabra Gol. Yā'qob and Abuna Pēṭros were killed.

The Jesuits now felt that their time had come and that, contrary to Bāḥr nagāš, this time they had placed their stakes with the right man to become Emperor. Indeed, Susenyos was an admirer of Father Paez, who professed his ideas with great vigour and enthusiasm. On the other hand, Abuna Sem'on, it is claimed, lived in open adultery with the wife of an Egyptian domiciled in the country and he kept a large ḥarīm of native girls. When one of these gave birth to a child, the Abuna had it exposed to be eaten by hyenas.[59] Moreover, the indigenous church was at that time split on account of the Tawāḥdowočč-Qebātočč controversy.[60]

In order to strengthen his power, Susenyos decided to pursue a policy of decentralisation and nepotism, entrusting the most powerful offices of the land to his brothers, Se'ela Krestos, Yamāna Krestos, Malke'ā Krestos and Afa Krestos, besides a few other relatives. To reduce the power of the Ethiopian Church, he attempted to cut its income by giving Church G^wults in Dāmot, Gožžām and Agawmeder to such Oromo who had helped him to power. He also preferred the faith of the Europeans, as the Tārika nagaśtāt state, and gave Father Paez and his colleagues a free hand, especially in the Northwest, where Paez was also charged with architectural work, as the relation that the Europeans built palaces in Danqaz and G^wargorā/Gorgorā confirms. The palace of Māryām Gemb, a rectangular building of stone and loam, with decorative façades, columns and a high terrace, was built by Paez between 1619-21.[61] The palace of the Emperor in Danqaz, also built by Paez was described by Almeida after his visit in 1624:

> "It is now 4 or five years since the Emperor, when stone-masons came from India, brought by the Patriarch, built a palace of stone and lime, a structure that was a wonder in that country and something that had never been seen nor yet imagined, and it was such as would have value and be reckoned a handsome building anywhere."[62]

Both buildings must have left a somewhat awesome impression on native Ethiopians. They demonstrated for everyone to see the European presence in Ethiopia.

Like Za-Dengel, Susenyos augmented his pro-European policy by writing letters to Europe to Pope Paul V (1605-21) and King Philip III of Spain and Portugal (1598-1621) in the years 1607, 1610 and 1615, making approximately the same offers.

However, the manifestations of his pro-European attitude brought Susenyos more and more animosity and even rebellion from the Ethiopian Church, the country-folk and Mak^{w}ānnent. Susenyos was continuously on the warpath not only subduing Agaw and Oromo tribes[63], but also several false Ḥadē Yā'qob who had become the symbol of Ethiopian Orthodoxy and found support among the peasantry[64] and many of the noblemen, *inter alios* the Dagāzmač Yolyos, Yamāna Krestos and Yonā'ēl whose cause of rebellion is explicitly mentioned: the Europeans.

Indeed, the battle of Ṣaddā on the 11th of April 1617 was a milestone in Susenyos' suicidal policy. Susenyos did kill not only Yolyos, but also many of the clergy, including Abuna Sem'on.[65] Now Susenyos had the dubious fame of having killed two Abuns in battle.

In this desperate situation Susenyos decided to play his last trump. Although it was an open secret[66] that he adhered to Catholicism, Susenyos thought he should now officially convert to Catholicism to gain military support from the Europeans. Yet these, remembering the promises of Lebna Dengel and Za-Dengel, had been hesitant so far to send assistance to the Emperor. Would they lend it now?

In May 1622 Susenyos, his brother Rās Se'ela Krestos, and Ṣaḥafē Te'ezāz (Azzāž) Ṭino and several other high officials submitted to baptism and were converted to Catholicism.[67] Instead of the desired support, though, Susenyos had to accept a large number of missionaries from the Society of Jesus[68] for whom, due to the attitudes of the Ottomans who controlled the Red Sea and of the indigenous population trying to obstruct their routes to and within Ethiopia, a special passageway had to be found, as passage No.6 confirms.

After the death of the astute and moderate Paez in 1622, his successor, Patriarch Safonsu/Afonsu, i.e. Dom Afonso Mendez, reached Ethiopia in 1625. With this event the onslaught on Ethiopian "orthodoxy" reached its "climax". Mendez tried to force the Ethiopians to adopt all facets of the Roman Catholic Church, theology, liturgy and feasts, and to prohibit, *inter alia*, the rite of circumcision, divorce and the observance of the Sabbath. The Mak^Wānnent and clergy he treated as pagans and by having the persons seeking an audience with him bow before his throne he usurped the role of an Abun.

When Susenyos tried to introduce the Roman Catholic faith to the Lāstā Agaw, a rebellion ensued that was to bring his fall. James Bruce[69] has argued that there had been scarcely a common layman in Lāstā who could distinguish between the Alexandrian and the Roman faith and that the struggle for Orthodoxy served merely as a pretext. Yet, if so, this pretence to oust the 'alāwi neguś (= the heretic Neguś) as he was known throughout the country served the ends of the Lāstā Agaw very well. As before, the confession of faith was also the profession of national identity. When Susenyos decided to change his faith, he was, in the view of his subjects, selling the country to the Europeans, thus disqualifying himself as their sovereign. There was no need for common men to know the intricacies of faith to understand the change. Mendez' attempts to alter their daily routine, through measures such as the prohibition of the observance of the Sabbath, made the "treason of Susenyos" apparent. The rebel's conviction that their resistance was "legitimate" is confirmed by their adoption of Malke'ā Krestos, a man of Solomonic descent and a brother of the Emperor, as their leader who assembled an army of 25,000 men. This was, as Pankhurst[70] observed, "remarkable in that Lasta was the reputed home of the Zagwé dynasty whose descendants were reputedly still governors of Wag."

While, in this context, the details of the Lāstā rebellion cannot be dealt with in great length[71], it should be noted that its importance was the inability of Susenyos to cope with it and that everywhere the rebel's success inspired the population further to rebel. Finally, even the last supporters of the Emperor, his own soldiers, mutinied in 1632 and refused to go on fighting. This is where his son's appeal, [Fāsiladas, who had become a Catholic himself], to restore the Alexandrian faith comes in. Realizing, finally, that the principle of *cuius religio, eius regio*[72], was an essential for any Emperor ruling Ethiopia, Susenyos agreed to his "abdication" in favour of Fāsiladas on 25 June 1632. So the Alexandrian faith as the official religion of the country was restored.[73]

As the *Tārika nagaśtāt* asserts, Fāsiladas pursued a policy of strengthening the Alexandrian faith and persecuting Europeans and Ethiopians of Roman Catholic faith. So Fāsiladas had his uncle, Rās Se'ela Krestos, come to his palace in Danqaz to persuade him back into the Alexandrian faith, promising him a high position. When the Rās refused, he was, as the Chronicle confirms, banished to Šawadā and subsequently liquidated. His remains disappeared.[74]

Patriarch Mendez and the missionaries were ordered to assemble and leave the country. Some of them who tried to go into hiding were caught and killed by the Neguś' henchmen or the peasantry. Mendez and other officials preferred to pretend obedience, hoping to find protection through Bāḥr nagāš Yoḥannes Akāy. The latter demonstrated, however, the change of Ethiopian attitudes towards Europeans, handing them over to the Pasha of Sawākin who in turn kept them prisoners until they were ransomed. In fact, the hatred of the Europeans went so far that Fāsiladas concluded a treaty with the Pasha stipulating the closure of Ethiopia to the Portuguese and other Franks, especially missionaries. What a remarkable turn of events, the enemies of the Empire, the Muslims, now became the guards that prevented Europeans from entering the Christian kingdom of Ethiopia from the sea![75]

That Fāsiladas meant business can also be seen in the episode of the French Capuchins trying to come to Ethiopia after the Pope made several efforts to calm down the Emperor, *inter alia*, by changing the missionary order. When Fāsiladas was informed of their arrival, he ordered the Pasha of Sawākin not to let them enter Ethiopia. The Pasha decapitated them upon their arrival in Sawākin.[76]

The reign of Fāsiladas marks the beginning of a rather rigid isolation from Europe for more than a century. No longer were sizeable groups of Europeans able to establish themselves in Ethiopia because the indigenous population, and especially the clergy, would not tolerate them.

The development of Ethiopian attitudes towards Europeans up to this stage has been characterized most suitably by Charles Jacques Poncet[77] who visited the country in the beginning the 18th century:

> "The horror which the Ethiopians have for the Mahometans and Europeans is almost equal. The occasion was this. The Mahometans, having render'd themselves powerful in the beginning of the 16th age, made themselves masters of the government. The Abyssinians, not being able to support so hard and so odious a yoak as that of Mahometans, call'd in the Portuguese to their assistance; who at that time were famous in the Indies, where they had newly establish'd themselves. These new conquerors were overjoy'd to find a free entrance into Ethiopia. They march'd against the Mahometans, encounter'd them, defeated them entirely, and resettl'd the imperial family upon the throne. So important a service render'd the Portuguese considerable [power] at the court in Ethiopia. Many of them planted themselves there and enjoy'd the principal employs. Their numbers increas'd, corruption of manners crept in, and they gave themselves such liberties that they raised jealousie [i.e. suspicion] in the Ethiopians that they design'd to make themselves masters of their country and subject it to the crown of Portugal. Upon this suspicion the people were in a fury against the Portuguese. They took up arms in all places and made a terrible slaughter of them, at the time they thought themselves most securely establish'd in that empire. Those who escap'd from this first commotion had a liberty allow'd to retire. There departed out of Ethiopia seven thousand Portuguese families, who dispers'd themselves thro' the Indies and upon the coasts of Africa. Some few remain'd in the country, and from these families do the white Abyssins descend who are amongst them and from whence they pretend the present Empress [Malakotawi[78]] . . . draws her origin."

The anti-European feelings were as Poncet[79] observes not limited to Catholics and the Portuguese:

> "At the time I was at the court of Ethiopia, I was inform'd that the Hollanders had attempted more than once to engage in commerce with the Ethiopians. But, whether it be difference in religion or whether it be the

154

great power of the Hollanders in the East Indies, that gives them a jealousy [i.e. suspicion] 'tis certain the Ethiopians wou'd never enter into any league with them and I have heard them say they would never trust any Christians who did not fast, or invoke the saints, or believe that Christ is really present in the holy sacrament."

The latter statement is obviously directed towards Protestantism. As Van Donzel[80] has pointed out:

"We might say that after the dramatic experiences with the Portuguese a general xenophobia prevailed, and if this was principally directed against Roman Catholics, this was simply because Protestants were practically un-known before the arrival of Heyling."

It was in this context as well as through the patronage of Abuna Marqos that Peter Heyling, a German Protestant, from Lübeck entered Ethiopia during Fāsiladas' reign. That was seemingly contradictory to Fāsiladas' general policy of keeping Europeans out. Heyling succeeded, however, through his teaching of Protestantism and especially of Protestant dogma, his discussions with the local clergy, and his translation of religious prayers and hymns into Amharic, to make himself and Protestantism known in Ethiopia and to provoke anti-European feelings also to Protestants, such as the Dutch, as the above report of Poncet shows.

Heyling's role is summed up by Ḥoǧa Murād[81] quite suitably[82] in his answers given to Ludolf:

"Petrus Heylingh of Lubeck is said to have departed from Egypt to Ethi-opia with the Patriarch Markus about 60 years ago, giving himself out as a medicus, with which profession he is said to have made good profits over the period of 14 years; but since his great patron, the above-mentioned Patriarch Markus, fell into disgrace with the emperor, was attacked by the common people and put into prison, this Petrus Heylingh had to leave the country; the more so because he quarrelled too much with the Abyssinians about differences in religion and tried to propagate there the doctrine of Luther. This Petrus is said to have been murdered on his return journey by the Turks of Suaquen because of his great wealth and treasures."

It is clear that Heyling accompanying Abuna Marqos came to Ethiopia in the 4th year of Fāsiladas' reign (= September 1635 - September 1636). The patronage of the Abun and the fact that he was allowed in his entourage must have given the Ethiopians the impression that Heyling was a Copt, or at least non-Catholic, and that he must have been accorded a certain amount of "immunity".

However, when Heyling showed his interest in converting Ethiopians, as it was now, to Protestantism, his status soon wavered. His interference in the Qebātočč-Tawāḥdowočč contro-versy was obvious by statements such as:

"Now if he [Christ] has worshipped [God], as you say, Christ, thus, when he received the Unction in his function (Wesen) as a human being, bowed before the divine nature, how can it be wrong to say, Christ as a human being has worshipped himself as God?"[83]

However, no one dared to touch him as long as he enjoyed the protection of Abuna Marqos and the Emperor. When, however, Abuna Marqos had been deposed in 1649-50, i.e. in the 17th year of Fāsiladas' reign[84], the protection for Heyling dissipated, as Ḥoǧa Murād has it, after he had stayed in Ethiopia for 14 years. What happened to Heyling is still uncertain.[85] However, similar to Ḫoǧa Murād, a Franciscan Father relates that in 1650 the Pasha of Sawākin de-capitated a Dutchman by the name of Pietro Leone[86], that was Peter Heyling.[87]

Fāsiladas' son, Emperor Yoḥannes (1667-82), the second Gondarine Emperor, decided to take an even harder line towards the Europeans, as a passage in the *Tārika nagaśtāt* indicates. He followed a rigid policy of religious segregation. His first step was to expel most remaining Euro-peans out of the country. As his chronicle[88] confirms:

> "In those days, there arose great excitement among the monks, because of the Europeans. 'We should have had more prosperity,' they said, 'since the time of their arrival until the present, and now they should go for our sake and not stay with us any day or night longer.' Thereafter the Emperor sent them back, 133 years since their arrival during the reign of our Emperor Wanag Sagad, 1 year and 8 months after our Emperor Yoḥannes had ascended to the throne."

In conjunction with said religious segregation affecting also the Muslims and the Falāśa, Yoḥannes decreed regarding the Europeans in an *'awāǧ*[89]:

> "that the Europeans must return to their homeland and leave ours; how-ever, those who have come to our faith and have received our baptism and our Communion may stay here with us, if they prefer so, they can go."

There is some indication that Emperor Iyasu I (1682-1706), Yoḥannes' successor, adopted a more liberal attitude towards the Europeans. This may have been due to the influence of his concubine, Malākotāwit, who, as Poncet suggests, was supposed to be of European stock[90], and it was manifest at the occasion of said doctor Charles Jacques Poncet's arrival at the Ethiopian court at Gondar in 1700. He had been brought into Ethiopia by Ḥaǧǧi 'Alī via Sennar.

The change in foreign policy became also apparent in the contacts Iyāsu resumed and main-tained with the Holy See, as well as the cordial reception of an ambassador of the Pope, Father Joseph of Jerusalem, by the Emperor in Gondar in 1702.[91]

However, despite the friendly sentiments of the Emperor and some of the Mak^wānnent[92] and even the Abun[93], the Ethiopian people as a whole, especially the peasantry, were not pre-pared to accept non-Orthodox Europeans to the country for any protracted period of time. This is obvious from the answers given by Poncet during his interrogation through the French Consulate at Cairo[94] on the 23rd of June 1701, by which he confirmed:

> "1. That he was kept in seclusion all the time that he was in Ethiopia, and had many times been in danger of losing his life; insomuch that once, see-ing the risk the King ran in protecting him, a Frank, he had declared that he would rather kill himself than allow His Majesty to suffer on his behalf.
>
> 2. That the King was obliged to visit him in secret, using for this a private passage.
>
> 3. Asked whether it would be possible to introduce some missionaries into that country, he replied that he himself, though a mere layman, had had difficulty in preserving his life, and for others it would be almost imposs-ible. He added that two Fathers of the Propaganda, having since his depar-ture had the temerity to penetrate into that country and having been de-tected, had been forced to hide themselves in the house of the uncle of Mons. Murat, and that they would be very fortunate if they succeeded in making their escape from the country without being stoned to death.
>
> 4. Asked whether, if Mons. Murat were received in France and well

treated, if would be possible to induce the King of Ethiopia to receive a French envoy, he answered that such a reception did not depend on the King but on the monks, who were implacable enemies of all Franks. Asked whether such an envoy would be safe, he replied that he did not think so."

Indeed, life was hazardous for all Europeans in Ethiopia, not only by Poncet's opinion. The answers related from the said Monsieur Ḫoǧa Murād to the questions of two Dutch assistant-merchants, Hugo Hendrik van Bergen and Theodorus Zas, in Surat on 17 December 1797 pertaining to the possibility of Dutch citizens entering Ethiopia, corroborate this fully:[95]

"Concerning our mission to the king his master, he said that, when His Right Honourable the Governor-General had made a proposal to him about this, he in clear terms had declared that no success whatever could be expected in this matter, circumstantially explaining the reasons, namely: the prohibition that no Western foreigners were admitted into the kingdom; this [prohibition] had progressively been exacted from the kings after the Portuguese had been expelled and was carried out so strictly that the transgressors could not imagine anything being more sure than a fatal conclusion, of which there were several examples."

This is confirmed by the report of the *Tārika nagaśtāt* that Sāmu'ēl (= Samuele de Beano), Dāwit (= Liberatus Weiß of Konnersreuth) and Mikā'ēl (Michele Pio da Zerba of Padua) were stoned to death under Emperor Dāwit in 1716. The three missionaries had come to Ethiopia via Sennar and had settled in Aynā Egzi'e in Wālqāyt, an area which was later to serve as a place of imprisonment.[96] His predecessor, Yoṣṭos (1711-16), had frequently absconded while he was out hunting and visited these priests, watching them celebrate mass, while he believed he was incognito. Yoṣṭos, who had already been accused of being a "usurper"[97], was soon stuck with the reputation of having left "Orthodoxy" for Catholicism and was thus called a "heretic". When the new Emperor, Dāwit, came to power it was only logical that after the "heretic" had died, those who had, so to say, seduced him to conversion would have to die also.

Characteristic for the power structures within the Empire at that time was that the Emperor chose to let the clergy pass judgement over these missionaries in a Synod, the outcome being a foregone conclusion. When the three missionaries professed themselves to be followers of Pope Leo I (440-61) and supporters of the Council of Chalcedon (451), it was easy to imagine how the Ethiopian clergymen would get excited and perturbed. Their fanaticism went so far that a six year old boy, being called Michael and apparently the son of Michele Pio da Zerba, who had broken his vows by taking a Ethiopian wife, was stoned with them.[98]

Only one category of European seems to have been accepted within the country, those who as the *'awāǧ* of Emperor Yoḥannes prescribed converted to the Alexandrian faith and through intermarriage became Ethiopianised. Indeed such persons could hold high offices, as was already mentioned with regard to Empress Malākotāwit or the European Fāsil who was given a daughter of Emperor Fāsiladas for marriage, the death of their daughter being mentioned in the *Tārika nagaśtāt*.

Even if they had wished so, during the first half of the 18th century no Ethiopian Emperor could have afforded to allow Europeans to come into the country openly. A case in point is an incident during the reign of Emperor Iyāsu II (1730-55). Iyāsu apparently cultivated contacts with Europe and had Europeans, even missionaries, secretly enter the country. At any rate, in 1733 the Abun and the Eč̣aǧē came to the Neguś with the accusation that two Europeans were staying at the royal palace. Fortunately, as far as Iyāsu was concerned, two Egyptians named Demēṭros and Giyorgis, who had built a new type of boat for his predecessor Bakāffā (1721-60)[99], were still in the country. Sly as he was, Iyāsu let the two Egyptians come, who, as their name suggests, were Copts and upon the interrogation of the two church officials were proven to be adherents to the Alexandrian faith and, through derobing, seen to have been circumcized.[100] The meticulousness of the clergymen shows the predicament of the Neguś and the hatred of Europeans.

However, further on in Iyāsu's reign, a Franciscan expedition led by the Czech Remedius Prutský, accompanied by his countryman Martin Lang and a Syrian Antonius of Aleppo, arrived at Gondar on 19th March 1752. They were able to stay nine months with the Neguś' tolerance.[101] This was in many ways the beginning of new contacts with Europe, a change in the attitudes of some sections of the Ethiopian nobility towards the Europeans. This will be discussed in another study.

Significant for Ethiopian attitudes towards *Afranǧ* became two sayings in Amharic:[102]

ፈረንጆች እንደ ፈትል መርፌ ይገቡ እንደ ወርካ ይሰፉ ፨

farangočč enda fatel marfē yegabbu enda warka yesaffu = "The Europeans go in like a thread through a needle's eye, they spread like a sycamore."

የፈረንጅ አሽከር ነጭ ለባሽ ከላይ ወደ ታች የሻሕን አመላላሽ ፨

ya-franǧ aškar nač labāš kalāy wadda tāč ya-šaḥan[103] *amalālāš*= "The servant of a European in white suit is not allowed to do anything but carry the plates up and down."

Certainly such attitudes are marked by experiences which cannot have been merely positive, and, like most expressions of such kind, aforesaid sayings contain a kernel of truth.

Basically, *all* aliens coming to Ethiopia before the "Age of Colonialism" discovered that the independence[104] and religious character of Ethiopia were not to be tampered with and sooner or later all who refused to abide by these taboos faced massive Ethiopian resistance.

Especially, Ethiopian-European relations and Ethiopian attitudes towards aliens were characterized by periods of opening and closing the country for Europeans, as the Emperors saw fit. While Europeans could help the Emperors in solving their internal and external problems, to facilitate trade, especially to procure arms and other kinds of armour, they also brought many new problems, testing the tolerance of the indigenous population. Every Emperor knew that entering into relations with a European power also meant a potential encroachment on Ethiopia's sovereignty.

On the other hand, the Ethiopian Emperors were able to pursue a more consistent policy towards such *Oriental* foreigners (including Armenians, Arabs and other Muslims, as well as Greeks considered to be Orientals) who came to stay as immigrants or traders. For these had, in general terms, no interest in missionizing Ethiopia, but were mainly concerned with their economic activities and gains which proved also to be of advantage to the country of their hosts. Through their knowledge of Oriental languages and their ability to travel throughout the Near and Far East, Ethiopia's foreign trade and policies were greatly facilitated.

NOTES

1. A more comprehensive study is reserved for a monograph.

2. Variants of *afranǧ: franǧ* and *faranǧ*. On the use of "Frank" for European see: E. Littmann, "Fränkisch" in *Aufsätze zur Sprachgeschichte vornehmlich des Orients. Festschrift für E. Kuhn* (Breslau 1916), pp.237-43; F. A. Dombrowski, "Ṭānāsee 106: Eine Chronik der Herrscher Äthiopiens" in *Äthiopistische Forschungen*, Vol.12 (Wiesbaden 1983) (henceforth Ṭānāsee 106), p.156, note 40 (with further literature).

3. On the relationship of the various *Tārika nagaśtāt* to one another see Ṭānāsee 106, pp.25-29, 346. The following passages are by no means complete and, unless it is indicated otherwise, they were mainly taken from my monograph Ṭānāsee 106. For a comparison of the text with other *Tārika nagaśtāt* see the footnotes of my book.

4. Ṭānāsee 106, pp.36, 155 f., especially note 40.

5. Ṭānāsee 106, pp.45-47; 170-74.

6. I. Guidi, "Di due frammenti relativi alla storia di Abissinia" in *Rendiconti della Accademia dei Lincei. Classe di scienze morali, storiche e filologiche* (= *Rendiconti*) (Rome 1893) (henceforth Guidi, frammenti) p.586.

7. Ṭānāsee 106, pp.47 f.; 175 f.

8. Guidi, frammenti, p.587.

9. Ṭānāsee 106, pp.55; 192-94.

10. F. Béguinot, *La cronaca abbreviata d'Abissinia: nuova versione dall'Etiopico* (Rome 1901) (= Béguinot, cronaca), p.45.

11. Ṭānāsee 106, pp.53; 194.

12. Ṭānāsee 106, pp.53 f.; 195 f.

13. In the sense that the majority of the people, especially in the remote areas, had not seen Europeans, but only heard of them.

14. Béguinot, cronaca, p.47.

15. Ṭānāsee 106, pp.54; 196 f.

16. Béguinot, cronaca, p.48.

17. Ṭānāsee 106, pp.54; 197.

18. Béguinot, cronaca, p.48.

19. Ṭānāsee 106, pp.59; 205.

20. Ṭānāsee 106, pp.102; 264 f.

21. Ṭānāsee 106, pp.129; 286.

22. See Ṭānāsee 106, p.156, note 40.

23. Concerning Matthew and the role of Armenians in Ethiopia see the forthcoming part III of this study.

24. This ideal was still propagated in the 20th century, when Pope Pius XI gave his blessing to Mussolini's invasion of Ethiopia in 1935.

25. Like Rubenson's title (see note 104), Donald Crummey's *Priests and Politicians. Protestant and Catholic Missions in Orthodox Ethiopia 1830-1868* (Oxford 1972) is an appropriate characterization for times still further back.

26. On the campaign against Māḥfūẓ see C. Conti Rossini, "Storia di Lebna Dengel re d'Etiopia sino alle prime lotte contro Ahmad ben Ibrahim" in *Rendiconti* Ser. V, Vol. III (Rome 1894) pp.633-36.

27. See Ṭānāsee 106, pp.290-95.

28. See for instance the report of Miguel de Castanhoso in E. Littman, *Die Heldentaten des Dom Christoph da Gama in Abessinien. Nach dem portugiesischen Berichte des Miguel de Castanhoso* (Berlin 1907) (= Littmann, Heldentaten).

29. Littmann, Heldentaten, p.1.

30. Littmann, Heldentaten, p.84.

31. Ṭānāsee 106, pp.175 f., note 204.

32. *Ibid.*

33. This was certainly an oversimplification.

34. Manuel Fernandez, Gonçalo Gualdamez, Gonçalo Cardoso, Antonio Fernandez and Francisco Lopez (See Ṭānāsee 106, p.176, note 206).

35. Cf. H. Ludolf, *Ad suam Historiam Aethiopicam antehac editam Commentarius* (Frankfurt 1691), pp.237-41.

36. Ṭānāsee 106, p.48.

37. See the article "Patriarch" in Bibliographisches Institut, *Meyers Enzyklopädisches Lexikon*, Vol.18 (Mannheim 1976), pp.297 f.

38. See note 37.

39. So, for instance, the Turkish title of *Pasha* became *bāšā*, the title for a fusilier (cf. Ṭānāsee 106, p.300) and that of *Wazīr* for an official of medium rank (cf. Ṭānāsee 106, p.305).

40. E. Cerulli, "Gli abbati di Dabra Libānos, capi del monachismo etiopico, secondo la 'lista rimata' " in *Orientalia NS* (Rome 1944) p.153.

41. A. Bartnicki and J. Mantel-Niećko, *Geschichte Äthiopiens*, Vol.I (Berlin 1978), pp.141 f.

42. Ṭānāsee 106, pp.48; 177 f.

43. The 14th Eçagē who sat in the chair from 1552 until the 23rd of March 1559.

44. Of Dabra Māryām.

45. Originally I translated *tamawwe'e* with "you will gain victory" (Ṭānāsee 106, pp.48; 178), but the sense of "survive" is also known (see A. Dillman, *Lexicon linguae Aethiopicae* (Leipzig 1865, repr. New York 1955), col.205.

46. F. M. Esteves Pereira, *Historia de Minas, Ademās Sagad (1559-63)* (Lisbon 1881), p.39.

47. Ṭānāsee 106, pp.179, notes 222 and 226.

48. So he is known in the Chronicles (cf. Ṭānāsee 106, p.188, note 227).

49. He wrote letters to King Dom Henrique I and later to Philip II of Spain, who ascended to the Portuguese throne in 1580.

50. Cf. F. A. Dombrowski, *Ethiopia's Access to the Sea* (Leiden 1985) (= henceforth Dombrowski, Access).

51. F. A. Dombrowski, "Observations on Crown-Pretendership in 17th Century Russia and Ethiopia" (= Dombrowski, Crown-Pretendership) in S. Rubenson (ed.), *Proceedings of the Seventh International Conference of Ethiopian Studies* (Arlöv, Sweden 1984) (= Rubenson, Proceedings), p.235.

52. Dombrowski, Crown-Pretendership, p. 235.

53. *Ibid.*

54. Dombrowski, Crown-Pretendership, p.236.

55. Dombrowski, Crown-Pretendership, p.235.

56. On *warañña* see Dombrowski, Crown-Pretendership, pp.233-41.

57. Dombrowski, Crown-Pretendership, p.235.

58. *Ibid.*

59. E. A. W. Budge, *A History of Ethiopia, Nubia & Abyssinia (according to the Hieroglyphic Inscriptions of Egypt and Nubia and the Ethiopian Chronicles)* (London 1928; repr. Oosterhout N.B., Niederlande 1966), Vol.2, p.389.

60. Ṭānāsee 106, pp.290-95.

61. Ṭānāsee 106, p.328.

62. C. F. Beckingham and G. W. B. Huntingford, *Some Records of Ethiopia 1593-1646. Being Extracts from the History of High Ethiopia or Abassia by Manoel de Almeida. Together with Bahrey's History of the Galla = Works Issued by the Hakluyt Society*, Vol.CVII (London 1954) p.188.

63. For the different tribes involved see Ṭānāsee 106, p.190 f., note 289.

64. Dombrowski, Crown-Pretendership, pp.233-41.

65. F. M. Esteves Pereira, *Chronica de Susenyos, Rei de Etiopia* (Lisbon 1900), Vol.II, pp.126-30.

66. See above passage No.4.

67. Ṭānāsee 106, p.193, note 300.

68. See the chart in Dombrowski, Access, p.25f.

69. J. Bruce, *Travels to Discover the Sources of the Nile in the Years 1768-1773*, Vol.II (Edinburgh 1790), p.371.

70. R. K. P. Pankhurst, "Wag and Lasta: An Essay in the Regional History of Ethiopia from the 14th Century to 1800" in Rubenson, Proceedings, p.215.

71. On the rebellion in Lāstā see Pankhurst, *op. cit.*, pp.214-18 and Ṭānāsee 106, pp.195-98.

72. Cf. Dombrowski, Crown-Pretendership, p.241.

73. Ṭānāsee 106, p.196, note 324.

74. Ṭānāsee 106, p.197, note 329.

75. Dombrowski, Access, p.30.

76. Dombrowski, Access, p.30, note 4.

77. W. Foster, *The Red Sea and Adjacent Countries at the Close of the Seventeenth Century as Described by Joseph Pitts, William Daniel and Charles Jacques Poncet = Works Issued by the Hakluyt Society*, 100 (Cambridge 1949) (= Poncet) p.124 f.

78. *Ibid.*, p.120, note 2.

79. *Ibid.*, p.154 f.

80. E. Van Donzel, *Foreign Relations of Ethiopia 1642-1700. Documents relating to the Journeys of Khodja Murād* (Istanbul-Leiden 1979) (= Van Donzel, Foreign Relations) p.2.

81. *Ibid.*, p.99.

82. Certainly M. Kropp ["Ein äthiopischer Text zu Peter Heyling: Ein bisher unbeachtetes Fragment einer Chronik des Fāsiladas" (= Kropp, Heyling) in Rubenson, Proceedings, p.243] is stretching his point when he assesses the value of Ḫoğa Murād's reports on Heyling as "die spärlichen und recht wirren Aussagen die der Ḫwaga Murād, ein Gesandter des äthiopischen Königs und die Holländer in Batavia machte; er beantwortete einen Fragenkatalog Ludolfs über Äthiopien!".

83. Kropp, Heyling, p.248.

84. Van Donzel, Foreign Relations, p.228, note 93.

85. See Kropp, Heyling, pp.249 f.

86. Cf. Kropp, Heyling, pp.251 f., note 45.

87. *Ibid.*

88. I. Guidi, "Annales Ioḥannis, Iyasu I, Bākāffa" in *CSCO* 23 and 25 (1903) (= Guidi, Annales), p.9.

89. *Ibid.*, p.8.

90. See note 78 above.

91. Dombrowski, Access, p.36.

92. For instance see Poncet's report.

93. Poncet, pp.122 f.

94. Poncet, pp.174 f.

95. Van Donzel, Foreign Relations, pp.111 f.

96. Especially during the rule of Bakaffa (1721-30); cf. Tanasee 106, pp.312 f.

97. Concerning Yoṣtos' legitimacy see the discussion in Dombrowski, Access, p.27, note 41.

98. Ṭānāsee 106, p.265, notes 790-93.

99. Guidi, Annales, pp.336-39.

100. I. Guidi, "Annales Regum 'Iyasu II et Iyo'as" in *CSCO*, 62 (1912), p.80.

101. Dombrowski, Access, p.38.

102. In I. Guidi, *Vocabulario amarico-italiano* (Rome 1901; repr. Rome 1953) col.374.

103. = Arabic *saḥn*, "bowl, dish, plate". Cf. H. Wehr-J. M. Cowan (eds.), *A Dictionary of Modern Written Arabic* (3rd ed.: Ithaca, N.Y. 1976), p.505.

104. In many respects Sven Rubenson has been fortunate with the title of his book *The Survival of Ethiopian Independence* (London 1976).

THE TA'ĀMRA 'ĪYASŪS:

A Study of Textual and Source-Critical Problems

S. Gerö

Biblical apocrypha constitute a particularly fascinating genre of ancient Ethiopic literature. Though Old Testament apocrypha are better known — here one can mention, for example, the Book of Enoch, the Book of Jubilees, the Fourth Book of Ezra or the Ascension of Isaiah — several works which can best be subsumed under the designation "Apocryphal New Testament" are equally valuable for the student of early Christian literature and traditions. Here one should note, in particular, the so-called Epistle of Apostles, extant in a fragmentary Coptic and also a complete Ethiopic version, the original of which work apparently goes back to the second century. There is a plethora of other pseudo-apostolic literature, much of which is not of narrative or apocalyptic but of canonical, legal character; and Ethiopic version of the Didascalia, the Sinodos, and the very rich pseudo-Clementine collection, the Qalēmenṭos.[1] There are also some texts which can be designated as apocryphal gospels; narratives pertaining to the period of the passion of Jesus, such as the "The Gospel of Gamaliel", which is connected with a larger group of Marian homilies; there are of course a large number of nativity legends pertaining to the Protevangelium, the story of the conception and birth of Jesus and the flight to Egypt, which can be broadly classified under the heading of Marian legends. But — and this bears emphasizing in connection with the immediate subject of this paper — the famous collection of the Miracles of Mary, the *Ta'āmra Māryām* (henceforth abbreviated to *TM*), by contrast should *not* be classified as a New Testament apocryphon. Rather, this collection of wonders performed to reward the devotee of the cult of the Virgin, often expressed in the form of veneration of her image, should be classified as hagiography, with the posthumous wonders, *ta'āmer* of martyrs or collections of miracles of angels. (Furthermore, it is well known that the *TM*, to a great extent, go back to a twelfth-century western source, via an Arabic intermediary[2] : the sources of our text, the *Ta'āmra 'Īyasūs* are older and — with one significant exception, to be discussed later — as far as identifiable, "oriental".)

The collection entitled Miracles of Jesus, *Ta'āmra 'Īyasūs* (henceforth abbreviated to *TI*) is, to be sure, not a straightforward gospel narrative; it is a compilation which includes much material not of a directly biographical nature, as well as long apocalyptic discourses. Though not all aspects of Jesus' life and work are treated in equal detail, and the chronological sequence of the episodes is at times confused, the work is nevertheless a "complete" gospel, insofar as it provides information ranging from the events of the nativity to those of passion and the resurrection. This is particularly noteworthy, because "complete" apocryphal gospels are relatively few, in contrast to texts which are devoted to only one particular portion of Jesus' life. The core is formed by a sequence of miracles performed by Jesus which, in contrast to the global and, so to speak, timeless perspective of the *TM*, take place in the concrete geographical setting of Palestine prior to and during the period of Jesus' public ministry. Though healing wonders are by no means absent, more characteristic are the miracles in which Jesus demonstrates his mastery over the animal world and the forces of nature in general. Furthermore, it is of particular interest, and will concern us later, that in the majority of the manuscripts of the *TI* one finds embedded a version of the so-called infancy gospel of Thomas, miracles performed by the child Jesus between the ages of five and twelve, or, alternatively, isolated episodes from another affiliated cycle of infancy legends.

The *TI* is a work which has been somewhat neglected in modern research; this neglect is all the more strange in view of the popularity and the liturgical employment of the work, reflected in the large number of extant manuscripts. The *TI*, when mentioned at all in histories of Ethiopic literature, are usually lumped together with the *TM* and similar collections.[3] The very title of the *TI* — which disguises the basically biographical framework of this composition — may well have been influenced by that of the *TM*. Research to be sure was and still is hampered by the lack of a complete critical edition. Only about two thirds of the text has been published in a European edition[4]; even long before the death of the editor, Sylvain Grébaut in 1955, the edition had been interrupted (the last instalment of the text appeared in 1923) and there is no sign of its continuation to be seen. The contents of the work have been, to be sure, generally made known for a longer time through Grébaut's preliminary description[5] and his publication of some extracts of particular interest.[6]

Some of the *TI* material is also included in the well-known printed lectionary for Passion Week, the *Gebra hemāmāt*.[7] The liturgical usage of the *TI* is indicated by the numbered divisions and the incorporation of stereotyped blessings of various individuals at the beginning and end of each *te'emert*; these individuals can only in part be identified with possessors of the several Ethiopic manuscripts. The actual division of the text into numbered miracles, however, may have been already a feature of the Arabic *Vorlage*. It is by reason of liturgical employment of the text that one finds an interweaving of *TM* and *TI* material in some late manuscripts (in particular, Uppsala Nr.32, with the title *Ta'āmra Māryām wa-'Iyasūs*).[8]

Grébaut had early conjectured in a general fashion that the *TI* were either translated from an Arabic text or at least were based on Arabic sources; he overlooked the fact that an Arabic fragment of a collection of miracles of Jesus, published already in 1899, admittedly from a single, late manuscript, dated A.D. 1599, gives a text close to a portion of the Arabic original of the *TI*.[9] The complete Arabic text, was subsequently identified and published[10], on the basis of a manuscript in the Biblioteca Ambrosiana in Milan, dated A.D. 1342[11]; the work is presented there only as the apocryphal book, of the apostle John not, as in Ethiopic, under the specific title of "miracles of Jesus". Subsequently it was discovered that there is an even older Arabic manuscript of this work, which gives in places a better, more complete text, *Sinaiticus arab.* 441, dated A.D. 1196 and that at least one further manuscript of early date contains extracts from the work (*Sinaiticus* 531, dated A.D. 1232).[12] That an Arabic text close to the one in the Milan manuscript, though not identical with it, underlies the *TI* has been satisfactorily demonstrated, though no systematic collation of the *TI* text with the entire Arabic material at our disposal has as yet been undertaken.[13] The Arabic text, in turn, was either translated from Syriac, as it is explicitly claimed in the colophon at the Milan manuscript[14], or, as is more likely, it is based in part on Syriac sources. The date of compilation or composition is difficult to fix precisely, but on the basis of some very slender indices (employment of an 8th-century source; possible references to the caliph al-Hakim) it has been dated to the late 10th or 11th century.[15] In any case it is now abundantly clear that the *TI* as a whole is no late medieval Ethiopic compilation. It has been conjectured that the text was translated from Arabic into Ethiopic in the fourteenth century, during the time of Abba Salama (1348-88)[16]; the earliest Ethiopic manuscript can be dated in any case to the fifteenth century and the *TI* is registered in a list of books given by Zar'a Ya'qob to the monastery Dabra Karbē.[17] It is important to note, however, that in the Arabic manuscripts one section of the *TI* does not appear at all, namely the eighth "miracle" of the Ethiopic text, the infancy gospel of Thomas material. For this no other Arabic *Vorlage* has as yet been identified, though the infancy gospel has an unusually rich direct textual tradition in Syriac, Greek, Latin, Georgian and even Church Slavonic, as well as reworkings in Arabic and Armenian.[18]

Grébaut for his edition collated only a small number of manuscripts readily available to him, and as the basis he chose, unfortunately, a manuscript (d'Abbadie 168) which exhibits a deviant type of text; the continuation of the edition should be based on more reliable manuscripts, closer to the now available Arabic original.[19] A preliminary listing by Conti Rossini already indicated no less than 26 manuscripts in European libraries which include the *TI*; in the meanwhile more have come to light, not to speak of all of the many manuscripts in Ethiopia itself.[20] The oldest manuscript, as noted already, dates from the 15th century, but most are of course considerably more recent. Nevertheless, the development of the text can be reconstructed with some degree of probability. The original translation from Arabic did not include any of the infancy gospel material, though the oldest manuscript already has one "infancy"-type addition.[21] This early (14th century ?) translation, divided into 42 sections, is represented by a relatively small number of manuscripts. It was on the one hand abbreviated by excising some of the sections and on the other hand was supplemented through the addition of the infancy gospel material. The "vulgate" version, printed by Grébaut, includes a complete version of the infancy gospel; this was at first appended at the end of the collection, but later was inserted at a chronologically more appropriate place.[22] A second group of manuscripts has only a few isolated stories of a group of three infancy miracles; for the sake of convenience at least, we can call this a second recension of the infancy gospel.[23]

Let us first turn to the "vulgate' version and the sources of this special infancy gospel material. The sequence of episodes is as follows: (1) Jesus forms birds out of mud and makes them come alive; (2) Jesus curses the son of Hanna the scribe, who withers up; (3) Jesus curses the boy who struck his shoulder and the boy dies. Joseph reprimands the child Jesus; (4) Jesus is sent to school, he expounds the riddle of the alphabet; (5) Jesus rouses the boy Zeno, who fell off the roof; (6) Jesus carries water in his cloak; (7) Jesus stretches and shortens pieces of wood to help Joseph in his trade; (8) the further variant versions of the story of Jesus in School and the arcane meaning of the alphabet; (9) Jesus heals Jacob, the son of Joseph, bitten by a viper; (10) paraphrase of the canonical story, from the gospel of Luke, of the child Jesus in the Temple. Finally two very short episodes: (11) Jesus rides on a sunbeam; and (12) he reaps a miraculously great harvest.

Now quite generally one can say that this Ethiopic infancy material corresponds most closely to the old Syriac version of the Gospel of Thomas, as preserved in Brit. Libr. Add. 14484, dating from the sixth century, rather than to the extant Greek and Latin versions and their derivatives, attested by much more recent manuscript evidence. Only one miracle of the Ethiopic is lacking in the Syriac, our No.10, Jesus riding on the sunbeam; this episode in amplified form appears also in the second recension and will be further discussed in that connection. The appearance of the miraculous harvest episode as an appendix in the Ethiopic, rather than at an earlier point, as in the Syriac and other versions, finds no ready explanation. To be sure, there are differences in the exact wording of the Ethiopic and the old Syriac, and on occasion the Ethiopic has banal, secondary readings. But on the whole the agreement is very close indeed, and in the Ethiopic we have a text-form close to one which was current in the 5th-6th centuries and a complete witness, comparable to or superior in value to the fragmentary Georgian version.[24] Direct translation from Syriac is possible but unlikely, especially since the names of the first letters of the alphabet are given as *alpha* and *beta*, Greek forms rather than Syriac or Ethiopic. It is tempting to suppose that the immediate *Vorlage* of the Ethiopic text incorporated in the *TI* was a lost Greek text which faithfully corresponded to the old Syriac, in contrast to the text of the reworked Greek manuscripts, and that this translation from the Greek dates from the pre-Islamic period.[25] The problem, of course, is that there is no trace of the independent existence of such an early translation of the infancy gospel, unless one takes the occurrence of the episode of Jesus in school in the *Epistula Apostolorum* to be such. The alternative hypothesis, of course, would be to assume a late — fourteenth or fifteenth century? — translation of an Arabic version of the infancy gospel; there is no evidence for such a version elsewhere, and it would not explain the very real textual affinities with the old Syriac.

Matters are less clear when it comes to the second recension, since here one cannot point to a single *Vorlage*, be it in Syriac, Arabic or in Greek. The sequence of the three episodes, when all are present, is: (1) Jesus rides on the sunbeam[26]; (2) Jesus makes birds of clay and animates them; and (3) Jesus mixes and separates the red and black ink of his teacher. Leaving aside the first episode for special treatment, it seems that (2) and (3) depend on, and elaborate, material from the corresponding episodes of the first recension. In (2) the story is really about the wish of other children to imitate Jesus' miraculous ability, and Jesus' reluctant granting of the request, but only once, to a particularly importunate child. There is no parallel material from other versions, and we may well deal with an Ethiopic elaboration of the legend. The situation seems to be similar in (3); a redactor, who found the wrath of the teacher inadequately motivated by the words of Jesus about Alpha and Beta, interpolated a childish prank, with the miraculous denouement, and for good measure put the acknowledgement of the fulfilment of the Emmanuel prophecy into the mouth of the teacher. It is possible that the unscrambling of the coloured inks is a variant of the miracle of the dyer, found not in the infancy gospel proper, but in some later texts, in particular in Arabic and Armenian[27], as well as in one Coptic manuscript fragment.[28]

In the episode of the sunbeam, as found in this second recension, the connection with an episode in the vulgate version is again present – instead of making the children play on a roof, the text here makes their attempt to imitate Jesus in riding the sunbeam the source of the fatal accident, for which the parents blame Jesus. The simple miracle of Jesus on the sunbeam by itself is, as noted, found in the vulgate version. Are we then dealing with a simple combination of the two episodes in the course of the development of the Ethiopic text itself? This is, of course, a possibility; but curiously the very same combination occurs, not in the major Greek and Syriac versions, but in "fringe" versions, in Latin texts (one late recension of the Latin pseudo-Matthew and the *Liber de infantia salvatoris*), in the Armenian infancy gospel and, very curiously, the closest parallel, one Slavonic version[29], which may here depend exceptionally on a Latin, rather than a Greek source. So it could well be that the story migrated from west to east and – perhaps via a hypothetical Arabic intermediary – entered the Ethiopic tradition. If this is the case, then the shorter variant in the vulgate version – found, one should recall, in an appendix, not in the body of the narrative – should be regarded as a later extract from this more original version in the second recension.

In this necessarily brief and partial survey of the problems posed by this text of the *TI*, several hypothetical connections have been proposed; much more extensive and detailed study of the *TI* and the parallel material would be needed to put some of the hypotheses on a firm footing. The *TI* is a potentially important and interesting text, which has demonstrable links to apocrypha of an earlier period. The dependence of the *TI* on the extant Arabic *Vorlage* indicates interesting medieval cultural connections with Syria and Palestine, not with Egypt for once, perhaps via the clearing house of Sinai monasticism. The analysis of the infancy gospel section showed that the text, even though the translation and redaction have to be dated fairly late, goes back to early Syriac textual traditions. In short, in the *Ta'āmra 'Iyasūs*, we have a jewel of Ethiopic apocryphal literature which clearly deserves, and surely would reward, further study.

NOTES

1. See in general E. Hammerschmidt, "Das pseudo-apostolische Schrifttum in äthiopischer Überlieferung", *Journal of Semitic Studies*, 9(1964), pp.114-21.

2. E. Cerulli, *Il libro etiopico dei miracoli di Maria*, (Rome, 1943), pp.17ff.

3. For example in I. Guidi, *Storia della letteratura etiopica*, (Rome, 1932), p.63.

4. S. Grébaut (ed.), "Les Miracles de Jésus", *Patrologia Orientalis*, 12 (1919), pp.550-652; 14(1920), pp.767-844; 17(1923), pp.783-857, breaking off with "miracle" no.30 (Baptism and Temptation of Jesus).

5. S. Grébaut, "Aperçu sur les Miracles de Notre Seigneur", *Revue de l'Orient Chrétien*, 16(1911), pp.255-65, 356-67; 21(1918-19), pp.94-99.

6. For example, S. Grébaut and A. Roman, "Un passage eschatologique des Miracles de Jésus", *Aethiops*, 3(1930), pp.35ff, 132ff.

7. E. Hammerschmidt, art. "Gebra hemāmāt", in J. Aßfalg and P. Krüger (eds.), *Kleines Wörtebuch des Christlichen Orients*, (Wiesbaden, 1975), p.117.

8. O. Löfgren, *Katalog über die äthiopischen Handschriften in der Universitätsbibliothek Uppsala*, (Stockholm, 1974), p.105.

9. W. Scott Watson, "A Syriac-Arabic Narrative of Miracles of Jesus", *American Journal of Semitic Languages*, 16(1899/1900), pp.37-46.

10. I. Galbiati, (ed. and Latin trans.), *Iohannis evangelium apocryphum arabice . . .* (Milan, 1957). For a critique of this edition see O. Löfgren in *Orientalische Literaturzeitung 56 (1961)*, pp.230-33; the same author also published a complete Swedish translation (*Det apokryfiska Johannesevangeliet*, [Stockholm, 1967]).

11. For a description of the manuscript, which includes some other texts also, see O. Löfgren and R. Traini, *Catalogue of the Arabic Manuscripts in the Bibliotheca Ambrosiana*, (Milan, 1975), pp.9-10.

12. M. van Esbroeck, "A propos de l'évangile apocryphe arabes attribué à Saint Jean", *Mélanges de l'Université Saint Joseph*, 49(1975-76), pp.597ff.

13. See O. Löfgren, "Ergänzendes zum apokryphen Johannesevangelium", *Orientalia Suecana*, 9(1960), pp.140-41.

14. I. Galbiati, *op. cit.*, p.267, line 2.

15. O. Löfgren, "Zur Charakteristik des apokryphen Johannesevangeliums", *Orientalia Suecana*, 9(1960), pp.128-29.

16. O. Löfgren, *op. cit.*, p.113.

17. See *Annales d'Éthiopie*, Vol.1, p.107.

18. See my article "The Infancy Gospel of Thomas: A Study of the Textual and Literary Problems", *Novum Testamentum*, 13(1971), pp.46-80.

19. O. Löfgren, "Ergänzendes . . .", p.142.

20. For a listing of manuscripts see V. Arras and L. van Rompay, "Les manuscrits éthiopiens des 'Miracles de Jésus'. . . ", *Analecta Bollandiana*, 93(1975), pp.133ff.

21. *Vat. Cerulli Etiop.*, 238. See Arras and van Rompay, *op. cit.*, p.142.

22. *Op. cit.*, p.144.

23. *Op. cit.*, p.145.

24. L. van Rompay, "De ethiopische versie van het Kindheidsevangelie volgens Thomas de Israeliet", in A. Théodoridès *et al.* (eds.), *L'enfant das les civilisations orientales*, (Louvain, 1980), pp.120ff. My own earlier brief evaluation dismissing the textual value of the Ethiopic as but a secondary witness ("The Infancy Gospel of Thomas", p.55) is accordingly to be corrected.

25. Van Rompay, *op. cit.*, p.132, n.47.

26. I am grateful to Prof. van Rompay for putting a photocopy and his Latin translation of the portion of *Vat. Cerulli Etiop.*, 125, folios 122v-123r, containing this episode, at my disposal. The other episodes of the second recension are readily accessible in A. Grohmann, "Reste einer neuer Rezension der Kindheitsgeschichte Jesu in den Ta'āmra 'Iyasūs", *Wiener Zeitschrift für die Kunde des Morgenlandes*, 28(1914), pp.1ff. The epi-

sode of the coloured ink was also edited *inter alia* by S. A. Turaev, "Efioskie melkie teksty", *Khristianskij Vostok*, 1(1912), p.57.

27. See "The Infancy Gospel of Thomas", p.58 (No.18).

28. W. E. Crum, *Catalogue of the Coptic Manuscripts in the Collection of the John Rylands Library, Manchester*, (Manchester, 1909), p.44.

29. "The Infancy Gospel of Thomas", p.57 (No.6*).

THE MEDITERRANEAN CONTEXT FOR

THE MEDIEVAL ROCK-CUT CHURCHES

OF ETHIOPIA*

Michael Gervers
University of Toronto

Numerous theories have been proposed to explain the widespread phenomenon of medieval rock-cut ecclesiastical architecture in Ethiopia. Some writers have suggested that it owes its origins to the influence of foreign ascetics coming from Egypt and Syria, where holy grottos and rock-cut places of worship are not unusual.[1] Others have looked to the Indian rock-cut temples as a source of inspiration, while still others see a transformation of previously pagan sites to Christian ones.[2] There may be some truth in all of these, but the problem of origins and influences is further compounded by the lack of a reliable chronological framework. With the exception, perhaps, of the monuments at Lalibela, Ethiopia's rock-cut churches have to this point proved to be undateable. It is now generally accepted that architectural style can be traced back to the early capital at Axum,[3] but this link is unsatisfactory for questions of dating because the influential buildings there predate the introduction of Christianity to the area in the fourth century. In the absence of corroborating archaeological materials, researchers have had little to go on other than local tradition. Such evidence is, however, far from satisfactory and one must be careful not to build too heavily on these questionable foundations.

In an attempt to explain the existence of rock-cut ecclesiastical architecture in Ethiopia, we note that rock-cut monasteries, churches, chapels and cells are common to both eastern and western Christian worlds and seem to stem from the eastern Mediterranean, more specifically from the Holy Land. Thus, we find them in Spain, France, Germany, Hungary, Italy, Malta, Greece, Bulgaria, Roumania, various provinces of Anatolia, Armenia, the Ukraine, Georgia, Syria and Egypt.[4] Ethiopia's close and early ties with Coptic Egypt and Syria would be sufficient to provide access to the traditions current in the rest of the Christian world and it is those traditions which seem most likely to have been responsible for encouraging the introduction of rock-cut ecclesiastical architecture to the area.

Such influences could, indeed, have been present from the fourth century, and they would have been regularly, if not constantly, renewed by contacts with Egypt, Ethiopia's gateway to the Mediterranean. Those contacts would have emphasized the ascetic and often anchoretic quality of Christianity in Egypt, itself derived from the influence of the early Desert Fathers. Dr. Richard Pankhurst, and others, pointed out already long ago how the revered Ethiopian ascetic, Moses the Black, lived during the late fourth century in the desert of Scetis.[5]

Important for the history of monasticism in Ethiopia is the tradition associated with the Nine Saints who evangelized the country in the late fifth and sixth centuries. According to tradition, one of these, St. Aragawi, founder of Debre Damo in the late fifth century, received his habit directly from St. Pachomius (c. 290-346).[6] Meinardus claims that the other eight who accompanied him came from the monastery of St. Anthony.[7] The veracity of this legend notwithstanding, the ties between them and Saints Anthony and Pachomius were reportedly close. This group may well have translated into Geez Pachomius' Rule. Similarly, the nine are thought to have translated Athanasius' *Life of St. Anthony* as well as the *Life of St. Paul the Hermit* (+c. 347).[8] Both of these highly respected Desert Fathers ended their long lives in caves.[9] The physical environment of these figures cannot have been overlooked by the Ethiopian monks, many of whose lives, or *gadl*, describe as having also lived in caves. Saints' lives are known generally to be derivative and to have borrowed much of their content from the biographies of the early Christian Fathers. Be that as it may, there is a sufficient number of rock-hewn sites in Ethiopia to enable us to conclude that the Ethiopian ascetic had a particular predilection for living in caves or grottos. R. Sauter has even proposed that some of the country's rock churches were the handywork of missionary saints who evangelized the area from the sixth to the fifteenth century. He cites in particular Saint Aron who, with his disciples, having first visited Lalibela, went south to Takazze where for several years they undertook the excavation of churches from the rock.[10]

For lack of a long-called-for inventory of medieval rock-cut ecclesiastical sites in Ethiopia, it is impossible to determine the numbers involved or even to draw any conclusions about their popularity in comparison with free-standing structures, many of which have disappeared. Needless to say, several hundred have been documented and these alone are sufficient to make Ethiopia one of the most important areas for this architectural phenomenon in the Christian world. One may suspect that the motivating factor behind their creation lies in the continuously renewed influence which the ascetic strain of desert monasticism had on the kingdom. In the absence of anything but occasional urbanization, and of the accumulation of wealth in rural areas, this ecclesiastical life style became symbolic of the Christian Church in Ethiopia.

Nothing of what has been said to this point explains why so many individual monks and monastic communities excavated churches, chapels and cells from the rock when they might just as well have built free-standing monuments. One argument might be that since rock-cut architecture requires no structural support, it could be created with little architectural knowledge other than a sense of design and proportion. In other words, one could copy interior form from free-standing monuments without having the technical or engineering skills to build them. This argument bears some plausibility in the context of a society, especially a small monastic one, which lacked architects. But, from what we know about medieval free-standing ecclesiastical architecture in Ethiopia, it is clear that technical know-how was available. Furthermore, when confronted with the complex of monolithic structures at Lalibela, and the symbolic meaning which can be attached to that place, it is difficult to imagine that the idea of working in the rock was anything but specific and intentional, the availability of architects notwithstanding.

Whatever the reason for creating a rock-cut church, Lalibela very probably stood behind the inspiration for other rock-cut churches in the country, whether they were built earlier or later. We have already pointed to a tradition which was almost certainly introduced by the early missionary saints coming from, or via, Coptic Egypt. In view of the widespread occurrence of medieval rock-cut architecture not only in Ethiopia, but more particularly in Christian lands elsewhere, one must ask what it was that led Christians to this architectural medium in the first place. We have mentioned the ascetic tradition, but it too must have had specific origins.

The earthly or terrestrial Jerusalem, confused from early Christian times with the Heavenly City described by St. Paul, was considered in the middle ages to be the centre of the world. There was always a strong attraction to that city, hence the layman's desire to go there to obtain salvation of his soul by physical association with the site of Christ's passion, and particularly with his burial place, the Holy Sepulchre. When he preached the crusade at Clermont in 1095, Pope Urban II is purported to have said: "Let the Holy Sepulchre of our Lord and saviour . . . especially arouse you . . . Enter upon the road to the Holy Sepulchre . . ."[11]

Obviously, not all Christians could make their way to the Holy City. They, like those who had been there, fervently desired to associate themselves with it *in absentia*. Like a relic, they wanted to have Jerusalem in their midst and, because association with the holy brought them closer to salvation, they honored those who in one way or another had experienced the mysteries of the Holy Sepulchre, the site of Christ's Resurrection. In order to bring Jerusalem home they created symbolic images of that site in many ways and in many places outside the Holy City. It may be argued that one such image took a monumental form in the shape of the rock-cut church or chapel.

Taken as a whole, medieval rock-cut ecclesiastical sites demonstrate one aspect of an early pan-Mediterranean monastic culture, which, as Peter Brown has pointed out, was unaware of any distinction between East and West. "It is important to stress," said he, "the horizontal unity of the Mediterranean."[12] The churches also demonstrate the great veneration which early Christians reserved for the places connected with Christ's life.

The ground plans of many of the Spanish and south Italian rock-cut churches, show that they resemble each other in their Byzantine form, frequently a cross-in-square plan. Attention has frequently been drawn to their architectural similarities with the many rock-cut monastic complexes in Cappadocia, and there are obvious historical grounds for believing that the earliest examples in Italy's once Byzantine province of Basilicata are attributable to Basilian monks.[13]

The same cannot be said of the French rock-cut churches, whose ground plans and architectural form seem, like those in Ethiopia, to be inspired above all by free-standing local models. Formal disparities arising from differences in historical and liturgical development, not to mention size, (one of the French examples represents over 15,000 cubic metres of excavated space), thus render it impossible to speak in terms of a common Byzantine origin. To make any sense of the problem at all one must look further afield and consider medieval rock-cut ecclesiastical architecture as a whole.

With the exception of the many sites located in southern Italy, the numbers occurring in Europe are relatively small. But, from the shores of the Bosphorus, northwards to Kiev, eastwards from Phrygia in Anatolia to Armenia, to Syria and south-east to Ethiopia, they represent an integral part of medieval ecclesiastical architecture. In short, their occurrence can for all practical purposes be associated with the territory of the later Roman Empire and its border and border-influenced areas, a factor which suggests that their appearance is neither coincidental, nor the unconscious result of a haphazard series of circumstances. Appearing for the most part in areas dominated by Orthodox Christianity, they would appear to derive from an ancient tradition, which drew renewed vitality from the very words of the Gospels themselves.

In pursuit of this argument, we remember from the gospels according to Matthew that Christ was buried in a rock-cut tomb, whence he was resurrected.

> And when Joseph had taken the body, he wrapped it in a clean linen cloth, and laid it in his own new tomb, which he had hewn out in the rock. (27: 59-60)

Rock-cut churches are not tombs, although, judging from the number of rock-cut burials associated with them, the idea of the martyrium is by no means absent. One may postulate, on the other hand, that they are a symbolic expression both of Christ's tomb, and also of his birthplace, situated by tradition and early apocryphal scripture in a grotto at Bethlehem. The following quote is from the second century *Protevangelium* of James (ch.12.10 to 14.12):[14]

> And Mary said to Joseph, Take me down from the ass, for that which is in me presses to come forth . . . And he found there a cave, and let her into it. And leaving her . . . in the cave, Joseph went forth to seek a Hebrew midwife in the village of Bethlehem . . . And the midwife went along with him, and stood in the cave. Then a bright cloud overshadowed the cave . . . But on a sudden the cloud became a great light in the cave, so that their eyes could not bear it. But the light gradually decreased, until the infant appeared, and sucked the breast of his mother Mary.

The iconographical potential of this story was not overlooked by medieval Byzantine artists who frequently represented the Nativity in a cave. If tradition rather than reality placed Christ's birthplace there, the result was to serve as a prefiguration of the Entombment, and consequently the Resurrection.

The image of Christ's birth as portrayed in the *Protevangelium* is that of the introduction of light, or enlightenment, to darkness, that is, to the cave which is the world of mankind in microcosm. In this context Christ continues an Oriental tradition of the sun god, represented in Zoroastrianism, for example, by Mithras who was born miraculously from a rock in a cave.[15] He further continues the ancient association of gods with rocks and mountain cults.[16]

The cave has another meaning in eastern cosmology and that is clearly expressed in the second half of the third century A.D. by Porphyry (A.D. ca. 232-305) in his *De antro nympharum*' There, he writes that "The Persians call the place a cave where they introduce an initiate to the mysteries, revealing to him the path by which souls descend and go back again".[17] Grottos, says he, "are proper to genesis and departure from genesis."[18] In other words, one enters life through the darkness of the cave, and departs from it in the same fashion. Prophyry was writing in terms of the Mithraic cave, but one can see how a similar symbolic meaning was conveyed through the popular tradition of Christ's birth, or genesis, in a cave, and his burial, after death, or departure from genesis, in a rock-cut tomb. It was only natural that from that rock-cut tomb he should be born again, or resurrected.

Specific grotto sites were already venerated as the places of Christ's birth and burial when, in the second quarter of the fourth century, Constantine built the monumental centrally planned martyria sanctuaries as part of the churches of the Nativity in Bethlehem and of the Holy Sepulchre in Jerusalem.[19] From these beginnings, based on scripture, grew the association of grottos and rock-cut sanctuaries with Christ's birth and death. His resurrection from the tomb was to attach to such formations, whether natural or man-made, the theme of salvation and deliverance. How better then could a monk or hermit prepare himself for the life to come than to pass the rest of his days in a rock-cut environment? How better to experience the birth and passion of Christ than to live, if not to die, in surroundings His own body had experienced. It was a step, albeit an ascetic one, towards the life everlasting, and far more meaningful for a monk than to sully himself by going on pilgrimage to the terrestrial Jerusalem.

The period which saw the appearance of the first rock-cut churches as such is undetermined, although Christians undoubtedly made use of caves for celebrating the Eucharist from very early on. A valuable description of an early *European* cave church occurs in the ninth-century account of the dedication of St. Michael's church at Siponto, on Mount Gargano in Italy's Apulia:

> The holy church of St. Michael is situated upon the high summit of a
> mountain, and appeared in the form of a cave . . . That house was
> made cornerwise or oblong, not quite after the custom of men's
> work, so that the walls should be straight, but it appeared rather like
> a cavern; and frequently the stones projected steeply as from a cliff.
> The roof also was of various heights — in one place a man might
> hardly reach it with his hand, and in another easily touch it with his
> head . . .[20]

Judging from the description, this church was quite unaltered from its natural obviously cavernous state.

The French scholar Nicole Thierry has convincingly dated the paintings in a Cappadocian rock-cut church to the fifth or early sixth century. She further postulates "that monks inhabited rock-cut dwellings from the inception of monasticism in Asia Minor",[21] that is to say, the 3rd century. The Cappadocian examples differ from the description of St. Michael's at Siponto in that most were carefully fashioned in imitation of free-standing Byzantine architecture. Their formal appearance notwithstanding, there seems sufficient evidence that rock-cut and cave churches (to be distinguished from oratories and chapels) had entered the Christian architectural repertory of Asia Minor by the sixth century, and southern Europe by the eighth.

The dating of Byzantine rock-cut architecture has invariably been based on the style of the paintings which adorn their interiors. Many of these, such as the simple red crosses with geometric borders, point to the Iconoclastic period, and it may well be that the same period which saw monks fleeing to Italy also resulted in a significant increase in the rock-cut ecclesiastical architecture of Phrygia and Cappadocia. Dating through decorative style can also be applied to monuments in such major Italian centres of rock-cut religious architecture as Matera, where the earliest paintings are thought to be Carolingian in origin.[22]

The evidence of painting can, however, only provide the latest possible date for a monument, for it would have been applied after, perhaps a long time after, the original excavation had taken place. As a consequence, and for lack of additional documentary or archaeological information, one is obliged to turn to the less satisfactory method of dating by style and by a comparison of local sites. The dating of any rock-cut structure by architectural style, however, is deceptive, since a natural rock surface tells little if anything about prior stages in a monument's development. If, with the passage of time, the interior were enlarged, the original 'walls' would be the first to disappear under the workman's chisel. It would thus be unwise to assume that extant rock-cut churches, with the exception of the monoliths such as one finds especially in Ethiopia, were originally conceived in the form in which we know them today.

In Ethiopia, as elsewhere, the existence of rock-cut monastic sites consisting of a church or chapel and a series of monks' cells and storage chambers may have developed out of reverence for a holy person who had retreated to a solitary cave to carry on undisturbed his contemplative life. To the retreat of this single ascetic, others were attracted. Cell upon cell was fashioned from the rock and eventually entire communities arose. The rate of development and degree of expansion varied, hence some remained as insignificant hermitages while others grew into major rock-cut ensembles. It is through this association of the grotto with the holy man and more importantly, if not indirectly, with the birth and Resurrection of Christ, that the origin of rock-cut Christian architecture may also be traced.

A good deal of what has been said concerning the nature and origins of rock-cut churches may be applied in more general terms to the crypt as it occurred in early Christian churches of both East and West. It has as its origin the subterranean burial chamber of the early Christians and, by imitation and association, came to symbolise the circumstances of Christ's own burial. With the official encouragement of Christianity in 313, and the subsequent erection by Constantine and his immediate successors of memorial churches with centrally planned martyria upon the traditionally accepted sites of Christ's birth and entombment, as well as over martyr's tombs, the subterranean burial chamber or crypt was to become an integral part of church architecture. Frequently, it too was carved out of the living rock. Once the association was established, the imitative theme prevailed and the crypt everywhere was reserved as a place to venerate holy relics of especial esteem. Furthermore, these relics, and the crypt itself, could recall the grotto scene of Christ's birth. As an example one may cite the crypt of Chartres Cathedral in France. In the late ninth century, the Emperor Charles the Bald presented to the church the tunic that the Virgin Mary was said to have worn at the birth of Christ. It was kept in the crypt, which by association was, and still is, called "la grotte", or the grotto.[23]

The Anastasis of the Church of the Holy Sepulchre in Jerusalem was built by Constantine or his sons as a memorial to the Resurrection. I would submit that the grotto or crypt, over which it was built, together with the grotto of the Nativity in Bethlehem, served as the direct inspiration for the tradition of rock-cut ecclesiastical architecture in the Christian world. That tradition was one way, and a significant one at that, of spreading the popular image and ideal of the Holy Land and especially of Jerusalem, throughout Christendom. The desire was strong to be a pilgrim, in spirit if not in body, and in such manner to participate vicariously in Christ's passion. It was not by coincidence that the biographers of Saints Anthony and Paul the Hermit describe these most influential examples of Christian asceticism as living their lives out in caves. The monks and hermits who followed them and their example envisaged a direct contact with the Holy Land in their rock-cut renditions of the sites of Christ's birth, entombment and, most important of all, his Resurrection. The Anastasis of the Church of the Holy Sepulchre commemorated and protected the site of the Resurrection. At points distant from the Holy Land, the rock-cut ecclesiastical site and the rotunda symbolized it.

While the Holy Land lay constantly in the focus of the medieval Christian, events of the eleventh and twelfth centuries placed renewed emphasis on the popular image of Jerusalem. The destruction of the Holy Sepulchre in Jerusalem by the Caliph Hakim in 1009, the schism between the Roman and Byzantine Orthodox Churches in 1054, the defeat of the Byzantine army at the hands of the Turks at the Battle of Manzikert in 1071, the triumph of the papacy in the Investiture Controversy, combined with an increasing sense of religious optimism and of Roman Orthodox righteousness led to a desire, if not a strong psychological need, first to liberate the Holy Land from the Moslems and then to bring Jerusalem home. The first objective was met through the institution of the crusade. The second, through the introduction, or rather re-introduction of images symbolizing Jerusalem and the Holy Sepulchre. One of the first projects of the conquering Franks was to rebuild that holiest of church tombs. The result, in Jerusalem, was a much foreshortened version of the original basilica, *cum* rotunda, in which the Anastasis rotunda predominated visually. This monument to the Resurrection became central to twelfth-century Christian thought. Said St. Bernard of the Holy Sepulchre in his apology to the Templars, written in the second quarter of the twelfth century:

> Somehow the Holy Sepulchre seems to be the most attractive of Holy places . . . I think that those who are actually able to see even with their bodily eyes the bodily resting place of the Lord must experience the strongest emotions . . . Even though this place is now empty of its sacred contents, it remains full of delightful mysteries for us — for us, I say, because it is our resting place.[24]

He then quotes from Romans 6: 4-5:

> If we have been buried together with him in the likeness of his death, so shall we be raised up with him.[25]

Bernard, on the other hand, was well aware that the Jerusalem which stood as the capital of the then Frankish Kingdom was not the Heavenly city described by St. Augustine. He, like St. Jerome centuries before him, would not have encouraged pilgrims to go to the Holy Land for the sake of improving their spiritual understanding of God. That understanding could as well, if not better, be obtained at home.[26]

Many must have felt it was better, and certainly safer and cheaper, to find their Jerusalem at home, but relatively few had the necessary mental discipline to do so through spiritual concentration alone. For these, a clearly defined physical context was required for the object of their devotion. Some found it in the symbolic rock-cut environment previously described, others in round churches reminiscent of the Holy Sepulchre, and still others in imaginative large scale copies of the Holy City. One of these, little known but highly significant in the present context, is carved out of an unusual rock formation in Germany called Externsteine, situated near the city of Horn in Kreis Detmold (Figures. 1, 2). The rocky outcrop is first mentioned in 1093, when it became the possession of Abdinghof Abbey in Paderborn. The complex contains two chapels. It has been suggested that the lower chapel, which was dedicated in 1115 by Bishop Heinrich of Paderborn, was an imitation of the grotto of the Finding of the Cross, or of an Adam-chapel. The upper chapel is referred to as the Golgotha chapel. In addition, there is a "Holy Sepulchre", a simple rock-cut sarcophagus in a niche at the north end of the complex (Figure 3). Finally, there is a large stone relief of the Descent from the Cross, dateable to ca.1130 (Figure 4).[27] There can be little doubt that Externsteine served as a place of pilgrimage. The rock-cut setting of "Golgotha" and of the "Holy Sepulchre" speak for themselves.

Returning to the opposite end of the Christian world, 2000 km. south of Jerusalem, to Ethiopia, we find a similar attraction to the Holy City and a desire to establish that object of pilgrimage locally. Sometime during the second half of the twelfth century, and probably before the reconquest of that city by Saladin in 1187, Lalibela of Ethiopia (1160-1211?) is said to have gone to Jerusalem and to have spent a number of years there before becoming king. If the attributions are correct, it was he, upon his return to Ethiopia, who had planned, and built, the Jerusalem complex of rock-cut churches at Roha. In so doing King Lalibela continued and reinforced a tradition which was already long established in his kingdom. Simultaneously, he brought to Ethiopia the symbolic Jerusalem that a renewed twelfth-century, enthusiastic religious consciousness saw spreading throughout Christendom.

A considerable amount of work remains to be done to determine the extent of the symbolism represented by the life of King Lalibela himself and the monuments at Roha which have long been attributed to his patronage, but some points are obvious.

We learn from the king's *gadl* for example that, motivated by jealousy, Lalibela's brother attempted to poison him. As though dead, he slept for three days. It was during this period that God's angel commanded him to build the Roha churches. Miraculously, he arose from his death-like sleep.[28] This story makes of King Lalibela a symbol of Christ incarnate. The 3-day sleep represents Christ's 3-day "death" prior to the Resurrection. The miraculous reawakening is symbolic of Easter, that is to say both of rebirth and of the Resurrection. The king then builds the Church of Golgotha, and furnishes this "copy" of the Church of the Holy Sepulchre, as his near contemporaries did at Externsteine, with the tomb of Adam and the tomb of Christ. He then chooses this as his own burial site.[29] Whether these royal burials were situated in rock-cut settings by popular tradition or in fact is immaterial to the symbolic sense of Resurrection attached to the site. By having himself buried next to Christ's sepulchre in the new Jerusalem at Roha, King Lalibela further associated himself with the attributes of Christ's person. Lalibela had already, by tradition, risen once from the dead on the third day; now from his tomb he might do so again. As a burial site this place was much sought after by others who wished to follow the example of King Lalibela. In the words of G. Gerster, "the desire to make one's last journey from this sacred place transformed Lalibela into one great cemetery."[30] If the king's contemporaries had not read the words of St. Bernard, to the effect that Christ's sepulchre was their resting place too, they sought the same objective of sharing in, or being part of, the Resurrection.

There is, of course, much more to the pilgrimage centre of Roha than the Church of Golgotha, although one may see that embodiment of the Holy Sepulchre as the most significant monument of them all in terms of symbolic meaning. Related to it in the context described above is the little rock-cut rotunda associated with the Church of Emanuel called, or serving as, Bethlehem. If, as Gerster has indicated, this was "the bakery for the preparation of the Eucharistic bread", then the name taken from the Hebrew, for "House of Bread", was meant very literally. On the other hand, a three-fold symbolic meaning can be given to this chapel. In the first place, it symbolizes Christ. The point is again underscored by Saint Bernard in his description of the Holy sites, as he quotes heavily from Scripture:

> Before all else, for the nourishment of holy souls you have Beth-
> lehem, the house of bread. It was there that he first appeared — he,
> the living bread come down from heaven, born of the Virgin.[31]

Secondly, there is the rotunda, reminiscent of the memorial octagon built over the Grotto of the Nativity by the Emperor Constantine in the fourth century. Thirdly, there is the rock-cut setting, a reflection of the cave, proper to genesis, in which Christ was popularly believed to have been born, in the presence of a bright light.

The evidence suggests that the origins of Ethiopia's rock-cut churches lies in a tradition of cave dwelling which arose from and was perpetuated by a strong attachment to the ascetic example of the early Christian Fathers. They in turn could associate their grotto dwellings with the grottos of the Nativity in Bethlehem and of Christ's burial in Jerusalem. Each of these grottos was a reminder of the Resurrection.

The step from saintly grottos to rock-cut chapels and eventually to churches was only a matter of time. When King Lalibela created his rock-cut complex at Roha he continued what was clearly a well-established phenomenon in his land. At the same time, he was responding to a renewed interest in pilgrimage which ran through Christendom in the twelfth and thirteenth centuries. He gave to the highlands of Ethiopia a New Jerusalem, and emphasized the theme of the Resurrection in the monuments which he caused to be hewn from the rock.

The subject of medieval rock-cut ecclesiastical architecture is broad and its origins far-ranging. Much work remains to be done to enable us to understand the symbolic and iconographic meaning which lies behind the structures and to interpret the motivations which prompted their excavation. Profitable research could, and should, be undertaken on the association of gods with rocks and caves, with the link between light and resurrection on the one hand and darkness and death on the other, and the tracing of such ancient traditional beliefs from the earliest evidence of polytheism to medieval monotheism. The evidence will undoubtedly confirm that in Ethiopia, as elsewhere, there is a common source for all rock-cut religious architecture, both monolithic and rupestrean.

NOTES

* The author is indebted to Carla Hegstrom and Mary McTavish, Reference Librarians at the University of Toronto, for their assistance in obtaining source materials for this paper.

1. Roger Sauter, "Où en est notre connaissance des églises rupestres d'Ethiopie," *Annales d'Ethiopie*, 5(1963), pp.288, 291.

2. *Ibid.*, pp.283, 284, 287.

3. David Buxton, "Ethiopian rock-hewn churches", *Antiquity*, 20 (1946), pp.60-69; "Ethiopian Medieval Architecture", *Ethiopian Studies*, Papers read at the Second International Conference,1963, Manchester, 1964, p.243; *The Abyssinians*, New York: Praeger, 1970, p.104. Beatrice Playne, *St. George for Ethiopia*, London: Constable, 1954, pp.17, 60-61. Roger Sauter, *op. cit., Annales d'Ethiopie*, 5 (1963), p.287.

4. ANATOLIA: C. H. Emilie Haspels, *The Highlands of Phyrigia: Sites and Monuments*, 2 vols., Princeton: Princeton University Press, 1971; Guillaume de Jerphanion, *Une nouvelle province de l'art byzantin. Les églises rupestres de Cappadoce*, 5 vols., Paris, 1925-1942; Spiro Kostof, *Caves of God: the monastic environment of Byzantine Cappadocia*, Cambridge, Mass.: M.I.T., 1972; Marcell Restle, *Byzantine Wall Painting in Asia Minor*, 3 vols., Greenwich, Conn.: New York Graphic Society, 1967; Nicole Thierry, *Peintures d'Asie Mineure et de Transcaucasie aux Xe et XIe siècles*, London: Variorum Reprints, 1977.
ARMENIA: Alexandr Sahinian, Armen Manoukian, T. A. Aslanian, *Gheghard*, Documents of Armenian Architecture, vol. 6, Milan: Edizioni Ares, 1973; Edouard Utudjian, *Les monuments arméniens du IVe siècle au XVIIe siècle*, Paris: Editions Albert Morancé, 1967, Figs. 212-218.
BULGARIA: Georgi Tschavrakov, *Bulgarische Klöster*, Sofia: Nauka i Iskustvo, 1975, pp.152-159.
FRANCE: M. le Marquis de Fayolle, "Les églises monolithes d'Aubeterre, de Gurat et de St. Emilion," *Congrès archéologique de France: Angoulême 1912*, vol. 2, Paris: Picard, 1913, pp.365-397; Michael Gervers, "The Cave Church at Gurat, Charente", *Gesta*, 6 (1967), pp.10-20 and "L'èglise rupestre de Gurat", *Archéologia*, 148 (1980), pp.42-53; Marc Thibout, "Les grottes de Jonas et les peintures murales de leur chapelle", *Cahiers Archéologiques*, 2 (1947), pp.115-128.
EGYPT: A. J. Butler, *Ancient Coptic Churches of Egypt*, vol. 1, Oxford: Clarendon Press, 1884, pp.346, 350-351; Otto F. A. Meinardus, *Monks and Monasteries of the Egyptian Desert*, Cairo: American University, 1961, p.65; Serge Sauneron, *Les ermitages chrétiens du desert d'Esna*, 4 vols., Institut français d'archéologie orientale du Caire, 1972.
GEORGIA: Ghivi Gaprindashvili, *Ancient Monuments of Georgia: Vardzia*, Leningrad: Aurora Art Publishers, 1975.
GERMANY: Georg Dehio, *Handbuch der deutschen Kunstdenkmaler*, new ed., by D. Kluge and W. Hausmann, Munich: Deutscher Kunstverlag, 1969, vol.2: *Westfalen*, pp.252-253.
GREECE: Maria Panayotidi, "L'église rupestre de la Nativité dans l'île de Naxos. Ses peintures primitives", *Cahiers archéologiques*, 23 (1974), pp.107-120.
HUNGARY: J. Csemegi, "A tihanyi barlanglakások", *Archaeológiai Értesitö*, 3rd series, vols. 7-9 (1948), pp.396-407.
ITALY: P. Luigi Abatangelo, *Chiese-Cripte e Affreschi Italo-Bizantini di Massafra*, 2 vols.,

178

Studi Francescani Salentini Sezione Storica 1, Taranto: Cressati, 1966; Edward Allen, *Stone Shelters*, Cambridge, Mass.: M.I.T., 1974 (1969), pp.31-75; La Scaletta, *Le chiese rupestri di Matera*, Rome: De Luca, 1966.

MALTA: Mario Buhagiar, "Medieval Cave-Dwellings and Rock-Cut Churches in Malta", *Atrium: Mediterranean and Middle East Architectural Construction Review*, 3 (n.d.), pp.17-22.

ROUMANIA: I. Burnea, "Les monuments rupestres de Basarabi en Dobroudja", *Cahiers Archéologiques*, 13 (1962), pp.187-208

SPAIN: Theodor Hauschild and Helmut Schlunk, "Die Höhlenkirche beim Cortijo de Val-decanales", *Madrider Mitteilungen*, 11 (1970), pp.223-229; B. Madariaga, "Notas acerca del origen de las iglesias rupestres", *Altamira*, vols. 1-3 (1968-1971), pp.153-170.

SYRIA: Otto F. A. Meinardus, "A note on some Maronite Monasteries in the Wâdi Qadîsha", *Orientalia Suecana*, 21 (1972), pp.9-25.

UKRAINE: Nikolai Dejevsky, "Kievan Cave Monastery", in *The Modern Encyclopedia of Russian and Soviet History*, ed. Joseph L. Wieczynski, 16 (1980), pp.220-223; S. K. Kilesso, *The Kievo-Pecherskaya Lavra*, Moscow, 1975; Nikolai Voronin, "The Monastery of the Caves", *Architectural Review*, 94 (1942), pp. 142-143.

5. Richard Pankhurst, "Caves in Ethiopian History, with a survey of cave sites in the environs of Addis Ababa", *Ethiopia Observer*, 16 (1972), pp.15-16.

6. Otto F. A. Meinardus, *Christian Egypt Ancient and Modern*, Cairo, 1977 (1965), p.22.

7. *Ibid.*

8. Sergew Hable Sellassie, *Ancient and Medieval Ethiopian History to 1270*, Addis Ababa, 1972, p.120.

9. St. Anthony's cave is described as being "a natural cavern in the sheer face of the cliff with a ledge in front, and seems one of a number of caves inhabited by the early anchorites". See A. J. Butler, *Ancient Coptic Churches of Egypt*, 1, p.346.

10. Roger Sauter, *op cit.*, *Annales d'Ethiopie*, 5 (1963), p.291.

11. Robert the Monk, *Historia Hierosolimitana*, I, 1-3 (*Recueil des historiens des croisades, Historiens Occidentaux*, III, Paris, 1866, p.728).

12. Peter Brown, "Eastern and Western Christendom in Late Antiquity", in *Society and the Holy in Late Antiquity*, Berkeley, Calif.: University of California Press, 1982, p.169.

13. It has been estimated that as many as 50,000 monks fled to Italy to avoid the antimonastic atmosphere which was widespread not only in Constantinople, but all over Anatolia during the Iconoclast controversy of A.D. 726-843. See A. A. Vasiliev, *History of the Byzantine Empire, 324-1453*, 2nd ed., vol.1, Madison, Wisc.: University of Wisconsin Press, 1970 (1952), p.262.

14. *The Aprocryphal New Testament, being all the Gospels, Epistles and other pieces now extant, attributed in the first four centuries to Jesus Christ, His apostles, and their companions, and not included in the New Testament by its compilers*, London: printed for William Hone, 1820, pp.32-34. For the dating of James see Jacqueline Lafontaine-Dosogne, "Iconography of the Cycle of the Life of the Virgin", in *The Kariye Djami*, vol.4: *Studies in the Art of the Kariye Djami and its Intellectual Background*, ed. Paul A. Underwood, London: Routledge and Kegan Paul, 1975, pp.163-194, esp. p.163.

15 Michael Gervers, "The Iconography of the Cave in Christian and Mithraic Tradition", in *Mysteria Mithrae*, ed. Ugo Bianchi, Leiden: E. J. Brill, 1979, pp.579-596, esp. pp.587-589.

16. Janet and Colin Bord, *Earth Rites: Fertility Practices in Pre-Industrial Britain*, London: Granada, 1982, pp.49-67; Arthur Bernard Cook, "The Mountain-Cults of Zeus", in *Zeus, a study in ancient religion*, vol.1, Cambridge, 1914, pp.117-186 and vol.2, pt.2, Cambridge, 1925, pp.868-987; M. W. de Viser, *Die nicht menschengestaligen Götter der Griechen*, Leiden: E. J. Brill, 1903, pp.1-9, 54-107; Mircea Eliade, trans. R. Sheed, *Patterns in Comparative Religion*, London: Sheed and Ward, 1958, pp.216-238; Ernst Fietz, *Von alten Kultmalen in Oberösterreich: ein Beitrag zur Heimatkunde*, Linz, 1974; E. Harrison, "ΔΙΑ ΑΙΘΟΝ and IOVEM LAPIDEM", in *Essays and Studies presented to William Ridgeway*, Cambridge, 1914, pp.92-98.

17. Porphyry, *The Cave of the Nymphs in the Odyssey*, a revised text with trans. by Seminar Classics609, Buffalo: State University of New York, 1969, p.9.

18. *Ibid.*, (24) p.25.

19. The site for the latter was probably chosen from what Richard Krautheimer describes as "one of a number of tomb chambers of traditional Jewish type in a rocky cliff, its entrance facing the rising sun". See *Early Christian and Byzantine Architecture*, Penguin Books, 1965, p.39.

20. *Liber de apparitione sancti Michaelis in Monte Gargano* . . . , in *Monumenta Germaniae Historica, Scriptores rerum Langobardicarum et Italicarum saec. VI - IX*, ed. G. Waitz, Hannover, 1878, pp.541, 543.

21. Nicole Thierry, "Peintures paléochrétiennes en Cappadoce; l'église no.1 de Balkandere", in *Synthronon: art et archéologie de la fin de l'antiquité et du Moyen Age*, Bibliothèque des Cahiers archéologiques, vol.2, Paris, 1968, p.59.

22. La Scaletta, *Le chiese rupestri di Matera*, pp.24-25.

23. Robert Branner, ed., *Chartres Cathedral*, New York: W. W. Norton and Co., Inc., 1969, pp.70, 107-114.

24. Bernard of Clairvaux, "In Praise of the New Knighthood", in *Treatises III*, Cistercian Fathers Series, no.19, Kalamazoo, Mich.: Cistercian Publications Inc., 1977, p.154.

25. *Ibid.*, p.162.

26. For Bernard, the terrestrial Jerusalem was his own Abbey of Clairvaux, through which, "by whole-hearted devotion" one could be "united to the one in heaven". *Ibid.*, p.115.

27. Georg Dehio, *Handbuch der deutschen Kunstdenkmaler*, 2: *Westfalen*, pp.252-253.

28. J. Perruchon, *Vie de Lalibela roi d'Ethiopie*, Paris, 1892, as referred to in Georg Gerster, *Churches in Rock: Early Christian Art in Ethiopia*, London: Phaidon, 1970, p.88.

29. He was not the first in his lineage to be buried, like Christ, in a rock-cut tomb. Jan Seyoum, his father, is reported as having been buried in the rock-cut church of Sarzina Michael; see Sergew Hable Sellassie, *Ancient and Medieval Ethiopian History to 1270*, p.266.

30. G. Gerster, *Churches in Rock*, p.90.

31. Bernard of Clairvaux, "In Praise of the New Knighthood", *op. cit.*, p.146.

Fig. 1
Externsteine, near Horn in Kreis Detmold, Germany.
General view of the Jerusalem complex.
Photo: R. P. Kintner

Fig. 2
Externsteine. View of the eastern face, lower portion of peak 1.
Photo: R. P. Kintner

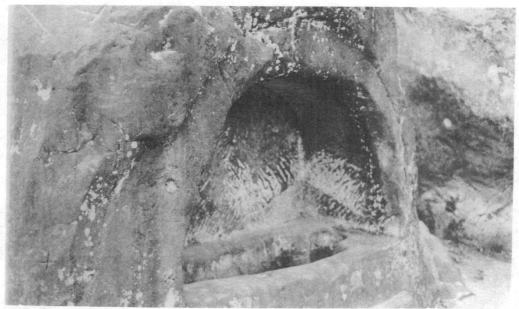

Fig. 3

Externsteine. Grotto of the Holy Sepulchre, located at the north end base of peak 1, facing north.

Photo: R. P. Kintner

Fig. 4

Externsteine. 12th-century relief sculpture of the Descent from the Cross, located at base of peak 1.

Photo: R. P. Kintner

INTRODUCING AN ARABIC HAGIOGRAPHY FROM WALLO

Hussein Ahmed

The recent revival of interest in hagiographical studies in Western Europe and the development of new methodological and analytical approaches to tap these sources, testify to the importance and relevance of the subject for an understanding of mediaeval religious and social history.[1] Popular veneration of saints and visits to their shrines, of which hagiographies are but a literary expression, constitute a *living* tradition which requires and deserves a proper investigation. It is now clear that works on the lives of saints and on their cults are not merely biographies of pious men; they also provide an insight into the pattern and dynamics of the religious life of the communities in which they lived and into the social and cultural milieux in which they operated.[2]

Ethiopianists have long recognized the significance of some Christian hagiographies for a partial reconstruction of the history of mediaeval Ethiopian society. The result of this scholarly awareness has been the translation, edition and publication of a large number of the extant Christian hagiographies.[3] Some have made extensive use of these and other unpublished ones in their treatment of some crucial aspects in the development of the Christian state and church.[4] What has not been noticed, however, is the existence and potential significance of a parallel hagiographical tradition within the Muslim communities of the country. Nonetheless, the availability of published Christian hagiographies is a source of inspiration for undertaking similar studies of Muslim hagiographies and provides a useful background and perspective for a comparative approach.[5]

The present contribution is aimed at bringing this fact to the attention of specialists in Ethiopian mediaeval history through what can be tentatively described as a preliminary commentary on a late nineteenth-century account on the life of a Muslim saint, *Shaykh* Ja'far Bukko of Gattira, once the main centre of the chiefdom of Lägä Gora, in present-day Wällo. The paper will focus on discussing the most important sections of the document which reflect its overall significance in the context of both the religious and literary development of indigenous Islam. In the concluding part, a brief comparison between the text and a couple of local Christian hagiographies will be attempted.

In the course of my fieldwork in Wällo and Shäwa in 1982/83, I had the good fortune to come across a number of manuscripts in Arabic, composed by past and contemporary Muslim scholars. One of these is the present hagiography with which this is concerned. This contribution is based on a fairly recent copy of the hagiography in the possession of one of my informants, who kindly let me consult and make photocopies of it.[6] According to him, the copy was made by his father[7] in the 1950s from the original text, which is in the hands of the author's brother in Gattira.[8] The manuscript is about 63 pages long and is written on long and lined foolscap paper. Each page contains between 27 and 33 lines.

Perhaps one of the most unusual features of this manuscript is that it does not have a colophon with the title and author's name inserted as in most Arabic manuscripts. Instead the reader finds the full title buried in the text itself when the author introduces it for the first time in the eighth section of what he calls *al-mabādī*[9] (lit.: principles, fundamental concepts). Hence, it can be argued, though only tentatively at this stage, that such a feature marks an early phase in the development of local Arabic literature.

The full title of the text is *Misku'l-Adhfar fī Manāqib Sayfu'l-Ḥaqq ash-Shaykh Ja'far (The Pungent Mask on the Virtues of Shaykh Ja'far, the Sword of Truth)*. The manuscript is not paginated and it was left to the present writer to put page numbers so as to facilitate reference while preparing this study. The entire narrative is in straight prose, except for a few places where some lines of verse are introduced.[10] These are inserted in the text in a very conspicuous way that makes sure they will be easily recognized by the reader. As to the prose narrative, the changes from one topic to the next are not clearly marked, except in the introduction. The arrangement of anecdotes and sections does not follow a strict chronological and thematic sequence and the entire text reads like a disorderly catalogue of episodes in the lives of the author's father and of his contemporaries, together with related events in and around the region in which they lived.[11] The language used is classical Arabic, with several colloquialisms and a number of unusual and highly localized forms of vocabulary frequently thrown in.[12]

After the doxology, the author introduces his work by thanking God for having caused him to "emanate from the loins of this man [his father]": *"aḥmaduhu an akhrajanī min ṣulbi hadhā'r-rajul"*, and by asking for His protection in this life and the hereafter. He refers to himself as a servant [of God] in need of His bounty, and as a poor man.[13] The author's full name is *Faqīh* Muḥammad ibn Sayf al-Ḥaqq[14] *ash-Shaykh* Ja'far Bukko[15] ibn Ṣiddīq Bukko of Gattira[16], who is a Shāfi'ī (follower of the Shāfi'ī *madhhab*, the predominant school of Islamic jurisprudence) and an Ash'arī (follower of the theological school founded by Abū'l-Ḥasan al-Ash'arī, *fl.* 873/4-935/6).

The preface (*muqaddimah*) spells out the immediate reason which prompted the hagiographer to compose the *manaqīb* (lit.: virtues)[17] of his father. In the course of a conversation with a fellow-traveller, the latter referred to the author's father as an *abba gar*[18] just like his own father, since people used to 'fear and obey' him. *Faqīh* Muḥammad was amazed at such 'disgusting ignorance' (*al-jahl al-faẓī*). In order to prove that the association of his father with a traditional ritual leader was an insult to his spiritual and saintly stature, he quotes a saying: "Only the masters know [other] masters": *"falā ya'rifu al-'ārifīn illā'l-'ārifūn.* He takes the point further by quoting what other contemporary scholars have said in praise of his father. Two things need to be underlined in connection with these laudatory remarks made about *Shaykh* Ja'far. Firstly, they testify to the high esteem in which he was held by his contemporaries and to the extent of his fame and influence. Secondly, they provide us with bits of very useful data on other scholars (indeed the text is rich in such material), about whom there is little available written information. No less than twenty names of scholar-saints are mentioned in this section and subsequently throughout the text, of which four refer to personalities who were very distinguished in their own right: *Sayyidu'l-Bā*[19], *Shaykh* Muḥammad Shāfī[20], *Shaykh* Sharafu'd-Dīn [Ibrāhīm] of Dägar[21] and *Faqīh* [Jamālu'd-Dīn] Muḥammad of Anna.[22]

The contemporary ruler of Lägä Gora, Adära [Billé][23] is also mentioned. This would certainly help in establishing the period in which the subject of the hagiography flourished.[24] Adära is described as a chief who was constantly engaged in military campaigns of conquest, and this provides some clues as to his position in the local power struggle. Although he was advised by one of the contemporary Muslim clerics to be on good terms with *Shaykh* Ja'far, a strong dispute between the two followed and the author ascribes Adära's deposition and death to the curse of the *shaykh*.[25]

There is an interesting reference to a visit by a man from Baṣrah, Iraq, who came to pay his respects to *Shaykh* Ja'far after his death.[26] This anecdote, if true, would shed light on the degree of contact which could have existed between the Muslim community in the region and the Muslim world at large. *Shaykh* Ja'far is presented as a champion of orthodoxy in his struggle against the religious leaders of his time, who used to unlawfully collect the poll-tax, animal skins and *aṣ-ṣumūr* (?), apparently for their own use, instead of distributing them amongst the poor. We are told that this earned him their hatred.[27] The preface is concluded with the date at which the composition of the work began: Dhū'l-Qa'dah, 1302 A.H.[28]

The first important section of the hagiography consists of ten guiding principles (*mabādi'*), which are described briefly in the next several pages.[29] The first is a reiteration of the merits of excellence in (pious) works and virtues, which strengthen the weak-minded. It is very interesting to note that he opposes this to (the barrenness of) pure theology and dogma. In this same subsection, the hagiographer states his source: oral data which he collected from his father's companions, as well as from members of his own family.[30] The second section explains why he gives precedence to the information about his father as related to him by a certain Shāfi'ī scholar of Argobba, another from Harṭumma, his own brother, *Shaykh* Muḥammad Ṣādiq, and uncle, *Shaykh* Qāsim, all of whom knew *Shaykh* Ja'far much more personally and intimately than did others. The third part includes a comment on the formation of local agnomens (*kunyah*): *Abba*, followed by the person's proper name, and some examples. The most interesting subsection, and perhaps one of the original contributions of the hagiographer, is his discussion of the problem of transliterating from Arabic to Amharic and vice-versa. He proposes and explains his own system in some detail and remarks on the absence in Amharic of sounds equivalent to those represented by the Arabic letters such as *thā', khā', dhāl, ṣād, ḍād, ẓā', 'ayn* and *ghayn*. He also reminds us that Arabic lacks the sounds represented by the Amharic letters like *čä, ǧä, ñä* and *gä*. For *čä,* he proposes to add a fourth dot to the three dots in the Arabic letter *shīn*, and calls the new letter "*shīn* of the horse" (*shīn al-khayl*) because *čä* in Amharic is also used to spur on a horse. He does the same for the others: *gä* is represented by a *kāf* with three dots over it and it is called *kāf al-'ajam*. He also comments on the linguistic affinity between Amharic and Arabic. Elsewhere in the text, when he introduces a local place name or an Amharic phrase for the first time, he either writes it with the signs of vocalization or spells out completely the vocalization in words.[31]

The fourth subsection is a further elaboration of the first and the author quotes a tradition attributed to Abū'l-Qāsim al-Junayd[32], who said that the "account of the pious is the foundation of [their] disciples' strength". The point is illustrated with a verse from the Qur'ān: "*wakullā naquṣṣu 'alayka min anbā'i'r-rusul mā nuthabbitu bihi fū'adaka*"[33], and with a *hādīth* according to which the Prophet said: "*inda dhikri'ṣ-ṣāliḥīn tanzilu'r-raḥmah*"[34]. The author then refers to 'Abd ar-Raḥmān ash-Shāfi'ī's *Nuzhatu'l-Majālis*, which covers various disciplines including *manāqib*.[35] The sixth principle states that the spiritual state of saints is inherited from that of prophets and that God casts light on the hearts of those who love Him and on those of the believers. He then refers the reader to his epistle called *Risālatu'l-Fawā'id*. The seventh subsection is a reminder to his readers that they should also pay attention to the accounts of people other than his own father, and the next one introduces the title of the work.

The second major part (*faṣl*) is an account of his grandfather, Ṣiddīq Bukko. This section appears to be out of place structurally, as it is inserted immediately after the eighth *mabda'*. However, the writer's intention is apparently to put the account of his father in a chronological and genealogical context and to show that *Shaykh* Ja'far is heir to the illustrious line of a saintly family. In this section, the hagiographer makes a reference to *Shaykh* Ṣābir, one of the companions of *Imām* Aḥmad ibn Ibrāhīm (Grañ), according to what was related to him by *Shaykh* Sharafu'd-Dīn of Dägär. Allusion is also made to a *zāwiyyah* (mosque-hospice) which had been built for *Shaykh* Ṣābir.[36] *Shaykh* Ja'far's conception and birth is linked to an encounter between his father and al-Khiḍr[37], who gave him a sheepskin full of water for him to use for the ritual ablution, as well as to drink and rub his wife with it. Al-Khiḍr also prophesied that a child of consequence would be born to him. Then follows an anecdote in which *Shaykh* Ja'far's father performs the miracle of bringing the dead back to life after praying to God (this being the first reference in the text to such a miracle) and another about his refusal to receive gifts from one of the local chiefs. All of these come up frequently in the subsequent sections which deal with the account of his son, *Shaykh* Ja'far Bukko. *Shaykh* Ṣiddīq also cursed Berru Lubo, the governor of Qallu (d. 1855/56) for having inadvertently replied in the negative when he asked him if he was Lubo's son. The *shaykh* is supposed to have had an unusually long life, and died in 1215 A.H./1800-01. He was buried in Gärado which became, according to the author, a salubrious and habitable place after his body was laid to rest there.[38]

The ninth subsection opens with the saying that "knowledge of virtues authorizes the one who has such knowledge to write it down and recite it". The tenth spells out the proprieties necessary for reciting *manāqibs*: reading of the Fātiḥah, the opening chapter of the Qur'ān; the need for total absorption and seriousness; ritual cleanliness of one's body and place; and totally refraining from mingling the reading of the *manāqib* with mundane anecdotes. The author then alludes to yet another work composed by himself, called *Fatḥu'ṣ-Ṣamad*, in which he discusses sainthood in great detail. He quotes the sayings of *Faqīh* Muḥammad al-Annī on the subject and mentions that, under him, he completed his training in *dhikr* (ritual recitation and repetition of formulas in praise of God) on Friday, 4 Muḥarram 1299 (26 November 1886) at the age of 29.

After a long prayer formula, the hagiography proper, namely the account of his father from his birth to adolescence, begins in a new *bāb* (chapter). The date of *Shaykh* Ja'far's birth is given as 1208/1793, and his birthplace as a village called Gudamo in Gärado. He died on Monday, in the month of Jumādā'l-Ākhir 1276 (1 January 1860) in Jamma, less than a year after he had escaped from imprisonment[39], following the devastation of the region by Téwodros. Then the author lists the names of important people buried near his grave and of those who attended his funeral. He also claims that his father completed the study of the Qur'ān in a year and that he had "seen the Night of Power" (*Laylatu'l-Qadr*).[40] *Shaykh* Ja'far's teachers in the various branches of knowledge are mentioned by name. For instance, he studied commentary of the Qur'ān, according to Jalālayn[41], under a disciple of *Muftī* Dāwūd of Däwwäy (d. 1234/1818-19), also known as *Muftī'l-Anām* (the Grand Judge of Mankind).

Inspired by al-Khiḍr[42], the *shaykh* travelled widely in Wällo and spent several years in various places in Lägä Gora, before finally settling in Jamma. There is also an allusion to a prophecy about the coming of Téwodros to devastate the area.[43] Then follows a lengthy tradition on sainthood and the need to be descended from Fāṭimah, the Prophet's daughter, is one is to have legitimate claims to sainthood. *Shaykh* Ja'far's agnomen is given as *Abba* Qundal, and this is interpreted by the author as a symbol of prominence. At a gathering of religious notables at *al-Ḥāj* Bushrā's place, the *shaykh* distinguished himself by answering a difficult question put to him by his host. Although those from Argobba attempted to refute his answer, he was able to defend himself by quoting the relevant verse from the Qur'ān.[44]

There is a brief description of the role which *Shaykh* Ja'far played in bringing about peace between *al-Ḥāj* Bushrā and *al-Ḥāj* Madanī, another prominent personality of the time, who were about to fight each other because the former did not apparently know that the latter was a *walī* (saint). *Shaykh* Ja'far subsequently said of him: "If he is not a *walī*, then Allāh does not have one on earth". We also come across yet another prophecy made by a local clairvoyant about Téwodros, followed by a long account on *al-Ḥāj* Madanī and his prophecy about the rise and death of Téwodros in the hands of "people from the West".[45]

A glimpse of *Shaykh* Ja'far's personality can be obtained from a brief description of him given by the hagiographer. He said that he used to sit on his elevated seat, which he never let anyone else sit on, and that other guests could only sit around or under his seat. Only for a certain *Shaykh* 'Abd al-Karīm did he make an exception, because the *shaykh*'s spiritual rank was higher than his.

A substantial part of the narrative is then devoted to a description of the life of one of the companions of *Shaykh* Ja'far, *Shaykh* Amān of Gissir, introduced at the beginning of the text. He was a great teacher, well-versed in the classical disciplines such as *Fiqh* and Qur'ānic exegesis, and his reputation was well-established in Qallu, Däwwäy and even in the Oromo regions. He was also a militant leader, who used to incite chiefs and soldiers to wage a *jihād* against unbelievers. He died in 1276 (1860).[46]

Then follows an account of the early education of *Shaykh* Ja'far. One is struck by the diversity of the subjects he studied: theology, *Fiqh*, interpretation of the Qur'ān, Sufism, *dhikr* and other more specialized branches, each under a different master. We also read of an encounter with al-Khiḍr, who instructed him to travel to the area beyond the Borkänna River, thus hinting at the region where he had to carry out his spiritual mission.[47] *Shaykh* Ja'far is described as an ascetic (*zāhid*)[48] and a traveller (*sayyāḥ*), who used to construct a *zāwiyyah* wherever he went, leaving a trustee to look after it, and who had established many *awqāf* (religious endowments) in Qallu and other parts of Wällo, like Wärrä Himäno.[49] He had a great appetite for knowledge and bought costly books and had rare works copied out (on one occasion he is said to have exchanged a ten-volume work for his own horse). A medium of exchange referred to, is what the hagiographer called *milḥah* (from *milḥ*: salt), 40 or 50 [bars of] which were equivalent to a "*riyāl*" (thaler?).

We are told that *Shaykh* Ja'far used to speak of three kinds of the heart and soul: the sound or perfect (*ṣaḥīḥ*), the broken (*munkasir [sic]*: *maksūr*) and the inverted (*maqlūb*). The three belonged, respectively, to the believer, the hypocrite and the unbeliever. He also discoursed about "paradise in this world", which, according to him, is manifested in the recognition of Allāh and is superior to "paradise in the hereafter". The hagiographer then includes the prayer formulae which his father used to recite on particular occasions, and mentions the fasts he used to keep. These are discussed in some detail.

Shaykh Ja'far used to consume *qāt*[50], but he was very critical of people referred to in the text as *qämati, fuqra* and *abba gar*[51], all of whom showed an excessive devotion to the substance of, and the rituals associated with, *qāt* and regarded it as an object of − not a means to − worship. The *shaykh* worked miracles on two occasions: the burning down of the house of someone who refused to sell him sheep and the resuscitation of a dead man.

The second big section of the hagiography deals with anecdotes relating to the *qämati* and the *abba gar*, to the practices of whom the author had already made a reference towards the end of the last section, in which we are told that *Shaykh* Ja'far strongly condemned their veneration of a ritual metal plate (*sīniyyah*). According to an account related to him by *Shaykh* Maḥmūd, grandson of *Shaykh Faqīh* Zubayr (a prominent scholar of Yäjju), *Shaykh* Ja'far once spent two months continuously in a *čat* session, seeking God's permission to wage his struggle against the *abba gar* and the *qämati* (a group specializing in the organization of *čat* rituals), and against reciters of the Qur'ān and the judges. The principal argument used against the *qämati* is the fact that to them, *qamāḥah*[52] was like an article of faith in itself. The hagiographer then describes the leading personalities of the ritual and their functions: *abba gar*, who was the leader; *nay*, the distributor of the *čat;* and *gobädän*, the special ceremonial site where they gathered and was itself an object of exaltation. It was usually located in an isolated spot under big trees. The *čat* leaves were picked with "passionate excitement" from trees in faraway places and those responsible for fetching it were known as the *awračča*. If they were ritually unclean, they would perform the primary ablution out of respect for carrying the *čat,* not out of a sense of duty to perform the obligatory ritual ablution. They claimed that when they were in a state of ecstasy, the *čat* would tell them what did and would happen. The fact that these people are associated by the author with the Oromo, suggests that, although the Oromo in the area were Islamized at the time, the process of thorough Islamization was apparently still going on. In fact, he claims that in addition to invoking Allāh's name, they also used to refer to Him as 'Waq' (the 'sky-god').

The *qämati* had complex proprieties and rules of conduct which governed what they called *Wädaja*.[53] In addition to the *abba gar* and *nay*, there were also other senior ritual men like the *surissa* and *mahässa*, who were held in awe by the ordinary people for whom they were seeking divine help. Although their prayers were effective and beneficial, their excessive veneration of *čat* and coffee and of expiatory gifts (*tulfänna*), and their belief that, in a state of semiconsciousness (*yäni*), they possessed the power to see what would happen, were all considered by *Shaykh* Ja'far as idolatrous. They also mingled other corrupt practices in their beliefs, such as mixing freely with women, who used to smear their hair with oil and perfume. Their claims to tell fortunes by looking into the flesh of slaughtered animals and that the *čat* could speak to them, were challenged by *Shaykh* Ja'far, who also disapproved of people soliciting their help and giving them gifts, and of the adultery which they sometimes committed.

The hagiographer speaks of an assembly of women called *Ruffo*, which performed functions analogous to the men's, and of the rivalry between the two. He cites the saying attributed to *al-Ḥāj* Bushrā about the veneration of *čat* and coffee: "whoever worships other than Allāh is a tempter (to error)", as a justification for the position taken by *Shaykh* Ja'far. Other similar legal opinions made by various scholars are also quoted. The *shaykh* did not stop at verbal condemnation: he openly declared war on, and burned down the ritual houses of, the traditional officiators. Forty of the leading ritual men appealed to Adära for justice, but he shrewdly refused to intervene by saying that he was "afraid of him [*Shaykh* Ja'far] as much as of them". However, this did not save him from a sharp reprimand from the *shaykh*. In the event, most of them were got rid of except one who repented and another who entered the *shaykh*'s service, having distributed his ill-gained wealth among the poor.

It was not only *Shaykh* Ja'far who condemned the un-Islamic practices of the religious and political notables. To *al-Ḥāj* Muḥammad Amān of Fällana[54], the recitation of the Qur'ān and of intercessory prayers in honour of the Prophet in the houses of the traditional nobility such as Adara, was *ḥarām* (a forbidden act). This was because grave sins such as adultery were committed and un-Islamic practices like the seclusion of the ruler behind a partition prevailed there. Because of this he spoke of the country as a whole as an "abode of injustice" ("*dār al-ẓulmah* [*sic*]: al-ẓulm"). This did not entirely please *Shaykh* Ja'far because it seemed to deny that pious people also existed. *Al-Ḥāj* Muḥammad said that these were exceptional people who were able to save their own lives (through piety), and that no just leader would rule the country except the *mahdī*.[55]

There follows a short but very interesting anecdote about a campaign against Wälqayt, led by one Sayyid ibn al-Badawī "from the West", who fought and defeated the 'infidels' miraculously, by throwing a spear into the ground: out of the hole came a large swarm of bees which played havoc with the enemy. He is said to have demanded tributes from the *ḥaṭī* (emperor) in Gondär, which he eventually received, and continued to do so for seven years, during which time he restored the *Sharī'ah* in the region. The historicity of this episode may be open to question but, in any case, as a tradition, it may well be a good indication of the extent of Muslim influence upon that region.

The hagiographer then returns to the discussion of the conflict between his father on the one hand, and the judges and reciters of the Qur'ān on the other, over the question of the disposal of skins, kidney and fats of animals slaughtered at funerals, all of which they used to keep for themselves. He also mentions that *Shaykh* Ja'far condemned certain traditional customs of the Oromo, such as women being deprived of their inheritance rights and bridal money. Adultery and other practices not sanctioned by the *Sunnah* (Prophetic Traditions), like the succession of a *qāḍī* by his own son, and the complete dependence of the religious officials on the favours of the secular rulers, were singled out as objectionable. There is also a contentious reference to how Grañ's death was caused by a plot organized by the conservative elements amongst the traditional clerics, because he tried to establish the rule of the *Sharī'ah* and forbid them to drink wine. There is a second mention of the *mahdī*.

A second section on coffee and *qāt* begins with the statement that the very consumption of *qāt* and drinking of coffee is, in itself, a permissible act. The author draws on traditions which he claims derive from the *Ḥadīth* to illustrate the point and enumerates some of the benefits accruing from their proper use: They open the eyes, ears and hearts of the servants of God and cause inattention (*ghaflah*) to disappear. They drive away the burden of the heart and body as well as 'the sickness of the mothworm' (*maraḍ as-sūs*). The author claims that the use of coffee began towards the end of the 8th/14th century and became known in Arabia in the beginning of the 9th/15th century. The man who introduced the drinking of coffee was *Shaykh* 'Alī b. 'Umar al-Khālidī. *Shaykh* Ja'far said that there is no vice in consuming *qāt*; it is mixing with women with no partition separating them from the men, and the use of *qāt* together with people who are not of the same faith and who think only of things of this world and not of the hereafter, that should be rebuked. As for the drinking of coffee, there are certain rites to be observed. The author refers the reader to a book on the subject called *Anīs aṣ-Ṣifwah fī Sharāb al-Qahwah*. Abū Muḥammad is quoted as having said about *qāt*: "A negligent amongst our novices who chews a portion of *qāt* is better than he who repeats God's names but who does not chew [*qāt*]". The hagiographer explains the key terms — *al-ghāfil, adh-dhākir* and *muridīn* — in the saying just quoted. He also refers to a saying attributed to *Shaykh* 'Alī b. 'Umar ash-Shādhilī, according to which he saw the secrets of the greatest names of Allāh inscribed on every leaf of the *qāt*. Other similar traditions are quoted to show the high esteem in which *qāt* should be held. The author lists in some detail the different uses of *qāt*.

The next big section is an account of what happened between *Shaykh* Ja'far and those chiefs, judges and others who went astray. It is related that once, while he was studying in Wärrä Babbo, the ruler of Yäjju, Guji[56], invited him and his teacher. *Shaykh* Ja'far refused to eat the food brought to him but asked instead for some *qāt*. As Guji was about to ask for their blessings just before pouring out some coffee, the *shaykh* ritually spat on his face and Guji wiped it off in contempt. This offended *Shaykh* Ja'far, who told Guji, in words couched in *double entendre*, about his imminent death. The *shaykh* is also supposed to have had the power of conversing with and appeasing the *jinn*s. In a separate incident, he got involved in a dispute with the Christian clergy in Dawunt, over the burning down of a church with which he was charged. We also read of an account of one of the few cases in which he defended in a vision a chief of Boräna, who was presumably his patron, against an attempt by *Shaykh* 'Abd Allāh Fātiḥah to slay him with his sword.

Shaykh Ja'far constantly exhorted Adära to rule according to Islamic law. The hagiographer remarks that most of the people in the region were polytheists, and that the Muslims still followed pre-Islamic customs. In the area called Aheyya Fäjj, on the Wällo-Shäwa border, militant religious leaders like *Shaykh* Muḥammad Shāfī attempted to establish Islam both by coercion and persuasion. However, a local saint later buried in the area had forbidden further incursions into the region because the community venerated his shrine. But secular leaders like Ḥasan and 'Alī Wädajé of Därra did try unsuccessfully to bring it under their control. An incident involving a military confrontation between 'Alī and some of the *'ulamā'* is discussed in some detail, although the reason for *Shaykh* Ja'far's reluctance to fight him is not clear. He also intervened on behalf of a saint-scholar in Yäjju to have land given to him by a local chief.

After the death of Adära, a meeting of judges and scholars was convened by *Shaykh* Ja'far, who charged them with unlawfully amassing and embezzling alms which should have been distributed among the poor. One of those charged said that, according to their rite (*madhab*), they could not be considered guilty, but one of the participants, *Shaykh* Amān, quoted the appropriate verse from the Qur'ān[57] which entitled the needy and the poor to receive charitable gifts. The debate continued until finally *Shaykh* Ja'far declared his opponents defeated. In the meantime, they admitted their errors and confessed that they had been under the influence of the rulers. They were then removed from office. One of them appealed to the woman ruler, Wärqitu[58], but she was unable to reverse his dismissal. *Shaykh* Ja'far then proceeded with the appointment of new and fair officials and judges, and distributed amongst the poor what had earlier been collected. The hagiographer admits that *Shaykh* Ja'far's attempts to reform the existing system of the administration of justice and the disposal of charitable alms did not fully succeed until the time of Téwodros — when 'Alī Adära and Amadé Berru were taken prisoner. The *shaykh* saw 'Alī's misfortune as a divine retribution for his untrustworthiness, corruption and oppressive rule. In a related and much earlier anecdote, he was able to claim and obtain from a former *qāḍī* what was to have been his share of gifts owed to him by *Shaykh* Ja'far's family upon the death of his father. The restoration was made officially known through an edict issued by *Däjjach* Berru of Qallu.

It is also related that a certain man once appeared before him seeking a settlement of a dispute with his wife, who wanted a divorce. When *Shaykh* Ja'far asked him to grant her the divorce and pay her bridal money, following the divine law, he refused an walked away; but when he asked him to do the same in the name of Adära, he turned back. After rebuking him for his 'hypocrisy', *Shaykh* Ja'far had him tied up and, despite his protests, a sentence was passed on him. The hagiographer quotes *Shaykh* Ja'far as saying that he had sworn to fulfil three things: never to be afraid of men, whether rulers or otherwise; to instruct his children; and not to share his life with a woman who complained about his means of livelihood.

Shaykh Ja'far is reported to have been considered a *quṭb* (divine axis: the highest rank in the Ṣūfī hierarchy of saints) and the author speaks of a prophecy made about his own birth. There is a brief reference to women saints and some description is given of the established ritual prayer performed by them. Curiously enough, *Shaykh* Ja'far once took part in a ceremony while two of his companions refrained from doing so, and the woman saint is said to have cursed them. Reference is also made to a skirmish in which he fought on the side of a local chief in Dawunt against Gugsa of Yäjju.[59] This is followed by a short account of *Shaykh* Abū Muḥammad of Birrinsa Qori in Däwwäy and the names of celebrated *'ulamā'* associated with him are also mentioned.

The last important anecdote related in the hagiography is the conflict between *Shaykh* Ja'far and Adära and his refusal to return a woman kept as a slave in Adära's house but who had been brought to the *shaykh* by her brother, seeking his protection. Subsequently, *Shaykh* Ja'far refused to recognize Adära's legitimacy as a ruler.

Having summarized the most outstanding anecdotes and themes in the hagiography, it now remains to put it in the perspective of older Christian hagiographies, as well as in the context of the institutional and literary development of indigenous Islam. It is obvious that there are striking similarities between the present *manāqib* and any one of the Christian hagiographies, in terms of the general aims which they were supposed to fulfil: glorification and idealization of a saint's life. The two traditions are committed to 'teaching religion by example'.[60] Both are composed in the classical languages of their respective religious tradition: Arabic and Ge'ez, and not in any of the vernacular languages. Their literary style, symbols and metaphors, as well as their references to earlier examples of piety and devotion on which should be modelled the life-style of the faithful in general and the main characters of the hagiography in particular, are very similar. There are also some structural similarities. While the saint remains the central figure of the narrative, other related anecdotes are introduced, and often discussed in detail, to shed light on particular aspects of his life or to seek scriptural sanction for his behaviour and actions. As the author of the present hagiography noted, the work is not only a biography of his father, but also of his contemporaries.

Of the four essential parts of a Christian hagiography, namely the story of the saint's life, the *kidan* or pact, miracles and *mälk'* or short hymns[61], the only one absent from the Arabic text under discussion is the pact. We find elements of the remaining three in our text, although the amount of coverage and the degree of emphasis on each of these parts are not as detailed and as high as in the Christian hagiographies. This is especially the case with miracles. There are fewer references to them in the present work than, for instance, in the hagiography on Täklä Haymanot.

Like the Christian hagiographers, who tended to use their work to enhance the prestige of a given saint and of his monastic establishment[62], our author had the intention of defending the position taken by his father on certain issues concerning Islam. There is repeated reference to the conflicts between *Shaykh* Ja'far and the religious and political establishment of his time. Although we are not told in sufficient detail about the nature of those conflicts — whether they were sectarian, theological, or simply clashes within the leadership or a struggle for influence — the general tone of the narrative and the particular issues which gave rise to the conflicts, clearly suggests a tense situation characterized by frequent confrontations between the reforming zeal of *Shaykh* Ja'far and others like him on the one hand, and the conservative reaction of the religious and political élite on the other.

One of the major differences between the present hagiography and works on Christian saints, such as Täklä Haymanot and Mäb'a Şeyon, is that in the case of the latter, there is a close association between a saint, or his monastic centre, and the Christian state: in terms of royal patronage or the support each sought from the other for theological and political reasons. This is not, however, to imply that this special kind of relationship was a permanent feature and that there were no clashes between the two. On the other hand, in the hagiography just reviewed, the relationship between the saint and the religious and political notables was precarious, to say the least. This is the general pattern, although *Shaykh* Ja'far at times sought help from, or defended, one or two of the secular rulers. The second difference has to do with the background of the saints. Although *Shaykh* Ja'far has once been referred to as a *zāhid*, there is no other hint in the text that he led, either early or later in his career, an austere and secluded life. On the other hand, in the case of both Täklä Haymanot and Täklä Maryam, there are many references to their strict ascetic life, long sojourns in the wilderness, and celibacy and chastity, as the hallmarks of their saintliness.

NOTES

1. The new revival is most evident from the range of topics and depth of analysis of papers read at congresses and from published collaborative works. See, for instance, *Hagiographie, Cultures et Sociétés IVe-XIIe siècles (Actes du Colloque organisé à Nanterre et à Paris, 2-5 mai 1979)* (Paris: Études Augustiniennes, 1981), in which 33 papers dealt with the narration and transmission of hagiographies, typology and cult of saints and hagiography and history. The most recent collection of relevant studies on the subject is Stephen Wilson (ed.), *Saints and their Cults, Studies in Religious Sociology, Folklore and History* (Cam-

bridge: Cambridge University Press, 1983), whose annotated bibliography lists 1309 titles of works, including two from Ethiopia. See also Michael Goodich, *Vita Perfecta: The Ideal of Sainthood in the Thirteenth Century* (Monographien zur Geschichte des Mittelalters, Band 25) (Stuttgart: Anton Hiersmann, 1982), pp.vii, 1-20.
For a critique of existing approaches to the study of hagiographies, see Evelyne Patlagean, "Ancient Byzantine hagiography and social history" in Wilson, *op. cit.*, pp.101-104; William H. Heist, "Hagiography, chiefly Celtic, and recent developments in folklore" in *Hagiographie, Cultures et Sociétés, op. cit.*, p.134 *ff.* For more general studies, see Hippolyte Delehaye, *Cinq Leçons sur la Méthode Hagiographique* (Subsidia Hagiographica 21) (Bruxelles: Société des Bollandistes, 1934); René Aigrain, *L'Hagiographie, ses sources, ses méthodes, son histoire* (Poitiers: Bloud & Gay, 1953), p.195 *ff.* and Baudoin de Gaiffier, *Études Critiques d'Hagiographie et d'Iconologie* (Subsidia Hagiographica 43) (Bruxelles: Société des Bollandistes, 1967), pp.289-310.

2. Wilson, *op. cit.*, pp.1, 6, 37; Goodich, *op. cit.*, pp.vii, 1-2, 5.

3. Among which, to mention but a few: René Basset, "Vie d'Abba Yohannī", *Bulletin de Correspondance Africaine* (1884), pp.433-53; J. Perruchon, *Vie de Lalibala, roi d'Éthiopie* (Paris, 1892); Ignazio Guidi, "Il Gadla Aragawi", *Memorie della Reale Accademia dei Lincei*, ser.5, vol.ii, pt.I (1896), pp.54-96; Carlo Conti Rossini, "Il 'Gadla Takla Haymanot' secondo la redazione Waldebanna", *MRAL*, ser.5, vol.ii, pt.I (1896), pp.97-143; E. A. Wallis Budge, *The Lives of Mabâ' Seyôn and Gabra Krestos* (London: W. Griggs, 1898); and *idem, The Life and Miracles of Takla Hâymânot* (London: W. Griggs, 1906).

4. Taddesse Tamrat, *Church and State in Ethiopia 1270-1527* (Oxford: Clarendon Press, 1972); *idem*, "Hagiographies and the Reconstruction of Medieval Ethiopian History" in Harold G. Marcus and Donald E. Crummey (eds.), *Rural Africana* (East Lansing, 1970), pp.12-20; and Steve Kaplan, "Hagiographies and the History of Medieval Ethiopia", *History in Africa*, 8(1981), pp.107-23, which is an assessment of Ethiopian Christian hagiographies in the light of methodologies used for analyzing similar West European sources.

5. As suggested by Wilson, *op. cit.*, p.41.

6. A copy of the manuscript has been deposited at the Institute of Ethiopian Studies, Addis Ababa University.

7. *Shaykh* Muḥammad Nūr 'Umar (September 29, 1983). Also confirmed by *Shaykh al-Ḥāj* Muḥammad Tāju'd-Dīn Aḥmad (interviewed in Kombolcha, March 29, 1982).

8. In this connection, it is perhaps worth mentioning that there is an unpublished abbreviated version of this manuscript (which I have seen but not studied), prepared by *Shaykh al-Ḥāj* Aḥmad b. 'Umar of Därra, northwestern Shäwa (d.1905/6) and entitled *Nashru'l-'Anbar, Mukhtaṣar Misku'l-Adhfar*. The present text has also been a source of inspiration for the composition of similar works by other authors.

9. *Misk*, p.5. It was *Shaykh* Muḥammad Nūr himself who wrote the title as it now stands on the front page of the manuscript.

10. *Misk*, pp.3, 24-25, 25, 38.

11. It is possible that, as Taddesse argues concerning Christian hagiographies (in *Church and State*, p.3), these sections were written at different times.

12. For instance, the frequent use of the colloquial interrogative pronoun *eysh* (for the more formal *mādhā*), forms of *khalā* (to abandon) and *rāḥa* (to go), and unusual verbal nouns: *kaffāryāt* for *kaffārah* (atonement), *qamḥah/qamāhah*, *sirriyyah* (kept woman) and many other linguistic peculiarities.

13. *Cf.* Gäbrä Mäsqäl, the author of the life of Täklä Haymanot, who refers to himself as a "sinful and evil man"; Budge, *The Life and Miracles*, p.3.

14. This is one of the *laqabs* (sobriquets) of *Shaykh* Ja'far which was given to him, according to the author, *Misk*, p.2, by *Shaykh* Muḥammad Shāfī. It means the 'Sword of Truth'. The other is *Sayfu'l-Qāḍā* ('Sword of Destiny or Canonical Law'). On *Shaykh* Muḥammad Shāfī, see *infra*, n.20.

15. Family name of *Shaykh* Ja'far. It is an Oromo word meaning 'sceptre'.

16. Arabic: *al-Gāttirī*. This is the most widespread means of appelation by which celebrated scholars and saints are known to the community. Only those closest to them and other scholars know their proper names. It is also a mark of respect. *Cf.* the case in Western Europe where places are named after saints: Wilson, *op. cit.*, p.12.

17. *Cf. gädl* (Act) in Ethiopic, and *aretai* (virtues) of pre-Christian mythological figures and heroes: Heist, "Hagiography", p.122. For a striking resemblance in the contents of the prologue between our text and mediaeval Ethiopian and West European Christian hagiographies, see Taddesse, "Hagiographies", p.15 and Goodich, *op. cit.*, p.62.

18. A word of Oromo provenance which means a leader of a ritual ceremony. See *infra* for further description.

19. Honorific title of *al-Ḥāj* Bushrā Ay Muḥammad of Gäta, southeast of Kombolcha (hence also known as Gäteyy or the *shaykh* of Gäta) where his shrine is a famous centre of pilgrimage. He also has another prestigious sobriquet: *Abū'l-Fayḍ* ('Father of [spiritual] Emanation') and is the author of a religious treatise called *Minḥa^{tu}'l-Ilāhiyyah wa'l-Fayḍa^{tu}'r-Rabbāniyyah* (Cairo, n.d.). He died on 3 February 1863.

20. A well-known scholar and militant leader (hence the epithet by which he is usually known: *al-mujāhid*), whose shrine at Jäma Negus in Albukko attracts thousands of pilgrims annually. Author of several, as yet unpublished, tracts. He died in 1221 A.H./1806-07.

21. Dägär is in Boräna.

22. In Rayya. Considered to be the most prolific writer of all the Muslim scholars in north-central Ethiopia. He died on 3 February 1882.

23. On Adära, see for instance, J. Lewis Krapf, *Travels, Researches, and Missionary Labours during an Eighteen Years' Residence in Eastern Africa* (London, 1860), *passim* and C. W. Isenberg and J. L. Krapf, *The Journals of C. W. Isenberg and J. L. Krapf*, new edn. (London, 1968), pp.39, 322, 324 *ff.* He died in 1853/54, according to local Arabic sources.

24. There are other clues in the text itself which are helpful for dating it.

25. *Misk*, p.2.

26. *Ibid.*, p.3.

27. *Ibid.* For more on this, see *infra.*

28. *Ca.* the third quarter of 1885. The events subsequently described actually fall between 1840 and 1870. Hence only four and a half generations separate these events from the date of composition.

29. *Misk*, pp.3-10.

30. The author is so explicit about his sources that he even distinguishes between acquaintances of his father and other informants, and members of his own family. No anecdote is in fact discussed without being introduced with expressions such as '*balaghanī anna*' ('it was related to me that'), '*akhbaranī*'('he informed me'), etc.

31. For instance, the full vocalization in Arabic of Birr'insa Qori, a village in Däwwäy, is written out thus: *kasrah* (sound of *i*) on *bā'*, *sukūn* (sign of vowellessness) on *rā'*, *kasrah* on the *hamzah*, *sukūn* on the *nūn*, *fatḥah* (sound of *a*) on the *sīn*, *ḍammah* (sound of *u*) on the *qāf*, *kasrah* on the *rā'*, and *sukūn* on the *yā'*: *Misk*, p.59.

32. A leading mystic of Baghdad, d.910 A.D.

33. "All that we relate to thee of the stories of the Apostles — with it we make firm thy heart." Qur'ān XI: 120.

34. "The mercy [of God] descends upon the commemoration of the virtuous."

35. It is quite possible that the structure of the present manuscript may have been influenced by the author's reading of this and other works.

36. There is a place about 3 miles northwest of Kombolcha called Säśśabir, which is a corruption of *Shaykh* Ṣābir. Informants say that it was one of the centres for the propagation of Islam in the surrounding areas after the end of Grañ's conquest.

37. Or al-Khaḍir. A figure who plays an important role in popular legend and story. In Ṣūfī circles he is actually regarded as a *walī* (saint) *par excellence.* In central Ethiopia, among the Muslims, Saturday is popularly known as the day of al-Khiḍr (*Sayyid* Khaḍr, as he is called locally), and is observed with a variety of ritual ceremonies (curiously enough even by Christians). His help is sought in matters relating to wealth and is therefore a patron saint of traders. He is supposed to be still alive because he had drunk the 'water of life' (*mā'u'l-ḥayāᵗ*).

38. *Misk*, p.9.

39. *Ibid.*, pp.10-11. In fact he had spent some time in Albukko before his death: *ibid.*, p.19.

40. 'Night of Power': Qur'ān XCVII. According to popular belief, it is associated with an angel, who would appear to those who are fortunate enough to see him towards the end of Ramaḍān. His appearance is preceded by a sudden outburst of glowing light and whoever manages to gaze at him and ask for his favours is rewarded accordingly.

41. 'Abd ar-Raḥmān b. Abī Bakr Jalāl ad-Dīn as-Suyūṭī(d. 1505) and Jalāl ad-Dīn Maḥallī (d. 1459), whose joint commentary on the Qur'ān, called *Tafsīr al-Jalālayn*, is regarded as a standard text.

42. *Cf.* the appearance of St. Michael to Täklä Haymanot (d. 1313) at certain crucial stages in his life: Budge, *The Life and Miracles, passim.*

43. *Misk,* p.12.

44. The question posed related to what *Shaykh* Ja'far would say if 'Abd al-Qāder [al-Jīlānī] (1077-1166) came up to him and asked him if he could recognize him, to which the *shaykh* replied in the negative. The verse quoted is: "*Qul 'in kuntum tuḥibbuna Allāh fa'ttabi'ūnī yuḥbibkumu Allāh wayaghfirlakum dhunūbakum wa'llāhu ghafīr^{un} raḥīm^{un}*" ("Say: 'If ye do love God, Follow me; God will love you and forgive you your sins; For God is Oft-Forgiving, Most Merciful'."): Qur'ān III: 31.

45. *Misk,* p.16. The 'people from the West' is clearly a reference to the Napier Expedition of 1868.

46. Thursday, 25 Ramaḍān 1276 (13 May 1860).

47. See n.42 above.

48. A rare reference to *zuhd* (ascetism) which is more of an exception to local Sufism than the rule.

49. Apparently given to him by the local chiefs or patrons.

50. *Catha edulis* or *celastrus edulis*; Amharic: *čat*; Arabic: *qāt.* The leaves are chewed and the juice has a stimulating effect. Although there is some literature on its origin and botanical characteristics, there is as yet no proper study devoted to the role it plays in the social and religious life of the Muslim communities in Ethiopia. For a different tradition about its origins and dissemination, see J. Spencer Trimingham, *Islam in Ethiopia* (London: Oxford University Press, 1952), p.228, n.1 and the article on *Ḳāt* in *The Encyclopaedia of Islam*, new edn. IV (Leiden: E. J. Brill, 1978), p.741.

51. On the meaning of these terms, see below, in the relevant section of the text.

52. Also spelt differently elsewhere in the text. From *qamḥah* (lit: wheat kernel or grain); in the jargon of the *qamāti*, it means the whole ceremony of group consumption of *čat* and the rituals associated with it.

53. Ceremony of prayer and supplication. Synonymous with *qamḥah* or *qimḥah.* The earliest reference to it is found in Krapf, *op. cit.,* p.323. On its role in the religious life of the Wällo Oromo Muslims, see Trimingham, *op. cit.,* pp.198, 258, 262.

54. A contemporary of Adära Billé. He died in AH 1273 (1856-57).

55. The tradition about the coming of the *mahdī* is not strong amongst Ethiopian Muslims. For a recent study of the phenomenon largely, but not exclusively, in the context of Ethiopian Christianity, see Merid W. Aregay, "Millenarian Traditions and Peasant Movements in Ethiopia 1500-1855" in Sven Rubenson (ed.), *Proceedings of the Seventh International Conference of Ethiopian Studies, University of Lund, 26-29 April 1982,* (Addis Ababa, Uppsala, East Lansing, 1984), pp.257-61 and B. G. Martin, "Mahdism, Muslim Clerics, and Holy Wars in Ethiopia, 1300-1600" in Harold Marcus (ed.), *Proceedings of the First United States Conference on Ethiopian Studies, Michigan State University, 2-5 May 1973,* (East Lansing, 1975), pp.91-100.

56. *Fl.* in the first decades of the 19th century.

57. *"Innamā'ṣ-ṣadaqātu lil-fuqarā'i wa'l-masākini . . ."* ("Alms are for the poor and the needy . . ."): Qur'ān IX: 60.

58. One of the contemporary so-called 'queens' of Wällo.

59. Died 1825.

60. Goodich, *op. cit.*, p.64.

61. Taddesse, *Church and State*, pp.2-3.

62. Taddesse, "Hagiographies", p.15; Kaplan, *op. cit.*, pp.113-14.

SOME HEBREW SOURCES ON THE BETA ISRAEL (FALASHA)

Steven Kaplan*

The Hebrew sources on the Beta Isra'el (Falasha) have only been studied by a few scholars. Although A. Z. Aeščoly[1] compiled an almost complete collection of these texts, this article which presents the sources in Hebrew and is itself in the same language, is obviously of limited value to most Ethiopianists. While some of the Hebrew sources have been translated into various European languages, the translations are scattered, incomplete, and of varied quality. Although a few sources, most notably Eldad HaDani, Benjamin of Tudela, Obadiah of Bertinoro, and Elijah of Ferrara are readily available and frequently cited, other less accessible sources have been almost ignored.[2] As part of a project under the auspices of the Ben Zvi Institute for the Study of Jewish Communities of the East, I am currently engaged in preparing a comprehensive English translation and commentary on approximately two dozen Hebrew sources on the Beta Isra'el which date from before the 19th century. In this paper I would like to offer a brief general overview of these sources, as well as a more detailed examination of some important 16th century sources.

With one or two doubtful exceptions, the Hebrew sources contain no firsthand accounts of Falasha life within Ethiopia. Rather, the authors were dependent upon information gleaned from travellers, pilgrims, legends, or Ethiopian Jews who themselves reached the Middle East. Egypt, as a major station in the Middle Eastern slave trade and in the wanderings of diaspora Jewry, proved to be an important locale for contacts between the Falasha and Jews of other countries. Obadiah of Bertinoro, Yitzhak Sholal, Abraham Ha-Levi, and David Abi ibn Zimra are four examples of important figures who had the situation of the Falasha brought to their attention during their stay in Egypt.

In other cases, Egypt served as a way station for Ethiopian Jews who later made their way to Jerusalem. Abraham Bail, Moses Basola, and Israel of Jerusalem all provide accounts of Ethiopian Jews in Jerusalem which are not found in Cerulli's magisterial work, *Etiopi in Palestina.*[3]

The Hebrew sources on the Falasha are, without exception, brief and fragmentary. No author appears to have made any attempt to provide a comprehensive history or description of the community. Rather, each has selected the particular feature or features which were of greatest relevance to his broader interest and included this snippet of information. For some the Falashas' ability to retain a degree of military and political autonomy was the most noteworthy feature of their existence. Thus, the 15th century Italian scholar, Elijah of Ferrara, wrote from Jerusalem: "It seems to me that I have already informed you of what a Jewish youth told me about the people of his country: that they are their own masters and are not subject to others".[4] Almost a century later another European immigrant to the Holy Land reported, in the name of the R. Yitzhak Cohen Sholal, a tale of Falasha heroism.

> "And the nagid said to us that one time four thieves came on the roof at night and they were very frightened. And the one who they were hosting (a Falasha) said, 'Why are you upset?' And they explained it to him. At once he grasped a sword in his hand and bounded like a lion by himself after them until they fled. And he said to them (his hosts), 'If it had been ten (thieves) it would have been the same to me because every day we kill many of them when they come to fight us."[5]

Alongside this tendency to celebrate Beta Israel courage and successes, there also existed a "school" of authors who sought to place the Jews of Ethiopia firmly within the framework of the long history of Jewish suffering. R. Obadiah of Bertinoro, best known for his commentary on the Mishnah, compared the situation of the Falasha in his day to that of the Jews under Antiochus.

"Prester John prevailed over Ephraim and struck them a tremendous blow, and entered their lands and destroyed and desolated them. And the memory of Israel was almost lost in those places and on those who remained in them various decrees were passed to convert them, like the decrees which the Greek King passed in the days of the Hasmoneans."[6]

The 16th century kaballist, Abraham Ha-Levi, sought to place the sufferings of the Falasha within the broad context of Jewish suffering and contemporary messianic speculation.

The Jewish authors were not alone in attempting to place the travails of their Ethiopian brethren in a broader historical framework. The Ethiopian Christian author of the chronicle of Emperor Sarsa Dengel (reigned 1563-1597) made explicit comparisons between the fate of the Jews in Ethiopia and those who fought the Romans in the second Temple period. Thus, the voluntary martyrdom of the Falasha who threw themselves off of cliffs, leads him to recall the comrades of Josephus who committed suicide rather than submit to the Romans, and Sarsa Dengel's defeat of the Jews is favorably compared to Titus and Vespasian's destruction of the Jewish Kingdom.[7]

A third prominent theme in the Hebrew texts is the question of the religious practices of Ethiopian Jews. Elijah of Ferrara appears to have been the first author to comment on this subject.

"They have the torah and oral commentary on it, but they do not have the talmud or our interpreters. I inquired of him (a Falasha) about some commandments. In some they tend towards our opinion and, in some, towards the opinion of the Karaites. They have the book of Esther but not Chanukah."[8]

Obadiah reported in similar vein:

"I could not determine from them if they observe the law of the Karaites or the Rabbinic Law for in a few respects it appears that they observe the law of the Karaites: for they said that no fire is found in their houses on the Sabbath and the rest appears as if they observe Rabbinic Law."[9]

The 16th century Karaite author, Abraham Ben Bali, confirms this report with regard to Sabbath candles.

"And when as prisoners they were brought to Egypt the Rabbis redeemed them and on Sabbath Eve when they saw they they (the Rabbis) light candles, they cried a great cry and covered their faces so as not to see the light of the candles."[10]

In the light of the preoccupations of later generations with the questions of Falasha origins and Jewishness, it is perhaps worth noting that none of our authors appear to have been greatly concerned with either of these questions. The Jews of Ethiopia were, according to an unbroken consensus, descendants of the Ten Lost Tribes. While authors may have differed as to the precise time or circumstances of their arrival in Ethiopia, none appear to have challenged their Jewishness. The one time in which some question is raised on this issue, the letters addressed to Rabbi David Abi ibn Zimra, the verdict is in favor of the Falasha.[11] In fact, it appears probable that no claim on the part of any Jewish authorities against the Falashas' Jewishness was ever put forward before the late 19th century.

The first decades of the 16th century appear to have been a period of increased contact between the Falasha and the Jews of the Middle East. The unsettled conditions in the Horn of Africa appear to have resulted in an increased number of Falasha slaves reaching Egypt and, after receiving their freedom, Palestine. The three authors whose comments are presented below all wrote between 1517 and 1528 and offer interesting information on Falasha, both in Ethiopia and outside.

I. MOSES BASOLA (1521-3)

Moses Ben Mordecai Basola was born in Pesaro, Italy in 1480 and served as a rabbi in that city. Among his students was Immanuel Benevento, who is remembered for his publication of the *Zohar*. Towards the end of 1521, Basola went on a pilgrimage to the Holy Land, where he remained for a year and a half.[12]

The short passage presented below is taken from his account of his trip to Palestine, *Shivhei Yerusahlayim* (Praises of Jerusalem). According to the distinguished historian, Cecil Roth, "the work is remarkable for its clarity, critical faculty, and clear delineation of economic and social issues".[13] The text was edited by Jacob D. Hayyim and published in 1938 by Yitzak Ben Zvi, who was also the first to identify Basola as its author.[14] Basola's account offers a highly condensed version of the material related by Israel of Perugia (see *infra*). Since Basola's visit to Jerusalem overlapped with Israel's, the two must have known each other, although it is doubtful if he was familiar with Israel's letter.

The passage appears in the appendix to Basola's book, in which he discusses the Ten Tribes and the Sambatyon river.

Moses Basola 1521-3

And when I was in Jerusalem the Holy City a Jew came from the land of Cush who was imprisoned among the Gentiles for 10 years. And he was bought by Ishmaelites who sold him to Jews in Egypt. And he came to see Jerusalem and the *nagid* spoke with him and he said clearly that there are many Jews there in the South, kings and princes, and they occasionally fight with the Indians (Ethiopians). And he said that among them are some from the First Temple. And the *nagid* R. Yitzhak Cohen Sholal recounted that for 30 years now he has hosted in his house a man from the tribe of Shimon. And he (the Falasha) said that in his land there are four tribes: one of them the tribe of Ischahar, is concerned with Torah and the prince over them is from the same tribe and he calls them and they answer him.

II. ISRAEL OF JERUSALEM (DEC. 1521)

The second text presented is an excerpt from a letter written by Israel, an Ashkenazi Jew who had moved to Jerusalem with his three sons, and is addressed to Abraham, a colleague in Perugia, Italy. Israel's narrative is in part confirmed by the testimony of Moses Basola (see above). Aeścoly, who was apparently unaware of Basola's report, discounts the historical value of Israel's letter.[16] Certainly, he is correct in questioning the claim that the Falasha knew Hebrew, although it must be noted that the text makes the more limited assertion that *a* Fälasha knew Hebrew. The tribal division of the Falasha and the heavenly revelations granted them are further troublesome points, although the phenomenon of a tribe devoted to religion could perhaps refer to monasticism. The account of the frontier towers is reminiscent of both Eldad Ha-Dani and the letters of Prester John.[17] Given Israel's relatively straightforward account of the first Falasha's arrival and *his* report, one is tempted to view the imaginative renderings found in the later sections of the letter as the product of either the *nagid* or his house guest, which Israel faithfully recorded.

While generally discounting the tale of the Portuguese Jew, Aeścoly notes it may be related to the episode of David Reubeni.[18]

U. D. Cassuto, who believed Reubeni was a Falasha, in part bases his argument on Israel's letter. His argument is problematic throughout. Firstly, he dates Israel's letter to December 1522.[19] To do so, however, he must ignore some of Moses Basola's evidence and argue that Moses lied about the dates of his stay in Jerusalem![20] In fact comparison of Israel's letter with that of Moses reveals that Israel's letter was written in December 1521. According to Moses, a

Falasha arrived while he was in Jerusalem, i.e. between 11 November and 30 December, 1521.[21] Israel refers to the same arrival as "last week during Chanukah", i.e. 25 Nov-2 Dec. Thus, his letter must have been written in mid-December 1521. Cassuto further argues, rather tortuously, that Israel misunderstood the events of Chanukah week and that the Jew who arrived was, in fact, the same person as had resided with the *nagid*, i.e. Reubeni! Again he must ignore Basola's testimony that the house guest resided for 30 years!

Israel of Jerusalem 1521

And last but not least, last week during Chanukah there was a Jew who was a prisoner at sea and was sold from hand to hand until he was sold in Alexandria, Egypt; and the Jews gave a large ransom until they redeemed him; and he was almost like a Cushite. He told us that in his land there are several thousand, tens of thousands of Jews and they have a great king who makes war with the Christians near him every day. And he is by the Nile, the River Nile of Egypt except for (?) another king who is in Singalan[23] which is 40 days from Aden and there are Ishmaelites and Christians subject to him. And this is certain because I talked with many people from his city and all the people of Jerusalem testify that they have 40 families. And today I spoke with our Lord the *nagid* R. Yitzhak Cohen Sholal[24] concerning the matter of the 10 tribes and he said that a Jew stayed in his house who had (spoke) Cushite, Hebrew and Arabic[25]; that he said that in their land they do not have a written book of the oral tradition and in all their judgements it is said: Joshua said in the name of Moses and in the name of the Mighty; and that in his land there are four tribes, the tribe of Shimon, the tribe of Ischahar, and two others whose name he didn't remember. And the tribe of Ischahar is busy with the Torah day and night. And (in) the other tribes some of them are involved with Torah and some with war for they are neighbour tribes to the Christians. And they have many fortresses on the border and in every single fortress the bravest youth of Israel to be found are gathered. And every time (the Christians) approach during the day they send up smoke as a signal and at night fire, and immediately everyone gathers to fight them. And he said that in time of need they ask and they are answered from heaven. The prince of the tribe of Ischahar wraps himself in his *talit*[26] and goes in the corner of the synagogue (where) they pray. And when they are answered at once fire descends from heaven and is apparent to everyone. And it descends on the head of the prince but the answer they do not hear, only the prince (hears).

Once the Cushites brought them a Jew from Portugal and they enquired of him concerning the exiles, Jerusalem, and the Temple. And he said to them, "We are in great distress going from nation to nation in captivity and sadness and the Temple is in ruin and Jerusalem is desolate and is in the hand of strangers". And immediately they tore their garments and cried a great cry for many days and decided to congregate and go to Jerusalem in strength until the prince said to them, "Wait until I asked what is taught to me from heaven". And he asked in his usual manner and they answered him from heaven "The time of salvation has not yet arrived and no one should leave his place, but salvation is coming near". And then ten rich men jumped up and volunteered to go from kingdom to kingdom and from nation to nation until they reached Jerusalem and they travelled by boat with the Cushite unto the lands which the King of Portugal had conquered and the King of Portugal summoned them, and when they told him of the honour of their wealth and the matter of their strength and their bravery and that they have the strength to fight against Prester John, and that they are answered from heaven, he was embarrassed that he had expelled (the Jews) and did not want it to be heard in his kingdom that there was still a hope and remnant of the nation of Israel and immediately decreed that they not be allowed onto land and the merchants of the state would come to them until he distanced them from the settlement on an island where they remained several months. Afterwards he sent (a message) to them saying, "What do you intend to do?" And they said to him, "We intend to go to Jerusalem". And he said to them, "If so then come into my ship and I will take you to Jerusalem". And when they were at sea, pirates came upon them and imprisoned their women and their children and stole all that they had and sold them as slaves. And after some time one came who was going round to find his wife and children and he was hosted in the house of the *nagid*

R. Yitzhak Cohen Sholal. And the *nagid* said to us (that) one time four thieves came on the roof at night and they were very frightened. And the one whom they were hosting said, "Why are you upset?" And they explained it to him. At once he grasped a sword in his hand and bounded like a lion by himself after them (the thieves) until they fled. And he said to them "If it had been ten (thieves) it would have been the same to me because every day we kill many of them when they come to fight with us".

III. ABRAHAM BEN ELIEZER HA-LEVI (C.1460-C.1528)

Abraham Ben Eliezer Ha-Levi (called Ha-Zaken: the Elder) was born in Spain, where he lived until the Spanish exile in 1492.[28] After the expulsion he lived briefly in a number of places, including Italy, Greece, Turkey, Egypt and perhaps Portugal. In Egypt he was befriended by the head of the Jewish Community, whom he accompanied to Jerusalem around the year 1517.[29] The precise date of Ha-Levi's death is unknown, but his last writings are dated 1528.

Ha-Levi was a prolific writer of apocalyptic Kabbalistic works. Like other Kabbalists of his time, he believed the coming of the Messiah to be near and devoted much energy to proving this and preparing the Jewish people for the end of days.

Ha-Levi's mystical orientation gives his writings on the Falasha a far different tone from those of either of his contemporaries, Moses Basola or Israel of Jerusalem. While they are primarily interested in the existence of the Falasha as evidence of the survival of the Ten Lost Tribes and a remnant of Jewish independence, Ha-Levi is at pains to portray events in Falasha history as signs of the dawning of the messianic era. Although Aešcoly is inclined to question Ha-Levi's reliability and his interpretation of events must be suspect, he nevertheless appears relatively well informed with regards to the Falasha and his various writings appear quite reliable.[30]

The first passage presented below is taken from Ha-Levi's commentary on *Nevu'ot Nachman*, also known as *Nevuot ha-Yeled* (The Child's Prophecy). In 1517 Ha-Levi wrote an extensive commentary on this work, a medieval Hebrew story which tells of a 5th century wonder child named Nachman.[31] In the excerpt cited below, Ha-Levi recounts the defeat of the Falasha by Na'od in 1506. Eight years later he was to repeat this story with greater detail (see passage C below).

A.   "And it is also possible that the reference in all this is to the people of the kingdom of Al-Habesh for they, also were our afflicters and spillers of our blood and butchered us. For near the land of Al-Habesh there was one kingdom of the kingdoms of the Jews. And in the year which the men of the sinful kingdom the kingdom of Portugal rose against the Marranos in that very year (1506) and at that time there arose a war between the Habeshites and the Israelites. And because the star of Jacob sank, and fell and was dark and blacked out at that time the hand of Samael[32] triumphed over the Jews and the Habeshites defeated them. And the hand of the Habeshites was severe, severe and hard on the Jews who were in this kingdom until they eliminated their name from the Kingdom. And those who remained fled to the mountains and there they strengthened themselves and defended themselves."

Passage B is taken from Ha-Levi's *Iggeret Sod ha-Geullah* (The Epistle of the Mystery of Redemption — 1521), an interpretation of portions of the Mystical work known as the *Zohar*.[33] In his commentary, Ha-Levi recounts for the first time the story of the Falasha victories of 1519/20. This material, which was not included in his earlier work (see above) has a ring of authenticity and reappears in later works in greater detail.

B.   "According to my understanding of one section in the *Ra'aya Meheimna*[34], after study and research on it, this year, which is the year 5280 (1519/20), there is redemption for a few of our countrymen in one country out of the (many) countries, far or near to us, but not through the Messiah, and this is the first redemption for there are four redemptions . . .

The copyist said: This is the redemption of 1520, according to what was told to us was in the land of Habash as is written in the interpretation to the 4th prophecy of the prophecies of Nahman.[35] According to chapter 50 (?): "And (in) the year 5280 (1519/20) the Jews were strengthened and they raised up a banner and broke the yoke of the Gentiles from upon them and succeeded against them in their wars"."

Passage C appears in a letter written in 1525 in which Ha-Levi expresses himself on the Falasha and the appearance of Martin Luther. The text presents, with considerable additional detail, the stories of Falasha defeat, revival and victory, contained in passages A and B above. Ha-Levi apparently first learned of the Falasha defeat of 1506 from a woman (bought as a slave?) he met during his stay in Egypt. The Falasha's changed fortunes and military successes came to his attention at a later date. Although he does not specify the source, he may have obtained some of his information from the Falasha who arrived in Jerusalem near the end of 1521 and is mentioned by Moses Basola and Israel of Jerusalem. There appears to be no reason to accept Aescoly's claim that the attribution of the name Gad to the Falasha King represents a confused abbreviation of Gideon, and his suggestion that the text might refer to the overthrow of the Zagwe is totally untenable.[36] Ha-Levi's description of the Ethiopian political system in which the central authorities sought to support loyal claimants to regional thrones appears quite accurate. As Taddesse notes, in areas under only indirect control, the Solomonic Kings appointed "members of the old hereditary families who ensured the regular payment of the annual tributes and the continued loyalties of their people . . .".[37] Finally, the text would appear to provide further confirmation of the weakened condition of the Solomonic Kings in the years just prior to the invasion of Ahmed Gragn.

C. 1525.

And concerning the matter of the first redemption in the year 5280 (1519/20) I will tell you that we have already recalled (this) in the fourth prophecy of the prophecies of Nahman, may he rest in peace[38] for near the land of Al-Habesh there was one kingdom of the Kingdoms of the Jews and in the year which the men of the sinful kingdom, the Kingdom of Portugal, rose against the Marranos among them to destroy them and to annihilate them in that very year. And at that time there arose a war between the Israelites in that kingdom and the people of Al-Habesh. And because the Star of Jacob was dark, and blacked out and sank and fell as if from heaven the nation of Israel fought in that year and therefore the hand of Samael triumphed and the Habeshites defeated them.[39] And because I did not explain there why a war broke out among them I will write it here to you as it was told to us:

And it is that the King who rules this kingdom is named Gad. And I saw in Egypt a woman from this land who would say that her brother was one of the ministers of King Gad and in the same year as the people of the sinful Kingdom of Portugal rose against the Marranos, King Gad died and left three sons. And between two of them a rift occurred and a war broke out over the kingship because each of them would prophesy to say, "I will be king". And one of the brothers[40] fled and went to the King of Al-Gabish (*sic*) and converted and said to him "Give me soldiers and a great army in plenty and I will give you all my brother's kingdom." And he did this and came with many people and strong hand[41] against his brother and perpetrated a great massacre against the Jews about 100 thousand men in addition to children according to what is heard and he also seized his brother the king, threw him in one of the holes.[42] And the power of the Habeshites continued to grow over the Israelites until they destroyed their name and in this kingdom there did not remain (any) except for a few people in a small weak and poor nation and it is a pillaged and despoiled nation and they are servants. And behold we have been told that in the year 1520 the people of that kingdom were strengthened again and defended[43] themselves and avenged (themselves)[44] and raised up and anointed a shield and broke the yoke of the Habeshites from upon them and succeeded against them in their wars and God helped[45] them and saved them for his name ('s sake). And therefore they were redeemed in that year in which God redeemed them from the hand of the enemy and if thus the matters were as was told to us. And these are those who were the most distant of foreign nations.

Text D is an excerpt from a letter written by Ha-Levi in 1528, shortly before his death. Although there are a few major differences between this letter and that written in 1525, a number of points make this a text of special interest. Firstly, and perhaps most importantly, this text is the first Hebrew document to refer to the Jews of Ethiopia as Falasha (Falasa). This compares favourably with early Ge'ez and Arabic references from the 16th century, and is extremely suggestive as to the date of origin of the term.[46] The first Hebrew reference to Salima (Salamt) is also noteworthy. The mention of the Portuguese which appears at the end of the text may be a reference to Alvarez's expedition, but it might also be a reflection of the contemporary Jewish preoccupation with that land (cf. Israel of Jerusalem).

D. 1528[47]

From Egypt to a place called Suakin[48] is a 50 (days) journey. And from there some say it is three days and some say it is five days to Falasa and the journey is very difficult. And Falasa is a strong Kingdom of Jews who are valiant who travel and live in hair tents to shepherd their flocks. For they are pastoralists and the land is wide before them and it is situated on high mountains and peaks and no one can ascend there to make war. And from there they descend to another land called Salima[49] (in Hebrew: Shalem) and it is another kingdom under the rule of Balasa (sic).[50] And it is a land flowing with milk. Near these kingdoms is another Kingdom of T'shaelites (sic)[51] called Gubar[52] and they pay taxes to the King of Falasa. It is still not clear to us from what tribe these Jews are, because the Ishmaelites from Gubar told us that they are neighbours of Gad and Dan, in the name of the two brothers who rule it, the King is called Gad and his brother Dan is the prince. And it was made clear to us by the Ismaelites from Gubar and Christians from Cush which is called Al-Habesh that their (Gad and Dan's) father was named Pinhas and they called him Son of the Lion because of his bravery, the interpretation of son of the lion is "shatterer and breaker of kings". (Many) people of Al-Habesh died in his wars and he died in battle[53] and left three sons: Gad, Dan and Todros (Theodorus). And a war broke out between them and Todros fled from his brothers and went to the land of Al-Hapesh (sic) and converted and brought from there a great army and powerful force according to the power of the kings who were his allies. And he suddenly entered the Kingdom of Salima and slaughtered many Jews, about 160,000 died. But into Falasa they could not (enter) because all the ascenders could not ascend them (the mountains). And after some days Todros fell into the hands of his two brothers who killed them. And this killing was in the year 5264 (1504).[54] Afterwards, the two brothers were strengthened and went out against their enemies, they were strengthened and did as they wished with their foes and the war was very great and the blow against the Habeshites was very great. And another time King Gad was seized in war by one of the kings and honoured him although he was captured by him. And they came to a compromise. King Gad would give him each year 40 ounces (of gold?) on condition that he would not let the Portuguese enter their land, because from there they come. Thus far.

NOTES

1. A. Z. Aešcoly "Yehudē habaš ba-siffrut ha-ivrit", *Zion*, 1 (1936), pp.316-36, 411-35. For a valuable bibliography of these sources see *idem* "The Falashas (bibliography)", *Kiryath Sepher*, XII, numbers 22-58.

2. E. N. Adler, *Jewish Travellers*, (London, 1930).

3. Rome 1943-7, vol.I, 234, 320-24.

4. Aešcoly, *op. cit.*, p.332. Unless noted otherwise translations are my own.

5.   Cf. *infra*.

6.   Aeškoly, *op. cit.*, p.332.

7.   C. Conti Rossini (ed.), *Historia Regis Sarsa Dengel (Malak Sagad)*, CSCO Scrip. Aeth. 3, Louvain.

8.   Aeškoly, *op. cit.*, p.331.

9.   *Ibid.*, pp.332-3.

10.   *Ibid.*, p.334.

11.   *Ibid.*, pp.334-5.

12.   At the end of his journey, Basola returned to Italy and settled in Ancona. Sometime after 1555, he returned to the Holy Land, where he died in 1560.

13.   *Encyclopaedia Judaica*, IV, p.310.

14.   *Masot Erez Yisrael le Moshe Basola*, (Jerusalem, 1938).

15.   Yitzhak Ha-Kohen Sholal, d.1524, was the last *nagid* (head of the Jewish community) in Egypt under Mamluk rule. After the Turkish conquest of Egypt in 1517, he settled in Jerusalem. All three of the authors cited in this article were acquaintances of his.

16.   Aeškoly, *op. cit.*

17.   *Ibid.*, pp.324-6, 328-9, and cf. the recent critical edition by E. Ullendorff and C. F. Beckingham, *The Hebrew Letters of Prester John*, (Oxford, 1982).

18.   Aeškoly, *op. cit.*, p.417.

19.   U. D. Cassuto, "Mi hayah David Ha-Reuveni?", *Tarbiz*, XXXII, (1963), p.345, n.7 and 344.

20.   *Ibid.*, p.345, n.7 and 344.

21.   A. Yaari, *Masot Erez Yisrael*, Tel Aviv, 1946, p.126.

22.   Cassuto, *op. cit.*, p.346.

23.   Possibly a reference to Cranganore in India, which the Jews of Cochin called Singili or Singoli. Cf. Adler, *op. cit.*, pp.372, 376.

24.   Cf. note 15 *supra*.

25.   For this reading cf. Cassuto, *op. cit.*, p. 345, n.34.

26.   Prayer shawl.

27.   Reading *tikvah* for *tiknah*.

28. On Ha-Levi see G. Scholem, *Kiryat Sepher*, 2(1925/6), pp.101-41, 267-73; *ibid.*, 7(1930-1), pp.440.56.

29. Cf. note 15 *supra*.

30. Aeškoly, *op. cit.*, pp.412-4.

31. Scholem, *op. cit.*, 1925/6, pp.115-9, 135-41.

32. The evil angel.

33. Scholem, *op. cit.*

34. Medieval Zoharic work written in the late 13th or early 14th century.

35. *Ibid.*

36. Scholem, *op. cit.*, 1930/31, p.442.

37. *Church and State in Ethiopia 1270-1527*, (London, 1972), p.297.

38. From this point until note 39 the text is almost identical with that published as Text **A** above.

39. End of passage from Text **A**.

40. In a later work, Ha-Levi identifies him as Todros.

41. Cf. Numbers 20:20.

42. Following Scholem's reading.

43. Hebrew verbs are singular (?).

44. Cf. Ezekiel 9:10, 11:21.

45. Following Scholem's reading.

46. See S. Kaplan, "The Fälasha and the Stephanite", *BSOAS*, XLVIII/2, (1985).

47. Aeškoly, *op. cit.*, pp.415-6.

48. *On the Red Sea in Modern Sudan.*

49. Ṣalamt.

50. Perhaps evidence, as Ha-Levi testifies that his information came from Muslim (Arabic) sources.

51. Read Ishmaelites, cf. below.

52. Location unclear, perhaps a reference to the Muslim kingdom of Jabara (Jabarta).

53. Lit. on his lance, perhaps meaning committed suicide.

54. The date here differs from that reported in the previous letters. This may reflect the additional information gleaned by Ha-Levi.

* I would like to thank the Harry S. Truman Research Institute for the Advancement of Peace and the Ben Zvi Institute for the Study of Jewish Communities of the East for their assistance in the preparation of this paper.

THE PROBLEM OF THE FORMATION

OF THE PEASANT CLASS IN ETHIOPIA

Yu. M. Kobischanov

The classics of Marxism-Leninism regard the peasant class as a whole as characterized by the following features: (1) small agricultural production, subsistence or semi-subsistence; (2) the specific place in the socio-economic relations, namely: the position of the producers of rent, feudal or semi-feudal; (3) a certain class unity prevailing over the caste and clan gradations. V. I. Lenin has developed the definition of peasantry as a class of feudal society in transition to the capitalist formation, and disintegrating under the influence of capitalist relations.[1]

Besides, there are a number of features complementary to these basic and cultural-historical ones which can characterize peasantry as a socio-cultural whole that has been in existence during a long multi-century and even multi-millennia historical development period. What we have in mind here is the specific peasant psychology, the interest and aspirations characteristic of the peasantry and also the traditions of class struggle which, as a rule, assumed a specifically "peasant" form.

The development, as such, and a degree of the development of the socio-economic and cultural-historical features, depends on the historical "age" (the degree of maturity and period of existence) of feudalism in some or other society. In this respect, Ethiopia occupies an intermediate place between Northern and Intertropical Africa, between the feudal-peasant society of the traditional Egypt, Tripolitana, Tunis and the "proto-peasantry" societies of the Niletic, and other peoples. At the same time, it should be noted that the mountain feudal-peasant Ethiopia occupied an "island" position, and was surrounded on all sides by a wide circle of less developed tribal, pre-class societies in which the feudal relations were at a comparatively low, or even at the inchoate, level of development. In relation to the Ethiopian civilization, those societies occupied a peripheral position.

However, in relation to the ancient and medieval feudal-peasant society (since the 9th-10th centuries Islamic civilization became a centre for Ethiopia and the greater part of other African countries) the Ethiopian feudalism was itself a peripheral phenomenon. In the period between the 16th and 19th century, Ethiopia leaves this system of feudal-peasant societies and "switches over" to a new system which was emerging together with the capitalist market; the country retains its peripheral position but as part of the feudal and the colonial periphery of European capitalism. As for the former centres, (in particular the Islamic ones: Egyptian Asia Minor, Iran and others), they themselves turn into a semi-colonial periphery of this world capitalist system.

At the same time, Ethiopian feudalism was, in itself, a deeply specific phenomenon. Many of its features were marginal in character over a long period of time. This was accounted for by the many century-long and diverse contacts of feudal Ethiopian society with the pre-class and early feudal societies which surrounded it, and also by its position of a "mountain fortress" against which the Islamic states conducted an offensive and which, in the second half of the 19th century, carried out a reconquest and consolidation of the entire country of Ethiopia around the Amharan centre.

Until the advent of the epoch of imperialism, which became a colonial period for Africa and the Arab East and in Ethiopia, which retained its independence — a period for creation of a feudal-absolutist Empire and the "second edition of self-ownership"[2], the majority of Ethiopian peasants were personally free. In many respects these feudally-exploited land-cultivators were close to the privileged warrior land-cultivators, who formed the greater part of the military estate. The influence of the so-called "Amharan military culture"[3], which emerged in the feudal medium, upon the Amharan peasantry was noted by many researchers. Travellers in the second half of the 19th century and the beginning of the 20th century wrote about the marginality of the social groups in Amharan ("Abyssinian") society, where social mobility increased at that time.[4] Though the fact that the society of Christian Ethiopia from the 16th to the beginning of the 20th century was feudal in character was not doubted by either the European travellers who observed it, or among the researchers of our time, it can truly be said that at that time the majority of Ethiopian peasantry was not wholly typical of the peasantry class in the epoch of feudalism, in contrast to such representatives of this class as Egyptian *fellahin*, Middle Asian *dehkani*, Russian *krepostniye krestyanie*, Polish *chłopy*, Japanese peasants, etc.

At the same time, this class was developing either at an accelerated pace or at a slower pace, sometimes even regressively, throughout the entire history of Ethiopia, in connection with the development of small subsistence production, feudal production relations and a feudal system of "extra-economic" compulsion.

Unfortunately, the archaeological study of Ethiopia, which is highly inadequate, does not allow the development of agriculture in this country — the major sphere of petty subsistence production — to be traced in the earlier pre-literate stage. However, this shortage of archaeological data is compensated for, to a certain extent, by the data provided by other sciences. It was only by N. I. Vavilov that the Ethiopian seat of agriculture was discovered, and its notable originality and evident ancient quality discovered.[5] To a large extent, the concept advanced by N. I. Vavilov has been confirmed by modern science, which at the same time identified still further major seats of specific agriculture in Ethiopia — one in the South West and another in the East of the Ethiopian uplands.[6] The analysis of ethnographic materials has prompted F. J. Simoons to assume that all its basic elements were received by the Ethiopian agriculturalists well before the migration of Semites to Africa. The grain crops, terracing of mountain slopes, irrigation, and probably, the ploughing implement (*maresha*) of ancient Egyptian times were known to the ancient Agaw.[7] Linguistic studies (made especially by the Soviet scientist A. Yu. Militaryov) point to the wide incidence in the ancient world of the Agaw language, whose presence can be found in the language of the Geez and in the Meroitic language. This provides evidence about the links the Agaw peoples maintained with the ancient cradles of civilization in the Nile Valley and the Tigre Plateau.

We can consider that in the first centuries of the first millennium before our era, the Agaw peoples already had the rudiments of a state and classes (land cultivators — proto-peasants, and also privileged aristocratic clans and lineages and lower proto-castes of hunters and artisans). Such a structure of society was characteristic for the majority of Kushitic (and also Omotic, Paranilotic and other neighbouring peoples) in the New Times.

About the middle of the first millennium B.C., the migration to the Tigre Plateau of land cultivators and merchants from South Arabia brought to Ethiopia the Semitic language (the ancient South Arabian written language), the monumental architecture and sculpture, a comparatively highly developed polytheistic religion and, evidently, provided new valuable elements for local agriculture, livestock-breeding and trade. Since that time, the merchant and cultural ties between Tigre civilization and those of Meroë and ancient South Arabia leave one in no doubt as to their existence. Approximately in the 5th century B.C. an early state existed on the Tigre Plateau[8], whose rulers have left us inscriptions in the ancient South Arabian (Sabaeic) language. Thus, in Northern Ethiopia at that time there already existed a probably rather primitive system of "extra-economic" compulsion of small producers. The major part of the latter consisted, evidently, of the land cultivators — ploughmen — irrigators — whose ethnic features and social position are not known to us at all. Therefore, there is nothing to confirm the view (which has become commonplace in works on the history of Ethiopia)[9] according to which the ancient Semitic colonists subjugated the local Kushitic population and turned them into their serfs.

In the period between the 4th century B.C. and the 1st century A.D., there was not a strong state in Ethiopia. But then, there emerged a millennium-long kingdom of Axum (from about the 2nd century to the beginning of the 11th century) which played a central role, not only in Ethiopia, but also in world history. However, as far as the immediate producers of Axumite society are concerned, we know very little of them. Their social status is not known and we can judge it only on the basis of indirect data. Thus, we know about the existence of slavery and vassalage in Axum. According to the sources, there were domestic slaves and trusted slave secretaries of the tsar Axum (the 4th century)[10] and also of foreigners who lived in Adulis (the 6th century)[11]. The Meccan Muslims who emigrated to Axum at the beginning of the 7th century were engaged in trade as clients (*jār*) of the king.[12] These data do not relate to the immediate producers engaged in agriculture, but it is quite possible that slavery as a status, indicating a considerable personal dependence of the vassals, was also, to a certain extent, in existence. The distribution by King Ezana of the 25,000 head of cattle among the six tribes of Beja[13] resettled by him, points to the existence of a relation of dependence with respect to cattle among the peoples of North Eritrea, Gurage country and other areas of Africa[14]. However, we know nothing more definite about the land-cultivators and livestock-breeders of the Axum kingdom. Certain indirect data (the widespread official formula *ahzabä aksum*, "peoples/ tribes of Axum") which even found its way into the South Arabian sources; the similar formula *'ngd mtn kl* (DAE 8, 13-14) or *kl 'gd 'gb* (with assimilated *n*); the phenomenon of *gefol* or *feorm* when the king ascended the throne, and probably in other cases[15], also the ethnic nick-name[16], special for each king — all these evidently confirm the considerable role played by free community members, which was characteristic of early feudal society. Probably, the warrior land cultivators made up the major portion of the Axum armies which conquered the sources of rent and trade routes for the kings and nobility. Smaller producers, land cultivators and large stock breeders, not only provided food, the products of their labour, for kings and their courts and nobility but also provided them with grain and large stock necessary to supply the caravans to the gold-bearing country of Sasu from whence gold was brought and also for ships to India which supplied artisan products and luxury goods. In this way, the Axum proto-peasantry (it could hardly be peasantry in the full meaning of this word) created the economic and military basis for the development of trade on the caravan and sea routes.

Did peasant monks and peasants exploited by monasteries exist in the Axumite kingdom? We have no direct data for answering this question.

Priesthood as a special social category probably existed among the ancient Kushites. Evidently among the ancient Agaw, Beja, and Kunama there were priest-chiefs/rainmakers who exploited, by charging a primitive rent, their "subjects" (land cultivators and livestock breeders). The polytheistic religion of Semitic immigrants was undoubtedly connected with several categories and ranks of priesthood and also *ieroduloi*. As far as the polytheistic religion of the Axumites is concerned, there were probably certain features in its social organization which were preserved by Ethiopian Christendom, for example, temple communities, or such mountain sanctuaries as Däbra-Damo before its Christianization. The social group of *ieroduloi*, or *debteras*, etc. The spread of Christianity and its synthesis with the Axumite civilization determined for a thousand and a half years ahead the composition of the Ethiopian clergy, which was very numerous and not always clearly separated from the laity: (a) the higher clergy: bishops, father superiors of churches and monasteries; (b) junior priests, their unmarried sons (deacons) and daughters (deaconesses) — the last category only disappeared in modern times — and *debteras*; (d) rank-and-file monks of hostel monasteries; (e) senior monks (*kelliotes*), and the novices in their service. Added to this should be wives, bondmaids and slaves of priests. It can hardly be doubted that the majority of junior clergy and members of their families were engaged in land cultivation and livestock breeding although, because of their special social status, they did not constitute part of the peasantry. As for the higher and medium-level clergy, they lived at the expense of the slave-owning (using as domestic servants) and the feudal exploitation of the lower clergy and members of their parishes.

It is evident that in the Axumite Kingdom the formation of peasantry as a class was not completed and this was, in general, characteristic of other early feudal societies.

This process was also incomplete in the "dark ages" of Ethiopian history (11th - 13th century). The decline of trade, the disappearance of urban life, the political disintegration — all this signified a regression in development and, probably, the intensification of archaic elements in the early feudal social system.

A new stage in the development of feudalism in Ethiopia began during the 13th - 14th century, after the unification of a considerable part of Ethiopia under the Christian Empire of Iyekuno-Amlak and his descendants and also within the Islamic confederation of Eastern and Southern Ethiopia under the hegemony of the Walasma dynasty.

Both the Christian Empire and the Islamic confederation[17] which were connected by diverse ties, including economic (trade, tribute) and political retained, in the main, the economic, political and religious ideological structures characteristic of the early feudal states. However, the feudal relations were developing within them at an accelerated pace. The consolidation of the feudal class was taking place who, at least in the Empire, were turned into *gulteñña*. The greatest degree of centralization of this feudal state was reached during the reign of Zara-Yaqob I (1434-1468). The Emperor's permanent residence of Däbrä-Byrhan – the capital of the Ethiopian Empire – makes its appearance and also capital taxation institutions of "right and left", etc., and the administrative apparatus in the provinces accountable to them and immediately to the king. As it was justly remarked by S. B. Chernetsov: "Possessing a military force and the growing domain apparatus it was not difficult for the kings . . . to turn once free community peasants who lived in the domain into feudal-dependent population. This process of enslavement of the local population was accelerated when lands were distributed as *gult* to royal servants or church institutions which, since they were closer to the rural population under their power, could exploit it more intensively."[18]

The colonization of lands with a non-Christian agricultural population[19] by military units and by the monasteries, the growth of Moslem cities on the sea coast and in the East on the Ethiopian highlands, and also the appearance of Moslem merchant groups of the caste type on the territories populated by non-Moslem agricultural populations, promoted the creation of privileged social groups which, in some cases, retained their agricultural pursuits but socially opposed the aboriginal land cultivators and, in many respects, connected with the local feudal rulers and with the imperial power more closely than with the latter. In relation to them, all personally 'free' land cultivators became all the more a class of feudally exploited peasantry. In the centralized feudal empire of Zara-Yaqob the numerous warriors from many tribes who retained the 'languages of their countries'[20], apart from the Amharic language, already constituted a fully formed estate. It retained its features also in latter times. The same can be said about the Christian clergy (within which priests and deacons composed one caste group and the *debteras* another), despite the competition offered by monastic order, individual monasteries, etc.[21]

The peasants of various ethnic groups and provinces already represented a certain class whole. This was recognized by Bahrey, the Ethiopian thinker of the 16th century, the author of *The History of the Galla*. Having set himself a limited task, to determine the military potential of feudal Ethiopian society, as compared to the potential of the military democracy of the Oromo, Bahrey identifies within it peasantry (*gäbyr mydyr*) and other social groups exempt from military service.[22] The peasant estate had two main distinctive features: pursuit of arable agriculture and payment of rent in the form of taxes and duties. On the basis of those features, there was determined also the socio-economic position of persons who were officially outside the peasant estate. Thus when the warriors of the Emperor Särtsä-Dyngyl captured Radai, brother of the ruler Sämen, in 1579, all his wealth consisted of several shirts "for he was a peasant growing grain".[23] When in 1604 Emperor Za-Dyngyl tried to levy taxes on military colonists, he issued an edict: "Let the people be warriors and (at the same time) peasants (*hara wä-gäbyr mydyr*)". In response to this the regiments of military settlers, "Mizān" and "Qurbān" rose in rebellion.[24]

However, in the rebellions and other events of the troublesome period of the 14th - 16th centuries no independent actions of the Ethiopian peasantry can be discerned. The demand to institute a "cheap church" presented by the followers of Ewostatewos did not emanate from the peasants (though it did not run counter to their interests).[25] Can the religious movements of the Stefanites and Michaelites be considered peasant movements? Or the struggle of the Falashas against the Emperor's power? It is easier to connect the actions of the Stefanites, Michaelites, Falashas and the Kemants and other confessional groups, with regional or ethnic interests, rather than with class struggle in the true meaning of the word. It is a characteristic fact that before the 17th century, in the plots and rebellions against the central power, an active part was taken, above all, by the feudal rulers of regions and principalities, by their warriors, etc. But the exploited land cultivators were an object of plunder and violence, or fled from the brigand soldiers in an effort to save their lives and their families.

The gory and destructive wars waged between Christian Ethiopia and the Imamate of Harar were accompanied by uprisings of the Moslems, Falashas and non-Christian Agaws who were subjugated by the Empire and oppressed by it; by the support of the Moslem armies by the latter; and by mass conversions of Christians to Islam. In a number of cases, land cultivators exploited by the Christian Amharic feudalities provided the driving force of those movements. At the same time, those peasants were supported by their 'own' representatives of feudal nobility who professed the same religion and belonged to the same tribe. This nobility was limited in their privileges by the imperial power and ousted from the sources of rent by Christian (Amharic and Tigraian) feudal lords. On the other hand, many Amharic and Tigraian feudal lords, together with their retinue and servants, changed from Christianity to Islam in order to retain their possessions and titles.[26] For the same reasons, they once rebelled against the Emperor and once recognized his power. Their actions had nothing to do with the class struggle whose elements, in the tragic events of that time, one could only judge on the basis of general considerations.

Those religious wars were only one link in the chain of events which took place between the 5th century and the middle of the 17th century. The events which, to a great extent, determined a further development of Ethiopian feudalism and particularly the peasant class. Other important events at the end of the Middle Ages in the North-East of Africa and the Red Sea region include the irruption of the Portuguese and Turkish Conquistadores, which was of worldwide historical importance, and the events of purely regional importance: the great migration of the nomadic tribes of the Oromo and the evolution of the Medieval Ethiopian Empire into the Gondar period.

Having settled the vast territories in various parts of the Ethiopian highlands, the Oromos interrupted their development for a long period of time, in a close contact with the Ethiopian and Islamic civilizations. This was possible because the pre-class society of the Oromos needed such contacts comparatively rarely. The aboriginal agricultural population fled in part from the invasion of the Oromos and in part was assimilated by them.

The Kushitic-speaking, Omotic-speaking and Semitic-speaking peasants of the lands conquered by the Oromo were exempted by them from feudal exploitation and, in some way or another, incorporated into the Oromo pre-class society. The regeneration of pre-feudal and preclass relations took place in the vast territories which had been the agricultural nucleus of Islamic Ethiopia and in the richest boundary provinces of Christian Ethiopia, the most suitable for agriculture.

However, the steady development of feudalism took place in the Amharic, Tigraian and Agaw regions which remained part of the Christian Ethiopian Empire. The rebirth of urban life took place after almost a thousand years of interruption. Attempts were made to reform the state management in the spirit of a larger centralization. The feudal immunity was developing at the same time. The process of consolidation of the feudal class around the royal clan (the socalled Solomonic dynasty) on the basis of a ramified and unified system of titles and holdings and the institution of vassals. The fully-formed class of feudal lords intensified the exploitation of the peasantry, which responded to that with a stronger class struggle. The 17th century saw the first anti-feudal peasant uprisings known to us. They were led by representatives of the working masses — peasants and artisans.

Like leaders of other peasant uprisings of the epoch of feudalism, the leaders of the peasant movements in the Ethiopia of that time posed before their followers as prophets or self-styled righteous monarchs who miraculously saved their 'lives' (compare the characteristic examples from the history of Russia in the 17th-18th century, Medieval Germany, and other countries). A prophet who called himself Christ appeared in Amhara-Saynt in the year 1603-1604. He gathered a host of followers. The movement was crushed only by the Emperor's troops. In subsequent years, Sämen and Shire were engulfed in anti-feudal uprisings. In the year 1608 or 1609, there appeared here an imposter who posed as the Emperor Yaqob (who died in 1607). He, too, rallied many people to his cause. This movement was crushed by the troops of the

Emperor Susynyos. But later, in the North of Ethiopia, another two false Yaqobs appeared. In 1617, the peasants of Shire, ruined by the local ruler, left their plots and fled to Serae. The intervention of the Emperor and also the church was called for once again to reintroduce order. In 1687-1688, the main Amharic provinces were engulfed in a peasant movement of "the poor and the vagabonds", headed by some Yishaq who was, according to the official version, a smith (i.e. representative of the despised artisan class) and the "instigator" (*wareñña*). Being defeated, Yishaq and his followers tried to find refuge with the Oromo-Tulama, but he was captured by a ruse, brought before the court in the presence of the Emperor Iyasu I and, of course, executed. A. Bartnicki and I. Mantel-Niećko note that this was the largest of the rebellions (*najwichszy z buntów*) or peasant rebellions (*bunty chłopskie*) in Ethiopia in the 17th century.[27]

Chronicles contain only the most important episodes in the class struggle of Ethiopian peasantry. And we can only guess that, apart from these, similar events took place which were lesser in scope.

But the socio-economic and cultural development of the former Southern and Eastern provinces and the peripheral possessions of the Ethiopian Empire continued. The proto-peasantry was also developing. In the early feudal kingdoms of Yamma, Walayta, Mocha, Kafa in South-West Ethiopia, there took place a process of formation of the peasantry class though it was still very far from completion. As a rule there existed in them the "non-impure" caste group of proto-peasants (land cultivators who opposed the higher and pure castes which exploited their labour) and also the lowest and "unpure" castes of artisans, hunters, etc. Thus, in the principality of Dimum (ethnos Dime, the group of ethnoses Gemu), the poll-paying land cultivators opposed the higher castes of the chiefs and priests and the lower castes of ritual servants (*kaysaf*), smiths, tanners and also hunters, who are the most autonomous group within the society of Dime.[28] This process of development of proto-peasantry into the peasant class progressed most of all in South-West Ethiopia, in the kingdom of Kafa, which included or subjugated a number of principalities whose population belonged to another ethnic group.

In the Gondarian Empire there took place the integration of Agaw ethnic groups into the Ethiopian feudal society (which was especially tangible in the example of the feudal lords of Kwara and the peasants of Falasha, Kemant and the Agaw of Gojjam). However, of greatest importance was the development of tribal society among the Oromo. Under the influence of their neighbours and the assimilated aboriginals, the proto-peasants of the Oromo went over to the pursuit of arable and in places (as Ito) irrigated agriculture. The Oromo borrowed many elements of the 'general Ethiopian' peasant sub-culture from Ethiosemitic peoples (the Amhara, the Gurage group, Harari, Argobba, Gafat in the valley of the river Abbay, Tigray in the South of Tigre). Those borrowings included those in the field of agricultural production, social organization, etc., (in parallel to it and beginning from the rule of the Gondarian Emperors Bäqaffa and Iyasu II, but especially intensively in the 19th century, the penetration of Galla customs into the Amharic military sub-culture took place). The formation of the 'tribal' states begun in the 18th century among the Yeju, in the first half of the 19th century among the Wallo, and among the Oromo tribes of Ynnarya (Jimma[29]) and, partly, Limu[30], etc., have been studied more than others. At the end of the 19th century, the Russian traveller A. K. Bulatovich wrote about the considerable development of feudal relations in the society of the Oromo, Leka, Wallaga and Jimma where, according to him, even serfdom made its appearance.[31] A more detailed consideration of this question reveals that Jimma and other Oromo states were, in accordance with many signs, early feudal. And lastly, part of the Oromo tribes before accession to Ethiopia (or in the extreme South — to the British colonial possessions) had not experienced feudal exploitation and political power.

The recrudescence of the Ethiopian Empire in the second half of the 19th century, and its consolidation within it of all Ethio-semites, Ethio-Kushitic and Omotic peoples (including almost all Oromo, except those living in the extreme South) took place only in the form of feudal conquest. The proto-peasants of the subjugated lands were turned into personally dependent, feudally exploited peasants (the *gabbar* system). There arrived the final stage in the formation of Ethiopian peasantry as a multi-million strong polyethnic class which was opposed by a rather consolidated feudal class.[32] After the *gabbar* system was annulled, this process accelerated. Despite the penetration of elements of capitalism into Ethiopian villages, the feudal nature of the exploitation of the Ethiopian peasantry by the state, landlords, church rent possession was retained and even intensified. The class self-consciousness and class struggle of the peasants was developing, though extremely unevenly, in various parts of the country. The class struggle of the peasants reached its apogee in the period of the 1974 revolution and in subsequent years. As it was justly remarked by V. S. Yagya: "The participants of the peasant rebellions were mainly rural inhabitants of the commercial agriculture area. The peasants of the traditional economy area as a rule stood aside from the turbulent events of 1974. However . . . the hopes entertained by reaction that the backward part of peasants would support them did not come true. The peasant masses did not come out in defence of the throne."[33]

It was precisely on the eve of the revolution and during the revolution that Ethiopia, in the person of her thinkers, writers, and revolutionaries, realizes that it is predominantly a peasant country. The eloquent symbol of this is the peasants' wooden plough (*maresha*) in the centre of the state arms emblem of socialist Ethiopia. Thus, in the history of the Ethiopian peasant class we identify the following main stages:

a. the "proto-peasant" stage, whose beginning coincides with the spread of agriculture, and is completed at the middle step of feudal formation in the conditions of developed and mature feudalism;

b. the stage of peasant society proper when peasantry mainly emerged as a class. In Tigre, this process began earlier than in other areas, but, on the whole, among Tigray, Amhara, Argobba and Falasha, and other ethnic groups of Northern and Central Ethiopia, it became clear only during the 15th-16th centuries and was only completed in the Gondarian period, while in the Southern part of Ethiopia — only after its accession to the Ethiopian Empire in the second half of the 19th century;

c. the stage of a comparatively uniform polyethnic class of peasants on the scale of the entirety of Ethiopia — the result of the socio-economic development of the country in the 20th century; and

d. the new stage in the development of the peasant class in Ethiopia opened by the 1974 revolution.

REFERENCES

1. "Inasmuch as in our countryside serf-owning society is being eliminated by "present-day" (bourgeois) society, insomuch the peasantry ceases to be a class and becomes divided into the rural proletariat and rural bourgeoisie (big, middle, petty and very small). Inasmuch as serf-owning relationships still exist, insomuch the "peasantry" still continues to be a class, i.e., we repeat, a class of serf-owning society rather than of bourgeois society." (V. I. Lenin, *Collected Works*, Vol.6, Progress Publishers, Moscow, 1964, *The Agrarian Programme of Russian Social-Democrats*, p.116).

2. Similar phenomena could be observed in other countries, including African countries, as they were drawn into the world capitalist system as its feudal (semi-feudal, feudal-colonial, semi-colonial) periphery.

3. Donald N. Levine. *Wax and Gold. Tradition and innovation in Ethiopian culture*. Chicago: Milwaukee, 1965.

4. In particular, the Russian travellers A. K. Bulatovich (A. K. Bulatovich. *Together with the troops of Menelik II. From Entoto to Baro. Report about travel to the South Western Areas of the Ethiopian Empire in 1896-1897*. Moscow, 1971, p.94 and further in the text),

N. P. Brovtsyn (N. P. Brovtsyn, *Materials on the Anthropology of Ethiopia. Abyssinians of Shoa Province.* St. Petersburg, 1909, p.71 and further in the text), A. I. Kokhanovsky and others. (In Russian)

5.   N. I. Vavilov. *The World Seats of the Most Important Cultural Plants – Selected Works*, Vol.2. Moscow - Leningrad, 1962. (In Russian)

6.   R. Portères. "Berceaux agricoles primaires sur le continent africain", *Journal of African History* (London), 1962, Vol.III, No.2, p.204 ff.

7.   F. J. Simoons. "Some Questions on the Prehistory of Ethiopia", *Journal of African History*, 1965, Vol.VI, No.1.

8.   About the earlier state, see Henri J. M. Claessen and Peter Skalnìk (eds.). *The Early State*. The Hague - Paris - New York, 1978.

9.   From the classical works, see Carlo Conti Rossini. *Storia d'Etiopia*. Bergamo, 1928; and Mordechai Abir. *Ethiopia and the Red Sea. The rise and decline of the Solomonic dynasty and Muslim-European rivalry in the region.* London, 1980, p.XV.

10.   Rufinus Turrianus. "Historia ecclesiastica", lib.X, cap.10 in Eusebius. *Historia ecclesiastica*. Th. Mommsen (ed.). Leipzig, 1908, t.II, pars 2, pp.972-973.

11.   Procopins Caesariensis. *De bello persico*, I, 20, 106.

12.   *Annales quos scripsit Abu Djafar Mohammed ibn Djarir al-Tabari*. Cum allis od M. J. de Goeje. Lugduni Batavorum, 1879, Ser.I, p.1189; Ibn Ishaq. *Sirat an nabiyy*. Cairo, 1963, pp.223-224.

13.   DAE 4 + 6 + 7.

14.   Yu. M. Kobishchanov. "African feudal societies: Reproduction and Unevenness of Development in Africa", *The Genesis of Backwardness and Ways of Development*. Moscow, 1974, pp.227-231. (In Russian)

15.   Yu. M. Kobishchanov. "Poludye in North-East African States" in *IV Congresso Internazionale di Studi Etiopici (Roma, 10-15 aprile 1972)*. Roma, 1974. Vol.I, pp.538-543.

16.   Yu. M. Kobishchanov. "The 'Armies' of king Ezana (the vestiges of military democracy in ancient Axum)". *Vestnik of Ancient History* (Moscow), 1962, No.1, p.98. (In Russian)

17.   Mordechai Abir. *Op. cit.*, p.26ff.

18.   S. B. Chernetsov, *Ethiopian feudal Monarchy in XIII-XVI centuries.* M., 1982, p.100. (In Russian)

19.   Taddesse Tamrat. *Church and State in Ethiopia: 1270-1527*. Oxford, 1972, p.99ff.

20.   B. A. Turayev. *The Abyssinian Chronicles of the XIV-XVI centuries*. Moscow - Leningrad, 1936, p.65.

21.   Taddesse Tamrat. *Op. cit.* For the Gondarian period see Jean Doresse. *La vie quotidienne des éthiopiens chretiens (aux XVIIe et XVIIIe siècles)*. Paris, 1972, p.143 et suiv. For the

second part of the 19th-20th century see John Markakis. *Ethiopia. Anatomy of a Traditional Policy*. Addis Ababa - Nairobi - New York, 1975, p.92ff.

22. Ignazio Guidi. Historia Gentis Galla. – Corpus Scriptorum Christianorum Orientalium. *Scriptores Aethiopici*. Series altera. T.III. Parisiis, 1907; K. P. Kalinovskaya. *The age groups in the peoples of Eastern Africa*. Moscow, 1976, p.141. Cf. F. Alvarez. *Narrative of the Portuguese Embassy to Abyssinia . . . L.*, 1881, pp.307-308.

23. Carlo Conti Rossini. Historia regis Sarsa Dengel. Corpus Scriptorum Christianorum Orientalium. *Scriptores Aethiopici*, Series II. T.III. Parisiis, 1907, p.93.

24. "A Brief Chronicle" of alaqa Lemlem, based on the manuscript kept in the Leningrad Department of the Institute of the Peoples of Asia, Aethiopica, 30 in *Africana. The Culture and Peoples of Africa*. Moscow-Leningrad, 1966, p.41 (the text in the Geez), 46 (Russian translation).

25. At the same time, it is highly indicative that the movement of the Ewostatewos rose and developed in Tigre, the ancient cradle of Ethiopian feudalism. Unfortunately, it is impossible to prove the correctness of the view advanced by S. B. Chernetsov to the effect that in this movement "arose and . . . organizationally was formed the anti-feudal protest . . . of the feudally dependant population" (S. B. Chernetsov. *Op. cit.*, pp.84, 98).

26. R. Basset. *Histoire de la conquête de l'Abyssinie (XVIe siècle) par Chihab ed-Din a Ahmed den Abd el-qader sur-nomme Arab Faqih*. Paris, 1897; B. A. Turayev. *The Abyssinian Chronicles*, p.126; F. Alvarez. *Narrative of the Portuguese Embassy to Abyssinia During the Years 1520-1527*. Ed. by Lord Stanley of Alderly. London, 1881, pp.308-309.

27. Andrzej Bartnicki, Joanna Mantel-Niećko. *Historia Etiopii*. Wroclaw - Warszawa - Kraków - Gdansk, 1971, pp.157, 158.

28. D. M. Todd. "Cast in Africa". *Africa* (London), 1977, Vol.47, No.4, p.404ff.

29. H. S. Lewis. *A Galla Monarchy: Jimma Aba Jifar, 1830-1932*. Madison, 1965.

30. Enrico Cerulli. *Etiopia occidentale*. Vol. I-II. Roma, 1933.

31. A. K. Bulatovich. *Op. cit.*, p.80.

32. The system of military-feudal, court and local administrative titles and holdings (*gult*), and also the marriage policy of the rulers of the country and its individual lands, the Christianization and Amharization of the traditional aboriginal nobility and warriors, served the purpose of consolidation of the feudal class. John Markakis noted important differences in the formation of classes in the Ethiopian society of that time in the North and South of the Empire (John Markakis. *Op. cit.*, pp.75-103). For the composition of the feudal class and the peasantry of Ethiopia in the second half of the 19th - the beginning of the 20th century, see also G. V. Tsypkin. *Ethiopia from fragmentation to political centralization (Second half of the 19th - the beginning of the 20th century*, Moscow, 1980, p.28 and on). G. V. Tsypkin remarked that during the entire period under study "no evidence of class actions of the main producing class of traditional Ethiopia – peasants against feudals – has come down to us" and (*Ibid.*, p.37). (In Russian)

33. V. S. Yagya. *Ethiopia in the newest times*. Moscow, 1978, p.257. (In Russian)

34. In this connection, in Amharic and other languages of Ethiopia, there has emerged the process of rethinking of old and introduction of new (foreign and artificially created) words for the designation of peasantry, farm labourers, kulaks, (thus in the Amharic text there has appeared the Russian word 'kulak'), the working people of the countryside, etc. (D. N. Levine. *Wax and Gold: Tradition and innovation in Ethiopian culture.* Chicago, London, 1965, p.81ff; S. B. Chernetsov. Certain observations on the peculiarities of the new lexicology and revolutionary phraseology in modern Amharic and the linguistic situation in Ethiopia. See *Africana*, XII, Leningrad, 1980, pp.183-186.).

THE SƏR'ATA GƏBR

A Mirror View of Daily Life
At the Ethiopian Royal Court in the Middle Ages

Manfred Kropp

Gəbr — the Royal banquet — is one of the most important portrayals of royal wealth and power, known to us from numerous descriptions of Gäbrä-Səllase, the chronicler of emperor Mənilək[1] as well as by detailed instructions for the later times in Maḫtäma-Səllase Wäldä-Mäsqäl's *Zəkrä nägär*.[2] As a social manifestation it belongs to the idea of conspicuous consumption which plays an important economic role in medieval Ethiopia. But for correct interpretation of our text — *śər'atä gəbr* — it is necessary to consider not only the meaning of *gəbr* as banquet but also its double counterpart: tribute and corvée.

The hitherto unpublished text of the *śər'atä gəbr* has been incorporated as part of a critical edition of the Ethiopian Royal chronicles which includes as well the *śər'atä mängəśt* accompanied by a series of historical documents elucidating its development and political practices.[3]

Manuscripts of the *śər'atä gəbr* are rare. The ms. Oxford 29 in Dillmann's catalogue of the Ethiopic manuscripts in the Bodleian Library is certainly one of the most famous and complete collections of Ethiopian chronicles.[4] Completed by the following ones, Oxford nr.30, 31 and 32, it can be regarded as a complete *corpus* of Ethiopian historiography from the times of 'Amdä-Ṣəyon till the end of the reign of Iyo'as. Ms. Oxford 29 has served as the basic Manuscript for the edition of the Old-Amharic Royal songs, the chronicles of Gälawdewos and Särṣä-Dəngəl.[5] It is the basic text for my new editions of the chronicles of 'Amdä-Ṣəyon, Zär'a-Ya'qob, Bä-Ədä-Maryam and his successor Əskəndər.[6] Pedro Paez was already thoroughly acquainted with the *śər'atä gəbr* and drew heavily upon it in his description of the Royal court and its life.[7] Dillmann in his masterly catalogue of the Bodleian manuscripts made some brief remarks about its contents.[8] The text has been used and cited in several monographs and articles on Ethiopian medieval history, for example in the valuable work of Taddesse Tamrat.[9]

However, the text as a whole has remained unedited, a fact which has hampered its use as a valuable historical source on medieval Ethiopia. The other manuscripts of the text are to be found:

— in the collection of chronicles made by Däǧǧazmač Ḫaylu and his friend and secretary Abägaz as represented in the following mss.[10]

d'Abbadie 118, fol.43 rc, 16-47 ra, 18[11]
Frankfurt Orient 38 (formerly Rüppell 1a), fol.20b, 17-30, a, -4[12]
London BM Or. 821, fol.99 rb — 108 vc[13]
Paris BN 143, fol.80, rb — 88 rb[14]

— as two further fragments outside the Ḫaylu-compilation in:

d'Abbadie 52, fol.66 v — 69 vb[15]
Mondon-Vidailhet 27, fol.53, vb, 4-54, ra, 18[16]

As a result of text critical examination the following observations can be made: the Oxford manuscript and the Ḫaylu-collection form a bifid stemma for the whole text. They are closely related as shown by common mistakes and lacunas. Within the Ḫaylu-collection A118 is the best copy; slightly inferior ms.BM Or 821; then comes ms.BN 143 which however, in other parts is defective; ms. Frankfurt 38 is a very bad, incomplete and defective copy.[17] For the beginning however, the fragment d'Abbadie 52 represents a third, independent and rather distinct tradition which allowed the discovery of the common lacunas in Oxford 29 and the

Haylu-collection. Ms Mondon-Vidailhet is a small fragment of very poor quality. Therefore the beginning of the text has a rather good critical basis. The remainder is less reliable, a fact which causes additional difficulties for interpretation.

(Some copies of my provisional draft of the edition were put at the disposal of the participants of the 8th ICES, one copy has been deposited in the Library of the IES.)

The following is a first attempt to shed some light on this obscure document which resisted detailed research and investigation till now. The contents of the text is a collection of detailed instructions for officers of the Royal mobile camp which encompass diverse aspects of daily life. Officers concerned in these instructions may be the *Fit-Awraris* as those who had to choose the place of encampment and to supervise the position of the whole camp. Then comes the *Ṣərag-Masäre*, the master of ceremonies who had to arrange banquets and to determine the contributions to them together with the Käntiba. Since the text gives all sorts of details about the complicated procedures in the Royal kitchen and household it is probable that it was a *Sərag-Masäre* himself who wrote this extraordinary document. I wish to cite the chronicle of Emperor Zär'a-Ya'qob which expressly states that the *Ṣərag-Masäre* in this case named Yoḥannəs, is an expert source for all further details on events at the court not mentioned in the chronicle itself.[18]

The contents of the *śər'atä gəbr* can be enumerated as follows:[19]

a) the division of the camp is organized in reference to the Royal tents in the centre including its enclosure (*mäkkabäbya*) and various gates. It can be established that there were fourteen gates in the inner enclosure, not twelve or thirteen as has been assumed.[20] In most of the previous lists the *Bä-Ṣärr-Waǧät-Däǧǧ* to the right rear of the camp has been forgotten (see Figure 1). There is also a description of the second enclosure (*ǧägʷäl* or *mägaräǧǧa*). The use of these terms is not very consistent in the document. Several times all the three mentioned words are used indistinctly. The second enclosure is concentric to the first, but the gates of this second cycle are only partially corresponding in position and names to those of the first enclosure; but perhaps the rest is simply not mentioned (see Figure 2). The use and guarding of these gates is strictly regulated according to rank and file of the dignitaries and vassals living in the camp, as well as to the troops serving there. The gates next to the central front gate called respectively *Wəddənaš-Däǧǧ* in the inner enclosure and *Bet-Anbäsa-Däǧǧ* in the outer enclosure are more prestigious.[21]

b) the tribute arriving is classified according to textiles, leather goods, metal vessels, arms and other categories of merchandise. Each ware is stored separately in sixteen tents or storehouses bearing the respective names of its contents which are repeated in the title of the keeper. The names of these tents are: 1. *Mängəst-Bet*, 2. *Məǧəlle-Bet* (from the Arabic *maǧalla*? It should be noted that the parchment is stored there), 3. *Märäbba-Bet*. 4. *Wärq-Bet*, 5. *Fətḥ-Bet*, 6. *Bä'alä-Ṣärḥ-Bəzzət-Bet*, 7. *Mäḥabas-Bet* (from Arabic *maḥbas* – "prison"?), 8. *Ingʷäǧa-Bet*, 9. *Qäsəy-Bet*, 10. *Bä'alä-Qəb.-Bet*, 11. *Ḥarb-Bet*, 12. *Ṭəqaqən-Ḥarb-Bet*, 13. *Mätälat-Bet*, 14. *Sänsälät-Bet*, 15. *Dər'-Bet*, 16. *Ṭəqaqən-Dər'-Bet*. Many Arabic loanwords used for these goods prove their foreign origin. The list of Arabic loanwords in ancient Amharic established by W. K. Brzuski[22] can be extended by a number of new words, for example: *wäšärbät*, corresponding to *mäšärbät*, derived from Arabic *mäšriba*, a kind of jug for drinking. This word occurs in the title of one of the five queens mentioned in the *śər'atä gəbr*, designating one essential part of her contribution to the banquet.[23] At the conclusion of these paragraphs there is a very obscure note stating that it was emperor 'Amdä-Ṣeyon who gave all these instructions about the storehouses, working for ten days over them in the *Märwe-Bet* and (last words of the sentence):[24]

ወዘሕኔ ቤተ ንጉሥ በአመቾ በሕኔ መመኮርይ ፶ ።

A tentative rendering: "And the Royal (store)house of His Majesty was 50 yards (in length? in height?) measured in His Majesty's standard measure".

c) the special tribute of certain troops consists mostly of firewood (*ənčät zä-mäkarämya*, literally wood for the camp during the rainy season) and wood for construction of fences and tents (*yä-mäsqäl ənčät*). Besides this the actual construction of the tents and the fences is carried out by the same troops called *Aqet Žär*. The probable Cushitic etymology of this name as "soldier for construction", supports this occupational function.[25]

d) a detailed list of the daily royal table is given which is astounding for its variety of bread, vegetables and drinks. Interestingly enough we find *yä-Afrəng̃-əng̃ära*, "foreign, European(?) bread", in these regulations dating at least from the times of Bä-Ɨdä-Maryam. The preparation of any of this food is the task of a special cook or brewer bearing the respective title. The list of these titles is the true reflection of the products prepared in the kitchen and the brewing houses.

Different cuts of the slaughtered animals are distributed according to rank and function; for example the liver, considered a desirable cut, is the due part of the 'Aqabe-sä'at. This institution is called *aman mäwabya* and easily derived from the root *wähabä*, "to give" and *aman*, "certainty". The place of distribution in front of the inner central gate is called *čəmmər aman* which I will explain later, and the ceremony itself *sər'atä aman*. The *sər'atä aman* is mentioned in the chronicle of Bä-Ɨdä-Maryam, but no further explanation is given there.[26] It was delayed because of bad news from the front. Now it is clear that this special ceremonial division of the slaughtered animal at the court is meant. Even for later times it is well attested that certain parts of the animals were the rights of various dignitaries, functionaries or groups of persons in the household of Ethiopian noblemen.

The animals brought for slaughter are sometimes ornamented in a special manner called *Bäläw-Särawər*. The rest of the animals were not thrown away but rationally used. The tendons were sent directly to the *Mängəst-Bet* (storehouse), to be precise, to the *Qäsəy-Bet*, where they were used for the costruction of umbrellas (*dəbab*). The hides were sent to another storehouse, the *Dər'-Bet*, where leather files (*wäflaq*), urgently needed for the transportation system of the camp, and stirrups (*ərkab*) were made.

e) then follows a description of the great banquet to be held at the end of the rainy season in the first days of Mäskäräm, during the feast of the prophets Mose and Jeremia. That is why it is called *mahbär zä-näbiyat*, or at other times *mahbärä Muse*. Here we can distinguish the rank and wealth of higher dignitaries of the court by counting and comparing the composition of their different contributions to the banquet (see Table 3). The common menu consists of rations which have a regulated numerical relation to each other. The definition of the singular terms can partially be derived from the context, but are submitted to further correction. For example, one menu consists of: 1 *mogärya* (hard bread used as a dish?) or *mogägarya* ("sauce-pan"?), 1 *wedat* (vessel?) of *wəşəh* or *wətt* to 3-4 *mäblə'* (literally food, "meat"?), to 7-8 *əng̃ära* (bread of *teff*) to 4-6 rations of beer (*sälla*) and mead (*şäg̃g̃*). The contributions of the higher ranks — besides the quantity — are distinguished by addition of better quality bread (for example *mofi*) and special vessels in silver or gold (perhaps horns) filled with mead (*şäg̃g̃*). Most of the names for these vessels are for the moment unintelligible, as for example *'abiyan, ağäl, sansa*, but for one of them I may try to find an interpretation: *färre i-yəs'əma*, "one who fears shall not kiss it".

The banquet takes place over a period of two days or several periods of two days. The first day is called *mätamya* (*mätä'amya*), let us say the tasty prelude to the double-portioned second day. Only higher ranking officials are allowed to eat from dishes employing knives. The hierarchical division is further indicated by black earthenware or terracotta dishes without ornaments (*leta gäbäta*) for the lower grades, silver and gold ornaments for the higher ones. The totals of the rations for the preliminary *mätamya* are about 945 *mogärya* and rations of *wətt* and approximately 3,450 rations of meat, *əng̃ära*, beer and mead, as well as 50 cows and 50 sheep, and double that for the next day. If the number of *mogärya* represents in any manner the number of places in the tents (*säqäla*), then, compared to the number of participants which should approximately be the same as the total number of the troops in the camp, it is clear that shifts were needed in order to eat. This is confirmed by the modern tradition and by pictures of royal banquets in popular painting. The last ones stress especially the importance of the kəlkəla-service, the guard duty required for the organization of the eating shifts. The number of rations fully complies to the number of soldiers in the camp, about 33,000, a number already mentioned by European eye-witnesses in the late Middle Ages.[27]

The Royal court proves to be an enormous train in the country which supports itself only temporarily, even from rich and fertile areas. Let us take the case of firewood – an even more serious problem for African towns these days: it is clear that a three-month stay during the rainy season will exhaust the natural resources of the environment considerably.[28] For the Betä-Nəgus̄, the private Royal household alone, the number of 450 mule burdens of firewood is given as the ration for the rainy season. If one could find out the numerical relation of the private household to the whole camp, then find an average measure of a mule's burden by extrapolating it from modern facts and compare the result to the average density of vegetation in Ethiopia, it should be possible to indicate a maximum stay in a given region in function of this parameter. Those facts seem to be the main reason why the king held a special council with his dignitaries in order to establish the location of the camp during the rainy season at the beginning of Säne[29]; at the time the däbtäras received their new clothes at the court. This is treated in a special paragraph in the s̄ər'atä mängəs̄t which till now was not correctly understood. Paragraph III, 18 should be translated as follows:[30]

> Regulation for the Raq-Masäre and Käntiba: After the council in the month of Säne of the king and his noblemen, (where to place the camp for the rainy season) and after the fixing of the number (of troops who should rest in the Royal camp), the Raq-Masäre fixes the contributions (of the different officials and dignitaries) for the Royal banquet (gəbr); and all the rest (of the contributions and corvées for the stay in the rainy season) is fixed by the Käntiba.[31]

f) the regulation of hygiene in the camp includes the cleaning and sweeping of the roads and open spaces, especially the removal of dung. The different areas of the camp are allotted to several troops.[32] For people there are rules regarding the latrine and draconic measures for those who break them: the culprit is stripped of his clothing, be he a man or woman, and as a punishment smeared with his own excrement. The name of the latrine as a fine example of euphemism in the camp argot will be explained at the end of the paper.

g) the regulations for breeding of mules were vital for the mobility of the camp, since the whole burden of tents, personal belongings, stores of every kind and treasuries were transported by mules. Six different races are named. The origin of these regulations is explicitly traced back to emperor 'Amdä-Şəyon and his son Säyfä-Ar'ad, later they were completed by Zär'a-Ya'qob. We already mentioned the regulations of the storehouses ascribed to 'Amdä-Şəyon. Special land-holdings all over the country are reserved for the breeding of mules under the supervision of ten dignitaries (Liqä Mäkʷas), all of them distinguished by attributes belonging to the sphere of riding, as bridles, stirrups and so on. It should be noted that during the rainy season most of the horses and mules are relocated as well in various land-holdings for one and the same reason and this is scarcity of food provisions for such a lot of animals over such a long period.

The concluding two paragraphs of the s̄ər'atä gəbr do not really belong to it. These are detailed lists of officials who accompanied Mənilək I from Jerusalem to Ethiopia. This part is closely related to the opening paragraphs in the s̄ər'atä mängəs̄t, but the titles differ notably between the two texts. But by comparing the attributes and functions of the officials one can establish a complete list of equivalents of titles which is rather useful for the interpretation of quite a lot of obscure passages in the different s̄ər'at and related documents. The main problem of these and the following lists (see *šärʿatä mängəšt*, part II) is the meaning of the juxtaposition of titles and towns or provinces. Apart from the problem of the practical value of these catalogues — do they reflect a historical and practical reality? — it does not become clear if jurisdiction over the respective countries is meant or just the tax revenues or something still different from these possibilities.

Did these sections not belong to the core of the *šärʿatä gäbr* we must on the other hand realize that the regulations are far from being the complete corpus of practical regulations in the Royal camp; for example the chronicle of Zärʾa-Yaʿqob contains a regulation for the sewing of robes of honour, which by style and contents certainly belongs to the *šärʿatä gäbr* but is not incorporated in the actual collection.[33]

In summary: as compared to the *šärʿatä mängəšt*, the *šärʿatä gäbr* is more detailed and more practical. It concerns itself essentially with the lower echelons in the Royal camp, while the *šärʿatä mängəst* describes the more important and grandiose ceremonies of the court which give it the character of a constitution. The court is, with its organization and with its regulated life and functions, a microcosm of the empire and the empire itself nothing less than a projection of the Royal court and household. Actually there is a threefold projection: the Royal private household in the inner enclosure of the camp is projected and paralleled in the greater household of the whole camp (see the parallels in the gates) and this is repeated in the virtual projection of the Royal camp into the whole empire. As a logical consequence there are no real state offices, but only household offices among many others, a further striking parallel to the kingdoms of early medieval Europe, especially the Carolingian one. Naturally many of these titles remain obscure and are difficult to interpret, but if we know that they possibly are related to household activities, then we have a means of solving the problem.

We have already given a short account of the official who could have written the *šärʿatä gäbr* which certainly reflects a long oral tradition; and this tradition has been written down only partially and preserved for us, as has been proven by parts of the *šärʿatä gäbr* to be found in the chronicle of Zärʾa-Yaʿqob and lacking in the texts itself. We have compared the style and the vocabulary of this text with other Ethiopian historical texts and have found that the chronicles of Zärʾa-Yaʿqob and Bä-Ǝdä-Maryam are nearest related. But it is only by chance that texts of this kind have been preserved by writing them down. We can't expect a systematical collection of all the regulations; by the way the same is true for the Amharic Royal songs and we just do not know what type of person found some interest in such lowly administrative "trifles" which should be learned by heart certainly and known by the respective functionaries, but which were in no way appreciated by the educated class.[34]

In view of the theme it is clear that the main difficulties of the *šärʿatä gäbr* lie with the vocabulary. Much of the above-mentioned subject matter is not acceptable in the literature and consequently does not turn up in the common dictionaries of Gəʿəz, nor those of Amharic and other semitic languages of Ethiopia. In the latter case, as these languages are not known only by literary tradition as Gəʿəz is, there is evidence for a change in the respective vocabulary in Amharic or, in some cases much more likely, the use of a certain argot in the text, which faded away with the medieval court of Ethiopia or, most lately, with the breakdown of the Gondarine court. Gäbrä-Səllase's descriptions on related subjects of the 19th century employ a very different vocabulary. For the language of the text it must be noted that often only the basic words of the sentences are Gəʿəz, the remainder are Amharic; that is to say the text is written in an extreme form of the *ləsanä tarik*. This makes the text of the *šärʿatä gäbr* an important document of Old Amharic. Therefore a careful philological analysis of the text will be a rewarding task.

The emphatic ṣ and ṭ are nearly always separated. This could be interpreted as the fact that the pronunciation of ṣ had not already changed to ṭ, or more likely, given the other known facts of Old Amharic, indicates the local variant of the Amharic used in the text. Most of the gutturals are nearly always written according to the etymological forms of the words, at least the different consonants h/ḥ / ẖ are not merged into one. This sheds some new light on disputed titles; for example *Iqaqetäč* is written *Yä-qaqyä-tähač*. The function of this official is to hear the complaints of the people in the place called *tahtay fit*. A tentative explanation could be:

those in the *taḥtay (fit)*, "those who hear the speeches". In any case, the proposed connection to *Aqet* is ruled out.[35] Also the Zâyeyahâx of Paez now becomes clear as *yä-ṣägg̃ yäḥaž*, "the one who takes care of the mead", that is to say the officer who later became known as *yä-ṣägg̃-azzaž*. Paez' description proves in other examples that he knew fairly well the *śǝr'atä gǝbr* or a nearly related document and compared it to the actual reality of the Ethiopian court in his times.[36] Other titles remain of obscure etymology, as for example *bähaltiyat* (queen), also written as *bä'altiyat* and *bä'altiḥat*. But the unstable orthography proves that already at the time the *śǝr'atä gǝbr* was written down the original form and the original meaning of the term had become obscure.

The nominal forms ending in -o and -ya (for instruments and other objects) occur from roots where these forms are not attested in modern Amharic. This is an indication of a type of argot, as W. Leslau stated in his studies about Ethiopian argots.[37] Examples are *ṭǝbso, lǝṭo, čǝqʷačǝqo* and many others. In general we encounter roots well attested in Amharic, but not in the nominal forms they occur in the text. The sense can be derived in many cases by analogy from the root-sense, but the morphological form has to be registered carefully in a glossary of Old Amharic.

Furthermore, there are examples of unknown words where it is impossible to find an etymon in the common dictionaries of Ethiopian semitic languages. The solution to many of these problems could be found a) by presupposing an hitherto unknown root, or b) according to the hypothesis of a special argot in the deformation of certain radicals of a root as a specific procedure in these artificial languages.[38] Sometimes unusual words seem to be explained in the text itself, as for example *läcän yä-ḥärd lahm*, "cow for slaughter".

Some further evidence for the use of a special argot is to be found in metaphors, a well-known phenomenon in this type of language. There are certainly quite a lot of these rhetorical devices we cannot understand, but for the sake of illustration I will give some intelligible examples. In treating the regulations of the latrine the metaphor *gǝmǧa meftah* is used and means literally "the place where one opens the fine robe". Euphemism is employed for the poor who can only afford to carry water to the banquet. It is with a slight contempt that he is called *wändǝmaččǝn*, "our brother". *Bareta*, literally a "urinal" designates a vessel of gold of a high dignitary. We would dare to consider it an ironic metaphor as used in the argot of soldiers. Another is to be found in the chronicle of Zär'a-Ya'qob where the royal standard is called *ṣärq*, literally "textile" or "rag".[39] In the Ethiopian argots quite a lot of negative sentence-designations are to be found. In the *śǝr'atä gǝbr* we can find some example for the same linguistic phenomenon: *Aysänfo*, "whose foot shall not trip"; *i-tarfǝd*, "do not come too late", a sort of beer only served with the king's consent; *färre i-yǝs'ǝma*. "one who fears shall not kiss it" as a designation of a drinking vessel.[40]

Ludolf, informed by his friend Abba Gregorius, already stated that in different parts of the Royal camp different slangs were spoken. He cites an example, the word for "to put, to impose". In the *fit* of the camp *dolä* is used, while in the *ḥʷala*, the rear of the camp one says *čämmärä*.[41] There is a place in the camp where the slaughtered animal is distributed and where the *ras* and the *däbtära* are allowed to eat. It is in front of the inner central gate (*wǝddǝnašdägg̃*) and before the great tent (*säqäla*). Now once this place is called *dulät däbäna*, clearly derived from *dolä*, the word used in the *fit* of the camp.[42] Another time it is called *čämmǝr aman*, clearly derived from *čämmärä* used in the rear of the camp.[43] All in all this is a confirmation of Ludolf's statements and of Abba Gregorius' reliability.

NOTES

1. Cf. Guébré Sellassié, *Chronique du règne de Ménélik II*. Paris, 1930. Tom.1, p.4, n.4 and pp.215-231 (chapter 34 of the Amharic text) the description of the banquet for the foundation of the church Ǝnṭotto Maryam; cf. as well the index s.v. *guebeur*. It is interesting to note the ideological interpretation of the Royal banquet compared to one of the miracles of Mary and the miracle of Qana in the Bible.

2. Cf. Maḥtäma-Səllase Wäldä-Mäsqäl, *Zəkrä nägär*. Addis Abeba, 1942 a.m. à 1950 n.Chr., pp.38-67.

3. Till new editions of the chronicles of ʿAmdä-Ṣəyon, Zärʾa-Yaʿqob, Bä-Ǝda-Maryam and successors, as well as the three introductory chapters of the chronicle of Särṣä-Dəngəl (treating Ləbnä-Dəngəl, Gälawdewos and Minas) are prepared to appear in the CSCO. A new critical edition of the *Sərʿatä mängəśt* with translation and commentary is to appear in the *Äthiopistische Forschungen*.

4. Cf. A. Dillmann, *Catalogus codicum manuscriptorum Bibliothecae Bodleianae Oxoniensis*. Pars. VII: Codices aethiopici. Oxford, 1848. pp.76b-82b.

5. Cf. I Guidi, *Le canzoni geez-amariña in onore di Re Abissini*. In: RRAL. ser.4., vol.5. Roma, 1889. pp.53-66; W. Conzelman, *Chronique de Galâwdêwos*. Paris, 1895; C. Conti Rossini, *Historia regis Sarṣa-Dengel (Malak Sagad)*. Leipzig (usw.), 1907. (CSCO. script. aeth. ser.2, tom.3. (= new numeration CSCO. script. aeth. 3-4). For the last text however, mss. d'Abbadie 42 and 52 (cf. Conti Rossini, *Notice sur les mss. éthiopiens de la collection d'Abbadie*. Paris, 1914. Nrr.194 and 195) are of great value and independent from the textual tradition represented by ms. Oxford 29 and the copies of the Ḥaylu-compilation. Consequently they are used in my edition of the introductory chapters to that chronicle and a collation to the rest of the text will be prepared.

6. The beginning of the ms. contains an abbreviation of the universal history of Wäldä-ʿAmid (al-Makīn) and several lists of the kings of Abyssinia. This text served as an introduction to many of the "Short chronicles".

7. Pedro Paez, *Historia Aethiopiae*. Livro I., capit.IV in: C. Beccari, *Rerum aethiopicarum scriptores occidentales (RAESO)*. Repr. Bruxelles, 1959. II. pp.51-59.

8. A. Dillman, *Codices aethiopici*, pp.77b-78a.

9. Taddesse Tamrat, *Church and State in Ethiopia, 1270-1527*. Oxford, 1972. pp.269-275.

10. For Däǧǧazmač-Ḥaylu see the contribution of Tekle-Tsadik Mekouria, *Histoire abrégée de Haylou Eshete (Degiazmatche)* in these proceedings. His life and works are treated in the introduction to my (unpublished) thesis: *Zəkrä Nägär. Die äthiopischen Königschroniken in der Sammlung des Generals Ḥaylu*. Heidelberg, 1984. His great compilation of chronicles was planned after the burning of the Royal archives at Gondär cf. I. Guidi, *Annales regum Iyasu II et Iyoʾas*. Paris, 1910-12 (CSCO. script. aeth. ser.2., tom.6 = CSCO. script. aeth. 28.29). Text, p.245; trans. p.254; H. Zotenberg, *Catalogue des mss. éthiopiens de la Bibliothèque Nationale*. Paris, 1877. p.220b (ms. Nr. 143) in the year 1769. The first copy was finished in 7278 a.m. = 1785/86 A.D.; cf. ms. d'Abbadie 118, fol.214 va; ms. Frankfurt, Or.38, p.459a; ms. Paris. BN 143, fol.322 rb; ms. London, BM Or.820, fol.30 va; BM Or.821 (with later changes in the datesı). But the compilation, or original chronicle of the times of Däǧǧazmač-Ḥaylu written by his friend and secretary Abägaz was continued until the death of Ḥaylu in the year 1809 A.D. The aforesaid mss. are the most important copies of the great compilation, having some different appendices for events after the year 1809 A.D.; they are of different origin and quality; one of them is most probably a fragment of the original, see my forthcoming article: *"Fragmente aus dem Landarchiv des Ḥaylu und das Original seiner Chronikensammlung"*.

11. Cf. Antoine d'Abbadie, *Catalogue raisonné des mss. éthiopiens*. Paris, 1859. pp.133-36, Nr.118; Conti Rossini, notice, nr.197, pp.199-200. This ms. till now has not been used in any edition. It is better than BM Or.821 (cf. Weld Blundell), *The Royal Chronicle of*

Abyssinia, 1769-1840. Cambridge, 1922, who unfortunately did not use it. Anyhow, Blundell's edition is to be remade on the basis of the original ms. which was preserved for the later parts of the compilation.

12. Cf. L. Goldschmidt, *Die Abessinischen Handschriften der Stadtbibliothek zu Frankfurt am Main* (Rüppellsche Sammlung). Berlin, 1897. nr.16, pp.58-62.

13. Cf. W. Wright, *Catalogue of the Ethiopic mss. in the British Museum, acquired since the year 1847.* London, 1877. pp.315a-138b; ms. nr. CCCXCII (but correctly CCCXCIII).

14. Cf. H. Zotenberg, *Catalogue*, pp.216a-221a.

15. Cf. A. d'Abbadie, *Catalogue*, p.63; Conti Rossini, notice, pp.197-198, nr.194. It is a most valuable ms., the more it is regrettable that only a fragment of the *śər'atä gəbr* is contained. Quite a lot of textual problems in the later passages of the *śər'atä gəbr* would be resolved if we had this tradition completely.

16. Cf. M. Chaine, *Catalogue des mss. éthiopiens de la collection Mondon-Vidailhet*. Paris, 1913. nr.27 (BN éth.213). It is not a copy of the Ḥaylu-compilation as indicated in the catalogue. The text of the chronicles is of poor quality. The fragment of 'Amdä-Ṣeyon's chronicle beginning at page 71 of the printed text (Perruchon's edition). The last part of the ms. does not represent the annals of Iyasu I (as indicated in nr.10, fol.172 of the catalogue). It is in fact an enlarged version of the *gädl* of Iyasu I; cf. the shorter version in Conti Rossini, *Iyasu I, re d'Etiopia e martire*, in: RSO.20, 1941, pp.65-128.

17. This classification of the mss. is — *mutatis mutandis* — valid for the other parts of the compilation. Thus the judgements of the previous editors who used these mss. in different texts are to be revised.

18. Cf. J. Perruchon, *Les chroniques de Zar'a Ya'əqob et de Ba'eda Maryam.* Paris, 1893. p.86.

19. I arranged the material according to subject matter and did not follow the rather free disposition of the material in the document itself, where the author often proceeds by mere association; for example, the mention of one name of *ṭälla* makes him give the whole list of brewers and brewhouses in the camp, out of context; the numbers of the guards is to be found on fol.31 rc for the right side of the camp, but only some pages later, fol.33 vc for the left side.

20. Cf. Taddesse Tamrat, *Church and State*, figure on p.270.

21. Here a rough list of the different users of the gates (ms.0 29, fol.33vc ff.):
    To the *left*:
    Sərgʷan-Däǧǧ: only to be used by the king's order; reserved for guests of the state and high dignitaries; some are named: Žan-Bäläw-Ras, Liqä-Mäṣane, Qaqetač.
    Šəlləmat-Däǧǧ: Bäġrond of the Šəlləmet-Bet, Gəra-Bä'altiḥat, Raq-Masäre of the Gəbr-Bet of the Gəra-Ba'altiḥat; Žan-Säfäna, Bä'alä-Ḥaräfä, Däqqä-Särgʷe, (Toni?) of the Gəra-Žan-Bet-Ṭäbaqi, the wäyzazər to the left.
    Mägaräǧǧa-Däǧǧ: guards: Gəra-Ras.
         users: ?
    Wullaǧ-Däǧǧ: Ṭəran-Ṭäbaqi, Žan-Däräba.
    Iyäsus-Däǧǧ: Gəra-Bəḥtwädäd, Gəra-Ras-Bä'aldäräba, Ṭəqaqənočč, Däǧǧ-Qäläbas.
    Mär'əd-Däǧǧ: guards: Däräba- Mu'ay-Ras.
         users: Rom-Nägat, Əskəndər-Ḥarsa.

To the *right*:

SərgWan-Däǧǧ: only to be used by the king's order.

Mäblə'-Däǧǧ:Qäñ'-Bä'altihat, Qäñ-Wäyzazər, Bä'altä-Šəhna, Bäǧrond of the Bäräkät-Bet, Raq-Masära of the Hase-Žär-Haddas of the Gəra-Bä'altihat, Raq-Masära of the Bä-'altä-Šəhna, Bä'alä-Haräfa of the Žan-Bet-Tabaqi.

Mägarägga-Däǧǧ: guards: Qäñ'-Ras.

users: ?

Mäsqäl-Däǧǧ: Pappas, Žan-Sərar, Təqaqənočč.

Bä-Särr-Waǧät-Däǧǧ: Qäñ'-Bəhtwädäd, Waǧät-Qäñ'-Žan-Däräba, Təran-Tabaqi (to the right?).

Bä'alä-Gəmǧa-Maryam-Däǧǧ: 'Aqabe-Sä'at, Mäzämməran, Qes-Hase, Liqä-Däbtära.

QWəlf-Däǧǧ:(opposite to the front central gate which seems to be reserved for the king's use.)

Hase-Ennat, Ras-Gäzet, Wäsärbät-Gäzet, Gälagəl-Gäzet.

Endədočč-QWamočč to the right and the left.

The areas of the guards are further defined for the gates of the outer enclosure. The Kätäma-SərgWan gates to the right and left are to be guarded by the Bet(ä)-Ansa troops, the Kätämä-Mägaräǧǧa gates to the right and left by the Bet(ä)-Hays troops.

The position of gates does not always correspond to the disposition of the encampment of the users within the camp.

22.   Cf. Witold Kazirmierz Brzuski, *Zapożyczenia Arabskie w dawnym i współczesnym języky Amharskim*. Warszawa, 1983. Other examples are: *kämr* from Arabic: *hamr* (wine) and *kəbz* from Arabic: *hubz* (bread).

23.   It is a jar for mead which can be made of silver or gold or can be plain and without ornaments (*leta*). The title of the queen is Wäsärbät-gäzet; cf. too J. Perruchon, *Chronique de Zar'a-Ya'əqob*, p.38 (corruption in the text there!). *Wäsärbät* is used as a measure as well and then corresponds to half a *madəgga*.

24.   *mämäkkWärya* could be a nominal derivative from *mokkärä* (cf. Guidi, *Vocabolario*, 96) with a metathesis and would then mean "an instrument to prove, to control". In the context a Royal standard measure for the yard for measuring incoming tributes of textiles, etc., could be meant. Cf. the king's yard (*dirā'al-malik* or *dirā'āl-hāšimī*) in Islamic countries.

Note the parallel in the chronicle of Zär'a-Ya'qob (ed. Perruchon, pp.26-27) where the chronicler gives the measures in yards for the height of the enclosures and expressly states that he himself did not measure it. To my knowledge this is the first hint of such a standard measure in Ethiopian chronicles.

25.   For *Aqet* as "soldier" loan word from Bilin cf. C. Brockelmann: *Abessinische Studien*. Berlin, 1950. (Berichte über die Verhandlungen der Sächs. Akademie d. Wissenschaften zu Leipzig. Phil-hist. Kl. 97,4), p.9. To the second element *zär* cf. Gaetano da Thiene: *Dizionario della lingua Galla*. Harar, 1939. p.211: *igiaru*, "edificare, costruire". For the sense in Amharic cf. Guidi, *Vocabolario*, 449.

26.   Cf. Perruchon, *Chronique de Ba'eda Maryam*, pp.166-167.

27.   Cf. C. F. Beckingham and G. W. B. Huntingford, *Some records of Ethiopia*. London, 1954. p.77; 30,000 to 40,000 men are given; cf. also R. Pankhurst, *History of Ethiopian Towns* (= *Äthiopistische Forschungen. 8.)* Wiesbaden, 1982, pp.41-48 for the mobile royal camp. The numbers according to their nominal roll (*kətab* from Arabic *kitāb*) are

given in the *śər'atä gəbr*, fol.31 rc and 33 vc: To the *left*: Zä-Gəra-Raq-Masära of the 40 Bet(?): 500; Bä'al-Diho: 1000; Aysänfo: 1000; Bä-Šäwa: 1000; Bä-Amhara: 1000; Bet-Ansa: 1500; Gəra-Nəsr-Qana Žan-'Of: 1777; Argänon: 500; Žan-Azzaž-Qana: 850; Adal-'Of: 500; Gəra-Bä'al(ä)-Waš/ka: 1000; Däräba-Mu'ay: 500; Bägamač: 500; Bä-Šärr-Nəhəb: 1500; Zä-Gəra-Bä-'altihat Gäd-Yəstän: 1000; Liqä-Saf: 1000; Lola-Mäžäkät: 1200. Totals to the left: 15,327.

To the *right*: Zä-Qän-Raq-Masära: 500; Žär-Haddas-Raq-Masära: 500; Bä 'altä-Šəhna Gäd-Yəstän: 500; Bä'al-Damo: 1000; Zä-Qän-Nəsr-Qana Wäsän-'Of: 1000; Bä-Dəl-'Of: 500; Žan-Qana: 500; Ayär-G^wəhna: 200; Mänkär-Qana: 150; Bä 'al-Harb-Ras: 1000; Žan-Wämbär-Ras: 500; Qän-Säqäla-Bä'alä-Waša: 500; Bet(ä)-Hays: 2000; Žan-Bäläw: 1000; Maryam-Wälta: 1000; Muǧa-Särre: 700; Žan-Täšäkama: 500; Bəstəgre: 1000; Aräg^wagät-Ras-Nəsr-Qana: 1550. Totals to the right: 14,600.

It is quite difficult to establish a numerical relation to the rations given for the banquet and the number of participants on the basis of highly speculative dates. The number given by Mähtämä-Səlasse. Zəkrä nägär, p.57 can only give a rough idea: 1 sheep = 5 *däst* (saucepan) = ration for 50 men; 3 cows = *wətt* for 1000 men. If for example *mäblə'* as the ration of meat could be equivalent to modern *däst* (for 10 men) we could count 34,500 participants of the banquet (cf. table 3). On the other hand the mentioned 50 cows were certainly not used for *wətt* but eaten as *bərəndo*; compare to this figure the 88 cows a day for the banquet in the Royal palace listed by Mähtämä-Səllasse (*Zəkrä nägär*, p.56). The rations in lower numbers as for example *mora*, *mofi* (from somali *mofo*, "bread"?) and the different kinds of *şäǧǧ* were certainly high quality food reserved to the king and high dignitaries or guests.

28. Cf. *Some records*, p.82; Ludolf, *Historia aethiopica*. Frankfurt, 1681. II, chapter 13. nr.11 gives 3-4 years as a maximum stay of the camp in one place.

29. Cf. Perruchon, *Chronique de Ba'eda Maryam*, p.130; unpublished chronicle of Gälaw-dewos in ms. Oxford 29 (p.4, 24 in my edition); Pereira, *Chronica de Minas*. Lisboa, 1887, p.767 f. The councillors always looked for a place with *tädla* i.e. abundant in supplies of every kind.

30. Cf. J. Varenbergh, *Studien zur äthiopischen Reichsordnung*. Straßburg, 1915. p.22; 38; I. Guidi, *Il Ser'ata Mangešt*. (= *Contributi alla storia letteraria dei Abissinia.1.*) in: RRAL. ser.5., vol.31.1922(1923).. p.82; Bairu Tafla and H. Scholler, *Ser'ata Mängest*. In: *Verfassung und Recht in Übersee*. 4.1976. p.495.

31. Cf. G. Coates, *Staatliche Einrichtungen und Landessitten in Abessinien*. Berlin, 1909. p.3.

32. The inner enclosure (*mäkkabäbya*) is cleaned by the Təran-Täbaqi and the Žan-Bet-Täbabqi. The Kätäma (here in its special sense as the space between inner and outer enclosure) is roughly divided into a front and rear region. The first one, including the open space before the Bet-Anbäsa-Däǧǧ (central front gate of the outer enclosure), is cleaned by the Bet-Ansa. The rear part of the *kätäma* is the duty of the Bet-Hays. Paez knew these regulations for the "Beita-Haiz" (cf. RAESO. II. p.54).

33. Cf. Perruchon, *Chronique de Zar'a-Ya'əqob*, p.37 f. Users of the Kätäma-Lahm-Däǧǧ are, according to the *śər'atä gəbr*, the princes who are educated in Gänz in the residence of the Gänz-Gärad. This customary education-place for royal princes is attested for the time of Bä-Ədä-Maryam; cf. Perruchon, *Histoire d'Eskender*. In: JA. ser.9., tom. 3, 1894. pp.32, 48.

34. Cf. Littmann's remarks about Kəflä-Giyorgis' reluctance to have a look at the Amharic Royal songs (*Amharische Kaiserlieder*. Straßburg, 1914. p.7.)

35. Cf. Guidi, *Il Serʿata Mangešt*, p.74 n.2; Guidi, *Vocabolario*, col.449.

36. Cf. RAESO. II. pp.51-57, especially p.54.

37. Cf. W. Leslau, *Ethiopian argots*. (à *Ianua linguarum*. Series practica. 17) The Hague, 1964. p.9; for Ethiopian argots in general see also Guidi, *Vocabolario*, col.672 s.v. *däbtära* and col. 892 s.v. *fidäl*.

38. Cf. W. Leslau, *Ethiopian argots*, p.8 (augmentation of roots); p.10-11 (substitution of radicals).

39. Cf. Perruchon, *Chronique de Zarʾa Yaʿəqob*, p.61 and note 4.

40. Cf. Leslau, *Ethiopian argots*, p.34.

41. Cf. H. Ludolf, *Lexicon Amharico-Latinum*. Frankfurt am Main, 1698. col.81; 94; Ludolf, *Historia*, II, chapter 13, nr. 11. Ludolf's descriptions in chapter 12: *de aula regis, apparatu et mensa et officiis aulicis* as well as chapter 13: *de castris regiis* are still a mine of information.

42. Cf. Perruchon, *Chronique de Zarʾa-Yaʿəqob*, p.25; 29. (*laʿlay fit*); the whole passage — description of the banquet — is clearly inspired by the *šarʿatä gabr*.

43. Ms. Oxford, 29 fol. 33 ra *passim*.

TABLE3: Contributions to the Royal Banquet maḥbārä Muse or zä-näbiyat in the first days of Mäskäräm. (Ms. Oxford 29, fol.32 ra - 32 va).
First number: rations for the first day (mäṭamya)/second number (generally double) rations for the second day (sanita).
The different contributions are given in their Ethiopian names without further comments.

DIGNITARY	CONTRIBUTIONS											
	Mogärya	Wedat	Mora	Mäblə'	Ingära	Mofi	Tälla	ordinary	Sägg 'Abiyan	Sansa	Agal	Färre Iyəs' ema
Gəra Bä'altiḥat	50/100	50/100	100/200	200/400	500/1000	–	200/400	100/200	5/10	5	5/10	–
Qäñ Bä'altiḥat	50/100	50/100	100/200	200/400	500/1000	–	200/400	100/200	5/10	5	5/10	–
Bä'altä-Şoḥna	50/100	50/100	100/200	200/400	500/1000	–	200/400	100/200	5/10	5	5/10	–
Wäšärbät-Gäzet	50/100	50/100	100/200	200/400	500/1000	–	200/400	100/200	5/10	5	5/10	–
Gälägəl-Gäzet	50/100	50/100	100/200	200/400	500/1000	–	200/400	100/200	5/10	5	5/10	–
(These five aforesaid dignitaries are named queens; there is a note that the totals of their rations should be 7799 between mogärya and mäblə')												
Gəra Bəḥtwädäd	50/100	50/100	–	200/400	500/1000	–	200/400	100/200	5/10	10	5/10	10/20 (10 silver) (10 leṭa)
Qäñ Bəḥtwädäd	50/100	50/100	–	200/400	500/1000	–	200/400	100/200	5/10	10		
Səraǧ-Masäre, Qes Ḥaşe, Liqä-Däbtära	(Their rations not clearly defined in the text; possibly the same as the Qäñ-Bəḥtwädäd, then)											
	50/100	50/100	–	200/400	500/1000	–	200/400	100/200	5/10	10	–	–
Gəra Ḥədug Ras, Gəra Geta, Gəra Žan-Bet-Ṭäbaqi	20/40	20/40	–	100/200	300/600	–	100/200	50/100	–	–	–	–
Qäñ Ḥədug Ras, Qäñ Geta, Qäñ Žan-Bet-Ṭäbaqi	20/40	20/40	–	100/200	300/600	–	100/200	50/100	–	–	–	–
Gəra Raq-Masära (zä-gəra Bet-Gabr?)	10/20	10/20	–	50/100	100/200	–	60/120	50/100	–	–	–	–
Qäñ Raq-Masära zä-Qäñ Bet-Gəbr	10/20	10/20	–	50/100	100/200	–	60/120	50/100	–	–	–	–
Bä'alä-Damo (Ras)	20/40	20/40	–	100/200	200/400	–	120/240	100/200	–	–	–	–
Bä'alä-Diho (Ras)	20/40	20/40	–	100/200	200/400	–	120/240	100/200	–	–	–	–
Aysänfo, Žär-Aqet-Dägafi	20/40	20/40	–	100/200	200/400	–	120/240	100/200	–	–	–	–
Qäñ-Nəsr-Qana	20/40	20/40	–	100/200	200/300	–	120/240	100/200	–	–	–	–
Gəra-Nəsr-Qana	20/40	20/40	–	100/200	200/300	–	120/240	100/200	–	–	–	–
Dämsasočč of the 9 Bets	180/360	180/360	–	900/1800	1800/2700	–	1080/2160	900/1800	–	–	–	–
? (1)	?/10	?/10	–	?/50	?/50	–	?/50	?/50	–	–	–	–
? (1)	10/20	10/20	–	50/100	50/100	–	50/140	50/100	–	–	–	–
Bet(ä)-Ḥayş	10/20	10/20	–	50/100	50/100	–	70/140	50/100	–	–	–	–
Žan-Masäre, Žan-Ḥaşana	20/40	20/40	–	100/200	100/200	–	100/200	100/200	–	–	–	–
Däräba-Mu'ay	10/20	10/20	–	50/100	50/100	–	20/30	50/100	–	–	–	–
Bä'alä-Waša (Waqa?)	10/20	10/20	–	50/100	50/100	–	20/30	50/100	–	–	–	–
Bəstegre	10/20	10/20	–	50/100	50/100	–	20/30	50/100	–	–	–	–
Qäläbas	150/300	150/300	–	(2)	600/countless	300/600	600/1000	500/600	–	50/50	–	–
Approximate totals (first day only!)	965	965	500	3450	8600	300	4480	3250	40	55	30	10

1)The text here is evidently corrupted and presents a lacuna of at least two dignitaries.

2)The mäblə' proves to be the ration of meat by the fact that the Qäläbas does not present those rations, but has to give animals for slaughter, as follows:

50 cows the first day, 30 ornamented with bäläw-särawər; the same the second day.
50 sheep the first day, 2 ornamented with bäläw-särawər; the same the second day.

In addition to this he has to bring a horse, ornamented with bäläw-särawər, two spears and some other weapons.

230

FIGURE 1: THE GATES OF THE INNER ENCLOSURE

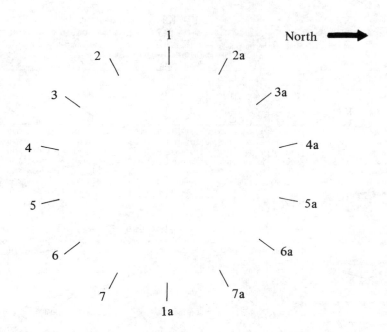

Central gates:

    1. Wəddənaš-Däǧǧ in front
    1a. Qʷəlf-Däǧǧ in the rear

Gates to the left:

    2. Ṣərgwan-Däǧǧ
    3. Səlləmat-Däǧǧ
    4. Mägaräǧǧa-Däǧǧ
    5. Wullaǧ-Däǧǧ
    6. Iyäsus-Däǧǧ
    7. Märʿəd-Däǧǧ

Gates to the right:

    2a. Sərgʷan-Däǧǧ
    3a. Mäblə ʿ-Däǧǧ
    4a. Mägaräǧǧa-Däǧǧ
    5a. Mäsqäl-Däǧǧ
    6a. Bä-Ṣärr-Wäǧat-Däǧǧ
    7a. Bäʿalä-Gəmǧa-Maryam-Däǧǧ

FIGURE 2: THE GATES OF THE OUTER ENCLOSURE IN CORRESPONDENCE TO THE GATES OF THE INNER ENCLOSURE

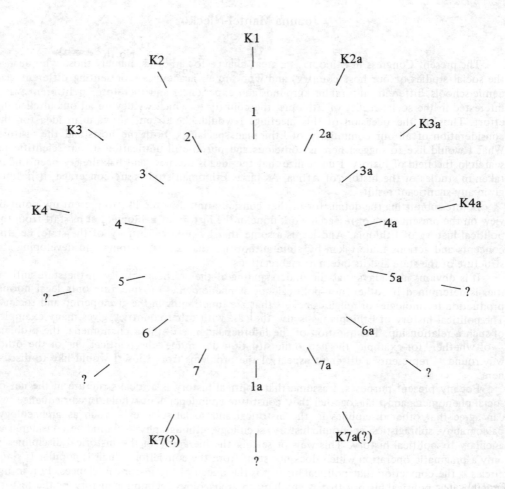

Central gate: K1: (yä-Kätäma) Bet(ä)-Anbäsa-Däǧǧ (to the west)

Gates to the left:

Gates to the right:

K2. Yä-Kätäma Sərgʷan-Däǧǧ	K2a. Yä-Kätäma Sərgʷan-Däǧǧ
K3. Yä-Kätäma Lahm-(?)-Däǧǧ	K3a. Yä-Kätäma Lahm-Däǧǧ
K4. Yä-Kätäma-Mägaräǧǧa-Däǧǧ	K4a. Yä-Kätäma Mägaräǧǧa-Däǧǧ
K7. Bet-Ḥayṣ-Däǧǧ	K7a. Bet-Ḥayṣ-Däǧǧ

Location and correspondence of K7 and K7a are not certain.

AUXILIARY HISTORICAL DISCIPLINES IN STUDIES OF
THE HISTORY OF ETHIOPIA

Joanna Mantel-Niecko

The present Congress in Ethiopia is a great chance for all of us, namely those who deal in the social studies of our host country, and who are all academics representing different academic schools, different cultural backgrounds and experiences and therefore, in different ways, interested in the social reality of Ethiopia, the country to which we devote all our intellectual effort. Thus on the occasion of this meeting, I would like to put forward an idea for the consideration of all our community of Ethiopian specialists, both the hosts and the visitors. What I would like to suggest here is conscious and purposeful unification of our scientific research in the field of history. I do realize that the idea is not new and has already been undertaken in studies of the history of Africa. As far as Ethiopian studies are concerned, it has not given any significant result.

Before submitting the details for further consideration, I would like to present my point of view on the present state of research work done in the history of Ethiopia. Let us start from the political history of Ethiopia. And let us assume that by political history of the state, i.e. the concepts and actions undertaken by state authorities that aim at shaping and developing the structure of the state and its international relations.[1]

It is obvious nowadays that the understanding of the political activity of the state authorities is determined by other, non-political, social phenomena – to mention only legal norms, production technologies or religious beliefs that are functioning in the given period and society. The political history of Ethiopia, as is also the case with other countries, gives many examples of such a relationship. The question of the interdependence of these phenomena, the problem – of whether, for example, the economic situation determines the political one or the other way round – represents a different aspect of the problems from those I would like to discuss here.

For my present purposes, I assume that political history is a focal structure in the net of social phenomena and that together they constitute an independent whole. In consequence, we can agree that other disciplines in the historical and social sciences – such as archaeology, paleography, sphragistics, economic history, sociology, ethnography – should be considered as ancillary to political history. This way of setting the hierarchy in the historical disciplines is only a pragmatic operation which does not stem from the conviction which is popular is some circles – the conviction that political history is the queen of the historical sciences. For, in my opinion, it is political history that is auxiliary to archaeology, economic history or the history of peasant movements. It is ancillary in the sense that the researcher would use the results of the science *without a closer look at its method* and he would not apply the method himself in his own considerations. *He would use the results* just to understand better the mechanisms and laws observed in the area of history he studied. Thus any domain of the social sciences that has got its own research methodology can be considered as auxiliary to another field which has a different methodology for investigating social reality. I accept this definition of auxiliary disciplines, for I am convinced that Prof. Witold Kula is right when he states that "scholarship has known polyhistores in the sphere of facts but has not heard of polyhistores in the domain of methods".[2]

I thought it necessary to present this reasoning in order to avoid the possibility of misunderstanding that could take place if one jumped to a conclusion that I might prefer one discipline of history to another and that I might consider philological studies of written historical records as subsidiary disciplines in research into the political history of Ethiopia, although it could as well be considered the main field, while the others would become subsidiary.

Thus, accepting only as a working hypothesis, the view that the political history of Ethiopia understood as history of the state authorities is the main discipline, it is time to pose a question about the sources of our knowledge. It is indisputable that historical written evidence of a given country — and Ethiopia has a long historiographic tradition — provides one of the most important sources of our knowledge. The analysis of these sources, their degree of credibility, while reproducing the history of past events, is of primary importance for the veracity of our opinions about the political history of Ethiopia. Let us then have a closer look at the state of Ethiopian historiography and begin with the generally known, catalogued collections of Ethiopian manuscripts which can be found in libraries in Ethiopia and Europe. Let us ignore the Aksum period and the period of the rule of the Zagwē dynasty and concentrate on the times from Yikuno Amlak's reign until the fall of the empire, i.e. the period from 1270 to 1974. If we consider, for example, the catalogues section under the entry "history", while ignoring other manuscript works that can also be a source of historical knowledge — for instance, hagiographies — we shall get the following results of a survey, unfortunately incomplete, of the catalogues:[3] in the 30 catalogues examined, historical evidence is missing of 12 emperors out of 66 that reigned in the period from 1270 to 1974. The reign of the remaining 54 emperors has a historical record in manuscripts, even in a few versions. So far it would seem that Ethiopian historical manuscripts recording the reign of only 37 emperors have been published. Thus, if the author of the work quoted here has managed successfully to obtain access to literature on the subject, then the lacunae in our knowledge based on accessible sources will include the reign of the emperors in the periods 1270-1314, 1344-1434, 1706-1721, 1769-1872 and 1913-1974.[4] The missing evidence covers 289 years in all. In the case of some rulers there are no native sources (historical writs), in others not all manuscripts have been published. It is obvious that it is not a manuscript, but a published source, that counts in the academic work of a historian. We are, therefore, in the position which does not allow the researcher of the political history of Ethiopia to use relatively accessible sources — i.e. those kept in libraries — not to mention the manuscripts which can be found in private and church collections.

This therefore gives rise to my first postulate — intensification of philological studies of Ethiopian historiography. It would be more appropriate not to use the word "intensification", but rather prevention of decreasing interest in Ethiopian philological studies. Philology is indispensable for setting the foundations for the real political history of the Ethiopian Empire, i.e. not only what is referred to as *histoire évenementielle*, but history that would also discover long-term tendencies in the structure of the state, the direction and factors of structural changes in various periods, a discipline that would make it possible to establish *caesura* in the political history of Ethiopia and that would be based on more profound criteria than those recognized today. It seems that all academics who, in various ways, are trying to study the past of Ethiopia would need to gather all the evidence that some of us have at our disposal, irrespective of catalogued information on the subject of the state of manuscript Ethiopian historiography and of the present state of its general accessibility through publishing. We need the now defunct *Monumenta Aethiopiae Historica* to organize knowledge about the existing sources and also about their old publications, which are dispersed all over the world and are not accessible in all the libraries; they could thus be forgotten altogether. The *Monumenta* would also be very important for they would help to organize and make the further research easier. We could then concentrate on the most important and urgent tasks, i.e. on filling in the gaps. This philological, bibliographic and archival work, auxiliary to the political history of Ethiopia, demands specialists if it is to bring some benefits. Therefore, perhaps, it would be reasonable to take advantage of our meeting and find out who has the possibilities and what they are like — to undertake a cooperative work on collecting and organizing in a systematic way all Ethiopian historiography and its publications which are dispersed in various libraries all over the world.

The postulate of undertaking work on *Monumenta Aethiopiae Historica* will entail some further consequences. The catalogues of Ethiopian manuscripts distinguish among the Ethiopian historical records: inventory lists of emperors, genealogies, chronologies, chronicles, annales and histories.[5] It is not clear though what the authors of the catalogues understood by the above-mentioned terms. It is generally understood that in European historical records there are three types of writing. They are annales, histories and chronicles.[6] The annales are considered to be papers which include a matter-of-fact description of events, chronological presentation of facts not commented on by the author. A chronicle includes a description of events where the relation between the cause and effect of the described facts is presented and given some justification, it is a description of events as they happen without acknowledging their further development and course of their results. And a history is a record devoted to past events, where causes and effects can be discussed and estimated by the author. The authors of the catalogues of Ethiopian manuscripts have evidently disregarded the differences in the notions, using them interchangeably. It happened that the same manuscript is referred to by one author of the catalogue as a chronicle, and by another as annales or a history.[7] We do not know today if the types of Ethiopian historiography can be identified with the above-quoted types of European historiography. And classification of the types of historical records is of primary importance for the history of culture, as well as for estimating the quality of the sources and the problem has already been raised by James McCann at the Vth International Conference of Ethiopian Studies[8], but I do not know if his postulate for professional analysis of Ethiopian Historical records, the problem of authorship, structure, types, etc., has been answered anywhere. If not – I would like to raise the problem again. I am convinced that without a specialist organisation and specification of what we know about the written historical sources of Ethiopia, our examination of the past history of this country faces serious difficulties or may lead nowhere.

And here it is not necessary to convince anybody that the present day conflicts of any country have their roots in the past, or that the past of all the societies in the world results in the present state of human tragedies. We must state a correct diagnosis, without which one can not find the key to present problems in one country or on a global scale – if there is any solution at all; to present a correct diagnosis means to know and understand how it all happened. And that is our task. Thus, if we are to know the history of Ethiopia a bit better and sooner, we should organize our work. Let us start from a step that may seem distant from major enquiries into the laws governing the development of Ethiopian history. Personally, I do not believe in any social theory that originates from historiosophic assumptions and not empiric investigations. It is the missing empiric studies that mean that historians of Ethiopia cannot make documented contributions to world discussion on the subject of social and economic systems of pre-industrial societies. We use the term "feudalism", not because we can prove the existence of feudalism in Ethiopia, but due to the fact that the social and economic system of the empire, which we do not fully understand, seem to show features of feudalism that existed in other regions of the world. And that is absolutely too little evidence.

Therefore, I suggest that we should start from the foundations, that is, from systematisation of written Ethiopian historical records which can be found in both European and Ethiopian libraries. This work will present a lot of problems that we probably cannot even anticipate and which can open some new prospects and perspectives of our knowledge. This has already been proposed by J. McCann in the previously quoted work.

Addis Ababa is the natural centre of Ethiopian studies. Beside it, there are only very few of us who work dispersed in different countries, too few to face all the problems and to examine the entire material – unable to create an academic community that would be connected by everyday research and discussion. And Ethiopian manuscripts are similarly dispersed all over the world. They are in Addis Ababa, Paris, London, Rome, Leningrad and other cities all over the world. It is a serious obstacle to the organization but it is not impossible to overcome. To make my statements more genuine, I would like to submit a concrete offer. I would like to offer the possibility of publishing in Warsaw the materials in the disciplines auxiliary to the political history of Ethiopia and the possibility that the research in this field could be carried out by the students and graduates of the Ethiopian Studies Division of the University of Warsaw. Warsaw is situated far away from Ethiopian libraries or centres. Thus the form of contact would have to be discussed among those who would like to engage in such work.

NOTES

1. In the reflections presented here on political history and auxiliary historical sciences, I was inspired by: W. Kula, *Problemy i metody historii gospodarczej (Problems and Methods in*

Economic History), Warsaw, 1983, and J. Topolski, *Methodology of History*, Warsaw, 1976.

2. W. Kula, *op. cit.*, p.60.

3. M.A. thesis by J. Krol, *Documentation of the History of Ethiopian Emperors of 1270-1974 in the Native Historical Records (Based on Catalogues of Ethiopian Manuscripts)*, unpublished typescript, Warsaw, 1984, University of Warsaw, Institute of Oriental Studies, Department of Languages and Cultures of Africa. The thesis illustrates the problem but does not exhaustively answer the question (out of 73 existing catalogues, we have only 30 at our disposal in Warsaw).

4. J. Krol, *op. cit.*, p.120. Collected and abridged chronicles were not included here.

5. *Ibid.*, p.24 *et passim*.

6. J. Topolski, *op.cit.*, p.46 *et passim*.

7. J. Krol, *op. cit.*, p.35.

8. J. McCann, "The Ethiopian chronicles as documentary tradition: description and methodology", *Proceedings of the Vth International Conference of Ethiopian Studies, Session B*, ed. by R. L. Hess, University of Illinois, Chicago, 1979, pp.387-396.

HUNTING IN GOJJAM:

THE CASE OF MATAKAL 1901-1932

Abdussamad H. Ahmad

Hunting in Ethiopia was performed both for the prestige and status it could bring hunters and as a traditional sport. It also had some economic significance, as it was the only way to obtain ivory, a valuable commodity. It was primarily carried out by the aristocracy and the military class of the Ethiopian highlands, who made expeditions to the lowland areas for this purpose.

From the Gondarine chronicles, one can see that hunting was conducted in earlier times. For example, King Iyassu I (1682-1706) conducted hunting expeditions to the Sudanese border from his seat at Gondar. At one time, he hunted a buffalo on the Blue Nile on the Sudanese border. It is also mentioned that he killed a large elephant around the Takazze river to the north of Gondar.[1] Pleased at his success in hunting game and to encourage the traditional aristocratic drive for hunting, Iyassu I himself gave horses to all the guards who accompanied him.[2]

In more recent times, and probably in the days of Iyassu I as well, elephants were particularly prized for the value of their tusks, but many other animals were also killed. Mansfield Parkyns, who visited the valleys of the Marab and the Takazze rivers in the 1840s, mentioned the availability of wild animals like elephants, rhinoceros, ostriches, giraffes and buffaloes.[3] He also stated that these animals were found in certain seasons only and noted that the hot and dry season which prevailed from mid-October to early May was considered to be the best period to hunt lions.[4] My informants recounted that during the rainy season from June to October wild animals generally would confine themselves deep in the forested areas. From mid-October to early May, however, wild animals would ascend and descend the streams of the less inhabited areas in order to get access to grass and water.[5] It was, therefore, from mid-October to early May that hunting was conducted.

The military class from Gojjām and Begemdir, the two northwestern provinces of Ethiopia, traditionally hunted animals in the lowlands of Matakal. Matakal is a vast district within Gojjām and covers approximately the western one-third of the entire province.

Matakal has gently undulating plains, which are broken here and there by smoothly flowing rivers. These rivers are Ardi, Durā, Tilliq and Gilgal Balas and Dinder, to mention just a few of the major ones. All are tributaries of the Blue Nile. Near the Dinder river and in the lowlands of Ayimā, which extended to the Sudanese border, there dwelled wild animals such as elephants, lions, buffaloes, giraffes, monkeys and apes.

The most numerous group of people in Matakal are the Gumuz, known to the highlanders as "Shānqellā", a generic and pejorative name for dark-skinned lowlanders. Dr. Abraham Demoz has critically observed that: "Ethiopia is the despair of the compulsive classifier".[6] Nonetheless, Marvin L. Bender, undaunted by this, places the Gumuz under what he calls the Nilo-Saharan family of languages.[7] Another group inhabiting Matakal are the Shināshā, whom Fleming relates to the Gonga, Anfillo and Kaffā, further to the south in Wallagā and Kaffā.[8] Historically dominant over the Shināshā and the Gumuz in Matakal were the Oromo. The Oromo had come, about four generations ago, from the areas to the south of the Blue Nile, according to information gathered in 1925 by R. F. Cheesman, the British consul at Dāngillā.[9] At the time of their arrival, they invaded the southern Matakal areas, known as the Wambarā highlands and Kitar hills, which apparently had formerly been occupied by the Shināshā. With better spears and reinforcements from Limmu to the south of the Blue Nile, the Oromo successfully drove the Shināshā to the lowlands. However, in the end, the ultimate losers were the Gumuz, who in turn were pushed to still lower lands by the Shināshā.[10]

Once they were successful in defeating the Shināshā, the Oromo began to advance further towards the Zigam, Balāyā and Dāngur highlands, which were inhabited by the Agaw. The Oromo advance was checked by a certain Agaw leader, Ajaz Jangwā, in the late nineteenth century. Thus, the Agaw kept the fertile lands under their control.[11] Although some of the Shin-āshā were pushed to the less desirable areas like Bulan, Gwāngwā, Kabo or Zaro and Kursha, some others remained near the Kitar hills and the Wambarā highlands, and some even inter-married with the Oromo.[12]

Other ethnic minorities, like the Kunfal and Gongā, still survive in the area. These minorities, like the Gumuz, were driven to the hot valleys to struggle against malaria and other diseases.[13] In the final analysis, in the struggle to keep the most fertile and highly watered areas of Matakal, the worst losers were the Gumuz, the Kunfal and Gongā.

In the late nineteenth century the Oromo attempted to penetrate further north from Wambarā, but were checked by the Amhara under King Takla-Haymanot of Gojjām (1881-1901). Having received the submission of the Oromo, the king treated them well. He christian-ized them and built the Dabra Zayt Church at Wambarā. The Oromo chief, by the name of Itu, was baptized and given the Christian name Gabra Māryām, with the title of *Fitāwrāri*.[14]

Not only were *Fitāwrāri* Itu and his chiefs baptized, but the king himself also affirmed their lordship over the Shināshā. The king also gave the Agaw chiefs the power to collect taxes from the Gumuz and other ethnic minorities. The Amhara military class served as rulers, super-visors of taxes and controllers of trade in coffee, civet, gold and especially ivory. The military class built towns (*Katamā*) in the elevated and most healthy areas of Matakal and resided there.[15]

After king Takla-Haymānot had died in 1901, his son *Rās* Haylu began to rule Gojjām. Haylu appointed administrators to control the remarkable resources of Matakal, a district which supplied coffee, civet, gold and ivory to the commerce of Ethiopia.[16] Haylu also vested these officials with the authority to control access to the rich hunting areas of Matakal and required that members of the Amhara military class of Gojjām and Begemdir who wanted to hunt, first obtain permission.[17]

Some officials, like *Fitāwrāri* Zalaqa Liqu, were said to have bought their lucrative offices for money. Zalaqa himself bought his office for two thousand Maria Theresa thalers from *Rās* Haylu. Zalaqa was in charge of hunting game in Matakal and resided at Balāyā mountains in the northwestern part of Matakal, right on the route taken by hunters of both Gojjām and Beg-emdir. Balāyā was a good jumping-off point for the lowlands of Awjamis and Omedla and beyond them to the Sudanese border lands.[18] Zalaqa was responsible for licensing the military class of Gojjām and Begemdir. He received two Maria Theresa thalers from every hunter before he could leave for the hunting field. The money was appropriated by Zalaqa himself. When the hunters came from the hunting field, Zalaqa was also responsible for collecting tribute from them in ivory. One out of every two tusks of an elephant was given to Zalaqa.

Zalaqa's camp resembled a military garrison, stationed to give service to the incoming hun-ters. Zalaqa had about a hundred professional hunters, known as *admā* (literally "rebels"), who served as excellent guides to incoming hunters. The *admā* had come from Agaw Midir and Dāmot and settled in the camp of Zalaqa. They were poor people who farmed during the rainy season and supplemented their income with tips which they received from the military class for helping its member secure and then sell the lucrative tusks. In return for their services, Zalaqa armed each one of them with spears and some were given rifles. Other local officials, like *Fitāw-rāri* Itu, also had *admā* under them. Itu, for example, had about fifty Oromo and Shinasha hun-ters. These were people personally employed by him. Itu gave them plots of coffee land in the Wambara highlands and Kitar hills. In addition to this, he armed them with spears and rifles. Whenever Itu himself went out hunting, his *admā* accompanied him to the hunting grounds of Matakal. In the event that Itu and his *admā* would kill an elephant, both tusks would be taken by him. Itu would then send one tusk as a part of his tax and the other for sale to the courtyard of Zalaqa at Balāyā. It is interesting to note that, unlike Zalaqa's *admā*, the *admā* under Itu did not serve as guides to incoming hunters.[19]

The *admā* under Zalaqa had mastered very well the ins and outs of the desert environment and the localities in which elephants abounded.[20] This was due to their experience in the hunt-ing field. They were originally *rist* (land use right) holders, but had become poor. This was be-cause they did not have enough oxen to plough their land with. They returned to hunting to eke out an existence. As pointed out earlier, they came one by one to settle in Balāyā. Their numbers grew from time to time so that they eventually formed a community.[21]

It should be pointed out that the *admā* did not have much experience in firing rifles as compared to the military class. This was due to the fact that they could not afford to buy bullets and Zalaqa did not want them to misuse his. Whenever they went out hunting with the military class, it was the latter who would pay for the price of the bullets. What is remarkable is that the *admā*, too, boasted of their skill in manipulating rifles.[22]

ከአፈሙዙ ከስይፋ ቀና ፡   With the muzzle down and the stock up,
እኛም እውቀንበት በፈርንጅ መላ ።   Indeed, we too, have mastered the technique
                         of the Faranji (i.e. foreigners).

Members of the military class of Gojjām and Begemdir met every year in October at Chāgni, capital of Matakal. Hunters from Begemdir joined those of Gojjām by way of Alafā, Tāqussā, Qwārā and the Dinder river. Others, following the Gonder, Bāhir-Dār, Dangur and Omedlā route, joined the hunters of Gojjām at Omedlā.[23] Before proceeding to Omedlā, hunters of Begemdir sent Zalaqa the customary two Maria Theresa Thalers fee required from every hunter. Zalaqa, in turn, would send them receipts for their payment. Hunters were predominantly members of the nobility who hunted for sport, prestige and status and, certainly, for the modest economic benefit it could bring them. To the *admā*, as it has been argued, the economic consideration was uppermost.[24]

Hunting was a sport in which the military class engaged every year. The hunting year was defined by the hot and dry season, when the lowlands were no longer feverish, the rivers were fordable and the wild animals were readily available. In Matakal, the game hunting areas extended from the Rās Dāsh highlands and Balāyā to the lowland country of Awjamis on the Sudanese border. This vast game area also extended from Amorā Mulā mountain across Ayimā river to Omedlā on the Sudanese border and all along the entire course of the Dinder river, which flows to the Sudan from the northwestern corner of Gojjām province.[25] Hunters from Gojjām and Begemdir could roam this area as far as the borderlands of the Sudan. However, they did not enter the territory of British Sudan.[26]

Hunters, like ordinary soldiers, used traditional weapons like spears, bows and arrows. Like an army band, they also had their own generals. Each hunter would enter the game hunting field with a shield and two spears. Horses also played a major role in hunting by terrorizing animals with their noise. The hunters performed very difficult manoeuvres chasing elephants, putting themselves at great risk. Accidents occurred when a horse stumbled against a tree and when the rider was knocked from his mount by the branch of a tree. This would result in the hunter's death, as the pursued animal would turn and trample his would-be killer to death.[27] The importance of horses did not change much from the days of Parkyns, who wrote that gallant horsemen got near animals and threw their lances. Parkyns also pointed out that the killing of a buffalo was equivalent in merit to killing twenty men.[28] My informants recounted that the killing of an elephant was equivalent to killing forty men.[29]

Horses ceased to be important around the 1920s, when the relatively sophisticated rifles such as *Wačafo* (Wetterly), *Dimotfor* (Lee Metford) and *Mawzer* (Mauser) were imported in great numbers.[30] Until the 1930s hunters continued to use *Sinādir* (Schneider hunting rifle) and muskets which had been popular in the nineteenth century. The muskets took a long time to fire, as powder had to be inserted before each shot and this was a slow process. Moreover, my informants claimed that elephants often smelt the fuse and escaped safely before the bullet left the barrel.[31] The advent of the Wetterly rifle, called *Wačafo* in Amharic (literally "running rapidly", the term signifies the speed of the rifle when fired), gave an immense boost to hunting. The rapidity with which the bullets left the barrels made it extremely difficult for elephants to escape. The reliability and accuracy of the *Wačafo* rifle is expressed by the following poem, collected in Matakal.[32]

With the help of the *Wačafo* rifle
The hunter claimed the lives of many

From the turn of the twentieth century till 1932, when *Rās* Haylu was sent to prison in Shewā by Emperor Haile Silasse, hunters destined for the hunting grounds of Matakal obtained permission from *Fitāwrāri* Zalaqa, ruler of the district. These hunters halted at Balāyā to make arrangements. Lists of hunters and the specific days each one of them was to begin shooting were registered by the *taqotātāri* (literally "accountant"; a person appointed by Zalaqa to register hunters and follow them to the field). The hunter who would start the day's shooting would be named *gadāy* (literally "killer") and the trophy of the day, say the lion's mane, the giraffe's tail or the elephant's tusks, would be given to him. Having agreed on such procedures, hunters led by the *admā* would proceed to hunt. However, the *admā* were not allowed to start the shooting. They had to wait until the hunter for the day fired the first bullet. Then they would extend their help, sometimes by firing their rifles, but most of the time by throwing their spears and shooting their arrows. This was done to save their bullets, as bullets were very expensive. In addition to this, the physical skills of accurately using spears and arrows were highly prized in traditional hunting. Hence, the *admā* as well as the hunters used spears and arrows after the firing of the first bullet by the assigned man of the day.[33] What really mattered, as Parkyns noted, was who first wounded the animal; it mattered little who really killed it. The credit was always attributed to the one who first drew blood from the animal.[34]

The *admā* resorted to their rifles when the quarry happened to be an elephant. They would attempt to give a fatal shot to the animal. Manoeuvres would be repeated many times until the animal was secured. Accidents occurred when the wounded elephant attacked its killers. But such accidents were not frequent as the *admā* coordinated their attack against the animal. Informants recounted that about twenty to thirty bullets were needed to kill an elephant, as hunters wanted to assure themselves that the animal was indeed killed, because they feared that a wounded animal would become furious and cause accidents.[35]

Throughout the 1920s, Ethiopian as well as foreign hunters were accompanied by the *admā*. Henry Darley, who led a hunting expedition in southwestern Ethiopia on the Sudanese border in the 1920s, was escorted by about four hundred warriors. The warriors were all natives of the game hunting area. He was also accompanied by a gun-bearer.[36] He mentioned that they guided him into a good position to attack a herd of elephants on the Ethio-Sudanese borderlands.[37] In Matakal as well, most of the game was being hunted on the Sudanese borderlands, as the British consul, R. F. Cheesman, reported in 1925.[38] Elephants most often were found in the forested areas of Matakal, which bordered the Sudan and was inhabited by the Gumuz. This did not change much from the days of James Bruce, the Scottish traveller, who reached Ethiopia by way of Egypt and the Sudan in 1769. Bruce noted that tusks of elephants were obtained from the country of the "Shanqella", as he called the Gumuz.[39]

To protect themselves at night from dangerous animals, whenever they camped, hunters procured fire by friction using a hard dry wood known as desert wood (*yabarahā inčat* in Amharic), after the flame was produced, large logs were added to it. Such a fire would keep dangerous animals away from the hunters' camp.[40] However, some hunters were so bold as to kill elephants by moonlight, while the animals drank water in the nearby streams. This was partly due to the relative largeness of the elephants, which made them visible during the night. Others succeeded in killing animals at dawn by following the tracks of the animals from their drinking site.[41] Hunters who succeeded in killing elephants by moonlight and at dawn attributed their success to the perfection of their hunting skills.[42]

The particular hunter who first shot and drew blood from the animal would be specially honored by being called *gadāy* for the night. He would be given the opportunity to take the mane of the lion, the tail of the giraffe, the horns of the buffalo and the tusks of the elephant as trophies. Hunters would be allowed to boast of their success, shouting out their bravery. They would wager that their deeds surpassed those of others before them.[43] The following poems exemplify the boasting of the hunters.[44]

በራት ቀደምቶቼ ያልሠሩትን ሥራ ፤
በጨለማ ገዳይ መብራት እያበራ ፨
ቀጭኔ ቢጓደኝ ማንብሎታል ጉዳይ ፤
ዝሆንስ ቢጓደድ ማንብሎታል ጉዳይ ፤
እባሮ አንከራቶ በጨለማ ገዳይ ፨

> Those who preceded me performed no such deeds
> I killed at night with the light I ignited
> I did not fear the giraffe which walked by
> I did not fear the elephant which walked by
> I followed their tracks and killed them at night

On the return journey from the hunting field to Balāyā, hunters and the *admā* raided Gumuz villages for cattle, large sheep, goats and, above all, for slaves. Their raiding tactics were simple. They would attack the villagers at dawn or any time during the day. It is worth noting that such attacks were not conducted at night. This was mainly due to the fact that the Gumuz, whose skill in using bows and arrows exceeded that of the hunters and the *admā* would make reprisal by attacking their enemies' camps during the night. The nights were conducive to such reprisals as hunters' camps were identified by their fires. During the night, therefore, the hunters did not attack the Gumuz. They even selected strategic camping sites for the night to protect themselves against Gumuz attacks.[45]

The hunters attacked Gumuz villages by calling their horse-names such as *gizāchaw* (literally "rule them"), *dānāchaw* (literally "judge them"), etc., and shouting out their valour with the traditional *fukarā* (literally "boasting"). They then took cattle and young boys and girls from the defenceless Gumuz villagers. Such raiding parties proceeded to Balāyā, to the court of *Fitāwrāri* Zalaqa Liqu.[46]

At Zalaqa's court, hunters were awarded honours comparable to soldiers victorious in wars. In return hunters would give Zalaqa large sheep, goats and Gumuz slaves, which they had captured from Gumuz villagers. Slaves were appropriate for this purpose because hunting parties also engaged in slave raiding expeditions in Gumuz localities and captured individuals as booty. Although the authorities in Addis Ababa were making efforts to suppress the international slave trade, internal slavery in Gojjām and the rest of northwestern Ethiopia continued.[47]

The honored hunters, as indicated earlier, gave some money for the *admā* who had cooperated with them to make the hunting expeditions successful. Some hunters got the money to pay the *admā* from the sale of tusks. Others got the money from contributions made by their near relatives. It was part of the tradition that relatives of successful hunters shared in their prestige and took pride in their achievements; hence their willingness to contribute money to support the hunters.[48]

Elephant killers in particular paid a tax of one out of every two tusks obtained. These tusks were sent to the court of *Rās* Haylu (1901-1932) at Dabra Mārqos by Zalaqa. Even the one tusk which was the hunters' share was bought by *Fitāwrāri* Zalaqa at Balāyā, who himself determined the price. He also paid the hunters the required amount of money on behalf of the *Rās*. The *Rās*, in turn, gave Zalaqa half the price for all the tusks which were received as tax. The *Rās,* who vested Zalaqa with the power to collect the customary two Maria Theresa Thalers fee required from every hunter, also allowed him to take the money. In this way, Haylu and his *Fitāwrāri* exercised a monopoly over the lucrative ivory trade in his domains. Hunters most often killed elephants for the chance of procuring ivory, but they were not allowed to take the tusks. This was because ivory could only be exported by authorized merchants who were agents of Haylu.[49] However, hunters were allowed to take the manes of lions, the tails of giraffes, and the horns of the buffaloes. They used the trophies to adorn their houses.[50]

When the hunters returned home, they would invite the villagers to a feast. Putting on the *qamis* (literally "tunic", special clothes worn during such occasions) and putting butter on their heads, they would shout their bravery with the traditional *fukarā*.[51] Some of the *fukarā* ran:

ኮልጓይ በሜማ ኮልጓይ በሜማ ፤
ተስዶ ገዳይ በዐረብ አውድማ

> I travelled on foot, I travelled on foot
> As far as the Arab borderlands [the Sudan]
> and became a killer.

The wives of the successful hunters were awarded honours comparable to the wives of the victorious soldiers in wars. They, too, sang in front of the villagers. Some of the songs explain the respect and the admiration these wives had for their husbands.[53]

እንኳን ገደለ እንጂ ደፈረለት እጅ ፣	Good that he shot and killed
ለመወዝወዙግ ምን ሆኘ ወዳጄ	I [his wife] am ready to dance [in front of the villagers]
ዱርም ስንጋ ይኸዉ ነዉ ነዉ ዉላችን ፣	the villagers]
በአደና በግርጣ ሲ.ሥራ ቤታችን ፨	Our marriage contract was such
	That our house was to be adorned with trophies.

A woman who was happy about the hunting success of her husband was said to have put butter on his head. She then began to ridicule the unsuccessful hunters or those who did not go out hunting at all, as the following verse demonstrates.[54]

እምቢ አለች ላሚቱ አልታለብ ብላ ፣	Even the cow refused to be milked
ያልገደለ ጉበዝ ይቀባኛል ብላ ፨	Fearing that the unsuccessful hunter may put her butter on his head.

Hunting, like the army, involved people of all ranks. While the nobility dominated and set the style, many lower rank people like the *admā* did a lot of hard work for scanty return. Hunters who belonged to the military class supplemented their income from the sale of tusks to Zalaqa, but their income was modest, too. It was *Rās* Haylu and *Fitāwrāri* Zalaqa who got the lion's share from hunting activities. To the rulers of Gojjam, the primary drive in encouraging hunting as a traditional sport was undoubtedly economic. The hunters themselves seem to have been motivated primarily by the status hunting would bring them, and by their relish for a traditional sport.

NOTES

* I wish to express my warm appreciation and gratitude to my advisor, Professor Donald Crummey, for his suggestions and critical comments on this paper. The paper is dedicated to the memory of Zakaria Abdullahi, who joined the University of Illinois before me, in pursuit of Ethiopian studies, but whose life was cut short by cancer on 25 April 1983.

1. Richard Pankhurst, *The Ethiopian Royal Chronicles*, (London: Oxford University Press, 1967), p.113.

2. *Ibid.*

3. Mansfield Parkyns, *Life in Abyssia: Three Years' Residence and Travels in that Country*, (New York: 1853), p.247.

4. *Ibid.*, p.92.

5. Informants: Ishate Mohammad, Makuriyā Bizunah and Tāddesse Jambare. Ishate Mohammad was a hunter and ivory merchant. He was interviewed at Dāngillā on 6 and 7 Sept., 1979. He was 82 at the time of the interview. Makuriyā Bizunah provided information about the hunting areas of Matakal. He was interviewed on 3 Sept., 1979. Tāddesse Jambare was ruler of Dibāti, a sub-district in Matakal. His knowledge of the entire district was invaluable to me. He was interviewed on 1 and 3 Sept., 1979. Makuriyā Bizunah and Tāddassa Jambare were 55 and 57, respectively, at the time of the interview. Both were interviewed at Chāgni. The former was Agaw and the latter was Amhara.

6. Abraham Demoz, "The Many Worlds of Ethiopia", *African Affairs*, v.68 (Jan., 1969), p.49.

7. Marvin L. Bender *et al., Language in Ethiopia*, (London: Oxford University Press, 1976), p.54.

8. H. C. Fleming, "Kaffa (Gonga) Languages", in Marvin L. Bender *et al., The Non-Semitic Languages of Ethiopia*, (East Lansing, Michigan, 1976), pp.351-76.

9. R. F. Cheesman, *Lake Tana and the Blue Nile*, (London: New Impression, Frank Cass and Company Limited, 1968), p.328.

10. Informant Dāmtaw Gobannā was interviewed at Chāgni on 4 Sept., 1979. He was a Shin-āshā by his mother and an Oromo by his father.

11. Informants: Makuriyā Bizunah and Tāddesse Jambare.

12. *Ibid.*

13. Weld H. Blundell, "Exploration of the Abai Basin in Abyssinia", *The Geographical Journal*, (June, 1906), p.535.

14. Informants: Makuriyā Bizunah and Tāddesse Jambere.

15. *Ibid.*

16. *Ibid.*

17. *Ibid.*

18. *Ibid.*, and Ishate Mohammad.

19. *Ibid.*

20. *Ibid.*

21. *Ibid.*

22. *Ibid.*

23. *Ibid.*

24. *Ibid.*

25. *Ibid.*

26. *Ibid.*

27. *Ibid.*

28. Parkyns, *op. cit.*, p.281.

29. Informants: Ishate Mohammad and Makuriyā Bizunah.

30. *Ibid.* See also my B.A. thesis, Addis Ababa University, Aug., 1977, p.23.

31. Informants: Makuriya Bizunah and Taddesse Jambare.

32. Ishate Mohammad.

33. Informants: Ishate Mohammad and Makuriyā Bizunah and Tāddesse Jambare.

34. Parkyns, *op. cit.*, pp.282-83.

35. Makuriyā Bizunah.

36. Major Henry Darley, *Slaves and Ivory in Abyssinia*, (New York: Robert M. McBride & Co., 1935), p.8.

37. *Ibid.*

38. Cheesman, *op. cit.*, p.46.

39. James Bruce, *Travels to Discover the Source of the Nile*, (Edinburgh University Press, 1790), p.172.

40. Informants: Ishate Mohammad and Makuriyā Bizunah.

41. *Ibid.*

42. *Ibid.*

43. *Ibid.*

44. *Ibid.*

45. *Ibid.*

46. *Ibid.*

47. *Ibid.*, and Tāddesse Jambare.

48. *Ibid.*

49. *Ibid.*

50. *Ibid.*

51. *Ibid.* See also Cheesman, *op. cit.*, p.354.

52. Informant: Makuriyā Bizunah.

53. Informants: Ishate Mohammad and Makuriyā Bizunah, See also Abdussamad, *op. cit.*, p.23.

54. *Ibid.*

TATAYYAQ MUGET:

THE TRADITIONAL ETHIOPIAN MODE OF LITIGATION

Aberra Jambere

The body of law that was indigenous to Ethiopia and which marked a significant development in the last century and the first three decades of this century was the regime of law known to modern legal science as Civil and Criminal Procedure laws. It was transmitted from generation to generation by oral tradition.

This procedural law included the law of evidence which incorporated a highly sophisticated technique of interrogation and cross-examination known as *Tatayyaq Muget*. The term *Tatayyaq* literally means 'be interrogated'. Technically, however, it is the traditional mode of litigation in court proceedings. *Esette-Ageba-Muget*[1] was used interchangeably with *Tatayyaq* to denote features of court proceedings and the same mode of litigation. *Muget* means litigation and includes all procedural aspects of the administration of justice.

General Virgin summarised his vivid eye-witness account of court proceedings conducted according to the indigenous mode of litigation of Ethiopia, in the following manner:

> "The Abyssinian is a born Speaker and neglects no opportunity of exercising this talent. A law-suit is a heaven-sent opening and entails as a rule a large and appreciative audience. Now threatening with shrugged shoulders, now, tearfully, he tells of his vanished farthing, and points a menacing, trembling finger towards the accused.
>
> The judge in the midst of a circle of spectators, having listened to the eloquence with a grave and thoughtful mien, now invites the accused to reply. Like a released spring he leaps up, and with raised hands calls heaven to witness his innocence, then falls on one knee, rises, stands on tiptoe, drops back on his heels, shakes his fist under the nose of his adversary and approaches the judge with clasped hands while all the time an unceasing stream of words pours from his lips."[2]

This theatrical exposition of court proceedings shows how the *Tatayyaq* mode of litigation which forms part and parcel of the great cultural heritage of the Amhara operates. The customary law of the Amhara, together with the *Tatayyaq* mode of litigation, had become the prevailing law in a good part of Ethiopia by 1935. This could have been due to the fact that the Amhara have enabled them to superimpose their own values over other ethnic groups of Ethiopia.

What are the major features of the institutions involved in the application of the *Tatayyaq Muget* and how does it actually operate?

I. FEATURES OF COURT PROCEEDINGS

Litigation at its initial stage, by and large, was a voluntary and spontaneous form of arbitration among Ethiopians.

A party to a dispute was entitled by law[3] to call upon any passer-by to decide his case. If the parties to the alleged dispute were satisfied by the rulings of the 'road side' courts, the matter would be considered settled. However, if a decision satisfactory to either or both of the parties could not be obtained, they would go to court or sometimes the person who acted as a 'road side' judge would take them to the lowest official judge.

The lowest official judge could be the *Chika Shum*[4] or the *Melkegna*[5]. The *Chika Shum* and the *Melkegna* were basically administrative officials who exercised judicial power. The concept of separation of power was alien to the then existing society. Every government official was, thus, referred to as *Dagna* (judge).

The *Techiwoch*[6] (assessors) stand next to the *Dagna* in importance. Some of them were selected by the contending parties and some by the regular court from among those people attending a court session.

The third typical feature of the judicial process is *Wass* (guarantee). The most frequent forms of guarantee were:

1) *Yeqebeqabe Wass* or *Yemegazia Wass* — a form of guarantee secured for good conduct by a resident in a community;

2) *Yesene-Ser'at Wass* — a guarantee produced by both parties to ensure respect of all procedural requirements in the proceedings of a case and appearance on the day fixed for its hearing;

3) *Yegefi Wass* — a guarantee produced by a party to prove the points he alleges;

4) *Yedagnenet Wass* — a guarantee for securing the payment of court fees by the party who lost the case;

5) *Yewurered Wass* — a guarantee to secure the payment of a wager (bet) payable on the settlement of a contested issue;

6) *Yebesella Wass* — a guarantee to secure the payment of the value claimed in civil suit;

7) *Yettelefa Wass* — a guarantee to secure the appearance of a person; and

8) *Yeje-Tebik Wass* — a guarantee to secure proper behaviour where a person had alleged that his life had been threatened by another; it was the latter who would be required to produce such a guarantee.

The fourth element of a legal process was the *Negere-Fej*. He was a person who usually had a fair knowledge of the law and who had agreed to represent another person before a court.

Let us now come to the crux of the matter and show how the *Tetayyaq* mode of litigation operated, i.e. how court proceedings were conducted at courts of all levels.

II. COURT PROCEEDINGS

A. Case Initiation

A court proceeding began with securing *Yesr'at Wass* by both the plaintiff and the defendant. The judge would then require the plaintiff to put forward his claim. After the full claim had been stated, the defendant would be required to admit or deny it.

If the claim was denied, the lawyer for the plaintiff would, moving with his stick to and fro in the court room, present the principal and side issues of the case.

The defendant, in his turn, would in like manner present his defence.

B. Wurrered Metekel: Laying Wager or Bet

At this stage, the plaintiff lays a wager to prove his claim. The defendant may require the plaintiff to reduce the amount of the wager, for instance, from a mule to a horse. If further reduction is required, it might be reduced to 'honey'.[7] The defendant would then lay the same amount of 'honey' as laid by the plaintiff. Alternatively, he should admit the claim, but deny some of the assertions, as the saying goes: " አምኖ ይሟገታል ከረከሰበት ይሸምታል " (Litigate after admitting the facts, where it is cheap).

The defendant, if he does not intend to deny the assertion, would respond by saying: "*Agurah tennagne*", meaning "I admit your contention".

If such admission is secured, the plaintiff would say: " በእጉራሁ ጠናኝ የተረታ—መሐል አገዳውን የተመታ " (A person who loses the litigation by admission is like a person who has lost his leg). He would then request that judgement be entered against the defendant. The party that invoked *agurah tennagne* would be required to pay one Birr as a court fee.

No appeal was allowed from such a ruling.

C. Introduction of Oral or Documentary Evidence

If the defendant denied some of the facts alleged against him, the facts which were denied had to be proved. The plaintiff may, therefore, introduce oral or documentary evidence or both to prove his allegation.

After both parties had laid their bets and the issue between them had been determined, at least three witnesses from both sides would be heard. The witnesses would openly testify before the court in the presence of the parties or their legal representatives. Where available, documentary evidence would have to be submitted to the court.

If, for reasons of old age or serious sickness, a witness was prevented from appearing before the court, the depositions of such a witness had to be taken by a judge commissioned for this purpose, who was known as *Yechibette Dagna*. This judge would be informed by the court as to the issues raised and would be required to report back the testimony of the witness. This judge would, therefore, go to the locality where such a witness lived, together with the parties to the dispute. He would then hear the testimony of the witness in the presence of the parties, four observers selected by both parties, and the local *Chika Shum*. On his return, and in the presence of the parties, he would report orally the testimony to the judge who had given him the assignment.[8]

If the *Chibette Dagna* made errors in transmitting the testimony, the method of correction that was used was as follows:

> "If he added to, or missed something from, what was stated by the witnesses, the interested party may state: Remember your honour! As God has endowed you with the power to remember, so let God help you to recall what has been so testified by so and so."[9]

If the *Chibette Dagna* stuck to his version, the observers would be required to given their own. Their version would be held as the correct one and, on that basis, depending on which one was proved correct, either the *Chibette Dagna* would be reproved, or the party which had made the allegation would pay compensation to the *Chibette Dagna*.[10]

In principle, a witness was not required to tender an oath prior to his testimony. He would, however, be required and warned to testify the truth and only the truth.

Failing this, the party against whom the witness testified had the right to request the court to require such a witness to tender an oath and this was done during mass, particularly when the holy communion was offered. The witness would close the door of a church or hold the Holy Bible, saying the following:

> "May he perforate me like His cross,
> May he erase me like His picture,
> May he chop me down into pieces like His flesh,
> May he spill me like His blood, and
> May he choke me up as His Altar is closed."

If he had already testified, out of court, the other party may impeach the credibility of his testimony or may claim that it may not be admissible at all.

Consanguinous relationship and other relationships, such as Godfather, adopted child, Godchild and the like, were grounds that could be invoked to bar a person from testifying or to discredit his testimony.[11]

The party which called the witness would, before asking him to testify, warn him as follows:

"One may go to hell after death;
One may be reduced to bones lying sick in bed;
One may also be a permanent inmate of a hospital;
So one is obliged to tell the truth."[12]

In a similar manner, the defendant will advise the witness to tell the truth and to testify that he knows nothing against him.

After all the witnesses have given their testimony, the party that felt that most of the witnesses have testified in his favour would claim:

"As a threshing ground would go to the one who prepared it, judgement
should be made in favour of one who had been proven right."

There were instances where each party to the suit would claim that the testimony given stood in his favour. In such a situation, contentions were settled by mere allocation of the testimony to this or that party by persons selected as observers. These persons were known as *Irtibe Emagne*.[13] Later on, however, the witness who had given the testimony which had become the object of contention would be recalled to ascertain as to whom his testimony favoured.[14] His answer would automatically untie the gordian knot.

D. Tatayyaq: Interrogation

In the past, parties to a civil case had no use of such legal institutions as defence witnesses. For the cause of action alleged by the plaintiff, there always lay a claim by the defendant that it should have been he who ought to have had the right to establish whether the alleged cause of action existed or not.[15]

On this point, Russelle and Michael, commenting on the ancient mode of litigation, have written the following about 140 years ago:

". . . lawyers stand on either side of the plaintiffs and the defendants
pleading in a loud tone of voice their several causes during which process
wagers of mules, cows, sheep and gold are continually laid by the orators
that they will prove such and such charges contained in the liable . . ."[16]

The use of such procedural right used to be invoked either by the party to the case personally, or by his counsel. Where such questions of law arose, the other party would say *Kafe*[17] or *Kettebekaye*.[18]

On the day fixed, the hearing would proceed with the questions of both parties.

The plaintiff, before proceeding to the interrogation in accordance with the rules of the *Tatayyaq Muget*, would ask whether or not the rules of procedure were correct. The defendant would answer in the positive, and the plaintiff would go on throwing various questions to show the implications of the claim set forth.

One is allowed to pose only one question at a time and the contending party has to give a single and direct answer to every question asked. If two questions are posed, two answers should, likewise, be given. In this manner, question and answer go back and forth between the adversaries. A bet is laid to sanction this rule of procedure. To answer anything less or more than what is required is tantamount to violating the rules of procedure.[19]

If one party violated this rule of procedure, he would be required to produce a guarantee for the payment of the wager made earlier. Whether or not a party had violated these rules was established by the *Techewoch*. Even where a party readily admitted the commission of such a fault, he must all the same pay the bet.

When the plaintiff finished his question, the defendant would start posing questions in turn.

E. Wurd Menzat or Bela Labelah: Art of Advocacy and Challenge

After the examination and cross-examination have been finalized, the parties would resort to *Wurd Anezaz*, the art of advocacy to convince the judge and the persons attending the court session by the use of poetry and eloquent expressions.

At the same time, each party would endeavour to ridicule and harass the other party by exposing some of the disgraceful deeds committed by the opponent and shameful events in his family background.

This technique was used to discredit the adversary by making public his weak points. Roughly, the presentation would run like this:

"Tell me and I will tell you the system of the *Atse Ser'at*[20] and the truth
of Abraham.
 Never will I speak a lie,
 but the truth and only the truth.
 On one side, the judge, . . .
 On the other me, . . . with deep fault grudge,
 there shall never be such fitting edges.
 The judgement rendered by judge . . .
 and an animal slaughtered by the knife of an Adal;
 never shall the judgement be quashed,
 so wouldn't there be a soul to hash.
 Daring to bet, to pay honey,
 pulling down the enemy to his own knee.
 If I have performed bad,
 that is sad.
 But if I have done well,
 you should never let me fail."[21]

In a similar manner, the other party in his turn would endeavour to convince the judge and to ridicule his adversary.

These are a lot of emotion-laden words, though they resemble the present legal concept of judgement opinion given just before the judge sums up the proceedings and gives his judgement.

One of the purposes of *Wurd Menzat* is to win over the judge. In this regard, a *Wurud* made by a certain Basha Mullatu Wolde Yohannes is believed to have greatly impressed *Afe-Negus* Nessibu:

"A leather thrown into the fire,
A bed splendid with leather attire,
So would Nessibu roast one found to be a liar,
as the piece of leather thrown in the fire,
Warm and soft, he is for the truth,
keeps it in the bosom of the bed,
that it may have the warmth."[22]

Once litigation had passed the *Wurd Anezaz* stage, *Techewoch* (assessors) would be asked to give their opinion in ascending order of seniority.

F. Opinion Giving and Rendering of Judgement

Techewoch or judges would tender the following catch when giving their opinion as to how the case should be disposed of:

> "Let me face my trial and let it be brought before the wronged.
> If I did anything and justice is shunned.
> Let the enemies of my lord be sent to the sword,
> let those close by the lord be beheaded,
> and those far off smashed."[23]

The observers, after giving their analysis, would recommend a decision.

Finally the judge would give his reasoned judgement. He would finally say to the plaintiff or the defendant, as the case might be:

> "I have decided against you, pay court fees and the bet."[24]

This would be the end of the matter, unless an appeal was made to the next higher court.[25]

G. Appeal

An appeal may be based on substantive or procedural issues, including interlocutory matters. Every complaint lodged against the judgement or interlocutory decisions of a court was examined not only by judges sitting in higher courts, but also by *Korquaris*, i.e. assessors attending the court session.

Appeals made on interlocutory order were not frequent. However, if one of the parties felt that such interlocutory decisions would be prejudicial to the principal issue, he was justified in making an interlocutory appeal. If on a question of ownership of title on land, a ruling was given as regards a will which was the basis of the right, this might be considered as a justifiable ground for lodging an interlocutory appeal.

Another matter that was taken to a higher court, particularly that of the *Afe-Negus*[26], was the question of interpretation of law. The *Yeyegebal kirker*, a dispute on who has the right to prove an allegation, and questions of interpretation of law were submitted to the *Afe-Negus*, who was assisted by the *Ras Wembers*.[27] For instruction or guidance as to how a set of facts or questions of law were to be interpreted, it was to this court that judges of lower rank referred.

III. CONCLUSION

The system of litigation conducted in accordance with the rules of the *Tatayyaq Muget*, during the last century and the beginning of this century, was indigenous and unique to Ethiopia.

In general, one may observe *inter alia* the following points of divergence between the present rules of Criminal and Civil Procedure Codes of Ethiopia[28] and the rules of the *Tatayyaq Muget*:

a) Court fees were paid out of the proceeds of bets laid down by the disputants.

b) Witnesses were introduced at the final stage when a claim is disputed, whereas presently evidence and witnesses are brought forward at the trial stage hearing.

c) The accused is required to prove his innocence. Under the present law, the accused is presumed to be innocent.

d) Cross-examination and examination-in-chief were exchanged between private complainant and the accused under the *Tatayyaq Muget*. Under the modern system, however, cross-examination is made by the accused or his counsel to the witness and the witness may be re-examined by the Public Prosecutor, while examination-in-chief is made after the case has been opened for trial.

c) In the *Tatayyaq Muget* the contending parties were allowed to digress in the process of litigation when trying to harass their adversaries or idolize the judges. No such mode of court 'battle' is allowed today. Instead, the parties are under pain of penalty required to stick to the issue raised and to support their argument with the relevant legal provisions and relevant facts.

A close observation of the old laws of Ethiopia reveals that the procedural laws were more developed than the substantive laws. This is attributable to the teachings of scholars of the *Fetha Negast*[29], experiences gained in the practice of the legal profession and the traditional value attached to the practice of bringing up young men as apprentices in the court of the governors and in the imperial court. The fact that litigation was, at least in the 'road-side' courts, a voluntary and spontaneous form of arbitration has greatly contributed in making the administration of justice a civic obligation of any law-abiding citizen. This and other factors combined together have succeeded in making the procedural laws relatively well developed.

NOTES

1. *Esett-Ageba* means one bets, agreeing to pay the amount or the kind of wager offered by the adversary.

2. Shibeshi Lemma, *Yettentu Esat Ageba Muget*, senior research paper submitted to the Department of Ethiopian Languages, Addis Ababa University (unpublished, Law Faculty Archives, 1965 EC).

3. In the preamble of most of the proclaimed laws, there was a stipulation to the effect that one had the right to bring a case to a passer-by, and the passer-by had the power to act as a judge and render justice.

4. *Chika Shum* is a local chief.

5. *Melkegna* is a governor of a locality.

6. At different levels of courts, different members of *Techiwoch* or *Korkaris* (assessors) were selected by both parties and the judge.

7. This was a kind of wager paid in cash, i.e. four Birr for every bet of *Mar* (honey).

8. Mahteme Selassie Wolde Meskel, *Yegnam-Allou Eniwaqachew*, (Addis Ababa, Institute of Ethiopian Studies, 1958 EC, unpublished).

9. *Ibid.*

10. *Ibid.*

11. Interview with Fitawrari Abebe Gebre, former judge and a high government official knowledgeable about the traditional mode of litigation.

12. *Ibid.*

13. Assessors nominated afresh for that particular hearing.

14. Mahteme Selassie, *op. cit.*, p.40.

15. *Ibid.*

16. Shibeshi Lemma, *op. cit.*, p.2.

17. It literally means 'with my mouth': technically, however, it is a request for leave to appear with a counsel, such plea entitled one to a three days leave.

18. It was a request for leave to appear with a counsel and it entitled one to a seven days' leave.

19. Mahteme Selassie, *op. cit.*, p.40.

20. It literally means 'the Law of the King'. It was a way of invoking the customary principles of law that had been applied and recognized by courts as either substantive or procedural law of the country.

21. Mahteme Selassie, *op. cit.*, pp.40-41.

22. Interview with Bitwoded Zewde Gebre-Heyot, former high government official.

23. Mahteme Selassie, *op. cit.*, p.39.

24. Interview with Fitawrari Abebe Gebre, cited above, note 11.

25. The hierarchy of regular courts prior to 1935 was:
    1) The *Zufan Chilot* (Crown Court)
    2) The *Afe-Negus Court* (Court of national jurisdiction)
    3) The *Shalleka Court* (Court of the Governor)
    4) *Yakal Dagna* (District Court)
    5) *Yesir* or *Yafer Dagna* (Court of first instance).

26. The Chief Justice.

27. Justices appointed by the central government to assist the *Afe-Negus* with appellate jurisdiction, sitting in six divisions to hear appeals coming from areas allotted to each of the divisions.

28. Criminal Procedure Code of 1961 and Civil Procedure Code of 1965.

29. The Law Book known as *The Law of the Kings*. It was incorporated into the legal system of Ethiopia between the 15th and 16th century.

A BRIEF HISTORICAL SURVEY OF THE

ETHIOPIAN ASKARIS (NATIVE COLONIAL SOLDIERS)

Amanuel Sahle

INTRODUCTION

The object of this paper is to examine the interaction between an imperialist power and an independent African people. It is the motto of all imperialist forces to divide in order to rule. The Italian invaders succeeded in their scheme, first in subduing the province of Eritrea and, after securing a strong foothold there, in trying to use the vanquished people to do the fighting for them in their imperialistic expansion in Eastern and North Africa.

The Askaris, or Ethiopian colonial soldiers serving under the Italian flag, were recruited with this aim in mind, i.e. to fight against their brothers beyond the Mereb and against "uncivilised people", who were again Africans like themselves.

This imperialist experiment, however, failed for many reasons, the most important being:

a. Ethiopia's long-standing independence and its historical political and cultural unity.

b. The unforgettable lessons of Dogali and Adua which had destroyed the notion that the white man was invincible.

c. The racism of the Italians themselves, which alienated many of its staunch supporters among the native people.

The era of the Askaris is a very interesting one and many curious happenings can be gathered from that period that might be of interest to the political, as well as the social, scientist, viz. the white coloniser's confused attitude towards a black people whom he recruits to fight against a black brother on the other side of a river; the attempt to use black Askaris to fight a capitalist war in Europe and a colonial war in Libya; the embarrassment of a white power made to witness a complete defeat at the hands of a black army in Adwa where, to add insult to injury, it had to look on helplessly as thousands of its native soldiers were being mutilated by the victor; the constant defections and desertions of the askaris who sympathised with their brothers beyond the Mereb.

This paper examines these points and also tries to depict the social implication of the Askari era, when songs and ballads were the common means of expression regarding the situation that was created in Northern Ethiopia at the time.

To write this paper, the author had to rely on:

a. Italian historical documents, mostly of fascist bias, and

b. Local informers, who seemed to have only a vague memory of so important and so recent a period in the history of the northern region of Ethiopia.

This being the case, the author does not pretend to have presented a complete and final survey of the period in question. However, the history of the Ethiopian Askaris has been too often overlooked by many historians, and giving just a glimpse of the life and adventures of these soldiers of fortune would be a good beginning for a further research in that direction.

ORIGINS

The word 'ascari', anglicized into 'askari', signified a native soldier of Eritrea (Christian or Moslem) or of Somalia or even of South Arabia, who enlisted of his own will in the Royal

Corps of Colonial Troops of Eritrea. Strictly speaking, the word 'askari' is a plural form, with the singular 'ascaro', but in official use 'askari' continued to be used as singular. The word is of Arabic origin and means simply 'a soldier'. Along the Zanzibar coast this was used to designate any person escorting a caravan without having any connection with the country's militia. The word diffused into central Africa along with the explorers while still retaining this meaning. When German East Africa was founded in 1890, however, the name 'askari' was given officially to the coloured troops enlisted by the colonial government (*schutztruppen*) and also to the native police force.[1]

The formation of indigenous troops in Eritrea almost coincided with the occupation of Massawa (5 Feb., 1885). A few days after landing in Massawa, Col. Tancredi Saletta formed two irregular indigenous detachments from the Bashi Bazuk serving with the Egyptian governor, dividing it into two 'hordes', one internal and destined for garrison services, the other external and assigned to the territory around Massawa, with a total force of a thousand strong, headed by native chiefs and officers. When the number increased to 2000 a certain Colonel Giovanni Battista Begni was given command. The native contingent was divided into three units: internal, external and mobile. The first result of this reorganization was to be seen soon in the battle of Sahati (25 Jan., 1887), when the Bashi Bazuk fought alongside the two Italian troops under Major Giovanni Boretti against Ras Alula, prior to the disaster of Dogali.

Later a certain General Asinari di san Marzano instituted a more systematic organization of the indigenous troops: two battalions were formed, each consisting of three companies and each company, in turn, comprising two half-companies and each half-company containing two 'hordes' or *buluks* or squads. The first battalion (or Halai) was posted in Munkulu, the first company (or Tabour) in Arkiko and the remaining two companies in Munkulu and Otumlo respectively, commanded by native officers. Soon after, General Baldissera inaugurated further reforms and thus on 1 Oct., 1888 there was established in Taulud (Massawa) the 4th battalion of native African Regiment with Somalis, Yemenites and Askaris of the 'Horde'. Egyptian Bashi Bazuk and disbanded Abyssinian local armies.

Finally, the royal decree of 30 June, 1889, No.6215, established the native corps of troops for the African garrisons and the name 'askari' appeared in the governmental decree of Eritrea of 30 March, 1891, No.12[2], Art.26, of the proclamation of 29 September, 1908 further states that "having joined his majesty, the king of Italy's army of his own free will, the Askari must adapt himself soon and with zeal to the hardship of his condition regarding his various military activities".[3]

THE BANDAS

Along with the formation of regular native detachments came the enrolment of the Bandas or irregulars. The Bandas were spared the military rigours of the regular army and they were more loyal to their respective chieftains than to the Italian government. The first Bandas to be enrolled under Col. Saletta were those of Kegnzmatch Hadgembess Gulwet of Adi Teclesan in 1885. In 1888 there were also formed in Ottumlo, by order of Major Di Majo, some Bandas from beyond Mereb with a force of 800 men. Others also joined from the region of Keren.[4]

The Bandas wore red bands on the head. Such an identity mark became necessary after the Battle of Coatit in 1895, when two Banda units fought each other, thinking that they were fighting against the army of Ras Mengesha of Tigray. During the governorship of Gondolfi in Eritrea (1890-92) the number of the Bandas increased to about 2000.[5]

THE ZAPTIAS*

The Zaptias (the word is Turkish, meaning 'policemen') were a sort of native military

---

* The Zaptias are remembered for their cruelty towards the indigenous people in a novel written by Abba Ghebreyessus Hailu — *Hade Zanta* (Asmara, 1951).

police force who helped in paying, or as interpreters or informers. The Zaptias were formed from the Bashi Bazuk by Marshal Cavedagni in 1885 in Massawa. They were distinguished by the red band which they wore around the waist and the blue ribbon on their turbans. They participated in the Libyan war but soon after, in 1918, they were relieved of their military duties and were assigned to security service. After the Italian invasion of 1936, schools for Zaptias appeared in Asmara, Gondar, Addis Ababa and Jimma, among others. However, the Zaptias resumed military service in 1941, fighting against Ethiopian liberation forces.[6]

THE COAST GUARDS OR THE NAVY

Native personnel were also enlisted in the Italian navy to serve on land as coastguards or on board ships as firemen, cooks, etc . . . in Massawa, Assab, Kisimayu and Mogadisho. But their number was insignificant.[7]

RECRUITMENT AND GENERAL CONDITIONS OF THE ASKARIS

Art.2 of the Eritrean Colony Legislation of 29 Sept., 1908*, states that to be accepted in the Royal Native Army, one has to be over 16 and under 24 years old and must sign for one years' service in the army. Preference was given to young men born in Eritrea, but for the artillery regiment, which required special qualifications, the preference was for Sudanese nationals.[8]

Youngsters whose origin was in regions beyond Mereb were accepted only under particular circumstances. These indigenous people joined the army out of hunger, in search of adventure and fortune, and for the security that was obtained by joining a strong colonial force.[9]

Such was the state of affairs until the battle of Adwa. Following the humiliating defeat of the Italians, the Askaris showed signs of reluctancy to volunteer. The Libyan war of 1912-1933 should be taken as an exception, because it was a foreign war to the Askaris. Even then the zeal that propelled them to march to North Africa was to wane once more during the Fascist invasion of the motherland in 1935. It was then that the Italians started to hunt for 'Volunteers' by paying premiums to local chiefs. When the British forces arrived in 1940, the situation worsened: the Italians were desperate and resorted to illegal means of conscription.

In the *Lettera Aperta Del' Africa Orientale Italiana* published in 1942, it is stated thus:

> "The speedy and forced conscription of the Askaris who were conducted *en masse* to the recruitment centers with threats and beatings from their chiefs who were all too greedy for the 10 lire reward they obtained from the Italian government for each conscripted Askari, changed the physiognomy of the native battalions so much that from this formless mass of lazy, underpaid, badly dressed, uncontrollable, badly trained and poorly armed men were to appear the first desertions right from the beginning."[10]

Regarding the treatment of the Askaris by Italians, Ferdinando Martini, the Governor of Eritrea (1897-1907) writes in his famous *Diary* that the annual pay of the Askari was superior to that of the soldier beyond Mereb. While the former got four thalers, a *gabi* (heavy cotton garment) and *surri* (a pair of khaki shorts), the latter got one lire and 75 cents a day or 50 lire a month or 600 lire a year. He adds that for this particular reason alone many had joined the Italian colonial forces.[11] This shows that the Italians were, from the beginning, dealing not with real soldiers but with mercenaries.

But the Askari was also required to show utmost love for Italy and its king if he wanted to be rewarded. An Askari could be promoted to Muntaz (lance corporal) only after two years of loyal service and for wartime merits; and the Muntaz could be promoted to Buluk Bashi (corporal) and the Buluk Bashi to Shumbashi (sergeant) for almost similar reasons.[12]

---

* The articles were not however static but changed as circumstances dictated.

On the other hand, punishment was severe but not brutal. Askaris were liable to receive five to fifty lashes of the whip. The 'Ceppo' was also administered, i.e. offenders were put in the stocks for punishment from one to five days.[13] Looking at the social aspects of the Askaris' condition, it is stated in one of the army regulations that the native army should be permitted with respect to religion, language, race and tribe in such a way that one half should be Christian and the other half Moslem.[14] This was probably a 'divide and rule' tactic. Furthermore Arabs and Africans were not mixed, as the former despised the latter as infidels.

There were two kinds of native troops. The *puri* (pure), who were from the province of Eritrea and who signed for one year's service in Libya, and the *misti* (mixed) composed of elements from beyond the Mereb, from Arabia and Somalia, who signed *for two years'** service. The battalions composed of pure and mixed askaris continued to fight in the Libyan war: from 1923-1928 in Tripolitana and from 1923-1933 in Cirenaica.[15]

But the Italians favoured the Sudanese more than the Eritrean Askaris to handle heavy artillery. They considered the Sudanese more serious and intelligent. The reason behind this was, however, the suspicion of the Italians towards the Christian highlanders who were related to the people who lived beyond the Mereb. The religious differences that existed in Ethiopia were, however, exploited by the colonisers. Contrary to military ethics, the canned meat given to the Askaris was prepared with strict regard for Christian and Moslem religious ritual**. This kind of food segregation sealed off any sort of contact between followers of the two religions. Army chaplains were even sent to Libya with a handsome pay to administer the last rites to the Christian Askaris.

In matters regarding loyalty, the Askaris were highly *praised* by the Italians for their heroic exploits in the field of war. Some detachments even had the privilege of passing in review before the king of Italy in Rome. Martini writes in his diary that "the Askaris fought under our officers valiantly and faithfully at Mai Daro against Lij Yilma, at Agordat against the Dervishes and on March of the same year (1891) near the waters of Halat".[16] But this loyalty was not built on solid ground. It was loyalty shown to the winner by the loser.

Accordingly, the military victories of the askaris gained during the initial incursions to subdue the province of Eritrea were greatly praised by the Italians. These first colonial victories were known as Agordat I, June 27, 1890; Sero Beit, June 16, 1892; Agordat II, December 21, 1893; Casala, July 17, 1894; Halai, December 19, 1894, where Bahta Hagos was killed; Coatit, January 13/14, 1895 against Ras Menghesha; and Senafe, January 15, 1895, where Menghesha was made to flee. The prestige of these victories opened the door for Agame and Tigray from which regions came new contingents of volunteers and bands with their respective chiefs.[17] Furthermore, the first Askaris to land in Libya on February 9, 1912 did demonstrate remarkable bravery in Tanjure, Zanzur, Bucamez, and Misurata, obtaining the honor of imperial blessing in Rome.

Ferdinando Martini writes that Italian officers described the manner of fighting as "fleeing forward". The Askaris were said to have fought like tigers but to have lacked the resistance of the Sudanese.[18] This may be attributed to the fact that, while the Askari was deep at heart a patriot and waited for chance to join his brothers, the Sudanese, on the other hand, resisted with all his might for he was a foreigner.

---

*   Some local people explained this fact by saying that those who signed for two years did not get any pension or severance pay after the termination of their service, this was why they were 'privileged' to serve for two years. Those who signed for one year only fared better after the service.

**   The meat was processed at the ex-Caramelli slaughterhouse in Asmara. The canned meat originating from an animal slaughtered by a Moslem was labelled and stamped with a seal approved by the Moslem Sharia, destined to be eaten only by Moslem Askaris; while the one destined for Christian Askari had to be authenticated by the representatives of the Monastery of Debre Bizen. (From local interview and from the *Diary* of Ferdinando Martini.)

Frankly speaking, the Italians never truly trusted the Askaris. The ghost of the black African defector and traitor continued to haunt the Italian officers' minds. For example, a large native army was considered unruly and dangerous. Attempts to form the Askaris into regiments were viewed with suspicion and were, therefore, abandoned. Martini writes that the Italians were all the time doubtful of the absolute sincerity of the Askaris but they could get consolation from the conviction that the Askaris would not join their brothers beyond the Mereb, owing to the very low pay of the Ethiopian soldiers.

The main headache for the Italians were, however, the Bandas, whose allegiance to Italy was more often than not flimsy. Although they fought for the coloniser with the permission of their respective chiefs and were paid by the Italian government, they nevertheless were the main sources of defection and desertion. Among Bandas led by *Dejazmatch* Tesfamariam (of Addi Quala), *Dejatch* Kidanemariam (of Deki Tesfa), *Dejatch* Sebhatu (of Hamasien), only those of *Dejatch* Tesfamariam remained faithful to Italy. The two most important Tigrean allies of the Italians, *Ras* Sebhat and *Dejatch* Hagos Teferi, defected to the Ethiopian side with 600 men only two weeks before the battle of Adwa, all the fighting men having been armed and paid by the Italian government.[19] Nevertheless, the colonial government was not slow to take corrective measures and these unruly irregulars were gradually put under control.

The Askaris were not, to say the least, free from actions that 'tarnished' their image in the eyes of the Italians. During the battle of Adwa, there were reports that Eritrean Bashi Bazouks refused to enter the battle with the excuse that "though we eat their money, we will not fight our country and our king".[20] Again, during the Battle of Tembien (1936), a certain Shumbashi Andom Tesfazion was ordered to bury the dead Italians and leave the Eritreans where they had fallen. Filled with indignation, Tesfazion insisted that these men who had fought side by side with the Italians had an equal right to a grave. Sentenced to punishment for insubordination, the Shumbashi went over to the Ethiopians with a hundred Askaris; other Eritreans followed this example and on the eve of the Battle of Mai Chew, Tesfazion's band was over a thousand strong[21]; and further to the south in the Neghele area, 904 Askaris deserted in a single night.[22]

The history of the Askaris is full of such defections and desertions of nationalists who informed on the Italian troops and who supplied wrong and misleading intelligence to the Italian army.[23] However, the Battle of Adua (1896) can be regarded as a landmark in Askari-Italian relationships. It was this battle that made the Askaris look at the white coloniser with a critical eye and a suspicious mind. The long-standing notion that the white man stood for all that was infallible and invincible was to be shattered in the minds of the native soldiers. The Italians were, from the beginning, careful not to mix freely with the Askaris, lest their weaknesses be revealed to the Askaris who considered them as omnipotent masters. When the Italians looked on, helpless, as hundreds of captive Askaris were mutilated by orders of Menilik for their part in the Battle of Adua, the seeds of future desertion and defection were already sown.

This unforgettable punishment left a gruesome memory in the minds, not only of the Askaris, but also of the local people in general. It is to be noted that during the Italian offensive of 1935, many a parent hid his sons for fear that the Italian government might take them as soldiers. Naturally, the Italians explained this reluctance by claiming that the Ethiopians on the other side of the Mereb were threatening the Askaris with cruel vengeance. Although there might have been other factors that had caused the native people not to venture in such a dangerous military mission alongside the Italians (for example the alienation of Eritreans in a fascist-dominated colony and the desire for solidarity with their brothers beyond the Mereb), the memory of Adua could have sufficed to warn the people of retaliatory action. While, during the Libyan wars of 1912-1934, people sold their cows and oxen to get enlisted in the native colonial army, the 1935 Italian offensive against Ethiopia had the opposite effect. Many were those who left land and property and crossed the border to join their brothers in their hour of need. But many (unfortunately) were also the unrepentant souls who crossed the Mereb to fight against their brothers.

On the other hand, the Italo-Libyan war of 1912-1933, where the Askaris played an important role, is a history in itself. Here the Ethiopian Askaris showed excessive zeal and emotion in volunteering *en masse* for a faraway adventure with hopes of heroism and fortune and did not have the least misgivings about helping the Italians to fight a people who, after all, were in race, religion and geography very different from them.*

The experience of the 'Trubuli', with their heroic exploits, changed the attitude of the Northern Ethiopian people towards mercenary war and towards the white colonial ruler. So popular was the war among the native people that many a Gojame, Wolloye and Oromo joined the native colonial army for fame and fortune.

There was also some international reaction regarding the Askaris and their activities in the Red Sea area. The passing of the first Eritrean detachment through the Suez Canal gave a pretext for Egypt to oppose the war on grounds of Islamic solidarity. It thus protested diplomatically against the recruitment and displacement of native peoples from the Red Sea regions occupied by Italy without the explicit agreement of Egypt, who claimed legitimate sovereignty. The protest remained without effect.[24]

THE SOCIAL ASPECT OF THE WAR

The formation of indigenous troops in a region detached from its motherland, the lessons of Adwa, the Libyan war, the Italian fascist aggression against the motherland and the famine of 1913-1917 in Northern Ethiopia, combined to create a society with complex social and economic life.

During the Libyan campaign, a large number of Eritrean nationals enlisted in the native colonial army. Consequently, the Italian government in Eritrea had to issue restrictive measures in its enrolment regulations. This was to discourage the large-scale volunteering that caused the weakening of the work force in Eritrea. But each restriction in Eritrea was largely compensated for by the mass enrolment of people from Tigray, Amhara, Gojam, Shoa and even from the Oromo region, who moved into Eritrea to get enlisted in the native colonial army.

The importance of this demographic change in Northern Ethiopia may be seen in the settlement of the people of Gojam, Shoa and the region of the Oromo in such Eritrean colonial towns as Ghinda, Nefasit and Keren.

Some aspects of the reactions to the war situation in a colonised country can be gathered from the folk songs which depicted the times more eloquently than anything else. This, for example, is a song which was sung to remind oneself of the slow but steady destruction of life caused by the internal, as well as the external, war:

> One by one
> Our boys are sent
> To their early graves

The reaction by the people to the Libyan war is best exemplified by the following song. Unfortunately, the Askaris did not share the feelings that produced the song:

> The train has come (from the port of Massawa)
> covered with smoke
> We are crying in vain for our missing sons
> (For the train brings to Asmara only the
> lucky ones
> Who had escaped death in the Libyan war

---

* According to *Hade Zanta*, it seems that Italian fascists massacred Ethiopians alleged to have killed some Italian workers in Hamedo, Tigray in 1936. The killers were actually Libyans brought to Ethiopia to fight alongside the Italians.

It is a historical fact that the Askaris were well paid by their masters, but this did not prevent their parents from seeing the absurdity of a desert war in which neither the country nor the people were near enough to be considered a threat. Hence the song:

> The son has gone to Libya to seek fortune
> His father spent it all on food
> Our tongues are alive indeed
> It is our sense of pride that is dead

The Askaris, with their gaudy uniforms, looked more like their bosses, the Italians, than their brothers. Naturally, they acted like their masters towards their black brothers, who regarded them with anger and suspicion:

> O God, have mercy, mercy!
> I see the Askari, putting on
> A white mask
> Over his black skin
> To scare me!

Even religious leaders are appealed to in the following song, to try and put an end to the foolhardy volunteering of the young boys who went to fight in the Libyan campaign:

> O village priest
> How can you shut your eyes
> When the blood of our dear sons
> Is shed all over the deserts of Libya

This last song vividly depicts the Askari's feeling of remorse in having to leave his country in order to fight a foreign war:

> I have left my fertile land behind
> Left my home behind
> Left the evergreen trees
> The sparkling streams
> Of the world of my youth
> Though fragrant breezes from the valley
> Embrace my heart and soul
> Yet will I march to those unknown lands
> To die and rot on those scorching sands (of Libya)

After the British occupation of Eritrea (1942) the Askaris were disbanded. Some served in the police force and others were posted in government organizations as guards and janitors.

But the Italian colonial mentality did not fade altogether. Smarting from their defeat in 1941 and getting all the tolerance they needed from their new white British brothers, who were grieved at heart to see a European power reduced to such a condition of humiliation, the Italians began to treat their former native soldiers in the most ungrateful and ungentlemanly way. In June 1941 the Zaptias, who had gone without pay for three months, sent a delegation to the Headquarters of the British Administration in Asmara to air their grievances. They were met by the chief of the Italian carabinieri. The latter, unable to swallow the humiliation caused by the Zaptias who, before the defeat of the Italians by the British, had never dreamed of confronting their masters in public, opened fire and killed a certain Tesfasslassie Habte. The rest fled, leaving another of their colleagues dead near the Catholic church of Kidane Mehret in Asmara.

In February 1944 members of the Eritrean police force protested against the fact that they were still administered by Italian colonial laws (they were obliged to wear the fez or Turbush, reminiscent of the Askari period; and were forbidden to wear shoes). But this protest went unheeded by the British and consequently the leaders of the protest, namely Inspector Assefaw Agostino, Inspector Ghebremariam, Inspector Yesus, Sergeant Tecleghiorghis Temelso, were imprisoned at Forto Baldissera in Asmara.*

This was the Italian way of biting the hand that helped them to build their shaky empire.

Today the ex-Askaris remember the colonial days with mixed feelings: those were the years of heroism, fortune, adventure and manhood. But they will never accept the fact that they themselves were, after all, mere mercenaries of the Italian government. That they were merely mercenaries, however, was an accepted fact among the Italians, who had never trusted them right from the very beginning.

CONCLUSION

The main reasons why the Italian government in East Africa established the colonial native troops were because native armies cost less, they were better adapted to the climate, they knew the terrain well and were useful in giving valuable information in exploration, thereby reducing the task of logistical services.

An additional explanation advanced by the Italians for establishing native troops in their colonies was that enlisting the natives in the colonial army killed the formation of politically-minded guerrilla bands that might later prove uncontrollable for the colonial power.[25] Thus the Italians treated early symptoms of an independence movement in the country they ruled. The native population was enticed to join the army and the Bandas, who were led by local chiefs, were used to fight rebels and bandits in the colony.[26] But this tactic did not last long. The series of betrayals, defections and desertions culminated in the 1935 mass reluctance of the Eritreans when a large number of them refused to follow the Italians in their war of aggression against the motherland.

The Battle of Adua was a landmark in the Italo-Askari entente, and although the Libyan war blinded many an Askari as to the real nature of Italian imperialist machinations, the 1935 Italian aggression opened their eyes once and for all.

Although the Italians praised their Askaris and poured medallions and prizes on them to the point of taking some of them to Italy to pass in review before their king and even had plans for using them in Italy in the 1914 war (this plan was dropped because the European climate proved too cold for the Askaris)*, the Italians did not have complete trust in them.

If the Askaris conception of Italy as a mighty nation was shattered in Adua, the belief that it could rule the seas through its naval prowess was to be discarded when the 7th Battalion of

---

* From oral interview.

Askaris went to the bottom of the sea with the Italian warship which was carrying them to Libya. Nevertheless, the era of the Askaris did produce valiant deeds and adventurous exploits but it did not result in decisive allegiance to a colonial power. Any economic or social or even sentimental attachment with the whites took more a form of expediency than political loyalty. To the Askaris, the Italians seemed more brotherly than a Moslem from his own country, for the Italians were Christians and the Askari could eat the meat that the Italians ate. If they accepted to fight a war the nature of which they dimly knew, it was for heroism and fortune. Nevertheless, the Italians "could fool some of the people most of the time, but they could not fool all of the people all of the time", and the result was to be seen in the 1935-41 war.

NOTES

1. *Enciclopedia Italiana*, 1931.

2. Angiolo Mori, *Manuale di Legislezione della colonia Eritrea*, Vol.6 (Roma, 1914), p.344.

3. Massimo A. Vitale, *L'Italia in Africa − L'opera dell'esercito (1885-1943)*, Vol.1. (Roma, 1960), pp.125 ff.

4. *Ibid.*, p.131.

5. *Ibid.*, p.131.

6. Massimo A. Vitale, *L'Italiana in Africa − L'opera dell'esercito (1911-1943)*, Vol.3 (Roma, 1964), pp.19-20.

7. Guiseppe Gioravanzo and Gurdi Vitti, *L'Italia in Africa (L'Opera della Maria) 1886-1943*, Vol.2 (Roma, 1959), p.95.

8. Mori, *op. cit.*, p.366.

9. Siro Perischelli, *Eroismo eritreo nella, storia d'Italia* (Domodosolar, 1968), p.15.

10. *Lettera Aperta dall'A.O.I.* (Asmara, January 1942), p.31.

11. Ferdinando Martini, *Nell'Africa Italiana (impersioni e recordi)*, (Milano, 1895), pp.115-116.

12. Mori, *op. cit.*, p.270.

13. *Ibid.*, p.360.

14. *Ibid.*, p.372.

15. Alberto Polera, *L'Abissinia di Leri*, (Roma, 1940), p.294.

16. Martini, *op. cit.*, p.115.

17. Polera, *op. cit.*, p.291.

18. Martini, *op. cit.*, p.116.

19. Sven Rubenson, *Survival of Ethiopian Independence*, (London, 1976), p.405.

20. *Ibid.*, p.405.

21. Angelo del Boca, *The Ethiopian War 1935-1941*, (Milan, 1965), p.122.

22. *Ibid.*, p.50.

23. Perischelli, *op. cit.*, p.140.

24. Vitale, Vol.3, *op. cit.*, pp.12-20.

25. Rodolfo Corselli, *La guerra in Colonia (manuali Coloniali)*, (Roma, 1914), p.29.

26. *Ibid.*, p.102.

A HISTORICAL SURVEY OF SOCIAL

AND ECONOMIC CONDITIONS IN WALLO,

1872 - 1917*

Asnake Ali

ETHNIC COMPOSITION

Until the early 17th century, highland Wallo was inhabited by Christian Amhara, from whom it had derived its name. The Afar, who were Muslims and pastoralists, occupied the lowland areas of Ambassal and Qalu to the east and south and the whole of Awssa. The 17th century saw the gradual entry and settlement of the increasingly Islamized Oromo in both the highland and lowland areas.[1] The Amhara were pushed into the highland provinces of Sayint and Wadla Dalanta bordering Gojam and Bagemidir to the west and north-west, respectively. Interspersed with the Oromo, they also remained clustered in the other parts of highland Wall, particularly in Warra Himano and Ambassal. The Afar continued to inhabit the lowland province of Awssa, and also interspersed with the Oromo, in the lowland districts of Ambassal and Qalu.

The Oromo occupied a large part of Wallo. They became the dominant inhabitants of Borana, Warra Ilu, Warra Himano, Qalu and Ambassal. In the 17th, 18th and 19th centuries they seem to have been in continuous interaction with their Amhara neighbours. Because of this, by the middle of the 19th century, it had already become difficult to differentiate between Amhara and Oromo in the highland provinces of Wallo. The missionaries, Isenberg and Krapf, who travelled through most of highland Wallo in 1842 wrote that very few of the Wallo Oromo spoke the language. They ascribed this to the constant intercourse of the Oromo with the Amhara to their north and south.[2] In the last quarter of the 19th and in the early 20th century, none of the highland Wallo Oromo spoke the language. They had been Amharized to the extent of forgetting their original language and identity. However, those who inhabit the lowland districts of Qalu and Ambassal are still Oromo. They speak the language. They identify themselves as Galla and not as Oromo.[3]

While the Amhara of Sayint and Wadla Dalanta remained Christians, most of those in the highland areas of Wallo seem to have been converted to Islam. Observing the existence of Christian Amhara communities in Warra Himano during their visit of the area, Isenberg and Krapf wrote that many of them in this province and the other had been forced or persuaded to adopt Islam by the Oromo in the earlier years.[4] Another place where Christians clustered in the middle of the 19th century was the island church of Lake Haiq in Tahuladare. They were very few in number. According to Isenberg and Krapf the benefits they used to receive from the surrounding districts were withdrawn from them by the Muslim Oromo.[5] Thus, in the second half of the 19th century, except Sayint and Wadla Dalanta, the other parts of highland and lowland Wallo were predominantly inhabited by Muslims.

According to informants, the various ethnic groups and particularly the Oromo and Afar fought among themselves incessantly through most of the 19th century.[6] This hampered social interaction and discouraged trade. The main cause for the conflict was the *Wajirat* tradition of the Oromo, who inhabited the edge of the escarpment extending from the Azabo and Rayo Oromo districts of present-day Wallo-Tigray border into the lowland districts of Yajju, Awssa, Ambassal and Qalu. The tradition entailed raids by the Oromo against the Afar of the lowland areas and sometimes against the Amhara of the highland districts. In the raids, properties, particularly cattle, were taken and in the process people lost their lives. In their turn, the Afar and Amhara organized raiding parties to avenge the destruction.[7] Because effective imperial authority did not yet extend into the lowland areas of the Oromo and Afar until the last decade of the 19th century, the tradition seems to have continued unabated.

With his rise as the dominant figure in Wallo in the 1890's *Ras* Mikael undertook the pacification of his lowland districts. The *Wajirat* tradition, if not brought completely under control, was minimized. Troops from the regional government at Dasse were stationed at key points in the area to prevent the Oromo and Afar from raiding each other.[8] This development inaugurated a new pattern of relationship between the peoples of the region. Social and economic intercourse was enhanced. The local market of Bati started to gain importance at this time. Located on the edge of the escarpment which falls sharply into the hot lowlands of Awssa, it became a meeting place for Amhara, Oromo and Afar merchants from the various parts of Wallo.[9] This facilitated the social, political and economic integration of the lowland Oromo and Afar with the other peoples of the region on the one hand, and among themselves on the other.

LAND TENURE

My informants claim that until the end of the 18th century, their ancestors had direct ownership of the land they tilled. They made only occasional gifts to their respective rulers in lieu of taxation. No one was imposed upon them for whom they had to meet obligations, such as sharing their produce and rendering labour services.[10] This changed in the 1790's. After he returned from a campaign to Gondar *Ca.* 1799, *Kollase* Amade of the Mammadoch is said to have made land grants to those officials who had joined him in the campaign according to their respective rank. The peasants who did not join him were turned into *gabbar*. They had to pay a portion of their produce to *Kollase* Amade's officials to whom the land was granted. Such a land was popularly referred to as *Yazamach* (campaigner) or *Alanga* land.[11] The period was one in which the Mammadoch carved out for themselves extensive domains by conquering most of the highland provinces of Wallo including Amhara Sayint. They were also coming into closer relation with Gondar. Therefore, the introduction of a new system of land tenure, implying the process of the feudalization of the Muslim-Oromo, was probably a result of the increasing contact with Amhara-Sayint and Gondar.

The system of land tenure established by *Kollase* Amade seems to have continued right down to *Ras* Mikael's days with little or no variation. However, with the process of Christianization and greater integration of Wallo into the empire, a more complex system of land tenure and local administration seems to have gradually emerged. As of the last quarter of the 19th century, it is possible to have a fairly clear picture of a stable social hierarchy in Wallo.

At the very top of the hierarchy were the members of the Mammadoch ruling family dominated at the time by *Ras* Mikael, his immediate relatives and associates. Each province and district in turn had its own local ruling family or hereditary *balabat* who were dependent on the Mammadoch prince, paid tribute to him and accompanied him during campaigns. Coming directly under the local hereditary rulers, there were a large number of *mislanes* who were *balabat* in their own right at the district level. Under them came many *chiqa shum*, who as the lowest officials in the feudal hierarchy were most closely connected with the mass of the peasants. The *mislane* and *chiqa shum*, between themselves, were responsible for the administration of justice at the local level and for the collection of taxes. They also made sure that the peasants of their localities met their obligation of work on *hudad* (crown lands) and other projects such as the construction of churches, bridges and palaces either for the local rulers or for members of the Mammadoch family.[12]

All the officials in the political and social hierarchy, who were hereditary *balabats*, enjoyed a great deal of authority over the peasants within the limits of their territories. Except the *chiqa shum*, all of them had their own retainers and soldiers, the number of which depended upon their rank and wealth. At the district and provincial level, it is reported that a local *balabat* could sometimes have troops and retainers numbering from 500 upwards to 10,000 and household servants numbering between 100 and 500.[13]

With his numerous soldiers and household servants, the *balabat* lived on the labours of the peasants of his respective district. Usually much of the land in the district under his jurisdiction directly served his needs. The peasants living on and cultivating the land were made his *gabbar*. They had to hand over a large share of their produce to him. The intimate nature of the dependency of the *balabat* on the labours of peasants is underlined by the appellation given to such pieces of land. Since the produce of these pieces of land serve the immediate needs of the *balabat*, the land was called *mad bet* (literally, "kitchen) or *gana gab* (literally, "for the lord's store"). Besides these, the *balabat* owned vast tracts of *hudad*. These were often in the most fertile areas and belonged directly to him. No free peasant was allowed to settle in them. They were cultivated for the *balabat* by his household servants and the peasants living within his jurisdiction. The *mislane* and *chiqa shum* were responsible for ensuring that the peasant *gabbar* of their respective localities contributed their appropriate share of labour in the cultivation of the *hudad*.[14]

The rest of the land in a district was partitioned among the soldiers and servants of the *balabat* according to rank. The peasants inhabiting the area were made their *gabbar* to serve their needs in much the same way as that of the *balabat* himself. Soldiers of rank who were granted relatively large tracts of land with many peasants as *gabbar* were popularly referred to as *abba bidra* ("chief"). Another category of soldiers may be seen in what one could call the "peasant soldiers". These were given pieces of land which they cultivated themselves and the produce of which they did not have the obligation to share with anyone. The land was given to them in lieu of salaries. In return for this, they always had to be available for campaigns whenever called upon by the regional or local ruling house. Finally there was another group of soldiers of low rank who were given very small pieces of land. They were allowed to live off the peasants of a given locality, each peasant contributing a small measure, usually one *qunna* (traditional measure), of his cereal produce for their up-keep. Hence, such soldiers were popularly called *Ya qollo*, meaning that they were only given contributions of grain by the peasant.[15]

Despite the internal differentiation of the categories of soldiers, they all had a common obligation of serving in the campaigns of their local rulers. If they failed to do so, their land or any other rights they had as such would be given to other soldiers and they could be reduced to the status of *gabbar*. As long as they observed their obligation, however, the soldiers could transmit their rights to their descendants, who likewise enjoyed the privileges of their fathers as long as they fulfilled their duties.[16]

A new type of landowner was created in the region with Yohannes' policy of proselytization. Churches were reestablished and land grants were made to them. This gave them rights similar to those of the *balabat* and the higher echelons of the soldiery. Pieces of land thus given to churches were generally referred to as *yasamon maret*, meaning land given in lieu of daily religious services, and was of two types. The first type was given to priests in lieu of salary for services rendered to the church. The second type of church land was *hudad* which belonged directly to the church concerned. Its produce was used to buy materials necessary for religious services and to hold feasts during holidays.[17] It was cultivated by the free labour of the peasantry of the neighbourhood.

In general in Wallo there were two categories of land: *gabbar* and *galla*. In the *gabbar* land, the farmer owned the land he tilled and had the right to pass it over to his children. His obligation was that he had to share a portion of his produce, usually one third, with any one of the following: a regional or local *balabat*, a soldier, a church or its priests.[18] Many informants also claim that a farmer of a *gabbar* land rendered labour services, such as constructing houses, fences and providing firewood.[19]

A *galla* land was of two types: *quami* ("permanent") and *tanaqay* ("removable"). A farmer who worked in a *quami galla* land was not evicted unless serious misunderstanding arose between him and the owner of the land. *Tanaqay galla* land was government owned and was given to individuals favored by it.[20] According to informants, farmers in both types of *galla* land did not have the right to transmit them to their children.[21] Besides sharing their produce with the owners of the land, they had also to render various types of labour services similar to those in the *gabbar* land.[22]

The farmer shared his produce or made his payments directly to the *balabat*, soldier or church. The share or payment due to the provincial and regional lords on the other hand was collected by the *mislane* and *chiqa shum*.[23] In some of the districts where honey and butter were produced in abundance, the farmer was obliged to make his payment in these products. Such was the case of Jama in Warra Ilu and Haiq in Ambassal.[24]

According to my informants, the type of taxes levied on the Wallo peasantry by the regional and central governments differed from time to time. Thus, a farmer was required to pay an *asrat* ("tithe"), one tenth of his agricultural produce, to the central government. Minilik had instituted this additional levy in 1892 in some parts of his empire. In the same decade *Ras* Mikael instituted other types of taxes in Wallo. A farmer who owned cattle had to pay a *chira* ("tail") tax of one thaler or one bar of salt in proportion with the number of his oxen and cows. One who owned sheep had to pay in kind what was called *bag milmil* ("the best sheep") to the regional government every year. Besides one who had his own hut for a residence had also to pay *ya tis* ("smoke tax) of one bar of salt every year. The *mislane* and *chiqa shum* were responsible for the collection of all these different taxes in their districts and villages.[25]

There were also other places in Wallo which had their own systems of land tenure, different from the other parts of the region: such were the districts of Argobba and Chafa in Qalu. The inhabitants of Argobba claim to have come from Ifat in Shawa in the remote past. They owned their land communally. Though an individual had rights of usufruct over his plot of land, he did not have right of ownership over it. It belonged to the community as a whole. Provided that he stayed in the district for some months, any newcomer was given farm land the produce of which went solely to himself.[26] The Argobba people, besides being farmers, were also weavers. Because of this they paid tax to the regional government in *shamma* blankets. This was done, not on an individual basis, but communally through their elected *chiqa shum*, in the name of each village. The material needed for the production of such blankets was contributed by all members of the community.[27]

In the 1880's and 90's the Oromo people of Chafa owed their allegiance to both Wallo and Shawa. The part to the north of the town of Albuko, extending eastwards, was called Rique and was part of Wallo. The land tenure system and the condition of life of the people there was similar to that found in the greater part of Wallo.[28] The rest of Chafa was under the loose control of the Shawan rulers. It was relegated for a long time in the late 1880's and 1890's to the chieftaincy of Ali Shafi, an Oromo. The area was divided into a number of localities each of which was under a minor chief popularly referred to as *dagna* ("judge"), who was responsible to Ali Shafi. Through the judges each farmer paid a tribute of one thaler or five *qunna* of maize to Ali Shafi every year. Besides this, on every *Masqal* day ("day of the cross"), each locality through its judge made a payment of an ox. After appropriating a portion of both types of tax payments, Ali Shafi relayed the rest, the major portion, to Minilik in Addis Ababa. Other than the above payments, the people of Chafa were free from other dues. There were no landlords imposed on them at the time. Because there was no scarcity of land, any individual had the right to clear an area and start a farm. However, Chafa was infested with mosquitoes and so outsiders avoided settling in it for a long time.[29]

In 1896, a few months after the battle of Adwa, Minilik granted that part of Chafa which belonged to Shawa to *Ras* Walde of Efrata, one of his lieutenants. The informant ascribed this to Ali Shafi's failure to accompany Minilik on the campaign to Adwa against the Italians.[30] *Ras* Walde changed the traditional system of taxation in the area and made the people pay a quarter and in some cases as much as half of their produce as tribute to himself. In addition, each farmer was also asked to pay between five and ten thalers every year. This new system of taxation led to a rebellion which was easily suppressed by *Ras* Walde's troops stationed at key points in the area. After this the land was divided between the sons, relatives and retainers of *Ras* Walde and the *gabbar* system began to be fully operative in the area.[31]

Craftsmen: gold, silver and iron-smiths, tanners, potters and weavers had their own quarters in most of the districts of Wallo. Members of the ruling house and provincial *balabat* had their craftsmen at their courts, particularly smiths of all types who produced instruments of labour, war and ornaments. As a subsidiary to their major occupation, craftsmen also engaged in agriculture. They had their own land. In such cases, they paid tax only for their handicraft products in cash and not for the land which they farmed. Probably this indicates that they did not own much land. The tax a craftsman paid ranged from one to three thalers a year. Excepting the weavers, who enjoyed a better status, other craftsmen were social outcasts and occupied the lowest position in the social hierarchy.[32]

TRADE

Before the 17th century, Wallo, which was then called Amhara, had a central place in the internal trade of Ethiopia. Its inhabitants played a significant role as commercial intermediaries between the northern and southern regions.[33] However, from the 17th century when the region started to be securely settled by the Oromo, until the last quarter of the 19th, trade became a negligible activity among the Wallo. The process of Oromo settlement in the region, which could not have been a peaceful process; the big wars fought among the lords of northern Ethiopia; and the small incessant wars which raged among the various *balabat* of Wallo made both interregional and local trading hazardous. Local trading activity, particularly between the highland Amhara and Oromo and the lowland Afar near the coast was all the more difficult, because of ethnic conflict referred to above.

It was probably the general political condition affecting the pursuit of normal and secure life which prevented the growth of a trading class prior to the late 19th century. According to an informant, few Wallo men were engaged in trading at a local level; none could be referred to as long-distance traders.[34] Most probably, this was what made the Wallo rulers in the last years of the 18th and the early 19th centuries bring merchants with experience in long-distance trade from places in other regions which had developed the tradition earlier. During his brief conquest of Gondar in the late 1790's *Kollase* Amade brought a group of Muslim merchants from there and settled them at Ada in Warra Himano. These seem to have started local trade in Wallo and long-distance trade with the northern regions and the coast. This is said to have given the first impetus to the development of an indigenous trading class. Of the merchants brought from Gondar, *Haj* Salih is still remembered. His sons and his grandsons in the middle and last two decades of the 19th century became prominent merchants in the region. One of his sons is said to have been referred to popularly as Ali *Gondare*.[35]

Most of the long-distance merchants in Wallo who were prominent in the last two decades of the 19th and in the first twenty years of the 20th centuries also had their origin in Bagemidir and Tigre. My informants, some of whom were the sons and grandsons of these merchants, report that their ancestors were brought to Wallo by Emperor Yohannes, when he was in the region in the late 1870's and the 1880's. He settle them at Boru Sillase, Ito Madhene Alem and Ancharo which became prosperous trade centres during this period.[36] Yohannes did this probably to revive the region's importance in the transit trade between northern and southern Ethiopia and to facilitate his drive for the re-unification of the country.

The general political development in Ethiopia during the last two decades of the 19th century extending into the 20th made the period a heyday for the revival of trade in Wallo. The rise of *Ras* Mikael as the sole ruler of Wallo ended the incessant local struggle for power in the region. The pacification of the lowland districts brought the ethnic conflict between highlanders and lowlanders under control and opened the route for traders to the coastal towns of the Red Sea and the Gulf of Aden. The incorporation of the southern and south-western regions into the Ethiopian state made the rich commodities of these places available in abundance to northern merchants. The trade routes in Wallo and those leading to other regions and the coast were made relatively safe and secure for traders. Wallo merchants organized in caravans from the various trade centres in the region started to trek to many parts of Ethiopia and the coast.

Long-distance trade by Wallo merchants was conducted in four main directions: to the southern and south-western regions of present-day Sidamo, Kaffa, Gemu Gofa, Illubabor and Wallega; to the northern regions of Tigre and Eritrea; to the western regions of Gojam and Bagemidir; and to the coast. There is no statistical data to help us estimate which of these routes were of greater importance to Wallo merchants. From the statements of informants, however, it seems that the ones leading to the south-west and to the coast were particularly frequented by Wallo merchants.[37] The south-western regions and the coast were the source of the commodities for the trade in the local markets in Wallo and in the western and northern regions. The contribution of Wallo in producing the real commodities for the trade was negligible. Only hides and skins were locally produced and sent to the coastal trade centres for export. What the Wallo merchants handled was essentially transit trade. To all places they went to, they carried the natural commodities from the south-western regions and manufactured good brought from the outside world which they received from Asmara, the ports of Assab and Tajura.[38]

In the period under discussion, the Maria Theresa Thaler had come into increasing use as a medium of exchange in commercial transactions. However, its use was limited only to the major trade centres. This was because of its extreme scarcity. Of course, the amount of Thaler available had increased.[39] But still it was found only in the possession of the politically powerful and the wealthy merchants. My informants emphasise that the coin was so important and scarce that a person with 500 Thalers was considered very rich.[40] Starting from 1894, coins minted by Minilik, with his effigy, were also in circulation. Their success, however, was not substantial. Their use was limited only to the major trade centres.[41]

Besides its being an indispensable food item, salt was still the major medium of exchange in transactions. It was one of the items of trade carried by Wallo merchants to the southern, south-western and western regions. Wallo merchants obtained salt from trade centres in Tigre, brought by Tigrean merchants from Taltal in the Danakil depression. They also obtained it at the markets of Bati and Dawe in the lowland areas of Awsa and Qalu, respectively. It was brought to these places by Afar merchants from the lakes in Awsa.[42]

As a medium of exchange, there were different types of salt bars, varying in size, which determined their value. Without recalling the value in Thalers of each type, informants remember their names: *Ganfur, Limadaw, Eyale, Wayro* and *Amole*.[43] Along with other types, the value in Thalers of some of these salt bars is recorded in written sources. Carlo Annaratone has recorded the following types with the weight of each in kilograms and value in Thalers:

Name	Weight in Kilograms	Value per Thaler	
		Minimum	Maximum
Lemedau	2,200	4	3
Eiale	800	10	7
Tera Ciau	2,000	4	4
Sabara	800	13	10[44]

An Italian geographical mission of the early 20th century has also recorded the following types with a brief description: *Amole*, which measured about 25 centimetres long, five centimetres wide and five centimetres thick; *Abroita*, which was an *Amole* cut in two; *Ganfur*, a piece three times as big as an *Amole* and used only for consumption.[45]

For the trade to the southern and south-western regions, Wallo merchants used two different routes to take them to Shawa. One led across the highland districts of Warra Ilu via Ahiya Fej into Shawa. The most important stations on this route were Kabe, Qeyafer, Ahiya Fej, Jirat, Jiru, Zinjaro Wuha, Aleltu, Jib Washa, Addis Ababa. The other route led across the hot, lowland country of Chafa. Important stations were Ganda Qore, Dulum Qotam, Chafa Robit, Karaqore, Ansokia Meda,[46] Jaweha, Shawa Robit, Chira Meda, Mush, Dabra Birhan, Chacha, Jib Washa, Addis Ababa. The former route was the most frequently used. Because it traversed hot, lowland areas, the latter was used rarely.[47] From Addis Ababa, southwards, a single route across the Waliso country was used. The journey to the trade centres of the southern and south-western regions and back to Wallo took four to five months.[48]

The most important commodities carried by the merchants to the trade centres of the southern and south-western regions were salt, and various types of European goods brought from the coast: coloured cloth, silks, beads, kohl and perfume. In exchange for these goods, important commodities brought from the south were coffee, spices, hides and skins, gold, ivory and slaves.[49] A small amount of these commodities were sold at local markets in Wallo and in Bagemidir and Gojam. The bulk was carried to Asmara and to the coastal towns of Assab and Tajura for export to the outside world.[50]

Written sources as well as my informants indicate that the volume of trade in slaves until the mid 1890's was large. *Ras* Mikael himself is referred to as a great exporter of slaves who sent numerous slave caravans to the coast. He and his nobles also kept many male and female slaves at their courts.[51] Minilik's half-hearted attempts to prohibit slave trading in the 1880's and early 1890's were completely ineffective. After 1895, he resorted to stronger measures to abolish the trade. Even though unable to eliminate it, this greatly curtailed the volume of trade in slaves in the late 1890's and in the early 20th century.[52] In this period only a small number of slaves was smuggled by Wallo merchants from the southern and south-western regions. This was usually done by bribing the local governors and the guards at the customs gates through which the trade routes passed. At other times, the merchants with the human cargo simply avoided the normal routes where the customs gates were located, often by passing them at night.[53] My informants indicate that Wallo merchants did not participate substantially in slave raiding. They bought them from professional slave raiders, usually Gojamme, who operated in the remotest parts of the southern and south-western regions.[54] Most of the slaves brought to Wallo were sold secretly at local markets and were used for household services. A few found their way to the Arab world. This was mostly across the lowland trade routes leading from Dawe to Tajura. A notorious slave merchant who dominated the slave traffic along this route, *Haj* Garad, is still remembered by my informants.[55] The slaves were brought to Dawe secretly by those merchants who brought them from the southern and south-western regions. The journey from Dawe to Tajura was also made in secrecy, usually at night.[56]

The direct access which Wallo merchants had to the ports of Assab, Tajura and Djibouti on the Red Sea and the Gulf of Aden was of crucial importance. It was through these ports that they exported most of the trade items brought from the southern and south-western regions including some local products. Afar merchants handled most of this trade, receiving the commodities from the highland merchants at Bati and Dawe. Because of the harsh climate, very few of the highland merchants dared to trade up to the coastal towns.[57] On the other hand, Afar merchants did not venture to the highland markets of Wallo or other parts of the country. They only relayed the commodities they brought from the coast to the highland merchants at Bati and Dawe.[58]

In addition to the items brought from the southern and south-western regions, the commodities exported through Assab, Tajura and Djibouti consisted of cattle and mules, mainly from Wallo. In exchange for these, the Wallo merchants relayed foreign goods collected at the coast to the southern, south-western and central regions, as already indicated above. *Ras* Mikael and Emperor Minilik also had firearms brought through these ports by the same merchants.[59] On their way back from Tajura, Afar merchants also ventured to the lakes of Awssa to get salt, which they themselves extracted and carried to Bati and Dawe.[60]

The trade route which led to Asmara across Tigre was also one of the most frequented by Wallo merchants. The major stations and trade centres on this route were Jari, Wuchale, Waldia, Gobiyye, Qobo, Alamata, Koram, Maichaw, Miqmawir, Maqale, Adigrat, Adiqeyih and finally Asmara. Sometimes, from Alamata traders followed the route through the lowland country until they reached Maqale. On this route between Alamata and Maqale, the important stations were Enda Makoni and Sanel Wuha.[61] Some of the merchants also claim to have carried their goods as far as Massawa on the Red Sea. They did this before reaching Asmara, from Adiqayih across the district of Koatit. It was at Adiqeyih that they made the transaction with the Arab and Italian merchants from Massawa who provided them with the camels to transport the goods across the hot, lowland country. Usually the merchants covered the distance from the various trade centres in Wallo to Asmara and back in five to six months. This was in the early 20th century.[62] It was mainly the commodities they brought from the south and south-west, particularly coffee and skins, that the merchants carried to Asmara and Massawa. They brought back European goods and salt.[63]

Wallo's trade with the neighbouring regions of Gojam and Bagemidir was negligible. Few merchants went to trade in these areas. Those who went to Gojam did so through the Borana province crossing the Abay river and usually attended only the market at Dabra Marqos.[64] Those who ventured into Bagemidir visited only Gayint and Dabra Tabor. They travelled through Wadla and Chachaho.[65] The important commodities carried into these regions consisted of salt, coffee and some of the foreign goods brought from the coast. These were exchanged mainly for butter, pepper and honey, which were consumed locally.[66]

The trade routes leading to the various parts of the country were dotted with a number of customs houses, where the merchants had to pay taxes for the goods they carried. These were particularly numerous on the two routes leading to Asmara and Addis Ababa.[67] In the Italian colony of Eritrea and in the south and south-west, there were few customs houses.[68] On the routes to Tajura and Assab from Wallo, there were customs houses only at Dawe and Bati. Besides, at various places in Awssa, the merchants were taxed irregularly by the local rulers through whose areas they happened to pass. In the eyes of the merchants, these rulers usually acted as *shifta* and the merchants had to negotiate the amount to be paid.[69] On the route to Dabra Tabor, there were customs houses at Wagal Tena and Chachaho and the revenue was appropriated by *Ras* Mikael and the governor of Gayint, respectively.[70]

The *nagadras* of the various caravans were usually responsible for the payments made at each customs house. In many of the places it was made in Thalers, ranging from one to three for each animal load.[71] In some places, particularly at Wagal Tena and Chachaho, the payment was made in bars of salt ranging from two to five.[72] For the payments they made, the merchants received receipts at each customs house. These were shown at others through which they had to pass.[73]

In the 1890's and early 20th century, most of the market-villages in the region tended to grow rather rapidly and a sizeable number of their population began to be engaged in trading activity. Most of these lived in a separate quarter which often constituted the local market. Such a quarter was popularly referred to as *atari ganda* ("a merchants' quarter").[74] Such centres predominantly inhabited by merchants cropped up in the various parts of Wallo. These soon became major trade centres, some of which were attended by traders not only from the various parts of Wallo, but even from places as far as Gondar. Such market-villages were Adas, Boru, Ancharo in the highland provinces and Bati and Dawe in the lowland areas.

Located in the district of Lugot in Warra Himano, Adas is reported to have been one of the earliest trade centres in Wallo. It had its beginnings in the late 1970's in the time of *Kollase* Amade, who brought merchants from Gondar and settled them here. Its location near Tanta, the centre of the early Mamadoch rulers, gave it prominence in this early period. In the last two decades of the 19th century, however, the shift of the centre of Wallo to Dasse seems to have brought about the decline of Adas. Its importance in this period and afterwards was more as a residential village of wealthy merchants than as a centre of trade.[75]

Ten kilometres to the north of Dasse, the Boru market was first established when Emperor Yohannes had the church of Sillase constructed at this place in the late 1870's. At this time the Emperor brought wealthy merchants from Bagemidir, Tigre and Gojam and settled them here. Among these merchants were *Nagadras* Zerihun and Lamlam from Gondar and *Nagadras* Habtu from Adwa.[76] Before its transfer to Boru, the market was held at Sulula, a nearby village, which was only a local and relatively unimportant market.[77] For quite a long time, even after Dasse had become the regional capital, it was at Boru that most of the caravans which trekked along the various routes were organized. Most of the goods brought by the caravans from the various places they visited were exposed at the market held every week on Saturdays. It was visited by merchants from the various provinces of the region and also from Gojam and Bagemidir, who brought local products for exchange.[78]

To the south-east of Dasse, near present-day Kombolcha, Ancharo started to gain prominence also in the time of Yohannes. Most of the merchants from Gojam, Bagemidir and Tigre settled here by Yohannes were Muslims; they included *Nagadras* Babur, *Haj* Siraj and *Haj* Birru.

Those settled at Boru were Christians.[79] Ancharo's popularity, however, was more as a merchant's quarter than as a centre of trade. When compared with the market at Boru, the market at Ancharo was a minor one. Only a few people from the neighbouring districts visited it.[80]

East of Dasse, Bati became an important centre of trade in the 1880's and 1890's, after the pacification of the Oromo and Afar of the lowlands. It got its name in this period.[81] However, its beginnings as a place for exchange between the ethnic groups of the area go back into the distant past. Before it came to be known as Bati, the Afar and Oromo called it "Dinsaro", which means "a night cloth" in Afar. An Afar merchant claims that the lowlanders got their cloths from the highlanders at this spot.[82] As it became the most important market town on the trade routes leading to Assab and Tajura in the 1890's and early 20th century, Bati was administered by a *nagadras* appointed from Dasse. It served as a depot for goods to and from the coast brought there by highland Wallo and Afar merchants, respectively. Moreover, it served as a local market, which was held weekly on Mondays. Exchange of local commodities took place between the highland and lowland people of the region here. The Afar brought oxen, butter and salt; the Amhara and Oromo supplied the market with horses, coffee and honey. However, because of the distance and the hostile climate, the market was not attended by merchants from other regions.[83]

Dawe was another centre of trade on the edge of the escarpment descending into the lowland area which became important in this period. It is located in the province of Qalu, to the south-east of Dasse. A route which led to Tajura passed through it. Like Bati, though smaller in size, Dawe served as a depot for goods to and from the ports. Its market was visited by the peoples of the neighbouring highland districts of Qawat, Manz and Ifat in Shawa. They brought local commodities such as grain and pepper and carried back salt.[84] Dawe was popular, however, more as a place through which slaves were transported to the port of Tajura than as a market for other commodities.[85]

Though the period was one of relative peace and security *Shifta* and highway men were still prevalent in the region. This was one of the factors which necessitated merchants, active in long-distance trading, to organize themselves in big caravans which sometimes contained up to 600 pack animals. Individuals and smaller groups from various places attached themselves to such a caravan. In such caravans some of the merchants had their own rifles and the wealthier even had armed retainers. Because of this, bandits rarely attempted to raid such well organized and armed caravans. However, even if the bandits dared to attack them, except at time of grave danger, the merchants did not use their arms. There was the fear of getting their properties destroyed and their pack animals killed. Because of this, the merchants usually preferred to appease the bandits with gifts in cash or in kind.[86]

Caravans were most of the time organized around popular and wealthy merchants who usually owned a large number of pack animals. The *nagadras* were responsible for all affairs that affected traders in the caravan. For example, they were responsible for the settlement of all duties at customs posts which they in turn collected from the individuals in the caravan. They also negotiated with bandits encountered along the trade routes.[87]

In the 1890's and early 20th century, when trade flourished, rulers started to develop increasing interest in controlling trade routes and centres. They did this by appointing various *nagadras* to important trade centres and routes.[88] Thus the social title of *nagadras* was transformed into a political one. Besides being a principal merchant in his area, a *nagadras* collected customs revenue and started to act as a magistrate and judge in local civil and commercial cases.[89] *Ras* Mikael is said to have appointed two wealthy merchants, Warqiye and Kassa as *nagadras*. Warqiye was made responsible for the route from Dasse to Tajura and Kassa to Asmara. Without recalling the specific trade centers and routes over which they were appointed, informants said that other wealthy merchants were also made *nagadras*.[90]

Because of the intimate relations they created with him, *Ras* Mikael is said to have made land grants to wealthy merchants. Dasta Gade and Salih Ali, the latter the grandson of the merchant by the same name brought from Gondar by *Kollase* Amade *Ca.* 1799, were granted land at Jari and Adas, respectively. *Ras* Mikael also made a similar land grant to another wealthy merchant, Mohammed Suraq at Bake.[91] Informants did not say whether or not these merchants were appointed as *nagadras*. They only said that the merchants had intimate relations with *Ras* Mikael and some of them traded for him. *Ras* Mikael is said to have gone to the extent of referring to Salih Ali as "my merchant". At one time in the 1890's Salih Ali is said to have traded for *Ras* Mikael. To a large extent, he is said to have been involved in the arms trade from the ports of Assab and Tajura.[92]

Thus, the importance of Wallo for trade in Ethiopia had considerably changed since the last quarter of the 19th century. It had then assumed great significance as the land of merchants. So much so that the people of Wallo later became most intimately associated with long-distance trade. This was facilitated naturally by Islam as the religion of most of the Wallo people.

NOTES

* This paper is drawn from my M.A. thesis entitled "Aspects of the Political History of Wallo: 1872-1917", presented to the School of Graduate Studies of Addis Ababa University in June 1983.

1. Zergaw Asfera, "Some Aspects of Historical Development in Amhara, Wallo; *Ca.* 1700-1815", unpublished B.A. thesis (Addis Ababa University, 1973), pp.1-6.

2. C. W. Isenberg and J. L. Krapf, *The Journals of Isenberg and Krapf* (London: Frank Cass and Co. Ltd., 1968), pp. 346, 411.

3. Informant: Mohammed Hartuma.

4. Isenberg and Krapf, *Journals*, p.362.

5. *Ibid.*, p.411.

6. Informants: Ababa Ayicheh; Hussein Yusuf; Mohammed Hartuma.

7. *Ibid.* Wajirat is the name of a district on the Wallo-Tigray border. That the raids are called after this district obviously reflect their significance in the area. Even though it was also found among the lowland Oromo of Awssa, Ambassal and Qalu, informants say that the *Wajirat* tradition was particularly strong among the Azabo and Raya, whose land is adjacent to Wajirat. Robert Markham in his *History of the Abyssinian Expedition* (London: Macmillan and Co., 1869), p.246, seems to corroborate this point. He says that the Azabo Galla made incessant raids on the Christian inhabitants of the neighbouring highland districts, among which Wajirat was one.

8. Informant: Ababa Ayicheh.

9. Informants: Hussein Yusuf; Ababa Ayicheh.

10. Informants: Ali Wadajo; Sheikh Madfu.

11. Informants: Ababa Ayicheh; Wandimagan Amhad; Ali Wadajo. The term *alanga* is derived from a leather whip used to urge horses on, for instance on long distance campaigns. This is also the meaning given by Gabra Wald Engida Warq, *Ya Ethiopia Maretina Gibir Sim* (Addis Ababa, 1956), p.51.

12. Informants: Hussein Abire; Molla Balachew; Ababa Ayicheh.

13. *Ibid.*

14. Informants: Ali Wadajo; Hussein Abire; Ababa Ayicheh.

15. *Ibid.*

16. *Ibid.*

17. Informants: Molla Eshate; Tagan Mankir.

18. Gabra Wald, *Ya Ethiopia Maret*, p.47; Mahatama Sillase Walda Masqual, *Zikra Nagar* (Addis Ababa, 1962), p.153; Informants: Wandimagan Ahmad; Fijaw Lamma; Molla Eshate.

19. Informants: Wandimagan Ahmad; Fijaw Lamma; Molla Eshate.

20. Gabra Wald, *Ya Ethiopia Maret*, p.47; Mahatama Sillase, *Zikra Nagar*, p.153.

21. Informants: Wandimagan Ahmad; Fijaw Lamma; Molla Eshate.

22. *Ibid.*: Gabra Wald, *loc. cit.*; Mahatama Sillase, *loc. cit.*

23. Informants: Fijaw Lamma; Molla Eshate.

24. Informants: Shawil Ayanachaw; Tasfa Farada.

25. Informants: Kabbada Mohammed; Yusuf Mohammed; Yusuf Sadiq; Ali Wadajo; Fijaw Lamma; Makonnan Zawde.

26. Informants: Ali Hashim; Yusuf Mohammed. Ali Hashim claims to have been the governor of Argobba from 1960-64.

27. *Ibid.*

28. Informant: Mohammed Hartuma.

29. *Ibid.*

30. *Ibid.*

31. *Ibid.*

32. Informants: Ababa Ayicheh; Yusuf Mohammed; Yimar Wiraqe; Molla Dilnasse; Bayana Achame.

33. Taddesse Tamrat, *Church and State in Ethiopia, 1270-1527* (London: Oxford University Press, 1972), pp.80-81 *and* "The States in Ethiopia and the Horn", *The General History of Africa*, Vol.IV, Chapter 17, ed. D. T. Niane (UNESCO, in Press).

34. Informant: Sheikh Madfu.

35. *Ibid.*

36. Informants: Wandimagan Ahmad; Haile Farris; Bogala Warqe. *Ato* Bogale Warqe claims to

be a grandson of one of the merchants brought from Gojam by Emperor Yohannes and settled at Boru.

37. Informants: Siraj Mohammed; Haile Farris; Maminaw Assafa; Bogala Warqe; Sheikh Madfu.

38. *Ibid.*

39. Richard Pankhurst, *Economic History of Ethiopia, 1800-1935* (Addis Ababa: Haile Selassie I University Press, 1968), p.472.

40. Informants: Hussein Zainu; Ababa Ayicheh.

41. Richard Pankhurst, *Economic History*, pp.481-82.

42. Annaratone, *In Abissinia*, p.405; Pankhurst, *Economic History*, p.243; Hussein Zainu; Daud Hassan.

43. Informants: Hussein Zainu; Ababa Ayicheh.

44. Annaratone, *In Abissinia*, p.406. The transliteration is quoted from Annaratone himself.

45. Pankhurst, *Economic History*, p.240. While written sources give some details about the other types of salt bars, nothing is said about *Wayro*.

46. In R. Basset (trans. and ed.), *Histoire de la Conquete de l'Abyssinie* (Paris: Ernest Leroux, 1897-1901), p.59. Ansoqia is recorded as one of the cities of the Christian state of Ethiopia during the wars of Ahmad Gran in the 1530's.

47. Informants: Hussein Yassin; Haile Farris; Maminaw Assafa; Siraj Mohammed.

48. *Ibid.*

49. *Ibid.*

50. Fijaw Lamma; Maminaw Assafa; Haile Farris.

51. Annaratone, *In Abissinia*, p.130; Pankhurst, *Economic History*, p.106; Sheikh Madfu; Omar Ali; Mangistu Walda Sillase.

52. Pankhurst, *Economic History*, pp.106-107.

53. Informants: Mangistu Walda Sillase; Maminaw Assafa. *Ato* Maminaw Assafa is an 83 years old ex-slave who is now a farmer at Boru. He has an intimate knowledge of how the slave trade operated at the time. As a slave he belonged to one of the important Tigre merchant families brought to Wallo by Yohannes. He is still called after his master, *Nagadras* Assafa, son of *Nagadras* Habtu.

54. Informants: Mangistu Walda Sillase; Maminaw Asafa.

55. Informants: Hussein Yassin; Daud Hassan.

56. *Ibid.*

57. Informants: Ababa Ayicheh; Daud Hassan; Hussein Yusuf; Omar Ali.

58. *Ibid.*

59. Informants: Daud Hassan; Hussein Yusuf.

60. *Ibid.*

61. Informants: Ahmad Tuha; Hussein Zainu; Hussein Yassin; Haile Farris.

62. Informants: Haile Farris; Hussein Yassin. *Ato* Haile Farris was involved in the Wallo-Massawa trade.

63. *Ibid.*

64. Informant: Maminaw Assafa.

65. Informant: Fijaw Lamma.

66. Informants: Maminaw Assafa; Fijaw Lamma.

67. Informants: Hussein Yassin; Haile Farris; Hussein Zainu; Mangistu Walda Sillase.

68. *Ibid.*

69. Informant: Daud Hassan.

70. Informant: Fijaw Lamma.

71. Informants: Hussein Yassin; Haile Farris; Hussein Zainu; Mangistu Walda Sillase; Daud Hassan.

72. Informant: Fijaw Lamma.

73. Informants: Haile Farris; Daud Hassan; Mangistu Walda Sillasse.

74. Informants: Ababa Ayicheh; Kabbada Ali. Sano Gabya in Dasse was such a place and even nowadays it is known as *atari ganda*. The weekly market of Dasse is also held at this place. While they have been unable to give the etymology of the term *atari*, informants agree that it is used in reference to merchants. *Ganda* means a village, a locality.

75. Informants: Sheikh Madfu; Ababa Ayicheh.

76. Informants: Ahmad Tuha; Wandimagan Ahmad; Bogale Warqe.

77. *Ibid.*

78. Informants: Ahmad Tuha; Wandimagan Ahmad; Bogale Warqe. The merchants from Gojam, Bagemidir and the other parts of Wallo brought local produce such as grain, butter, honey, pepper, skins and cattle to the market at Boru.

79. Informants: Ahmad Tuha; Hussein Abire; Kabbada Ali.

80. *Ibid.*

81. Informants: Hussein Yusuf; Ababa Ayicheh.

82. Informant: Hussein Yusuf.

83. Informants: Hussein Yusuf; Ababa Ayicheh; Omar Ali.

84. *Ibid.*

85. Informant: Daud Hassan.

86. Informants: Daud Hassan; Hussein Yassin.

87. Informants: Hussein Zainu; Ababa Ayicheh; Haile Farris.

88. *Ibid.*

89. Peter Garretson, "Some thoughts on towns and the Naggadras in Feudal Ethiopia in the late 19th and early 20th centuries", *Paper prepared for the conference on Ethiopian Feudalism* (Addis Ababa, March 1976). p.1; Hussein Zainu; Ababa Ayicheh; Haile Farris.

90. Informants: Hussein Zainu; Ababa Ayicheh; Haile Farris.

91. Informants: Haile Farris; Daud Hassan; Mangistu Walda Sillase; Sheikh Madfu.

92. *Ibid.*

SOME ASPECTS OF POST-LIBERATION ETHIOPIA

(1941-1950*)

Bahru Zewde

"If one Ethiopian robbed another by
profiteering, at least the money
remained in Ethiopia."

> Mekonnen Habte Wold
> December 1944

The period of Ethiopian history after 1941 has deservedly attracted considerable attention. Many works have been published on it, most, if not all, of them rotating on the personality of Emperor Haile Selassie. The general drift of the literature has been in the line of what the Emperor himself had pronounced when he was restored to the throne (words that remained enshrined on the title pages of *Addis Zaman* until his political demise) — the opening of a new era. Beginning with the monumental study of Perham and ending with Gilkes' *The Dying Lion*, so uncomfortably poised astride Absolutism and Revolution, the focus of attention has been on the consolidation of autocracy after 1941. Much more recently, and drawing considerably on American and British archival material, Harold Marcus has produced a fairly detailed study of the period, albeit characteristically weighted on the diplomatic side.[1] This has now been followed by John Spencer's personal and intimate account of the period.[2]

There is no denying the fact that the period 1941-74 constitutes a significant one in modern Ethiopian history. It marks, not only the consummation of autocratic rule, but also the articulation of classes and class contradictions eventually leading to the Revolution. But the logic of historical perspective, if nothing else, demands that this period be seen, not in isolation, but in relation to the preceding periods. The antecedents of 1941-74 are to be sought, not only in 1917-35, but also in 1936-41. I have tried to deal elsewhere with the formative significance of the Regency and the five years of imperial rule before the Fascist aggression.[3] A proper assessment of the historical significance of the Italian Occupation for the political economy of Ethiopia is still pending.[4] But it is quite evident that the Italian legacy cannot be merely subsumed, as has been the custom, under road-building and prostitution. Rather, it would include a host of other elements at both the infra-structural and superstructural levels which had a direct bearing on Ethiopian economy and society after liberation.

What is attempted in this paper is one more contribution to the study of post-Liberation Ethiopia. While highlighting some of the unique characteristics of the period, an effort will at the same time be made to place them in the context of the history of twentieth-century Ethiopia in general. The terminal date is dictated as much by the material at my disposal, as by a feeling that the American domination that follows ushers in a new chapter of post-Liberation history which merits separate investigation.[5]

With regard to Ethiopia's relations with the imperialist powers, the most fundamental change that the period witnessed, in comparison with the pre-1935 period, is the shift from tripartite competition (between France, Britain and Italy) to unilateral domination (by the British). This quite obviously was a result of the role that Britain, by force of circumstances, came to play in the final act of liberation from Fascist occupation. It was enshrined in the two agree-

---

*   The material for this preliminary study is largely derived from the pertinent Foreign Office Archives of the Public Record Office in London (which I gathered in the summer of 1983) and some archival and unpublished material here in Ethiopia. I gratefully acknowledge financial assistance rendered to me by the British Academy and the British Council for the London end of the research.

ments of decreasing stringency (1942 and 1944) that Haile Selassie was forced to sign with his powerful ally, as the price for his restoration to the throne. And it was characterized by far-reaching British control of Ethiopian finance and administration.

This control, one should emphasize, did not go without protest. And herein lies one of the essential features of this period: the conflict between the British policy of creating a semi-protectorate in Ethiopia and the Emperor's desire to restore his autocratic rule in alliance with, but not under, the British. As he wrote in August 1941:**« በኛ በኩል እገራችን አማካሪ እንደሚያስፈ ልጋት እናውቃለን ነገር ግን ነጻነቷ ሳይነካ ካልሆነ ከጣልያን ቀምበር ወጥታ ወደ ሌላ ቀምበር ትዛራለች ማለ ት የማይታሰብ ክንቱ ነው ።** [6]

An important element of the whole situation was that while the war was over for Ethiopia, the Second World War was still raging. This provided a convenient pretext for the British to institute stringent control over Ethiopia on "imperial defence grounds". On the other hand, to strip the Emperor of even the outer trappings of power would have been self-defeating and would have fed political opposition to the British as well as to the Emperor. The precise formula of the relationship between the British and the Emperor was adumbrated in the Foreign Office in the fall of 1941. Gradually, the position of the War Office, which had amounted to one of establishing a protectorate over Ethiopia, was abandoned and that of the Foreign Office, which urged a more subtle, but nonetheless effective control, prevailed.[7] The two agreements embody the latter position.

Although the 1942 agreement was said to have been given "cordial reception"[8] by the Emperor, he soon became acutely aware of the constraints that it imposed on his power. Far from reconstituting his power on a new and strengthened basis, it circumscribed it considerably in such important spheres as finance, the army and foreign policy. The result was increasing estrangement between the two allies, which, the second agreement of 1944 notwithstanding, led the Emperor to continue to seek — and eventually find — a new ally, the United States. A new light is thrown on this whole situation by the letters that the Emperor wrote to his Minister in London, Blatta Ayele Gebre, in the years 1943-45.[9]

As it emerges from the letters, the minister was to be more than anything else a press officer, rallying the rather powerful Pro-Emperor lobby in Britain to counter the machinations of the British Government. Ayele's accreditation was not only for the task of facilitating the immediate task at hand, i.e. the agreement negotiations, but also to monitor what was being planned for or against Ethiopia after the War **(የታሰብልንን ፣ የታሰብብንን)**. For this purpose, he was to get in touch with representatives of governments-in-exile in London.[10]

Apparently impressed by the power of the press during his five-year exile in England, the Emperor urged his representative to do everything possible in this direction to put across to the public the Emperor's case. Following the Emperor's refusal to accept the British subsidy at the end of 1944 (on the grounds that it was too small), a vigorous campaign was launched charging, among other things, that slavery was still widespread in Ethiopia. Ayele was then instructed to make protests, have the *awaj* banning slavery in Ethiopia published in the papers **(« ሌሎች ጋዜ ጦች እንኳ እናትምም ቢሉ በትን'ሸም፣ጋዜጣም ቢሆን ማሳተም ገንዘብም ሰጥቶ ቢሆን »)**[11], write letters to editors, and raise the issued in parliament through friendly delegates if newspapers refused to publish the letters.[12] In this connection, he was to work closely with the most ardent campaigner for the Emperor's cause, Sylvia Pankhurst, giving her adequate, but discreet, financial support.[13]

It is clear from the letters that the Emperor felt quite dismayed at the turn his relations with the British had taken and the posture of opposition that he had been forced to assume. He therefore went out of his way to protest his gratitude for past services and commitment to future friendship. In January 1945, he wrote in a tone of desperation and futility: **« ቢያምንም ባያምንም የተቻለንን ያህል በእንግሊዝ የምንሰውጠው እንደሌላ ሳታረጻም አልቀረህም »**[14]. Already in 1943, he had clearly spelled out the nature of the Anglo-Ethiopian partnership he envisaged: **... በጠቅላላው ለሚመጣው ጊዜ የእንግሊዝ ሕዝብ በኢትዮጵያ ተጠቅሞ ላጉሩ ጥቅም የሚተውበትን በሕዝቡ ጥቅም መገናኛ፣ተራምዶ ሁሉቱ መንግሥት የማይናወጥ የወዳጅነት መገናኛ የሚመሠረትበትን**

278

ኢትዮጵያ ራስዋ ብቻዋን ጉዳይዋን አደራጅ ለመሆን የሚበቃ አትም ስለማታገኝ የዛሬውም የዓለም መን ግሥታት መገናኛ በኢንተር ናቸናል ጉዳይ ተነዋላ ለመኖር የማይፈቅድላተም እርሷም የማታወደው ነገር ስለሆነ ነጻነቷዋና ግዛቲዋ ተጠብቆላትጥቅሟን በማካፈል ሪጋት አስተናባሪ የምታገኝበትን ማሰብ ነው ። [15]

One element that tended to cloud the relationship of the Emperor and the British was the latters' suspicion that the former was courting the Americans. The suspicion was not ground-less. But the Emperor was at pains to assure the British that he had no intention of turning his back on them. As he wrote in May 1943:

ክአሜሪካ ጋር ስላላን ወደፈትም፡እየሱፉ እንዲኊዴ ስለምንጥርበት ግንኙነት ወዳጀቾችን በደህና ዓይን የተ መለከቱት አይመስልም ... ክአሜሪካ በመቀራረብ ምክንያት ከወዳጃችን ክእንግሊዝ ለመራቅ ምንም የ ምናስበው ነገር የለም ስለዚህ ጉዳይ በዚህ ያሉት የወዳጃችን አገር ሰዎች በሌላ ተርጉመው በዚያ ያሉ ትን እንዲያሳምኑዋቸው ነገሩ ባጋ ጠመወ ጊዜ ክአሜሪካን ጋር ከእንግሊዝ የተደበቀ ምንም ልዩ ጉዳይ አለ መኖራን እንድትሪዳው ነው ። [16]

Such protestations of loyalty aside, however, there were a number of factors which made continuation of the partnership between the two allies impossible. In the letter written on the same date as the note cited above, he recalled the reluctant acceptance of the institution of Occupied Enemy Territory Administration (OETA), with the curtailment of independence and sovereignty that it implied, and argued that the time was ripe for a new agreement.

Specific problems created by the 1942 agreement were the British exercise of judicial powers which was reminiscent of the capitulatory Klobukowski Treaty (1908), restriction of the country's military strength and its foreign relations, and the issue of currency.[17] The arrogant and often racist behaviour of the "Ethiopian Army", as the British troops came to call themselves, as well as their unilateral actions, such as the sequestration of Ras Haylu's property at Debre Marqos, emphasized the Emperor's powerlessness.[18] Pressures for grant of an area for hydraulic works at Lake Tana demonstrated that the British were ready to exploit their superior position to further their imperial interests.[19] Further, their reluctance to extradite Haile Selassie Gugsa, who had treacherously defected to the Italian side in 1935, was to remain, even in the words of Lord De La Warr, British negotiator of the 1944 agreement, a shadow on Anglo-Ethiopian relations.[20]

The Emperor looked forward to the new agreement as a means of escaping from the posi-tion of exclusive dependence on the British to which the politics of liberation had reduced him. The British were a niggardly but possessive master. They tied up his hands and deprived him of all the necessary means of reconstituting his autocratic power. At the same time they exercised political and military control incommensurate with the financial assistance they rendered. On the horizon was looming a better partner, the United States, which was ready to give (or at any rate was believed to be) a liberal supply of cash without entailing the discomfiture of direct political and military control, "to benefit from Ethiopia and at the same time bring benefit to the country" – the perfect neo-colonial arrangement. As he confided to his representative in London:

... ይህን ስምምነት ማቅረብ ያሳሰበን ፡ የሚሪካ መንግሥት መላክተኛውን ልኮ ለጋሲዮን ስላሳም ፡ ከዚህ መን ግሥት ጋር ስለ ገንዘብ ብድርና ስለሌላም እርዳታ የምንነጋገረው ሁሉ ፍጹም ለማግኘት እን ዲችል አስቀድሞ ከእን ግለዝ መንግሥት ጋር ባያረግነው ስምምነት የታገድነውን አንዳንድ የነጻነት መ ብት ማቃናት አስ ፈላጊ ስለሆንና ላ ራችን የሚጠቅም መስለው የታየንን ጉዳዮች በነጻነት ከሌሎች መን ግሥቶች ጋር ለመነጋገ ር እንዲመች ነው ። [21]

The Emperor's concern at the restrictions imposed on him by British presence is substan-tiated from an unusual quarter. In a rare moment of candour, the British Minister, Howe, wrote to Eden thus:

We have been content to let the country lapse into its 'native state' con-dition . . . We have wanted the least possible responsibility. We have been unwilling or unable to provide the minimum assistance in men and materials necessary to put the administration on its feet. We have turned down the Emperor's repeated requests for help for the roads and other communications. . . We cleaned the country of Italian equipment and refused to allow more than a handful of Italians to remain for essential services. We removed the currency reserves, both dollar and shilling, and with them the best means of holding the dollar rate. Ethiopia's export trade in hides, skins, beeswax has been crippled by our inability to give adequate prices.[22]

But the 1944 agreement, while improving the Emperor's position in some respects, hardly settled the issues outstanding between the two parties. A measure of the Emperor's frustration is his contrasting appraisal of Lord De La Warr. Although he had charitably characterized De La Warr as ፍስሐ ገጽ (of pleasing countenance)[23] on his arrival, he could not conceal his ire at his attitude after the conclusion of the agreement, in particular his joining in the chorus of public outcry in London at the Emperor's refusal to accept the British offer of subsidy. The Emperor was at pains to explain the grounds for his rejection of what he considered a paltry offer (£3 million rather than the £10 million recommended by British experts), drawing on a saying to drive his point home: እንዳያግ ጥሪው እንዳይበላ ግሩው ። [24]

On the two vital territorial issues, Ogaden and Eritrea, as well, the outcome of the agreement can only be described as frustrating. This feeling of frustration comes out very clearly in the memo that he submitted to Churchill in February 1945, on the occasion of his meeting in Cairo with the British Prime Minister and President Roosevelt:

በአዲሱም ውል ንግግር ጊዜ … ሕዝባችን ውጋዴን ወደ ኢትዮጵያ የሚመለስበት ጊዜ ደርሷል ብሎ በጋለ ተስፋ ተጠባባቆ ነበር ። እኛም ስለውጋዴን ከእንግሊዝ መንግሥት መላክተኞች ጋራ በጥብቅ ከተከራከርንበት በኋላ የተቾገርንበት ጉዳይ መሆኑን ለክቡርነትዎ በቴሌግራም አስታወቅን። ውጋዴን ወደ ኢትዮጵያ አስተዳደር መመለፅ ከመቆየቱ ሌላ በእንግሊዚ የጦር ሥራዊት እንድትተዳደር የተደረገበት የውሎቃል ሕዝባችንን ቅር ብሎ እታል ።እኛም እንደጠበቅነው አልሆነም ። [25]

The issue of Eritrea, too, remained pending. As is common knowledge, it was to require years of diplomatic ups and downs before she could even be federated to Ethiopia. In the meantime, the Emperor kept the issue very much in the forefront of his diplomacy, adducing both strategic and historical arguments for reunion. Without an outlet to the sea, he reasoned, Ethiopia's liberation would only be nominal, and hence a burden rather than a blessing.[26] In a second memo to Churchill during their Cairo meeting, he recalled former British official pronouncements on Ethiopia's rights to Eritrea and presented the issue of reunion, not as a matter of privilege, but as a matter of right. To enumerate the strong ethnic, historical, geographical and economic grounds for reunion, he argued, would be superfluous.[27]

Aside from these fundamental territorial issues, finance was another important source of friction between the Emperor and the British. The root of the problem was the incompatibility of the Emperor's need for extensive financial resources to reconstitute his power and the implacably orthodox fiscal policy of the British.[28] At the same time, on the questions of banking and currency, the issue boiled down to one of dependence or independence. This contradiction was reflected in the relations between the Emperor and his British advisers: Sandford for Interior, Stafford for Finance and Bethell for Commerce. Nothing illustrates better the mutual disenchantment of the two erstwhile partners than the antipathy that developed between the Emperor and Sandford, who only two years back had marched shoulder to shoulder from Khartoum to Addis Ababa. In a letter in which the former castigated his advisers, he reserved his severest critique to Sandford, not only for his overweening attitude towards the government and officials, but also for his instigation of the other advisers to write a joint letter of resignation on the issue of currency.[29]

From the outset, the British had directed all their efforts to kill the Maria Theresa thaler and tie the Ethiopian currency to sterling. The East African shilling that they introduced to further this objective proved unpopular however. It led to considerable friction between soldier and peasant, as the latter refused to sell grain for the currency in which the former were paid.[30]

Ultimately, of course, the Emperor himself was to turn against the thaler, but after he had instituted his own currency, based on the dollar rather than sterling. Thus, merchants were forced to sign a declaration behind locked doors that they would abide by the government ban on the thaler. Peasants coming to the market were likewise compelled to change their thaler into the new currency (at the rate of three 50 cent pieces or 'shillings' to the thaler).[31]

A related question was that of banking. As early as the fall of 1941, the famous Barclays Bank of London had tried to step in along the path so propitiously cleared by British troops. But it met a chilling rebuff when the Emperor did not even deign to receive its representative. Thereafter, the British fell back on a characteristic position: preventing the Emperor from establishing his own bank. An official of the British Treasury ventured the opinion that the primitive credit machinery of the country did not warrant the institution of a central bank. For some time they succeeded in persuading the Emperor to buy the idea of a Currency Board, which would be composed of the Ethiopian Minister of Finance and two other members to be nominated by the Treasury and appointed by the Emperor. Based in London, the Board was to act for all practical purposes like a bank, being responsible among other things for the issuance of the new currency (an Ethiopian pound equivalent to the East African Shilling) that the British were planning to impose on the country.[32]

The founding of the State Bank of Ethiopia in August 1942 dealt a final blow to the British bid for fiscal control. The bitterness of the pill was in no way mitigated by the appointment of Collier, a Briton and governor of the pre-1935 Bank of Ethiopia, as the governor of the new bank. The Treasury official mentioned above had already expressed regret that Collier had been allowed to return to Ethiopia, presumably because he was not readily amenable to British imperial interests.[33]

As if this were not enough, some three years later, an additional bank, an agricultural one (parent of the current AID Bank) was inaugurated against the explicit objection of British advisers. One British report described the whole venture as the brainchild of the Minister of Commerce and Agriculture, Ato Makonnen Habte Wold, and "his get-rich-quick friends".[34]

The characterization is a good illustration of British bitterness at Makonnen, who is dubbed "ultra-nationalist" in another report.[35] It had its origin in the tight control that he exercised over import-export trade through an organization that he had created for the purpose, the Ethiopian National Corporation (ENC). One of the most important economic realities of post-Liberation Ethiopia was the high demand for Ethiopian products, particularly cereals and coffee, in the world market and the false sense of prosperity that this created. Having been liberated from the clutches of Fascism first, Ethiopia was in a unique position to supply to the dislocated and war-torn markets of the Middle East at inflationary prices. The figures for Ethiopian export trade continued to show a progressive increase, reaching a total of £3,114,076 in 1944-45. Of these, cereals contributed to nearly £1 million, coffee to £1,200,000 and gold to £893,000. The total figure marked a favourable balance of trade to the value of £380,000, which was improved to £500,000 in the first half of the following year.[36]

Another predominant factor that conditioned the nature of the post-Liberation Ethiopian economy was the legacy of Italian occupation. Expatriate firms prominent in export-import trade had been among the first victims of the new order. The Ethiopian economy was appended to the autarkic economic system of the metropolis. While their ambitious agricultural projects evaporated with their military defeat, the Italians left behind an impressive network of roads (although some parts of it were damaged through military action in the final year), some one thousand lorries, a fairly extensive milling industry, a much more expanded cash economy and a taste, particularly among the elite, for consumer goods such as European dress and cars.[37] One observer has even claimed that the occupation had an emancipatory effect on women, as witnessed by the higher number of women to be seen dancing at receptions.[38]

An inclination to engage in commercial activities had not been unknown among members of the Ethiopian ruling class prior to the occupation. *Naggadras* Hayla Giyorgis, *Ras* Tafari, *Ras*

Haylu and *Ras* Dasta Damtaw are four prominent examples that one can cite in this context. What the occupation probably did was to encourage a pre-1935 trend in two important ways: the destruction of the expatriate firms and the spread of what one may call a corporatist economic ethos. Thus, Bethell, the commercial adviser, could write in 1944: "One striking feature is the number of Ethiopians, many of the upper classes, who have now turned to trade".[39] A report of the IBRD mission which visited Ethiopia towards the end of the decade concluded that the palace "seemed to have interests in nearly all commercial enterprises into which we enquired".[40] Not only was it involved in trade in coffee[41] and such luxury items as champagne and perfume[42], but it also "formed companies for the operation of the Colonalpi mill . . ., a brewery and alcohol distillery, and a shoe factory".[43]

The high-point of state participation in commerce can be said to have been reached with the formation of the above-mentioned ENC in mid-1943. Having a share capital of about 1,300,000 Maria Theresa thalers, it came to enjoy a lucrative monopoly over the supply of cereals to the United Kingdom Commercial Corporation (UKCC), which in turn exported them to the Middle East. An idea of the profits that accrued to the ENC and its members can be formed from the fact that the latter often acted as the former's dealers, buying cereals from the peasant at 6.50 thaler per quintal and selling them to the ENC at 10.50, the ENC would in turn sell it to UKCC at 12.[44]

Nor was it only the peasant who thus became a defenceless victim of the ENC. A powerful firm like A. Bess & Co., was compelled to sell grains it had purchased at 32 shillings per quintal to the ENC at 30 and subsequently re-buy for export to Aden at 35. The British report which gives this information comments wryly: "Not even 'private enterprise' could better this".[45] In a somewhat related development (although admittedly the role of the ENC here is not quite manifest), some rich Greek merchants who had been canvassed by the Greek chargé d'affaires to come to the rescue of a Greek construction company which was in serious financial difficulties were dissuaded from doing so when "hints were conveyed to them that it would be better for them" not to do so. Some of the firm's operations had apparently clashed with the interests of some high-placed officials.[46]

Makonnen's control of trade extended to the import side. Exploiting his position as Minister of Commerce, he made the granting of import licenses conditional on the delivery of all cotton goods to a new company that he had helped to create, the Ethiopian Society for Commerce and Transport (popularly known as *Mahber Bet*). The *Mahber Bet* was reported to be making "astronomical" profits through the sale of cotton goods in the black market. Its official patronage enabled it to weather the vagaries of the market. It could renege on engagements to buy goods from importers if the price for those goods was falling. It could also buy in shillings and sell in dollars.[47]

The British strongly resented the sway that Makonnen held on import-export trade. In December 1944, Bethell gave a three-month's notice of resignation and one of the reasons he gave for this step was what he described as the stranglehold that the ENC exercised on trade.[48] A commission was established early the following year to investigate his allegations, but it was inconceivable that it would make any serious enquiry into an enterprise that had proved so profitable to so many high-placed persons.[49] In one of the legation's reports to the Foreign Office, too, there is the following observation:

> Ever since the restoration of the Ethiopian Government, Ato Makonnen
> Habte Wold has been obsessed by the conviction that Ethiopia had always
> been bled by foreign merchants, and that he must devise a means of divert-
> ing their profits into Ethiopian pockets.[50]

The legation's main worry was that the profits so made by the ENC, instead of being recycled into the market, were being hoarded, thereby contributing to the shortage of money.[51]

The burden of this highly lucrative business venture was felt not only by the producing peasant and the merchant, but also (and probably most) by the consumer. The rising price of cereals entailed a high cost of living. "It is unfortunate", Bethell commented, "that his [i.e. the

Ethiopian's] first years of regained freedom should have coincided with a period of scarcity and high prices".[52] In November 1945, the Emperor donated 50 tons of cereals and 200 pieces of cotton-cloth to the people of Tigrai to meet the growing shortage in both. A British report rejected the official explanation of poor harvest and readily and, one may add plausibly, attributed it to the activities of the ENC.[53]

Almost as prominent as Makonnen Habte Wald in the Post-Liberation money-making spree was his namesake, Makonnen Walda Yohannes, brother of the powerful Minister of the Pen, *Sahafe Te'ezaz* Walda Giyorgis, and Custodian of Enemy property until his disgrace in 1955. In the latter capacity, he presided over the expropriation and administration of a number of Italian buildings and plants, including the electricity plant CONIEL (Compagnia nazionale imprese elettriche), which was rechristened the Shoan Electric Light and Power Authority and of which he became director.[54] Although such expropriated property was theoretically sold on the open market, potential competitors were discouraged by the fictitiously high prices quoted and the property in question ultimately found itself in the hands either of the Government or of Makonnen and his favourites.[55] A variation on this theme was reported in Jimma, where Makonnen's representative sold the best house in town for £10 — to himself![56] Other items inherited by Makonnen included a fleet of trucks, operated by what came to be known as the Imperial Motor Transport Company, the Lancia Garage (re-named Enaware Garage)[57], and the sugar plantation at the site of what later developed into the Wonji Sugar Estate.[58]

It was in the field of public transport that Makonnen was to reach the high point of his semi-official business career. This was particularly so with his helping to establish the General Ethiopian Transport (GET for short, more popularly known as Anbassa) in 1952 as a share company with a capital of 600,000 Ethiopian dollars, of which the Government and the Emperor, proxy of Makonnen, owned a third. Through his directorship of the Electric Light and Power Authority, Makonnen was in charge of a further 50,000 dollars. Genealogically, GET was successor to the less ambitious Public Transport department established within the Ministry of Communications in 1942/43. Under the energetic and enterprising directorship of the French-educated Mekbib Damte, abandoned trucks had been furnished with improvised seats and batteries, Italian drivers and mechanics hired and female conductors trained. The outcome was a fleet of some twenty buses that had come to provide both urban and inter-urban transport service.[59]

The origins of GET underline the Italian parentage of a number of industrial plants and a few public utilities. To the latter category should be added CONIEL, the precursor of EELPA. To the former belong the textile mills and cement factory in Dire Dawa, the fibre mills and four flour mills (including the famous Cerealia) in Addis Ababa, a number of saw mills spread throughout the country, and some timber and furniture works. In addition, in 1944, there were estimated to be some 1,321 commercial and 1,383 private vehicles of which 877 and 888 respectively were of Italian origin, mostly Fiat.[60]

How much of the wealth that the Makonnens so ingeniously amassed they kept to themselves and how much of it found its way into government and/or royal coffers is an intriguing question which is not so easy to answer. In spite of his eventual disgrace, the link with Emperor and Government is more apparent in the case of Makonnen Wolda Yohannes than in that of his more successful namesake, who appears to have been acting pretty much on his own. After all, the former acted as official representative of Emperor and Government in GET, rather than as a private shareholder. And steel reinforcers that he had expropriated from the abortive Italian sugar mills at Wonji were transported to the capital and used in the construction of the Jubilee Palace.[61]

The contribution of such money-making enterprises to Government revenue should not, however, be given undue prominence. Aside from the British subsidy, the three main sources of such revenue were: land tax, customs, and Adola gold. A 1944 report by Stafford, the financial adviser, estimated the total revenue at £2,843,600 and gave the following breakdown of the major contributions:[62]

Land	—	590,000
Customs	—	650,000
Gold	—	500,000

From the days of his regency, the rationalisation of land ownership (more precisely registration and privatization) had been among the Emperor's top concerns. The rationale behind this policy appears to have been an augmented revenue and a landed class enjoying security of tenure — both important bulwarks of the emerging absolutist state.[63] The privatisation of land gained even greater momentum after Liberation.[64] Correspondingly, successive regulations defined ever more sharply the landowner's tax obligations to the state.

The first Land Tax Proclamation after Liberation was promulgated in March 1942. This fixed the rate for measured land at 15 dollars per *gasha* for *lam* (i.e. half the 1935 rate), 10 dollars per *gasha* for *lam-taf* and 5 dollars per *gasha* for *taf*. On unmeasured land, the rate was to be half that of 1935.[65] The relative lightness of the burden can be said to reflect the insecurity of the Emperor's political position. Some three years later, however, a new proclamation was issued superseding the 1942 one. It represented a further step in the rationalization of land tax. It abolished corvee and replaced all forms of land tribute by a fixed *geber* on land and a tax in lieu of *asrat* (tithe), both to be paid in cash.

The rate imposed by the new proclamation was much higher than that of 1942: 50 dollars per *gasha* for *lam* (45 in the provinces of Wallaga, Sidamo, Illubabor, Gamu Gofa and Kafa), 40 for *lam-taf* and 15 for *taf*. It is interesting to note that all the increases on the categories of measured land were represented by the commuted *asrat* payment: 35, 30 and 10 dollars respectively. Unmeasured *gabbar* land was to pay 20 dollars. Unmeasured *rest* in "Shawa Amhara" was divided into three categories with payments of 20, 15 and 5 dollars. Gojjam, Tigrai and Begemder were to pay in cash *geber* equal to the 1935 rate and the *asrat* on current produce.[66]

This new legislation essentially followed the recommendations of the Tithe and Land Tax Committee submitted on 6 December 1943. These had included: annulment of the 1942 provision for payment at half the pre-War rate and reinstitution of the full rate; devising of means of extracting tax revenue from the fairly extensive *rest-gult* and *maderia* lands, which had hitherto gone untaxed and discouragement as much as possible of payment of *asrat* in kind.[67]

Centralized collection and administration of customs had been another overriding preoccupation of the Emperor before 1935. In this, he had the services of two enterprising and dedicated servants: the Ethiopian, Gabra Egziabher François, and the American, Colson.[68] After Liberation, the Emperor was understandably keen on the speedy reassertion of his control over customs. Gabra Egziabher seems to have got a worthy successor in Bafaqadu Walda Mikael, described by Stafford as "one of the best and most vigorous of the younger generation".[69] Though certainly not endowed with the money-making talents or the dedication of a Colson, a British customs adviser by the name of Underhill also came to be employed.[70]

The upshot of this renewed concern with customs revenue was the customs duties proclamation of July 1943, which fixed the duties to be paid on export and import items. The former were limited to hides and skins, coffee, civet and wax. The first three were to pay 10% *ad valorem* and the last item, 5%. The proclamation dealt primarily with import items, which were divided into fourteen categories and were to pay duties ranging from 10% to 75% *ad valorem* and in some cases fixed duties. Items not specified in the proclamation were to pay 20% *ad valorem*.[71]

Adola gold constituted the third most important source of government revenue. Viewed in historical perspective, it is interesting to note that the metal that has eluded so many concession-hunters before 1935 now came to the relief of the post-Liberation Government. In 1944/45, it came to constitute more than a quarter of total revenue. This did not include the substantial amount that found its way into the Palace coffers. Two factors contributed to the high income from gold: the inflationary prices it secured in Egyptian and Indian markets and the regime of tyranny and oppression imposed on the inhabitants and labourers of the mining district. With regard to the former, gold was said to have been sold at more than double its normal price in the said markets.[72] With regard to the latter, we have an eyewitness account of

1948, which talks of roadblocks at every village from Wando to Nagale and of soldiers accompanying every passing vehicle in the gold district to prevent any smuggling — conditions which in one form or another were to continue to prevail in subsequent decades. The report concludes:

> The local inhabitants look miserable and live in continual fear of arrest or molestation. If they so much as dig a yard of ground in the vicinity of their huts, they are brought before the Military Officers and accused of searching for gold. The whole impression left on the traveller is that of a penal settlement.[73]

Such, then, were some of the salient features of post-Liberation Ethiopia in the 1940s. They can be summed up as the irreconcilability of the constrictions imposed by British overlordship and the Emperor's desire to reconstitute his regained power on an even more strengthened and autocratic basis. The former emanated from a considered policy of returning the country to the pre-1935 position. The latter presaged the building of the absolutist state on even firmer foundations than that which obtained before 1935. This was the genesis of the partnership between the Emperor and the United States. It was to be the historical destiny of American imperialism to provide the infrastructural and superstructural support so essential for the consolidation of absolutism. Ethiopian Airlines, Imperial Highway Authority, Imperial Telecommunications Board, the various activities of the Point Four Programme and an armed force which came to be regarded as one of the strongest in Africa, were some of the results of the new partnership.

NOTES

1. Harold G. Marcus, *Ethiopia, Great Britain and the United States, 1941-1974* (Berkeley, 1983).

2. John H. Spencer, *Ethiopia at Bay: A Personal Account of the Haile Selassie Years* (Algonac, Reference Publications Inc., 1984).

3. Bharu Zewde, "Economic Origins of the Absolutist State in Ethiopia", *Journal of Ethiopian Studies*, XVII (1984, pp.1-29).

4. The only attempt so far that I know of is that of Alberto Sbacchi: *Italian Colonialism in Ethiopia, 1936-1940* , Ph.D. thesis (Chicago, 1975).

5. See Marcus, particularly chs. III and IV, and Spencer.

6. In a letter to his daughter, Tanagne Warq, then still in London: FO.371/27521. "We know that our country needs advisers. But this should not impinge on her independence; it is unthinkable that Ethiopia would free herself from the Italian yoke only to submit to another."

7. The relevant documents for this internal debate are to be found in FO.371/27514, 27521 and 27524.

8. FO.371/31597, GOC East Africa to War Office, 1.2.42.

9. IES Ms. No.1985.

10. *Ibid.*, letter of 7.9.35/15.5.43.

11. "Even if the big ones refuse to publish, paying the smaller ones to do so."

12. *Ibid.*, letter of 25.4.37/2.6.45.

13. *Ibid.*, letter of 19.10.35/26.6.43; 22.6.36/30.10.44; 27.3.36/6.12.43.

14. "Whether they believe it or not, we trust you have made it clear to them that we have no better friend than England." *Ibid.*, letter of 18.1.38/28.9.45.

15. "In general, we should aim so that the English may benefit from Ethiopia and at the same time bring benefit to the country, and on this basis of mutual benefit found the unshakeable friendship of the two governments. Since Ethiopia on her own does not have the strength to arrange her affairs and since in the present order of international relations neither can she live in isolation nor is she inclined to do so, we should seek an intermediary power to assist her and partake of her interests without violating her independence and territorial integrity." *Ibid.*, letter of 7.9.35/15.5.43.

16. "It appears that our friends are not happy about the relationship that we have with America and which we shall strive to expand even further in the future . . . By getting closer to the Americans, we have no intention of moving away from the British. We tell you this so that, when the occasion presents itself, you would be in a position to clear any misunderstandings that may be created because of false reports from here and to emphasize that, in our relations with the Americans, we have nothing to hide from the British." *Ibid.*, note of 7.9.35/15.5.43.

17. *Ibid.*

18. FO.317/31600, Haile Selassie to Platt, 13.10.42.

19. IES Ms. No.1785, letter of 3.11.35/11.7.43.

20. *Ibid.*, letter of 25.4.37/3.1.45, reporting on conversation with De La Warr. Cf. Haggai Erlich, "Tigrean Nationalism, British Involvement and Haile Selassie's Emerging Absolutism — Northern Ethiopia, 1941-1943", *Asian and African Studies,* 15 (1981), pp.213-216.

21. "What made us think of proposing a new agreement is the fact that the United States government has sent its representative here and established a legation. In order to conclude an agreement for Loan or other assistance, we have to remove some of the restrictions that the previous agreement with the British government has imposed on us and be in a position to negotiate freely with any government matters of interest to our country." IES Ms. No.1705, letter of 12.4.36/22.12.43.

22. FO.317/4448, Howe to Eden, 12.1.44.

23. IES Ms. No.1785, letter of 29.1.37/9.10.44.

24. "Invite him so that he won't complain, but prevent him from eating." *Ibid.*, letter of 2.5.37/10.1.45.

25. "During the negotiations for the new agreement, our people were eagerly anticipating the restoration of Ogaden to Ethiopia. We ourselves had also argued strongly with the British Delegation on the issue and had conveyed Our concern to you by telegram. Our people have been dismayed by the fact that not only has the Ogaden not been restored to Ethi-

opia, but also that it has been put under British military administration. Nor was this what We ourselves had expected." *Ibid.*, memo of Yekatit 1937/February 1945.

26. *Ibid.*, letter of 11.12.37/17.8.45.

27. *Ibid.*, memo of Yekatit 1937/February 1945.

28. See, for instance, the frustration of the financial adviser, Stafford, in FO.371/4470, enclosure in Howe to Eden, 4.1.44: "There is no tendency to achieve equilibrium as between State revenue and expenditure because of the expectation that the gap between the two will always be met by pennies from heaven, providential showers which, however, must not impose any obligation upon the beneficiaries".

29. IES Ms. No.1785, letter of 3.11.35/10.7.43.

30. *Ibid.*, letter of 7.9.35/15.5.43; FO.371/35626, Haile Selassie to Sandys, 9.1.43. For a detailed discussion of the currency issue, the reader is referred to Maria Genoino Caravaglios, "Ethiopian Currency during World War II according to the Unpublished Documents of the British and Italian Archives", *Proceedings of the Seventh International Conference of Ethiopian Studies*, ed. Sven Rubenson (1984). One looks in vain, however, for references to the Italian archival material promised by the title.

31. FO.371/53461, Addis Ababa Report No.49, November 1946. See also FO.371/63132, Addis Ababa Report No.51, January 1947.

32. See FO.371/31595 for the correspondence relating to this matter.

33. FO.371/31596, Rowe-Dutton to Mackereth, 20.2.42.

34. FO.371/46050, Addis Ababa Report No.33, July 1945; *The Development Bank of Ethiopia and Its Services* (Addis Ababa, 1967). For the text of the proclamation, see *Negarit Gazeta*, No.75, 1937 E.C.

35, FO.371/46050, Addis Ababa Report No.36, October 1945.

36. FO.371/41463, Bethell Report, enclosure in Cook to Bevin, 10.4.46.

37. *Ibid.*, enclosure in Howe to Eden, 2.9.44.

38. FO.371/41467, Cook to Eden, 17.5.44.

39. FO.371/41463, Bethell Report, enclosed in Howe to Eden, 2.9.44.

40. FO.371/80255, Crawford Report, 26.5.50.

41. FO.371/80232, Harar consular report, enclosure, 9.3.49.

42. FO.371/53461, Addis Ababa Report No.39, January 1946.

43. FO.371/35612, Quarterly Economic Report, enclosed in Howe to FO, 7.5.43.

44. FO.371/46049, Bethell to private secretary of the Emperor, 30.1.45.

45. FO.371/63132, Addis Ababa Report No.50, December 1946.

46. FO.371/69306, Addis Ababa Report No.64, April 1948.

47. FO.371/46049, Bethell to private secretary of the Emperor, 30.1.45. See FO.371/63132, Addis Ababa Report No.51, January 1947, for a slightly modified form of control of export of cereals and import of cotton goods.

48. FO.371/46049, Bethell to Minister of Commerce and Industry, 26.12.44.

49. FO.371/46049, Howe to Eden, 23.1.45.

50. FO.371/46049, Cook to Eden, 12.2.45.

51. *Ibid*. There is an element of hypocrisy here, as the British themselves had earlier contributed to such shortage by exporting a large amount of Maria Theresa thalers in their bid to kill this resilient currency.

52. FO.371/41463, enclosure in Howe to Eden, 2.9.44.

53. FO.371/46050, Addis Ababa Report No.37, November 1945.

54. Kebre-Ab Tesfai, "The History of General Ethiopian Transport Share Company (1944-1966 E.C.)". BA thesis (AAU, Dept. of History, 1984), p.17.

55. FO.371/53461, Addis Ababa Report No.41, March 1946; No.44, June 1946.

56. FO.371/63132, Addis Ababa Report No.50, December 1946.

57. Kebre-Ab, *loc. cit.*: FO.371/53461, Addis Ababa Report No.41, March 1946.

58. Bahru Zewde, "Environment and Capital: Notes for a History of the Wonji-Shoa Sugar Estate (1951-1974)", Paper presented at the Sixth Eastern Africa History Conference, (Ambo, 1984), p.7.

59. Kebre-Ab, *op. cit.*, pp.8-11.

60. FO.371/41463, Bethell report, enclosed in Howe to Eden, 2.9.44.

61. Bahru Zewde, "Environment and Capital . . .", *op. cit.*, p.7.

62. FO.371/41472, enclosure in Cook to Eden, 16.5.44.

63. Bahru Zewde, "Economic Origins . . .", *op. cit.*, pp.15ff.

64. An argument for increasing rationalization of ownership and security of tenure after Liberation was made in an extensive report by Sandford: FO.371/4470, "Memorandum on Land Tenure, Registration and Land Measurement in Ethiopia", 5.1.44.

65. *Negarit Gazeta*, No.8, 1934 E.C.

66. *Negarit Gazeta*, No.70, 1937 E.C.

67. FO.371/41470, "Report of the Tithe and Land Tax Committee", 6.12.43. The committee was composed of the Vice-Minister and the Principal Adviser of the Ministry of the Interior, the Financial Adviser, the Directors-General of the Ministry of Finance, of the

Lands Department and of Administrative Services, and a representative of the Ministry of Agriculture.

For a discussion of this and related fiscal issues, see Eshetu Chole, "Towards a History of the Fiscal Policy of the Pre-Revolutionary Ethiopian State", Paper presented for the East African History Conference (Nazareth, 1982).

68. Bahru Zewde, "Economic Origins . . .", *op. cit.*, pp.25ff.

69. FO.371/41472, enclosure in Cook to Eden, 16.5.44.

70. FO.371/35632, Howe to CPO, 9.1.43; Cook to Eden, 16.5.44; Stafford report, enclosed in Cook to Eden, 16.5.44.

71. *Negarit Gazeta*, No.39, 1935 E.C. Cf. Eshetu, pp.11ff.

72. FO.371/53446, Cook to Bevin, 9.4.46.

73. FO.371/69308, report of British consul, enclosed in Forester to Bevin, 15.3.48.

THE ANGLICAN CHURCH IN ETHIOPIA

Experiments in co-operation with the Ethiopian Orthodox Church

C. F. Battell

The attitude of successive rulers to foreign missionary endeavours in a country with a large indigenous Christian population has always been justifiably circumspect. Foreign missionaries were allowed to enter Ethiopia in the 19th century with certain reservations and were often valued for their technical skills and expertise more than for their missionary enterprise. Before he became Emperor, Tewodros had only been willing for missionaries to enter his territory "on condition that my subjects do not say 'I am French because I am a Catholic' or 'I am British because I am a Protestant' ". More recently in 1926, speaking to the League of Nations, the Regent gave expression to the same feeling: "Throughout their history they (the Ethiopians) have seldom met with foreigners who did not desire to possess themselves of Abyssinian territory and destroy their independence. For this reason prudence is necessary when we have to convince our people that foreigners . . . are genuinely innocent of concealed political aims".

It is also true that many of the attempts to start missionary work in Ethiopia in the 19th century did not lead to any permanent results, even though later missionaries may have gained from the previous experience and mistakes of their predecessors. The history of Anglican missionary endeavour in Ethiopia is different from that of other churches in so far as it is the only Church which has consistently worked with the Ethiopian Orthodox Church and has resisted all attempts to set up an Ethiopian branch of the Anglican Church, often despite encouragement to do so from individual Ethiopians themselves. Direct Anglican work has only been undertaken among expatriate residents, who were from an Anglican background or who chose to join the Anglican community here. Some other churches sent missionaries who arrived with the intention of following the same policy but for various reasons they all abandoned attempts to re-vitalise or reform the Ethiopian Orthodox Church in favour of setting up their own denominations. Again, it has to be admitted that this was often done with the full support and encouragement of some of their Ethiopian protégés.

The 19th century in Britain saw a growing awareness of the need to spread the Christian faith "o'er heathen lands afar" and although the missionary societies founded for this purpose met with some opposition, they did gradually succeed in winning approval for missionary endeavour. The Church Missionary Society, founded in 1799, was often in its early years short of volunteers for overseas missionary work and so it was that they came to recruit a number of German and Swiss missionaries for overseas service.

Among those so recruited was Samuel Gobat, a French-speaking Swiss, who in spite of his Lutheran ordination went on later (1846) to become the second Anglican Archbishop in Jerusalem. He had become interested in the Oromo people through reading Jesuit narratives of the 16th century and was sent by the Church Missionary Society (C.M.S.) to evangelise the Copts (sic) and Muslims of Egypt. While there, he met and became friendly with an Ethiopian monk called Wolde Giyorgis who taught him Amharic.

In 1827, through the Ethiopian links he had already established, Gobat was introduced to the Ethiopian monastery in Jerusalem where he found "a much greater reverence for the word of God" than among the other Christian bodies there. Through daily contact with the monastery, he became very familiar with Ethiopian culture and the Amharic language. Together with Christian Kugler, another C.M.S. missionary, Gobat planned an expedition to Ethiopia, but the unsettled conditions in the country prevented them from going there immediately. By 1829 they had become friends with the ambassador of the ruler of Tigrai who was in Egypt and had also acquired a stock of books which contained the Gospels, Acts and Romans in the Amharic translation of an Ethiopian monk. In the same year they set off for Ethiopia and on arrival established good relations with many clergy including the Itchege, the senior Ethiopian monk. The Church Missionary Society did not envisage any proselytism. Their objectives were the revival of the Orthodox Church and the hope that this would eventually lead to the conversion of Muslims and pagans. Such a policy clearly required great tact and patience since the acceptance of the Orthodox faith was by no means unqualified.

Gobat continued for some time to engage in frank and friendly discussions with the Orthodox clergy and made a good impression on many of them, not only because of his extensive knowledge of the scriptures, but also because he was willing to express his ignorance on a number of theological points and for the most part refused to take sides in contemporary Ethiopian theological controversies. The Orthodox Church at this time was deeply divided on a number of Christological and other issues and because of laxity stood in need of a great deal of reform if it were to remain faithful to its own tradition. By 1830, Gobat was able to put forward a programme of reform to the Orthodox Church which reflected his own Protestant prejudices and which met with a good deal of opposition. It should also be stated that there were some Orthodox clergy who were opposed to change of any kind.

In 1833, Gobat went to Europe and returned to Ethiopia two years later with a wife and accompanied by a gifted linguist, Dr. Isenberg. Gobat and his wife became so ill at Adwa that they were forced to leave in 1836 and were replaced in the following year by Dr. Krapf, who had also been trained at the St. Chrischona missionary training college. In the meantime, however, Dejjazmach Wube, the ruler of Simyen, had expanded the territory he controlled to Tigrai and with some encouragement from the Jesuits he was persuaded to expel the C.M.S. missionaries. Krapf went to the ruler of Shewa and found a life-time interest in the Galla people, while Isenberg returned to England to pursue his linguistic studies, composing the first Amharic dictionary and grammar in English. He was also responsible for the translation of the Church of England's Book of Common Prayer into Amharic, a work which was published by the Society for the Promotion of Christian Knowledge in 1842.

Some years passed before other missionaries were able to come to Ethiopia. Gobat who had shown great sensitivity towards local needs and aspirations retained his deep affection for the country and after he went to Jerusalem as Archbishop he resolved to send a group of people to Ethiopia, which technically came within his jurisdiction as far as Anglican work was concerned. There were some grounds for optimism about such a venture. The disunity and unrest which had so hampered the work before seemed to be at an end and a strong ruler had emerged in the person of Tewodros. Krapf and another Chrischona-trained missionary, Martin Flad, were sent to obtain permission for the sending of a team of missionaries. Before seeing Tewodros they met the Abuna who agreed to support the venture provided that all converts should be baptised Ethiopian Orthodox and that any missionaries sent should be lay people. He also advised that the team to be sent should not reveal themselves to the Emperor as missionaries but as artisans with valuable technical skills. This was accepted though in fact it was later to lead to much misunderstanding and bitterness. Gobat intended that the missionaries should support themselves and earn their own living, but the real purpose behind their coming was to influence the Orthodox Church so that there might arise from within it a desire for internal reform.

Flad was encouraged by the response to his ideas particularly among the Jews of Ethiopia, the Falasha, and this was reported to the Church's Mission to the Jews (C.M.J.), which had been founded in 1809 to try and convert Jews to Christianity. In 1859, this mission sent Henry Aaron Stern, himself a convert from Judaism, to make investigations and the following year he met Tewodros who gave permission for work among the Jews provided that anyone converted should be baptised into the Ethiopian Orthodox Church.

Stern persuaded Flad to join the Church's Mission to the Jews and Gobat agreed to his secondment from C.M.S. A number of schools and mission stations were opened and some converts made from among the Falasha. It was at this time too that the station at Jenda about fourteen miles north of Lake Tana was opened complementing the schools already opened at Gondar and at Gafat near Debre Tabor.

It was not long, however, before these modest beginnings were rapidly overtaken by political events. Stern was often insensitive towards Ethiopians. Nor did he attempt to conceal his contempt for the Emperor's "workmen" as he called the artisans at a time when the Emperor was honouring them as nobles. By 1863, Tewodros' plan to unite Ethiopia and make it wholly Christian seemed increasingly unlikely to succeed. He had even dreamed of conquering the Turks, of recapturing Jerusalem and winning the world for Christ and was suspicious of the French and British because of their refusal to co-operate actively in such grandiose and unrealistic ventures. The news that the Turks had expelled the Ethiopian monks from the Church of the Holy Sepulchre in Jerusalem, despite the appeal by Gobat to the British Consul to try to prevent it came as a final disappointment.

However, in October 1863, Stern who had been to England and returned with another Jewish convert Rosenthall, was preparing to leave feeling that the mission could be safely left in the hands of Flad and with high hopes for the future, oblivious of the storm that was about to break. After the first days' travel he came across Tewodros' camp. What followed is well-known and is outside the scope of this article.

Stern's attitude to the "natives" was all too colonial and contemptuous and he was particularly hostile to those of the C.M.S. artisans who had taken Ethiopian wives and become assimilated into Ethiopian society. His arrest by Tewodros for having unwittingly insulted him and the damning evidence revealed in his private journal in which he accused Tewodros of "cold blooded murder" ensured that his fate was sealed. Condemned to death at a public trial, Tewodros came to realise that Stern was of more use to him alive than dead and so he was imprisoned. The subsequent arrest of the British Consul Cameron and the other missionaries led inexorably to the Napier Expedition to free them and the suicide of Tewodros at Magdala.

It is a tribute to his tenacity that little more than two years after the release of the missionaries, Martin Flad was back in Ethiopia seeking permission from Yohannes IV to work with four of the Ethiopian converts who had been sent to St. Chrischona for training. The emperor replied that he would only allow Copts in his territory as religious teachers. Flad was given twenty days to organise the mission at Jenda before leaving. Work was continued on a small scale by indigenous converts who were often suspect in Orthodox eyes because of their Protestant tendencies and Flad worked on an Amharic version of the Bible and other translation work from outside. The British withdrawal from Sudan in 1883 and the outbreak of the Ethio-Mahdist wars after 1885 made journeys to Ethiopia difficult but Flad managed to return to Massawa in 1890 with a quantity of Amharic literature and met with some of his Ethiopian evangelists. He returned for the last time in 1894 to find much of the work in disarray and there were serious doubts about whether the work, which had been further hampered by a Jewish mission to the Falasha, would survive. In fact there were no further converts until 1909.

After the First World War, Ras Tafari asked for foreign help of all kinds including missionaries, and in 1922, after a long delay the necessary permits were obtained and Frederic Flad, son of Martin, came to Ethiopia. He met one of his father's devoted followers, Aragawi, who had been educated in Germany and later at St. Chrischona at the expense of Consul Cameron, and visited the mission at Jenda. Later in 1927, two C.M.J. missionaries Heintze and Baur were given a permit to go to Jenda. For a time they worked together but later they separated and Baur started work among the Qimant while Heintze believed that the Gospel could be spread more effectively by working among the more educated Ethiopians. This work continued on a modest scale in co-operation with the Ethiopian Orthodox Church until all missionaries were ordered to leave the country following the attempted assassination of Marshal Graziani.

During the late 1920s Alfred Buxton, a pioneer missionary to the Congo, set his sights on the evangelisation of the Horn of Africa and arrived in Addis Ababa from Kenya.

There were few Orthodox Churches among the pagan and Muslim tribes of southern Ethiopia and his first contact with the ancient Church was at Yavello, where he was welcomed by the priest in charge. In his diary he wrote, "There is no doubt that the Church needs the breath of God, but at the same time I am convinced it is the key to Ethiopia . . .". At first, however, he was fairly sceptical about the possibility of revival within the Orthodox Church, but as he came to know the Orthodox Church better his conviction grew that the right policy for the new mission was not to establish Protestant or Anglican churches as he had done in his earlier missionary work, but to work for the revival of the national Church. He made a number of proposals for work that he could usefully undertake but was eventually persuaded to begin with a Bible School for young Orthodoxmen. This was opened in Addis Ababa together with an elementary school in Fiche and medical work in Asbe Teferi. A number of Ethiopian evangelists were trained and employed and were at first enthusiastically received in Orthodox Churches in Addis Ababa and Zuquala but later there was opposition from more conservative priests.

Buxton and his associates were also behind the project for an authorised translation of the Bible in Amharic by Scholars of the Orthodox Church. One of these men was Belatengeta Herui, the Minister of Foreign Affairs, who translated the Gospels and Acts from Ge'ez into Amharic. The existing Amharic version of the Bible at this time was produced by Protestants at the end of the 19th century and was not acceptable to the Ethiopian Orthodox Church. When the Italian invasion began in 1935, Buxton arranged for the four Gospels and Acts to be hastily printed and distributed to the Ethiopian soldiers who were fighting Mussolini's troops. When the Italians reached Addis Ababa, the manuscript of the Amharic Bible was smuggled out by Buxton and was later printed but it proved inadequate as a translation and never gained wide acceptance.

Buxton was killed in a bombing attack on London in 1942, but in 1940, one of his team, David Stokes, joined the Ethiopian forces in Sudan and took part in the liberation of Ethiopia. He returned in 1942. Later Stokes wrote a number of Bible commentaries in Amharic and through his contacts with a wide number of churchmen he was able to break down some of the opposition and mistrust of foreign missionaries which was an inevitable result of the Italian invasion. Such was the trust built up by him and by other missionaries working for the Bible Churchman's Missionary Society that by the 1960s they were teaching in church schools at the Holy Trinity Cathedral, the Church secondary school in Mekele and the convent in Sebeta. Other Anglican missionaries in recent times such as Eric Payne and Roger Cowley by their deep knowledge of the Orthodox Church and respect for its traditions have exercised a remarkable influence on a number of people who now hold prominent positions within the Ethiopian Church. The work of the Church's Ministry among the Jews and the Bible Churchman's Missionary Society (B.C.M.S.) continued to be undertaken until as late as the mid-1970s.

Much of the work was on a relatively small scale. A considerable amount of literature was produced for the Orthodox Church and because of their linguistic skills, which were always regarded as an essential part of their endeavours, they exercised a good deal of influence. It is not possible to measure this influence easily. As one of the missionaries was later to write: "The fruit of our persistence (in working only with the Ethiopian Orthodox Church) over more than forty years may not be very evident to human eyes today, but the work was undertaken to the glory of God and for the good of Ethiopia and only God can judge its ultimate worth".

As well as undertaking to work directly through missionary societies for the good of the Ethiopian Church, the Anglican Church also established a Chaplaincy in Addis Ababa in 1926, which is the only remaining Anglican work in Ethiopia today. The first Anglican Chaplain was John Ethelstan Cheese, an eccentric clergyman, who had a deep interest in evangelising Somalis. The new minister in Addis Ababa, Charles Henry Bentinck, in 1925, had wanted the services of an Anglican priest and had come into contact with Cheese who was then in Aden. He arrived in Addis Ababa in March 1926 and held the first Anglican Service in the capital on March 21st. Cheese returned to Aden but by this time the British community, which then numbered about thirty, were considering employing an Anglican Chaplain, who would also assist the Orthodox Church in whatever ways presented themselves.

The Archbishop of Canterbury's Mission had already made a good job of assisting the Assyrian Church and Anglicans had a good record of non-proselytising friendship with other Orthodox Churches. It was also thought possible that Cheese might be able to undertake missionary work among Muslims to which he was greatly attracted. Thus it was that correspondence between Randall Davidson, the Archbishop of Canterbury, Llewellyn Gwynne, Bishop of Egypt and Sudan and the Reverend Stacy Waddy, Secretary of the Society for the Propagation of the Gospel, led to the setting up of an Anglican Chaplaincy for expatriates with

Cheese as the first Chaplain. Cheese became a well-known figure about the city and was regarded by many of the local inhabitants as the kind of "holy man" familiar to the Orthodox tradition. Being peripatetic by nature, he visited British Somaliland from his Addis Ababa base and even thought of setting up his headquarters in Harar though this was not at all what his sponsors had intended. In Addis Ababa, he held services in the Durbar Hall of the residence of the British Minister and at Mulo Farm where Colonel and Mrs. Sandford were already settled. Austere and idiosyncratic, as he was, it soon became clear that he refused to be confined to Addis Ababa, and the pull of Somalia proved too great. His bishop wrote despairing letters about the "peripatetic friar" and the Society for the Propagation undertook to find a more permanent Chaplain. By June 1928, Bentinck was describing him as "utterly impractical" and as "a bit of a joke", in a very critical letter to his bishop.

In 1928, the search of the Society for the Propagation for a more reliable person as Chaplain led to the appointment of Austin Frederic Matthew, a former missionary in Nyasaland with the Universities Mission to Central Africa. Like Cheese, he was a bachelor, but five years younger and of a very different temperament. After spending some time in Cairo getting used to the diocese and the Islamic scene, he travelled to Addis Ababa via Djibouti, arriving on 5 October 1928, where he was met by Cheese and Sandford. Cheese spent five days showing Matthew round and then disappeared into Somaliland. Matthew stayed for forty years.

As well as holding services for the expatriate community, Matthew was deeply concerned to establish good relations with the Ethiopian Orthodox Church. Within two years of his arrival he had acquired a good knowledge of the Orthodox Church which he viewed both sympathetically and realistically. Thus, at this time he was able to write:

> The difficulty in the way of establishing friendly relations is that the Abyssinian Church has no desire to have any relations with any other Church except only the Coptic Church. After centuries of isolation from all but the Coptic Church except for a period of contact with the Roman Catholic Church, which to put it mildly did nothing to awake a desire for further contact, the attitude of the Abyssinian Church today is one of self-sufficiency and suspicion — self-sufficiency as being unaware that it has anything to learn from contact with other bodies of Christians and suspicion that any attempt to cultivate friendly relations is based on an idea of introducing new ways leading to the abandonment of the customs of old days which are held to be all that can be desired.

Matthew resisted attempts to start a school as he thought this would look like an attempt to draw boys away from the Ethiopian Orthodox Church. He noted that while missions were tolerated by the government for their educational and medical work, they were looked on with the gravest suspicion by the indigenous Church. He saw that the best way in which he could establish influence was through personal contact and by gradually enlarging his circle of acquaintances. This was a slow way in which to proceed. He envisaged a long period when he would do nothing to upset the prejudices and traditions of the local Church but would try to accumulate knowledge of its faith and practice in the hope that one day "we shall be able to give much needed help". He saw that there would be no hope of achieving this unless it was crystal clear that the Church of England had no intention of proselytising and was sometimes suspicious even of the other Anglican missions on this account. He disagreed with those Protestants who dismissed the Orthodox Church as being beyond hope of internal reform and even kept aloof from them lest he should be thought to be associated with their views. As early as 1930 he could write with great breadth of vision:

> I cannot believe that the Abyssinian Church, ignorant and superstitious and degraded though it is, is quite as bad as people make out. It is very easy to see the weak points of any institution and the weaknesses of the Church here are patent to the most casual observer. It required knowledge and sympathetic enquiry to find out what good underlies its obvious faults. It would not be hard for a visitor to England to find out

the faults of the Church of England; to estimate its influence would require more knowledge of English life and the English Church than a visitor in a short time could acquire. The criticisms of the Abyssinian Church which I have read in books on Abyssinia seem to me to be the superficial comments which anyone might make. I have not seen any attempt at appreciation with sympathy and understanding. I am not prepared on the partial evidence before me to agree with the other missionaries that the Church is dead and that the only thing to do is to replace it with other purer forms of Christianity. I am not ready to give up hope of revival which will enable it to undertake its own missionary work.

He compares the situation of the Church to that of the Church in pre-Reformation England and had hopes that the secular authority might press for improvements from within. In all of this his attitude was fundamentally different from that of the other missionaries. He was keen to show that the Church of England was not as narrow as men like Cheese with his cheap jibes about mariolatry had made it out to be. Unlike most of the other Anglican missionaries he wanted to show that the Church of England as well as being reformed claimed to be the Catholic Church of the land, at one with the apostolic Church.

He received encouragement from some leading members of the British community such as the British minister, Sir Sydney Barton, and from Colonel and Mrs. Sandford, who were well aware that such pioneering work should be supported and that no one else within the British Community knew much about the Ethiopian Orthodox Church at all.

By the time of the Italian invasion he found himself wholly on the side of the Ethiopians. His house was looted though his servants preserved some of his manuscript notes on the Orthodox Church. He refused to put up a notice in Italian advertising Church services, as the law required, and wrote later that "though I had little to do with the Italians, that little did not impress me favourably". On 21 July 1936 he was ordered out of Ethiopia on the orders of Graziani himself on the grounds that he was "not a friend of Italy". During the years of Occupation he went to Jerusalem where he worked in assisting Ethiopian refugees. On his return, he wrote in the *Ethiopian Star* about Ethiopia before the invasion "to correct the impression prevalent that everything in the country except the native huts was built by the Italians and that they are responsible for everything here which is any way reminiscent of western civilisation".

In his attitudes, Matthew received little official recognition from his own Church. Indeed, he made himself unpopular by his attitude, for example, to the B.C.M.S. to whose coming he was basically opposed because he disapproved of their methods. His bishop thought that what Matthew envisaged was unrealistic because it would "take many centuries" to achieve anything. Matthew even advised his own bishop not to visit Ethiopia unless he could revise his negative attitudes towards the local Church. He advised this because he thought that Gwynne's coming "would raise doubts about the good faith of the Church of England which through its Archbishop has expressed sympathy with the Ethiopian Church and a desire to help it and would strengthen the feeling against foreign missions thereby helping to defeat our object".

Knowing the conservatism of the Orthodox Church, he tried to encourage modest reforms which were realistic and was keen that a good Amharic version of the Bible should be readily available together with translations of the liturgy as well. He was one of the team of scholars who worked on the modern Amharic version of the Bible when it was commissioned and after retiring as Chaplain he continued to live in Ethiopia continuing his translation work and eventually dying here in 1968.

The policy of Anglicanism within Ethiopia has little to show in human terms, but often its influence has been wider than might at first appear to be the case. It has attracted a number of men who were deeply committed to Ethiopia and its Church and to assisting that Church without much regard for self-interest. They gave themselves unstintingly to this country in the belief that Ethiopia had much to teach as well as learn from the rest of Christendom and in the belief that "Ethiopia would still stretch out its hands unto God".

NOTE ON SOURCES

In the preparation of this article I have had recourse to a number of the standard works on the earlier period such as Donald Crummey's *Priests and Politicians* and G. Aren's *Evangelical Pioneers in Ethiopia*. Eric Payne wrote a history of C.M.J. in Ethiopia entitled *Ethiopian Jews – the story of a Mission*. I am grateful also to Mr. Michael Blair for providing me with material on the work of B.C.M.S. in the country and also to the Reverend Philip Cousins for kindly sending me the chapter from his unpublished biography of Ethelstan Cheese relating to Ethiopia. For the section on Canon A. F. Matthew, I used his own reports which are kept in the archives of U.S.P.G., London. I wish to express my gratitude to all the above sources while accepting blame for any shortcomings as my own.

QUELQUES NOTES SUR LE ROLE D'ABBA JEROME GABRA-MUSE

DANS LA DIPLOMATIE ETHIOPIENNE DE L'ENTRE-DEUX GUERRES

Berhanou Abbēbé

Dans *Guirlande*, travaux offerts à Abba Jérôme Gabra-Musé par ses élèves et ses amis, mon maître Joseph Tubiana remarque que celui que le monde savant a perdu depuis[1], est resté toujours évasif sur ses missions en Europe avant la conquête italienne.

A-t-il accompagné les émissaires éthiopiens dans les capitales des Puissances victorieuses à la fin de la Première Guerre Mondiale?

A-t-il pris part aux négociations préparant l'admission de l'Ethiopie à la S.D.N?

Etait-il à Genève lors de l'admission?

Sans le concours du hasard, la perspicacité de M. Tubiana qui a deviné presque tout, parce qu'elle a su tout supposer — ne nous aurait pas procuré des certitudes sur tout une tranche de la vie d'Abba Jérôme, que celui-ci s'amusait à occulter. C'est le hasard en effet qui a voulu qu'un Ethiopien de nos amis nous remît en Février 1980, un cahier (0.20 x 0.25 cm), couverture de toile cirée noire, de provenance italienne (Cartiere Binda, Milano), et contenant 34 feuilles de notes hétérogènes à l'encre et au crayon, où l'italien, l'amharique, le français et le tegriññā se côtoient sur les sujets les plus diverses.

"Ce cahier", dit Ato Fesseha, "doit avoir appartenu à un homme instruit du temps jadis . . . . Je vous l'offre".

Quelle ne fut pas notre surprise quand nous découvrîmes à la suite d'une lecture attentive l'ébauche d'une lettre à Abba Takill[2], datée: Nice, 20 Février 1920, signée Abba Jérôme, et portant la mention "cachetée et expédiée en recommandée".

Après cette page 61, tout devint clair: Nous étions en possession d'un carnet de notes d'Abba Jérôme — probablement du seul document de sa main — permettant de jeter un peu de lueur sur la zone d'ombre qui persiste sur son passage d'Asmara à Addis-Abeba et sur sa carrière d'émissaire politique.

Les notes couvrent la période 1915-1921 et figurent dans le désordre le plus complet. Il a fallu tout recopier, classer par ordre chronologique les parties datées et replacer dans leur contexte celles qui ne l'étaient pas.

Les données receuillies dans *Guirlande*, ainsi que des documents et livres consultés aux fins d'une recherche sur l'Ethiopie et la Société des Nations (*Adhuc sub judice lis est!*) nous ont permi d'éclairer le texte de faits collatéraux et accessoires permettant de nous situer dans les circonstances du moment et de montrer par transparence quelques aspects de la vie intellectuelle et politique à Addis Abeba en ce début de siècle.

Comme nous n'avions pu apporter notre brin de roseau à cette *Guirlande* tressée par M. Tubiana, nous avons pensé qu'il ne déplairait pas aux Ethiopiens et aux Ethiopisants qu'un enfant du pays s'acquitte, ici, d'obligations non pas d'étiquette et de politesse, mais de communion avec Abba Jérôme.

Notre société, une société à histoire, ne peut s'empêcher d'intérioriser l'histoire de ce pionnier des temps modernes — Abba Jérôme — pour en faire le moteur de son développement.

Cette communication se propose de noter quelques points de repère qui jalonnent une longue existence désormais seculière et volontiers secrète d'où s'échappent par endroits les velléités indistinctes du réformateur et l'habile sagacité du diplomate.

1. L'Intellectuel rebelle "nouvellement venu"

En 1915 Abba Jérôme est à Asmara.

Les premières pages de son cahier de notes sont couvertes d'adresses d'imprimeries et de maisons d'édition, toutes italiennes. En tête de celles-ci " l'Istituto Orientale di Napoli, via Duomo, 219, Napoli" traine comme un chagrin, car il n'y remplaça pas Afawarq.[3]

En 1916, toujours à Asmara; entre le 7 et le 10 Mars, il se constitue une garde-robe impressionnante: pelisse, imperméable, manteau noir, jarretière, montre, cravates, épingle d'or, sac de voyage, le tout à commander à l'Unione Cooperativa de Milan. (Via Maravigli, 9-11).[4]

Pendant deux ans et trois mois aucune note.

" Addis Abeba le 18 Juin 1918", date calligraphiée en tête de page et précédée d'un cachet à l'encre rouge, plutôt empâté représentant un personnage à la chevelure en "arbañña" (style "afro"), tenant un coutelas de la main droite et montant la garde devant un donjon; ni rond, ni cornu, ce cachet se distingue de nos sceaux habituels par l'absence de contour. Mais quelle en est la signification? Abba Jérôme, gardien de Lalibela? Il peut bien se réclamer de ses ancêtres![5] Il fait également songer au rêve merveilleux de Jacob à Béthel, un peu ce que William Simpson a imaginé dans *An artist jotting in Abyssinia* au sujet du titre "Dağğazmač".[6]

Lorsque, nous référant au document reproduit ci-contre, nous observâmes le cachet de plus prés, nous découvrîmes que la coiffure était, en fait, une auréole, le coutelas une palme! De là à courir à une Histoire des Saints il n'y avait qu'un pas. Mais l'iconographie du Saint réformateur de la Vulgate rendue familière par la caverne de Betlehem, par les tableaux du Titien, du Gréco et de Jordaens, celui du Carpaccio à Venise dont l'histoire du vieillard qui retire une épine de la patte d'un lion, nous ramena aux années de catéchisme à l'italienne, n'a rien de commun avec la figuration de notre cachet. Une note de la main d'Abba Jérôme, en première ligne de la page 22 du cahier sur l'existence d'une île Jérôme (ou *it.* Girolamo) dans l'Adriatique ne nous aida pas davantage. Finalement nous eûmes recours à une histoire des Saints plus complète[7] et y découvrîmes un Saint Jérôme Emiliani, dont le mérite principal semble avoir été l'évasion de la prison de Castelnuovo di Friuli où il était incarcéré en 1511 par Monsieur de la Palisse! D'où le donjon et la palme, complétant la concordance avec notre cachet. . .

Faut-il y voir le symbole de l'évasion d'Abba Jérôme d'Erythrée, alors colonie italienne, projet qu'il devait nourrir de longue date. Pourquoi pas. Après tout, les noms prédestinés, ne voilà t-il pas un fait culturel trés éthiopien: ስም ይመርሕ ንበ ግብሩ (le nom inspire [l'action]). Au fond, pourquoi Abba Jérôme appelle-t-il constamment le Ras Tafiri "Abba Takill"? (l'intégrateur). N'est-ce pas en raison d'une vague prophétie qui voulait qu'un jour ce Prince réalisât l'union de l'Erythrée à son royaume d'origine?[8] L'onomastique éthiopienne est riche de ces noms prédestinés, Minilik et Théodoros (que A. Z. Aéscoly rapproche) étant les plus chargés d'interprétations millénaristes. Notons qu'Abba Jérôme a continué de se servir de son cachet au moins jusqu'en 1920.

Abba Jérôme à Addis, on ne saurait rien imaginer de plus radieux et de plus étincelant que ce nouveau venu, élégant, savant, poliglotte, (qualité prisée entre toutes). Les échos d'une vie nouvelle, innombrable et fougueuse montent du carnet. Le carquoi colonial rompu, cette âme qui ne pouvait accepter les demi privilèges de la prétrise coloniale s'insère avec aisance dans le vie séculière de la partie libre de son vaste pays, l'Ethiopie. Tout concourt à faire de lui un heureux citoyen.

D'abord, Wasanē Zamanuēl, Consul d'Ethiopie à Asmara a été nommé "Kantibā" d'Addis Abeba. Abba Jérôme l'y suit; il achète les meubles, aménage les locaux, désinfecte, rénove et s'exclame: " Si nous ne pouvons décréter que toutes les maisons de la ville soient repeintes, donnons au moins l'exemple en blanchissant la Municipalité à la chaux".[9] Il demande aussi que les cartes qu'il a achetées pour le Consulat d'Asmara soient apportées (celle des commissariats d'Erythrée, celle des provinces, celle de la région Hāmāseñ-Makalē) ainsi que ses livres . . . On a finalement l'impression qu'à Asmara il jouait un rôle, de loin, plus important que "les leçons d'Italien"[10] qu'il prétend donner à Wasanē Zamanuēl.

Son apparition à la Municipalité d'Addis ne peut s'expliquer par un simple concours de circonstances.

L'accueil que le Gouvernement lui réserve est aussi exceptionnel. Dés le 15 Sanē (22 Juin) de cette année il s'exerce sur son cahier à rédiger une lettre de remerciements au Prince Héritier pour le choix qui lui fut offert entre cinq propriétés urbaines.[11] Ses préparatifs pour se constituer un nouvel appareil intellectuel sont impressionnants. Lors de sa première visite à Ato

Iyāsu Daneēl[12] originaire de Keren et libraire de son état, il achète pas moins de quatre-vingt quatre livres d'occasion d'une étonnante variété: médecine, géographie, agriculture, littérature, histoire, etc. Il parcourt la ville pour en acheter d'autres destinés au Kantibā Wasanē; se propose de consulter le recueil de recettes médicales de l'Empereur Menelik.[13]

Pendant ce temps il se familiarise à l'amharique et à la géographie du Choa, notant à loisir les expressions qui lui échappent (*ambokbuākkā ant boqbwāqqā* = lâche que tu es), les chef-lieux de cette province, la généalogie des Rois du Choa, assortie de la durée du régne de chacun.[14]

Cette effervescence est interrompue pour une raison qui paraît à peine réelle de nos jours: "Un homme de l'Azzäž qui nous a emprunté notre plume et notre encre tarde à nous les rendre; nous voilà dans un désœuvrement complet . . . depuis dix jours".[15]

Abba Jérôme s'occupe déjà de soldats "venus de l'autre côté", certains avec armes et bagages et qui faisaient de la détention préventive en vertu d'un soi-disant accord conclu par le Daggač Gabra-Sellasé avec les Italiens. Abba Jérôme n'en croit rien.

Mais Ato Heruy prétend qu'une telle obligation existe. Mikāēl Berrou[16] confirme et la rattache à l'Arrangement tripartie de 1906. "Ils ont tous tort! Armés ou pas, les prévenus en question ont le droit de traverser la frontière", réplique Abba Jérôme.

Il en informe le Prince Héritier, et lui signale, au passage, qu'il est indispensable qu'un recueil de Traités et Conventions intéressant l'Ethiopie soit traduit, imprimé et mis à la disposition des autorités.

Ce souci des relations extérieures a-t-il inspiré le Prince Héritier à se servir d'Abba Jérôme à une époque où les tristes évènements *hedar bašitā* ont privé le Prince des loyaux services de Kantibā Wasané qui avait acquis une grande expérience en la matière, et d'un autre jeune intellectuel catholique, Ato Gezaw, fort instruit en histoire universelle, connaissant le latin, jouissa d'une bonne réputation de mathématicien et chargé de la traduction du "Code Civil Européen" (ou droit international privé).[17] L'épidémie faillit même emporter le Prince.

En date du 21 Nahasé (26 août) Abba Jérôme note: "Avvertire il raggiro del popolo circa lo stato attuale d'infirmità . . . (del Ras) . . .[18] C'est que le spectre de Iyāsu est vivace!" A partir de Maskaram 1911 (Septembre 1918) il est chargé de la correspondence diplomatique avec Jérusalem, Alexandrie, Rome et le Comte Colli Di Felizzano, alors Ministre d'Italie à Addis Abeba.[19]

Le 9 Janvier 1919 il est reçu en audience par le Prince Héritier qui lui demande de traduire le Droit International Public, et ensuite le Privé, à partir d'un texte italien que lui procurerait le Comte Colli.[20] Que la tâche lui soit confiée à peine deux mois après le décés d'Ato Gezaw, survenu le 20 Novembre 1918, dénote une certaine urgence.

Avec l'inauguration, le 18 Janvier, de la Conférence de la Paix, la politique mondiale et éthiopienne venaient de se doter d'une nouvelle dimension: l'Internationalisme.

Abba Jérôme, chargé de suivre les évènements, traduit des articles de journaux relatant, non seulement les évènements qui se déroulent au sein de la Conférence de Paris, mais aussi à celle de Berne où la Conférence Socialiste s'est tenue depuis le 3 Février 1919. Digression légitime, car on se demandait à l'époque si cette dernière conférence ne fut pas tenue pour balancer la Conférence de la Paix et pour peser sur ses décisions.

Dés lors ses visites s'orientent vers les commis de politique étrangère: Capucci, Heruy, Chefneux.

Ses lectures même sont empreintes de certaines finalités politiques: le drapeau national, l'emblème éthiopien, les rudiments d'une constitution éthiopienne. Abba Jérôme essaie de forger un néologisme pour diségner la Constitution:

ሥነ ኍባሬ ሥርዓተ መንግሥት ኢትዮጵያ

የኢትዮጵያ መንግሥት ኩነት ፤ ትዳር ። [21]

S'y trouvent posés les principes de l'absolutisme des droits impériaux; les justifications du titre Negusa-Nagast, (L'Empereur ayant prépondérance sur les Monarques des différents royaumes de l'Empire); le lion, symbole impérial; la signification des trois couleurs du drapeau éthiopien.

La liste des ouvrages à acheter se restreint essentiellement à des articles de politique immédiate du pays; les titres sont marqués à la hâte, au crayon, notamment "Gli avvenimenti in Ethiopia e la questione del 'Trattato a tré' " paru dans *l'Africa Italiana* en Octobre sous la signature d'Enrico Cerulli, et " Il colpo di Stato in Ethiopia" de Vico Mantegazza que publiait *Lettura* du 1er Décembre 1916.

Cette année-là les grands du pays avaient été convoquées pour débattre en Conseil l'adhésion de l'Ethiopie à la Société des Nations.

> "Pour le Ras Tafari, Régent de l'Empire, comme pour l'Impératrice et le Gouvernement éthiopien tout entier, demander l'admission de l'Ethiopie dans la S.D.N. était une opération infiniment délicate au point de vue intérieur abyssin. Les grands Chefs se rendaient compte que l'Ethiopie allait prendre là des engagements solennels qui viendraient forcément peser sur leur indépendance traditionnelle; mais ce qui les inquiétait surtout et j'ai eu l'occasion de le constater dans des conversations en traversant les plateaux abyssins, en 1920, c'est de pouvoir sûrement tenir les engagements qu'ils prendraient en entrant dans la S.D.N. Je peux dire que cette préoccupation était la principale dans leur esprit."[22]

On pourrait compléter utilement l'observation de Michel Côte en y ajoutant l'inquiétude générale que causait l'attitude du Prince novice dont on ne savait jusqu'où le modernisme pouvait aller trop loin.

Ras Tafari qui avait senti que le Conseil d'Empire n'en finissait pas de tergiverser sur l'adhésion ordonna le 7 Ter 1911 (15 Janvier 1919) que ceux qui n'étaient pas en mesure de s'exprimer sur le champ le fassent par écrit.[23]

Les motions vinrent en abondance, dont les plus représentatives furent les suivantes:

> "Une fois mis au joug, le boeuf n'a guère plus qu'un choix: marcher au risque de se voir infliger des coups de fouet".

C'était l'opinion exprimée par le Ras Kasa, connu pour ses idées ultra-conservatrices.[24]

Deux prélats cauteleux et prudents, le Mamher Dasta et le Malaka Berhan Şegē, font des distingués subtils dans une motion conjointe:

> " La foi éthiopienne se distingue par sa dévotion particulière à Notre Dame Marie. Cela interdit l'union religieuse avec certains, mais il est loisible de nouer des liens d'amitié avec tous."[25]

On devine l'allusion à peine voilée au protestantisme que, de surcroît, le Clergé associe volontiers à l'Angleterre.

Finalement celle d'Abba Jérôme, qui projette une lumière crue, nourrie d'expériences personelles sur "le monde extérieur" et qui en a aux palabres oiseuses qui se déroulent sous ses yeux. L'opinion qu'il exprime se place au dessus de la mêlée et se préoccupe, par delà les intérêts de classe et de secte, de préparer la défense du pays contre le réquisitoire auquel il doit s'attendre avant d'accéder à la S.D.N.

Voici la traduction du texte intégral:

"DE L'OPPORTUNITE DE L'ENVOI D'UNE DELEGATION

Une grande assemblée est en passe de se réunir en Europe. Il s'en suivra le partage de la terre entre les Puissances. Tous les Grands de ce monde son réunis à Paris pour plaider la cause de leurs pays respectifs. Nous devons y déléguer nos personnalités éminentes.

Nos ennemis qui ont l'intention d'envahir notre pays s'apprêtent à nous mettre au banc des accusés. Nous saurons nous en défendre.

Les chefs d'accusation qu'ils entendent susciter contre nous sont connus:

1. L'esclavage en Ethiopie,
2. Le trafic d'armes avec nos voisins en violation de la Convention de Bruxelles,
3. Le manque de surveillance dans les zones frontalières,
4. Le danger de nous voir gêner le cours du Nil Bleu,
5. Les conflits de lois,
6. Les insuffisances de notre règlementation commerciale.

Pour régler toutes ces questions il est indispensable que le Prince Héritier accompagné de certaines dignitaires de l'Empire se rende en Europe.

La sauvegarde de notre indépendance ainsi que la coopération durable et fructueuse avec les Européens dépendra du succès de la défense que le Prince Héritier et les dignitaires qui l'accompagnent auront opposés aux accusations colportées sur le compte de notre pays.

Pour parvenir aux fins qui sont les nôtres, nous pourrons trouver des amis parmi les Français et les Américains car ces deux gouvernements ne prétendent pas que l'occupation de l'Ethiopie soit une condition *sine qua non* de la défense de leur intérêt national.

Si nous pouvions les rallier à notre cause, la balance pencherait de notre côté, ou tout au moins, l'équilibre serait rétabli entre nos intérêts et ceux des Italiens et des Anglais.

Les journaux représentent une force avec laquelle il faut compter, car en Europe, les journalistes sont nombreux. Il sera donc bon d'offrir à ceux-ci des bagues en or, afin que précédé d'une bonne presse, le prestige de notre pays soit rehaussé aux yeux des représentants de tous les gouvernements qui se sont donnés rendez vous à Paris. L'or pur d'Ethiopie est très prisé par les Européens; c'est celui qu'ils préfèrent. Il convient aussi de se faire accompagner d'un bon choix d'objets manufacturés tapis de soie et de laine, tauges d'apparat, vanneries, tauges de dignitaires (*ğano*), boucliers incrustes d'or, sabres, lances, harnais marqués aux armes impériales. Avec ces objets, et d'autres qui ne sont pas mentionnés ici, on pourra faire une exposition de l'artisanat éthiopien.

Les décorations, les défenses d'éléphant, les cornes de rhynocéros et de buffle, les peaux de lion, tels sont les cadeaux agréables aux "Farang̃". Prenez garde de croire que ceux-ci n'aiment pas les pots de vin.

N'abusons pas des délibérations comme nous avons accoutumé de faire. Rappelons nous ce qui advint à Noë.

Quiconque refuse d'approuver ces vues n'aime pas sa Patrie.[26]"

Avant la soumission de ce memorandum qui a "changé l'âme du combat", nous avions trouvé qu'Abba Jérôme notait fiévreusement les titres de certains articles politiques tout récents, qui n'étaient peut-être pas disponibles à Addis Abeba. Pourquoi les aurait-il notés sans cela?

Le 16, il marque l'adresse de Max-Léon et de Herma Plazikowski, aussi bien à Aroussi (entre le Mont Cilalo et le lac Zuway) qu'en Europe, aux bons soins d'Eugène Mittwoch (orientalischer Seminar der Universität — Berlin).[27] Préparait-il un voyage?

Précisément à cette époque, les projets de lettres de l'Impératrice Zawditu sont prêts; tous datés du 15 Miazya 1911 (23 Avril 1919). Ces messages de félicitations destinés aux Etats Unis d'Amérique, à la France, à la Grande Bretagne, à l'Italie et à la Belgique reprennent invariablement cette formule: "Nous regrettons vivement que nos délégués n'aient pas pu partir plus tôt, faute de navires pour les transporter."[28] Les délégations qui doivent les remettre aux Puissances victorieuses hâtent leurs préparatifs. Ils sont manifestement en retard.

On ne peut s'empêcher de penser à "ce qui advint à Noë . . ."

La délégation chargée de remettre le message à Poincaré et au Roi des Belges se compose de: Daǧǧač Walda-Gabréēl, Daǧǧazmač Šibaši et de Naggādrās Zawgé.[29]

Abba Jérôme n'y figure pas et le cahier est obstinément silencieux sur cette mission.

2. L'Emissaire du Prince

Le 18 Août 1919, nous le retrouvons à Olten en Suisse. Là il s'est muni du cours de *Droit Diplomatique* de Pradier (1900) et du *Manuel Diplomatique et Consulaire* de Monnet (1910). Il note que l'ouvrage de Keller sur Alfred Ilg est digne d'intérêt et qu'il convient de se le procurer.[30]

Or, entre le départ des délégués en Mai 1919 et l'apparition d'Abba Jérôme à Olten en Août, des évènements trés importants se sont déroulés en Europe: la signature de la Convention de Saint Germain-en-Laye (Septembre 1919), la démission du Cabinet de Clémenceau (18 Janvier 1920), le départ de Lloyd George et de Nitti de Paris où les ambassadeurs des Alliés vont être substitués au Conseil Suprême (21 Janvier).

Nouveau silence du cahier pendant six mois presque, jour pour jour, et Abba Jérôme fait surface à Nice, le 20 Janvier 1920.[31] A cette date une page du cahier est couverte d'une critique serrée du livre de Pierre Alype: *L'Ethiopie et les convoitises allemands*.[32] Il est particulièrement frappé par cette citation: "Ainsi isolement extérieur et morcellement intérieur, tels sont les traits qui dominent la Géographie de l'Abyssinie"[33], et Abba Jérôme de réagir:

> "Regardez donc sur le tableau ci-joint le nombre d'Ambassadeurs, de Consuls et d'Agents que la Suisse, dont le territoire national n'est guère plus étendu que la province du Kaffa, a dépêchés auprés de la Société des Nations!
> Si *Behèra Ag'àzi*, (expression favorite d'Abba Jérôme pour désigner l'Ethiopie) entend maintenir sa souveraineté et rehausser son prestige et son inviolabilité, elle se doit d'en faire autant."[34]

Puis se référant à la page 68 où Pierre Alype combat la crainte que suscite auprès des Ethiopiens par les nouvelles alarmantes d'une action militaire italienne, Abba Jérôme semble faire fi des déclarations rassurantes qu'ont pu faire de Martini (alors Ministre italien des colonies) et le Marquis de San Giuliano, Ministre des Affaires Etrangères. Pour démontrer "la probité de l'attitude italienne"[35], le témoignage de ces deux personalités italiennes ne suffit pas; ne sont-ils pas juges et parties? Et Pierre Alype, lui, n'invente-t-il pas sous contrainte des arguments patriotiques en faveur de l'Allié italien, à une époque où l'on ne pouvait pas deviner encore le sort de la guerre?

Plus actuel et plus juriste, Abba Jérôme rétorque que la seule garantie de l'Ethiopie repose désormais sur les principes nouveaux du Droit International, notamment du Préambule et de l'article 21 du Pacte de la Société des Nations.[36]

"Or, l'Ethiopie . . ." ne fait pas encore partie de cette Organisation qui pourra lui garantir la paix et la sécurité. Il a suspendu sa phrase; c'est nous qui croyons pouvoir deviner la suite logique. Revenant enfin à la page 39 où Pierre Alype reproche à l'Allemagne d'avoir dénoncé l'enclavement de l'Ethiopie, le trust anglais du caoutchouc et le monopole ferroviaire français, il regrette que l'autorité de Zawditu et du Prince Héritier ait pu être mise en doute:

> "Qui est derrière cette publication? Nous indiquerons dans le prochain courrier ceux qui font courir les faux bruits."[37]

Mais ces observations d'Abba Jérôme ne peuvent pas nous interdir d'être justes à l'égard des *Convoitises* qui ont paru au beau milieu de la guerre, en 1917, à une époque où l'on envisageait même d'engager les armées éthiopiennes dans la grande aventure, aux côtés des Alliés. Par ailleurs, le thème des *Convoitises* était d'actualité. Dans son discours d'ouverture de la Conférence de la Paix, Raymond Poincaré ne disait-il pas:

> "C'est l'étendu des *Convoitises Allemandes* qui a ainsi amené tant de peuples, petits et grands, à se liguer contre le même adversaire."

Encore que son titre ait fait fortune, il ne fait pas de doute que l'ouvrage était complètement dépassé au moment où Abba Jérôme le découvre, en Février 1920, puisqu'achevé en 1916, il paraît en 1917 avec une préface datée du 30 Juin 1916, qui en est encore à se louer de ce que Leğ Iyāsu "est parvenu à stabiliser sa puissance et recevra bientôt le titre de Negus; qu'aussitôt après cet évènement historique, son père le Ras Mikaël, personnage le plus éminent de l'Empire se propose de faire un voyage en Europe et de séjourner à Paris, à Londres et à Rome."[38]

Certes, la visite prévue chez les signataires de ce que Pierre Alype appelle "le loyal arrangement" du 13 Décembre 1906, ne pouvait manquer d'irriter Abba Jérôme, partisan de Tafari, qui supportait mal la diffusion d'un ouvrage dont le contenu était rendu caduc par la célérité des évènements qui ont suivi le coup d'Etat du 27 Septembre 1916. On dirait poutant qu'Abba Jérôme ne peut souffrir ces vérités abstraites et extraordinaires de la *realpolitik* qu'il regarde comme des spectres qui lui font peur! Plus justifiable est l'appréhension que suscite le danger potentiel de "l'Arrangement" que l'on avait déjà opposé à Abba Jérôme au sujet des rescapés d'Erythrée et dont il note, ce 23 Février 1920:

Art.19   በቶሎ ተተርጉሞ ፡ ከሎንደን የ1906 ታኅሣሥ 13 አገባጥሞ

የሚጽፍ ፡ ውሉም በመላው ይጽፍ ።

የማይስማማ ውል ተዋውለውበት የሆነ እንደሆነ ያለውን

Art.20   ቀድቶ በሰፈው ማፍሰስ ።[39]

En d'autres termes Abba Jérôme fait deux observations. Dans la première il envisage "l'Arrangement" à la lumière de l'Article 19 de la Charte qui statue que "l'Assemblée peut de temps à autre inviter les membres de la Société à procéder à un nouvel examen des Traités devenus inapplicables ainsi que des situations internationales dont le maintien pourrait mettre en péril la paix du monde."

Dans la seconde, il se réfère à l'Article 20 qui dispose que "les membres de la Société reconnaissent, chacun en ce qui le concerne, que le présent abroge toutes obligations ou ententes *inter se*" incompatibles avec ses termes et s'engagent solennellement à ne pas contracter à l'avenir de semblables.

Si avant son entrée dans la Société, un membre a assumé des obligations incompatibles avec les termes du Pacte, il doit prendre des mesures immédiates pour se dégager de ces obligations.

Les conclusions qui découlent de ces deux observations sont claires:

— Un nouvel examen de "l'Arrangement" est possible,
— Il incombe aux signataires d'abroger celui-là.

Abba Jérôme est-il seul à Nice lorsqu'il rédige cette note, ou faut-il y voir la main invisible de Lagarde qui avait donné sa démission jugeant, bien à l'excès semble-t-il, son œuvre détruite par la participation de la France à la Conférence de Londres de 1906, relative au Chemin de Fer Ethiopien.[40]

La note d'Abba Jérôme et une lettre du Ras Tafari du 15 Yekkàtit 1911 (22 Février 1919) se croisent. Voici la traduction de celle du dernier que nous présentons intégralement parce qu'elle permet de voir à la fois la fréquence et le caractère strictement confidentiel de la correspondance qu'Abba Jérôme entretient avec le Ras:

> "A Abba Jérôme,
> Comment te portes-tu? Je vais bien, Dieu merci. Tes lettres me sont par-

venues ainsi que les dépêches chiffrées qui les précèdent. Comme la clé de ton chiffre est égarée, tu m'en enverra une copie. Je t'avais fait dire qu'à l'avenir nous conviendrions d'un autre code.

J'ai parcouru le livre sur les conditions d'admission à la S.D.N. que tu m'as envoyé. Je maintiens à ce sujet le projet que nous avions formé ensemble.

J'avais cru que tu m'aurais envoyé, comme convenu, des traductions de documents ayant trait à la Conférence de la paix, ou à défaut, d'ouvrages utiles au pays.

Il serait, au demeurant, tout aussi utile que tu reviennes momentanément afin que nous puissions nous consulter. Le 15 Yekkàtit 1912"[41]

A peine un mois après cette date, le 13 Magabit (22 Mars), Abba Jérôme envoie la clé de son code.[42] Il note sur son cahier[43] – probablement en vue de répondre aux vœux exprimés par le Ras – les livres qu'il se propose de traduire en Amharique (un livre de Médecine légale, un autre de Jurisprudence et un Abrégé des Traités et Conventions de l'Ethiopie avec l'Europe) et la suggestion qu'il doit lui faire d'adhérer à la "Croix Blanche", l'association de Marguerite Rolland dont le but est de sauver les enfants et de leur prodiguer une éducation.

Ce même jour, le Prince Héritier répondait à sa lettre relative au livre de Pierre Alype, ainsi qu'à une publication suisse intitulée *Un message historique boîteux*...

"Envoies-moi le gros livre paru en Suisse (*sic*) qui contient des diffamations sur l'Ethiopie ... Ledit individu (l'auteur) a-t-il toujours l'intention de revenir en Ethiopie, ou y renonce-t-il définitivement?[44]

Je désire acquérir des ouvrages parus depuis la fin de la Guerre mondiale; tâche de me constituer une liste avec indication des prix ...

Ce que je regrette vivement, parce que j'y comptais beaucoup, c'est que nous ayions manqué les achats d'armement, faute d'un agent qui nous aurait représenté pendant les enchères. Quoi qu'il en soit, je ne me ferai par faute d'établir une représentation en France et en Angleterre, dès que possible. Quant aux servantes et domestiques qui partent pour la France, je ferai en sorte que leur nombre soit désormais limité."[45]

Dans une troisième lettre du 11 Miàzià 1912[46] (19 Avril 1920), Ras Tafari accuse réception de la clé du code, et poursuit:

"Tu m'as dit que tu traduisais le Droit International, envoies-moi la partie achevé.

Dorénavant consacre-toi à la traduction de la ሰዋየደናብረን (lisez "Loi de l.homme.., donc Droits de l'homme), probablement du Code Napoléon[47] que tu te procureras sans tarder. Quant au Droit International, je l'ai déjà fait traduire ici même."

Répondant au désir du Prince Héritier, Abba Jérôme a sans doute effectué un bref séjour à Addis Abeba, puisque les 5 et 6 Juin nous le découvrons entre Suez et Port Said venant de Djibouti et voguant vers l'Europe.

Il devait donc être à Addis Abeba au mois de Mai quand Sir Frederik Lugard, ancien Gouverneur du Nigéria et son compagnon le Colonel Sandford quittaient la capitale à la suite de l'échec rapide de " L'Abyssinian Corporation" que certains considèrent comme une ouverture du Foreign Office donnant le change à un sombre dessein anglais d'occupation de l'Ethiopie par la Somalie Britannique.[48]

Il ne pouvait pas ignorer qu'un monopole anglais de l'exploration minière de la province du Harrar c'était la mort de Djibouti, de même que l'échec de cette enterprise devait éclaircir l'horizon des relations Franco-Ethiopiennes. Son passage à Djibouti est d'ailleurs révélateur de ce soulagement. Le brouillon, daté Port Saïd, 6 Juin 1920, d'une lettre qu'il adresse au Prince Héritier et que le cahier nous a conservé en témoigne.

A peine arrivé à Djibouti, Abba Jérôme se rend à la résidence du Gouverneur, lui présente les salutations orales du Ras Tafari qui n'a pu lui écrire parce que c'était dimanche et qu'il s'était rendu à l'église. Il n'a aucune peine à convaincre son hôte que le Ras était le gardien de l'amitié franco-éthiopienne. Bref il réussit à s'embarquer le jour même sur une recommandation du Gouverneur ... et sans avoir eu à faire viser son passeport par la police de Djibouti.[49]

Il est à Paris en Juillet 1920[50], et point de trace depuis, pendant prés de sept mois.

Le 7 Février 1921 Pierre Alype adresse au Prince Héritier une trés longue note[51] (11 bonne pages dans la traduction amharique achevée le 26 Miàzià — 4 Mai 1921): explication sur-abondante des intentions britanniques et des conséquences que le maintien de "L'Abyssinian Corporation" aurait pu entraîner dans les relations franco-éthiopiennes (violation de l'Article 2 du traité Klobukowski — 1908) et dans celles franco-britanniques (atteinte aux dispositions des Articles 2 et 4 de l'Arrangement du 13 Décembre 1906).

Pierre Alype se montre aussi farouche ennemi des convoitises allemandes que du plan anglais: il fait une analyse exhaustive des conséquences qu'aurait pu entraîner le maintien de cette "Corporation". Du point de vue territorial, le plan anglais aurait abouti à l'extension de la Somalie britannique; à l'utilisation du Chemin de Fer Franco-Ethiopien comme voie de pénétration militaire; à l'encerclement total de l'Ethiopie privée de Djibouti, son accès à la mer; à l'isolement de la Côte française des Somalie, emputée de son hinterland.

Du point de vue diplomatique le maintien de la concession en dépit du traité Klobukowski aurait discrédité l'Ethiopie aux yeux de la S.D.N. qui en aurait conclu à l'incapacité de ce pays de garantir l'exécution de ses engagements.

Encore que tardive, cette note a dû impressionner le Ras Tafari qui avait révoqué la concession de "l'Abyssinian Corporation", éclairé par des amis français sur son caractère inamical et insolite.[52]

Le 14 Septembre 1921, le Comte Linan de Bellefonds adresse au Prince Héritier une lettre par laquelle il engage sa personne ainsi que celles de ses collaborateurs, dont Pierre Alype, à coopérer sous l'égide du Prince dans l'intérêt de l'Ethiopie. Il spécifie que l'offre lui était parvenue aux bons soins de "son émissaire", Abba Jérôme.

La révocation de "l'Abyssinian Corporation" ne laissait pas que d'irriter le Gouvernement britannique. On connait les articles du *Westminster Gazette*[53] et du *West Africa*, véritable campagne de déstabilisation de l'Ethiopie, que le *Bulletin de l'Afrique française* devait combattre énergiquement.[54]

Malgré tout, la déclaration suivante de Sir Frédérik Lugard qui avalisait la campagne autour de l'esclavage en Ethiopie devait peser d'un grand poids sur la détermination des adversaires de l'admission de l'Ethiopie à la S.D.N. dont la demande devait parvenir à Genève, le 12 Août 1923:

> "Le Ras Tafari, je crois, était désireux de solliciter cette admission dés que la formation de la Ligue lui était connue, parce qu'il estimait, ce faisant, qu'il obtiendrait une garantie d'indépendance; mais lorsqu'on lui fit entendre qu'il ne pouvait y entrer qu'à la condition que l'esclavage cessât, il renonça à son idée, car il n'avait pas le pouvoir nécessaire pour remplir cette condition."[55]

La France de son côté s'étant donné le rôle d'introductrice de l'Empire d'Ethiopie dans la S.D.N. se posait en protectrice morale et cherchait à s'assurer une situation prééminente. Mais elle avait mis en garde l'Ethiopie contre cette pratique, l'esclavage, avant même que la demande d'admission ne fût introduite. C'est le Nagàdras Zawga qui nous laisse ce témoignage remarquable:

> "Le Ministre français des Affaires Extérieures nous dit que cette guerre avait modifié l'équilibre antérieur et que les Gouvernements du monde

allaient bientôt se réunir pour établir un nouvel ordre. Il importe, nous dit-il, que votre Gouvernement soit informé de l'intérêt que représente sa participation à cette assemblée. Le seul ecueil c'est l'esclavage qui discrédite votre pays; il faut l'abroger . . ."[56]

On s'explique donc que ce soit la France qui fit en sorte que la question fût liée au procès de l'esclavage dans le monde, que Genève avait entrepris sur l'initiative de l'Angleterre.

La manœuvre française ne fit en somme que proclamer la nécessité d'introduire dans les débats le prévenu principal, l'Ethiopie, dont automatiquement la présence était considérée nécessaire!

Carlo Cito de Bitetto qui évoque cette époque avec amertume ajoute: "C'était le coup du gangster qui se soustrait à ses ennemis en se laissant mettre en prison . . ."[57]

Le comte Bonin-Longare, délégué de l'Italie pré-fasciste qui soutint l'admission de l'Ethiopie était-il maffioso?

Ainsi une nouvelle triplice (France-Italie-Ethiopie) s'était formée dont les manœuvres dirigées par la France l'emportèrent en mettant l'Angleterre en minorité.

3. Le Retrait de l'Emissaire

De toute évidence le combat continue, mais les protagonistes changent de camp. L'émissaire solitaire et furtif ne pouvait tout voir par lui-même, maintenant que la terre est si grande et le monde si compliqué. L'équipe nouvellement recrutée qui bénéficie d'un meilleur accès aux affaires se donne aussi de nouveaux relais.

De Bellefonds et Pierre Alype ont choisi de se servir de l'entremise d'André Jarosseau, vicaire apostolique à Harrar, éducateur et homme de confiance de Ras Tafari et ami de Lagarde.

A Addis Abeba, le Ras est entouré d'anciens élèves des Missions catholiques. "La direction des services modernisés des Postes, Télégraphes et Douanes"[58] est entre leurs mains. Le propre secrétaire particulier du Prince Héritier, Ato Walda Mariam, est de la partie.

On conçoit mal qu'Abba Jérôme, cet homme libre, ennemi du paternalisme et qui avait, de surcroît, abandonné l'état écclésiastique, pût collaborer avec ce milieu très catholique.

Toujours est-il que les accusations portées contre l'Ethiopie lors des débats qui précédèrent son admission à la S.D.N. étaient prévues par Abba Jérôme, bien à l'avance. Que tout ce qui est "international", droit comme opinion publique, fut inspiré par lui; que la Constitution avant la lettre fut l'objet de ses préoccupations. Mais à Genève, le jour de l'admission, Daġġāzmač Nādaw en šammà était accompagné du Comte Linant de Bellefonds, portant un caban de laine bleue qui faisait le plus grand effet, suivi d'un petit secrétaire de délégation qui a fait ses études dans un des lycées les plus renommés de Paris.[59]

Image, prémonitoire de l'Ethiopie du lendemain, où le conseilleur s'insinue entre le pouvoir et le savoir.

Au lendemain de Genève, Abba Jérôme qui œuvra pour que son pays ne soit exclu du "concert des Nations", jouit d'un prestige incontestable. Il n'ignore certes pas que lorsque l'Ethiopie admise à dans la Société des Nations en 1923 avait signé une déclaration par laquelle elle prenait, vis-à-vis de cet organisme l'engagement formel, en ce qui concerne l'importation des armes et munitions, de se conformer aux principes énoncés dans la convention de St-Germain du 10 Septembre 1919 et particulièrement aux stipulations de l'art. 6 de ladite convention. Dans cette déclaration il est dit aussi que "l'Ethiopie est demeurée prête à fournir au conseil toutes information et à prendre en considération toutes recommandations . . ."

Cette adhésion — condition nécessaire de l'admission de l'Ethiopie dans la S.D.N. — équivalait à la reconnaissance que son territoire faisait partie de la zone prohibée par l'acte général de Bruxelles (1890). Car, s'il est vrai que l'acte en question ne liait pas directement l'Ethiopie qui n'y vait pas adhéré, il n'en demeurait pas moins que par le traité conclu avec l'Angleterre le 14 Mai 1897 et avec la France le 10 Janvier 1908, elle s'y engageait indirectement.

De surcroît, la convention relative à la contrebande des armes à la côte des Somalis conclue à Londres le 13 Décembre 1906 par l'Angleterre, la France et l'Italie, dans le but de prévenir tout désordre dans leurs territoires respectifs dans la région éthiopienne et sur le littoral de la mer Rouge, du golfe d'Aden et de l'océan Indien contenait des restrictions à l'autorisation de transit d'armes et munitions destinées à l'Ethiopie et faisait obligation aux trois Gouvernements d'agir auprés du Négus afin que le trafic des armes et des munitions soit interdit en territoire éthiopien, suivant les prescriptions de l'acte général de Bruxelles.

L'ardeur de l'Ethiopie pour se faire admettre à la S.D.N. s'explique donc par sa volonté de se dégager de ces contraintes . . . librement consenties ou subis à son corps défendant.

Or, la convention de St-Germain n'est qu'une nouvelle contrainte qui présente l'inconvénient d'être internationale. "Etre au carcan a son charme. Tout le monde voit que vous êtes infâmes", dit Victor Hugo.[60] Mais heureusement, la convention de St-Germain n'est pas entrée en vigueur. Elle a même cessé d'être un projet susceptible de réalisation, puisque depuis 1925 elle a été remplacée par la convention de Genève.

L'Ethiopie est donc restée après son admission dans la même situation où elle se trouvait auparavant, en vertu des traités passés par elle avec l'Angleterre et la France et la Convention tripartie de contrebande.

Faute de satisfactions suffisantes la convention de Genéve de 1925 n'aboutit pas, non plus!

Par une note en date du 2 Mars 1928 les gouvernements Britanniques, Italien et Français invitent le gouvernement Ethiopien à se faire représenter à une conférence qui se tiendara à Paris.

L'année s'écoule sans que rien ne se passe.

Le Bitwodded Guétatchéou Abaté qui venait de présenter ses lettres de créance au Président Doumergue le 3 Mai est désigné premier dilègue à la conférence le 16 Juillet. Sur ces entre faites le trés officiel *Berhanenna Salam* annonce que "Son Excellence" Abba Jérôme, nommé adjoint au ministre d'Ethiopie en Italie a quitté Addis Abéba le 7 Juillet 1929, avec le Liqa Makwas Mangacha, Ministre.[61]

Hélas, la coexistence entre le Ministre et son adjoint ne fut ni durable ni pacifique et se termina par un coup de dent qui faillit priver Abba Jérôme d'un doigt de la main. On n'a jamais su les raisons de la dispute[62], mais on devine aisément que le Ministre se soit trouvé en trés mauvaise posture pour en venir à un expédient fort déconsidéré dans un combat virile.

Toujours est-il qu'Abba Jérôme quitte Rome pour Paris où il pourra bénéficier de la protection de Mme l'Ambassadrice qui n'est autre que Woyzero Aster Mangacha, la propre petite fille de l'Empereur Johannes IV. Son arrivée ne devait pas déplaire non plus au Bitwodded Guétatchéou que sa jeune équipe composée d'Andargatcheou Messay, d'Efrem Tewalda Medhen et d'Ayala Sebhat fût renforcée d'un vétéran, particulièrement informé, dans des circonstances où les délicates négociations avec les trois puissances limitrophes rendaient son concours indispensable. Finalement, c'est sur un succés complet pour l'Ethiopie que la conférence réunie à Paris pour la réglementation de l'importation et de l'exportation, du transit et du commerce des armes en Ethiopie terminera ses travaux le 14 Décembre 1929.

Fin mars de l'année suivante c'est la campagne de Qwana où l'Ethiopie utilisa pour la première fois un avion à des fins belliqueuses. Le Négus-Régent remporte une victoire aisée contre le Ras Gougsa Wolé qui fut tué au combat. Le traité de Paris avait porté ses fruits. Deux jours après l'Impératrice Zawditou, épouse de Ras Gougsa, vint à mourir de maladie au Guebi d'Addis Abéba. La fièvre des préparatifs du couronnement du Négus-Régent fixé au 2 Novembre relégua bientôt au second plan ces évènements funestes et les bruits non moins macabres qui couraient sur l'empoisonnement de l'Impératrice.

Abba Jérôme invité aux fêtes du couronnement s'appretait à voguer vers l'Ethiopie lorsqu'à l'embarquement à Marseille la douane française découvrit une mitrailleuse dans ses valises . . . diplomatiques. On devine l'embarras où cette affaire jeta le Bitwodded Guétatchéou qui était dans le même navire et ignorait tout de l'objet mystérieux. La presse monta en épingle cette affaire qui venait à point nommé après le traité sur la contrebande à peine vieux de quelques mois. Dans les jours qui suivirent un diplomate turque fut pris en flagrant délit de trafic de drogue. Ce bruit couvrit l'autre et Abba Jérôme regagna son pays, désolé d'avoir manqué l'occasion d'offrir un cadeau trés apprécié a nouvel Empereur, car c'est à lui que la mitrailleuse était destinée![63]

En 1929, Abba Jérôme qui œuvra pour que son pays ne soit exclu du "concert des nations" — (autant dire du marché aux armes, car le fin mot des démarches éthiopiennes pour l'admission à la S.D.N. se réduit à cela) prend congé de la diplomatie aussi discrètement qu'il y était entré. Il a vecu assez longtemps pour voir que la norme de la justice sans la force préconisée par le Pacte ne pouvait assurer le sécurité collective. Sa mitrailleuse nous dit assez long sur ses convictions. Décidément, cet homme en savait trop; il en avait trop vu. On comprend qu'il ait choisi d'être un sage.

Ces quelques lignes qui évoquent des faits glanés dans son cahier de notes et ailleurs ne retracent assurément qu'une infime tranche du rôle diplomatique qu'il a su jouer au cours d'une décénnie riche en évènements, mais on conviendra que même si elles étaient seules de cette venue dans son œuvre, elles suffiraient à lui faire place parmi les grands Ethiopiens de sa génération.

NOTES

1. Le 15 Octobre 1983 à Cannes, à l'âge de 102 ans.

2. Nom de cheval du Ras Tafari Makonnen, héritier du trône et Régent à l'époque. Voir note 8 ci-après.

3. *Guirlande*, p.33.

4. Cahier, pp.1, 2, 7.

5. Guirlande, p.36

6. *Good Words*, 1908 (Oct. 1), p.607, col.1.

7. *Butler's Lives of the Saints*, London (1956): July 20, St. Jeromi Emiliani, pp.150-151.

8. Un versificateur, Tašala Mangestu aurait écrit en 1920 éth (1927-1928).
   "La génisse Erythrée ne se fait qu'à son taureau;
   Lequelle la ramènera qu'on le veuille ou non."
   Cité par Ballaṭa Gabre in *Zenawi Pārlamān* (1946 éth), p.43.

9. Cahier, p.3.

10. *Guirlande*, p.33.

11. Cahier, p.16.

12. Iyāsu Dāyr de son nom d'origine (1865-1953 éth). Cf. Strelcyn, *Prières magiques éthiopiennes pour délier le charme*. Roeznik Or. p.LXII. Vers 1926 Ato Iyāsu tenait à Addis une boutique de luxe où les ras, les değğāzmač et les grandes dames se payaient des manteaux de qualité, importés d'Europe. *Berhanenna Salam* du 7 Janvier au 22 Avril 1926.

13. Cahier, pp.67-68.

14. Cahier, pp.13, 16, 18, 22, 23, 26, 27, 29, 30, 31, 39.

15. Cahier, p.3.

16. Originaire du Walqāyet, un des nombreux délégués à l'Exposition universelle (1900), interprête au Consulat anglais.

17. Cahier, pp.42, 37. Heruy, *Biographie*, p.96. A travers le "moucho" (poéme funèbre) de Kantibā Wassané qu'il nous a conservé, Cahier, on devine aisément qu'Abba Jérôme venait de perdre l'irremplaçable ami qui savait partager ses convictions irredentistes et unitariennes au regard de l'Erythrée colonisée.

18. Cahier, p.42.

19. *Ibid.*, p.48.

20. *Ibid.*, p.21.

21. *Ibid.*, p.17: on remarquera que sémantiquement son néologisme évolue autour de l'idée de "Status" et de "Constituo" (action de se tenir, posture, placer debout, dresser) ce qui trahit le latiniste.

22. Charles Michel Côte, extrait de *l'Afrique française* cité dans une brochure anonyme parue sous le titre *Une route impériale française menacée en Mer Rouge*. Imprimerie de "L'Entreprise", Paris, 1934, pp.60-61. L'article de base intitulé "Les négociations franco italiennes et l'Ethiopie" est sûrement de Pierre Alype.

23. Arch. Nat. Dossier 493. Chemise 3.

24. *Ibid.*

25. *Ibid.* St. Classeur 359. Chemise 3. Pièce No.65. Mamher Dasta n'est autre que le future Abuna Abraham. Quand au Malalka Berhan Sege, il était Jurisconsulte ou lecteur du Jatha Nagast, auprès de l'impératrice Zawditu.

26. *Ibid.*, Classeur 493. Varia. Document non numéroté.

27. Cahier, p.11.

28. Arch. Nat. Classeur 493. Varia. Document No.2.

29. *Ibid.*, Classeur 359. Chemise 3. Document No.64.

30. Cahier, pp.11, 36, 38.

31. *Ibid.*, p.61.

32. Pierre Alype: "Les Grands Problèmes Coloniaux", *L'Ethiopie et les Convoitises Allemandes: La Politique Anglo-Franco-Italienne*, Paris – Nancy (1917).

33. Tirée d'Angoulavant et Vigneras, *Djibouti – Mer-Rouge – Abyssinie* (1902). Notons que ceux-ci s'inspirent de *l'Afrique à l'entrée du XXè siècle* de Henri Lorin.

34. Cahier, p.61.

35. Expression dont se sert Pierre Alype.

36. Abba Jérôme nous a laisseé une ébauche de traduction amharique de deux dispositions. Cahier, p.64.

37. Cahier, p.61.

38. *L'Ethiopie et les convoitises allemandes, op. cit.*, p.XXX.

39. Cahier, p.65: "Traduire d'urgence l'article [de la Charte] et rétablir sa correlation avec l'Arrangement de Londres du 13 Décembre 1906; recopier le texte intégral de l'arrangement. Reprendre l'art 20 [de la Charte] qui a trait aux ententes incompatibles avec les termes de celle-ci et l'analyser exaustivement."

40. Gaëtan Bernoville, *L'Epopée missionnaire en Ethiopie, Monseigneur Jarosseau et la Mission des Gallas*, (Paris; Albin Michael, 1950), p.285.

41. Arch. Nat. Classeur No.104, p.454.

42. Voir la reproduction photographique.

43. Cahier, p.45.

44. Pierre Alype est venu pour la 1ère fois en Ethiopie en Février 1919 et y a effectué, par la suite "de fréquents voyages d'études". Cf. Pierre Alype, *L'Empire du Negus*, 1925, p.1 et Préface du même, p.XIII.

45. Arch. Nat. Classeur No.104, p.527.

46. *Ibid.*, No.622.

47. C'est à dire le Code Civil Français. Interprétation conjecturale d'un terme obscur.

48. "Une route impériale française menacée en Mer-Rouge" (1934) (extrait d'un article de Michel Côte paru dans le *Bulletin de l'Afrique française*, pp.60-61. Aussi Carlo Cito de Bitetto, *Méditerranée Mer Rouge – Routes Impériales*, Grasset (1937), p.72. Nous signalons à ce sujet un article de Bahru Zewdé paru dans les *Proceedings of the Seventh International Conference of Ethiopian Studies*, sous le titre "The Fumbling Debut of British Capital in Ethiopia", pp.331-39, qui est une communication fondée sur une documentation de première main.

49. Cahier, p.28.

50. *Guirlande*, p.302.

51. Arch. Nat. Dossier 493, divers.

52. Pierre Alype, *L'Empire du Negus*, p.186.

53. Articles du Major Darley et du Dr. Sharp, parus en Janvier 1922 et réunis en brochure; ainsi que celui du Dr. Martin Warquah (Apologie de l'esclavage en Ethiopie) 16 Sept. 1922.

54. Mai 1922 – Signés *Daǧǧāzmač*, alias Ch. Michel Côte et Pierre Alype.

55. *Westminster Gazette*, 9 Mai 1922.

56. Note écrite de Zawgà au Conseil d'Empire, lors des débats relatifs à l'envoi d'une délégation à la S.D.N. Zawgà a été en France en 1900 (Exposition Universelle) et en 1919 avec la délégation qui porta les félicitations aux Puissances victorieuses.

57. Bitetto, *op. cit.*, pp.76-77.

58. Gaëtan Bernoville, *op. cit.*, p.279.

59. *La fouille d'avis*, Lausanne. Cité dans *Une Route Impériale*, p.38.

60. Victor Hugo, *Les travalleurs de la mer*, 1, VI, 6.

61. *Berhanenna Salam*. 5e année. No.29. Jeudi 18 Juillet 1929, p.236, col.1.

62. M. Abate Guaétatchéou qui m'a confié ses souvenirs d'enfance à l'Ambassade de Paris voudra bien trouver ici l'expression de ma gratitude.

63. *Ibid.*

THREE AMHARIC DOCUMENTS OF MARRIAGE

AND INHERITANCE FROM THE

EIGHTEENTH AND NINETEENTH CENTURIES

Donald Crummey
University of Illinois

THE DOCUMENTS*

Document 1. UNESCO Dima 10:2.6; folio 1 of readings for Ṭer-Genbot (Original text in Pl.I)

I have made Gälawdéwos my first born; let him be the leader (*aläqa*) in the house of my mother and of my father.

I have two portions at Agäṣ,(which I received) when I shared with my sisters. I have given him one (of them) with its house; Čelṭan; Yäsaga; Sar Fogära; Wäyngé; Gafat, together with the house; Arga; Asana; Aräfa; Gafat; Denj; Dima; Samet; (and) all the soldiers which are in the land. Except for what Marta has taken, (let him have) Nazrét, Nabra, Enädeb. Two-thirds he should take. The remaining one-third he will share equally with Marta, Enqwelal, and Näčo's daughter. From my *rim* and from my *gult*, let him be satisfied with what is due to him as a member of the gentry, and let him share one-third. Except for the soldiers, let Gälawdéwos and Enqwelal share Shäläkwet. I have given Dagut, Yäṭequré, and Gwena to Näčo's daughter, in addition to her share. I have given him all the land which I have given him with oxen ready for the plow. I have given him the house in Gondär.

I have given him: a Mälk'e; one Psalter; one Wedasé Amlak with a Sem'on Zä'amed; five horses; five mules; two sets of water vessels; two large chairs; one large cooking pot; one bathing vessel and basin; all the tents; from the ordinary swords let him choose ten swords; one large and one small sabre; two cushions; thirty milking pots; twenty drinking vessels (*berälé*); and let none of them share the female slaves or the male slaves with him.

What remains after he takes these things, let him divide equally with them; and let him be satisfied with what is due to him as leader (*aläqa*). Whoever violates this (agreement), my son, on my behalf, shall deny and expel him. And let him be cursed by the mouth of Peter and Paul.

Document 2. British Library, Orient 778, folio 1ᵛ, columns 1 and 2. (Original text in Pl.II)

When the children of *Ras* Wäldä Giyorgis and *Wäyzäro* Wälätä Rufa'él married; – when the son of *Ras* Wäldä Giyorgis, *Abéto* Gälawdéwos, married the daughter of *Wäyzäro* Wälätä Rufa'él, *Wäyzäro* Wälätä Ṣeyon; having determined the value of the *aläqenat*, *Ras* Wäldä Giyorgis gave the *aläqenat* to *Wäyzäro* Wälätä Ṣeyon. And *Wäyzäro* Wälätä Ṣeyon gave (it) to *Abéto* Wäldä Giyorgis. When *Balambaras* Ešété married *Abéto* Wäldä Giyorgis's daughter, *Wäyzäro* Wälätä Rufa'él, having determined the value of the *aläqenät*, both *Abéto* Gälawdéwos and *Abéto* Wäldä Giyorgis gave the *aläqenät* to *Balambaras* Ešété.

Those who witnessed this settlement: *Liqé* Täklä Haymanot, *Liqé* Bätré, *Liqé* Fäsilo, *Liqé* Yesayeyas, *Azaž* Kokäbä Leda, *Azaž* Abésélom, *Azaž* Bahrey, *Liqé* Näčo, *Abunä* Yohännes, *Eččage* Hénok; and from the nobility: *Däjj Azmač* Benyam, *Azaž* Lulé, *Balambaras* Men Täsenot, *Azaž* Samu'él, *Qäñ Azmač* Näčo, *Käntiba* Neṣakessos; from the sons of the gentry: *Abéto* Haylu, *Abéto* Zär'a Ṣeyon, *Abéto* Birarra, *Abéto* 'Awey Kiwos, *Abéto* Abésélom, *Abéto* Ya'qob, *Abéto* Faliq, son of *Abéto* Aṣmä Giyorgis, *Blattén Géta* Täklä Abib, *Yäšaläqa* Armasqos, *Abéto* Gälawdéwos, *Blattén Géta* Ṣäga Sellasé; from the *aläqas* (leaders) of the endowed churches: from Iyäsus the *aläqa*, *Ṣerag Masäré* Häbtä Dengel; from Gemja Bét, *Liqä Ma'meran* Neway; the *aläqa* from Däbrä Berhan, *Aläqa* Awsé; from Abunä Täklä Haymanot,

Märi Géta Qenwat; from Rufa'él, *Aläqa* Fasil; from Aṣṣaṣṣamé Qeddus Mika'él, *Mälakä Gänät* Yohas; from Hämärä Noh, *Mälakä Sälam* Wäldä Le'ul; from Qeddus Giyorgis, *Aläqa* Eskender.

When he gave this *aläqenät*, it was in the presence of his son.

The settlement of this matter was written in the year of Matéwos, in the second year of the reign of our King Iyo'as.

Document 3. UNESCO Dima 10:2.5, folio 532 ʳ. (Original text in Pl.III)

Däjjamač Haylu, when he died, gave the *aläqenät* to *Wäyzäro* Merṣit. And when he gave it, his father confessor, *Mämheré* Täklä Haymanot, Amaré Wäldä Täklé, Habtä Kiros Wäldä Arägay, and *Blatta* Enkwayähu were present. *Abéto* Gošu took her to court over this *aläqenät*, appealing to the judgment of *Däjjamač* Gugsa. *Abéto* Gošu lost the case. After this they were reconciled, with these relatives acting as arbitrators and making the judgment: from Gwozzam; Säblu Gošu, *Abéto* Séruh, Kinu Wäldä Iyäsus; and from Bégämeder; Metek Aṣqu, Hirut Wäldä Nagwodgwad, Wäldä Nér Haylu, *Azaž* Mehrka, Ragu'él Gošu, *Azaž* Aṣqu. And the agreement was that *Wäyzäro* Merṣit, having assumed the *aläqenät*, should allocate the land and cattle. (In the case of) a military expedition, *Wäyzäro* Merṣit should campaign. Whoever violates this (must pay a fine of) 10 *waqét* in the case of the cattle, and 50 *waqét* in the case of the land. After paying (the violator) is still bound by the agreement.

In the year of Marqos, 25 of *Ṭer*, it was written down in front of: *Mämher* Wäldä Maryam, *Qésä Gäbäz* Wändem Hun, *Mägabi* Eséy, *Eraq Maseré* Heṣanu, Däbrä Ṣemuna, *Mämher* Natan, and all Dima.

For this agreement, *Wäyzäro* Merṣit's guarantor — *Abéto* Séruh; *Ato* Gošu's guarantor — *Azaž* Aṣqu; and the backup guarantor — *Ato* Sedät.

The judge who disassociated himself from the group: Metek Aṣqu.

COMMENTARY

The Manuscripts

These documents come from three separate manuscripts. Documents 1 and 3 come from different copies of the Synaxarium held by the Qeddus Giyorgis Church at Däbrä Dima in Gojjam. The Dima materials were filmed by the UNESCO project and I have had access to them through the microfilm copy held by the Institute of Ethiopian Studies. The project numbers are 10:2.6 for Doc.1 and 10:2.5 for Doc.3. I have not had direct access even to the microfilm, but am indebted in the first instance to the good offices of the late Volker Stitz and Tesfayohannes Fissahaie, and more recently to Dr. Taddesse Tamrat, for supplying me with photocopies. Tesfayohannes drafted the translations of these two documents. Document 2 comes from British Library, Orient 778, a manuscript of the *Mäṣḥäfä Hawi*. It was held for many years by one of the major Gondär churches, probably by Aṣṣaṣṣamé Qeddus Mika'él, which is frequently mentioned in its marginalia concerning land. The manuscripts thus come from churches separated by hundreds of kilometres. Nevertheless, they detail the affairs of a closely-related set of Ethiopian nobles, and trace the transmission within that set of a family institution over a period of five generations. In itself it is significant that manuscripts of such widely separated provenance should deal with such closely related affairs. This confirms an impression gleaned from the Ethiopian chronicles of the eighteenth and nineteenth centuries, and some of the European travellers of the nineteenth, that the Ethiopian nobility did form a national ruling class and that its activities and dealings ranged widely over the northern Ethiopian plateau.

The Documents: form and language

The documents share a terse, spare style. They are distinguished the one from the other by a number of features.

Document 1 is the most distinctive. It is highly unusual in the marginalia stemming from

316

the Gondarine period in that grammatically it assumes the first person form; and in that it is anonymous, is undated, and lists no witnesses. It is also unusual in mentioning slaves, the only one of our three documents to do so. Not that slaves themselves were rare. On the contrary, they probably played a social role of some importance in eighteenth century Gondär. However, it is a fact that slaves are rarely mentioned either in the chronicles or in the marginalia dating from the eighteenth century. Doc.1 is conventional in its emphasis on land, and by no means unique in its subsequent listing of other items of moveable property. So far as form is concerned we should note that this document closes with a curse found in many other analogous documents of the period. It is difficult to identify with confidence most of the places mentioned in Doc.1; and I assume the bulk of them to have been of local significance in Gojjam proper. Gafat is tantalizing since we know it once to have referred to a much wider area, and also to be used locally near Däbrä Tabor. The propagator of this document (who, as we know from our other sources, was *Ras* Wäldä Giyorgis) held property both in the vicinity of Dima and in Gondär, thereby establishing the link already remarked upon.

The language of Doc.1 bears examination. It introduces the use of the term *aläqa*, a common enough title or element of titles, but one not previously discussed in this context. This term is the linguistic and substantive thread that runs through all three documents. My rendering of "leader" reflects the way in which it parallels the use of that English term. Doc.1 also mentions *rim* and *gult*. The latter term is pretty well understood as the generic term for fief, but the former merits closer attention, since the vast bulk of the lands documented in the marginalia of Ethiopian manuscripts of the eighteenth and nineteenth centuries are of this type.[1] *Rim* has received little attention from scholars, yet clearly played a prominent role in the eyes of some Ethiopians at that time. *Rim* land was fief land held by churches. In many respects it functioned just as *gult* land did. However, it was the only land in Christian Ethiopia readily susceptible to sale, and we have records of several thousands of such sales in the eighteenth and nineteenth centuries.

Doc.1 also contains two phrases of note: *yäçäwa serat yebäqaw*; and *yaläqa serat yebäqaw*. I have rendered these somewhat lengthily as: "let him be satisfied with what is due to him as a member of the gentry"; and "let him be satisfied with what is due to him as leader". I find the use of *serat* interesting here. It corresponds very closely to the Western idea of "establishment", without its modern or contemporary overtones. In the present context it strongly implies the existence of social standards, almost a consensus, as to what an appropriate standard of living was for one who held the role of leader, or for one who was *çäwa*. *Çäwa* is also interesting. In its most colloquial modern usage, *yäçäwa lej*, it indicates a person of refinement. In its earliest recorded usage it meant "regiment" or "soldier". In certain contexts it may mean "lay" as opposed to "clergy". I believe these various usages may be reconciled if we posit a period in which military colonists, or members of regiments, had evolved into local nobilities. Eventually the term would have become somewhat synonymous with nobility in general, and with the lesser nobility in particular since military service continued into the twentieth century to be a conspicuous part of Ethiopian noble life. Grandees and title-holders had their own labels, *mäkwannent* and *mäsafent*, thereby leaving *çäwa* to play a residual role. For this reason I have rendered it as "gentry". As we will see, Doc.2 distinguishes *çäwa* from more elevated social ranks.

Document 2 is rather more conventional when set against the body of marginalia from which it comes. It has two key elements widely found in the marginalia: it is dated (to the second year of Emperor Iyo'as, i.e. 1757-8 AD); and it features witnesses. It also employs the normal third person voice. Doc.2 introduces the abstract term *aläqenät* thereby indicating that we are dealing with an office, or an institution.

The abstract noun, *aläqenät*, appears in most of the dictionaries, but their definitions are vague, and sometimes inaccurate.[2] So far as I know, the term *aläqenät* has never been discussed in scholarly publications. However, the nineteenth century French traveller, Antoine d'Abbadie, addressed it in an unpublished passage.[3] Given the paucity of references, and the importance which I attribute to the institution, I believe it is worth quoting d'Abbadie at length:

On the death of one of the spouses, if there are children, they take the father's goods, the eldest son of a religious marriage taking the *alakaennette* (*sic*) . . . The *alakaennete* (*sic*) is the quarter which is constituted into a special inalienable property (= *majorat*) and which is passed intact with its military obligation from generation to generation. The remainder, which is called *dehennette*, is divided according to the number of descendants, up to infinity . . . If the eldest is a daughter and her siblings male, she cannot be made *alaka*.

D'Abbadie had a tendency throughout his work to see Ethiopian things in a romantic Catholic medieval mold, and to over-systematize Ethiopian customary law. Nonetheless, his gist here is clear: the *aläqenät* was an institution of inheritance which favored one child over the others by giving that child a substantially larger, and better-defined, share of the inheritance. With the *aläqenät* went an obligation to military service. We will find that d'Abbadie's account of the *aläqenät* helps us understand all three of our documents. *Dehennette*, the term which he uses to refer to the remaining inheritance, literally means "poverty", further emphasizing the unequal character of this pattern of inheritance.[4] D'Abbadie's concluding remark about the rights of women in this situation is questionable. We will see that Doc.3 concerns a woman's being appointed as *aläqa*, and turning back the legal challenge of someone who appears to have been her brother. In parts of his discussion expunged from the translation d'Abbadie does contrast strongly the lesser rights of bastards as opposed to the legitimate children of an Ethiopian religious marriage. Our record does not tell us whether or not bastardy was an issue in Doc.3; but there is little in the other documents which I have seen from this period, or in the standard accounts of customary law, to justify so strong a distinction as d'Abbadie makes.

So far as the documents in hand go, they provide few tangible details about the *aläqenät*. For example, there are no mentions of land in Doc.2 which hark back to Doc.1; and only family connections allow us to suppose that these two documents are related, and refer to the same institution. Nonetheless, further information *is* implicit in Doc.2 about what an *aläqenät* was like. Firstly, the *aläqenät*, far from being simply a position of seniority, had definite material value. Doc.2 strongly suggests that this value could be assessed in monetary terms. Doc.2 goes on to indicate that this value was sufficiently great to make it the key element in the marriage settlement of a highly-placed nobleman.[5] *Balambaras* Ešété was a blood relative of Empress Mentewwab, the only woman in Ethiopian history prior to Empress Zäwditu of whose coronation we have a record, and a prominent and active member of her court. In its listing of the witnesses Doc.2 classifies them with the use of two terms worthy of remark: *mäkwannent* and *čäwa lejoč*. In general I would want to render *mäkwannent* as "nobility", and in this instance the titles held by those embraced under this rubric would surely justify such a usage. The term does seem limited in its use to those very high on the social scale and close to the centers of power. The *čäwa lejoč* clearly occupy a step or two down the social ladder and I have tried to indicate this by use of the term "gentry". My conviction that this document originated in Gondär is strengthened by the fact that the eight churches mentioned as having their leaders amongst the witnesses are all to be found in that town.

Document 3 shares a number of conventional features with Doc.2. It lists witnesses and it is dated. The style of dating is, unfortunately, a common one: day and month and year indicated only by reference to the cycle of four evangelists. Doc.3 is the only one of our documents to list guarantors to a settlement. Such guarantors were, in fact, very common, not just in the settlement of litigation, but also in sales of property. Doc.3, however, is one of the very few documents of which I am aware from the Gondarine period to specify fines for infringement of the settlement. Note that Doc.3 repeats the use of the abstract *aläqenät* and makes it the subject of litigation and judicial ruling. It also introduces another institution, the *zämäča*, and assigns the right to campaign to a woman. We know of other women warriors in Ethiopian history: Empress Männän against whom Emperor Téwodros campaigned before his coronation; and some of the patriots who resisted Italian occupation in the late 1930s; but this is the first time of which I am aware that scholarship has documented an Ethiopian woman having been given precedence over a man in military affairs, and belonging as it does to the first quarter of the nineteenth century, it must also be the earliest such instance. Finally, so far as the geography of our documents is concerned, it is noteworthy that Doc.3 mentions both Gojjam and Bégamder.

Personalities and Relationships

Document 2 is the linchpin of my reconstruction. It alone spells out the relationships of the people mentioned in our documents and allows us to bridge the gap of five generations separating Wälä Giyorgis and Wälätä Rufa'él at the beginning from Merṣit and Gošu at the end. It alone allows us to deduce the name of the propagator of Doc.1: *Ras* Wälä Giyorgis. I have drawn out the relationships which run through and link all three documents in Figure 1. In this case graphic representation is made all the more important by the combination of spare syntax and the fact that we have two pairs of individuals sharing common names, separated in the one instance (Wälätä Rufa'él) by three generations, and in the other (Wälä Giyorgis) by two. A summary of what happened follows.

At an uncertain point in time, but possibly around 1700, *Ras* Wälä Giyorgis and *Wayzäro* Wälätä Rufa'él arranged the marriage of their daughter, Wälätä Ṣeyon, to *Abéto* Gälawdéwos, who appears briefly in the chronicles.[6] As part of this process Wälä Giyorgis adopted Gälawdéwos as his legal heir making him the *aläqa* in the affairs of his family, and endowing him richly in order for him to play this role. The *aläqenät* was the principal endowment of the marriage of Gälawdéwos and Wälätä Ṣeyon, who had at least one son whom they called Wälä Giyorgis, after his grandfather. To this son Wälätä Ṣeyon passed the *aläqenät*. Wälä Giyorgis in his turn had a daughter, Wälätä Rufa'él, whom he named after his maternal grandmother. On the occasion of this young woman's marriage sometime in 1757 or 1758 to the prominent court notable, *Balambaras* Ešété, her father and grandfather arranged for the *aläqenät* to serve as the principal endowment of their marriage.[7] Ešété played a prominent role in court affairs all through the 1750s and 1760s.[8] Wälätä Rufa'él and Ešété had a son Haylu. Haylu, in his turn, is discussed at length in the chronicles for the 1770s and 1780s.[9] Haylu bequeathed the *aläqenät* to his daughter Merṣit who successfully defended her right to the *aläqenät* against the legal challenge of her brother Gošu. This challenge was adjudicated by *Ras* Gugsa who ruled the province of Bégämder from around 1800 to 1825.[10] Merṣit was still alive in 1833.[11]

This bare account passes lightly over many problems, and calls out for frequent commentary. A good starting point would be the identities of *Ras* Wälä Giyorgis and *Wayzäro* Wälätä Rufa'él, co-originators of this line. Wälätä Rufa'él was a daughter of Emperor Iyyasu I and evidently a formidable political intriguer.[12] Wälä Giyorgis is shadowier. Apparently he died in June 1706, which means that Doc. 1 must be earlier.[13] Wälätä Rufa'él survived both her husband and her daughter. Wälätä Ṣeyon died in 1718, while her mother survived at least until September 1721.[14/15]

A second matter calling for comment is the substance of the inheritance which Wälä Giyorgis gave to Gälawdéwos, and which is detailed in Doc.1. With the *aläqenät*, Wälä Giyorgis gave his son-in-law the lion's share of his property. The other beneficiaries named in the will were all female: Marta and Enqwelal, presumably full siblings of each (and also of Wälätä Ṣeyon?), and the daughter of an apparently deceased brother of Marta and Enqwelal, called Näčo.[16] The basic principle of partition of property appears to have been by thirds, not the quarter mentioned by d'Abbadie; and in this instance the favored beneficiary received two-thirds, the others sharing the remaining one-third. Within the remaining one-third, which, as we earlier saw, d'Abbadie referred to as *dehennette*, the principle of equal partition came into play. The will dealt in *rim* and *gult* lands; that is to say in administrative rights over, and to the revenue of, agricultural lands. This appears also from the bequeathal of what we must see as administrative rights over " all the soldiers which are in the land". In Doc.3 military leadership became explicit. Doc.1 rather touches, however lightly, on agricultural production, when Wälä Giyorgis passed on a key form of capital in "oxen ready for the plow". The exalted social position, and hence noble rank of Wälä Giyorgis, is indicated by his wealth in possessing books, of which he passed on three to his son, as well as ten horses and mules, and the tents necessary for the nobility's favored activities of hunting and warfare. Finally Wäldä Giyorgis bequeathed slaves. Altogether it was a rich endowment.

It is not entirely clear how we are to reconcile the different accounts of the transferral of this endowment which Documents 1 and 2 contain. Doc.1 claims that the transfer was direct from father to son-in-law, Wäldä Giyorgis to Gälawdéwos, and makes no reference to Gälawdéwos's marital status. However, Doc.2 has the *aläqenät* being formally given to Wälätä Şeyon on the occasion of her marriage to Gälawdéwos. This discrepancy may be explained if, as is probable, Doc.1 is earlier than Doc.2. Be that as it may, Doc.2 goes on to recount how Wälätä Şeyon gave it to her son by Gälawdéwos, Wäldä Giyorgis. Finally, Doc.2 had Gälawdéwos return to play an active role in transferring the *aläqenät* on the occasion of his granddaughter's marriage. We could easily explain the divergent roles played by Gälawdéwos and Wälätä Şeyon if we supposed that the death of Wälätä Şeyon had intervened between her giving of the *aläqenät* to her son, and the subsequent passing of it on the occasion of her granddaughter's marriage. We might also explain the anomalies in these accounts by positing either that while Wälätä Şeyon received some formal access to the office of *aläqenät*, she never received an *exclusive* right to it; or that while Wälätä Şeyon did receive an exclusive *right* to the office, Gälawdéwos remained its behind-the-scenes effective occupant. The evidence is ambiguous.

One obscure link in the documents, and in my reconstruction from them, requires external clarification. Gälawdéwos and Wälätä Şeyon, whose marriage is one of the key events in Doc.2, had a son whom they named after Gälawdéwos's father and benefactor, Wäldä Giyorgis. This relationship is far from explicit in our documents, and only becomes clear from a genealogy of a later descendant, Ešété Haylu, contained in one of the royal chronicles.[17] This second Wäldä Giyorgis, in his turn, had the daughter, Wälätä Rufa'él, who confusingly was named after her maternal great-grandmother. Wälätä Rufa'él married *Balambaras* Ešété, second cousin to the reigning empress, Mentewwab, and active national figure in his own right.[18] At this point Gälawdéwos returned to bequeath, along with his son, the *aläqenät* to Wälätä Rufa'él's husband, Ešété. From here on the *aläqenät* appears in the documents only as an office, without mention of the specific lands and places detailed in Doc.1. We do have records of the property dealings of two of the grandchildren of Ešété and Wälätä Rufa'él, in the senior line of inheritance, but it is impossible to relate the properties dealt back to those of Doc.1.[19]

The links between Doc.3 and the other documents are also obscure and require external clarification. From the *Royal Chronicle* we learn that the most influential surviving son of Ešété and Wälätä Rufa'él was Haylu, known through his connection to his father as Ešété Haylu.[20] This same Haylu also had a daughter, Merşit.[21] Moreover, Merşit and a brother, Gošu, were active buyers and sellers of land in the earlier nineteenth century, in a church and an area associated with their father, Mahdärä Maryam in Bégämder.[22] This information allows us to place Doc.3 firmly in a line with Documents 1 and 2.

As Doc.3 tells us, Haylu bestowed the *aläqenät* on his daughter, Merşit. This time it was an effective, not a figurehead, *aläqenät* which was in question. In earlier cases in this line it is hard to weigh the influence of women on the office. Doc.2 tells us that Wälätä Şeyon received the *aläqenät* at the time of her marriage, and that she passed it on to her son; but the effect of this is blurred by the knowledge that subsequently her husband and son bestowed the office on a man, Ešété. Merşit's rights were explicit, and endorsed by judicial sanction. She had the authority to allocate land and cattle on behalf of her father's family; and she got the duty of leading troops on campaign. Two generations earlier another woman had insinuated herself into the most powerful position in the country: Mentewwab had had herself made empress and ruler. Nonetheless, such rule by a woman is rare in the documentation on Ethiopia.

Two things strike me as significant. On the one hand, it was rare, and to some extent abnormal. We have seen that in every generation prior to this one men entered the scene actively when affairs of the *aläqenät* arose. The two clear earlier holders of this office were both men: Gälawdéwos and Ešété, and I think we can deduce that Haylu succeeded his father Esété in office. Male dominance of this family's institution accords well with the dominance which men exercised in the world of politics, the military and the church. Both chronicles and foreign sources indicate the pervasiveness of men in these spheres. On the other hand, rare or abnormal as it may have been, female leadership did occur in Ethiopia in the eighteenth and nineteenth centuries. Männän was a very prominent leader of the 1840s and earlier 1850s. Mästawat and Wärqit held forth in Wällo in the 1860s; and no one should take lightly the political influence or capacity for independent action of Ṭaytu at the century's end.

Merṣit's brother Gošu challenged his sister's assumption of the *aläqenät*. Our record of the case, which was taken to *Däjjazmač* Gugsa, ruler of Bégämder in the first quarter of the nineteenth century, gives us no real indication of the basis of Gošu's case; it is written from the standpoint of the trial's outcome, vindication of Merṣit's claim. But it is hard not to see a wounded male ego in the plaintiff Gošu, who now disappears from the scene.

Aläqenät and Class

In the institution of the *aläqenät* we seem to be in the presence of a key device whereby the Ethiopian nobility constituted, and recreated, itself as a class. We have paid insufficient attention to this question. On the one hand we have a heavily rhetorical approach to class formation in historic Ethiopia. On the other hand we have a closely focused, textual tradition, which, allied to historical studies which have been narrative in form and empiricist in conceptual underpinnings, ignores such broad questions. The two approaches should talk to each other a little more.

I see the problem as follows. In historic Ethiopia we are dealing with a hierarchical, unequal society which reproduced itself with remarkable facility over a number of centuries. We need to be cautious about continuity since both our documentation and our studies are discontinuous. However, I am prepared to argue that there is a high degree of continuity in culture and social practice over the period covered by the documents presented here; and I would extend that continuity to include the whole of the eighteenth and nineteenth centuries, in spite of some dramatic political changes during the same time. Continuity of such societal inequality would seem to require the notion of class: a dominant group or groups with an interest in this inequality, who recreate it against other groups with conflicting interest.

Most observers concur in recognizing a distinctly "feudal" flavor to historic Ethiopian society and polity, and it is difficult indeed to conceive of a feudality without a dominant nobility, or of a dominant nobility without a subject peasantry. Cutting against this image is our knowledge about patterns of inheritance, the workings of the *rest* system.[23] *Rest* as a prevailing value or concept pervades the culture and dictates equality in inheritance. Equality in inheritance is levelling, and directly contradicts a principle of class formation: accumulation. No class can dominate another class without accumulating power over that class and material resources to maintain that power. Consequently, in historic Ethiopia there had to be institutions and devices which contradicted the *rest* principle and which allowed accumulated positions of power and of material resources to be transferred from one generation to another. There had to be devices which allowed for the *reproduction* of the noble class as a class. The *aläqenät* was such an institution.

The *aläqenät* allowed Ethiopian noble families to preserve their corporate identity through harboring their resources. We may speak of "Ethiopian" noble families with particular confidence here since of our two cases in which prominent noble lineages invoked this device as part of marriage arrangements, one came from an Amareñña-speaking milieu, and the account of it was written in Amareñña; while the other involved the most dominant Tegreñña-speaking nobleman of the eighteenth century, Mika'él Sehul. The latter marriage, not previously referred to, is recorded in a document published by Richard Pankhurst, and took place on September 2, 1755 AD.[24] It united Wäldä Hawaryat, the son of Mika'él, with Alṭaš, the daughter of Empress Mentewwab. Mika'él was the ruler of all northern Ethiopia. On the occasion of the wedding he gave his son rich lands in Tegré province, some derived paternally and some maternally. He also donated guns, swords, slaves and oxen; and concluded the deed as follows: "And he has given the *aläqenät* to *Abbéto* Wäldä Hawaryat. From this that is written the brothers will not share."[25] In this case, as in the cases recorded in the documents presented here, the *aläqenäts* were part of more general wills or settlements which endowed one favored child, or in-law, with a major proportion of the family's position and holdings, together with the position of *aläqa*. The office of *aläqenät* ensured the continuing identity of the "family", and especially of the holdings which it had built up, through control of corporate resources and through power to reconcile conflicting claims to those resources.

At this point, in a curious way, the ambilineal descent system may have come to reinforce noble "family" corporate continuity. Hoben has emphasised how the lack of family names and the full identification of individuals with both father's and mother's lineages, meant that Amhära "families" hardly existed beyond the primary household stage.[26] And yet something very similar to the noble "families" of medieval western Europe or medieval Japan did exist in Ethiopia: groups of people linked by descent and marriage arrangements, clustering around centers of accumulated power and wealth. These groups recreated and reconstituted themselves generation after generation through physical procreation and marriages, and through the deployment of their power and wealth. The ambilineal descent system meant that it was comparatively easy to "spin off" those kin for whom resources were inadequate. Seen from the other side, the ambilineal descent system encouraged individuals who were faring poorly by association with one set of kin, and one center of power, to activate a different set of kin, and a different set of *rest* claims, and to move elsewhere: to change "families". The ambilineal descent system thus provided a highly fluid mechanism for continuously adjusting resources and claimants on and to those resources. It did *not* necessarily erode those resources or work in a levelling fashion.

The *aläqenät* is a key institution affording us a glimpse of the dynamics of how the Ethiopian nobility reproduced itself as a class. We should expect to find the *aläqenät* featuring prominently in both wills and marriage arrangements of the nobility. In truth, we do not have frequent mentions of it; but this is true of many other important institutions as well. The two cases we do have, that of the lineage emanating from *Ras* Wäldä Giyorgis presented in the documents above, and that of *Ras* Mika'él Sehul documented by Richard Pankhurst[27], in the eminence of their participants make up for what they lack in frequency of repetition. Both cases on hand date from the eighteenth century. Surely we can expect to find wills and marriage settlements involving the *aläqenät* from both nineteenth and twentieth centuries.

Bairu Tafla has discussed some of the key interests at work in the marriage arrangements of the Ethiopian nobility during the era of Emperor Menilek.[28] I think we can now flesh out that picture a little more fully by talking about the various property arrangements which inspired such marriage alliances. These arrangements involved *gult* claims in a generic sense, and touched on a host of claims to offices and to rights over land and cattle. In organizing these claims and in resolving internal family disputes over them, the *aläqenät* was a key institution. It is not surprising that it played a role in historic marriages amongst the Ethiopian nobility. I think we can expect to find additional examples.

NOTES

* For their advice in the translations, I am deeply indebted to Professor Abraham Demoz, Dr. Getatchew Haile and Ato Abdussamad H. Ahmad.

1. D. Crummey, "Gondarine *Rim* Land Sales: an introductory description and analysis", *Proceedings of the Fifth International Conference of Ethiopian Studies* (Chicago, 1979). For *gult*, see A. Hoben, *Land Tenure Amongst the Amhara of Ethiopia. The Dynamics of Cognatic Descent* (Chicago, 1973), 5-6, 75-9.

2. I. Guidi, *Vocabolario Amarico-Italiano* (Rome, 1901), 415, which uncharacteristically is wrong; J. Baeteman, *Dictionnaire Amarigna-Francais* (Dire-Daoua, 1929), 46; Tasamma Habte Mikael, *Käsaté Berhan Täsämma. Yä Amareñña Mäzgäba Qalat* (Addis Ababa, 1951 EC), 694.

3. Vatican Library, *Carte d'Abbadie*, Cartone XVIII, f. 367ᵛ. I have substantially altered the punctuation. D'Abbadie uses the untranslatable term *majorat*, which the *Petit Larousse Illustré* (1984) defines as: "bien inaliénable attaché à la possession d'un titre de noblesse, qui, au 19ᵉ siècle, était transmis, avec le titre, au fils aîné d'une famille." I am grateful to Severine Arlabosse for her assistance here.

4. Guidi, *Vocabolario*, 643.

5. R. Pankhurst, "An Eighteenth Century Dynastic Marriage Contract between Empress Mentewwab of Gondar and Ras Mika'el Sehul of Tegre", *Bulletin of the School of Oriental and African Studies*, XLII, 3(1979), 457-66. Pankhurst's marriage contract concludes by bestowing a family *aläqenät* as a key element of a marriage contract; it also mentions slaves.

6. I. Guidi, *Annales Iyasu II et Iyo'as* (Rome, 1912), 48.

7. Richard Pankhurst correctly dates Doc.2, but errs in having the wedding of Gälawdéwos and Wälätä Ṣeyon occur at this time: "Marriage Contract", 462, n.39.

8. Guidi, *Iyasu II*, pp.161-239 *passim*.

9. H. Weld Blundell, *The Royal Chronicle of Abyssinia 1769-1840* (Cambridge, 1922), 304-50 *passim*. See also the closely related texts published by I. Guidi: "La storia di Hayla Mika'el", *Rendiconti della Reale Accademia dei Lincei*, S.5, XI (1902), 3-79.

10. C. Conti Rossini, "La cronica reale Abissina dall'anno 1800 all'anno 1840", *Rendiconti della Reale Accademia dei Lincei*, S.5, XXV (1916), 864-97 *passim*; and *idem.* "Nuovi documenti per la storia d'Abissinia nel secolo XIX", *Atti dell'Accademia Nazionale dei Lincei*, S.8, II (1947), 359-67 *passim*.

11. W. P. E. S. Rüppell, *Reise in Abyssinien* (Frankfurt-am-Main, 2 vols., 1838-40), II, 197.

12. For this identification I am indebted in the first instance to Richard Pankhurst and his article, "Hamasén and the Gondarine Monarchy: A Reappraisal of Oral Traditions", *N.E.A. Journal of Research on North East Africa*, I, 1 (1981), 49, footnote 50. For the sources, see R. Basset, *Etudes sur l'Histoire d'Ethiopie* (Paris, 1882), 153, 167, 175, 186, 194; James Bruce, *Travels to Discover the Source of the Nile in the Years 1768, 1769, 1770, 1771, 1772 and 1773* (Edinburgh: 5 vols., 1790), II, 600-601.

13. Basset, *op. cit.*, 175.

14. *Ibid.*, 194-5, Bruce, *op. cit.*, 600-601.

15. *Ibid.*

16. *Abéto* Qosṭé is *not* mentioned: see above, and Guidi, *Iohannis I*, 333. Was he no relation at all? Or have we here only a list of full siblings; the children of one mother, Wäldä Giyorgis's wife by a religious marriage?

17. Weld Blundell, *Royal Chronicle*, 304. D. Crummey, "Family and Property Amongst the Amhara Nobility", *Journal of African History*, XXIV, 2 (1983), 207-20, draws on the documents under discussion here and establishes this point.

18. Guidi, *Iyasu II*, 9-11, 161-239 *passim*; see also James Bruce, *Travels to Discover the Source of the Nile* (Edinburgh, 5 vols., 1790), especially Vol.II, 609, where the relationship between Mentewwab and Ešété is incorrectly put.

19. Cambridge University Library, Additional Manuscript 1570, marginalia, *passim*, for the activities of Merşit Haylu and Gošu Haylu.

20. Weld Blundell, *Royal Chronicle*, 304.

21. *Ibid.*, 332.

22. Cambridge, *Add. Mss.* 1570 *passim*.

23. Hoben, *Land Tenure*. Social scientists working on Ethiopia have failed adequately to come to terms with this seminal book.

24. Pankhurst, "Marriage Contract". *Bull. SOAS*, XLII, 3 (1979), 457-66.

25. *Ibid.*, 463.

26. A. Hoben, "Family, Land and Class in Northwest Europe and Northern Highland Ethiopia", pp.157-70 in H. Marcus (ed.), *Proceedings of the First United States Conference on Ethiopian Studies. Michigan State University, 2-5 May 1973* (East Lansing, 1975).

27. Pankhurst, "Marriage Contract".

28. Bairu Tafla, "Marriage as a Political Device: an appraisal of a socio-political aspect of the Menilek period 1889-1916", *Journal of Ethiopian Studies*, X, 1 (1972), 13-21.

FIG. 1: RELATIONSHIPS

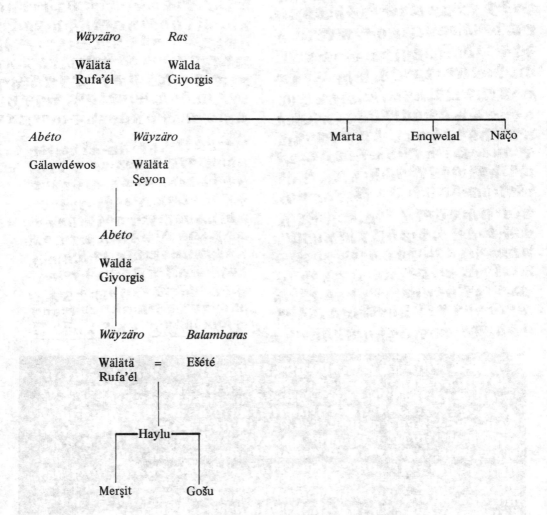

እራክ፡ወለዱ፡ጊዮርጊ፡ክዮ፡ወይዘሮ፡
ወለተ፡ፋተ፡ኤል፡ልጅ፡ሲ፡ጋቦ፡የራ፡ክ፡ወ
ለይ፡ጊዮርጊ፡ክ፡ልጅ፡እቢተ፡ገለውይ
ዋ፡ክ፡የወይዘሮ፡ወለተ፡ተተ፡ኤ፡ልፍ፡ልጅ
ወይዘሮ፡ወለተ፡ጽዮግ፡ን፡ሊ፡እገ፡ው፡እለ
ትነተን፡ጥጋ፡እድር፡ገው፡እራ፡ክ፡ወለዱ፡ጊ
ዮርጊ፡ክ፡ለወይዘሮ፡ወለተ፡ጽዮግ፡ን፡እ
ትነተን፡ስጡ፡ወይዘሮ፡ወለተ፡ጽ፡ዮ፡ገ፡ዎ
ሳ፡ቢተ፡ወለዱ፡ጊዮርጊ፡ክ፡ስጡ፡ያ፡ቢቶ
ወለዱ፡ጊዮርጊ፡ክ፡ን፡ልጅ፡ወይዘሮ፡ወ
ለተ፡ተተ፡ኤ፡ል፡ን፡ገገም፡ባ፡ራ፡ክ፡እሒ፡ቀ፡ሒ
እገው፡እለ፡ቀ፡ነ፡ት፡ዋ፡ወ፡ን፡እ፡ድር፡ገው፡እ፡ቢ
ቶ፡ገ፡ገ፡ወ፡ይ፡ዎ፡ክ፡ም፡እ፡ቢ፡ቶ፡ወ፡ለ፡ዱ፡ጊ፡ዮ
ራ፡ክ፡ም፡ስ፡ገ፡ገ፡ም፡ገ፡ገ፡ራ፡ክ፡እ፡ሒ፡ቶ፡እ፡ለ፡ቶ
ነ፡ት፡ን፡ስ፡ጡ፡ይ፡ህ፡ን፡ፍ፡ጼ፡ሜ፡የ፡ለ፡ሙ፡ሊ
ቶ፡ተ፡ክ፡ለ፡ሃ፡ይ፡ማ፡ኖ፡ት፡ሊ፡ቲ፡በ፡ት፡ሪ፡ሊ
ቶ፡ፋ፡ሊ፡ሉ፡እ፡ሊ፡ቶ፡ይ፡ሳ፡ይ፡ያ፡ክ፡እ፡ዛ፡ጋ፡ር፡ክ
ክ፡ስ፡ል፡ዱ፡እ፡ዛ፡ጋ፡ር፡እ፡ቢ፡ሊ፡ሉ፡ም፡እ፡ጋ፡ር፡ብ
ሕ፡ር፡ይ፡ሊ፡ቀ፡ነ፡ረ፡እ፡ኩ፡ነ፡ዮ፡ሐ፡ት፡ክ
ጨ፡ጊ፡ሃ፡ዎ፡ክ፡ክ፡መ፡ክ፡ገ፡ገ፡ን፡ት፡ም፡ይ፡ጅ፡እ
ዝ፡መ፡ች፡ብ፡ገ፡ያ፡ዎ፡እ፡ዛ፡ጋ፡ር፡ሱ፡ሊ፡ገ፡ሳ፡ው
ባ፡ራ፡ክ፡ዮ፡ዋ፡ተ፡ክ፡ኖ፡ት፡እ፡ዛ፡ጋ፡ር፡ሳ፡ው፡ኤ፡ል

ቁ፡ሽ፡እ፡ዘ፡ማ፡ች፡ጉ፡ሮ፡ን፡ክ፡ን፡ቲ፡በ፡ን፡ክ፡አ፡ክ
ክ፡ቢ፡ዋ፡ል፡ጀ፡ች፡እ፡ቢ፡ት፡ሃ፡ይ፡ለ፡እ፡ቢ፡ት፡ዘ
ር፡ቅ፡ሽ፡ዎ፡ን፡እ፡ቢ፡ቶ፡ቢ፡ራ፡ር፡እ፡ቢ፡ት፡ቀ
ይ፡ኪ፡ዎ፡ክ፡እ፡ቢ፡ት፡እ፡ቤ፡ች፡ሊ፡ሱ፡ም፡እ፡ስ፡ተ
ያ፡ዐ፡ቀ፡ብ፡ያ፡ቤ፡ት፡እ፡ጽ፡ም፡ጊ፡ዮ፡ር፡ጊ፡ክ፡ል
ጅ፡እ፡ቢ፡ት፡ፈ፡ሊ፡ት፡ብ፡ባ፡ቴ፡ን፡ጊ፡ተ፡ተ፡ክ፡ለ
እ፡ቢ፡ብ፡የ፡ሽ፡ለ፡ት፡እ፡ር፡ማ፡እ፡ቀ፡ክ፡ያ፡ለ፡ት፡ገ
ላ፡ው፡ይ፡ዎ፡ክ፡ብ፡ባ፡ቴ፡ን፡ጊ፡ተ፡ጸ፡ገ፡ሥ፡ላ፡እ
ክ፡እ፡ድ፡ባ፡ራ፡ት፡እ፡ለ፡ቶ፡ች፡ክ፡እ፡የ፡ሱ፡ክ፡እ፡ለ
ታ፡ጸ፡ግ፡ማ፡ስ፡ሬ፡ህ፡ባ፡ት፡ድ፡ን፡ግ፡ል፡ክ፡ገ
ም፡ጅ፡ቢ፡ት፡ሊ፡ቀ፡ማ፡ዕ፡ም፡ሬ፡ን፡ገ፡ዋ፡ይ፡ክ
ይ፡ብ፡ረ፡ብ፡ር፡ሃ፡ን፡እ፡ለ፡ታ፡ክ፡ፍ፡ሉ፡ማ፡ር፡ሃ፡ዎ፡ም

ክ፡ተ፡ከ፡ቲ፡ዎ፡እ፡ለ፡ታ፡እ፡ው፡ሊ፡ክ፡በ፡ሁ፡ተ
ክ፡ለ፡ሃ፡ይ፡ማ፡ኖ፡ት፡መ፡ሬ፡ት፡ጊ፡ተ፡ት፡ገ፡ዋ፡ት
ክ፡ፉ፡ተ፡ኤ፡ል፡እ፡ለ፡ታ፡ፈ፡ሊ፡ል፡ክ፡ጸ፡ን፡ጽ
ት፡ጹ፡ክ፡ሚ፡ካ፡ኤ፡ል፡መ፡ጋ፡ክ፡ገ፡ነ፡ት፡ዮ
ሐ፡ስ፡እ፡ሐ፡መ፡ረ፡ን፡ዋ፡መ፡ባ፡ክ፡ሕ፡ፈ፡ም
ወ፡ለ፡ድ፡ል፡ው፡ል፡ክ፡ት፡ዱ፡ክ፡ጊ፡ዮ፡ር፡ጊ፡ክ
እ፡ለ፡ታ፡እ፡ክ፡ብ፡ፈ፡ዮ፡ክ፡ይ፡ህ፡ን፡ሕ፡ስ፡በ፡ው፡እ
ለ፡ት፡ነ፡ተ፡ን፡ል፡ጀ፡ች፡ዎ፡ን፡እ፡ስ፡ተ፡ም፡ኡ፡ን
ወ፡እ፡ዝ፡ን፡ት፡ች፡ፈ፡ጸ፡ም፡ን፡ን፡ገ፡ር፡ተ፡ጽ፡ሕ፡ረ
በ፡ዘ፡መ፡ነ፡ማ፡ቲ፡ዎ፡ክ፡በ፡ፄ፡ጓ፡መ፡ተ፡መ፡ን
ጋ፡ሥ፡ት፡በ፡ን፡ተ፡ሪ፡ስ፡ነ፡ኢ፡ዮ፡አ፡ክ

SOME NOTES ON THE ROLE OF VILLAGE SCHOOLS

IN GRAFTING PROTESTANTISM IN WOLLEGA: 1898-1935

Daniel Ayana

The incorporation of Wollaga under the rule of Menelik II was accompanied by the introduction of Christianity and had the effect of bringing, among other things rudimentary church education to the region. This was achieved through the few church schools which were established along with Orthodox churches. These church schools had their origins in the traditional church education practised in the northern part of Ethiopia since the introduction of Christianity.

These traditional church schools had the aim of preserving and transmitting the cultural heritage of the Christian Ethiopian population. Besides, the immediate task of this traditional church education seems to have been to train some of the youth for church service as deacons, priests and scribes. Aimed at preserving and transmitting the cultural heritage, these traditional church schools did not have the aim of widening the pupils' conception of the world. Rather they were institutions to mould the young to accept the *status quo* as transmitted from generation to generation and then bequeath it to the next generation. This necessitated acceptance of all teaching without question. Consequently, creativity and curiosity on the part of the pupils were considered as flaws that should be corrected with all their manifestations. Thus, besides the training of the youth to enable the church to maintain its functions, traditional church education in Ethiopia seems to have been geared towards shaping the young to conform to established authority.

The curriculum of primary traditional church education in Ethiopia basically comprised of the learning of alphabets and memorizing the Acts of the Apostles and the Psalms. As part of shaping the pupils, it also included the teaching of morality: obedience, humbleness, respect for the elders by carrying out some duties for them. In fact a few students could continue their studies beyond the primary stage, although for most of the pupils this primary traditional church education was the end of their formal education. After this stage of education the pupils served the churches or they rendered services to the emperors or the nobility.[1] Some of them seem to have returned to farming.

When these church schools were introduced to Wollaga they were referred to as *kutir bet*. As in the northern half of Ethiopia the *kutir bet* were in most cases a one-room hut with thatched roof. It could be the church premises itself or a building attached to the church. Sometimes it was conducted under a tree near the church.[2] These *kutir bet* were few in number as were the churches and the priests. They were used by the few churchmen to train the sons of Government officials, the priests and the local chiefs. It was aimed at producing young men who could support and later take over the tasks of the priests. As such their curriculum seems to have been modelled upon the curriculum of the traditional church education practised elsewhere in Ethiopia.[3] However, the curriculum and the teaching itself seem to have been superficial due to the absence of qualified teachers.

As mentioned above, the pupils were from the local priestly families and children of central government officials and of some of the local chiefs who did not bother to employ tutors for their children. At the *kutir bet* they were taught how to read and write and were required to memorize prayers, the Psalms and the Acts of the Apostles. After completing what the available teachers could teach them, most of those from the priestly families gradually took over the duties of their fathers. The others were employed as secretaries to the local chiefs or governors.[4]

Among the northern Ethiopian nobility there was the tradition of employing tutors for their children. In the process the sons of the nobility were exposed to primary traditional church education in which they learned the alphabets and memorized some portions of religious literature.[5] Usually the sons of the nobility were not given the chance of furthering their education beyond this stage. By the time they reached the age of twelve or thirteen the children of the nobility were channelled, deliberately or by circumstances, to traditional sports as befitted their social class and to the practise of feudal etiquette. As a result most of the sons of the nobility were not educated much in the traditional church education.[6]

One can find a parallel development with respect to the education of the sons of the local chiefs in Wollaga after the incorporation. Some of the local chiefs employed tutors for their children. These tutors were mostly priests or relatives of the priests or individuals who had come to the newly incorporated areas to improve their lot. Naturally they had to have a basic knowledge of how to read and write. These tutors were given *qalab*, an agreed amount of grain, by their employers for their services. The tutors would then teach the sons of the chiefs how to read and write and help them to memorize some portions of the Bible. Beyond reading and writing, they were generally required to embrace Orthodox Christianity. After they had finished what the tutors could teach them, they were told by their parents to practise horse-racing and to observe other time-honoured feudal etiquette. There is no indication that they had the interest or the encouragement to pursue their studies even after modern schools were introduced. The ultimate objective seems to have been to train them to read and write and then prepare them to take over the duties of their chiefly families.[7]

However, by the end of the last century, village schools had been introduced in Wollaga by the Protestant missions or their Ethiopian counterparts. These village schools were one of the main institutions through which the missionaries expanded Christianity in Africa. They contributed a lot in providing converts and indigenous leaders. As the pioneer missionaries confronted the traditional religions they sought for points of contact between them and the local people, where the latter could be influenced. Village schools were established by the missionaries to provide such points of contact to implant the new religion. Throughout their history missionaries had considered educational work as a means for the evangelical objectives. Thus, it was as an indirect means of expanding Christianity that village schools were established.[8]

During the initial stage the difference between Bible preaching and secular teaching was blurred. In most cases one premise was used both for Sunday service and for teaching. The content of the curriculum was either religion-oriented or had conversion as its objective. Besides, village schools were used as a corrosive force against the established traditional religion and practices. Since the missionaries were directly or indirectly teaching against the traditional customs, values and beliefs the pupils were gradually being detached from the traditional way of thinking and invariably converted. And through these village schools new ideas, ways of life, expectations and new ways of explaining the world were built in the minds of the students. For this purpose it was usually not the adults but the children, in whose minds the traditional way of thinking was not deeprooted, who were chosen to be taught and to form the nucleus of the rising generation.[9] Thus, unlike traditional church education in Ethiopia, village schools had the objective of destabilizing and destroying the established social system and tradition.

Most of these village schools had literacy programmes to get their converts to read the Bible for themselves. In the early stages village schools did not give training in special branches of knowledge. The main aim was to shape "the personal and spiritual character of the pupils attending the school . . . ". To effectively implement this objective, teaching was introduced in the vernacular language. And the missionaries themselves learned the vernacular of the people among whom they were working. They then reduced the vernacular into a written form to facilitate reading and understanding by the local people. This method appears to have been very effective "for . . . the language of a people is the expression of its soul, by which alone a key to their thoughts could be found."[10] Relevant religious literature was then translated into the vernacular,[11] for use in the village schools to counter what the society informally taught its young members.

Through their traditional religion, the Oromo children had been taught informally the society's moral values and they had grown up with them. Thus, one of the main tenets of informal education was that one was always expected to speak the truth. An individual found lying repeatedly would lose respect in the community. In this regard, it has been written that if one was found to be a liar he was despised and would be denied a say in public meetings.[12] Whether this is true or an exaggerated statement it provides us with a notion of how lying was unacceptable in traditional Oromo society.

The other important traditional moral value was that an individual was expected to respect his parents and the elder members of the community. Respect does not seem to have been limited to the traditional deference that juniors ought to show their seniors. It included helping one's parents and elders in times of need and feeding them when they were unable to work. An individual who failed to discharge this duty was considered irresponsible and became an object of curse and contempt in the community.[13] Consequently, respect for elders constituted one part of the informal traditional education in Oromo society.

Related to the above is the tradition that the young were always expected to be humble. They should not be proud in their relationships, especially with the elders. To this effect the elders casually inquired about the character of every young man in the community. If they were told that he was proud or wicked they commented that he was going to fail in his life.[14]

Abstention from illicit sexual intercourse was another traditional moral value which was imparted to the young informally. Members of the community were expected to avoid fornication and adultery, although strict observance of this differed from region to region. This was necessary to smooth the relationships between members of the community. Besides, persons who claimed descent from *borana*, "pure" Oromo, were expected to avoid fornication with *gabaro*, though this was seldom respected. Members of occupational castes were not allowed to marry or have affairs outside their castes.[15] This seems to have been aimed at restricting the occupational castes to a degraded position which they could have circumvented through intermarriage. Thus it was maintained in the informal education.

Murder was also forbidden according to the traditional moral values. In cases of murder the culprit had to pay blood price, known as *gumma*, to the relatives of the slain. If he could not pay *gumma* the relatives of the murdered could avenge their kinsman by taking the law into their own hands.[16] In this respect the attitude towards murder for personal motive seems to have been different from the interclan or intertribal fratricidal wars which were done for the interest of the clan or the tribe. In such cases bravery in wars was encouraged and constituted one of the informal points of education.

Stealing was also forbidden. This seems to have arisen with the growth of private property. Consequently theft was to be compensated in amount by more than what was stolen.[17]

These were some of the tenets of the traditional informal education which the young had to know in the process of becoming full-grown members of the society. Besides these the young were also informally taught to observe and discharge some of the duties that had to be performed in the traditional societies and offerings dedicated to the different spirits. The assumed value of every sacrifice and offering that was dedicated to each spirit in the traditional religion was informally taught to the young as they witnessed the ceremonies.[18]

At home parents naturally looked after the behaviour of their children; while outside the young were informally supervised by members of the community. Violation of the tenets of moral values, which at the same time were part of the traditional laws, led to admonition or punishment by the parents. But repeated violation entailed reprimand by the elders in the community whose cooperation was requested by the family of the incorrigible. In extreme cases, the youth was flogged by the able-bodied members of the community.[19]

There was also another mechanism to ensure that the younger members of the community observed what they were taught informally. This was fear of curse and a need for blessing and respect from the community. Blessing or curse was considered to be operative by the traditional Oromo and most young men took it at its face value. Especially the blessing or the cursing of the elder members of the community was believed to be effective sooner or later. Consequently, the younger members of the community needed blessing as a contribution to the fulfilment of their aspirations.[20] Thus, through such informal teachings of the traditional moral values, it was aimed at preserving the cultural heritage of the society and transmitting it to the succeeding generation.

Socially and politically, the 19th century witnessed the weakening of the *gada* system in Wollaga due to the rise of petty chiefs who established their personal rule in the different localities. The decline of the *gada* system and the rise of chiefs was accompanied by new kinds of laws and moral values that corresponded to the newly evolved indigenous political structure. However, before this new political structure strengthened itself Shoan expansion made Orthodox Christianity the official religion in Wollaga. With the introduction of Christianity the undermined traditional laws and religious practices were outlawed by decree. However, the local people generally continued practising their old customs and beliefs.[21] It was at this juncture that the Protestants started preaching another brand of Christianity in Wollaga.

When the Protestants arrived Orthodox Christianity was disrupting the already undermined traditional religion. But it had not made much headway in superseding the traditional religion. However, it had introduced new values which were the result of the newly introduced administration. Accordingly baptised people were considered as those who belonged to the religion of the rulers. People who had learned how to read and write were considered knowledgeable and appointed or employed in different capacities.[22] Although this should not mean that there were no groups who rejected or despised the new system and its values, the fact that it was from above gradually made it time-honoured.

This condition favoured the Protestants who systematically used, among others, village schools to preach Protestantism. The Protestant missions or their Ethiopian counterparts used village schools to establish themselves among the local people. Prior to 1935 the Swedish, the American and the German Protestant missions were active in Wollaga. The presence of these missions enabled most parts of this region to have schools. Thus, in the pre-occupation period there were eight schools out of which five belonged to the Protestants.[23]

These schools were in most cases centres where the missions trained students who became teachers in the village schools. Although founded by different mission groups these schools had almost the same curriculum. The lessons included Bible study, stories, Church history and Amharic and sometimes English if there was a qualified teacher. Some of them had introduced Ge'ez along with Amharic. The German mission taught German instead of English. The reason given was that the pupils after learning English could desert them to find better employment, ignoring the mission's objective of expanding Protestantism. Instead the pupils were required to learn German to serve later as translators.[24]

The teachers in these early schools were mostly from the "English School" in Addis Ababa established by the Swedish medical missionary K. Cederquvist. Some of them were trained at Asmara or Massawa by the Swedish missionaries to work among the Oromo. Still others were local pupils who had earlier attended the lessons offered by the missionaries or the above teachers. Besides these, there were also Orthodox priests who were employed to teach Amharic and/or Ge'ez. This was possible since until after 1935 doctrinal differences were in most cases shelved or smoothly handled by the missions so as not to arouse opposition.[25]

However, in some areas where there was no direct supervision by the missions and where the local people had taken over the leadership, doctrinal differences were brought to the fore and there was opposition by the local Orthodox clergy. However, thanks to the autonomy that local rulers enjoyed in administration after the incorporation, they managed to protect the teachers, whose teaching was more comprehensible since they taught in the vernacular and hence more attractive. After 1916 the missions and their Ethiopian followers were given freedom to work.[26]

The problem of reducing the Oromo language into a written form was tackled by the Swedish Evangelical Missionaries. This mission group had wanted to work among the Oromo in the 1860s and 1870s; but it could not reach them through the central highlands of Ethiopia because of the unsettled political situation during the last years of Tewodros' reign and because of Yohannes' religious policy. They then temporarily settled at Massawa and waited for an opportune moment to proceed to southern Ethiopia. It was during this time that the missionaries met freed enslaved Oromo at Massawa. These freed slaves were trained by the missionaries to go back and preach in their respective areas. As part of this plan the freed slaves translated the Bible and other religious literature into Oromo. Besides translating they also prepared some books that could help them in teaching. This literature was published and made available for teaching.[27]

Using the religious literature prepared in Oromo, instructions in the schools established by the different mission groups was conducted in the same language instead of Amharic which the government wanted. The curriculum was naturally directed towards converting the pupils. Therefore, to enable the pupils to understand easily they were first taught to read and write in the vernacular. The books that were used for teaching and which were distributed among the students were prepared in such a way that their training could lead their thoughts towards accepting the new religion — Protestantism.[28]

Initially it was the sons of the local chiefs who started attending these schools although there were pupils of peasant background. However, for most of the sons of the chiefly families it seemed *infra dignitatem* to attend school. Consequently, the sons of the local peasantry gradually replaced them and diligently attended instructions given by the Protestant teachers,[29] probably considering it as a means of improving their social status.

After completing what was taught at these schools, most of these students returned to their respective villages and established what could be called branch village schools. This does not mean that they built a house to teach in. Rather they worked in their families' residences. Here they taught interested individuals, usually in the evenings or afternoons, when there was free time. Or sometimes they taught in the homes of the interested individuals turn by turn. These teachers were closely supervised by the missions or their Ethiopian followers and encouraged to impart whatever basic knowledge they had. Since these teachers had books written in Oromo, which were seen as something novel, they were not short of an audience. Out of curiosity interested people began learning how to read and write. By the time they knew how to read and write they were channelled to the village schools established by the missions, if they wanted to pursue their studies. Here they would get additional training to become village teachers or to assist the teacher in the village from where they had come. If they did not want to pursue their studies by going to the mission village schools they were provided with portions of the Oromo Bible and at times the Oromo Bible itself. To improve their reading ability the pupils invariably continued reading during their leisure time. In most cases when they read, there were some people who sat with them to listen to the reading. Most of the readers and the listeners were finally converted and constituted followers of Protestantism in the villages. And most of the village schools were later transformed into indigenous Protestant churches.[30]

In some instances when branch village schools were not established, the pupils went back to their respective villages and tried to win over their peers to attend the village schools founded by the missions. Besides they taught them casually to arouse their interest. If they could not attend the schools they were invited to Sunday service which was usually held after the Orthodox Church service was over. In such cases they would have to walk a distance of an hour or two. This led to the establishment of a church in their own villages with the first pupil who attended the mission village school as the village leader. If they happened to be closer to the mission station they became members of the church established in or around the mission station.[31]

On the other hand the village school, which was established in or around the mission station, continued functioning. As time went on the enrollment in these schools increased and they were gradually transformed into modern elementary mission schools with regular classes. The pupils in these schools were not pressed to go back to their villages to expand Protestantism. Neither were they forced to adhere to Protestant doctrine. Those who could find the means of furthering their education went to Addis Ababa for further learning. For instance when Tafari Makonnen School was officially inaugurated in 1925 thirty students from Wollaga joined this school. Besides, the availability of these schools in the region seems to have changed the attitude of the local chiefs towards encouraging the young to attend the new schools and to pursue their studies further. In fact they had already gone beyond urging their dignitaries to send their children to the schools. Accordingly *dajazmach* Habta-Mariam Gabra-Egziabher sent twenty-three students to the newly established Tafari Makonnen school, paying "their school fees", while *fitawrari* Mardassa Jote selected forty students from the Gidami *Kutir bet* and enrolled them in the school established by the American mission at Sayo in 1919. According to some sources, in the late 1920s and before 1935 the number of students in Wollaga had exceeded the number of students int the capital.[32]

The sons of the dignitaries of the local chief who had attended these mission schools were employed in the government offices from where they directly or indirectly helped the Protestant teachers. Most of the sons of the peasantry who could not pursue their studies went on preaching Protestantism. In the process they became indigenous leaders. In the performance of this task the availability of Oromo literature supplemented whatever training they had.

But above all the nature of the traditional religion of the Oromo had also helped the indigenous leaders. While they were being trained by the missionaries or their Ethiopian trainees, what these pupils were taught informally by their families was not entirely discarded. In fact most of the basic Oromo traditional values found their parallels in the Biblical Ten Commandments. Besides most of the concepts of the traditional religions of the Oromo were equated with some of the Biblical concepts in the process of translation.[33]

In the same manner while teaching in the villages the teachers were facing an audience which was not entirely new to the teaching. Concepts such as *Waqa*, which the traditional Oromo worshipped, was equated with God. The traditionally understood omnipotence of *Waqa* was elaborated in the Oromo Bible with Oromo language proverbs and adages which found parallels in the Bible. The traditional belief in *Waqa* as the creator had its counterpart in the book of Genesis.[34]

Belief in the life hereafter was not known among the traditional Oromo. However, there was the concept of *lubu*, soul, and a belief that after death *lubu* goes to the abode of truth. And *Waqa* was traditionally considered as the guardian of truth. For the indigenous leaders stretching and adapting this traditional belief to Biblical principles does not seem to have been hard. Traditionally righteous life was necessary to contribute to success in worldly life, in contrast to wickedness and vice which led to failure. Therefore, the indigenous leaders easily transformed this belief to the necessity of virtuous life, in accordance with the principles of Christianity. On the other hand, traditional beliefs which were found contrary to the new teaching were denounced and gradually dropped.[35]

Based on the available data village schools seem to have served as centres for reinterpreting and readjusting the traditional religion of the Oromo along the principles of Protestant doctrine. In the process village teachers evolved as indigenous leaders in grafting the new doctrine onto the traditional religion.

NOTES

1. Girma Amare, "Aims and Purpose of Church Education in Ethiopia", *Ethiopian Journal of Education*, I, 1 (1967), pp.4-10.

2. *Ibid.*

3. *Ibid.* Interview: Mamhire Wuhib Gabru, Naqamte; Mamhire Wondimu Worqineh Buliso; Marigeta Makonnen Balate, Bojji.

4. *Ibid.*

5. Interview: Mamhire Wuhib Gabru; Qanazmatch Abdissa Mossa, Afa-Mamhire Gabra Kidan Bishaw, Naqamte; Ato Tasissa Homma, Ato Yoseph Yishaq, Nejo.

6. C. W. Isenberg and J. L. Krapf, *The Journal of Isenberg and Krapf Detailing their Proceedings in the Kingdom of Shoa and Journey in other parts of Abyssinia in the Years 1839, 1840, 1841 and 1842* (London, 1843), p.86.

7. Bairu Tafla, "The Education of the Ethiopian Mekwannent in the 19th century", *The Ethiopian Journal of Education*, VI, I (1973), pp.19-20.

8. Interview: Qan. Abdissa Mossa, Mamhire Wuhib Gabru, Naqamte; Marigata Makonnen Balate, Ato Galata Bojji, Bojji; Mamhire Wondimu Wondium Worqineh, Ato Dabsu Billi Guliso; Agafari Gutama Diko, Najo.

9. B. Holmes, ed., *Educational Policy and Mission Schools: Case Studies from the British Empire.* (London, 1967), p.270; R. I. Rotberg, *Christian Missionaries and Creation of Northern Rhodesia 1880-1924*, (Princeton, 1969), p.43.

10. J. W. C. Dougall, *Christians in the African Revolution* (Edinburgh, 1963), pp.11, 15, 18; E. A. Ayandele, *The Missionary Impact on Modern Nigeria, 1848-1891; The Making of a New Elite* (London, 1965), p.137.

11. Ayandele, *op. cit.*, p.340.

12. Rotberg, *op. cit.*, p.108; Dougall, *op. cit.*, p.11; Holmes, *op. cit.*, pp.2, 26, 271; C. G. Baeta, *Christianity in Tropical Africa, Studies Presented and Discussed at the Seventh International African Seminar*, (London, 1968), p.17.

13. Isenberg and Krapf, *op. cit.*, p.152.

14. Dinsa Lepissa Abba Jobir, "The Gada System of Government and Sera Chafe Oromo" (LLB Thesis, A.A.U., 1975), p.180.

15. Interview: Ato Sorri Selle, Ato Jorgo Senno, Aira; Ato Bati Hembele, Ato Balcha Denta, Dambi Dollo; Ato Maggarssa Salbanna, Hadiya.

16. Dinsa, *op. cit.*, pp.178-188; Interview: Ato Sorri Selle, Ato Jorgo Senno, Aira; Ato Dibaba Lota, Dambi Dollo; Ato Magarssa Salbana, Hadiya.

17. Dinsa, *op. cit.*, p.120. Mitiku Tucho, "Impacts of Pastoralism on the Oromo of Qellam, Wollaga" (B.A. Thesis, A.A.U. (1983), p.57.

18. Dinsa, *op. cit.*, pp.178-185.

19. Daniel Ayana, "Protestant Missions in Wollaga: A study of the Activities of the Missions and their Local Converts" (M.A. Thesis, A.A.U., 1984), pp.29-44.

20. *Ibid.*

21. *Ibid.*

22. *Ibid.*, p.51.

23. Daffa Jamo, *A'dda Oromo Wollaga* (Addis Ababa, 1974 E.C.), pp.54-55; Interview: Ato Magarssa Salbanna, Hadiya; Ato Sorri Selle, Ato Jorgo Senno, Aira.

24. *Idem.* "A Short History of Western Synod", p.18. Besides these there was one government school and three Catholic mission schools.

25. D. Wassman. *Pionierdienst unter den Galla in west Abessien* (Hannover, 1938), pp.58-61.

26. *Ibid.*, pp.64-67. Daffa Jammo, "A Short History", p.12; Interview: Ato Galata Bojji, Jaleta Wasse, Qes Namara Challa, Bojji; Ato Tasissa Homma, Ato Yoseph Yishaq, Najo.

27. G. Aren. *Evangelical Pioneers in Ethiopia: Origins of the Evangelical Makane Yesus Church* (Uppsala, 1978), pp.25, 439.

28 Daniel, *op. cit.*, pp.69-77.

29. Wassman, *op. cit.*, pp.98-99; Interview: Agafari Gutama Diko, Ato Tasissa Homma, Ato Joseph Yishaq, Najo; Ato Dibaba Lata, Ato Bati Hambele, Dambi Dollo; Ato Gilo Waqayo, W/o Nagare Boku, Naqamte.

30. Gidada Solon, *The other Side of Darkness* (New York, 1972), pp.12-16; Wassman, *op. cit.*, pp.81-83; "Evangelical Church Makane Yesus Inception and Development", pp.34-35; Interview: Qes. Namata Bojji, Bojji.

31. *Ibid.*

32. Seid Mohammed, "The History of Tafari Makonnen School, 1924-1974" (B.A. Thesis, A.A.U., 1983), p.18; Nagaso Gidada, "Impact of Christianity on Qellem Awraja, Western Wollaga, 1886 to 1941" (B.A. Thesis, H.S.I.U., 1971), p.28; V. Haldin Norberg, *Swedes in Haile Sillassie's Ethiopia 1924-1952: A Study in Early Development cooperation* (Uppsala, 1977), pp.118-119; Interview: Ato Gamtessa Amuma, Ato Bacha Denta, Ato Bati Hembele, Dambi Dollo; Qes Tassissa Duressa, W/o Qanatu Karorssa, Aira; Qes Namara Chala, Qes Jalata Wasse, Bojji.

33. Daniel, *op. cit.*, pp.108-110. Tarfassa Digga, "A Short Biography of Onesimos Nesib (c.1850-1931)", (B.A. Thesis, H.S.I.U., 1973), pp.12-17.

34. Daniel, *op. cit.*, pp.110-114.

35. *Ibid.*, *Proceedings of the Second Annual Seminar of the Department of History, A.A.U.*, Vol.I, (Addis Ababa, 1984): Daniel Ayana, "The Concept of *Waqa* and the Missionaries: A preliminary Study in the Grafting of Christianity on a Traditional Belief in Wollaga", pp.105-122.

RAS IMMIRU:

IL SUO RUOLO DURANTE LA GUERRA ITALO-ETIOPICA

Angelo Del Boca

Forse nessuna amicizia è durata tanto a lungo, è stata cementata da tanti episodi, come quella fra l'ultimo imperatore d'Etiopia e suo cugino, ras Immirù Haile Sellase. Nati entrambi nel 1892, in un villaggio non lontano da Harar, essi "crebbero insieme − come ricorda Hailé Selassié I nella sua autobiografia − come se fossero stati gemelli".[1] Dal casato illustre essi ebbero tutti i privilegi e gli onori: l'opportunità di formarsi culturalmente attraverso studi relativamente solidi, di apprendere lingue straniere, di affinarsi nell'arte del comando, di frequentare la corte del grande Menelik. Doni e privilegi che appaiono ancora più vistosi, eccezionali, se si rapportano alla società etiopica di fine secolo, ancora totalmente contadina e retta da un'oligarchia di tipo feudale.

Germogliata nella prima infanzia, l'amicizia fra i due aristocratici scioani dura un'intera e lunga esistenza, ottant'anni. Un'amicizia che sopravvive anche quando il destino colloca Hailé Selassié sul trono di Salomone e ras Immirù in una posizione subalterna. Un'intesa che resiste anche quando i due uomini si fanno portatori di filosofie politiche diverse e rivelano una differente visione dei metodi da adottare per far uscire l'Etiopia dalla notte medioevale. Una fraternità che non viene neppure scalfita quando forze rivali, nel 1960, ma anche prima, cercheranno di opporre l'uno all'altro. Una simpatia reciproca che passa indenne attraverso ottant'anni di congiure di palazzo, di colpi di stato abortiti, di rivoluzioni mancate. E quando, infine, gli uomini del *Derg* spazzeranno via la monarchia millennaria con tutte le sue strutture arretrate, sarà ancora ras Immirù a confortare l'imperatore deposto, ad accompagnarlo fuori del palazzo imperiale, a seguirlo sino alla *Volkswagen* blu che deve portarlo in prigionia.

Pur con alti e bassi, e pause causate dalla reclusione in Italia e dagli incarichi diplomatici all'estero, ras Immirù svolge nei confronti del sovrano un ruolo di confidente e di consigliere, che sarà sempre improntato alla massima lealtà. Ciò non significa, necessariamente, che Hailè Selassiè lo ascolti sempre e che faccia tesoro dei suoi suggerimenti. Più volte, anzi, di fronte a scelte di capitale importanza, l'imperatore ignora i consigli del cugino ed agisce in senso opposto. Al liberalismo di ras Immirù contrappone sempre, caparbiamente, un riformismo estremamente cauto, persuaso che l'Etiopia deve uscire dal suo sottosviluppo senza traumi e scosse violente. Giungerà anche, quando la popolarità del cugino comincerà a dargli ombra, a ripagare la sua lealtà e franchezza con l'esilio, seppure dorato, di Washington, Mosca e New Delhi. E certo non può apprezzare la decisione di ras Immirù, presa negli anni '50, di distribuire le sue terre ai contadini, un gesto che accresce la sua fama di progressista e lo indica ai rivoluzionari in potenza come l'uomo del ricambio.

Questo saggio, comunque, non si propone di esaminare la storia di un'amicizia fra aristocratici al vertice del potere, ma la vicenda personale di ras Immirù, con particolare riferimento alla sua esperienza di comandante militare nel conflitto italo-etiopico del 1935-36 e nella successiva fase della guerriglia. Un periodo particolarmente difficile per l'Etiopia, nel corso del quale il ras scioano rivela doti insospettabili di capo e di soldato, qualificandosi come il miglior generale dell'impero ed anche il più fortunato. La sua offensiva contro il campo trincerato di Adua-Axum e contro le stesse basi italiane di rifornimento in Eritrea, eseguita con truppe raccoglitïcce, male armate e in parte anche non fidate, non soltanto tolse il sonno a Mussolini, ma costituisce il solo esempio di tattica vincente in una guerra dove, per tradizione e per motivi di prestigio, si preferisce la battaglia campale alla guerriglia, facendo così il gioco dell'avversario, già tanto più forte.

Prima di cimentarsi come soldato, ras Immirù si era distinto nel ruolo di amministratore, governando con raro equilibrio e fermezza una regione estremamente complessa e turbolenta come il Goggiam. Si era anche imposto come uomo di diritto, difendendo nel 1930 la prima Costituzione etiopica elaborata da Teclè Hawariate dagli assalti di altri aristocratici, come i ras

Cassa, Hailù, Sejum, Gugsa Araia, che si battevano per conservare intatti i loro privilegi.[2] E quando si era trattato di riarmare il paese, dinanzi alle minacce dell'Italia fascista, ras Immirù aveva preso la strada dell'Europa capeggiando le missioni in Francia e in Svizzera che avrebbero procurato all'Etiopia le prime armi moderne.

Quando, all'inizio degli anni '30, Mussolini autorizza la campagna di sovversione che ha lo scopo di sgretolare le istituzioni etiopiche in vista di una campagna militare, agenti italiani avvicinano un gran numero di capi abissini, tanto al centro dell'impero che alla periferia, con il proposito di corromperli, di neutralizzarli, indebolendo così il potere centrale e il nascente nazionalismo.[3] All' "offensiva dei talleri" non resistono notabili come lo stesso genero dell'imperatore, degiac Hailè Selassiè Gugsa, come l'ex governatore degli Azebò Galla, degiac Aberrà Tedla, come il figlio di ras Hailù, ligg Mammo e decine di capi minori.

Pur con la massima discrezione, anche ras Immirù viene avvicinato. Il contatto è stabilito a Debrà Marcòs, capitale del Goggiam, nel corso del 1934, da un giovanissimo diplomatico, il barone Filippo Muzi Falcone. Ma il tentativo fallisce. Ras Immirù accetta volentieri di misurarsi con il barone sul campo di tennis ed è particolarmente generoso nel contraccambiare i doni di sua moglie Marion; tuttavia, non soltanto non raccoglie le allusioni del console italiano, ma, pur colmandolo di cortesie, gli fa il vuoto intorno. In un rapporto del 20 ottobre ai suoi superiori, riconoscendo la sua assoluta impotenza dinanzi alla disarmante tattica del ras scioano, Muzi Falcone precisa che, fino a quando il Goggiam resterà alle sue dipendenze, ogni tentativo di infiltrazione e di sovversione si rivelerà inutile: "In lui ho trovato il primo abissino, fra tutti quelli con cui ho avuto a che fare, che sappia talvolta dire un 'no' sulla faccia, senza ricorrere ai soliti mezzucci dei 'ni' e degli 'isci naga'. Le questioni che lo fanno maggiormente imbestialire sono quelle in cui vede o crede di vedere dei tentativi di propaganda. 'Gli italiani — ebbe una volta a dirmi — sono peggio degli inglesi: dove entrano fanno come una macchia d'olio' ".[4]

Diverso è invece il comportamento del degiac Ajaleu Burrù, governatore dell'Amhara settentrionale e considerato in Etiopia come uno fra i più prestigiosi uomini di guerra. Anche se per ben tre volte egli ha dato, fra il 1916 e il 1930, il suo contributo determinante al successo di Hailè Selassiè contro i suoi avversari, Ajaleu Burrù non è riuscito ad ottenere dal negus il titolo di ras e il comando su più vasti territori, e ciò lo amareggia e lo rende particolarmente sensibile alle promesse degli agenti italiani. Circuito in un primo tempo dal console italiano a Gondar, Raffaele Di Lauro, il quale non perde occasione per ricordare al degiac la sua mancata promozione a ras[5], in un secondo momento, quasi alla vigilia del conflitto, viene colmato di lusinghe e indotto in tentazione dall'ex governatore dell'Eritrea, Jacopo Gasparini[6], il quale sa benissimo che, in caso di guerra con l'Italia, al degiac verrà affidata un'armata e che sarebbe oltremodo importante renderla in parte o del tutto inoffensiva.

Ma allo scoppio della guerra, forse per il suo contegno sospetto, Ajaleu Burrù non riceve dall'imperatore il comando di un'armata, ma viene sottoposto a ras Immirù, al quale è stato assegnato il compito di operare nello Scirè, all'estrema sinistra dello schieramento etiopica. Questo nuovo affronto costituisce probabilmente le goccia che fa traboccare il calice, che spinge l'esitante Ajaleu Burrù ad accantonare le ultime riserve e a prendere in seria considerazione l'ipotesi di cambiare di campo. E' in questo stato d'animo che il degiac autorizza il figlio Zeudè a prendere contatto con gli italiani, ad appena un mese dall'inizio della guerra e mentre il generale De Bono è fermo ad Adua e a Macallè. Di questo contatto, che evidentemente ritiene della massima importanza, De Bono informa Mussolini il 24 novembre 1935 con un telegramma "segreto assolutamente personale", nel quale precisa che "gli armati di Ajaleu sono sparsi ed il figlio assicura che non si riuniranno nè faranno atti di ostilità. Essi vorrebbero che noi fossimo più celeri, ma noi dobbiamo piegarci ad alcune imprescindibili necessità dovendo per ora muovere delle masse. La mia opinione è che se non faremo passi falsi e non avremo insuccessi bellici anche parziali potremo ritenerci tranquilli dal lato di Ajaleu Burrù".[7]

Gli accordi fra Ajaleu Burrù e gli italiani vengono perfezionati a fine novembre, quando un messo di Jacopo Gasparini, Mohamed Iman, raggiunge il campo del degiac nella regione dello Tzeghedè. In questa regione boschiva e ben protetta dall'osservazione aerea, Ajaleu Burrù sta ultimando, su pressione del negus e di ras Immirù, il concentramento dei suoi uomini, che ammontano a 30 mila uomini, ma sono, per sua stessa ammissione, in parte armati con vecchi fucili e in parte addirittura disarmati.[8] Al messo di Gasparini il governatore dell'Amhara settentrionale pone, per il suo passaggio nel campo italiano, queste precise condizioni: 1) la nomina a ras; 2) il comando sul Beghemeder e il Semien; 3) l'invio urgente di armi moderne, di munizioni e di talleri. In cambio, egli si impegna ad arrestare la marcia di ras Immirù, che sta per raggiungerlo con 12 mila uomini bene armati, ed a far insorgere contro il potere centrale il Goggiam e il Beghemeder. Ma c'è un'ultima condizione che il degiac pone ed è le più pesante. Non fidandosi, evidentemente, della parola di Gasparini e neppure di quella di Bagoglio, che nel frattempo è succeduto a De Bono nel comando delle operazioni, egli esige, "per essere sicuro", una lettera autografa dello stesso Mussolini.

Per quanto il documento richiesto da Ajaleu Burrù sia estremamente compromettente e non certo in armonia con la sicumera e le pose imperiali del duce, il 6 dicembre 1935 Mussolini accetta le condizioni poste dal degiac e gli invia questa lettera impegnativa: "Giunga al degiac Ajaleu Burrù. A lei salute. Sono contento che lei abbia in progetto di accordarsi col Governo d'Italia e che abbia manifestato tale suo progetto a S. E. Gasparini. Se ci accordiamo, ella, nominato Ras, riceverà oltre a tutto il suo attuale comando anche il comando del Beghemeder. Per tutto quanto si riferisce al nostro accordo ella accetti le parole di S. E. Gasparini come mie parole. Mussolini."[9] La lettera, affidata al solito messo di fiducia di Gasparini, non giungerà a destinazione che a fine dicembre, troppo tardi per impedire lo scontro fra gli uomini di Ajaleu Burrù, pungolati da quelli di Immirù, e le forze di invasione fasciste. Ma prima di soffermacci su questo scontro, che si conclude con una netta vittoria etiopica, dobbiamo fare un passo indietro ed occuparci di ras Immirù e della sua lunga marcia verso il fronte.

"Poco dopo l'inizio delle ostilità con l'Italia, — testimonia lo stesso ras Immirù — ricevetti l'ordine dall'imperatore di portami con i miei uomini nello Scirè e alle spalle di Adua. Il *chitet* aveva fruttato nel mio governatorato 25 mila uomini. Diecimila li aveva raccolti il degiac Ajaleu Burrù nei suoi domini e altri 5 mila alcuni capi minori. Potevo così contare su 40 mila uomini[10], ma il grosso delle forze, che aveva come base di partenza Debrà Marcòs e la regione del Tana, avrebbe dovuto compiere più di 500 chilometri per portarsi al fronte. Fu una marcia difficile ed estenuante, che durò settimane e settimane. Ai primi di dicembre, poco prima che raggiungessimo Dabàt, fummo sorpresi dagli aerei e sottoposti a un violentissimo bombardamento. Era la prima volta che ci accadeva e il trambusto fu tale che, quando tornò la calma, m'accorsi che il degiac Ghessessè Belau aveva fatto dietro-front ed era tornato con i suoi armati nel Goggiam. Non fu, del resto, la sola diserzione che dovetti lamentare; senza contare il fatto che non potei fare alcun affidamento sui diecimila uomini di Ajaleu Burrù, che sapevo in trattative con gli italiani per passare dalla loro parte e che nei consigli di guerra non portava che una nota di disfattismo. Cosicché, quando giunsi ai guadi del Tacazzè, potevo contare all'incirca su metà degli uomini con i quali ero partito."[11]

La situazione in cui ras Immirù si viene a trovare nella prima quindicina di dicembre, alla vigilia dello scontro di Dembeguinà, è ancora più grave di quanto il ras non riferisca nella sua testimonianza. Il degiac Ghessessè Belau e altri capi minori goggiamiti non si sono limitati a disertare, ma al loro ritorno nel Goggiam si porranno in stato di aperta ribellione, paralizzando le vie di rifornimento di Immirù e costringendo l'imperatore ad impiegare parte delle sue riserve per domare la rivolta.[12] Quanto al degiac Ajaleu Burrù, la sua condotta è talmente strana ed ambigua da suscitare sospetti anche in un uomo meno avveduto di ras Immirù. Nel memoriale che egli consegnerà a Gasparini il 13 maggio 1936, all'atto della sua "sotto missione", il governatore dell'Amhara settentrionale si vanterà di aver ostacolato in tutti i modi il suo superiore, sia marciando lentissimamente verso il fronte ("ho impiegato più giorni per fare la strada che poteva essere fatta in cinque ore"), sia impedendo ai suoi uomini, in qualche circostanza, di combattere.[13] Ma il tradimento è ancora più palese quando Ajaleu Burrù, su consiglio di Gasparini, indirizza ras Immirù ai guadi del Tacazzœ, dove gli apparecchi da bombardamento di Ajmone Cat sono pronti a rovesciare, nella stretta valle percorsa dal fiume, tonnellate di tritolo e di iprite. "I risultati delle ricognizioni aeree — telegrafa Badoglio a Mussolini, l'11 dicembre 1935 — stanno infatti provando che ras Immirù si mantiene sinora in detta direzione."[14]

Ma l'agguato al Tacazzè, almeno in un primo tempo, non avviene. Marciando nelle ore notturne ed eludendo così la sorveglianza aerea, le avanguardie di ras Immirù e del degiac Ajaleu

Burrù attraversano il fiume nella notte fra il 14 e il 15 dicembre e, senza rendersene ancora conto, danno inizio ad un'offensiva che valicherà anche le frontiere dell'Eritrea. I due contingenti che guadano il Tacazzè in due punti, a Mai Timchet e a Addi Aiticheb, sono costituiti da 2 mila uomini di Ajaleu Burrù e da 3 mila di ras Immirù: truppe regolari, queste ultime, che vestono una divisa cachi e sono dotate del miglior armamento (mitragliatrici pesanti, fucili *Mauser*, mitra di fabbricazione belga, bombe a mano). Esse non rappresentano soltanto il nerbo dell'armata di ras Immirù, ma hanno anche il compito di controllare le forze irregolari di Ajaleu Burrù, di spingerle al combattimento, di impedire nuove defezioni. E' per questo motivo che, suo malgrado, Ajaleu Burrù viene a trovarsi tra i vincitori di Dembeguinà.

Dopo aver guadato il Tacazzè e aver preso contatto con il Gruppo Bande del maggiore Luigi Criniti, che stava in osservazione sul fiume, i due contingenti etiopici costringono gli italo-eritrei a ritirarsi celermente, ma non tanto da riuscire a sfuggire ad una manovra di accerchiamento, che si conclude nella stretta di Dembeguinà. Qui, i mille ascari di Criniti, anche se appoggiati da uno squadrone di carri veloci al comando del capitano Crippa, vengono decimati, sommersi dagli abissini, che calano dalle alture ad ondate successive. Quando, a sera, il combattimento si spegne, sul campo sono rimasti, fra morti e feriti, 9 ufficiali e 22 soldati italiani e ben 370 ascari eritrei. Criniti è riuscito, con un assalto alla baionetta, a rompere l'accerchiamento, ma non ha portato con sé che 420 uomini, di cui 125 feriti in modo grave. Dei carri armati di Crippa non uno si è salvato, distrutti a colpi di pietra, sventrati con sbarre di ferro, da uomini che sino al giorno prima non avevano mai visto simili ordigni di guerra.[15]

Su questo inizio fortunato dell'offensiva etiopica nello Scirè, ascoltiamo le testimonianze di entrambe le parti. "Non fu soltanto importante perché riuscimmo a catturare 50 mitragliatrici e un forte quantitativo di fucili — sostiene ras Immirù — ma perché la rotta degli italiani fu tale che le nostre avanguardie, lanciate all'inseguimento, poterono occupare Endà Selassiè e più tardi Selaclacà. In pratica avevamo riconquistato, grazie a quel fatto d'arme, buona parte dello Scirè e stavamo incuneandoci alle spalle dello schieramento italiano."[16] Badoglio, che sul momento avverte tutta la pericolosità della mossa di ras Immirù, tanto da precipitarsi ad Axum due giorni dopo lo scontro e da cercare di addossare tutta la responsabilità dell'insuccesso sul generale Maravigna, un anno dopo i fatti, quando mette mano alle sue memorie e può a suo piacimento manipolare la storia della campagna africana, scrive: "Questo episodio . . . era di scarsa importanza se riferito al quadro generale della situazione; esso costituiva però sempre un nostro insuccesso che l'avversario, come era logico prevedere, aveva cercato di ingrandire. L'episodio avrebbe potuto, e perciò dovuto, essere evitato, qualora la stretta di Dembeguinà fosse stata occupata e l'impiego del Gruppo Bande fosse stato, conformemente al suo compito, limitato all'osservazione."[17]

A botta calda, la reazione di Mussolini è veemente, esasperata, furiosa. Come ricorda Lessona, il duce giunge persino a criticare aspramente l'opera di Badoglio in pieno Gran Consiglio e ventila l'ipotesi di una sua sostituzione.[18] In un telegramma a Badoglio, poi, parlando del fatto, precisa di averne ricavato "la più penosa impressione" e di giudicarlo come "un grave insuccesso, col quale gli etiopici hanno preso e conservato sino ad oggi l'iniziativa sulla nostra destra."[19] Quanto a De Bono, egli ringrazia il cielo di essere stato esonerato in tempo dall'incarico di comandante superiore in Africa e scrive nel suo diario segreto, alla data del 19 dicembre: "Lo scontro di Dembeguinà non è stato poca cosa. Badoglio ha chiesto 2 divisioni; gliele manderanno? Pare inviino le 2 libiche. Ma ci vorranno 15 giorni almeno prima che siano impiegabili. E in questi 15 giorni? O possono tenere le posizioni che hanno e allora le due divisioni sono inutili, o devono ritirarsi o modificare le posizioni per preparare la controffesa . . . . e allora è un affare serio."[20]

Oltre alla richiesta di due nuove divisioni per fronteggiare l'offensiva di ras Immirù, Badoglio chiede a Mussolini, che la concede, l'autorizzazione a fare largo impiego degli aggressivi chimici, che sino al dicembre erano stati usati soltanto in pochi casi, come deterrente o per "punizione". Dal 22 dicembre al 18 gennaio vengono lanciati, soltanto sul fronte nord, oltre 2 mila quintali di bombe, una parte rilevante delle quali caricate a gas. La zona più battuta è la valle del Tacazzè, con i suoi guadi, luoghi obbligati di transito per le truppe di ras Immirù, che soltanto il 25 dicembre si saranno trasferite tutte sulla riva destra del fiume ad alimentare l'offensiva. Battuto sul campo, ad armi regolari, Badoglio cerca ora nell'iprite, un'arma proibita dalle convenzioni internazionali, lo strumento micidiale per arrestare l'avanzata delle "orde abissine". E l'iprite, in effetti, almeno nei primi tempi, gioca un ruolo importante, anche se non decisivo.

Sugli effetti del solfuro di etile biclorurato, uno dei gas tossici più letali perché provoca rapidamente la necrosi del protoplasma cellulare, abbiamo la testimonianza dello stesso ras Immirù: "Fu uno spettacolo terrificante. Io stesso sfuggii per un caso alla morte. Era la mattina del 23 dicembre, avevo da poco attraversato il Tacazzè, quando comparvero nel cielo alcuni aeroplani. Il fatto, tuttavia, non ci allarmò troppo, perché ormai ci eravamo abituati ai bombardamenti. Quel mattino, però, non lanciarono bombe, ma strani fusti che si rompevano, appena toccavano il suolo o l'acqua del fiume, e proiettavano intorno un liquido incolore. Prima che mi rendessi conto di ciò che stava accadendo, alcune centinaia fra i miei uomini erano rimasti colpiti dal misterioso liquido e urlavano per il dolore, mentre i loro piedi nudi, le loro mani, i loro volti si coprivano di vesciche. Altri, che si erano dissetati al fiume, si contorcevano a terra in un'agonia che durò ore. Fra i colpiti c'erano anche dei contadini che avevano portato le mandrie al fiume, e gente dei villaggi vicini. I miei sottocapi, intanto, mi avevano circondato e mi chiedevano consiglio, ma io ero stordito, non sapevo che cosa rispondere, non sapevo come combattere questa pioggia che bruciava e uccideva."[21]

Nonostante l'iprite, il grosso dell'armata di ras Immirù riesce a valicare il fiume e va a rafforzare le avanguardie che intanto, dopo lo scontro di Dembeguinà, hanno espugnato il passo di Af Gagà, costretto la divisione Gran Sasso a ritirarsi da Selaclacà ed ora premono sul campo trincerato di Adua-Axum. Badoglio cerca allora di rendere la zona compresa fra Selaclacà e il Tacazzè una terra bruciata intensificando il lancio dell'iprite e delle bombe incendiarie. Di questa azione e dei suoi effetti avvisa Lessona con un telegramma del 9 gennaio, che dice: "Impiego iprite si è dimostrato molto efficace, specie verso la zona del Tacazzè. Circolano voci di terrore per effetti del gas."[22] Cinque giorni dopo, in un dispaccio diretto a Gasparini, che è a Tessenei, Badoglio scrive: "Prego avvertire noto personaggio (Ajaleu Burrù) che fra qualche giorno avverrà un inaudito bombardamento nella zona a nord del Tacazzè; pertanto egli si sposti a sud del Tacazzè con tutta la sua gente per non essere danneggiato."[23] In un altro telegramma, sempre diretto a Gasparini, Badoglio precisa: "A giorni farò un'emissione di gas che avvelenerà tutto fino al Tacazzè."[24]

E' in queste settimane, tra la fine di dicembre del 1935 e i primi de marzo del 1936, che ras Immirù rivela tutte le sue qualità di stratega, di organizzatore, di mediatore. Egli non soltanto riesce a tenere insieme un esercito assai poco amalgamato e in parte anche malfido per il tradimento di Ajaleu Burrù, ma è in grado di portarlo al combattimento e di mietere successi. E se Badoglio ha fatto dello Scirè una terra bruciata, ras Immirù si rifornisce più lontano, in regioni non ancora contaminate dall'iprite, facendo muovere le carovane soltanto di notte e su nuove piste che, con molta lungimiranza, ha fatto costruire. Il ras è anche il solo, fra i comandanti d'armata etiopici, ad organizzare un efficiente servizio di informazioni. Grazie soprattutto al clero di Axum, Immirù viene a conoscere l'esatta composizione, dislocazione e armamento del II corpo d'armata di Maravigna, che per due mesi, stretto nella morsa etiopica, non riuscirà a prendere alcuna iniziativa limitandosi a rinsaldare le fortificazioni del campo trincerato di Adua-Axum. Ma gli informatori di Immirù non sono soltanto ad Axum, ma nella stessa Eritrea, da dove partono tutti i rifornimenti diretti al fronte e dove sono dislocati gli immensi depositi che debbono alimentare il più grande esercito coloniale che la storia ricordi.

Non soddisfatto di aver rioccupato quasi tutto lo Scirè, in base alle informazioni raccolte, ras Immirù tenta una manovra ancora più audace, quella di invadere, attraverso l'inospitale Adi Abò e le valli dell'Obel e del Rubà Catinà, la stessa Eritrea, non con l'ambizione di occupare Asmara, ma con quella più modesta di portare il subbuglio nelle retrovie italiane attaccando i depositi e le colonne di rifornimento. Per queste azioni, egli adotta la tattica della guerriglia, costituendo reparti mobilissimi di non più di 4-500 uomini, i quali riescono ad infiltrarsi fra le maglie della linea di protezione del confine, che Badoglio di è affrettato a costituire, con due intere divisioni, la Cosseria e la 1e Febbraio, non appena ha intuito il disegno di ras Immirù di aggirare il fianco destro dello schieramento italiano.

Per circa due mesi, poche migliaia di etiopici al comando del degiac Mesfin e dei fitaurari Chidanè Marian, Melaù, Tesfai e Chenfè, tengono in continuo allarme e paralizzano le due divisioni italiane schierate nel Dechi Tesfà, passando e ripassando il Mareb, risalendo le valli dei torrenti Obel e Catinà fino alle posizioni delle camicie nere, oppure portandosi alle spalle di Adua per intercettare i convogli che provengono da Addi Qualà. Per fare qualche esempio, il 13 febbraio attaccano il cantiere della Gondrand, a Mai Lalhà, e lo distruggono uccidendo 85 operai italiani. Il 20 febbraio sorprendono nell'alto Adi Abò alcuni reparti del XXVII battaglione eritreo e li annientano con i loro ufficiali italiani. Due giorni dopo penetrano per una trentina di chilometri in Eritrea e attaccano il deposito di munizioni di Mai Scium facendo saltare in aria 5 mila proiettili da artiglieria e decine di migliaia di cartucce per armi portatili.

Su queste azioni di guerriglia, specie su quelle condotte in territorio eritreo, Badoglio ordina che sia tenuto il più rigoroso silenzio, perché non si vuole assolutamente ammettere che gli etiopici sono in grado di portare la guerra in Eritrea. Grande pubblicità viene invece data all'attacco al cantiere della Gondrand a Mai Lahlà, sia perché il numero dei morti italiani è troppo alto perché il fatto possa essere tenuto nascosto, sia perché l'episodio, con l'uccisione di operai e persino di una donna, si presta benissimo a riproporre al mondo l'immagine di un'Etiopia barbara e sanguinaria.[25] Nel riferire l'episodio, corredandolo di "immagini raccapriccianti", tuttavia, la stampa italiana si guarda bene dal riferire questi particolari: 1) gli operai italiani erano in parte armati ed erano comunque militarizzati; 2) l'organizzazione di sicurezza era scadentissima, nonostante che il cantiere fosse in zona di operazioni; 3) la donna uccisa, moglie dell'ingegner Rocca, capo del cantiere, si trovava abusivamente a Mai Lahlà; 4) le repressioni, dopo l'eccidio, furono tali e indiscriminate da sollevare le proteste dello stesso capo dell'ufficio politico del II corpo d'armata, Alberto Pollera, il quale avvertiva i suoi superiori che la reazione degli operai e soldati italiani perdurava "con esplosioni di brutale, ingiustificata violenza", "malgrado le severe misure prese dall'autorità militare".[26]

Nel luglio del 1936, a guerra finita, il comandante etiopico del fronte nord, ras Cassa Hailù, respingerà le accuse italiane di atrocità e preciserà, dopo aver elencato alcuni episodi di generosità degli etiopici: "Si preferiva citare i casi eccezionali di alcuni nostri soldati, le cui mogli e figli erano stati atrocemente ustionati dai gas, che si erano vendicati dei loro selvaggi aggressori massacrando un campo di operai tra il Mareb e Darò Taclè. Si è presentato questo episodio come un vile attacco a civili senza difesa . . . Per quanto ingaggiati da un'impresa privata, questi operai erano equiparati ai soldati del genio; essi costruivano strade che conducevano nella nostra patria i cannoni e i rifornimenti dell'aggressore".[27] Ras Immirù, dal canto suo, sarà ancora più esplicito, assumendosi l'intera responsabilità dell'episodio: "Ho dato io stesso al fitaurari Tesfai l'ordine di attaccare il campo di Mai Lahlà. Lo ritenevo e lo ritengo ancora un atto legittimo di guerra, perché gli operai erano in zona di operazioni ed erano armati di moschetto. Infatti essi si difesero accanitamente infliggendoci dure perdite. Cosa che non potevano certo fare le nostre popolazioni, quando venivano attaccate e decimate dall'aviazione fascista".[28]

Mentre ras Immirù, come lo stesso Mussolini riconosce, continua a mantenere l'iniziativa nello Scirè, sugli altri fronti le cose si mettono male per gli etiopici. Ras Mulughetà è stato battuto sull'Amba Aradam e lungo la ritirata ha perso anche la vita. Ras Cassa e ras Sejum, che avevano sfiorato la vittoria nel Tembien, in una successiva battaglia sono stati sbaragliati e costretti alla fuga. Quanto a ras Destà, fallita la sua offensiva su Dolo, ha perso quasi tutti i suoi uomini nella tragica ritirata su Neghelli. Di questi fatti ras Immirù ha notizie imprecise, perché non possiede alcuna stazione ricetrasmittente e deve servirsi soltanto dei corrieri a cavallo. Negli ultimi giorni di febbraio, comunque, egli riceve una lettera dell'imperatore, che lo invita ad abbandonare lo Scirè e a ripiegare sull'Amba Alagi, perché egli prevede che gli italiani cercheranno di isolarlo e di prenderlo in trappola. Questo timore, del resto, è condiviso anche da ras Immirù, il quale si è accorto, grazie alla sua rete di informatori, che non deve soltanto fronteggiare il II corpo d'armata di Maravigna, ma presto anche il IV corpo d'armata di Babbini, che ha lasciato il Dechi Tesfà e seppure lentamente, attraverso la regione desertica dell'Adi Abò, sta avanzando per minacciare il fianco sinistro dello schieramento etiopico.

Avendo subito chiara la visione della manovra a tenaglia ideata da Badoglio, ras Immirù decide perciò di ripiegare sul Tacazzè. Ma per evitare che la ritirata si trasformi in un disastro, a causa soprattutto dei martellamenti aerei, decide di compiere lo sganciamento in due tempi. Mentre forti contingenti di truppe regolari resteranno di copertura sulle alture fortificate di Adi Haimanal, di Coietzà, di Af Gagà, e impegneranno il II corpo d'armata, se Maravigna si deciderà ad attaccare, il grosso dell'esercito, con le salmerie e le donne, si ritirerà in buon ordine verso i guadi del Tacazzè, muovendosi di notte e seguendo le piste meno esposte all'osservazione aerea.

Badoglio non sospetta minimamente che ras Immirù abbia intuito il suo piano e che già abbia predisposto ogni cosa per limitare i danni della ritirata. Ammette, anzi, di avere scarse informazioni sull'avversario e scrive: "Incerte e contraddittorie erano le notizie sulla forza complessiva di tale armata: secondo taluni aveva mantenuto a numero i 50,000 uomini con i quali risultava avesse passato nel mese di dicembre il Tacazzè, secondo altri superava di poco i 25,000. Concordi erano invece le informazioni che segnalavano le non buone condizioni morali e materiali della massa avversaria, e la ripercussione che la notizia della vittoria da noi conseguita nell'Endertà aveva avuto, scuotendo la fiducia nel successo finale. Sembrava inoltre vi fosse un latente conflitto tra i due comandanti, non soltanto dovuto a rivalità di comando, ma anche al contegno del degiac Ajaleu Burrù, il quale aveva, in alcune circostanze, dimostrato di non essere alieno dal sottomettersi al nostro governo."[29]

Incerto sul numero degli avversari ed avendo anche ormai perso la speranza in una defezione di Ajaleu Burrù[30], Badoglio decide di giocare la partita gettando nella battaglia dello Scirè due interi corpi d'armata, cioè 47 mila uomini, più tutta l'artiglieria disponibile, comprese alcune batterie da 149 che hanno già fatto un eccellente lavoro arando profondamente i fianchi dell'Amba Aradam. L'attacco viene lanciato all'alba del 29 febbraio dai 30 mila uomini di Maravigna, mentre i 17 mila di Babbini proseguono la loro marcia attraverso l'Adi Abò per realizzare la manovra a tenaglia. Ma l'azione non si svolge come Badoglio aveva previsto. Babbini, per cominciare, procede troppo lentamente e giungerà sul campo di battaglia ad operazioni concluse, pur avendo determinato, con la sua minaccia a distanza, il ripiegamento degli etiopici. Il secondo contrattempo è causato dagli uomini di ras Immirù, che si battono splendidamente, prendendo spesso l'iniziativa, come riconosce anche Badoglio: "All'altezza delle alture dell'Haimanal, (la Gavinana) veniva improvvisamente attaccata da forti nuclei nemici, valutati ad alcune migliaia di uomini che, insinuatisi attraverso il terreno rotto e coperto, le cagionavano gravi perdite, e cercavano di avvolgerla".[31] E ancora: "Il nemico opponeva, fra le 13 e le 17, tenacissima resistenza e tentava, in forze, un contrattacco condotto da regolari, appoggiati da numerose armi automatiche".[32]

Con appena 10-12 mila uomini, senza artiglierie e senza aviazione, ras Immirù tiene a bada per tre giorni un avversario numericamente tre volte superiore e capace di un volume di fuoco infernale se si considera che, durante lo scontro, le artiglierie hanno sparato più di 21 mila colpi, che sono state lanciate 148 mila bombe a mano e consumato più di un milione di proiettili per fucile e armi automatiche, senza contare il concorso dei carri armati e dei reparti lanciafiamme e il lancio, da parte dell'aviazione, di 247 quintali di bombe.[33] Smentendo Badoglio, che, come abbiamo visto, ha definito gli etiopici "in non buone condizioni morali e materiali", il comandante della Gran Sasso, generale Adalberto di Savoia-Genova, scrive al contrario: "La tenacia con cui gli armati del ras Immirù resistettero per tre giorni e la violenza dei contrattacchi, dimostrarono come quegli Amhara fossero particolarmente agguerriti nello spirito, perché l'abissino combatte generalmente una sola giornata, in capo alla quale o ha vinto o si considera vinto".[34] Dal canto suo il tenente Paolo Cesarini, che nel combattimento perde una gamba, riferisce: "Ritengo che quella dello Scirè sia stata la battaglia più dura, proprio per le qualità strategiche di ras Immirù e per la tenacia dei suoi uomini. Egli ci inflisse le perdite più alte subite in una battaglia: fra morti e feriti 63 ufficiali, 894 italiani e 12 eritrei".[35]

Ed è soltanto nelle ultime ore del 2 marzo che gli italiani si accorgono che ras Immirù li ha beffati. "Nonostante gli sforzi sovrumani degli ufficiali e delle truppe — riconosce il colonnello Dino Pollacci della Gavinana — gli obiettivi non sono stati raggiunti e ci appare sempre più certa l'ipotesi che ras Immirù abbia lasciato ad ostacolarci un'adeguata aliquota con compiti di retroguardia, e stia riparando ordinatamente col grosso e con le impedimenta a sud del Tacazzè".[36] All'alba del 3 marzo, infatti, non soltanto non scatta la manovra a tenaglia, perché Babbini è ancora a tre giorni di marcia dal luogo dei combattimenti, ma il II corpo d'armata di Maravigna, quando si rimette in movimento, dopo un'intensa preparazione d'artiglieria, si trova dinanzi il vuoto assoluto. "Immirù aveva manovrato bene." – ammette Giovanni Artieri, con un atto di cavalleria, abbastanza raro negli anni del ventennio – "Occorre rendere giustizia a questo generale, sbaragliato come gli altri, ma dimostratosi intenditore di guerre."[37] E Luca dei Sabelli è ancora più circostanziato nel riconoscimento: "Alle mosse dei nostri, ras Immirù oppose una resistenza che, per la prima volta dall'andamento della campagna, era ispirata a un abile concetto operativo. Egli scaglionò, sul percorso delle nostre truppe, delle forti avanguardie, dietro le quali tenne in mano il resto delle forze controllandone abilmente l'impiego".[38]

Anche se ras Immirù è riuscito ad imporre la sua volontà e la sua bravura dalle prime fucilate del 29 febbraio alle ultime del 2 marzo, il costo dell'operazione, per gli etiopici, è però altissimo. "Perdite del nemico accertate sul campo, circa 4000" – riferisce Badoglio – "a queste devono aggiungersi quelle inflitte dall'aviazione durante l'inseguimento, valutate complessivamente ad oltre 3000."[39] Per vendicarsi della mancata vittoria sull'avversario e non essendo ormai più in grado di riagganciarlo con le stanche e provate divisioni di Maravigna, il maresciallo Badoglio lancia infatti 120 caccia e bombardieri all'inseguimento degli armati di ras Immirù, che sono già giunti ai guadi del Tacazzè e hanno ormai a portata di mano il sicuro labirinto montuoso dello Tsellemtì, e li tempesta con 636 quintali di esplosivo e di iprite, completando l'opera con bombe incendiarie, che trasformano in un solo rogo i fianchi boschivi della valle del Tacazzè "rendendo quanto mai tragica" – precisa Badoglio – "la situazione del nemico in fuga".[40]

"Riuscii a condurre in salvo, al di là del fiume, circa diecimila uomini" – racconta ras Immirù – "ma essi erano talmente scossi e demoralizzati che non fui più in grado di tenerli insieme. Era mia intenzione organizzare la guerriglia fra i monti dello Tsellemtì e del Semien, che si prestano meravigliosamente allo scopo, ma quando ne parlai con il degiac Ajaleu Burrù, che era uno dei pochi capi che fossero rimasti in vita, non ne volle sapere e decise di ritirarsi con i suoi uomini e con quelli del fratello Admasù più indietro, nel Beghemeder. Ogni giorno che passava dovevo lamentare nuove perdite, provocate sia dalle incursioni aeree che dalle diserzioni. Cosicché quando giunsi ai piedi del Ras Dascian, non mi restavano che trecento uomini, la mia guardia del corpo."[41] Le massicce diserzioni sono anche provocate da un altro fatto, che ci viene riferito da Hailè Selassiè: "Gli italiani cominciarono ad inviare, settimana dopo settimana, un gran numero di apparecchi che colpirono, con bombe incendiarie, capoluoghi di provincia come Dabàt nel Semien, Gondar nel Beghemeder, Debrà Marcòs nel Goggiam. Quando i soldati originari di queste regioni appresero il fatto, si lasciarono cogliere dal panico, non furono più in grado di restare al fronte e alla spicciolata ritornarono alle loro case."[42]

Anche nel resto dell'impero, del resto, la resistenza è ormai alla fine. A difendere gli accessi alla capitale è rimasto soltanto l'imperatore con 31 mila uomini e poche speranze. Il 23 marzo, una settimana prima di impegnarsi nello scontro finale e sfortunato di Mai Ceu, Hailè Selassiè scrive una lunga lettera a ras Immirù nella quale fa una sintesi degli ultimi avvenimenti: "Come avrete certamente inteso, un esercito così numeroso che aveva già respinto e intimidito il nemico riuscendo a riconquistare Macallè, s'è disfatto senza che avesse subìto gravi perdite e senza avere affatto tentato di resistere. E questa è una cosa che fa dolore. Il nostro esercito, famoso per tutta l'Europa per il suo valore, ha perduto il suo nome; condotto alla rovina da alcuni traditori s'è ridotto così." Poi, dopo aver precisato che "il ras Cassa e il ras Sejum sono con noi, ma non hanno con loro alcun armato", il negus esorta Immirù ad agire, se gli è possibile, nel suo settore, oppure a trasferirsi a Mai Ceu "per morire insieme a noi".[43]

Ma la lettera imperiale non giungerà mai a destinazione poiché cadrà nelle mani di Badoglio. Quanto a ras Immirù, egli prosegue il suo ripiegamento muovendosi soltanto di notte perché l'aviazione italiana lo tallona con implacabile costanza. "Avevo urgenza di mettermi in contatto con l'imperatore" – racconta il ras – "e puntai su Dabàt, dove c'era il telefono, ma stavo avvicinandomi alla città quando appresi che gli italiani erano alle sue porte. Allora decisi di proseguire per Gondar, ma anche questa città era stata occupata e poco mancò non cadessi prigioniero."[44] La diserzione di Ajaleu Burrù e di altri capi minori ha infatti consentito alla colonna Starace di raggiungere Gondar senza sparare un solo colpo di fucile. Ma il tradimento di Ajaleu Burrù non verrà premiato, perché, come precisa Badoglio in una lettera a Gasparini, il degiac ha troppo tergiversato e i suoi soldati "ci strenuamente combatto sul Tacazzè e in Scirè".[45]

Sfuggendo alla colonna guidata da Achille Starace, il segretario del partito fascista, ras Immirù arriva il 2 aprile a Dankaz, a sud di Gondar, da dove riparte cinque giorni dopo. "Non mi restava che raggiungere Debrà Marcòs" — continua a narrare ras Immirù — "ma quando vi arrivai, dopo più di un mese di marcia e dopo aver sostenuto alcuni scontri con bande di ribelli pagate e armate dagli italiani, appresi che l'imperatore era andato a Gibuti e che Addis Abeba stava per cadere. Allora radunai un po' di uomini e mi preparai alla guerriglia".[46] Il governatore del Goggiam lascia Debrà Marcòs verso la metà di maggio, allorché apprende che, dopo la caduta di Addis Abeba, è stato costituito un governo provisorio nella lontana Gore, capoluogo dell'Ilù Babor, e che a presiederlo è stato designato il presidente del Senato, il vecchio degiac Uolde Tzadek.[47] Con appena 500 uomini, ed affrontando una nuova marcia di settecento chilometri, ras Immirù raggiunge Gore, dove si sono rifugiati gli uomini più compromessi con il regime del negus, molti disertori eritrei e parte degli allievi ufficiali della scuola di Oletta. "Questi ultimi" — ricorda ras Immirù — "erano impazienti, volevano a tutti i costi battersi, ma io che avevo ormai una lunga esperienza di guerra contro gli italiani, ritenevo che fosse una follia e che fosse preferibile sconfinare nel Sudan per attendervi tempi migliori. Anche perché a Gore, per quanto fossimo, attraverso Gambela, in comunicazione con il mondo esterno e persino con Londra, continuavamo a non ricevere aiuti e nemmeno le munizioni indispensabili per continuare la lotta".[48]

Tanto ras Immirù che il degiac Uolde Tzadek sono inoltre persuasi che non œ possibile preparare una controffensiva partendo da Gore, una regione abitata da Galla e perciò completamente ostile, ed informano l'imperatore, che si è rifugiato in Gran Bretagna, che ogni tentativo di rivincita è destinato al fallimento. Ma Hailè Selassiè, nonostante che la Società delle Nazioni lo abbia abbandonato al suo destino e l'Inghilterra si limiti a concedergli un'avara ospitalità, preme per un'ulteriore resistenza e chiede al cugino un nuovo sforzo: impedire agli italiani l'avanzata nelle regioni dell'Ovest e, se sarà possibile, in un secondo tempo marciare su Addis Abeba.

Pur con la morte nell'anima, perché sa perfettamente che la sua missione è votata alla catastrofe, ras Immirù si accinge a preparare la spedizione e a metà ottobre emana un proclama, che dice: "Chiamati da molte migliaia di voci per la libertà dell'Etiopia a marciare su Addis Abeba, io da Lechemti, il bituodded Uolde Tzadek da Bunnò e il degiac Tayè Gululatiè da Gimma, dobbiamo marciare aiutandoci a vicenda. Voi che verrete, ricordando la libertà della nostra madrepatria, sarete accolti con gioia. Questa spedizione non è obbligatoria ma volontaria, da fratelli, e non sembra che forze nemiche possano arrestarci".[49] Non raccoglie che 1200 volontari. E il 10 novembre, prima di lasciare per sempre Gore, invia ad Hailè Selassiè l'ultimo suo messaggio: "Abbiamo disposto di metterci in marcia per unirci alla nostra gente che ci attende e per difenderci dal nemico".[50] Dal suo esilio di Bath, l'imperatore gli invia un telegramma, che ha il tono biblico di altri suoi messaggi: "Colui che vede la sua Patria nelle mani del nemico è condannato ad essere afflitto per tutta la sua vita. Sono addolorato che in questa ora non mi trovi tra di voi. Che Iddio vi assista dal cadere in mani del nemico".[51]

Con la partenza di ras Immirù, si chiude anche l'esistenza dell'effimero governo provvisorio di Gore, che ha turbato il trionfo di Mussolini e reso inquieto il viceré Graziani. Ras Immirù si pone in movimento proprio mentre Graziani, liquidata la guerriglia intorno ad Addis Abeba, ha tutte le forze disponibili per accingersi alla conquista dell'Ovest. Il momento è perciò particolarmente sfavorevole, poiché il ras si trova a combattere contemporaneamente gli italiani e le popolazioni galla che hanno fatto causa comune con essi. Pur essendo stato più volte aggredito dai galla, ras Immirù non dispera di poterli ricondurre alla ragione e perciò diffonde un proclama che dice: "O popoli dell'Uollega e del Liecà! Gli italiani che, contro il diritto, hanno ucciso i nostri soldati col veleno e con le bombe, sono forse venuti ora per guardarvi col cuore commosso, per farvi vivere tranquilli? Lo credete voi? Che gli italiani non abbiano cuore, ve l'hanno già detto i nostri fratelli che andarono in guerra. Se gli italiani avessero un cuore buono e sapessero governare, non avrebbero dovuto combattere per 25 anni a Tripoli. Se credete che essi vi lasceranno vivere sui vostri terreni e che non li prenderanno con la forza, domandatelo ai vostri fratelli eritrei. Di fronte al pericolo di morte li hanno mandati avanti, ma non li hanno resi partecipi dei loro onori. Gli italiani ci vogliono togliere il paese che i nostri avi resero prospero. Cercano ogni pretesto per sterminarci".[52]

Ma i galla sono stati sottomessi dagli scioani da troppo poco tempo per aver acquisito un patriottismo etiopico. Gli appelli cadono perciò nel vuoto e ras Immirù, vistasi preclusa la strada di Lechemti, inverte la marcia e si dirige verso il Caffa nella speranza di unirsi alle forze del degiac Tayè Gululatiè. "Tra novembre e dicembre" — ricorda il ras — "ci scontrammo più volte con gli italiani nella regione dell'Uollega, ma dopo ogni combattimento le nostre riserve di proiettili diminuivano paurosamente. Spinto lontano da Gore, con una buona parte dei miei uomini che aveva contratto la malaria nelle zone paludose, decisi di spostarmi verso Gimma per poi raggiungere Magi e la frontiera con il Sudan. Ma gli italiani mi avevano già tagliato la strada e fui costretto, combattendo di continuo, a tornare sui miei passi".[53] Battuto il 12 dicembre 1936 dalla colonna Princivalle, quattro giorni dopo deve arrendersi al colonnello Malta, quando si scopre in trappola, stretto fra gli italiani e il fiume Gogeb in piena. Il giornalista Vittorio Gorresio che lo incontra poche ore dopo la cattura, così lo descrive: "Sotto il tendone della mensa di Bonga l'atmosfera era piuttosto cavalleresca e lo sconfitto Immirù, piccolino, minuto, il volto tondo incorniciato da capelli crespi e da una breve barba, lo sguardo quieto, non mancava di qualche regalità".[54]

Nonostante che Mussolini abbia disposto che ogni capo etiopico ribelle venga immediatamente passato per le armi dopo la cattura, in questa circostanza Graziani fa di testa sua e non applica, nei confronti di ras Immirù, le "misure di rigore", sia per il modo con il quale il ras si è arreso, sia perché, spiega a Lessona, la sua esecuzione sommaria avrebbe una ripercussione sfavorevole proprio mentre sono in corso le trattative per la resa di un altro capo ribelle, ras Destà Damtèu.[55] A Roma, però, c'è qualche incertezza sulla sorte da riservare al miglior generale di Hailè Selassiè. Molti non hanno dimenticato la giornata nera di Dembeguinà, l'eccidio del cantiere Gondrand, le puntate offensive in Eritrea, l'altissimo costo in vite umane della battaglia dello Scirè e per ultima la sfida dalla lontana Gore, e vorrebbero che ras Immirù pagasse. La sentenza, comunque, la pronuncia di lì a qualche giorno Mussolini: "Ras Immirù dovrà essere considerato prigioniero di guerra e in tale condizione trasferito appena possibile ad Addis Abeba, indi in Italia, ove sarà confinato a vita".[56]

In Italia ras Immirù ci va con il piroscafo "Colombo", carico di truppe che rientrano in patria. Spesso lo lasciano salire sul ponte, in compagnia di altri capi minori, che cercano di proteggerlo dagli obiettivi e dagli sguardi indiscreti. "Quando arrivammo a Napoli, ai primi di gennaio del 1937" — racconta il ras — "c'era il Principe di Piemonte ad attendere i soldati. Noi restammo chiusi in cabina fintantoché durò la cerimonia. Poi salì a bordo un ufficiale, il quale mi lesse una lettera di Mussolini, con la quale mi comunicava che sarei stato confinato nell'isola di Ponza. L'indomani, infatti, accompagnato da un colonnello dei carabinieri, fui imbarcato su di una motovedetta militare e trasferito a Ponza, già gremita di detenuti politici italiani e nella quale mi avrebbero raggiunto, nei mesi successivi, molti altri capi etiopici".[57]

A Ponza ras Immirù vive in una casetta bassa, nella quale, per l'ironia del destino, sette anni dopo andrà ad alloggiare Mussolini, prigioniero di Badoglio, che gli aveva regalato l'impero, e che lui aveva colmato di titoli e di onori. Lo trattano con molti riguardi, specialmente il "commissario Salvadore", di cui il ras serba un gradito ricordo.[58] Anche il direttore della colonia penale va spesso a fargli visita, con il preciso incarico, affidatogli da Mussolini, di convincerlo a dichiararsi formalmente "sottomesso". Se ras Immirù rilasciasse una dichiarazione pubblica in questo senso, con molta probabilità potrebbe ritornare in patria, come è già accaduto a ras Sejum e a tantri altri. Ma il ras non si piega. E un giorno, al suo interlocutore, pone con fermezza questo quesito: "Ma che giudizio dareste voi di un italiano che durante il Risorgimento avesse fatto atto di sottomissione all'Austria?".[59]

A Ponza ras Immirù rimane sino al 1939. Dalle lettere che il suo segretario, il futuro ministro Ilma Deressa, scrive alla moglie Cheddest, sappiamo che la vita nell'isola, per i confinati etiopici, scorre lenta, monotona, tristissima. Non è il clima che li disturba ("Qui non fa molto freddo;" — scrive Ilma Deressa — "anche durante l'inverno non fa più freddo che ad Addis Abeba") e neppure le restrizioni e il cibo diverso. Ciò che li riempie di angoscia è la lontananza dalla loro terra e dai loro famigliari, il filtro severo della censura militare che impedisce loro di capire che cosa accade nel lontano impero.

Alla fine del 1939 ras Immirù viene trasferito a Lipari, dove trascorre altri tre anni di confino, più o meno nelle stesse condizioni di vita che a Ponza. Poi, nel 1942, l'ultimo trasferimento, a Longobucco, un grosso paese di montagna calabro, tra la Sila Greca e la Sila Grande. Qui gli è concessa una maggior libertà, forse perché la guerra sta andando molto male per l'Italia ed in Etiopia, invece, è tornato Hailè Selassiè e nelle sue mani ci sono decine di migliaia di ostaggi italiani. Gli è consentito di tenere una radio, di muoversi per il paese, di avvicinare la gente. Così, per la prima volta, ha modo di conoscere gli italiani. E scopre che, anche se hanno vinto l'Etiopia e l'hanno sottomessa per cinque anni, essi sono poveri e infelici come gli etiopici, contadini senza terre come gli etiopici. E' forse a Longobucco, osservando una realtà tanto simile a quella del suo paese, che l'aristocratico scioano, il cugino e confidente di un imperatore per designazione divina, comincia a rivedere la propria scala dei valori ed a maturare quei cambiamenti che lo porteranno, dieci anni dopo, a regalare le sue terre ai contadini e a fare pressioni su Hailè Sellassiè perché imbocchi la via delle vere riforme.

"La mia prigionia finì nell'autunno del 1943, quando gli Alleati sbarcarono in Calabria" — racconta ras Immirù — "Scrissi una lettera ad Eisenhower, segnalando la mia presenza a Longobucco, e due settimane dopo vennero due ufficiali inglesi a prelevarmi. Fui condotto a Bari e poi, con un aereo, al Cairo ed infine ad Addis Abeba. Il mio confino, in tutto, era durato sette anni e non tutta la vita, come aveva decretato Mussolini."[61]

Quando l'incontriamo noi, il 13 aprile 1965, nella sua modesta casa di Addis Abeba, in cima ad una collina nel quartiere di Arada, ras Immirù ha ormai 73 anni. E' un uomo di bassa statura, con il viso tondo e bonario, a raggiera, come quelli di Einstein. Quando ci riceve, nella sua stanza di lavoro, dopo aver preso congedo dall'Abuna, indossa un doppiopetto color fumo di Londra e sulla camicia candida porta una cravatta nera. Gli italiani che lo hanno visto dipingere come un tiranno avido e crudele da Achille Starace, faticherebbero molto a riconoscerlo in questo personaggio compito, garbato e sereno, che vive ormai nella leggenda. Ha accettato di rispondere alle nostre domande sulla parte che ha avuto nel conflitto italo-etiopico, e lo fa con una modestia che incanta e con una precisione che stupisce. Quattro ore di racconto e poi, alla fine: "Ci siamo piegati davanti ai carri armati, agli aeroplani, ai gas. Non avevamo scampo. Ma è acqua passata. Oggi è tornato il sereno. Vede, gli italiani sono qui e sono i nostri amici".[62]

Oggi ras Immirù Haile Sellase riposa nella chiesa della Trinità, in Addis Abeba, dove sono sepolti altri capi storici della resistenza etiopica al fascismo ed anche Sylvia Pankhurst, l'intellettuale inglese che spese tanta parte della sua esistenza per difendere la causa dell'Etiopia. E' il solo aristocratico che sia passato indenne attraverso la bufera della rivoluzione del 1974[63]; il solo che abbia ricevuto, alla sua morte, avvenuta il 18 agosto 1980, gli onori militari. Ha scritto *The Ethiopian Herald* il giorno dei funerali: "Egli ha vissuto una vita straordinaria di amministratore, di giudice, di combattente per la libertà, di ambasciatore al servizio del suo popolo. Era anche conosciuto per la sua partecipazione alle sofferenze dei più umili e per aver fatto del suo meglio per migliorare il loro stato." I famigliari avrebbero voluto che sulla tomba ci fosse un busto del congiunto e ci incaricarono di trovare in Italia uno scultore di fama disposto a farlo. Ma gli scultori interpellati chiesero cifre impossibili. Il fatto che ras Immirù avesse donato tutto il suo ai poveri non li toccava.

NOTE

1. Haile Sellasie I, *My life and Ethiopia's progress, 1892-1937*, (London: Oxford University Press, 1976), p.15.

2. *Ivi*, p.180. In precedenza, ras Immirù era stato governatore dell'Harar e dello Uollo.

3. Angelo Del Boca, *Gli italiani in Africa Orientale. La conquista dell'impero*, (Roma-Bari: Laterza, 1979), pp.231-44.

4.   ASMAE, *Etiopia*, b.24, f.1, pos.1/5.

5.   Raffaele Di Lauro, *Tre anni a Gondar*, (Milano: Mondadori, 1936), pp.138-41.

6.   Cfr. Luigi Goglia, "La missione del senatore Jacopo Gasparini nell'Amhara" in *Storia contemporanea*, n.4, 1977, pp.791-822.

7.   ASMAI, pos.181/13, f.60.

8.   *Ivi*. Dall lettera inviata da Ajaleu Burrù a Gasparini. Che l'armata dello Scirè avesse un armamento piuttosto scadente lo conferma anche il negus nelle sue memorie (*op. cit.*, p.267): "Soltanto il 10 per cento possedeva fucili *Mauser*. Il 90 per cento disponeva di armi che avevano più di quarant'anni, come il *Gras* e lo *Schneider* e altri fucili antiquati dello stesso tipo".

9.   ASMAI, pos.181/13, f.60.

10. Su queste cifre le fonti discordano. Hailè Selassiè, ad esempio (*op. cit.*, p.266), assegna a Immirù soltanto 10 mila uomini. Ajaleu Burrù, dal canto suo, pretende, come abbiamo visto, di averne mobilitati 30 mila, anche se poi riconosce che parte di essi sono disarmati.

11. Testimonianza di ras Immirù Haile Sellasse, rilasciata all'Autore il 13 aprile 1965 ad Addis Abeba.

12. Ghessessè Belou, nonostante che il negus gli avesse mandato contro il fitaurari Alamireu con un piccolo esercito, continuò a mantenere in vita la ribellione fino all'arrivo nel Goggiam degli italiani. Egli veniva rifornito di armi e denaro da Badoglio con aviolanci.

13. Il memoriale è nell'archivio Gasparini ed è riprodotto in L. Goglia, *op. cit.*, pp.811-15.

14. ASMAI, pos.181/13, f.60.

15. Cfr. A. Del Boca, *Gli italiani in Africa Orientale.*, *op. cit.*, pp.477-80.

16. TaA di ras Immirù, *cit.*

17. Pietro Badoglio, *La guerra d'Etiopia*, (Milano: Mondadori, 1936), pp.45-46.

18. Alessandro Lessona, *Memorie*, (Firenze: Sansoni, 1958), p.237.

19. Documentazione sull'Etiopia presso l'Autore, *Telegrammi di Mussolini AO*, Segreto, n.230, del 6 gennaio 1936.

20. Cit. in G. Bianchi, *Rivelazioni sul conflitto italo-etiopico*, (Milano: CEIS, 1967), p.114.

21. TaA di ras Immirù, *op. cit.*

22. ASMAI, AOI, pos.181/15, f.74.

23. *Ivi*, pos. 181/13, f.60.

24. *Ibid.*

25. Per una completa ricostruzione dell'episodio di Mai Lahlà, si veda: A. Del Boca, "La verità sul massacro della Gondrand", in *Storia Illustrata*, n.311, ottobre 1983, pp.68-74.

26. ASMAI, AOI, pos.181/24, f.116. Lettera del 24 febbraio 1936.

27. *La vérité sur la guerre italo-éthiopienne. Une victoire de la civilisation, par le Négus*, supplemento di "Vu", Paris, luglio 1936, p.37.

28. TaA di ras Immirù, *op. cit.*

29. P. Badoglio, *op. cit.*, p.137.

30. Pur avendo creato a ras Immirù ogni genere di difficoltà, il governatore dell'Amhara settentrionale non trovò il coraggio (o ne fu impedito) di ribellarsi e di passare nel campo avversario.

31. P. Badoglio, *op. cit.*, p.142.

32. *Ivi*, p.144.

33. Per una dettagliata ricostruzione della battaglia, si veda: A. Del Boca, *Gli italiani in Africa Orientale.*, *op. cit.*, pp.588-601.

34. Adalberto di Savoia-Genova, *Mistica fascista in Africa Orientale*, Quaderni di dottrina fascista a cura della Scuola di mistica fascista, Milano 1937, p.30.

35. Testimonianza all'Autore di Paolo Cesarini, rilasciata il 29 aprile 1965.

36. Dino Pollacci, *Con la Gavinana in Africa Orientale*, Pistoia: S. A. Arte della stampa, 1942, p.275.

37. Giovanni Artieri, *Cronaca del Fronte Nord*, Milano: Salocchi, 1937, pp.234-35.

38. Luca dei Sabelli, *Storia d'Abissinia*, Vol.IV, Edizioni Roma, Roma 1938, p.290.

39. P. Badoglio, *op. cit.*, p.146.

40. *Ivi*, p.145.

41. TaA di ras Immirù, *op. cit.*

42. Haile Sellassie I, *op. cit.*, p.270.

43. La lettera è riprodotta in P. Badoglio, *op. cit.*, pp.176-77.

44. TaA di ras Immirù, *op. cit.*

45. ASMAI, AOI, pos.181/11, f.1.

46. TaA di ras Immirù, *op. cit.*

47. Per le vicende del governo provvisario di Gore, si veda: A. Del Boca, *Gli italiani in Africa Orientale. La caduta dell'impero*, Roma-Bari: Laterza, 1982, pp.26-38.

48. TaA di ras Immirù, *op. cit.*

49. ACS, *Fondo Graziani*, b.20.

50. ASMAI, AOI, pos.181/34, f.161.

51. *Ibid.*

52. Rodolfo Graziani, *I primi venti mesi dell'impero*, manoscritto inedito in ACS, *Fondo Graziani*, b.56.

53. TaA di ras Immirù, *op. cit.*

54. Vittorio Gorresio, *La vita ingenua*, Milano: Rizzoli, 1980, p.131.

55. R. Graziani, *op. cit.*; dal telegramma n.32507 di Graziani al ministro Lessona.

56. *Ivi.* Tel. n.18216. Con un successivo telegramma a Graziani (n.50183), Lessona precisava tuttavia: "S. E. il Capo del Governo intende però che dopo questo ultimo esperimento tutti i capi ribelli che d'ora innanzi cadranno comunque nelle nostre mani siano immediatamente passati per le armi. Assicurare".

57. TaA di ras Immirù, *op. cit.*

58. *Ibid.*

59. Cit. in V. Gorresio, *op. cit.*, p.131.

60. ASMAI, pos.181/54, f.253.

61. TaA di ras Immirù, *op. cit.*

62. *Ibid.*

63. Per altre notizie sull'attività di ras Immirù dal 1943 alla sua morte, si veda: A. Del Boca, *Gli italiani in Africa Orientale. Nostalgia delle colonie*, Roma-Bari, 1984.

THE FIRST ETHIOPIAN CABINET:

BACKGROUND AND SIGNIFICANCE OF THE 1907 REFORM

Svein Ege

On 26 October 1907 Menilek informed the foreign powers represented at his court that he intended to reform his government by appointing ministers on a European pattern. So far he had nominated seven ministers: *Afänegus* Näsibu (Justice), *Fitawrari* Habtä-Giyorgis (War), *Aläqa* Gäbrä-Sellasē (*Sähafē-te'ezaz*, Minister of the Pen), *Bäjjerond* Mulu-Gēta (Finances), *Liqämäkwas* Kätäma (Interior), *Näggadras* Haylä-Giyorgis (Trade and Foreign Affairs) and *Käntiba* Wäldä-Şadeq (Agriculture).[1]

The move was unexpected indeed. Ethiopians and foreigners alike were taken by surprise. The autocratic style of Menilek's government, the feudal organization of the state, and the lack of educated administrative personnel had seemed to preclude any initiative of the kind.[2] The European representatives were impatient for replies to their numerous demands to Menilek and were not prepared for an Ethiopian-initiated reform of government. The reaction was one of surprise, even indignation, particularly by the Italian representative, Count Colli di Felizzano:

> "In my judgement the formation of the Ethiopian Cabinet does not in any way modify the conditions of the country in itself nor in its relations with the other powers; the total lack of any internal organization corresponding to the new institution and the ministers' complete lack of any education and preparation or any idea about their tasks and functions, give the pompous initiative of the Negus the character of a parody and excludes any importance or seriousness."[3]

The British representative, Hohler, was less categoric in his rejection of the reform, and had to admit that Menilek probably had serious intentions, but his description of the immediate results of the formation of a cabinet abounds with irony:

> "I sent round today to ascertain what progress its members were making with their various functions, and they were found to be engaged as follows:- The Minister of War was in bed, being unwell. The Privy Seal was busy gathering in hay. The Finance Minister was in attendance on the King. The Minister of Justice was seated under a tree administering justice. The Minister of Agriculture was engaged in quarrying and collecting stones for the construction of a new road, while his colleague of the Interior was supervising the laying down of those stones. The Minister for Foreign Affairs was weeding one of His Majesty's cornfields."[4]

Only the French representative was not surprised, and he commented on the reform as an important initiative, and added with complacency that Menilek had asked for four or five French advisers.[5] The contrasting reactions indicate that the interests of the European powers were involved.

The significance of the reform is not, however, limited to the context of foreign policy. The nomination of ministers constituted a new element in the development of Ethiopian political institutions, a reform of potentially great consequences. Whereas Euro-American historians have tended to play down the novelty and significance of Menilek's initiative[6], Ethiopian writers have given it considerable emphasis. *Aläqa* Gäbrä-Sellasē, first Minister of the Pen and Menilek's biographer, describes it in the context of Menilek's good works and modernizing policy. Mahtämä-Sellasē sets out the functions of each ministry.[7] From the way they present the material, they seem to underwrite the judgement of Aba Paulos Tzadua that:

351

"The introduction of the ministerial system was a most remarkable innovation, and at the same time it indicated a decisive turn in the history of the administrative organization of the Empire. Overcoming traditional systems, a new structure of central administrative organization comparable to that of other countries had been initiated."[8]

EXTERNAL BACKGROUND

After the routing of the Italian army at Adwa, thereby putting an end to one of the major colonizing efforts in Africa, the survival of Ethiopian independence was affirmed, but not guaranteed, even in the short term. Under the camouflage of friendship and assistance against Italian and British expansion, France was gaining influence in Ethiopia, obviously aiming at some kind of protectorate. The Anglo-Egyptian campaign against the Mahdist state in Sudan was progressing rapidly, and taken together with British expansion in Kenya and the Somaliland protectorate, represented a strong pressure on the Ethiopian sphere. The Italo-Ethiopian peace treaty of 1897 marked the end of an acute crisis in Italian colonial policy, during which even retirement from Eritrea had been considered, and introduced a period of consolidation of Italian colonizing strength.[9]

None of the powers aimed at immediate conquest of Ethiopia, but sought influence through cooperation and pressure. The central bone of contention between the powers was the projected railway Jibuti—Harrar—Addis Abäba—the White Nile. Various schemes — buying up the French company, constructing alternative railway lines, blocking the progress of the Jibuti railway, internationalizing the railway — were tried or considered. Despite, or because of, intense diplomatic activity, the situation was characterized by stalemate. Due to the contradiction of interests, the European powers counterbalanced each other and were played off against each other by Menilek.

The three main European rivals in Ethiopia tried to settle their disagreements by the Tripartite Agreement of 13 December 1906. The aim of the agreement was to introduce a new policy of cooperation among the three powers by settling the main outstanding differences — the railway question, mutual information by the representatives, how to handle demands for concessions and, ominously, how to partition Ethiopia.[10] Despite "the common interest of France, Great Britain and Italy being in maintaining the integrity of Ethiopia"[11], the main difficulty during the negotiations had been to agree on how to divide Ethiopia in case of disintegration.[12]

The foreign policy of Menilek in the period 1896-1906 had been based on the contradictions between the European powers. Thus he had been able to seek assistance from the French against the Italian attempt at colonization, then against British expansion in the Nile valley towards the end of the century, and finally from the British against a predominant French influence through the railway. Agreement between the three powers undermined this policy and could only result in the gradual decline or abrupt loss of Ethiopian independence. Increasing contacts with Germany, the United States and Belgium could in no way turn the tide. Therefore the reaction of Menilek to the Tripartite Agreement was negative, despite the attempts of the European representatives to persuade him that the agreement, mentioning the integrity of Ethiopia, was in his interest.[13]

The three powers sought to exploit the new situation in different and conflicting ways. The British representative urged for a new era of "white policy" in Ethiopia, a project which he discussed also with French and Italian colonial authorities. The aim was to establish European hegemony in Ethiopia, under British leadership, by agreeing on procedures to solve differences and thus exclude the Ethiopian side from such disagreements. The Ethiopians were to meet a united front in demands for concessions, for reforms of interest to European enterprise, for a favourable settlement of the emerging problem of succession after Menilek.[14]

Italy supported the white policy, although not British leadership. The French continued and even strengthened their policy of friendship to Ethiopia. Their main objective in signing the Tripartite Agreement had been to break the stalemate and be able to continue the Jibuti railway to Addis Abäba, thus gaining a predominant position *vis-à-vis* Ethiopians and rival European powers alike. In order to get Menilek's consent to the railway project, they played on his fear of their own partners, Great Britain and Italy, and acted as the only true upholders of Ethiopian independence. Furthermore, a united Ethiopia was the best economic basis for the expensive railway.[15]

Menilek realized the danger represented by the Tripartite Agreement, but he also noticed the continuing contradictions between the powers. His policy indicates that he did not simply act under pressure, nor obediently followed advice, but took independent and effective countermeasures.

A key element in the success of his foreign policy was the collection of information on the European equation. For a couple of decades Alfred Ilg had advised him on foreign policy, until he left Ethiopia in 1906. Various other Europeans acted as advisers for shorter terms.[16] But the most important source of information was probably the foreign diplomatic representatives themselves, usually more than willing to provide Menilek with information that would hurt rivals.

From the Ethiopian side the European threat had two elements, one general concerning Ethiopian independence and another dealing with the specific problem of succession. The general problem was met by a policy of settling the frontiers with the European colonies and by reforms to strengthen the state. The last years of Menilek's active reign saw the establishment of the first modern school, reform of the apparatus of justice, membership in the International Postal Union, the introduction of numerous technical novelties and, notably, the appointment of ministers.[17]

An obvious objective of these initiatives was to counter criticism of Ethiopian backwardness, demonstrate decision to modernize independently, in other words to relieve the European powers of the 'white man's burden'. In this context the appointment of ministers may well be considered a paper reform, implying very little direct change in the central administrative apparatus, but it was by no means a meaningless reform.

The establishment of a cabinet also formed part of the attempt to ease the problem of succession. From 1907 to 1909 there emerged a succession package consisting of the cabinet and the nomination of the young prince, *Lej* Yasu, as successor and *Ras* Täsämma as his guardian, later also plenipotentiary of the government. Although the succession package did not prevent the crisis, it worked for several years. It did not work well, but it is difficult to imagine any other Ethiopian solution that would have stood a better chance. The contrafactual hypothesis of what would have happened to Ethiopia if there were no cabinet is worth considering, even if no specific answer can be given.

THE INTERNAL BACKGROUND

Ethiopian government during the Menilek period and before was autocratic, with power centered in the person of the monarch. This is the picture established by Darkwah for the period when Menilek was only *negus* of Shawa, and continued by Marcus for the later period.[18] Indeed, after the victory over the Italians and the decline and later fall of his main rival, *Ras* Mängäsha Yohannes of Tegray, Menilek's power reached new heights, a degree of concentration of power perhaps never previously attained in Ethiopian history.

As late as 1907, when Menilek was already seriously ill and the succession crisis had emerged, the French representative, a sharp observer of central Ethiopian politics, commented:

> "There is not a detail of his administration of which he does not occupy himself; he wants to see and order everything. While he is discussing an order for a million, one comes to ask him permission to take a sack of flour or a plank; twice a week he gives justice and audiences, for five to six hours, without interruption."[19]

Ethiopian government was autocratic, but a picture of the central power apparatus consisting only of Menilek is clearly misleading. The concept of the omni-present autocrat is real, as ideology is real — it was the way his subjects should see him. But certainly he had numerous subordinate chiefs, administrators, advisers, all claiming their share of power. His policy, in his role as centre of the political system, was to attach the principal positions of power to his court. This he achieved by making people closely related to himself the leading figures of the empire. The *rases* Dargē, Mäkonnen, Wälda-Giyorgis, and Täsämma are cases in point. Another group was formed by those not biologically related, but representing families closely attached to the Shawan court through a tradition of loyal service, *Bäjjerond* Mulu-Gēta and *Dajjazmach* Abatä probably being of such extraction.[20] Finally there were certain adopted members of the court, originating from the conquered peoples, such as *Fitawrari* Habtä-Giyorgis and *Däjjazmach* Balcha.[21] Such persons formed the centre of the power block around Menilek.

Menilek's rule was personal. In a feudal political system of the Ethiopian kind, any government by impersonal institutions was out of the question. There was a large state apparatus, but the king was the active centre of the state. For cohesion to hold good, he had to be able to center the aspirations of his subjects on himself, to be the centre of pressures and compromises, remunerations and punishments, to hold the fate of his subordinates in his hand. Thus Menilek's activity was not limited to high state affairs; he was "omni-present", and highly successful.

In the period 1896-1906 Menilek lost his closest advisers; *Ras* Dargē, *Azzaj* Wäldä-Ṣadeq and *Ras* Mäkonnen died, while Alfred Ilg left Ethiopia in 1906. This created a vacuum in the government. The response was to promote new people to become the guarantors of the stability of the state. The conspicuous rise of *Fitawrari* Habtä-Giyorgis must be seen in this context; likewise, the careers of *Ras* Täsämma and of the *däjjazmaches* Abatä and Balcha are strictly related to the problem of the renewal of the governmental system.

However, promotions could not solve the real problem, the ailing centre. The irrevocable decline of his health made it clear that the central manipulator of the political system, its focus, would soon have to be replaced. By appointing ministers, Menilek initiated an institutional reform that might serve to ease the burden of administration on himself, but above all be a bulwark for the young *Lej* Yasu against external and internal pressures. *Lej* Yasu, even if assisted by a guardian, could hardly act as the centre of the empire — only perhaps as the centre of his ministers. Thus the cabinet can be seen as a shield against Ethiopian and European demands and intrigues, as well as a reform of the executive. The structural reform therefore had its internal rationale, although the European titles, the "peacock's feathers", were a function of foreign policy considerations.

The idea of the reform may well have originated with Harrington's pressure for European advisers and *de facto* control of the broad lines of Ethiopian politics. It was probably also related to the decline of Ilg's position, Menilek's own European adviser, and designed as a useful guarantor *vis-à-vis* Europe. His fall was closely linked to the railway question and he had been the object of much intrigue. The nomination of Ethiopian ministers came only approximately one month after what appears as the final confirmation of his disgrace, the confiscation of his house.[22]

The initiative, which had thus been maturing for some time, was probably directly inspired by Klobukowski, despite his claims to the contrary.[23] It represented a major success of his:

> "conciliating policy tending to suggest in a friendly way reforms for the benefit of Abyssinia, and to lead a sovereign, whom it is necessary to persuade and not to intimidate, gently, methodically on the road of progress and civilization."[24]

This contrasted with the British and Italian view that the three powers should:

> "exercise a friendly pression on the Ethiopian government in all circumstances where the interests of our citizens are concerned."[25]

But the reform may also have had an Ethiopian inspirer, *Näggadras* Haylä-Giyorgis, a new favourite of Menilek who received both the ministries of trade and foreign affairs in the first cabinet. As chief administrator of the trade of Addis Abäba, he was much in contact with Europeans, particularly the small traders.

> "From these he picks up scraps of information and ideas, and poses as being an authority on European ways, manners, and systems. Tricked out with these peacock's feathers, he easily imposes himself on the king, who has no means of knowing better, as being the true bird."[26]

Indeed there is consistency in Hohler's description of the cabinet as a paper reform and of *Näggadras* Haylä-Giyorgis as being tricked out with peacock's feathers. Both represented to the imperialist the same cardinal sin, attempts to wrench from him the basis of his superiority.

THE REFORM AND ITS EFFECTS

The nomination of ministers was communicated to the European representatives on 26 October 1907, on which occasion Menilek stressed his desire to bring his government up to European standards:

> "We have long been thinking of establishing European organization in our country, in Ethiopia; and you have always said that it would be good for Ethiopia to start to introduce European organization; and now, if it is God's will that my life be long enough, I have started to appoint ministers."[27]

A few weeks later he addressed his ministers, motivating the formation of the cabinet by the European criticism of lack of law and ordered government, and of the insufficiency of rule by one man. He particularly admonished the ministers not to quarrel or envy, but to act always in agreement. In this way they would help him to administer Ethiopia for the good of Ethiopians.[28]

In January 1908 (15 *ṭeqemt* 1900) Menilek made the reform public. The functions of each ministry were outlined in some detail.[29] Although Menilek's government was still as autocratic as ever, the practical establishment of the cabinet progressed during 1908. In July the first meeting of the cabinet as a collective body was held[30], and Menilek was soon considering, with French assistance, the advisability of appointing a prime minister, the strongest candidate being *Fitawrari* Habtä-Giyorgis.[31]

The crisis suffered by Menilek in August acted as a further spur. There were rumours about the nomination of a prime minister, a measure receiving widespread support. The ministers were reaching a certain level of organization, first concentrating on the delineation of their respective economic responsibilities and benefits.[32] The progress was so marked that even the Italian representative had to admit that the scheme had some chance of success. The nomination of *Ras* Täsämma as guardian of *Lej* Yasu further strengthened the conviction that Ethiopia was not inevitably bound to succumb.[33]

Little is known about the development of the early ministries. The administrative side of the reform was secondary to solving the succession crisis, to protect the state against external pressure and internal conflicts and revolts. Probably the ministers continued to exercise their duties as *fitawrari, bäjjerond*, etc., much as before. In the provinces the apparent effects of the reform were even less. Armbruster, travelling through western Bägēmeder and Gojjam commented:

> "In regard to the Imperial Ethiopian Government, of which we read in the European press, I have to state that in these territories it simply does not exist. I have read in a serious newspaper of Decrees about education in the Ethiopian Empire promulgated at Adis Ababa, of Ministers for Education,

for Finance, for Posts and Telegraphs, and Ministers with I know not what portfolios. Whatever profound operations these personages may be effecting at Adis Ababa, neither they nor their works have ever been heard of in any part of Abyssinia I have visited. In the course of conversation with many individuals from different parts of the country I frequently inquired about these matters and met with nobody who knew anything of either Minister or Decree."[34]

The appointment of ministers did not lead to change in provincial administration, but it changed the balance of power between the centre and the provinces. The pre-reform prospects for developments after Menilek consisted of provincial rebellions and power struggle until one chief was able to assert himself by military power, foreign intervention apart. One or more Tegray chiefs were almost certain to rebel, if successful perhaps even claim emperorship on the basis of descent from *Aşē* Yohannes. After the death of the strongest candidate for Shäwan succession, *Ras* Mäkonnen, several of the leading Shäwan chiefs could lay about equal claims to the throne or had the opportunity to support a pretender as their candidate. Unrest in the conquered south added to the instability of the situation.

Furthermore, there was the problem of Empress Taytu, a strong politician, seeking to build up a faction around herself to prolong her power after the death of her husband. She was consistently working against the candidacy of *Lej* Yasu until her fall in March 1910. The appointment of ministers to carry on Menilek's policy, strengthened by the nomination of *Ras* Täsämma as guardian and his agreement with *Ras* Mika'ēl, father of *Lej* Yasu, curtailed Taytu's independent power. Without this institutional innovation her control of court politics might easily have been greater, with certain consequences for the struggle for power.

The establishment of the cabinet introduce a new central element in Ethiopian politics. Its importance was not so much the administrative effects, as the fact that it existed independently of the life of the king. The cabinet and the prominence of chiefs with a strong central background are important factors when explaining why Ethiopian integrity was not seriously threatened from within in the ensuing period.

The view that the reform was not important was partly based on the claim that the ministers appointed were almost all persons of no consequence and would therefore not be able to assert themselves. Admittedly, only *Fitawrari* Habtä-Giyorgis commanded a large territory. As minister of war he also gained control of the emperor's army and became by far the single most powerful chief. His was a case of highly successful advancement from palace service to provincial command.[35]

The ministers were recruited from the personnel of the palace, many of them not well known to the Europeans. *Afänegus* Näsibu was an exception, as his presidency of the supreme court was a conspicuous and obviously influential position.[36] *Aläqa* Gäbrä-Sellasē, Menilek's secretary, was a highly trusted official and much respected adviser.[37] *Bäjjerond* Mulu-Gēta belonged to a prominent Morate family and was related to *Ras* Täsämma.[38] *Käntiba* Wäldä-Ṣadeq had been the trusted secretary of *Ras* Dargē and had married into the Dargē family.[39] *Näggadras* Haylä-Giyorgis was in charge of the customs of Addis Abäba, and probably also of much of Menilek's commercial activity, thus occupying one of the economically most important positions in the empire.[40] Quite naturally the ministers were not recruited from the powerful regional chiefs, but from the *balämwals* of the court. They were court administrators who had gained the favour of Menilek. Finally, most of them already occupied traditional positions roughly corresponding to their new duties.[41]

Menilek had advised his ministers to act in agreement, as a cabinet. Even so, it is quite probable that he deliberately composed his cabinet of rivals. The systematic use of contradictions to prevent anybody from gaining too much power was a typical aspect of the feudal state. At least conflicts soon emerged between the ministers[42], and were to characterize the cabinet and the Ethiopian political scene until the collective deposition of the ministers in 1918.

The cabinet, quite obviously, did not function in the same way as in a state with a parliament or a strongly developed bureaucracy. The ministers sought to maintain and improve their positions through factional politics; the reform could not break the logic of the Ethiopian political system. But they participated in the game of power as a distinct central element. In fact the later European complaints of factionalism, inactivity and corruption is evidence of the continued activities of the ministers and belies the original prophecy of non-existence.

The European criticism of the reform had played on an implicit comparison with ministries in Europe, by which means it was easy to deride the "paper reform". However, in the field of foreign policy, these "peacock's feathers" were quite effective. The nomination of ministers was also a plausible, and not wholly unsuccessful, attempt to solve the approaching succession crisis. Although in many cases ministerial nomination only meant a change of title, the institution of a cabinet, a collective body, was an element that soon gained a momentum of its own and was to colour Ethiopian politics for a decade.

NOTES

Abbreviations used in the notes:

ASMAI   Archivio storico dell' ex Ministero dell'Africa Italiana (Rome).

FO   Foreign Office (in the Public Record Office, London).

JES   Journal of Ethiopian Studies.

MAE   Ministère des Affaires Etrangères (Paris).

NS   MAE, Nouvelle Serie (1897-1914); all references to "Ethiopie".

––––––––––––––––

1.   MAE, NS 1 f. 174r., Klobukowski to Pichon, Addis Abäba 27.10.07; FO 401/10, No.236, p.163, Hohler to Grey, Addis Abäba 28.10.07; ASMAI 38/4/38, Colli to Ministro Esteri, Addis Abäba 30.10.07, No.104, f. 1r; Mahtämä-Sellasē Wäldä-Mäsqäl, Zekrä Nägär (Addis Abäba, 1962 EC), p.54. Colli mistakenly describes Aläqa Gäbrä-Sellasē as Minister of Education and Käntiba Wäldä-Ṣadeq as Minister of Public Works.

2.   FO 401/10, Hohler ibid., pp.162-3.

3.   ASMAI 38/4/38, Colli ibid., f. 1r-v.

4.   FO 401/10, Hohler ibid., p.163.

5.   MAE, Klobukowski ibid., f. 174r-v.

6.   Cf. Harold G. Marcus, The Life and Times of Menelik II. Ethiopia 1844-1913 (Oxford, 1975), pp.227-28; Richard Greenfield, Ethiopia. A New Political History (London, 1965), p.131; also S. Rubenson, "Modern Ethiopia", in Joseph C. Anene and G. N. Brown (eds.), Africa in the Nineteenth and Twentieth Centuries (London, 1966), p.227; Margery Perham, The Government of Ethiopia (Evanston, 1969) pp.87, 88-89.

7.   Guèbrè Sellasié, Chronique du règne de Ménélik II, ed. by M. Coppet (Paris, 1931), Vol.2, pp.527-28; Mahtämä-Sellasē, Zekrä Nägär, pp.68-69, 194, 223, 318.

8.   Aba Paulos Tzadua, "Organisation of the Central Administration in Ethiopia", un-

published Ph.D. thesis, quoted in James C. N. Paul and C. Clapham, *Ethiopian Constitutional Development. A Sourcebook,* Vol.1 (Addis Abäba, 1972), p.321.

9. Cf. Marcus, *Life and Times*, pp.174-213; Angelo del Boca, *Gli Italiani in Africa Orientale, Vol.1. Dall'Unità alla marcia su Roma* (Bari, 1976), pp.751-76.

10. ASMAI 41/1/10, "Arrangement concernant l'Abyssinie entre la France, la Grande-Bretagne, et l'Italie", paraphrased at the Foreign Office, 6 July 1906.

11. *Ibid.*, p.1.

12. Cf. Marcus, *Life and Times*, pp.205-11; *idem*, "A preliminary history of the Tripartite Treaty of December 13, 1906" in *JES* (1964), Vol.2, No.2, pp.21-40.

13. See, as examples, FO 401/9, No.177, Di San Giuliano to Grey, London, 12.10.06; FO 401/10, No.173, Hohler to Grey, Addis Abäba, 25.09.07; ASMAI 41/1/11, Ciccodicola to Esteri (via Asmara), Addis Abäba, 8.12.06, No.115.
Menilek's judgement seems sound and it is difficult to agree to the interpretation that "Although Ethiopia had not been a participant in the negotiations, the empire gained considerable stability from the treaty which marked the end of active British and French imperialism in the region, and eliminated, for a time, the likelihood of Italian expansion" (Marcus, *Life and Times*, pp.212-13).

14. FO 401/10, No.21, Memorandum by Harrington, Paris 18.02.07; ASMAI 38/4/35, "Punti sui quali si è stati d'accordo col Colonnello Harrington nel colloquio da lui avuto con il Ministro degli Affari Easteri, col Marchese Di San Giuliano e col Comm. Agnesa", Rome, February 1907, p.1.

15. MAE, NS 1, f. 162 v., Klobukowski to Pichon, Addis Abäba, 23.09.07; FO 401/10, No.237, Hohler to Grey, Addis Abäba, 29.10.07; ASMAI 37/2/15, Colli to Ministro Esteri, Addis Abäba, 1.10.07, f. 2r.; ASMAI 38/4/37, Salvago Raggi to Esteri, Asmara, 6.09.07, transmitting from Colli.

16. Cf. R. Pankhurst, "Menilek and the utilisation of foreign skills", in *JES*, (1967), Vol.5, No.1, pp.48-49; Bairu Tafla, "Civil titles and offices in the reign of Emperor Menilek II, 1889-1913", in *IV Congresso Internazionale di Studi Etiopici* (Rome 1972), Rome 1974, Vol.1, p.605.

17. Cf. Marcus, *Life and Times*, pp.200, 227-28.

18. R. H. Kofi Darkwah, *Shewa, Menilek and the Ethiopian Empire 1813-1889* (London, 1975), pp.111-40; Marcus, *Life and Times*, pp.214-15.

19. MAE, NS 1, f. 140 v., Klobukowski to Pichon, Addis Abäba, 21.07.07.

20. Heruy Wäldä-Sellasē, *Yä-heywät tarik* (Addis Abäba, 1911 EC), p.11; Mahtämä-Sellasē Wäldä-Masqal, "Yä-ityoppeya bahel ṭenat", in *JES* (1969), Vol.7, No.2, p.251.

21. Bairu Tafla, "Two Ethiopian biographies", in *JES* (1968), Vol.6, No.1, pp.125-26; *idem*, "Four Ethiopian Biographies: Däjjazmač Gärmamē, Däjjazmač Gäbrä-Egzi'abehér Moroda, Däjjazmač Balča and Käntiba Gäbru Dästa", in *JES* (1969), Vol.7, No.2, pp.14-17.

22. ASMAI 38/4/38, Colli to Esteri (Addis Ababa), 30.09.07, No.115.

23. MAE, NS 16, f. 238r., Klobukowski to Pichon, Addis Abäba, 28.11.07; ASMAI 38/4/38, Colli to Ministro Esteri, Addis Abäba, 30.10.07, No.104, f. 2r-v.

24. MAE, NS 16, f. 171r., Klobukowski to Pichon, Addis Abäba, 11.10.07.

25. *Ibid.*, ff., 170v.-171r.

26. FO 401/10, N.236, Hohler to Grey, Addis Abäba, 28.10.07; see also Heruy, *Yä-heywät tarik*, p.41. Heruy emphasizes the innovating tendency of Haylä-Giyorgis.

27. ASMAI 38/4/38, Menilek to Colli, Addis Abäba, 14 *ṭeqemt* 1900, enclosed in Colli to Ministro Esteri, Addis Ababa, 30.10.07.

28. MAE, NS 1, f. 178r. "Allocution de S. M. Menelick II à ses ministres", enclosed in Klobukowski to Pichon, Addis Abäba, 20.11.07.

29. Mahtämä-Sellasē, *Zekra Nägär*, p.54.

30. Guèbrè Sellasié, *Chronique*, Vol.2, p.528, n.12.

31. MAE, NS 1, f. 220r., Brice to Pichon, Addis Ababa, 9.07.08. The new French representative was more open than his predecessor about his policy of influencing internal Ethiopian developments through Dr. Vitalien:
"Dans les longs entretiens que j'avais eus avec le docteur, nous avions souvent discuté de l'intérêt qu'il y aurait à amener les titulaires des divers portefeuilles à échanger leurs vues et à ne pas se tenir isolés les uns des autres. Nous avions rêvé de réunions périodiques pour consolider et unifier l'action gouvernementale dans ce pays. . . . Tous ce qui était de nature à grouper les efforts de chacun des Ministres me paraissait oeuvre utile et à encourager. Le Dr. Vitalien l'avait bien compris et avec son habileté ordinaire, tout en donnant ses soins au Negus, il l'a amené à partager cette idée lui laissant croire qu'il en était l'auteur."
Ibid., ff. 220r.-v.

32. ASMAI 37/3/18, Miniscalchi to Ministero Esteri, Addis Abäba, 2.10.08, p.3.

33. *Ibid.*, pp.3-4; ASMAI 37/3/18, Miniscalchi to Ministero Esteri, Addis Abäba, 19.11.08, pp.1-2.

34. FO 401/11, No.221, p.183, Armbruster to Major Phipps (report on journey in northwestern Ethiopia), n.d., enclosed in Graham to Grey, Cairo, 26.09.08.

35. Bairu Tafla, "Two Ethiopian Biographies", pp.125-26.

36. FO 401/10, No.236, Hohler to Grey, Addis Abäba, 28.10.07, pp.162-63; Heruy, *Yä-heywät tarik*, p.45.

37. Heruy, *op. cit.*, p.91.

38. *Ibid.*, p.11.

39. *Ibid.*, p.74; Mahtämä-Sellasē, "Yä-ityoppeya bahel ṭenat", p.267.

40. Heruy, *op. cit.*, p.41; FO 401/10, No.236, Hohler to Grey, Addis Ababa, 28.10.07, p.163.

41. Cf. Bairu Tafla, *op. cit.*, p.597.

42. ASMAI 37/3/18, Miniscalchi to Ministero Esteri, Addis Abäba, 2.10.08, p.4.

RAS ALULA, RAS SEYUM, TIGRE AND

ETHIOPIA'S INTEGRITY*

Haggai Erlich

The existence of Ethiopia as an independent state which survived the modern challenge of western imperialism is a subject of great historical interest. The phenomenon of an African entity, situated on a strategic junction facing successfully such an external challenge and even emerging stronger, larger and better united, was usually conceived by observers as an abnormality. Scholars were always looking for explanations: European politicians often acted on the assumption that the phenomenon was merely a temporary episode.

Their dilemmas in facing this enigma were beautifully summarised by British Colonel Cheesman, who in the midst of one relevant historical process reported to his superiors in the British Foreign Office:

> "During the reign of Menelik and since then" — wrote Cheesman — "the foreign policies of England, France and Italy in regard to Ethiopia have been based on the assumption that she must break up, yet she did nothing of the sort. She has survived the reigns of Lij Yasu, Zawditu and Haile Sellasi, and showed a united if ineffectual front to the Italians in 1935-1936. Yet the *theory of disintegration* [emphasis mine, H.E.] persisted . . . It is not surprising that [many westerners] could not realise that a *national unity* existed in Ethiopia and that a government that was not visible and that was so different from their own could possibly last more than a few months.
> The crazy structure of the Ethiopian empire is held together by a *mysterious magnetism* [emphasis mine], which is incomprehensible to one who has no more than a superficial knowledge of Ethiopia."

What indeed is this "crazy structure" based on such "mysterious magnetism" which has repeatedly stood the test of the "theory of disintegration"? Why did Ethiopia survive, in terms of political unity even benefited from, the challenges which shattered and destroyed the political structure of other African and Asian societies? The answer to this question can not be clear and simple. For, like most other important historic phenomena, it is a question of a multidimensional nature. In this paper I do not pretend to be able to deal with more than just one relevant aspect. I shall do it by way of summarising briefly two cases connected with the history of the Tigre province.

The province of Tigre has always played a central and pivotal role in the story of Ethiopia's integrity. This was true to such an extent that some foreign politicians who were pursuing the promotion of Ethiopia's dismemberment used to label their strategy "Tigrean politics". Indeed the old political rivalry between Tigre and Shoa, couched as it was with linguistic, religious and other differences, tempted many casual observers to believe that the inevitable breaking point of Ethiopia was somewhere between these two provinces. This concept motivated the Ethiopian policy of Khedivial Egypt under the expansionist Ismail; of Italy from Crispi to Mussolini; of some of the British during the Second World War period, not to mention some participants in contemporary politics. Yet — as I shall demonstrate below — in the most crucial junctions of history the *theory of disintegration* was proved erroneous also, indeed especially, in Tigre, which remained all throughout part and parcel of Ethiopia's "crazy structure". Let me now refer briefly to two relevant cases.

The first one is the story of *Ras* Alula and Ethiopia's integrity. I do not intend to dwell here on its sequence and details. My attempt at constructing in detail his role within his period is presented in my book: *Ethiopia and Eritrea during the Scramble for Africa; a political biography of Ras Alula 1875-1897* (co-published by MSU and Tel Aviv University, 1982).

The threat that existed at that period to Ethiopia's integrity and independence needs no extensive reminding: Italy, in full imperialist steam in the late 1880s, tore Eritrea off Ethiopia, was trying through patronizing diplomacy to obtain protectorship over the whole country, and resorted simultaneously to the subversive *politica tigrigna*. *Ras* Alula's role in Ethiopia's story of facing this challenge was important throughout.

As long as Emperor Yohannes was alive, Alula was the architect and caretaker of the tough military resistance to Italian encroachment. Having scored various victories in the battlefield, he gained at that time his nearly legendary name as the champion of Ethiopia's integrity. But after the death of his master Yohannes, when the empire's center was transferred by Emperor Menelik to Shoa, Alula's role underwent a fundamental change. He refused to accept the fact that, due to the new circumstances he was reduced to a mere local chief in a somewhat remote and impoverished province. He therefore spent the following five years (1889-1894) in a relentless effort to maintain Tigre's independence from Shoa. From the point of view of Ethiopia's integrity it was a very dangerous game. *Ras* Alula did not hesitate, for this purpose, to turn Tigre into an uncontrollable buffer-zone, to openly defy Emperor Menelik recognition of his authority to prevent Yohannes's heir, *Ras* Mangasha, by force from submitting to the Emperor, and even to strive for cooperation with the Italians in Asmara. One can only speculate what could have been the future of Ethiopia had Alula persisted in this line to the end. I guess that in such circumstances a victory at Adwa would never have occurred; and that the Italian imperialists would have successfully proceeded with their policy of provincial subversion at the expense of Ethiopia's integrity and independence.

Seen from this angle the turning point of our story came two years prior to the Adwa victory, in June 1894. On the 4th of that month, amidst a huge ceremony, the big chiefs of Tigre, headed by *Ras* Alula and *Ras* Mangasha, swore allegiance to Menelik. Thus the authority of the emperor, the great unifier of southern Ethiopia was extended over the strategically vital Tigre and the north. From this point onward history was shaped in a direction culminating with the shattering of the "theory of disintegration" in Adwa and the recognition by the powers of Ethiopia's sovereignty within her modern boundaries.

The coming of the Tigrean chiefs to Addis Ababa and their recognition of the central authority of the Emperor was the result of a decision taken by Alula. Subsequently the *Ras* returned to Tigre to play the role of great defender of the country's integrity. He led the imperial army in the clashes preliminary to Adwa and acted as the emperor's personal adviser and chief-of-staff during the decisive battle. After the victory he remained in Tigre as Menelik's man trying to promote unification in the troubled north. What caused Alula to decide at that moment of truth of June 1894 to act for the return of Tigre to a reunited Ethiopia? Let us leave this question for a while and turn to our second case-study — the story of *Ras* Seyum, Yohannes's grandson, and Ethiopia's integrity.

From the point of view of our discussion, the general background to this story, though taking place some five decades later, was similar. In the year 1941 Ethiopia was facing a threat to her integrity no less serious than that of 1894. The British army had defeated the fascist conquerors of the country who five years earlier had occupied Ethiopia and erased her name from the maps. Yet the British liberators were not unanimous on the future of Ethiopia and the region. On the one hand, there was their officially declared policy. It was formulated by Foreign Secretary Anthony Eden, who promised publicly to restore Ethiopia's pre-war territorial integrity and full sovereignty under Emperor Haile-Sellasse. But there was a war situation in the region and the world and the British Foreign Office was hardly in a position to determine policy. Eden's men in Ethiopia at the time were a few ex-advisers and ex-diplomats, who could do very little to help the Emperor, himself lacking visible means of power, to restore Ethiopia's statehood. On the other hand there were in the British camp the men of the British army and the War Office, who as the actual occupiers had at that time the real military, political and financial control of the region. Their ideas and plans — as revealed from documents available now — were entirely different from those of Eden and the Foreign Office.

They implied in essence the dismemberment of Ethiopia and a rearrangement of the whole region according to British long-range strategic considerations. One such consideration was that the Sudan, not Egypt, was to serve in the post-war period as the main British stronghold on the junction of the Middle East and Africa. This necessitated two things relevant to our story:

a. The annexation to Sudan of western Eritrean territories inhabited by Muslims.

b. The creation under British mandate of a "Tigrai state" consisting of the main parts of the Eritrean highlands and of Tigre province.

This was a new version of the old Italian *politica Tigrigna*, though a far more sophisticated and modernised one, thanks to the efforts made from British Asmara to spread in the relevant regions a notion of "Tigrean nationalism". Indeed, as the liberating British army marched inward, in May 1941 *Ras* Seyum, grandson of Emperor Yohannes and a leading chief in Tigre for some three decades, was contacted and appointed by the British as the governor of Tigre (together — by the way — with none other than the great traitor *Dadjazmach* Haile-Sellasse Gugsa). The appointment was made without even informing the Emperor, and signified, together with the appointment of lesser chiefs in the province, the British military's determination to prepare the ground for the execution of their regional strategy. Emperor Haile-Sellasse protested to London upon hearing of the developments, but his detailed telegram reached Churchill the very same week in June 1941 when the Nazis invaded the USSR. No wonder then that the British war cabinet brushed aside matters such as Haile-Sellasse's complaint against D.C.P.O. Eritrea, Kennedy-Cooke, for arresting the Emperor's nominee in Agame and replacing him with one *Shalaqa* Kassa . . . Indeed the outcome of the whole issue was determined neither in London nor in Addis Ababa, but in Tigre and by *Ras* Seyum. In early July he made his move: much to the frustration of the British political officers he went to Addis Ababa where, on July 8th, 1941, he swore allegiance to the Emperor.

From this moment onward history took a direction proving again the fallacy of "the theory of disintegration". Seyum's step was decisive for the ensuing struggle over Tigre between the Emperor and the Asmara based British military. The description of the whole complicated affair is outside the scope of this short paper. I have attempted to reconstruct the facts in my article " 'Tigrean nationalism', British involvement and Haile-Selasse's emerging Absolutism". The general consequences are well known. In the ensuing years the Emperor managed not only to preserve Tigre but also to outmanoeuvre the British military administration to the extent that they themselves helped him to quell the "Woyane" revolt in Tigre. Furthermore, the regaining of Tigre opened the way for a later struggle for the restoration of Eritrea to Ethiopia. As for Seyum, he was made governor of Tigre in 1947 and went on serving the Emperor and the government of Ethiopia till his death in 1960.

Again, we are left with speculations only as to what would have been Ethiopia's story had Seyum decided to opt for the British in Asmara. Who can say what shape history would have taken? I, for one, can hardly see what could have stopped the British from accomplishing a good part of their scheme. Equally, I can hardly see how, in such circumstances, Ethiopia could have maintained Tigre, let alone regain Eritrea, and emerge out of the chaotic World War II, as she had done out of the "scramble for Africa" even stronger and better united than before.

Studying these two stories in detail was for me an experience of great value, especially in trying to understand the more general question of Ethiopia's survival. For they shed light I think on this "mysterious magnetism" which in Cheesman's words "holds together the crazy structure of Ethiopia". What is then this "magnetism"? What is really the reason behind this recurrent story of Ethiopia's reunification and survival? In other words what motivated Alula and Seyum, as well as thousands of other Ethiopians in thousands of other moments of truth, to opt for a united country?

Was it a sentiment of national patriotism?

My answer is: no. Of course, no one can deny that a strong and a sincere sense of national affiliation was very much alive in the hearts of our heroes, as well as in the hearts of all Ethiopians of the various provinces. But, as we have seen, in daily politics they were not directly motivated by this sentiment. I presume that in a paradoxical way the notion of Ethiopia's eternal existence was so deeply entrenched that it was simply taken for granted by many of the Ethiopian participants in the politics of traditional Ethiopia. It was probably against the background of such a sense of security that so many historical figures allowed themselves to cooperate with Ethiopia's enemies in order to promote their position in internal politics. Examples to this effect include no lesser figures than Emperors Yohannes and Menelik. I have mentioned already Alula's cooperation with the Italians against Menelik in the years immediately after Yohannes's death. *Ras* Seyum had a somewhat similar record in the years prior to Mussolini's invasion and during the period of occupation. Indeed, in the cases discussed above both of our heroes had the option of continuing their alliance with Italian or British Asmara, and in the framework of traditional politics – without tarnishing their image as great leaders.

Was it because of the military strength of the capital, Addis Ababa?

My answer here is absolutely in the negative. At least from the point of view of the north, Ethiopia's center was never able to enforce its authority on the provinces by sheer force. Emperor Tewodros who tried to do this failed completely; Yohannes gave up the idea from the start; while Menelik scored some success in the north but only through flexible diplomacy and marriage connections. Even Haile-Sellasse, who in the post-World War I period managed to disarm the leading families in the north, preferred to follow Menelik's policy. In the 1890s Menelik was simply unable to force a military solution in Tigre, while Haile-Sellasse in 1941 had no army whatsoever. Both Alula and Seyum, from the strictly military aspect, had very little to fear from Addis Ababa.

If not sentiments from the periphery and not power from the center, what then is "the mysterious magnetism" which held Ethiopia together? The question – in my mind – leads us back to Alula's and Seyum's moments of truth. I say this not just because they took decisions of dramatic importance, but mainly because their stories are just a sample of thousands such moments and decisions made by thousands of leaders of various ranks and importance throughout Ethiopia's history.

What motivated them to opt for Addis Ababa, and not for provincial separatism? At the risk of sounding cynical let me put in bluntly – it was worthwhile. It was worthwhile for Alula to enter the service of Menelik as it was the same for Seyum in joining the government of Haile-Sellasse. Both took no risk in doing so after years of disobedience or of rebellion. They knew perfectly well, aware of the country's centuries-old *flexible pragmatism*, that they would not only be forgiven but also be allowed to participate in the all-Ethiopian political game. Indeed, to my understanding, this was the main ingredient in the "mysterious" formula of "magnetism" – the notion shared by all Ethiopians of political ambition that the country's socio-political system, as it radiated from the capital, was pragmatic, open, and flexible. It was pragmatic enough to disregard their past and background; open enough to let them transfer ambitions from provincial politics to the all-Ethiopian sphere; and flexible enough to let them compete there in a political game relatively free of dogmas and stigmas, fulfilling ambitions according to personal abilities. *Ras* Alula in his time had all the reasons to believe that in Addis Ababa he would be pardoned and would be promoted, because of his ability, from a chief in a remote province to a central position in the imperial forces. *Ras* Seyum in his time knew that his chances to become a *Negus*, and real master in his home province of Tigre, lay in the capital. Both realised that because of the flexibility and openness of the all-Ethiopian game they would do better to join in it than separate from it.

One other important illustration of the argument that the "magnetism" of Ethiopia stemmed primarily from this flexibility of her system is the case of Eritrea's reunification in the

1940s and 1950s. The province was reannexed not because Addis Ababa had the power to force it, but essentiallly because the strong elements in Eritrean society of the time wanted it. They did so mainly because they wanted to participate, spiritually and materially, not in the life of a provincial Eritrea but in the life of a great Ethiopia, which promised them better possibilities in various fields. Very many of them did indeed, as they still do, participate and excel in the national economic, cultural and political life of the country. It was only when the decaying regime of Haile-Sellasse in the late 1960s lost its patience with the local drop-outs and, instead of promoting flexibility, imposed a military regime and resorted to the exercise of force in the province that the successful reannexation changed course and luck.

Ethiopia's traditional flexibility, like all other phenomena related to human affairs, was a matter of many aspects and implications. It was not only a reason for national unity, it was also, at the same time, a reason for stagnant conservatism and lack of revolutionary progress. For who is the person of strong character who would like to revolt against a system which enables him to fulfil his ambitions? Ethiopia's socio-political pragmatism united the country, by letting her most able sons into leadership; but it was simultaneously because of this very system that no significant class-struggle or ideological competition took place in pre-revolutionary Ethiopia to shape a new society built on modern concepts.

NOTE

*   This article is a summary of one of the themes appearing in my compositions listed below:

Ethiopia and Eritrea during the scramble for Africa, Political Biography of Ras Alula, Michigan, 1982.
"Tigrean Politics 1930-1935 and the approaching Italo-Ethiopian War", in Goldenberg (ed.), *Proceedings of the Sixth International Conference of Ethiopian Studies*, Rotterdam Balkema, 1986, pp.101-131.
"Tigrean Nationalism, British Involvement and Haile-Sellasse's Emerging Absolutism — 1941-1943 in Northern Ethiopia", *Asian African Studies* (Israel), 1981, pp.191-227.
The Struggle over Eritrea 1962-1978: *War and Revolution in the Horn of Africa*. Stanford Hoover Institutions, 1983.

HARAR AU TEMPS DE ARTHUR RIMBAUD'

1880—1891

Emile Foucher

Rimbaud dans une lettre aux siens, datée du 13 décembre 1880, annonçait son arrivée à Harar:

> "Je suis arrivé dans ce pays après 20 jours de cheval à travers le désert Somali. Harar est une ville colonisée par les Egyptiens. La garnison est de plusieurs milliers d'hommes. Ici se trouve notre agence et nos magasins. Les produits marchands du pays sont le café, l'ivoire, les peaux, etc . . . Le pays est élevé, mais non infertile. Le climat est frais et non malsain. On importe ici toutes les marchandises d'Europe, par chameaux."

Les années 1880-1891 furent pour la vieille et indépendante cité de Harar riches en événements qui changèrent le cours de son histoire. Ce fut d'abord l'occupation égyptienne, puis le règne éphémère d'un émir local et enfin la prise du territoire par les armées de Menelik, roi du Choa.

Partie I: 1880-1883

Le dernier émir de Harar, *Mohammed bin 'Ali bin Abdushakur* (1856-1875), régna d'une manière despotique. Il fabriquait de fausses monnaies, monopolisait entre ses mains tout le commerce. Il défendit à ses sujets de manger du riz et des dattes sous prétexte qu'il n'appartenait qu'au roi de consommer des mets si delicieux, la bouche des gens du peuple étant trop grossière pour apprécier à leur juste valeur un aliment aussi succulent. Il est inutile de dire qu'avec une pareille attitude le commerce devait languir.

Les Harariens envoyerent en Egypte une délégation de 4 personnes pour demander au Khédive Isma'el aide et protection. Ce dernier organisa un corps expéditionnaire sous le commandement de *Mohammed Raouf Pacha*. Les troupes égyptiennes, composées en bonne partie de Turcs, après avoir rencontré une certaine resistance, dans la plaine de Combolcia, de la part de tribus Oromo, arriverent en vue de Harar le 10 octobre 1875. Le 11 octobre, selon un rapport de Raouf Pacha, on fut informé que l'émir desirait se rendre. Deux officiers furent dépêchés avec les drapeaux égyptiens qu'ils hissèrent à une heure de l'après-midi sur le palais et sur une des portes. Accompagné de l'émir, Mohammed Raouf Pacha fit son entrée par la porte de Fallana, au moment de la prière d'aser, "à 3h.40 p.m.", lit-on encore dans le rapport. Si on s'en tient à une tradition orale, le soir du même jour on célébrait le ZIKRI au battement du tambour. On fit croire aux Egyptiens que c'était le rappel de la population pour les attaquer. Les soldats pénétrèrent alors dans la ville. Trouvant les rues désertes, ils allèrent directement chez l'émir qu'ils étranglèrent. Des traditions écrites locales plus près de la verité, semblet-il, parlent de l'entrée des troupes le 10, ou même le 14 du mois de Ramadan et de l'exécution de l'émir le 26 ramadan, le 27 selon certains, donc deux semaines plus tard, au moment de derham, c'est-à-dire entre 10 et 11 heures du matin. L'émir récitait le Coran.

Un des successeurs de Mohammed Raouf Pacha au gouvernement de la ville fut l'énergique *Mohammed Nadi Pacha* que l'on nomma à ce poste en juin 1880. C'était un bel homme agé de 45 à 50 ans. De haute stature et bien proportionné, il dépassait son entourage de presque toute la tête. "Vernissé d'une certaine politesse et droiture d'âme", il favorise le commerce avec l'étranger. Des marchands indiens, grecs, italiens arrivèrent. C'est alors que la maison Viannay-Bardey de Lyon-Aden établit à Harar une succursale. Son agent fut le poète bien connu Arthur Rimbaud. Ce dernier prit possession de son poste, comme on vient de le dire, au début de décembre 1880.

Mohammed Nadi Pacha donna dans une ville où régnait un ardent fanatisme un exemple de tolérance en accueillant les premiers missionaires catholiques: "Je n'eus qu'à me louer de la réception que me fit Salim-Bey", le vice-gouverneur, note Monseigneur Taurin. Ce dernier avait déjà rencontré Mohammed Nadi Pacha à Zeila que lui avait fait le meilleur accueil, car il avait reçu du Khédive d'Egypte des instructions concernant la mission.

Sous Mohammed Nadi Pacha le total des troupes stationées à Harar s'élevait de 4.000 à 5.000 hommes.

> "A mon arrivée, en 1880", écrit Bardey, "le corps d'occupation comptait une brigade, soit un régiment égyptien et un régiment soudanais, deux batteries d'artillerie, 300 bachi-bouzouks ou troupes de choc, un peloton de chasseurs à cheval et un peloton de carabiniers casqués; pour produire une impression sur les indigènes Mohammed Nadi Pacha créa toute une administration qui occupait plus de 150 fonctionnaires, secrétaires, employés de douane."

Il organisa la police, releva les murs et les fortifications. Homme de discipline, son attitude sévère provoqua des protestations. C'est ainsi que, lorsqu'il fit son entrée à Harar le 23 septembre 1881.

> "il y eut un essai de résistance de la part de Salim-Bey; plusieurs soldats viennent protester devant moi", écrit Mgr Taurin, "contre la conduite du Bey; va-t-on se battre? S'il y avait une lutte sérieuse entre les deux partis ce serait une bonne occasion pour les fanatiques de Harar de profiter du tumulte pour se jeter sur notre maison. La majorité se declara pour Mohammed Nadi Pacha, les soldats, forçant les portes, l'introduisirent triomphalement, du reste, il n'a jamais prononcé que des paroles pacifiques."

Harar était une ville de 30.000 a 40.000 habitants où le commerce florissait. Ses marchands partaient au loin dans le sud de l'Ethiopie pour ouvrir des marchés.

Les environs de la ville avaient des jardins bien cultivés où poussaient le sorgho, le café, le kat, le tabac, la canne à sucre et des légumes que les Egyptiens avaient introduits. Ils inaugurèrent la culture de la vigne et toutes les variétés de céréales et légumineuses du delta.

Sous l'administration khédivale le commerce augmenta considérablement. Le principal revenu de la région était le café, les peaux de chèvres, de boeufs, le warz, sorte de safran, que l'on envoyait au golfe Persique ou en Arabie, où il servait de teinture et de cosmétique pour les dames.

Au temps des Emirs n'arrivaient à Harar que 70 caravanes, les routes étaient tres peu sûres. Des qu'une caravane était annoncée, les Oromo exactement informés par leurs espions se portaient à sa rencontre et lui demandaient une rançon; si la caravane était riche, elle devait, sous peine d'être pillée complètement, s'exécuter sur le champ. Si elle était pauvre, il fallait attendre avec patience le moment où les pillards reviennent à de meilleurs sentiments en ne leur laissant qu'une partie des marchandises. Par contre, sous les Egyptiens, on comptait 400 caravanes de la côte à Harar. Ces derniers assuraient la sécurité des voies de communication; des stations et des postes militaires avaient été établis sur tout le parcours.

Même une malle d'Europe, la "malle égyptienne", arrivait regulièrement.

Bardey notait que les douanes rendaient assez pour l'entretien des 4.000-5.000 hommes de troupe et fonctionnaires. Harar envoya même quelques fois au Caire des surplus d'impôts.

Le commerce aurait pu être plus developpé, "si le pays n'était entouré de brigands qui coupent les routes des meilleurs débouchés. Ce n'était pas toujours facile d'atteindre les marchés intérieurs" (Rimbaud).

> "En 1881", raconte Bardey, "j'engageai des gens de la tribu des Nole et leurs chameaux pour se rendre à Boubassa (sud de Harar), où mon agent

Rimbaud était allé créer un marché. Salim-Bey, gouverneur par intérim, dans sa sollicitude pour nos existences, chercha à nous dissuader de faire ce voyage. Il dit aux Nole: le prix de votre location de chameaux sera votre sang. Les Nole me dirent que si j'allais, ils me suivraient. Nous y allâmes et rien de fâcheux ne nous arriva."

Les craintes de Salim-Bey étaient néanmoins fondées. Peu de mois auparavant, l'explorateur francais Lucereau avait été assassiné à Warabele au voisinage de Kulubi. L'année 1881 fut marquée par une famine affreuse qui ralentit l'expansion économique. Mgr.Taurin écrivait le 20 mai 1881:

"Nous arrivons ici en pleine famine. Les récoltes ayant manqué l'année dernière et les routes ne sont pas assez bien ouvertes pour que les denrées nous arrivent de l'exterieur, aussi la population meurt-elle de faim. On comptait chaque jour 30 a 40 personnes expirant dans les rues et sur les places publiques."

Ali Rida Pacha

Mohammed Nadi Pacha quitta Harar le jeudi 11 janvier 1883. Le nouveau gouverneur tarda à venir. 1er octobre 1883, on publia officiellement la nomination du pacha Ali Rida qui venait de débarquer à Zeila. Il en partit le 6 novembre 1883 à 3 heures de l'après-midi et fit son entrée solennelle à Harar le 19 novembre à 9 heures du matin.

"De chez Rimbaud", écrit Mgr Taurin, "nous assistons au défilé des troupes devant le Pacha. Il est Turc, d'origine Kurde, fit sa carrière dans l'artillerie où il est général de division. Ceux qui l'ont approché jusqu'ici en disent du bien, c'est un vieillard de 70 ans à figure martiale, encore bien conservé."

"Homme d'une grande piété", dit Paulitschke, "il gouverna d'une façon passive et fut apprecié des musulmans. Il combattit l'influence des 'hommes de médecine' et 'docteurs de miracles'. Il fit détruire leurs drogues qui avaient fait beaucoup de mal par l'inoculation de certains vaccins. Il voulait aussi trouver les trésors qui, d'après lui, devaient exister dans les tombeaux de l'immigration argobba, au sud de Harar, trésors qu'on ne parvint pas à découvrir."

Pendant les derniers mois de 1883, les routes devaient être relativement sûres pour que Rimbaud ait pu explorer l'Ogaden (le rapport sur l'Ogaden daté de décembre 1883), et eut songé à créer un poste sur la rivière Wabi, à Imeh, à 8 jours de distance de Harar par caravanes.

Sous le gouvernement de Ali Rida se dessine déjà la pénétration des armées de Menelik vers Harar. Le 15 juin 1883, Mgr Taurin signalait que "les chefs amhara semblent s'être contentés de soumettre le pays au tribut jusqu'a la frontière des Oborra, située à une centaine de kilomètres à l'ouest de Harar". Rimbaud confirme en partie ces faits. Il écrivait en effet le 25 septembre 1883: "nous croyons que l'Itou sera definitivement annexé à l'empire de Menelik au commencement de 1884 . . . pour la cité de Harar, elle est hors du plan de l'Abyssinie". Pour dire vrai, il aurait pu ajouter: "momentanément".

Partie II; 1884-1886
"Subsidiaire alliance avec l'Angleterre" (Bardey)
"Un timide essai d'occupation" (Borelli)

Ce fut une période d'incertitudes. Les Egyptiens quittent. Les Anglais vont-ils venir? Vont-ils rester? Enfin de compte, ils decideront de passer le pouvoir a Abdullahi, fils du dernier émir que les Egyptiens avaient exécuté. Rimbaud ne sera pas le témoin de ces évènements. Il partit le 10 mars 1884 pour Aden et ne reviendra à Harar qu'en 1887 " où il ne fera d'ailleurs que passer

. . . la maison, se trouvant gênée (et les troubles de la guerre se répercutant ici), est en train de me faire liquider cette agence de Harar" (janvier 1884).

Ridouan Pacha

L'officier de marine, *Ridouan Pacha*, revint a Harar le 24 novembre 1884, après en avoir été gouverneur de mars 1878 à juin 1880. Il était accompagné d'officiers anglo-indiens et de la police indienne qui avaient pour mission de diriger les mesures d'évacuation.

Qu'est-ce qui amena les Egyptiens à abandonner Harar? Bardey écrivait: "qu'après les évènements d'Egypte de 1882, l'Angleterre obligea les Egyptiens à évacuer Harar, Berbera et Zeila. L'intention évidente de l'Angleterre était de se subsistuer aux Egyptiens en mettant l'ancienne colonie égyptienne en 'subsidiaire alliance' suivant son terme".

Le 24 février 1884 deux officiers anglais arrivent, toute la ville va les voir par curiosité et non par sympathie car depuis qu'on a entendu ici qu'ils étaient en route tous ont été préoccupés, qui sont-ils? Pourquoi viennent-ils? Et voici l'incident arrivé au major Hunter.

> "Hunter, n'étant pas content de la maison qu'on lui avait donnée, est venu loger chez Rimbaud. Le Pacha, l'ayant su, lui a intimé l'ordre de partir le soir même et aurait défendu aux habitants d'aller le voir. C'est sans doute pour apaiser la déconvenue de Rimbaud que le major fit acheter chez lui pour 500 thalaris de marchandises."

"Le drapeau britannique (le drapeau des Indes, relate le père Ferdinand) flotte continuellement sur l'ancien comptoir de Bardey et les Harari sont furieux parce qu'il y a une croix au milieu."

De toute façon, Ridouan Pacha lança un ordre du jour enjoignant à toute la population d'obéir aux ordres du délégué anglais et se mettre entièrement a sa disposition. Le premier soin du délégué fut d'enrôler des soldats indigènes et on réussit à former en quelques jours une troupe d'une centaine d'hommes, Somali et Harari. On fait réparer les forteresses et les routes. On fit élever hors de la ville des batteries, chacune de ces batteries recevra une garnison de dix soldats indiens et le nombre de ces forts sera de dix.

Un ordre d'Egypte arrive en août 1884, disant qu'il fallait évacuer la ville le plus tôt possible et que si le temps manquait, il faudrait se mettre en dehors des murs sous des tentes. Les soldats égyptiens commencent alors à faire leurs paquets des objets les plus précieux. Il n'y a plus d'argent. Beaucoup sont de mauvaise humeur, car ils n'ont pas été payés. Tous les officiers, forcés de partir et qui étaient, apres dix ans de séjour, devenus propriétaires et chargés de famille, ont abandonné leurs meubles et immeubles pour rien aux indigènes et pour accélérer l'évacuation on leur a donné des "bons de propriété au Harar" qu'ils ne trouveront à se faire rembourser nulle part. Les chameliers qui ont chargé les bagages retournent à Harar, furieux contre les Egyptiens. Ils ne donnent rien à manger, disent-ils, et nous font faire des marches forcées.

Ridouan Pacha, lui, quittera le 26 mai 1886. Il quitta la ville escorté de toutes les autorités et salué par le canon. L'occupation égyptienne appartenait désormais au passé.

Les Britanniques n'avaient nullement l'intention d'annexer Harar. Ils désiraient seulement préparer le transfert du pouvoir à un chef local. Ripon, l'ex vice-roi des Indes, était opposé à l'occupation anglaise de Harar. Les Anglais actuellement ne s'en occupent que dans la crainte de voir s'y implanter les Français. Leur but est d'évacuer Harar et de la remettre aux indigènes sous leur protection. Voici la raison principale qu'en donnait Rimbaud: "La côte du Somali et le Harar sont en train de passer des mains de la pauvre Egypte dans celle des Anglais, qui n'ont d'ailleurs pas assez de forces pour maintenir toutes ces colonies". Peu avant, le père Ferdinand avait déjà remarque: "faute de soldats, les anglais ne peuvent pas occuper Harar". Mgr Taurin notait lui aussi: "On dirait qu'ils ont travaillé à se débarrasser de Harar tellement leurs procédés sont contradictoires avec leurs intérêts".

Règne de l'émir Abdullahi

Walsh, gouverneur anglais de Berbera et Zeila, aurait dit, en septembre 1884, que les Egyptyiens quitteraient Harar dans 6 mois, qu'on nommerait un émir, choisi parmi les indigènes avec un résident anglais et une armée anglo-indigène. En janvier 1885, on publie que l'élection d'un émir, issu de la famille princière, sera décidément abandonée aux votes de la population de Harar et peut-être des tribus oromo voisines. Le nouvel Emir prit le parti de régner seul sans la tutelle anglaise: consternation du consul anglais qui comptait fermer le diwan immediatement et gouverner au nom de son gouvernement.

L'agent de Bardey raconte l'avènement du nouvel emir:

> " Le 20 mai (1885) a eu lieu le couronnement de l'émir, assisté de ses 15 frères, armés de sabres et revêtus d'immenses robes de madapolam, et en présence du pacha et du consul anglais, en tenue officielle. Dans la cour du diwan avait été disposée une estrade couverte de tapis, sur laquelle monta le bachikateb égyptien pour lire le firman du khédive, conseillant spéciale-ment au nouveau souverain de protéger le commerce et de garder la patrie de l'invasion. Sur ce, aux cris de la population acclamant l'émir, le drapeau vert du defunt émir fut hissé sur le diwan, et après les prières de grâces à la coupole de l'illustre Abadir et a l'antique mosquée des émirs, Abdullahi entre et vint siéger au Diwan en place du Pacha, résolu à gouverner seul comme le lui accorde le firman, et sans aucune intervention du consul anglais. Il est certain que la troupe indigène, étant du côté de l'émir et maîtresse des forts, de l'artillerie et des munitions, le consul sera expulsé s'il ne prend le parti de se taire."

Le 10 juin 1885, les deux délégués anglais quittent Harar en emportant leur drapeau. C'est ainsi que l'émir dejoua les plans de l'Angleterre: "mettre Harar en subsidiaire alliance".

Partie III: 1887-1891
Harar passe sous le contrôle de Menelik

D'après certaines confidences reçues de Menelik, on pensait depuis longtemps que celui-ci prendrait Harar un jour ou l'autre. Ne disait-il pas à son entourage: " L'Harar comme les autres pays de Jimma, Kaffa etc . . . appartenait à l'empire éthiopien en 1500, et fut perdu par les vic-toires de Gragn". Ce fut l'affaire Porro qui fournit à Menelik le prétexte d'attaquer Harar. Mgr Taurin écrit dans son journal que le massacre de l'éxpedition italienne eut lieu à Artou (pres de Geldessa), sans doute le mercredi 7 avril 1886:

> " . . . les étrangers auraient remis leurs armes sur la promesse d'être con-duits sûrement a l'émir. On se serait mis en marche et vers Artou on aurait tiré sur eux. Le compte Porro, fuyant a cheval, fut tué par un Issa . . . on dit que l'émir n'avait pas donné l'ordre de ce massacre." Il semble bien que les envoyés harariens, si on s'en tient à la tradition locale, avaient seule-ment reçu l'ordre d'empêcher la mission Porro de pénétrer sur le territoire Oromo.

La confrontation des armées choannes de Menelik avec celle de l'émir Abdullahi eut lieu le 7 janvier 1887, fête du Noel éthiopien (tahsas 29). Rimbaud raconte le combat au directeur du journal le *Bosphore égyptien*:

> "Menelik avait depuis longtemps l'intention de s'emparer du Harar, où il croyait trouver un arsenal formidable, et en avait prévenu les agents poli-tiques français et anglais sur la côté . . . d'un côté, l'émir Abdullahi, depuis

le départ de Ridouan Pacha . . . organisait une petite armée et revait de devenir le Mahadi des tribus musulmanes du centre de Harar. Menelik se mit en marche lui-même d'Antotto avec une trentaine de mille guerriers. La rencontre eut lieu a Chalanko, à l'ouest de Harar . . . l'émir n'avait que quelques centaines de Remington, le reste de la troupe combattant a l'arme blanche. Se trois mille guerriers furent sabrés et écrasés en un clin d'oeil par ceux du roi du Choa . . . l'émir, (qui avait eu le bras cassé dans le combat - Mgr Taurin -), put s'enfuir au Harar d'où il partit la même nuit pour aller se réfugier chez le chef de la tribu des Guerrys dans la direction de Berbera . . . Menelik entra ensuite (9 janvier) au Harar sans résistance, et ayant consigné ses troupes hors de la ville, aucun pillage n'eut lieu. Le monarque se borna à frapper une imposition de 75.000 thalers sur la ville et la contrée, à confisquer, selon le droit de guerre abyssin, les biens meubles et immeubles des vaincus morts dans la bataille, et alla emporter lui-même des maisons des Européens et des autres tous les objets qui lui plurent. Il se fit remettre toutes les armes et munitions en dépôt en ville . . . . . et s'en retourna pour le Choa laissant 3.000 de ses fusilliers campés sur une hauteur voisine."

Au moment de la prise de Harar, Rimbaud arrivait à Antotto avec son chargement de fusils. Là, il attendit le retour de Menelik qui fit son entrée victorieuse "précédé de musiciens sonnant à tue-tête des trompettes égyptiennes trouvées à Harar, et suivi de sa troupe et de son butin, parmi lequel deux canons Krupp transportés chacun par 80 hommes".

Le gouvernement de Makonnen

Rimbaud partit d'Antotto le 1er mai 1887, en compagnie de l'explorateur français Jules Borelli. Il allait à Harar rencontrer Makonnen, le nouveau gouverneur, qui lui versa 8.500 thalers sous forme de traites. Le long du chemin, il traversa, le 20 mai 1887, le champ de bataille de Chalanko où "des squelettes gisent de toutes parts et nous foulons sous nos pieds de ossements humains" (Borelli).

A Harar, Rimbaud ne fera qu'y passer, puisque le 30 juillet, au plus tard, on le trouve à Aden. Ce qu'il verra a été décrit par Borelli:

"Le gouverneur Makonnen me reçoit bien et me donne un logement. A son arrivée, Menelik avait interdit l'entrée de la ville à ses soldats . . . après son départ les tentes ont été abandonnées, et ils ont fouillé les silos et enlevé toutes les provisions. Les malheureux spoliés se sont plaints à Makonnen qui n'osait pas sévir dans la crainte d'une rebellion . . . le séjour à Harar est funeste aux gens du Choa: 4.000 soldats et 2.000 serviteurs sont rassemblés dans la ville. Il en perit beaucoup. La mortalité à pour cause immédiate la mauvaise qualité du dourah (sorgho) qui fermente dans les silos."

Rimbaud revient pour de bon à Harar le 3 mai 1888. Il en repartira, malade et infirme, le 7 avril 1891, allongé sur une civière.

Une lettre officielle, datée du 15 mai 1888, l'engage à suspendre provisoirement "le débarquement des armes pour le Choa". Il renonce alors au commerce des armes et décide de fonder à Harar, pour son compte, une agence commerciale. Il est "bien pourvu de fonds et de marchandises", "somme toute on est en paix et sûreté relatives", "les affaires, elles, vont tantôt bien, tantôt mal". La route de Zeila reste, quand même, peu sûre. "Les routes sont à chaque instant fermées par des guerres, des révoltes, qui mettent mes caravanes en péril."

La voie d'acces au Choa était désormais ouverte et Rimbaud commerce avec cette région par l'intermédiaire de Ilg, le ministre suisse de Menelik.

"Le roi Menelik avait fait, entre-temps, une nouvelle et formidable contribution extraordinaire. Comment payer cette somme? L'épizootie a tout détruit ici, la récolte du café est nulle . . . les européens ont été condamnés à payer leur part." (Rimbaud).

Dans la seconde moitié de 1889, Makonnen partira en ambassade en Italie. Le 2 août, il s'embarquera de Zeila à bord du croiseur italien Christophe Colomb pour arriver le 21 à Naples. Makonnen resta toujours attaché à Rimbaud. Témoin cette lettre qu'il lui écrivit pendant sa dernière maladie: " J'apprends avec plaisir que vous vous proposez de revenir à Harar pour continuer votre commerce. Cela me fait plaisir, oui, revenez vite en bonne santé. Je suis toujours votre ami".

Malgré tous les tracas, inévitables aux négociants de cette période, et quelques mois avant son départ, apparaît enfin, dans une lettre que Rimbaud adressa à sa mère, une note optimiste: " J'envoie à la côte des caravanes de produits de ces pays: or, musc, café etc . . . enfin on y est libre et le climat est bon".

SOURCES

Journal du Père Ferdinand (MS), archives, Harar.

Journal de Monseigneur Taurin Cahagne (MS), archives, Rome.

Lettres de Monseigneur Taurin Cahagne (MS), archives, Paris.

Bardey, Alfred. Notes sur Harar, (Bulletin de géographie historique et descriptive, Paris, année 1897).

Bardey, Alfred. *Barr-Adjam, souvenirs d'Afrique Orientale.*

Borelli, Jules. *Ethiopie Méridionale*. Paris, 1890.

Douin. *Le règne du Khédive Ismael: la conquête du pays de Harar*. Le Caire, 1936-1941.

Mohammed Mukhtar. *Notes sur le pays de Harar*. Le Caire, 1876. (Bulletin de la soc. Khédivale du Caire).

Paulitschke, F. *Le Harar sous l'administration égyptienne: 1875-1885* (bull. de la soc. Khédivale du Caire, série 2, no.10).

Rimbaud, Arthur. *Oeuvres complétes*. Paris, La Pléiade, 1975.

MARKETS, LOCAL TRADERS AND LONG-DISTANCE MERCHANTS IN SOUTHWESTERN ETHIOPIA DURING THE NINETEENTH CENTURY

Guluma Gemeda

The prevailing political conditions in southwestern Ethiopia during the nineteenth century were not very conducive for the conduct of trade. The reports of foreign travellers, merchants and missionaries who visited some parts of Ethiopia in the middle of this century indicate that the Oromo in southwestern Ethiopia were in a constant state of warfare. This prevalent state of war and the resulting sense of insecurity all over the region inhibited the movement of merchants. Charles Beke, who visited some places in Gojjam in the early 1840s, remarked for example: "The constant state of warfare in which the Gallas live renders it . . . utterly impossible for a single traveller to penetrate through their country".[1] At the same time, Plowden, who witnessed the difficulties that caravan merchants faced in Gudru, noted the long time they spent while negotiating with local authorities, because "each man on his father's land is a master".[2]

Further to the south, in the territories of the Oromo monarchies in the Gibe valley, the situation was more or less similar to what Plowden observed in Gudru. The only difference was probably the existence of relatively well-organized monarchies, and the safety of merchants at least within the confines of these kingdoms. In the Gibe valley, the number of local authorities demanding duties was largely minimized. But even here, the constant state of emergency and the conflicts which harassed Ethiopian society in general also affected this area. The constant fighting among the Oromo monarchies themselves on the one hand, and the wars against the Omotic kingdoms on the other impeded the movement of merchants.[3]

But this does not mean that trade was totally absent. Despite all the obstacles, merchants managed to move about through these lands. Even before the turn of the nineteenth century, James Bruce, one of the very few foreigners who visited Ethiopia in the eighteenth century, noted that Muslim merchants had found out the means of trading with the Oromo in the west partly through "courage, patience and attention".[4]

This trade throughout the nineteenth century was quite similar to the pre-colonial trade patterns in other parts of Africa. Passing through different areas under the control of the local chiefs, the long distance merchants had to negotiate for the safety of their lives and their properties. The local political authorities, on the other hand, provided protection to the caravan merchants in return for gifts of valuable luxury items or the monopoly of buying and selling the commodities they needed.[5] Moreover, as elsewhere in Africa, long distance trade in Ethiopia was largely seasonal. Here, more than the obstacles created by the local political conditions, movement during the rainy season was hindered by the heavy rains and the overflooded rivers. But people engaged in trade were not idle even during the rainy season. The amateur traders who operated on a small scale between the various local markets simply turned to their agriculture. The more important caravan merchants spent the time planning and organizing themselves for the next commercial expeditions.[6] Thus, the end of the rainy season was marked by the launching of new commercial expeditions in different directions.

As a result of this trade, many foreign goods and salt, the most important product of northern Ethiopia, reached the Omotic and Oromo kingdoms in the southwest while commodities like gold, ivory, slaves, musk, coffee, wax and honey were exported from the area. The trade in these commodities in the nineteenth century facilitated the emergence of some markets along the main trade routes. Although these markets gained more importance in the nineteenth century due to the revival of trade, some of them were probably not new. They seem to have served as centres of local exchange for many centuries. Some of these markets that flourished in Gudru in the mid-nineteenth century had already been noted by A. Triulzi.[7] These markets served mainly for the transit trade between northern and southwestern Ethiopia. As witnessed by Massaia in the 1850s, some of them, like Asandabo, attracted many people from the surrounding areas, their number reaching about one hundred thousand on market days;[8] while others were attended by at least three thousand to five thousand people.[9]

During the same period, a number of such markets also flourished in the southwest, in the Omotic and Oromo territories. Billo, for example, emerged as a leading market in the eastern Leqa region.[10] This market served as a meeting place for merchants coming from the Sibu and Leqa chiefdoms in the west; Bunno and Dapo in the southwest; Kafa and the Gibe Oromo monarchies in the south. To the west of Billo grew markets like Sire (in the eastern Sibu region), Neqemte and Boneya (in Leqa), Arjo and Getema.[11] But even more important were those that emerged in the Gibe valley, in the Oromo monarchies and Kafa. In Limmu, the most northerly branch of the Oromo monarchies, were markets like Saqa, Atnago, Chaffe, Dambi (Suntu) and Sappa.[12] Among these Saqa was by far the most important market in the region. Charles Beke considered it a ". . . universally recognized . . . principal market" in the country.[13] Limmu, during his visit to Gojjam, was "the main source of the trade of Abyssinia".[14] It was at Saqa that the long-distance and local traders exchanged their goods. By the middle of the nineteenth century, both Krapf and Harris estimated the population of this market place to be about twelve thousand inhabitants.[15] But this figure seems to have increased on market days and when new caravans arrived from the north. On the arrival of a fresh caravan from the north, Antoine d'Abbadie writes: ". . . huts are bought and carried sometimes from the distance of several miles, [but] when the caravan is gone, most of the Saka huts are taken down".[16]

Besides Saqa there were also other important markets in the Gibe region. These included: Hirmata, Qumbi and Ono (all in Jimma), Sayo (in Gomma), Challa (in Gera), Bonga (in Kafa) and Gombota (in Guma).[17] Most of these markets were visited by the long-distance merchants or their agents. Farther in the west the revival of trade through the Bertha region in the second half of the nineteenth century led to the emergence of some important exchange centres both in Bela Shangul and the western edges of the Oromo territory.[18]

In the middle of the nineteenth century these markets were linked by trade routes which were frequented by both long-distance merchants and local traders. One of the major routes connecting the markets in the Oromo region south of the Abbay with those in Gojjam and beyond passed through Asandabo, in Gudru, to Basso in Gojjam. Going from Asandabo southwards, this route led to Lagamara and Billo in the eastern Leqa region.[19] From Billo, merchants passed through the Nonno territory before reaching Saqa. But because of the prevalent hostilities between Limmu and Nonno, long-distance merchants were forced to stay in the latter country. Sometimes, when relations between the two were tense, as they were in 1842-3, merchants were delayed there for months.[20]

But on their arrival in the kingdom of Limmu, long-distance merchants enjoyed the protection of the king of that country, Abba Bogibo (r. 1825-1861). For the protection that he extended to merchants and travellers who visited his kingdom, Abba Bogibo earned much popularity.[21] The strength of his kingdom and the generous gifts that he sent to the chiefs who controlled the trade routes at different points made him the most influential chief in southwestern Ethiopia in the middle of the century.

Abba Bogibo is, however, often accused of prohibiting merchants from going beyond his kingdom.[22] Thus, merchants coming from northern Ethiopia were allowed to exchange their goods with those coming from the surrounding areas at the markets under his control. This means that the markets in Limmu were, at least for some time, the focal points to which merchants came from the north and the south — Kafa, Jimma, Guma, Gomma, Gera, Kambata, and even as far south as Walayta, Kullo and Konta.[23] Abba Bogibo was able to turn Saqa, his capital, into an important trading centre in the Gibe region. Through this trade, Saqa was able to attract many Muslim merchants, some of whom later on settled there permanently. It is, however, important to note that some of the caravan merchants were able to reach other

Fig.1 The Gibe Monarchies and the Trade Routes in the 19th Century

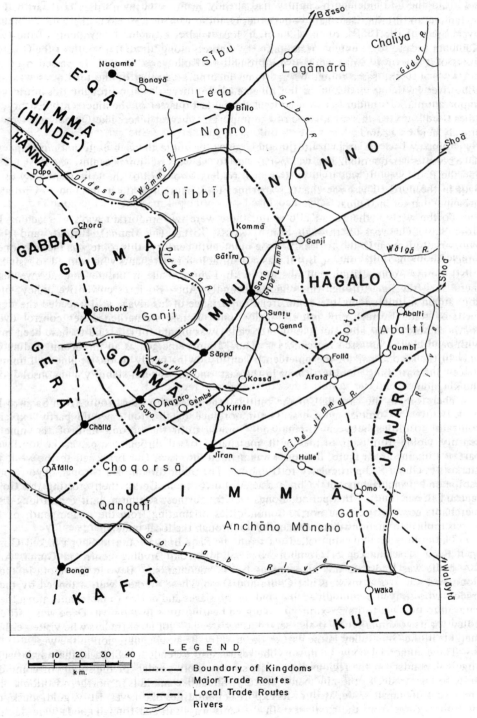

LEGEND

——·——·—— Boundary of Kingdoms
———————— Major Trade Routes
— — — — — Local Trade Routes
〜〜〜〜〜 Rivers

markets in the south, in spite of the attempts made by the rulers of Limmu to stop them.

Passing through Saqa further to the south, the route was divided at least into four branches. One of these appears to have passed through Folla, in the northeastern part of Jimma, to Janjero and Bosha, and then to the other Omotic principalities along the banks of the Omo river. From the left bank of the Gibe river, local traders brought the products of the Gurage, Kambata and, to some extent, Walayta to the markets along the route. South of the Gojeb, products of the surrounding regions were brought to Kullo, and from there passed over to the north through the same route. When Jimma incorporated most of the territories west of the Gibe river in the second half of the nineteenth century, she also brought this route and its important markets under her own control. In the last quarter of the nineteenth century, when Jules Borelli visited this area, some of the important market places like Qumbi and Omo were already held by Jimma.[24]

Compared to the other routes in the region, the route through eastern Jimma appears to have been less frequented. This was partly due to the wars of Jimma against the Bosha, Janjero and the Badi clans. It was used by the local traders who most of the time went only as far as Saqa in the north. These merchants sometimes took another route from Omo to Hirmata, the principal market in Jimma.

To the west of the Saqa-Kullo route, there were two important ways of reaching Bonga from Saqa. One passed through Sontu, Kossa, Kiftan (in Manna), Hirmata and through Choqorsa to Bonga. In the first half of the nineteenth century, this route was the only one over which Jimma had full control. But it was not suitable for merchants who wanted to visit Bonga. First, Jimma's competition and hostility with Limmu made it unsafe and inconvenient for merchants travelling through this region. Secondly, Abba Bogibo's preventive policy, presumably aimed at minimizing the commercial importance of his rivals, also impeded the development of trade through this route. Finally, until Jimma strengthened her control over the southern borders the area along the Gojeb valley was unsafe for it is said to have been infested with bandits who harassed merchants.[25] Thus, Jimma emerged as an important trading centre only in the second half of the nineteenth century owing partly to the decline of Limmu; her success in controlling more territories in the east; and the general stability and consolidation of the kingdom.[26]

Therefore, in the first half of the century, the most important route from Saqa to Bonga passed through Gomma and Gera. The importance of this route would partly explain the constant hostilities between Jimma and Gomma until the second half of the nineteenth century. Going from Saqa to the south, merchants passed through Sappa, in the southwestern part of Limmu. From there, the route was divided into two. One branched to the west, to the markets in Guma and particularly to Gombota. The other directly led through Sayo (Gomma's capital and principal market), Challa and Afallo (both in Gera); then crossing the Gojeb, it reached Bonga. During this period, Bonga was the farthest southern limit for all long-distance merchants coming from the north. Commodities originating from the region south of Bonga were supplied to the long-distance merchants through the local traders.

The other route that branched off from the Saqa-Bonga route at Sappa linked Gombota with Saqa. The market of Gombota was an important trading centre in Guma. Antoine d'Abbadie was told that this market was full of merchants.[27] Beyond Gombota in the west flourished some local markets like Chora and Dapo. These markets were attended by the local traders who relayed commodities like gold, ivory, slaves and coffee to merchants along the main caravan route. Due to its proximity to the gold bearing areas in the west, Dapo was particularly noted for its gold market.[28] It also served as a watershed for local traders who visited either the markets in the Gibe valley in the east or those in the Bela Sahngul region in the west.

The commercial network in the Gibe region also extended to Shoa in the northeast. Shoa largely depended on the regions west of its southwestern border for the supply of commodities in its foreign trade. In the nineteenth century, Shoa, like markets in northern Ethiopia, carried out a kind of transit trade. Most of its export commodities like slaves, ivory, gold, musk, coffee and others came from the southwest. In the same way, salt and foreign goods were distributed to the western region.[29] For the exchange of these commodities, Shoa had some important markets on its southwestern border. Among these, Rogge, near the Yerer mountain, and Endodi, near the upper Awash were particularly very important for its trade with the southwestern region.[30] Local traders from the Gibe valley came to these frontier markets with the products of their region and exchanged them for those coming from the north (salt) and the coast (foreign goods). This trade was largely left to the local traders because of the commercial policy of the Shoan rulers. As part of their efforts to maintain the commercial importance of the kingdom, these rulers did not very often allow the long-distance merchants to penetrate to the west.[31] However, through the commercial network established between the small markets and the activities of the local traders, Shoa obtained the marketable products of the Gibe region.

Although not very clearly established and probably less regular,[32] there were two routes that linked the Gibe region with Shoa. One of these went from the Gibe region (Jimma or Limmu) through Hagalo and Nonno territories to the Dandi mountain, near the source of the Guder river. From there, it led to the Shoan markets of Rogge or Endodi.[33] The second route led from northeastern Jimma or Saqa to the Chabo country; and then passing through the Soddo market it reached Endodi and Rogge.[34] During his visit to the Gibe region in the early 1840s, Antoine d'Abbadie was told that some merchants from the west were going to the Soddo market to sell slaves and other products of the Gibe region.[35]

On the other hand, very little is known about the penetration of Sudanese merchants into southwestern Ethiopia. Some foreigners who visited the region in the middle of the nineteenth century were informed about the coming of Sudanese merchants to the edges of the western Oromo territories.[36] In the early 1840s, Antoine d'Abbadie, for example, heard of the coming of Arab merchants, presumably through Sennar, to the market of Goji (Bojji?), a place two and a half days journey north of Sayo.[37] He was also told that some of these merchants sometimes went as far south as Sayo, Anfillo and Gacho (?).[38] At the same time Beke, who was informed from a distance about the penetration of the Sudanese merchants as far as the Gibe region via Wellega, wrote: "The currency [in Kafa] consists of pieces of rock salt brought by the Sennar merchants by way of Wallaga, and common glass beads, thirty of which are equivalent to a piece of salt".[39] Massaia even mentions the coming of merchants from Fazogli to Billo market where they are said to have sold their gold and ivory.[40]

This, however, seems unlikely. Although entertained by merchants and missionaries,[41] the opening of a direct route from the Sudan to the Gibe region was prevented by various factors. Merchants were prevented from entering the region south of Sayo and Anfillo mainly by the hostile environment, that is the prevalence of malaria and *gandi* which killed human beings and the beasts of burden respectively.[42] And even more important, the general absence of security for the life and property of the merchants prevented them from passing through the western Oromo lands to Kafa and the Oromo kingdoms in the Gibe region. Testifying to this, a respectable Christian merchant from Gojjam told Antoine d'Abbadie that:

> Tout le Wallaga est un pays trés peu sûr. On y tue tout étranger qui montre une objet de quelque valeur, même une toge blanche. Le meurtrier n'a ensuite qu'a parcourir une petite distance pour entrer dans un pays different ou il est à l'abri des poursuites. Cet état d'insecurité est la principale raison qui empêche les marchands du Sannar de pénetrer jusqu'a Inarya . . . Les negres tuent souvent les arabes en route, ce qui explique le peu du developpement du commerce de ce côte là.[43]

But this again does not mean that the products of the southwestern region failed to reach the main trading centres either in the west or the east. Although Sudanese merchants were not able to penetrate through the western Oromo region, commodities from the interior were supplied through a relay system by the Sibu and Leqa merchants: local traders collected the export commodities from the interior and supplied to the Sudanese merchants coming to the Bela Shangul markets. In exchange they received salt, beads, cloths and other goods which they distributed into the interior.[44] In spite of the limitations this trading system provided the Sudanese merchants with the commodities of southwestern Ethiopia. It also served as an alternative route when the Sudanese merchants were unable to proceed to the Gibe region directly through Gondar.[45]

The trade of the Gibe region through the southeast is even more obscure. Items like sea salt are said to have reached Kafa through the southeast.[46] Kafa and the other peoples along the Omo valley are also said to have had trade relations with the Borana.[47] But at the same time the Somali trading system through this region appears to have hardly penetrated beyond the lakes. Abir believes that the Somali caravan system did not extend beyond the chain of lakes in southern Ethiopia.[48] This was because the Borana were opposed to the penetration of the Somali caravans to the west beyond their region. Thus, the trade of the Benadir coast with the interior was carried out through ". . . relays of indigenous trading systems, passing the trade goods of the far interior from one set of trading people to another until they finally reached the coast".[49] Here essentially the same pattern of the relay system that was seen in the direction of Bela Shangul existed in the southeast.

Thus, at least in the second half of the nineteenth century, southwestern Ethiopia had been brought into the wider network of commerce and commercial relations with northern and northeastern Ethiopia on the one hand and, even if indirectly, with Sudanese and Somali trading centres in the northwest and southeast respectively. But it would be wrong to attribute the creation of these commercial relations to the existence of long-distance merchants only. In this trade a very important role was also played by the local traders.

In the nineteenth century, trade in southwestern Ethiopia was carried out on two levels and involved two groups of merchants. At the local level it was conducted by small traders who do not seem to have been full-fledged merchants. They were amateur traders who operated with limited funds within a limited area. Nevertheless, this group of traders played a very important role in the commercial network of the period. For the local people, they were the only source of valuable goods from remote and inaccessible markets. They acted as middlemen between the people who lived in places far away from the major markets and the long-distance merchants. The local traders visited the small markets, to which the long-distance merchants had no access. Sometimes they also seem to have operated in relatively distant areas. A number of the itinerant traders whom Antoine d'Abbadie met during his visit to Saqa in 1843, and whom he calls the *afcala* seem to have belonged to this group of traders.[50] Some of these travelled as far as Sayo or Anfillo in the west. One such merchant was a certain Dawd, a native of Limmu, who gave his itinerary to Antoine d'Abbadie, after he returned from a commercial expedition towards Anfillo.[51] According to Dawd, the journey from Saqa to Anfillo took ten and a half or eleven days.[52] Abba Qawe, another informant of the French traveller, also seems to have visited the region west of the Gabba river to collect export commodities before he settled down in Saqa as one of Abba Bogibo's riflemen.[53]

During his stay in Limmu, d'Abbadie also met other local traders coming from Kafa, Kullo, Tambaro and even Walayta.[54] These traders brought the export commodities abundantly found in their respective areas, and exchanged them for goods coming from other areas. Kullo merchants, for example, brought slaves, mules, and locally made cotton cloths and exchanged them for salt, beads and other northern commodities.[55]

In the 1850s, Massaia also met some local traders at the market places along the caravan route between Basso and Saqa. At Billo, for example, he met a certain Jijo, shortly after he returned from a commercial expedition to Dapo.[56] It seems that there were many such local traders who were stationed at different centres, along the main caravan routes. Taking these centres as points of departure, many of them travelled to markets either inaccessible to or thought unprofitable by the relatively wealthy caravan merchants. But with their better knowledge of the area and their good local connections, these traders seem to have returned with reasonable profits. In doing this, they provided the long-distance merchants with the products of the interior which could not have reached the major markets otherwise. The local traders also played an active role in distributing the goods brought by the long-distance merchants. Thus, the two groups of merchants to some extent depended on each other.

Nevertheless, not all local traders were satisfied with the profits that they earned by selling their goods to the long-distance merchants. In an attempt to get more profits, some of them travelled to some markets in northern Ethiopia. Although they could not compete with the wealthy long-distance merchants, the small traders could earn some profits by making many and quicker trips between the north and southwestern regions.[57] Their trips were not only facilitated by their small size and local connections but also by the amount and type of commodities they dealt with. Because of their limited funds, the size of their merchandise was small and less expensive. For example, the small traders dealt with commodities like wax, coriander and coffee which were less expensive and less sought after by the wealthy merchants, who instead were concerned more with ivory, gold and slaves. Both the size and prices of the goods in which the small traders dealt had some practical advantages. Due to the small size of their merchandise and the cheaper prices they offered, they could easily dispose of their goods.[58] As Massaia suggests, some of the local traders from Gudru were able to make good fortunes by going to the Gibe region where they could buy coffee, wax and coriander with the salt they saved while serving the wealthy long-distance merchants.[59] These merchants had their Christian counterparts in the north. The latter, Beke claims, largely dealt with rock salt (amole), and travelled much faster than the Muslim merchants who dealt with slaves.[60] Like the small local traders in the south, the Christian amole merchants were able to dispose of their salt very easily since it was highly needed in the south.

Apparently, some of the local traders in the southwest during the nineteenth century were also agents of the big caravan merchants and local rulers. Abba Bogibo, for instance, is said to have sent some of his commercial agents to Sayo to exchange salt for horses.[61]

On the other hand, unlike the local traders, the bigger caravan merchants dominated the long-distance trade and the important trading centres. This group consisted of relatively wealthy and predominantly Muslim merchants. These merchants operated with big funds and visited only the major markets along the main caravan route. Some of them also had store houses at different places.[62] Beyond the major markets, they dealt through their agents and local traders to get the supplies from the distant places. Their penetration into places beyond the main trading centres was hampered by various political factors; insecurity due to unfavourable political conditions; frequent local wars; existence of hostile populations; absence of strong and cooperative chiefs to patronize them; or the prohibitionist policies of some local rulers. Owing to such problems, the Sudanese merchants who came to the Bela Shangul markets were not able to proceed beyond the Bertha region; while in the southeast, the Somali merchants from the Benadir coast were unable to penetrate beyond the Borana region. Similarly, due to the protective policy of the Shoan rulers, the Harari, Somali and Afar merchants were stopped at Aliyu Amba, Shoa's principal market. Therefore, even though the existence of the long-distance merchants was a stimulus for the revival of trade in the region, the active and more decisive role was played by the local traders.

MAJOR ITEMS OF TRADE

In the nineteenth century, the trade items taken to the southwest by the caravan merchants were mostly foreign goods. Merchants from Godnar took glasses, beads, cloths of different size and colour (especially blue calico), knives, scissors, cooking wares and, of course, salt to markets in the Gibe valley.[63] From the markets of Limmu, these and other local products were carried farther south to Kafa and the surrounding areas.

Among the major items taken to the south from the markets in the north, salt (amole) was by far the most important commodity. It was needed everywhere in Ethiopia, but its relative scarcity in the south and southwest increased demand for it even more. Thus, it was an indispensable item for both long-distance merchants and local traders.

The high demand for amole in southwestern Ethiopia during the nineteenth century can be deduced from its relative prices in northern Ethiopia, in Shoa, in Limmu and Kafa. In the 1840s Krapf estimated that a thaler could buy twenty pieces of salt in Shoa; while the same amount could only purchase five pieces in Kafa.[64] At the same time, in Limmu a piece of salt was exchanged for either large quantities of coffee, or three great pitchers of honey, or several sacks of wheat.[65] Almost four decades later, the Italian explorer, A. Cecchi, noted that a waqet (c.28

grams) of gold was needed to buy sixty to eighty *amoles* in the eastern Leqa market of Billo;[66] while in the early 1880s, another Italian traveller, Augusto Franzoj, observed that a thaler could purchase twenty-five to thirty *amoles* in Soqota; fifteen in Gondar; thirteen in Dabre Tabor; eight in Ankobar; seven in the Gibe Oromo kingdoms and six in Kafa.[67]

Salt was the principal item that the Sudanese merchants brought to the Bela Shangul markets in the west. In the last quarter of the nineteenth century, the import of salt to the Bela Shangul region was estimated at 70,000 pounds a year.[68] There, it was exchanged for the products of the western Oromo and the gold of Bela Shangul.

With the exception of some regional specializations, the markets in southwestern Ethiopia offered more or less similar products to the long-distance merchants. The principal items exported from this region included slaves, ivory, musk, gold, coffee and other natural products.[69] Of all these products, slaves constituted the major part of the trade in the nineteenth century.[70] The unfortunate victims were obtained through various ways; but the continuous internal wars might have been the major source of this trade.[71] Many slaves were brought to the markets of the Oromo monarchies of the Gibe valley from the surrounding Omotic principalities. Kafa was one of the major sources of slaves. Slaves from this region are said to have been passive and excellent when taken outside of their areas.[72]

It is very difficult to estimate the number of slaves annually sold from the southwest. But Beke at least gives us a rough estimate of the number of slaves reaching Basso in the early 1840s from the Oromo areas south of the Abbay. According to him, the weekly average was about two hundred slaves and he puts the annual figure nearer to about 6,000 to 7,000.[73] Probably half this number were also sold through Shoa.

Another important commodity originating from the southwest was ivory. Although not as rare as it was in the later years, big herds of elephants are said to have been found in this region in the middle of the nineteenth century.[74] But they were found more abundantly in the areas south of the Gojeb.[75] Before the commercial importance of ivory was recognized, elephants were killed mainly as a sign of bravery and for the exhibition of one's prowess. But even in the 1840s about seventy-five pairs of elephant teeth were weekly reaching Basso from the southwestern region.[76] The increased demand for ivory during this century seems to have led to the extensive search for and hunting of elephants.

Musk also constituted a considerable part of the export trade.[77] The main sources of this item were the Kafa and Oromo kingdoms of the Gibe valley.[78] In addition to the great demand for it in the caravan trade, musk was also of much medicinal value among the local people in the Gibe region.[79]

The civet cat from which the musk was obtained lived in the forests. In the Gibe region, these cats were caught by trapping and then kept in cages, where they were fed on meat and corn.[80] They were then exposed to heat, sometimes by burning fires daily in front of the cages to make the cats perspire.[81] The precious trade material was collected from the bladder in the hidden part of its body every eight days, if the cat was in a good condition, or every fifteen days in the case of malnourishment.[82] The musk thus collected was put into horns and sold to merchants. In the mid-nineteenth century, the industry of musk collection did not exist north of Limmu.[83]

Gold was another important item sought for by the long-distance merchants. In spite of Enarya's old reputation for the abundance of its gold, the Oromo kingdoms, which later on took over the region, did not possess mines of this precious item. Kafa also possessed no gold; it was brought there from the neighbouring areas like Sheka.[84] The trading centres along the northern caravan route and the markets in the Gibe valley got their gold supplies from the region west of the Didessa river or Wellega through local traders. Besides its importance as a precious item of trade, gold was also in great demand in the Gibe valley where it served as regalia of kingship among the Omotic and Oromo kingdoms. Its trade and possession was also strictly monopolized by the rulers. Due to this it is very difficult to assess the volume of the gold trade.

The major items of trade briefly listed above were mainly handled by the big caravan merchants. Besides, there were also other commodities like coffee, honey, wax, coriander, cotton and other local products.[85] At the local markets such items as cotton cloths, iron, cattle, mules and horses were also exchanged.[86] In Limmu, according to Antoine d'Abbadie, a good mule was sold for fourteen *amole*; a donkey for ten; a cow for six.[87] As regards local manufacturing, Limmu was also noted for its ". . . . daggers with well wrought blades, and ivory handles very elegantly inlaid with silver as well as cloths with ornamental borders".[88]

Among the commodities largely handled by the local traders, the demand for coffee was increasing in the second half of the nineteenth century. As a wild plant, coffee appears to have existed for many centuries in the forests of southwestern Ethiopia. Tradition in fact points at the highlands of Kafa as the original home of coffee.[89] Undoubtedly, today Ethiopia is considered as the original home of *Coffee arabica*.[90]

Since time immemorial coffee seems to have been used in Ethiopia both as food and as beverage. For this purpose, not only the beans but sometimes the whole fruit and the leaves were used in different ways.[91] Although both the cultivation and the consumption of coffee was interdicted for many centuries in the northern Christian areas, including Shoa, it had become a universal beverage among the inhabitants of the Gibe region by the middle of the nineteenth century.[92]

Both oral tradition and the relatively scanty references in the accounts of the nineteenth century travellers indicate that coffee was emerging as an important trade item only in the second half of the nineteenth century. Until this period, the matured and the best quality beans of the wild coffee were collected (in the months of September, October and November) and preserved for family consumption. During his visit to the Gibe region, Massaia witnessed the abundant existence of wild coffee in the region and lamented that it could not be a source of any great wealth for the local population because of the difficulty of transporting it to the coast.[93] Massaia also says that because of its limited demand coffee was rarely found in the markets.[94]

In general, the price of coffee was very low in the nineteenth century. In Saqa, for example, an *amole* bought about seven to fifteen pounds of coffee in the 1840s.[95] Coffee was then so cheap that it was sold in terms of whole load and there were no smaller units with which to measure it.[96] In the 1850s it was generally exchanged for an equal amount of grain.[97] Our informants also confirm that the price of coffee was very low in the past. They contend that the measurement of coffee by cups or other smaller units was totally unknown in this region until very recently. The smallest unit of coffee sold was a sack of goatskin, which the coffee merchants collected by very rough estimates.[98]

Apparently, the big caravan merchants did not bother to buy too much coffee in the first half the last century. If they bought some, as Massaia says, it was for their own consumption on their journey or to pay for the hospitality of the people who facilitated their progress on the route.[99] Thus, like wax and coriander, coffee was largely left to the local traders, who, however made some reasonable profits from its trade.[100] During his stay in Gojjam, Beke saw a Christian merchant who became an independent trader after returning to Basso with four donkeys loaded with coffee. This man claimed that he bought the coffee for two thalers in Saqa together with the donkeys[101] Abba Bogibo is also said to have sold a mule load of coffee for a mere thaler.[102]

Beyond collecting the wild coffee from the forests, the cultivation of coffee was rare before the second quarter of the nineteenth century. According to tradition, the cultivation of coffee began in Gomma about one hundred and fifty years ago.[103] During his reign in the 1830s and 1840s, Abba Rebu of Gomma is said to have ordered all his subjects to cultivate coffee. But the dignitaries were opposed to his decree due to the belief that the expansion of coffee forests would endanger the number of their cattle. However, they finally accepted the decision of the monarch when they were threatened with the confiscation of their wealth, and the loss of their positions in the kingdom.[104]

In the second half of the nineteenth century, further progress was made in the cultivation of coffee. In the 1850s, Abba Bogibo is reported to have possessed vast fields of coffee plantations.[105] Other Oromo chiefs in the southwest are also said to have been planting more coffee trees during the same period. On his way to Kafa, Massaia observed large coffee forests owned by the rulers of Gomma and Gera; and during his short stay in Kafa he himself planted about three thousand coffee trees around the Catholic station at Shappa.[106]

These very small beginnings in the cultivation of coffee in the nineteenth century eventually made the southwestern region probably the most economically valuable part of Ethiopia. By the beginning of the twentieth century the trade in coffee started to grow very significantly probably due to the improving means of transportation, i.e. the opening of the Gambela water transport system and the Jibuti-Addis Ababa railway.[107]

NOTES

1. C. T. Beke, "Abyssinia - being a continuation of routes in that country", *Journal of Geographical Society*, XIV (1844), pp.19-20; also *idem.*, "Diary of Journey in Abyssinia, 1840-1841", British Museum MS, ADD, 30251, p.265.

2. W. C. Plowden, *Travels in Abyssinia and the Galla Country* (London, Longmans, 1868), p.308. See also A. Triulzi, "The Gudru Oromo and their neighbours in the two generations before the Battle of Embabo", *Journal of Ethiopian Studies*, XIII:1 (1975), pp.54-55.

3. Informants: Abba Warri Abba Kabe (Agaro, 30 Aug. and 4 Sept. 1982). This informant gave some details on the wars fought between Jimma and Gomma during the reign of Abba Rebu (c. 1854-58) in Jimma. Limmu's constant wars against Hagalo and Nonno is also attested to by Limmu informants: Abba Dula Abba Magal (Ambuye, 26 Sept. 1982); Ato Shafi Abba Godu (Saqa, 24 Sept. 1982); Sheikh Aliye Abba Diko (Saqa, 23 Sept. 1982); Abba Warri Abba Garo (Ambuye, 27 Sept. 1982). See also E. Cerulli, "Folk Literature of the Galla of Southern Abyssinia", *Harvard African Studies*, III (Cambridge, 1922), pp.18-20.

4. J. Bruce, *Travels to discover the Sources of the Nile in the year 1768, 1769, 1770, 1771, 1772 and 1773*, 5 vols. (London, Gregg International Publishers, 1972), II, pp.222-3.

5. For example, see J. Vansina, *The Tio Kingdom* (London, International African Institute, 1973), pp.252-3.

6. G. Massaia, "My Thirty-Five Years of Missionary Work on the Ethiopian Plateau", 12 vols. III, p.50. This is a literal English translation of *I Miei Trentacinque anni di missione in alta Etiopia* (Rome, 1886-95). The translation was done by Father Aurelian Leverly in Addis Ababa, 1975-77. See also M. Abir, *Ethiopia: The Era of the Princes; the Challenge of Islam and the Re-unification of the Christian Empire* (London, Longmans, 1968), pp.50-51.

7. Triulzi, "The Gudru Oromo", p.53.

8. Massaia, "My Thirty-Five Years of Missionary Work", III, p.9.

9. Plowden, *Travels in Abyssinia*, p.310.

10. On Billo market, see Massaia, "My Thirty-Five Years of Missionary Work", IV, p.175; VI, pp.71-72; A. Cecchi, *Da Zeile alle frontiere de Caffa*, 3 vols, (Rome, 1885-7), II, pp.556-63.

11. Tesema Ta'a, "The Oromo of Wollega: A Historical Survey to 1910", M.A. thesis, Addis Ababa University (1980), pp.55-61. Tesema believes that there was a direct trade route linking Gojjam and the Gibe kingdoms through Neqemte. But this route had not yet

developed in the middle of the nineteenth century. See C. T. Beke, "Abyssinia . . . continuation of Routes", pp.39-40.

12. Informants: Ato Taddesse Solomon (Atnago, 21 Sept. 1982); Abba Dula Abba Godu (Saqa, 23 Sept, 1982).

13. C. T. Beke, *An Enquiry into M. A. d'Abbadie's Journey to Kaffa in the Year 1843 and 1844* (London, 1851), p.51.

14. C. T. Beke, "On the Countries South of Abyssinia", *Journal of the Royal Geographical Society*, XIII, (1843), p.259.

15. J. L. Krapf, *Travels, Research and Missionary Labours* (London, Frank Cass, 1968), p.64; W. C. Harris, *The Highlands of Ethiopia*, 3 vols. (London, Gregg International Publishers, 1968), III, p.53. Today Saqa remains outside the main Addis Ababa-Jimma road and has less commercial importance. During my field trip in Sept. 1982, its population was estimated to be only 500 to 700 inhabitants.

16. Antoine d'Abbadie, "Remark on Dr. Beke's Paper 'On the countries south of Abyssinia' ", in C. T. Beke, *Enquiry*, Appendix I. This statement was made in reaction to Beke's claim that Saqa was "the great emporium of Enarea". See *Enquiry*, p.51.

17. Informants: Abba Jobir Abba Boga (Agaro, 2 Sept. 1982), Abba Dura Abba Bora (Gera, 10 Sept. 1982). Abba Wari Abba Kabe.

18. See A. Triulzi, *Salt, Gold and Legitimacy; Prelude to the History of a no-man's land, Bela Shangul, Wallaga, Ethiopia* (c. 1800-1898) (Napoli, Instituto universitario Orientale, 1981), pp.125-38.

19. The route from Basso to Saqa has been mentioned by some nineteenth century travellers. For example, Ant. d'Abbadie, *Géographie de l'Ethiopie* (Paris, 1890), pp.54-55 and *passim*; C. T. Beke, "Diary of Journey in Abyssinia", British Museum MS, 30248, p.57; Plowden, *Travels*, p.308.

20. Beke, "On the countries South of Abyssinia", p.256.

21. Antoine d'Abbadie, *Géographie,* p.6; Massaia, "My Thirty-Five Years of Missionary Work", IV, p.185.

22. Massaia, "My Thirty-Five Years of Missionary Work", IV, p.185. See also R. Pankhurst, "An Inquiry into the Penetration of Firearms in Southern Ethiopia in the Nineteenth Century prior to the Reign of Menelik", *Ethiopia Observer*, XII:2 (1969), p.130.

23. Note should also be made of a similar policy of the rulers of Shoa during the same period. To maintain the commercial importance of the kingdom, they are very often said to have prohibited the merchants coming from the coast from travelling to the southwest and similarly the local traders coming from the southwest were prevented from going to the coast. At Aliyu Amba, the Harari, Afar and Somali merchants stayed in some sort of ethnic groupings. See R. H. Kofi Darkway, *Shewa, Menelik and the Ethiopian Empire* (London, Heinemann, 1978), pp.162, 172-5.

24. J. Borelli, *Ethiopie Meridionale* (Paris, 1890), pp.320, 331.

25. Harris, *The Highlands of Ethiopia*, III, pp.60-1.

26. Hailemariam Goshu attributes the commercial importance of Jimma in the latter part of the nineteenth century to the development of its local "industry" entrepreneurs and the stability of life in the kingdom: "The Kingdom of Abba Jifar II (1861-1934)", B.A. Thesis, Addis Ababa University (1970), p.11.

27. Antoine d'Abbadie, *Géographie,* p.77.

28. On Dapo (Dabo) and its gold trade, see Massaia, "My Thirty-Five Years of Missionary Work", VI, p.82.

29. Darkwah, *Shewa*, pp.156-8.

30. *Ibid.*, pp.157-60.

31. See note 23.

32. Ant. d'Abbadie says that one of the three commercial outlets of Limmu was Shoa through Agabdja which was regular and almost all coffee was exported by that route. "Remarks on Dr. Beke's paper", quoted in Beke, *Enquiry*, p.42. But Beke says merchants from Shoa only occasionally went to Limmu and there was "no regular trade between the two countries": "On the countries south of Abyssinia", p.259.

33. For example, see the itineraries of A. Aubry, "Une mission au royaume de Choa et dans les pays Galla", *Archives des missions scientifiques et literaries*, XIV (1888); and A. Franzoj, *Continente Nero* (Torino, 1885). See also Darkwah, *Shewa*, p.157.

34. Darkwah, *Shewa*, p.157.

35. Antoine d'Abbadie, *Géographie,* p.221.

36. *Ibid.*, pp.81-82. For other references see Triulzi, *Salt, Gold and Legitimacy*, p.131.

37. Antoine d'Abbadie, *Géographie,* pp.225-6.

38. *Ibid.*, p.97; cf. p.226.

39. Beke, "On the countries south of Abyssinia", p.262.

40. Massaia, "My Thirty-Five Years of Missionary Work", IV, p.175; VI, pp.71-72. However, he does not tell the route.

41. Antoine d'Abbadie, *Géographie,* p.203; G. Massaia, in a letter written in Kafa, 12 Oct., 1860, in *ibid.*, p.252; and "My Thirty-Five Years of Missionary Work", VI, p.82.

42. Antoine d'Abbadie, *Géographie,* p.213.

43. *Ibid.*, p.203.

44. Triulzi, *Salt, Gold and Legitimacy*, p.130.

45. *Ibid.*, pp.126-7.

46. Antoine d'Abbadie, *Géographie,* p.112; Beke, "One the countries south of Abyssinia", p.264.

47. R. Pankhurst, "The Trade of Southern and Western Ethiopia and the Indian Ocean Ports in the nineteenth and early twentieth centuries", *Journal of Ethiopian Studies*, III:2 (1965), p.37.

48. *Ibid.*; Abir, "Southern Ethiopia", in R. Gray and D. Birmingham, eds., *Pre-Colonial African Trade* (London, Oxford University Press, 1970), p.128.

49. Abir, "Southern Ethiopia", pp.130-1.

50. Antoine d'Abbadie called these traders *afcala*. He says that they were Oromo traders from Lofe, north of Saqa, Leqa and the surrounding areas. As he travelled from Basso to Saqa in 1843, with one group of these traders, he noticed the speed with which they conducted trade. He observed that they travelled between Saqa and Basso in a matter of five or six days, while it took long-distance merchants at least three months to complete this journey. According to Antoine d'Abbadie, the *afcala* were not satisfied with a single trip per year between Basso and the markets in the southern regions; they went and returned each time, selling their goods very quickly at reasonable profit. Antoine d'Abbadie, "Papiers d'Abbadie", F.N.A. 21300, p.296; *idem. Géographie*, pp.(6), 115. See also Abir, "Southern Ethiopia", pp.126-7; *idem.*, "The Emergence and Islamization of the Galla kingdoms for the Gibe and north Ethiopia's trade with these kingdoms 1800-54" (mimeographed, Addis Ababa, 1963). Today there are only very few informants who know the activities of the *afcala*. One informant, Abba Kabe, claims that *afcala* is probably a corruption of *abshala* (literally, "clever"). Interestingly, his description of the *abshala* corresponds to d'Abbadie's *afcala*. In the newly published Oromo dictionary, Gragg makes the meaning of these words the same. G. B. Gragg, ed., *Oromo Dictionary* (East Lansing, Michigan State University, 1982), p.9.

51. Antoine d'Abbadie, *Géographie*, pp.91-92.

52. *Ibid.*

53. *Ibid.*, p.147.

54. *Ibid.*, pp.80-89, 111-2.

55. *Ibid.*, p.112.

56. Massaia, "My Thirty-Five Years of Missionary Work", VI, pp.81-3.

57. Abir, "Southern Ethiopia", p.127.

58. The big caravan merchants had the problem of finding customers for their larger merchandise. Antoine d'Abbadie, for example, witnessed one wealthy long-distance merchant, Omar Badri, from Harqiqo, who had stayed two years in Jimma before he could dispose of his goods. Antoine d'Abbadie, "Remarks on Dr. Beke's Paper", quoted in Beke, *Enquiry*, p.51.

59. Massaia, "My Thirty-Five Years of Missionary Work", V, pp.78-9.

60. Beke, "Abyssinia . . . continuation of Routes", p.29.

61. Antoine d'Abbadie, *Géographie*, p.113.

62. Massaia, for example, met a certain Desta Guangul, son of a wealthy long-distance merchant from Gondar, at Lagamara. Massaia claims that this merchant had store houses at Massawa, Soqota, Ifag and Kafa: "My Thirty-Five Years of Missionary Work", IV, p.169.

63. Krapf, *Travels*, p.66; E. Combes and M. Tamisier, *Voyage en Abyssinie, dans les pays des Galla, de Choa et d'Ifat, 1835-1837*, 4 vols. (Paris, 1838), IV, p.97.

64. Krapf, *Travels*, p.58.

65. *Ibid.*, p.66.

66. A. Cecchi, *Da Zeila*, II, p.559; Triulzi, *Salt, Gold and Legitimacy*, p.131.

67. A. Franzoj, *Continente Nero*, p.58. For *amole*-thaler exchange rates in the nineteenth century, see R. Pankhurst, *Economic History of Ethiopia, 1800-1935* (Addis Ababa, 1968), pp.463-4.

68. Triulzi, *Salt, Gold and Legitimacy*, p.131.

69. Krapf, *Travels*, p.66.

70. Harris, *The Highlands of Ethiopia*, III, pp.55-6; Abir, *The Era of the Princes*, pp.53-62; Pankhurst, *Economic History*, pp.82-92.

71. Leon des Avancheres, in E. Massaia, *Lettere e scritti Minori anni 1827-1889*, 6 vols. (Rome, 1978), I, pp.28-9. See also Abir, *The Era of the Princes*, pp.54-5, and Guluma Gemeda, "Historical Traditions of the Gibe States: A preliminary Review of the Jimma Oral Tradition Project", B.A. thesis, Addis Ababa University (1980), pp.18-19. Tekalign W. Mariam is currently studying the slave trade in Jimma. See his M.A. thesis, "Slavery and the slave trade in the Kingdom of Jimma (ca. 1800-1935)", Addis Ababa University, 1984.

72. Massaia, *Lettere*, III, p.241.

73. Beke, "Abyssinia . . . continuation of Routes", p.19.

74. Informant: Abba Dula Abba Mogal (Ambuye).

75. Krapf, *Travels*, pp.66-7.

76. Beke, "Abyssinia . . . continuation of Routes", p.19.

77. Harris, *The Highlands of Ethiopia*, III, pp.55-6.

78. Beke, "On the countries south of Abyssinia", p.262.

79. Krapf, *Travels*, p.66.

80. *Ibid.*, pp.66-7; Massaia, *Lettere*, III, p.240.

81. Krapf, *Travels*, pp.66-7.

82. Massaia, *Lettere*, III, p.240.

83. *Ibid.*

84. Beke,"On the countries south of Abyssinia", p.262.

89. Harris, *The Highlands of Ethiopia*, II, p.429; III, p.55; Beke, "On the countries south of Abyssinia", p.262; Krapf, *Travels*, p.66. See also H. P. Huffnagel, *Agriculture in Ethiopia* (Rome, FAO, 1961), p.204.

90. Huffnagel, *Agriculture in Ethiopia*, p.204.

91. *Ibid.*, p.205.

92. Harris, *The Highlands of Ethiopia*, II, pp.411, 427, 429.

93. Massaia, "My Thirty-Five Years of Missionary Work", V, p.78.

94. *Ibid.*

95. Harris, *The Highlands of Ethiopia*, II, p.429; III, pp.55-6; Beke, "On the countries south of Abyssinia", p.258; *idem.*, "Diary of Journey in Abyssinia", pp.312-3.

96. Cf. Antoine d'Abbadie, "Remarks on Dr. Beke's paper", quoted in Beke, *Enquiry*, p.40.

97. Massaia, "My Thirty-Five Years of Missionary Work", V, p.78.

98. Informant: Abba Warri Abba Garo (Ambuye).

99. Massaia, "My Thirty-Five Years of Missionary Work", V, p.78.

100. *Ibid.*

101. Beke, "On the countries south of Abyssinia", p.258.

102. *Ibid.*

103. Informant: Abba Warri Abba Kabe (Agaro).

104. *Ibid.*

105. Massaia, "My Thirty-Five Years of Missionary Work", IV, p.187.

106. *Ibid.*, V, p.75. Antoine d'Abbadie was also told that the king of Jimma was planting coffee trees in the second quarter of the nineteenth century. "Remarks on Dr. Beke's paper", quoted in Beke, *Enquiry*, p.40.

107. Pankhurst, *Economic History*, pp.431, 451.

Alemayehu Lirenso

INTRODUCTION

GRAIN MARKETING IN POST–1974 ETHIOPIA: POLICIES, PROBLEMS AND PROSPECTS

Alemayehu Lirenso
Institute of Development Research
Addis Ababa University

INTRODUCTION

Generally speaking, agricultural marketing plays a crucial role in linking the spatial and temporal distance between rural production and urban consumption of farm outputs. But this depends on how it is organized in space and time, based on a specific economic policy (Beaujeu-Garnier and Delobez, 1979). Marketing of staple crops is a particularly important activity for rural-urban relationships as the market demand for food crops originates both in the urban and rural sectors of the economy. It is, therefore, plausible to say that the first priority of economic activity must be food supply because other economic activities can only exist if the need for food is met first (Schneider, 1984, 12). By the same token, it is understood that food marketing should be efficiently organized in order to make the various sectors of the economy function well.

The fact that food is a basic need and an important link between the rural and urban sectors of the economy has drawn the attention of many scholars to the study of the "food system" in many developing countries. Of these, Lele (1968), Jones (1972) and Croll (1983) may be noted. Most of these studies focused on the search for efficiency in the domestic food marketing system. Lele studied the grain markets in India and found that the Indian grain marketing system is competitive and seems to function well, whereas Jones gave an opposite conclusion from his study of Nigeria, Sierra Leone and Kenya. Exceptionally, Croll discovered that the Chinese marketing system has increased the stabilization of food rationing in spite of a rapid population increase.

Some empirical studies had also been undertaken on the structure of grain marketing in Ethiopia in the 1960's and 1970's. For example, a study of profit margins of grain merchants in the open market of Addis Ababa in 1966, showed that private investment in the grain trade yielded better returns than private investment in crop production (de Young, 1967). Also, during 1967-69 the Standford Research Institute studies marketing of grains and pulses and estimated the domestic supply - demand volumes for cereals (Thodey, 1969). Following this, Cornell University undertook a major analysis of the grain marketing system in the light of the assumed "market imperfections" in the early 1970's. The study concluded that the marketing of agricultural commodities works effectively, except at the village level (Manig, 1972, 66). A comprehensive field study of grain marketing was, also, undertaken for the whole country in 1971/72 based on observations of market practices in 90 market towns and on interviews with 2,500 grain dealers and farmers in those towns (Eubanks, 1973). The studies gave a general picture of the national grain market system and analysed how the private grain marketing system functioned up to the mid-1970's. Moreover, the studies were used as a framework for the Extension and Project Implementation Department's (EPID) marketing program in 1975/76, a plan to establish a farmer-based output marketing system within EPID (Wickstrom, 1973).

But after the February 1974 Revolution, similar empirical studies have not been undertaken, except that the situation of grain marketing was analysed by Holmberg (1977) for the year 1976 (i.e. the year after the land reform). Unfortunately, we lack a comprehensive and reliable body of literature showing the situation of grain marketing in the post-1974 period, during which several changes have been introduced into the erstwhile grain marketing system.

This paper makes a cursory review of the policy changes which took place in the field of grain marketing after 1974 and attempts to show the major operational difficulties faced by the state marketing agency, viz: the Agricultural Marketing Corporation (AMC) in the process of grain procurement from the peasant sector.

Field surveys have not been conducted for the purpose of this study. Most of the data contained here are, therefore, obtained from various documents. However, it is worth mentioning that the data on the operational problems of AMC at local level, are partly based on my earlier case study of the AMC branch at Hossana (Alemayehu, 1984).

GOVERNMENT PARTICIPATION AND CHANGES IN GRAIN MARKETING POLICY

Until 1960, most of the grain sold in local, regional and terminal markets was handled by private traders. Eubanks estimated that the number of middlemen engaged in the grain trade ranged between 12,500 and 25,000 in rural areas, and between 4,000 and 8,000 in urban areas (Eubanks quoted by Holmberg, 1977, 9). Competition was high among the middlemen at local and regional levels. As a result, grain prices in local markets were determined by market forces, although they were influenced by retail prices in the terminal markets (Manig, 1973, 64).

On the other hand, the grain producers lacked storage facilities and market information, and hence used to sell their produce during the harvest season at lower prices. In fact, their hasty sales of surplus grain were basically due to urgent need for cash to pay tax and debts (Agri-service Ethiopia, 1976, 7). In this regard, the grain producers were exposed to price exploitation by grain merchants.

According to Thodey, in 1966, the marketed surplus of cereal grains was 630,000 MT. Out of this, 15% went to the terminal markets of Addis Ababa and Asmara, and 40% to other regional markets, whereas the rest remained in the local markets. The market dependent population was 17% of the whole population in 1966. From the total marketed surplus 27.8% was constituted by *teff*, 21% by barley, 17.1% by sorghum, 16.3% by maize and 15% by wheat, suggesting that cereal grains constituted the bulk of the diet of the urban population in Ethiopia (Thodey quoted by Wickstrom, 1973, 5).

Government participation in the grain trade started in 1950 with the establishment of the Ethiopian Grain Board (EGB), which was set up as an autonomous agency to undertake export licensing, quality control and overseas market intelligence. However, it was weak in control of the domestic grain trade mainly because it did not hold stocks and could not stabilize the domestic market prices (Holmberg, 1977, 10).

In 1960 the government established the Ethiopian Grain Corporation (EGC) with the object of intervening in grain marketing as a big buyer (General Notice No. 267 of 1960). But the strong position of private traders in local markets undermined the role of the EGC. Hence, its market share could not exceed 5% of the marketed surplus until 1975/76 (Holmberg, 1977, 10). Moreover, the EGC lacked both working capital and a price policy, and suffered from limited market information at local level because its operations were mainly limited to large towns.

During the Third Five Year Development Plan (1968-73) grain marketing was included in the Comprehensive Agricultural Package Programs of the Chilalo Agricultural Development Unit (CADU), the Wolamo Agricultural Development Unit (WADU), and the Ada District Development Program (ADDP). The Package Programs aimed at protecting the farmers in their regions from the price exploitation by local traders, by purchasing cereals at harvest time at prices higher than local markets and storing them until prices of terminal markets were favourable. But the programs were ineffective due to the strong influence of middlemen, and served an insignificant proportion of the target population.

Active participation by the government in grain marketing developed only in the post-revolution period. In 1975, the Provisional Military Administrative Council (PMAC) had declared its general economic policy which listed eighteen activities that could be undertaken by the private sector, subject to government regulations. Among these were the wholesale and retail trades (PMAC, 1975, 11). The present grain marketing Policy is derived in part from the 1975 economic policy.

The establishment of the Agricultural Marketing Corporation (AMC) in 1976 was the first measure taken by the PMAC to enter into grain marketing (PMAC, Proc. No. 105, of 1976). According to Article 7 of Proclamation No. 105, the AMC was given several powers and duties which included purchase of agricultural products for domestic consumption, procurement and distribution of inputs and maintenance of a national grain reserve.

Until 1978/79, the AMC performed its grain procurements from peasants through competition with private traders in local markets. But following the introduction of the National Revolutionary Development Campaign (NRDC)[2] and the establishment of the Central Planning Supreme Council (CPSC), in 1978, the major objectives of the AMC in the field of grain marketing were restated as follows:

a) stabilisation of producer and consumer prices for grains;

b) encouraging grain production through price incentives; and

c) ensuring an adequate food supply for the public distribution system.

To achieve these goals, the AMC obtained the full support of the government (material as well as administrative), and used a quota purchase scheme and fixed prices as its key marketing strategy. Its working capital was, for example, 78,500,000 Birr in 1981/82 (NRDC & CPSC, 1982, 165). Bank loans accounted for 83% of the total value, whereas the rest was generated by the Corporation (10.2%), and granted by the government (6.8%). The major administrative support was, of course, the establishment of the Grain Purchase Task Force (GPTF) at all levels of the administrative hierarchy since 1977/78. The GPTF is an administrative body mainly composed of representatives from the Ministry of Interior, the Ministry of Domestic Trade, the Ministry of Transport and Communications, the Ministry of Agriculture and the Chairman of Peasant Associations at the respective levels of the administrative hierarchy. The major task of the GPTF at *woreda* level is the allocation of grain delivery quotas to peasant associations and service co-operatives, and the control of private grain traders in order to facilitate the AMC's operations at local level. The woreda administrator is Chairman of the woreda GPTF, whereas the AMC representative in the AMC's operational area is Secretary of the Woreda GPTF.

IMPLEMENTATION OF THE CURRENT GRAIN PROCUREMENT POLICY

Since 1979, the AMC has been assisted by at least four procurement policies for the achievement of the national goals of grain marketing. These are:-

a) control of private grain trade through licensing and supervision of the movement of private traders;

b) annually fixed (quota) purchases;

c) fixed and uniform grain procurement prices; and

d) giving purchase priority to grains supplied by service co-operatives over other suppliers.

The implementation of these policies at the regional and local levels and their effects are briefly discussed below.

Grain Licensing Policy

In accordance with the 1975 economic policy merchants have the right to engage themselves in wholesale and retail grain trade, however, the grain wholesalers remain under strict government control through the licensing policy of 1975 (PMAC, Proclamation No.76 of 1975). According to Article 5 of this proclamation, a trading license may be issued to a wholesaler with a working capital of less than 300,000 Birr. Moreover, the information obtained from the Domestic Business Activities and Price Control Administration of the Ministry of Domestic

Trade in December showed that a wholesaler has to pay 200 Birr as an annual fee for license renewal and one Birr per 1,000 Birr of his working capital for registration. Again, according to Article 6 of Proclamation No.76 of 1975, a license may be issued to a retailer is his working capital does not exceed 200,000 Birr.

At present, the number of grain wholesalers to be licensed every year is determined by the GTPF in each region, and the Domestic Business Activities and Price Control Administration issues licenses only to those grain wholesalers recommended by the GPTF. To be favourably recommended by the GPTF and to maintain their trading licenses grain wholesalers should not engage in any other activity besides wholesaling, should not violate the grain prices fixed by the CPSC, and should not move grains illegally (i.e. without getting moving permission from the local/regional GPTF). However, some wholesalers did not respect these regulations in the last six years, and some are said to have lost their trading license for not complying with the GPTF regulations in various regions. A case of AMC's branch at Hosana for example indicated that four out of thirty wholesalers lost their licenses in 1981/82 because they were alleged to have moved grains illegally, ignored the AMC's fixed grain prices and also earned incomes from farmland outside their home towns (Alemayehu, 1984, 63). By December 1984, there were 2153 licensed grain wholesalers and 2789 licensed grain retailers throughout the country. In Gojjam, one of the grain-surplus regions, over 1100 grain wholesalers and retailers were banned as of 1982/83 (Table 1).

TABLE 1

Number of Licensed Grain Merchants by Administrative Region
(1982/83)

Region	Wholesalers	Retailers	Total
Gojjam	None	None	None
Gondar	212	277	489
Wellega	121	98	219
Wello	136	303	439
Sidamo	63	180	243
Hararghe	165	222	387
Tigrai	179	114	293
Gamo Gofa	–	4	4
Illubabor	5	21	26
Keffa	35	110	143
Bale	40	8	48
Asseb	3	33	36
Addis Ababa	865	881	1746
Arssi	289	73	362
Eritrea	40	181	221
Total	2153	2789	4942

Source: Domestic Business Activities and Price Control Administration,
    Ministry of Domestic Trade, 1984.

Apart from the licence controls, restrictions on grain movements are enforced in various localities. For instance, a wholesaler has to get a letter of permission from the GPTF prior to his purchase of grains in local markets and his leave for other centres. Checkpoints are set up along major routes of grain-flow. Such local or regional restrictions placed on grain traders are alleged to be those going well beyond the central government's grain purchase directives (e.g. see the report of the Government of Ethiopia/World Bank Mission, 1983, 48).

Quota Delivery Policy

Since 1979/80, AMC's grain procurements at regional and sub-regional levels are based on quota purchases. Each year, grain quotas are set for each crop and each region by the CPSC, and then given to the GPTF and the AMC for implementation. The regional quotas are assessed largely on the basis of the number of peasant associations and service co-operatives, and on the basis of rough production estimates of each region. Assessment of quotes at farm unit level has not yet been developed.

The minimum grain quota for a peasant association was 100 quintals in 1979/80 but this floor was raised to 150 quintals in 1980/81 mainly because the peasant associations had delivered less grain than expected. On the other hand, all licensed grain wholesalers had to supply a minimum of 30% of the purchases in 1979'80, but since 1980/81 each trader is required to deliver at least 50% of his annual purchases to the AMC. After supplying the required quota the trader gets clearance from GPTF which enables him to sell the rest in the free market. Distinctively, state farms and producer co-operatives are supposed to deliver all their marketed output to the AMC.

TABLE 2

Regional Share of Grain Quotas (1979/80 - 1981/82)

Region ('000 quintals)	Allocation of quotas for cereals (1000 quintals)	% Share
Shewa	1,802.1	36.6
Gojjam	1,260.3	25.6
Arssi	888.3	18.0
Gondar	200.1	4.1
Wello	150.1	3.1
Keffa	146.4	3.0
Sidamo	139.2	2.0
Wellega	138.6	2.8
Bale	130.2	2.6
Illubabor	68.4	1.4
Total	1,923.9	100

Source: AMC, *Statistical Data on AMC Operations*, 1983

Over 80% of the grain quotas, between 1979/80 and 1981/82, had been allocated to three major grain surplus regions, viz. Shews, Gojjam and Arssi; the rest had been distributed among other regions (Table 2).

The allocation of quotas for different crops, also showed that over 45% of the total grain quotas between 1979/80 and 1981/82 was for *teff*, the rest being divided among other crops (Table 3).

The use of quota delivery systems has increased the purchase of the AMC rapidly since 1979/80. Hence, the quota delivery policy has contributed to the increase in AMC's procurement (Table 4).

The actual purchases of different cereals also indicated that AMC has been procuring more *teff* than other crops (Table 5).

TABLE 3

Share of Grain Quotas for Major Cereals
(1979/80 - 1983/84)

Crop	Quota allocation for different regions ('000 quintals)	% Share
Teff	4,374.6	44.4
Maize	1,343.9	13.6
Wheat	1,708.0	17.3
Barley	921.4	9.4
Sorghum	1,504.5	15.3
Total	9,852.4	100

Source: AMC, *Statistical Data on AMC Operations*, 1983.

TABLE 4

Changes in AMC's Grain Procurements
From Domestic Sources (1976/77 - 1982/83)

Year	Grain Procurement (in million quintals)	% Change
1976/77	1.2	—
1977/78	1.4	16.7
1978/79	1.5	7.1
1979/80	2.7	80.0
1980/81	4.4	62.0
1981/82	4.6	4.0
1982/83	5.7	23.9

Source: AMC, Annual Reports of various years, Addis Ababa

TABLE 5

AMC's Purchase of Cereals from Traders, Peasants
and Co-operatives (1978/79 - 1983/84)

Crop	Quantity purchased ('000 quintals)	Percent
Teff	3.682.0	36.3
Maize	2,113.5	20.8
Barley	1,557.2	15.3
Wheat	1,985.3	19.6
Sorghum	815.6	8.0
Total	10,153.6	100

Source: AMC, Addis Ababa.

TABLE 6

Distribution of AMC Grain Collection Centres
By Region (1981/82)

Region	Number of collection centres	Percent
Gondar	74	8.6
Gojjam	184	21.5
Shewa	311	36.3
Arssi	49	5.7
Wellega	40	4.7
Wello	48	5.6
Keffa	17	2.0
Bale	93	10.9
Illubabor	29	3.4
Sidamo	11	1.3
Total	856	100

Also, the implementation of quota delivery systems in the grain surplus regions has required large numbers of grain collection centres since 1977/78. The geographic expansion of the AMC's network in the grain-surplus regions showed a total of 856 grain procurement (collection) centres by 1981/82 (Table 6).

Fixed and Uniform Price Policy

Nowadays, there are both free market and controlled prices for grains. The development of controlled grain prices in the post-1974 period has three distinct phases. In the initial phase (1975/76 - 1978/79) grain prices were fixed by the Ethiopian Grain Board (EGB) and the Ethiopian Grain Agency (ECA) on the basis of prices of central markets such as Addis Ababa, Jimma, Gondar, Dessie, Dire Dawa, Mekele, Gimbi and Shashemene. After the price of the central markets (with radii of 250 kms.) had been fixed the prices of subsidiary markets were determined by adding the cost of transport. However, this system of price fixation was abandoned in 1978 because it was disadvantageous to peasants living far away from central markets, and selling their produce at cheap prices but purchasing consumer manufactures at higher prices compared to those peasants living closer to the central markets. In 1977/78 attempts were made to fix grain prices rationally for producers on the basis of the cost of production and for consumers on the basis of the average inflation rates in major urban centres. But the endeavours to implement the fixed prices by the EGA were disrupted mainly by the Ethio-Somalia war.

Secondly, in 1979/80, the discretion to fix producer prices in each region was given to the regional GPTF, which is supposed to have a better knowledge of the conditions of grain production in each region. However, this system of price discentralization was cancelled in 1980/81 because the GPTF showed inconsistencies in fixing prices. For example, prices in some regions were once set in favour of urban consumers, whereas in others they were fixed in favour of farmers. Other times, producer prices were set in favour of AMC because the GPTF wanted to maintain the AMC's profit margin (usually 2.5% of the wholesale price).

Thirdly, in 1980/81, the government adopted a fixed and nationwide pricing policy as part of its central planning. This system of pan-territorial pricing is still in force and provides peasants throughout the country with the same price for the same type and quantity of products. Private traders, service co-operatives and producers' co-operatives get 5 Birr per quintal greater than the producer price. The prices paid to state farms is, however, 20 to 50 percent higher than that of the peasants indicated in Table 7.

The producer prices, as shown in Table 7, have been stagnant during the last four years except for marginal increases of 8.3%, 13.6% and 17.6% on the prices of *teff*, sorghum and maize, respectively.

TABLE 7

AMC Purchase Price (Birr/quintal)

	PEASANTS		SERVICE CO-OPS AND TRADERS	
	1980/81 - 1981/2	1982/83	1980/81 - 1981/82	1982/83
White teff	41	45	46	50
Mixed teff	35	38	40	43
Brown teff	32	34	37	39
White wheat	34	24	30	39
Mixed wheat	30	30	35	35
Black wheat	29	29	34	34
White barley	28	28	32	32
Other barley	26	26	30	30
White sorghum	23	27	27	31
Other sorghum	21	23	25	27
Maize	17	20	21	24

Source: NRDC and CPSC, Addis Ababa.

Purchase Priority to Grains Supplied by Service Co-operatives

Very recently, the AMC has shown a tendency to give purchase priority to service co-operatives over other suppliers. This is done for two main reasons. First, the government's policy encourages co-operative marketing in order to socialize trade in the long-term. Secondly, AMC makes purchase arrangements with service co-operatives more effectively than with other suppliers. The AMC branch at Hosana, for example, distribute sacks to service co-operatives, give them weighing services and purchase grain from them on a credit basis in cases when the branch's overdraft is protracted due to the long process of replenishment (Alemayehu, 1984, 61). AMC does not withdraw its overdraft from the bank all at once due to fear of high interest charges (i.e. 9.5% per annum).

In the Ten Years Development Plan it is envisaged that the market share of AMC in marketed surplus will increase from 55% in 1982/83 to 80% in 1992/93, with an annual growth rate of 2.5%. It is also expected that by 1992/93 the AMC would purchase grains only from state farms (78.6%), settlement farms (1.5%) and producers' co-operatives (19.6%), leaving the private traders and peasant associations (CPSC, 1984, 207). However, the experience of AMC in the last three years shows that merchants have been important suppliers of grains to the AMC compared to other suppliers.

TABLE 8

AMC's Grain Purchases from Different Sources
(1979/80 - 1981/2)

Suppliers	1979/80		1980/81		1981/2	
	quintals	(% share)	quintals	(% share)	quintals	(% share)
Service co-operatives	252,245	9.8	579,500	25.7	870,318	28.4
Producer's co-operative	13,242	0.5	53,389	2.4	82,383	2.7
Peasant associations	592,547	23.1	98,167	3.9	149,375	4.9
State farms	23,232	0.9	20,047	1.3	73,483	2.4
Private traders	1,688,246	65.7	1,505,824	66.7	1.889.091	61.6
Total	2,569,512	100	2,256,927	100	3,064,650	100

Source: AMC, Addis Ababa

PROBLEMS ARISING FROM THE IMPLEMENTATION OF GRAIN PROCUREMENT POLICIES

My own earlier field studies, and various documentary sources indicate that the following are major operational problems of grain marketing.

1. The first attempt to control the private grain trade at local level lacked central directives and witnessed some confusion among the peasants and grain collectors in rural areas. For example, all grain collectors in local markets of Kembata and Hadiya awraja (Shewa administrative region) have not been licensed. Despite this fact they have been playing an intermediary role as assemblers of grains for the local and regional wholesalers. They collect grains from remote areas using pack animals and limited working capital. However, by the time the AMC started purchasing grains from local markets the peasant association officials tended to prevent the grain collectors from buying grain in local markets and taking it to wholesalers in big market towns.[3] This happened mainly because the officials either considered that it was only the AMC which was empowered to buy all the grain coming from farms to local markets, or they were unclear if a small scale private trade was illegal or not (Alemayehu, 1982, 20).

2. The GPTF members at lower levels usually live at awraja or woreda capitals where the offices of respective ministries are found. But this resulted in a spatial disaggregation of the GPTF activities due to inadequate communications between the GPTF members living in different towns. As a result, the GPTF which is an important institutional mechanism to implement grain marketing policy at local level remained weak in controlling private trade.

For example, in Kembata and Hadiya awraja, a woreda administrator residing in the woreda capital could not frequently meet and work with the AMC representative living in the awraja capital due to lack of transport. As a result, the grain traders attempted to move grain illegally without having permission from the woreda GPTF (Alemayehu, 1984, 81).

3. The regional allocation of grain quotas seems to follow the general cropping patterns of administrative regions. But its sub-division to lower levels fails to correspond with the actual cropping patterns in various localities. For example, the *teff* quota for Kembata and Hadiya awraja constituted 49% of the AMC's planned purchases at the Hosana branch in 1982/83 crop year. But it was estimated that only 10% of the cropped area of the awraja was under *teff* (CSO, 1970, 23). The difference between the cropping patterns and the planned purchases was, therefore, reflected in under-quota purchases at the end of the year. The case study revealed that the actual purchase of *teff* was only 33% of planned purchases (Alemayehu, 1984, 53). Such under-quota performances usually cause dissatisfaction among the AMC branch managers and the purchase officers whose interest is to procure more *teff* than other crops, and suggest that central planning of grain marketing is not based on the geographic patterns of crop production, due to inadequate, up-to-date local information on cropping patterns.

4. The rapid expansion of the AMC network since the introduction of grain quotas has imposed tremendous strains on the operations of AMC, and hence created shortage of manpower (e.g. purchasers, accountants, etc.) and marketing facilities (e.g. roads, trucks, weighing scales, tarpaulins, sacks, stores, etc.). For example, the case study of the AMC's branch at Hosana revealed that AMC's trips to inaccessible service co-operatives involved high transport costs due to damage of trucks on very rough roads. The grain storage capacity at farm level in some woredas could handle less than 40% of the AMC grain purchases in 1982/83, the rest being stored in the open air with wastage and quality deterioration until the AMC collected it (Alemayehu, 1984, 74). Also, some international agencies have considered the large expansion of grain collection centres without roads as a major cause of AMC's operational inefficiency (World Bank, 1984, 6).

5. Unlike the free market prices the AMC prices have not shown spatial and temporal variations. Moreover, the AMC producer prices remained to be substantially lower than the price offered by private traders. A case study in Arssi region, for instance, revealed that the 1981/82 average AMC prices were lower than the average local market prices by 72.2% for sorghum, 52.9% for maize, 51.8% for *teff*, 29% for wheat and 18.5% for barley (Ministry of Agriculture, 1982, 18-19). As a result, AMC could not compete with private traders and could not attract many peasants. This is reflected in decreasing supply-share of peasant associations from 23% in 1979/80 to 4.9% in 1981/82 (See Table 8). The 1980 annual report of the Ministry of Domestic Trade noted the negative reaction of peasants to the lower producer prices offered by the AMC. The report also indicated that some producers of cereals, particularly of *teff*, showed reluctance to sell over-quota grains to the AMC in local markets, and even tended to withhold grain from the markets. Others did not like to deliver high quality *teff* (i.e. white *teff*) to the AMC and, hence, mixed low quality *teff* (i.e. brown *teff*) with the high quality to fulfil quotas. Besides, some peasants delivered low value crops (e.g. maize) as substitutes for high value crops (e.g. *teff*) claiming that they had not produced them. It can, thus, be argued that fixed prices have discouraged peasants from selling some of their grain to the AMC and diverted the flow of grains to the private traders, who turned out to be important suppliers of grains to the AMC. This contradicts with the long-term goal of socialization of grain trade. Moreover, imposition of grain quotas on peasants with relatively low levels of producer prices and abandoning of private trade is supposed to affect the revenues of grain producers adversely.

CONCLUDING REMARKS

This paper has briefly indicated the changes that have occurred in grain marketing in post-1974 Ethiopia. It has also indicated the major operational problems that grain marketing is facing in the post-1974 period. The existence of the operational problems and their undesirable effects, in turn, calls for remedies to be sought by central planners in order to encourage grain production in rural areas, to increase the efficiency of grain procurement and hence to meet the ever-increasing food needs in urban areas of Ethiopia.

It is, therefore, important to take into account the following points for the improvement of the grain marketing system in Ethiopia.

1. In rural Ethiopia where the basic marketing infrastructure is as yet undeveloped the use of primitive transport is indispensable. AMC purchases can be increased and its operational costs can be reduced if the peasants in inaccessible areas are encouraged to transport grains by pack animals to the roadside bulking centres until these areas are served by motor roads. The incentive can be developed by compensating for the cost of transport which the peasants have incurred, in addition to the producer prices offered by AMC.

2. In fixing and allocating grain quotas a maximum effort should be made to ascertain the correspondence between the planned purchases and the cropping patterns at local levels. It is also essential to ascertain whether or not grain quotas maintain a balance between the grain requirements of the state and the needs of the producers. Experience of the quota purchase schemes in other countries (e.g. Peoples Republic of China) show that attempts are always made to create a balance between the claims of the state, the requirements of the collective and the needs of the producers. To reduce the adverse effects of compulsory quotas there the Above-Quota Purchase (AQP) and the Discussion Purchase (DP) schemes are used as optional quota deliveries (Anthony and Stone, 1980; Croll, 1983, 74).

3. In determining the AMC purchase prices care must be taken to make the prices reflect the cost of production in various regions (localities) with and without locational and natural advantages. Attempts should also be made to minimize the difference between the returns that peasants get from selling grains to the AMC and to the private traders.

4. It should be clearly known that rational and realistic grain marketing plans can be formulated if data showing actual marketing conditions are available. The current Central Planning of grain marketing lacks vital local and regional information on grain markets in rural Ethiopia. At present the private traders are required to supply 50% of their annual purchases to the AMC without assessing the quantity and value of their annual purchases. It is also important to study the potential impact of grain quotas and fixed prices on grain producers so that the necessary adjustments could be made on the current quota and pricing policies.

NOTES

1. Ethiopia was a net exporter of food grains until 1947, and self-sufficient between 1947-1958. But, it has started importing food grains since 1958/59.

2. NRDC was a campaign launched to boost production based on annually set targets by the CPSC, now the Office of National Committee for Central Planning (ONCCP).

3. In Kembata and Hadiya awraja, this was a serious problem at that time because the local government discouraged double occupations and hence insisted farmers engaged in part-time trade (e.g. grain collection) to choose only one of the two occupations.

BIBLIOGRAPHY

Agri-Service (1976). *Rural Markets and Prices in Wolaita Awraja: Some features and prospects*, Socio-economic Section Paper No. 5. Addis Ababa.

Alemayehu Lirenso (1982). *Problems of Rural Employment: A preliminary assessment of factors affecting local traders in Kembata and Hadiya*, Background Paper presented to ILO/JASPA, Ethiopia Employment Advisory Mission, August, 1982.

———————— (1984). *State Commerce and Service-Co-operatives in Kembata and Hadiya: An economic geographic analysis* (M.A. Thesis, Unpublished) Addis Ababa University.

Anthony, T. and Stone, B. (1980) *Food Production in Peoples Republic of China*, Washington, D.C. IFPRT, RR 15.

Beaujeu-Garnier, J. and Delobez, A. (1979). *Geography of Marketing*, London, Longman.

Croll, E. (1983). *The Family Rice Bowl: Food and the domestic economy in China*, London, Zed Press.

CSO (1970). *Report On A Survey of Shewa Province*, Report No. 1, Addis Ababa.

de Young, M. (1976). "The internal Marketing of Agricultural Products and its influence on Agricultural Productivity and income." *Ethiopia Observer* Vol.11 No.1.

Eubanks, K. (1973). *Market Structure Study Related to Those Commodities that Provide the Basic Subsistence for the People of Ethiopia*, Ministry of Agriculture, Addis Ababa (draft Manuscript).

Government of Ethiopia/ World Bank Mission (1983). *Review of Farmers' Incentives and Agricultural Marketing and Distribution Efficiency* (Confidential).

Jones, W. C. (1972). *Marketing Staple Food Crops in Tropical Africa*, Ithaca, Cornell University Press.

Lele, U. (1968). *Food Grain Marketing in India, Private Performance and Policy*, Cornell University Press.

Manig, W. (1973). *Marketing of Selected Agricultural Commodities in Baco Area, Ethiopia*, Cornell University Press.

Ministry of Agriculture (1982). *Cost of Production of Major Crops and Grain Selling Prices*, ARDU Publication, No.2.

Ministry of Domestic Trade (1980). *AMC's 1973 E. C. Plan*, Addis Ababa (Amharic edition).

NRDC & CPSC (1982).	*1974 E. C. Plan Performance*, Addis Ababa, (Amharic edition).
————————— (1983).	*The Ten Year Development Plan 1983/84 - 1992/93*, Addis Ababa (Amharic edition).
PMAC (1975).	*Declaration of Economic Policy of Socialist Ethiopia*, Addis Ababa, Berhanena Selam Printing Press.
—————————	*Proclamation Relating to Commercial Activities Undertaken by the Private Sector*, Negarit Gazeta, Proclamation No.76 of 1975.
Schneider, H. (1984).	*Meeting Food Needs in a Context of Change*. Paris, OECD.
Thodey, A. R. (1973).	*Marketing of Grains and Pulses in Ethiopia*, Standford Research Institute, Report No.16.
Wickstrom, Bo. (1973).	*Increasing Efficiency in the National Grain Marketing System of Ethiopia: A policy guideline*. EPID Publication, No.14. Addis Ababa.
World Bank (1984).	*Ethiopia: Opportunities and constraints in peasant farming*. (A working paper).

THE SINO-SOVIET CONFLICT AND THE CONFLICT

IN THE HORN OF AFRICA (1956-1976)

Aleme Eshete

For this particular study the conflict in the Horn will be limited to the issues of Greater Somalia and Eritrean secession, and will involve Ethiopia, Somalia, the Sudan (and Egypt), and marginally, Kenya.

INTRODUCTION

The Soviet Bolshevik revolution was well known in Ethiopia since its origin. By accident of history, about the same time there was a popular uprising in Ethiopia demanding the removal of corrupt ministers. The movement led by the central regiment known as the Mehal Sefari was referred to at the time by western diplomats as the movement of the "Soviets", and Ras Teferi, (later Emperor Haile Selassie), then regent and crown prince, had to quote the example of Russia in order to warn the people to stop such a mass demonstration against the established government.

With the rise to power of the Bolsheviks, Russo-Ethiopian diplomatic relations were suspended and the last chargé d'affaires, P. K. Vingoradof, mortgaged the buildings of the legation in 1919 in order to pay his fare back to Europe. The legation became Ethiopian government property and was later rented to the Belgian Embassy.

A good number of White Russian refugees had come to Ethiopia — a royalist Orthodox Christian nation similar to Tsarist Russia. And it was through these princes and nobles, engineers and doctors, that anti-communism was perpetuated in Ethiopia. It was thus that, in 1929, White Russians employed in the office of the Ethiopian national security claimed to have discovered a Bolshevik network in Ethiopia. Dr. Gavriloff, a Russian refugee, was expelled in this connection. The British representative at Addis Ababa, quoting his Italian colleague, wrote at the time: "A certain Dr. Magaritti, an Albanian subject and a lawyer by profession, is the Addis Ababa agent of the Soviet Government, and indulges in a considerable amount of secret propaganda . . .".

The newspaper *Berhannena Selam* of 30 May 1929 had as an editorial: *Expulsion of Dr. Gavriloff for having tried to teach Bolshevism in Ethiopia*. The paper accuses Dr. Gavriloff of indoctrinating patients "in teachings that were destructive to the country and the public. But the God-fearing Ethiopian people, respectful of the King, instead of listening to his advice went and denounced Gavriloff to the Security Police of the Municipality." According to the same paper, investigation of Dr. Gaviloff produced a letter from Sofia (Bulgaria). This letter (later discovered to be a forgery) gave the Security Police unequivocal proof that Dr. Gavriloff was the agent of the Bolsheviks in Ethiopia. Gavriloff's mission, according to *Berhanena Selam*, was to find an occasion where the Empress, the King, the princes, the high clergy, and the supreme judges would assemble, in order to throw bombs and destroy them.

Other arrests of White Russians and a few Ethiopians (including Fitawrari Tekle Hawariat) were made in connection with this alleged Bolshevik network.[1]

This fascinating story which at first sight appears rather far-fetched, becomes more intriguing when one examines the issue in the light of a similar discovery of a "Bolshevik network" about the same time, in neighbouring Sudan, then a British colony. In an article entitled "Communist activities in the Middle East with special reference to Egypt and the Sudan", Jeafar Muhammad Ali Bakheit gives the details of a Bolshevik network in the region, not very dissimilar from the one alleged to have been discovered in Ethiopia.

The problem began to unfold its dimensions when the author was examining archival documents on the background of the White Flag League — a secret nationalist organisation composed initially of army officers and government officials (its insignia, the white flag with a map of the Nile), and directed mainly against British Colonialism, and supporting independence for and cooperation with Egypt. It was established in 1923 following a scission of the Sudanese Union Society. While the Union had as its principal arm the distribution of pamphlets against the British and the local Muslim religious and political aristocracy, the White Flag League wanted to go beyond the mere war of words. It was active both in the rural and urban areas. Subsequently accepted as the spokesman of the Sudanese workers, the League organised a series of anti-British demonstrations. And British massive arrests, dismissals, transfers and deportations of Egyptians in the Sudan, only provoked more demonstrations.

The author found in the archives of the White Flag League, an Arabic periodical addressed to the President of the League, Ali Abdel Latif. It was printed in Stockholm, posted in Berlin and issued by an Egyptian Union of Students in Germany. One of its articles on the colonial problems in the Nile Valley listed colonial abuses and exploitation: the colonisers lived in luxury while the natives dragged in their chains and poverty. The article ended with a call for "the formation of a Moslem peasant Republic in the Sudan". And it was known that Ali Abdel Latif called on the peasants in similar terms, to unite and revolt for liberty.

The British had at the time suspected, as was then ordinarily the case, a communist network behind the mass agitation and demonstration of the White Flag League. They suspected on one hand the influence of the "professional communists" of Armenian, Central European and Baltic extraction, working in the administration in Atbara, while on the other they suspected a Wafdist[2] – Communist Egyptian infiltration.

The organisational structure and composition of the White Flag League took subsequently the form of a "Front", representing the army, the students, the workers, the peasants, the petit-bourgeoisie and the nobility, perhaps a Sudanese version of Lenin's "Front". The White League's highest performance was the successful anti-British mass protest and demonstration of 1924, referred to as "revolution" by Sudanese historians. How does the summer of 1924 popular demonstration link up with communist activities in the region? Towards the end of 1924 a circular was issued by the district committee of the communist parties in Palestine, Syria and Lebanon. It incited workers to strike on the 1st of May (1925), and to celebrate the occasion. "The English and French authorities," the circular read, "occupy our countries by force (of arms) . . . so that they may guard themselves against any revolution which may emanate from the majority of the unjustly treated nations." The circular attacked Britain, for "having put out the fire of revolution in the Sudan", and killing innocent people, closing the Egyptian parliament and endeavouring to deprive the labourers and peasants of the right of election.

The British Intelligence claimed to have found out, at length, that the centre of communist activities in the region was the Soviet Embassy at Jeddah! The Embassy had linguists, erudites in oriental languages and studies, lawyers, etc., engaged full-time in the spread of Bolshevism in the region. Intelligence work was intensified in Egypt and the Sudan in search of a communist network. In May 1925 alleged communists were rounded up in Cairo and Alexandria following the arrest of a certain Dimitri Andryeve. A printing press and a quantity of literature were discovered. Copies of communist circulars which circulated in large numbers in Egypt and the Sudan were seized. The Wafd party was accused of collaborating with the communists. Evidence was found to testify to attempts by the Egyptian communist party to establish new centres of agitation following the defeat of the White Flag League in 1924, by sending money and material to Khartoum. Moreover the Egyptian communist party was assigned to keep in close touch with communist parties and revolutionary organisations in the whole of this area, both in the independent and subject states. A conference of communist and revolutionary organisations of the region was to be organised in order to unite the workers and peasants in a common struggle against the imperialists of Spain, France, Italy and England.

Following this, the Communist party in Egypt was suppressed and so also communist activities in the Sudan.

SOVIET DIPLOMATIC RELATIONS IN THE HORN

What we saw up to now was the domain of real or imaginary revolutionary agitation in the Horn in the early years of Soviet power. But there were also official Soviet attempts to establish diplomatic relations with Ethiopia soon after the Bolshevik Revolution. Indeed, in 1921, the Soviet government had sent I. A. Zalkind of the Foreign Office to Addis Ababa. Zalkind had managed to make his way through Djibouti, by rail, to Addis Ababa with the help of the personnel of the Ethiopian monastery in Jerusalem. However, Zalkind's attempt to convince the Ethiopian government to accept the resumption of diplomatic relations was not successful, mainly because of western opposition and fear of the aristocracy. Again in 1925, the Soviet Consul in Jedda (Hejaz) is said to have arranged "talks" between Ethiopia and the Soviet Union for the same purpose, but again without success. However, the true nature of these "talks" and contacts could only be revealed by a direct examination of the Soviet archives.[3]

Diplomatic relations were established between Ethiopia and the Soviet Union in 1943 after the liberation of Ethiopia from Fascist occupation; but exchange of ambassadors was resumed only in 1956. Relations developed favourably and on the basis of an Ethio-Soviet trade agreement the Soviet Union accorded Ethiopia a loan of US.$100 million. Further, a cultural and scientific cooperation agreement was signed and more aid was accorded by the Soviets in this field. But superpower politics and Ethiopia's alliance with U.S. was a stumbling block for a deep and lasting Ethio-Soviet relationship. On the one hand, the Soviets were bent on dislodging the Americans from their base in Asmara, and on the other, they intended to counterbalance the U.S.-Ethiopian pact by a Soviet-Somali entente. Indeed Soviet involvement in the Somali Republic was further aggravated by Sino-Soviet rivalry and competition in that country. Hence, on one hand the Soviet direct or indirect support to Eritrean secession, and on the other, support to Mogadisho's expansionist project of Greater Somalia, contributed as factors of friction between the Soviet Union and Ethiopia.

As far as Eritrea was concerned, the Soviet Union had at the close of the Second World War advocated independence for Eritrea during the Four Power Commission and United Nations debates on the disposal of the then Italian colonies, and gave lengthy arguments in support of their stand. Since the establishment of the Eritrean secessionist movements in the 1960s there were repeated reports of Soviet indirect aid to these movements – done in very covert ways so as not to incite Ethiopian animosity, and with the principal objective of dislodging the Americans from their strategic Red Sea base. The ELF got Czech and Soviet arms from Libyan stocks and these were shipped via Saudi Arabia to Eritrea. Soviet arms were also getting to the ELF and later EPLF through the Sudan, Libya (after 1969), PDRY, Syria and Iraq. Until 1967 Cuban military advisers had also been training Eritrean cadres based in Aden (PDRY).[4]

As far as Somalia was concerned, the Soviets are said to have had relations with the Greater Somalia propagators since before independence either directly or through the Italian Communist Party.[5] As late as 1963 an article in the Soviet newspaper, *Izvestiya*, considered Somali pursuit "of the unification of all Somalis into an independent Somali State" to be "natural".[6] The Somali Republic resumed diplomatic relations with the Soviet Union soon after independence in 1960, and also with China in the same year.

The Peoples Republic of China, like the Soviet Union, had contacts with Greater Somalia propagators in pre-independence days, when she supported leaders of the Greater Somalia League whose Chairman was in China in September 1960[7] and the Somali National Union, both of which failed to emerge as significant post-independence political forces. Even after Somalia's independence, China had for some time continued to support these "rebels" considered to have been more ardent militants of the Greater Somalia objective, and was even reported to have approached on their behalf some Ogaden chiefs.[8] But China cooperated more closely with the established government in Somalia since 1960. And as China, unlike the Soviet Union, had no diplomatic relations with Ethiopia (and Kenya until December 1963) to fear their reaction, China had no inhibitions in supporting Somalia's territorial demands.[9] It was indeed suggested that China used Somalia as the headquarters for the dissemination of her political influence in the Horn and East Africa. The huge Chinese Embassy on the outskirts of

Mogadisho was staffed with a large personnel, 230 officially registered. The Embassy ran a school for its staff in the languages of the region, including Afar, Somali, Amharic and Swahili.[10]

As Somalia's expansionist ambitions became more evident, and as western nations (on good terms with Ethiopia and Kenya) showed less and less willingness to underwrite them, Prime Minister Shermarke turned to Peking. He visited China in August 1963 when China granted £1.05 million to help to balance the budget, and an interest free loan of 7.2 million, repayable over seventeen years with a seven year grace period. Ethiopia and Kenya must have viewed Sino-Somali connections with suspicion. And right after Shermarke's visit, a Kenyan (KANU) delegation arrived in Beijing. In view of the Somali Prime Minister's visit and speculation over a reported Chinese promise to give military aid to Somalia, the Chinese Foreign Minister, Chen Yi, assured the Kenyan delegation that no weapons would be sent and that he had advised Dr. Shermarke to negotiate with Kenya over their territorial dispute.[11]

Reaction from the Soviet Union to China's aid and loan to Somalia was swift. She made aid offers worth £20 million as a immediate counter, and in October 1963 concluded what China had refused, an estimated £15 million military aid agreement with Somalia. The Russians agreed to train 20,000 soldiers, all with Soviet equipment.[12] Somali officers were sent to the Soviet Union and Russian equipment began to arrive. A team of Russian technicians and experts soon followed. The Soviet Union had offered more scholarships to Somalia than to any other single African country at the end of 1964. Ethiopia and Kenya, who signed a defence pact, protested against the military aid agreement concluded in December 1963 and the Soviets appeared to have been worried about African hostility which the agreement had aroused. The Soviet ambassador in Addis Ababa assured the Emperor that the degree of military assistance had been exaggerated; the Soviets also reportedly sought assurances (which they did not get or which were not fulfilled, as the later years will prove) that the Somalis would use their Russian equipment only in self-defence, and not against other African states.[13]

Thus, as was said by different authors, Somalia was the winner in the Sino-Soviet conflict. The Chinese, whose influence was soon superseded by that of the Soviets, continued their aid to Somalia mainly in the field of agriculture, light industry, highways, medicine, etc. "All this aid was granted", Chou En Lai reported, "to reinforce Somalia's struggles to safeguard state sovereignty and consolidate national independence against control and interference by old and new colonialists."[14] Following the coup d'etat of 1969, which brought Siad Barre to power, "Scientific Socialism" was declared as the guideline of Somali politics, and this only helped to strengthen further the Soviet-Somali relationship — perhaps at the expense, among others, of the Chinese, who in the early 1970s had started, as we shall see, arming Ethiopia in order to offset Soviet military support to Somalia.

Sudan's diplomatic relations with the Soviet Union go back to 1959, three years after independence. The Communist Party of the Sudan was formed in 1946 — soon to become the strongest in Africa. But rather than facilitating the Soviet Union's relations with the Sudan, the existence of the Sudanese Communist party has rather complicated relations, due to the lack of cooperation, or even a *modus vivendi*, between the "national democratic" government and the Communist Party, or due to outright anti-communism of the former, as was the case under General Abboud (1958-64). Following the fall of Abboud in 1964, the National Front Government, including the Communist Party, was established. But the Front lasted only 102 days, during which a number of democratic reforms were proclaimed. The Sudanese government then turned to the right. Following the military coup of 25 May 1969 of General Giaffar Nimeiry, which proclaimed scientific socialism as its guideline, the Communist Party was again invited to cooperate, although without much enthusiasm on the part of the latter. Be that as it may, the Soviet Union was, between 1961-70, by far Sudan's main supplier of arms, offering military assistance estimated at US.$63,000,000 during the decade.[15] Gradually the cooperation turned into a bitter contradiction (following Nimeiry's attempt to incorporate the Communists into Sudan's Socialist Union, in the manner of the Egyptian Communist Party that was incorporated into Nasser's socialism). The contradiction between the two came to a head with the coup of July 1971 alleged to have been engineered in cooperation with the Communist

Party of the Sudan, and hence also allegedly with the Soviet Union. The result was the liquidation of the Communist Party of the Sudan and the massacre of thousands of Communists. Soviet-Sudan relations also suffered tremendously, and the Chinese exploited this misfortune without any regret for the Sudanese Communist Party. And yet the Soviets blamed the Sudan Communist leaders for Maoism! Soviet-Sudan relations were rendered still worse following Soviet-Egyptian falling-out, and expulsion of Soviet experts from Egypt in July 1972. The new Sudano-Egyptian western orientation (and in particular close alliance with the U.S.) turned out to the advantage of the People's Republic of China.

Sudan recognised the People's Republic of China in 1959, three years after independence. China did not have good relations with the pro-Soviet Communist party of the Sudan.[16] China, however, had good relations with the government in Khartoum. During Prime Minister Chou En Lai's visit to the Sudan in 1964, the Sudan expressed its support for China's membership of the United Nations, as well as for the convening of a second Bandung, in which China hoped to isolate the Soviet Union. Chou En Lai, on his part expressed profound support to the Palestinian struggle for the restoration of their homeland and for Arab unity. China did not support the Southern Sudan rebellion out of respect for her good relations with Khartoum, but also because of fear of Arab reaction. A deterioration of Sino-Sudanese relations could have jeopardised China's relations with Egypt, Algeria, Morocco and the Arab world. Indeed when after Sudan's support (together with China) to the Lumumbists in the Congo against Tshombe in 1964, and Congo's subsequent threat to help the Southern Sudan fighters, China had declared in August 1965 that it hoped the problem of the south would be solved within the framework of Sudanese unity and announced its readiness to help the Sudan against any foreign intervention aimed at undermining this. China also had good trade relations with the Sudan. But the first Sino-Sudanese economic aid agreement was signed by a Sudanese delegation visiting China only in June 1970. On this occasion, China granted the Sudan an interest-free loan of £14.5 million, repayable over fifteen years by the export of Sudanese crops. President Jaafar Nimeiry was himself in China in August 1970. Until the coup of July 1971, Nimeiry's government maintained good relations with both China and the Soviet Union, and had declined to align itself openly with either party to the Sino-Soviet conflict.[17] However, following the unsuccessful 1971 coup against Nimeiry, in which the Sudanese communists (branded as pro-Soviet) were involved, the Chinese sent a letter of congratulation and encouragement to General Nimeiry for crushing the coup.[18] Following the coup, General Nimeiry liquidated the Communist Party of the Sudan. A massacre of thousands of communists followed. Soviet-Sudan relationships suffered. Paradoxically, the Soviets accused the Sudanese Communist Party of adventurism and Maoism:

> Incitement to reject the United National Front as the foundation of non-capitalist development, simplify its class structure, repudiate the alliance with some bourgeois strata, and even to proclaim the greatest slogan of all — the dictatorship of the proletariat — can only bring revolutionary forces to defeat. *These are the kinds of adventurist slogans which Maoism is propounding* and, playing on their radicalness, is trying to spread its influence in the African and Asian countries.[19]

General Nimeiry thanked the Chinese for their stand on this occasion. Moreover he revealed that the Chinese had offered to give him arms and to train the Sudanese armed forces. Mao had told him that a Chinese offer of eight Mig.17s and enough modern tanks to equip a division were a present from the Chinese people. Chairman Mao refused any payment: "We do not sell arms used to fight imperialism. China is not an arms dealer." From this time onwards, Sudan took the Chinese side in the Sino-Soviet conflict.

SINO-SOVIET DIPLOMATIC RELATIONS

As was stated above, China's first contact with African political leaders took place at the Bandung Conference (Indonesia) held from 18-24 April 1955. The Chinese Prime Minister,

Chou En Lai, who represented his country, had then the opportunity to meet African leaders, such as Gamal Abdel Nasser of Egypt. Ethiopia's Emperor Haile Selassie did not attend the Bandung Conference as Afro-Asian politics was then hardly a preoccupation of the Ethiopian leaders. Ethiopia was represented by Blata Dawit Eqube Egzi, Vice Minister at the Ministry of Foreign Affairs, Lej Mikael Emru, Director General of Civil Aviation, Lej Endalkachew Mekonnen, Chief of Protocol at the Ministry of Foreign Affairs, and Ketema Yifru, Director of the American-Asian Department in the Ministry of Foreign Affairs.[20] There was apparently no African department in Ethiopia's Ministry of Foreign Affairs! Bandung does not appear to have been an important event in Ethiopian politics and Chinese contacts, if any, had not produced any diplomatic effects. This was no surprise in view of Ethiopia's alliance with the United States. The Ethiopian army had fought the Chinese volunteers in Korea by the side of the US-UN forces, and supported South Korea, between 1950-1953. And naturally, the Chinese did not have a good press in Ethiopia at this time. The first real contact with China took place in February 1964, when Prime Minister Chou En Lai, who was on a tour in Africa, came to Ethiopia following a surprise invitation by the Emperor. As the Sino-Soviet conflict was already underway since 1956, not only the U.S. but also the Soviet Union might have been opposed to the meeting. But alleged Chinese involvement in the Greater Somalia issue, as well as in Eritrean secession, were strong factors recommending a rapprochement with the People's Republic of China. At the reception, the Emperor, referring to the 750 million Chinese, pleased the Chinese Prime Minister by calling China a Super Power. But he was also frank in telling Chou En Lai where he differed with Chinese politics and declaring his support for the Nuclear Ban Treaty signed between U.S., the U.S.S.R. and Britain in August 1963, a treaty condemned by China, the Emperor said:

> Peace is indivisible. If war breaks out in one area, it could involve the whole world. If the Third World War breaks out it could destroy the whole world. We therefore do not believe that any one country could support such a war. Ethiopia therefore believes firmly in the reduction of arms. And Ethiopia has supported and become party to the Nuclear Test Ban Treaty in the conviction that it will contribute to arms reduction talks. We have been grieved to learn that some countries have rejected the nuclear test ban treaty. And this is one of the major points of disagreement between the People's Republic of China and Ethiopia.[21]

And as if to justify his decision to send a contingent of the Ethiopian army to Korea (to fight the North Koreans and the Chinese) in 1951-53, as well as to the Congo in 1961, again as part of the U.N. forces, (which China considered a U.S. invasion under the aegis of the U.N.), the Emperor said:

> Because of Ethiopia's fresh memory of Fascist aggression which, not stopped in time by the League of Nations, led to the Second World War, Ethiopia resolutely supports all United Nations operations.

At the termination of Chou En Lai's stay in Ethiopia, the two sides declared in a joint communique, that they had had open and "sincere" exchanges of opinion. The two sides had agreed that, although governments may have different political, social and economic doctrines, they could maintain relations and live in peaceful coexistence. Ethiopia and China agreed to keep the Bandung spirit and to support the liberation movements in Africa. They concurred on such points as non-aggression, peaceful solution of conflicts, respect for territorial integrity, world peace, nuclear disarmament, etc. Ethiopia pledged to support as before Chinese membership of the United Nations. One of the major reasons for Chou's African tour was to canvas African support for a second Bandung, excluding the Soviet Union, on the grounds that the Soviet Union was not, in essence, an Asian country and allegedly (although denied by China) on the basis of race — the Soviet Union was not black or coloured! The Emperor, who may not have been *au courant* with Chinese objectives, concurred with Chou that it was the right time to hold the second Afro-Asian congress. Finally the two sides agreed to take appropriate measures "in the near future" in order to strengthen their relationship.[22]

It has been said that the U.S. had put pressure on the Ethiopia Government against the signing of a joint Ethio-Chinese communique, and Chou En Lai is reported to have stated in a press conference in Somalia that Ethiopia, like Morocco, was controlled by foreigners and that a foreign hand was pressing down very heavily upon her: "The Ethiopian people, therefore, want and wish to escape from this and be free".[23]

Nothing is said about the Afro-Asian Peoples Solidarity Organisation (AAPSO), of which Ethiopia was a founding member (Cairo, 27 December 1957) and which had become the major arena of Sino-Soviet rivalry, each trying to attract as many supporters as possible and dominate the organisation, with varying success. Finally, the Soviet Union succeeded in obtaining major control of the organisation and used it against China. China finally withdrew from the organisation.[24]

Although the Sino-Ethiopian joint communique stated that relations would be established as soon as possible, years passed before this materialised. High politics and the international power system, as well as Ethiopia's alliance with the U.S., may have been the major stumbling blocks, but Haile Selassie also gave sentimental reasons for withholding the decision. By quoting Chiang Kai Shek's Nanking government non-recognition of the Fascist invasion of Ethiopia, the Emperor said that he found it difficult to abandon Taiwan, in order to recognise the People's Republic of China.[25] The PRC was, as is well known, opposed to the "Two China" policy.

Ethiopia and China established diplomatic relations in December 1940 on the basis of China's five principles of peaceful coexistence:

- mutual respect for territorial integrity and sovereignty
- mutual non-aggression
- mutual non-interference
- equality and mutual benefit
- peaceful coexistence[26]

A number of factors may have determined the Emperor to recognise China at this particular juncture. One factor may have been the Sino-American detente that had replaced the Soviet-American detente of the 1960s. Indeed, as the Sino-Soviet conflict, mainly the territorial controversy on the 4,150 miles of Sino-Soviet border, got worse China sought out a strong U.S. ally. Following the downfall of Kruschev, Sino-Soviet negotiations were resumed in 1964, but these led nowhere. And according to the Chinese claim, from the breakdown of negotiations in 1964 to March 1969, there were 4,189 border incidents. Two large clashes had erupted on 2 March and 14-15 March 1969, in the Chin Pao island in the Ussuri river. A number of soldiers were killed on both sides. Thousands of soldiers — a million, according to some estimates — were massed on both sides of the border. And at one point it was feared that the Soviets might strike at China's atomic installations and start an all-out war. By this time, (particularly since Nixon's election in 1969), U.S. policy had moved from entente and cooperation with the Soviet Union to entente with China, exploiting the Sino-Soviet split and under pressure to end the U.S. aggression in Vietnam. This meant the end of U.S. policy of containment and encirclement of China, and the end of the bipolarised world political system to one that was five-power centered: the U.S., U.S.S.R., China, Japan and Western Europe. Friendly declarations started to come forth from both the U.S. and China. The U.S. had told the Soviet Union that it would not approve aggression against China. Mao Tse Toung declared that he would like to see Nixon in Beijing, where the American President was indeed, on 18 February 1972.[27]

Other factors affecting Sino-Ethiopian rapprochement were related to regional politics and conflict, such as Soviet close relations with Somalia and the Sudan. China's aid to Eritrean secession was another factor that influenced the Ethiopian government to start diplomatic relations with Beijing. As in other cases, China pledged herself to stop all direct and indirect aid to Eritrean secession as a price for diplomatic recognition by Imperial Ethiopia[28], (and perhaps as a price also for detente with U.S.). Indeed, it was often reported in the 1960s[29] that China (as well as the Soviet Union and Cuba) gave military aid and training in guerrilla warfare to the Eritrean secessionist movement, the ELF, either directly or through Syria, and Yemen, channelled through the Sudan. And this was no more fabrication of the Ethiopian government to raise the spectre of communism and ensure American support, as Clapham says.[30] The ELF broadcasts themselves gave occasional thanks for support by China. According to other sources, Eritrean secessionists were among other Africans being trained by the Chinese on the Tanzanian island of Pemba.[31] Osman Saleh Sabe had also on one occasion told newsmen (1969) that "the Chinese People's Republic gives us military aid but there is no communist tendency in the ELF programme".[32] And in November 1971 an ELF spokesman confirmed that "Peking which had previously supported us as part of the International Revolution no longer does so because of China's policy of widening her international relations".[33]

At the same time, whatever aid the Chinese might have given to the Somali Republic in support of its Greater Somalia expansionist project must also have stopped, more so as its influence there was being superseded by that of the Soviets. The issue of Sino-Somalia relationship was indeed one of the causes preventing the establishment of diplomatic relations between China and Ethiopia.[34] And the surprise invitation forwarded to Chou En Lai in 1964 to visit Ethiopia before he visited Somalia was motivated by the Emperor's desire "to put his side of the Ethiopian-Somali dispute . . . The patched-up nature of the visit was emphasized by Chou being received, not in the capital Addis Ababa, but in Asmara".[35]

In October 1971 Emperor Haile Selassie visited China and in November, following a Technical Cooperation Agreement, Ethiopia received in loan some US.$100 million from China, the biggest sum accorded by China in Africa, after the Tanzam railway. In February 1973, an Ethiopian Air Lines flight to Shanghai was inaugurated, strengthening ties and connecting China with Ethiopia. In December 1973 it was reported that the People's Republic of China had offered heavy weaponry to Ethiopia on a free of charge basis. The weapons included tanks and fighter planes. This move is in conformity with "China's willingness to frustrate Soviet weapons pouring into neighbouring Somalia".[36]

CHINA AND THE ETHIOPIAN REVOLUTION: 1974-1976

CLOSE IDENTITY OF VIEWS

Maoist influence in the Ethiopian student movement is an interesting subject that has not been sufficiently explored. Randi Bonning Balsvik, in her thesis "Haile Selassie's Students, Rise of Social and Political Consciousness", wrote:

> The last years of Haile Selassie's regime confirmed the direction of the
> ideological development of the last year of the 1960s: the hard line leftists
> had now outspoken opposition. The USUAA was committed to the extent
> that union officials when sworn into office, promised to support and
> promote the ideological aspects of Marxism-Leninism Mao Tse Toung
> Thought.

And Ali Mazrui (notwithstanding his derogatory comments) noted in his "The Chinese Model and the Soviet Model in Eastern and Southern Africa" that the Ethiopian Revolution was led by intellectuals who gave ideological guidance to the military and who followed a "neo-Maoist" orientation.

Indeed, since the origin, the Ethiopian Revolution appeared to have been strongly attracted and influenced by Maoism and China. Since the outbreak of the Revolution, China had consistently given moral and material support (including some military hardware) to Ethiopia. High level Ethiopian delegations were successively sent to China. These included Derg delegations, ministerial delegations, University academic staff delegation, medical personnel, etc. Chairman

412

Mengistu himself, then First Vice-Chairman, is reported to have made an unofficial, and unpublicised trip to China during the period under consideration.

The very important National Democratic Revolution (NDR) programme proclaimed in Ethiopia on 20 April 1976, was heavily influenced by Mao Tse Toung's "On New Democracy" (1954), and was very similar to the NDR programme of Vietnam, Cambodia and North Korea. The role of underground movements such as MEISON (particularly through the Mass Organisational Office) in introducing Chinese or Maoist political institutions in Ethiopia, if any, is an area that needs to be explored with due emphasis. In the same way, the origin and relationship, if any, with the Chinese Cultural Revolution, of institutions such as ግጋለጥ (exposing reactionaries in public meetings), ሂስና ግለሂስ . . .(criticism and auto-criticism — usually in public) ውይይት (regular weekly, fortnightly and now monthly political education sessions), in public as well as private organisations etc., as well as in education and the arts (poster art, theatre, music, etc.) need also further exploration.

To appreciate the extent of the influence of China on the Ethiopian Revolutionary process, suffice to see the recommendations of a Derg delegation after a trip of one month (towards the end of 1976) in China. The group was given briefings on the formation of the Communist Party of China, about the Chinese Revolution, land reform, economic construction, the militia, on how China abolished unemployment and prostitution, on socialist education, on the nationality issue, on mass organisation, and finally on China's foreign policy, including the Sino-Soviet conflict. And upon their return, the members of the delegation recommended the application of Chinese solutions to the Ethiopian situation, in several sectors.

In the sector close to us, socialist education, the delegation had specific recommendations drawn from the Chinese experience. It is to be remembered that the Great Proletarian Cultural Revolution of China (1966-1969) contended that a lot of time was spent in class education, had thus recommended that the number of years spent in elementary, high school and university education should be reduced, that manual labour and political education should be incorporated with book education, that there should be no entrance examination, that mass organisations and not the University should determine enrolment and acceptance of students according to revolutionary commitment and not only by virtue of academic grades, etc. These values of the Cultural Revolution were followed in China, even beyond 1969-70, by the so-called "gang of four", who lasted until Mao Tse Toung died, i.e. September 1976. We know that following the death of Mao Tse Toung the "gang of four" were removed. So also the values that they introduced. The present leaders of China, who have extended the Cultural Revolution period (formerly limited to between 1966-1969) to include all the period extending to 1976, and hold Mao Tse Toung (who at its earlier stage patronised the "gang of four") as responsible for this period of "subjective thinking divorced from reality", and which "was responsible for the most severe setback and the heaviest losses suffered by the Party, the State and the people since the founding of the People's Republic".[37] And the China that the Ethiopian delegations saw was the China of the "gang of four" and their recommendations, therefore, reflected images of the Chinese Cultural Revolution.

When Mao Tse Toung died on 9 September 1976, the reaction of the Ethiopian government shows the extent of the influence of China and Mao Tse Toung thought on the leaders. It is imperative that we get a clear idea of the forces in power at this particular stage of the Ethiopian Revolution.[38] It was later declared that these forces favoured EPRP and perhaps collaboration with the West (particularly the U.S.). What was the position of China in this internal struggle for power within the Derg, and what were its relations with EPRP? These are questions that get clarified at a later stage but which will require profound exploration. Or was there a consensus on this issue at the time. In any case the PMAC broadcasted an official proclamation:

"The death of Chairman Mao is not only a bitter loss for the people of China, but to all oppressed peoples of the world who followed his revolutionary teachings. The thoughts of Chairman Mao Tse Toung have helped the Ethiopian oppressed masses in their struggle against feudalism, capitalism and imperialism."

413

"Chairman Mao Tse Toung is of the rank of the revolutionary leaders Marx, Lenin and Engels . . . "

"If China is today a model to all oppressed peoples who undertake an anti-imperialist revolution, it is because of Chairman Mao's refined and profound revolutionary philosophy."

"In his lifetime Chairman Mao has by applying Marxism Leninism to our epoch, rendered it a revolutionary guide for the liberation of the oppressed peoples. Mao Tse Toung has written many works and several of these works are now in the hands of the Ethiopian revolutionaries. Of particular importance to peoples similar to Ethiopia is his work *On the New Democracy*, a unique revolutionary guideline!"

"The scientific thought of Chairman Mao is light that leads the oppressed peoples of the world to victory."

"He will therefore not be forgotten."

"The death of Chairman Mao does not only distress the Chinese people but also all the oppressed people in fresh revolutionary transition. We therefore declare that the grief of the Chinese people is also that of the people of Ethiopia."

A three day mourning period was announced, with flags at half-mast. Several newspaper articles praised Mao Tse Toung and his work. An article in *Addis Zemen* (Meskerem 8, 1969) praised Mao as the great man of the epoch, without match. According to the editorial, Mao's New Democracy was the only path for backward feudo-bourgeois regimes in the era of imperialism:

... ሊቀ መንበር ግአ የዓለምን አንድ አራተኛ ሕዝብ ታሪክና ዕድል የቀየሱ ፤ ለዓለም ጭቁን ሕዝቦች ሁሉ የተስፋ ችቦ የፈነጠቁ ለአብዮታውያን ሁሉ የትግል አርአያ የሆኑ ተወዳዳሪ የሌላቸው የክፍለ ዘመናች ን ታላቅ ሰው ነበሩ ።
ሊቀ መንበር ግአን የመሰለ ታጋይና ፈላስፋ በሆያኛው ክፍለ ዘመን መድረክ ላይ ባይወጣ ኖሮ የሶስተኛው ዓ ለም ጭቁን ሕዝቦች የአዲሱ ዲሞ ክራሲ አብዮት ምን መልክ ይይዝ እንደነበር ለመገመት ያስቸግራል

"የጓላት"

* * * * * *

Exactly two years later, in September 1978, Chairman Mengistu made his famous Revolution Day speech:

"The Communist Party of China continuously retrograding, has surprised the World by the stand it has taken regarding Cuba, Chile, Egypt, the Sudan, Vietnam, and the Angolan revolution . . ."

"This reactionary line of the Chinese Communist Party has got worse from day to day, that China has now taken the side of reactionary leaders and supporting their lines by suffocating liberation movements and revolution . . ."

"Regarding China's attitude towards our Revolution she appeared supportive at the beginning. But soon she started to take divisive measures among revolutionaries and weakening the Ethiopian Revolution. China in collaboration with the CIA, armed secessionists and EPRP, caused the death of many who stood for the oppressed masses."

"Following the declaration of "Red Sea-Arab Lake" by few Arab countries in the hope of creating a cause for conflict with Ethiopia, China supported them whole-heartedly."

"When the reactionary Somali army invaded our country and massacred the Ethiopian masses, China gave bullets to the invading army . . ."
"She accused the Cubans, who were with us defending our Revolution and territorial integrity, as mercenaries . . ."

Relations with China have drastically been damaged. Mao's books were stopped from enter-ing Ethiopia in the future. Of the millions of Marxist books that entered Ethiopia in the post-revolution period, Mao's works had a respectable share. But in the future no more, those in Government bookshops were withdrawn. Ethiopia has turned her face for a moment against China.

Relations with the Soviet Union flourish and prosper. What has happened? This will be the subject of the next chapter.

NOTES

1.   Aleme Eshete, "Ethiopia and the Bolshevik Revolution: 1871-1935", *Africa*, Vol.XXXII, No.1, March 1977.

2.   The Wafd was the nationalist party contesting the British colonial presence in Egypt be-fore and after 1922 – the date marking a shared administration of Egypt by the British and a constitutional monarchy. After 1923 the Wafdist party contested both the British and the Egyptian monarchy. The Wafd was initially considered a mass part with some communist affiliation.

3.   Anatoly A. Gromyko, *Soviet Ethiopian Relations*, Moscow 1979.

4.   Rama Bhaiwadj, *The Dilemma of the Horn*, (1979), p.105; Roy Lyons, "The USSR, China and the Horn of Africa", *Review of African Politics*; Hagai Erlich, *The struggle over Eritrea*, (1983); P. Henze, *Arming the Horn*, (1982).

5.   Zbigniew Brzezniski, *Africa and the Communist World*, (Stanford, 1963), p.193.

6.   Nimrod Novik, "On the shores of Bab el Mandeb: Soviet diplomacy and regional dyna-mics", *Foreign Policy Research Institute*, Pennsylvania (1979), p.25.

7.   Ogunsanwo A, *China's Policy in Africa: 1958-1971*, (Cambridge, 1974), p.83.

8.   Larkin B, *China And Africa: 1949-1970*, (London, 1971), p.175n.

9.   Brzezniski, *op. cit.*, p.193.

10.   Hutchinson, *China's African Revolution*, (London, 1975), p.91.

11.   Ogunsanwo, *op. cit.*, p.121.

12.   150 Mig.17 fighters according to one (perhaps exaggerated) estimate, *Middle East and North Africa*, 1970-71, 150 T-34 medium tanks and Soviet-made 100mm field guns. (Agunsanwo, *op. cit.*, pp.225-226). Between 1961-70, Somalia had received, according to P. Henze, a total of US$47,000,000 worth of Soviet military assistance. (P. Henze, *op. cit.*).

13. *Africa Confidential*, No.1, 1964; see also Hutchison, *op. cit.*, pp.90, 102.

14. Ogunsanwo, *op. cit.*, pp.154, 225-226, 245, 276.

15. P. Henze, *op. cit.*

16. Hutchison, *op. cit.*, p.120.

17. Ogunsanwo, *op. cit.*, pp.173-74, 246.

18. *Ibid.*, p.246.

19. David Morison, "Moscow and the Problem of Third World Communism: The Lesson of the Sudan", in *Mizan*, Vol.XIII, No.3, December 1971, quoting Ulyanovsky, "Third World Problems of Socialist Orientation".

20. *Addis Zemen*, Miaza 8, 1947 (April 1955).

21. However, when later on, on the occasion of Chinese nuclear testing, Ketema Yifru of the Foreign Office was asked about his reaction, he is reported to have said: "Every country has the right to defend itself and China is no exception". Larkin, *op. cit.*, p.79.

22. *Addis Zemen*, Tir 21, 25, 1956.

23. Hutchison, *op. cit.*, pp.65, 119; Ogunsanwo, *op. cit.*, p.125, quoting Somali Radio, 4 February, 1964.

24. China withdrew from the organisation on 17 March 1967, declaring: "It must be pointed out that the present secretariat of AAPSO in Cairo is already in the control of Soviet revisionists. Correct propositions put forth by the secretaries of different countries who defend the revolutionary line of solidarity against imperialism and stand for what is just have long been arbitrarily suppressed. As a matter of fact, the Permanent Secretariat has already degenerated into a tool of Soviet revisionists for implementing their counter-revolutionary line. We, therefore, declare that we shall henceforth have nothing to do with this organ". B. Larkin, *op. cit.*, p.141.

25. Larkin, *op. cit.*, p.16, n.3; see also R. Greenfield, *Ethiopia a New Political History*, (London, 1968), p.249.

26. *Addis Zemen*, Hedar 23, 1963; see also Ogunsanwo, *op. cit.*, p.5.

27. China was admitted to the United Nations in October 1971. Diplomatic relations also followed soon with conservative Arab countries of the Middle East, such as Iran and Kuwait, followed by a corresponding decline in Chinese aid to liberation movements of the region (Palestine, Dhofar, etc.).

28. Hutchison, *op. cit.*, p.166.

29. See for example *The Observer*, 22/6/69 — "Chinese arms for Ethiopian rebels" reporting the arrival of two shiploads of Chinese arms bought with Saudi and Kuwaiti funds for the ELF.

30. C. Clapham, *Haile Selassie's Government*, (London, 1969), p.80.

31. *Africa Report*, May 1971; Hutchison, *op. cit.*, p.119; Ogunsanwo, *op. cit.*, p.242; Hagai Erlich, *The Struggle over Eritrea*, (1983); Yitzhak Shichor, "The Middle East in China's Foreign Policy", (PhD. Thesis, 1976), p.345.

32. *Problemes Africains et du Tiers Monde*, No.496, Jeudi 29 Mai, 1969.

33. Hutchison, *op. cit.*, p.166.

34. *Ibid.*, p.119.

35. *Ibid.*, p.70.

36. *The Washington Post*, 30/12/73; *Corriere della Sera* (Italy), 31/12/73; *Al Anwar* (Beirut), 31/12/73.

37. *Resolution on CPC History: Authoritative Assessment of Mao Zedong, The Cultural Revolution* . . . (Beijing, 1981), p.32 sqq.

38. December 1976, reorganisation of PMAC and the February 1977 coup.

A REVIEW OF LIMNOLOGICAL RESEARCH IN

ETHIOPIA: A HISTORICAL PERSPECTIVE

Amha Belay

INTRODUCTION

(1) Limnology as a Subject

It is perhaps appropriate to introduce the subject of limnology briefly before presenting the review proper. Limnology is the study of inland waters — lakes, rivers, swamps etc. It is concerned mainly with the study of the functional relationships and productivity of freshwater communities in so far as they are affected by their physical, chemical and biotic environment. The subject has its main practical applications in fisheries, public health and water pollution. Much of hydrology which is a subject devoted to the study of geological, chemical, physical and climatic aspects of water resources is also included in limnology since these factors affect the distribution and productivity of aquatic organisms. Thus the subject is not a single discipline. It is a synthesis drawing upon many disciplines and owing its substance to the contributions of workers from diverse scientific fields like physics, chemistry, geology and biology.

(2) The Inland Waters of Ethiopia

Located between $3°$ and $18°$ N latitude and $33°$ and $48°$ E longitude, Ethiopia is one of the largest countries in Africa, covering nearly 1,300,000 km^2. The country abounds with several important and perennial rivers traversing more than 6,000 km of land and contains many lakes covering a total area of about 7,000 km^2.

The major rivers are the Abbay or Blue Nile, the Wabi Shebele, the Awash, the Ghenale, the Ghibe-Omo, the Tekezie, the Mereb and the Baro rivers which flow for 800, 1,000, 1,200, 860, 760, 650, 440 and 227 km in Ethiopia, respectively. These major rivers have a total annual discharge of 63 billion m^3, of which the Abbay (Blue Nile) accounts for about 80 percent.

The major lakes include Lake Tana and the seven Rift Valley lakes — Zeway, Abiata, Langano, Shala, Awasa, Abbaya and Chamo. Lake Tana has a surface area of more than 3,570 km^2 while the seven Rift Valley lakes cover a total area of about 2,960 km^2. The important man-made lakes include Koka and Fincha which cover a total area of 425 km^2. In addition, there are a number of small crater lakes, particularly those of the Debre Zeit lakes and a few groundwater fed lakes. The location and the morphometric characteristics of the major lakes are given in Figure 1 and Table 1 (at the end of the paper).

Despite the existence of such a vast aquatic resource, limnological research has not yet been conducted in an organized and coordinated fashion. The research so far conducted is fragmentary in nature and of short term duration. With the exception of some hydrological studies very little limnological work has been made on the vast majority of Ethiopian rivers. In the following, therefore, an attempt is made to review some of the important limnological literature on Ethiopian lakes. For a more comprehensive list of references on Ethiopian limnology the reader is referred to Amha Belay (1984).

GEOLOGICAL AND PALAEOLIMNOLOGICAL STUDIES

Geological and palaeolimnological studies are important in limnology because they shed light on the origin and subsequent history of lake basins and hence on the evolution of their flora and fauna. In addition the surrounding geology has a bearing on the nutrient status and hence the productivity of lakes.

In this connection, extensive studies have been made on the geology of Ethiopian lakes. The geology and mode of origin of Lake Tana has been described by Dainelli (1943) and Mohr (1962) while those of the Rift Valley lakes have been reported by Dipadola (1972) and Mohr

(1962 a; b; 1966; 1971). The geology and origin of the Bishoftu crater lakes have been described by Mohr (1961).

Extensive studies have been made on the evolution of some Ethiopian lakes particularly those of the Afar Depression and the Rift Valley lakes. The studies involve reconstruction of former climatic and environmental conditions from evidence gathered using sediment analysis, diatom analysis and palynological investigations. Mention should be made here of some of the important works done on the Afar lakes, notably Lake Abbe, Asal and Afrera by Gasse (1974; 1975; 1977a and b), Gasse and Stietltjas (1973), Gasse and Street (1978a and b), and Gasse, *et al.* (1980). Palaeolimnological work related to the evolution of some Rift Valley lakes has been reported by Descourtieux-Conqueugniot (1982), Grove and Dekker (1976), Grove and Gouide (1971a and b), Grove, *et al.* (1975), Street (1979; 1980; 1981; 1982). Palynological studies made on the Omo basin and Lake Rudolf (Turkana) by Bonnefille (1970; 1972a and b) show that climatic fluctuations have been a feature of the Rudolf basin for more that two million years.

PHYSICAL AND CHEMICAL STUDIES

The physical and chemical environment of lakes such as meteorological and hydrological factors, the depth distribution of light, temperature, oxygen and nutrients affect the abundance, distribution and productivity of freshwater organisms. Thus knowledge of such limnological events is important in lake research.

Hydrological data on Ethiopian lakes are plentiful though these have rarely been used to explain other limnological events (Daniel Gemechu, 1977; Dugdale, 1964; Mesfin Woldemariam, 1972).

Very little attention has been given to the seasonal course of thermal events as indeed to the seasonality of other limnological events in Ethiopian lakes. The only seasonal studies of temperature and oxygen made are those of Wood, *et al.* (1976) on the Bishoftu crater lakes and Kassahun Wodajo (1982) on Lakes Abiata and Langano. Nevertheless data on short term and diurnal studies of temperature and oxygen distribution have been made available by Amha Belay and Wood (1982), Baxter, *et al.* (1965), Morandini (1940), Prosser, *et al.* (1968) and Riedel (1962).

The optical properties of Ethiopian lakes have not been adequately studied. Talling (1976a) has provided data on the optical properties of Lake Tana while those of some Rift Valley lakes have been reported by Amha Belay and Wood (1982), Kassahun Wodajo (1982) and Wood and Prosser (1978). Baxter and Golobitsch (1970) have given some information on the optical characteristics of Lake Hayq.

The published information on the chemistry of Ethiopian lakes is very scattered and of varying detail and reliability. With the exception of the work by Kassahun Wodajo (1982) on Lakes Abiata and Langano, and Wood, *et al.* (1984) on the Debre Zeit lakes, virtually no study has been made of the seasonal course of chemical events. Data on the chemistry of Ethiopian lakes are found scattered among various early reports. Bini (1940) has reported on the chemistry of Lake Tana and Brunelli, *et al.* (1941) and Loffredo and Maldura (1941) have conducted chemical investigations on the Rift Valley lakes. More recently, Pitwell (1971) has done extensive chemical analysis of Ethiopian waters. Prosser, *et al.* (1968) and Getachew Teffera (1980) have looked into the chemistry of some of the Debre Zeit lakes. Talling and Talling (1965) give valuable information on the chemistry of African lake waters including those of some Ethiopian lakes. The chemical composition of Lake Tana has been summarized by Talling (1976a) from results obtained in earlier studies. A detailed study of the chemical composition of Lake Shala has been performed by Baumann, *et al.* (1975). More recent studies by Amha Belay and Wood (1982) and Kassahun Wodajo (1982) provide information on the chemical composition of Lakes Abiata, Langano, Abbaya and Chamo. The chemical limnology of some Ethiopian mountain lakes have also been studies by Baxter and Golobitsch (1981) and Loffler (1977, 1978).

420

Biological studies are the central theme of limnology since all other limnological parameters are investigated to see their effect on biological productivity and interrelationship of aquatic organisms with their abiotic and biotic environment. Such studies as the spatial and temporal distribution of freshwater organisms, their productivity or trophic links are thus essential to an understanding of aquatic ecosystems.

Studies on biological limnology in Ethiopian lakes have concentrated mainly on the description of the flora and fauna. The temporal and spatial distribution of Ethiopian freshwater algae are inadequately studied while reports on types and distribution of aquatic macrophytes are scanty (cf. Brunelli and Cannicci, 1940). The presence of a variety of algal communities in the Rift Valley lakes has been documented in some of the earliest reports (Cannicci and Almagia, 1947; Lowndes, 1930; Vatova, 1940; Zanon, 1942). The seasonal distribution and abundance of phytoplankton has been studied in Lake Abiyata and Lake Langano by Kassahun Wodajo (1982). Amha Belay and Wood (1982) have provided information on the horizontal distribution of phytoplankton in Lake Chamo during a period of an algal bloom. The phytoplankton of Lake Tana have been described by Rzoska (1976) and Talling (1976b).

There is very little work done concerning primary production in Ethiopian lakes. Studies involving direct measurements of primary production include those by Talling, *et al.* (1973) on two Bishoftu crater lakes and those by Kassahun Wodajo (1982), and Amha Belay and Wood (1984) on some Rift Valley lakes. In addition, Wood, *et al.* (1978) and Amha Belay and Wood (1982) have attempted to estimate algal biomass in some Rift Valley lakes from chlorophyll concentration.

The zooplankton of some Ethiopian inland waters have been described by Brunelli and Cannicci (1940), Cannicci and Almagia (1947), Lowndes (1930, 1932), Rzoska (1967) and Talling and Rzoska (1967). With the exception of the work by Kassahun Wodajo and Amha Belay (1984), there is no study made on the seasonal distribution and abundance of zooplankton in Ethiopian lakes.

The ichthyofauna of Lake Tana has been documented by Bini (1940b) and a more recent review of the fish in this lake is given by Greenwood (1976). Riedel (1962) gives information on the fish fauna of Lake Abbaya. Shibru Tedla (1973) has compiled most of the information on the distribution of freshwater fish in Ethiopian inland waters.

Not much research has been done on the breeding and production biology of the commercially valuable fish of the country. However, Woldemichael Getaneh and Maria Getaneh (1981) have attempted to investigate the breeding period and fecundity of *Tilapia nilotica* in Lake Zeway. Estimates of potential fish yield have been calculated from the morphoedaphic index by Wood, *et al.* (1978) while Kassahum Wodajo (1982) has attempted to estimate fish yield in Lake Abiata and Lake Langano from the morphoedaphic index and from primary production data. Recently, Gopa Consultants (1982) have done fishstock assessment in Lakes Zeway and Abbaya from echo sounding and actual catch data.

To put the foregoing review in a historical perspective, it can be said that limnological research started in Ethiopia in the late 1930's mainly by Italian scientists who made exploratory missions to Lake Tana and the Rift Valley lakes (Bini, 1940 a.b; Brunelli and Cannicci, 1940; Brunelli, *et al.*, 1941; Cannicci and Almagia, 1947; Dainelli, 1943; Loffredo and Maldura, 1941; Morandini, 1940; Vatova, 1940; Zoanon, 1942). Virtually no work was done after that until the late 1960's when there was a revival of limnological work through the contribution of some of the expatriate members of the departments of Biology, Chemistry, and Geology, Addis Ababa University. Their work is still being published almost twenty years after (Baxter and Wood, 1965; Baxter, *et al.*, 1965; Mohr, 1961; 1962a; b; 1971; Pitwell, 1971; Prosser, *et al.*, 1968; Wood, *et al.*, 1976; Wood and Prosser, 1978, to mention a few). Since then limnological research has progressed slowly but steadily until this point in time when significant contributions are being made by Ethiopian researchers particularly by staff members and graduate students of the Addis Ababa University.

It is evident from the foregoing review that very little coordinated and integrated limnological research has been undertaken until very recently. The published information is of a fragmentary nature and not up-to-date. Seasonal studies of limnological events are lacking and most of the studies made are qualitative or semiquantitative.

PRESENT STATUS AND FUTURE PROSPECTS

FOR LIMNOLOGICAL RESEARCH IN ETHIOPIA

A look at the foregoing review reveals that very little contribution has been made by indigenous staff in the field of limnology in Ethiopia until very recently. We have thus not yet developed an indigenous capability to conduct research on the many fronts of this field.

Nevertheless, the contribution from Ethiopians has increased slightly in the last few years mainly due to the efforts made by the Addis Ababa University to encourage scientific research in general. A lot of unpublished data have already been generated mainly by Ethiopian researchers and graduate students.

The future seems very bright for limnological research in Ethiopia thanks to a cooperative project that has recently been established between the Biology Department, Addis Ababa University and the Biology Department, University of Waterloo. Through this project the necessary equipment and facilities to conduct limnological research have already been acquired. It is envisaged that up to five staff members of our department will be trained at a Ph.D. level. These staff members will be doing their research component of the Ph.D. programme in Ethiopia, thereby generating the needed limnological information on Ethiopian lakes while at the same time strengthening our indigenous research capabilities. In addition, staff exchange between the University of Waterloo and Addis Ababa University will allow us to train young limnologists at the M.Sc. level. This may go some way towards satisfying the need for limnologists in the country.

CONCLUSION

The demands on water resources are increasing exponentially and necessitate a corresponding increase in management, as well as a degree of manipulation. Unless we comprehend the rudiments of their functional operation, any hope of using them effectively is lost. Limnological research is thus vital to the national economic development of developing countries in general as it provides the necessary background for the effective and rational utilization of existing freshwater resources. For instance, the increasing nutritional importance of fish as a source of protein will alone make the scientific management of some of our freshwater resources essential.

A great deal thus needs to be known about the functional operation and fundamental behaviour of our lakes and rivers. Fundamental, that is, not in the sense of esoteric, obscure academic research but to the wise, long-term use of our existing freshwater resources.

ACKNOWLEDGEMENTS

This work was made possible through a research fund obtained from the Research and Publications Office, Addis Ababa University.

REFERENCES

Amha Belay, 1984

A Bibliography of Ethiopian limnology (To be published), *SINET, Ethiopia, J. Sci.*

Amha Belay and R. B. Wood, 1982

Limnological aspects of an algal bloom on Lake Chamo, Gamo Gofa Administrative Region of Ethiopia in 1978. *SINET, Ethiopia, J. Sci.* 5(1): 1-19.

Amha Belay and R. B. Wood, 1984

Primary productivity of five Ethiopian Rift Valley Lakes (In press) *Verh. Internat. Verein. Limnol.*

Baumann, A., U. Forstner and R. Rohde, 1975

Lake Shala: water chemistry, mineralogy and geochemistry of sediments in an Ethiopian rift lake. *Geol. Rundschau*, 64: 593-609.

Baxter, R. M. and D. L. Golobitsch, 1970

A note on the limnology of Lake Hayq, Ethiopia, *Limnol. Oceanogr.*, 15: 144-149.

Baxter, R. M. and D. L. Golobitsch, 1981

Observations on Garba Guratch, an Ethiopian mountain lake, *SINET, Ethiop., J. Sci.*, 4(1): 63-68.

Baxter, R. M. and R. B. Wood, 1965

Studies on stratification in the Bishoftu crater lakes, *J. appl. Ecol.*, 2: 416.

Baxter, R. M., M. V. Prosser, J.F. Talling and R.B. Wood, 1965

Stratification in tropical African lakes at moderate altitudes (1,500 to 2,000 m), *Limnol. Oceanogr.*, 10: 511-520.

Bini, G., 1940a

Ricerche chimiche nelle acque del Lago Tana: 9-52. In *Missione di Studio al Lago Tana*, Vol.III, Ricerche Limnologiche, part 2: Chimicha e biologia. Reale Academia d'Italia.

Bini, G., 1940b

I Pesci del Lago Tana: 135-206. In *Missione di Studio al Lago Tana*, Vol.III, Ricerche Limnologiche, part 2: Chimicha e biologia. Reale Academia d'Italia.

Bonnefille, R., 1970

Premiers résultats concernant l'analyse pollinique d'échantillons du Pléistocène de l'Omo (Ethiopie). C. R. Acad. Sc., Paris 270: 2430-2433.

Bonnefille, R., 1972a

Associations Polliniques Actuelles et Quaternaries en Ethiopie. Thèse, Univ. de Paris VI, CNRS A 07229 T. I, 513p.

Bonnefille, R., 1972b

Considérations sur la composition d'une microflore pollinique des formations Plio-pléistocène de la basse vallée de l'Omo (Ethiopie), pp. 22-27. In E. M. Van Zinderen Bakker (ed.), *Palaeoecology of Africa*, V., 7., A. A. Balkema, Cape Town.

Brunelli, G. and G. Cannicci, 1940

Le characteristiche biologiche del Lago Tana: 69-133. In *Missione di Studio al Lago Tana*, Vol.III, Ricerche Limnologiche, part 2: Chimicha e biologia. Reale Academia d'Italia.

Brunelli, G., G. Cannicci,

Esplorazione dei laghi della Fossa Galla. Collezione Scientifica e

| S. Lofredo, C. M. Maldura, G. Morandini, P. Parenzan, A Vatova and G. Zolezzi, 1941 | documentaria dell'Africa Italiana II. Airoldi. Verbania. 2 vols. 258pp. |

| Cannicci, G. and F. Almagia, 1947 | Notizie sulla "facies" planctonica di alcuni laghi della Fossa Galla. *Pesca Piscicolt, Idrobiol* 23, 2NS: 54-77. |

| Dainelli, G., 1943 | *Geologia dell'Africa Orientale*, 4 vols. R. Acc. Italia, Rome. |

| Daniel Gemetchu, 1977 | *Aspects of climate and water budget in Ethiopia.* Addis Ababa University Press, Addis Ababa. pp.71. |

| Descourtieux-Coqueugniot, C. 1979 | Les diatomées du Sondage du lac Abiya (Ethiopie) systematique et paléoécologie. Unpublished. Thèse 3e cycle, Université de Paris VI; 76pp. |

| DiPaola, G. M., 1972 | The Ethiopian Rift Valley (between $7°\ 00'$ and $8°\ 40'$ lat north). *Bull. Volcanol.*, 36(4): 517-560. |

| Dugdale, J. S., 1964 | Ethiopian climates and vegetation: the state of our present knowledge. J. *Semetic studies*, 9: 250-256. |

| Gasse, F. and L. Stieltjes, 1978 | Les sédiments du Quaternaire recent du lac Asal (Afar Central, Territoire français des Afars et des Issas). *Bull. Bur. Rech. Géol.*, min. 2e ser., 4(4): 229-245. |

| Gasse, F., 1974 | Diatomées des sédiments holocènes du lac Afrera (Afar septentrional, Ethiopie). Essai de reconstitution de l'évolution du milieu. *Int. Rev. Ges. Hydrobiol.*, 58: 941-964. |

| Gasse, F., 1975 | L'évolution des lacs de l'Afar Central (Ethiopie et T.F.A.I.) du Plio-Pléistocène a l'Actuel: Reconstitution des paléomilieux lacustres à partir de l'étude des diatomées. Université de Paris VI, 406pp., 3 vols. |

| Gasse, F., 1977a | Evolution of Lake Abbe (Ethiopia and T.F.A.I.) from 70,000 b.p., *Nature*, 265: 42-45. |

| Gasse, F., 1977b | Les groupements de diatomées planktoniques: base de la classification des lacs quaternaires de l'Afar Central: 207-234. In *Recherches françaises sur le Quaternaire hors de France*. Etude. Quatern. Comité National française de l'INQUA. Bull. Ass. Fr. Suppl. 1.50. Paris. |

| Gasse, F. and F. A. Street, 1978a | Late Quaternary lake – level fluctuations and environments of the northern Rift Valley and Afar region (Ethiopia and Djibouti). *Palaeogeogr. Palaeoclimatol Palaeoecol.* 24: 279-325. |

| Gasse, F. and F. A. Street, 1978b | The main stages of the late Quaternary evolution of the northern Rift Valley and Afar lakes (Ethiopia and Djibouti). *Polskie Archum Hydrobiol.* 25: 145-150. |

| Gasse, F., P. Rognon and | Quaternary history of the Afar and Ethiopian Rift lakes: 361- |

F.A. Street, 1980 — 400. In M. A. J. Williams and H. Faure (eds.) *The Sahara and the Nile*, Balkemma, Rotterdam: 607pp.

Getachew Teffera, 1980 — A limnological note on Lake Chelekleka, *SINET, Ethiopia, J. Sci.*, 3(2): 143-152.

Gopa Consultants, 1982 — Fisheries Development Project: Research Programme Final Report. Ministry of Agriculture, Department of Fisheries, Addis Ababa, Ethiopia. 56 pp.

Greenwood, P. H., 1976 — Fish fauna of the Nile: 127-141. In Rzoska, J. (Ed.), *The Nile, biology of an ancient river*. Junk., The Hague: 417 pp.

Grove, A. T. and A. S. Goudie, 1971a — **Late quaternary lake levels in the Rift Valley of Southern** Ethiopia and elsewhere in tropical Africa. *Nature*, 234: 403-405.

Grove, A. T. and A. S. Goudie, 1971b — Secrets of Lake Stefanie's past. *Geogr. Mag.*, 43: 542-547.

Grove, A. T., F. A. Street and A.S.Goudie, 1975 — Former lake levels and climatic change in the Rift Valley of Southern Ethiopia. *Geogr. J.*, 141: 177-202.

Grove, A. T. and G. Dekker, 1976 — Late quaternary lake levels in the Rift Valley of Southern Ethiopia. In "Proceedings, VII Panafrican Congress of Prehistory and Quaternary Studies". (B. Abebe, J. Chavaillon and J. E. G. Sutton, Eds.) pp.405-407. Ethiopian Ministry of Culture, Addis Ababa.

Kassahun Wodajo, 1982 — Comparative limnology of Lake Abiata and Lake Langano in relation to primary and secondary production. Unpublished M.Sc thesis. Addis Ababa University. 127 pp.

Kassahun Wodajo and Amha Belay, 1984 — Species composition and seasonal abundance of zooplankton in two Ethiopian Rift Valley lakes — lakes Abiata and Langano. *Hydrobiologia*, 113, 129-136.

Lezine, A. M., 1982 — Etude Palynologique des sédiments quaternaires du lac Abiata (Ethiopia). *Paleoecology of Africa*. Balkema, Rotterdam, 14: 93-98.

Löffler, H., 1977 — Beobachtungen Zur Anatidenfauna der Bale-Berge (Äthiopien). *Egretta* 20 (1): 36-44.

Löffler, H., 1978 — Limnological and paleolimnological data on the Bale mountain lakes (Ethiopia). *Verh. int. Limnol.* 20: 1131-1138.

Lofredo, S. and C. M. Maldura, 1941 — Risultati generali delle ricerche di chimica limnologica sulle acquae dei laghi dell'Africa orientale italia esplorati dalla Missione ittiologica: 18-200. In G. Brunelli *et al.*, (eds.) *Esplorazione dei laghi della Fossa Galla*, Vol.I: Collezione scientifica e documentaria dell'Africa Italiana III. Airoldi Verbania, Rome. 258 pp.

Lowndes, A. G., 1930   Freshwater Copepoda from Abyssinia collected by Mr. J. Omer-Cooper. *Proc. Zool. Soc. Lond.*, 161-179.

Lowndes, A.G., 1932   Report on the Ostracoda. Mr. Omer-Cooper's investigation of the Abyssinian freshwaters (Dr. Hugh Scott's Expedition). *Proc. Zool. Soc. Lond.*, Part 3, 677-708.

Mesfin Wolde Mariam, 1972   *An introductory geography of Ethiopia.* Addis Ababa. 215 pp.

Mohr, P., 1961   The geology, structure and origin of the Bishoftu explosion craters, Shoa, Ethiopia. *Bull. Geophys. Obs.*, Addis Ababa, 2: 65-101.

Mohr, P., 1962a   The Ethiopian Rift System. *Bull. Geophys. Obs.*, Addis Ababa, 3: 33-62.

Mohr, P., 1962b   *The geology of Ethiopia.* University College, Addis Ababa Press, Addis Ababa, Ethiopia.

Mohr, P., 1966   Geological report on the Lake Langano and adjacent plateau regions. *Bull. Geophys. Obs.*, Addis Ababa, 9: 59-75.

Mohr, P., 1971   *The geology of Ethiopia.* Haile Selassie I University Press. (Now Addis Ababa University Press), 268 pp.

Morandini, G., 1940   Ricerche limnologiche, Geografia-Fisica, Vol.III, 1, *Missione di Studio al Lago Tana*, p. 319.

Pitwell, C. R., 1971   Analysis of Ethiopian and other natural waters, H.S.I.U., Addis Ababa.

Prosser, M. V., R. B. Wood and R. M. Baxter, 1968   The Bishoftu Crater Lakes: A bathymetric and chemical study. *Arch. Hydrobiol.*, 58 (4): 435-468.

Riedel, D., 1962   Der Margheritensee (Sudabessinien) Zugleich ein Beitrag zu Kenntis der abessinischen Graben seen. *Arch. Hydrobiol.*, 58 (4): 435-468.

Rzoska, J., 1976   Lake Tana, headwaters of the Blue Nile: 223-232. In Rzoska, J. (ed.) *The Nile, biology of an ancient river.* Junk. The Hague: 417 pp.

Shibru Tedla, 1973   *Freshwater Fishes of Ethiopia.* Department of Biology, H.S.I.U., Addis Ababa. Mimeo. 101pp.

Street, F. A., 1979   Late Quaternary precipitation estimates for the Zeway-Shala basin, Southern Ethiopia. *Paleoecology of Africa.* Balkema, Rotterdam, 12: 135-144.

Street, F. A., 1980   The relative importance of climate and local bydrological factors influencing lake-level fluctuations. *Paleoecology of Africa.* Balkema, Rotterdam, 12: 137-158.

Street, F. A., 1981   Chronology of late Pleistocene and Holocene lake-level fluctuations, Zeway-Shala basin, Ethiopia. In R. E. Leakey and B. A. Ogot (eds.), *Proceedings VIII Panafrican Congress of Prehistoric and Quaternary Studies.* International Louis Leakey Memorial Institute for African Prehistory, Nairobi. 143-146.

Street, F. A., 1982   Twentieth century fluctuations in lake-level in the Zeway-Shala basin, Ethiopia. *Paleoecology of Africa.* Balkema, Rotterdam. 15: 99-110.

Talling, J. F., 1976a   Water characteristics: 357-384. In Rzoska, J. (ed.), *The Nile, biology of an ancient river.* Junk, The Hague: 417pp.

Talling, J. F., 1976b   Phytoplankton: composition, development and productivity: 385-400. In Rzoska, J. (ed.), *The Nile, biology of an ancient river.* Junk, The Hague: 417pp.

Talling, J. F. and J. Rzoska, 1967   The development of plankton in relation to hydrological regime in the Blue Nile, *J. Ecol.* 55: 637-662.

Talling, J. F. and I. B. Talling, 1965   The chemical composition of African lake waters. *Int. Revue. ges. Hydrobiol. Hydrogr.*, 50 (3): 421-463.

Talling, J. F., R. B. Wood, M. V. Prosser and R. M. Baxter, 1973   The upper limit of photosynthetic productivity by phytoplankton: evidence from Ethiopian Soda lakes. *Freshwater Biol.*, 3: 53-76.

Vatova, A., 1940   Notizie idrografiche biologiche sui laghi dell'Africa Orientale Italiana. *Thalassia* 4 (9): 25 pp.

Woldemichael Getaneh and Maria Getaneh, 1979   Breeding period and fecundity of *Tilapia nilotica* L. in Lake Zeway. *Eth. J. Agr. Sci.*, 1 (1): 13-21.

Wood, R. B., R. M. Baxter and M. V. Prosser, 1984   Seasonal and comparative aspects of chemical stratification in some tropical crater lakes. Ethiopia (In press) *Freshwater Biol.*, 14.

Wood, R. B. and M. V. Prosser, 1978   Optical characteristics of the Rift Valley lakes of Ethiopia, *SINET, Ethiopia J. Sci.*, 1 (2): 73-85.

Zoanon, B., 1942   Diatomee dei Laghi Galla (A.O.I.), *Atti R. Accad. Ital. Memorie* 12: 431-568.

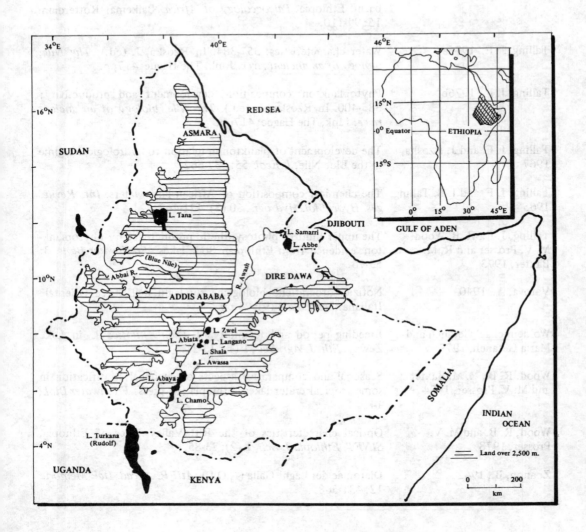

TABLE 1: MORPHOMETRIC CHARACTERISTICS OF THE MAJOR ETHIOPIAN LAKES

	Tana	Zwei	Abiata	Langano	Shalla	Awasa	Abaya	Chamo
Location	12° N; 37°20′ E	8°3′ N; 38°50′ E	7°36′ N; 8°48′ E	7°36′ N; 38°45′ E	7°30′ N; 38°30′ E	70°3′ N; 38°24′ E	6°2′–6°35′N 37°40′–38°5′E	5° 40′N; 37°37′E
Altitude	1829	1848	1573	1585	1567	1708	1285	1280
Surface Area (km²)	3170	440	205	230	409	130	1161	551
Maximum Length (km)	78	32	21	23	27	17	70	36
Maximum Width (km)	67	20	12	16	17	11	28	23
Maximum Depth (m)	14	7	14	46	266	22	13	30
Mean Depth (m)	8.9	2.5	7.6	17	86	11	7	–
Volume (m³)	28×10^9	1.1×10^9	1.6×10^9	3.8×10^9	37×10^9	13×10^9	8.2×10^9	–
Shore line (km)	385	102	62	78	110	52	225	118
Shore Devt.	–	1.37	1.22	1.45	1.53	1.29	1.86	–
Watershed area (km²)	13350	7025	1630	1600	3920	1250	17300	–
Watershed area Lake Volume ratio (m²:m³)	0.48	6.39	1.02	0.42	0.11	0.96	2.11	–

PATTERNS AND TRENDS OF CRIME IN ETHIOPIA:

A COMPARATIVE ANALYSIS OF THE CRIME PROBLEM

IN THE PRE- AND POST-REVOLUTION PERIODS

Andargatchew Tesfaye

Travellers and writers on Ethiopian affairs have emphasized that litigation is an endemic feature of Ethiopian society, of proportion similar to the ones observed in any peasant society. Some even ventured to claim that for Ethiopians litigation is a psychological disposition. Though there is an apparent failure on the part of these writers to indicate why it had been so, the raw police crime statistics and the number of court cases seem to bear out their allegations.[1] Apart from these passing comments and a few reports based on secondary materials, crime in Ethiopia is one of the most neglected areas of research. The extent and causes of crime are yet to be studied.

In this paper attempts will be made to analyze the patterns and trends of crime in the pre- and post-revolution periods. In Part 1, the volume of crime and the prevailing patterns of crime in the pre-revolution period will be dealt with. In Part II, the available data will be analyzed to see whether the assumptions by the police, that the crime rate, after the revolution, has been declining[2], holds true or not. Finally, in Part III, attempts will be made to see, from the existing data, if there has been any change in the patterns and trends of crime in Ethiopia after the 1974 Revolution.

In this paper the term 'pattern' means the traits or the observable features that characterize the crime problem in Ethiopia. On the other hand, the term 'trend' refers to the prevailing tendency of the crime problem. Does the crime problem show any tendency to take a different direction away from what used to be observed in the past, is one of the questions to be answered.

PART I.

Ethiopia had remained, for centuries, a feudal society characterized by a distinct stratification, with the Emperor as the head of the political, social, economic and even religious systems. Next to the Emperor came the royal family, the nobility, high government and ecclesiastical officials. At the bottom of the hierarchy were the majority of the people, consisting of small merchants (traders) and priestly classes, and a large majority of the peasantry engaged in subsistence agriculture.[3]

Subsistence agriculture has been the mainstay of over 80% of the population. Yet more than two thirds of the total land belonged to the Ethiopian Coptic Church, the Emperor and his family, the nobility, high government and church officials. The masses were not only confined to the remaining one-third of the land, but were also subjugated to a life of tenancy and corvee labour. In addition, they had to pay up to 75% of their produce to the landlords.[4]

The majority of the people were deprived of other essential services as well. The literacy rate was only 10%, while health services were available to 20% of the total population at most. Even those meagre services were inequitably distributed, as Eshetu Chole put it:

> "Addis Ababa with less than 3% of the total population, accounts for over 50% of all doctors, and it also accounts for more than 20% of teachers in all government schools. Figures could be added at length, but the essential feature, that of a vast rural-urban split, is one that should not be lost sight of."[5]

The socio-economic conditions that obtained in the country had a number of serious consequences. The unparalleled coercion and exploitation of the peasant farmers by the establish-

431

ment and the never improving socio-economic conditions in the rural areas, resulted in occasional protests, revolts and various kinds of behaviour by the masses which were labelled 'illegal' acts by the government.[6] As a result of the archaic economic system, rural-urban split, rural-urban migration, unemployment and under-employment, crime, delinquency and prostitution had become rampant.

Though their accuracy may be questionable, available police statistics over the past several years indicate that crimes had been increasing up to 1973/74, when they gradually started to decline. After 1978/79 they began to pick up slightly, as can be observed in Table 1.

TABLE 1

Frequency of Crimes by Category, as Percent of Total Indictments*

Year	Crimes Against the Person		Crimes Against Property		Other Crimes**		Total
	No. of Crimes	Percent of Total	No. of Crimes	Percent of Total	No. of Crimes	Percent of Total	Total
***							
1964/65	35,568	34.19	26,882	25.84	41,575	39.97	104,025
1965/66	37,071	33.36	29,180	26.26	44,863	40.38	111,114
1966/67	34,018	29.85	28,517	25.02	51,420	45.12	113,955
1967/68	34,702	32.02	26,257	24.23	47,407	43.75	108,366
1968/69	33,128	33.99	23,737	24.35	40,610	41.66	97,475
1969/70	30,155	31.80	23,185	24.45	41,479	43.75	94,819
1970/71	30,883	30.74	26,620	26.49	42,970	42.77	100,473
1971/72	29,163	29.81	27,016	27.67	41,473	42.47	97,652
1972/73	28,608	23.33	25,687	25.89	68,682	55.85	122,977
1973/74	26,004	24.33	28,387	26.56	52,503	49.12	106,894
1974/75	26,599	22.26	27,772	23.24	65,137	54.50	119,508
1975/76	23,759	23.48	22,204	21.94	55,239	54.58	101,202
1976/77	19,181	27.27	16,071	22.95	35,089	49.88	70,341
1977/78	11,961	33.59	8,547	24.00	15,105	42.41	35,613
1978/79	10,222	31.07	12,305	37.40	10,372	31.53	32,899
1979/80	14,872	33.52	15,654	35.29	13,837	31.19	44,363
1980/81	17,474	35.87	15,207	29.16	17,038	34.97	48,719
1981/82	18,673	36.05	18,671	36.09	14,457	27.91	51,801
1982/83	17,771	35.48	18,268	36.47	14,055	28.06	50,094

*   Compiled from Unpublished Annual Police Reports
**   Other crimes include mainly crimes against the state, and crimes against state and municipal regulations.
*** The years are given as 1964/65, etc., because all criminal statistics are available for the Ethiopian calendar year, which begins in September and has seven to eight years difference from the Gregorian Calendar.

Crimes in Ethiopia can be broadly categorised as crimes against the person, crimes against property, crimes against the state and crimes against state regulations (mainly municipal and trade regulations). In this paper we will be concerned mainly with the first two categories.

In Ethiopia, crimes against the person and crimes against property, in most cases, make up more than 50% of the total crimes as the figures in Table 1 show. This proportion is more or less maintained for a number of years. For instance in 1964/65 crimes against the person and crimes against property consisted of 34.19% and 25.84% of all crimes, respectively.[7] Ten years later, in 1973/74, the same proportion was more or less still holding. It was 24.33% and 26.56% respectively, with a slight reversal, that is crime against property was slightly higher.

Such proportions are not generally observed in many other countries. Usually crimes against property are much higher than crimes against the person. A brief comparison of the conditions in some African countries will illustrate this (there is no special reason for selecting these countries except for the availability of the data). In Ethiopia in 1970 the number of crimes reported to the police were 28,066 offences against the person and 23,899 offences against property.[8] For the same year in Kenya 10,468 and 14,998 offences against the person and property, respectively, were reported.[9] Similarly in Ghana, for the same year, 42,052 and 47,049 against the person and property, respectively, were reported.[10] In 1968 in Uganda 25,575 offences against property were recorded.[11] These comparisons can be more vividly observed in Table 2.

TABLE 2.

Ratio of Crimes Against the Person and Against Property in a few African Countries

1	2	3	4	5
Country	Year	Crime Against the Person	Crime Against Property	Ratio of 3 to 4
Ethiopia	1970	28,666	23,899	1.2:1
Kenya	1970	10,468	14,998	0.7:1
Ghana	1970	42,052	47,049	0.89:1
Uganda	1968	25,575	44,892	0.57:1

From the figures (the ratios) it is clear that, though in general the crime rate appears to be lower compared to the population size of the three other countries, the ratio of crimes against the person in Ethiopia is much higher than crimes against property. In the three other countries invariably the ratio of crimes against property is higher than crimes against the person.

To emphasize the difference in the patterns of crime in Ethiopia, comparative figures showing the worldwide conditions are given in the following four charts.

CHART 1:- Criminal offences by Major Categories expressed as percent of 100,000 population for 1970-1975 worldwide.*

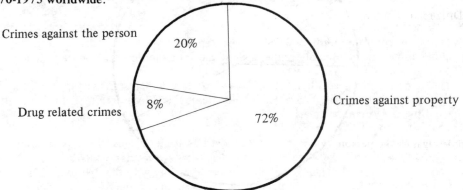

Crimes against the person 20%

Drug related crimes 8%

Crimes against property

72%

* Charts 1 to 3 are taken from *Crime Prevention and Control: Report of the Secretary-General* (UN document No/A/32/199 September 1977), pp.9-14.

From Chart 1 we can see that 72% of all the crimes committed throughout the world for the years 1970-75 were crimes against property, while crimes against the person and drug related crimes accounted for 20% and 8%, respectively. The overall rate of criminal offences for the period was approximately 900 per 100,000 population.[12]

CHART 2:- Crime Rates (per 100,000 population) by Major categories for Developed countries for 1970-1975

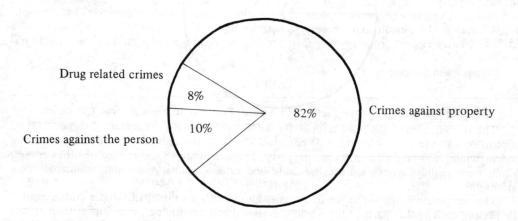

The overall crime rate in the developed countries was 1000 per 100,000 population for 1970-1975. As shown in Chart 2, 82% of the total crime accounted for crimes against property. Crimes against the person and drug related crimes constituted only 10% and 8%, respectively.[13]

CHART 3:- Crime Rates (per 100,000 population) by Major categories for Developing countries for 1970-1975

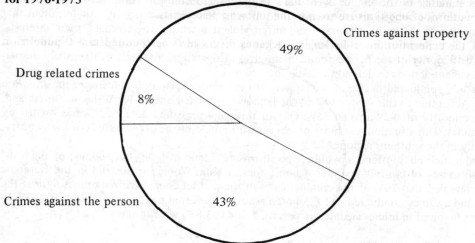

In the developing countries the overall crime rate was approximately 800 per 100,000 population. 49% of the crimes for 1970-1975 were crimes against property. Crimes against the person and drug related crimes consisted of 43% and 8%, respectively.[14]

CHART 4:- Crime Rates (per 100,000 population) by Major Categories, for Ethiopia, 1970-1975*

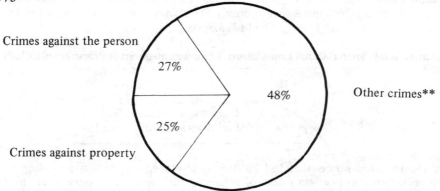

Crimes against the person

27%

48%   Other crimes**

25%

Crimes against property

The overall crime rate for Ethiopia for 1970-1975 was approximately 395 per 100,00 population. As the figures in Chart 4 indicate 27% of all the crimes were crimes against the person, while 25% were crimes against property. The remaining 48% consisted of other crimes, which were mainly crimes against the state and crimes against state and municipal regulations.[15]

The comparative figures, in the four charts above, indicate that in Ethiopia crimes against the person, unlike other parts of the world (developed and developing), were higher than crimes against property. This unique pattern was invariably maintained over a number of years, as the figures in Table 1 and the four charts clearly show.

What theoretical implications can be read in this apparent anomaly? Why are crimes against the person higher than crimes against property in Ethiopia? Could it be due to the communal nature of some crimes against the person, or could there be much deeper implications? For instance, in 1974/75 for 119,508 crimes reported to the police, 188,513 persons were apprehended as culprits. This figure implies almost two (1.58) persons per crime.[16]

Usually a simple quarrel over property, particularly a piece of land, may spark off serious cases of assault or even homicide, in which families and relatives may be involved. Ethiopian feudal society placed a great deal of value and prestige on land ownership. Indeed, the measure of one's standing in society, or even one's manhood, especially in rural areas, had been expressed in terms of one's fortune to own and protect a piece of land. It is no wonder, then, that so many should resort to desperate and often violent attempts to safeguard their interests. Besides, the concentration of wealth in the hands of the few and the desperate conditions in which the majority of the people found themselves instigated many to resort to equally desperate and violent actions to defend the little they owned.[17]

A study conducted in one of the regions of the country (Hararghe) illustrates the situation vividly. According to this study, 44% of the landowners owned only 2.4% of the measured land, while a minority of 0.2% owned 75%. Out of this total measured area, 95.4% was owned by two families. This situation was more or less similar in most of the other regions of the country, especially in the southern regions.[18]

Under such circumstances, would it be surprising if land disputes became one of the most common causes of crime? A study of court files in Kuni Woreda (a district in the Hararghe region) revealed that 20% of the criminal cases in the district court involved crimes against the person and a survey conducted in 1975 in ten randomly selected prisons indicated that of 3,638 prisoners involved in crimes against the person, 2,504 (63.8%) were farmers.[20]

*   Calculated from the figures in Table 1.
**   Consists mainly of crimes against state and crimes against state and municipal regulations. Minor crimes, such as drug related crimes and others, are also included. Since the statistics are available only in this manner, it does not allow further breakdowns.

The figures in Table 3 illustrate more clearly the extent to which land related disputes dominated court cases.

TABLE 3.

Percentage of Land Related Court Cases Before Land was made State Property in 1975*

1) 36.50% of all cases held over from 1973
2) 22.41% of all cases filed in 1974
3) 19.55% of all cases decided in 1974
4) 43.55% of all cases adjourned until 1975

Certain socio-cultural norms that had inevitably developed due to the prevailing social structure led people to adopt certain modes of behaviour. Ethiopia is a country where bravery and courage are greatly admired qualities. A 'man' is not supposed to lose in a fight, especially in connection with his family or property. Therefore, aggressiveness and violence become the main means of protecting one's 'name', rights and property in the absence of the rule of law.[21] However, one wonders whether in this case the aggressiveness is a sign of bravery or, rather, of hopelessness and a struggle for survival in a society where justice has been highly personalized and is too slow in redressing the aggrieved party.[22]

The second largest group of crimes, as shown in Table 1, had been crimes against property and these crimes took place mainly in urban areas. The rate of rural-urban migration has been very high, mainly caused by under-employment and lack of prospects in rural areas, and cities have been estimated to grow at about 10% per annum. For instance, the population living in 165 municipalities increased from about 1.4 million in 1962, to about 2.3 million in 1970.[23] As in various parts of the developing world, urbanization has been having its own toll in Ethiopia as well. People, young and old have been uprooted from the relatively close, static patterns of rural life and have been thrust into the uncertain turbulence of the city, where every man is a stranger. They have been forced to learn to survive in an environment that is completely artificial and inhospitable. They did not know how to regain the sense of community they had lost in the transitional process.[24]

Since the absorption capacity of Ethiopian cities is limited, a large number of unemployed people roamed the city streets. In the early 1970s the unemployment rate was estimated at 15-20% of the labour force.[25] It was reported that 84,135 job seekers were registered in the various employment offices between 1956 and 1961. Of these only 15% managed to obtain employment through the employment offices. 3326 workers were laid off by private enterprises in 1968.[26] The huge gap that existed between the number of people in search of employment and the employing capacities of the various organizations could be seen from the fact that in 1972/73 all enterprises employing 10 or more people only had a total of 54,965 people on their payroll.[27] Under such circumstances, it is inevitable for such unfortunate people to be fertile ground for deviant activities, such as theft, robbery, burglary and other similar crimes. After all it is a matter of survival. This condition is well illustrated by the 1975 study of 6687 prisoners which indicated that 1191 of them were committed for property offences. Prior to their commitment 29.58% were farmers, 28.97% were employed in various services and 20.49% did not have any specific occupation.[28] These are usually the least remunerative areas of employment in the country. As a result of all this, people were forced to adopt certain survival patterns which were labelled as 'anti-social'. Some became beggars[29] or prostitutes in order to survive[30], while others resorted to a life of crime. Society was quick to brand these types of behaviour

---

* Taken from Girma Wolde Selassie, "The Impact of Ethiopian Revolution on the Laws and Legal Institutions of the country" in Sven Rubenson (ed.), *Proceedings of the Seventh International Conference of Ethiopian Studies*, University of Lund, 26-29 April 1982, p.574. The figures include both civil and criminal cases.

anti-social and criminal, yet did absolutely nothing to develop an understanding of why people behaved in the way they did. Criminals were passed through the grinding mill of justice and dumped into the dehumanizing prison systems.

PART II.

This is how it was in pre-revolution Ethiopia. How has it been since the revolution? The overall changes that have been instituted since 1974 have affected, not only the political, but also the social, economic and cultural lives of people in general. The nationalization of rural land, urban land and extra houses, and the creation of Peasants' Associations and Urban Dwellers' Associations have radically changed the old social, political, economic and, to some extent, legal systems. To begin with, the creation of these bodies is supposed to have brought political and legal power to the doorsteps of people in both the rural and urban areas. Peasants' Associations and Urban Dwellers' Associations have been empowered by law to establish, not only judicial tribunals to attend to minor civil and criminal cases in their localities, but also to have their own defence squads and public safety committees to keep peace and order.[31]

The creation of these mass organizations seems to have brought about a fall in the volume of crime. According to police statistics, (see Table 1) in 1972/73, the year just before the Revolution, 100,597 crimes were reported to the police. Five years later, in 1977/78, crimes reported to the police fell to 35,642 and in 1982/83 they went up slightly to 50,094. Is this fall in the crime rate, as reported by the police, real or apparent? Were there circumstances that inevitably led to the fall of the crime rate immediately after the Revolution? Would this fall be lasting or temporary? Are the noticeable changes in the crime condition related only to the volume of crime, or are there also changes in the patterns and trends of crime? Attempts shall be made in this paper to answer these and similar questions in order to show that to some extent the fall in volume of crimes is more apparent than real. On the other hand, attempts will also be made to show that as a result of the structural changes that have taken place since 1974, there have been subsequent changes in the patterns and trends of crime.

The creation of Peasants' and Urban Dwellers' Associations, together with their judicial tribunals and revolutionary guards, had an impact on the volume of crime, especially during the earliest stages of the Revolution. These associations were given wide ranging powers under the respective proclamations by which they were created, as summarised by Raul Valdes Vivo:

"The Kebele's responsibilities in activities for the well-being of the people,
in defense operations and in administration of justice are well defined . . .
A proclamation issued in October, 1976 . . . gave them the power to establish their own courts of justice and defined the radius of action of those
courts and their procedures in civil and criminal cases."[32]

At the initial stages, because their own survival was at stake, these associations were very active and carried out their law and order responsibilities very enthusiastically. Strict controls were placed on population movements of both the rural villages and urban neighbourhoods through the issuance of identity cards. Revolutionary guards and/or members of the neighbour-hood associations were put on patrol duties both during the day and night. Definitely this had an effect in discouraging certain categories of crime, such as petty theft and burglary.

On the other hand, breaches of the law such as intimidation, offences against the privacy of domicile, dangerous vagrancy, assault, public indecency and outrages against morality, failure to bring up and to maintain children, etc., as defined under the Penal Code and most of the pro-visions of the Code of Petty Offences were put within the jurisdiction of the judicial tribunals of the Peasants' and Urban Dwellers' Associations.[33] They handle these cases without referring to either the police or to the Attorney General's Office, unless the cases are beyond their juris-diction. However, if individuals have to be detained until they appear before the tribunals, they have to be referred to the police stations for detention purposes, especially in the urban areas. Therefore, the cases that are dealt with by the tribunals are not reflected in the official statis-

Table 4
Crime Rates for the Major Categories of Crime for 1976/77 to 1982/83

Categories of Crime	1975/77	%	1977/78	%	+1978/79	%	1979/80	%
Homicide	3892	—	3410	− 12.38	2355	− 30.94	2647	+ 12.04
Attempted Homicide	2723	—	1849	− 32.10	1280	− 30.77	1251	− 2.27
Manslaughter	66	—	85	+ 28.79	123	+ 44.71	146	+ 18.70
Assault	12085	—	6284	− 48.00	5449	− 13.29	9133	+ 67.61
Robbery	812	—	341	− 58.00	260	− 23.75	426	+ 63.85
Burglary	1080	—	630	− 41.67	469	− 25.56	449	− 4.26
Theft	10136	—	5744	− 43.33	8276	+ 44.08	10635	+ 28.05
Fraud	1161	—	740	− 36.26	1076	+ 45.41	1247	+ 15.89
Breach of Trust	1383	—	1348	− 2.53	2224	+ 64.99	2897	+ 30.26
Violations of various State and Municipal Regulations	13163	—	6332	− 51.09	8748	+ 38.16	12088	+ 38.18
TOTAL:	46501	—	26763	− 42.45	30260	+ 13.07	40919	+ 35.22

Categories of Crime	1980/81	%	1981/82	%	1982/83	%
Homicide	2706	+ 2.23	2895	+ 6.98	2977	+ 2.83
Attempted Homicide	1333	+ 6.55	1520	+ 14.03	1511	− 0.59
Manslaughter	163	+ 11.64	185	+ 13.50	195	+ 5.41
Assault	11499	+ 25.91	12326	+ 7.19	11286	+ 8.44
Robbery	452	+ 6.10	526	+ 16.37	556	+ 5.07
Burglary	538	+ 19.82	622	+ 15.61	580	+ 6.75
Theft	11868	+ 11.59	12793	+ 7.79	12520	− 2.13
Fraud	1349	+ 8.18	1375	+ 1.93	1270	+ 7.64
Breach of Trust	3223	+ 11.25	3344	+ 3.80	3312	− 0.96
Violations of various State and Municipal Regulations	12123	+ 0.29	12614	+ 4.05	12218	+ 3.14
TOTAL:	45254	+ 10.59	48200	+ 6.50	46425	− 3.07

Source: Adapted from Unpublished Police Annual Reports.

tics. In other words, the data are not included in either the police statistics or in the court statistics compiled by the Ministry of Law and Justice. They may have been included, partially, in prison records, but unfortunately these are not available to the public. Thus, there is no visible mechanism by which the judicial tribunals are supposed to report to a central register where all crimes are recorded. Could not this be one of the reasons why the crime rate appears to have been declining?

Another contributing factor for the decline of crime could be the political turmoil that followed the military coup of 1974, which led to internal struggle between the Provisional Military Administrative Council (PMAC) and underground movements that wanted political control of the country. This struggle eventually led to what was known as the period of white and red terror, which resulted in killings and counter-killings.[34] As a result, strict control was imposed on people's movements. A dusk to dawn curfew was imposed throughout the country. The period of terror was at its peak in 1977 and, as Table 1 shows, this was the period when the rate of crime began to decline. In addition, it could be observed from Table 4 opposite that certain crimes declined during this period of time.

As the figures indicate, in 1977/78 the overall decline of certain categories of crime was 42.45% when compared to the previous year, 1976/77. Crimes like robbery, violations of state and municipal regulations, assault, theft and burglary declined by 58%, 51%, 48%, 43% and 41% respectively. In fact, except for manslaughter, all categories of crime had declined. Could there be any reason for a decline other than the overall tense political situation?

People, especially potential criminals, may have been too scared and refrained from illegal acts because the probability of being apprehended was too high. Even victims of crimes and/or witnesses may have failed to report crimes because of the overall tense conditions prevailing then. People seemed to be scared of being caught in the cross-fire. Besides, under such circumstances, one cannot be too certain about the rule of law.

From the figures in Table 4, one can observe that the crime rate gradually picked up as the political condition improved after 1979/80. In fact, in 1979/80, except for attempted homicide and burglary, the rates for all other major crimes increased compared to the previous year. The overall crime increase over the previous year was 35%.

The wars with Somalia in the East and South, and the royalist groups in the West and the Eritrean rebels in the North of the country seem to have indirectly affected the crime rates, especially in the mid-1970s. As a result of these wars a large number of the members of the police force were deployed to the war fronts. Besides, though not openly stated, there appeared to be a tendency to assume that there will be no need for a strong police force, in the long run, as peasants' and urban dwellers' associations would eventually take over the role of the police. Consequently the future role of the police seemed to have been played down and the size of the force was left to decline gradually.[35] This situation can be seen clearly from the figures in Table 5, which compares the size of the police force for 1971/72 and 1981/82 in relation to the size of the population and the area covered by a police patrol.

On the average in 1971/72 a policeman covered about 43 square kilometers and about 930 people. But in 1981/82, ten years later, the situation had completely changed. The area a police patrolman had to cover had increased by 253% to 152 square kilometers and the size of population per policeman had increased to 3763 or an increase of 304.6%. The change in proportion, both in the area and population covered by a policeman is even more dramatic in some administrative regions. The case of Shoa administrative region is typical (see Table 5, number 10).

The figures in the Table indicate that the number of the police posts for 1971/72 and 1981/82 were almost the same. But in 1981/82 out of the 26,451 posts only 16,896 were on actual police duty. Of the existing number of policemen, only 8039 or 47.6% were on actual police duty. The rest were deployed in administrative or other supportive services.[36] It was only after 1982, it seems, that it was realized the country could not do without a strong police force and the training of new recruits was restarted.[37]

One of the consequences of this shortfall in the size of the police force was the closure of some police stations, especially in areas that were affected by war conditions. The figures in Table 6 show the number of Awrajas (provinces) and Woredas (districts) that were unmanned.

Table 5
Comparison of Police Force in Relation to Population & Area Covered by a Patrolman for 1971/72 and 1981/82

Region	+ 1971/1972					1981/82					
	Area in Square K.Meters	Population (1972)	Number of Police-men	Average Area Per Police	Average Population Per Police	Population (1979)	NUMBER OF POLICEMEN			Average Area Per Police	Average Population Per Police
							Number of Positions	Number on Payroll	On Actual Police Duty		
1) Arssi	23,500	852,900	686	34.3	1243.3	1,119,300	467	400	173	135.8	6469.9
2) Bale	124,600	707,800	2005	62.1	353.0	856,100	1374	685	259	481.1	3305.4
3) Gondar	74,200	1,355,800	901	82.4	1504.8	1,999,600	884	624	271	273.8	7378.6
4) Eritrea	117,600	1,947,600	6337	18.6	307.3	2,362,600	3496	1903	888	132.4	2660.6
5) Gamo Goffa	39,500	698,800	1453	27.2	480.9	977,100	1005	573	336	117.6	2908.0
6) Gojam	61,600	1,750,100	866	71.1	2020.9	1,984,400	650	576	253	243.5	7843.5
7) Hararghe	259,700	3,359,200	5417	47.9	620.1	3,043,200	3382	2448	1202	216.1	2531.8
8) Illubabour	47,400	688,800	818	57.9	842.1	789,500	714	425	113	419.5	6986.7
9) Keffa	54,600	1,693,000	1570	34.8	1078.3	1,573,000	1167	837	343	159.2	4586.0
10) Shoa	85,200	5,369,500	2296	37.1	2338.6	6,195,300	1431	1211	409	208.3	15147.4
11) Addis Ababa	200	912,100	1792	0.1	509.0	1,216,300	1817	1151	969	0.2	1255.2
12) Sidamo	117,300	2,479,800	1355	86.6	1830.1	2,734,700	1142	772	442	265.4	6187.1
13) Tigrai	65,900	1,828,900	1080	61.0	1693.4	2,105,400	857	588	310	212.6	6791.6
14) Wolega	71,200	1,269,100	739	96.3	1717.3	1,966,300	5514	436	210	339.0	9363.3
15) Wollo	79,400	2,459,900	1153	68.9	2133.5	2,544,100	832	631	338	234.9	7526.9
16) Others	—	—	—	—	—	—	6719	3536	1518	—	—
TOTAL	1,221,900	27,373,300	28,468	42.9	961.5	31,466,900	31,451	16,796	8034	152.1	3916.7

TABLE 6.

Awrajas and Woredas With and Without Police Stations

Year	Awrajas				Woredas			
	With Police		Without Police		With Police		Without Police	
		%		%		%		%
1) 1971 EC (1978/79)	90	88.2	12	11.8	217	37.9	335	62.1
2) 1972 EC (1979/80)	95	93.1	7	6.9	408	71.3	164	28.7
3) 1973 EC (1980/81)	96	94.1	6	5.9	402	70.3	170	29.7
4) 1974 EC (1981/82)	94	90.5	8	7.8	418	73.1	154	26.9
5) 1975 EC (1982/83)	97	95.1	5	4.9	448	78.3	124	21.7
Average:	94	92.2	8	7.8	379	66.3	193	33.7

Source: Compiled from unpublished Annual Police Reports for the years 1971 to 1975 EC (1978/79 to 1982/83).

On the average, eight Awrajas (7.8) and 193 Woredas (33.7) did not have policemen from 1977/78 to 1982/83. This means that in most cases crimes from these areas were never reported, except when the crimes were very serious and the administrators of these areas referred cases to the nearest police station.[38]

Considering the situations discussed above, the assumption that crime has been declining after the Revolution, as reported by the police, is rather difficult to accept. When one considers the fact that (a) all criminal cases handled by the peasants' and urban dwellers' associations (however petty they may have been) were not reported and therefore not included in official statistics; (b) on the average, 7.8% of the 102 Awrajas and 33.7% of the 572 Woredas did not have policemen and therefore no crimes were reported from these areas for a number of years; and (c) in general all the administrative regions had a much reduced number of policemen and the average land area and population size each patrolman had to cover had been greatly increased, as compared to the pre-revolution period, it becomes very difficult to endorse the police assumption that crime in general had declined in the post-revolution period.

Further investigation is definitely called for. However, this would be possible only when all concerned agencies maintain accurate records and a mechanism for uniform reporting is developed. The kind of statistics the Central Statistical Office has been reporting on law and order are of little value for further research.

PART III.

Though it is rather difficult to show for sure that the crime rates are declining on the basis of available statistics, it seems possible to show that at least the patterns and trends of crime in the post-revolution period are gradually changing. These changes appear to be the direct result of the changes that have been taking place in the country since 1974. Such radical changes as obtained in Ethiopia affected the whole structure of society. Radcliffe-Brown had rightly pointed out the effect of such changes:

> ". . . change occurs when a society as the result of disturbances induced
> either by internal developments or impact from without, changes its struc-
> tural form . . . However slight . . . it is a change such that when there is

sufficient of it, the society passes from one type of social structure to another."[39]

Such has been the change that has been taking place in Ethiopia, where the old social structure has been completely shattered and new setups are taking the place of the old ones. In the process of such changes, previous social control mechanisms are weakened because of the internal conflicting norms that develop. In such a revolutionary situation class bonds become loose. Social changes of this nature may have both disorganizing and organizing consequences.[40]

In a politically and socially confused state, social mobility becomes relatively for some groups at least, even if it may be short-lived in some cases. In the process of such social mobility, some fast and unscrupulous individuals hold on to certain positions, not necessarily by virtue of their abilities and qualifications, but simply because they quickly identify themselves with the new condition in order to gain advantage. This situation is made possible by the fact that such a revolutionary condition is likely to generate a certain amount of nationalism, which unites certain sectors of society around certain ideal goals. Some 'partisans', however, are likely to use this condition to their own advantage.

On the other hand, such a revolutionary upheaval and change in the old structure undermines traditional means of social control. While loyalties are centered around a central goal at the higher level, ties at the lower levels, such as the family, the community or the village, weaken or break down. As a result, social control mechanisms such as gossip, criticism, ridicule, reprimand, lose their effectiveness and some individuals take advantage of the prevailing conditions and grab at the bandwagon of success, be it political, social or economic, at the expense of both their fellow 'partisans' and the society at large.[41] Horton and Leslie summarised this appropriately when they stated that:

> ". . . In the resultant confusion, old rules were both debated and ignored, yet no new rules were generally accepted. Change had disorganized — disrupted the organization — the former system of behaviour."[42]

Until new rules and practices are developed and a new equilibrium is created, the confusion will have its own toll socially, economically and politically.

In the rural areas of Ethiopia, the nationalization of rural land and the creation of thousands of Peasants' Associations, changed the social and political power structure that had existed for centuries. Newly elected officials from among the peasants, who had very little experience in administrative, judicial and management functions, were suddenly entrusted with heavy responsibilities for local administration. In such situations, the possibilities for misuse of power and other responsibilities, be it deliberate or otherwise, could be expected. Misuse of association funds and other properties have been apparent from the regular media reports. Similarly, in the urban areas, the nationalization of urban land and extra houses and the creation of urban dwellers' associations brought about similar structural changes and brought into power people from the masses. During the early stages of the revolution especially, people who had owned any kind of property were directly or indirectly barred from holding offices in these associations. The outcome was that the people with little experience took over the management of urban dwellers' associations and their cooperative shops. The result, in many cases, was mismanagement, at times from sheer lack of know-how and experience, as the Ottaways have pointed out:

> "To be sure the functioning of these associations varied greatly. Some were in the hands of rich peasants; in some local priests had a large say; and in others elected officials were beginning to act like balabbats. Some radical critics found the associations more 'petty bourgeois' than socialist in orientation, and their members more interested in private ownership of land than fired by a new spirit of collectivity."[43]

Similar conditions prevailed in the nationalized industries. The government gradually proceeded to nationalize imports and exports, retail business and services; however, control mechanisms, at least at the earliest stage, did not develop as fast as they should have.[44] Hence, misappropriation and embezzlement of government and public agency funds became quite common, as reported by the media. In November 1981, the newspapers reported that in a period of about five years (1967 to 1974 EC) cases of misappropriation and embezzlement worth Birr. 7,930,896.65 were brought before the courts.[45] In addition, the Prosecutor of the Special Military Court reported in November 1981 that breach of trust had been increasing since 1978. He pointed out that in 1980, in a period of six months, cases of misappropriation and embezzlement involving Birr. 2,300,303.69 were referred to his office.[46]

In fact it is in this connection that COPWE (Commission for the Organization of the Party of the Working Peoples of Ethiopia) passed the following resolution in February 1981, aimed at curbing wastefulness and misappropriation of public property.

1) All workers should vigilantly protect public property and bring to the attention of the law those that misuse and misappropriate public funds;

2) The general tendency that seems to prevail in government and public agencies regarding tardiness in work, misuse of property, failure to keep proper accounts, failure to collect taxes and other harmful tendencies should be nipped in the bud;

3) Strong measures should be taken, with the assistance of the public, against those who take bribes, embezzle and cheat.[47]

In this connection, one of the High Court judges stated in 1981 that cases of breaches of trust, as a result of the fast expanding government controlled enterprises and the creation of various public agencies, were overcrowding the courts.[48]

This condition can well be summarised with the words of Harry Elmer Barnes — "need and greed explain most crimes".[49] In a state of social confusion some people greedily seek material success at the expense of others or the system. People want to quickly gratify their wants and desires. This appears to be the case in Ethiopia, when one observes the patterns and trends of crime since the 1974 Revolution[50] as documented by the figures in Table 7.

The figures in the Table show the comparative crime conditions for the pre-revolution years (1969/70 to 1972/73) and the post revolution period (1978/79 to 1982/83). A cursory look at the figures shows that the crime rate has been going down during the post-revolution period. However, this has been fully dealt with in earlier pages. On the other hand, a closer look at the figures in Table 7 shows some changes in the patterns and trends of crime. If we take ten of the prevalent types of crimes, as shown in the Table, of the two periods and compare them, some changes in the patterns and trends of crime can be observed. This can be shown more clearly in a tabular form (Table 8).

The ten prevalent types of crime in the pre-revolution period make up (on the average for the four years) about 70% of the total crime, while in the post-revolution period (average for the five years) they make up about 97% as shown in Table 8. There seems to be a tendency, in the post-revolution period, for crimes to concentrate around much fewer acts of breaches of the law. However, one should be cognizant of the possibility of some crimes being lumped together by the police in the process of compiling the statistics. But this does not appear to be the main reason for the difference between the two periods.

There is another clear contrast between the two periods. As it can be observed from the figures in Table 8, in the pre-revolution period 25.46% of the total crimes (the average for the four years) were crimes against property and 33.65% were crimes against the person. While in the post-revolution period, it is 37.08% and 34.43% respectively. As discussed earlier, in Ethiopia generally crimes against the person had been more frequent than crimes against property. This trend was true for the pre-revolution period, as the figures in Tables 7 and 8 indicate.

Table 7
Patterns & Trends in Crime in the Pre-Revolution Period

Types of Crime	1969/70 No	%	1970/71 No	%	1971/72 No	%	1972/73 No	%
1) Homicide	1872	2.00	2922	2.81	2972	3.05	3225	2.62
2) Attempted Homicide	3447	3.68	3442	3.31	3528	3.62	2828	3.11
3) Manslaughter	117	0.12	90	0.09	96	0.10	101	0.08
4) Accidental Bodily Injury	144	0.15	78	0.08	76	0.08	86	0.07
5) Assault	18128	19.35	18184	17.49	17726	18.17	20705	16.84
6) Threats	2149	2.29	2412	2.32	2479	2.54	24902	20.25
7) Abuse (Insult)	1556	1.66	1768	1.70	1616	1.66	1642	1.34
8) Arson	1563	1.67	1891	1.82	1375	1.41	1781	1.45
9) Damage To Property	3638	3.88	4253	4.09	4258	4.36	4284	3.48
10) Armed Robbery (Banditry)	904	0.96	1073	1.03	1031	1.06	976	0.79
11) Robbery	928	0.99	937	0.90	915	0.94	1173	0.95
12) Various Types Of Burglary	2478	2.65	2339	2.25	2033	2.08	2183	1.78
13) Pickpocketing	352	0.38	356	0.34	370	0.38	457	0.37
14) Various Types Of Theft	13938	14.88	16706	16.07	15599	15.99	14740	11.99
15) Receiving Stolen Goods	98	0.10	99	0.10	81	0.08	93	0.08
16) Abduction & Rape	362	0.39	2412	2.32	376	0.39	387	0.31
17) Other Sexual Offences	291	0.31	1768	1.70	292	0.30	276	0.22
18) Fraud	1235	1.32	1244	1.20	1249	1.28	1258	1.02
19) Forgery	25	0.03	15	0.01	19	0.02	15	0.01
20) Crimes Against Public Health	33	0.04	39	0.04	20	0.02	24	0.02
21) Crimes Against The Economy	31	0.03	24	0.02	14	0.01	19	0.02
22) Crimes Against The State	152	0.16	163	0.16	33	0.03	11	0.01
23) Breach Of Trust	892	0.95	1082	1.04	1131	1.16	1033	0.84
24) Possession Of Unauthorized Arms	357	0.38	435	0.42	390	0.40	257	0.21
25) Violation Of Regulations	10560	11.27	11004	10.59	10767	11.03	10034	8.16
26) Abandoning Infants (Babies)	—	—	—	—	—	—	—	—
27) Illegal Use Of Drugs	—	—	—	—	—	—	—	—
28) Homosexuality	—	—	—	—	—	—	—	—
29) Illegal Abortions	—	—	—	—	—	—	—	—
30) Other Crimes	28435	30.35	29214	28.10	29132	29.86	29487	23.98
TOTAL	93685	100	103950	100	97578	100	122977	100

Table 7a
Patterns & Trends in Crime in the Post-Revolution Period

Types of Crime	1978/79		1979/80		1980/81		1981/82		1982/83	
	No	%	No	%	No	%	No	%	No	%
1) Homicide	2389	7.60	2707	6.10	2770	5.69	2954	5.70	3053	6.10
2) Attempted Homicide	1280	3.89	1251	2.82	1333	2.74	1520	2.93	1511	3.02
3) Manslaughter	667	2.03	999	2.25	1047	2.15	1024	1.98	1140	2.28
4) Accidental Bodily Injury	—	—	—	—	—	—	—	—	—	—
5) Assault	5449	16.56	9133	20.59	11499	23.60	12326	23.80	11286	22.55
6) Threats	—	—	—	—	—	—	—	—	—	—
7) Abuse (Insult)	—	—	—	—	—	—	—	—	—	—
8) Arson	—	—	—	—	—	—	—	—	—	—
9) Damage To Property	—	—	—	—	—	—	—	—	—	—
10) Armed Robbery (Banditry)	—	—	—	—	—	—	—	—	—	—
11) Robbery	260	0.79	426	0.96	452	0.93	526	1.02	556	1.11
12) Various Types Of Burglary	469	1.43	449	1.01	538	1.10	622	1.20	580	1.16
13) Pickpocketing	—	—	—	—	—	—	—	—	—	—
14) Various Types Of Theft	8276	25.16	10635	23.97	11868	24.36	12793	24.70	12510	24.99
15) Receiving Stolen Goods	—	—	—	—	—	—	—	—	—	—
16) Abduction & Rape	359	1.09	598	1.35	648	1.33	680	1.31	614	1.23
17) Other Sexual Offences	—	—	—	—	—	—	—	—	—	—
18) Fraud	1076	3.27	1247	2.81	1349	2.77	1375	2.65	1270	2.54
19) Forgery	—	—	—	—	—	—	—	—	—	—
20) Crimes Against Public Health	13	0.04	17	0.04	4	0.01	8	0.02	9	0.02
21) Crimes Against The Economy	1193	3.63	1210	2.73	1344	2.76	1577	3.04	1504	3.00
22) Crimes Against The State	425	1.29	533	1.20	336	0.69	259	0.50	322	0.64
23) Breach Of Trust	2224	6.76	2897	6.53	3223	6.62	3355	6.48	3312	6.62
24) Possession Of Unauthorized Arms	—	—	—	—	—	—	—	—	—	—
25) Violation Of Regulations	8748	26.59	12088	27.25	12123	24.88	12614	24.35	12218	24.41
26) Abandoning Infants (Babies)	24	0.07	38	0.09	32	0.07	30	0.06	62	0.12
27) Illegal Use Of Drugs	6	0.02	6	0.01	5	0.01	7	0.01	11	0.02
28) Homosexuality	41	0.12	106	0.24	125	0.26	100	0.19	75	0.15
29) Illegal Abortions	—	—	23	0.05	16	0.03	31	0.06	21	0.04
30) Other Crimes	—	—	—	—	7	0.01	—	—	—	—
TOTAL	32899	100	44363	100	48719	100	51801	100	50054	100

However, the trends seem to be gradually changing in the post-revolution period, as can be observed from the figures in Tables 7 and 8.

TABLE 8

The Ten Most Prevalent Crimes for the Pre- and Post-Revolution Periods

Pre-Revolution Period		Post-Revolution period	
1) Assault	17.96%	1) Violations of regulations	25.50%
2) Theft	17.73%	2) Theft	24.64%
3) Violations of regulations	10.26%	3) Assault	21.42%
4) Threats (against persons)	6.85%	4) Breach of trust	6.60%
5) Damage to property	3.95%	5) Homicide	6.17%
6) Homicide	3.82%	6) Attempted homicide	3.08%
7) Attempted homicide	3.43%	7) Crimes against the	
8) Burglary	2.19%	economy	3.03%
9) Abuse (insult)	1.59%	8) Fraud	2.81%
10) Arson	1.59%	9) Manslaughter	2.14%
		10) Abduction and rape	1.62%
Total	69.37%		
		Total	97.01%

A look at the figures in Table 8 indicates that the trends in crime are dramatically changing. For instance violation of regulations had been quite common in the pre-revolution period, but it has more than doubled in the post-revolution period. These crimes are mainly connected with the hoarding of basic consumer goods, the breach of price regulations, failure to pay taxes, dealing with black-market goods, etc. As the Government is gradually moving into retail business, individual traders and businessmen try to create price destabilization either by hoarding or by demanding exorbitant prices for certain basic commodities, and the government has been intensifying some forms of control mechanisms. Consequently, a large number of people are being prosecuted, as reported daily by the mass media. Police reports also confirm the fact.[51]

Another crime which in the pre-revolution period hardly accounted for 1% of all crimes but has increased almost six times since the Revolution is the breach of trust or the misappropriation of public property. The creation of a large number of public agencies, such as peasants' associations, urban dwellers' associations, the creation of large number of enterprises in the areas of nationalized industries, the establishment of numerous corporations in the areas of retail business, and the creation of a large number of state farms and their subsidiaries, etc., led since the Revolution to the appointment of large numbers of people in responsible positions. This sudden mobility seems to have created more greed. As a result, embezzlement seems to have become the order of the day. In fact the PMAC has taken the problem very seriously and has issued a special proclamation and has established a special court to deal with the problem of corruption and abuse of power. Emphasizing the seriousness of the problem of embezzlement, Tameru Wondimagegnehu stated that out of the cases that were referred to the Special Court or to the office of the Special Prosecuter, 50% dealt with breaches of trust. In fact, even the statistics of cases handled in the regular courts between 1978 and 1982 indicate that breaches of trust stood in the fourth place, next to theft, assault and homicide.[52]

The seriousness of the problem can be assessed not only from the fact that the media have been condemning the act, but also from the fact that the government has been forced to create a Special Court, and People's Control Committees in practically all governmental and quasi-governmental agencies and enterprises. This has been aptly summarized by Girma Wolde Selassie:

446

"Post-revolution Ethiopia has also seen a rise in the volume of cases relating to certain types of disputes. I will mention only one such category — embezzlement. I chose this category of crime, not only because of its dramatic increase since the Revolution, but also because the dangerous proportion it has assumed has recently attracted the attention of the government.

My own study of a few provincial courts shows that misappropriation of public funds has risen considerably. The Sidamo Police records, for instance, reveal that the number of embezzlement cases reported the year preceding the outbreak of the Revolution was only 90. Six years later, however, the figure rose to 249 — an increase by 276 percent. Media reports relating to the campaign recently launched by the government to fight corruption and other official misconduct indicated that the nationwide picture is probably worse."[53]

To cite another example, a crime which hardly accounted for half a percent in the pre-revolution period but has increased threefold in the post-revolution period, is crime against the economy. This crime mainly consists of sabotage in various governmental and semi-autonomous enterprises. According to reports by the police, the chief motive of the various crimes against the economy is mainly political, especially in the early stages of the Revolution.[54]

Other crimes that have become more common in the post-revolution period could be cited (see Table 8), but the examples discussed above should suffice to illustrate the contention that the patterns and trends in crime have been changing in the post-revolution period. It is important to note that these changes do not affect only the volume of certain crimes. In fact the most important change occurs in the patterns of crime dominance. Crimes against property seem to be more prevalent than crimes against the person in the post-revolution period as compared with the pre-revolution period. Consequently, crimes that were insignificant (in volume) in the pre-revolution period seem to be increasing much more rapidly than the most traditional crimes that were more dominant in the past. Therefore, the assumption that the radical changes that were brought about by the Revolution in the social structure of society, and the fact that new social, political and economic institutions are emerging, have brought about changes, at least in the transitional process, in the patterns and trends of crime in Ethiopia, seems to be borne out by the available data.

NOTES

1. See Donald N. Levine, *Wax and Gold: Tradition and Innovation in Ethiopian Culture*, (Chicago: The University of Chicago Press, 1965), p.248; Herbert S. Lewis, "Wealth, Influence and Prestige Among the Shoa Galla", in Arthur Tuden and Leonard Plotnicov (eds.), *Social Stratification in Africa*, (New York, The Free Press, 1970), p.172.

2. See the *Police Gazette*, "The Police and Its Progress", Hidar 15, 1975 EC, 17th year Number 2, and the various unpublished Annual Police Reports for the years 1970 to 1975 EC.

3. See Robert L. Hess, *Ethiopia: The Modernization of Autocracy*, (Ithaca, Cornell University Press, 1970), pp.75-77; Donald N. Levine, *op. cit.*, pp.150-155.

4. See G. A. Lipsky, *Ethiopia, Its People, Its Society, Its Culture*, (New Haven, Harf Press, 1962), p.34; Irving Kaplan *et al.*, *Area Hand-book for Ethiopia*, (Washington D.C., US Government Printing Office, 1971), pp.103-114.

5. Eshetu Chole, "The Mode of Production in Ethiopia and Realities Thereof", in *Challenge: Journal of the World-Wide Union of Ethiopian Students*, Vol.XII, No.1, 1971, pp.8-9.

6. Peter Schwab (ed.), *Ethiopia and Haile Selassie*, (New York, Facts on File Inc., 1972), pp.115-135; Kaplan *et al., op. cit.*, pp.289-304.

7. Andargatchew Tesfaye in Dae H. Chang (ed.), *Criminology: A Cross Cultural Perspective*, (New Delhi, Vika, 1976), pp.401-406. See also Table 1.

8. See Table 1.

9. Erasto Muga, *Crime and Delinquency in Kenya*, (Nairobi, East African Literature Bureau, 1975), p.8.

10. D. N. A. Nortey, "Crime Trends in Ghana", *Ghana Social Science Journal*, Vol. 4 No.1, May 1977, p.108.

11. Marshal B. Clinard and Daniel J. Abbot, *Crime in Developing Countries: A Comparative Perspective*, (New York, John Wiley and Sons, 1973), p.18.

12. United Nations, *Crime Prevention and Control: Report of the Secretary General*, (UN A/32/199, 22 September 1977), p.9.

13. *Ibid.*, p.11.

14. *Ibid.*

15. Calculated from the figures in Table 1 for the years 1969/70 to 1974/75. In calculating the crime population ratio per 100,000, the population for Ethiopia was taken to be 27,102,100, as reported in the *Statistical Abstract For 1976*, p.21.

16. Ministry of Interior, Provisional Military Government of Socialist Ethiopia, Statement Prepared in 1978 for an International Symposium (Unpublished), p.19.

17. Steven Lowenstein, "The Penal System of Ethiopia", *Journal of Ethiopian Law*, Vol.II No.2, 1965, p.392.

18. Mesfin Kinfu in *Proceedings of the Social Science Seminar*, 1974 (unpublished), Institute of Development Research, Addis Ababa University, p.159.

19. *Ibid.*, pp.164-165.

20. Prisons Study Committee, Ministry of Interior of the Ethiopian Socialist Military Government, (unpublished official document), 1975, p.126.

21. Donald Levine, *op. cit.*, pp.248-249.

22. John Markakis, *Ethiopia: Anatomy of A Traditional Polity*, (Addis Ababa, Oxford University Press, 1975), pp.297-298.

23. See *Statistical Abstract*, Central Statistics Office, Addis Ababa. Compiled from the various issues of 1963 to 1970.

24. Andargatchew Tesfaye, "Juvenile Delinquency: An Urban Phenomenon" in Marina Ottaway (ed.), *Urbanization in Ethiopia: A Text with Integrated Readings*, (Addis Ababa University, Dept. of Sociology, 1976), p.336.

25. Planning Commission, *Imperial Ethiopian Government, The Employment Problem in Ethiopia*, (Addis Ababa, 1972, Unpublished), p.19.

26. International Labour Organization, *Report to the Imperial Ethiopian Government of the Exploratory Employment Policy Mission*, (Geneva, 1973), pp.52-59.

27. Duri Mohammed, "Industrialization and Income Distribution in Ethiopia" in J. F. Rweyemamu (ed.), *Industrialization and Income Distribution in Africa*, (Dakar, Codesria, 1980), p.29.

28. Prison Study Committee, *op. cit.*, p.126.

29. See Robert N. Bowen, *Begging in Addis Ababa*, (Unpublished), Honolulu, Hawaii, April 1968.

30. Laketch Dirasse, "Survival Techniques of Female Migrants in Ethiopian Urban Centers", unpublished paper prepared for the Third International Congress of Africanists, Addis Ababa, December 9-14 1973.

31. "Peasant Association Organization and Consolidation Proclamation", Proclamation No.71 of 1975, *Negarit Gazeta*, No.15, December 4 1975, Chapter 3, Article 21-40. "Urban Dwellers' Associations Consolidation and Municipalities Proclamation", Proclamation No.104 of 1976, *Negarit Gazeta*, No.5, October 9 1976, Chapter 3, Articles 10-12.

32. Raul Valdes Vivo, *Ethiopia, the Unknown Revolution*, (Havana, Social Science Publishers, 1977), p.104.

33. Proclamation No.71 of 1975, *op. cit.*, 21; Proclamation No.5 of 1976, *op. cit.*, Art.11(2).

34. Marina and David Ottaway, *Ethiopia: Empire in Revolution*, (New York, African Publishing Company, 1978), pp.142-148.

35. This problem was indicated in the unpublished police Annual Reports for 1970 to 1975 EC (1977 to 1983). The 1970 EC report specifically indicates the number of policemen killed and wounded in action, those who were abducted (or taken prisoner) and those that deserted.

36. See unpublished Annual Police Report for 1973 EC, p.9.

37. Interview with Colonel Feleke Tabbor, Head, Training Department, Revolutionary Police Force.

38. See unpublished Annual Police Report for 1975 EC, p.12.

39. A. R. Radcliffe-Brown, *A Natural Science of Society*, (Glencoe, Illinois Press, 1975), p.87.

40. Marshal B. Clinard and Robert P. Meier, *Sociology of Deviant Behaviour*, (New York, Holt, Rhinehart and Wiston, Fifth Edition, 1978), p.66.

41. See Dae H. Chang, *op. cit.*, pp.31-32. Clinard and Meier, *op. cit.*, pp.18-23.

42. Paul B. Morton and Gerald R. Seslie, *The Sociology of Social Problems*, (New York, Appleton Century Crafts, 4th Edition, 1970), p.32.

43. Marina and David Ottaway, *op. cit.*, pp.181-182.

44. Tameru Wondimagegnehu, "Some Features of the New Law Against Breaches of Trust", in *Law and Justice*, Vol.1, No.1, pp.43-50. This is a bi-annual journal published by the Special Court. The article is in Amharic and the translation is mine.

45. *Addis Zemen*, Hidar 8, 1974 EC.

46. *Ibid.*, Hidar 9, 1974 EC.

47. A free translation of the text as it appears in *Addis Zemen*, Yekatit 7, 1973 EC, p.10.

48. *Addis Zemen*, Megabit 9, 1973 EC, pp.3-4.

49. As cited by Mabel A. Elliott and Francis E. Merrill, *Social Disorganization*, (New York, Harper and Brothers, 4th Edition, 1961), p.121.

50. See unpublished Police Annual Reports for 1975, p.36.

51. *Ibid.*

52. Tameru Wondimagegnehu, *op. cit.*, p.43.

53. Girma Wolde Selassie, "The Impact of the Ethiopian Revolution on the Laws and Legal Institutions of the Country" in Sven Rubenson (ed.), *Proceedings of the Seventh International Conference of Ethiopian Studies*, University of Lund, 26-29 April, 1982, p.569.

54. See unpublished Police Annual Report for 1975 EC, pp.12-18.

GEOGRAPHIC MOBILITY IN URBAN ETHIOPIA

THE CASE OF SHASHEMANNE

Gunilla Bjeren

1. Introduction: The study and the paper

The findings reported in this paper are part of the results from a case study of migration to and from Shashemanne before 1974 which was published in the first half of 1985.[1] Since little research had been done on migration in Ethiopia at the time when the Shashemanne study was planned, it was designed as an exploratory study, aimed at investigating the mechanisms behind migration to Shashemanne.[2] There were consequently no formulated hypotheses to be tested; rather, the aim of the study was to formulate hypotheses, or at least guidelines, that could be used for further research into urban migration in Ethiopia.

The aim of this paper is to give an indication of the mechanisms behind migration to Shashemanne, particularly the relation between the ethnic structure of the central southern region of Ethiopia and urban migration. I will do this by first outlining the general character of the migration pattern of Shashemanne. After that I will divide the overall migration pattern into different types of "migration career". We will then go on to see how migrants from different ethnic groups dominate different career patterns. Finally, we will look at the profiles[3] of the ethnic groups in Shashemanne in order to make the relation between migration and ethnic structure intelligible.

2. Migration patterns of Shashemanne: Summary of the patterns of overall migration to and from Shashemanne before 1974

In this section we will have a look at the *overall* picture of migration to Shashemanne, up to April 1973 when data collection ended. Our concern here is with aggregate migration patterns; in the coming section we will look at the migration patterns of different groups.

The material

The analysis of migration to Shashemanne is based on migration histories collected from persons included in two samples of households. The first sample consists of persons who were first interviewed by the CSO[4] in 1965, in the First Round of the Urban Sample Survey, and then reinterviewed by myself and an assistant in May-July 1972. This sample represents a group of relatively permanent town dwellers about whom we know for certain that they had lived in Shashemanne longer than 6.5 years at the time of the 1972 interview. In 1965, 10% of the households in Shashemanne had been included in the CSO survey. This was 186 households, containing 755 persons. In 1972, we were able to trace 649 (86%) of these individuals. In the study of migration I concentrated on the migration careers of heads of household and wives. I was able to collect 178 migration histories from persons still alive and remaining in Shashemanne.

The second sample consists of a 5% random sample of households in Shashemanne in 1973. The sample was drawn from an enumeration of all dwelling units in the town carried out by the Malaria Eradication Service in December 1972. The interviews were carried out during February -April 1972 by a team of locally recruited interviewers.[5] Background data were collected for all household members of 141 households, totalling 564 persons. Detailed migration histories were collected from heads of household and wives in 138 households. Altogether 222 migration histories were collected, from 105 men and 117 women.

It is not uncommon for migration studies to limit the population under study to heads of household. The justification given for this limitation varies; heads of household are often considered "primary decision makers" (Mullenbach, 1976: 145), implying that their decisions have

451

determined the migration of all members of the household at all times. Studying only heads of household neglects the particular characteristics of the migration of women. Even if a minority of female heads of household are present in most urban locations, they are often so few that a researcher of migration may feel justified in ignoring them.[6] However, in Ethiopian towns women are represented to the same extent as men — in fact, until the last decade women were often a majority of town dwellers. This means that the migration of women cannot be ignored if one is to understand urban migration. And "women" in this context must include both female heads of household and wives. Many urban women move between these two statuses during their lifetime[7] and one cannot, therefore, assume any important differences in migration careers between women of the two categories.

Because of the inclusion of the migration histories of the survivals from the 1965 CSO study, the material contains more information about migration prior to 1965 than after 1965. Bearing in mind the great uncertainty of all time estimates, the migration histories pertain to arrival dates of the following approximate distribution:

TABLE 1: Approximate date of arrival in Shashemanne for heads of households and wives, interviewed in 1972 and 1973

	Arrived in Shashemanne			
	Born in Shashemanne No.	1965 or earlier No.	1965/66 or earlier No.	Total No.
1. *Survivals from 1965 study*				
Male heads of household	10	77	—	87
Female heads of household and wives	6	85	—	91
Total	16	162		178
2, *Respondents from 1973 survey*				
Male heads of household	10	48	47	105
Female heads of household and wives	12	53	52	117
Total	22*	101	99	222
TOTAL, both samples	38	263	99	400
Proportion of all respondents	10%	66%	25%	101%

* Four respondents were born in Shashemanne but had gone away and later returned. They were thus both "born in town" and migrants. In the table above they are in the "born in town" category.

452

Table 1 shows that the entire migration material consists of 400 migration histories, of which two thirds pertain to respondents who either were born in Shashemanne or who had arrived in town prior to 1965/66, and one fourth to respondents who had arrived in Shashemanne after 1965/66. 90% of the respondents had migrated to Shashemanne; 10% were born in the town.

Summary description of the aggregate migration pattern of Shashemanne

The most salient characteristics of the aggregate migration patterns of Shashemanne can be summarized in the following manner:

1. Approximately 90% of adult men and women[8] in Shashemanne in the period from the middle of the sixties and the beginning of the seventies were migrants to the town.
2. Approximately 60% of the adult migrants were born in some rural area.
3. About 50% of the migrants were born within 100 km. radius of Shashemanne.
4. Although the majority of the adult migrants were born in rural areas, 67% had another town as their last place of residence before coming to Shashemanne.
5. Of the 33% rural-urban migrants, two-thirds had come to Shashemanne from an area extending no more than 150 km. from the town.
6. The inter-urban migrants came from about 60 different towns (both samples). Addis Ababa was the most important single point of departure for the migrants in both samples.
7. Together with Addis Ababa, another 13 towns accounted for nearly 70% of all urban-urban migration. The sending towns could be divided into four groups:
    A. First Addis Ababa, the national capital, 250 km. away from Shashemanne. 22% of the migrants came from Addis Ababa.
    B. The second group consisted of towns of approximately the same size as Shashemanne, located within 200 km. of Shashemanne. About 30% of the inter-urban migrants came from these towns.
    C. The third group consisted of four very small towns close to Shashemanne. 12% of the migrants came from these small towns.
    D. The fourth and last group consisted of three important industrial towns 200 km. or more away from Shashemanne. 6% came from these towns.
8. At the same time as Shashemanne received large numbers of migrants from other towns and the surrounding rural areas, there was a stream of migration *away* from the town.
9. The migration away from Shashemanne had to a large extent the same destination as the last places of residence for migrants to Shashemanne. This means that in many instances Shashemanne in fact had a *migratory exchange* with other towns.
10. Addis Ababa appears to be the largest single recipient of migrants *from* Shashemanne, just as the capital was the most important sender for migrants *to* Shashemanne.

3. Different ways of moving to Shashemanne

Nearly all, or 90%, of the heads of household and wives who were included in the two samples described in the previous section had moved to Shashemanne from somewhere else. But there was considerable variation in the manner that people had come to the town — some had moved to Shashemanne straight from their birth-places, others had lived in several other towns before arriving, etc. I have chosen to call the manner in which a person has moved to Shashemanne his or her *migration career*. A migration career does not include a description of the exact places that someone has lived in along the road, but consists of an outline of his mobility that makes it possible to classify his movement along with those of others.

Different criteria may be used to distinguish between types of migration career. Below I have used the following criteria:

1. born in Shashemanne and never moved;
2. moved directly to Shashemanne from *rural* birth-place;

3. moved directly to Shashemanne from *urban* birth-place;
4. lived in one place other than birth-place before arriving in Shashemanne;
5. lived in two places[9] other than birth-place before arriving in Shashemanne;
6. lived in three or more places other than birth-place before arriving in Shashemanne.

The table below shows the distribution of the heads of household and wives included in the 1973 sample over different types of migration career.

Table 2: Types of migration career of heads of household and wives included in the 1973 sample survey of Shashemanne[10]

Type of migration career	No.	%
M1: Born in Shashemanne, not migrated at all	18	8
M2: Born in rural area moved directly to Shashemanne	57	26
M3: Born in urban area moved directly to Shashemanne	34	16
M4: Lived in one place before Shashemanne	49	24
M5: Lived in two places before Shashemanne	25	11
M6: Lived in three or more places before Shashemanne	36	16
Total	219*	101

* Detailed migration histories could not be ascertained for three individuals in the sample.

Table 2 tells us that there is a great deal of variation in the way in which different persons had arrived in Shashemanne in 1973. In order to think about the mechanisms behind the movement to the town we must, however, go beyond the aggregate picture presented above. One can disaggregate the total pattern of migration careers in several ways. One can look at the way persons with different occupations have moved, how people born in different types of places have moved, differences between educated and non-educated, etc. The discussion below is based on the difference in migration patterns between persons belonging to the different *ethnic groups*[11] represented in Shashemanne. This is because ethnic differences subsume many other, in themselves relevant, differences between people.

4. The relation between ethnic identity and migration career

The population of the central region of southern Ethiopia is characterized by great ethnic complexity. This was reflected in the ethnic composition of Shashemanne in the beginning of the 70's. In the sample surveys made in the town in 1970 and 1973, 10 different ethnic groups were represented. Of those, four made up about 15% or more of the population.

People belonging to the same ethnic category share parts of, or an entire, cultural repertoire and speak mutually intelligible languages. Some ethnic categories contain many million people, living in almost all parts of Ethiopia. Persons of such categories may share little more than language with urban coethnics from regions other than their own. But in a given town, people of an ethnic category are likely also to belong to the same ethnic *group*, in a more narrow sense, and therefore to have kinship, lineage or clan links in addition to their cultural and linguistic affinity.[12] People of the same ethnic identity in the same town are likely to have their rural origin in the same region and to share the same migration pattern. J. C. Caldwell, who is responsible for the most comprehensive study of rural-urban migration so far undertaken in Africa, has pointed out the supreme importance of geographical origin in the formation of individual migration careers:

> Much of the propensity for migration depends not so much on who the individual is or what has been done to him, as on where his residence is and what has historically transpired in the area (Caldwell, 1969: 212).

Even though Caldwell does not make the connection between ethnic identity and region, it is clear that in a country where the geographical map is laid out on a social "map" made up of a criss-cross of peoples with different social structure, economic systems and history in relation to the state, geographical origin *per se* may not be very enlightening in the analysis of migration patterns; the important thing is to know the ethnic (and therefore geographic) origin of the migrants and the economic, social and political peculiarities of the ethnic groups in question.[13]

The four largest ethnic groups in Shashemanne in the 1973 sample were Amhara (35%), Gurage (18%), Wolaita (16%), and Oromo (14%). In addition, there were smaller groups of Tigrai, Kembata, Dorze, Arabs, and "Keffa"[14].

In the table below I have summarized the distribution of ethnic groups over the different types of migration career.

TABLE 3: Ethnicity and types of migration career

Ethnic Group:	1	2	3	4	5	6	7	Total
No. in sample of hh + wives	81	43	35	27	15	10	8	219
% in sample	37	20	16	12	7	5	4	101
Remove others, corrected proportion	38	20	17	13	7	5	—	100
No. in type of migration career: M1	7	3	1	6	0	0	—	17
No. in M2	9	15	19	7	0	5	—	55
No. in M3	13	4	9	1	5	2	—	34
No. in M4	23	10	5	4	2	2	—	46
No. in M5	13	5	0	5	1	0	—	24
No. in M6	16	6	1	4	7	1	—	35
Total	81	43	35	27	15	10	—	211

Key to ethnic groups: 1 = Amhara, 2 = Gurage, 3 = Wolaita, 4 = Oromo, 5 = Tigrai/Eritrean, 6 = Kembata, 7 = Other.

Key to type of migration career: M1 = Born in Shashemanne, never migrated; M2 = Born in rural area, moved directly to Shashemanne; M3 = Born in other urban area, moved directly to Shashemanne; M4 = Moved once before migrating to Shashemanne; M5 = Moved twice before migrating to Shashemanne; M6 = Moved three or more times before migrating to Shashemanne.

In Table 3 I have removed the "other" category from the division into separate migration types since it included few individuals in turn belonging to different ethnic groups. In the tables below I have also joined migration career types 5 and 6. Table 4a gives the proportion of migrants from the different ethnic groups *within* each type of migration career. It shows, that is, what proportion of the persons in migration type 1, etc. belonged to the Amhara, Gurage, etc. group. The bottom line shows the proportion of each group in the entire sample (less the persons belonging to the "other" category).

TABLE 4a: Ethnic proportions in different migration types

Ethnic Group:	1	2	3	4	5	6	No.	Total
Migration career:								
M1	41.2	17.61	5.9	35.3	0	0	17	100.0
M2	16.4	37.3	34.5	12.7	0	9.1	55	100.0
M3	38.2	11.8	26.5	2.9	14.7	5.9	34	100.0
M4	50.0	21.7	10.9	8.7	4.3	4.3	46	99.9
M5 + M6	49.2	18.6	1.7	15.3	13.6	1.7	59	100.1
Total							211	
Proportion in samples	38	20	17	13	7	5		100.0

Key to ethnic groups: 1 = Amhara, 2 = Gurage, 3 = Wolaita, 4 = Oromo, 5 = Tigrai/Eritrean, 6 = Kembata.

Key to type of migration career: M1 = Born in Shashemanne, never migrated; M2 = Born in rural area, moved directly to Shashemanne; M3 = Born in other urban area, moved directly to Shashemanne; M4 = Moved once before migrating to Shashemanne; M5 = Moved twice before migrating to Shashemanne; M6 = Moved three or more times before migrating to Shashemanne.

Table 4b shows in diagrammatic form when the proportion of a given ethnic group deviates more than 5% in either direction from the proportion in the sample.

TABLE 4b: Relative frequency of different ethnic groups in different types of migration career

	1	2	3	4	5	6
Mig. career 1	0	0	−	+	−	−
Mig. career 2	−	+	+	0	−	0
Mig. career 3	0	−	+	−	+	0
Mig. career 4	+	0	−	−	0	0
Mig. career 5 + 6	+	0	−	0	+	0

− : deviates more than −5% from proportion in sample
0 : within +/−5% of proportion in sample
+ : deviates more than 5% from proportion in sample

Key to ethnic groups: 1 = Amhara, 2 = Gurage, 3 = Wolaita, 4 = Oromo, 5 = Tigrai/Eritrean, 6 = Kembata.

Key to type of migration career: M1 = Born in Shashemanne, never migrated; M2 = Born in rural area, moved directly to Shashemanne; M3 = Born in other urban area, moved directly to Shashemanne; M4 = Moved once before migrating to Shashemanne; M5 = Moved twice before migrating to Shashemanne; M6 = Moved three or more times before migrating to Shashemanne.

Two ethnic groups are over-represented in career type 5+6, that is, among those who have moved twice or more times before migrating to Shashemanne. Both groups are correspondingly *under*-represented in type 2, which represents the traditional rural-urban migration. The two groups are the Amhara and the Tigrai. Both groups have their rural homelands at considerable distance from Shashemanne. This is particularly true of the Tigrai/Eritrea group from the two northernmost provinces in the country, but also for the Amhara one has to calculate at least 300 km. as the minimum distance to genuine "Amharaland". It is therefore quite understandable that the two groups have come to Shashemanne primarily from other towns. It is less easy to explain why the Tigrai/Eritreans also are over-represented in the group that has come to Shashemanne *directly* from some other urban area. Since they stem from areas farthest away one would expect them to have touched down at least some place on the road to Shashemanne. The Amhara and Tigrai/Eritrean groups make up 45% of the sample and their migration patterns therefore dominate the aggregate migration pattern to Shashemanne.

Two groups are over-represented among career type M2: the traditional rural-urban migrants. These are the Gurage and the Wolaita, who together make up about 35% of the sample. The Gurage are under-represented among the migrants who have come directly from some other urban area — a reflection maybe of there being few towns in Gurageland — but are otherwise proportionally represented in the remaining career types. The Wolaita on the other had are over-represented in both direct-moving migration types — and under-represented in the three others. The fact that they are few among the persons born in town could be an indication *either* of the Wolaita being relative newcomers to Shashemanne *or* of the group not settling in the town to the same extent as other groups.

The Oromo present a confusing picture. On the one hand, they form the only group over-represented among the persons born in Shashemanne, but on the other hand they are *not* under-represented among the migrants who have moved many times. This contradiction may be an effect of the composite nature of the Oromo group. In it are included both Arsi persons from the ethnic sub-group originally inhabiting the Shashemanne area, and Shoa-Oromo from the same rural homelands as some of the Amhara.

The Kembata finally are the smallest group in the sample. They are under-represented only among the persons born in town; they are proportionally represented in the remaining 4 types of migration career.

We will now look at the same figures in another way, namely to see how the different types of migration career are represented within each ethnic group.

TABLE 5: Relative frequency of different migration careers in different ethnic groups

Ethnic Group:	1	2	3	4	5	6	Prop. in Sample
Mig. career:							
M1	8.6	6.8	2.9	22.2	0	0	8.1
M2	11.2	34.9	54.2	25.9	0	50.0	26.1
M3	16.0	9.3	25.7	3.7	33.3	20.0	16.1
M4	28.4	23.3	14.3	14.8	13.3	20.0	21.8
M5 + M6	35.8	25.6	2.9	33.3	53.3	10.0	28.0
Total	100.0	99.9	100.0	99.9	100.0	100.0	100.1
No.in sample	81	43	35	27	15	10	211.0
Average number of moves* [15]	2.3	2.0	1.2	1.6	2.5	1.1	
* including the move to Shashemanne.							

Key to ethnic groups: 1 = Amhara, 2 = Gurage, 3 = Wolaita, 4 = Oromo, 5 = Tigrai/Eritrean, 6 = Kembata.

Key to type of migration career: M1 = Born in Shashemanne, never migrated; M2 = Born in rural area, moved directly to Shashemanne; M3 = Born in other urban area, moved directly to Shashemanne; M4 = Moved once before migrating to Shashemanne; M5 = Moved twice before migrating to Shashemanne; M6 = Moved three or more times before migrating to Shashemanne.

With this table the relation between the different ethnic groups is somewhat modified. The Amhara and the Tigrai/Eritrean still form a group of their own — few direct rural-urban migrants, a high proportion having moved twice or more (about 65%), and a high average number of moves per person.

But it no longer appears appropriate to group the Gurage and Wolaita together. The connection to the local region is much stronger for the Wolaita than for the Gurage: 83% of the Wolaita against 51% of the Gurage were born in town or direct rural-urban or inter-urban migrants. As a consequence, the Wolaita had only made 1.2 moves per person on average and the Gurage 2.0. The Wolaita instead appear relatively similar to the Kembata who had made 1.1 moves to Shashemanne on the average, and where 70% were direct migrants.

It seems then that we can divide the ethnic groups into four different migration patterns. One, represented by the Amhara and Tigrai/Eritreans, consists of persons who on the average have made several moves, with only about a third of the migrants being born in or moving directly to Shashemanne. One, represented by the Wolaita and Kembata, consists of persons who have made few moves on the way to Shashemanne, with 70% or more coming directly to the town. The Gurage and the Oromo have their own distinct patterns, in between the two other groups.

5. Discussion: Some mechanisms behind migration to Shashemanne

As a social phenomenon, migration is very much a *derived phenomenon*.[16] Despite the fact that scholars for a long time have tried to formulate universal laws about the characteristics of human migration[17], a process of migration is always embedded in a particular context. The migration histories of people cannot be understood except in terms of the political, economic and social history of the country and region where the migrants have lived.

In central southern Ethiopia, the context is multi-ethnic where the many different ethnic groups have had their own particular place in a regional history which before 1974 was characterized by economic and political diversity, conquest and subjugation followed by the introduction of a universal political and economic system where one ethnic group, the Amhara, to a large extent dominated the others.[18] The towns that developed after the conquest for a long time remained administrative and military outposts of the Ethiopian state, poorly integrated with the economic and social life of the different peoples of the region. The rapid growth of many small towns along the Addis Ababa-Nairobi highway at the end of the sixties and the beginning of the seventies, was induced by changes in the region that were largely initiated *outside* the region: processes leading to consolidation of large landholdings, mechanization of agriculture, the development of the transport system, increase in long-distance trade, etc.

At the beginning of the seventies, the relative position of the ethnic groups represented in Shashemanne was a reflection of the regional history of central southern Ethiopia. The Amhara and Wolaita represent two extremes. Despite the fact that the rural homelands of the Amhara were far away, the Amhara were most numerous and also dominated the most prestigious occupations in the town. In the Second Round of the Urban Survey[19] the Amhara made up about 40% of the male heads of household, but 70% of all white-collar workers in the town and 80% of the military and the police. In the 1973 migration study, 60% of the men above 20 years of age among the Amhara were able to read and write, and 23% of the women. The geographic origins of the heads of household and wives were distributed over all of central Ethiopia, from the northern province of (then) Begemdir[20], to the southern province of Sidamo. Respondents born in southern Ethiopia were practically all children or grandchildren of soldiers. There was a surplus of women compared to men, the sex quota being 85.[21]

The Wolaita on the other hand were as few as the Gurage and Oromo in the 1970 study, about 15%, despite the considerably shorter distances between rural areas dominated by each group respectively and Shashemanne than the distance between rural areas dominated by Amhara and the town. But of the daily labourers in Shashemanne the Wolaita made up almost 75% (the Amhara were represented by 8%), among the military and police there were *no* Wolaita and only individual instances of Wolaita being white-collar or other kinds of skilled workers. In the

1973 material, 4 of the Wolaita men above 20 years of age were able to read and write, and none of the women. All of the Wolaita came from one province, Sidamo, and most from a specific geographic locality, the (then) Wolamo[22] *awraja*. All fathers of Wolaita husbands and wives were farmers. There was a considerable surplus of men, the sex quota being 122.

What emerges then is a kind of ethnic "complex" or "syndrome" where many different factors related to geographic mobility and position in the social and economic hierarchy of towns are linked to one another. This in itself is not surprising. Studies from African countries have shown that one aspect of ethnic affiliation is precisely that it affects many different areas of life.[23] What the Shashemanne study shows, is that geographic mobility is yet another factor that is related to ethnic affiliation, and the form this relation had in the town in the beginning of the 70s.

Finally, I want to remind my readers of the fact that the study I have discussed here was made in a specific region and at a specific time period. I believe that the mechanisms behind migration to Shashemanne could be observed in other multi-ethnic southern towns of Ethiopia before 1974. But the relative position of the ethnic groups would have varied; in Soddo, in Wolaita *awraja*, the situation of the Wolaita was probably quite different from the situation in Shashemanne, for instance. However, the mechanisms behind migration to northern, ethnically homogeneous, towns must have been quite different and could probably best be analysed in terms of social and economic class.[24]

Then there is the matter of period. After the many events, political, military and ecological, of the last decade it is an open question what relevance the approach indicated here has for a study of contemporary urban migration. Even so, the study of Shashemanne in the 1970s provides one of a very few[25] starting points for future research in the field of urban migration in Ethiopia.

NOTES

1. *Migration to Shashemanne: Ethnicity, Occupation and Gender in Urban Ethiopia*, Uppsala, 1985.

2. Shashemanne was chosen for study because of its rapid growth rate coupled with the absence of any "obvious attraction for rural-urban migrants", such as industries, plantations, aid schemes, etc. When planning the study, I saw it very much in terms of a study of rural-urban migration.

3. In terms of various occupational and demographic characteristics.

4. The Central Statistical Office of the (then) Imperial Ethiopian Government.

5. The interviewers worked as teachers in the local Elementary and Junior High schools.

6. See Obbo, 1980: Chapter 1, for a discussion of the neglect of women in African urban studies.

7. In the 1973 sample, 45% of the wives and 60% of the female heads of household, above 30 years of age, had been married more than once.

8. I use the characteristics of the migration of heads of household and wives to approximate the characteristics of the migration of all adults in Shashemanne in the summary.

9. The places on the road between the birthplace of a migrant and Shashemanne were in nearly all instances other towns. I have avoided all reference to time when defining the different types of migration because of the uncertainty of time estimates in social surveys

in Shashemanne. Bjeren, 1985, includes a discussion of the kinds of variables that can safely be used in urban social surveys in Ethiopia.

10. The discussion below is based on material from the 1973 survey only. This is because the questionnaire addressed to the 1973 sample included specific questions about migration career in a way that the 1972 questionnaire did not, and because it is clear to which population the 1973 sample can be referred.

11. I am using the term "ethnic group" where others may choose to use the terms "nationality" or "tribe".

12. Hjort in his study of Isiolo town, northern Kenya, has an instructive discussion of the difference between ethnic group and ethnic category, and refers to the extensive discussion among social anthropologists about the nature of "ethnicity" (Hjort, 1979: 176pp).

13. The same point has been made by Samir Amin.

14. I am not certain to what ethnic group the three persons claiming to be "Keffa" should be added.

15. Number of times moved between birthplace and Shashemanne.

16. I owe this formulation to Mullenbach, 1976, who in turn quotes Friedmann and Wulff, 1975.

17. Beginning with Ravenstein, 1889. An interesting more recent formulation is that by Lee, 1969.

18. For a recent description and analysis of the ethnic history of the region see Braukämper, 1980.

19. The figures about relative position in different occupations are calculations from the primary material of the Second Round of the Urban Survey. The data were collected in Shashemanne by the CSO in 1970 and covered 991 households. I have used the data from this survey rather than from my own in 1972 and 1973 because the patterns of ethnic stratification of the economy can only be seen in a sufficiently large material.

20. Now Gondar.

21. Number of men per 100 women.

22. Now Wolaita *awraja*.

23. See for instance Mitchell 1970, where he shows how ethnic identity coincides with other characteristics such as occupation, level of education and religion in Zambia and Zimbabwe, or the discussion in Hanna & Hanna, 1971.

24. Underneath the ethnic analysis presented in this paper there is, of course, a class dimension. But since ethnic identity and class coincide to a considerable extent I have not touched upon this here.

25. There are few empirical studies of urban migration in Ethiopia easily available. When writing about Shashemanne I have found the chapters on migration in the dissertations by Mullenbach, 1976 and Lakech, 1978 useful.

REFERENCES

Amin, Samir, 1974

"Introduction" in Amin, Samir (ed.), *Modern Migrations in Western Africa*. London.

Bjeren, Gunilla, 1985

Migration to Shashemanne: Ethnicity, Occupation and Gender in Urban Ethiopia. Uppsala.

Braukämper, Ulrich, 1980

Geschichte der Hadiya Sud-Äthiopiens, *Studien zur Kulturkunde*: 50. Wiesbaden.

Caldwell, J. C., 1969

African Rural-Urban Migration: The Movement to Ghana's Towns. Canberra/London.

Friedmann, J. and Wulff, 1975

The Urban Transition. London.

Hanna, W. J. and Hanna, J. L., 1971

Urban dynamics in black Africa. Chicago, New York.

Hjort, Anders, 1979

Savanna Town. Rural Ties and Urban Opportunities in Northern Kenya. Stockholm.

Lakech Diresse, 1978

"The socio-economic position of women in Addis Ababa: The case of prostitution". Unpublished PhD dissertation: Boston University.

Lee, E., 1969

"A theory of migration" in Jackson, J. A. (ed.), *Migration*, Cambridge.

Mitchell, J. C., 1970

"Tribe and social change in South Central Africa: A situational approach" in *Journal of Asian and African Studies*, Vol.5, pp.83-101.

Mullenbach, H. J., 1976

"Akaki Beseka: Urban Processes in an Ethiopian Industrial Town". Unpublished PhD dissertation: Northwestern University.

Obbo, C., 1980

African Women: Their Struggle for Economic Independence. London.

Ravenstein, E. G., 1885

"The Laws of Migration", *Journal of the Royal Statistical Society*, 48:2. Cited in Lee, above.

POLITICAL POWER AND SOCIAL FORMATION IN ETHIOPIA
UNDER THE OLD REGIME: NOTES ON MARXIST THEORY

Dessalegn Rahmato

INTRODUCTION

This work should not be taken as a political or social history of the Old Regime, but rather as a modest attempt at participation in the current Marxist debate on the state in developing societies. We are concerned with Marxist political theory partly for reasons of personal preference, and partly because the scholarly exchange in this area is of recent origin and promises to be a long and stimulating one. We have chosen the Old Regime as material for a case study because now that it is dead and gone, an academic *postmortem* presents itself, offering researchers opportunities for a more dispassionate investigation.

Such an investigation is necessary in the light of developments at the time of the fatal crisis of the Old Regime. In particular, the manner in which the allegedly unassailable power of the monarchy, and of the classes that it was claimed to represent, disintegrated in the face of what was only a fragmented opposition, now casts serious doubts on many of the arguments of liberal as well as radical pundits of the time. The events of 1974 and after are too well known, though yet to be rigorously examined, to need recounting here, but for our purposes the following points are worth noting: 1) the state collapsed suddenly and without the least resistance; 2) the nobility, considered to be the most powerful class in the country, vanished from the political scene almost overnight; 3) neither crown, church, nor privileged class was found to be necessary for the construction of a new state in the country; and, 4) the disappearance of crown and nobility *per se* did not unleash centrifugal tendencies threatening the integrity of the country.

We draw these conclusions only with hindsight, but having done so, the next step should be a re-assessment of the structure of power and social formation of the Old Regime. The re-evaluation which we are attempting here will, it is hoped, also serve as a basis for raising questions regarding current theories of political development.

THE STATE IN DEVELOPING SOCIETIES:
A BRIEF REVIEW OF THE DEBATE[1]

The state in developing societies is said to be characterized by what is called an "over-developed" political structure. This structure, it is argued, was not originally the work of an ascendant, or dominant indigenous social force (a native bourgeoisie, for instance), but rather a creation of the colonial power, or more specifically, the metropolitan bourgeoisie of the "mother" country. The main purpose of this particular apparatus originally was the effective subjugation of all sectors of colonized society and the more efficient extraction of economic surplus. At independence, this apparatus is captured by an indigenous social force — a petty bourgeois elite, according to some (Mamdani, Shivji, Saul, and generally all who have examined the east African experience), a military-bureaucratic oligarchy according to others (Alavi), a national or bureaucratic bourgeoisie (Boron, Samoff), etc. — which employs this same apparatus for similar purposes, namely political subjugation and economic control.

The apparatus of the state is "over-developed" — i.e. it supports a massive bureaucracy, a large force of coercion, etc. — in that it is not congruent with nor necessary for the needs of the rather backward and simple social and economic structures typically found in such societies. This is partly because, it is argued, the bases of the state lie in the metropolitan structure itself from which it is separated at the time of independence. According to Alavi, who is credited for having popularized this notion of "over-development", the excessive accretion of the "powers of control and regulation that the state has accumulated and elaborated extend far beyond the

463

logic of what may be necessary for the orderly functioning of the social institutions of the society over which the state presides".[2]

Another characteristic that all developing polities are supposed to share in common is dependency. Just as developing economies are said to be articulated to international capital, or incorporated in a subordinate form into the world system, so too are Third World states. Indeed, some insist that these states are a creation of the world system, and are sustained by it, their essential function being to facilitate, and at times to participate in, the extraction of surplus from native society by international capital.[3] Others have viewed the dependent state as a medium for transmitting to indigenous society the structure of material and power relations inherent in the world capitalist system. In the context of external dependence, it is claimed, the "state in underdeveloped capitalist societies is primarily an agent of transmitting the global dynamics of the international division of labour to the national level and of reproducing the internal class and political power structure according to these dynamics".[4]

The theory of dependency has been extended further, and is thought to be the key determinant of the form of the state itself, i.e. whether it is liberal, populist, authoritarian, etc. Going one step further, some analysts have even seen the hand of international capital in the rise of extreme forms of political despotism, such as that of Idi Amin in Uganda.[5] A slightly more subtle proposition contends that the greater penetration and consolidation of capitalism in developing societies (i.e. greater dependency) has been accompanied not by the democratization of society but rather by the intensification of authoritarianism.[6]

Another concept which is also currently in vogue, and which is considered to be an important contribution to Marxist political theory is the concept of "relative autonomy". It is puzzling that Marxists should "discover" this concept now, when it has been there all along in many of Marx's political writings. The argument is that what distinguishes developing from developed societies is that the former contain a multiplicity of what are called fundamental classes, or social strata, but no one of these social groups is said to be capable of exercising direct control over the state. The state, in other words, is not the instrument of any one class, and hence acquires relative autonomy.[7] It has a wider freedom of action as well as sphere of involvement than states in other social forms, and its power to set policy and make decisions is not restricted by sectional or class interests. However, relative autonomy does not prevent the state from being involved in the sphere of production — directly owning and operating economic enterprises, participating in joint-venture schemes with local or international capital, etc.; indeed, in this respect, it is shown to be far more interventionist than other kinds of states outside the Soviet system.

So much in brief about current theories regarding developing polities. In place of a detailed criticism, we shall present a few general comments, indicating where the weakness of these theories lies.

As we tried to show above, current Marxist theory insists that society and state in the developing world are externally determined, that is, their structure, character and behaviour are shaped or conditioned by global social and economic forces. The indigenous social organism is said to possess no life of its own, and the indigenous political actors are considered blind instruments of alien powers, variously labelled as the metropolitan bourgeoisie, international capital or the world market. Where classical Marxism sought the determinants of the state primarily in the interplay of social and economic processes *intrinsic* to the society in question, contemporary theory denies altogether that developing societies have characteristics innate to themselves. On the contrary, it argues that these societies are merely mediums through which external world forces express themselves, or reproduce the conditions of their dominance.

Secondly, contemporary analysis fails to consider the relation between the state on the one hand, and society on the other as having an important bearing on the political system itself, and on the structure of power. The relations that are given emphasis instead are the relations between the state in question and external powers, and those among the indigenous social classes viewed, in this case, through a crudely conceptualized schema of class struggle. It is further stressed that the so called fundamental classes do not act on their own free will, as they are appendages of global social forces. The theory glosses over the innately resilient nature, as well as the centrifugal impulse, of precapitalist processes in many developing societies, and fails to examine how these affect the deployment of political power. It forgets that each developing society possesses a social "architecture" inherent to itself, and a self-developed political culture — though this may not still exist in its pristine form — and both play an important role in determining the complexions of the state.

In short, the literature on the state is clearly inadequate to the tasks it has set for itself, highly tendentious, and still suffering, like the societies it is trying to investigate, from underdevelopment. In the attempt to place its subject, i.e. developing polities, firmly in the world context and thus to provide an alternative scheme of analysis to the rather "isolationist" approach of liberal theory, radical theory has ended up by transforming world capital into an omniscient and omnipotent power.

We believe that for a number of developing countries, which are characterized by what we shall call the *fragmentation of society*, the state-society relation, and the analysis based on it, should provide fruitful results. This does not exclude consideration of the role and effects of external factors, but only relegates them to a subordinate status, where they in fact belong. It needs to be borne in mind that the consolidation of society and of production is often a necessary condition for the intrusion of world capital into that society.

The theory of social fragmentation cannot be discussed here in any detail because of limitations of space, however, the following are examples of fragmentation, which have a determining effect on the structure of power.

In a number of developing societies there are tendencies inhibiting the concentration of capital, the centralization of production, and the articulation of the economic formation. There prevails instead a system of generalized petty production with its attendant parcelization of means of production, and individualization of the labour process. This is what we call the *fragmentation of the economy*. These same societies further reveal the insufficient development of self-assertive, modern (i.e. post-traditional) social classes, and in consequence, the class struggle is muted and fails to play a significant role in the political process. This gives rise to and is in turn sustained by the *fragmentation of the social structure*. A multiplicity of primordial loyalties and interests — ethnic, religious, regional, etc. — which cut across class lines and which are permeated with particularism, narrowly-conceived corporatism, etc., act as powerful, socially disintegrative forces. In this condition, it is often the state which stands for the general interest in opposition to society. Here we have what we call the *fragmentation of the political culture*.

In short, where society as a whole is fragmented — the degree of fragmentation of course varies from one experience to another — the tendency is for the state to become correspondingly over-dominant, that is, to subordinate all social forces, to assume all authority, and to be the major active element. The argument that the so-called overdeveloped state is originally the work of external forces forgets that this form of state was already present, in substance, in a number of societies before the advent of colonialism, as a cursory glance, for instance, at African history will show, and would have been constructed any way without the colonial experience as the political history of the Old Regime demonstrates. It is also curious that over 100 years after independence in the case of Latin America, and nearly four decades in that of the Indian subcontinent, the colonial legacy should continue to exercise such a decisive influence. The point simply put is this: in post-colonial conditions, the weakness of society magnifies the strength of the state. This is basically the meaning of Gramsci's observation that in conditions of general backwardness "the State [is] everything, civil society . . . primordial and gelatinous; in the West, there [is] a proper relation between State and civil society, and when the State trembles a sturdy structure of civil society [is] at once revealed".[8] The main task of political development theory should be to analyze precisely why society is "gelatinous", and to explain how it has enabled the state to superimpose itself on it.

In this paper, the focus is on the state and the structure of the economic formation, leaving out any discussion of the two other problematics noted above. But first, let us see how the structure of power in the Old Regime is to be defined.

The political system of the Old Regime has been variously described as traditional or feudal autocracy, absolute monarchy, constitutionalized absolutism, or feudo-bourgeois monarchy.[9] But a careful re-examination of the subject shows the inadequacy of earlier analysis, and the need for fresh theorization. It is certainly true that in outward form, the political system contained a great deal that was feudal: politics involved a hierarchically-constructed system of personal dependency relationships, a rigidly ordered behaviour, Byzantine language, etc. However, in substance and viewed "structurally", the polity revealed a different character, at least in one major respect: whereas feudal polities are inconceivable without the parcelization of sovereignty, the centralization of authority and the construction of an integral politico-social order was the most important achievement of the old state.[10] Indeed, the political history of the Old Regime contains clear landmarks where the state made a determined shift from feudatory monarchy to "absolutism", the earliest of this being the 1931 constitution.

One work which of late has come to influence studies about the Old Regime is Perry Anderson's *Lineages of the Absolute State*, which may be considered an important contribution to Marxist political history.[11] In this work, the author argues that the absolutist state in post-medieval Europe was essentially the instrument of a resurgent nobility whose power was being threatened by the new men of commerce and industry — the rising bourgeoisie. This is in sharp contrast to the earlier, more orthodox Marxist interpretation, which considered the state under absolutism as a mediating force whose main task was to balance the power and influence of the two bitter rivals, the nobility and the bourgeoisie. For Anderson, however, absolutism involved the re-deployment of the forces of the state to preserve the economic interests of the landed classes and to consolidate feudal domination which had earlier been undermined by changes in property and class relations.

The absolutist state, which for the first time created a centralized political apparatus, a standing army, a uniform fiscal system — in a word, the structure of the modern nation-state — was at the same time the servant of the traditional landed powers: in western Europe, it was employed to reassert the authority of the nobility over an increasingly restive peasant population, in eastern Europe, to consolidate the re-infeudation of the rural producers. There is an obvious paradox here which Anderson does not entirely resolve, which is that absolutism is conceived as an attempt at the fusion of two opposed tendencies, namely, that which is new with that which is traditional. It is also curious that the "unorthodox" Anderson should try to reinstate the orthodox, class-reductionist view of political power.

We shall define the structure of political power in the Old Regime as "absolutist", but *NOT* in line with Anderson's analysis. We believe that the foundations of Ethiopian absolutism, the articulation of classes in the society, and the relations of the state to the dominant social elements were distinctly different from the European experience, and Anderson's central thesis therefore is *not pertinent* to our case.

Before we present the arguments, let us just make a few general comments. All things considered, Ethiopian absolutism, as we wish to call it, marked a progressive advance over all earlier forms of state. It must in particular be given credit for the following: a) the centralization of the structure of power which brought to an end the fragmentation of political authority with all its attendant ills; b) the building up of a modern, professional standing army replacing the ragtag mass levies controlled by regional warlords; c) the elaboration of a uniform, centrally administered fiscal and tax system which laid the groundwork for the rationalisation of the economy; d) the setting up of a similar administrative and judicial practice throughout the country. Without these accomplishments, the territorial integration of the country, such as it was, would not have been possible.

Royal power shared authority with no one, i.e. with no independent social or political forces, but instead bestowed on itself, through both the 1931 and 1955 constitutions, supreme authority assuming in practice the role of chief legislator, policy maker and administrator. But it is, we believe, a mistake to define the state in terms exclusively of royal power and to see the two as being one and the same, as some analysts have done, for the latter would not have been effective and viable without its support staff in the civil and military bureaucracy.[12] In the context of the Marxist debate, the specificities of Ethiopian absolutism may be described as follows:-

1. Royal absolutism held unquestioned supremacy over all classes in the country. It was by no means the arbitrator between contending social forces (as orthodox theory suggests), for no such forces did in fact exist, nor was it the instrument of a resurgent nobility (Anderson's argument), because the Ethiopian nobility was effectively shorn of its power and reduced to a subordinate status early in Haile Selassie's reign. From its very inception, Ethiopian absolutism had to separate and distance itself from its traditional class base and, indeed, exercise strict control over the nobility in order to be able to reconstruct the unitary state.[13]

The concentration of preponderant authority was achieved early in the history of the old state, i.e. in the course of the modernization of the political system, which previously was fragmented, with power in the hands of a host of semi-autonomous regional warlords. At this early period, the tension between society on the one hand, whose centrifugal tendencies impelled it towards "autonomization", and the state on the other, whose imperatives drove it in the opposite direction, was resolved in favour of the latter. This victory was made possible in part by the building up of a relatively elaborate state apparatus and by concentrating in the hands of the state, authority in all matters pertaining to revenue collection, tax administration and the allocation of material resources.[14]

Absolutism not only subordinated the aristocracy, but also brought about a significant change in the character of the class itself. The further consolidation of the state saw the aristocracy gradually discard its traditional militaristic preoccupations — which thus saved the country from the perennial depredations of civil strife — and evolve into a more stable and settled class of landed nobility. Although this meant greater dependency on royal power, it also brought with it a relatively greater economic security for the noble class as a whole. In the process, however, and with its increased involvement in the apparatus of central government, the nobility became more and more detached from its regional links and traditional base of political support. By the end of the 1950s, the nobility was virtually a spent force, although this was not evident until the crisis of 1974, when it abruptly and ignominiously collapsed.

2. Although the absolutist state was not the instrument of any one class, it does not mean that it regarded all classes equally. Of the variety of interests considered by the state, those of the nobility were accorded a most-favoured status. This was the basis of the nobility's standing and influence in society. However, this class was not an independent social force capable of making autonomous decisions, or independently reproducing the conditions of its own social position. Its power was a *derived* power which was conditional on the personal dependency relationship that its members maintained with the monarchy. The nobility was not an "economic" class, i.e. it was not a force in production, nor did it play a significant role in economic activity. Furthermore, the class was not in reality a coherent class, it was instead fragmented by internecine conflicts, rivalries of interest, etc. It was unable to elaborate a meaningful ideology, which is so essential for the inner coherence of a class, nor did it inspire a transcendant political culture that went beyond its narrow, corporate interests.

A reading of Marx's observations about the Asiatic mode of production suggests that a distinction ought to be made between a *ruling* class and a *proprietary* class. The first is a social force whose economic position has enabled it to capture state power, or to shape it decisively in its own image, the second, one which is dominant only in the economic sphere. The state in the latter case is independent of all classes, proprietary or otherwise, and exercises domination over all of society.[15] Ethiopian society under absolutism shares this feature in common with society in the Asiatic mode, namely that the nobility was *not* a ruling but rather merely a *proprietary* class.

3. The apparatus of absolutism was hierarchical, bureaucratic and relatively overblown, but this apparatus was a conscious creation of the state itself. The point needs to be emphasized in

the light of the theoretical debate we are considering, which is that the forging of the machinery of state was accomplished not through imperialism, which was threatening the country at the early period of the rise of emperor Haile Selassie, but rather against it. It needs to be noted also that the history of Ethiopian technocracy, that is, that discrete professional group primarily engaged in the routine management of government affairs, is coterminous with the history of absolutism.

4. Ethiopian absolutism did not in particular encourage the further infeudation of the peasantry, nor did it attempt to do away with feudal property relations where these were in force. Essentially, it favoured the preservation of the system of generalized petty production which consisted, as we shall show below, of a disarticulated amalgam of rural and urban economic forms. The state itself was an economic power not just because it determined the process of accumulation, but also because it was the biggest landlord, industrialist, financier and employer. The economy was, of course, surrounded by the world-capitalist economy, and foreign capital did play some role in it, but we are not convinced that therefore the country should be described as capitalist or peripheral capitalist.

A unitary state, a segmentary social formation, the first drawing its strength because of the second — such was the political complexion of the Old Regime. Viewed "structurally", the content of absolutism has more in common with modern-day post-colonial states than post-medieval monarchies of either western or eastern Europe. However, in form and outward appearance — royal power, aristocratic privilege, legitimacy based on Biblical mythology, pomp and ceremony at court, etc. — the old state was largely medieval and out of step with the real world. But then, the Old Regime was, in this as in many other respects, characteristically Janus-faced: it was at once modern and traditional, contemporary and anachronistic.

THE FRAGMENTATION OF THE ECONOMY

There have been in the past a number of claims that the Old Regime had undergone, or was in the process of undergoing, the transition to capitalism, although it has not always been agreed exactly when the process actually began. The initial impulse has been located by some as far back as the turn of the century, and by others as recently as the early post-war period.[16]

The best attempt so far to justify the capitalist transition argument empirically has been made by UNCTAD, [*Major Issues in Transfer of Technology in Developing Countries: A Case Study of Ethiopia*, Geneva, 19 June 1974 (esp. ch. III)]. However, a close examination of the evidence presented in the document shows that the authors' position cannot really be sustained. This position, in fact, is based not on the relation of the capitalist sector to the surrounding pre-capitalist economies, and on the strength of the former vis-a-vis the latter, but rather on the growth of the modern sector in the post-war period, and the strong position of foreign interests in it. The authors themselves recognize that capitalist production was very small — a fact which leads them to characterize it as an "enclave economy", i.e. one which has a tenuous link with the larger economy surrounding it.

We shall argue that the old economic formation consisted of an assemblage of several discrete modes of production, jointed loosely together more by political than economic bonds, and each capable of near complete self-sufficiency. In this formation, pre-capitalist production in general was predominant, and was responsible for the decentralization of production and of capital — in a word, the fragmentation of the economy.

The ensemble of pre-capitalist economic forms we shall group under the label "system of generalized petty production". The term "mode of production" refers in this paper to the material aspect of social life, i.e. the way in which individuals in society appropriate nature, and produce their subsistence. A number of modes of production (or economic forms) constitute an *economic formation*, or social formation, if the juridical and political spheres are included.

Samir Amin has identified five modes of production which he believes are pertinent to peripheral societies. These are: the primitive communal, the tribute paying (which, in its advanced form, is said to give rise to a sub-mode called the feudal), the slave owning, the simple petty-commodity, and the capitalist modes of production. The capitalist mode is invariably the dominant force around which others are articulated.[17] The articulation of modes of production, which is currently popular among some Marxist scholars, may be stated briefly as follows: an economic formation consists of a dominant economic form together with several subordinate ones, and the former (usually capitalist) organises the others around itself and uses them as a source of accumulation. The latter can no longer be fully pre-capitalist because they have become subverted by capital through their articulation with it.

The term "articulation" does not of course appear in Marx, but the concept is not foreign to him, and is to be found in a number of his works. He rejected the notion, however, that capital assumes a dominant role in an economic formation as a matter of course; on the contrary, he believed that under certain circumstances, capitalist production can become subordinated to or enfeebled by older economic forms. He pointed out, for example, that in societies predominantly characterized by independent, subsistence and small-holding peasant production:

> . . . The agricultural population has a great numerical preponderance over the urban population, i.e. that even if the capitalist mode of production is dominant it is relatively little developed, so that the concentration of capital is also confined to narrow limits in the other branches of production, and a fragmentation of capital prevails.[18]

Marx stressed that the transformation of pre-capitalist economies was not only a slow and gradual process but that for a time capital itself may even be conditioned by them and confined to narrow limits. This, we believe, is precisely what happened in the Ethiopian case. How quickly and effectively capital transforms or reconditions older economies depends on a host of factors, among which Marx singled out the resilience and intrinsic organization of the economies themselves as the most significant. How far capital "leads to the dissolution of the old mode of production depends *first and foremost* on the solidity and inner articulation of this mode of production".[19]

The following six modes of production which, we believe, constituted the economic formation of the Old Regime, reveal how deep the heterogeneity (and fragmentation) of the formation was, and how serious were the obstacles against the advance of capitalism.

The Rural Sector

1. Feudal production. This mode of production, which at the most primary level involves landlordism, tenancy and rent as a form of surplus extraction, was endemic in the southern regions of the country. Enough has been said about this and tributary production discussed below, and there is no need to dwell on both here. However — and this fact has not been sufficiently stressed in the literature — side by side with tenancy and dependent cultivation in these areas, one found a system of independent peasant proprietorship where the cultivator himself was the owner of his plot which he employed for his own subsistence. I have shown elsewhere that independent, petty-proprietorship was slightly more widespread in the country as a whole than tenant cultivation. Although one hesitates to categorize this as an autonomous mode of production, one ought to caution, at least, against its complete submersion within feudalism.[20]

2. The tributary mode of production. This economic form corresponds to what in the Ethiopian literature on the land system was often called the "communal system", and covers the same areas in northern Ethiopia, including highland Eritrea. We are not convinced that, as Amin and some others have suggested, this form should be considered simply a variant of feudal production, because it reveals distinct characteristics in at least two major aspects, namely property ownership and mode of surplus extraction. The tributary system entailed a corporate-family or kinship form of ownership — as opposed to landlordism in feudalism — and surplus was extracted from the producers by means of tribute rather than rent, as in the latter.

3. *Pastoral production*. We shall be concerned here with nomadic pastoralism for this was and still is by far the most dominant form in the country, although pockets of sedentary pastoralism and transhumance are also to be found in several areas. Ethiopian pastoralists occupy an area of about 40 million hectares, which is one-third of the land area of the country, and are estimated to constitute between 10% and 15% of the total population.[21]

The question whether or not nomadic pastoralism constitutes a distinct mode of production has not yet been conclusively settled, despite the fact that the features common to all pastoral societies, and the specificity of pastoral production are no longer in dispute. Among Marxists, there is not yet a general consensus on the definitions of pastoralism, its historical roots, or evolutionary potential. Marx himself did not consider pastoralism as a separate economic form but on several occasions he made references to it, references which are however of a descriptive kind.[22] Among those Marxists who have identified mobile stockbreeding as a discrete economic form, Anderson must be singled out, although this view has recently been shared by others as well. Anderson has argued that nomadic pastoralism "represents a distinct mode of production, with its own dynamic, limits and constraints, that should not be confused with those of either tribal or feudal agriculture". He points out that pastoralism, as an original historical path of evolution, branched off from primitive agrarian cultivation and "represented in certain respects a more highly specialized and skilled exploitation of the natural world than pre-feudal agriculture".[23]

Both Marx and Anderson are, of course, describing a form of pastoralism in which the herder and the herd roamed across vast stretches of land in search of fresh pasture and water. This is the "pure form" of nomadism, which is not at all the dominant form either in Ethiopia, or elsewhere at present. Finally, it should be noted, as an element in the debate, that some Soviet writers, whose country contains a large pastoral population (still!), refuse to consider this activity as separate and distinct, preferring to look at it as a variant of feudalism, or "patriarchal feudalism" to be exact.

For us, Ethiopian pastoralism clearly reveals characteristics and dynamics that are not found in the other economies, and definitely constitutes a form of production *sui generis*.[24] In contrast to Anderson, who insists that the pastoralist's basic means of production is livestock and Soviet writers, who argue that it is land, we consider instead that both livestock and land constitute the primary means of subsistence. The chief purpose of economic activity here is the production and reproduction of livestock, but this is carried on under extremely inhospitable natural conditions, in which productive endeavour consists in the maximal utilization of these conditions through adaptation to them. Production therefore does not call for the control or transformation of nature, but rather the adjustment of human effort to the ecological conditions and to the cyclical occurrences of nature.

The production unit is the extended family which consists of the household head, his numerous wives, his children and several adult relatives. The division of labour is very rudimentary and is in fact based on gender and, in those communities who practice the age-set system, on age gradation. As technology is virtually unknown, the size of the family is proportional to the wealth (i.e. the herd size) of the household. Production takes place within the community and by utilizing the resources of the community. Access to water points, pasture, salt licks, etc., which is provided to all members on an equal basis, is however a condition of membership in the community, which always consists of a cluster of grazing families who constitute a "corporate" body — the *rera* of the Boran, the *degma* of the Somal, or the *Kidhu* of the Afar. It is this "corporate" body that owns the natural means of production within a defined geographical setting.

Thus the pastoralist is an individual owner in so far as his herd are involved, but a collective owner in so far as the natural means of production are concerned, and individual production takes place through the collective appropriation of natural resources. Production, on the other hand, involves in large measure the organization and management of herds through the technique of periodic mobility. Mobility, which is built into pastoralism, involves the movement of both people and herd, and is the most important technique employed for the maximal utilization of resources, the efficient reproduction of the herd, and the minimization of risk to capital. But to this must also be added that mobility also allows depleted natural resources to be replenished so that they can be used or consumed again; thus it is not just livestock that are reproduced, as Anderson has argued, but the material conditions of production as well.

Pastoral society is highly egalitarian, partly because it is also deeply segmentary — the exceptions may be small pastoralists such as the Geleb in the Omo delta, and the Beni Amir in north-west Eritrea. Social differentiation based on access to resources and relations to means of production are absent, by and large, although distinctions based on wealth, i.e. the size of one's herd, are not uncommon. Indeed, some have seen in the social organization, or rather absence of organization, of pastoralist societies such as the Afar forms of individualism and self-assertion bordering on anarchism.[25]

4. Peripheral-communal production. The analysis of this economic form presents some difficulties in that the literature on the subject is rather limited, and what is available consists for the most part of ethnographic and linguistic material.[26] The production mode under discussion is not exactly analogous to Marx's primitive communism (or tribal form of ownership) for, in many respects, peripheral-communalism is more structured and "evolved" than what Marx had in mind. The area under this economy covers a large expanse of territory stretching the full length of western Ethiopia along the Sudanese border. It also includes most of the highlands of Gamo Goffa, central Keffa and Illubabor, and western Wollega. It is very difficult to determine how many people are engaged in this form of subsistence activity, but it may not be an exaggeration to say that they constitute between 5% to 8% of the total population of the country.

The people in the peripheral system are predominantly sedentary agriculturalists, who also practice hunting and fishing, gathering, stock breeding and, at times, apiculture. It is not always the case, however, that cultivation constitutes the dominant form of activity, on the contrary, among some of the nationalities, grain production is supplemental to other endeavours such as hunting, gathering or stock breeding.

In the majority of cases it is swidden agriculture — i.e. shifting, slash-and-burn cultivation — which is practiced, and the implements employed are correspondingly rudimentary, the most widely used being the digging stick, the hoe and a hand tool for clearing land. Slash and burn cultivation is, from the ecological point of view, terribly destructive but it offers the practitioner the largest rewards with the least input of labour and the most primitive technology. The system of property ownership here reveals a dual characteristic: it combines, very often, individual *possession* with communal *ownership*. Each family cultivates the land that it has managed to clear at any given moment and enjoys possessory right over this plot until the land is abandoned due to the demands of the particular agricultural system adopted by the community. The community on the other hand is the real owner of the land, and possession or the right of usufruct is accorded to the individual as a member of the collectivity. Private possession, communal property; society here, we believe, shares a lot of things in common with the system Marx called the Germanic community.[27]

As with property ownership, so also with production, the private and the communal are interrelated and interdependent. The actual process of production, i.e. the clearing of the land, the preparation of the soil and, at times, harvesting, is often carried on collectively and through communal labour, whereas the fruits of this effort are appropriated individually. As one writer has put it, the guiding principle here is "collective input, individual output".[28]

Society under peripheral-communalism is, almost without exception, uniformly undifferentiated, revealing in some instances even more than pastoral societies, almost complete social homogeneity. Each family shares the same material culture, possesses the same means of production, has equal access to all of the community's resources and utilizes the same know-how as every other family. But this egalitarian form of social relation is contradicted by the patriarchal nature of domestic life and individual relations and, as in the case of pastoral societies, the democracy that exists is only for the chiefs of households and generational superiors.

The Urban Sector

5. Handicraft and household production. This is in many respects quite similar to what Amin has termed "simple, petty-commodity production". The basic prerequisites of this economic form — which we shall also refer to as cottage industry — are the following: a) as Amin has pointed out, handicraft production cannot exist by itself, but rather in symbiosis with other economies; b) often, it requires the growth of urban centres for its own development, for rural cottage industry can only have a limited market and potential and c) it flourishes where capitalist production has not firmly established itself in the social formation.

A host of activities, often based in the home or in small workshops, come under the category of handicraft and household production: the manufacture of craft products including household utensils, woven cloth, traditional implements and weapons, and jewellery; the processing of finished or semi-finished goods — tailoring, tanning, woodworking; the provision of skilled services, such as thatching, plastering, etc. in traditional house building, and the production and vending of traditional food and drinks.[29] This economy continues to this day to be the mainstay of a large portion of the population in both urban and rural areas, although its real strength and magnitude may never be accurately known. Official surveys in the early 1970s — which were however restricted in their coverage — showed that by the end of the last Plan period handicraft and household production consisted of over a quarter of a million enterprises, provided employment for well over 310,000 people and contributed slightly more to GDP than manufacturing industry. These figures would be raised higher if we were to include in this economic form — and there are good grounds for doing so — small-scale industries. One study conducted in two southern provinces found that 6% of the population of these regions depended in whole or in part on craft production for its livelihood and it suggested that this figure should actually be taken to be valid for the whole of the country.[30] We believe however that a more careful and inclusive investigation would reveal that those who depend on this activity for their basic subsistence constitute, then as well as now, far more than 6% of the total population.

6. *Capitalist production,* especially manufacturing industry — we shall deal with this below.

These six modes of production, held together not so much by the imperatives of generalized exchange, as by the state, defined the diversity of the country's *material* culture and the heterogeneity of its system of production. The relation among the various economic forms was for the most part superficial, since a majority of them were pre-capitalist, subsistence oriented and self-sufficient economies. Capitalist production, far from being the leading element around which the others were articulated, was instead submerged within the system of generalized petty production.

A classification of the Ethiopian people on the basis of modes of production, rather than the standard linguistic or ecological one, would produce interesting results for, as has been suggested above, each economic form very often cuts across ethnic and linguistic boundaries. The same people from the point of view of language and ethnic origin were to be found under different modes of production and thus separated by different material cultures; on the other hand, people of entirely different ethnicity shared commonalities for precisely the same reasons. The people we have grouped under peripheral-communalism, for instance, would be represented, in Levine's scheme of classification, by the Sudanic and Omotic groups, and by the cultures in the southern end of the Lacustrine group.[31] From the point of view of material culture and social needs, the Beni Amir pastoralists of north-western Eritrea have more in common with the Oromo-speaking Boran pastoralists of southern Sidamo than the latter have with the sedentary Oromo agriculturalists in the highlands who, ethnically and linguistically, are descended from the same roots.

The fragmentation of industrial production.* Even by the standards of sub-Saharan Africa, capitalist production in the Old Regime was exceedingly small; it provided just about 52,000 jobs, and contributed about (really less than) 5% to the GDP in the early 1970s.[32] The total paid up capital of all manufacturing enterprises was US$136 million, and total fixed capital as-

---

* All monetary figures in US$, and US$1.00 has been taken to be Eth.$2.50.

sets, US$145 million. On the strength of one or the other of these two factors alone, the entire manufacturing industry of the country could be compared to a medium-sized American business firm. Light industries, producing basic consumables such as processed food, textiles, beverages, leather and wood products, employing obsolete or rather antiquated technology, greatly dominated the sector.

If we look at the distribution of enterprises by size, we find that a good portion of industry was made up of small, minimally mechanized establishments. Of the 420 enterprises making up the totality of the manufacturing sector, one-third consisted of small establishments, employing *up to* 50 persons and using, in many instances, low motive power or manually operated equipment. Those that may be called medium-to-large enterprises, that is employing between 200 to 500 persons, numbered only 40, whereas those that by local and international standards could be considered large, meaning employing over 500 persons, totalled a mere 18.

Furthermore, of the more than 100 food processing enterprises, about 70% consisted of bakeries, small edible-oil presses and flour mills, mostly family owned and family operated. About 40% of all textile enterprises consisted of small, again family owned, knitting and related outfits. In the wood industry, 80% consisted of sawmills scattered in many rural areas and operated mostly by expatriates. In addition, 50%, 30% and 70% of the enterprises in these three industries respectively had fixed capital assets of less than US$100,000. The point, in brief, is that capitalist production was still infantile and suffered seriously as a result — from structural segmentation.

The fragmentation of foreign capital. Despite the fact that government policy offered foreign investors the most attractive guarantees and the most tempting incentives, international capital remained unimpressed, if not downright disdainful. Western multi-nationals found the country with its backward economy, undeveloped market, negligible investment opportunities, poor infrastructure, unskilled labour force, etc., distinctly unattractive and were quite content to leave whatever small pickings there were to be had to the small expatriate businesses and petty capitalists. According to the Ministry of Commerce and Industry document already noted, 42% of the total paid up capital of manufacturing industry — i.e. about $57.6 million — was foreign owned, with 35%, or $48 million, belonging to the government. The figure does not of course represent the full extent of foreign capital in the country but serves as a measure. The flow of private capital into the country may also serve as another yardstick: between 1954 and 1974, total private capital inflow was valued at $141 million.[33] For comparison, between 1940 and 1960, Liberia attached $420 million in private capital.

To obtain a more realistic picture, one ought to make a distinction between expatriate capital and foreign-based capital. The reason for this is obvious: expatriates were long time residents of the country and, in a good number of cases, obtained their capital and retained their earnings locally. Although to distinguish which is foreign-based and which is expatriate capital in the available records is an impossible task, the point should nevertheless be kept in mind as the empirical evidence is analyzed.

A breakdown of the ownership of foreign capital by country and sectoral distribution brings out clearly two facts: a) that the dominant forces of international capital, and of imperialism, were at best of negligible importance judged by their share of assets in Ethiopian industry; this means that the relation between the country and the dominant external powers was not conditioned by economic considerations and b) that the fragmentation of foreign capital was such as to preclude the control of the domestic economy by external forces.

The list of "foreign" interests involved in manufacturing is fairly long; the holdings and sectoral involvements of the major interests are the following: in first place, Italian capital (both foreign and expatriate) which was involved virtually in all branches of industry, totalled $14 million, followed in second place by Dutch capital (sugar plantation and refinery) with $10.8 million. The rest of the interests were petty: Japanese holdings (textiles, synthetic fibre, tyres, metal) $3.8 million; U.S. (agriculture, food processing) $3.5 million; Greek, foreign and expatriate (in distillery, food processing, textiles, etc.) $3.0 million; British (agriculture mainly) $2.5

million; and Indian (textiles) $1.5 million. Minor interests (Israeli, Scandinavian, West German, Swiss, etc.) were valued at less than one million dollars each.[34]

The basic argument we are posing may now be summed up as follows: first, the empirical evidence reveals that the fragmentation of foreign capital was such that no one interest or economic power had a dominant enough position *to exercise strategic leadership* in production, or in the process of industrialization. Indeed, such strategic leadership *devolved upon the state* on account of its dominance of the economy. Second, the penetration of international capital into the country was distinctly superficial and the preponderance of the pre-capitalist system continued to hold.

The dominance of the state in the economy. As the single most important owner of means of production, the state was the prime mover in all matters related to economic activity. In consequence, indigenous capital could only be peripheral to, and foreign capital, dependent on it. The state here fully emerges as a direct force — a pre-eminent one at that — of accumulation, supplanting or overshadowing all other independent agents of accumulation, including those of foreign origin. Some writers have labelled this the "entrepreneurial state", however the label can have significance only if interpreted politically or seen in terms of power relations.

REFERENCES

1. The following is a partial list of the theoretical literature:
    H. Alavi, "The State in Post-Colonial Societies: Pakistan and Bangladesh", *New Left Review*, No. 74, 1972; Alavi, "State and Class under Peripheral Capitalism" and "The Structure of Peripheral Capitalism", both in Alavi and Shanin (eds.), *Introduction to the Sociology of Developing Societies*, New York, Monthly Review Press, 1982; A. A. Boron, "Latin America: Between Hobbes and Friedmann", *New Left Review*, No. 130, 1981; R. D. Duvall and J. R. Freeman, "The State and Dependent Capitalism", *International Studies Quarterly*, Vol. 25, No. 1, 1981; H. Goulbourne (ed.), *Politics and State in the Third World*, London, Macmillan Press, 1980; W. Hein and K. Stenzel, "The Capitalist State and Under-development in Latin America: The Case of Venezuela", in Goulbourne (ed.); B. Henderson, "The Chilean State after the Coup", *Socialist Register 1977*; S. Langden, "Multinational Corporations and the State in Africa", in J. Willamil (ed.), *Transnational Capitalism and National Development*, Hassocks, Harvest Press, 1979; Colin Leys, *Underdevelopment in Kenya*, London, Heinemann, 1975; Leys, "The 'Overdeveloped' Post Colonial State: A Re-valuation", *Review of African Political Geonomy*, No. 5, 1976; M. Mamdani, *Politics and Class Formation in Uganda*, New York, Monthly Review Press, 1976; R. Munck, *Politics and Dependency in the Third World: The Case of Latin America*, London, Zed Books, 1984; J. Samoff, "Class, Class Conflict and the State in Africa", *Political Science Quarterly*, Vol. 97, Spring 1982; John S. Saul, *The State and Revolution in Eastern Africa*, New York, Monthly Review Press, 1979; I. G. Shivji, *The Class Struggles in Tanzania*, New York, Monthly Review Press, 1976; T. Skocpol, *States and Social Revolutions*, London and New York, Cambridge University Press, 1979; W. Ziemann and M. Lanzendorfer, "The State in Peripheral Societies", *Socialist Register 1977*.

2. Alavi, "State and Class . . .", p.302. This notion has been criticised, though superficially, by Leys (1976), but accepted in substance by almost all.

3. Duvall and Freeman; Langden; Ziemann and Lanzendorfer; Munck and, of course, Alavi.

4. Hein and Stenzel.

5. Goulbourne (Ch.11); Saul in his treatment of the "unsteady state" (esp. p.294).

6. Boron (this work deals in part with Argentina but it was written before the coming to power of Alfonsin); Henderson, though slightly different.

7. The relative autonomy concept has been endorsed by almost all writers, except a few writing on Latin America; Alavi and Saul are its most enthusiastic proponents, but Skocpol (pp.24-33) has argued in favour of more than "relative" autonomy.

8. A. Gramsci: *Selections from the Prison Notebooks*, Q. Hoare and G. N. Smith, trans., New York, International Pub., 1971, p.238.

9. Among the standard political works are: Addis Hiwet: *Ethiopia, from Autocracy to Revolution*, London, R. A. P. E., 1975; C. Clapham: *Haile Selassie's Government*, New York, Praeger, 1969; P. Gilkes: *The Dying Lion, Feudalism and Modernization in Ethiopia*, London, Julian Friedmann, 1975; R. Greenfield: *Ethiopia, A New Political History*, New York, Praeger, 1965; R. Hess: *Ethiopia, the Modernization of Autocracy*, Ithaca, N.Y., Cornell Univ. Pr., 1970; John Markakis: *Ethiopia, Anatomy of a Traditional Polity*, Addis Ababa, Oxford Univ. Press, 1974; L. Mosley: *Haile Selassie, the Conquering Lion*, Englewood Cliffs, Prentice-Hall, 1965; M. Perham: *The Government of Ethiopia*, Evanston, Northwestern Univ. Press, 1969 (1st ed., 1948); P. Schwab: *Decision Making in Ethiopia*, Rutherford, Teaneck, 1972.

10. Clapham, Gilkes and Markakis have described the state as "traditional or feudal autocracy" (Mosley termed it "paternalism"), Addis Hiwet has often used "absolute monarchy", but quite loosely, "constitutionalized absolutism" is Hess's contribution; "feudo-bourgeois monarchy" is the current, official description.

11. London, NLB, 1974 (pp.18-42 and 194 ff.). One example of orthodox interpretation is A. D. Lublinskaya, "The Contemporary Bourgeois Conception of Absolute Monarchy", in Wolpe, ed., below. For an attempt to apply "absolutism" to Ethiopia, see Bahru Zewde, "Economic Origins of the Absolutist State in Ethiopia (1916-1935)", History Dept., AAU, 27-30, 1983.

12. Clapham, who represents the extreme side in this respect, has insisted that in the "imperial system" the emperor, and he alone, constituted the state (see ch.3).

13 For the story of the struggle between monarchy and aristocracy see Mosley. That the state was not the instrument of the nobility was first made within "Ethiopian Marxism" by Henock Kifle, but in the context of "relative autonomy" theory; see his unpublished paper; "Theories of the State in Peripheral Capitalism, a Critique with Reference to the Post War Ethiopian State", Amherst, Mass., Sept. 1980.

14. The fiscal and administrative reforms of the pre-war period severely curtailed the aristocracy's power over the peasantry. The land "reforms" also relieved the rural producers of some of the onerous burdens imposed on them by the landlords. In the immediate post-war period, the state was strengthened by a series of legislation which further eroded the power of the aristocracy. For the early period see Balambaras Mahteme Selassie: *Zikre Negger*, Addis Ababa, 1942 Eth. C. For the post-war legislations, see *Consolidated Laws of Ethiopia*, Addis Ababa, Faculty of Law, Haile Selassie I Univ., 1972.

15. The controversy among Marxists over the Asiatic mode of production (AMP) is still unsettled. Anderson repudiated the theory and suggested that it be given the "decent burial it deserves" (*Lineages . . . ,* pp.462-549). A. Gouldner saw it as an anomaly, "a moment of aborted creativity" in Marxism (*The Two Marxisms*, New York, Seabury Press, 1980, Ch. II). M. Rodinson rejected it as inadequate (*Islam and Capitalism*, New York, Pan-

theon Books, 1973, pp.58-68). On the other hand, the most vigorous defence has come from U. Melotti (*Marx and the Third World*, London, Macmillan, 1977). H. Draper has also added his voice in support: *Karl Marx's Theory of Revolution*, Vol. I, New York, MR Press, 1977 (chs. 21 and 22). M. Godelier accepts the AMP as an important concept but asks that it be purged of certain "dead elements", "The Concept of the 'Asiatic Mode of Production' and Marxist Models of Social Evolution", in D. Seddon (ed.), *Relations of Production*, London, Frank Cass, 1978. For Marx's views, see *Pre Capitalist Economic Formations*, E. J. Hobsbawm, ed., New York, International Publishers, 1965 (hereafter cited as *Formations*).

16. Addis Hiwet suggest the former view, for the latter, F. Halliday and M. Molyneux, *The Ethiopian Revolution*, London, Verso, 1981, pp.69-74. J. Markakis and Nega Ayele have described the economy as "peripheral capitalist", *Class and Revolution in Ethiopia*, Spokesman Books, 1978, ch. 3.

17. *Unequal Development: An Essay in the Social Formation of Peripheral Capitalism*, Hassocks, Harvester Press, 1976, pp.13-26. For the articulation debate, see H. Wolpe (Ed.), *The Articulation of Modes of Production*, London, Routledge, 1980, esp. introductory essay.

18. *Capital*, Vol. 3, Penguin edn., 1981: "The establishment of capitalism in a social formation necessarily implies the transformation, and in some sense the destruction of formerly dominant modes of production", (Wolpe, p. 93). How absurd! If this were true, one would not be talking about "social formation" or "articulation".

19. *Ibid.*, p.449 our emphasis. Ch. 20 of this volume, and in vol. 2 (any edition), ch. 1, section II, and ch. IV are also relevant.

20. I have discussed this and the land system in general in my *Agrarian Reform in Ethiopia*, Uppsala, Scandinavian Institute of African Studies, 1984, Section 2. For the literature on the land system see bibliography in this work.

21. There is a fairly extensive literature on pastoralism, but the list here is partial as we have left out ethnographic studies, works relating to the treatment of pastoralists by public and private agencies, articles in journals, etc. *East African Pastoralism*, Addis Ababa, I.L.C.A., (?) 1977; T. Monod (ed.), *Pastoralism in Tropical Africa*, London, Oxford Univ. Pr., 1975; *Pastoral Production and Society*, London, Cambridge Univ. Pr., 1979. All three are proceedings of international conferences bringing together the works of distinguished scholars on the subject. Each contains one or more articles on Ethiopian pastoralism, and also an extensive bibliography. U. Almagor, *Pastoral Partners*, Manchester, Manchester Univ. Prs., 1978; C. Carr, *Pastoralism in Crisis*, Chicago, Chicago Univ. Prs., 1977. Both these are about the Dassenetch for Geleb of south-west Ethiopia. N. Cossins, *Green Heart of a Dying Land: A Study of the New Cotton Wealth of the Old Afar Sultanate of Aussa*, Unpublished ms., Addis Ababa, 1973; Cossins, *No Way to Live: A Study of the Afar Clans of the North-East Rangelands Area of Ethiopia*, Addis Ababa, 1972. Both prepared for Livestock and Meat Board (LMB). J. Helland, *Five Essays on the Study of Pastoralists and the Development of Pastoralism*, Bergen, Univ. of Bergen (Norway), 1980; includes articles on the Boran and Afar. Livestock and Meat Board (LMB), *Southern Rangelands Livestock Development Project. Part II, Studies and Surveys, Vol 2, Sociology and Pastoral Economy, Summary Report*, Rome, Agrotec, 1974. LMB, *Ibid. Appendix I, Borana Plateau, Appendix 2, Western Somali Lowlands. Ibid., Relief and Rehabilitation Commission: A Study of Nomadic Areas for Settlement. Study Report, Parts I, II, and III*, Addis Ababa, Sept. 1974.

22. For the debate on pastoralism, see *Pastoral Production* . . .For Marx's view, *Formations*, pp.88-89.

23. *Passages*, pp.217-228; the quotation on p.218 and 219 respectively. For a similar argument, see introductory essay in *Pastoral Production*. It is curious that Amin is silent about pastoralism, although this form of economic life is very widespread in many parts of the Third World.

24. C. Carr in her study of the pastoralist Dassenech (or Geleb) of the Omo delta, describes pastoralism as a "primitive mode of production"; see the analysis in ch. 5 of her book.

25. Cossins, whose studies of the Afar are most informative, characterized Afar society as a cluster of semi-anarchic individuals.

26. Only a few references will be given here, leaving out ethnographic and socio-linguistic works, articles, etc. For an extended bibliography see M. L. Bender (ed.), *The Non-Semitic Languages of Ethiopia*, East Lansing, Mich., African Studies Center, Michigan State Univ., 1976. Also, each of the articles in Donham and James (eds.) contains lengthy references. D. L. Donham and W. James (eds.), *Working Papers on Society and History in Imperial Ethiopia: The Southern Periphery from the 1880s to 1974*, Cambridge (England), African Studies Center, June 1980. I have borrowed the term "peripheral" from this work. F. J. Simons, *Northwest Ethiopia: Peoples and Economy*, Madison, 1960 (for the Gumuz of Gonder province). I. A. Strecker, *Selected Aspects of Socio-Economic Organization in Southern Gamu Goffa*, a Report Submitted to the Southern Gamu Goffa Design Team (USAID), Addis Ababa, Oct. 1976; Strecker, *Traditional Life and Prospects for Socio-Economic Development in the Hamer Administrative District of Southern Gamu Goffa*, a Report to the Relief and Rehabilitation Commission, Addis Ababa, 1976; A. R. Tippett, *Peoples of Southwest Ethiopia*, South Pasadena, William Carey Library, 1970. For an introduction to the area and the people, see E. Cerulli, *Peoples of South-West Ethiopia and its Borderland*, London: International African Institute, 1956. For a cultural history of the people, J. S. Trimingham, *Islam in Ethiopia*, London, Frank Cass, 1965 (1st edn. 1952).

27. *Formation*, esp. pp.75-80. We disagree with the position held by some that it is pastoral society that resembles the Germanic community — see *Pastoral Production* . . .

28. Strecker, RRC Report, p. 102-3.

29. The literature on the subject includes: — CSO, *Advance Report on the 1972-73 Rural Survey of Cottage and Handicraft Industries*, Addis Ababa, April 1975. Ministry of Commerce and Industry, *Report on a Seminar on Small-Scale, Cottage and Handicraft Industries*, Addis Ababa, Sept. 1975. HASSIDA, *Report on a Survey of Small Scale Industries in Eleven Towns (1976-77)*, Addis Ababa, March 1979. ILO, *Report to the Government of Ethiopia on Handicraft and Small Scale Industries*, Geneva, 1964. D. Karsten, *The Economics of Handicrafts in Traditional Societies: An Investigation in Sidamo and Gemu Goffa Province, Southern Ethiopia*, Munchen, Weltforum Verlag, 1972. Planning Commission Office, *The Third Five Year Plan: An Assessment and Implementation Report, Vol. II, Annex I - VII*, Addis Ababa, Oct. 1973 (Annex V for Handicrafts), hereafter cited as PCO document.

30. Karsten, p.133.

31. D. Levine, *Greater Ethiopia: The Evolution of a Multi-Ethnic Society*, Chicago, Chicago Univ. Pr., 1974; the classification appears on pp. 33-39.

32. The evidence for what follows is based on the following:— Ministry of Commerce and Industry and C.S.O., *Survey of Manufacturing Industry 1971/72*, Addis Ababa, August 1975; unpublished document, C.S.O., *Statistical Abstracts 1975*, Addis Ababa, 1975. Planning Commission Office, *op. cit.*, (P.C.O).

33. Computed from PCO document, and "The Balance of Payments Constraint and Economic Development in Ethiopia", *Market Report*, Commercial Bank of Ethiopia, March - April 1975.

34. Befekadu Degefe gives slightly different figures; see his "Industrialization, Investment Policy and Foreign Capital in Ethiopia 1950-1974", *Proceedings of the Seminar on Industrial Transformation*, Held in Nazareth, January 18-20, 1980. Institute of Development Research, July 1983.

SOME LEADING ISSUES OF RURAL TRANSFORMATION

IN ETHIOPIA

Fassil G. Kiros

INTRODUCTION

The contents of this short paper might be described as reflections on development. They are based on experiences which are quite familiar to students of development and practitioners alike. It is believed that the broad outline that this paper endeavours to provide can play a useful purpose at this stage of transitional development of Ethiopia. It might help minimize the hazard of confusion always present in the intricate process of socio-economic change. For, under such circumstances, it is possible at times to confuse symptoms with basic ills, causes with consequences, means with ends. Hence the modest contribution of this paper may be to help regain perspective, whose contours may otherwise be blurred in the turbulent environment of socio-economic change.

The development problems that face a country like Ethiopia are many, and they are highly intractable. This paper will draw attention to only a few of those basic issues which pertain in the first instance to the question of rural transformation.[1] How is it possible to separate such basic issues from all other development issues? This question is not easy to answer under the circumstances of a developing country which suffers little from the dearth of development problems.

Indeed, there is likely to be disagreement about the ranking of the issues. To some, the politically minded in particular, the leading issues may appear to be those which, if unresolved, might threaten political stability. To others, the students of development in particular, the leading issues would appear to be those whose resolution, or the lack of it, would likely influence the course and tempo of future development. To one the criterion is the present and the immediate future, to the other the long-term future. This paper is oriented toward the latter perspective. Nonetheless, by the general criterion of the student of development alone, many issues are likely to compete for "leadership". Hence, one of the contributions of this short paper might be to trigger a debate on the question of which development issues constitute the most basic in the circumstances of Ethiopia today. However, it is important to bear in mind that all development issues are interlinked in one way or another. No matter the issues to be considered, all other issues are likely to lurk in the background.

What then are those issues of rural transformation outlined in this paper? The first among them has to be with the question of reconciling the aim of long-term development with the immediate needs of raising the level of living of the population. Second is the issue of institutional transformation in agriculture. Third is the problem of utilization of human and material resources. Fourth is the problem of devising development strategies appropriate to the highly diverse conditions prevailing in the rural environment. And fifth is the danger posed by the pathology of bureaucratization. As indicated above, it will be found that other issues are subsumed within those stated, some of which may surface in the course of our discussions.

LONG TERM DEVELOPMENT AND MEETING BASIC NEEDS

Ethiopia, like many developing countries is committed to long-term socio-economic development and to the urgent task of improving the level of the population. These are fundamental goals. However, a basic question that often arises is whether and under what conditions both goals can be realized.

Long-term development requires the generation of surplus beginning at an early stage. Most of the surplus in the circumstances of countries such as Ethiopia must come from the peasant sector whose production constitutes a large part of the Gross Domestic Product (GDP).

Poverty, however, weighs heavily on the peasant population and it is the peasantry which frequently suffers from the scourge of famine. How then can surplus be extracted from the peasant sector without, as it were, killing the "goose that lays the golden egg"?

The question becomes problematic because countries on the road of socialist development tend to attach importance to the long-term transformation of peasant agriculture on which the development of all other sectors depends. The basic dilemma of the transition must however be resolved. The key for its resolution lies in the recognition of the fact that in the case of the large segment of the rural population of Ethiopia, improvement of the level of living would only mean the alleviation of deep poverty and suffering. The opportunity cost of the measures required for this purpose does not consist of "surplus" foregone. For, the latter is virtually non-existent under the conditions of mass poverty which prevail today.

It is not difficult to see that the extraction of much surplus from the peasant sector is almost impossible under the conditions prevailing in Ethiopia today. Surplus can be generated only if productivity increases, and in the circumstances of Ethiopia this can result from "increased consumption" as it does from investment as conventionally understood.

Hence, in the initial stage of development, priority should be assigned to the task of alleviating poverty. This strategy of endeavouring to improve the living conditions of the rural population might be understood as an "enabling strategy" of development. The approach accepts the fact that rural transformation is a long-term process but that the process can only be sustained by "motivation" from within. Such motivation can result from the initial improvement of the conditions of life.

In essence, the "enabling strategy" of development is a strategy which aims to enhance the physical capability of rural man and to stimulate his creative powers so that he is enabled to become himself the agent of development. Such a strategy can better motivate rural man to bear the costs and the sacrifice of development.

The question might be raised as to where the resources would be acquired to provide the initial stimulus. Such a question can certainly not be taken to imply that the society entirely lacks the necessary resources for this purpose. Furthermore, it must be realized that being a late-comer in the development sphere has not been devoid of any advantage whatsoever. One can rightfully state that perhaps at no time in world history have nations been more inclined to support the cause of development than in the last few decades. A common desire to alleviate poverty in developing countries prevails today. There is, therefore, no compelling reason in every situation to strive to "raise oneself by one's own bootstraps" as it were. This statement is made with full awareness of the debate of "dependency vs. self-reliance" which has preoccupied many students of development. It is felt that there is nothing inherent in international aid that will inevitably lead to "dependence" or that will of necessity undermine "self-reliance". It all depends on the type of assistance and how effectively it is put to use. Careful planning and intelligent use of external resources can lead to increasing surplus generation without necessarily further impoverishing the rural poor.

THE ISSUE OF INSTITUTIONAL TRANSFORMATION IN AGRICULTURE

It is well known that peasant production in Ethiopia continues to be dominated by family based subsistence production. On average, probably no more than 10% of each peasant household's produce finds its way to the market. There is therefore hardly any question about the necessity to alter this primitive self-sufficient mode of production. The issue that we address ourselves to here is not concerned about the desirability of institutional transformation of peasant agriculture. The issue rather is how well to achieve such transformation.

Probably no other issue has been as fundamental as the issue of "socialist transformation" of agriculture in predominantly peasant societies. The first country to confront it was, of course, Russia. The specific aspects of the issue have to do with its importance and urgency in the face of the likely slow process of change that is attainable, the temptation to apply political pressure and coercion where such an approach might impede steady progress, and the emphasis on ideology and rhetoric where the problem requires greater practical skill in the translation of words into action.

Perhaps no other than Lenin himself has shown greater appreciation of this issue:

> We know very well that in countries where small peasant farming prevails the transition to socialism cannot be effected except by a series of gradual preliminary stages . . . We fully realize that such tremendous changes in the lives of tens of millions of people as the transition from small individual peasant farming to collective farming, affecting as they do the most deep-going roots of the peasants' way of life and their mores, can only be accomplished by long effort and only when necessity compels people to re-shape their lives.[2]

In the case of Ethiopia, measures have already been taken in the creation of mass organizations in the agricultural sector consisting of the peasant associations and their service cooperatives. These new institutions are transitional in character since they constitute associations whose members are individual cultivators, the ultimate end sought being the creation of producers' cooperatives. Judging from the functions assigned to them however, it would be correct to regard the peasant associations and the service cooperatives as "schools for peasant cooperation". Among the powers and duties of the peasant associations defined by the "Proclamation to provide for the Consolidation of Peasant Associations" are the following:

Every peasant association formed at any level shall have the powers and duties to:

1. in cooperation with those concerned, *agitate, educate, coordinate the peasantry* and render the necessary assistance thereto with a view to expanding and strengthening agricultural producers' cooperatives which are the bases for socialist construction in rural areas;

2. *agitate, educate and coordinate the peasantry*, with a view to liberating it from backwardness, by establishing and strengthening agricultural service cooperatives, increasing production and expanding social services . . . ;

3. in cooperation with the appropriate government and mass organizations, coordinate the peasantry and make the necessary efforts for the betterment of the lives of peasants living in lands that are overpopulated or of poor productivity and that of nomads;

4. in cooperation with those concerned, *coordinate the peasantry with a view to liberating it from archaic modes of production and backward practices and cultures* by advancing its ideological outlook and developing its initiative and thereby enhance productivity; render the necessary assistance thereto,

5. follow-up and supervise the proper tilling and development of cultivable land and the augmentation of production;

6. in cooperation with those concerned, make the necessary participation in the effort *to enable the peasantry to gain rapid progress in education, health, transport and similar social services* . . .

7. *participate fully in the effort to satisfy the educational needs of the peasantry*; implement plans devised to this effect by the Government from time to time . . .[3]

The service cooperatives too have been assigned functions which are designed to stimulate initial cooperation among the peasantry. Their functions include the following:

1. to procure crop expansion services;
2. to market the produce of members at fair prices;
3. to give loans at fair interest rates;
4. to give storage and savings services;
5. to supply consumer goods to the members according to their needs;
6. to give education in socialist philosophy and cooperative work in order to enhance the political consciousness of the peasantry;
7. to supply improved agricultural implements and provide tractor services . . .;
8. to give flour mill services;
9. to organize craftsmen in order to promote cottage industry; and
10. to provide political education with a view to establishing agricultural producers' cooperative societies by forming, promoting and consolidating mutual aid teams like *debo* . . .[4]

Now all this is fine. And if the "schools of cooperation" do carry out their duties, there is little doubt that they would facilitate promotion of the peasantry to the stage of producers' cooperatives as envisaged by the "Policy on Agricultural Producers' Cooperatives".[5] The issue that is being raised here is however whether the full potential of these transitional associations is being realized. How effectively can the development of producers' cooperatives be motivated by dint of example resulting from participation in peasant associations or service cooperatives? How are the functions of peasant associations or service cooperatives monitored? How is it ensured that these institutions respond to the felt needs of the peasantry? And how closely do the individual peasants in turn identify themselves with the objectives of their organizations?

Certainly, the role that peasants organizations have played in many areas cannot be overemphasised. The purpose of raising these questions is only to direct greater attention to the pivotal role that the mass organizations can play in the transformation of peasant agriculture in Ethiopia. Left to themselves, they may not achieve their function of promoting producers' cooperatives in reasonable time. Indeed, in the experience of Russia for example, Lenin tells us that:

> . . . it has frequently happened that the communes have only succeeded in provoking a negative attitude among the peasantry, and the word 'commune' has at times become a call to fight communism . . .[6]

As Goran Hyden has argued, it would be well to remember that the peasantry in Africa has the power of eluding capture. "Small is powerful in Africa", wrote Hyden, "because it is sustained by an active peasant mode of production with its own alternative economy".[7] Hence, the peasant association model of Ethiopia must be seen as an experiment to overpower a system of production which has continued to resist change elsewhere in Africa.

THE PROBLEM OF RESOURCE UTILIZATION

The most basic resources of a rural society are the people, the land, and all the animate and inanimate forces emanating from the land. These basic resources are unfortunately pitifully under-employed.

It is generally assumed that something around 45% of the potential labour force is either unemployed or underemployed in countries like Ethiopia. Although the accuracy of this figure may be questioned, it does indicate the likely order of magnitude of unemployment and underemployment that may exist in these countries. This is a fundamental problem in all developing countries, and must be considered even more so in "socialist" societies where labour power is taken to be the only source of surplus value.

The approach for dealing with this basic problem will depend on the analysis of the nature of underemployment. We can in this regard gain useful insight from the analysis of Karl Marx. Marx tells us that the magnitude of surplus value (and of the price of labour power) are determined by three circumstances: (1) the length of the working day or the extensive magnitude of labour; (2) the normal intensity of labour, or its intensive magnitude; and (3) the productiveness of labor dependent on the development of the conditions of production.[8]

How might these circumstances be interpreted in the situation of rural Ethiopia? Let us consider the case of the extensive magnitude of labor. It may be more pertinent in the case of peasant production to speak of the length of the working year instead of the length of the working day. It is well known that a substantial segment of the work-year is unutilized in many parts of rural Ethiopia due, among other things, to religious holidays and social ceremonies. One study, for instance, has found that in some parts of the country 37% of the work-year was unutilized due to religious holidays and social functions alone.[9]

The need for extending the working year is, therefore, readily appreciated. This may however be difficult to realize in a short time given the tenacity of beliefs, especially in the celebration of religious holidays. This author once asked a sample of peasants, as part of a major rural survey, whether they would be prepared to work on certain religious holidays, on which they had never worked before, if His Holiness the Patriarch (Head of the Ethiopian Orthodox Church) were to grant it. Many of the respondents answered in the negative. Then the following question was put to one peasant: "Why would you not accept the authority of the Patriarch regarding this matter?". His prompt answer was that a Patriarch who advocated violation of religious holidays should be allowed to be Patriarch no more! Clearly, this indicates the difficulty that is likely to be encountered in the attempt to change established beliefs. There is however little doubt that the change will take place in the course of the transformation of rural society. In the first place it must be realized that not all religious holidays are celebrated with equal fervour in all communities. Furthermore, experience shows that many former believers have begun to give up the celebration of certain religious holidays when taking up occupations in industry or in Government. Fasting, too, has often become a thing of the past once such people become a part of a new environment.

It is also important to recognize that there are other social functions which may be reformed or adjusted with much less resistance on the part of the peasantry. It might be a wise policy to focus attention on these phenomena, not only because the chances of success are better, but also because such success can pave the way for better results in the attempt to alter the more deeply rooted cultural beliefs.

The intensive magnitude of labor is difficult to measure. It might be possible to make a judgement that the magnitude of energy expended per unit of time is relatively high under conditions of factory production, where the worker performs repetitive machine-paced operations. In contrast, it is not difficult to observe that certain occupations (bureaucratic occupations for example) especially in developing countries are not always taxing, it may sometimes be possible to eliminate an entire post without adding much strain of work on those workers that remain.

The drudgery involved under the conditions of peasant production is likely to demand much exertion during certain phases of the production cycle. This may however not be comparable to the demands of many hours a day of repetitive activity over a period of many months in an iron foundry, for example. Yet, given the poor physical condition of the average peasant producer owing to dietary deficiency, it would be too optimistic under prevailing conditions to expect the sustained outpouring of labour-power for land cultivation. While this point might be debatable, there may at least be agreement on the fact that there is no certainty as in the case of factory work that the normal intensity of labor will be consistently high under the conditions of family-based peasant production. Here therefore is again a case for making "workers" the "peasants".

It hardly needs to be repeated that the productiveness of labor is extremely low under the conditions of peasant production. This is explained by the primitive instruments of production employed by the peasantry. There may however be many other factors that determine the productiveness of labor, factors which will not be discussed here.

It is clear from the above that a chronic problem of unemployment and underemployment of labor prevails in countries such as Ethiopia. It must be appreciated that unemployed labor is latent surplus. Nor is this only to invoke the "labor theory of value". As Nyerere has said:

> We don't need to read Karl Marx or Adam Smith to find out that neither the land nor the hoe actually produces wealth. And we don't need to take degrees in Economics to know that neither the worker nor the landlord produces land. Land is God's gift to man — it is always there. But we do know, still without degrees in Economics, that the axe and the plough were produced by the labourer. Some of our more sophisticated friends apparently have to undergo the most rigorous intellectual training simply in order to discover that stone axes were produced by that ancient gentleman 'Early Man' to make it easier for him to skin the impala he had just killed with a club, which he had also made for himself.[10]

But that which Nyerere refers to as "God's gift to man" is also underemployed. One popularly quoted figure by students of economics in Ethiopia has been that only about 11% of the potentially arable land of the country is being utilized. Nobody can vouch today that this figure is accurate. It matters little however if one chooses to double or even triple the number.

Why is the land unutilized? Part of the answer lies in the pattern of the geographical distribution of the population. The distribution of the population of Ethiopia is approximately as shown in Table 1. The regional distribution of the population is therefore uneven. Large variations are found within each region and sub-region as well. It is recognized of course that arable

TABLE 1

Regional Distribution of the Population of Ethiopia

Region	Number	Density Persons per km^2
Arsi	1,662,223	67.6
Bale	1,006,491	7.8
Eritrea	2,704,000*	23.0
Gamo Gofa	1,248,034	31.1
Gonder	2,905,362	39.6
Gojam	3,244,882	50.4
Harerghe	4,151,706	16.3
Ilubabor	963,327	19.0
Kefa	2,450,369	46.2
Shewa	8,090,585	94.6
Sidamo	3,790,579	32.5
Tigrai	2,409,700	36.7
Welega	2,369,677	33.9
Welo	3,609,918	45.7
Addis Ababa	1,412,575	7063
Total	42,019,418	34.3

* Includes Asab Administration.

Source: Population figures were obtained from *Population and Housing Census, Preliminary Report*, Central Statistics Office (ESO), 1984, p.15; Area of Administrative Regions were obtained from *Statistical Abstract*, CSO, 1980.

land is not evenly distributed, so that it may be argued that the density of the population would tend to vary reflecting the presence or absence of such land. Alas! This has not been shown to be the case. Certainly, it is not possible to argue that the density of the population of Wello and Tigrai is relatively high and that of Bale low because the former abound in fertile land while the latter does not.

There is clearly a case for a policy of resettlement of much of the population of rural Ethiopia. The issue is not that the need for a resettlement policy is not recognized. It is rather that there are social and cultural, political and ethnic, and economic and financial problems associated with the task of human resettlement. This calls for a long-term national strategy and for careful planning aiming to attain more full and effective utilization of two of the most basic resources — land and labor.

The special problem of the settlement of nomadic and semi-nomadic people must also be given a central position in Ethiopia. It is recognized that there are those who propose a "rationalisation program" for nomadic activity instead of the settlement of the people. This however cannot be accepted as a long-term solution to the problem. This segment of our population, whose number is unknown, endures harsh and precarious conditions of existence. This situation alone is sufficient to justify economic and financial sacrifice to enable nomadic people in time to lead a settled life. There is, however, more to it than this. The nomadic people of Ethiopia control a substantial portion of the large herds for which the country is reputed (Table 2). This immense potential resource will continue to be poorly utilized, and many even gradually be decimated by persistent natural calamity, unless nomadic herding gives way to settled husbandry.

The settlement of nomadic people however calls for even more careful planning. In the first place, we know very little about the nomadic people of Ethiopia. What is their number? What is their pattern of movement? What is the appropriate strategy that must be pursued in habituating nomadic people to settled living? These are basic questions and must be answered satisfactorily if settlement is to be carried out with any degree of success. And "success" is important in settlement and resettlement activity, for otherwise future efforts are certain to meet strong resistance.

NEED FOR RELEVANT STRATEGIES OF RURAL DEVELOPMENT

The economic and social landscape of rural Ethiopia is extremely variegated. Agro-ecological conditions, systems of production, and social circumstances vary widely even within relatively restricted geographical areas. Broadly speaking, the systems of production include seed-farming, inset-planting, and pastoral complexes. Each one of these categories is assumed to contain many sub-systems.[11]

TABLE 2

Estimates of the Ethiopian National and Nomadic Herd ('000)			
Types of Animals	National	Nomadic	Percent Noma-dic/National
Cattle	26350	6350	24
Sheep	21280	4890	23
Goats	15850	5170	33
Equines	6730	1350	20
Camels	1000	1000	100

Source: *The Nomadic Areas of Ethiopia, Study Report*, UNDP, RRC, 1984, Part III B, Average computed from the 4 reports summarized in Table 7, p.29.

The fact that the rural sector consists of heterogeneous production systems indicates that no single approach of development can be equally relevant in all rural areas. The prevailing problems of production, and the potential of future development differ from region to region. Under such circumstances, the overall approach of rural development would have to be one that seeks to respond to the problems and needs in particular regions and communities.

In the past, certain rural development projects, an outstanding example of which was the Chilalo Agricultural Development Unit (now Arsi Rural Development Unit), were initiated in Ethiopia with a long term aim to replicate the development experiences gained there to other parts of the country. Such a strategy could have, however, only limited success under the varied conditions of peasant agriculture in Ethiopia. The particular experience gained in one region may have no direct relevance to another region. Indeed, a survey undertaken in the Chilalo *Awraja* itself has shown that the conditions of production within that area are highly varied:

> Comparison of the farm tables reveals considerable differences in cropping patterns reflecting [the] gradation. For example, local barley is grown in all areas, but the proportion of the total cropped area under this cereal steadily increases with increasing altitude, as does the proportion of farmers who cultivate it. The mean area per farm under barley also bears a positive relationship to altitude rank. Maize and *teff* were not found at all in [some areas] and the percentage of total acreage devoted to both crops . . . the percentage of farmers growing these two crops . . . and the fields of both crops tend to [vary]. Wheat provides another example.[12]

Hence, a rural development strategy which is based on the delivery of a few standard inputs of production risks a chance of failure. Studies in Ethiopia have shown in fact that "agricultural development packages" devised outside the specific rural milieu may be incongruent with the actual need. In a survey undertaken in Ada *Wereda*, for example, it was found that there was inconsistency between the types of inputs delivered to the peasants and the perception of what the latter considered to be the actual problems of production for which solutions were required. (Compare Tables 3 and 4.)

This has two important implications. One is that because of the absence of even rudimentary information about the conditions and problems of production, there is clear need to involve the producers themselves in the identification of problems and in the setting of priorities. There is no intention here to dwell upon the desirability of the participatory approach of development. It must be pointed out however that in practice participation has been limited to the involvement of the peasantry in the "implementation" of rural development activity rather than in the planning of it. As emphasized by Lenin:

> The idea of building a communist society exclusively with the hands of the communists is childish, absolutely childish. We communists are but a drop in the ocean, a drop in the ocean of the people. We shall be able to lead the people along the road we have chosen only if we correctly determine it not only from the standpoint of its direction in World History but also determine it for our own native land, for our own country . . . [otherwise] the peasants will say: 'You are splendid fellows, you defended our country. That is why we obeyed you. But if you cannot run the show, get out!' Yes, that is what the peasants will say.[13]

The second implication has to do with the research-*cum*-experimentation strategy which needs to be followed in countries such as Ethiopia. First, a rural development research system would need to be evolved correspondingly to the prevailing agro-ecological and production systems of the country as best as these can be defined at present. The Institute of Agricultural Research follows such an approach on a limited scale. What is called for however is a more comprehensive system of research geared toward meeting the long-term requirements of the various regions and sub-regions of the country. Secondly, the research system that is needed might be one characterized as an "open" system. This means research which in the first instance is much less preoccupied than has been the case in the past with the search of the "miracle" varieties of grain seeds and animal breeds, but is more broadly aimed at "rural development". This means research into the socio-cultural, technological, and institutional as well as the economic aspects of development. The term "open" system is also used to indicate an approach which does not erect a wall around itself separating it from the rural society within which it functions. One often hears agricultural researchers speak of yields obtained under the "conditions of the researcher" as contrasted with those obtained under the "conditions of the peasant". It is suggested here that there is at present only one relevant condition of production and that is the peasant condition of production. The initial challenge to the researcher is how to increase production under that condition, thereby to augment the surplus required for long-term rural transformation and national development.

TABLE 3

Problems of Agricultural Production as Perceived by the Peasantry	
Problems	Percent Respondents Ranking Problem as 1 and 2
Pests	64.8
Weeds	58.0
Wild Animals	38.3
Climatic Variation	14.9
Decline in Soil Fertility	7.2
Others	3.4

Source: Fassil G. Kiros, "Search for Alternatives of Agricultural Development Strategy Under Varied Conditions of Peasant Agriculture in Ethiopia — A Case Study in Ada *Wereda, Ethiopian Journal of Agricultural Science*, Vol.2, No.2, June 1980, p.119.

TABLE 4

Extent of Use of Selected Inputs in the Survey Area	
Inputs	Percent Respondents Reporting Usage at least once
Fertilizer	68.8
"Improved" seeds	12.9
Pesticides	20.3
Herbicides	7.1

Source: Fassil G. Kiros, *Ibid.*

THE "PATHOLOGY OF INSTITUTION BUILDING"

The title of this section of the paper is borrowed from Dan Mudoola, who had coined it in connection with the problem of over-bureaucratization in Tanzania. As that author has put it:

> The fetish for institution-building has created problems of over-bureaucratization. Because the State seeks to penetrate many areas of socio-economic and political life, it has created an atmosphere governed by bureaucracies. To enumerate a few — there are the Party, Government, mass organizations and parastatal bureaucracies, in addition to the bureaucracies of the armed and security forces. This degree of bureaucratization may create a situation where these organizations may seek to serve and service interests which are peculiar to themselves at the extreme expense of the goals for which they have been established and may lead to inter- and intra-bureaucratic conflicts that again may lead to institutional immobilisme.[14]

The relatively rapid expansion of the State machinery in Africa is explained by the fact that the State in these countries assumes major responsibility for national development. As stated above, a problem which is of serious concern in this relation is the "bureaucratic malaise" which more often than not accompanies the expansion of the State sector. Many of the new institutions absorb a substantial part of the national budget, but their contribution to national development is often very much in doubt. Indeed, some of these institutions are not only inefficient, but often become the breeding ground for corruption and wasteful practices.

The expansion of the State sector is obviously greatest in those developing countries which follow the socialist road of development. Rarely are such institutions the result of careful planning . They are often created *pro forma* with little effort at adaptation to the needs and circumstances prevailing in particular countries. And once created, such institutions soon become part of the established order and grow relatively rapidly, feeding vampire-like on the limited public resources and leaving only a reduced amount for investment in production activities.

The particular concern here is, of course, the problem of bureaucratization as it pertains to rural development. In Ethiopia, one of the dramatic developments in recent years has been the great number of Governmental institutions and mass organizations that have been created. Many of these bodies have a role to play in rural development. Each is usually organized hierarchically from a head office in Addis Ababa down to the level of the *Awraja, Wereda* or even lower. Each operates according to its own administrative rules. But for most the target to be served is the rural population. The basic issue that must be faced has therefore to do with how the existing institutional infrastructure can be made to serve the goal of rural transformation and national development effectively and economically. This calls for a systematic and critical evaluation of the system as a whole, bearing in mind the conditions that prevail in the present and the needs of future development.

Most important in terms of the long-term requirements is the introduction of planning in the sphere of institution-building. Many questions can be answered in the process of such planning. What can a new institution perform better than existing institutions? What are the costs and what are the benefits? What are the critical linkages envisaged with other institutions or mass organizations and how are they to be made more effective? How well and on what basis have the detailed *modus operandi* been designed? What is the projected level of long-term institutional growth and what are the determining factors and objectives of such growth? These and other questions can be answered through a system of planned institutional development. And as implied above, the earlier such a system is introduced the better, for institutions have the capacity to endure long after they have outlived their usefulness.

CONCLUDING REMARKS

The aim of this paper has been to rethink experience and by this to help regain perspective in dealing with some of the basic issues of rural transformation confronting countries such as Ethiopia. The issues pertaining to rural transformation are many and are likely to be highly intractable. However, an attempt has been made to indicate the approaches for dealing with those basic issues raised in this paper.

Hence, it is suggested firstly that, under the conditions of mass poverty that prevail in countries such as Ethiopia, the need to provide for the basic necessities of life becomes a matter of great urgency, since no sustainable long-term development is otherwise attainable. Nor is this proposition to be taken as a plea for a "social welfare" program for rural society, but rather as an "enabling strategy" of development designed to stimulate and motivate a process of dynamic socio-economic change. Secondly, in the case of institutional transformation of peasant agriculture, there is need to take full advantage of the achievements scored thus far, thereby to generate the economic surplus that is required for the building of the future society. Thirdly, although the problem of underutilization of human and material resources is at the heart of the development problem, it rarely seems to be addressed directly and effectively in many developing countries. Here, there is need to design and implement what may be referred to as a "resource-based" strategy of development aiming to make full and efficient use of the basic resources which in a poor country consist of land and labor. The "resource-based" strategy is also relevant in dealing with the fourth problem, which pertains to the highly varied agro-ecological and social conditions prevailing in the rural sector. This situation calls for a development approach designed to deal with the particular conditions and circumstances which manifest themselves in various areas. There is here need to resist the temptation to apply simple and uniform solutions to complex and dissimilar development problems. And finally, capacity-building is imperative in order to deal effectively with the many facets of the development challenge. There is,however, need to avoid the danger of overbureaucratization. A *planned approach* of institution-building is called for, especially in countries which pursue the socialist path of development. Indeed, all the issues identified in this paper point to the need to pay greater attention to the task of planning. It may be argued that the current socio-economic crisis in Africa has not been due to the failure to accept *development* as a dominant national goal, but has rather been due to the ineffectiveness of the means employed in pursuing this goal, i.e. due to weakness in planning or the lack of commitment to a planned process of socio-economic change.

NOTES

1. No attempt is made here to provide any special definition of "rural transformation" but only the suggestion that such a process is the fundamental requisite for national development in countries such as Ethiopia and necessitates coordinated economic, social, political, institutional and technological changes.

2. Lenin, *On the Socialist Transformation of Agriculture*, Novosti Press Agency Publishing House, Moscow, 1975, pp.187-88.

3. Peasant Associations Consolidation Proclamation No.223 of 1982, Provisional Military Administrative Council (P.M.A.C.).

4. Peasant Associations Organization and Consolidation Proclamation No.71 of 1975, PMAC.

5. *Policy on Agricultural Producers' Cooperatives*, Provisional Military Administrative Council, Addis Ababa, June 1979.

6. Lenin, *op. cit.*, p.202.

7.   Goran Hyden, *Beyond Ujama in Tanzania, Underdevelopment and an Uncaptured Peasantry*, Heineman, London, p.33.

8.   Karl Marx, *Capital*, Vol.1, Progress Publishers, Moscow, Chapter XVII.

9.   Fassil G. Kiros, "An Estimate of the Proportion of the Potential Work-Year Allocated to Socio-Cultural Observances in Rural Ethiopia", *Ethiopian Journal of Development Research*, vol.2, No.2, Oct. 1976.

10.   Julius Nyerere, *Ujama, Essays on Socialism*, Oxford University Press, London, 1968, p.4.

11.   E. Westphal, *Agricultural Systems in Ethiopia*, Center for Agricultural Publishing and Documentation, Wageningen, 1976.

12.   Gerald J. Gill, *Farm Technology Pilot Survey*, Research Report No.23, Institute of Development Research, Addis Ababa University, pp.13-18.

13.   Lenin, *op. cit.*, pp.71-72.

14.   Dan Mudoola, "The Pathology of Institution-Building — The Tanzanian Case" in *Challenging Rural Poverty*, Fassil G. Kiros (ed.), Africa World Press, 1985.

ADDIS ABABA UNIVERSITY:

A STUDY OF AN INSTITUTION 1961-1981

Fisseha Haile

INTRODUCTION

This paper presents an overview history of Addis Ababa University from 1961-1981. The paper deals mainly with:

a) early stages of the University development (1950-1960),
b) the period between 1961-1974 (pre-revolution),
c) the growth and development aspect of the University program, and
d) the development aspect after the revolution.

The paper was part of a research study conducted to determine the "institutionality" of Addis Ababa University. For the purpose of the study, institution refers to organizations staffed with personnel capable of carrying out defined but evolving programs, contributing to social and economic development and having continuing resource and application of new methods and values (Balse 1973: 255).

The Academic Institution-Building Model (AIBM) was the research framework used. The study considered both the internal mechanisms and the external linkages of the University, using pertinent variables to classify information.

Hence, the model and variables that were selected to discuss and analyze the data to determine the institutionality of Addis Ababa University are presented below:

Institutional Variables	Mission Fulfilment	Environmental Linkages
Leadership Doctrine Program Resource Structure	Transaction	Enabling Functional Normative Diffused

Resource Acquisition

The data that was collected and interpreted through the use of AIBM was finally evaluated by means of five analytic judgements suggested by Esman (1972) and further modified by Chamberlain (1979). The evaluative variables and their definition was as follows:

1. *Technical capacity*. The ability of the institution to deliver the services required by the constituency at an increasing level of technical competence, whether it is teaching, research or service.

2. *Normative commitments*. The extent to which the attitudes and beliefs for which the institution is responsible are internalized and accepted by faculty, staff and students; for example, promotion criteria for faculty, or participative roles for students in institutional decision making.

3. *Innovative thrust*. The ability of the institution to innovate so that the sanctioned beliefs and attitudes for which it is responsible will not be frozen in their original form, and the

institution can continually learn and adapt to new technological and political opportunities.

4. *Environmental image.* The extent to which the institution is valued by the constituency. This can be demonstrated by the ability to (a) require resources based on the institution's intrinsic worth, (b) operate in ways that deviate from traditional patterns, (c) defend itself against attack or criticism, and (d) influence decisions in its sphere of action.

5. *Spread effect.* The degree to which the beliefs and attitudes of the institution have been integrated into ongoing activities of other organizations.

These standards were adopted for this study as a means for drawing conclusions concerning the level of institutionality achieved by Addis Ababa University. The following conclusion was drawn on the basis of the findings of the study.

1. The study suggested that Addis Ababa University has reached a level of institutionality during the first decade of its founding.

2. Addis Ababa University has become the major producer of trained manpower for the country.

3. The Academic Institution-Building Model methodology as adapted by Chamberlain has been found to be a useful instrument for screening information that was considered pertinent to academic institutions.

Finally, though the findings of the study were found to be positive, there were certain aspects of the institution that were found to be weak. Some of the points raised included (a) the lack of a clearly defined relationship between the University and its sponsoring agent, (b) the lack of well developed contacts between the University and other foreign or local functional organizations and agencies up to the period of this study (1984); the relationship was largely based on a personal basis and (c) the participation of the students both in the academic and administrative affairs of the University was found to be minimal, particularly after 1977. (For a detailed treatment of the topic please refer to Fisseha Haile, *A Study of Institutionality: Addis Ababa University: 1961-1981*, Ed.D. dissertation, Indiana University, Bloomington, 1984.).

OVERVIEW HISTORY OF ADDIS ABABA UNIVERSITY: 1961-1981

Just as Ethiopia had developed her literature and schools long before her first contact with Europe, so it was of her own volition, as an independent self-governing country, that she introduced modern education with emphasis on the study of modern science, and techniques of teaching of foreign languages.
(*Ethiopia Observer*, 1958, p.13)

For decades prior to the introduction of modern education in Ethiopia in 1908, the orthodox church and the Moslem mosque controlled the system of traditional education. Commenting on the contribution of the church, Girma wrote:

Ethiopia's vital forces throughout her long stretch of history has been the Church. This powerful institution represented the old order with which it was identified. It gave the nation a unity of purpose.
(Girma, 1964, p.4)

Addis Ababa University (AAU) is located in Addis Ababa, the capital city of Ethiopia. The

University was founded as a public institution, created by general notice no.284 on February 28, 1961. From its inception to 1974 it was known as Haile Selassie I University, but following the revolution in 1974, its name was changed to Addis Ababa. To avoid confusion in this study the University will be referred to only as Addis Ababa University.

Early Stage of Development

In his book, *Ethiopian Journey*, Henze described the situation as follows: "The twentieth century has penetrated Ethiopia in many ways and places; power stations, port facilities, factories, hospitals, radio and TV broadcasting, schools, airlines and modern highways". On the other hand, he continued: "Many highways end in trails and one steps quickly from the twentieth century back into the tenth or into Biblical times" (Henze, 1977, p.21).

Ethiopia has been ruled for centuries by Rases (the equivalent of English dukes), with power shifting periodically from one center to another. It is only in the final decade of the 19th century that Emperor Menilik II reunified the empire and consciously began moving it into the so-called modern world.

Discussing class and ethnicity in Ethiopia, two known scholars of the region made the following observation:

> In terms of class structure, there was no other black African country like
> Ethiopia with its 2000 year old tradition of monarchy, a semi-autonomous
> provincial nobility, and millions of downtrodden peasants paying to their
> landlords rents, taxes and services.
> (Ottaway, 1978, p.14)

Therefore, the Ethiopian character is born as the result of centuries of a feudal tradition which has influenced Ethiopian life, habits and attitudes.

Agriculture is the backbone of Ethiopia's economy. In addition to raising livestock for domestic use, as well as for export, there are also small industries and distributive services that contribute to the economy.

During the decade 1950 to 1960, prior to the founding of Addis Ababa University, five colleges were founded by the Ethiopian government with the assistance of foreign countries. The colleges, founding dates, and sponsors are listed in Table 1.

TABLE 1: ETHIOPIAN COLLEGES, 1950-1960

	College	Year	Governing Ministry	Foreign Sponsor or Agency
1.	*University College of Addis Ababa (U.C.A.A.)	1950	Chartered	
2.	Alemaya College	1953	Agriculture	U.S.A.
3.	Engineering College	1953	Education	
4.	Building College	1954	Education	Sweden
5.	Gondar Public Health College	1954	Public Health	W.H.O. and U.N.I.C.E.F.

* Not to be confused with Addis Ababa University.

493

These colleges were founded to meet the immediate needs for qualified civil servants, trained professionals and technicians necessitated by the development of the government bureaucracy and the growth of the country's economic sector. There was strong competition among these colleges to recruit the best students and to obtain the biggest budget from the government (Three Decades of University Education, 1980, p.11). Most of the colleges offered only diploma-level courses. Students who successfully completed their studies were sent abroad, usually to western Europe and North America, where they received further training in their respective fields. The state of higher education in Ethiopia in 1960, prior to the founding of Addis Ababa University, can best be understood by the following statement:

> Viewed within the proper perspective, the first decade of higher education
> had many fruitful results: five colleges with fairly high academic standards;
> over 1300 graduates, a student population at the end of the period (1961)
> of almost 1000; and a student body with increasing consciousness of its
> obligation towards the broad masses of Ethiopia.
> (Three Decades of University Education, 1980, pp.10-11)

Addis Ababa University, 1961-1974

The growth and development of Addis Ababa University, beginning with its founding, can be divided into two phases, the pre-revolution and post-revolution periods, 1961 to 1974, and 1974 to the present, respectively. Between 1961 and 1974, the University followed the structure and function of the North American model of higher education. The first 4 years of its existence, 1961 to 1965, were essentially a period of reorganization of the various colleges, that were brought together under one charter to form the University. The initial tasks confronting the new administration were (1) to absorb its existing centers and develop integrated policies governing academic standards, administration, and planning, and (2) to expand higher education into new fields to meet critical new manpower needs (Presidential Commission on Planning, Reorganization and Consolidation, 1968, p.3).

The mission of the University, as presented to the Chancellor's Advisory Committee (the government) was (1) to rank among the leading universities of the world, (2) to advance knowledge and to seek truth, and (3) to be exemplary to future universities of Ethiopia. During the convocation celebrating the founding of the University on December 18, 1961, the Chancellor (head of the government) noted in his message that:

> The spread of knowledge is the bastion of liberty. . . To this great cause we
> have been able to secure financial and professional help from the United
> States of America. This institution will now coordinate and make more
> fruitful our existing centers of learning, both the U.C.A.A. and various
> technical colleges.
> The attainment of a goal is only a temporary achievement. The challenges
> to you, the faculty and students of this University, have only begun. New
> opportunities for enabling yourself to set ideas of achievement are waiting
> to be seized. We charge you to make the most of them through humility,
> toil and perseverance that gives education its deepest meaning.

Addis Ababa University inherited several separate systems of higher education, each with its own history, its own purpose, its own form and style of organization, and its own administration. This diversity was potentially beneficial, as they were all in place, but they also presented major problems in terms of fashioning these institutions into a coherent, purposeful, and integrated university (Aklilu, 1977, p.59). The task of coordinating the systems of higher education under a centralized administration was seen to be a major challenge.

The founding of the University was seen also as politically significant. The University was founded during a period when most African countries were gaining their independence from centuries of colonial rule. Ethiopia, one of the countries that had remained independent, was playing the leading role in the organization of African Unity, whose headquarters were later established in Addis Ababa. Thus, the founding of the University was important, not only as a means for achieving the developmental needs of Ethiopian society, but it was also a symbol of the achievement of modern status for the nation, seen as necessary as airports, highways and hospitals.

In a climate of continuous change, the main campus of the University was placed in the old palace, which the Emperor chose to abandon after the attempted *coup d'etat* of 1960. Though the setting of the University was in a beautifully kept location, it was functionally useless for academic activity. Not only was the palace inherited, but most of the palace personnel were left behind and became University employees in various administrative positions. Accordingly, the social and psychological behaviour of the University was, at least for a while, aristocratic. The first Ethiopian president, Lij Kassa Wolde Mariam, was a member of the royal family, who served as a "useful" transitional link between the government and the University in acquiring financial resources and, at times, settling troubles aroused by radical students and staff members.

When the University was established, the academic staff consisted largely of foreigners, Ethiopians comprised only 25% of the total academic staff of 176 (Trudeau, 1964, p.89). "Ethiopianization" of the staff was begun through a staff development program, which sent over 50 individuals each year to Asia, Europe and North America.

The Ethiopian government shouldered most of the expenses of the University. During the first academic year, 1961-62, the government appropriation was approximately $6,000 per student, per year. In 1969, the appropriation per student was less than 3,000 Birr, but foreign assistance provided another $1,000 per student per year (Summerskill, 1970, p.126 – U.S.$1 = Eth. Birr 2.07). About a third of the University's expenses were covered through foreign assistance. Several proposals to increase revenue were considered, including charging fees to students whose families were well-to-do. However, this latter plan was never put into effect and education has always remained free.

Beginning in 1961, the United States government, through various agencies (A.I.D., UNICEF, Ford Foundation, Fulbright, etc.), participated in the build-up of the University, especially in its administrative organization. The initial priorities were staff development, physical expansion, policy formation and local and international relations. The University followed the American model of a land grant university. Emphasizing the influence of the United States government, Legesse wrote: "Not only was U.S.A. training predominant among Ethiopian faculty members, but also U.S. nationals held dominating positions among expatriate faculty members in the Addis Ababa University" (Legesse, 1979, p.337).

From 1965, many committees were formed at various levels to study and recommend ways of meeting the various problems and challenges faced by the University while maintaining its academic standards. In 1965, the Chancellor's Advisory Committee was formed (government sponsored), which consisted of seven foreign experts from around the world. Most of them had previous experience as consultants and advisors for higher education in developing countries. All of them had Ph.D.'s or its equivalent and had extensive experience both in teaching and academic administration. Their names and countries are listed below:

1. Cos, Sir Christopher W. M., British Educator
2. Eurich, Alvin C., American Educator
3. Husen, Torsten, Swedish Educator
4. Kerr, Clark, American Educator
5. Kenetsch, George, German Scientist and Educator
6. Wells, Herman B., American Educator
7. Oluwasanmi, H. A., Nigerian Educator

(University Catalog, 1968)

495

Growth and Development of Programs

The period between 1961 to 1965 was one of continuous expansion, due to the demands created by the increased number of students completing 12th grade and fulfilling admission requirements for the University.

The need to expand the University was also determined when it became apparent that those African countries that had recently gained their independence had better institutions of higher education, despite their many years of colonial rule. Commenting on this, Dr. Teshome wrote: "When for the first time in our history we began to interact directly with other sovereign African States and to compare educational notes with them, the comparison was to bring traumatic shocks and salutary new motivations [sic]" (Teshome, 1979, p.147).

The Ethiopian government, therefore, was willing to help the University in its effort to attain high standards and gain recognition by foreign universities and governments that could provide professional expertise and financial backing. Foreign experts, mainly from the United States, were placed at the University to help organize and plan future developments of the University. The best students from Uganda, Kenya, Tanzania, Ghana and Sudan were given scholarships by the Ethiopian government to study at the University.

As the University continued to expand its programs and increase enrolment, the need for foreign assistance in human, material or financial aid was even more apparent. Though the colleges that were brought together to create the University were now under one centralized administrative system, their settings, academic structures and functions remained largely untouched. These colleges continued the original relationship with their individual foreign sponsors or agencies and were attached to the University mostly on administrative aspects for a long time.

During the 1961-62 academic year, the University began a range of new programs and institutes, such as Ethiopian Studies and the Institute of Development Research (IDR). Besides the regular academic programs, the Extension Program was founded in 1962 to provide University programs to students other than regular full-time day students. Renamed the Continuing Education Program, it became so successful that it began to serve almost equal numbers of students as the daytime regular program, without any cost to the University.

In addition to the Continuing Education Program, the Ethiopian University Service, which was started in 1965, also became an important means of rendering services by the University by taking the services of the University to people in the countryside. For many regular university students working in this program, and who were largely children of urban dwellers, the EUS provided their first real understanding of the way of life of the typical Ethiopian rural community. The University service was a program that required one year's work from each University student after completion of his third year of college. The program, however, was terminated in 1974, following the revolution.

Among the early committees that were formed to study and guide the day-to-day and future operations of the University, were the following standing committees:

1. Academic standards
2. Board of admissions
3. Development and finance
4. Ethiopian university service
5. Extension
6. Curriculum
7. Faculty affairs and promotion
8. Freshman advisory committee
9. Editorial board
10. Library
11. Scholarship

Each committee of at least 10 members from various faculties and departments as deemed appropriate for the purpose.

Developmental Aspects After the Revolution

Until 1974, continuous effort was made to study social and economic trends that could affect the growth of the University, and to engage in short and long term planning for both academic programs and physical expansion. However, in 1974, when the University seemed to be maturing as an institution, a radical revolution took place in the country and the University was closed for 2 years, resulting in the loss of many of the human, material and financial resources that it had been accumulating during the previous decade.

The Provisional Military Government that overthrew the monarchy, aware of the potential influence of the University, immediately used it as headquarters for the Development-Through-Cooperation Campaign, known as *Zemecha*. All university students and staff were required to participate in the Campaign. The experience gained earlier through the Ethiopian University Service became the model for *Zemecha*. The trained manpower, the students and the material resources became most indispensable to the government's initial effort to implement the various new policies that followed the demise of the monarchy. The importance of the University as an institution for public service was well demonstrated by the willingness and competence of its staff and students and the flexibility and adaptability they showed during the turbulent period.

The first step taken by the government was to proclaim the establishment of a Commission for Higher Education in 1977, under Proclamation No.109/1099, to coordinate all existing institutions of higher education behind specified purposes and objectives. The planning and establishing of the Commission were done at the University.

When the University opened its doors for the first time after the revolution in the fall of 1976, it had lost many of its staff members and there was a great lack of financial assistance from friendly countries, due to the government's political policies. Elaborating on this, Legum and Lee, in their book *Conflict in the Horn of Africa*, said:

> Centuries-old friendship with western nations, even those heavily engaged i development and aid projects in Ethiopia, were erased almost at a stroke; relations with the U.S., Britain, and Sweden swiftly degenerated into open hostility. The new ties were firmly with the Soviet bloc — with Russia, with East Germany, Czechoslovakia, Poland, Hungary, Bulgaria, as well as with Cuba and Yugoslavia.
> (Legum and Lee, 1977, p.94)

The new government had to meet all the expenses needed to run the University, at least for a while.

During the period of revolution and transition, the lack of clear development guidelines, the lack of human and material resources, and the lack of leadership, had left the University with very little for it to be able to carry on its responsibilities. Despite all of this, it continued to function with the old curriculum, while a new curriculum was being prepared. Soon a new admission policy was set in place and other administrative policies generally were incorporated.

The problems that besieged the new government were also reflected in the University. Though the quality of instruction was rumoured to have deteriorated, due to less qualified students and a lack of competent staff and financial resources, still every effort was made to keep the University going.

Despite the political turbulence in the country at this time, there was no interference by the government in matters regarding the University's instructional program. There were shifts in leadership from time to time, reflecting the government's intention to keep an eye on the only institution of higher education in the country, but these were nominal and had little effect on the actual programs at the University.

Addis Ababa University, in the 20 year period under review, has existed in an environment of rapid social, economic, cultural and political change. As a result, a complex process of interactions has taken place between (1) the various academic and administrative units of the University, and (2) the external environment. This interaction has determined its character as an educational institution, and the nature of its continued existence.

BIBLIOGRAPHY

Addis Ababa University, (1973)
Consolidated Legislation of the Faculty Council, with Revisions up to September 17, 1973. Mimeographed.

——————— (1965)
Convocation celebrating the founding of Addis Ababa University, Monday, December 18, 1961, Addis Ababa: Artistic Printing Press.

——————— (1968)
General catalogue 1968-69, Addis Ababa: Central Printing Press.

——————— (1980)
Three decades of university education, Addis Ababa: Artistic Press.

Ethiopian Observer (1958)
Journal of independent opinion, economics, history and the arts, Vol.II, No.4, Sylvia Pankhurst (ed.), England: Perry Brothers Ltd.

Girma Amare (1964)
Education and conflict of values in Ethiopia: A study of the socio-moral problems arising out of the introduction of modern education in Ethiopia. Ph.D. dissertation, Southern Illinois University, 1964.

Henze, P. B. (1971)
Ethiopian Journey: Travels in Ethiopia 1969-72, London: Ernest Benn Limited, 287pp.

Legesse Lema (1979)
Political economy of Ethiopia 1875-1974. Agricultural educational and international antecedents of the revolution. Ph.D. dissertation, Department of Economics, Notre Dame, Indiana, 1979.

Legume, C. and B. Lee (1977)
Conflict in the Horn of Africa, New York: Africana Publishing Company, 1979.

Lipsky, A. C. (1962)
Ethiopia: Its people, its society and its culture. Prepared under the auspices of the American University, New Haven: Hraf Press, 376pp.

Ottaway, M. and D. (1978)
Ethiopia: "Empire in revolution", New York: Africana Publishing Company, a division of Holmes & Meier Publishers, Inc., 250pp.

Summerskill, J. (1970)
Addis Ababa University: A blue-print for development. Mimeographed. Addis Ababa: The Ford Foundation.

Teshome Wagaw (1979)
Education in Ethiopia: Prospect and retrospect, Ann Arbor: The University of Michigan Press, 256pp.

Trudeau, E. (1964)
Higher education in Ethiopia. Ph.D. dissertation, Columbia University Teachers College.

HEALTH RESEARCH AND ITS ORGANIZATION IN ETHIOPIA

Fisseha Haile Meskal

INTRODUCTION

In the early years of health research most emphasis was placed on understanding pathogenesis, finding new drugs and developing treatment methods in order to combat disease circumstances. That was perhaps one of the reasons why health research was then referred to as *Medical Research*. With the development of broader views to health promotion, that is the control and prevention of diseases which include vaccination, vector control, environmental sanitation, etc., health research extended its domain from medicine to biological and other natural sciences. This was perhaps one of the reasons for the introduction of the broader term *Biomedical Research*.

Accumulated experience and new developments indicate that health promotion is dependent not only on medical and biomedical research, but also on investigations in biobehaviour, sociology, anthropology, economics, etc. That the solution to health problems lies not only on biomedical sciences is made evident in statements of several distinguished health worker including those of Professor T. A. Lambo, who recently stated that: "The health consequences of poverty, such as malnutrition, obesity, smoking, drug abuse, apartheid, crime, suicide, are more likely to be controlled or even prevented by behavioural and environmental modification than by our knowledge of clinical science".[1] Improvements of the health delivery activities including routine office works in health departments, is also regarded as contributing to health development. All these gave rise to what is known as *Health Service Research*. The scope of health service research includes, as indicated in a workshop report on Health Service Research by the Ethiopian Science and Technology Commission, "the critical evaluation of current health status and health service, the design of alternate health care delivery systems, the implementation of such systems and the evaluation of the effectiveness and efficiency of alternate designs of health care delivery".[2]

Before we started to develop a complete understanding of health service a new terminology, with its own conception, came into the picture. This is *Health Systems Research*. I do not claim to have yet fully grasped the concept embedded in this terminology. But in a paper on health systems research, Taylor states that: "In primary Health Care the need is for the simplest, least expensive and most widely usable technological procedures, and health systems research should make special effort to ensure that appropriate technology is available at the periphery".[3] According to the same author, health systems research requires the participation of "experts from a variety of disciplines". In February 1983 a WHO study group stated that health system research is generally directed towards solving problems in the organization, management, financing or delivery of health services in order to improve their efficiency and effectiveness.[4] In a paper on national health systems, Kleczkowski *et al.* indicate that health systems research has been defined as "the systematic study of the means by which biomedical, sociomedical and other relevant knowledge is brought to bear on the health of communities under a given set of conditions".[5]

The little health research carried out in Ethiopia is limited mainly to medical and biomedical research with perhaps a beginning in health services research. I am not yet aware of any single work on health systems research in Ethiopia, unless this is the same as health services research. The scope of the present paper is limited to presenting a bird's eye view of health research organization and activities in Ethiopia with the primary aim of initiating discussions on some outstanding issues.

The paper is not the result of any rigorous systematic investigation on health research in Ethiopia. It is based mainly on my own personal experience both as a researcher and managing officer of a research institution. Some information has also been used from a review of relevant literature and interviews with heads of other research institutions in the country.

ORGANIZATION OF HEALTH RESEARCH IN ETHIOPIA

Health research activities in Ethiopia take place in University research institutes and faculties, in institutions of the Ministry of Health, and in organizations partially or exclusively supported by external agencies. Almost all research work conducted within the higher education system is organized in the faculties of Medicine, Natural Sciences, Pharmacy and a research institute (Institute of Pathobiology), of Addis Ababa University. Two institutions in the Ministry of Health, including the Central Laboratory and Research Institute, and the Ethiopian Nutrition Institute, have research as an important component of their function. The All Africa Leprosy Rehabilitation and Training Centre (ALERT), and the Armauer Hansen Research Institute (AHRI), both situated in the same compound and run almost entirely by external organizations, are responsible for clinical and immunological research into leprosy.

The University faculties have research as part of their overall responsibility in promoting knowledge, but are not required or encouraged to limit themselves to specific research areas of practical value to the country. The choice of research problems is based mainly on the interest and capability of the individual researcher and the major driving force behind is the common slogan: "Publish or Perish".

Institutions of the Ministry of Health were occupied, in the past, with routine services and the little research work done before the popular revolution of 1974 was conducted mostly by expatriates with little participation of nationals. As stated in a report of the Health Research Council, the findings of the expatriate researchers were published in diverse periodicals and sometimes in languages not understood by most Ethiopian health workers.[6]

Immediately after the popular revolution, research started to receive due recognition in national development. Thus in 1975 a Science and Technology Commission was established for the first time with the primary responsibility "to encourage, strengthen and guide" research.[7] Four years later, a council for health research was established within the Commission to help promote research in the health sector.

After 10 meetings of the Council over the past 4 or 5 years, we now have a better understanding of health research priorities, as well as a clearer delineation and coordination of research activities among the institutes. The major health problems of Ethiopia are now grouped by the Health Council into three categories, including Nutrition Problems, Communicable Diseases and a group of special health problems of which perinatal and childhood problems are most outstanding.[6]

ORGANIZATION OF NUTRITION RESEARCH

Research related to nutrition is mainly the responsibility of the Ethiopian Nutrition Institute (ENI) whose research objectives include: a) development of new recipes, particularly for weaning food; b) identification of staple foods and food taboos; c) preparation of dietary profile; d) the improvement of food processing procedures at the domestic level; e) identification of vitamin deficiency; and f) surveillance of prevailing food and nutrition problems and devising intervention programmes.[8] Other activities of the institute include training nutrition educators, preparation of teaching materials, and participation in data collection for the "Early Warning System". Managed by a director who is responsible directly to the Permanent Secretary of the Ministry of Health, ENI has at present 31 scientific, 25 technical and 75 supportive staff. It enjoys financial support from the Ethiopian Government, international organizations like UNICEF and ECA, and bilateral assistance from Sweden and Canada.

RESEARCH IN MOTHER AND CHILD HEALTH

Research in childhood and maternity problems was in the past conducted almost entirely by expatriate scientists in the Ethio-Swedish Pediatric Clinic. This is now effectively taken over by national professionals in the Ethio-Swedish Childrens' Hospital and the Gynaecology/ Obstetrics Department of the Faculty of Medicine in Addis Ababa. These units, in collaboration with the Mother and Child Health Coordinating Office in the Ministry of Health, have recently formed a WHO Collaborating Centre for Perinatalogy. The objective of the Centre is the development of perinatal care through research and exchange of technical information.[9] The ongoing and planned research activities include: trends in birth weight distribution over a decade, maternal body energy balance and pregnancy outcome, gravidogramme based on risk profile, risk approach in MCH care delivery, etc.

THE ALERT/AHRI RESEARCH COLLABORATION

Originally established as a corporation in 1965, the main objective of the All Africa Leprosy Rehabilitation and Training Centre (ALERT) includes the provision of training (mainly to African health workers) in all aspects of leprosy including treatment, control and rehabilitation.[10] In addition to hospital services, training and control activities, the ALERT staff also undertake clinical research in leprosy.

The Armauer Hansen Research Institute (AHRI — named after the Norwegian doctor who discovered the leprosy bacillus in 1873) was established in 1969 by the Norwegian and Swedish Save the Children foundations. [11] It is affiliated with ALERT with which it shares the same compound.

In 1981 a joint ALERT/AHRI Research Committee was established to coordinate research activities in the two institutions. ALERT provides the clinical facilities necessary for AHRI's research activities, and the latter in return provides laboratory diagnostic services for physicians and leprosy supervisors, and collaborates in the clinical research programme of the ALERT staff. Both ALERT and AHRI are designated WHO collaborating centres for research in leprosy.[12]

HEALTH SERVICE RESEARCH (HSR)

Based on a working group report of the Ethiopia-Sweden-WHO Collaboration in HSR, an office for the coordination of health service research was established in 1982 within the Planning and Programming Bureau of the Ministry of Health. The HSR Unit is assisted by a committee which develops guidelines and determines priority areas for research. The committee also reviews individual research projects and monitors their progress. It is chaired by the Head of the Planning and Programming Bureau, and the Unit leader acts as the secretary.

The main objective of the HSR in Ethiopia is "to generate scientific information that could be utilized in the formulation of policies, planning, programming and organization of health systems based on PHC to achieve HFA/200".[13] The collaborative group mentioned above identified nineteen HSR projects to be executed in 1982-3, with financial support from WHO, SIDA and SAREC. The unit had encountered staggering difficulties in the initial phase, and little has been achieved in 1982-83. With a reorganization of the unit and the committee in September 1984, there appears some prospect for the unit to be more productive.

ORGANIZATION OF RESEARCH IN COMMUNICABLE DISEASES

Research in infectious and communicable diseases (including microbiology, epidemiology and vector biology) takes place in several institutions including the medical faculties in Addis Ababa and Gondar, the Pathobiology Institute, the Faculty of Science and the Central Laboratory and Research Institute. As the last mentioned institute is the main research arm of the Ministry of Health, and as the present writer is more familiar with research work in this than in the other institutions, we shall present below the status of health research in this institute and the common constraints encountered.

THE CENTRAL LABORATORY AND RESEARCH INSTITUTE

Establishment and Function

The Central Laboratory and Research Institute (CLRI) is one of the oldest scientific institutions in Ethiopia. It was first established during the Italian occupation (1936-1941) under what was then called Ministro de la Sanita. Immediately after independence, the laboratory was reorganized by a team of British scientists and the name "Imperial Medical Research Institute" was given to it. In 1950 the technical and administrative responsibilities of the Institute were transferred, on a contractual agreement, to a French team of scientists from the Pasteur Institute of Paris, and the name was changed to "Institute Pasteur d'Ethiopie". On completion of their second contractual term in 1964, the French team left the institute and handed over the technical and administrative responsibilities to a few Ethiopian scientists and technicians.[14]

The present activities of the institute include referral diagnostic laboratory service, microbiological and toxicological analysis of consumable products, quality control of prophylactic, diagnostic and therapeutic substances, production of biological preparations like vaccines and diagnostic antigens, training in medical laboratory technology, and applied research in support of disease control and prevention. Because of its relatively long life and the wide variety of services rendered to the public, the institute is usually referred to as "the Laboratory" for almost any laboratory determination. Table 1 illustrates the diversity and volume of work at the Institute.

TABLE 1

Type and volume of work at CLRI[15]		
Type of Service	Volume of work in	
	1982-'83	1983-'84
1. Diagnostic determinations	171,938	204,240
2. Quality Control	2,111	1,866
3. Vaccines against cholera, typhoid and rabies as well as diagnostic antigens, in litres	486.9	445.34
4. Technicians trained,	21	25
5. Research projects completed	11	16

Research accomplishments in the 1983-'84 fiscal year are the highest ever in the history of the institute. A brief look at the annual reports for the past few years reveals a steady, though modest, growth of research activities at the institute. Table 2 gives the titles of research projects completed in the 1983-'84 fiscal year.

TABLE 2

Research projects completed in 1983-'84 fiscal year[16]

1. Endemicity of urinary schistosomiasis in the Enta-dyota village of the Gewani flood-plain.

2. Comparative evaluation of centrifugation and Nytrel filtration technique in the recovery of *Schistosoma haematobium* eggs.

3. Prevalence of onchocerciasis in Bebeka, Keffa Administrative Region, Ethiopia.

4. Preferred site for skin snipping in the detection of microfilaria of *Onchocerca volvulus.*

5. Urinary Schistosomiasis in the Upper Middle Awash Valley, part I, Epidemiology.

6. The correlation between *S. haematobium* infection and proteinuria, Leukomaturia, hematuria.

7. The spectrum of HB.V. infection in Ethiopia.

8. The distribution of the subtypes of HBsAg in Ethiopia.

9. Retrospective study of acute Hepatitis A and B among Ethiopian children.

10. The immune status of young adult female population to Rubella virus infection in Ethiopia.

11. Monthly incidence of rota infection in young children in Addis Ababa.

12. Beta-Lactamase producing *N. gonorrhoea.*

13. Human pulmonary mycosis: A preliminary survey.

14. Drug susceptibility of *Mycobacterium* tuberculosis isolated in Asmara.

15. The use of sonicate preparation of mycobacterium tuberculosis (New Tuberculin) in the assessment of BCG vaccination.

16. Skin-test sensitization by tubercle bacilli and by other mycobacteria in Ethiopian children.

Strategies for the development of research at CLRI

Until quite recent years, CLRI did not have clearly defined research objectives nor strategies for the development of health research. The steps taken now for strengthening the research capability of the institute include:

a) identification of research objectives of the institute and determining priority areas of research,

b) development of the critical mass in research manpower,

c) strengthening the organizational set up of the institute, and

d) acquisition of basic facilities in working space and scientific equipment.

We shall hereafter dwell a bit on each of these strategies, describing prevailing situations and focusing some attention on selected constraints.

The general objectives of health research at CLRI presently include the development of accurate information on prevailing diseases and the development, adaptation or adoption of appropriate technology for their control and prevention. Specifically the institute aspires to:

a) determine the prevalence and intensity of major endemic infectious and communicable diseases in large state farms, settlement areas, and other centres of high human concentration,

b) develop satisfactory understanding of the pattern of occasional epidemic outbreaks and provide health workers with information and technological know-how to prevent the outbreak, and

c) manipulate available knowledge for the development of local capabilities in the prevention and control of diseases.

Manpower development

Physicians with clinical experience and a training in epidemiology and/or microbiology would have been most suitable for research in the control of diseases. At the moment there are very few people of this qualification in Ethiopia and whenever available they are attracted to the university system. Difficulties are great in training physicians in epidemiology or microbiology. In the first place, very few clinicians opt for these subjects to specialize in. In the second place, the Ministry of Health has not been keen to release practising physicians for further studies, understandably, because of their limited supply and the high risk of losing them during studies abroad. The alternative adopted to manpower development for CLRI has been recruiting candidates with qualifications in biological sciences, and giving them the opportunity to train abroad in such specialized fields as microbiology, immunology, vector biology, and epidemiology.

As shown in Table 3, efforts in manpower development over the past seven years resulted in a satisfactory improvement of the quality and number of scientific and technical staff of the institute.

TABLE 3: CLRI Staff Development, 1977 to 1984

Staff Category	Qualifications	Number in	
		1977	1984
Scientific	Ph.D or equivalent	1	4
	M.Sc.	6	12
	B.Sc.	15	28
Technical	Senior technicians	17	36
Administrative and supportive staff		159	195
Total		198	275

Candidates in biology are available, but the risk of brain drain appears equally high in this as well. Alternatives are being explored to develop mechanisms of training at home the required research manpower.

Physical facilities

Suitable laboratory rooms, appropriate equipment, adequate reagents and means of transport are some of the essential physical requirements for effective undertakings in health research. The equipment and supply needed for routine diagnostic services at the institute are bought with part of the revenue collected from such services. Most of this equipment like microscopes, centrifuges, incubators and deep freezers are also used for research. Correspondingly, equipment purchased on research funds is sometimes utilized for advanced diagnostic services. Thus the mutualism between service and research has to a certain extent enabled the institute to overcome constraints in basic equipment. It has also resulted in the efficient and effective utilization of these expensive laboratory materials.

Acquisition of spare parts is the main constraint in maintaining congenial working conditions in laboratories. Research equipment these days is more and more sophisticated, and maintenance is absolutely impossible without importing every little spare part. What makes this even more complicated and frustrating is the frequent changes of model, thus rendering expensive equipment useless after a limited period of service. Complete reliance on all imported spare parts not only contributes to the drainage of limited foreign exchange, but has also a dampening effect on the creativity of our scientific and technical personnel.

SOME OUTSTANDING PROBLEMS OF HEALTH RESEARCH IN ETHIOPIA

The story of health research in Ethiopia will not be completed without mentioning a few of the most outstanding constraints encountered in the management of research. As stated earlier, health research in post-revolution Ethiopia is much more organized and given better support. However, there are still a number of constraints to overcome before a satisfactory mechanism for the promotion and development of research is ensured. Thus:

- research priorities are not yet adequately identified;

- there is no strong financial commitment in support of health research;

- no suitable arrangements exist within the Ministry of Health for effective implementation of research findings;

- there is no sufficient coordination and guidance for health research, particularly within the higher education system and among expatriates;

- existing rules and regulations pertaining to personnel and financial management are not conducive to the promotion of health research;

- there is still little attention given to the significance of socio-behavioural and anthropological studies in health systems; and

- there is very little research incentive, and no compensation for field research in hardship conditions, etc.

To sum up, we have briefly reviewed the scope and type of health research in general, and the kind of health research activities taking place in Ethiopia. We have also briefly described existing facilities and limitations in health research. It is hoped that this will serve as a starting point for a further development of health research in support of Primary Health Care in Ethiopia.

ACKNOWLEDGEMENTS

My grateful thanks go to Dr. Nebiat Teferi of the Perinatology Unit, Ato Zewdu W. Gabriel of the Ethiopian Nutrition Institute, Dr. Yayehyirad Kitaw, Board Member of ALERT, and Dr. Taye Tadesse, Director of the All Africa Leprosy Rehabilitation and Training Centre, for their cooperation in supplying me with needed information on their respective institutions.

REFERENCES

1. Lambo, T. A., 1983, "Advisory Committee on Medical Research, The First Major Landmark", *World Health (The magazine of the World Health Organization)*. December, 1983, pp. 2-4.

2. Ethiopian Science and Technology Commission. *Report of the National Health Service Research Workshop* (undated), mimeo.

3. Taylor, C. E., 1983, "Health systems research: How can it be used?", *World Health Forum*, 4 (4): 328-335.

4. WHO Study Group Report, Feb. 1983, *Research for Reorientation of National Health Systems*.

5. Kleckowski, B. M., Roemer, N. L. and Van der Werff, A., 1984, "National Health Systems and their Reorientation towards Health for all", *WHO Public Health Papers*, No. 77, p.19.

6. Health Research Council, 1980, *Research and Experimental Development Policy in Health (1980-84)*, Draft 2, Mimeo. Ethiopian Science and Technology Commission, Addis Ababa.

7. Proclamation No.52 of 1965. A Proclamation to Establish an Ethiopian Science and Technology Commission. *Negarit Gazeta*. Berhanena Selam Printing Press, Addis Ababa.

8. Gabriel, W. Zewdu, Personal Communication, 1984.

9. Ethio-Swedish Children's Hospital. Plan of work for the WHO Collaborating Centre. Perinatal Health Care Development, March 1983. Mimeo ESCH/1/84. Addis Ababa.

10. Tadesse, Taye. Personal Communication, 1984.

11. Annual Report for 1984. All Africa Leprosy Rehabilitation and Training Centre, Addis Ababa.

12. Annual Report for 1983. All Africa Leprosy Rehabilitation and Training Centre, Addis Ababa.

13. Report of a Working Group of Ethiopia, Sweden and WHO Collaboration, 1982. Health Service Research in support of Primary Health Care. Draft mimeo HSR/ETHIOPIA/82.1.

14. Gebre, Zerihun. Personal Communication, 1984.

15. Annual Report for 1983-84. Central Laboratory and Research Institute, Addis Ababa.

16. *Ibid.*

MEDIATED AGRICULTURAL EDUCATION IN ETHIOPIA

John Gartley

INTRODUCTION

Over the last several decades, the goal of socio-economic development has been pursued with a zeal matched only by the degree of failure of such efforts. Lately, communication theorists and mass media technicians have been included as a necessary component of the development industry. Unfortunately, the rate of success for development projects which take media processes into account is arguably no better than for those which ignore this component. What has emerged over the last two decades is a dialogue that questions all aspects of the dominant beliefs about culture, communication and development. The fundamental relationships between man and his environment — both physical and cultural — are being scrutinized. Even the forms of the questioning/learning process itself have been critically inspected, and found lacking. The utilization of media in Ethiopia for education, development and agricultural evolution addresses itself directly to this on-going dialogue. In fact, the structure of the media system in Ethiopia is unique on the African continent and, as such, the media utilization for development purposes has the potential for answering the questions asked by critical scholars and for actualizing a truly "grassroots" approach.

An understanding of what is meant by the term "paradigm" and how the process of paradigm change has occurred throughout history is necessary before an exploration of the need for a paradigm-shift in communication can be carried out. Both definition and process are treated by Thomas Kuhn in *The Structure of Scientific Revolutions*. In this work, Kuhn states that a paradigm refers to:

> . . . the sources of the methods, problem-field, and standards of solution accepted by any mature scientific community at any given time . . . paradigms provide scientists not only with a map but also with some of the directions essential for map making. In learning a paradigm the scientist acquires theory, methods and standards together, usually in an inextricable mixture.[1]

In this sense, a paradigm structures how we look at the world, what questions are deemed worthy of exploration, and what methods are used to explore reality.

Even though Kuhn examines the quantitative sciences in his work, his observations about paradigms and paradigm-shifts are equally valid for humanistic or socio-cultural fields of study as well.[2] There is also evidence that the belief systems man develops affect not only how he approaches a problem, or what problems he chooses to pursue, but also his perceptual sense as well.[3]

> Individuals give meaning to a visual perception by interpreting in light of what they have learned beforehand. Otherwise, the eye registers an image, but the brain fails to attribute significance to it. It is the cognitive map — the record of experiences, previous perceptions and learned concepts stored and arranged in the brain — that allows us to 'see'. Just as an object will remain meaningless or perhaps be misinterpreted by someone who has no place for it in a personal frame of reference, so too members of a culture will fail to see things that are completely outside their cultural experience or will interpret what they see in terms of their own cultural reference frame.[4]

The above statement is the core of the thesis concerning the utilization of media for development within a cultural mode. Indeed, it should be obvious that the structure of a paradigm is of paramount importance to any study of communication, especially since "... something like a paradigm is prerequisite to perception itself. What man sees depends both upon what he looks at and also upon what his previous visual-perceptual experience had taught him to see"[5], which points to a duality that exists in any study of communication. Since our understanding of communication processes arises out of our creation of models of these processes, any communication paradigm has two modes:

> In one mode communication models tell us what the process is; in their second mode they produce the behavior they have described. Communication can be modelled in several empirically adequate ways but these several models have quite different forms of social relations.[6]

These ethical implications necessitate that any empirical study of communication also examines the paradigm which underpins the study.

An examination of the literature supports the contention that mainstream communication theory and practice — whether labelled the "transmission" or "effects" model — originated with the United States and from there were exported throughout most of the world.[7] This model, in turn, grew out of the Western liberal *Weltanschaung* and is connected to the various processes of modernization which resulted in what is today loosely called "Western Society: the growth of democracy, science and industrialism". The driving force behind the development of Western Society is a belief in three basic assumptions: individuals, science and progress.[8]

The belief in individualism has resulted in a communication model which defines the individual, in isolation from social forces and institutions, as a basic unit of analysis.[9] This is best illustrated by the overriding concern with the persuasive, or "cost-effective", aspects of the communication process by mainstream researchers.[10] Communication theorists turned to those disciplines which placed an overriding emphasis on the individual — psychology, social psychology and behaviorism — as the primary source for their models of society.[11]

The belief in the organic progress of man provides Western communication practitioners with the ethical and moral force necessary to justify a model preoccupied with persuasion, and at the same time, provides a major goal of communication projects — the changing of the attitudes and behaviors of the individual. Empirical science is the "only" tool which can lead the way to the achievement of this goal. It is belief in the Western liberal paradigm which grounds all aspects of mainstream mass communication theory, research and practice.[12]

Just as there is general agreement over the philosophical and geographical origins of "effects" research and the transmission view of communication, there exists general agreement in the literature as to what the specific components of the transmission model are. First and foremost, communication is defined as a process that entails the transfer of information, attitudes, behaviors and/or technological innovations from a sender, or source, to a receiver, or receivers.[13] As mentioned earlier, the primary goal of this process is persuasion.[14] Generally, adherents to a transmission view of communication are asking the basic questions: "What do the media do to people".[15] In an attempt to better answer this question, and to obtain the maximum level of "effect" to the source's message, called "feedback", is incorporated into the transmission model as a message adjusting device.[16]

The emphasis which adherents of the transmission model place on information transfer, media channels, feedback and effects, is indicative of the adoption of a physical (as opposed to humanistic) and mechanistic view of the process of communication. This reduction of communication to a mechanical process is a necessary outgrowth of the need to develop a data base which is sufficiently empirical and quantitative in nature to allow for scientific manipulation.

As an outgrowth of the concern with media systems, adherents of the transmission model structured their model of communication vertically — information is disseminated from the top, downward. More specifically, the flow of information originated from industrialized, urban centers is disseminated outward. Thus, the flow of communication, when defined as information transfer, is heavily unidirectional.[17]

The same paradigmatic beliefs which structured communication theory and practice were heavily influential in structuring the direction of post-World War II development efforts as well.

The Western liberal model of modernization, which had a history of "success", particularly in England and the United States, was adopted without question as the correct model for the world.[18] As with communication theory, development policies originated almost exclusively in the United States and were then disseminated outward.[19] These policies all adhered to a definition of development centered around economic growth,[20] and the development of industrial, urban centers from which modernizing forces might spread to ". . . backward, archaic and traditional areas".[21] The main thrust of development efforts was to break down the dichotomy between the traditional and the modern, through the penetration of technology and industry into traditional areas.[22]

Several factors worked together toward inclusion of mass media systems into the development effort:

> The pressures of economic development goals, the size and dispersion of target audiences in developing areas, the availability of modern communication technology, and an interest in selling expensive communication equipment all worked to make the media an important element in rural development programs.[23]

The common paradigmatic origins of Western communication development theories ensured that the cost-efficiency of mass media systems would be fully exploited in the attempt to transmit information about social, economic and technological innovations to "underdeveloped" people. At the same time this reliance enabled researchers to take advantage of the numerous "cause-effect", or "persuasion" studies which had already been carried out in the United States.[24] Through the examination of development projects which contain a communication component, the dominant *applied* (as opposed to theoretical) communication models could be identified and outlined.

In the 1970s, the Third World began to call for a more equitable and just use of media in their countries. Growing from the concerns outlined by the *dependencia* writers and the concerns emanating from the failures of many development schemes utilizing media, media theorists began to evaluate the possibilities of a new and cultural approach to the study of human communication — a communication based on the premise that communication involves more than the successful transfer of information from sender to receiver. The transmission model, with its reliance on mechanistic, "scientific" models, was considered unable to account for major activities of man — such as his participation in rituals, the creation of myths and art forms, and manners, for instance — that are quite obviously communicative in nature.[25] This recognition, that communication is a cultural process that operates through a variety of interconnected forms, is not a new generative idea however:

> The ritual view of communication, while a minor thread in our national thought, is by far the older of those views; old enough in fact for dictionaries to list it under 'Archaic'. In a ritual definition, communication is linked to terms such as sharing, participation, association, fellowship, and the possession of common faith. This definition exploits the ancient identity and common roots of the terms commonness, communion, community and communication. A ritual view of communication is not directed toward the extension of messages in space, but the maintenance of society in time; not the act of imparting information but the representing of shared beliefs.[26]

The process of communication, when defined as the creation of meaning through participation in cultural forms, always embodies dual elements that are inseparable. At the most basic level, the creation and use of a primary symbol, what is meant to be descriptive label, inherently carries within itself a web of associations. These webs of significance develop in the individual users a set of attitudes toward and connections with the object, action or concept so named.[27] This is nothing more than a recognition that symbols operate both denotatively and connotatively, always and at the same time. Thus, the cultural approach to the study of communication views the human response to reality as a constructive, and not a passive process.[28] Regardless of the various metaphysical schemes that have been invented to explain this phenomenon, one fact remains clear: the creation and use of symbolic forms lies at the heart of what it means to be human.[29]

> To exist humanly, is to *name* the world, to change it. Once named, the world in its turn reappears to the namers as a problem and requires of them a new *naming*. Men are not built in silence, but in work, in action-reflection.[30]

Although Friere refers only to oral communication, his basic premise applies to all the various symbolic systems developed by men. Art, ritual, magic — these are all cultural forms which employ symbol systems to organize and express attitudes and beliefs about reality.[31] It is a basic premise among those who are calling for a qualitative, culturally oriented approach to the study of communication that politics, economic systems, religions, as well as all sociocultural forms, are merely interrelated symbolic systems — in short, forms used for human communication.

> There is more than a verbal tie between the words common, community and communication. Men live in a community in virtue of the things which they have in common; and communication is the way in which they come to possess things in common. What they must have in common . . . are aims, beliefs, aspirations, knowledge — a common understanding — likemindedness as sociologists say. Such things cannot be passed physically from one to another like bricks; they cannot be shared as persons would share a pie by dividing it into physical pieces . . . Consensus demands communication.[32]

It is the concept of the community of mankind and the need to incorporate the indigenous cultural values, communication systems and local languages which is the foundation for this paper. There is an opportunity in Ethiopia to produce a truly grassroots, culturally based mediated educational system. It would be the first in Africa and one of the first in the world.

THE POTENTIAL FOR MEDIATED EDUCATION IN ETHIOPIA

The possibilities for a truly "grassroots" or cultural approach to mediated development grows out of a historical and cultural analysis of media in Ethiopia as well as material gained by interviews conducted in March of 1984. The conclusions and proposals generated are designed to facilitate the utilization of mass media for agricultural development in Ethiopia within the proposed interim stage between MPP II and the initiation of the proposed Peasant Agricultural Development Project (PADEP).

The suggested utilization of mass media for agricultural development is based on the Government of Ethiopia's (GOE's) stated policy of decentralization, and on the concept of "grassroots" of participatory media. The foci of local media programming and the local development agency (DA) are to be interrelated and interlinked. The diffusion of information on agricultural techniques and technology, therefore, will be reinforced by the interrelated activities of the DAs, audio cassettes which can be utilized in the field, posters and radio. In addition, the mass media components of the particular projects would be designed in such a manner that they incorporate regionally appropriate nationality languages and indigenous cultural values and communication techniques. The central concept, then, is that the media which would be utilized in this project should be designed to reinforce the DA's message. In addition, the agricultural media programs would serve to provide information in times of emergency, e.g. broadcasting locations where relief assistance can be obtained during, or as a result of, weather related problems, and as a means of sharing information between farmers often separated by distance and/or topography but who share common agricultural problems or concerns.

PRELIMINARY RADIO UTILIZATION RESEARCH

In early 1984, Ato Makonnen Tefera of the PADEP office in Addis Ababa conducted basic research on the utilization and the availability of radio in the Kefa Administrative Region.[33] Kefa was chosen because of the level of local agricultural development and acceptance of innovations. Utilizing a questionnaire developed by the PADEP task force, three awrajas and six weredas were randomly selected (from a total of six awrajas and thirty-eight weredas) and a total of 250 farmers were interviewed. Ten farmers were taken from each producer cooperative and each peasant association. In total, nine producer cooperatives and sixteen peasant associations were represented in this research.

Of the total farmers interviewed, forty-eight owned a radio (20%).[34] However, only thirty-two of the forty-eight radios were functioning properly. Of the farmers who owned functioning receiver sets, twenty-three (72%) stated that they regularly listened to the agricultural education programs broadcast by the Ministry of Information and National Guidance.

When asked why they did not own a radio receiver, the major reason given was that the farmers had spent their money on more essential items such as clothing, food and shelter. However, 40% of the farmers who did not own receiver sets listened to agricultural education programs on a receiver set located in the home of a relative or friend, in a producer cooperative or, most often, at a central location in the peasant association.

A majority of the farmers interviewed listened to the agricultural education programs as mentioned above. However, the majority of the farmers contended that the transmission time for the programs (Tuesday or Thursday mornings) were inconvenient in that the farmers were already working in the fields at that time. The farmers have proposed that the transmission time be changed to Saturday afternoon and/or Sunday.

Language was a major consideration mentioned regularly by the farmers. The programs are broadcast in Amharic and Oromigna, while the majority of the farmers interviewed speak Keffigna and Gimirigna. Many farmers stated that they would appreciate agricultural education programming which was broadcast in local languages in order that they might more readily understand what they considered to be important and significant information.

In addition to the radio programs, agricultural education in the area under study is reinforced by the use of posters placed in producer cooperatives, peasant associations and at the Ministry of Agriculture wereda offices. When the farmers from the sample weredas were questioned by Ato Makonnen, 30% had seen or noticed the posters. However, many of the farmers who had observed the posters were confused as to their meaning. Some confusion seemed to have been caused by language problems, by inappropriate utilization of slogans or logos which signified indigenous iconographic meanings contrary to those for which the posters were designed, or by messages which did not address the specific agricultural problems of the farmers of that region. Of the farmers who did state that they had acquired some knowledge from the posters, the two messages which were most successful were those concerned with weeding and grain storage. According to Ato Makonnen, however, "posters could play an important role in teaching the farmers about the [sic] new techniques and innovations of agriculture". There is a need, therefore, "for the wereda workers (especially DAs) to explain what they [the posters] mean, otherwise it will be a waste of money, time and labor producing the posters".

As a result of Ato Makonnen's field research, we have some indication of the degree of radio receiver saturation and of the general reactions of the farmers of the sample weredas to both agricultural programming and the utilization of posters used to reinforce the mediated development messages. It was surprising to note that 20% of the farmers interviewed owned a set. However, there were concerns voiced about timing of the broadcasts, the nature of the broadcast content which did not address the specific agricultural concerns of the Kefa Administrative Region (because the broadcasts originated centrally in Addis Ababa), the utilization of inappropriate language. In addition, Ato Makonnen's research seems to indicate that the utilization of posters to reinforce agricultural development aims needs to be re-evaluated. Ato Makonnen will be conducting a similar research project in Harrage Administrative Region in the near future. It will be interesting to compare the results with those gained from his research in Kefa.

PRESENT ACTIVITIES OF AGENCIES
INVOLVED IN THE PROPOSED PROJECT

The Ministry of Agriculture: At present, the Ministry of Agriculture, under the T & V concept, is involved in limited mediated agricultural education. Centered almost exclusively on the utilization of posters, the activities have been concentrated at the wereda level with limited national or regional coordination. The Ministry is also involved in generating information through its public affairs arm for the Ministry of Information and National Guidance agricultural programming.[35]

The Ministry of Information and National Guidance: The agricultural programs of the Ministry of Information and National Guidance have been broadcast on a regular basis since the pre-revolutionary period.[36] Produced by Ato Gebeyhu Woobe, the programs are broadcast nationally twice a week from the Gedja transmitter located near Addis Ababa. Until recently, two thirty-minute programs were broadcast weekly. At present, three programs of fifteen minutes duration are broadcast weekly.

Of the three programs, two are designed to address issues of agricultural development at the level of the peasant association of the individual farmer. Broadcast at 7:10 A.M. on Tuesdays and Thursdays, these programs tend to concentrate on topics generated from the Ministry of Agriculture in Addis Ababa. When transport is available, field interviews are conducted with individual farmers concerning major agricultural research concerns such as new crops, livestock development and the benefits gained from the adoption of new techniques and technologies. The third program, also originating in Addis Ababa and broadcast nationally every Wednesday evening at 9:15 P.M., concentrates on the dissemination of information to the general public, to ministries and to state farms about general agricultural policy and new policy initiatives developed by the Ministry of Agriculture.

The program format for all three programs includes features with traditional music being utilized to bridge the various program segments. In addition, interviews generated in the field or in the studio are incorporated regularly. The production staff includes Ato Gebeyhu Woobe and an assistant producer. Technical facilities and additional staffing needs are provided by the Ministry of Information and National Guidance.

As noted in Ato Makonnen's field research in Kefa, the broadcast times generally do not coincide with the listening habits and lifestyles of the farmers in Ethiopia. By 7:10 A.M., for example, most farmers are already in the fields. In addition, because of a paucity of receiver sets which necessitates travel to listening centers, the lateness of the evening broadcast time is also inconvenient. The evening broadcast is, therefore, most likely to be heard by urban listeners. Because of programming priorities of the national service, however, there is little opportunity for altering broadcast times. Within the Ethiopian context, educational broadcasts have been given priority within the complimentary service of DEMM (Department of Educational Mass Media).

Department of Educational Mass Media: It seems important that some historical background on DEMM be presented before discussing the present role of the agency in Ethiopian mediated education. The history of this agency is additionally significant because, unlike the situation in many developing countries, DEMM has a long and established involvement in the process of providing educational media support. The Mass Media Centre, as it was known until 1970, actually grew out of the Audio Visual Centre established by the Point Four Program under the Ministry of Education in 1953.[37] Located in the present premises of DEMM and designed to provide audio visual support material for various governmental development projects, the specific duties of the center were photographic and film production along with the printing of textbooks and teaching materials for schools and other development agencies. By the late 1950s, the printing responsibilities were moved to the Berhannena Selam Printing Press. It is interesting to note, however, that the facilities and some of the equipment and staff have remained and are now part of the Department of Educational Mass Media. Two of the present photographers/cinematographers at DEMM, for example, have been at the center since the late 1950s or early 1960s.

After the GOE decision to establish an Ethiopian Television Service in 1964 at the time of the organizational meetings of the OAU, serious thought was given to expanding programming to educational television. Supported by AID and The British Council, space was procured in the same compound as the old Audio Visual Centre. Several producers, some of whom are presently involved in the development of programming at DEMM, were sent for training at CEDO (Center for Educational Development Overseas) in London; others, such as the present Director of Training and the present Director of Utilization and Evaluation, were hired at the same time. In 1966, Ethiopian Educational Television was established. Transmissions were live at that time, and were broadcast to schools in Addis Ababa with coverage which eventually reached nearly 95,000 students. Teachers' guide books were developed and distributed by the Centre to complete the educational package.

1969-71 was a significant period in the evolution of the center. The entire compound was devoted to educational media, educational radio was developed, studios for radio and television were constructed and additional staff was hired, including the present Director of DEMM and the present Head of the Radio Division.

At present, educational programming is disseminated by radio only, the television service having ceased programming operations in 1981.[38] Programs are produced at the studios in DEMM and then the tapes are physically transported to the eleven regional broadcast stations. These eleven medium wave stations (Alemaya 567 kHz, Asmara 810 kHz, Bhar Dar 744 kHz, Debre Markos 612 kHz, Dessie 549 kHz, Ghimbi 540 kHz, Gore 756 kHz, Legedadi 720 kHz, Makalle 549 kHz, Robe 801 kHz, Wollayetta Sodo 738 kHz) then transmit the programs in their respective regions. At present, each of the regional transmitters broadcasts on only one kw. of power. Within the next year, through the auspices of an IDA VI education credit, each of the eleven stations will be able to broadcast on an additional ten kw. transmitter.

Each of the above mentioned one kw. transmitters are utilized for the transmission of school broadcasts, 8:00 A.M. − 4:00 P.M., Monday through Friday. Programs in Amharic language, science, social studies and English language are transmitted to elementary schools throughout the country. The programs are designed to illustrate material with the curriculum established by the Ministry of Education. In addition, programs concentrating on educational methodologies have been developed for teachers. Radio sets and batteries, which have been donated by UNICEF and other organizations, are distributed to the schools and are maintained by DEMM. In addition, DEMM produces and distributes teachers' guides for each program and is in charge of the evaluation of the programs.

National adult education programs concentrate in two areas: literacy training and correspondence education. The literacy programs are developed in cooperation with the Department of Adult Education (administratively within the Ministry of Education [MOE]). The decision was made that, because of lack of personnel, evaluation of the mediated literacy programming in each of the nation's literacy centers was impractical. Therefore, for effective utilization and programming evaluation, model centers have been established. The literacy programs are broadcast 7:15 A.M. − 8:00 A.M. and 5:00 P.M. − 6:15 P.M., Monday through Friday.

Correspondence education is presently in an experimental stage as it enters its third year and is not yet cost effective because of the small size of the audience (students are required to formally enroll for these courses). At present, DEMM, in cooperation with the Correspondence Education Section of the Department of Adult Education produces a program series on biology. In 1984, production will begin on a series of language instruction programs (Amharic and English). The programs are designed to provide students with curriculum related materials in order for them to eventually earn a secondary school certificate. Following the pattern of traditional distance education programs, materials generated from the students' workbooks (which are produced and distributed by DEMM) are forwarded to the Correspondence Education Section in Addis Ababa for grading and evaluation.

Additional programming of a non-formal nature is transmitted from the Legadadi station. Concentrating on agricultural and home science education, the programs are transmitted from 3:00 P.M. – 5:30 P.M. on Saturdays and 10:30 A.M. – 1:00 P.M. on Sundays.

Additionally, there are significant non-production activities and responsibilities carried out at DEMM. These responsibilities and activities include training, distribution of equipment and support materials and evaluation and utilization.

The Training Officer coordinates regular training sessions for program producers, often in cooperation with, or with the assistance of, outside organizations. A Mr. Peter King, from The British Council, for example, ran a training course for radio producers in March of 1984.

Equipment distribution as well as the distribution of other materials is coordinated through the assistance of the Ministry of Education. There is a permanent media coordinator in each of the ministry's offices at the administrative region level. In addition, the ministry provides a media coordinator at the awraja level for more localized coordination.

Utilization and evaluation are significant aspects of any media organization, especially one which produces the amount of programming regularly generated by DEMM. Although this department is understaffed (it has only two staff members assigned to it) the amount of material generated from program and utilization research is significant. While the research that it generated is basic survey research, additional investment in personnel and materials would be necessary to allow this department to produce any significant analysis of the materials they generate.

Involved in site evaluation and program pre-broadcast testing, the evaluation and utilization officers assist in determining the present and future success or failure of programming. The major aspect of their work, however, is the coordination of the activities of the media officers at the regional and awraja levels. It would be impossible with the limited staff of this office to visit all of the schools involved in the formal education program. As a result, a sample group of schools has been selected for constant monitoring. Questionnaires are collected and coordinated by the regional media officers who then send the information to the DEMM office in Addis Ababa. The result is two publications – *Evaluation of Educational Radio in Ethiopia* and *Utilization of Educational Radio in Ethiopia*.

There are two reasons why DEMM provides a significant opportunity for the development of mediated agricultural education programming. First, DEMM is unique within the African context and within most of the Third World in that it is a part of the Ministry of Education and, therefore, is separated from the Ministry of Information and National Guidance. While the two ministries often compliment each other in their programming, the separation does mean that there is no competition on the DEMM station for educational programming time while in most governmental stations, education must compete for time, staff and facilities with other governmental priorities. Secondly, DEMM and many of the staff involved at DEMM have been active in the dissemination of mediated educational and development related programming for almost twenty years. While a long-term commitment does not necessarily guarantee that an educational program such as the one proposed later in this document will be successful, it does mean that there is a level of experience and knowledge of the field available which will make realistic and feasible planning possible.

Agri-Service Ethiopia: Agri-Service Ethiopia (ASE) is a non-governmental organization sponsored to a large extent by NOVIB, a Dutch development foundation. (It is anticipated, however, that the Ministry of Agriculture will play an increasing role in the support of ASE in the future.) Since 1977, ASE and DEMM have been involved in the development and implementation of the radio farm forum concept in various regions of the country. The rural farm forum concept, growing out of the successful utilization of radio for the dissemination of agricultural and home service material in Canada, utilized the concept of group leaders and satellite groups. In the Ethiopian context, a group leader is defined as a literate farmer who is trained by ASE through its correspondence education section and who has the responsibility for forming and leading the satellite group. A satellite group is defined as a group of farmers composed of both literate and illiterate individuals who are trained by a group leader so that "each member can acquire skills transmitted through the radio program".[39]

The group leader for each satellite group (or rural farm forum) is trained by ASE and DEMM in the operation of the receiver set and in techniques of small group discussion. The training deals with issues such as "the objectives of ASE and DEMM, the communication process, radio and its contribution to development, how to use timetables, how to care for radio sets and how to erect an antenna and the role of group leaders in a rural farm forum".[40] It is felt that, if an individual from the area of the rural farm forum is the group leader, greater commitment will be made to the project because, as part of the community, the leader will have a vested interest in the success of the activity.

The rural farm forum groups meet in producer cooperatives, peasant association meeting centers, in skill training centers, in literacy centers or other locations in which it might be convenient for the members to meet. Individuals who wish to become a member of a rural farm forum group are enrolled and attendance is kept for each session. (There is, therefore, a record of all individuals who are or have been members.) Some demographic information is generated by the attendance sheet including sex, marital status, occupation, age and education level. Each rural farm forum averages between 25-40 members.

The radio program content is developed by the staff of ASE and the programs are produced by DEMM. Broadcast from the regional transmitters during the early morning and late afternoon adult education program slots, the fifteen minute programs on agriculture, health and civics are transmitted in the majority language(s) of the area covered. For example, in the Wolayta Sodo area, programs are broadcast in Amharic, Oromigna and Wolaytigna.

The agricultural education programs produced by ASE and DEMM can be divided into two major categories: agricultural education and home science or health education. Agricultural programs broadcast in 1983 covered topics such as farm planning, growing corn, teff and sorghum, soil conservation, contour ploughing, fertilizers and cultivating potatoes. Home science and health education programs included balanced diet, foods of Ethiopia, malnutrition and resultant diseases, food and water sanitation, environmental sanitation, home and family management, selecting home sites, making shelving and elevated storage, and constructing a washing table.

At present, there are 199 rural farm forums in Ethiopia[41] which have been established by ASE and programmed by ASE and DEMM. The distribution and plans for expansion are as follows:

Shewa Region — 42

Kambata-Hadia — 30 (awraja)	Ambo — 12 (awraja)
Angache — 11 (wereda)	Ambo Zuria — 12 (wereda)
Lemu — 4	
Gibmichu — 15	

60 additional rural farm forums are planned in Shewa Administrative Region for 1984.

Bale Region — 77

Genale — 27	Mendeyu — 50
	(four settlement areas)
Harolaunte — 5	
Ejerssa Mudemtu — 4	Abmtu — 20
Ketta — 3	Aminga — 10
Burro Chele — 3	Sabaja Goda — 10
Bakku — 4	Ratteba — 10
Berresa — 4	
Derracha — 4	

60 additional rural farm forums are planned in Bale Administrative Region for 1984.

Sidamo Region — 49

Wolayta Sodo — 49
(awraja)

Damot Gale — 7 (wereda)	Sodo Zuria — 7
Koysha — 6	Bolosso — 7
Humbo — 6	Domot Woyede — 5
	Offa — 3

Arsi Region — 39

Chilalo — 39
(awraja)

Kofele — 1 (wereda)	Munnesa — 5
Gilegeasasa — 2	Zuway Dugda — 4
Limu and Bibilo — 7	Hetossa — 6
Digelu and Tijo — 7	Dodota — 7

80 additional rural farm forums are planned in Arsi Administrative Region in 1984.

There is a planned expansion of the rural farm forum project into Gojjam Administrative Region by developing 80-100 rural farm forums there during 1984.

Beyond the activities involved in the rural farm forums, ASE is concerned with other aspects of adult education in the agricultural and home science fields. Picture albums are produced for those who are not literate.[42] The pictures illustrate basic agricultural and home science concerns. In 1983, twenty-one posters were produced; the subjects illustrated were nutrition, home improvement, mother and child, prenatal care, and baby and child care. Flip charts are developed for use by the ASE field agents in addition to a series of booklets, each of which is concerned with a particular aspect of agricultural development or home science. Subjects such as bee keeping, livestock, new crops, fertilizers, contour planting, crop rotation, etc., are treated in each booklet. The peasant, after reading the booklet, takes the test which is included and, if the answers are satisfactory, receives a certificate of completion. Twelve pamphlets are produced for both agriculture and home science. ASE also produces a newsletter. Eighty thousand are printed and distributed to farmers four times a year. Presently, the newsletter is published in three languages, 40,000 in Amharic, 20,000 in Oromigna and 20,000 in Tigrigna.

CONCLUSION

A cultural-grassroots approach to mediated development in general and agricultural development specifically is a possibility within the Ethiopian context. The existence of regional stations, the commitment of the MOA to decentralized grassroots development and relative independence of DEMM in terms of personnel, production facilities and scheduling has created a situation in which theory may be translated into practice. The benefits for the peasant farmers would include the increase in the amount of knowledge which would be generated and transmitted concerning agricultural techniques and technology. Integrated with the activities of the DAs, localized media development projects would evaluate ways to best provide farmers with information on the objectives, scope and opportunities available through an agricultural extension project. In addition, being integrated with the objectives of MOA through the DAs, a strengthened line of communication would be established between MOA and the individual peasant farmers. Based on a grassroots approach which incorporates indigenous cultural values, national languages and traditional communication techniques, the activities would meet the needs of local populations.

In addition, programming could provide a source of information on visits of the DAs to local producer cooperatives, service cooperatives and peasant associations, as well as information in times of distress such as local outbreaks of disease and famine. One cannot ignore the fact that radio can also provide the potential for bringing together distanced individuals and families who share common problems and concerns. The sharing of information by peasant association service cooperatives and producer cooperatives, as well as individual peasant farmers, will potentially ameliorate difficulties for the farmers and will develop among them a greater sense of common identity — of community — which has been defined above as true communication.

NOTES

1. Thomas S.Kuhn, *The Structure of Scientific Revolutions*, 2nd ed. (Chicago: The University of Chicago Press, 1970), pp.103, 109.

2. See Juan E. Diaz Bordenave, *Communication and Rural Development*, (Paris: United Nations Educational, Scientific and Cultural Organization, 1977), p.9; Susanne K. Langer, *Philosophy in a New Key: A Study in the Symbolism of Reason, Rite and Rt*, 3rd ed., (Cambridge, Mass.: Harvard University Press, 1957), Chap.1 and Robert Misbet, "Introduction: The Problem of Social Change" in *Social Change*, Robert Misbet, ed., (New York: Harper and Row, 1973), pp.1-45.

3.   See Rudolf Arnheim, *Art and Visual Perception: A Psychology of The Creative Eye*, rev. ed., (Berkley: University of California Press, 1974) and Marshall Segall, Donald T. Campbell and Melville J. Herskovits, *The Influence of Culture on Visual Perception*, (Indianapolis: Bobbs-Merill Company, 1966).

4.   James Mangan, "Cultural Conventions of Pictorial Representation: Iconic Literacy and Education", *ECTJ: Educational Communication and Technology*, Vol.26, No.3, pp.245-246.

5.   Thomas Kuhn, *op. cit.*, p.112.

6.   James W. Carey, "A Cultural Approach to Communication", (unpublished monograph, Institutes of Communication Research, University of Illinois at Champaign-Urbana, 1973), published in *Communication*, 2, 1975.

7.   Luis Ramiro Beltran, "Alien Premises, Objects, and Methods in Latin American Communication Research", *Communication Research*, Vol.3, No.2 (April 1976), p.109; and Juan Diaz Bordenave, "Communication of Agricultural Innovations in Latin America: the Need for a new Model", *Communication Research*, Vol.3, No.2 (April 1976), p.145.

8.   This historical connection is outlined in detail by Lawrence Grossberg, "Interpreting the 'Crisis' of Culture in Communication Theory", *Journal of Communication*, Vol.29, No.1 (Winter 1979), pp.59-62; Diaz Bordenave supports Grossberg's thesis concerning mainstream communication theory; see also Langer, *op. cit.*, pp.14-15, 23-24.

9.   Beltran, *op. cit.*, p.118; Grossberg, *op. cit.*, p.60; and Everett M. Rogers, "Where Are We in Understanding the Diffusion of Innovation?", Wilbur Schramm and Daniel Lerner, eds., *Communication and Change: The Last Ten Years — and the Next*, (Honolulu: University of Hawaii, 1976), pp.212-213.

10. Luis Ramiro Beltran, "Rural Development and Social Communication: Relationships and Strategies", in Robert H. Crawford and William B. Ward, eds., *Communication Strategies for Rural Development: Proceedings of the Cornell-CIAT International Symposium*, (Ithaca, N.Y.: New York State College of Agriculture and Life Sciences, 1974), pp.13-14.

11. Grossberg, *op. cit.*, p.60; and Emile G. McAnany, ed., *Communications in the Rural Third World: The Role of Information in Development*, (New York: Praeger Publishers, 1980), pp.143-144.

12. Grossberg, *op. cit.*, p.61.

13. Beltran, "Rural Development", pp.13-14; Diaz Bordenave, "Communication of Agricultural Innovations", p.137; and Everett M. Rogers, *Modernization Among Peasants: The Impact of Communication*, (New York: Holt, Rinehart and Winston, 1979), p.7.

14. Beltran, "Rural Development", pp.13-14.

15. David L. Swanson, "The Continuing Evolution of the Uses and Gratification Approach", *Communication Research*, Vol.6, No.1, p.4 (paraphrasing Elihu Katz).

16. Beltran, "Rural Development", pp.13-14.

17. Bryant E. Kearl, "Communication for Agricultural Development" and Harry T. Oshima, "Development and Mass Communication — A Re-Examination", both works in Schramm

and Lerner, eds., *op. cit.*, pp,171 and 28 respectively; and Herbert I Schiller, *Communication and Cultural Domination*, (White Plains, N.Y.: International Arts and Sciences Press, 1976).

18. For a history of development theory and practice in general, see James Petras, *Critical Perspectives in Imperialism and Social Class in the Third World*, (New York: Monthly Review Press, 1978). For analyses dealing specifically with Latin America, see Ronald Chilcote and Joel C. Edelstein, eds., *Latin America: The Struggle with Dependency and Beyond*, (New York: John Wiley and Songs, 1974); James D. Cockcroft, Andre Gunder Frank and Dale L. Johnson, *Dependence and Underdevelopment: Latin America's Political Economy*, (Garden City, N.Y.: Doubleday and Company, Anchor Books, 1972); Celso Furtado, *Economic Development of Latin America: A Survey from Colonial Times to the Cuban Revolution*; Suzette Macedo, trans. (Cambridge: Cambridge University Press, 1970); and Juan Diaz Bordenave, "Communication" and *Communication and Rural Development*; among other works.

19. Beltran, "Rural Development", pp.12-19.

20. Everett M. Rogers, "Communication and Development, the Passing of the Dominant Paradigm", *Communication Research*, Vol.3, No.2, (April 1976), p.214.

21. Chiltoge, *Latin America*, p.3.

22. *Ibid.*

23. Diaz Bordenave, *Communication and Rural Development*, pp.13-14; see also Kearl, *op. cit.*, p.167.

24. Fortner, p.2.

25. Langer, *op. cit.*, p.38.

26. *Ibid.*

27. George Herbert Mead, "A Behavioristic Account of the Significant Symbol", *Journal of Philosophy*, 19: 157-63 (1922), p.162.

28. Langer, *op. cit.*, 24-25; Harold A. Innis, *Empire and Communications*, (Toronto: University of Toronto Press, 1972), pp.19, 26, 43.

29. Langer, *op. cit.*, pp.28-43.

30. Paulo Friere, *Pedagogy of the Oppressed*, Lyra Mergman Ramos, trans., (New York: The Seabury Press, 1970), p.76.

31. Langer, *op. cit.*, p.45.

32. Carey, *op. cit.*

33. PADEP Task Force (unpublished questionnaire).

34. Interview: Ato Makonnen Tefera, March 1984.

35. *Ibid.*

36. Interview: Ato Gebeyhu Woobe, March 1984.

37. General information on DEMM generated from *Educational Mass Media*, (Addis Ababa: EMPDA, 1981).

38. Interview: Ato Abebe Berhanu, Director of DEMM, Ato Abdu Mozayen, Former Director EMMS and special consultant.

39. *Annual Report, Agri-Service Ethiopia, 1982*, (Addis Ababa: Agri-Service Ethiopia, February 1983), p.19.

40. *Ibid.*

41. Interview: Staff of Agri-Service Ethiopia, March 1984.

42. Agri-Service Annual Report (Addis Ababa: Agri-Service Ethiopia, 1983), pp.2-3.

SOVIET-ETHIOPIAN RELATIONS TODAY

Anatoly A. Gromyko

Esteemed Mr. Chairman,
Esteemed participants in the eighth International
  Congress of Ethiopian Studies,

On behalf of the delegation of Soviet scholars allow me first of all to express sincere appreciation to the Organizing Committee of the eighth International Congress of Ethiopian Studies for its considerable effort that went into preparing our meeting, as well as our particular respect to Dr. Taddesse Tamrat, Chairman of the Organizing Committee and of the Congress, Director of the Institute of Ethiopian Studies of Addis Ababa University, who together with Dr. Douri Mohammed, President of the University, and his colleagues, made an impressive contribution to the organization of this representative forum.

Our congress has been convened in Addis Ababa at a time so significant for Ethiopia. Last September a constituent congress of the Workers' Party of Ethiopia was held, a congress of historic importance. The Congress adopted the Statute and the Programme of the Party which are based on the principles of Marxism-Leninism providing for the WPE's vanguard role in the struggle for completing the national democratic revolution and building a socialist society. Having just celebrated the tenth anniversary of its revolution, the country has entered a new stage of development. I find it necessary to emphasize that Ethiopian studies as a science have deep historical roots and a rich literature. Work in that field will undoubtedly continue. At the same time, Ethiopian studies cannot fail to reflect the realities of the current revolutionary process of breaking down the age-old foundations of the former petrified empire.

I would venture a suggestion that historians, sociologists, ethnographers, linguists, and economists will increasingly focus their studies on modern and recent history, bringing them closer to our time and to the Ethiopian people's revolution which has brought about truly progressive socio-economic and political changes in the life of the Ethiopian people.

Distinguished colleagues,

In my country Ethiopian studies have a rich history, and it is no accident. That reflects among other things the solid historical foundation underlying Soviet-Ethiopian relations.

The most remarkable feature of relations between our two countries is perhaps the fact that they have never been troubled by anything in all their history. Russian and Soviet people have always had the friendliest feelings towards Ethiopia while the Ethiopians have always pronounced with respect the word *maskob* — Russian, Soviet (derivative from the word "Moscow") because in the people's memory that word has been associated with Russian doctors — *khakims* who back in the last century attended to sick civilians and wounded soldier patriots of their country; it has been associated with Russia providing humane assistance to Ethiopia, with the Soviet Union raising its voice against the fascist occupation of this African country and with Soviet people demonstrating their solidarity with the Ethiopian revolution by giving it comprehensive moral, political and economic support on the part of the USSR.

Relations between the peoples of the Soviet Union and Ethiopia before the 1974 Ethiopian revolution. Ethiopian studies in the Soviet Union over the same period.

Relations between the peoples of the Soviet Union and Ethiopia are deeply rooted in history. Since the main stages of these relations have been covered in sufficient detail both in Soviet and foreign literature I shall address only some of them, with a special emphasis on the development of Soviet-Ethiopian relations at the present stage and on Ethiopian studies in our country, which also have their own history.

The peoples of the Soviet multinational state have long taken interest in Ethiopia with its age-old culture and peculiarities of its languages, script, literature, art, and religion and with its eventful and complex history. This is true of the Russians and Ukrainians, Armenians and Georgians, Estonians and Azerbaijanians, and many other peoples of our country. Archives and museums not only in Moscow and Leningrad, but also in Yerevan, Tbilisi, Tartu, Uzhgorod, Odessa, Krasnodar, Sverdlovsk, Taganrog, Kiev and other cities of the Soviet Union, as well as libraries of various cities of Europe, Africa and Asia contain manuscripts, documents, and books many of which are still unknown or little known to the world scientific community. Some of them are becoming the subject of scientific research only now. They contain a wealth of information about the history of political, scientific, and cultural contacts between our two countries.

Initial information about Ethiopia appeared in our country over 7 centuries ago, while the very first attempts at establishing official political relations between Ethiopia and Russia date as far back as the end of the 17th century. Iov Ludolf, a Saxonian scholar and a leading student of Ethiopian history and language of his time, was the first to advocate closer relations between Ethiopia and Russia. However, a joint Russian-Saxonian expedition to Ethiopia conceived by him did not materialize.

Judging by archive documents, Emperor Peter I of Russia later made an attempt to establish closer contacts between Russia and Ethiopia.[1] While under Peter I a Russian expedition to Ethiopia did not materialise, the idea itself is of a certain interest. Indeed it was Peter I who sent Abraham Hannibal, an Ethiopian by origin and the great-grandfather of Alexander Pushkin, the great poet and the genius of world literature, to a school of military engineers.

Over time the Russian scientific community's interest in Ethiopia grew noticeably. First attempts at studying the Ethiopian languages and the Ethiopian script were probably made in the mid-18th century. It is noteworthy that those efforts were associated with the great Russian scholar, Mikhail Lomonosov. The USSR Academy of Sciences has in its Archives an extract from the Register of the Academic Chancellory dated 2 November 1755 indicating the need to prepare "Abyssinian or Ethiopian syllables" for Lomonosov's *Russian Grammar*.

In the 1820s the Ethiopian language became a subject of university education in our country. At first a course in the Ethiopian language was introduced at the oriental languages department of Kharkov University where it was taught by a Petersburg academician and well-known orientalist, B. A. Dorn. Subsequently he studied the manuscript collections of the Public Library and the Asian Museum of the Academy of Sciences which marked the beginning of a description of the Ethiopian manuscripts collections of the Public Library and the Asian Museum, which by that time began accumulating in our libraries.

The last third of the 19th century is generally known to have been a time of severe trials for the peoples of Ethiopia. The country proved to be the only African state which at that time succeeded in preserving its independence in an armed struggle against the colonialists. In its fight to stay independent the government of Ethiopia sought Russia's support. The stand taken by Russia, as is now generally recognized, objectively contributed to the struggle of Ethiopia for preserving its freedom. At the height of the Italo-Ethiopian war of 1895-1896 the Ethiopian government dispatched an extraordinary mission to Russia.

At a time of adversity for Ethiopia the sympathies of progressive Russians were on the side of the Ethiopian people fighting for their independence. In those days the great Russian writer, Lev Tolstoy, wrote an article, full of anger and pain, in which he denounced the action by the Italian government that had unleashed the war against Ethiopia.[2] In 1896 funds were raised in Russia for providing medical assistance to wounded and sick Ethiopian soldiers. The Russian Red Cross Society sent a group to Ethiopia, which provided medical aid not only to the wounded in the Ethiopian army, but also to civilians and started medical training courses for Ethiopians. Many members of that group were awarded orders and medals by the government of Ethiopia.

In the 19th-early 20th centuries a large number of travellers, physicians and diplomats representing different peoples of our country visited Ethiopia. Among them were Y. P. Kovalevsky, V. F. Mashkov, A. V. Eliseyev, N. S. Leontyev, K. S. Zvyagin, A. K. Bulatovich, N. P. Brovtsyn, P. V. Schusev, L. K. Artamonov, A. I. Kokhanovsky and others who brought back not only most interesting ethnographic material, but also valuable data on the socio-economic structure of the Ethiopian society of that period. It should be stressed that the Russian expeditions to Ethiopia of that time, aside from contributing to the establishment of diplomatic relations between Russia and Ethiopia in 1897, helped develop cultural ties between our two countries. During the same period, Ethiopian young men who had come to Russia with members of the Russian expeditions studied at various educational establishments of the country. Particularly beneficial to Ethiopians was the work of our physicians, doctor's assistants and orderlies who for a decade provided help to the local population at a hospital established at the Russian mission in Addis Ababa.

Towards the end of the 19th century when Russia's interest in Ethiopia, its history, philology and ethnography increased, two prominent scholars in our country, V. V. Bolotov and B. A. Turaev, made a significant contribution to Ethiopian studies in the world. For his scientific accomplishments V. V. Bolotov was awarded the title of corresponding member of the Petersburg Academy of Sciences. He was a major authority in the field of Ethiopian history and literature and had an excellent knowledge of the Ge'ez and Amharic languages. Research done by V. V. Bolotov on the history of Ethiopia's Christian church is particularly interesting.

B. A. Turaev was the first to resume university teaching of the Ethiopian language after B. A. Dorn. In 1902, he published his work on Ethiopian studies entitled *Investigations in the Field of Hagiological Sources of Ethiopian History*. He also published a number of literary monuments of Ethiopian culture. Following Dorn, Kokovtsev and Bolotov, he continued the description of Ethiopian manuscripts and in 1906 issued a complete catalogue of the entire Petersburg collection of Ethiopian manuscripts. Because of his untimely death he did not finish his work on preparing for publication historical chronicles of Ethiopia of the 14th-16th centuries. That study was completed by another noted Soviet orientalist, I. Y. Krachkovsky. There is every reason to say that academician Turaev laid the foundation for Ethiopian linguistic studies in our country to be subsequently developed by a galaxy of Soviet scholars. Turaev and Krachkovsky were scientists who worked at a time of transition from one social era to another.

In October 1917 the Great October Socialist Revolution took place in Russia. And it must be said that the Soviet Government and our people have always come out in support of the Ethiopian people at all subsequent stages of their history.

In the difficult revolutionary years the Soviet state was seeking to establish friendly ties with Ethiopia. According to the recently discovered archive documents, in June 1921 I. A. Zalkind from the Peoples' Commissariat of Foreign Affairs of the Soviet Republic was sent to Ethiopia on a diplomatic mission and managed to reach Addis Ababa where he held talks with the leaders of the Ethiopian state on reestablishing formal relations between the two countries and dispatching a diplomatic mission from Soviet Russia to Ethiopia. Those plans found a favourable response from the Ethiopian leaders, but they did not conceal their apprehension regarding the position of the Entente Powers on this matter. Relations between Soviet Russia and Ethiopia were not reestablished at that time and in 1922 the Soviet diplomat returned to the USSR.

Upon his return, I. Zalkind published an "Abyssinia" article in the *Novi Vostok* journal, under the pen name of I. Vanin, which contained some telling conclusions. He wrote that Ethiopia was at a crossroads and at that time the choice depended more on the country itself than on any influence and pressure on the part of Europe. The alternative was either to take the road passing through the white-hot crucible of capitalism, to go through every stage of covert or overt colonization or *to enter the era of growing productive forces under the aegis of the power of the working people, with a minimum of sacrifice and a maximum of assistance from those countries where new social forms had already triumphed* (my emphasis).[3]

Subsequently Ethiopian public opinion clearly advocated the establishment of relations with the Soviet Union. But in those years Soviet-Ethiopian relations were not established both because of the opposition from the Entente countries and, certainly, because of the negative attitude shown by Ethiopia's feudal reaction.

However, despite the obstacles raised by West European powers, social contacts between the two countries continued to develop. For instance, the newspaper *Ethiopie commerciale* published at that time in Addis Ababa often covered events in the Soviet Union.[4] In 1927 a

Soviet agrobotanical expedition headed by an outstanding Soviet scientist, Academician N. I. Vavilov, worked in Ethiopia. The expedition contributed to world science by discovering an original site of plant domestication.[5] Trade ties also began to develop between the USSR and Ethiopia.

In 1935, the government of fascist Italy unleashed a war against Ethiopia. The position of the Soviet Union during that period is well known. That is why I will dwell only on some points.

Even before the Italian fascists attacked Ethiopia the Soviet Union came out strongly for its defence. The Soviet representative at the League of Nations declared that his country abided by the principle of Ethiopia's equality and independence. That was a consistent stand of Soviet diplomacy throughout the struggle of the peoples of Ethiopia against the fascist aggression. The Soviet Union was pressing for an effective application of sanctions against fascist Italy and was denouncing before the eyes of the world the colonial and aggressive nature of the war, and the policy of "appeasement" or, in fact, encouragement of the aggressor, pursued by some Western powers. The working people of the Soviet Union followed with sympathy the nationwide struggle waged by Ethiopia against the Italian invaders.

The Soviet Union was not only one of the states that did not recognize the fascist annexation of Ethiopia, but it also persevered in its efforts to support the people of that country even after its occupation by Italy. Thus, at the Plenary of the League of Nations on July 1, 1936, the head of the Soviet delegation insisted that only effective actions against the aggressor could save the victim. At a meeting of the Council of the League of Nations in May 1938, the USSR representative stressed that recognizing the results of forcible actions, especially when a country which had fallen victim to aggression continued its struggle for independence, was tantamount to direct assistance to the aggressor and to a stab in the back of the victim.[6]

The consistent anti-colonial stand of the Soviet Union was an important moral and political encouragement for Ethiopia in struggle. In July 1944, the newspaper *The Ethiopian Herald* wrote that the country still remembered that despite the fact that there had been no formal relations between Ethiopia and the USSR, the latter had not hesitated to come out in defence of the interests of Ethiopia at the League of Nations.[7]

During the fascist aggression against Ethiopia and the occupation of that country Soviet students in African affairs published a number of works dedicated to the peoples of Ethiopia, of which a collection of scientific articles, *Abyssinia (Ethiopia)* edited by D. A. Olderogge and published in 1936 by the Institute of Anthropology, Archaeology and Ethnography of the USSR Academy of Sciences, deserves special mention. This book is a major study on Ethiopia's history, ethnography and economy in the 1930s. Like many other publications of that period, the book exposed the true nature of the fascist aggression in Ethiopia and the policy of connivance at that aggression pursued by a number of governments.

In the mid-1930s the teaching of the Amharic language was first introduced by linguist N. V. Yushmanov at Leningrad University. In those years he published his scientific work *The Structure of the Amharic Language*, as well as general surveys of the languages in Ethiopia, which appeared as articles in the journal *Sovetskaya Etnographia* (issue No.1, 1936) and in the above-mentioned collection, *Abyssinia (Ethiopia)*.

Diplomatic relations with the Soviet Union were established on April 21, 1943, after Ethiopia's liberation from the fascist occupation.

The victory of the Soviet Union over Nazi Germany in the Great Patriotic War gave a tremendous impetus to the evolution of the world revolutionary process. Africa was gradually throwing off the shackles of colonialism and Soviet-Ethiopian relations were further developed.

In 1936, the Governments of the Soviet Union and Ethiopia agreed to raise their diplomatic mission in Addis Ababa and Moscow to embassy level and to exchange ambassadors. Since then economic and cultural ties between the two countries have been developing successfully. A Soviet-Ethiopian trade and economic agreement was signed in July 1959. The Soviet Union extended to Ethiopia a long-term credit in the amount of 90m. roubles to develop the country's industry and agriculture. In the summer of 1962 a contract was signed to design and build an oil refinery in Assab. Commissioned in the spring of 1967, the refinery was called by the Ethiopian public a pioneering effort in the development of the country's heavy industry.

In 1960, the first agreement on cultural cooperation between the USSR and Ethiopia was signed and since 1961 protocols on cultural events have been signed on a regular basis. Since 1960 Ethiopian and Soviet art exhibitions have been exchanged. Ethiopian dancers and singers toured the Soviet Union and Soviet artists performed in Ethiopia. Russian translations of Ethiopian authors have appeared while Russian classics and Soviet authors have been translated into the Amharic language. It should be noted, however, that before the 1974 people's revolution Soviet publications allowed in Ethiopia were mainly fiction, whereas political literature and the classics of Marxism-Leninism were strictly prohibited in Ethiopia.

In the late 1950s a new generation of Soviet scholars specializing in Ethiopian studies began their work and they include a majority of those doing research today. They are characterized by both greater specialization and a wider range of research. One of the older generation scholars still working at that time was academician I. Y. Krachkovsky, the author of a unique work entitled *An Introduction of Ethiopian Philology* (L., 1955) in which he made a comprehensive analysis of almost every work by foreign and national specialists in Ethiopian linguistics and literature. Linguist V. P. Starinin doing research on the Ge'ez language also worked at that time.

In the 1960s and 1970s there were systematic publications and research in the USSR of its own sources (Russian, Armenian, Georgian, etc.) as well as of Arabic, Greco-Roman and Syrian sources on the history of Ethiopia and its neighbouring countries. Among those works mention could be made of studies relating to notes and documents of Russian travellers to Ethiopia in the mid-19th and early 20th centuries (works by M. V. Right, I. S. Katsnolson, L. E. Kubbel and others), to the archives of the Russian diplomatic mission to Ethiopia at the end of the 19th century (a monograph by I. I. Vasin), Georgian sources (work by V. G. Macharadze), Armenian documents (works by A. G. Turtyan, O. K. Topusyan), Arabic sources on Ethiopia (articles by L. E. Kubbel, V. V. Matveyev, Y. M. Kobishchanov), etc.

Considerable attention was given to studies of Ethiopian history: its ancient history (works by A. G. Lundin, Y. M. Kobishchanov, K. P. Kalinovskaya, S. B. Chernetsov); modern history (works by Y. M. Kobishchanov, M. V. Right, V. A. Trofimov); recent history (D. R. Voblikov, V. A. Trofimov, M. V. Right, V. S. Yagya and others); as well as of Ethiopia's economy (A. G. Kokyev, A. Y. Elyanov). Ethiopia was an important subject dealt with in such regional studies as *The History of Africa in the 19th-early 20th Centuries* and *The Recent History of Africa*, carried out by several authors. Research was also done in the field of ethnography, ethnic history of the peoples of Ethiopia (K. P. Kalinovskaya, Z. P. Akisheva, Y. M. Kobishchanov, M. V. Right, V. S. Yagya) and linguistics (E. B. Gankin, E. G. Titov).

Soviet-Ethiopian relations and Ethiopian studies in the USSR after the 1974 revolution

The beginning of the national democratic revolution in Ethiopia in 1974 is associated with expanding Soviet-Ethiopian relations which are becoming truly comprehensive. While receiving Comrade Mengistu Haile Mariam, Chairman of the PMAC and COPWE and at present General Secretary of the WPE Central Committee, in Moscow on March 29, 1984, Comrade Konstantin U. Chernenko, General Secretary of the CPSU Central Committee, said: "It was only after the victory of the Ethiopian revolution . . . that these relations have really blossomed and sparkled with new facets".[8]

A new impetus has also been given to the development of Ethiopian studies in the Soviet Union which have since focused on examining the causes and prospects of the Ethiopian revolution and the nature of its driving forces, as well as the dynamics and trends of revolutionary developments.

A number of interesting studies concerning Ethiopia were published in the Soviet Union in the 1970s and 1980s. Among them mention should be made of the following monographs: "National Democratic Revolution in Ethiopia", Moscow, the Institute for African Studies of the USSR Academy of Sciences, 1976; "Ethiopian Studies. History and Culture", Moscow,

Nauka, 1981; G. L. Galperin, "Ethiopia: Population, Resources and Economy", Moscow, *Nauka*, 1978; G. A. Tsypkin, "Ethiopia: From Division to Political Centralization", Moscow, *Mysl*, 1978; S. B. Chernetsov, "Ethiopian Feudal Monarchy in the 13th-16th Centuries", Moscow, *Nauka*, 1982; a collective monograph by Soviet, Ethiopian, Czechoslovak, Hungarian and Bulgarian scholars, "Contemporary Problems and Foreign Policy of Ethiopia", Moscow, *Mezhdunarodniye Otnosheniya*, 1982; books by A. G. Kokyev, "Ethiopia is Building a New Life", Moscow, *Znaniye*, 1977; V. I. Korovikov, *Ethiopia – Revolutionary Years*, Moscow, Novosti Press Agency, 1979; articles by V. K. Vigand, G. L. Galperin, E. K. Denisov, Y. M. Kobishchanov, A. G. Kokyev, M. V. Right, S. B. Chernetsov, K. I Sharayev and many other scholars. These works are indicative of the continuing interest shown in Ethiopian studies in the USSR for Ethiopian culture, ethnic problems and the history of establishing a united Ethiopian state.

Quite a few of the Soviet studies attest to an interest in the basic concepts and main trends of the revolutionary process in the country, differentiation between the general features and specific characteristics of the Ethiopian revolution, practical experience of the Ethiopians in establishing government bodies, a vanguard party and social organizations, as well as in the democratization of political life in the country.

Soviet scholars, including those at the Institute for African Studies of the USSR Academy of Sciences who are engaged in research into the problems of Ethiopia, see their task, *inter alia*, in assisting Ethiopian scholars and the working people of this country in a progressive restructuring of their life by analyzing the processes taking place in Ethiopia, disseminating truthful information about these processes in the USSR and abroad, as well as synthesizing and disseminating the experience gained in the process of progressive transformations.

Some bourgeois authors in the West are trying to prove that the socio-economic orientation of Ethiopia, its socialist aspirations and ideals have no prospects. Unfortunately, these views are at times shared by some researchers rejecting the objectives and ideas of revolutionary democrats who are leading the country along the path of socialist orientation chosen by the Ethiopian working people and who have proclaimed their adherence to Marxism-Leninism.

It is evident that such views are untenable. Indeed, they are refuted by the successes of socialist-orientated Ethiopia and by the fact that it has joined the ranks of the most progressive developing countries.

Ever since the national democratic revolution began in Ethiopia in 1974, it has stimulated the development of political relations between the USSR and Socialist Ethiopia. Two government delegations from Ethiopia visited the Soviet Union in January/February and in July 1976. The joint communique on the results of the last of these two visits pointed out that there were prospects for deepening relations between our two countries.

Regular contacts between the leaders of the Provisional Military Administrative Council (PMAC) and the Commission for Organizing the Party of the Working People of Ethiopia (COPWE) and the leaders of the CPSU and the Soviet state which take the form of visits and personal messages have acquired particular significance for the further development of these relations.

Comrade Mengistu Haile Mariam, Chairman of the PMAC and COPWE and now General Secretary of the WPE Central Committee, paid several official and working visits to the Soviet Union, the latest being in March this year.

High-level Party and Government delegations from the USSR visited Addis Ababa in connection with the celebration of the anniversaries of the Ethiopian revolution and to participate in the constituent congress of the WPE.

The ministries of foreign affairs of the two countries have a regular exchange of information. Our friendly relations have been put on a firm legal contractual basis. On May 4, 1977, the USSR and Socialist Ethiopia signed the Declaration on Basic Principles of Friendly Relations and Cooperation, and on November 20, 1978, they concluded the Treaty of Friendship and Cooperation which has become fundamental basis for developing all-round relations between the two countries in various fields.

Interparty ties based on common ideological principles have always been of utmost importance for deepening Soviet-Ethiopian cooperation. The CPSU has invariably sympathized with the WPE from the very first days of its activities.

Already, in the course of the visit of Comrade Mengistu Haile Mariam to the USSR in October 1982, the Agreement on Cooperation between the CPSU and the COPWE and the Plan of Ties between them for 1983-1984 were signed. This plan is now being implemented. Thus, the Soviet Union is assisting Ethiopia in training cadres of political organizers and activists: together with Ethiopians, Soviet instructors are teaching social sciences at the Yekatit-66 Political School in Addis Ababa. On several occasions the CPSU presented our Ethiopian friends with large collections of Marxist-Leninist literature. Active contacts are also being maintained between social organizations of the USSR and Ethiopia, i.e. between the All-Union Central Council of Trade Unions and the All-Ethiopia Trade Union, the Young Communist League and the Association of Youth of Revolutionary Ethiopia, the Soviet Women's Committee and the Revolutionary Ethiopia Women Association.

The commonality of ideological principles based on the Marxist-Leninist theory has brought about close diplomatic cooperation between the two countries. At various international forums, Ethiopian and Soviet representatives oppose imperialism, neocolonialism, racism, apartheid, zionism and advocate peace, international detente, the establishment of a new international economic order, turning the Indian Ocean into a zone of peace, peaceful settlement of disputes existing between neighbouring states, non-interference in the internal affairs of states and maintenance of normal relations between states with different social systems on the basis of the principles of peaceful coexistence.

Soviet people and Soviet scientists highly appreciate the vigorous support on the part of the people and government of Ethiopia for the peaceful policy course of the CPSU and the Soviet government, and its policy of the struggle against imperialism. Today Soviet-Ethiopian cooperation has entered a new stage which makes happy all of us, friends of Socialist Ethiopia. Soviet-Ethiopian friendship effectively contributes to cohesion of anti-imperialist forces and strengthens peace and international security.

Soviet-Ethiopian economic cooperation

Faithful to its internationalist principles, the Soviet Union is rendering Socialist Ethiopia considerable assistance in reconstructing and developing its national economy, strengthening its public sector in industry, power production, agriculture, in training national cadres, and improving the systems of national economic planning, public health and education. On March 29, 1984, during their meeting in the Kremlin, Konstantin U. Chernenko, General Secretary of the CPSU Central Committee, and Mengistu Haile Mariam, Chairman of the PMAC of Socialist Ethiopia and the COPWE, expressed their satisfaction at the successful development of relations between the Soviet Union and Socialist Ethiopia and pronounced themselves in favour of their further strengthening.[9]

The Soviet Union not only grants credits on easy terms to friendly Ethiopia, but also strives to provide financial, economic and technical assistance in such a way as to enable Ethiopia to become economically independent as early as possible, raise its productivity of labour and meet material and spiritual requirements of the working people of the country moving along the chosen road towards socialism, which in the final analysis means nothing but meeting the interests of the working masses.

Soviet-Ethiopian economic cooperation is based on a whole series of agreements and protocols signed in accordance with the principles of the Treaty of Friendship and Cooperation between the two countries. An Intergovernmental Soviet-Ethiopian Commission on Economic, Scientific and Technical Cooperation and Trade has been set up to improve the mechanism of economic and technical cooperation. The basic principles underlying our cooperation in these, as well as in other fields, are equality, respect for national sovereignty, non-interference in the internal affairs of the partners.

The choice of specific areas and projects of our economic and technical cooperation is determined by priorities in the Ethiopian economy.

Agriculture is known to be at present one of the highest priorities with the Ethiopian leadership. That is why the Soviet Union is assisting the country in building a system to irrigate 10 thousand hectares of land in the region of Baro-Akobo (Gambela), constructing six refrigerating plants with a combined capacity of over 4 thousand tons, granaries with a combined capacity of 306 thousand tons (of 50 granaries under construction in recent years, 18 are already commissioned), six repair shops for tractors and other agricultural machinery (each with a capacity of 500 repairs a year), several machine rental stations, including stations for grain treatment and winnowing, and training centers for farm machine operators. The USSR also rendered assistance to Ethiopia in building a tractor-assembling plant which became operational in summer 1984.

No country, having set before it the goal of building socialism, can do without industrial development. Being well aware of that, the Ethiopian leaders give priority to such industries as power and building materials, whose development will ensure a rapid growth of other industries, such as machine-building, metallurgy and chemistry at a later stage. Together with the GDR and Czechoslovakia, the Soviet Union is assisting Ethiopia in building a hydropower station in the region of Melka Vakena (150 thousand kw) and a power line as well as a cement plant with a capacity of 600 thousand tons a year in Dire Daua. Besides, the Soviet Unions is providing help in consolidating the Ethiopian State Building Organization, sending its specialists and supplying it with construction equipment and transport facilities.

Development of mineral resources is of great importance for the future of the Ethiopian economy. And here, too, Soviet organizations are helping their Ethiopian friends with mineral prospecting and extraction, in particular of gold and hydrocarbons. At present we are assisting in the reconstruction of the oil refinery built with Soviet aid in the town of Assab and in the building of 10 oil tanks with a combined capacity of 66 thousand m^3.

Training of national specialists occupies a prominent place in Soviet-Ethiopian cooperation. Our country sends dozens of school and university teachers to Ethiopia, supplies Ethiopian vocational training centers with equipment and specialists. Our country continues to provide equipment and instructors to the Bahar Dar Politechnical Institute built by the Soviet Union and presented to the Ethiopian people.

In addition, our organizations are training technicians and workers at all Soviet-assisted projects. All in all, 650 Soviet specialists work on projects of Soviet-Ethiopian cooperation.

We are successfully developing our cooperation in planning, whose organization and improvement is indispensable for a socialist economy. A Permanent Soviet-Ethiopian working group on cooperation in planning is functioning in accordance with the agreement of October 1981 between the State Planning Committee of the USSR and the Supreme Central Planning Council of Ethiopia.

On September 8, 1984, a long-term programme of economic cooperation between the Soviet Union and Socialist Ethiopia was signed, which puts the development of economic relations between the two countries on a planned footing. The purpose of Soviet assistance is to contribute to the development of key branches of Ethiopia's economy.

Soviet-Ethiopian cultural and scientific cooperation

Presently, cultural and scientific cooperation between the USSR and Ethiopia is based on the Agreement of May 6, 1977, followed up by the signing of a whole series of documents governing the development of bilateral ties. For example, the agreements currently implemented are the Agreement of Friendship and Cooperation between the Executive Council of the Kishinev City Soviet of the Moldavian Soviet Socialist Republic and the City Council of Addis Ababa of April 29, 1977 (Kishinev and Addis Ababa are twin towns), the Agreement on Cultural Cooperation between the Union of Soviet Friendship Societies and the Committee of Ethiopian-Soviet Friendship of May 3, 1978, the Agreement on Information Exchanges between TASS and the Ethiopian News Agency (ENA) of February 5, 1976, the Agreement on Cooperation in the Field of Television and Broadcasting between the State Committee of Television and Radio of the USSR and the Ethiopian Radio and Television of June 10, 1977, the

Protocol on the Recognition and Equivalence of Educational Certificates, Scientific Degrees and Titles of May 24, 1978, the Protocol on Training Specialists for Ethiopia at Higher and Specialized Secondary Educational Establishments of the USSR in 1980-1984 of February 15, 1980, and the Agreements on Exchanges and Cooperation between Addis Ababa University and Kiev and Vilnus Universities of August 1982. Two-year protocols on cultural and sports co-operation are signed on a regular basis.

Agreements on cooperation between the writers' and journalists' organizations of the two countries have been signed and are being implemented. Traditional friendly ties are maintained between the Russian and the Ethiopian Orthodox Churches. The Patriarch of the Russian Orthodox Church paid a visit to Ethiopia in January 1974. In recent years a number of delegations of the Ethiopian Church have visited the Soviet Union. Contacts between the Muslims of the two countries have also become more active.

The Committee of Ethiopian-Soviet Friendship and Solidarity has been functioning in Ethiopia since 1977 and the USSR-Ethiopia Friendship Society has been active in the USSR since 1978.

There are exchanges of delegations in the fields of culture, science and public health, visits of writers, journalists and artists, as well as exchanges of performing groups, exhibitions, etc.

A Permanent Soviet Exhibition (i.e. a cultural center and a mission of the Union of Soviet Friendship Societies) has been open in Addis Ababa since 1945. It has a cinema hall seating 330 people and a library of 15 thousand books. The center sponsors a Russian language course, with an annual student body of almost 400 Ethiopians.

Since 1947 a hospital of the Soviet Red Cross and Red Crescent Society, which was awarded the Soviet Order of Friendship of Peoples on February 23, 1973, has been operating in Addis Ababa.

Annually the Soviet Union provides over 500 scholarships for Ethiopian students and post-graduates to study in the USSR. There are now nearly 2500 Ethiopians studying in our country.

Scientific and technological ties between the USSR and Ethiopia are governed by the Programme of Scientific and Technological Cooperation signed on December 13, 1981 which covers such fields as energy, water economy, agriculture and meteorology.

Scientific cooperation between our countries is also expanding. Under the agreement of May 3, 1972, the Soviet side built a phytopathological research laboratory in Ambo, where Soviet and Ethiopian agronomists and specialists in plant disease control are working together.

An Agreement on Cooperation was signed in August 1982 between Addis Ababa University and the Institute for African Studies of the USSR Academy of Sciences which we are representing here. That instrument provides for exchanges of scientific materials, mission of scholars, etc.

Those two institutions have exchanged delegations; the Institute for African Studies and the Institute for Ethiopian Studies of Addis Ababa University have started to exchange scholars.

Of special mention are the Soviet-African Scientific and Political Conference held in Moscow in 1981, in which a delegation of Ethiopian scholars took a most active part[10], and the First All-Union Conference on Ethiopian Studies (Moscow, June 1979) attended by guests from Ethiopia, Czechoslovakia, Bulgaria and Hungary.[11]

The Institute for Ethiopian Studies of Addis Ababa University and its Director, Dr. Taddesse Tamrat have played an important part in those conferences and in contacts and cooperation between Soviet scholars specializing in African studies and Ethiopian scholars.

Speaking at the constituent congress of the Workers' Party of Ethiopia, Mengistu Haile Mariam described the current stage in Ethiopia's relations with socialist countries as follows: "The Soviet Union and other socialist countries . . . sided with the Ethiopian revolution and rendered it firm support when international imperialism launched a war against us on all fronts in the attempt to check, relying on reactionary forces, the progress of our revolution and to violate the territorial integrity of the country. We have reached the current stage at which we are in a position to form a vanguard party due to the heroic struggle of Ethiopian revolutionaries and the people and thanks to the boundless support of our brothers true to the principle of proletarian internationalism."[12]

The current state of Soviet-Ethiopian relations and the achievements in Ethiopian studies in the Soviet Union show that friendship and cooperation between the Soviet Union, the first socialist country in human history, and Socialist Ethiopia have been steadily developing ever since the 1974 national democratic revolution in Ethiopia and hold good prospects for the future.

NOTES

1. K. Kharlampovich, "On the History of Church Solidarity in the 18th Century", *Journal of the Public Education Ministry*, 1910, New Series, p.92 (Rus. ed.).

2. L. N. Tolstoy, *Complete Works*, vol. 31, pp.193-198 (Rus. ed.).

3. I. Vanin, "Abyssinia", *Novi Vostok*, 1922, No. 2, p.541 (Rus. ed.).

4. A quote from D. A. Makeev, "Soviet-Ethiopian relations in the 1920-30s", *Narody Azii i Afriki*, 1975, No.5.

5. N. I. Vavilov, *Wheats of Abyssinia and their place in the general system of wheats*, M., 1931.

6. *Foreign policy of the USSR. Collected Documents, Vol.IV (1935-June 1941)*, M., 1946, p.352 (Rus. ed.).

7. A quote from V. S. Kozlov, "Italo-Ethiopian War of 1935-1936". Candidate's thesis, M., 1981, p.219-220 (Rus. ed.).

8. *Pravda*, 30.3.84.

9. *Ibid.*

10. See *Soviet-African Scientific and Political Conference, 13-16 October 1981*, Moscow, 1982.

11. See *All-Union Conference on Ethiopian Studies, Moscow, 19-21 June 1979. (Abstracts of Reports)*, Moscow, 1979. See also An. A. Gromyko, *Soviet-Ethiopian Relations. Ethiopian Studies in the USSR*, Institute for African Studies, USSR Academy of Sciences, Moscow, 1979.

12. *Pravda*, 8.9.84.

THE ECONOMIC DEVELOPMENT OF KENYA AND ETHIOPIA, 1950-1974

An Essay in Comparison

Paul B. Henze

INTRODUCTION

Ethiopia and Kenya have more features in common than either has with any other African country. Geographically, both consist of temperate highlands surrounded by desert and tropical lowlands. The highlands have been the principal center of development, and highland peoples the main source of economic and political dynamism in both countries. Both countries' economies have been based on agriculture and animal-raising, with a great variety of crops and methods of exploitation. Even with rapidly increasing populations, both countries have the potential of feeding their people and simultaneously exploiting agriculture as a source of ever-increasing export revenue. In the absence of major mineral discoveries, agriculture will have to be the basis of self-propelled economic development — with agricultural exports earning capital for investment in infrastructure and industry, and agricultural production providing the basis for a wide range of domestic industry. Processed and manufactured goods, in turn, can meet not only domestic requirements, but are also a potential source of additional export earnings. In the absence of petroleum, the problem of securing dependable energy supplies for an expanding economy confronts both countries with similar challenges. Large and rapidly increasing populations in both countries represent both a risk and an opportunity. If high rates of economic growth can be maintained so that the population can be adequately fed, educated, organized and motivated, human capital can be developed to bring many returns. The increasing consumption requirements of an expanding population can fuel the productive process.

There is no basic rivalry or intrinsic source of political tension between Ethiopia and Kenya. Neither represents a problem for the other. This fortunate relationship is unique in the region. There is thus a natural basis for cooperation and mutual interaction which can be beneficial to both, especially in relation to these countries' priority goals: modernization and provision of the prerequisites for a higher standard of living and more satisfying social conditions for their people. In light of these circumstances, it is remarkable that there has been so little exchange of experience in economic development between Ethiopia and Kenya. The situation is no doubt in large part to be explained by the very different political evolution of the two countries. Ethiopia, a long-independent, traditional state, evolved in isolation from the rest of Africa. Ethiopians, when they became concerned with modernization and economic development in the 20th century, thought of their situation as unique. Their brief experience of Italian colonialism left them with little inclination to regard colonial methods of development as a model for their own efforts. They tended to reject colonial powers' priorities. Kenya, on the other hand, came to nationhood only as a result of colonial development. Its people had no choice in economic development decisions in a colony long regarded as unusually favourable for European settlement. Development effort was for a long period concentrated on creation of an economy dominated by a small group of white settlers and infrastructure was originally built according to their priorities and future plans.

The net result, nevertheless, was the creation of a strong base on which an independent state, giving priority to the needs of its African population, could build. This result was not fore-ordained, however. The leadership under which Kenya became independent had the wisdom to preserve the positive features of its inheritance and build upon them. The political and economic background becomes less important as time passes, and should not inhibit study of the experience of each country — Ethiopia and Kenya — by the other. It is for this reason that I have undertaken a comparative study of the economic development experience of these two countries from the 1950s onward. In this essay I present some of the tentative conclusions I have reached from examination of the experience of both countries during the quarter century, 1950-1974. We can already study this period with the benefit of ten more years of hindsight. Thus we can see how the policies pursued and results achieved during this quarter century enabled these countries to meet the problems of the subsequent period in which both are now deeply enmeshed. I will not go into these in the present paper, however, but will examine them in a second, later stage of this study.

MAIN FEATURES OF KENYAN DEVELOPMENT, 1950-74

Economic development in Kenya during the period examined in this essay falls into two almost equal parts with 1963, the year in which the country first achieved self-government (1 June) and then independence (12 December), the watershed. The pace of development accelerated markedly following independence. A World Bank study published in 1975 concluded:

> During the first decade of independence Kenya has been remarkably successful in . . . achieving rapid economic growth. Virtually every indicator of performance . . . is well above the average for a country at Kenya's stage of development. GDP grew at an average rate of about 7% a year between 1964 and 1972, and few developing countries can better this kind of performance over an eight-year period.[1]

Though independence brought a sharp break with many of the economic policies that had characterized the colonial period, it was by capitalizing on the advantages Kenya had gained from the positive aspects of colonialism that the surge of growth during the first decade of independence was achieved. These included establishment of infrastructure: transport and communications networks, power generating facilities, modern trade networks and a wide range of manufacturing industries supplying local needs. It is true that development until the late 1950s had occurred in the framework of an approach which envisioned a society in which white settlers might go on increasing and retain dominance indefinitely. With less than 20,000 Whites before the Second World War, Kenya counted nearly 30,000 in its 1948 census. The White population had risen to almost 70,000 by 1960 and played a major role in development of both large-scale agriculture and industry. The economic effect of the MauMau rebellion was much less than the political effect. The Asian population of Kenya had also increased rapidly during this same period. From a prewar total of approximately 45,000, it was approaching 200,000 on the eve of independence. The Asian population dominated small and medium-scale trade, was active in many small and medium-size industries and provided clerical and medium-level managerial personnel for both public services and larger-scale industrial and commercial developments.

Kenya's African population had a much lower economic status than Europeans and Asians. Colonial Kenya had a highly stratified society with sub-groups among the major population divisions playing special roles as well. While the country's per capita GNP stood at $85 on the eve of independence,[2] the level for the 97% of the population who were African was estimated at no more than $50, the same level or perhaps even a bit lower than Ethiopia's at that time. Nevertheless, the African population of Kenya had already benefited substantially from the accelerated pace of colonial development.[3] This can be demonstrated in many ways, but a few basic statistics demonstrate rapid population increase as a result of improved health conditions and the expansion of education and literacy.

According to the census of 1931, Kenya's total population stood at 3,261,000. The 1948 census counted and/or estimated a population of 5,408,000, an increase of 66% in 17 years, only a very small proportion of which can be attributed to European or Asian immigration. By 1969 the population had risen to 10,943,000, an increase of 102% in 21 years! In 1960 adult literacy already stood at 20%, while 47% of children of primary school age were actually in school. During the same year only 7% of Ethiopia's primary school age were attending classes.

The greatest challenge Kenya's new leaders faced on achieving independence was Africanization of the country's most productive agricultural region, the so-called "White Highlands". This task was accomplished in an orderly fashion and in accordance with carefully devised legal principles by the end of the 1960s with no adverse impact on agricultural production. In fact, the agricultural sector as a whole grew at a rate of about 5% a year between 1964 and 1972.[4] Agricultural exports, constituting about 70% of total exports, increased from £37,000,000 in 1965 to almost £50,000,000 in 1971. Coffee and tea were the prime export earners with coffee exports increasing 49% in volume and 52% in value in just four seasons — 1968-1971. Tea exports doubled between 1965 and 1971.[5] Increased production came from both large- and small-scale agriculture.

Agricultural development policy rested on encouragement of the small farmer as the main producer of the country's basic food needs and on expansion of large estate agriculture with both indigenous and foreign capital as a source of exports and supply for domestic agro-industry. In industry as well, newly independent Kenya looked to the private sector to provide the main impetus for development though, contrary to the impression created by some critics of Kenyan economic development policies, the government never adopted a complete *laissez-faire* approach.[6] Government policy encouraged labor-intensive production in small-scale agriculture, for example, at the expense of lowered productivity in comparison with estate agriculture.[7] Labor, which was plentiful, was also absorbed in building and construction industries, which grew at the average rate of 12.3% per year while manufacturing rose at a rate of 7.6% per annum during the period 1964-1972. Tourism, already comparatively well developed by African standards at the time of independence, continued to be encouraged and became a significant foreign-exchange earner.

Resources for development came from two primary sources. An unusually high rate of domestic savings (an average ratio of 19-20% during the 1964-1972 period) — a level higher than that achieved by South Korea during the same period and exceeded in Africa only by the Ivory Coast.[8] Kenya also attracted a large and growing volume of official aid, receiving about $8 per capita per year during the period 1965-1971. The annual level of total disbursements more than doubled during the first independence decade, from £10,000,000 in 1964 to £21,000,000 in 1972.[9]

Meanwhile education expanded rapidly at all levels, public health and other social services to the population were extended well beyond the level prevailing at independence throughout the most heavily populated parts of the country and there was steady improvement of roads and communications. Outlying parts of the country tended to be neglected. Africans replaced Europeans and Asians in most areas of the economy with very little disruption of essential functions and only temporary reduction of efficiency. Competitiveness for prestigious jobs ensured a relatively high level of African performance.

Accelerated development brought many problems as well: pressure on available land in the central highlands, not always successful efforts to bring new land into cultivation in areas of moderate to low fertility and uncertain rainfall, heavy influx of population to urban centers, especially Nairobi, with consequent exacerbation of problems of underemployment and unemployment. Handicrafts and small rural industries, good sources of employment and training of labor, developed unevenly. Government performance in encouragement of some areas of development left a good deal to be desired.[10] On balance, however, what is surprising is not that there were problem areas and failures, but that a government so new and relatively inexperienced performed so well in coordinating divergent interests and avoiding over-bureaucratization.

The international energy crisis which began at the end of 1973 and resulted in a worldwide rise in inflation soon had an impact on Kenya. As the quarter century being surveyed here came to an end, Kenya's leaders found themselves in a forced pause in the pace of development. They and Kenya's foreign aid donors and investors had to evaluate the experience of the previous decade and reconsider goals and methods of operation in light of rising political pressure for greater equality in distribution of gains as well as criticism of inefficiencies in utilization of resources:

There was some evidence that the benefits of development since independence had been confined primarily to the 30% of smallholders in the most favoured rural areas, to wage earners in the modern sector . . . and to the African elite having advantages of capital, formal education or influence. In Kenya's relatively open society these inequities had attracted much scholarly analysis and political debate.[11]

Agriculture, if rationally developed and properly supported, was widely agreed to be the area where the greatest improvements in utilization of resources could be made. The aim would be both to secure greater equalization of wealth and to increase consumption among the whole population and at the same time to increase export earnings. Export earnings would be used both to offset the cost of increased energy imports and to provide capital for continued industrialization.

MAIN FEATURES OF ETHIOPIAN DEVELOPMENT — 1950-1974

A definitive study of the economic impact of the Italian occupation of Ethiopia remains to be done. While it is obvious that the country gained from the expansion of the highway system, from urban construction and civic improvements and from establishment of a few small industries, electric generating plants, waterworks, etc., there was no manpower or educational development. This confronted liberated Ethiopia with a serious problem in 1941. The problem was recognized in Haile Selassie's appeal to individual Italians to remain and help develop the country. It also played a role in Ethiopia's desire to regain Eritrea. There was, in fact, substantial expansion after 1941 in industry and service facilities in Eritrea and improvements in transportation and communications facilities for the use of Allied military forces to support the campaigns in the Middle East. This added significantly to the effect of Italian colonial development in Eritrea. Thus after Federation in 1952, Eritrea made a contribution to Ethiopia's economy considerably larger than its population and size would indicate, not only because it possessed almost half the industrial and service capacity of the country, but because it served as a reservoir of educated and trained manpower. Eritrea continued to make a heavy contribution to Ethiopian manpower requirements even after educational and training programs generated a continually increasing supply of talent from other parts of the country.

At the beginning of the period being surveyed here, agriculture did not loom large in thinking about economic development in Ethiopia. Concern was for development of industry. There were hopes that the country would prove to have exploitable mineral wealth. Before much development could take place, however, it was clear that infrastructure had to be given high priority: transportation, communications, electric power. The establishment of Ethiopian Airlines in 1946 was a far-sighted step, both for the economic development and political integration of the country. Initially the highway program concentrated on maintenance of roads built or improved during the Italian occupation. In the 1950s the program shifted to new construction — an effort which continues today in accordance with plans originally developed three decades ago. In highway development Ethiopia, with even more difficult terrain, compares well with Kenya, and has been far ahead of neighbouring countries such as Sudan and Somalia.

A ten-year industrial plan was formulated in 1944. Foreign capital was encouraged and development aid sought from many friendly countries as well as from UN and other international programs. Foreign specialists were widely employed and helped draw up the first 5-year plan which went into effect in 1956. It gave emphasis to infrastructure development. Industry was emphasized in the second 5-year plan, which extended from 1962-1967. Even before the 5-year planning system became a permanent feature of Ethiopian economic development efforts, several important institutions had been established: the Highway Authority, the Power and Light Authority, the Telecommunications Board, the Ethiopian Investment Corporation and the Central Statistical Office. Planning and development require statistics. This had been an extremely underdeveloped area in Ethiopia, in contrast to Kenya where colonial administration had felt this need quite early. It is only in the 1960s that we can use aggregated statistics as a measure of Ethiopian development.

By 1967 Ethiopia's GDP had increased approximately 50% over the absolute level of 1961. Allowing for inflation, calculated at slightly more than 2% per year, average annual growth during the period had been about 5%, per capita GDP had reached $60 with an estimated population of 24 million. Population was estimated to be increasing at 2% per year, but since no census had been taken, all population statistics were based on small samples and estimates. Modern manufacturing had increased rapidly, growing at an average rate of 17.6% per year between 1961-1967. In spite of substantial increases in production by expanding commercial farms, which were being encouraged but accounted for only an extremely small proportion of cultivated land, agriculture was expanding at a much slower rate than the rest of the economy, averaging about 2% growth per year. It was evident that it was thus no more than keeping up with population growth and could not, without major expansion of productivity, provide for increased consumption by the population, let alone supply the needs of agro-industry or even provide large increases in primary exports.

Though expenditure on medical and health services increased at 12.1% per year during this period, the base had been so low and the needs so great that initial progress merely served to emphasize the challenging requirements yet to be faced. The same was true in education, where a revolution of rising expectations was already under way. About 530,000 students attended primary and secondary schools in the 1967-1968 school year. By this time the universities in Addis Ababa and Asmara, along with specialized colleges at other locations, had 3200 students. Nearly 2000 Ethiopian students were studying abroad. Public education outlays increased at an average annual rate of 16.3% during the decade of the 1960s, substantially above the level for Africa as a whole. Nevertheless, in spite of expanding adult literacy campaigns, literacy in the population as a whole was estimated to be no greater than 10% by 1970.[12]

External economic aid appeared large in absolute terms and rose steadily during the 1950s and 1960s. It was, on the whole, well used. In view of Ethiopia's large population, per capita aid was nevertheless very low in comparison with most of the rest of Africa – an average of $13.80 per capita during the entire decade of the 1960s, in contrast to $56.90 for Kenya and $90 for Somalia! In view of these contrasts, it is obvious that the size of external economic assistance had little relationship to the efficiency of its use. It is quite likely that it was being used more efficiently in Ethiopia than in Kenya, e.g., for while Ethiopia grew during the 1960s at half Kenya's rate, on a per capita basis it received only one quarter as much as its southern neighbor. Direct foreign investment in Ethiopia was not large, but some projects were notably successful, especially the great sugar estates in the Awash valley developed with Dutch capital in the 1950s which came into production during the 1960s. Commercial cotton growing to supply expanding textile mills also increased rapidly with both foreign capital and local resources being invested.

The composition of Ethiopia's exports nevertheless remained what they had traditionally been: coffee, hides and skins, and other elementary agricultural products. Coffee exports expanded from 21,000 tons in 1950 to 63,000 tons in 1963, worth approximately $43,000,000 and rising to over 90,000 tons in the early 1970s with earnings approaching $200 million in a period of high world coffee prices.[13]

By the time the Third Five Year Plan was being drawn up in 1967, deepened realization of the importance of agriculture to Ethiopia's economic and social development had set in. The large traditional subsistence sector combined with the modern agricultural sector continued to occupy more than 90% of the country's population. Unless agriculture could be made more productive, market access expanded and elementary processing of agricultural produce improved (grading of coffee, upgrading of hides and skins), the country could never hope to develop the foundations for sustained modernization and improvement of living standards. Both foreign specialists and the now substantial group of young, educated Ethiopian technocrats agreed on the seriousness of the problem. Within both groups, however, there were increasingly divergent opinions as to how to tackle it. Government policy favored development of commercial agriculture and facilitated imports to speed its development: agricultural machinery imports almost quadrupled between 1962 and 1966; fertilizer imports increased almost ten times between 1962 and 1965.[14] Large increases in coffee production and exports were achieved by improved collection and processing methods. The superficial illusion was created that expansion of agricultural production could be painless and extremely rewarding. The 1967 Arab-Israeli War disrupted plans for large-scale export of fruits and vegetables from Eritrea via the Suez Canal, but prospects for increased trade with parts of the Middle East appeared good.

Nevertheless, agriculture as a whole remained seriously undercapitalized. The Ministry of Agriculture accounted for only a small proportion of total governmental development expenditure. Foreign donors took the initiative in drawing up pilot development projects, some on a very large scale, such as CADU. Intense controversy gradually developed about land reform. In retrospect, it can already be seen that the advice the Ethiopian government received on land reform from foreign specialists was often contradictory. Political and economic considerations were not clearly differentiated. The great bulk of the Ethiopian peasantry remained, as far as could be determined, largely indifferent to the land reform debate. In this, Ethiopia was very different from Kenya, where the process of "re-occupation" and development of the White Highlands had energized the most dynamic segment of the highland peasantry and engaged them actively in the economic development process.[15]

Except in selected commodities and in commercial estate agriculture, productivity increased slowly in Ethiopia. The country as a whole did not benefit markedly from the incipient Green Revolution. Problems of erosion, overpopulation and addiction to primitive methods of cultivation, especially in the northern highlands, were identified and in part diagnosed, but corrective programs were barely set in motion by the time severe famine conditions developed in 1973.[16]

Critics of Ethiopia's slow pace of economic development — both domestic and foreign — frequently singled out military expenditures as a major inhibiting factor. While Ethiopia spent an average of 2.4 times as much of its GNP on defense during the 1960s as Kenya, its military outlays were approximately the same level as the average for Africa as a whole during this period. Ethiopian military expenditures were far below those of Sudan and Somalia.[17]

Like Kenya, Ethiopia was severely affected by the petroleum price increases of 1973-1974. The psychological effect in Ethiopia was greater than in Kenya, for Ethiopians were already becoming concerned with what appeared to be relative economic stagnation and the inability of their government to formulate economic policies that would ensure self-sustained growth. The concrete financial effect of the price increases was more severe in Kenya because the rapid pace of development there had encouraged higher expectations. The need to scale these down created a serious political problem. More conservative financial management, long characteristic of Ethiopia, mitigated the financial effects of the crisis.

SOME STATISTICAL COMPARISONS[18]

GDP/GNP

In absolute terms, Kenya's GDP was approximately 80% of Ethiopia's in 1960. It surpassed Ethiopia's in 1969. On a per capita basis, Kenya's GDP was already 2.3 times that of Ethiopia in 1969. By 1974 the disparity had increased further (in spite of a more rapid population increase in Kenya), almost reaching 3:1. Ethiopia had $126 per capita GDP in 1974 as against $357 for Kenya (calculations are in 1981 dollars). Ethiopia began to experience stagnation in GDP growth in 1973, before the petroleum price increase. Kenya did not experience the same stagnation until the following year. In both countries the proportion of GDP growth generated by industry and services was substantially higher than that from agriculture. In Ethiopia, however, agriculture grew at approximately half the rate of Kenya in the early 1970s. Larger absolute GDP and a higher rate of growth generates more resources for investment: during the decade of the 1960s, the gross domestic investment rate in Ethiopia was 5.7% as against 10.3% for Kenya.

Energy

Production and consumption of energy developed at a much more rapid pace in Ethiopia than in Kenya, in large part because the Ethiopian economy was beginning from a much lower base. Ethiopia is, however, much more richly endowed with hydroelectric power resources. During the period 1960-1974, e.g., energy consumption increased in Ethiopia at an annual rate of 22.7% while the increase in Kenya was only 9.3%. Energy consumption per capita, though at a much lower level in Ethiopia, approximately 1/11 of that of Kenya, increased to approximately 1/8 that of Kenya by the mid-1970s. Energy imports as a percentage of total merchandise imports were substantially lower in Ethiopia than in Kenya, 11% vs. 18%, in 1960. This ratio was maintained essentially unchanged through the end of the period surveyed.

Trade and Balance of Payments

Though Ethiopian trade was at a much lower level than Kenya's (total trade turnover – i.e. imports and exports combined – was exactly one-third that of Kenya in 1974), it was very close to being in balance. Ethiopia's imports exceeded exports in value by only 5% in 1974. Kenyan imports exceeded exports by 55% in the same year. An imbalance in food needs was already becoming apparent in statistics at this time. Ethiopia imported 118,000 tons of cereals in 1974 as against 15,000 tons imported into Kenya the same year. Of this amount, 59,000 tons was donated food aid in the Ethiopian case; only 2,000 tons were donated to Kenya. Comparatively, however, the level of agricultural development in Kenya had already substantially exceeded that of Ethiopia. One measure is the consumption of fertilizer (primarily imported in both cases) per hectare of arable land: 4/10 of a kilogram for Ethiopia as against 22.4 kilograms for Kenya.

Capital Inflow

In 1970 Kenya was attracting external capital at a rate only slightly higher than Ethiopia – $30,000,000 as against $27,000,000. Principal repayment requirements in that year were identical, $15,000,000, for both countries. Ethiopian inflow was thus $13,000,000 in comparison with $15,000,000 for Kenya. Ethiopia's outstanding and disbursed foreign indebtedness in 1970 stood at $169,000,000 in comparison with Kenya's $313,000,000. Ethiopia's debt represented 9.5% of GDP while Kenya's represented 20.3%. Ethiopia's interest payments in 1970 stood at $6,000,000 per year, while Kenya's were $11,000,000. Debt service as a percentage of GDP for Ethiopia in 1970 was 1.2%, for Kenya 1.7%. Debt service as a percentage of exports of goods and services was 11.4% for Ethiopia, 5.3% for Kenya. Ethiopia's extremely low debt service ratio enabled her to weather the period of petroleum price increases more easily than Kenya did. At the same time they revealed a much lower level of economic dynamism.

Defense

As of 1974, Kenyan defense expenditure represented 1.4% of GDP and 6.7% of the national budget. It amounted to $5 per capita. Expenditure on the military in Ethiopia in the same year absorbed 3.8% of GDP, 20.2% of the national budget. Given the country's much larger population, however, it represented an outlay of only $4 per capita. Kenya's armed forces totalled 9000 men in 1974, one-fifth of Ethiopia's 45,000.

CONCLUSIONS

Kenya achieved greater dynamism in economic development during the quarter century being surveyed. The general level of well-being of the country's African population may well have been below that of Ethiopia's at the beginning of the period, but by 1974 it was substantially above it. Kenya's dynamism came from two main sources: (1) the gains resulting from colonial development and (2) the stimulus provided by independence. In addition, Kenyan political leadership after independence was more intensely focused on economic development as a high priority national goal and less concerned with exercising African or international leadership than Ethiopia's.

Agriculture came to be recognized in both countries as a key problem as well as a prime area of opportunity. Ethiopians took subsistence agriculture for granted as a way of life much longer than Kenyans did. The stimulus of repossessing the White Highlands while capitalizing off the development that had occurred in them during the colonial period gave forward momentum to Kenyan agriculture which proved largely self-sustaining in spite of contradictions and problems that became apparent by the end of the period. No similar challenging development channelled thinking about agriculture in Ethiopia or focused governmental attention on the problem, though the introduction of commercial farming and regional development projects in several areas of the country provided substantial stimulus of local importance. In at least three areas of Ethiopia agricultural development reached levels as high as, or even higher than, Kenya: Eritrea; the Awash Valley; and the central coffee-growing regions of the province of Kaffa.

Neither Kenya nor Ethiopia had, by 1974, achieved a high level of sustained agricultural growth that could either ensure (1) an adequate food supply for rapidly growing population or (2) a basis for continually expanding exports of either primary products or dependable supplies of raw materials for agro-industry.

Both Kenya and Ethiopia commendably avoided excessively large and showy industrial schemes and "white elephant" projects of the kind that have embarrassed many African countries and wasted major resources. The development experience of both Ethiopia and Kenya provides examples that could be profitably studied and applied by the other: e.g. the expansion of tea growing in Kenya; the success of Ethiopian Airlines; expansion of tourism in Kenya; lowland development projects in Ethiopia such as Tendaho and Setit-Humera. Both countries need to speed up development of non-petroleum energy sources: geo-thermal and solar, for example.

Regional disparities have continued to be at least as great in Kenya as in Ethiopia and some of Kenya's peoples are far from playing a role in national life or participating in development at all. Neither country had by 1974 developed broad programs for dealing with overpopulation in highland areas threatened by erosion, self-exhaustion and other forms of environmental degeneration.

The slower pace of Ethiopian development — resulting from more cautious development policies — probably ensured more efficient utilization of capital inflow (foreign aid and investment), but also discouraged investment at a time when investors were looking for new opportunities. The other side of this coin, however, is the fact that the *economic* effect of petroleum price increases after 1974 was more serious on Kenya than on Ethiopia. Kenya's larger indebtedness naturally confronted the country with more serious debt management problems when international terms of lending became less advantageous for developing countries. The more conservative approach to borrowing which characterized Ethiopia during the quarter century under examination, and conservative fiscal management habits as well, left Ethiopia better able to cope with the financial strains of the ensuing decade.

All of these observations must be tested against the experience of the decade 1975-1984, as well as against the results of more intensive research. They are offered essentially as hypotheses and to stimulate debate.

NOTES

1. John Burrows (coordinating author), *Kenya, into the Second Decade*, Johns Hopkins Press, Baltimore, 1975, p.5.

2. Unless otherwise specified, figures are "then-year" US dollars.

3. Robert L. Tignor, *The Colonial Transformation of Kenya*, Princeton University Press, Princeton, NJ, 1976.

4. Burrows, *op. cit.*, p.448.

5. Burrows, *op. cit.*, p.449.

6. Colin Leys, *Underdevelopment in Kenya*, University of California Press, Berkeley and Los Angeles, 1974, and Nicola Swainson, *The Development of Corporate Capitalism in Kenya, 1918-1977*, University of California Press, Berkeley and Los Angeles, 1980, are among the most comprehensive critical studies of Kenyan development experience during this period. A review of the first book by Arthur Hazlewood, "Kenya: Income Distribution and Poverty — an Unfashionable View", *Journal of Modern African Studies*, 16/1, 1978, pp.81-95, would be less unfashionable today than it seemed in 1978 in the light of African economic stagnation during recent years. As Hazlewood observed then: "Economic growth has been out of fashion as a target of economic policy . . . " (p.83). It never fell out of fashion among Kenya's leadership, unfashionable as it may have been with many Western and African intellectuals.

7. G. D. Sawyer, "Trends in Kenyan Agriculture in Relation to Employment", *Journal of Modern African Studies*, 11/3, 1973, pp.393-403.

8. Burrows, *op. cit.*, p.355.

9. Burrows, *op. cit.*, p.417.

10. Ian Livingstone, "An Evaluation of Kenya's Rural Industrial Development Program", *Journal of Modern African Studies*, Sept. 1977, pp.495-504.

11. Irving Kaplan (ed.), *Area Handbook for Kenya*, DA Pam 550-56, Washington, USGPO, 1976, p.256.

12. Data in the preceding paragraphs is derived largely from "Basic Data on the Economy of Ethiopia" prepared by the American Embassy, Addis Ababa and issued by the US Department of Commerce, August 1973; Irving Kaplan (ed.), *Area Handbook for Ethiopia*, DA Pam 550-28, USGPO, Washington, 1971; and Imperial Ethiopian Government, *Third Five Year Development Plan, 1961-1965 E.C. (1968-1973)*, Addis Ababa, 1968.

13. Mesfin Wolde Mariam, *An Introductory Geography of Ethiopia*, Addis Ababa, 1972, pp.159ff.

14. Mesfin Wolde Mariam, *op. cit.*, p.120.

15. See, e.g., Michael Stahl, *Ethiopia: Political Contradictions in Agricultural Development*, Stockholm, 1974. The most comprehensive survey of foreign specialists' advice has been done by John M. Cohen, "Foreign Involvement in Land Reform: the Case of Ethiopia", a paper prepared by the International Conference on Land Reform in Mexico City, January 1983.

16. Mesfin Wolde Mariam pointed out in 1972 that Ethiopia was already tending to become a net importer of food — *op. cit.*, p.127.

17. My paper presented at the VIIth International Conference of Ethiopian Studies in Lund, Sweden, in April 1982, "Arming the Horn, 1960-1980", goes into this subject at greater length.

18. The statistics in the section which follows are all derived from World Bank, "World Development Reports", published annually for the World Bank by Oxford University Press.

MEDICAL GEOGRAPHY:

ITS ROLE IN DISEASE CONTROL IN ETHIOPIA

AND OTHER AFRICAN COUNTRIES

Helmut Kloos
Department of Geography
Addis Ababa University

INTRODUCTION

Medical geography clearly overlaps with and supplements epidemiology. Whereas epidemiology is concerned primarily with the distribution of disease and physiological conditions in populations and the underlying factors of such distributions, geography is the study of spatial patterns and processes and the identification and explanation of links between humans and the environment. As a subfield of geography, medical geography focuses on the spatial distribution of disease and health care, with associative analyses of environmental (physical, biotic, social and cultural) influences. Although geographic variation is one well recognised factor in epidemiology, few epidemiologists are educated sufficiently in the areas of climate, vegetation, soils, land use, population distribution, culture, social organisation and statistical and methodological techniques that geographers commonly use in spatial analysis. Most medical geographers, on the other hand, know little about disease processes and pathogenesis. The dialogue between researchers in these two disciplines has been relatively weak in the past in spite of "the complimentarity between epidemiology and geography" and "the potential intellectual and social benefits of interdisciplinary collaboration have not been realized".[1] Recent approaches in health care and disease control world-wide, particularly Primary Health Care, and the persistence of drought and other environmental problems in many African countries, can provide the rationale and the necessary opportunities for increased interdisciplinary research and training not only involving epidemiologists and medical geographers but also medical sociologists, medical anthropologists and medical economists. The World Health Organisation, recognising the need for interdisciplinary collaboration between the biomedical and social sciences, has established a socio-economic section as part of the Special Programme for Research and Training in Tropical Diseases.[2]

The objectives of this paper are to 1) give a brief historical account of the development of medical geography; 2) discuss the conceptual basis of medical geography in order to answer the question: "Why can medical geography contribute to disease control and health development?"; 3) review selected medical geographical studies, mostly by geographers, in Africa and at the same time discuss some methodologies and techniques commonly used by medical geographers to answer the question: "Where and how can medical geography contribute to disease control and health development?"; 4) suggest some areas for further research; and 5) briefly describe the medical geography programme in the Department of Geography of Addis Ababa University.

HISTORICAL DEVELOPMENT AND PRESENT STATUS OF MEDICAL GEOGRAPHY

In a review of the development and present status of medical geography, Pyle[3] noted that although interest in the study of the geographic distribution of disease dates back at least to the Greek physician Hippocrates (5th century B.C.), the term medical geography did not come into use before the 18th century. In the mid-19th century, after Pasteur's discovery of disease-causing organisms as the basic cause of infectious disease, the dominance of the germ theory of disease causation focused great attention on disease agents and resulted in the neglect of man in the totality of his environment and thus medical geography. The development of highly successful pesticides and pharmaceutical drugs also delayed the adoption of a broader approach to health analysis based on man-environment interaction.

Since the 1950s adoption of a broader approach to health analysis has benefited medical geography. Thus a combination of 1) environmental systems analysis of health problems; 2) the appearance of drug-resistance in pathogens and insecticide-resistance in mosquitoes and other vectors; 3) sharp increases in diseases of industrialisation and urbanisation, such as cancer and cardiovascular diseases; and 4) difficulties in meeting health care and nutrition needs in developing countries, have resulted in a shift of emphasis toward holistic medicine. As a result, both the social and physical environment, as well as human behaviour, nutrition, immunity and health care, were finally recognised as interacting factors in health and disease.[4]

Although differences in the scope of medical geography and techniques used in different countries do not permit a single definition of this discipline, the one offered by Hunter[5], as "the application of geographical concepts and techniques to health-related problems" is in agreement with most work by medical geographers. Since its development as a distinct discipline in Europe, the U.S.S.R., the United States and Japan during the 1930s, medical geography has been added to the curricula of geography departments in most industrialised countries. More recently programmes in medical geography have been developed in African and other developing countries, including Mexico, India, Kenya, Zambia, Nigeria and now in Ethiopia, and geographers are increasingly becoming involved in health-related research in these countries.[6] A recent bibliography lists more than 1,800 references of medical geographical works world-wide.[6]

In Ethiopia, the monographs by Schaller and Kuls and by Zein Ahmed and Kloos[8] and papers by Kloos[9], Roundy[10], and Yelizarov[11], are recent contributions to medical geography but medical geographical writings in this country can be traced further back in time. In the 19th century several physicians attempted to analyse the geographic distribution of infectious diseases in different parts of Ethiopia[12] and knowledge of the altitudinal distribution of malaria, typhus and acute upper respiratory infections is reflected in the treatises of *debteras*.[13] Although these and other studies, mostly by physician/epidemiologists, revealed marked spatial variation in disease occurrence and transmission, few of them evaluated new opportunities and problems in disease control and health development resulting from the Ethiopian Revolution. For an example, changes in health infrastructure and priorities in socialist Ethiopia, with an emphasis on primary health care, as formulated in the 10-Year Plan (1984-1993), the literacy campaign, the land reform and large-scale resettlement of populations from drought affected areas may all influence disease transmission and the provision of and access to health care.[14] Recurrent droughts and famines since the early 1970s add yet another dimension to the present health and disease situation in Ethiopia.

CONCEPTUAL BASIS

Essential to an understanding of the conceptual basis of medical geography is the realisation that geography is interdisciplinary and synthesising. Moreover, it is generally accepted that the environment and disease as well as health-seeking behaviour and health care delivery are interacting systems. Because geography is strongly synthesising and eclectic, it is committed to interdisciplinary cooperation with other social and environmental sciences as well as the biomedical sciences. As a discipline that bridges the social and environmental sciences, geography derives its integration and coherence from systems-related analysis of man-environmental interaction in space and time. Disease may be defined as an *interaction* of disease-causing agent, host and environment (physical, biotic, social and cultural).[15] Disease control measures ideally focus on breaking the weakest link in the transmission cycle or causal chain but this is only possible when all relevant geographic, economic, sociocultural, logistic and administrative factors in a given area are studied comprehensively. The reviews by Knight[16], Meade[17], Howe[18] and Learmonth[19] of medical geographical studies with a disease ecology perspective examine basic conceptual and methodological issues in infectious and non-infectious disease ecology and distribution.

In addition to disease ecology, health care planning, delivery and utilisation have received much attention by medical geographers in recent years. Central place theory and related concepts of locational analysis that allow for consideration of such factors as travel distance, duration and cost of travel to health facilities, their size and cost of treatment are all commonly evaluated in the development of location/allocation models.[20] Unfortunately, nearly all existing models were developed in countries depending primarily on modern medical systems and few geographers have attempted to study health care in Africa, where the majority of the population in most areas continues to use primarily traditional medicine. Good[21], noting that traditional medical systems have been neglected by geographers, outlined areas of research needing attention.

REVIEW OF STUDIES AND METHODOLOGICAL CONSIDERATIONS, BY SUBFIELD OF MEDICAL GEOGRAPHY

An increasing number of subfield specialisations in medical geography have been recognised. Only some of the subfields are treated here. They were selected on the basis of some of the most pressing public health needs in Africa, particularly Ethiopia. Other subfields are biometeorology, mental health and environmental pollution. It is well accepted, however, that the complexity of most health problems and the difficulties usually encountered in their solution defy simple classification and the categories identified here should be viewed as preliminary.

1. *Historical:* Historical studies of the occurrence and diffusion of disease in developing countries, long neglected due to scarcity of published information, are increasingly being pursued by geographers and other social scientists. The broad surveys by McNeill[22], Ackerknecht[23], and Henschen[24] of the history of disease distribution world-wide, Patterson[25] and Hartwick and Patterson[26] represent major contributions to our knowledge of health development in Africa. Papers by Hunter[27], Kwofie[28], Adesina[29] and the monographs by McKelvey[30] and Stock[31] also provide needed information on the changing geography of diseases in Africa and develop useful methodologies. In Ethiopia, Pankhurst's[32] reviews of travel accounts and chronicles and Zein Ahmed Zein and Kloos's disease atlas[33] indicate the impact and persistence of major diseases in this country.

2. *Infectious Diseases:* Several infectious diseases, including trypanosomiasis, measles, tuberculosis and leprosy, although reduced in prevalence in many areas, still constitute a major drain on human and economic resources. Schistosomiasis, malaria and some forms of filariasis are even increasing in many endemic areas. Ecological upsets related to water resources development, population movements, development of drug resistance in *Plasmodium* spp., insecticide resistance in *Anopheles* and the adaptation of filariasis-transmitting mosquitoes to sewage and latrines in cities and other man-made habitats are major factors in this alarming situation.[34] In non-vectored infectious diseases medical geographical studies typically focus on population movements and density indices for analytical purposes due to the person-to-person mode of transmission. Ferguson and Leeuenburg[35], in one of the first studies of the dynamics of non-vectored diseases in Africa, are working toward a simulation model of measles in a rural area of Kenya. In vectored diseases, the need to understand the requirements of appropriate vectors and intermediate, reservoir and definitive hosts in the disease transmission cycle necessitates the use of broader systems analysis. In schistosomiasis, for example, it is imperative for control purposes that the life cycle and ecology of both the parasite and the snail intermediate host; the demographic, socio-economic and behavioural aspects of the human host; as well as the interactions of all three subsystems in space and time[36] be considered in Ethiopia, water temperatures in areas above 2,000 metres are generally too low for the survival of *Schistosoma mansoni cercariae* and too high for the survival of the *Biomphalaria pfeifferi* snail host below about 800 metres, where the

more tropical snail *Bulinus abyssinicus* transmits *S. haematobium* in swamps rather than streams and canal systems.[37] In our study of schistosomiasis in the Awash Valley between 1973 and 1976 we were able to predict the geographic distribution of both types of schistosomiasis, based on climatic temperature, agricultural development parameters and population movements[38] as confirmed by recent epidemiological studies.[39] Studies of the flight pattern of *Simulium* sp. in relation to onchocerciasis prevalence[40] and of the spatial correlation between cracking black soils, habitat preference of the sand fly vector and leishmaniasis prevalence in southwest Ethiopia[41] also illustrate the predictive value of medical geographical research. The geographic distribution of leishmaniasis in Ethiopia is probably less understood than that of any other vectored disease.[42]

The appearance and spread of drug-resistant malaria in East Africa and pesticide-resistant vectors of malaria, onchocerciasis and trypanosomiasis in various parts of the tropics[43] is another problem in need of medical geographical research. Beales[44] recommended mapping of the changing geographical distribution of drug-resistant malaria as a means of monitoring its diffusion and as an aid in the development of appropriate control measures. International, regional and local population movements[45] all may result in the spread of resistant parasites in Ethiopia, where the recent studies have detected chloroquine resistance along the Sudan and Somalia borders.[46] Conceptual and methodological issues in the study of population movements in relation to disease transmission and control were discussed by Kloos[47], Mayer[48], Meade[49] and Prothero.[50] An equally relevant area of man-made disease is the spread of schistosomiasis and malaria in economic development projects. The creation of large reservoirs and canal systems and congregation of large human populations with their attendant housing and sanitation problems pose major challenges to planners and health officials.[51] Plans call for irrigation development in all major river basins in Ethiopia[52], in most of which malaria and schistosomiasis are already endemic. This requires that well designed epidemiological and medical geographical studies be undertaken during the planning stage of agricultural and hydro-electric projects if these and other water borne diseases are to be controlled.[53]

3. *Chronic, Noninfectious Diseases:* Disease associated with ageing, industrialisation, urbanisation and related stress and pollution, sedentarisation, dietary changes and modern life styles in general, including cancer, heart disease, bronchitis and diabetes, are most prevalent in industrialised countries. They have received relatively little attention by medical geographers in the developing world, although urban populations are increasingly affected. Analysis of extensive hospital data shows that African urban populations have significantly higher morbidity and mortality from cancer of the colon, hypertension, diabetes and heart disease than their tribesmen in rural areas who adhere to a traditional subsistence way of life.[54] Several other non-infectious diseases, however, including liver cancer, tend to be more prevalent in rural populations consuming mouldy foods (aflotoxins) and certain traditional herbal medicines.[55]

Naturally occurring geochemical constituents of soils and water are increasingly associated with chronic diseases.[56] In Ethiopia's Rift Valley, use of deep-well water containing high concentrations of fluoride has resulted in severe forms of fluorosis.[57] In the highlands of Ethiopia, Kenya, Uganda and Cameroon, where red latosol soils of basaltic origin prevail, swollen feet and lower legs of barefooted rural people have been associated with absorption, through the skin, of iron oxide, alumina and silica, which are thought to produce a toxic reaction in the lymphatic system.[58] If this hypothesis can be proven to be correct, then simply the wearing of shoes could prevent this type of elephantiasis.

Cancer, cardiovascular and many other chronic noninfectious diseases are mainly caused by a combination of environmental factors, many of which remain to be identified. Statistical analysis of spatially patterned disease occurrence and environmental factors may reveal causal relationships.[59]

4. *Nutrition:* Although the nutritional state of an individual or a population has a significant

impact on physical and mental development, well being and resistance to infection[60], medical geographers have paid relatively little attention to the geography of malnutrition and dietary patterns.[61] May's extensive work[62] on the regionalisation of dietary and nutritional patterns in Africa, Newman's review[63] of protein calorie malnutrition in Sub-Saharan Africa and Anneger's work[64] in West Africa provide a conceptual basis for medical geographical studies of diet and nutrition at the regional level. A valuable bibliography of dietary patterns cross-culturally comes from Freedman.[65] Grivetti[66] identified sveral themes needing further attention by geographers, including religious food taboos and the relative roles of culture and the physical environment in famines. In-depth studies of the food ecology of individual ethnic groups can provide culture-specific information on food needs and nutritional levels in different areas and communities.[67] The seminal work by Simoons[68] on the geography of specific meat, fish and milk avoidances in different parts of Africa has many nutritional implications and should be useful to development planners and relief organizations providing food aid to disaster areas. The avoidance of fish and fish products by many pastoralists in Africa, including the Afar, Somali and some Oromo groups[69] and the preference for *teff* and *ensete* in different parts of the highlands are more obvious examples from Ethiopia. The importance of food habits is indicated by the recent delay of food aid by voluntary organizations to the drought stricken areas in Wolayta Awraja, partly due to lack of information on food preferences of the local population.[70] Moreover, diets normally change slowly and the use of new, unaccustomed foods has been associated with various health effects.[71]

Seasonality of food shortages, malnutrition, infection and mortality is increasingly considered as an important aspect of rural poverty.[72] The effects of more persistent drought conditions also require that medical geographical research findings be applied to solving pressing health problems.[73] Measuring food intake[74] and nutritional levels in populations[75] continue to be controversial issues in empirical studies. In spite of these methodological problems, medical geographers increasingly use anthropometric and other empirical measurements of nutritional levels.[76]

Numerous factors affecting the availability and consumption of foods and nutrition in Ethiopia remain to be studied in depth. They include economic policy[77], transportation systems and other distribution factors, such as domestic and foreign trade and markets, pricing structures and the development of production systems along socialist lines. Recurrent drought and famine in several regions[78] constitute a serious health problem to the solution of which applied climatologists, agricultural geographers, regional planners and other geographers can make contributions. For example, through collaborative studies with the Relief and Rehabilitation Commission (RRC), which monitors food supply in drought prone areas, geographers may help to delineate food deficit areas. A similar approach was successfully used in Nigeria.[79]

5. *Health Care Delivery:* The spatiality of health care services in regard to planning, delivery and utilisation, has become one of the major subfields of medical geography.[80] Primary objectives of studies in these areas are: 1) optimum *location* of all kinds of health care facilities, ranging from rural health centres, clinics and drug shops to large national teaching hospitals, in order to minimise patients' travel time and cost; 2) optimal *allocation* of new or added hospital beds and medical services for local, regional and national facilities. Planners of health care facilities must consider: 1) the range of services to be provided; 2) the size of the catchment area of any given medical facility; 3) the size and distribution of the potential patient population (usually defined as the 'population at risk') as determined from their demographic structure and the prevalence and incidence of specific diseases, and 4) anticipated population changes due to natural increase or decrease and migration. The location of practitioners, whether physicians, dentists, midwives, village health workers or traditional healers, should be known since this is an important factor in the efficiency of health care delivery. Equitable distribution of medical services has not been achieved in any

country but discrepancies between population distribution and accessibility to medical care are particularly pronounced in Africa.[81]

Most studies of health care services utilisation have considered distance, time and cost of patients' travel, type of facility as well as cultural and organizational factors. It is increasingly recognised that broader conceptualisation of health-seeking behaviour is needed that takes into consideration the various steps of the illness behaviour process, namely: 1) perception of the severity of illness; 2) determination of available treatment action sets; 3) assessment of treatment plans and benefits; 4) analysis of treatment costs and net benefits, and 5) selection of a treatment plan.[82]

The presence of two basic medical systems in Africa, the traditional and modern or cosmopolitan types, and marked variation in the geographic distribution of diseases in individual countries require the development of more holistic and culture-specific systems of health care in agreement with the Primary Health Care approach.[83] Although the modern system is generally most developed in urban areas and the traditional system continues to meet the health needs of the majority of rural people, traditional medicine is still widely employed in large African cities, including Nairobi and Addis Ababa.[84]

Major geographical problems faced by health planners include proper evaluation of the distance factor in utilisation of health care, high population mobility and low density in areas of pastoral nomadism and migrant labour[85] and absence of national census data in several countries. Geographers, in collaborative studies, may make important contributions to the study of distance and population parameters.

A third system of health care in Africa, usually described as the transitional system, has received little attention by social and medical scientists. Illegal drug peddlers, injectionists and women carrying out abortions are some of the practitioners constituting an apparently widespread although unofficial system.[86]

Traditional Ethiopian medicine[87] and the modern system[88] largely maintained their polarised position in the past with few attempts at integration. The new 10—Year Plan of the Ministry of Health emphasises primary health care and provides for the inclusion of certain aspects of traditional medicine in health care delivery. A revised health policy along with infrastructure now in place in rural areas, particularly farmers', women's and urban associations, may form the basis of a spatially more efficient national health care system. As part of this ambitious programme of health services expansion, the number of health workers, rural health stations and health centres is to be increased between two and threefold. Moreover, one community health agent and one traditional birth attendant are to be trained for each of the approximately 35,000 peasant associations by 1990, with community participation an important ingredient.[89] Location and staffing of the new facilities will have to be based on the usual location/allocation parameters discussed above.

6. *Data Measurement and Presentation:* Mapping of diseases, their vectors, hosts and environmental parameters is generally considered the first step in analysing medical geographical data. All mapping techniques commonly used in geographical research, including dot, chloropleth, isopleth, trend surface, interactance and computer maps, cartograms, diagrams and graphs, have been used. McGlashan[90] outlined some of the difficulties facing medical geographers analysing disease distribution data in Africa, particularly lack of adequate and reliable information. Stimson[91] urged geographers to pay greater attention to data reliability, particularly of statistically aggregated data. Commonly used methods of mathematical scaling, essential for quantifying and comparing health within and among populations, and derived from epidemiology, were reviewed by Pyle.[92]

Computer graphics can greatly increase speed and accuracy of statistical mapping. Particularly geographical associations between health related and environmental variables and service area studies incorporating information on patient origin and time/distance of travel are effectively carried out with computer assistance. Spatial correlation of relevant environmental and disease variables may assist in elucidating new causal relationships in cancer and other noninfectious diseases. Data can be stored and continuously updated and edited for recall to produce maps showing changing disease situations. Lack of adequate and comparable data, as well as their high cost, however, have limited the application of computer graphics largely to extensive or continuous mapping operations in a few countries.[93]

Remote sensing is a potentially useful technique in medical geographical research. Both geographers and epidemiologists have used it to predict vector occurrence and disease transmission. Cline[94] attempted to predict risk of hookworm transmission in Central American communities based on soil type, degree of shade cover, type of agricultural activities, altitude and slope as interpreted from aerial photographs. Recently Chinese geographers associated changes in water regime and beach development in lakes with the distribution of *Onchomelania* snails, transmitters of *Schistosoma japonicum* in East Asia.[95] Imagery available in Ethiopia could be used to define vegetation zones, geological structure, drought conditions and wetlands such as swamps and land use settlement patterns conducive to vector breeding and thus disease transmission.

Modelling can play an important role in predicting the spread of diseases and evaluating the impact of individual control measures and their cost effectiveness. The transmission and diffusion of infectious and noninfectious diseases and the incidence of malnutrition are the result of complex interactions in the physical, biotic and human environments as discussed above. The parameters selected for study will vary with each disease, from area to area, season to season, by disease prevalence and intensity, transmission characteristics, the stage of control campaigns and availability of resources. With changing situations, interventions will also have to change. Models can monitor inputs and outputs in this dynamic context, clarify decision-making and thus assist in evaluating the effectiveness of disease control programmes. However, before computer utilisation in disease modelling and rigorous quantification can become useful, it is necessary to develop reliable qualitative models.[96]

THE MEDICAL GEOGRAPHY PROGRAMME AT ADDIS ABABA UNIVERSITY

Since 1984/85, a medical geography programme at the Master's level is being developed in the Geography Department of Addis Ababa University. Its objectives are to provide students with concepts and techniques required for research and teaching of medical geography in Ethiopia as well as preparation for doctoral studies in other countries. All students are required to take courses in epidemiology and medical statistics and, depending on their area of specialisation, community health, nutrition, entomology or parasitology in the Medical Faculty of Addis Ababa University. In the Department of Geography all medical geography students are taking seminars in medical geography.

CONCLUSION

This review indicates that the potential contribution of medical geography to the control of tropical diseases and the development of health in Ethiopia and other African countries is considerable. Ethiopia particularly, due to its highly varied physical/biotic and human environment, the restructuring of its health care system and far-reaching socio-economic changes in the last ten years, offers many opportunities to motivated scholars. What seems to be most urgently needed now is: 1)increased awareness among geographers and other social scientists that they can effectively contribute to national health development; 2) the development of relevant courses in the respective curricula; and 3) greater interaction between social and biomedical scientists. The need for social science input is increasingly recognised by public health officials.[97] However, for social scientists to be most effective, it will be necessary that traditional attitudes that have resisted the multidisciplinary, collaborative approach worldwide for many years be discarded by both social and biomedical scientists.

REFERENCES

1. Mayer, J. D. "The role of spatial analysis and geographical data in the detection of disease causation", *Social Science and Medicine*, Vol.17 (1983), 1213-1221.

2. Rosenfield, P. L., Widstrant, C. G. and A. P. Ruderman. "Social and economic research of the UNDP/World Bank/WHO Special Programme for Research and Training in Tropical Diseases", *Social Science and Medicine*, Vol.15A (1981), 529-538.

3. Pyle, G. F. *Applied Medical Geography*, London: John Wiley and Sons, 1979.

4. Hunter, J. M. "The challenge of medical geography" in Hunter, J. M. (ed.), *The Geography of Health and Disease*, pp.1-31. Department of Geography, University of North Carolina at Chapel Hill, 1980.

5. *Ibid.*

6. Prothero, R. M. "Studies in medical geography in Africa", *Geojournal*, Vol.5.4 (1981), 298-303.

7. Akhtar, R. *The Geography of Health: An Essay and a Bibliography*, New Delhi: Marwah Publications, 1982.

8. Schaller, K. F. and W. Kuls. *Äthiopien-Ethiopia*. Geomedical Monograph Series, Heidelberg: Springer Verlag, 1972; Zein Ahmed Zein and H. Koos (eds.), *The Ecology of Health and Disease in Ethiopia*. Addis Ababa: Ministry of Health, 1988.

9. Kloos, H. "Schistosomiasis and Irrigation in the Awash Valley of Ethiopia". Ph.D. dissertation, University of California, Davis. Published upon demand by Microfilm International, Ann Arbor, Michigan, 1977; Kloos, H., Aklilu Lemma and G. DeSole, "Schistosoma mansoni distribution in Ethiopia: A study in medical geography", *Annals of Tropical Medicine and Parasitology*, Vol.72 (1978), 461-470; Kloos, H., Desole, G. and Aklilu Lemma, "Intestinal parasitism in seminomadic pastoralists and subsistence farmers in and around irrigation schemes in the Awash Valley, Ethiopia, with special emphasis on ecological and cultural associations", *Social Science and Medicine*, Vol.15B (1981), 457-46; Kloos, H., Tsegaye Chamo, Dawit Abemo, Kefale Gebre Tsadik and Solomon Belay, "Utilisation of selected pharmacies and drugs in Addis Ababa: a study in medical geography", *Ethiopian Medical Journal*, Vol.24 (1986), pp.105-111.

10. Roundy, R. W. "Hazards of Communicable Disease Transmission Resulting from Cultural Behavior in Ethiopian Highland-Dwelling Populations: A Cultural-Medical Geographical Study". Ph.D. dissertation, University of California, Los Angeles. Published upon demand by Microfilm International, Ann Arbor, Michigan, 1975; Roundy, "Altitudinal mobility and disease hazards for Ethiopian populations", *Economic Geography*, Vol.52 (1976), 103-115; Roundy, "A model combining human behavior and disease ecology to assess disease hazard in a community: rural Ethiopia", *Social Science and Medicine*, Vol.12D (1978), 321-329.

11. Yelizarov, V. A. "Data on the medical geography of Ethiopia", *Soviet Geography*, Vol.16 (1975), 321-329.

12. See for example Grossi, V., "La geografia medica dell'Abissinia", *in* Grossi, V. (ed.), *Questioni di Geografia Politica*, Torino, 1888, pp.75-84.

13. Strelcyn, S. *Medecine et Plantes d'Ethiopie: Les Traites Medicaux Ethiopie*, Warsaw: Panstwowe Wyawnictwo Naukwe, 1968.

14. Asfaw Desta. "Introducing NHDN (National Health Development Network) in Ethiopia". Paper presented at the 20th Annual Meeting of the Ethiopian Medical Association, 23-26 May, 1984.

15. May, J. M. "The ecology of human disease", *Annals of the New York Academy of Sciences*, Vol.84 (1960), 789-794.

16. Knight, C. G. "The geography of vectored diseases" *in* Hunter, J. M. (ed.), *The Geography . . . op. cit.*

17. Meade, M. S. "An interactive framework for geochemistry and cardiovascular disease". In Meade, M. S. (ed.), *Conceptual and Methodological Issues in Medical Geography*, Department of Geography, University of North Carolina at Chapel Hill, 1980, pp.194-221.

18. Howe, G. M. *A World Geography of Human Diseases*, London: Academic Press, 1977.

19. Learmonth, A. T. A. *Patterns of Disease and Hunger*, London: David & Charles, Newton Abbot, 1978.

20. Pyle, G. F., *op. cit.*

21. Good, C. H. "Traditional medicine: an agenda for medical geographers", *Social Science and Medicine*, Vol.11 (1977), 705-713.

22. McNeill, W. H. *Plaques and Peoples*, Garden City: Anchor Press, 1976.

23. Ackerknecht, E. H. *History and Geography of the Most Important Diseases*, New York: Hafner, 1965.

24. Henschen, F. *The History and Geography of Diseases*, New York: Delacorte Press, 1966.

25. Patterson, K. D. *Health in Colonial Ghana: Disease, Medicine and Socio-Economic Change, 1900-1955*, Waltham, Mass: Crossroads Press, 1981.

26. Hartwick, G. W. and Patterson, K. D. (eds.). *Disease in African History: An Introductory Survey and Case Studies*, Durham, N. Carolina: Duke University Press, 1978.

27. Hunter, J. M. "River blindness in Nangodi, northern Ghana: a hypothesis of cyclical advance and retreat", *Geographical Review*, Vol.56 (1966), 398-416.

28. Kwofie, K. M. "A spatio-temporal analysis of cholera diffusion in western Africa", *Economic Geography*, Vol.52 (1976), 127-135.

29. Adesine, H. O. "Explanation of the spatial diffusion process of cholera in Ibadan City, Nigeria". Paper presented at the International Geographical Union Symposium on the Geography of Health, Madras, 1981.

30. McKelvey, J. J. Jr. *Man Against Tsetse: Struggle for Africa*, Ithaca: Cornell University Press, 1973.

31. Stock, R. *Cholera in Africa*, London: International African Institute, 1976.

32. Pankhurst, R. "The history and traditional treatment of smallpox in Ethiopia", *Medical History*, Vol.9 (1965), 343-346; "The history and treatment of rabies in Ethiopia", *Medical History*, Vol.14 (1970), 378-389; "Some notes on the history of typhus in Ethiopia", *Medical History*, Vol.20 (1976), 384-389.

33. Zein Ahmed Zein and Kloos, *op. cit.*

34. Beales, P. F. "The containment of resistant falciparum malaria". Unpublished document, WHO/MAL/81.931 of the World Health Organisation, Geneva, 1981; Kloos, H. and K. Thompson. "Schistosomiasis in Africa: an ecological perspective", *Journal of Tropical Geography*, Vol.48 (1979), 31-46; Surtees G. "Effects of irrigation on mosquito populations and mosquito-borne diseases in man with particular reference to ricefield extension", *International Journal of Environmental Studies*, Vol.1 (1970), 35-42; Kershaw, W.E. "Filariasis" *in* Howe, G. M. (ed.), *op. cit.*, pp.33-60; Deom, J. "Water resources development and health. A selected bibliography". World Health Organisation Document MPD 82.2, Geneva, 1982.

35. Ferguson, A. and J. Leeuwenburg. "Local mobility and spatial dynamics of measles in a rural area of Kenya", *GeoJournal*, Vol.5.4 (1981), 315-321.

36. Kloos, H. and K. Thompson, *op. cit.*

37. Kloos, H., Aklilu Lemma and G. DeSole, "Schistosoma mansoni . . ." *op. cit.*; Kloos, H. and Aklilu Lemma. "Bilharziasis in the Awash Valley. III. Epidemiological studies in Nura Era, Abadir, Melka Sadi and Amibara irrigation schemes". *Ethiopian Medical Journal*, Vol.15 (1977), 161-168.

38. Kloos, H. "Schistosomiasis and Irrigation . . .", *op. cit.*

39. Institute of Pathobiology, Addis Ababa University. "Expanded programme of applied research and training towards prevention of schistosomiasis in Ethiopia". Progress report No.3 to the World Health Organisation, Addis Ababa, 1982.

40. DeSole, G. and H. Kloos. "Transmission patterns of onchocerciasis in south-western Ethiopia", *Parassitologia*, Vol.18 (1976), 53-65; Seyoum Taticheff, "Prevalence of onchocerciasis". Paper read at the 20th Annual Meeting of the Ethiopian Medical Association, Addis Ababa, 23-26 May 1984.

41. Fuller, G. K. "Kala-azar in Ethiopia: survey of southwest Ethiopia", *Annals of Tropical Medicine and Parasitology*, Vol.73 (1979), 417-431.

42. Teklemariam Ayele, Eyassu Habte-Gabr and Ayele Belehu. *Leishmaniasis in Ethiopia: a Handbook*. Proceedings of a Workshop held in Addis Ababa, Institute of Pathobiology, 25-27 May 1981. Addis Ababa: Graphic Printers,1982.

43. Hess, U., Timmersman, P. M. and M. Jones. "Combined chloroquine/fansidar-resistant falciparum malaria appears in East Africa", *American Journal of Tropical Medicine and Hygiene*, Vol.32 (1983), 217-220; Anonymous. "Pesticides for public health: collaboration with industry strengthened", *WHO Chronicle*, Vol.37 (1983), 212-214; Chapin, G. and R. Wasserstrom. "Pesticide use and malaria resurgence in Central America and India", *Social Science and Medicine*, Vol.17 (1983), 273-290.

44. Beales, P. F., *op. cit.*

45. Prothero, R. M., *op. cit.*; Roundy, R. W. "Altitudinal mobility . . .", *op. cit.*; Kloos, H. "Farm labor migrations in the Awash Valley of Ethiopia", *International Migration Review*, Vol.16 (1982), 133-168; Prothero, R. M. *Migrants and Malaria in Africa*. Pittsburgh: University of Pittsburgh Press, 1965.

46. Teklehaimanot, A., "Chloroquine resistant plasmodium falciparum malaria in Ethiopia", *Lancet*, No.8499 (July 1986), p.127.

47. Kloos, H. "Parasitism and selected rural-rural population movements: an attempt to develop a conceptual basis and methodological framework", *Proceedings of the Workshop on Human Population Movements and their Impact on Tropical Disease Transmission and Control*, Kandy, Sri Lanka: Kandy Offset Printers Ltd., 1984, pp.31-41.

48. Mayer, J. D. "Migrant studies and medical geography: conceptual problems and methodological issues" *in* Meade, M. S. (ed.), *Conceptual and Methodological . . . , op. cit.*

49. Meade, M.S. "Medical geography as human ecology: the dimension of population movement", *Geographical Review*, Vol.67 (1977), 379-393.

50. Prothero, R. M. "Disease and mobility: a neglected factor in epidemiology", *International Journal of Epidemiology*, Vol.6 (1977), 259-267.

51. Kloos, H., DeSole, G. and Aklilu Lemma. "Intestinal parasitism . . .", *op. cit.*; Herbert, D. and N. B. Hijazi. "Ill health and health care in Khartoum/Omdurman", *Social Science and Medicine*, Vol.18 (1984), 335-343; Hughes, C. C. and J. M. Hunter. "Disease and 'development' in Africa", *Social Science and Medicine*, Vol.3 (1970), 443-493; Hunter, J. M., Rey, L. and D. Scott. "Man-made lakes and man-made diseases", *Social Science and Medicine*, Vol.16 (1982), 1127-1145.

52. Goorian, P. "Irrigation policy in the Awash River Basin". Unpublished report prepared for WRDA and FAO, Addis Ababa, 1983, 97pp.

53. Rosenfield, P. L., Widstrant, C. G. and A. P. Ruderman, *op. cit.*; World Health Organisation. "Scientific Working Group on Social and Economic Research: Guidelines to assess the social and economic consequences of tropical diseases". Unpublished document TDR.SER-SWG (2) 80.3, Geneva, 1980, 58pp.

54. Trowell, H. G. and D. P. Burkitt (eds.). *Western Diseases, their Emergence and Prevention*, Cambridge, Mass.: Harvard University Press, 1981.

55. McGlashan, N. D. "Primary liver cancer and food-based toxins. A Swaziland example", *Ecology of Disease*, Vol.1 (1982), 37-44; Schoenthal, R. and A. Coaty. "The hepatoxicity of some Ethiopian and East African plants, including some used in traditional medicine", *East African Journal of Medicine*, Vol.45 (1965), 577-579.

56. Armstrong, R. W. "Medical geography and its geologic substrate", *Memoirs of the Geological Society of America*, No.123 (1971), 211-215.

57. Prothero, R. M. "Studies in medical geography . . . ", *op. cit.*; Kloos, H. and Aklilu Lemma. "Bilharziasis . . . ", *op. cit.*

58. Price, E. W. "The association of endemic elephantiasis of the lower legs in East Africa with soil derived from volcanic rock", *Transactions of the Royal Society of Tropical Medicine and Hygiene*, Vol.70 (1976), 288-295; Price, E. W., McHardy, W. J. and F. D.

Pooley. "Endemic elephantiasis of the lower legs as a health hazard of barefoot agriculturalists in Cameroon", *Annals of Occupational Medicine*, Vol.24 (1981), 1-8.

59. Glick, B. J. "The geographic analysis of cancer occurrence: past progress and future directions" *in* Meade, M. S. (ed.), *Conceptual . . . op. cit.*, pp.170-193.

60. Scrimshaw, N. S., Taylor, C. E. and J. E. Gordon. *Interaction of Nutrition and Infection*, WHO Monograph Series, Geneva: World Health Organisation, 1971.

61. Newman, J. L. "Dietary behavior and protein-energy-malnutrition in Africa south of the Sahara: some themes for medical geography" *in* Meade, M. S. (ed.), *Conceptual . . . op. cit.*, pp.77-92.

62. May, J. M. *The Ecology of Malnutrition in Middle Africa*, New York: Hafner, 1965; May, J. M. *The Ecology of Malnutrition in Northern Africa*, New York: Hafner, 1967; May, J. M. in collaboration with McLellan, D. L. *The Ecology of Malnutrition in the French-Speaking Countries of West Africa and Madagascar*, New York: Hafner, 1968; May, J. M. and D. L. McLellan. *The Ecology of Malnutrition in Eastern Africa and Four Countries in Western Africa*, New York: Hafner, 1970; May, J. M. *The Ecology of Malnutrition in Seven Countries in Southern Africa and in Portuguese Guinea*, New York: Hafner, 1971.

63. Newman, J. L., *op. cit.*

64. Annegers, J. F. "Geographical Pattern of Diet and Nutritional Status in West Africa with Special Reference to Calorie and Protein Deficiencies". Ph.D. dissertation, Department of Geography, Michigan State University, East Lansing, 1972.

65. Freedman, R. L. *Human Food Uses: A Cross-Cultural Comprehensive Annotated Bibliography, Supplement*, Westport, C. T.: Greenwood Press, 1983.

66. Grivetti, L. E. "Cultural nutrition: anthropological and geographical themes", *Annual Review of Nutrition*, Vol.1 (1981), 47-68.

67. Grivetti, L. E. "Dietary Resources and Social Aspects of Food Use in a Tswana Tribe". Ph.D. dissertation, Department of Geography, University of California, Davis, 1976; Newman, J. L. "Dimensions of Sandawe diet", *Ecology of Food and Nutrition*, Vol.4 (1975), 33-39.

68. Simoons, F. J. "Rejection of fish as human food in Africa: a problem in history and ecology", *Ecology of Food and Nutrition*, Vol.3 (1974), 89-105 *and* "Geography and genetics as factors in the psychobiology of human food selection" *in* Barker, L. M. *The Psychobiology of Human Food Selection*, New York: AVI Publications, 1982, pp.205-224.

69. Simoons, F. J. "Rejection . . . ", *op. cit.*; Kloos, H. "Development, drought and famine in the Awash Valley of Ethiopia", *African Studies Review*, Vol.25 (1982), 21-48.

70. Salole, G. M. "Muddy fields and ivory towers: the practice of anthropology and small scale development in Ethiopia". Paper presented at the Eighth International Conference of Ethiopian Studies, 26-30 November 1984, Addis Ababa.

71. Kloos, H. "Development, drought . . . ", *op. cit.*; Weil, C. "Morbidity, mortality and diet as indicators of physical and economic adaptation among Bolivian migrants", *Social Science and Medicine*, Vol.13A (1979), 215-222.

72. Chambers, R., Longhurst, R., Bradley, D. and R. Feachem. "Seasonal dimensions to rural poverty: analysis and practical implications", *Journal of Tropical Medicine and Hygiene*, Vol.92 (1982), 156-172; Hunter, J. M. "Seasonal hunger in a part of the west African savanna: a survey of bodyweights in Nangodi, northern Ghana", *Transactions of the Institute of British Geographers*, Publication No.41 (1967), 167-185.

73. Kloos, H. "Development, drought . . .", *op. cit.*; Garner, C. R. "Food production and development in the African savanna", *Geoview*, Vol. 2 (1977), 36-50; Edmondson, W. "Applied nutritional geography: priorities and practice", *Social Science and Medicine*, Vol.14D (1980), 133-137.

74. Kranzler, N. J., Mullen, B. J., Comstock, E. M., Holden, C. A., Schulz, H. C. and L. E. Grivetti. "Methods of food intake assessment — an annotated bibliography", *Journal of Nutrition Education*, Vol.14 (1982), 108-119.

75. Edozien, J. C. "Establishment of a biochemical norm for the evaluation of nutrition status in West Africa", *Journal of the West African Science Association*, Vol.10 (1965), 3-21.

76. Newman, J. L. "Some considerations in the field of measurement of diet", *Professional Geographer*, Vol.29 (1977), 171-196; Rossington, C. E. "Environmental aspects of child growth and nutrition: a case study from Ibadan, Nigeria", *GeoJournal*, Vol.5.4 (1981), 347-354; Turner, M. A. "Nutritional survey in Moshaneng, Ngwaketse, Botswana: preliminary findings and observations", *GeoJournal*, Vol.5.4 (1981), 339-346; Uyanga, J. "The regional correlates of child nutrition in rural southeastern Nigeria", *GeoJournal*, Vol.5.4 (1981), 331-338.

77. Koehn, P. "Ethiopia: famine, food production and changes in the legal order", *African Studies Review*, Vol.22 (1979), 51-71.

78. Mesfin Wolde Mariam. *Rural Vulnerability to Famine in Ethiopia*, New Delhi: Vikas Publishers, 1984; Dawit Wolde-Giorgis. "The current drought in Ethiopia". Paper presented at the Eighth International Conference of Ethiopian Studies, 26-30 November 1984, Addis Ababa.

79. Udo, R. K. "Food deficit areas in Nigeria", *Geographical Review*, Vol.61 (1971), 415-430.

80. Pyle, G. F., *op. cit.*; Mayer, J. D. "Relations between two traditions in medical geography: health systems planning and geographical epidemiology", *Progress in Human Geography*, Vol.2 (1981), 216-230; Shannon, G. W. "Space and time in medical geography", *in* Meade, M. S. (ed.) *Conceptual . . . op. cit.*

81. Pyle, G. F., *op. cit.*; Prothero, R. M. "Studies in medical geography . . ., *op. cit.*; Gish, O. "Resource allocation, equality of access and health", *International Journal of Health Services*, Vol.3 (1973), 399-412.

82. Fabrega, H. "Toward a model of illness behavior", *Medical Care*, Vol.11 (1973), 470-484; *see also* Shannon, G. W., *op. cit.*, for a brief description of this model.

83. Fayewonyomi, B. A. "An approach to effective health care delivery in a developing nation: a case of Nigeria", *Social Science and Medicine*, Vol.17 (1983), 525-530; Good, C. M., Hunter, J. M. and S. S. Katz. "The interface of dual systems in health care in the developing world: towards health policy initiatives in Africa", *Social Science and Medi-*

cine, Vol. 130 (1979), 141-154; Kighela, N., Bibeau, G. and E. Corin. "East Africa's two medical systems: options for planners", *World Health Forum*, Vol.1, No.1 (1981), 96-99; Neumann, A. K. and P. Lauro. "Ethnomedicine and biomedicine linking", *Social Science and Medicine*, Vol.16 (1982), 1917-1924; Stock, R. "Traditional healers in rural Hausaland", *GeoJournal*, Vol.5.4 (1981), 363-368.

84. Good, C. M. and V. N. Kimani. "Urban traditional medicine: a Nairobi case study", *East African Medical Journal*, Vol.57 (1980), 705-713; Kloos, H. "Medicine vendors and their products in markets in the Ethiopian highlands and Rift Valley", *Ethiopian Medical Journal*, Vol.16 (1978), 47-69.

85. Colson, A. C. "The differential use of medical resources in developing countries", *Journal of Health and Social Behavior*, Vol.12 (1971), 226-235; Gesler, W. M. "Illness and health practitioner use in Calabar, Nigeria", *Social Science and Medicine*, Vol.13D (1979), 23-30; Stock, R. "Distance and the utilization of health facilities in rural Nigeria", *Social Science and Medicine*, Vol.17 (1983), 563-570; Gish, O and G. Walker. *Mobile Health Services*, London: Tri-Med Books Ltd., 1977; Imperato, P. J. "Nomads of the west African Sahel and the delivery of health services to them", *Social Science and Medicine*, Vol.8 (1974), 443-457; Prothero, R. M. "Problems of public health among pastoralists: a case study from Africa" *in* McGlashan, N. D., (ed.). *Medical Geography: Techniques and Field Studies*, London: Methuen, 1972, pp.105-118.

86. Buschkens, W. F. L. and L. J. Slikkerveer. *Health Care in East Africa: Illness Behavior of the Eastern Oromo in Hararghe (Ethiopia)*, Assen: Van Gorcum, 1982; Landy, D. "Role adaption: traditional curers under the impact of western medicine" *in* Logan, M. H. and E. E. Hunt, (eds.). *Health and Human Condition: Perspectives on Medical Anthropology*, North Scituate, Mass.: Duxbury Press, pp.217-241; Van der Geest, S. "The illegal distribution of western medicines in developing countries: pharmacists, drug pedlars, injection doctors and others. A bibliographic exploration", *Medical Anthropology*, Vol.6 (1982), 197-219.

87. Kloos, H. "Medicine vendors . . . ", *op. cit.*; Giel, P. L. "Faith healing and spirit possession in Ghion, Ethiopia", *Social Science and Medicine*, Vol.2 (1968), 63-79; Strelcyn, S. *Médecine et Plantes d'Éthiopie: Enquete sur les Noms et l'Emploi des Plantes en Ethiopie*, Naples: Instituto Universitario Orientale, 1973; Paulos Milkias. "Traditional institutions and traditional elites: the role of education in the Ethiopian body politic", *African Studies Review*, Vol.19 (1976), 79-93; Rodinson, M. Magie. *Médecine et Possession en Éthiopie*, Le Havre: Moutin & Co., 1967; Young, A. L. "Medical Beliefs and Practices of Begemder Amhara". Ph.D. dissertation, Department of Anthropology, University of Maryland, 1970.

88. Young, A. L. "Internalising and externalising medical systems: an Ethiopian example", *Social Science and Medicine*, Vol.10 (1976), 147-156; Hailu Meche and Mehari Woldeab. "Reaching the people: some issues in the utilization of selected hospitals in Addis Ababa", *The Ethiopian Journal of Health Development*, Vol.1 (1984), 65-73; Conacher, D. G. "Medical care in Ethiopia", *Transactions of the Royal Society of Tropical Medicine and Hygiene*, Vol.70 (1976), 141-144; Nordberg, E. "Self-portrait of an average rural drug shop in Ethiopia today", *Ethiopian Medical Journal*, Vol.12 (1974), 25-32; Asfaw Desta. "National Health Planning in Ethiopia". D.P.H. dissertation, Department of Public Health, Johns Hopkins University, Baltimore, 1971.

89. Gish, O. "Some observations about health development in three African socialist countries: Ethiopia, Mozambique and Tanzania", *Social Science and Medicine*, in press.

90. Armstrong, R. W. "Computers and mapping in medical geography", pp.69-88; Forster, F. "Use of demographic base maps for the presentation of areal data in epidemiology", pp.59-68; Learmonth, A. T. A. "Medicine and medical geography", pp.17-42 *all in* McGlashan, N. D. (ed.), *op. cit.*

91. Stimson, R. J. "Research design and methodological problems in the geography of health", *in* McGlashan, N. D. and J. R. Blunden (eds.) *Geographical Aspect of Health*, London: Academic Press, 1983, pp.258-272.

92. Mayer, J. D. "The role of spatial analysis . . . ", *op. cit.*

93. Pyle, G. F. *op. cit.*; Francis, A. M. and J. B. Schneider. "Using computer graphics to map origin-destination data describing health care delivery systems", *Social Science and Medicine*, Vol.57 (1984), 499-512; Armstrong, R. W. "Computers . . . ", *op. cit.*

94. Cline, B. L. New eyes for epidemiologists, *American Journal of Epidemiology*, Vol.92 (1979), 85-89.

95. Jiagu, S. and L. Shenkal. "Application of Landsat Images to the researches of the environment for Onchomelania breeding in the Dongting Lake", *Proceedings of the Fourth Asian Conference on Remote Sensing*, Session B, Land Use, 1983, p.821.

96. Learmonth, A. T. A. *Patterns . . . op. cit.*; Hunter, J. M. "Man-environmental holism as an approach to the study of disease transmission and control". Unpublished document, HPD/PCT-TDR of the World Health Organization, Geneva, 1976, 35pp.

97. Fisseha Haile Meskal. "Health research and its organization in Ethiopia". Paper presented at the Eighth International Conference of Ethiopian Studies, 26-30 November 1984, Addis Ababa.

ANALYTICAL APPROACH

TO DISASTER PREPAREDNESS

Laike M. Asfaw

INTRODUCTION

Most natural disasters have their origins in primary processes deep in the earth's interior or in the solar-terrestrial interaction and as such are generally not accessible for control by man. However, their adverse manifestations on man and his environment have been the source of losses suffered by man all through the ages (Cornell, 1976).

Most of the losses in a situation of disaster are due to secondary and tertiary effects induced by primary natural processes. Although the primary processes are beyond the control of man, the secondary and tertiary effects are, to a large extent, amenable to mitigating actions by man.

In order to determine the nature of mitigating measures in a disaster-preparedness programme, it is important to understand the interaction of the primary processes with the man-environment system and the subsequent manifestations in the forms of secondary and tertiary effects.

The first task of an agency in charge of a disaster-preparedness programme is to delineate its domain of responsibility. This requires the existence of a mechanism for declaring a situation as that of a disaster both in space and time. Generally there is a lack of precision in the definition and application of terms employed to describe a situation of disaster. For example, terms like magnitude and intensity are used arbitrarily but should be made more precise. These parameters can usefully be employed to declare a situation of disaster and delineate the area affected. Such characterization can form the basis for defining the responsibility area of institutes established to handle situations of disaster. Furthermore, the variations of these parameters with space and time reveal important characteristics of disaster that can be utilized in formulating mitigating measures.

Site vulnerability analysis for endemic hazards and hazards induced by man as a result of development is a fundamentally important task in a disaster-preparedness programme. Once the disaster prone-ness of sites is determined, basic preliminary measures to mitigate their effects can be taken. These would include, among other things, public education and prediction of disasters when possible.

It is also important to have some means for evaluating the performance of any disaster preparedness programme. The rating of performances and an in-depth retrospective study of the whole disaster preparedness programme assists tremendously in the evolution of a better programme.

TERMS AND PARAMETERS

Cause and effects (manifestations)

We will consider continuously or suddenly growing adverse changes in the man-environment system and restrict ourselves to those that are the effects of natural causes. In this context, the primary effects of the natural causes will be the primary manifestations. Manifestations generated by the primary effects as the causes will be secondary effects or secondary manifestations. Tertiary, quaternary, etc. effects are defined in analogous manner.

Examples of the relative effects of such corollaries are shown on the following page, set out in tabular form (Table 1).

TABLE 1

Primary natural process	Solar-Terrestrial process	Solar-Terrestrial process	Processes Deep in the Earth	Processes Deep in the Earth
Primary effects or Primary manifestations	no rain drought	heavy rains floods	volcano lava and ash flows	earthquakes, faults, landslides
Secondary effects	crop failure	destruction by flood, deaths	burial of settlement	destruction of buildings, dam
Tertiary effects	epidemics death			flooding fire
Quaternary effects	cultural and spiritual disintegration			deaths

Loss and Cumulative Loss

Taking areas prone to adverse changes in the man-environment system, the adverse change will be referred to as the loss. The loss up to a given time will be the cumulative loss.

For example, the loss can involve the following manifestations:

Loss of human life
injuries
destruction of settlements
destruction of dams, bridges, etc.
loss of crops
loss of arable land
loss of property

The losses are generally associated with primary, secondary and tertiary effects. These losses can conveniently be expressed in a unified unit as is usually done.

Intensity and Cumulative Intensity

The loss over a given locality (per unit area) at a given time (per unit time) will be referred to as the intensity. The total loss over a given area (per unit area) up to a given time is the cumulative intensity.

Limit of Affected Area

The limit of the affected area is delineated by defining a threshold intensity. The iso-intensity line with the threshold value delineates the boundary of the affected area (Fig.1). The region within the threshold iso-intensity line forms the whole affected area. A similar definition can be made in terms of cumulative intensity.

Magnitude and Cumulative Magnitude

We will define the total loss over the whole affected area (LWAA) at a given time as the magnitude (Fig.2). The total loss over the whole of the affected area up to a given time is the cumulative magnitude.

Fig.1 Iso-intensity Map

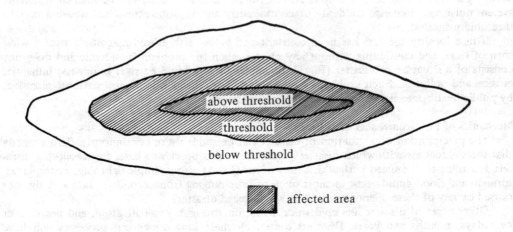

above threshold

threshold

below threshold

affected area

Fig.2 Magnitude (vertical line) and cumulative
magnitude (shaded area)

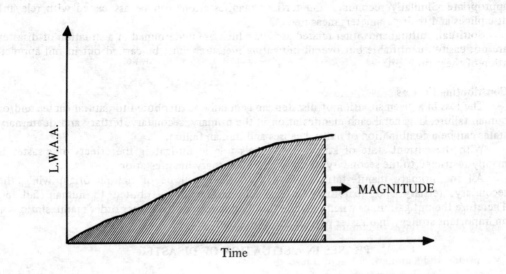

L.W.A.A.

MAGNITUDE

Time

Situation of Disaster

This will be defined as any sudden or continually growing adverse change above a given threshold magnitude in the man-environment system.

To avoid identifying small incidents as disasters there must be a threshold magnitude for declaring a situation as that of a disaster. For the realization of disaster, the man-environment system must either change suddenly or continuously and in both cases must above a certain threshold magnitude.

If in a locality the loss has been constant and below a threshold magnitude over a wide span of time, and continuing without any change, then the problem is endemic and does not consists of a situation of disaster (Fig.3). Examples of this could be river blindness, bilharzia, erosion and pollution. Such problems must be dealt with through long term national planning, by public health agencies and other appropriate bodies.

Mechanics of the Occurrences of Disaster

The precipitation of a situation of disaster can be suddenly or continuously. This suggests that the suddenness with which disasters occur varies and provides a basis for classifying disasters according to the speed with which they occur (Fig.4). For example lightning, earthquakes, tornado and flood could occur in short spans of time ranging from seconds to hours. A disaster caused by any of these phenomena will be a high speed disaster.

Other types of disaster like epidemics, pollution, drought, desertification, and pests occur over days, months and years. Disasters caused by these long drawn out processes will have speeds ranging between intermediate and low.

Classification of Disasters and Association of Parameters

The variety of manifestations associated with the change in the man-environment system can be studied by employing appropriate disciplines. We will classify the phenomena of disaster by discipline, and it is generally possible to speak of geophysical, biological, etc., disasters. In all cases, the man-environment system changes adversely to man. The identification of primary, secondary and tertiary manifestations with appropriate disciplines forms the basis for applying science and technology to the study of disasters.

The parameters to be measured in the study of disasters are properly defined in the appropriate disciplines. For example, if we are studying drought, meteorological parameters will be appropriate. Similarly secondary and tertiary manifestations can be associated with relevant disciplines and their parameters measured.

Spiritual, cultural and other related aspects which are undermined in a situation of disaster are not easily quantifiable but overall mitigating measures must be carried out in full appreciation of these problems.

Contributing Factors

The loss in a given situation of disaster can generally be attributed to natural causes and/or human failure. In general each manifestation in the primary, secondary, tertiary and quaternary states can be a combination of natural causes and human failure.

With the current state of knowledge, man's role in mitigating the effects of disaster is mainly restricted to the secondary, tertiary and quaternary manifestations.

All the primary manifestations we will consider will be of natural origin while the secondary, tertiary and quaternary effects can largely be attributed to human failures. Therefore the mitigation, or when possible the elimination, of the higher order manifestations is an important strategy in disaster preparedness programmes.

PHASES IN A SITUATION OF DISASTER

The monitoring of loss and therefore of magnitude at various points in time in a disaster-prone area in the light of a given threshold magnitude implies that the situation before a threshold is reached is a situation of pre-disaster. While the magnitude remains above the

Fig.3 Difference between disaster and endemic hazard

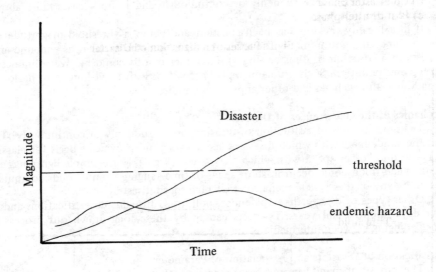

Fig.4 Speed of occurrence of disasters

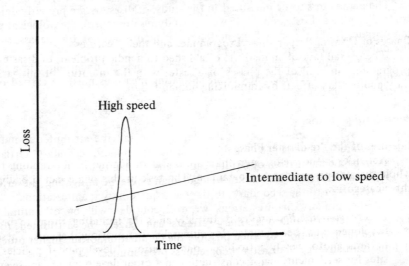

threshold value the situation is a co-disaster situation and when the magnitude falls below the threshold the situation will be a post-disaster situation (Fig.5). Therefore, generally, the phases involved in a disaster process can broadly be classified as:

a) Pre-disaster phase
b) Co-disaster phase
c) Post-disaster phase

Fig.5 Phases of a Situation of Disaster

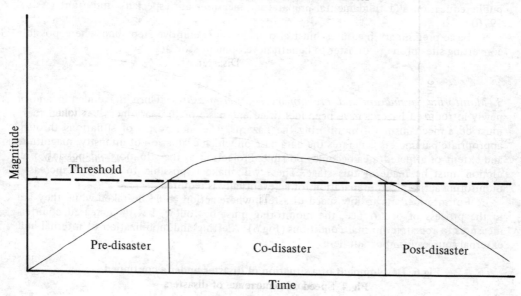

Phases of Disaster Preparedness Programmes and their Features

The overall task of an institute established to handle problems of disaster should consists of programmes in each of the phases of disaster with the intention of mitigating, mainly, secondary and tertiary effects by minimizing human failure.

Features of the Pre-disaster Phase

Activities in the pre-disaster phase are the most decisive in determining the outcome of the whole disaster preparedness programme. The task in this phase can broadly be classified into three categories.

1. Site vulnerability analysis: Initially all sites including those to be newly settled or developed must be evaluated for vulnerability to various hazards. These include endemic hazards and/or newly introduced ones. National development policies must ensure that sites for settlement, major construction and other developments are selected in full view of the disaster proneness of localities and what new variety of hazards the process of development could introduce.

For example, developing a quarry site could destabilize slopes, inducing landslides and subsequent loss of arable land. Another case in point is the intense pumping of sub-surface water leading to widespread land subsidence.

2. Basic preliminary measures: The next step following site vulnerability analysis is to take fundamental preparatory measures to reduce adverse manifestations in a possible eventuality. These can include, for example, making buildings safe from earthquakes, hurricanes, etc., and arable land safe from flooding, landslide, erosion, etc., in regions where these are identified to be the endemic and/or newly induced hazards. Generally the preparation must aim at reducing all possible secondary and tertiary effects.

Public education about the disaster proneness of sites is especially important in mitigating higher order manifestations. In the case of high speed disasters, where there will be no time to take counter-measures while the disasters are in the process of occurrence, public education and fundamental preparatory measures are especially important (Asfaw 1976).

Basic preliminary measures must also include pre-emptive steps and where possible converting sites prone to disaster to benefit development schemes.

3. Monitoring, evaluation and preliminary counter-measures: Once the endemic and/or newly introduced hazards have been identified and basic preliminary measures taken there must be a mechanism for monitoring the hazards. The monitoring of situations through appropriate parameters generates the data base on which evaluation of intensity, magnitude and extent of affected area becomes possible. Projection of the situation and possibly prediction must be made at this stage. These will make it possible to decide if increased monitoring activity and preparation for an eventually is required.

For intermediate to low speed disasters, where action could be taken while they are in the process of occurrence, the monitoring must be followed with increased counter-measures to reinstate normal conditions (Fig.6). Alerting and mobilization of internal and external sources is important here.

**Fig.6 Development of a situation of disaster under a continued
counter-measure**

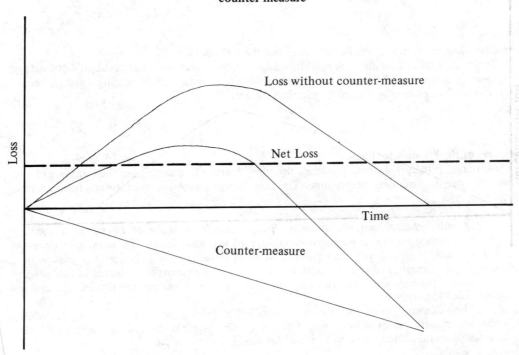

For high speed disasters, the onslaught starts suddenly and has a short duration so that there will be no time to take counter-measures while they are occurring. As indicated, this fact must make basic preliminary measures and public education most important in preparing for such eventualities.

Features of the Co-disaster Phase

This phase is entered as soon as the threshold magnitude is surpassed. The ground has been prepared for this eventuality in the pre-disaster phase, so that enhanced counter-measures can be taken over the whole affected area. The intensity distribution map can be one of the useful guides in the allocation of mobilized resources. Furthermore, especially in the case of intermediate to low speed disasters, the experience gained in the pre-disaster phase is an important asset in determining the course of action to be taken in the co-disaster phase. The immediate task in this phase is to bring the magnitude below the threshold value.

Features of the Post-disaster Phase

When the magnitude falls below the threshold value the post-disaster phase is entered. Generally, however, this phase is characterized by high cumulative loss (Fig.7). Activities in this phase must focus on decreasing the high cumulative effects to absolute minimum or zero. Long term reconstruction, reclamation and preparing for possible recurrence of the event are among the important features in this phase. Also, re-evaluation of the whole disaster-preparedness programme will be one of the major tasks in this phase. This phase passes over to the pre-disaster phase smoothly.

Fig.7 Net Cumulative Loss in a Situation of Disaster

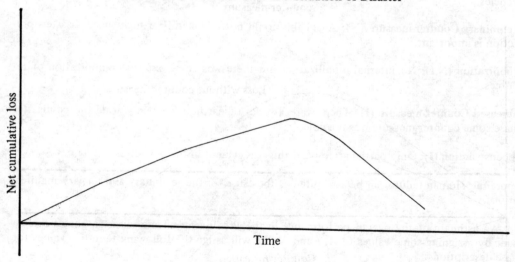

A SIMPLIFIED SCHEME FOR PERFORMANCE EVALUATION

The tasks in a disaster preparedness programme have been divided into various phases and the activities in each phase have been summarized. The utilization of resources and application of methods of science and technology, including the role they play, have also been clarified. The performances in a disaster preparedness programme must be judged against such standards. The requirements as laid out in the pre-disaster, co-disaster and post-disaster phases must form the basis for performance evaluation.

In the following table (Table 2) we will make performance evaluation for some Ethiopian disasters; however, in the absence of adequate data, the analysis presented here must be considered a preliminary one.

The evaluation is based on various reports by the Geophysical Observatory and the Relief and Rehabilitation Commission.

Performances in the pre-disaster and co-disaster phases must be evaluated separately. In the post-disaster phase, the co-disaster manifestations are evaluated relative to the pre-disaster performances.

To clarify matters, we will consider the 1969 Serdo earthquake (Dakin *et. al.*, 1971) — the first row in Table 2. Going from left to right we have:

Site Vulnerability Analysis (N.N.): No work carried out to identify endemic and induced hazards. The town of Serdo was built with no such consideration.

Basic Preliminary Measures (N): There was no public education and structures were not designed to resist earthquakes.

Monitoring, Evaluation and Prediction (N): Such activities did not exist. . .

Alerting (N): . . . as a result it was not possible to alert either the local people or external agencies.

Preliminary Counter-measure (N): Again this could not be taken. For high speed disaster, prediction is important.

Mobilization (N.I): No internal mobilization but there was some external mobilization of resources.

Increased Counter-measure (I): There were a series of earthquakes and during the co-disaster phase some counter-measure was possible.

Reconstruction (I): Only partial attempt of this was evident in the post-disaster phase.

Appraisal: Human failure can be attributed as the cause for the secondary and tertiary manifestations.

An estimate of the overall performance in the Pre-disaster and Co-disaster phases can be made by assigning some values to A, I and N. We will assign the following tentative values for these descriptions:

$$A = 2$$
$$I = 1$$
$$N = 0$$

Substituting these values for the pre-disaster and co-disaster performances we obtain:

$$\frac{0+0+0+0+0+0+0+1+1}{2+2+2+2+2+2+2+2+2} = \frac{1}{9} = 11.1\%$$

which is a very low value. Most certainly the secondary effects (24 deaths and 167 injuries out of a population of 420) were purely due to human failure. There was no site vulnerability analysis or public education and structures were not designed to resist earthquakes.

In the evaluation some items must carry more weight than others. For example, site vulnerability analysis for endemic and induced hazards must carry the maximum weight. Ignorance of the vulnerability of sites to a given hazard could imply maximum destruction in an eventuality.

The number of columns in Table 2 could have been enlarged. For example monitoring, evaluation and prediction could each have appeared in a single column; also basic preliminary measures include public education and other pre-emptive measures which are not listed in Table 2.

Generally the adverse manifestations constituting secondary and tertiary effects in the co-disaster phase could be mitigated by a well planned pre-disaster programme. In the appraisal during the post-disaster phase, the contribution of human failure to the aggravation of the problem should be based largely on the pre-disaster phase performance.

Adverse manifestations such as fire, collapse of buildings, deaths and injuries can be reduced by proper design consideration and public education in the pre-disaster phase. Inadequate design consideration and lack of public education programmes are human failures. On the other hand, if damage occurs in spite of good public education and utilization of all the know-how in science and technology within the limit of available resources, it should be attributed to nature. After the reducible limit, failures must be attributed to nature. In this manner the contributions of man and nature can be identified. The degree of human success is determined by 'the state of the art' in science and technology, and the resource to implement it and as such varies from time to time.

CONCLUSION

An institution which makes a determined effort to solve problems of disaster, in a self-reliant manner, will face the need to formulate its programme in a rational way. The rational response consists of applying science and technology within the framework of available resources.

'The state of the art' in science and technology determines man's ability to combat disasters and hence his rational response. The state of the art is advancing at a tremendous rate and the knowledge available is such that many natural disasters can be predicted with some precision in space and time. On the other hand, the practical application of this knowledge to minimise the effects of disaster requires resources and even where resources have been available implementation is lagging far behind. The problem of applying scientific and technological know-how using available resources must entirely be attributed to man and the amplification of a situation of disaster through secondary and tertiary effects is basically a human failure.

As science and technology advance, the possibility of increased human failures contributing to a situation of disaster could be a serious issue. Perhaps, ultimately science and technology could equip man with the necessary knowledge to stop disasters from occurring, but this knowledge must be utilized effectively.

The existence of constraints such as limited resources in solving a problem of disaster with a variety of manifestations implies allocation of resources in an optimum way. If unlimited resources are available, or reliance on others is to be institutionalized, then the *raison d'etre* for a disaster preparedness programme suggested here would be pre-empted. It is in the determined effort to be self-reliant that such a methodology finds meaning.

As indicated at the outset, basic preliminary measures should include pre-emptive steps and, where possible, converting what looks like an adverse situation to advantageous schemes. For example, the flood prone areas of Tefki and Teji in central Ethiopia imply that irrigation farms can thrive easily by damming the Awash river upstream and as such the cause for this disaster can be pre-empted.

Regarding continuous monitoring of high speed disasters, there can only be a period of increased activity based on prediction once basic preliminary measures have been taken. But the

TABLE 2: Performance evaluation for disaster preparedness programme

DISASTER LOCATION DATE	PRE — Site Vulnerability Analysis		DISASTER PHASE — Disaster Preparedness Based on (A) and (B)				CO-DISASTER — Mobilization		Increased Counter Measure based on (C) to (G)	POST-DISASTER — Reconstruction	Appraisal Human Failure / Nature
	Endemic hazard (A)	Induced hazard (B)	Basic Prelim. measures (C)	Monitor Evaluate Predict (D)	Alerting based on (D)	Prelim. Counter-measure (E)	Internal (F)	External (G)			
Earthquake Serdo 1969	N	N	N	N	N	N	N	I	I	I	100/0
Drought Ethiopia 1973	N	N	N	I	I	N	I	I	I	I	30/70
Landslide Gamo Gofa 1975	N	N	N	N	N	N	I	N	I	N	100/0
Flood Kelafe 1976	N	N	N	N	N	N	N	I	I	I	90/10
Flood Awasa 1980	N		N	N	N	I	I	N	I	N	100/0
Earthquake Awara Melka 1981	N	N	N	N	N	N	N	I	I	N	100/0
Landslide Hosana 1983	N	N	N	N	N	N	N	I	N	N	100/0

A = Complete and/or adeqate   N = Nothing attempted   I = Inadequate or partial attempt   Blank = not applicable onset of low to intermediate speed disasters cannot be clearly defined and monitoring should start at a much earlier stage than when the knowledge becomes widespread among the public. Full-fledged monitoring in the absence of the slightest symptoms, other than routine surveillance work, could be wasteful and unwarranted for an institute established to deal with situations of disaster.

REFERENCES

Cornell, J. (1976)
The Great International Disaster Book. Scribner's Sons, New York, p.382.

Dakin, F. M., Gouin, P. and S. Roger (1971)
"The 1969 Earthquake in Serdo". *Bull. Geophys. Obs.*, No.13, pp.19-56.

Laike M. Asfaw (1976)
"A survey of the participation of local people in the prevention and cure of Geophysical and Geological Disasters", *Proceedings of WASA*, Freetown.

CHARACTERISTICS OF AMHARIC IDIOMATIC EXPRESSIONS

Amsalu Aklilu[1]

INTRODUCTION

Peculiar uses of particular words, phrases and turns of expressions which, from long usage, have become stereotyped in a particular language are known as idioms.[2] The Amharic language is full of such idiomatic turns of expressions. So far, to my knowledge, Amharic idioms have not been studied and described. The aim of this paper, therefore, is to throw some light on this matter by showing the most relevant comments on the various types, when this is felt necessary. This does not mean, however, that I am attempting to show why particular idioms have assumed their present shape. This is a very difficult task and I don't think one can reach a satisfactory conclusion in such an endeavour.

AMHARIC IDIOM FORMATION

The groupings given below are not exhaustive, but are only an attempt to stimulate those who, in the future, will undertake a more rigorous research in this field.

Most of the Amharic idioms are a combination of words; that is, phrases or sentences. Combining names of the parts of the body with other words or phrases plays a significant role in the formation of idioms. For example, with the noun . . ልብ (heart), 117 idiomatic expressions are recorded in the collection cited above. It would be interesting to find out if this phenomenon is also similar in the other languages of Ethiopia, particularly within the Semitic group of languages.

I shall next try to show the various types of Amharic idiomatic formations. First, I shall treat the phrase or sentence formation types and next those that deal with the parts of the human body, followed by very common nouns and verbs that play major roles in this respect.

1. Phrase or Sentence Types

a) verb + verb + አለ

በል በል አለ	was instigated, incited
ሆይ ሆይ አለ	encouraged; intervened
በረክ በረክ አለ	shivered with fear

b) constructive status

ሁሉ አገርሽ	adaptable (person)
መቀስ አፍ	talkative (lit. scissors-mouthed)
ሕገወጥ	lawless (lit. an outlaw)
አጽም ርስት	family land (lit. the land of bone, perhaps due to the fact that the forefathers have died toiling on the land for generations since bone has also the implication of ancestors in Amharic)

c) + noun + noun

የሀገር ምሰሶ	an important man for the nation (lit. central pillar of a nation)
የሕልም ሩጫ	wishful desire (lit. running in one's dream)
የመስቀል ወፍ	a rare visitor (lit. Maskel's bird, apparently type of bird that only appears about September)
የሰው ሰው	a perfect man (lit. an outstanding man among many others)

571

d) noun + verbal adjective

ጆሮ ጠቢ
informer, spy (lit. ear sucker. This is because a spy informs about people he had spied on stealthily, i.e. coming near to somebody's ear)

ለዛ ሙጥጤ
graceless (lit. devoid of all human charm)

ጠፍር ነካሽ
caravan merchant (lit. one who bites off a strip of leather. This is because a caravan merchant bites the strip of leather with which he ties fast the load on the back of pack-animals while both of his hands are busy fastening the load. He thus uses his teeth for holding the strip of leather)

በር ከፋች
pioneer (lit. door opener)

e) noun + verb

ልቡ ሸፈተ
changed one's mind (lit. his heart has rebelled)

ሐረግ መዘዘ
traced one's ancestors (lit. pulled twine) cf. የዘር ሐረግ

ሀሞቱ ፈሰሰ
lost hope (lit. his bile was poured out) In Amharic the word 'bile' indicates courage, vigour and bravery due to its bitter taste. The pouring out of bile therefore means that he is devoid of any courage, vigour or bravery.

It is noteworthy to mention that this type of formation is more common than any other type.

f) adj. + noun

አውራ ምስክር
an eye-witness (lit. leading witness)

ሌባ ሚዛን
false scale (lit. a thief scale)

ሹል ቂጥ
restless (lit. one with a pointed bottom)

ቀጭን እመቤት
a well-to-do-lady (lit. a thin lady) also ቀጭን ጌታ well-to-do gentleman

g) verbal adj. + verbal adj.

አጥፈና ጠፊ
antagonistic (lit. destroyer and destroyable)

ቆራጭ ፈላጭ
all-powerful, omnipotent (lit. one who cuts and splits)

ተካይ ነቃይ
dictator, despot (lit. one who plants and roots out, i.e. one who does whatever pleases him)

አዛዥ ነካሽ
thankless, ungrateful (lit. one who bites the one that has carried him on his back)

h) verb + verb + አደረገ

ብር ብር አደረገ
made restless (lit. was made to fly constantly)

አገም ጠቀም አደረገ
was not very serious

ያዝ ለቀቅ አደረገ
was not very serious (lit. took hold of something and let it fall)

i) verbal adj. + noun

ትክል ድንጋይ
lazy (lit. planted stone)

ትኩስ ኃይል
youth (lit. fresh force)

ስልጡን እጅ
thief (lit. skilled hand)

j) gerund + gerund

ውሎ ውሎ
later on, at last

ቆስቁሶ ቆስቁሳ
having instigated (lit. gave the fire several pokes)

አልፎ አልፎ
occasionally

572

k) noun + noun + verb

ቄና ቄና ተነፈስ	panted (lit. breathed full of bushels)
ቆላ ደጋ ረገጠ	was perplexed (lit. walked through the lowlands and high-lands; that is, aimlessly)

l) noun + noun + አለ

እንባ እንባ አለው	was about to cry (lit. felt as if tears are coming)
ጋን ጋን አለ	was extremely drunk (lit. he smells like a clay jar, in which täg or tälla is brewed)

m) adj. + adj. + አለ

ቅዱስ ቅዱስ አለ	flattered (lit. he said "you are indeed a saint")
ሌላ ሌላ ኦለ	became putrid (lit. had an alien smell)
የታጣ የታጣ አለ	became putrid (lit. had an alien smell)

As mentioned above, these are not the only ways in which Amharic idiomatic expressions are constructed: there are also other forms that I have intentionally left out because they are less common. To mention just a few, there are forms such as: (hilarious); noun + noun e.g. ሰርግና ምላሽ Adj. + adj. e.g. የቅርብ ሩቅ easy-looking but difficult gerund + verbal adj. e.g. ሠርቶ አፍራሽ God. (lit. he that makes and destroys); gerund + adj. e.g. ቆርጦ ቀጥል a liar (lit. he who cuts and connects); ለፍቶ መና useless, ጆሮ ዳባ ልበስ turned a deaf ear to.

From the various examples cited above one can observe, generally speaking, two types of Amharic idiomatic expressions. The first type is that in which, from the very combination of the various words, one could guess their probable meaning. If, for example, we see the English idiom "hold one's tongue" we could guess what the probable meaning could be: "to remain silent". The second type is not as easy as this; for example, with the idiom "she has a tongue", the problem becomes more difficult, because the meaning is not as transparent as the former one. Here it means "she is a shrew". The same is true in Amharic. This could be illustrated with the following examples: የሀገር ምሰሶ literally means "central pillar of a nation". However the real meaning is "an indispensable man of a nation"; that is, an important man. On the other hand, an idiomatic expression such as ሐረግ መዘዘ which literally means "drew out the stem of a creeping plant" and whose real meaning is "traced back one's ancestors", is rather difficult to guess.

INGREDIENT WORDS OF THE MOST COMMON AMHARIC IDIOMS

Going through the Amsalu-Dagniatchew collection of 4000 Amharic idiomatic expressions, I noticed that a great number of idioms are composed of very common and very frequently used Amharic words. I have tried to put these into three categories for reasons of convenience. They are: names of important parts of the body; very common nouns; and verbs used in the language.

I. Names of Important Parts of the Body

Names of the parts of the body as ingredients of idiom formation are not unique to the Amharic language. The English language, for example, demonstrates the same characteristic. English nouns such as "hand", "heart", "head", "eye", etc., are extensively used in various idiomatic expressions.

a. ልብ : heart

ልብ ደንዳና	stout-hearted (lit. hard-hearted)
ልብ ተራራ	filled with great ambition over-confident (lit. mountain-hearted)
ልብ ቅን	kind-hearted (lit. straight-hearted)

ልብ ሙሉ	daring, courageous (lit. full-hearted)
ልብ ቀላል	hasty (lit. light-hearted)
ልብ አውልቅ	nagging (lit. one who dismantles the heart)
ልብ ሰፊ	tolerant, long-suffering (lit. broad-hearted)
ልቡ አበጠ	became extemely conceited, boastful (lit. had a swollen heart)
ልብ ደረቅ	cruel (lit. dry-hearted)
ልብ ድንጊያ	adamant, not easy to convince (lit. stone-hearted)
ልብ ድፍን	stupid (person), dull; daring, courageous (lit. whole-hearted)
ልቡ ቀረ	had an inclination towards s/t (lit. his heart stayed back)

As can be seen from the above few examples, the word "heart" in the Amharic language has a very extended meaning. It is used to express concepts like attitude, sentiment, disposition (bad or good), temperament, behaviour. It is this semantic versatility of the word that has made it play an important role in the formation of idioms. In the above mentioned collection of Amharic idiomatic expressions I have counted 117 cases containing this word.

b. አንጀት : intestine

አንጀቱ ደንዳና	patient (lit. big-hearted)
አንጀቱ ጥ7	cruel (lit. strong-hearted)
አንጀቱ ቅቤ ጠጣ	was highly satisfied
አንጀቴን አለበኝ	I am extremely hungry (lit. it milks my intestine)
አንጀቴ ራሰ	I became extremely happy (lit. my heart became wet)
አንጀቴ ናት	She is my love
ካንጀቱ ተናገረ	He spoke from his heart
አንጀት ላንጀት	mutual understanding

The word አንጀት like ልብ is very widely used in combination with other words and so many idioms are formed with it. This word conveys the concept of feeling, emotion, love, understanding or disposition. There are many instances when the word አንጀት is substituted by the word ልብ in an idiom, thus conveying nearly the same meaning; e.g. የልቡን ነገረኝ and ያንጀቱን ነገረኝ mean "he was sincere in what he told me", or ካንጀቴ እወዳታለሁ and ከልቤ እወዳታለሁ mean "I love her from my heart". Furthermore አንጀቴን ይበላዋል and ልቤን ይበላዋል could be interchanged meaning "I sympathise with him, አንጀት ላንጀት አልተገናኘ-ኹም could be also changed into ልብ ለልብ አልተገናኙም meaning "they could not reach a mutual understanding".

c. አፍ : mouth

ሹል አፍ	talkative (lit. protruding mouth)
አፈ ማር	eloquent (lit. honey-mouthed)
አፈ ርጭም	polite (in one's talk)
አፉን አዳጠው	had a slip of the tongue (lit. his mouth slipped)
አፉን ይበላዋል	he is talkative (lit. it itches his mouth)

Obviously idioms that are built with this word deal mainly with the process and manner of talking. Such notions as polite, impolite (in manner of talking), modest or immodest, calm or vociferous, are expressed by idioms composed from this word.

d. እጅ : hand

እጅ ሰፊ	generous (lit. one having wide hands)
እጅ ለጅ	hand in hand (a probable borrowing from English)
እጅ በጅ	paying in cash (lit. hand with hand)
እጁን ሰጠ	surrendered (lit. gave his hands)

| እጅ አደረገ | received (lit. converted into hand) |
| እጁ አጠረ | was short of money (lit. his hand became short) |

As could naturally be expected with the word "hand" the act of giving and taking, receiving, paying and helping are expressed. The concept of skill is also conveyed: e.g. እጅ ስንኩል unskilled (woman), እጅ ብልህ skilled.

e. እግር : foot

በእገሌ እግር	in place of so and so (lit. on somebody's foot, meaning when someone had left another one has taken his place)
እግረ ቀላል	swift (lit. light-footed)
እግረ ነጭ	unlucky (lit. white-footed. The colour white has a negative meaning in Amharic)
እግረ እርጥብ	lucky (lit. wet-footed. Wet as opposed to dry has a positive meaning e.g. means he is fortunate. In a country where most people are engaged in agriculture, wet weather is a sign of verdure and thus of plenty)
እግር በግር	one after the other (lit. foot after foot i.e. after someone has left another follows)

"Motion" is the central concept of idioms that are built with the word "foot". The concept of "luck" is also expressed. To give an example for the second concept, when we say አበበ እግረ እርጥብ ነው we mean "Abebe is a lucky man" i.e. after he arrived at a certain place he has found something desirable, e.g. a feast or wedding where a lot of food and drink is served.

f. ዓይን : eye

ዓይነ ደረቅ	shameless (lit. dry-eyed)
ዓይነ ገመድ	estimation (lit. the rope of the eye, since rope is used as a measuring device)
ዓይን ገብ	attractive (lit. something that goes into the eye)
ዓይኑ ቀላ	was envious (lit. his eyes have become red)
ዓይን አዉጣ	was shameless (lit. one who plucks at somebody's eyes)

The word "eye" is one of the most resourceful words in the formation of Amharic idioms. In the collection mentioned earlier, I have found some sixty-one idioms that are built with this word. Most of the idioms constructed with the word "eye" convey the notion of human behaviour such as shame, envy, cruelty, and disposition.

g. ጆሮ : ear

የጆሮ ምግብ	nice to hear (lit. food for the ears)
ጆሮ ስጠኝ	listen to me (lit. give me ear)
ጆሮ ጠቢ	spy (lit. ear sucker)
ጆሮ የሚጠልዝ	very loud (lit. that strikes the ear heavily)
ጆሮዉን ይዞ አሠራዉ	forced somebody to work (lit. he made him work, holding his ears)

As could be expected, most of the idiomatic expressions formed with the word "ear" in Amharic convey the notion of sound and listening. Sometimes in an indirect way it could also mean "time". In cases like ጆሮ የለዉም we mean that "he has no time", that is, he is so busy that he could not listen to any one.

h. ፊት : face

| ኮሶ ፊት | gloomy person (ኮሶ is a purgative for killing tapeworm, with an unpleasant taste) |

ፈተ ሰልካካ	beautiful
ፊቱን ጻጠረ	frowned (lit. tied his face)
ፊቱን ነፋ	was sulky (lit. inflated his face)
ፊት መመለሻ	bribe (lit. means for changing somebody's facial expression from gloominess to cheerfulness)

II. Very Common Nouns Used in the Language

a. ልጅ : child
የላም ልጅ	milk (lit. the child of a cow)
የበረት ልጅ	bastard (lit. stable child)
ልጅነቱን ያልጨረሰ	infantile (lit. one who has not passed his childhood)

b. ቃል : word
ቃል ሰጠ	promised (lit. gave a word)
በቃሉ ጸና	kept his promise (lit. was firm in his words)
ቃሉ ጎደለ	was disobeyed; did not keep his promise (lit. his words became half full)
ቃለ ከባድ	influential (lit. one with heavy words)

c. ቀን : day
ቀን ሲያዘነብል	when bad luck comes (lit. when the day inclines)
ቀን ወጣለት	he is having good days (lit. days have come up to his favour)
ቀኔ ነው ።	it is my lucky day (lit. it is my day)

d. ቤት : house
ሁለት ቤት	very close friends (lit. two houses i.e. friends who often visit each other and enjoy doing so)
ቤቱን ሰው እያወቀውም	he is a miser (lit. no one knows his house; that is, where he lives)
የሴት ቤት	house of prostitutes (lit. woman's house)
የሴት ጉድ	unbecoming behaviour (lit. secret of one's house, i.e. should not be divulged to outsiders)

e. ነፍስ : soul
በነፍስ	separately, per head
በነፍስ ድረስ	arrived when badly needed (lit. arrived when one is still alive)
ነፍስ ቢስ	extremely busy; restless (lit. soulless)
ነፍሴ ናት	I love her very much (lit. she is my soul)
ነፍስ ሆነ	became very expensive (lit. it has become a soul)

f. አፈር : soil, earth
አፈር ሆነ	died (lit. was converted into soil)
አፈር አልባሽ	husband or wife (one of the married couples who takes care of the burial of the one who dies first)
አፈር ገፊ	peasant (lit. soil pusher)
አፈር ጠራው	died back in one's homeland

Soil is the symbol of death in Ethiopian culture for the obvious reason that people are buried after they die. Therefore most idiomatic expressions formed with this word convey this notion. To illustrate this, some more idiomatic expressions could be given, e.g. አፈር መሬት ብላ

died; was extremely humiliated; አፈር ቀመሰ was buried; አፈር ይቅለሰው may God have mercy upon him (after death); አፈር ይብላኝ let me die instead of him; I am extremely sorry for him.

g. ውሃ : water

በውሃ ይለፍ	may it last long (dress; that is, by being washed rather than by being damaged or burnt)
ውሃ ቀጠነ	demanded the impossible (lit. the water has become thin)
ውሃ ሆነ	was caught by surprise; became very thin (lit. he has become water)
ውሃ ቅዳ ውሃ መልስ	futile exercise

h. ወሬ : news, gossip

ለወሬ ብሎ	hastily (lit. for the sake of hearsay)
ወሬ ዘራ	spread news (lit. sewed news)
የወሬ ወሬ	hearsay (lit. the news of news)

III. Very Common Verbs Used in the Language

I have divided this type of verb into two categories, since they show particular common characteristics among themselves. These are verbs of *motion* and those of *action*. It seems that these types of verbs play a big role in the formation of Amharic idiomatic expressions.

Verbs of Motion

a. ሞላ : was, became full

ለዓይን ሞላ	grew up; was magnified (lit. was full for the eyes)
ሰዓቱ ሞላ	it is time (lit. the time has become full)
ትዳሩ ሞላ	became prosperous (that is, ones marital life)
አባ ሙላት	generous (lit. the father of plenty)

b. ቀረ : remained; did not appear

ልቡ ቀረ	doubted (lit. his heart stayed back)
ቆሞ ቀር	old maid, spinster (derogatory, lit. she who stands forever without any change in her lifestyle)
ቋም አፍ	talkative, trouble-maker (lit. one with standing mouth, i.e. with active mouth)

c. ወደቀ : fell down

ልቤ ወደቀባት	I have fallen in love with her (lit. my heart has fallen upon her)
አወዳደቅ ያውቃል	he has a good eye for beauty (lit. he knows how to fall down)
ውድቅ ሆነ	was rejected (proposal; for example)
ውድቅድቅ አለ	became very old (lit. he has fallen completely, became wizened)
የማይወድቀው	greedy (lit. nothing falls down from him)

d. ወረደ : descended, went down; dismounted

ልብ ወረደው	was fatigued (lit. his heart has fallen down)
እዳውን ተወረደ	paid back one's debts
ታች አብሽ ወረደ	was humiliated, was disgraced
ውርድ ከራሴ	I shall not be responsible for the consequences!

e. ወጣ : went out, ascended; came out

ስም አወጣ	gave a name

577

ባፍንጫዬ ይውጣ	I am not interested at all (lit. let it go out of my nose)
አሥራ ሁለት ጠጉር አወጣ	became an extremely old person (lit. grew twelve kinds of hairs)
እጅ አወጣ	became a thief (lit. grew hands)
እጁን አወጣ	saved himself (lit. got his hands out)

f. ዋለ : spent the day; treated somebody

በውል ተገኘ	kept one's words (lit. was found knotted, that is, not loose)
እቤት ዋለ	became very old (lit. he spends the days at home)
ከፋ ዋለበት	mistreated somebody badly
ውለህ ግባ	have good luck (lit. come back after passing the day)
ውለኛ ሰው	a serious person (lit. a man with knots, i.e. not loose)
አይውሉ ዋለብኝ	he has mistreated me (lit. he did with me what he wouldn't do with others)

g. ዞረ : revolved, turned, turned around, went around

ራሴን አታዙረኝ /ው	don't make me mad, don't make me angry (lit. don't turn my head)
ዙሪያ ንግግር	circumlocution (lit. a round about speech)
ዙሪያ ገባው	the entire
ዞር ዞር	after a long time; at the end (lit. having rotated for several times)
አትዙርብኝ	don't start to quarrel with me (as you did with the others)
ዙሪያ ዙሪያውን አትሂድ	don't beat about the bush (lit. don't go round)

h. ደረሰ : arrived, approached

መድረሻ ቢስ	homeless (lit. somebody without destination)
አልደረስክህ-ብህም	I did not offend you (lit. I did not come near you)
የልቡ ደረሰ	was contented (lit. what he had thought has reached)
የይድረስ የይድረስ	hastily done

i. ገባ : entered, came in

ልቡ ገባ	consented, agreed to (lit. his heart has entered i.e. was tranquilized and rested)
ተለም ገባው	learned easily (lit. learning has penetrated him)
ልብ ገቢ	attractive (lit. something that goes into the heart)
መከራ ገባ	is in a difficulty (lit. disaster has come in)
ቃል ገባ	gave promise
ነገር ገባው	was preoccupied, felt uneasy (lit. a thing came into him)

Verbs of Action

a. መታ : hit, struck, beat

መታ ያለ	short and stout (lit. a little bit compacted)
ልቤን መታኝ	it occurred to me (lit. it struck my heart)
መላ መታ	came out with a good idea (lit. stroke an idea)
አድማ መታ	conspired (lit. stroke a strike)
እሳት መታው	was well-cooked, was over-cooked (lit. was hit by fire)
መንገድ መታው	was fatigued (from a long journey, lit. he was hit by the road)

b. ሰራ : worked

ሁለተኛ ተሰራ	was cured after a severe illness (lit. he was created for a second time)

578

ሰርቶ አፍራሽ	God (lit. he who builds and destroys)
ስራዬ ብሎ	intentionally (lit. taking it as one's duty)
ሁለተኛ ስራ	done slovenly (lit. done a second time)
ነገር ሰራ	contrived malice (lit. he worked something)

c. ሰበረ : broke

ዓይነ / አንገተ ሰባራ	shy (lit. broken eyes/neck)
ቅስሙን ሰበረ	broke somebody's spirit, vigour
ዋጋ ሰበረ	cheapened the price of s.th (lit. broke the price)
አንገቱን ሰበረ	was sad, became melancholic (lit. stooped)
ኬላ ሰበረ	contraband item (lit. border-breaker)

d. ረገጠ : tramped, trod

አስረግጠህ ንገረኝ	tell me the fact (lit. tramp the thing and tell me)
ገበታ ረጋጭ	impolite; somebody who does not observe table etiquette (lit. one who kicks the dining table)
ድንበር ረገጠ	demarcated (lit. trod on the border)
አንገቱን ረገጠ	oppressed him (lit. trod on his neck)

e. ቆረጠ : cut

ሆዬ ቆረጠ	became determined (lit. his stomach has made up its mind)
ምን ቢቆርጠኝ	I wouldn't allow myself
ቆርጦ ቀጥል	liar (lit. he who cuts and joins again)
ተስፋ ቆረጠ	lost hope (lit. cut hope)
የስጋ ቁራጭ	blood relation (lit. a small piece of meat)
የሰይጣን ቁራጭ	very cruel, vicious (lit. piece of the Devil)

f. ዘራ : sowed

ለዘርም የለ	disappeared completely (lit. there is nothing remaining for seed. This is said in comparison with a farmer that does not use all of his yield of crop for food but has to keep some to be used as seed for the next season)
ማንዘራሽ	prostitute; impolite (lit. no one knows who has sown you, i.e. not of decent parents; or "no one knows from where you have come")
ዕውር የዘራው	densely populated agricultural field (lit. sown by a blind man)
ዘር ማንዘር	the whole clan

g. ወለደ : gave birth to

ልብ ወለድ	novel (lit. created by the heart)
ሱሪ ቢጥሉባት የምትወልድ	fecund (lit. a woman who becomes pregnant even when one throws towards her a pair of trousers)
በሬ ወለደ	liar (lit. an ox has given birth to a calf)
ጊዜ የወለደው	vogue (lit. something that is born by time)

h. ዘጋ : closed

መጽሐፍ ዘጋ	swore (with the Bible, lit. closed the Bible. This is the way Christians swear in Ethiopia. They close an open scripture)
ዘግቶ በላ	avaricious, miser (lit. one who eats closing his doors so that no one could get in and share the food he is eating)
ፋይሉ ተዘጋ	was decided upon (lit. the file has been closed)

ዘጋው   ignored him (lit. closed him)
ቤቱ ተዘጋ   had a broken family (lit. his house has been closed)

CONCLUSION

From the above exposition of the characteristics of Amharic idiomatic expressions one notices that Amharic idioms are, generally speaking, of a descriptive nature. They mainly focus on describing human behaviour and ability. Attitude, temperament, emotion, disposition, as well as skillfulness, dexterity, success, and agility are the main foci of Amharic turns of expression.

The Amharic language, a language that has served as a medium of wider communication for many centuries in a multilingual society like Ethiopia although not used as a written language before the end of the nineteenth century, clearly demonstrates a very rich and diversified collection of turns of expression. One might wonder and ask oneself whether such a phenomenon could be ascribed to the nature and development patterns of any language. In other words, could we assume that a language with a plethora of different types of idioms could be rated as one that is more developed than another with less varieties of idiomatic expressions? I believe that a serious look at the question, if not treated before, could be a challenging linguistic venture of significant value.

Amharic turns of expressions are fascinating to collect and interesting to study. They reflect on our understanding of the verbal subtleties of the Ethiopian mind in expressing colourfully its surroundings, however abstract the notion could be. No doubt such a study will contribute to the understanding of the culture of the Ethiopian people.

NOTES

1. Two years ago my friend, Ato Dagniatchew Worku, and I agreed to undertake the collection of Amharic idiomatic expressions with the aim that such a collection, if organized and published in book form, would be of great use for schools, as well as for those who are not Amharic mother tongue speakers. The collection, alphabetization and translation of about 4000 idioms has materialized in almost two years, and this work is now in press.

2. W. L. McMordie, *English Idioms and How to Use Them*, London University, Oxford Press, 1954, p.5.

580

THE AGAW LANGUAGES:

A COMPARATIVE MORPHOLOGICAL PERSPECTIVE

D. L. Appleyard

INTRODUCTORY REMARKS

The Agaw languages form a small, clearly defined group whose membership of the Cushitic family has never been in doubt. Moreover, the internal relationships between the constituent members of the group, here conventionally represented by the four languages, Bilin, Khamtanga, Kemant, and Awngi[1], are essentially apparent to anyone acquainted with the material. To this extent, the object of this paper may seem to be to state the obvious. In another article[2], I attempted to examine the same question of internal Agaw relationships from the angle of comparative phonology, making use of the premise that the latter criteria alone may serve to formulate a "genealogical" scheme for a group of already demonstrably related languages. However, I did have occasion to note there that other levels of analysis should be used in conjunction with the former to define better the picture of interrelationship. This may, of course, be done with lexical comparison, and indeed this is generally the area with which linguists work first of all when endeavouring to establish a working scheme of language relationships in newly opened up fields. However, it may be argued that the lexicon is more open to innovation and comparatively rapid change and that modification in the lexical system of a language has less of an implication on the integrity of the linguistic system as a whole than in other more "fundamental" levels. If this is so, as I would argue, then lexical criteria for use in carefully structured comparative work are perhaps not the best data to employ. On the other hand, the most "fundamental" level, which is best suited to work of this kind, at least in highly inflected languages such as are the members of the Cushitic family, is the morphological system, both in its patterns and in the morphemes themselves used in the patterns.

It is, therefore, my intention to examine in this paper a selected number of morphological categories and patterns relevant to Agaw in order to see what kind of picture of internal relationships emerges and how this relates to the results of similar work in the phonological field already undertaken.

Ideally the entire morphological system of each of the languages under review should be examined. Indeed, over recent years I have begun to make such a full study. For the purposes of this paper, however, I have chosen three significant areas of the morphology only. There is, of course, a certain degree of subjectivity in the choice but, as I hope will become clear, these three categories are particularly interesting and yield clearly the sort of results anticipated. The three are:

  i)   the marking of gender in the morphology of case inflexions in nouns;
  ii)   the morphology of number in nouns;
  iii) the morphology of distinct main and subordinate paradigms in the inflexion of verbs.

Of these, items i) and iii) are especially distinctive features of Agaw, even within Cushitic. Similar features may exist in other Cushitic languages, of course, and the seeds of both may be traced back to Proto-Cushitic. The particular Agaw developments, however, are distinctive and represent specific innovations. Additionally, from the Agaw evidence alone, whilst it is possible to propose some formal reconstructions of the structures involved as part of the Proto-Agaw system, each of the four branches of Agaw shows sufficient individual development of this proto-system to enable these features to be used as criteria in the observation of the internal grouping of Agaw. Each branch of Agaw can thus be seen to have further developed or in some way altered the proto-system, in such a way as to permit the grading of shared change or retention and the consequent drawing up of lines of relationship between the four branches.

The second item on the list is slightly different from the other two, insofar as both the functional and the formal categories involved are clearly inherited from Proto-Cushitic. When we look at the individual forms in the various Agaw languages, however, there are very obvious divisions between languages as to how the inherited system has been developed and restructured.

Before proceeding to details, it is worth noting that the Agaw material described here and the reconstructions proposed are likely to be of direct relevance to comparative Cushitic studies as a whole. For instance, I have already suggested that gender distinction in case marking in nouns, whilst carried in Agaw to a degree not, I believe, observed elsewhere in Cushitic, has its roots in the case system that can be adduced for Proto-Cushitic in accordance with Sasse's reconstructions, for instance.[3] Again, it is evident that in part the system of verbal inflexion in Agaw derives from a Proto-Cushitic pattern, but that Agaw has mostly reorganised the inherited system, restricting the seemingly older suffix conjugation to certain subordinate functions and creating a new main verb set with a different formant. Here, though, traces of the older, more general function of the "original" pattern may be detected in Awngi. Furthermore, Agaw is not of course alone in Cushitic in having created new main verb paradigms, *viz.* Highland East Cushitic for instance.

1. THE MATERIAL

1.1. Gender marking in the morphology of case in nouns.

In common with other Cushitic languages, Agaw has a two-term gender system, in which the classes are conventionally referred to as masculine and feminine. In Agaw this "gender" system is best handled on the same level as the category of number to produce a single three-term combined gender/number system. I do not wish to deal here with the morphology of case inflexion in plural nouns, partly because the forms in question generally follow the same pattern as masculine nouns, though not exclusively so[4], but more especially because they do not provide a particularly good illustration for the exercise in hand.

In all Agaw languages except Awngi the gender of a noun cannot be regularly deduced from its citation form, i.e. the item as produced in isolation, but only from the operation of gender concord within a structured piece of speech, or, as relevant to the discussion here, from the observation of certain case forms.

In Awngi, on the other hand, a formal distinction between masculine and feminine is made in the citation form (here identical to the nominative form). So:

masc.	fem.
-C (consonant) ∿ -i ∿ -e ∿ -u	-a

I would suggest, however, that the Awngi system is the result of restructuring of the original Prot-Agaw pattern to a much greater degree than what can be observed in the other languages. Here the citation form (variously equated with the nominative or absolute case according to the other functions of the case, i.e. whether or not it is also used to indicate the subject) is as follows:

	masc.	fem.
Bilin	-C ∿ -a ∿ -i ∿ -e ∿ -u ∿ -o[5]	-a ∿ -i
Khamtanga	-C ∿ -a ∿ -i ∿ -u[6]	-C ∿ -a
Kemant	-C ∿ -a ∿ -i ∿ -u[6]	-C ∿ -a

The reconstructed pattern for Proto-Agaw might be some such as:

masc.	fem.
i)*-C	*-C ∿ *-i
ii) *-a	*-a

The masculine -i in Bilin is structurally different from feminine -i, as can readily be seen from the fact that the former becomes ɨ before other case endings, whereas the latter is maintained. Masculine -i ∿ -ɨ- is merely a cluster breaking vowel — all nouns of this type would appear to have two consonants or a long consonant preceding — -i being an allophone of ɨ in word final position.

In Agaw, with the exception of Awngi, gender distinction is not therefore generally marked in the base or citation form, but is expressed in many instances by the selection of discrete, gender-distinct case suffixes in the oblique (i.e. non-citation) cases. In Awngi, on the other hand, the case markers remain constant and the gender of the noun is conveyed in the final element of the stem, which is identical to the nominative or citation form. Thus, already there can be seen to be a clear structural difference between Awngi and the rest of Agaw in this one part of the morphology. The question arises as to how the two systems, the gender marked and the unmarked case paradigms, relate to one another, if indeed they do. There is in fact some correlation in the formal markers of case between the two, but the differences are sufficient to suggest that the Awngi pattern has developed independently from the other, and that the system of gender marking in case forms seen in the other languages is perhaps an innovation on their part, but a shared one nonetheless. Thus, looking at Awngi, I have already shown that gender is marked solely in the stem final (masc. -C ∿ -i ∿ -u ∿ -e; fem. -a). Leaving aside masculines in -u and -e, which are not common nor central to the argument here, whilst -C stems correspond to Proto-Agaw type i), the selection of -i as a masculine marker, at first sight at odds with the reconstructed pattern where -i is a feminine marker, most probably derives from the original subject case of masculine nouns type ii), still extant in Kemant, thus replacing the old absolute masculine ending -a, and leaving the latter vowel free to be interpreted solely as a marker of the feminine gender. Secondly, whilst some of the case markers of Awngi are plainly related to those of the other languages, others appear to have no cognates. Also, a few of the Awngi formants, though formally relatable to those of Bilin-Khamtanga-Kemant, show different functions: e.g. the locative -da and the comitative -li (see the table following).

Table 1

For the purposes of the table, I shall ignore the rarer vocalic stems in Bilin and in Awngi and conflate the Bilin masculines in -i with the -C stems, in accordance with my earlier remarks. In Bilin, Khamtanga, and Kemant, therefore, I shall deal with two masculine stem types: -C and -V (i.e. -a); the same types also occur in the feminine in Khamtanga and Kemant, whereas in Bilin there is only one feminine type, namely -V (i.e. -i and -a, where the stem vowels remain intact before the case suffixes).

From the table, the following are the most important and relevant points to note. The patterns in Bilin-Khamtanga-Kemant are fairly closely related and can be derived from a common source. The differences can be explained quite easily, for instance through the collapse of the old absolute: subject case contrast in Bilin and Khamtanga, or the intrusion of originally dative case endings in the masculine possessive in Khamtanga.

To sum up, therefore, there is a formal distinction in respect of gender in the formants of the object, possessive, dative, and to a lesser extent locative and comitative cases in the three northern languages. In the last two cases the distinction is only partially marked and consists of an infixed -t- (in Bilin and Khamtanga, and then only in the locative in both languages), or what can be shown to derive from an earlier infixed -t- (-y- in the Kemant locative). Incidentally, the origin of this infix would seem to be the same as the feminine possessive case, to which the locative "postposition" was added. In the other cases, however, the form of the case marker it-

TABLE 1

	Bilin	Khamtanga	Kemant	Awngi
Abs. m.	-C	-C	-C	
f.	-V	-V	-V	-C/V
Subj. m.	-V	-C	-C	
f.	-V	-C	-V	-C/V
Obj. m.	-Vs	-C	-Cis	-C/Vwa[8]
f.	-Vt	-Ct	-Cit	
Poss. m.	-i	-Ciz	-C	-C/V +(-u/w ~ -t ~ -kw)[9]
f.	-Vr	-Ct	-Ci	
Dat. m.	-Vd	-Ciz	-Cz(i)	-C/Vs(i)
f.	-Vsi	-Cs/tis	-Cš(i)	
Loc.[7] m.	-il	-Cil	-Cil(i)	-C/Vda
f.	-Vtil	-Ctil	?	
Com. m.	-Vdi	-Cjig/tijig	-Cdi	-C/Vli
f.	-Vdi	-Cjig/tijig	-Cdi	

584

self is different, cf. Bilin obj.m. -s, obj.f. -t; dat.m. -d, dat.f. -si, and so on. I propose that the protoforms of these three cases be reconstructed as follows:

	masc.		fem.
Obj.	*-s		*-t' (i.e. *-tt or *-t#)
Poss.	*-Ø ~ *-i		*-t
Dat.	*-z		*-s(i)

The locative case ending can be reconstructed as *-l(i) added to the possessive case, and the comitative as *-di added to the absolute, i.e. the bare stem.

The possessive, as reconstructed, derives directly from what can be proposed for Proto-Cushitic, allowing for the loss of Proto-Cushitic short final vowels and the reduction of long vowels in Agaw:

PC masc.	*-i ~ *-ii	>	PA	*-Ø ~ *-i
PC fem.	*-Vti ~ -VVti	>	PA	*-Vt

A difference in the old absolute and subject cases between masculine and feminine has been reconstructed[10] as a feature of Proto-Cushitic noun inflexion. It is, as has been seen, only in Kemant that these two categories of case have survived in Agaw, and there only in one type of noun (i.e. masculine -a stems, reflecting Proto-Cushitic *-VV). Elsewhere this system has been replaced by a nominative and object case pattern, where it is the object and not the subject case that is the marked form. In Kemant, as in other languages, a special definite object case has also been created: masc. *-s, fem. *-t' (this latter certainly of pronominal origin); Awngi -wa (cf. Kemant directional and allative suffix -wa).

Thus, whatever the restructuring of the inherited system, the roots of gender contrast in case marking are to be found in Proto-Cushitic and passed from there into Proto-Agaw. The Agaw innovation lies in having extended the principle to other cases, an innovation which the evidence would seem to suggest was not shared by Awngi, but which must therefore be dated to after the Proto-Agaw stage, but before the split up of the once homogeneous unit that preceded Bilin, Khamtanga, and Kemant.

1.2. The morphology of plural marking

In Bilin, Khamtanga, and Kemant, i.e. again with the exception of Awngi, plural marking in nouns is essentially heterogeneous. That is to say, there are various ways of forming noun plurals and the particular method employed in each individual case cannot be predicted from the form or meaning of the singular noun which acts as the base form. In Khamtanga and Kemant, furthermore, the two languages with which I am best familiar, there is not always a one-to-one relationship between a given noun and a certain plural formative device; many nouns have more than one plural form, apparently quite at random. The various devices employed by the three northern languages are for the most part very similar and derive from common inherited patterns. Leaving aside the few examples of irregular plurals, the devices in question are as follows:

i) some internal modification of the stem of the singular noun, typically in the form of consonantal ablaut;[11]

ii) reduplication, usually only partial reduplication and often combined with device i);

iii) the addition of a plural marking suffix to the singular stem.

A further pattern consists of a combination of i) and iii). Whilst the principles involved are shared by Bilin, Khamtanga, and Kemant, there is a fair amount of difference between the three in the actual forms concerned.

Thus, much greater use is made of consonantal ablaut in Bilin than in the other two languages; Bilin has a larger set of ablaut pairs than either Khamtanga or Kemant and a greater number of nouns follows this pattern; indeed, in Kemant ablaut is so infrequent and restricted to such a small set of nouns that it verges on what may be deemed an irregular, non-productive process. Nevertheless, the smaller set of ablaut pairs in Khamtanga and Kemant can be formally related to correspondents in Bilin and derive regularly from the same Proto-Agaw patterns. In Bilin, however, it appears that the device has spread and must have become a widely productive pattern at some stage in the language's history to explain its occurrence with types of consonant not subject to it in the other languages. The details of consonantal ablaut in noun plurals can be traced in the descriptions of the languages in question and have, in any case, been discussed elsewhere.[12] I shall, therefore, refrain from repeating here the mass of material that illustrates the patterns. What may be said here is that the commonest principle of ablaut, when framed in Proto-Agaw terms, is the opposition of voiced to voiceless consonant, and more especially stop consonant:[13]

$$*b \quad : \quad *f$$
$$*g \quad : \quad *k$$
$$*g^w \quad : \quad *k^w$$
$$*G^w \quad : \quad *q^w \text{ (presumably also } *G : *q).$$

Bilin also has sets deriving from Proto-Agaw *d : *t; *dz : *ts; *z : *s, but these may be analogical extensions of the pattern. Common to all three languages are also sets deriving from Proto-Agaw:

$$*x \quad : \quad *k$$
$$*t \quad : \quad *t' \text{ (i.e. } *tt)$$
$$*r \quad : \quad *l.$$

Consonantal ablaut as a plural marking device is totally absent from Awngi. Yet, its antiquity in Agaw is perhaps demonstrated by the fact that the apparent lack of any common phonetic process in each of the modern languages is solved only when the corresponding Proto-Agaw sets are reconstructed and there some system does appear. I would also hazard to suggest that the device may go back to a Proto-Cushitic pattern of short v. long consonant (C : CC), in some cases at least.

When we turn to device iii), plural marking by suffix, we observe a considerable amount of variation between languages in the form(s) of the plural suffix. Here, too, there is a major cleavage between Awngi and the rest of Agaw.

The three languages, Bilin, Khamtanga, and Kemant, all share a plural suffix involving the consonant t, which is indubitably of inherited Cushitic origin. In Awngi, however, there is only one instance of this suffix, as recorded by Hetzron, in the irregular noun čwá 'mother', which forms its plural by adding the usual Awngi plural suffix -ka to what is clearly an old plural in -t: čútká. In Bilin the suffix appears as -ti (i.e. with the cluster breaking vowel -i as on -CC stem final masculine nouns, the stem preceding the suffix -t always ending in a consonant): säbära : säbärti 'python', liɲin : liɲinti 'house'; or as -tit i.e. doubled: nan : nantit 'hand'. In Khamtanga it occurs as -t ∿ -t' and extended as -tan ∿ -t'an: síbra : sibŕt' 'snake'; ɲin : ɲint'án 'house'. In Kemant it appears as -ti, or with a further plural suffix as -tik: nan : nanti ∿ nantik 'hand'.

The usual Awngi plural suffix is -ka. The only apparent cognate of this is the Kemant plural suffix -k(i). The latter would seem to be a fairly recent innovation; not only is it more frequent in the material collected by myself a little over ten years ago than in that gathered by d'Abbadie and later analysed and published by Conti Rossini over seventy years ago, but also in my material it frequently replaces or is added to some other plural marking device. It is tempting to connect this "new" plural suffix with the practically identical enclitic -ki $\sim$ -ik 'all', which has cognates throughout Agaw. Just how this is to be related to the Awngi plural suffix, if at all, is not clear, particularly as the enclitic 'all' appears there as -gi with a voiced velar.

It would therefore seem that Awngi has largely simplified the heterogeneous system of noun plural marking. I would suggest that at the other extreme Bilin has expanded the consonant ablaut system. Kemant, on the other hand, has retained all the inherited devices, but has begun to modify the system by innovating a simpler, productive suffix, formally reminiscent of the Awngi suffix, but perhaps totally independently of the latter.

1.3 The morphology of main and subordinate verb inflexions

The common method of finite verb inflexion in Agaw comprises of the suffixation of composite elements to the lexical root, marking such categories as person, tense/aspect, modality, and certain other specific syntactic functions. It is generally agreed that these suffixed elements derive from old auxiliary verbs added to an invariable verbal noun of some kind. These erstwhile auxiliaries themselves originally inflected for person by means of prefixes, in certain persons combined with suffixes, after the pattern familiar from other Cushitic languages. In almost all Cushitic languages such traces as there are of independent prefix inflecting verbs are few and, indeed, in Agaw it is only Awngi which preserves any examples of this archaic inflexion pattern, once again confirming the separateness of this language from the rest of Agaw. The suffix inflecting pattern (i.e. with the old auxiliary) is a common Cushitic innovation, not only the pattern, but also the actual form of the basic auxiliary, represented by a single vowel -V subject to alternation of quality according to tense/aspect. So much is familiar. Where Agaw shows a further and individual development from this ancient Cushitic pattern is that the old -V auxiliary forms have, for the most part, become restricted to various subordinate forms and are typically combined with some further element defining the nature of subordination: e.g. Bilin qʷaldináxir 'you who saw'; qʷaldinínädin 'because you saw'; qʷaldinó 'you having seen'; where in each case just -din- represents the old auxiliary, 2nd person plural. In main verb function, that is in the capacity of the simple indicative verb, Agaw has created new forms built on a different auxiliary, but still inflected by the old prefix pattern and thus an innovation that can only have occurred when the prefix conjugation was still part of the morphological system. As it stands, this statement of a simple main (indicative): subordinate differentiation reflected in the "auxiliary" component of the verbal complex is essentially true for Bilin, Khamtanga, and Kemant — modal forms such as the jussive occurring in main verb position remain outside this statement. This situation in Awngi is rather more complex.

In Awngi there are two sets of main verb paradigms, which following Hetzron's terminology we may call the indefinite and definite aspects, imperfective and perfective. The indefinite aspect expresses an action or event that is uncertain and only vaguely situated in time and space, whilst the definite aspect indicates an undoubted action or fact. Such a distinction is not made in any of the other Agaw languages. Where this becomes relevant to the present discussion is insofar as the form of one of the indefinite tenses clearly descends directly from the old -V auxiliary conjugation. The other, namely the perfective indefinite, is formally identical to a subordinate form called the short converb by Hetzron and thus is not in itself originally parallel to the imperfective indefinite; it does nevertheless contain an old -V auxiliary like other subordinates.

In Awngi, too, the "new" main verb conjugations also exist, but not in a form immediately relatable to those found in Bilin, Khamtanga, and Kemant. In some respects the Awngi forms are more archaic and do not show the demonstrable innovations shared by the other languages. The perfective definite of Awngi is formally more readily relatable to its counterparts in the other languages. The imperfective definite, on the other hand, is identical to the subjectal relative, imperfective tense, and may be best handled as simply that, used in main verb position[14], though there is something of a case to be made that this identification is only secondary and that the original "new" auxiliary forms lie behind some, at least, of the paradigm. In what follows I shall therefore provisionally treat this paradigm as ultimately cognate with the imperfective or present main verb form in the other languages.

For the remainder of this discussion, I should like to concentrate on the forms of this "new" auxiliary conjugation. The auxiliary may be characterised in its most likely original form as *-Vk and is plainly identical to the independent root meaning 'be' appearing across Agaw: Bilin ʔak- : ʔax-;[15] Khamtanga aq- ∿ a-; Kemant aɣ-; Awngi -aɣ ∿ -aq.[16] The inflexion of the "auxiliary", however, differs from the current patterns of verb conjugation, not only in its following the old prefix system of inflexion, but also insofar as in Bilin, Khamtanga, and Kemant, at least, it shows a particular kind of consonantal ablaut according to tense/aspect. A very restricted set of roots in Bilin seems to exhibit the same kind of ablaut, and whatever the origin of this aspectual ablaut, it is doubtless to a similar process that the ablaut in the "auxiliary" must be traced. Thus, just as the following three Bilin roots show a velar stop in their imperfective aspect forms and a corresponding fricative in the perfective: nak- : nax- 'give'; šak- : šax- 'take'; ʔak- : ʔax- 'be', so the "auxiliary" in Bilin has -k^w in the present and -x^w in the past tense. A similar variation in the consonant of the "auxiliary" occurs in Khamtanga and Kemant, though aspectual ablaut does not occur elsewhere in those languages. The correspondence between the three languages is regular and permits the reconstruction of protoforms *-Vk^w (present/imperfective) : *-VG^w (past/perfective). There is no trace, however, of such an ablaut in the Awngi forms.

In Awngi, on the other hand, there is alternation in the consonant of the "auxiliary" between -ɣ (present etc.) and -ɣ^w (past etc.), i.e. between a simple voiced uvular stop and a labialised voiced uvular stop. The feature labialisation is present in both tenses of the "auxiliary" in the other languages, but is absent from the presumed cognate independent root. This needs to be explained.[17] If the auxiliary root in Pre-Agaw is reconstructed as **-Vk (i.e. the same as the independent root), with root vowel alternation according to aspect: **-a- (imperfective) : **-u- (perfective), in agreement with a possible Proto-Cushitic pattern, then in the first instance this might be expected to become Proto-Agaw *-aK : *-ɨK^w (where K = an undetermined velar/uvular). Thence the perfective could have developed to *-ɨG^w (for Proto-Cushitic *k > Proto-Agaw *G in weak, medial position, cf. the masculine gender clitic PC *ku > Proto-Agaw *-G^w). The imperfective aspect form would be expected to develop similarly to *-aG and thence directly to Awngi -aɣ. In the other languages aspectual ablaut seems to have been applied and the feature labialisation carried over from the perfective: *-aG > *-ak/-äk > *-ak^w/-äk^w.[18] Thus, so far, the stem shape of the auxiliary can be traced in Agaw, where there is already a divergence between Awngi and the other languages.

When we turn to the inflexion of the "auxiliary", there are further differences between Awngi and the rest, on the one hand, and between Bilin-Khamtanga and Kemant, on the other. The details are complex and are perhaps best illustrated at this point by Table 2 (opposite). The Awngi forms, except those bracketed, all contain a further suffix -a. The bracketed forms are not derived from the "auxiliary" paradigm of *-Vk, but contain the *-V "auxiliary" (imperfective) and the appropriate gender enclitic: masc. -w, fem. -t, plur. -k^w plus -í, and are identical to the subjectal relative forms. Indeed, so are the other persons, which raises the question I alluded to earlier: whether the Awngi imperfective definite is related to the main verb paradigms, or is in fact the relative used in main verb position. If so, the ending -aɣa, etc., is not to be analysed as auxiliary -aɣ + particle -a, but as *-V auxiliary (-a) + relative particle (1st and 2nd persons) -ɣa.

In Bilin, Khamtanga, and Kemant the most outstanding innovation on the presumed protopattern is the form of the 3rd person feminine, both tenses. Here the presumed original form of the auxiliary *-tak^w and *-tiG^w have been replaced by *-at·i and *-it·i, in which the element *k^w/*-G^w of the original seems to have been identified with the masculine gender clitic and thus substituted with the corresponding feminine clitic *-ti : *-tak^w > *-tati > -at·i (perhaps through metathesis), *-tiG^w > *-titi > *-it·i.

Another development in Bilin, Khamtanga, and Kemant, though only partial in the last, is the metathesis of the "auxiliary" consonant *k^w/*-G^w and the original *-n suffix of the 2nd and 3rd persons plural. Kemant preserves the older sequence in the present tense only, but

588

TABLE II

Present tense

	Bilin	Khamtanga	Kemant	Awngi
S. 1.	-äkʷin	-äkʷin	-äkʷ	-áɣá
2.	-räkʷ[19]	-räkʷ[19]	-yäkʷ[19]	-táɣá
3m.	-äkʷ	-äkʷ	-äkʷ	[-áwí]
3f.	-äti	-äč	-ät(i)	[-tátí]
P. 1.	-näkʷin	-näkʷin	-näkʷ	-náɣá
2.	-dänäkʷ	-irnäkʷ	-yäkʷin	-tányá
3.	-änäkʷ	-ŋäkʷ	-äkʷin	[-ánkʷí]

Past tense

	Bilin	Khamtanga	Kemant	Awngi
S. 1.	-xʷin	-un	-iɣʷ	-ɣʷà
2.	-rixʷ[19]	-ru[19]	-yiɣʷ[19]	-tíɣʷà
3m.	-ixʷ	-u	-iɣʷ	-ɣʷà
3f.	-ti	-ič	-it(i)	-tíɣʷà
P. 1.	-nixʷin	-nun	-niɣʷ	-níɣʷà
2.	-dinixʷ	-irnu	-iniɣʷ	-túnà
3.	-nixʷ	-uŋ	-(i)niɣʷ	-únà

follows the pattern of Bilin and Khamtanga in the past: present 2pl. *-takʷVn > Bilin -dänäkʷ, Khamtanga -irnäkʷ, but Kemant -yäkʷin; 3 pl. *-akʷVn > Bilin -änäkʷ, Khamtanga -ŋäkʷ, but Kemant -äkʷin; past 2 pl. *-tiGʷin > Bilin -dinixʷ, Khamtanga -irnu, Kemant -iniɣʷ; 3 pl. *-iGʷin, Bilin -nixʷ, Khamtanga -uŋ, Kemant -(i)niɣʷ (for these past forms cf. Awngi -tún+à and -ún+à, resp.). A similar metathesis may appear in Awngi 2pl. imperfective definite -tányá, if indeed this belongs here.

The final feature to be noted here is an isogloss which distinguishes Bilin and Khamtanga from Kemant, namely the suffix -in on the 1st person, singular and plural. I think this is clearly best regarded as an innovation rather than a retained archaism lost elsewhere as there is no evidence in Agaw for a 1st person suffix -n, nor, indeed, I believe, is there any such elsewhere in Cushitic.

2. CONCLUDING REMARKS

After examining the date from the three selected areas of the morphology, and proposing the most likely lines of development leading to the current systems in each language, it is now appropriate to draw the conclusions together and to see whether the evidence supports the internal relationship scheme obtained from the comparative phonological study.

The first and most obvious distinction between the languages is that which has been repeated throughout the discussion, i.e. that Awngi stands well apart from the rest of Agaw. It lacks gender differentiation in the marking of the oblique cases which is notable elsewhere. It has almost completely restructured the system of plural marking in nouns, lacking entirely the distinctive Agaw consonantal ablaut pattern. In the inflexion of the verb, as examined here in respect of main and subordinate paradigms, in some areas Awngi looks more archaic, having retained a trace of the -V auxiliary pattern in main verb function (indicative). The inflexion of the -Vk auxiliary is also more archaic, having neither reformed the 3rd person feminine nor metathesized the elements of the 2nd and 3rd persons plural. These three criteria alone, I would suggest, are fundamental and significant enough to identify Awngi as constituting a separate branch of Agaw in contradistinction to all the rest. Other instances from the morphological system not alluded to here could be adduced in support of this argument, *viz.* the retention of some instances of the old prefix conjugation in verbs; the negative verb system; certain features of the pronominal and demonstrative system; and so on.

Within the remaining three languages, a less striking division can be noted between Bilin and Khamtanga, on the one hand, and Kemant, on the other. In the case system, whilst all three share the same gender marking in oblique cases, Kemant has retained the old absolute: subject cases contrast, restructured elsewhere to a nominative: object case pattern. In common with Bilin, though, Kemant also has a marked object case used for definite direct objects. In the plural marking system, Kemant is basically similar to Bilin and Khamtanga, but has a further suffix in -k which is demonstrably an innovation. In the verb patterns discussed, Kemant lacks the -in suffix of the 1st persons in Bilin and Khamtanga, and has not everywhere metathesized the elements of the 2nd and 3rd plural of the -Vk auxiliary paradigms.

Finally, Bilin and Khamtanga contain enough similar features to permit their being grouped as the two most closely related Agaw languages, which is supported by historical tradition.

The kind of pattern that emerges from the morphological data is as follows, and is, in sum, the same as that drawn from phonological evidence:

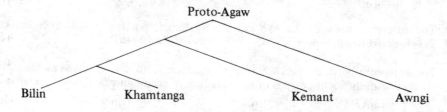

NOTES

1. I have argued elsewhere for the practical reality of working with these four. See in particular Appleyard 1984 (a), p.34.
   The Khamtanga and Kemant material cited is from my own fieldnotes, see Appleyard (forthcoming) and 1975, respectively. The Bilin material is drawn from Palmer 1957, 1958; the Awngi is from Hetzron 1969, 1978.

2. Appleyard 1984 (a).

3. Sasse 1984.

4. Bilin, Khamtanga, and Kemant, for instance, have a special possessive plural case in -ä.

5. Bilin items ending in -e, -u, -o mostly, if not exclusively, seem to be loanwords or proper names.

6. Khamtanga and Kemant also have a few masculine nouns ending in vowels other than -a, but these would all seem to derive from Proto-Agaw -C finals: Khamtanga ami, Kemant amu 'thorn' < PA *ʔamix ∿ *ʔamixᵂ.

7. In Bilin this case has allative function only.

8. Awngi object -wa combines with the preceding consonant or vowel as follows: -C + wa → -Cwa ∿ -Co; -i + wa → -e; -a + wa → -awa.

9. The Awngi possessive consists of the unmodified stem plus the gender clitic in agreement with the head noun. This type of possessive NP, which Hetzron calls the agreeing genitive, is structurally different from the "non-agreeing genitive" seen in the other languages, where the gender of the subordinate noun, i.e. the possessor, is marked. Agreeing genitives also occur in Bilin, Khamtanga, and Kemant, but constructed on the base of the possessive case to which the gender clitic is added.

10. Sasse 1984.

11. See Zaborski 1976.

12. *Ibid.*

13. In the absence of a phoneme *p, *f functions in Agaw as the voiceless counterpart of *b. This, of course, is a common feature to many Cushitic, and indeed Semitic, languages.

14. Relative verbs are used as main verbs in other Agaw languages in certain kinds of marked or focalized sentences.

15. The difference between the two stems is aspectual; essentially ʔak- is imperfective and ʔax- is perfective in aspect.

16. The difference between the two stems here differs from that observed in Bilin; the stems are used with different persons of the paradigm in accordance with what Hetzron calls the voice rule; see Hetzron 1969, p.7.

17. For an explanation with reference to Awngi see Hetzron 1969, p.72.

18. This aspectual ablaut may derive from an alteration of consonant length, not unlike the plural ablaut described above; thus, Pre-Agaw **-akk > Proto-Agaw *-ak (> *-ak^W/-äk^W), whilst Pre-Agaw **-uk > Proto-Agaw *-iG^W. If this is the case, then Agaw preserves here, albeit in a very restricted way, a very old Afroasiatic feature, whereby the imperfective aspect is marked not only by vocalization in *a, but also by consonant length inside the stem.

19. The 2nd person index also appears in Bilin as -d, in Khamtanga as -d or -dr, and under separate conditions in Khamtanga and Kemant as -tr and -t, respectively.

REFERENCES

Appleyard 1975   'A descriptive outline of Kemant', *BSOAS*, 38, 2, pp.316-50.

——————— 1984   (a) 'The internal classification of the Agaw languages: a comparative and historical phonology', in *Current Progress in Afro-Asiatic Linguistics, (Papers of the Third International Hamito-Semitic Congress), Current Issues in Linguistic Theory 28*, John Benjamins, Amsterdam, pp.33-67.

(b) 'The morphology of the negative verb in Agaw', *Transactions of the Philological Society 1984*, pp.202-19.

Appleyard (forthcoming)   'A grammatical sketch of Khamtanga'.

Hetzron 1969   *The verbal system of Southern Agaw, (University of California Publications, Near Eastern Studies 12),* University of California Press, Berkeley and Los Angeles.

—————— 1978   'The nominal system of Awngi (Southern Agaw)', *BSOAS*, 41, 1, pp.121-41.

Palmer 1957   'The verb in Bilin', *BSOAS*, 19, 1, pp.131-59.

—————— 1958   'The noun in Bilin', *BSOAS*, 21, 2, pp.376-91.

Sasse 1974   'Ein Subjektcasus in Agaw', *Folia Orientalia*, 15, pp.55-67.

—————— 1984   'Case in Cushitic, Semitic and Berber', in *Current Progress in Afro-Asiatic Linguistics . . . op. cit.,* pp.111-26.

Zaborski 1976   'Consonant apophony and consonant alternation in Bilin plurals', *Afroasiatic Linguistics*, vol.3, pt.6.

THE NEW TERMINOLOGY IN AMHARIC FOR

SCIENCE AND TECHNOLOGY

Assefa Gabre Mariam Tessema and Girma Zenebe

INTRODUCTION

Ethiopia, having opened herself to world influence since the late nineteenth century, has been exposed to modern ways and consequently to a large amount of foreign vocabulary, mostly scientific and technological.

Though, in the past, work on terminology was undertaken in the country, it was only by a few interested individuals and by even fewer organizations and institutions – primarily the Curriculum Department of the Ministry of Education, the Ethiopian Standards Institute and Addis Ababa University. These attempts, however, were *ad hoc* and decentralized and could cover only a very limited area. The role played by the Academy of Ethiopian Languages in this regard is quite remarkable. According to paragraph 4,4 of the Proclamation, the Academy is given power and duties:

"To conduct research into words emanating from modern science, technology and art and thus to establish Amharic equivalents or translations for technical terms serviceable in education, research and other fields."[1]

To this end, therefore, the Academy has recently started work on a Science and Technology Terms Translation Project (STTTP) in Amharic and the project is now in its final stage.

Since most of the theoretical aspect of the problem concerning technical terms in Amharic have been discussed in the paper presented at the Seventh International Conference of Ethiopian Studies[2], attention will now be given to the activities of the above-mentioned project.

1.0 The Science and Technology Terms Translation Project (STTTP)

About three years ago an agreement was signed (between the Ethiopian Government and the UNIFSTD (United Nations Interim Fund For Science And Technology For Development) to lend support to a project entitled "Development of National Capacity for Popularization and Training in Science and Technology through Language and Demonstration". Following this, another sub-project entitled "Development of Scientific and Technological Terminology in Amharic", was agreed upon by the Ethiopian Science and Technology Commission, the executing agency, and the Academy of Ethiopian Languages. The Academy was entrusted with the full responsibility of implementing the terminology project.

The overall objective of this project is to develop a scientific and technological vocabulary in Amharic geared to providing a medium through which scientific and technological knowledge can be easily disseminated to and absorbed by readers of high school level.

The Academy made an all-out effort and succeeded in bringing together a number of professionals in the various areas of science, technology and linguistics and drew up a clear cut program of work in several phases, in accordance with the principal project document.

The project was sub-divided into the following phases:

i)   Compilation of Terms
ii) Translation of Terms
iii) Preparation and production of illustrated booklets, popular literature and the compilation of an illustrated dictionary.

The day-to-day activities of the project were taken care of by the administrative section of the Academy. The direct participation of Addis Ababa University was sought and the Faculty of Science was selected as the centre for the execution of the project. The Academic Commission of the Faculty of Science recommended two staff members to serve as technical coordinators. In addition, a language senior expert and supervisor was later assigned to assist panels in their work.

Along with the phases of the project mentioned above, other important subsidiary activities have been undertaken, chief of which are:

- Study tours:
- Evaluation workshops:
- Distribution of Translated Terms for comments.

At the beginning, several experts, especially those from the linguistic area, were called upon to prepare theoretical background material and this was presented at a workshop held at Nazareth. The workshop in its closing plenary session spelled out some guidelines for execution.

1.1 An Outline of the three phases of the Project

1.1.1. Compilation of Terms

The systematic identification and documentation of the terms that needed to be translated into Amharic was the first challenge of the project. Though the overall objective is to bring about the dissemination of scientific and technological knowledge in the country, priority was given to terms that are being utilized from grades 1 to 12. These terms were taken out from the appropriate school textbooks, defined in their context and, where available, the Amharic equivalent was suggested. In some cases, particularly in the field of technology, appropriate terms were collected from places such as garages, construction sites, etc.

In three months more than 12,500 terms were compiled (by senior university students under supervision of the co-ordinators of the project and field specialists), in the following 12 disciplines.

1. Biology (Botany and Zoology)
2. Chemistry
3. Geology
4. Mathematics
5. Physics
6. Geography
7. Statistics
8. Agriculture
9. Medicine
10. Pharmacy
11. Nutrition
12. Technology (Electrical, Mechanical and Building

All terms in each discipline were then alphabetically arranged in a card system. The following criteria were used to determine which terms should be eliminated:

a) words whose Amharic equivalents are already well known;

b) names of units, laws named after individuals, names of most elements and compounds, internationally accepted scientific names of plants, animals, etc..

Each of the selected terms was then registered on a card with its definition and usage. The context of the term and its source was noted. These terms served for the subsequent phase of the project, namely the translation phase.

1.1.2. Translation of Terms

At the end of the compilation phase, translation workshops were organized for the members of the translation panels. Two workshops were held and they were successful forums where clear cut principles and guidelines for translation work were defined. This phase was the most critical and challenging part of the project.

In all, fifteen panels were formed in twelve disciplines, each panel consisting of three persons; two subject specialists and a linguist as chairman. Circulars were regularly prepared and distributed, not only to panel members but also to arouse interest and encourage cooperation in the immediate intellectual community.

In order to translate the terms compiled in phase one, the panelists used one of the four methodologies defined during the workshops:

1) Coinage;
2) Finding an equivalent term in other Ethiopian languages to fit the term to be translated;
3) Adaptation;
4) Adoption;

Over a period of ten months, the total number of science and technology terms translated was 15,695, as shown below:

Discipline	Terms translated
Biology	2,315
Chemistry	1,405
Geology	1,205
Geography	1,757
Mathematics	1,049
Physics	2,228
Statistics	585
Technology	1,945
Medicine (Pharmacy)	2,023
Nutrition	589
Agriculture	594
TOTAL	15,695

This total is larger than the number of terms compiled during the first phase; some essential terms which had not been included were added by the panelists during the translation work.

Although many problems arose, the end results were very satisfactory, both in the total number of terms translated and, above all, in the quality of the overall translation work.

1.1.3. Interdisciplinary Panel

During the translation period some previously unanticipated problems occured, but corrective measures were implemented.

Some terms, for example, found in two or more disciplines (physics, chemistry, mathematics, etc.) convey more than one concept. Since translating them differently in the different disciplines could lead to inconsistencies, an interdisciplinary panel of two linguists and seven subject specialists was formed, charged with monitoring any duplication and ambiguity in translation. One Amharic equivalent for each English term commonly used in different disciplines was sought, either by selecting one from the different alternatives given or by putting forward a more appropriate alternative. The recommendations of the interdisciplinary panel were incorporated into the final output of the various disciplines.

1.1.4. Popularization and Standardization of Concepts

This later phase entailed the preparation and production of illustrated booklets and popular literature together with the compilation of a dictionary. This challenging phase needed prior planning and thought in order to ensure success. In the original plan, great importance was placed on two study tours, to countries which had undertaken similar exercises. Because of financial constraints, however, one of the study tours was cancelled and as a substitute, an additional workshop was convened, to formulate detailed guidelines and methods of implementing this phase of the project. Recommendations on methodologies to be followed in the illustration of the newly translated Amharic scientific and technical terms and in the writing of popular literature in Amharic using these new concepts were drawn up.

The first task of this phase was the preparation of illustrated booklets. In accordance with one of the recommendations of the workshop, a sample illustrated booklet was prepared, using both descriptive and pictorial illustrations.

Following a general meeting of panelists, in which the booklet was assessed and further detail worked out on the recommended methodologies, illustration panels were formed in the twelve disciplines, each panel consisting of one or more subject specialists and a linguist, assisted by student helpers, a draftsman and the technical coordinators.

These illustrations greatly facilitate the acceptance of the newly coined terms by a wide readership. The illustrated booklets will serve as important raw material for the illustrated science and technology dictionary, which is expected to be prepared at the completion of the project.

After critical evaluation of the sample, popular literature was prepared, with the main objective of propagating scientific concepts and simultaneously popularizing the new Amharic equivalents. More emphasis is to be given to cementing into Amharic the newly coined scientific terms, while at the same time disseminating scientific concepts to a broad stratum of readers. The popular literature may also be aided by pictorial illustrations.

The final part of the project is the preparation of a science and technology dictionary in Amharic with an index in English.

2.0 Additional activities

In conjunction with the main translation work, several important additional activities have been undertaken, which have contributed considerably to the success of the project.

2.1 Study Tours

The problem created by the inability of a language to express scientific and technological concepts is not uniquely Ethiopian. Some countries, however, have solved the problem of making their languages a medium for science and technology.

Several decades ago Hebrew was almost on the verge of extinction but now, after such a short period of time, Israel has succeeded in making it a scientific and technological language. Similarly, some Arab countries have developed Arabic as a medium at university level. Both Hebrew and Arabic now have a basic vocabulary in the area of science and technology. Ethiopia, therefore, clearly needs to share the experience of such countries and a team of four people actively participating in the project went on a study tour.

The main objective of this tour was to gain first hand knowledge of how the languages were developed. Both Hebrew and Arabic are used as the medium of instruction in all the school systems, so that an assessment of how this has been achieved is of the greatest importance to the Ethiopian project. Furthermore, the linguistic relationship between Arabic, Hebrew and Amharic (all semitic languages) increases the relevance of the investigations on the means by which Hebrew and Arabic developed the capability of fulfilling basic communication needs in science and technology.

The team heard a series of lectures and they were given a number of booklets, pamphlets, dictionaries and other materials, all of which were useful in the second phase of the project.

In addition, the previous Secretary General of the Academy of Ethiopian Languages visited various institutions of language studies, including the Kiswahili Council, the Kiswahili Institute of Research and the Curriculum Department of the Ministry of Education of Tanzania. These institutions are all working together to standardize Swahili so that it meets the requirements of modern scientific and technological language.

2.2 Workshops

In the original plan, three workshops were planned to consolidate the activities of the project, but to date four workshops have been held. The role of these in increasing the tempo and quality of the project has been considerable.

At every workshop reports and study papers were presented on various themes. Of the different issues discussed the following were the most important:

— Papers on establishing Amharic equivalents for scientific and technical terms and on conditions in which terms in other languages could be adapted or adopted,
— Papers on translation methodologies,
— Papers on dissemination methods of the newly coined terms.

Furthermore, in all workshops the development of the project was analyzed, previous experiences shared, new guidelines and methodologies drafted; etc. The papers and reports presented, which were the basis of lively debates and discussions, helped all the participants to develop a coherent outlook.

Apart from panelists and those directly involved in the project, the workshops were attended by appropriate personnel from various institutions and organizations and by other selected individuals.

2.3 Circulation of Translated Terms

Efforts have been made from the outset to involve as many experts as possible in the project. In addition, since this kind of project needs wider evaluation, many more appropriate and concerned people have been included to participate and help with the clarification of the work.

Particularly in the translation phase, the major part of the project, it has been ensured that the findings of the different panels should reach the public for comment.

Circulars have been published regularly and circulated for comments and suggestions. These have generated interesting discussions and feedback has been channelled to the panels concerned. The monthly output of most panels has also been compiled in a series of Preliminary Lists covering all the terms translated and these have been circulated to a large number of individuals and institutions. For the basic school subjects, namely biology, chemistry, physics and mathematics, lists of new terms have been circulated to teachers in six carefully selected comprehensive high schools in Addis Ababa. The comments and suggestions obtained, though few, were very helpful.

3.0 Conclusion

Because of its multi-disciplinary nature and the extent of coverage, the magnitude of this project makes it one of the most comprehensive projects of its kind ever launched in Ethiopia. Although similar attempts have been made in the past, in particular by the Ministry of Education, these covered a few areas only and till now, no such systematic undertaking has ever been conceived and implemented. The project, therefore, was found to be very challenging. The study tour, the theoretical papers presented, the convening of the workshops, the regular meetings and discussions and, above all, the effort made by the participants have helped to overcome this challenge.

Translation of scientific and technological terms is an ever-continuing process. Furthermore, the completion of such a project can be realized only after being used effectively, which necessarily will need a considerable period of time. However, the project has succeeded already in bringing together a number of experts in the areas of science, technology and language and the experience must not be underestimated.

NOTES

1. *Negarit Gazeta*, 1972, p.127.

2. Assefa Gabre-Mariam Tesemma, "Technical Terms in Amharic: Problems and Solutions", *Proceedings of the Seventh International Conference of Ethiopian Studies*, University of Lund, 1984, pp.91-102.

TOWARDS A DEFINITION OF THE NOMINAL SPECIFIERS IN AMHARIC[1]

Baye Yimam

1.00 Introduction

This paper attempts to give a descriptive account of nominal specifiers. In the literature (Armbruster: 1908; Mersie-Hazen: 1935 (EC); Hebo: 1955; Takle-Mariam Fantaye: 1964 (EC); Leslau: 1967; Dawkins: 1969; Cohen: 1970; Harmann: 1981) mention is made of articles, quantifiers, demonstrative adjectives, possessive adjectives, indefinite pronouns, interrogatives, etc., all of which are related in one way or another to nouns. This paper recognizes only articles and quantifiers and includes them both under the category of specifier, and on syntactic-semantic grounds, it recategorizes all the other items as part of either one of these two sub-classes. It also argues that some independent pronouns, and what have been called measure and classifier phrases also belong to the category of specifier. In accordance with this analysis, it assigns articles and quantifiers to different nodes in the hierarchical structures of noun phrases.

Specifiers are lexical or grammatical formatives that occur with a noun head in phrasal structures in order to limit the referential or quantitative scope of the head. They may be single items or constituents. On the basis of their syntactic-semantic characteristics, they can be divided into articles and quantifiers.

1.1 Articles: These are suffixes or independent formatives which restrict or denote the referential range of a noun with which they occur. Without them nouns may be generic as instantiated by (1) below:

1a) *bäg (widd näw)*
     sheep expensive is-it 'sheep is expensive'

1b) *färäs (yä-bet insäsa nä-w)*
     horse house animal is-it 'horse is a domestic animal'

In both examples *bäg* 'sheep' and *färäs* 'horse' refer generically to the entire class, as opposed to other such classes of animals as *anbäsa* 'lion', *näbir* 'leopard', etc. This generic reference can be narrowed down by using one of two types of articles: definite or indefinite.

1.1.1 Indefinite Article: This includes what have traditionally been known as 'indefinite pronouns'. (Dawkins: 1969: 63) and the numeral *and* 'one'.

2a) *and bäg (motä)*[2]
     a sheep died-it 'a sheep died'

2b) *mannim tämari*
     any student 'any student'

2c) *yetimm agär*
     any country 'any country'

The reference of the nouns in (2) above is to any one member of the class denoted by the head noun. In pragmatic terms such structures as (1) and (2) are used to initiate discourse or to introduce new information into one which is already under way.

1.1.2 Definite Article: Unlike the indefinite article, the definite article does not initiate or introduce new information into discourse, but refers to a noun which has already been introduced into one and is understood by both parties of the discourse to be as such. The following are some examples:

3a) *bäg-u*   *(tillik nä-w)*
     sheep-the   big   is-it 'The/his sheep is big'

3b) *yɨh*   *bäg*
     this   sheep 'this sheep'

3c) *yä-ine bäg*
     my   sheep 'my sheep'

In 3a) /-u/, which is commonly known as a determiner, is referential or anaphoric to an antecedent noun which has been introduced into discourse, whereas the deictic elements of *yɨh* 'this' or *yä* 'that' point to a particular *bäg* 'sheep' which in terms of spatio-temporal relations could be near to or away from the speaker or the hearer. *yä-ine* 'my' in 3c) does much the same thing by limiting the reference of *bäg* to just the one possessed by me.

In addition to these, certain independent pronouns can be added to the list of deictics, since they too occur in prenominal positions and operate in the same way as demonstratives do. The following examples may illustrate this:

4a) *iňňa*   *tämari-woččč(in-zämt-allä-n)*
     we   student-pl. we-campaign-aux-we 'we students shall campaign'

4b) *innänta liǰ-očč*   *(yä-zare abäba-wočč na-čči-hu)*
     you   children.pl. gen.today flower-pl. are-pl.-you
     'you children are flowers of today'

4c) *issu*   *bäg*   *(yä-ine nä-w)*
     sheep   poss.I is-it 'that sheep is mine'

4d) *innässu bäg-očč (yä-ine na-ččä-w)*
     sheep-pl. poss.I are-pl. 'those sheep are mine'

Like demonstratives they restrict the reference to one in the vicinity of the speaker, or of the hearer, (second person) or of a third party. The reference to an object in the vicinity of the second person employs *issu* ∿ *issuwa* ∿ *innässu*.

Compare the following in relation to yourself as the speaker:

5a) *yɨh*   *bäg*
     this   sheep (close to speaker)

5b) *ya*   *bäg*
     that   sheep (far from both speaker and hearer)

5c) *issu*   *bäg*
     sheep (close to the hearer only)

Strictly speaking, therefore, third person pronouns are demonstratives (cf. Getachew: 1967). Moreover, the fact that they, and second person pronouns, like demonstratives exhibit the same affix to show plurality makes this assertion even more apparent. Let us observe the following paradigm:

2   *antä* (you) *innä-antä*

3   issu   (he)   innä-issu

1   ine   (I)   iňňa³

(ii)a   yih   innä-y(/z/) ih
        this   pl.   this

(ii)b   ya   innä-y(/z/) ia
        that   pl.   that

It is on account of such syntactic-semantic similarities that Lyons (1979: 639) says "third person personal pronouns are obviously dispensable in favour of demonstrative pronouns".

As is generally the case with elements belonging to the same category, there is only substitutability but not co-occurrence between any two of them, except when one wants to emphasize the head, in which case structures such as those of (6a) and (6b) but not those of (6c-e) could be employed.

6a)   Yih   yä-ine bäg
      this   gen.I sheep 'this sheep of mine'

6b)   Ya   yä-kasa bäg
      that   gen.K   sheep 'that sheep of Kasa'

6c)*   yih   bäg-u
       this   sheep-the

6d)*   issu   bäg-u
        ?   sheep-the

6e)*   yä   issu   bäg⁴
       that   ?   sheep

The presence of the demonstrative yih in (a) or ya 'that' in (b) does not make the head noun definite any more than it is made by the possessive yä-ine 'my' or yä-kasa 'Kasa's'. It only gives it some emphasis.

The anaphoric /-u⌣⁵ -wa/ is formally identical with the third person possessive affix /-un⌣ -wa/ and it is hardly possible to tell which one of the two is used in contexts such as:

7a)   bäg   -u
      sheep   the/his

7b)   bäg   -wa
      sheep   the(f)/her

But with kinship terms such as abbat 'father', innat 'mother' and certain other terms referring to hierarchically organized social roles such as geta 'lord' and aškär 'servant' a distinction is made between the two structures. Compare the following, for example:

8a)   abbat-u⌣   -wa
      father-his   her

8a¹)   abbat-iyyä-u
       father ?   the 'the father'

601

8b) *innat-u⌣-wa*
mother his her

8b¹) *innat-iyyä-wa*
mother the 'the mother'

8c) *wändimm-u⌣-wa*
brother his her

8c¹) *wändimm-iyyä-w (w'u)* 'the brother'

In the possessive structures, the affix /-u⌣-wa/ immediately follows the root/stem *abbat* 'father' just as it does in other nouns. But the anaphoric /-u⌣-wa/ does not follow the same root/stem *abbat* 'father' or *innat* 'mother' but a new stem *abbat/-iyya-* or *innat-iyya-* which may probably be glossed as 'a father' or 'a mother' as opposed to 'father' or 'mother' in general.

Outside the class of such nouns referring to human relations, this process is also apparent in two other nouns, namely, *säw* 'man' and *set* 'woman', which as we can see from the following examples have wide reference.

9a) *säw   yalä-migib   aynorimm*
man   without food   not-he-live-not 'man cannot live without food'

9b) *säw-u   täsäbässäbä*
man-the/his gathered together 'the/his men gathered together'

9c) *(and) säw   mätt'a*
a   man   came-he '(A) man/men came'

As is obvious from the gloss (9a) refers to the generic 'man' as opposed to, say, the generic 'lion'; (9b) refers to a number of people already known or made definite by the anaphoric or possessive /-u/; and (9c) to an unidentified person or persons. Since (9b) with the suffix /-u/ is interpretable only as 'the men' or 'his men'; in other words, as a definite plural, the definite particular or singular cannot be figured out from such structures. In order to make this reference, /-u/ has to be attached not to *säw* but to a different stem *säw-iyyä-* as in(9d) below, parallel to *abbat-iyyä-* above.

9d) *säw-iyyä-u (mät't'a)*
man ? the came-he 'the man came'

In the same way *set* may refer to 'woman' without any affix and to 'female' as opposed to 'male' with the affix /-wa/. The following examples are illustrative of this:

10a) *set   haylä̈ña   särratä̈ña   nä-čč*
woman strong   worker   is-she

10b) *set-wa   aššänäfä-čč-iññ*
female-the   beat-she-me

In order to refer to one particular woman, the affix /-wa/ has to be attached to the stem *set-iyyä-(o)-* on a par with *saw-iyyä-* as in (10c) below:

10c) *set-iyyä-wa   (iyyo' iyyä-wa)*
woman-? the   'the woman'

602

In the example cited above, it is only /-u‿wa/, not /-iyyä/, which shows definiteness, nor is it the case that /iyyäw/ or /iyyäwa/ is a single formative. This is evident from the ungramatical and the corresponding grammatical structures of (11):

11a)* yih säw-iyyä-w   a¹) yih säw-iyyä
     this man ? the   this man ?

11b)* and säw-iyyä-w   b¹) and säw-iyyä
      a man the   a man

11c)* yačči set-iyyä-wa   c¹) yačči set-iyyo
     that(f) woman? the(t)   that(f) woman?

11d)* issu säw-iyyä-w   d¹) issu säw-iyyä
      man ? the   man

In fact the occurrence of /-iyyä/ in the grammatical structures proves that it is not anaphoric on its own in the way that /-u‿wa/ is, for in that case, the structure in (11a¹ - d¹) would be ungrammatical as the nouns would already have been made definite by the elements preceding them. Then what is /-iyyä/?[6]

Since it is found only with nouns which are otherwise generic; pointing to a wide range of reference, its function is to form the stem for the particular singular, from which it may then be concluded that it is a kind of stem formative. Notice that it does not occur with plural nouns as in (12) below, which again supports this conclusion:

12a)* innäzia   säw-iyyä-wočč   but   innäzia   säw-očč
     those   men ? pl.   those   men pl.

12b)* innäzia   set-iyyä-wočč   but   innäzia   set-očč
     those   women pl.   those   women pl.

What we have seen so far are elements which in one way or another determine entities with respect to discourse spatio-temporal factors. In what follows, we will consider those others which denote quantity or mass.

1.2 Quantifiers: These are forms that occur preceding a noun head 'to produce expressions whose reference is determined in terms of size of the set of individuals or in terms of the amount of substance that is being referred to' (Lyons, 1977: 455). In other words they are forms that answer questions of 'how much/many?'.

Like articles, they can be divided into definite and indefinite types.

1.2.1 Indefinite Quantifiers: These include forms like bizu 'much/many'; t'ik'it 'few/small'; tinniš 'little', etc. On the basis of the type of noun they occur with, they can be further divided into two sub-types. In group (i) are those which occur with (+ count) nouns and in (ii) those with (- count) nouns:

                   (i)   (ii)

bizu	t'ik'it		bizu[7]	
'many/much'	'(a) few'		'much'	
ayyale	andimm	+ tämari	tinniš	+ witha
'several'	'none/no'	'student'	'little'	'water'
andand	hullu[8]		minimm	
'some'	'all'		'none'	

In both groups quantitative reference is not specified; the terms are relative to an imagined and fixed amount against which a mass of things or substance is compared and stated as being more or less.

In order to state the amount in specific and definite terms, we have to resort to the second type of quantifier.

1.2.2 Definite Quantifiers: These involve numerals directly or indirectly; directly because the amount can be figured out by direct counting, and indirectly by using other means such as units of measurement. Thus, they can be subdivided into numerals proper on the one hand, and measure and classifier phrases on the other.

1.2.2.1 Numerals: Here, only cardinal numbers are considered to indicate amount as figured out by direct counting. They occur only with (+ count) nouns; hence (13a and b), but not (13c), are grammatical.

13a) *sost bäg (-očč)*
       three sheep pl.   'three sheep'

13b) *hulät färäs (-očč)*
       two   horse pl.   'two horses'

13c) **sost duk'et*
       three flour

1.2.2.2 Measure phrases: The quantity of mass nouns such as *duk'et* 'flour' can be made definite by using certain units of measurements or in terms of their containers as the case may be. Both may vary according to what is measured. The following are some examples:

Liquid: The unit could be a measurement such as a litre or a container in which case varies from the smallest *birč'ikk'o* 'glass to the largest *gan* 'vessel':

14a) *sost birč'ikk'o t'älla*
       three glass   beer   'three glasses of beer'

14b) *sost litre zäyit*
       three oil   'three litres of oil'

14c) *sost gan t'älla*
       three vessel beer   'three vessels of beer'

Grain: the unit varying from *t'asa* 'can' to *gwätära* 'barn':

15a) *sost t'asa t'ef*
       three can   t'ef   'three cans of t'ef'
15b) *sost gwätära   t'ef*
       three barn   t'ef   'three barns of t'ef'

Sometimes amount is figures out in terms of quantifications of the means of transport, such as lorries or animals. Hence structures such as:

16a) *and mäkina   t'ef*
       one lorry-load t'ef

604

16b) *and   ahiyya   t'ef*
    one   donkey-load t'ef

are quite possible.

Length: units vary from *sinzir* 'span' to *gaššsa* (about 40 hectares)

17a) *and sinzir märet*
     span of land

17c) *sost gaššsa märet*
     three   land

17b) *sost kind märet*
     three cubit land

17d) *sost metir č'ark'*
     three metres cloth 'three metres of cloth'

Some count nouns occur with such measure phrases, too. Thus, corresponding to (17) we have (18):

18a) *hulätt   mäkina   wättadar (-occ)*
     two   truck   soldiers (pl.)

18b) *hulätt   bärät käbt*[9]
     two   pen   cattle

The head of the measure phrase is always in the singular; the idea of plurality being indicated by the preceding numeral. Hence (19) is ungrammatical:

19a)* *hulätt mäkinawočč wättadar (-očč)*

19b)**sost baratočč   käbt (-očč)*

19c)**sost birč'ikk'owočč t'älla*

The head of the measure phrase can occur without a preceding numeral only when the amount 'one' is understood. Thus (16) can be paraphrased as (20):

20) *sinzir märet*
    span-of land 'a span of land'

1.2.2.3 Classifier[10] **phrases**: These are like the measure phrases except that (1) the head of the classifier phrase is neither a unit of measurement nor a container; but one of a set of nouns which designates individuation, (2) the head of the entire or subordinate phrase is in most cases a mass noun of a type which, if need be, can be counted as a mass of individuated pieces.

The nouns that constitute the head of the classifier phrase subcategorize other nouns on the basis of such selectional restriction feature such as (+ plant) or (-animate). The following are examples of those with the feature (+ plant):

i) *igir:* 'leg'

21a) *and   igir bärbäre*
     one   ?   pepper   'one individual pepper plant'

21b) *hulätt igir šimbira*
     two   ?   chick peas   'two individual chickpea plants'

21c) *sost*   *igir*   *bunna*
     three   ?   coffee beans   'three individual coffee plants'

21d) *sost*   *igir*   *gešo*
     three   ?   geso leaves   'three individual gesho seedlings'

21e) *sost*   *igir*   *bahirzaf*
     three   ?   eucalyptus   'three individual eucalyptus trees'

In all such structures *igir* is obligatorily preceded by numerals as the idea is to itemize or enumerate each individual piece that constitutes the mass. Thus, (22) below is ungrammatical.

22a)* *igir*   *bärbäre*

22b)* *igir*   *bunna*

The form *igir* does not seem to cover everything that shares the feature (+ plant) as the following examples are dubious, if not ungrammatical:

23a) ?   *and*   *igir*   *k'ulk'ual*
        one   ?   cactus

23b) ?   *and*   *igir*   *k'inč'ib*
        one   ?   candle plant

There is no syntactic-semantic reason *per se* for (23) to be an exception as the nouns that constitute the heads of the phrases are names of plants like those in (21). Furthermore corresponding to (23) the following are possible without *igir*:

24a) *and*   *k'ulk'ual*   'one cactus'

24b) *hulätt*   *k'inč'ib*   'one candle plant'

The reason for the ungrammaticality of phrases including *igir* such as (23) seems to be one of salience, a feature which according to Comrie (1981:192) "relates to the way in which certain actants present in a situation are seized on by humans as foci of attention, only subsequently attention being paid to less salient, less individuated objects". This is an extra-linguistic phenomenon in the sense that "a lot of cultural bias" (*ibid.*) is involved in the characterization of nouns as being high or low in the hierarchy of salience. In this regard, those nouns in (21) refer to plants that are socio-culturally more important and, therefore, more salient than those in (23). The former can be planted and/or transplanted and looked after; while the latter may grow wild. It is such nouns with a high degree of socio-cultural relevance which attract, as stated above, our attention and recur in discourse situations as topics. Because of this extra-linguistic factor which leads to their receiving high position in the hierarchy, such nouns are likely to be marked more than their counterparts lower down in the hierarchy for such grammatical categories as number, gender or case. In this particular case where number is involved, it is those in (21) which are subject to enumeration as individuated entities. What this means is that what is culturally characterized as being high or more salient is also linguistically manifested as being marked in one way or another.

ii) *ras:* Within the category (+ plant), *ras* (literally 'head') occurs with nouns in much the same way and with the same purpose as *igir* does.

25a) *hulätt ras*   *šinkurt*
two   onion   'two heads of onion'

25b) *hulätt ras*   *bäkk'ollo*
two   maize   'two heads of maize'

25c) *hulätt ras*   *išat*
two   green sorghum   'two heads of sorghum'

The idea here is to itemize the head as a single entity without paying any attention to the individual seeds that a cob of maize may contain, for example, nor is the attention paid to the rest of the plant in general. If the reference is to the latter, namely to the seeds, the form used is a different one, as we will see later.

Although the original association is with the human head, not all 'roundish' things within the class are referred to by *ras*. Hence, the following are dubious, at least in the dialect of Wollo, on which this paper is based:

26a) ?   *sost ras*   *birtukan*
three   oranges

26b) ?   *sost ras*   *muz*
three   bananas

27c) ?   *sost ras*   *lomi*
three   lemons

In such cases only the numerals or other indefinite quantifiers are employed and the reference would be to the whole, rather than to each individual piece.

iii) *k'int'at* 'grain'. As stated earlier, *ras* refers to the head in general; thus, any reference to each seed that a cob of maize carries, for example, is made by *k'int'at* as in (27):

27a) *hulätt k'int'at*   *bäk'ollo*
two   pieces   corn   'two individual pieces of corn'

27b) *hulätt k'int'at*   *mašilla*
two   pieces   sorghum   'two individual pieces of sorghum'

27c) *hulätt k'int'at*   *bunna*
two   pieces   coffee bean 'two individual pieces of coffee bean'

k'int'at seems to presuppose smallness too, since the reference is to the seeds as opposed to the heads that contain them. Unlike *igir* or *ras*, it may occur without a preceding numeral, as in:

28a) *k'int'at*   *bak'k'ollo*
corn

28b) *k'int'at*   *mašilla*
sorghum

and even attains the function of a negative quantifier as these structures are paraphrasable as:

29a) *minimm*   *bak'k'ollo*
no   corn

29b) *minimm*   *mašilla*
    no   sorghum

This is more evident in structures such as the following where both occur with only a negative verb:

30a) *k'int'at*   *bäkk'ollo*   *al-bälla-hu-mm*
    single   corn   not-ate-I-not   'I have not eaten a single corn'

30b) *minimm*   *bäkk'ollo*   *al-bälla-hu-mm*
    no   corn   not-ate-I-not   'I have not eaten any corn'

30c)* *k'int'at*   *bäkk'ollo*   *bälla-hu*
    single   corn   ate-I

30d)* *minimm*   *bäkk'ollo*   *bälla-hu*
    no   corn   ate-I

Notice that the individuating *k'int'at* can occur with both forms of the verb as (31) is possible:

31) *hulätt*   *k'int'at*   *bäkk'ollo*   *bälla-hu/al-bälla-hu-mm*
   two   corn   ate-I   not-ate-I-not

Thus, the individuating *k'int'at* is different from the non-individuating one of (28-30).

What we have seen thus far is the syntactic process of individuating nouns that are assigned the feature (+ plant). In what follows, the same process is applied to those nouns that are (- plant) and (+ animate). We will consider here two forms.

i) *k'änd:* 'horn'. This form occurs with the mass noun *käbt* constituting the head of the phrase. In its narrow sense it denotes cows and oxen only. Other 'horned' animals, domestic or wild, do not seem to be characterized in the same way as the following examples suggest:

32a) *sost* *k'änd*[11]   *käbt*
   three head   cattle   'three head of cattle'

32b) *sost* *k'änd*   *bäg*
                   sheep

32c) *sost* *k'änd*   *nyala*

In (32b) *bäg* 'sheep' is (+ count) and may, therefore, be quantified with numerals or other indefinite quantifiers, but the case of (32c) may involve the feature of salience as well, since *nyala* is not as important as *käbt* 'cattle' is. As in the case of the previous forms, *k'änd* is obligatorily preceded by a numeral for structures such as (33) are ungrammatical:

33)* *k'änd käbt*

ii) *gamma:* 'mane'. Like *k'änd*, *gamma* is generally associated with *käbt*, but with particular reference to those with manes. The syntactic structure and the semantic interpretation is the same as that of the former.

34a) *and* *gamma*   *käbt*
   one   mane   cattle

34b) *sost   gamma   käbt*
     three mane   cattle

The reference here is primarily to horses and mules which, like those with horns, form part of what is designated by *käbt* 'cattle'.

Parallel to (34), (35) is possible but for a different purpose and with a different structure:

35a) *and   yä-gamma   käbt*
     one   gen.mane   cattle   gen. = genitive

35b) *sost   yä-k'änd   käbt*
     three gen.horn   cattle

Unlike *and gamma* which is a noun phrase by itself operating as a specifier, *yä-gamma* is a pre-positional phrase and, as such, a complement to the head noun *käbt* 'cattle'. For a more straightforward piece of evidence for this, let us compare it with *k'änd, igir,* etc.:

36a) *sost   yä-k'änd   käbt*

36b)* *sost   yä-igir   bärbäre*

36c)* *sost   yä-ras   šinkurt*

Corresponding to the ungrammatical (b) and (c), (37) is possible:

37a) *sost   kilo yä-šäwa bärbäre*
     three   gen.sawa pepper

37b) *sost   kuntal yä-Goǰǰam šinkurt*
     three sacks gen.Gojjam onion

Notice that parallel to *yä-gamma* or *yä-k'änd* what we have is *yä-šäwa* or *yä-Goǰǰam* and both show the source of the material but not its amount as itemized. This is done, as we have seen above, by the specifier phrase *and gamma* or *and k'änd*, etc. Hence, *yä-gamma* is the same as *yä-šäwa* and is different from *and gamma* or *and k'änd*.

The two specifier phrases we have considered so far are similar to other noun phrases in their configurations. There is always a head preceded by a numeral as shown in the tree below for *and igir.*

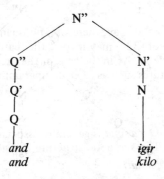

The indefinite quantifier can also be phrases as indicated by (Q"), in the tree, since we have structure involving the degree word *bät'am* 'very', as in:

38a)* *bät'am*   *bizu* *igir*
    very   many

38b)* *bät'am*   *igir*

which can be represented as:

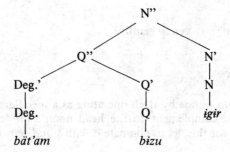

This means then that with the exclusion of numerals, other quantitative specifiers may be treated as constituents. Hence (N") above may be rewritten as:

$$N'' \longrightarrow \left\{ \begin{array}{c} \text{numeral} \\ Q'' \end{array} \right\} \quad N'$$

where (Q") stands for any of the three phrasal specifiers, namely quantifier, measure and classifier phrases.

Now since what we have labelled as articles occur as sisters of N", they should be treated as branching down from a higher node. Let us see the following structures:

39a) *hulätt*   *igir*   *gešo*
     two   gesho tree

39b) *innäziya*   *hulätt*   *igir*   *gešowočč*

This suggests then that (39b) is analysable as below:

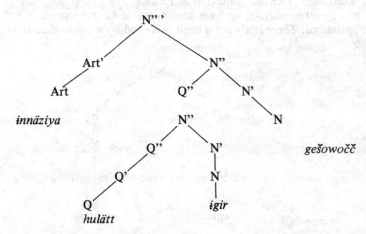

1.3 Conclusions: What we have seen thus far can be summed up as follows: The nouns phrase in Amharic can partially be treated as a constituent consisting of a specifier and a head. The specifier is either entity or quantity/mass denoting. The former is what has been called Article and has sub-divisions to which the terms determiners, possessives and demonstratives are assigned on syntactic grounds. The latter includes numerals, indefinite quantifiers, measure and classifier phrases. The two are also treated as belonging to different nodes in the hierarchy.

To this effect, a phrase structure rule of the type (41) can be formulated:

41a) N'' ' ⟶ (Art)'   N''

41b) N'' ⟶ (Q)''   N'

41c) N' ⟶ N

41d) Art' ⟶ Art

41e) Q'' ⟶ (Deg)'   Q'

41f) Q'' ⟶ Q

41g) Deg' ⟶ Deg

The rule generates only phrases of head and specifier configuration. It does not account for relative clauses, adjectives and prepositional phrases for these are complements of N' or N'' (cf. Jackendoff: 1977) and have not been included in this analysis.

NOTES

1. I am grateful to R. J. Hayward for his insightful comments and suggestions. I have bene-fited from the discussion we had. Responsibility is, however, all mine.

2. *and* here is an article and is regarded as different from the quantifier *and* 'one'.

3. Could *iňňa* be derived from *innä-ine* or *ine-innä*?

4. Possible only when the meaning 'this sheep of his' is intended.

5. There is also *itu* which, in addition to definiteness, shows diminutiveness, as in:

> *bet-itu*
> house-the-dim.   'the small house'

6. This is different from the distributive *iyyä* which is prenominal, as in:

> *bä-   iyyä säw -u   bet*
> in   each man 's   house

7. I assume (b i zu) to be bilexical. Here it means :much' and subcategorizes (- count) nouns.

8. *hullu* is post-nominal only when there is no pre-nominal article. Thus:

> *säw   hullu*
> man   all   'all men'

> *innäzih   hullu säw-očč*
> these   all   men-pl.   'all these men'

9.   Referring to 'oxen' and 'cows' only.

10. The term is used here in the sense of Lyons (1979: 462), where it is used as a device of individuation and enumeration.

11. *sost k'änd* is the same as the English expression 'three head' (of cattle); so it should be noted that 'heads' not 'horns' are counted.

BIBLIOGRAPHY

Armbruster, C. H. (1908)   *Initia Amharica – Introduction to Spoken Amharic*, Cambridge University Press.

Cohen, Marcel (1970)   *Traité de Langue Amharique (Abyssinie)*, Paris, Institut d'Ethnologie.

Comrie, Bernard (1981)   *Language Universal and Linguistic Typology*, Cambridge University Press.

Dawkins, C. H. (1969)   *The Fundamentals of Amharic*, Addis Ababa: Sudan Interior Mission.

Desta Tekle-Wold (1970)   *Yämariñña Mäzgäbä - k'alat*, Addis Ababa: Artistic Printing Press.

Friedrich, P. (1970)   "Shape in Grammar", *Language*, 46, 379-407.

Getachew Haile (1967)   "Demonstrative Pronouns in Amharic", *J.E.S.*, 5, 9-12.

Hartmann, Josef (1980)   *Amharische Grammatik*, Wiesbaden: Franz Steiner Verlag Gmbh.

Hebo, P. Agostino (1955)   *Grammatica Amharica*, Asmara: Scuola Tipografica Francescana.

Jackendoff, Ray (1968)   "Quantifiers in English", *Foundation of Language*, 4, 422-42.

——————— (1979)   *X̄-Syntax: A Study of Phrase Structure*, MIT Press.

Leslau, Wolf (1967)   *Amharic Textbook*, Wiesbaden: Otto Harrassowitz.

Lyons, John (1979)   *Semantics*, Vol.II, Cambridge University Press.

Mersie-Hazen Wolde-kirkos   *Yämariñña Säwasïw*, Addis Ababa, Artistic Printing Press.
(1935)

Parsons, T. (1972)   "The Analysis of Mass Terms and Amount Terms", *Foundation of Language*, 6, 362-88.

Teklemariam Fantaye (1964)   *Hohitä-T'ïbäb zä-Sinä S'ihuf*, Addis Ababa: Central Printing Press.

A DISCOURSE ANALYSIS OF AMHARIC NARRATIVE

Loren F. Bliese

INTRODUCTION

The following paper is an attempt to formalize research done on Amharic narrative texts by Dr. Mikre Sellassie Gebre Ammanuel, Mr. Peter Unseth and myself. Each of us analyzed several stories from texts printed in Edward Ullendorff's *An Amharic Chrestomathy* (1965, abbreviated below to EU), Kebbede Michael's *Yäéwqät Bélléc'éta* (1949 EC, below as KM), and B. G. Mahitema Sillasse W. M.'s *Énqélf Lämméne* (1960 EC, below as MS). We followed the charting method of analysis developed by Robert Longacre (1981, 1983) together with Stephen Levinsohn (1978). The aim of discourse analysis is to show how the development of the whole text determines such features as verb categories, participant reference and peak markers.

1. VERB SALIENCE

It has been shown in many languages that each discourse type has a preference for certain verb forms to show the prominent or salient material in the text, and that other verb forms can be graded for salience within each discourse type. For example, Robert Longacre has drawn up a diagram, "Etic bands of salience in narrative", from his discourse studies in many languages (1984, see also 1981 and 1982). These principles were applied to Amharic narrative texts. Various verb forms were placed on a cline of salience similar to Longacre's etic bands, with intuitively prominent forms at the top and less prominent forms in descending order.

Amharic Narrative Verb Salience Cline

1'. Pivotal events — direct speech quotes plus perfect aspect of *alä* 'say'

  1. Main events — perfect aspect, and consecutive gerunds preceding them

    2. Flashbacks — the gerundive or imperfect stem plus *näbbär* or *noro* 'was'

      3. Routine, script-predictable events — perfect aspect verbs with conjunctions *éyyä-, bä-gize* 'when', *sélä* 'because', *kä-bähwalä* 'after, *éndä* 'as soon as'

        4. Background activity — imperfect aspect with, and occasionally without, conjunctions *si-, bi* 'when'

          5. Setting — temporal conjunctions for time; *éndä* 'as' for place; and 'be'

            6. Collateral — negatives, purpose clauses and modals

              7. Evaluation — reason clauses with *sélä-* or *énna* 'because'

                8. Cohesion — relative clauses, temporal clauses which are constituents of relatives, *éndä* 'that', coextensive gerunds, and 'be, became'

Note:(1) Consecutive gerunds may be demoted to levels 2, 3, and 4 when they precede verbs in those levels.

    (2) Coextensive (stative) gerunds may be promoted to 5, 6, and 7 when they precede

verbs in those levels. (Those which make up one meaning with a following verb are dealt with as a unit, and classified according to the following verb. See 1.4 and 1.6 below.)

1.1' Pivotal Events

The highest level of salience in a narrative is found where there are pivotal events. These are clauses with heightened vividness often containing the unexpected. In the stories we analyzed, the most common grammatical feature at such points was the use of direct speech. For example, in the story "The Rich Farmer", the farmer passes his guests unnoticed while dressed in work clothes, but when he dresses in respectable clothes and returns, they stand and greet him. His response is, "I'm the previous one, say welcome to my clothes". The unexpected response is given heightened vividness by the cryptic direct speech quotation. The verbal marker for direct speech here is the perfect aspect verb *al-accäw* 'he said to them' (EU:59; also see KM:24).

1.1 Main Events

In a narrative text, main events are distinguished as those which are punctiliar and sequential, carrying the story-line forward. They are actions which happen at a specific time and are part of the series of events in the story. This main line of a narrative is often marked by a special verb form. In Amharic narrative texts the perfect aspect verb was invariably the final verb at the end of every sequence of events. Often two perfect verbs were also coordinated by the conjunction *-nna* 'and'. Furthermore, the independent perfect verb form is found only in the main line of the narrative. In the Amharic tense system the perfect verb is the only independent verb form which does not have an auxiliary. This lack serves to mark the perfect aspect independent verb as the narrative tense in Amharic.

However, instead of a series of perfect verbs, the gerund (or converb), or a series of gerunds, regularly preceded the final perfect verb whenever a series of events was closely related. Intuitively, they also carry the main line of the story. In most stories gerunds only precede perfect aspect verbs and can be added to the cline as another verb form for the main line (MS:18-19, 27-30; KM:23-24, 27, 40-41, 50-51, 97-99).

However, such consecutive gerunds (read with a final stress and followed by a pause) are found in any of the first four categories. The gerund, therefore, has a broader function than a marker of the main line in narrative texts. For example, in "A Feeble Monk" there is a series of two consecutive gerunds followed by a less salient script-predictable perfect aspect conjunction: *agébtäw* "having caused to enter" (a leopard into a sack), *albésäw* "having covered it", *éndä däbbäqut* "as soon as he hid it". It seems best to say that the gerunds are subordinate to the *éndä* clause rather than to the next gerund clause, "the hunters having come" (MS:25). In "A Wise Blind Man", a series of seven gerunds is followed by the conjunction *bi-mmäläkkätäw* "when he looked at it" (KM:31; also see KM:63 and 64). This excludes a neat definition that consecutive gerunds always precede perfect aspect verbs, and is the reason for the note above, allowing them to be demoted to levels 2, 3 and 4 when they precede verbs in those levels.

1.2 Flashbacks

Flashbacks are events out of chronological order in the sense that the story progresses to a certain point but then drops back to some event which began earlier. This is often connected to a shift in scene or subject. Flashbacks in Amharic are marked by a gerund plus *näbbär* or *noro* 'was' for punctiliar action, and an imperfect plus *näbbär* or *noro* for continuous action.

In "A Traveller" a man returns home from a trip unexpectedly. Before he enters his house it is stated that three men "were talking" *yécc'äwawwätu näbbär* with his wife (MS:145). The continuous action began before his arrival but is not described until after his arrival is told, so it is marked by the imperfect aspect plus *näbbär*.

Later, in preparation for the traveller's entrance, we find the flashback, *nafqo näbbär* "he had longed", referring to his previous longing as he now enters and kisses his family (MS:145).

In "A Wise Blind Man" his burying of a sack and return to his house is told. Then the story continues with a flashback that the neighbor *yét'äbbéqäw noro* "had been watching him" (KM:31).

If a sequential event precedes a flashback marked by *näbbär* it will be found as a gerund. For example, in "A Woman with Trading Skills", after the arrival of a rich customer to the woman prostitute is described, a flashback of her previous activities follows. The first two verbs are gerunds followed by the marked flashback: *éswam betwan ant'éfa täzägajjéta tét'äbbéqäw sélä näbbärä* "Because she having decorated her house and having prepared herself was waiting for him" (MS: 29).

1.3 Routine, Script-predictable Events

A category which is important in arranging verbs in a salience cline is that of routine, script-predictable events. These are events which, if left out of the story, would not leave a gap in the main line since the hearers share a common script and would fill in the information automatically. Such events, when included in the telling of the story, normally do not take the verb form which marks the main line. This was found for many predictable events in the stories analyzed.

Various conjunctions with perfect aspect verbs are used with routine, script-predictable events. One in the story of the rich farmer is *bä-gize* "when". After the statement, "in order to see his cattle", comes the clause, *wädä däj bä-wätt'a gize* "when he went out to the entrance". Since going out to the entrance is predictable from the preceding clause, it does not have the salience of a main verb (EU: 59).

Another conjunction in the same story which is used for a script-predictable event is *éyyä* "while". When the visitors saw him dressed up *éyyä-tänässu* "while getting up", having been startled they greeted him. The custom of standing up when a respected person enters a room is part of the common script for Ethiopians, so the event does not have to be treated as a main event and be marked by perfect aspect.

Kä-bähwala "after" is another temporal conjunction which is found in script-predictable clauses. In "A Woman with Trading Skills", a man brings a bundle of fresh grain as she had requested. The routine action follows, *kä-täqäbbäläc bähwala* "after she took it". The conjunction is used several times in the story for such routine events (MS:28-30).

Another perfect aspect clause in the same story is *t'éqit c'éwéwwét éndä yazum* "while they were involved in small talk", where the conjunction *éndä* denotes script-predictable activity (MS: 29).

Causal conjunctions with *sélä* and perfect verbs are also used for script-predictable activities. In the same story, the rich man was seated under a gourd of milk hanging on the wall. Later when the man was startled he jumped up. The story continues, "because he hit" *sélä mätta* his head on the gourd of milk it spilled on his head (MS: 29).

1.4 Background Activity

Background activity is any event that is given to clarify the main event line. In Amharic various conjunctions with imperfect aspect verbs are used for background activity. The verbs often are durative rather than punctiliar. For example, in "A Woman with Trading Skills", the rich man is first introduced with two gerund clauses and a *si-* "while" conjunction clause, all of a durative nature. Sitting on a pacing mule, having his servant carrying his gun, "while pacing along" *si-yasägér* he caught up with her (MS: 28). The first three clauses are background activities leading up to the final perfect aspect verb. Note that the gerunds take up the salience of the verb which follows them. (See also EU: 59, *si-yars* "while ploughing" he spent the day.)

The conjunction *bi-* also has temporal meaning and denotes background activities. In "A Partridge Chick Caught in a Trap", after the man takes the presumably dead bird out of the trap, his companion tells him to throw it up so he can see it. The next clause is *wädä sämay wärwär bi-yadärgat* "to sky throwing when-he did". This is background activity preparatory to the climax. The story then concludes with two more compound verbs emphasizing the escape (MS: 19-20).

In "A Story about a Drunkard", there is a series of an imperfect stem plus *-nna* "and", followed by two temporal conjunctions, two gerunds, and a final imperfect aspect verb. The whole series describes the habitual activity of a drunkard, *yét'ätt'abbät-énna éyyä-säkkärä simäsh hedo ' ' ' tänyéto yadéral* "He drinks with it and while being drunk when it becomes evening having gone . . . having lain down he spends the night" (KM: 98). The use of imperfect aspect is rare in the narrative texts we studied, but the first and last verbs of this series show that it can be used in background activity. The passage also has good examples of *éyyä* in a script-predictable clause, and *si-* in a setting clause. It also shows the use of two types of gerunds before the imperfect aspect verb. The gerund *hedo* is consecutive with final stress, while *tänyéto* "lying down" has no stress and makes up one meaning with the final verb "spends the night". (See Goldenberg's distinction in Hetzron: 1972, 99-100.)

1.5 Setting

Setting is expository material that tells where and when the story is taking place. It is not events like the above background activity. The subjects of setting clauses are often inanimate such as "evening, day, month", etc., or they are related to verbs of motion which change the place, or "be" verbs describing circumstances.

For example, in "The Rich Farmer" after the man spent the day ploughing, we find *bämässhä gize* "when it became evening" (EU: 59). In "A Traveller" referred to earlier, the first scene is the man leaving home. Then we have these words changing the time, *bézu wärat kasalläfä bähwala* "after he had spent many months" (See also KM: 24).

In the same story the man then returns to his country, and the next place for the setting is noted by the clause, *käbetum aqérabiya bä-därräsä gize* "when he arrived near his house" (MS: 145). In "A Woman with Trading Skills", while the woman was talking to the rich man the scene shifts briefly to the kitchen where her first customer was having a dream. This is done with the clause, *kä-majät éndä honä* "as he was in the kitchen" (MS: 29).

The situation of the characters may be illustrated by "A Tall Man and a Short Man". They are introduced as *wädajjoc honäw éyyätärädaddu abéräw linoru täsémammu* "being friends while helping each other they agreed to live together" (KM: 50). Both gerunds are of the co-extensive non-stressed type, and the situation of the characters is described by the subordinate clause "while helping each other" with the conjunction *éyyä*. In "Bad Air" the kind of day is described *qänum bäal noro* "and the day being a holiday (KM: 63). The use of the "be" verbs in the above three examples of settings is significant since they are on a lower salience level than action verbs in narrative discourse.

1.6 Collateral

Collateral is the term used for other than the existing circumstances. Negatives, purpose clauses, and modals are the usual verb forms in collateral. Since they do not tell anything that actually happens, they are low on the salience cline.

An emphatic negative is illustrated in "The Rich Farmer" when the visitors *s-a-ynnäsullät norém s-a-ylut qärru* "remain without rising or saying welcome" to the rich farmer when he comes in from the field (EU: 59). A normal negative is illustrated earlier in the same story when the rich farmer enters his house *säwénnätun s-a-yfäqéd* "without inspecting his body". In this case the negative verb with the prefix *-a-* is also in a *s-* "when" clause (EU: 59).

Collateral is also illustrated by purpose clauses. Amharic uses the preposition *lä-* plus the infinitive as one way to show purpose. For example, later in the same story the farmer goes to the door *käbt lämayyät* "in order to see his cattle". The conjunction *li-* also shows purpose as in *abéraw li-noru täsämammu* "they agreed to live together". The gerund *abéräw* is of the coextensive one-meaning type without stress (KM: 50). Another form for purpose clauses is with the conjunction énd-' In "A Fitting Revenge", after the rich man's bad turn of events, action was taken kagär éndi-wät'a "that he leave the country" (KM: 24).

Modals also show another possible set than the existing events. In Amharic the verb cal "be able" is ued with the infinitive to show a possible activity. For example, in "Bad Air" we find liyadénaccäw saycélu qärru "they were not able to save them" (KM: 64).

1.7 Evaluation

Evaluation is the term used to indicate the author's interjection of himself into the story. It is giving information directly to the hearer rather than going the normal route of the story line. Reason clauses with sélä- or -énna "because", are markers of evaluation in Amharic. For example, in "A Partridge Chick Caught in a Trap", after she is caught the author interjects the comment, "Well then, when trouble comes because the first thing they think of is their parents . . .". A little later another comment is added, "Since a mother is always wise enough to advise her child" (MS: 18). A similar evaluative comment from "Three Travellers" is, "Since a trickster never rests" (KM: 40).

In the short narrative which we examined a very common use of a verb in this category of evaluation was the final yébbalal "it is said" which ended most of the stories in Énqélf Lämméne (MS: 19, 24, 27), or in a few cases, came immediately after the introduction (MS: 40, 63). Excluding direct speech, this is the most regular use of the imperfect aspect verb alone in Amharic narrative discourse.

All the stories in Énqélf Lämméne and a few in Yäéwqät Bélléc'éta have a final hortatory statement which is best intepreted as evaluation. The verbs are mostly imperatives and "should" forms (MS: 17, 19, etc.; KM: 99).

1.8 Cohesion

Any text has a certain amount of repetition. This ties the story together and helps the hearer to follow since information is slowed down.

Relative clauses are a very common form, giving cohesion. For example, in "A Woman with Trading Skills", when the rich man came back to her house he is described as bäbäqélo yézwat yämätt'aw "the one who had brought her on his mule" (MS: 29). The coextensive gerund followed by the relative clause simply repeats the information already told earlier and is, therefore, put in this less salient form. The arrival of the first customer is described with a temporal conjunction followed by a relative clause: ya kägäbäya sétémät'a yäqätt'äräccéw éhél t'äbbaqi "that grain watchman to whom she had given an appointment when she came from market" (MS: 28). All of this information had already been given, so the function of the clause is merely to give cohesion by repetition. Gerunds and temporal clauses which precede relative clauses give known information and have the same salience as their relative clause.

The next word in the story shows another verb form used in cohesion: énd-azzäzäccéw "as she commanded him". The conjunction éndä "as" reminds the hearer of her earlier arrangements.

An example of cohesion with the verb "became" is found in "A Tall Man and a Short Man". After a series of three gerunds which repeat the previously told injuries of the short man, we find the summary akalä gwädälo honä "he became a maimed person" (KM: 50).

Coextensive gerunds marked by lack of final stress are also used in cohesion clauses. In the sotry of the rich farmer, two such gerunds are found describing the farmer: läbéso käbéro bayyut gize "when they saw him having dressed himself and having become honourable" (EU: 59). These are stative descriptions of something that had happened punctilily before. The function of the gerund here is to give cohesion, not to add new events. In contrast, the two previous examples in this story of läbéso "having dressed himself", are both punctiliar, consecutive events and have the distinctive stress on the final syllable, followed by a pause, so they are part of the main line events. This illustrates the interesting feature that consecutive (stressed) gerunds may be in any of the first four categories involving activities, and coextensive (unstressed) gerunds may be in any of the last four stative categories. This makes a nice dichotomy in the salience cline dividing action verbs from stative verbs.

2. PARTICIPANT REFERENCE

2.1 Introduction of Main Characters

The most common device used to introduce the main character in the narratives we studied was the numeral *and* "one" before some identifying noun. For example, "The Rich Farmer" begins, *and säw* "one man". A female main character will have a feminine suffix *and-it* as in "A Woman with Trading Skills" (MS: 27). The main character is normally introduced as the subject of its sentence as in the above two examples.

If there is more than one main character, *and* may be repeated as in "A Fitting Revenge" *and déha säw . . . and habtam säw* "one poor man . . . one rich man" (KM: 23). Note that adjectives are added to distinguish the two. Other numerals also are used in place of "one" when several people function as a group. For example, *hulät leboc* "two thieves" (MS: 48).

Besides adjectives, relative clauses are also used together with *and* in introducing main characters. The story "An Old Dog and a Jackal" begins with this clause, *édémewén mulu bäqénénnäténna bätamanyénnät lägetaw siyagélägél yänorä and aroge wéssha* "one old dog who had lived his whole life serving his master honorably and faithfully" (MS: 175).

In a few stories, the use of *and* is not in pointing out the main character but seems to be tied to the introduction of the story to mark it as a fable. For example, a story may begin with *and qän* "one day" (KM: 114) or *käélätat and qän* (KM: 50; MS: 145) with meaning similar to the English "once upon a time". The place setting may also take this indefinite form, which marks the narrative as a story where the place is imaginary or not important. For example, in the story "A Traveller", the introduction states that he was living in *and agär* "one country" (MS: 145; also see KM: 74). In the story, "One Old Man's Blessing", (MS: 33), the main character appears after an earlier scene where a father gives a last will and dies. But it is the father who is introduced with *and*, not the main character, the son who becomes prominent later.

An exception to the use of *and* was found in several stories which begin with animals without any other identification (MS: 43, 80, 102, 105 hyena; 64, 102 baboon; 80, 105 leopard; 74, Mr. chicken, etc). A few stories used *and* in introducing animals, for example "one hyena" (MS: 206), so animals may either have *and* or not have it.

The verb *näbbär* "was" is often found closing the initial sentence of the story when the subject is a noun clause modified by *and* and optionally other adjectives or relative clauses (see EU: 59). Other stories connect the introduction of the main character with the first events in the initial sentence without separating them by *näbbär* (See MS: 27).

2.2 Other Characters and Props

A common method of introducing other characters is as the direct object of the action of the main character. For example, the woman with trading skills "met a grain watchman", and later "met a goat herder" and "met one cow herder" (MS: 28).

In contrast, in the above story the fourth male character is the rich man who plays a more important role, and is introduced as the sentence subject with three subordinate verbs and a final *därräsäbbat* "he caught up with her" (MS: 28). Even in this case he is introduced in relation to the woman. Prominence is given to the introduction of a character by the grammatical form.

Minor characters and props are often introduced with no special identification. In the above story the servant is simply included in the introduction of the rich man, with the clause "having made his servant carry his gun" (MS: 28). In the story "A Fitting Revenge", the stone is an important prop. However, it has no special introduction : *déngiya anséto* "having picked up a stone" (KM: 23). In other stories, props are sometimes introduced with *and* "one" (MS: 27-28).

2.3 Definite Article

Once a character or prop is introduced, it becomes known to the hearer, and in all succeeding references is identified with a definite article or some other qualifier which makes it definite. For example, in "A Fitting Revenge", after the poor man and rich man are introduced with *and* "one", the following two references to each are with the definite article, *habtam-u* "the rich man", *déha-w* "the poor man" (KM: 23).

2.4 Reintroducing Participants

If a participant leaves the scene and then returns, a deictic, a relative clause of identification, or a definite noun can be used to reintroduce him. In "A Woman with Trading Skills", when the first and second men she made appointments with arrived, they are reintroduced with the deictic *ya* (MS: 28), and when she is reintroduced at the end of the story, we find the feminine deictic *yac* "that" (MS: 30).

In the same story, the return of the rich man is given more prominence with a relative clause (MS: 29; see 1.8). The two minor characters are reintroduced in the last two scenes of the same story simply by their identifying definite nouns: *baläféyälu* "the owner of the goat", and *baläwätätu* "owner of the milk" (MS: 29). Previously, the latter is similarly reintroduced as *balälamu* "owner of the cow" (MS: 28).

2.5 Switch Reference

A switch in subjects of main clauses is usually marked in Amharic. If the new subject is a new or reintroduced participant, the above markers ("one", deictics, and relative clauses) will make it unnecessary to further mark the new subject.

Similarly, if the time or place setting changes, this change will also be sufficient to not require another switch reference marker. Where these obvious markers are not present, Amharic has coordinating conjunctions which serve to mark the switch. The most common of these is *mm* "and" (written as a single -*m* when word final). Olga Kapeliuk has already noted this function when she writes, ". . . the presence of -*mm* marks a change of subject . . ." (1978: 274). Although -*mm* has another primary function to show paragraph cohesion, its importance in marking switch reference was observed in all the texts analyzed. For example, in "A Woman with Trading Skills" -*mm* is used thirteen times to show switch reference (MS: 27-30).

An example with a noun in "A Fitting Revenge" comes after the rich man throws the stone. The next sentence then begins, *dähawu-m* "and the poor man" (KM: 23). Examples of *mm* with pronouns are found in "A Woman with Trading Skills", after she greets the grain watchman, the next sentence signals the switch by *éssu-m* "and he". After he makes his appointment, the next sentence begins *ésswa-m* "and she" (MS: 27).

If a contrast is intended, *gén* "but" will come in place of -*mm*. For example, in "A Fitting Revenge", the rich man told the beggar to go away. Then the next sentence begins with *gén*: "but the poor man continued begging in his desire thinking he might get something" (KM: 23; lso see MS: 18).

Sometimes the change in subject is only marked by verb morphology. This is especially common in alternating speech quotations.

2.6 Various Names for the Same Character

Amharic narratives like to vary the names of the characters. The three names, "herder of cows", "owner of a cow", and "owner of milk" for the same person in "A Woman with Trading Skills" were already noted. The rich man there is called "duke", "nobleman", and "ruler" (MS:

28-30). In "An Old Dog and a Jackal" the dog is also called "the old guard", and his masters are called "house owners", "lords", and "overseers" (MS: 175-176).

3. PEAK

An effort was made to note anything unusual at the peak or high point in the stories analyzed. Some of the ways the stories marked peak are noted below.

3.1 Direct Speech at Peak

As was noted in 1.1', pivotal events are often marked by direct speech in Amharic narratives. In "A Woman with Trading Skills" the first scene of making arrangements has a lot of direct speech. The second scene of the arrival of her customers has none. The third scene has only one direct speech which is the peak of the narrative. The sleeping grain watcher cries out in his sleep "Stop! Beat him to the entrance!" (MS: 29). The contrast of this short direct speech cry with no other direct speech around it is a very effective marker of peak.

3.2 Crowded Stage at Peak

Most of the stories have as many of the characters as possible on the stage at peak. In the above story the cry of the sleeping man brings everyone out of hiding, crashing into and breaking things in their effort to get away (MS: 29). In "An Old Dog and a Jackal" all participants — the dog, the jackal, the owners and their baby — are involved at peak (MS: 176).

3.3 Grammatical Structure Change at Peak

One common method of marking peak is to vary the grammatical structure at the high point. In "The Rich Farmer" (EU: 59), the sentence before the peak has 27 words, and the one before it has 21. Both sentences have complicated structures with many gerunds and conjunctions. The farmer's climatic statement, however, is in a short sentence of only seven words containing two short sentences of three words each in the quote. This shift from complex to simple structure effectively marks the peak.

3.4 Lexical Vividness at Peak

Amharic has compound forms with the verb "say" and "do" which increase vividness. These are especially useful to mark peak. For example, in "A Woman with Trading Skills", the startled man hiding under the bed jumps up, knocking the bed over onto the water pot and other pottery which *énkétkét sébérbér bélo* "saying crush and smash" became potsherds (MS: 29; also see MS: 19-20 quoted in 1.3 above).

Amharic also has an intensive verb form which serves nicely for marking peak. When the rich man knocks his head on the gourd, spilling milk on his head, he "is startled". The verb form used is not the simple form *dänäggät'ä*, but the intensive *tädänaggät'ä*. The startled goat herder is described as "scattering" the baskets, not with the simple gerund *bätténo*, but with the intensive *bätatténo* (MS: 29).

3.5 Intense Activity at Peak

Peak is often marked in narratives by intense activity. The above story of all the men rushing madly to get out of the prostitute's house is a fine example.

BIBLIOGRAPHY

Grimes, Joseph E.	*The Thread of Discourse,* (The Hague: Mouton, 1975)
Hetzron, Robert	"Ethiopian Semitic: Studies in Classification", *Journal of Semitic Studies*, 2 (Manchester University, 1972).
Kapeliuk, Olga	"Particles of Concatenation and of Reference in Amharic", *Bulletin of the School of Oriental and African Studies*, 41.2 (London, 1978), pp.272-282.
Kebbede, Michael	*Yäéwqät Bélléc'ta* (Addis Ababa: Artistic, 1949 EC). Abbreviated above as **(KM)**.
Longacre, Robert	"A Spectrum and Profile Approach to Discourse Analysis", *Text*, 1.4 (1981), pp.337-359.
————————	"Verb Ranking and the Constituent Structure of Discourse", *Journal of the Linguistic Association of the Southwest*, 5.3, 4 (1982), pp.177-202.
————————	*Grammar of Discourse*, (New York: Plenum, 1983).
————————	"Etic bands of salience in narrative", (Mimeographed sheet presented in the Bible Society of Ethiopia Discourse Analysis Workshop, June, 1984).
Longacre, R. and Stephen Levinsohn	"Field Analysis of Discourse", *Current Trends in Textlinguistics* (Research in Text Theory 2), ed. W. U. Dressler (Berlin: Gruyter, 1978), pp.103-122.
(Bilaten Geta) Mahitema Sillasse Wolde Mesqel	*Énqélf Lämméne* (Addis Ababa: Artistic, 1960 EC). Abbreviated above as **(MS)**.
Ullendorff, Edward	*An Amharic Chrestomathy* (London: Oxford, 1965). Abbreviated above as **(EU)**.

SOME NOTES ON AMHARIC PERFORMATIVE VERBS

Demissie Manahlot

J. Austin (1962) claims that explicit performative utterances differ from statements. The following are examples of such utterances.

(1)   I order you to go

(2)   I promise to give you 5 birr

These expressions, according to Austin, are neither true nor false. They neither describe nor report about any thing. The speaker is a first person, whereas the addressee is a second person. The main verb is in the simple present tense. The saying/uttering of such an expression constitutes the performance of an action. For instance, in uttering:

(1)   an action of ordering is said to take place, while in uttering

(2)   an action of promising is performed. The main verb names the type of illocutionary force that results at the moment of utterance provided that certain conditions are satisfied. For example, the utterer of (1) has to be someone who is in a position to give orders, whereas the hearer has to be someone who obeys orders. Furthermore, the whole context of uttering the expression should be appropriate to ordering and obeying.

Now, whether Austin implies that such an explicit performative formula occurs in all languages is hard to tell. But let us see a few examples in Amharic. In Amharic the form of the verb which is more or less equivalent to the English present simple indicative is expressed in the imperfective form, which is generally 4-ways ambiguous with respect to the aspect of the verb. For instance, the clause:

(3)   *yɨ - bäl - all*
he - eat - aux[1]

can be interpreted as follows:

(a)   He eats   (simple present)
(b)   He eats   (habitual present)
(c)   He is eating   (progressive present)
(d)   He will eat   (future)

Therefore, if we translate English explicit performative utterances into Amharic using the imperfective form, it is difficult to make sure that the performative sense of the English is maintained in the Amharic version. Thus (1) may be translated as shown in (4).

(4)   *ɨndɨ - tɨ - hed   azz - ɨh - all äh^u*
comp[2] - you - go   order-you -aux - I
'I order you to go!'

The imperfective forms of certain verbs like *azzäz-* 'order' are understood only in the habitual present or future sense. Hence, the accurate translation of (4) should be either:

'I always order you to go!'   or   'I will order you to go'

This means that (4) cannot be understood as an order by the addressee and therefore it cannot be a performative utterance at all. It appears that the perfective form of the verb is more appropriate for verbs like *azzäz-* to express performative ideas. Thus (1) can be translated as shown in (5) below:

(5) *indi - ti - hed   azižž - e - h - all - äh^u*
     comp - you - go order - I - you - aux - I
     Lit: 'I have ordered you to go'

But (5) has to be said in an emphatic intonation to be understood as an order. Otherwise, it can be understood as a report. Usually an expression like (5) has to be followed by the imperative form of the embedded verb to avoid this ambiguity as shown in (6).

(6) *indi ti - hed   ižž - e - h - all äh^u, hid*
     'I have ordered you to go, go!'

To take another example of *azzäz-*type, consider (7):

(7) *yih-n-lij (bä) - aläk'a - nnät   Somm - e - w - all - äh^u*
     This OM[3] boy (at) monitor - ness appoint - I - him - aux - I
     Lit: 'I appoint this boy monitor'

The verb *šomm-* 'appoint' appears to be different from *azzäz-*type, for it lacks an embedded verb. But most likely, the embedded verb has undergone some kind of deletion rule.

Thus (7) can be expressed as in (8) by adding the verb *särra* 'to work, to serve'.

(8) *yih - n   lij   bä - aläk'a - nnät ind-yi - sära*
     This OM   boy as - monitor - ness Comp - he - work

     šomm - e - w - all - äh^u
     appoint - I - him - aux - I

     Lit: 'I have appointed this boy to serve as a monitor'
          'I appoint this boy to serve as a monitor'

To make either (7) or (8) sound more like a performative — i.e. to avoid the sense of reporting, a time adverbial like *k-ahun ǰämmiro* - 'from now on, as of now', could be added at the beginning of the sentence or elsewhere in the sentence, as shown in (9):

(9a) *k-ahun ǰämmiro, yih-n lij bä-aläk'a-nnät (ind - yi   - sära) šomm - e - w - all - äh^u*
      from-now starting this -OM boy as-monitor-ness comp-he-work appoint-I-him-aux-I

(9b) *yih-n lij k-ahun ǰämmiro bä-aläk'a-nnät (ind - yi   - sära) šomm - e - w - all - äh^u*

(9c) *yih-n lij bä-aläk'a-nnät (ind-yi   - sära) k-ahun ǰämmiro šomm - e - w - all - äh^u*

All three of these sentences can be translated as:

     Lit: 'I have appointed this boy monitor as of now!'
          'I appoint this boy monitor as of now as of this very moment!'

The performativeness of any utterance like (5) or (7) - (8) is of course determined by the circumstances under which it is uttered. Thus, if (7) is said by a teacher in the presence of

624

students in a classroom situation, its performativeness becomes obvious while its reportness is entirely avoided.

Now let us consider a different type of performative verb. The Amharic version of the English explicit performative utterance shown in (2) contains another type of Amharic performative verb which is different from the *azzäz*-type as translated in (10):

(10) *ammist birr l - i - sät' - ihk'ali - gä ba-all-äh^u*
5 bi rr Comp-I-give-you word I-enter-aux-I
Lit: 'I give you my word to give you 5 birr!'
'I promise to give you 5 birr'

As shown in this sentence, the performative verb *k'al gäbba-* 'give one's word, promise' is used in its imperfective form. It will definitely be a non-performative utterance if used in its perfective form as in the case of *azzäz-*. Consider (11) to see the difference.

(11) *ammist birr l - i sät' - ih k'al gäbičč - e - all - äh^u*
'I have promised to give you 5 birr'

In other words, the addressee understands (11) as a report, not as an act of promising. Nevertheless, (10) is not entirely free from ambiguity, for a future reading is slightly felt especially if uttered out of context. A future time adverb may be used to make the future reading of (10) more explicit as shown below:

(12) *ammist birr l - i - sät'- ih nägä k'ali - gäba - all - äh^u*
'I will promise tomorrow to give you 5 birr'

The syntactic difference between *azzäz-* and *k'al gäbba* lies mainly in the type of complementation that they allow. *azzäz-* allows an embedded clause marked with the complementizer *ind -* whereas *k'al gäbba* allows an embedded clause marked with the complementizer *l (i) -*. Furthermore, *k'al gäbba-* can occur with an infinitive embedded clause preceded by the preposition *lä-* 'for', whereas *azzäz-* may occur with *zänd*-clause.

Thus (10) can be expressed with *lä - mä -* clause while (5) can be expressed with a *zänd*-clause as shown in (13) and (14) respectively.

(13) *- antä ammirr lä mä - st'ät k'ali - gäb - all - äh^u*
to-you 5 birr for-comp-give word - enter - aux - I
'I promise to give you 5 birr'

(14) *ti - hed zänd azižž - e - h - all - äh^u*
you - go comp. order - I - you - aux - I
Lit: 'I have ordered you to go'
'I order you to go'

The unacceptability of the following sentences illustrate that embedding the *l(i)-* or the *mä* clause in *azzäz* is not allowed.

(15) *li - ti - hed azizz - e - h - all - äh^u*

(16) *ant ä - n lä - mä - hed azižž - e - h - all - äh^u*

apparently *k'al gäbba* allows all four types of embedding

(17) *??ammist birri - sätih - zänd k'ali - gäb - all - äh^u*

(18) *? ammɨst bɨrr - ɨndɨ   - sät' - ɨh k'alɨ - gäb - all - äh^u*

As we have seen so far, performative utterances with the *azzäz-* type of verbs are expressed in the perfective form followed by the auxiliary verb *all*, whereas utterances with the *k'al gäbba* type of verbs are expressed in the imperfective form followed by the same auxiliary verb.
Below are listed some examples from each type:

azzäz- type	*k'al gäbba-* type
fäk'k'äd- 'allow'	*lämmän-* 'beg'
wässän- 'decide'	*t'äyyäk'-* 'request'
šälläm-/s'ät'- 'award, give'	+*assassäb-* 'remind'
säyyäm- 'name'	+*astawwäk'-* 'notify'
šom- 'appoint'	*gälläs'-* 'report'
kad- 'denounce'	*däggäf-* 'support'
färräd- 'sentence'	*mal-* 'swear'
+*assänabbät-* 'dismiss'	+*amäläkät-a* 'apply'
+*awärräs-* 'bequeath'	+*amäsäggän-* 'thank'
wäggä^z- 'condemn'	*s'älläy-* 'pray'
gäzzät- 'threaten to excommunicate	*mäkkär-* 'advise'
	+*astänäk'k'k'ak'* 'warn'

+ = these are derived causative stems

The semantic difference between these two categories of verbs seems to be related to the difference in status between the speaker and the hearer. In the *azzäz-* type of verbs the speaker has a higher position than the hearer. According to Searle (1981: 7), such utterances "require extra linguistic institutions for their performance". He goes on to elaborate this point as follows:

> "There are a large number of illocutionary acts that require an extra lin-
> guistic institution and generally, a special position by the speaker and the
> hearer within that institution in order for the act to be performed. Thus,
> in order to bless, excommunicate, christen, pronounce guilty . . . it is not
> sufficient for any old speaker to say to any old hearer, 'I bless', 'I excom-
> municate', etc., one must have a position within an extra linguistic institu-
> tion."

In the second group of verbs, the speaker seems to hold a lower status than the hearer. Most of these verbs generally occur at the end of formal business letters and very rarely in actual conversational situations. In formal letters, they always appear in the imperfective form thus:

(19) . . . *innamäläkkɨtallän* . . . *amäläkkɨtalläh^u* - 'we/I apply'
. . . *int'äyyɨk'allän* . . . *it'äyyɨk'alläh^u* - 'we/I request'
. . . *innasassɨballän* . . . *asassɨballäh^u* - 'we/I remind'
. . . *innɨlämmɨnallän* . . . *ɨlämmɨnalläh^u* - 'we/I beg', etc.

These examples clearly indicate that the addressee is involved in making decisions with respect to the state of affairs explained in the body of the letter. The writer appeals for some kind of decision which has to be made sometime in the future. Hence, the usage of the imperfective form of the verb becomes pertinent. But in the case of the former group of verbs, the decision has to be made in the mind of the speaker before it is announced. Hence, the usage of the perfective form of the verb seems to be appropriate at the time of the announcement to the addressee. Thus, at the court, the judge would say to the guilty disputant:

(20) *y - and a mät issirat färd - än - ibb - ih - all*
      Lit: 'We have sentenced you to one year's imprisonment'
      'We sentence you to one year's imprisonment'

Another feature of these verbs is the fact that they are generally expressed in the passive form without an agent. Thus (20) would be expressed as shown in (21):

(21) *y - and amät issirat tä - färd - o - bb - ih - all*
      'you have been sentenced to one year of imprisonment'
      'you are (hereby) sentenced to one year's imprisonment'

An exception from the list under the *azzäz-* type is the verb *awärräs-* 'bequeath' which cannot be passivized at all in the same manner as the other members of the group. Compare (22) with (23) and (24) with (25):

(22) *kä - zzih biro assänabičč - e - h - all - äh^u*
      Lit: 'I have dismissed you from this office'
      'I dismiss you from this office'

(23) *kä - zzih biro tä-sänabt - äh - all*
      Lit: 'You have been dismissed from this office'
      'You are (hereby) dismissed from this office'

(24) *bet - e - n awriss - e - h - all - äh^u, (wisäd-äw)*
      Lit: 'I have bequeathed my house to you, (take it)'
      'I bequeath my house to you (take it)'

(25) **bet - e - n tä - wärs - äh - all*
      * 'You are bequeathed my house'

It appears to me that the passivization of the second group of verbs would make the utterance sound a bit sarcastic. Let us consider the active and passive forms of the verb *lämmän-* 'beg'.

(26) *bet indi - ti - sära - ll - inni - lämmin-ih - all - äh^u*
      'I beg you to build a house for me'

(27) *? bet indi - ti - sära - ll - inn ti   - llämmän - all - äh*
      'You are begged to build a house for me'

The utterance of (27) cannot be taken as a genuine request for help. In fact the sentence implies that the speaker has no confidence in the ability of the hearer to do what is requested of him. Such an utterance may sometimes be made to tease the hearer in a joking manner. However, most verbs in this group do not allow passivization at all performatively.

NOTES

1. aux = auxiliary

2. comp = complementizer

3. OM = object marker

REFERENCES

G. Gazdar (1979)   *Pragmatics*, Academic Press Inc., New York.

J. L. Austin (1962)   *How To Do Things With Words*, J. O. Urmson (ed.), Oxford, Clarendon Press.

J. R. Searle (1981)   *Expression and Meaning*, Voil-Ballou Press Inc., Binghamton, New York.

Kent Back and Robert M. *Linguistic Communication and Speech Acts*, The MIT Press, Harnish (1979)   Cambridge, London, England.

SEMITIC AND EAST CUSHITIC: WORD-INITIAL LARYNGEALS

Aron Dolgopolsky
University of Haifa

The purpose of the present study is to find regular proto-East Cushitic (EC) etymological correspondences of the proto-Semitic (S) laryngeal consonants (*ʔ, *h, *ḥ, *x, *ʕ, *ɣ) in the word-initial position and to reconstruct the underlying ancestral proto-system of laryngeals. The reconstructed proto-East Cushitic stems and roots are quoted from, or based on, the studies by H.-J. Sasse, P. Black and B. Heine (see References). In the proto-Semitic stems the reconstruction of the accent and of the post-tonic vowels is based on DPhS and DNE.

A. Semitic *ʔ- corresponds to East Cushitic *ʔ-:

(1) S *ʔanī́ (∿ *ʔana) 'I' [> Heb. ʔănī́, Aram. ʔănā́, Arab. ʔanā́, Eth. ʔana] = EC *ʔani/u 'I' [> Saho, Afar anu, Somali an, ani-, Rendille, Boni ani, Bayso ani/a, anni, Oromo ani (subj.)/ana (obj.), Konso an-ti/an-a, Gidole an-to/an(-a), Sidamo ane, ani, Darasa, Kambatta, Hadiya ani, Burji áni, Dullay an-o] (SE 26, D 210).

(2) S *ʔanta 'thou' m., *ʔanti 'thou' f. [> Akkad. atta m., atti f., Heb. ʔattā́ m., ʔattə f., Arab. ʔanta m., ʔanti f., Eth. ʔanta m., ʔantī f., etc.] = EC *ʔati/u 'thou' [> Saho, Afar atu, Somali adi-, Boni adi, Rendille, Bayso, Oromo, Darasa, Hadiya ati, Sidamo ate, ati, Konso, Gidole at-ti, Burji áši, Gollango ato, etc.]. Cp. also the pl. forms: S *ʔantim 'you' pl. m. [> Heb. ʔattém, Arab. ʔantumu, Eth. ʔantəmū, etc.], *ʔantim-na > *ʔantinna 'you' pl. f. = EC *ʔatin 'you' pl. [> Saho, Afar, Rendille atin, Somali idin-, Dasenech itti(ni), Tsamay atun-i, Burji ašínu, etc.] (SE 29, D 133-5).

(3) S *ʔayy- 'which?', stem of interrogative pronouns (and adverbs) [> Arab. ʔayy-, Eth. ʔay, Heb. ʔê-zē 'which?', Akk. ay(y)akam 'where?', etc.] = EC *ʔay 'who?' [> Saho, Boni ay, Somali ayy-o, Oromo ē-nnu 'who?', ē-sa 'where?', Konso ay-no 'who?', ay-ša 'where?', Gidole ay-no, Sidamo, Hadiya ay, ayye, Burji áyye 'who?'] (SE 30).

(4) S *ʔab- (ending-stressed: acc. *ʔabá, nom. *ʔabú, gen. *ʔabí) 'father' [> Arab. ʔab-, Heb. ʔaḇ, Eth. ʔab, etc., cf. DPhS 1-7] = EC *ʔabb- (∿ *ʔābb-) 'father' [> Saho, Afar abb-a, Somali ābb-e 'father', abb-ān 'protector', Rendille ab-a, Bayso ab-o, Oromo ābb-ō, Konso āpp-a, Hadiya ābb-a, Burji ābb-ó] (SE 21).

(5) S *ʔarw {∇y}- 'beast, large animal' [> Heb. ʔaryē 'lion', Eth. ʔarwē 'beast', Aram., Syr. ʔaryā 'lion', Arab. ʔarwīyat- 'wild sheep'] = EC *ʔawr- 'large male animal' [> Saho awr 'bull', Somali awr 'he-camel', Rendille or 'he-camel, bull', Boni ōr 'male elephant', Dasenech ʔawr-ič 'he-camel', Oromo ōrr-ō 'burden camels'] (SE 45-6).

(6) S *ʔarbaʕ- 'four' [> Arab. ʔarbaʕ-, Heb. ʔarbáʕ, etc.] = EC *ʔaf{a}r- 'four' [> Saho afar, Somali afar, Rendille afar, Bayso afar(i), Arbore afar-a, Oromo, Konso, Gidole afur, Dasenech ʔaffur]. The sequence of the word-medial consonants in S is to be explained by metathesis resembling that found in Oromo (Moreno) arfāni 'four persons', arfāfa 'fourth' (D 136, 231-2, B 104, 167, 153)

(7) S *√ʔry 'to gather, collect' [> Heb. √ʔry/w (pf. ʔārā) 'to pluck, gather', Eth. (Geez) √ʔry (pf. ʔaraya), Tigrinya √ʔry (pf. ʔaräyä) 'to collect', Tigre √ʔry (pf. ʔara) 'to collect, heap up', Akkad. arū 'granary'] = EC: proto-Sam *ùrùùri 'to gather' [> Somali ururi, Rendille u'rúri, Boni erúri]. Here proto-Sam *Ø- (zero) < EC *ʔ-. See H 75.

(8) S *ʔurr- 'sunshine, light' [> Akkad. *urru* 'day', Heb. ʔōr 'light', Ugar. ʔr 'beleuchten'] = EC **ʔur- > Afar *ur-* 'to burn' (itr.).

(9) S **√ʔrg > Arab. √ʔrǧ (pf. *ʔariǧa*) 'to smell fragrant', *ʔariǧ-* 'good smell, perfume, scent' = EC: proto-Sam *ur-* 'odor, smell' (n.) [> Boni, Rendille, Somali *ur-*]. Proto-Sam Ø- < EC *ʔ-. See H 75.

Occasionally EC *ʔV- (*ʔ- + vowel) corresponds to zero in S:

(10) S *p- 'mouth' (ending-stressed: acc. *p-á, nom. *p-ú, gen. *p-i) [> Arab. st. constr. nom. *fū*, gen. *fī*, etc., Heb. *pē* (<*pí* gen.), st. costr. *pī*, Samar. Heb. *fā*, st. c. *fī*, Ugar. *p*, Akkad. *pû-m*, OAkk. *pā'um, pī um*, OAram. *pm*, Bibl. Aram. *pum* < *pú-m* st. det., see DPhS 1-7] = EC *ʔaf- 'mouth' [> Saho, Afar, Somali, Rendille, Boni *af*, Dasenech ʔaf-u, Oromo *af-āni*, Konso *af-ā*, Sidamo, Darasa *af-o*, Hadiya *af-oʔo*, Burji *af-ay*] (SE 19, 51, SB 23, B 99, D 230).

(11) S *śikk-/*śukk-/*śawk- 'thorn' [*śikk-/*śukk- > Heb. *śek̲* (pl. *śikkîm*) 'thorn', *śukkā* 'sharp weapon', Jewish Aram. *sikkə̱tā*, Syr. *sekkə̱tā*, Arab. *šikkat-* 'sharp weapon'; *śawk- > Arab. *šawk-*, Eth. *śōk* 'thorn'] = EC *ʔilk- 'tooth' [> Saho *ik-o*, Somali *ilig*, pl. *ilk-o*, Rendille, *ilaḫ*, pl. *ilko*, Bayso pl. *ilko*, Boni pl. *ilke*, Elmolo pl. *ilkoʔ*, Arbore *ilkwa*, Oromo *ilk-āni*, Konso *ilk-ittu*, Gollango *ilke* pl. etc] (SE 12, B 190). Here EC *l goes back to *ś, cp. South Cushitic *ʔiśikᵂa 'tooth' (see E 17, 292, DLC #66).

In these cases the S stems are likely to have lost the initial *ʔ- together with the following vowel (under special prosodic conditions), e.g. Pre-Sem. *ʔap-V́ 'mouth' > S *p-V́.

B. Semitic *h- corresponds to East Cushitic *ʔ-:

(12) S *hárar- 'mountain' [> Heb. *har* 'mountain' (< *háraru*), pl. st. c. *harərê*, *hărārêhā* 'her mountains'', Phoen. *hr*, Old Canaanite (in Akkad. transcription) *xarri*] = EC *ʔurr-/*ʔirr- 'top, mountain' [> Burji *urr-a* 'mountain', Oromo *irr-a* 'on top of', Konso *irr-ōta* 'mountain', Dasenech ʔurr-u 'above, sky', Elmolo *urr-u* 'above', Saho, Afar *ir-o* 'outside, away, abroad'] (SB 134).

(13) S *√hll 'to begin to shine (heavenly body)', 'daylight' (→ 'spend the day' → 'be') [> Arab. √hll (pf. *halla*) 'to appear (new moon)', Heb. (caus.) impf. 3 sg. m. *yāhél*, 3 pl. *yāhéllû* 'to make shine, to shine', Eth. *hallawa* 'to be' (subj. *yahallū*), Arab. *hilāl-*, Eth. *həlāl* 'new moon'] = EC *ʔōl- 'to spend the day, to stay' [> Oromo, Konso *ōl-* 'to spend the day', Gidole (benefactive) *ol-aḍ-* 'to be late', Somali *ōl* 'did not stay'] (a blend with *√wʕl 'to stay, be' > Burji *wol-ʔ-* 'to pass the time, stay', Hadiya *wull-* 'to stand'?) (SB 188).

(14) S *√hbb 'flower, to bloom' > Syr. *habbə̱tā*, pl. *habbê* 'flower', *habbāb̲-ā* 'flower', *hab* (pf.) 'floruit' and possibly Amh., Argobba, Gafat, Masqan, Gogot, Soddo *abäba* 'flower' (if these are not borrowed from Cushitic) = EC (?) *{ʔ}ambab- 'flower' [> Saho, Afar *ambab* 'flower', Močča Oromo (Dolgopolsky) *ababo* 'flower (sp.)'. The stem is found in Agaw: Kemant (Conti-Rossini) *ambāb*, Bilin (Reinisch) *ambōba* 'flower'. Tigre, Tigrinya ʕambäbä 'to bloom' and Tigre ʕəmboba 'flower' are Cushitic loan-words (ʕ due to phonological reinterpretation in the process of borrowing?). Cp. D 235, LG III: 6.

(15) S: Arab. *hurnuʕ-, hurnūʕ-* 'louse' = EC *ʔingir- 'louse' [> Somali, Rendille *inʒir*, Boni *iśir*, Elmolo *iŋkir*, Arbore *ingir-a*, Oromo *inʒir-āni*] (B 182, SB 103). Does Saho (Reinisch) *ingaʕ* 'louse' belong here?

In some stems proto-East Cushitic lost the initial *ʔ- together with the following vowel:

(16) S *√hdp 'to push, thrust' (→ 'to hurry') [> Heb. √hdp 'to thrust, push, drive', Aram. √hdp 'to thrust, hurry', Tigre √hdf 'to come unexpectedly', hədf belä 'to do hastily, unexpectedly'] = EC *ḏīb- (< *ʔdīb-?) 'to push' [> Oromo ḏīb-, Burji ḏīb-, Sidamo ṯīb-].

(17) S *√hyʕ 'to flow' [> Sabaic √hyʕ 'to flow, run', hyʕ 'flow of water, libation', Arab. √hyʕ 'to fuse (lead), to flow, be spread, vomit', hayʕ- (n. act.) 'flow'] = EC *yaʕ- or *yaʕ- 'to flow away' [> Burji yaʔ- 'to flow', Somali yaʕ- 'to run away', Oromo yaʔ-, Gidole yeʔ- 'to fall down in particles, to sprinkle down'] (SB 192).

C. There is a correspondence between Semitic *ḥ- and East Cushitic *ḥ-:

(18) S *ḥall- 'clean, pure' [> Akkad. ellu 'clean, pure', Syriac ḥallel 'to clean', Jewish Aramaic (Targum) ḥallel 'to wash, rinse'] = EC: Somali ḥal- 'to wash' (Somali ḥ- points to EC *ḥ-).

(19) S *√ḥkk ∿ *√ḥkk 'to scratch' [*√ḥkk > Middle Heb. √ḥkk 'to rub, scratch', Syr. √ḥkk 'rasit, prurivit, fricuit', Arab. √ḥkk 'rub, scrape', Eth. (Geez) √ḥkk, Tigrinya ḥakäkä, Tigre ḥakkä 'to scrape, rub', Akkad. ekēku 'to scratch'; S *√ḥkk >Heb. √ḥkk 'to cut in', Phoen., Yaudic √ḥkk 'eingraben', Aram. √ḥkk, Arab. √ḥqq 'to furrow'] = EC *ḥek- ∿ *ḥok- 'to scratch' [> Saho ḥokuk-, Somali ḥoq-, Rendille ox-, Boni hoʔ-, Arbore hek-, Oromo hōk-, Gidole hek- 'to scratch', Burji hokok- 'to scratch oneself'] (SB 100).

(20) S **√ḥbw > Arab. √ḥbw 'to draw near, to give' = EC *-{ḥ}iw-, *-{ḥ}uw- ({ḥ} is *ḥ or *h) 'to give' [> Saho -oḥo-/-uḥu-, Afar -eḥe- (with a final morphophonemic /w/, as shown by R. Hayward), Sidamo uw(w)-, Burji uww- 'to give'] (SB 185).

(21) S *ḥadd- 'sharp' [> Heb. ḥad, pl. ḥaddîm, Arab. ḥadd- 'sharp', Akkad. eddu 'pointed'] = EC *ḥād- 'to shave' [> Elmolo het- 'to shave', hēt-o 'shaving knife', Oromo hād-, Konso, Gidole hāt-, Burji had- 'to shave'] (SB 37).

(22) S: Arab. √ḥlʔ 'to strike with a sword' = EC **ḥal- > Somali ḥalālay- 'to circumcise, to cut the throat'. The comparison is supported by a South Cushitic cognate: South Cush. **ḥal- 'to cut off' (> Dahalo ḥalīṭe 'knife', see E 334, DLC #26).

(23) S **ḥígz- or **ḥíg√z- > Arab. ḥigz- 'root' = EC *ḥizz- 'root, blood vessel' [> Somali ḥidid, Rendille ḥiy, Boni, Bayso hidid, Dasenech hiz, Elmolo hiwe, Oromo hidd-a, Konso hitt-ina, Gidole hitt-in, Arbore hiyds-o-koro, Harso ḥiss-e, Gawwada hitte, hitte, hisse 'root', Burji hidd-i 'root, blood vessel'] (EC *-zz- < *-gz- by assimilation) (SB 95, B 177, 200, 256, SE 20, 36, H 64).

(24) S *ḥúpn- or *ḥúp√n- 'hand, hollow of hand' [> Heb. ḥóφen 'hollow of hand', Aram., Syr. ḥuφnā 'hollow of hand, handful', Arab. ḥufn-at- ∿ ḥafn-at- 'handful', Akkad. upnu 'fist, hand'] = EC *ḥubn- 'limb, muscle' [> Somali ḥubin (pl. ḥubn-o) 'limb', Oromo humn-a 'energy', Konso hupn-a 'power, strength'] (SE 15, 58, B107).

(25) (?) S **√{ḥ}mk ({ḥ} is *ḥ or *ʕ) > Akkad. emūku 'strength' = EC: proto-Sam *hōg 'strength' [> Somali hōga, Boni hōg] (proto-Sam *ḥ- goes back to EC *ḥ-) (H 64).

(26) S biconsonantal base *ḥr-: *√ḥrϑ 'to plough, to dig' [> Heb. √ḥrš, Ugar., Arab √ḥrϑ, Eth. √ḥrs, Akkad. erēšu], *√ḥrṣ 'to cut in, cut down, dig (in)' [> Heb √ḥrṣ 'to sharpen, cut', Ugar. ḥrṣ 'furrow, wrinkle', Arab. ḥarṣat- 'a wound tearing the skin, a hole in a garment'; West Sem. → Akkad. √xrṣ 'to cut down, incise'] = EC *ha(a)r-, *harʔ- or *haʔr- 'to scrape' (→ 'to plough') [> Afar hār-is- 'to clean out contents of viscera', Rendille ḥar- 'to sweep', Elmolo her-r-, Konso har- 'to scoop soil from hole', Oromo har- ∿ hār- 'to

sweep, clear out', Gidole *hār-awwa* 'razor', Hadiya *hār-* 'to scratch', Burji *harʔ-* 'to plough, cultivate'] (SB 92).

(27) S **√*ḥyr* > Arab. *ḥiyar-* ∿ *ḥayar-* 'multa pecora et magnam familiam habens' = EC **ḥor-* 'to breed' [> Oromo *hor-ī* 'cattle, livestock', Konso *hor-ēta* 'wealth, livestock', Gidole *horet* 'cattle', *hor-* 'to multiply (domestic animals)', Hadiya *hoʔl-* (v. mid. < **hor-ḍ-*) 'to increase, breed', Burji *hor-ʔ-* ∿ *hor-aḍ-* 'to breed'] (SB 101).

In one root the S correspondence of the EC **ḥ-* happens to be **x-* (instead of the expected **ḥ-*):

(28) S *√*xyṭ* 'to sew' > Arab. √*xyṭ* (pf. *xāṭa*, impf. *-xīṭu*) 'to sew up', Middle Hebrew, Syriac √*ḥwṭ* (pf. *ḥāṭ*, impf. *-ḥūṭ*) 'to sew' = EC **ḥiḍ-* 'to tie' (→ 'to sew') [> Afar *ḥiḍ*, 'to attach camels in Indian file', *-idḥiḍ-* 'to sew', Somali, Rendille *ḥiḍ-*, Boni *hir-*, Oromo, Konso, Gidole, Burji *ḥiḍ-*, Dasenech *hiz/t-*, Yāku *hed-* 'to tie'] (SB 96, B 201, 260, 195, H 64).
   The ancient meaning is likely to be 'to tie', with a later semantic change 'to tie' → 'to sew' independently in Semitic and in Afar.
   The deviation of the regular correspondence of the initial laryngeals (S **x-* instead of **ḥ-*) is most probably due to the influence of the S word **xūṭ-* 'thread'.

D. In the presence of **g* East Cushitic **ḥ-* corresponds to Semitic **ḥ-:

(29) S *√*ḥgb* 'to cover' [> Arab. √*ḥǧb* 'to veil', *ḥiǧāb-* 'veil, screen', Jibbāli *ḥɔ́tgəb* 'to wrap and tie a cloth round one's knees and sit cross-legged'] = EC **hagōg-* 'to cover over' [> Saho *agōg-* 'to be covered with clothes', Somali *hagog* 'cloth draped over one's head', Rendille *agog-* 'to cover', Oromo *hagōg-aḍ-*] (SE 39, 40).

(30) S *√*ḥngr* > Arab. *ḥunǧūr-* 'larynx', *ḥanǧarat-* 'larynx', Jibbāli *ḥangɔ́rɔ́t* (pl. *ḥonúgər*) 'hollow under the Adam's apple' = EC: proto-Sam **hangúri* 'throat' [> Somali *hunguri*, Boni *ha ŋurᵉ*](H 63).

(31) S *√*ḥgw* 'to remain' [> Arab. √*ḥġw* 'to remain', Mehri, Ḥarsusi *ḥátgi* 'to stay with one's family', Jibbāli *oḥógi* 'to wait'] = EC **heg-/*hog-* 'to stand' [> Saho *og-us-* (caus.) 'to lift', *og-ut-* (refl.) 'to get up', Somali *hinȝ-i-* (caus.) 'to lift', Oromo *heȝ-* ∿ *eȝ-* 'to stand'] (SE 39).

In order to account for the undermentioned cognate set (38) (EC **hur-* 'to recover from illness' = S √*xrg* 'to go out') we must try a more accurate definition of the conditioning factor: EC initial **h* corresponds to S initial **ḥ* (rather than **x*) in the presence of a root-medial **g* in the Semitic root.

E. East Cushitic **h-* corresponds to Semitic **x-* (unless there is a root-medial **g* in Semitic):

(32) S **(-)xūr-* (√*xwr*) '(to be) weak, little' [> Arab. √*xwr* (pf. *xāra*, impf. *-xūru*) 'to be weak', Mehri *xawr*, Ḥarsusi *xerōn*, Jibbāli *xérín*, Soqoṭri *ḥareren* 'a little', (??) Akkad. *xūrū* 'son'] = EC **har-* 'to become tired or weak' [> Rendille *har-* ∿ *ar-*, Elmolo *anan-ar-e* 'to become tired', Konso *har-* 'to grow weaker or poorer'] (SE 40).

(33) S **xáraʔ-* 'dung, excrement' [> Heb. (pl.) *ḥărāʔîm*, Arab. *xarʔ-*, Syriac *ḥeryā*, Jewish Aramaic (transliteration) *ḥryʔ*, Tigrinya *ḥarʔī*, Amh. *ar*, etc. 'dung, excrement'] = EC: proto-Sam **hār-* 'diarrhoea, excrement' > Somali *har* 'human excrement', Boni *hār*, Rendille *har* 'diarrhoea'; Afar *hara* 'dung, excrement' is likely to be an Arabic loan-word (since in an inherited word an initial zero is expected); see H62.

(34) S *√xbl 'to injure' [> Heb., Aram. √ḥbl 'to injure', Arab. √xbl 'to corrupt, to disorder the brain, to cripple', Sabaic xbl 'ruin' (n.), Akkad. √xbl (inf. xabālu) 'to oppress, to ravage, to undo', xibiltu 'damage; wrong, evil deed'] = EC *hub- 'to injure' [> Oromo hub- 'to injure', Somali hub 'weapons', Sidamo (h)ub-, Hadiya ubb- 'to fall, raid'] (SE 40).

(35) S*√xdr (*'to sleep' →) 'to live (wohnen)', 'to be benumbed', 'to be dark' [> Arab. √xdr 'to remain and keep to (a place)', 'to be benumbed (limb)', Sabaic √xdr '(?) to remain', Eth. √xdr 'to live, dwell (wohnen)', 'to stay'], whence S *xádar- ∿ xíd∇r- 'sleeping place' → 'inner room, dark room, dark place' [> Biblical Heb. ḥéder 'inner room, chamber (private, as bedroom)', Epigr. Heb., Phoen. ḥdr '(funeral) chamber', Arab. xidr- 'inner room', xadar- 'dark place', Tigrinya xǝdró 'logement de nuit', Sabaic xdr 'chamber, funeral chamber'] = EC *-hdir-/*-hdur-/*hudr- 'to sleep' [> Afar -iḥdir-, Somali hurd-, inf. hurud, Rendille udur-/urd-, Bayso (h)udur- 'to sleep'] (SE 40-1, B 139).

(36) S: Akkad. xarr- 'watercourse (canal, wadi, ravine)', (?) Arab. xarxar- 'water flowing abundantly' = EC *har- 'pond, creek, brook' [> Saho ar-a 'river, brook', Somali har-o 'lake', Arbore har-u 'river', Oromo har-ō 'swamp, artificial pond', Eastern Oromo har-ō/i 'lake', (?) Burji har- 'to flow'] (SE 39, SB 91).

(37) S *√xbʔ ∿ *√xby 'to conceal, darkness' [> Akkad. xabû, Arab. √xbʔ (pf. xabaʔa, impf. -xbiʔ-), Eth. √xbʔ (pf. xabʔa, subj. -xbāʔ) 'to conceal', Heb. neḥbā (pass. of √ḥbʔ) 'to hide oneself', heḥbî (caus. of √ḥbʔ) 'to hide' (tr.), Syr. ḥubyā 'darkness', Sabaic √xbʔ 'to conceal'] = EC *hawn-/*hawēn- 'darkness, night' [> Yāku ʔaun 'darkness', Somali habēn, Boni hawēn, Rendille ibēn, Dullay awn-e 'night'] (SE 40).

(38) S*√xrg 'to go out' [> Arab. √xrǧ 'to go out', Ḥarsusi √xrg 'to go out, to die', Jibbāli √xrg 'to die', Middle Heb. ḥōrēg 'step-son' (← 'external' ← 'going out'); Bibl. Heb. √ḥrg 'to go quaking out' is a merger of two S roots: *√xrg 'to go out' and *√ḥrg 'to quake, fear' [> Arab. √ḥrǧ 'to be unable for fear and rage')] = EC *hur- 'to recover from illness' [> Saho, Afar ur-, Sidamo, Burji hur- 'to recover (from illness)', Somali hur- 'to begin to burn up well (fire)'] (SE 39, 40, SB 102).

(39) S: Arab. xubb- 'bark (of a tree)' = EC *huww- 'to cover' (→ 'to dress, wear') [> Somali huw-ad- 'to drape oneself in a garment', Wollega Oromo uww-is- (caus.) 'to cover, to dress', Konso, Gidole uww-aḍ- 'to wear'] (SE 38, B 173, 204).

(40) S *√xbr 'to raise a clamour' (→ 'to announce' → 'to know') [> Akkad. √xbr (inf. xabāru) 'to raise a clamour, to be noisy', Arab. √xbr (G-stem: pf. xabara, impf. -xbur-) 'to know', (D-stem : xabbara) 'to inform', Heb. √hbr (pf. hāḇar) 'beschwören' (Dt. 18:11, Ps 58:6), Eth. √xbr (pf. xabra) 'conspirare, conjurare' (merger with the verb *√xbr 'to tie' derived from *xîb⟨∇⟩r- 'knot, tie')] = EC *habār- 'to curse' [> Saho, Rendille, Oromo abar-, Somali, Boni habar-] (SE 39, 40).

F. Semitic *ʕ- corresponds to East Cushitic *ʕ-:

(41) S *ʕal- 'top' [> Heb. ʕāl, ʕal 'height', Arab. ʕalu 'upper part', etc.], whence S *ʕalay 'on' [> Heb. ʕal, ʕālê (ʕāláyiḵ 'on you' sg. f. < *ʕalay-ki), Arab. ʕalā, ʕalay-, Akkad. eli, etc.] = EC *ʕal- 'mountain, highland' [> Saho ʔal 'mountain', Somali ʕal 'any lofty coastal range of mountains', Rendille ḥal 'mountain', Dullay ʕal-e 'mountain, highland'] (SE 35-6).

(42) S: Arab. √ʕbb 'to swallow, drink the whole of' = EC *ʕab-/*-aʕab- 'to drink' [> Afar

-aʕab- (pf.), -aʕub- (juss.), Saho -ōʕob- (pf.), Somali ʕabb- 'to drink'] (B 150, D 139, 225-6).

(43) S *ʕawd- 'circle' [> Heb. ṣôḏ 'a going round, continuance', Eth. ʕawd 'circuit, circle'], whence *ʕawd-{i} (gen. form?) 'rursum' → 'again' [> Heb. ṣôḏ 'again', Bibl. Aramaic ṣôd 'again', Eth. ʕādi 'again, once again'] = EC *ʕawd- 'round place' → 'threshing ground, kraal' [> Bayso awd, Oromo ūd-a, Konso, Gidole awt- 'kraal', Kambatta, Alaba ōd-u, Hadiya ōd-oʔo, Burji óyd-a, Dullay ʕawt-o 'threshing ground'] (SB 157).

(44) S **√ʕll > Arab. √ʕll 'to drink for the second time' = EC *ʕalal- or *ʕalāl- 'to chew the cud' [> Somali ʕalāl- 'to chew, ruminate', Oromo alal-a 'cud', Konso, Gidole, Burji alal- 'to chew the cud'] (SB 25).

(45) S **√ʕlhṣ > Arab. muʕalhaṣ- 'raw' = EC **ʕayḍ- > proto-Sam *ʕayḍi 'unripe' [> Somali ʕaydin, ʕeḏin, Boni ēri, Rendille ḥēḏi] (< **√ʕṣĉ- < **√lhʕĉ-; see H 77; on *-lh- > *-ṣ- in Cushitic see DLC ## 84-86). Does Saho ʕelō 'raw meat' (RSh 62) belong here (-l- < EC *-l- < *-ṣ-)?

(46) S: Arab. ʕaylam- 'a well with much water' or 'a well with salted water' = EC *ʕel- 'water-hole, a well' [> Saho, Afar ʕel-a, Somali ʕel, Dasenech ʕel-, Borana Oromo ēl-a, Konso el-a, Gidole ēl 'water-hole, well', Burji ēl-a, Dullay ʕel-, Yāku ēl- 'water-hole', Sidamo ēl-a 'river', Hadiya ēr-a 'salt lake', Elmolo ēl 'grave'] (B109, 113, SB 67).

(47) S *√ʕwy 'to cry' [> Arab. عَلَى وَى ʕawā pf./yuʕāwī impf. (form III from √ʕwy) 'clamavit cum aliquo', Jibbāli √ʕwy (pf. ʕe, subj. yaʕbé) 'to bark, whine, howl (dog, wolf), to yap(child)'] = EC *ʕiyy- 'to cry' [> Somali ʕiyy-, Bayso iy-, Oromo iyy- 'to cry', Burji iy- 'to cry for help'] (SB 108).

(48) S **-ʕīg- > Arab. ʕyg (impf. -ʕīg-) 'to quench one's thirst' = EC *ʕig-/*ʕug-/*ʕag- 'to drink' [> Dullay ʕuk-, Boni -aʔak-/-iʔik-, Arbore -iyg-, Dasenech, Elmolo ʔik-, Konso uk-, Gidole uk-, Sidamo ag-, Yāku ek- (< *ʕag-)] (B 108, SE 17).

(49) S *ʕiś(√)b- 'grass, herbage' [> Heb. ʕéśeb, Bibl. Aram. ʕisbā, Syr. ʕesbā, Arab. ʕušb-, Akkad. išbabtu 'grass, herbage', Sabaic ʕs₃b 'pasture-land'] = EC *ʕaws- ∽ *ʕayš- 'grass' [> Saho, Afar, ʕays-o 'vegetables, grass', Somali ʕaws 'dry grass', Rendille ḥos, Boni āse, Bayso ēs, Dasenech ʔīš, Sidamo ays-o 'grass', Dullay ʕaš-ko 'grass', Oromo ēs 'a kind of corn'] (SE 44, 45, B215, H77). The reason for EC *š instead of the expected *l < *ś is not clear.

(50) S *√ʕyb 'defect, guilt, shame' [> Arab. √ʕyb (pf. ʕāba, impf. -ʕīb-) 'to have a blemish, a defect', ʕayb- 'vice, defect', Jewish Aram. ʕayyābā 'guilty', Syr. ʕayyeb 'irrisit, derisit, subsannavit', Eastern Neo-Aramaic (Zakho) ʕēba 'shame, reproach' (AH II/2:105)] = LEC (Lowland East Cushitic) *ʕeb- 'to be ashamed' > Somali ʕebay- 'to put to shame'. (B 109, 113).

G. Semitic *γ- corresponds to East Cushitic *ʕ-:

(51) S *√γyb 'to lack knowledge, to be hidden' [> Arab. γayb- 'whatever is hidden from one, mystery', Mehri, Ḥarsusi, Jibbāli √γyb 'to faint', (?) Soqotri √ʕyf (pf. ʕeyhof) 'to disappear'] and probably S *√γhb >Arab. √γhb 'to neglect, forget' = LEC *ʕeb- 'to be foolish' [> Konso, Gidole ēp- 'to be foolish' (merger with EC *ʕeb- 'to be ashamed', see above (50))] (B 109, 113).

(52) (?) S *√γll '(?) to be hostile' [> Arab. γill- 'enmity, rancour, malevolence',√γll (pf, γalla,

634

impf. -γill-)'to be filled with hatred', ʔaγalla 'to make a raid', Sabaic √γll 'to be angry'] =
EC *Ꞩol- 'war' [> Somali Ꞩol 'army, enemy', Boni ol, Rendille ḥol, Hadiya or-a 'war', Elmolo is-olol 'quarrel', Oromo lōl- (< *olōl- < *ꞨolꞨol-) 'fight'] (SE 21, B 243, H 77).

(53) S *√γly 'to boil (in cooking)' [> Arab. γly (impf. -γliy-) 'to boil (cooking pot)', Jibbāli
aγlé 'to put (milk) on to boil', γútli 'to boil, be boiling'] = LEC *Ꞩul- 'to smoke out in
order to clean' [> Somali Ꞩuley- 'branch, or grass, burned in order to clean a milk vessel',
Wollega Oromo, Gidole ul- 'to smoke out a beehive or container', Konso il- 'to smoke out
a beehive'] (B 108).

(54) S **√γlð > Arab. √γlð 'to be thick, heavy' = EC *Ꞩils-/*Ꞩuls- 'to be heavy' [> Afar Ꞩils-i,
Somali Ꞩulus, Boni ules, Dasenech iliš, Elmolo ils-iḍa, Arbore ilč-iyḍa, Oromo ulf-ataʔ
'heavy', Konso uls- 'heavy', Rendille ḥules 'weight'] (SE 5,6, B 139, 168, H 78, D 141).

(55) S *√γṣṣ 'to be narrow' [> Arab. γuṣṣat- 'obstructing the throat, stopping the breath (food,
anger, grief)', √γṣṣ 'to be choked by smth.', Jibbali maγṣéṣ, maγéṣ 'small path between
houses (← *'narrow place')] = EC *Ꞩ{u}ç∇ç- or *Ꞩ{u}ḍ∇ḍ- ({u} = *u or *i) 'to be narrow,
short' [> Somali Ꞩiḍīḍi 'narrowness', Saho uḍuḍ 'short'] (D 248).

(56) S: Arab. γayṭam- 'thick milk' = EC *Ꞩiṭ- 'curds' (< *Ꞩiṭ-t-?) [> Saho, Afar -i-t-Ꞩit- 'to
curdle', Afar Ꞩit-ta 'curds', Somali ḍit-o (< *tꞨit-to?) 'curdled milk', Bayso it-at- 'to clot
(milk, blood)', Oromo itit- 'to curdle', itit-tū 'curds'] (SB 108).

(57) S: Arab. √γϑr 'être rouge clair, rouge brun' = LEC *Ꞩas- 'red' [> Afar Ꞩas- 'to be red',
Somali Ꞩas 'red'] (B 203).

(58) S: Arab. √γδw 'to feed', γaδw- 'feeding' (n. act.) = EC *Ꞩa{z}- ({z} is *z or *d) > LEC
*Ꞩad- 'meat' [> Somali Ꞩad 'piece of meat', Saho hado, Afar ḥādo 'meat'] (B 219, D 161,
294).

(59) S *√γrr 'to be white' [> Arab. √γrr (pf. γarra, impf. -γarr-) 'to be white (complexion)', Jibbāli γórór 'pure, saltless water'] = EC *Ꞩarr- ∿ *Ꞩirr- '«white» (i.e. grey) hair' [> Somali
Ꞩirr-o, Oromo arr-ī, Dullay Ꞩarr-e 'grey hair', Burji arr-ē las 'to go grey (hair)'] (SB 28).

CONCLUSIONS

The correspondences of the initial laryngeals may be summarized as follows:

	Semitic	East Cushitic	Conditions
A	*ʔ	*ʔ	—
B	*h	*ʔ	—
C	*ḥ	*ḥ	—
D	*ḥ	*ḥ	in the presence of a root-medial *g in Semitic
E	*x	*ḥ	if there is no root-medial *g in S
F	*Ꞩ	*Ꞩ	—
G	*γ	*Ꞩ	—

For the first pair of correspondences (A and B) we must choose between two theoretically
possible explanations: (1) two ancient phonemes (labelled *ʔ and *h) have been preserved in
Semitic and have merged in EC, (2) one ancient phoneme has been preserved in East Cushitic
and has split in S, i.e. it has changed into two different phonemes under different conditions.
The latter hypothesis is acceptable only if there is complementary distribution between the
Semitic reflexes (*ʔ and *h) dependent on some conditioning factor. Since no such comple-

mentary distribution is observed, the latter explanation (split in S) is to be rejected, and the former hypothesis (merger in EC) is the only acceptable one. In other words, we must assume that in the proto-system (to be labelled "proto-Semito-Cushitic" = pSC) there were two phonemes: *ʔ- (> S *ʔ-, EC *ʔ-) and *h- (> S *h-, EC *ʔ-). *Mutatis mutandis*, the same is true of the pair of correspondences F and G: among the two theoretically possible explanations (merger and split) the former is the only acceptable one, so that we must assume two proto-phonemes: *ʕ- (> S *ʕ-, EC *ʕ-) and *γ- (> S *γ-, EC *ʕ-).

In the case of D (S *ḫ-, EC *h-) and E (S *x-, EC *h-) the situation is different. There is a conditioning factor (presence vs. absence of a root-medial *g in S) responsible for the complementary distribution of the Semitic reflexes. Hence we must accept the hypothesis of split in S: pSC *x- > pre-Sem. *x- and EC *h-, subsequently pre-Sem. *x- changed to *ḫ- in the presence of a root-medial *g (by dissimilation) and remained *x if there was no medial *g.

Our conclusions may be formulated in the following table:

	PSC	>	EC	S	
1.	*ʔ-	>	*ʔ-	*ʔ-	
2.	*h-	>	*ʔ-	*h-	
3.	*ḫ-	>	*ḫ-	*ḫ-	
4.	*x-	>	*h-	*x-	and (in the presence of a root-medial *g) *ḫ-
5.	*ʕ-	>	*ʕ-	*ʕ-	
6.	*γ-	>	*ʕ-	*γ-	

SIGNS AND SYMBOLS

In proto-Semitic and in Sem. languages: *x* stands for traditional *ḥ*, and *ś* for *š*.

In Hebrew: ˆ symbolizes long vowels spelled with *matres lectionis*, ˘ is used to denote super-short vowels (hăṭāphīm).

In Arabic: ǧ is ح , δ is ظ

In Geez: ś symbolizes Ŝawt.

In all languages: ʒ = Engl. *j*, č = Engl. *ch*, ḍ is injective *d*, ḍ is retroflex *d*, q is uvular *k*, ṭ is dental *t* (if opposed to alveolar or gingival *t*). ∇ stands for unspecified vowel. Consonantic roots are symbolized by √. In the reconstructions two types of "uncertainty brackets" are used: brackets { } denote dubious phonemes (* {h} means "*h or the like"), brackets ⟨ ⟩ are used when the very presence of any phoneme is questionable (*xíb⟨∇⟩r- means "*xíb∇r- or *xíbr-"). Glottalized (both ejective and injective) consonants (as well as Arabic uvularized consonants) are dotted: ṭ, ḳ, ṣ, ḍ, etc. Lateral obstruents ("hlaterals") are denoted by a circumflex ˆ: ŝ means "voiceless fricative lateral".

REFERENCES

AH = F. Rosenthal (ed.), *An Aramaic Handbook*, I/1-2, II/1-2 (Wiesbaden, 1961).

B = P. Black, *Lowland East Cushitic: Subgrouping and Reconstruction*, Doctoral diss. (Yale Univ., 1974).

D = A. Dolgopol'skij, *Sravnitel'no-istoričeskaja fonetika kušitskix jazykov* (Moscow, 1973).

DLC = A. Dolgopolsky, "South Cushitic Lateral Consonants as Compared to Semitic and East Cushitic", in H. Jungraithmayr and M. Müller (eds.), *Proceedings of the 4th International Hamito-Semitic Congress*, (Amsterdam, 1987).

DNE = A. Dolgopolsky, "Semitic Nomina Segolata in Ethiopian", in: G. Goldenberg (ed.), *Proceedings of the 6th International Conference on Ethiopian Studies.* (Rotterdam, 1986).

DPhS = A. Dolgopolsky, "On Phonemic Stress in Proto-Semitic", *Israel Oriental Studies* VIII (1978), pp.1-12.

E = Chr. Ehret, *The Historical Reconstruction of Southern Cushitic Phonology and Vocabulary* (Berlin, 1980).

H = B. Heine, "The Sam Languages. A History of Rendille, Boni, and Somali", *Afroasiatic Linguistic* VI (1978), pp.23-115.

LG = W. Leslau, *Etymological Dictionary of Gurage (Ethiopic)*, I-III (Wiesbaden, 1979).

RSh = L. Reinisch, *Die Saho-Sprache, II: Wörterbuch der Saho-Sprache* (Wien, 1890).

SB = H. -J. Sasse, *An Etymological Dictionary of Burji* (Hamburg, 1982).

SE = H. -J. Sasse, "Consonant Phonemes of Proto-East-Cushitic", *Afroasiatic Linguistics* VII (1979), pp.1-67.

SOCIAL TRANSFORMATION IN THE EARLY HISTORY

OF THE HORN OF AFRICA:

Linguistic Clues to Developments of the Period 500 B.C. to A.D. 500

Christopher Ehret

The establishment of Semitic languages in the Horn of Africa during the last millennium B.C. reflects a major set of social transformations. Languages new to an area do not displace other languages from use for trivial reasons of taste or fashion, but normally because the social formations associated with the new languages are spreading at the expense of previous social formations. The patterns of relationship among the Ethiopic languages show that two focal points of spread of the new tongues soon arose, the one much neglected by historians being probably the upper Awash River watershed. The patterns of word borrowing in the languages require that the Semitic speakers were initially a tiny minority and indicate that they added little, if any, new technological or agricultural knowledge to that already present on the south side of the Red Sea.[1] The establishment and spread of Ethiopic languages among the populations of the Horn cannot be attributed thus to technological advantage; rather, it seems probable that the Semitic speakers held the key ground in the spread of new kinds of relations of production or exchange.

I

The framework for historical reconstruction is provided by the subclassification of the Ethiopic languages. The classification which derives from cognate counting in basic vocabulary, and that of Hetzron (1972, 1975, 1977), based on the identification of shared innovations in morphology, are in agreement broadly and often in detail as well. The lexicostatistical matrix (see Appendix 1 for data and analysis, at variance with the proposals of Bender 1971) allows the following scheme of relationships (individual language names italicised):

Ethiopic
    I. North Ethiopic
        A. *Tigre*
        B. *Tigrinya*

    II. South Ethiopic
        A. Cross-Rift
            1. *Amharic, Argobba* (Western Cross-Rift)
            2. Eastern Cross-Rift
                a. *Harari*
                b. *Zway, Walani*
        B. *Gafat*
        C. *Soddo*
        D. Gurage
            1. Chaha-Mäsqan
                a. *Mäsqan*
                b. Chaha-Ennemor
                    i. *Chaha, Geto*
                    ii. *Ennemor*
            2. *Mesmes*

Hetzron includes some additional dialects and languages for which cognate counts are not available; but, for the same languages as those in the lexicostatistical classification, his scheme of relationships has the following form:

Ethiopic
    I. North Ethiopic
        A. *Tigre*
        B. *Tigrinya*
    II. South Ethiopic
        A. Transversal South Ethiopic [= Cross-Rift]
            1. *Amharic, Argobba* (Central Transversal)
            2. Eastern Transversal
                a. *Harari*
                b. *Zway, Walani*
        B. Outer South Ethiopic
            1. "*n* group"
                a. *Gafat*
                b. *Soddo*
            2. "*tt* group" [= Gurage]
                a. *Mäsqan*
                b. "3-tense group"
                    i. *Chaha*
                    ii. *Geto, Ennemor, Mesmes*

Hetzron's classification disagrees at just two points with the one based on cognate counting, one of these a difference only in degree of refinement and the other a contradictory placement.

Firstly, Hetzron feels able from apparent shared morphological innovations to combine Gafat and Soddo into one of two subgroups — the other being the Gurage of the lexicostatistical formulation — which together form an Outer subbranch of South Ethiopic coordinate with the Cross-Rift (Hetzron's Transversal) subbranch recognized by both classifications. The cognate percentages (see Appendix 1) give no indication that Gafat and Soddo are closer related to each other than to other South Ethiopic tongues, nor do they give any basis for establishing an Outer subbranch. The two languages appear from the percentages equally far from the Cross-Rift languages as they are from each other and from the Gurage ("*tt*") group. Neither can any lexical innovations diagnostic of an Outer subbranch be identified in the 100-word list of basic vocabulary. Assuming Hetzron's innovations for an Outer South Ethiopic grouping are not unrecognized archaisms, two histories are possible:

(1) Hetzron is correct is interpreting the shared features as innovations dating to a common proto-Outer South Ethiopic dialect, from which his Outer languages descend. In that case, the proto-Outer dialect was in existence only a very short time, not longer than one or two centuries, from the time of its divergence out of proto-Cross-Rift to that of its own divergence into proto-Gafat-Soddo and proto-Gurage. Proto-Gafat-Soddo would in turn have diverged equally rapidly into separate dialects ancestral to Gafat and Soddo. If any longer period obtained, the shared lexical innovations dating to the common periods of history would begin to be numerous enough to show up in elevated cognate percentages in basic vocabulary.

(2) The shared features are convergent developments, due to contacts dating subsequent to the initial splitting up of proto-South Ethiopic. Cases of such convergence certainly exist in the southerly Ethiopic speech areas as Hetzron (1969) has shown. In this kind of instance, the proto-South Ethiopic speech community would have begun at first to diverge into three or four sets of communities (Cross-Rift, Gafat-Soddo, and Gurage; or Cross-Rift, Gafat, Soddo, and Gurage), but with those communities which developed the particular shared innovations of Hetzron's Outer subbranch remaining for a period in close geographical con-

tact and influencing each other's dialects. In this way we might account for both the mutual divergence implied by the lexical counts and the lack of major lexical innovations indicative of a common proto-Outer period, and yet for the common adoption of a very few new morphological features at the same time.

Both histories require only a slight modification of the history implied in the cognate pattern – the addition of a brief span to the period of the break-up of proto-South Ethiopic social unity, during which some of the derivative communities remained a while in close contact, either as speakers of a common daughter dialect of proto-South Ethiopic, or of two or three mutually interacting dialects.

The second difference in the classifications concerns the placement of Geto, Ennemor and, Mesmes. For reasons discussed in Appendix 1, Mesmes is best placed as the lexicostatistical classification requires, while the relationships among Chaha, Geto and Ennemor might well be as Hetzron has proposed. In any case, the differentiation of the latter three into separate speech communities, with cognates in the eighty percents, lies in much later periods of time than concern us here.

II

From this evidence, plus that of the loanwords and of the geographical distribution of languages, it is possible to chart a series of early periods and locations of Ethiopic-speaking societies in northeastern Africa. The history of Ethiopic languages in the Horn begins with the proto-Ethiopic speaking community.[2] A significant set of innovations unique to that proto-language requires a period of its separate existence as a distinct language separate from its nearest relatives, the South Arabian tongues. Though its language can be shown, by the simple application of the standard least-moves principle of linguistic-historical inference, to have come from the Arabian side of the Red Sea, the proto-Ethiopic community took shape in Africa. The testimony takes the form of a prominent set of loanwords in proto-Ethiopic from an undoubtedly African language. The speakers of proto-Ethiopic probably lived in, or just off, the northern edges of the Ethiopian highlands, because the particular language from which the words were adopted belonged to the Agaw branch of Cushitic (see Appendix 2).

The Agaw loanword set fits the category of borrowing which has been called "intensive general" (Ehret 1981), the most notable characteristic of which is the significant penetration of loanwords into even the 100-word list of core vocabulary. This kind of word-borrowing has demographic and chronological implications. It implies, firstly, that the speakers of the borrowing language were a persistently minority community, for a long time fluent in the donor language as well as their own, before finally the majority population's language began to drop from use in favour of the formerly minority tongue. Secondly, borrowings in basic vocabulary under circumstances of intensive general influence tend to be added, it appears, at a rate of about one or two per century. There seem to be about six Agaw loans in proto-Ethiopic core vocabulary (Appendix 2), indicating that the proto-Ethiopic period had a length of perhaps three to six centuries. Fleming's earlier view that South and North Ethiopic separately derived from South Arabian (Fleming 1968) has some importance at this point. Fleming did not find a clear lexicostatistical indication of a separate proto-Ethiopic period; that lack suggests that a shorter chronology is to be preferred and that the period is likely to have lasted nearer to three centuries than to six.

The proto-Ethiopic period came to an end with the beginning of divergence of the proto-Ethiopic language into proto-North and proto-South Ethiopic dialects. The proto-North Ethiopic speaking society developed among those who remained inhabitants in the northern highland fringes. Over the next few centuries, the North Ethiopic communities may have remained for a while a minority before finally beginning to grow by extensive linguistic assimilation of Agaw populations. At least two more loanwords in basic vocabulary appear to have come into proto-North Ethiopic vocabulary (Appendix 2), indicative of possibly a continuing intensive general influence from Agaw lasting one or two centuries. Thereafter, however, only much less heavy types of word-borrowing appear in the evolution of the North Ethiopic tongues, showing that North Ethiopic speech communities had begun to take on the characteristics of a majority population in their particular regions of habitation.

The proto-South Ethiopic society coalesced around a group of Ethiopic speakers who settled far away to the south, in the upper Awash country. Two mutually confirmatory lines of evidence place them there. One is the linguistic geography of the South Ethiopic languages, with their division into a northern branch, Cross-Rift, the languages of which can be traced back to the areas straddling the Awash watershed, and a second branch or group of branches whose members, except for Gafat, concentrate in the areas immediately south of the upper Awash. The second line of evidence is provided by a major set of loanwords datable to the proto-South Ethiopic language. These loans come from an Eastern Cushitic language, probably related closest to the Highland Eastern Cushitic tongues, spoken still today in areas adjacent to those implied by the linguistic geography to have been the proto-South Ethiopic homeland. (See Appleyard 1975, 1978, for selections of these loans.)

There is also a smaller set of Agaw loanwords apparently limited to South Ethiopic. Their presence could be explained by assuming that the proto-South Ethiopic community first began to emerge as a separate group of people in the northern highland fringe before the movement around to the south, and that the loans were adopted then. But a more economical and satisfactory solution is that the first precursors of the proto-South Ethiopic society moved into a region where Eastern Cushitic- and Agaw-speaking territories conjoined, with the Agaw being perhaps a somewhat less important component in the amalgam of peoples which developed into the proto-South Ethiopic society than the Eastern Cushites. Agaw country in later times lay not so far to the west of the probable areas of original South Ethiopic settlement and could quite reasonably be presumed to have extended at one time as far east almost as the Rift, there touching on the Eastern Cushitic lands in and to the east of the Rift Valley.

The proto-South Ethiopic word borrowings have again the semantic distribution characteristic of the intensive general category of borrowing. The proto-South Ethiopic people must at first have formed a minority element, which only after a period of time began to amalgamate the larger indigenous population into the new society. At least four loanwords in core vocabulary come from the Eastern Cushitic people involved in this social history, and possibly as many as three from the Agaw (Appendix 2). Assuming these to be partially contemporaneous influences, the period of the establishment and subsequent growth of the proto-South Ethiopic society is likely to have lasted around three or four centuries.

The proto-South Ethiopic society thereafter began, over an additional period of one to three centuries (see suggestions as to time span in Section I above), to diverge into a set of four societies, by expansion into areas on the immediate south of the proto-South Ethiopic homeland. The Gafat, judging from their apparent location in medieval times (Shack 1974: 148), probably stem from a community which established itself off to the west, south of the Abbay. The pre-Soddo and the proto-Gurage presumably evolved in or near the areas immediately south and southwest of the upper course of the Awash, where their modern linguistic heirs reside today. The fourth society, the proto-Cross-Rift people, are best considered as made up of the South Ethiopic people who continued to reside in the proto-South Ethiopic homeland. Shortly thereafter, the proto-Cross-Rift society itself underwent a further split into two daughter communities. The Western Cross-Rift people, from whose dialect the Amharic and Argobba languages derive, probably arose among those who continued to occupy parts of the older proto-South Ethiopic country, while the Eastern Cross-Rift society took form perhaps just to the east or southeast in portions of the far upper Shebeelle River watershed. At approximately the same time, the proto-Gurage were also beginning to split into separate pre-Mesmes and proto-Chaha-Mäsqan sets of communities.

The secondary expansions of the early South Semitic peoples initiated a variety of contact situations with surrounding Cushites. Only a very uneven and tiny sampling of the evidence for such contacts has so far been identified, and except for core vocabulary items it is often not yet possible to know whether a particular root word has a wider distribution than has been noted for it or not. Gurage expansion continued the process of interaction with and absorption of

Highland Eastern Cushites which was begun in proto-South Ethiopic times; and the close relations between Gurage and Highland peoples extended right into recent times, as loanwords limited to narrow subgroups of Gurage attest (Appendix 2). Gafat has possibly some Highland Eastern Cushitic loanwords of its own; if so, this evidence supports its very early placement next to the proto-Gurage. The proto-Cross-Rift people and their descendants, the proto-Western Cross-Rift society, may have continued the dual interaction with both Agaw and Eastern Cushites; a number of loanwords have this implication providing they are actually innovations dating to those periods (e.g. roots for 'goat', 'bamboo', 'castrated animal' in Appleyard 1975). Such contacts would be in keeping with the indications of linguistic geography that the proto-Cross-Rift and proto-Western Cross-Rift peoples remained in much the same areas as those inhabited by their ancestral proto-South Ethiopic community. The early Eastern Cross-Rift peoples, on the other hand, entered generally into close interactions, as their easterly trend of expansion portended, with Eastern Cushites whose language or languages did not belong to Highland branch (Appendix 2). On the whole, loanwords were less commonly adopted into core vocabulary in the later eras, indicating that the South Ethiopic societies had become more numerous, established populations — no longer exceedingly small, though expansive minorities.

III

To put these developments into some kind of chronological framework, a subvariety of lexicostatistics called glottochronology must be brought into play. Glottochronology makes use of the observation that the proportion of change in the body of words used for the hundred meanings of a core list tends to a semblance of a normal distribution curve, when measured for different languages over a constant period of time. The proportion of such vocabulary a language can be expected to retain unchanged, in the absence of intensive language interference, will normally fall somewhere in the mid-eighty percent range after a thousand years. Two sister languages, after a thousand years of divergence out of their common mother tongue, should retain in common something in the lower mid-seventy percents of the core vocabulary with which they began. Glottochronology rose to prominence in the 1950s in a burst of fashionability; in an equally unscholarly manner, it became increasingly unfashionable by the later 1960s. The method, despite the inadequacies of the theory in which it is couched, in fact gives reasonably useful, though very rough datings, as work in a number of regions and language families has shown. Its datings of Ethiopic language history tend to be broadly consistent with dating expected from other kinds of evidence and with the time spans suggested by the loanword evidence.

The proto-Ethiopic split into separate South and North Ethiopic branches is marked by a cognate range in core vocabulary centering on 43-49%. In glottochronological reckoning this range would be equivalent to a divergence period of about 2500 years. One additional problem must be addressed, however, in proposing approximate dates in some Ethiopic cases. It has been found in other African examples that word borrowings into core vocabulary which have taken place since two languages have split from each other tend to depress their cognate percentage with each other in proportion to the frequency of the loans in the two vocabularies (Ehret 1971, 1980, and elsewhere). In view of the large number of loanwords which have entered North and South Ethiopic core vocabularies since the end of proto-Ethiopic times, the figure of 2500 years must be seen as the upper limit for the break-up of proto-Ethiopic, rather than a median figure. The end of the proto-Ethiopic period would therefore best be placed more recent than 500 B.C., perhaps in about the fourth or third century B.C.

The earlier existence of the proto-Ethiopic community would go back, as suggested from the evidence of the intensive general loanword set in its language, another three or four centuries in the northern Horn, at least to mid-millennium and perhaps to the seventh or even the eighth century. There is no need to press the proto-Ethiopic settlement back farther in time to account for the differences between early Ethiopic and Epigraphic South Arabian. The disparity between spoken and written forms of languages is too much a historical commonplace to require further comment. In any case, proto-Ethiopic need not have derived from the same dialect as that which formed the basis for EPA. Indeed, it is unlikely to have, for South Arabian settlers more probably were drawn mostly from the nearby Arabian coastlands just across the Red Sea — from seaports if they were traders — rather than the interior areas where the principal South Arabian populations and the governing centers tended to lie.

The proto-South Ethiopic society arose around an apparently small group of Ethiopic speakers who moved to the upper Awash areas at the end of proto-Ethiopic times, suggested above to be perhaps mid-way through the second half of the last millennium B.C. The later break up of the developing South Ethiopic society into several descendant communities is marked by a cognate range centering around 48-59%, its median point of 54% indicating a time of about 2000 years ago. In the South Ethiopic case, later word borrowing by South branch languages from each other has probably often raised the percentages of apparent cognates, partially compensating for the expected depression of cognates due to penetration of Eastern Cushitic loans into basic vocabulary. It would be not improbable, then, for the beginning of South Ethiopic differentiation to have fallen fairly close to the 2000 years implied by the cognate counts, perhaps thus sometime around about the first century A.D. This dating of the incipient South Ethiopic break up to about three or four centuries after the proto-Ethiopic split fits very well indeed with the independent evidence of borrowing in basic vocabulary, which suggested that the proto-South Ethiopic era lasted just about that long. The slightly higher ranges of cognate, centering in the very high fifty percents, between the two primary subgroups of Cross-Rift and the two primary subgroups of Gurage South Ethiopic indicate that the further divergence of South Ethiopic into at least six societies, spread out around the eastern, southern and southwestern sides of the upper Awash country — proto-Western Cross-Rift, proto-Eastern Cross-Rift, pre-Gafat, pre-Soddo, proto-Chaha-Mäsqan and pre-Mesmes — should have been complete by the fourth or fifth century A.D.

IV

The questions of how and why the Ethiopic tongues were able to become established as major indigenous languages in northeastern Africa can be answered as yet only by inference and speculative proposals. Some solutions can be discounted, however. The first Ethiopic speakers did not come as technologically advantaged conquerors. It may perhaps be possible that the South Arabian settlers introduced iron to the Horn; but what little as has yet been investigated of northeastern African iron-working terminology suggests that metallurgy in some form was already known and that the root (*bir-t) used for iron throughout the Horn today was borrowed into early Ethiopic from a Cushitic source (e.g. Appleyard 1975, Blakney 1963). Neither did the early Ethiopic groups apparently introduce any significantly different agricultural knowledge or practice to the regions of their settlement (Ehret 1979).

From the kinds of agricultural words borrowed we can say something, however, about relations of the early Ethiopic speakers with the peoples among whom they settled. They were, in the first place, not farmers. Understandably, the names of crops new to South Arabian immigrants, such as t'ef, finger millet, and nug, came into Ethiopic from Cushitic languages. But, to a surprising extent, even the names for crops and agricultural implements of ancient acquaintance to Semitic peoples in Asia were also borrowed from the indigenes (Appleyard 1975, Ehret 1979, and others). This lack of agricultural orientation is strongly attested for the proto-Ethiopic period, in which such terms as those for wheat, mashed chickpeas, flax, and ploughshare were all borrowed. It continued among the proto-South Ethiopic settlers of the upper Awash region, who adopted additional basic cultivating vocabulary, including words for barley, wheat bread, and chickpea. The early Ethiopic people surely all consumed the products of the local cultivators, but just as surely seem not to have been the cultivators themselves.

Two possibilities present themselves. The Ethiopic speakers may have formed a ruling class with a distinctive language of its own, supporting itself by extracting a surplus from the still Cushitic speaking cultivators. But such a situation is, linguistically speaking, an inherently unstable one, in which either the ruling class will in a relatively few generations take up the language of the ruled, or the ruled will begin increasingly to shift to the rulers' language. Alternatively the Ethiopic speakers may have followed a particular occupational specialization which allowed them for a long period to operate outside narrow social linkages to particular localities but obliged them to obtain their food by purchase from the cultivators.

Both possibilities could in fact have been operative in successive eras. A fundamental theme in Red Sea history in the last millennium B.C. is the expansion of long distance trade. The trade came at first overland through the western side of Arabia. But several principal products, among them tortoise shell and frankincense, were produced in the drier northern fringe of the Horn, and so the attention of traders would soon have been drawn to the areas across the Red Sea from South Arabia. It can be proposed that the early Ethiopic language was brought into the Horn by traders from South Arabia, who as transmitters of goods between societies would have stood outside the normal social networks of the cultivating Cushitic population and who would by occupation have been non-cultivators. In time, it can be speculated, some traders might have been able to contract marriage with daughters of local chiefs or notables, since such alliances would have benefited both traders and chiefs in channelling and securing the flow of trade goods. If so, then eventually opportunities could have arisen for the offspring of marriages of that kind to parlay their combined chiefly descent and familial access to the trade into a wider political power. Thus might a ruling class, whose home language was proto-Ethiopic, begin to evolve and its language thereafter begin to spread among the general populace.

The proto-South Ethiopic settlers, from the pattern of their word borrowings from sur-rounding peoples, seem in some way to have replicated the kinds of relations of the proto-Ethiopic period, but in a new and distant locale. It is tempting to wonder whether the proto-South Ethiopic people might not at first have been traders too, coming from the already estab-lished Ethiopic-speaking areas on the north edge of the highlands and seeking to open up new sources of supply of goods, such as ivory and rhinoceros horn, perhaps in response to the added Ptolemaic presence in the Red Sea and the growth of the Indian connection during the last three centuries B.C.

The social basis for the long-term maintenance of South Ethiopic speech is unclear, however. In the north, the rise of small kingdoms and eventually of a state, Aksum, in which the language of the dominant stratum and of the core areas of the state was Ethiopic, and the continuing major importance of trade as a source of revenue supporting the state, are well attested. But for the countries in and around the upper Awash, the evidence is lacking as yet for continuities between the much later state-building eras from the ninth century A.D. onward and the earlier period of South Ethiopic establishment. If the South Ethiopic settlers came for trade, the as yet unattested political consequences of their settlement may have been restricted to the more northerly and earliest areas of their settlement in the Awash country. In Gurage and perhaps elsewhere, South Ethiopic languages spread to peoples who, except for shift of lan-guage, see to have either carried on or soon reverted back to earlier Cushitic patterns of culture and governance, without major lasting change. Other social mechanisms of language shift than those associated with state-building will probably have to be sought if we are to explain the secondary expansions of the early South Ethiopic speech areas.

NOTES

1. I am especially indebted to the work of David Appleyard, who is, needless to say, not to blame for the conclusions I have drawn from his evidence.

2. In some theory, the proto-period is the instant in time at which the proto-language first be-gins to diverge into dialects. But in the real world no such single moment of divergence nor-mally exists. In practice, it is useful to allow the proto-period to cover the two, or three, or four centuries immediately preceding the unmistakable manifestation of divergence.

REFERENCES

Appleyard, D. L. (1975)   'The Semitic basis of the Amharic lexicon', Ph.D. thesis, School of Oriental and African Studies, University of London.

——————— (1978)   'Linguistic evidence of non-Semitic influence in the history of Ethiopian Semitic: lexical borrowing in Ge'ez and other Ethiopian Semitic languages', *Abbay* 9: 49-56.

Bender, M. L. (1971)   'The languages of Ethiopia', *Anthropological Linguistics*, 13, no.5, pp.165-288.

Blakney, C. (1963)   'On "banana" and "iron", linguistic footprints in African history'. Hartford: Hartford (Seminary) Studies in Linguistics, no.13.

Ehret, C. (1971)   *Southern Nilotic History: Linguistic Approaches to the Study of the Past*, Evanston: Northwestern University Press.

——————— (1979)   'On the antiquity of agriculture in Ethiopia', *Journal of African History* 20: 161-177.

——————— (1980)   *The Historical Reconstruction of Southern Cushitic Phonology and Vocabulary*, **Kölner Beiträge** zur Afrikanistik, Band 5. Berlin: Dietrich Reimer Verlag.

——————— (1981)   'The demographic implications of linguistic change and language shift'. In C. Fyfe and D. McMaster (eds.), *African Historical Demography*, vol.2. Edinburgh: Centre of African Studies, University of Edinburgh.

Fleming, H. C. (1968)   'Ethiopic language history: testing linguistic hypotheses in an archaeological and documentary context', *Ethnohistory* 15: 353-388.

Hetzron, R. (1969)   'The classification of the Ethiopian Semitic languages'. Unpublished paper, cited in Hetzron 1977: 22.

——————— (1972)   *Ethiopian Semitic, Studies in Classification*, Journal of Semitic Studies, Monograph No.2. Manchester: The University Press.

——————— (1975)   'Genetic classification and Ethiopian Semitic'. In J. and T. Bynon (eds.), *Hamito-Semitica*. The Hague: Mouton.

——————— (1977)   *The Gunnän-Gurage Languages*. Naples: Istituto Orientale di Napoli.

Shack, W. A. (1974)   *The Central Ethiopians*. London: International African Institute.

The matrix of cognates among Ethiopic languages in core vocabulary is taken from Bender (1971). (Since Bender does not segregate coherent ranges of cognate, which form an approximation of a normal distribution, from anomalously out-of-range scores, he comes up with a somewhat different and more equivocal classification from the data.)

```
Tigre

64  Tigrinya
─ ─ ─ ─
46  49  ┆ Gafat
        ┆ + + +
52  56  ┆ 65 + Amharic
        ┆    +
45  53  ┆ 57 + 79 Argobba
        ┆    + ○ ○ ○ ○
47  48  ┆ 52 + 61 56 ○ Harari
        ┆    +        ○ . . . . .
49  47  ┆ 53 + 59 56 ○     .
        ┆    +        ○ 70 . Zway
52  51  ┆ 59 + 60 57 ○ 70 . 79 Walani
        ┆    + + + + + + + + +
43  45  ┆ 54  56 57  59  55  59 + Mäsqan
        ┆                    +  . . . . .
44  43  ┆ 52  55 55  54  58  62 + 80 . Chaha
        ┆                    +       .
44  43  ┆ 51  53 52  52  55  58 + 76 . 89 Geto
        ┆                    +       . . . . . . . .
43  43  ┆ 49  50 53  54  55  55 + 70 . 81 83 . Ennemor
        ┆                    +  ○ ○ ○ ○ ○ ○ ○ ○ ○ ○ ○ ○
40  40  ┆ 48  45 50  49  55  49 + 58  56 59  68  ○ Mesmes
        ┆                    +  + + + + + + + + + + + + +
47  49  ┆ 62  66 64  61  61  63  69  70 69  66    58 + Soddo
```

A dash line sets off the scores which define the distinct North and South branches of Ethiopic, while a line of plus marks (+) encloses those counts to the right of the dash line which form the lowest range of cognate among the South Ethiopic tongues. Higher percentage ranges marking the successively later splits within the several branches of South Ethiopic are demarcated respectively by lines of small circles and lines of dots.

The subclassification implied by the matrix is the following:

Ethiopic (43-49%) [40%] [51-52%]
    I. North Ethiopic (64%)
        A. *Tigre*
        B. *Tigrinya*
    II. South Ethiopic (48-59%) [45%] [62%]
        A. Cross-Rift (56-61%)
            1. *Amharic, Argobba* (79%)
            2. Eastern Cross-Rift (70%)
                a. *Harari*
                b. *Walani, Zway* (79%)
        B. *Gafat*
        C. *Soddo*

        D. Gurage (56-59%)
            1. Chaha-Mäsqan (70-80%)
                a. *Mäsqan*
                b. Chaha-Ennemor (81-83%)
                    i. *Chaha, Geto* (89%)
                    ii. *Ennemor*
            2. *Mesmes*

The name Gurage has been resurrected for a group resembling the old Gurage in composition, except for the dropping of Soddo and the Zway-Walani-etc. group of dialects. Hetzron's Transversal has been replaced with Cross-Rift, a name of clearer geographical implication in common English and more easily translatable. Names of individual languages and dialects are italicised. Figures in parentheses give the core clustering of cognate counts between the primary subgroups in that particular level of grouping or, if just two languages are shown in the group, the percentage of cognate between the two. Percentages in brackets represent individual low and high scores which lie somewhat outside the core range within which the rest of the cognate scores for a particular group cluster. Together the figures in parentheses and those in brackets thus conform to the expectations of a normal distribution curve and so add an additional level of confidence in the validity of the classification.

It is apparent that a few scores, italicised in the cognate matrix, turn out to be anomalously high in comparison with the overall patterns. For these counts, even the possibility of explaining them as far extremes on the bell-shaped normal distribution curve is of vanishingly small probability. The alternative solution is that such counts reflect undetected word-borrowing between the languages involved. The borrowings may be undetected either because they were adopted early enough to conform to the regular patterns of sound shift, or because their fit with the sound shift history has not yet been closely enough examined. The four notably anomalous cases are those of Amharic with Tigrinya, Amharic with Gafat, Mesmes with Ennemor, and Soddo with the rest of South Ethiopic.

The direct effect of undetected word borrowing between related languages is the raising of the apparent cognate percentage of the borrowing language with the language from which the loanwords come, because the undetected loans will be counted as if they were valid cognates retained since the common ancestral period. The corrollary indirect effect, which helps determine the direction of borrowing and confirms the conclusion that borrowing is in fact involved, is the lesser raising of the score of the borrowing language with other languages especially closely related to the donor language. The reason for this secondary effect is that the closely related tongues will, because of their close relationship, have many (but not all) of the same words as those borrowed from their near relative and thus will have their scores with the borrowing language inflated to some extent, too. Amharic's over-high apparent cognate with Tigrinya can therefore in part be attributed to word-borrowing by Amharic from Tigrinya because Amharic also has an over-high score, though offset somewhat lower, with Tigre, Tigrinya's closest relative. On the other hand, Tigrinya has apparently adopted words from Amharic as well, since its count with Amharic's closest related language, Argobba, is similarly over-high, though again not as high as with Amharic, the inferred donor language.

The direction of influence is not so clear in the cases of Amharic and Gafat and of Ennemor and Mesmes. It is possible that some of the early expansion of Amharic, before 1500, may have been over areas speaking early Gafat or a closely related tongue; such a history might in part account for the inflated Gafat-Amharic percentage, while more recent loan activity from Amharic to Gafat in the centuries of Gafat's decline might further have raised the apparent cognate of the two languages. Both possibilities deserve careful investigation. Ennemor should be considered the more probable borrowing language in the Mesmes-Ennemor interaction because no disturbment of Mesmes' scores with Ennemor's nearest congeners seems visible. Heztron's genetic grouping of Ennemor and Mesmes depends on the presumption that the morphological criteria he has identified were not borrowed. Such borrowing is relatively infrequent, but it does take place. Here the lexical evidence strongly indicates intensive language interference between Mesmes and Ennemor and, except for the one score of Mesmes-Ennemor itself, a very sharp break between Mesmes and the rest of the group to which Ennemor belongs. Even the over-high cognates between the two languages is distinctly below the general range of cognates among Ennemor and its other near relatives. More likely than not, then, morphological interference accompanied lexical in this instance, making Mesmes seem more closely related to Ennemor than is actually the case.

Soddo provides the most striking case of anomalously high percentages. Its highest range is 66-70% with the Chaha-Mäsqan languages, among which it is geographically embedded; its range with the rest of South Ethiopic is also over-high, but offset lower at 58-66%. Its 47% and 49% with North Ethiopic languages clearly places it outside that group. Soddo can thus be accounted a South Ethiopic tongue with an extraordinarily high rate of word borrowing in basic vocabulary, probably on the order of about 15%, from Chaha-Mäsqan — a situation which reflects probably centuries of close social interactions between Soddo speakers and their immediate neighbors. The expected corollary effect of such a history is present: the Soddo scores with the nearest related languages of the donors — Gafat, Cross-Rift and Mesmes — are also raised several points over what otherwise would be expected, though not as high as with the indicated donor group, Chaha-Mäsqan.

APPENDIX 2

Loanwords in Core Vocabularies

Proto-Ethiopic

"cloud": *dämmänä — Agaw: Awngi *dummini*, Qimant *dɛmmɛna*, Bilen *dɛmna*, Xamta *dimɪna*

"fish": *ᶜasa — Agaw: Aw. *asi*, Qi. *a:sa*, Bi. *ᶜa:sɛ*

"smoke": *ṭis — Agaw: Aw. *tiša*, Bi. *tida*, Xa. *t'iya*

"hair": *ṣägʷär — Agaw: Bi. *šigʷir*; cf. also PEC *t'ogor*

"egg": *'V(n)k'ak'Vḥ — Cushitic: PSC *k'ok'aanḥ-*; EC: Oromo *ank'ak'u*, Gobeze *ukah*, Somali-II *'ukaḥ*, etc.

"to fly": *bärärä — Cushitic: PSC *pir-*; PEC *barar-*

"to know": *ᶜok' — Agaw: Aw. *aq-*, Qi. *a:xʷ-*

Proto-North Ethiopic

"skin": *k'arbät — Agaw: Qi. *kʷoreve*, Xa. *k'erbir*; also Qi. *kebera* "bark"

"meat": *siga (also in Amharic) — Agaw: Bi. *sixa*, Qi. *si:ye*, Xa. *si:ya*; cf. also Saho *saga* "cow"

? "to swim": *hambäsä — Agaw: Bi. *xambes-*

Proto-South Ethiopic

"dog": *wiša — Highland Eastern Cushitic: *wuš-*

"fat": *c'omma — EC: HEC *c'om-* (Oromo *c'o:ma*); Agaw: Qi., Bi. *c'omma* "knee": *g^wilbät — Cushitic: PEC *gulb-/*gilb-; Agaw: Aw. gulvi, Xa. girib; PSC *gili (preSC *gilib)

"tongue": *^{c}anräbät or *^{c}arnäbät — PEC *^{c}anrab-; PSC *^{c}aanda (preSC *^{c}aandab)

"sand": *hašäwä — Agaw: Qi. ašewa, Xa. ašewɛ, Dembiya ašo; also Beja haš, PSC *hats-

"tree": *zaf — Agaw: Qi. zaf, Xa. zäf, Quara ǧafa (Appleyard 1975)

"water": *'äk^{w}ä — Agaw: Aw. aɣu, Xa. aqw, Bi. ak^{,w}, Qi. a:ɣo

Proto-Western Cross-Rift

"tail": *jer (not identical with proto-Ethiopic *ṭira) — EC: Afar gera; Qi. jeray, Xa. jera (but these could be loans from an Amharic dialect without final -at)

"skin": *k'oda — Cushitic: PSC *kw'aad- "goatskin"

Amharic

"water": wäha — HEC: Sidamo wāhō, Kambatta wo'a, Hadiya wo'o, Alaba, Burji wa

Argobba

"mountain": gubba — EC: Dullay *gub-

Proto-Eastern Cross-Rift

"road": *'u(n)ga — EC: Gawwada unge, Gobeze u:nk-

"sun": *'air- — EC: Afar ayro; cf. wider PEC *'ar-?

Harari

"knee": gilib — separate borrowing of root from probably a Lowland Eastern Cushitic language

Zway-Walani

"fire": *ji:r- — PEC *gi:r- (HEC, Afar)

"heart": *wɛzen- — PEC *wazn- (HEC *wɛzɛn-) (Ometo wɛzɛn-: loan from HEC)

"white": *gumar- — EC: Bayso gumara; also HEC: Libido gobana

Zway

"bark": k'ɛ:nc'e — HEC *k'unc'e

"sun": ari:t — EC: proto-Soomaali *'arit

650

"black": *gembɛlla*
(separate adoption by
Mesmes?)

EC: HEC: Kambatta, Alaba *gembɛlla*; also Bayso *gamballi*

Soddo

"mountain": *geggera*

Cushitic: Oromo *ga:ra*; PSC **gar-* or **gad-* "forest"; Bilen *gira* "mountain"

Gafat

"other": *wilɛ*

HEC **wel-*

"mouth": *simotɛ*

HEC: Hadiya, Libido *su:me*

"good": *gunnɛ*
(presumed **gudnɛ*)

Agaw: Aw. *gud* (Aw. is a recent neighbor of Gafat)

Proto-Gurage

"red": **biša*
(also found in Soddo)

HEC: Kambatta, Alaba *bi:ša* "red" (PEC **bis-* "color")

Mesmes

"hair": *dugu:ra*

PEC **t'ogor-* (**t'* > ɖ in several Lowland Eastern Cushitic languages)

? "night": *haᵂonšo:de*

HEC: Sidamo, Darasa *ha:ša*

"black": *gombonna*
(separate loan in Zway?)

HEC: Kambatta, Alaba *gembɛlla*; also Bayso *gamballi*

Mäsqan

"good": *fäya*
(also found in Soddo as
fäyyan)

PEC **fiiᶜ-* or **fayᶜ-*

Comments:

This listing is restricted to what seem to be strong cases; a number of possible loanwords which could have been weakly proposed were left off. In many cases particular attestations of roots are given in the form that appears in Bender 1971; ɛ in such instances probably normally represents what is written more commonly in Ethiopian orthography as *ä*. PSC (proto-Southern Cushitic) reconstructions are from Ehret 1971; some PEC reconstructions are from the unpublished research of C. Ehret and M. N. Cali. Some of the loanwords will probably be found to have somewhat wider distributions in Ethiopic than is shown here, and so will date to earlier stages of Ethiopic differentiation.

Abbreviations: PSC, proto-Southern Cushitic; PEC, proto-Eastern Cushitic; EC, Eastern Cushitic; HEC, Highland Eastern Cushitic.

A TEXT ON THE SAINTS OF KÄDIḤ

Getatchew Haile

INTRODUCTION

The Saints of Kädiḥ are among the several groups of early saints of the Church of Ethiopia remembered vaguely in tradition. The Synaxary entry for them is limited to mentioning the date on which they are commemorated:

> Also on this day [the 24th of the month of *Taḥśaś*]took place the resting
> of the Saints of Kädiḥ on one day, as the angel told them.[1]

None of the other known sources, the *Arke*, the *Nägś* and the *Dəggʷa* are more informative than the *Sənkəsar*. The entries there are no more than hymns asking for the intercession of the Saints:

1. Hail, I say (to you), who became saints,
    refuges in the country of Kädiḥ.
    Wealthy fathers, who make the poor wealthy,
    adorn my ear(s) with the glory of earring(s)
    and anoint (my) eye(s) with the ointment of healing.[2]

2. With toil, hard work and exceeding diligence
    they entered the wide land of inheritance through the narrow way,
    adorned with purity like the angels,
    our fathers, the Righteous of Kädiḥ.[3]

The *Zəmmare*, too, makes a reference to the Saints, but the reference is, from the historical point of view, rather insignificant.[4]

Although it is not as informative as one would like it to be, the text under study, EMML 1479, ff.283r-285v, is by far the most extensive known source (to me) so far. Unfortunately, however, this text is so confused in some important places that my translation of it may not reflect the exact thoughts of its author(s).[5] The manuscript from which it is taken, EMML 1479, is dated, "6959 year of Mercy, during reign of Our King Zär'a Ya'eqob who is called Qwåṣṭänṭinos" (f.285v), that is, 1466/7 A.D.[6] The "corruption" in the language indicates that this date is not that of the composition of the text but of its copying, apparently from a manuscript which was already corrupt. In it one suspects a conflation of accounts. For example, the person of the subject changes in the middle of a paragraph. In some places, it is not even clear who the narrator is, the Saints themselves or another person who uses "we" as well as "they" when referring to the Saints and to those who buried them. Furthermore, it is difficult to determine from this text whether the Saints of Kädiḥ were one or several groups. The text does not make it clear whether the different sections are different traditions about one group of saints or stories about different groups of saints who have something in common so as to be called collectively *Ṣadqanä Kädiḥ* or "Saints of Kädiḥ". The number of persons in the group(s) is different in each section, but they all go to the "River Kädiḥ" and die there together. There are indications that they were slain, but, even though it seems very likely, it is not stated anywhere in clear terms that they were martyrs, *säma't*. Tentatively one may suggest that Christian missionaries may have met resistance to their evangelical activities from the non-Christian population of "Kädiḥ" who ambushed and massacred any group that was attempting to bring change to the religious culture of the region. Similar incidents may have happened over and over again until the inhabitants became Christians and then founded a monastery and built a church in the name of the Blessed Virgin.

This text also fails to tell us the time when Kädiḥ flourished as a Christian center and when the text was composed. Most of the places mentioned in this text are infrequent in Gəʿəz literature. My impression is that the Saints of Kädiḥ lived during or towards the end of the Aksumite period, but this hypothesis does not account for the mention of Ḥayq and Saf in a notice concerning saints of the Aksumite period. In any event, because of its age and unique content the text is, I believe, worth editing. However incomplete it may be, we owe to this text valuable information about the *Ṣadqanä Kädiḥ* and other facts connected with them, in particular, about the possible cave life of Ethiopian Christian communities at that time. It seems that the rock-hewn churches of Təgray served, or were served by, communities who lived in caves. This text seems to be the first sourse of information that can be used for writing history for that period of Ethiopia.

The text is reproduced as it appears on the microfilm of EMML 1479. As regards punctuation, the only change I have introduced is that I have reduced signs of more than four dots to four dots. Since the eliminated dots were mostly in red ink, they are not always legible on the black and white microfilm. The names of the original owner and abbot (?) have been erased and replaced by ʾƎnqʷå Bərhan and Säyfä Mika'el, respectively. These names and poorly legible words and letters are reproduced here in square brackets.

በስመ አብ ወወልድ ወመንፈስ ቅዱስ

ስምዑ ዘንተ ነገረ ዘኮነ ላዕለ ጻድቃን ከዲሕ እመ ዐሡሩ ወሰሙኑ ለወርኀ ታኅሣሥ ተንሥኡ እምሀገረ አብዓዛ ወ፳ ወ፺ [1] በጽሑ ኀበ ፈለገ ከዲሕ ወኀብረ ልቦሙ ። ወርእየ እግዚአብሔር እለ [2] በጥቡዕ ልቦሙ ወከመ አሐዱ መንፈሶሙ ። ወፈነወ መልአኮ ኀቤሆሙ ። ወይቤሎሙ ውእቱ መልአክ ወተናገሮሙ ከመ ሰብእ ዘይትናገር ወይቤለኒ [3] አዕርፉ ወቢቱ ውሰተ ዝንቱ ፈለግ ወቆምኒ ኀቡረ ወተናጸርኒ ለለ ባሕቲተኒ [4] ወነጸርኒ እንተ ቅድሜኒ ወኢርኢናሁ ወካዕበ ነጸርኒ ድኅሬኒ ወኢርኢናሁ ። ወካዕበ ይቤለኒ ኢትሰምዑኑ ። ወካዕበ ቆምኒ ኀቡረ ወተናጸርኒ በበይናቲኒ ወነጸርኒ የማነነ ወጸጋመነ ወኢረከብኖ።ወካዕበ ይቤለኒ ውእቱ ቢቱ ውስተ ዝንቱ ፈለግ።ወሖርኒ ኀበ አረፍተ ደብር ወቢትኒ ውስቴቱ ወቦቱ ዕፀወ ምሉእ ፍሬ ። ወኖምኒ ኵልነ ። ወይቤለኒ ውእቱ ኑሙ እስከ እገብእ ኀቤክሙ ወአንከርኒ ሶቤሃ ከመ [5] መልአክ ውእቱ ዘሎ ዘይትናገረኒ ። ወኖምኒ እመ ፳ ወ ፩ ለወርኀ ታኅሣስ ወተፈጸሙ [6] ወአእረፉ በሰላም ። ጸሎቶሙ ወትንብልናሆሙ ትዕቀቦ (ለዕንቈ ብርሃን) ወበረከቶሙ የሀሉ በኵሉ ጊዜ ምስለ (ሰይፈ ሚካኤል) ኀጥእ ወአስተብ ቍዖቶሙ ትመግቦ አሜን ።

ወሖረ ውእቱ መልአክ ኀበ እለ ይነብሩ አእመረ [7] ወአስተርአዮሙ መንፈቀ ሌሊት ወይቤሎሙ ሖሩ ወቅብርዎሙ ለእለ ኀረዮሙ እግዚአብሔር ወሖሩ ወረከብዎሙ አብድንቲሆሙ ወተሰምዐ ነገሩ ውስተ ኵሉ በሓውርት ወተጋብኡ ሕዝብ ዘአልቦ ኍልቈ [8] ጳጳሳት (?) ወመነኮሳት ወቀሳውስት ወዲያቆናት ወመሃይምናን ወዘመሩ መዝሙረ ወአዕረጉ ዕጣነ ወጸሎተ ኀበ እግዚአብሔር ። ወእመ ፳ ወ ፩ ለወርኀ ታኅሣስ እስከ ፳ ወ ፱ [9] ለመዐልት ነበሩ ወአልቦ ዘበልዖሙ ሥጋሆሙ ወኢአራዊተ ገደም ወኢአዕ (f. 283 v) ዋፈ ሰማይ ወይመስሉ ዘይነውሙ ። ወተማከሩ ኵሎሙ እለ መጽኡ ኀቤ ሆሙ ወይቤሉ ናንሥኦሙ ። ወተባሀሉ በበይናቲሆሙ [10] ወከረዩ ምድረ ወገብሩ ግበበ ዕሙቀ [11] ወቀበርዎሙ ወሐነጹ ዲቤሆሙ ቤተ ክርስቲያን ዘማርያም ።

ተአምሪሁ ኀበ ዝኀሮሙ ለጻድቃን መስቀል ዘወርቅ ተረክበ ። ወካዕበ ስምዑ [12] እለ መካነ መንግሢ ዘብዙኅ ዝኀሩ በዓት [13] እንዘ አፍራስስ ዓቃቤ ስዓቱ ወእስጢፋኖስ ዲያቆናዩ ። ወሖሩ ሰምዑ [14] ዘኮነ ተአምረ ላዕለ ፈለገ ከዲሕ ላዕለ ቅዱሳኒሁ ወኄሩያኒሁ ወጻድቃኒሁ ወፍቁራኒሁ ለእግዚአብሔር ። በኀበ መጠራ ፹ ወ፱ ወበኀበ መንግሢ ፸ ወ፯ ወበኀበ ዔዝን ፵ ወ፯ ወበኀበ ዓንባሴን ፺ ወ፭ ወኵሎሙ ተሳምዑ [15] ኀቡረ ለሐዊረ ፍኖት ዘቦቱ ምንኩስና ። ወቀሳውስት ወዲያቆናት ወደናግል ወመሃይምናን ወወራዙት ወአንስት ወወሐክት [16] ወኵሎሙ በአሚኖቱ ለእግዚአብሔር መጽኡ በይባቤ ወበትፍሥሕት ወቀሠፍዎሙ በምሩር [17] አመ ፳ ወ፬ ለወርኀ ታኅሣሥ ፻፺ ወ፺ ወ፱ ወበሰረገላ እንዘ የሐውሩ ወይጸውርዎሙ መላእክት እስመ ርቱዕ ሃይማኖቶሙ ። [18] ወጸውዕዎ ለአባ አፍራስስ ወይቤልዎ አባ አቡነ ትሰምዕኑ ። ወአጽምአ እእዘኒሁ [19] ወነጸረ ሰማየ ። ወይቤልዎ ሖር ከዲሐ እንተ ይብልዋ ምቱር ወበህየ ትረክብ ሥጋነ ወቅበረነ ። ወሖረ ከመ ይቅብሮሙ ወበጽሐ ኀበ ፈለገ ከዲሕ ወሰእነ አብድንቲሆሙ ረኪበ ። ወቀጸቦ መልአክ ለአባ አፍራስስ ወሰሐቦ በእዴሁ ወይቤሎ ነዐ ዝየ ኀበ ምቱር ። ወሖሩ ብዙኃን ድኅሬሁ ወረከቡ ብዙኃን አብድንቲሆሙ ወበከይነ ። ምስሌ (የ) [20] ሰብአ ከዲሕ ወይቤሉነ እለ ውሉተ ሀገር ወኮነ ክላሕ ዐቢይ ። ወተጋብኡ ኵሉ ሕዝብ ዘአልቦ

ኖልቴ እመ ጀ ወቼ ለወርነ [21] ታኀሣሥ ። ወተማኅሩ ካህናት ወመነኮሳት ምስለ ጠቢባን ። ወይቤሉ እፎ ንኅሥአሙ ወኢንክል ወተባህሉ በበይ ናቲሆሙ እለ ይሴሀቡ [22] ናንሥአሙ ወንትቤርም ። [23] ወእፎ ንክል በሕዱ ሰዓት ። ወተባህሉ በበይናቲሆሙ ናቅድም እለ ይሴሀቡ ናንሥእ ። ወእንዛሣናሆሙ አብድንቲሆሙ ለጀ (f. 284 r) ጀ ወቼ ወባዕዳነ ኈደናኖሙ አብድንት ዘእንበለ ንክሪ ግብበ እስከ ንፁጽሐ ጊብ ሀገር ። ወተከሥተ [24] መቃብራት ወእንበርነ አብድንቲሆሙ ወነጸርነ ዘተከሥተ መቃብራት ወቀበርናሆሙ ለጀጀ ወቼ ወካዕበ ገባእነ ጊብ አብድንቲሆሙ ወኢረክብነ ወኢአሐዱ ተከዝነ ምንት ውእቱ ዝንቱ ወተኀሥአ አባ አፍራስስ ወይቤ ናልዕል ልብነ [25] ጊብ እግዚአብሔር ጽምዕት ነፍስነ ከመ እንተ ትበውአ ማየ [26] ከርሣ ሰብእ ። ወሰቢሃ ትትፌሳሕ እምከመ ረውየት ወጸገብት ። ወሰቢሃ ትትፌሳሕ ። ወከማሁ ቦአት ውስተ አልባቢነ እለ [27] ሰማዕነ ነገረ ለአባ አፍራስስ ወአለዪ ቆምነ ቅድመ ሕዝብ ወተባህሉ በበይናቲሆሙ እንዝ ይብሉ ንግባእነ [28] ጊብ ውሱደን [29] ወእስተነ [30] ወክብርነ ወጋብ ተድላነ ወፍግዓነ [31] ወጊብ ኵሉ መብልዕነ ወመስቴነ ። ወሰቢሃ ተንሥአ ቀሲሰ ገበዝ ዘከሢሐ ዘስመ ምሉአ ስብሐት ወይቤ እፎ ንናፍቅ ላዕለ ፍኖተ እግዚአብሔር እንዝ መቃብራትኒ ለሊሁ [32] ይትከሥት [33] ወአብይንትዊ ዘነደግነ ኢረክብነ ። ወአራዊተ ገዳምኒ ኢበልዕዎም ሥጋሆሙ ምንተኑ [34] ውእተ ዝንቱ ተአምር ዘኮነ ። ወተባህሉ እለ ተጋብኡ ውስቱቱ [35] እመ ጀ ወቼ [36] ጸርነ [37] ታኀሣሥ ወቀልቀሎ [38] ለእለ ተጋብኡ ፰ጀፀ ወጀ ወእጽሐዋዊ ለዛቲ መጽሐፈ ከመ ትኩኑ ስምዓ ለደጋሪ [39] ከመ ያእምሩ በዝ ይደኅን ኵሉ ሰብእ ። ወእምይእቲ ዕለት መጽአ ፍቅር ወተፋቅሮ ላዕለ ኵሉ ሰብእ እለ የኀድሩ ፈለገ ከዲሕ ካህናት በኀብረተ ወተወከፉ ነዳያን ወምስኪናን ወነጋዲያን ወሴላሲያን እስመ ምዕራፎም ለዜሎም ርጉባን ወለጽሞኣን ወይተዌይፉ በኀብረታ ካህናት ፱ ወ (፺) [40] ወሀለው ውስተ ፭ ግብ

ወተአምሩ ጊብ አሬ መቃብሪሆሙ መስቀል ዘዘሩ እሉ ክለላን በጽድቅ ወተዓቀበ ዘንተ ነገረ ከመ ትኩኑ ውሉደ ብርሃን ። ወአንስቲያ ሆሙ እለ ክለላት በጽድቅ ። ወጊብ አሬ መቃብሪሆሙ መስቀል ዘዘርቅ ። ወእለ የኀድሩ ውስተታ ሕዝብ ወእንስት ወመዓብ ወአዋልድ ወአግብርቲ ሆሙ ተበዱ ከመ ይትባደር ሰብአ ለብሊይ ወለስቲይ ። ወከማሁ ተበዱ ውቱ (ም) ሆሩ ፍናተ እግዚአብሔር ለምሐር ወለወኂብ ወለተወከሮ (f. 284 v) ርጉባን ወጽሞአን ። ወኵሎም እለ ይንብሩ ውስተ ይእቲ ሀገር እምከመ ነገደ ወሐረ ርሑቀ ብሔረ ወይጉነዲ ወይመጽኡ ከመ አተ ይትፈሥሑ ደቂቁ ። ወከማሁ ይትፈሥሑ ከመ ይርእዩ ነጋዲያን ወሴላሲያን ወምስኪናን ወጽመዋን ። [41] መመንፈቅሙ ይጸውሩ አልሲ ሆሙ [42] ወመንፈቅሙ ይእኅዙ ሐዊሮም ወይስሕቡ ለለእብያቲሆሙ እስመ ከሉ ተጥሁሩ ገቢረ ሠናይ ። ወእንስትኒ ይነሥአ መብልዕ ውስተ አልባሲሆን ወወራዙትኒ ውስተ ሕጽኖሙ ወለዋልድን ይነሥአ መብል ጥዑመ ውስተ ቀወቶን [43] ወይሁቡ ጊብስተ በገዳም ለነጋዲያን ነለዳያን ወለርጉባን ወምስኪናን ወከሉሆም ክለላን በጽድቅ

ወይቤሎሙ [44] አባ ይድራሕ ሠናይ ዐቀቢ ሰዓት ለምሉእ ስብሐት ቀሲስ ገበዝ ። ወበዝ መዋዕሊን ዘንተ ማየ [45] ዘየማን ወዘጸጋም ዘቱሉ (?) ዘይውሕዝ ወዘይወርድ ውስተ ፈለገ ትፍሥሕት ወይኮውነ ሲሳየ ለጸቱ [46] መመብልዕ ወበየጋራ መዋዕል ሚመጠ (ነ) ሀላዊ ለዛቲ ሀገር ። ወይ ቤሎ ሰብአ ድራሕ ሠናይ ምሉእ ስብሐት በከመ ምግባሮም ወለሰመኒ ሠናይ ልቦሙ ይውሕዝ [47] አፍላጋ ዘየማን ወዘጸጋም ። ወለሰመኒ እኩይ ልቦሙ ወምግባሮም ሰቢያ ይትነተሙ እንጉዕት [48] አፍላጋ ዘየማን ወዘጸጋም ወከሉ ዘይወርድ ውስተ ፈለገ ሠናይ ። ወበውእቱ መዋዕሊ በውስተ ፭ ቅን ጾት ወበውስተ ፭ ሥርዓት [49] እኅል (?) [50] ስበላት [51] እኅል እስመ ናዝርግ ጸሉተን ወዕጣነን ወኀብስተን ወኀብረተን [52] ፭ ውእተ ወይ ኩን [53] ፭ ንብረትክም ወበአትክም ወወአጎኩም ብእሲ ወብእሲት አኮኑ ፤ ይሰከብ ውስተ ፭ ዓራት ወይመጽአሙ ፍትወት ወይነራከቡ ። ወኢ ምክመ ተወልደ ይኮውን ኈየ ጥዑመደ እስመ እምኅሊና ሠናይ ተገነ ወተወለደ [54] ወምስለ ሕሊና እኩይስ ዘይትወለድ እኩየ ይኮውን ።

እንተ [55] ይዶ ። ወሰፋ ። ወሐይቅ ። ወአራረ ። ወሐና ። ወናዝሬ ። ወብለት ። ወተራከበ በውስተ ፍኖት ። ፭ ወቼ እመ ፭ ለጠተምት ። ወመ ጽእ እስመ ስምዐ ዕዶብ ነገረ በእንተ ደርታን [56] ቦዲሐ ወመኡ [57] እንተ ዓቀበ ደጕብንት ወነልቁ እመ ፭ ለጠተምት እስመ አፍቀሮም እግዚአ ብሔር ወነሬሮም (f.285 r) ለጸድታን ከዲሕ ። ወይኮን ተገዝከሮሙ እመ (፭) [58] ለጠተምት ግብሩ ከመ አሙ ፭ ወ ፭ ለታኀሣሙ ግብሩ [59] ብጹዓን እለ ይትዓቀብዮ ለዝንተ ነገረ ወእለ ይገብሩ ግብሮም ለጸድታን ከዲሕ ። ብጹዓን እለ ይኮውን ክማሆሙ ወይበውሉ ውስተ ሀገር ቅዱሳት [60] እስመ ለከሎሙ አስተጋብአሙ እግዚአብሔር ለነዒዮህ [61] ብዑዕ ውእቱ ዘይትዓዘዝ ውስተ ዛቲ ሀገር በትሕትና ወበተፋቅሮ ወበ ወኅር ነዳያን ወምስኪናን ወነጋዲያን ወበአርሞ ወይመጽኡ ጸጸሳት ። [62] ወትአምኃ ። [63] ወነገሥትኒ መመኳንንትኒ ወካህናትኒ ወእንስትኒ ። ብዑዕ ውእቱ ዘይጸምዕ ነገረ ዝንተ መጽሐፈ ለእመ ጥቡዕ ልቡ ወይኮውን [64] ክማሆሙ ። ወይን ዕርፍ ለዛቲ መጽሐፈ ጊብ ማኅፈድ ጽኑዕ ከመ ኢትማስን ለዓለም ።

ወዘሀሎ ወርቅ ወብሩር ወዕንቁ ክቡር ውስተ ቅጽር ዘአልቦ ፕልቄ ። ወከደንዎ 65 ውስተ ገነአ 66 ወርቅ 67 ወብሩር ጎበ ቅጽራ ወመርናባቲ እንተ ሠረቁ ወእንተ ዐረብ እንተ የማና ወጸጋግ ውስተ ግበቢሆሙ ለመነኮሳት አልቦቴ ወርቅ ወኢብሩረ ወውስተ ግበቢሆም ለካህናት ወለሕዝብ አልቦ ፕልቄ ብርት ወነጺን ወዐረር ጎበ ዘሆኡ ግበበ ለለ በይናቲሆሙ ለካህናት ፩ ወለሕዝብ ፩ ወ ፪ ግበበ ወእጽምአት ታአምረ መግበርሙስ ለቅዱሳን ኢትገብሩ ወተሐጉሱ ዕሴተክሙ 68 ወእኩ እንዘ ሰብእ ይልእክዎሙ ለወይን ወወይን ይልእኩ 69 ለልብ ወልብ ይልእኩ ለለሳነ ወልሳንኒ ይልእኩ ለኵሉ ሕሊና ወኵሉ ፍትወት 70 ወይከውኑ ኩሎሙ በከ ወከንቱ ወከማሁ ኢረኩን ምግባርሆሙ ከንቱ ወበከ አላ እጽንዕዋ ለጥበብ በጥቡዕ ልብክሙ ዘእንበላ ኑፋቴ ከመ ትረፈ ምስሌሆሙ ምድር 71 ሐዲስ ወከብርተ ለዓለም ዓለም አሜን ።

ጎበ ሀለወ ካህናት ግበብ 72 ጬ ወ ፫ እመት ዕመቁ ወበውቴቱ መነደሪሆሙ 73 ፪ ወጬ እጋጋእት 74 ዘቦቱ ወርቅ ውስቴቱ ዉፀ 75 ወለሕ ዝብ ፪ ወ ፫ እጋጋእት ወቀሡት ። 76 ወግዕዠንታት ፬ ዘወርቅ በዘ ቀበርዎሙ ወሀለወ 77 ወእንበርኃ በየማን ምሥዋዕ ውስተ ግቡ ሆሎ ። 78 መዝንቱ ኩሉ ወርቅ ወብሩር ወዕን ቱ ክቡር ። ወከሎ ዘየመጽኡ ነገሥተ ወመኳንንት ወጸጸሳት 79 ወቀላው (f.285 v) ስት ወዲያቆናተ ወብ ዙኃን ሕዝብ ወመዘምራን ወእንስት ወደናግል ወአዋልድ ወኵሎሙ በውስተ ክሳውዲሆሙ ያመጽኡ አምኃ ለማርያም እስመ ማርያም ተንከተመ ጽድቅ ይእቲ ። እስመ ወርቅስ እብን ውእት ሜጡ ለክቡር ወኮሎሙ መፍቀርያን ወርቅ ሐጕሉ እስመ እብን ውእት ። ወንሕነሂ አእመርናሁ ከመ እብን ውእት ወኮልነ አግባእናሁ ለቤተ እግዚአብሔር ለዓለም ዓለም አሜን ። አሜን ። ወአሜን ።

TRANSLATION, EMML 1479, FF. 283r–285v.

In the name of the Father and of the Son and of the Holy Spirit.

Listen to this account of what happened to the Saints of Kädih. They set out from the town (hagär) of Ab'aza on the 18th of the month of Taḥśaś, and twenty and ninety (sic) (of them)[1] came as far as the River Kädih. Their heart(s) were united.[2] And God saw their determination and how their spirit was one.[2] He sent his angel to them. The angel spoke to them and addressed them as if he were a man speaking. He said to us (sic)[3], "Rest and spend the night at this river". We all stopped and looked at one another. We looked before us but we did not see him. Then we looked behind us but we did not see him. He again said to us, "Are you not listening?" Again we all stopped and looked at each other. We looked (to) our right and left but we did not find him. He again said to us, "Spend the night at this river". We went to the side of the mountain and spent the night there [lit. in it]. It [the place] had trees filled with fruits. We all slept. He [the angel] told us, "Sleep until I come back to you". At that time we wondered (knowing) that it was an angel who spoke to us all (that). We slept on the 24th of the month of Taḥśaś. They (sic)[4] were silenced and rested in peace. May their prayer and intercession guard ['Ǝnqwǎ Bǝrhan], and may their blessing be always with [Säyfä Mika'el], the sinner, and may their supplication nourish him. Amen.

That angel went to those who lived in A'əmär (?)[5] and appeared to them at midnight and said to them, "Go and bury those whom God has chosen". They went and found their corpses. And the news was heard in all districts. Countless people gathered, (including) bishops, monks, priests, deacons and the faithful. They sang song(s) and offered up incense and prayer to God. They [the Saints in their dead bodies] were there from the 24th of the month of Taḥśaś until the day of the 29th.[6] Nothing had eaten their bodies, neither wild animals nor birds (f.283v) of the sky. They looked as though they were asleep. All those who came to them took counsel (together) and said, "Let us remove them". They discussed[7] among themselves and excavated the earth and made deep graves and buried them. Over them they built a church (in the name) of Mary.

The miracle: A golden cross was found at the tomb of the Saints.

Also those of Mäkanä Mängwəti, whose many tombs were cell(s), heard, when Afrasəs was the aqqabe sä'at and Ǝstifanos the deacon. They went [because] they heard of the miracle that happened at [lit. to] the River Kädih, to the holy ones, the elect and the saints of God: from Mätära 89, from Mängwəti 77, from 'Ezən 47 and from 'Anbazen 91. They all agreed together to take the road of [lit. which has] monasticism.[8] Priests, deacons, virgins, laymen, young men and women and wǎhakt[9], all came trusting in God singing and rejoicing. The 392(?)[10] smote them at Mətur on the 24th of the month of Taḥśaś. And while they were departing in a chariot, (kernel of) grain[26] and from one (kernel of) wheat[27] (? come) sevenfold ears[28] because we offer up our prayers and incense, and our bread and our living are (in) common." Let your living, your coming in and your going out be (in) common. Do not husband and wife sleep in one bed, does not desire come to them and they meet? When (a child) is then born, he becomes a chosen one and a delight because he is conceived and born out of a good thought. But he who is born out of a bad thought becomes bad.

Those of Däyo, Saf, Ḥayq, Arari, Heno, Nazre and Bəlät, 25 (in all), met on the road (?) on the 20th (of the month) of Ṭəqəmt. They came because they had heard an astounding thing about the Righteous of Kädiḥ. They came to the ascent of Dägʷâyənt and perished on the 20th of Ṭəqəmt because God had loved and chosen the (f.285r.) Righteous of Kädiḥ. Let their commemoration be (made on) the 20th of Ṭəqəmt. Celebrate (it) like the 24th of Taḥśaś. Celebrate (it). Blessed are those who keep this account and those who do the deeds of the Righteous of Kädiḥ. Blessed are those who become like them and enter the city of the holy ones, for God has gathered all his chosen ones. Blessed is he who endures in this town in modesty, mutual love, receiving the poor, the needy and the strangers, and (lives) placidly. Bishops come and greet it [Kädiḥ], also kings, rulers, priests and women (do the same). Blessed is he who listens to the story in [lit. of] this book. If he is determined, he shall be like them. Let them place this book in a strong bastion that it may not be destroyed for ever, in an enclosure where there are countless gold, silver and precious stone(s). Seal it in a *gän'* [= big amphora] (like) gold and silver. But its [Kädiḥ's?] enclosure and compound in the east and west, on the right and left, in the caves of the monks, has neither gold nor silver. In the caves of the priests and the laity, [gold and silver?] are countless. The bronze, iron and lead are in every cave where one enters, one (cave) for each of the priests and twenty-eight caves for the laity.[29] You know how to listen to this, but the deeds of the holy ones you do not do, and (so) you lose your reward(s). Is it not so, that, when one directs one's eye[30], the eye directs the heart[31], and the heart directs the tongue and the tongue directs every thought and every desire, and every thing becomes useless and vain? Likewise, let not your deeds become vain and useless, but strengthen wisdom[32] with your determination, without doubting, so that you may inherit with them [the Righteous of Kädiḥ?] a new and a glorious land forever and ever. Amen.

The depths of the caves where the priests were is 31 cubits and in it is the dwelling of 28[33] (priests). The big amphoras (there) which have gold in them are 32.[33] (In the dwelling) for the laity there are 23 big amphoras and *qäsuts* [= vessels]. The six golden censers were/are where they buried them. There is/was also [?]. They placed it on the right side of the altar (which) is/was in the cave. All this is gold, silver and precious stone(s), all that kings, rulers, bishops, priests (f.285v.), deacons, and many (of) the laity, the psalmists, the women, virgins and girls brought. They all brought (them) on their shoulders, as a present to Mary because Mary is the bridge of righteousness. For gold is (mere) stone, the price of the glorious one.[34] All lovers of gold have perished because it is (mere) stone. We knew it, that it is (mere) stone. And we all brought it to the house of God forever and ever. Amen.

NOTES TO THE INTRODUCTION

1. See, for example, E. A. Wallis Budge, *The Book of the Saints of the Ethiopian Church*, 4 vols., Cambridge 1928 (reprint, Hildesheim, New York, 1976), p.411.

2. The *Arke* hymns are not yet edited, but see EMML 1297 (= IES, no.34) f.72ab, Getatchew Haile, *A Catalogue of Ethiopian Manuscripts Microfilmed for the Ethiopian Manuscript Microfilm Library, Addis Ababa and for the Hill Monastic Manuscript Library, Collegeville, vol.IV: Project Numbers 1101-1500*, Collegeville (Minnesota), 1979, no.3, p.303.

3. There are several collections of *Nägś* hymns, but none of them is edited. The composition quoted here is ascribed to Giyorgis of Gasəčča; see EMML 204, f.74a, William F. Macomber, *A Catalogue of Ethiopian Manuscripts Microfilmed for the Ethiopian Manu-*

the angels carrying them — because their faith was orthodox — they called Abba Afrasəs and said to him, "Father, *Abunä*, do you hear?" He opened his ears and looked up into the sky. They told him, "Go to Kädiḥ which is called Mətur. You will find our bodies there; bury us." He went to bury them. He came to the River Kädiḥ but was unable to find their corpses. The angel beckoned Abba Afrasəs and drew him by the hand, and said to him "Come here to Mətur". Many (people) followed him and many (people) found their corpses. We (*sic*)[11] cried. The people of Kädiḥ came with [me?][12], and the villagers spoke to us, [?].[13] And there was a great wailing. All the people, who were innumerable, came together on the 28th of *Taḥśaś*. The priests and monks took counsel with the wise saying, "How is it that we remove them but we are unable?".[14] They said to one other, "Let us remove the elders and bury [the rest][15], but how can we do (that) at the same time?" They said to one other, "Let us first remove the elders". We removed the corpses of the (f.284r) 2003.[16] As for the others, we left them dead, without digging graves (for them) until we came to town. (In the town) the tombs were opened (by themselves). We put down their corpses and looked into the tombs that were opened. We then buried the 2003. Then we came back to their [i.e. the rest of the] corpses, but we did not find a single one. We were grieved (wondering), "What is this?". Abba Afrasəs stood up and said, "Let us lift up our heart(s) to God. Our souls are thirsty. As one's stomach which receives water and rejoices at that moment, when it is filled and sated, (our souls) shall rejoice at that time".[17] Indeed [lit. likewise], (the words) entered the hearts of those of us who listened to the words of Abba Afrasəs and who were standing before the people.[18] They [the people] discussed among themselves saying, "May we go back to our children, wives, our dignity, and to our comfort and dissipation and to all our food and drink?". At that time, the *qäsisä gäbäz* of Kädiḥ,whose name (was) Məlu'a Səbḥat, rose up and said, "Why [lit. how] do we doubt about the way of God, when tombs open by themselves, and when we could not find the corpses that we left, although wild animals did not eat their bodies? What is this miracle which has happened?".[19] Those who were gathered on the 24th (*sic*) of the month of *Taḥśaś* disagreed among themselves on it (?). The number of those who were gathered was 779.[20] They had this book written to be a witness for posterity, so that (people) may know the way by which all people are saved. Since that day love and mutual affection[21] came to all the people who dwelt at the River Kädiḥ, the priests (who lived) in community, receiving the poor, the needy, the strangers and the anchorites, because it is a resting place for all the hungry and the thirsty. The fifty-six priests received (strangers) in unity.[22] They were there in one cave.[23]

And the miracle: At the door of their tomb there was a silver cross.

They were crowned with righteousness. Keep this account so that you may be children of light. Their wives, too, were crowned with righteousness. And at the door of their tomb there was a cross of bronze.[24] Those who dwelt in it were the laity. Women, widowers, girls and their servants hastened (to do good deeds) as one would hasten to eat and drink; in that manner they hastened and learned the way of God, to pity, to give, and to receive (f.284v.) the hungry and the thirsty. All the people who lived in that town were like one who travels and goes to a far away country and stays a long time. They come (to him) like his children (who) rejoice when he returns; they rejoiced in that manner when they saw [lit. to see] strangers, anchorites, the needy and the deaf (*sic*).[25] Some of them carried their clothes (?) and some of them took hold (of them by) their waist(s) and pulled (them) to their individual lodgings, for all had learned to do good deeds. The women carried food in their skirts, the young men [brought drink?] (carrying) against their chests, and the girls carried delicious food in their pots (?) and gave out bread in the wilderness to the strangers, the poor, the hungry and the needy. They were all crowned with righteousness.

Abba Yəmraḥ Śannay, the *aqqabe sä'at*, said to Məlu'a Səbḥat, the *qäsisä gäbäz*, "In this time of ours, (we see) the water(s) of the right and left, and all that flows and goes down into the river(s) is a pleasure; (all) is for provisions and food for all. But in the latter days, what will be the level of life in this region?". Məlu'a Səbḥat said to Abba Yəmraḥ Śannay, "(It will be) according to their deeds. If their hearts are good, the rivers of the right and left shall flow. But if their hearts and deeds are bad, then the sources (of) the rivers of the right and left shall be sealed. Every thing that goes down into the river(s) is good. In this time of ours, from one script Microfilm Library, Addis Ababa and for the Monastic Library, Collegeville, vol.I: Project Numbers 1-300, Collegeville (Minnesota), 1975, p.215.

4. *Amməstu Şäwatəwå Zemawočč*, Addis Ababa, 1965 E.C., p.444. The *Zəmmare* hymn here is rather about the redeeming Son who was sent from Heaven, . . . who is the glory of the *Şadqan* . . . *Şadqan*, which seems to be a reference to the Saints of Kädiḥ, occurs only once in the entire hymn.

5. Kinefe-Rigb Zelleke, "Bibliography of the Ethiopic Hagiographical Traditions", *Journal of Ethiopian Studies*, vol.13/2 (1975), no.128, p.87, mentions several "copies" of this *gädl*, including one at the Institute of Ethiopian Studies, Addis Ababa University. My attempts to locate one of them, especially that of the Institute, have been unsuccessful.

6. Described in Getatchew Haile, *op. cit.*, vol.IV, 1979, pp.593-8.

NOTES TO THE TEXT

1. Probably ወአም ፮ ወፄ

2. Probably ከመ

3. Note the change of person.

4. ለለ ባሕቲትነ (?)

5. እስመ or እስመ አእመርነ ከመ

6. Note the change of person.

7. አእመረ is a verb, "to know", but here the word seems to be አእመረ a possible place name with the adverb marker *ä*; cf. ሐር ከዲሐ (towards the end of f.283v.).

8. ጥል ቁ is the old form of ጎል ቁ

9. This is according to the note in the margin. The text has ፮ ወፄ (*sic*).

10. A word or phrase such as ንቅብርሙ is probably missing.

11. The adjective እሙቅ is singular, whereas the noun it describes, ግባብ is plural.

12. ስምዑ (?) "Furthermore, listen: Those from Mäkanä Mäng^{w}əti . . . went [because] they heard . . ."

13. The grammatical function of this word is not clear in this sentence.

14. Probably ወሐሩ እስመ ስምዑ

15. The form is not attested in the dictionaries (cf. Amharic ተስማሙ).

16. The word is not attested in the dictionaries. The form is plural, probably of ወንኪ or ውሐኪ (cf. ጸሐፈ → ጸሐፍት ፡ ንጉሥ → ነገሥት).

17. Probably በምቱር

18. For ሃይማኖቶሙ

19. For እዝኄሁ or አእዛኄሁ

20. Note the change of person.

21. The የ suffixed to ምስሌ has been erased. Perhaps the word ምስሌ , too, should have been erased.

22. For ለወርን

23. እለ ይልጕቁ is in the subject form, but with the help of the following sentence it seems possible to understand it as the object of the sentence, that is ለእለ ይልህቁ

24. Possibly ለገዐዳን is missing.

25. For ተከሥቱ or ተከሥታ (plural).

26. For ልብነ

27. Probably ግይ . To keep this form in the object form, the verb has to be ታብእ , understanding ክርሠ ሰብእ as the subject. The text in this section is corrupt.

28. ለእለ (?)

29. Probably ንግባእኪ

30. For ውሉድነ

31. For አንስቲያን or ብእሲትነ

32. For ወናግዕን

33. For ለሲሆን or ለሲሆሙ

34. For ይትከሡቱ or ይትከሡታ

35. The meaning of ውስቴቱ is not clear.

36. This is according to the text, as well as the note in the margin, but it should probably be ፮ወ፫ as above; see n.21.

37. For ለወርን

38. For ውጥልቆሙ

39. Perhaps መዋዕል or ትውልድ is missing.

40. The number ፯ is not visible in the text but occurs in the margin.

41. Probably ርኁባን ወጽሙዓን

42. For አልባሲሆሙ

43. Probably ቀሠፉን

44. Probably ወይቤሎ unless we understand ወይቤሎሙ as a polite form, and not plural.

45. Probably ወበዝ መዋዕሊነ ንሬኢ ዘንተ ማየ . . . ።

46. ለኵሉ inserted later in the wrong place; read ወይከውን ሲሳየ ወመብልዐ ለኵሉ

47. ይውሕዙ or ይውሕዛ in the plural.

48. Probably እንቅዕት አፍላግ or እንቅዕት ወአፍላግ

49. Probably ሥርናይ

50. The number ፯ appears only in the margin. The text has been erased and what seems to be the number ፮ (or ፬?) inserted.

51. Obviously for ሰበልቱ

52. For ወነብስትነ [with part of ነ that distinguishes it from ን erased] ወንብረትነ

53. For ወይኩን

54. For ወተወልደ

55. The significance of preferring the feminine እንተ to the masculine እለ is not clear. Although the verbs (e.g. ወተራከቡ , ወመጽኡ) are in the masculine plural, at least some of them could be groups of women. See also n.60 below.

56. For ጸድቃነ

57. For ወመጽኡ

58. The space is blank, obviously to be filled with ፯ even though it does not appear in the margin either.

59. This second ግበሩ is probably redundant.

60. This form (feminine plural) indicates that this paragraph is dealing with women; see also n.55 above.

61. ለጐራየሁ is apparently in apposition to ለኵሎሙ

62. Not clear ጸጻሳት (?)

63. For ወይትእምኅዋ

64. The ወ in ወይከውን and in other similar cases seems to have the meaning and grammatical role of the Arabic فَ (fa) in conditional sentences.

65. The object of the verb ከደነ is not clear. The word could be ከድንዋ referring to መጽሐፍ like ያንብርዋ in the preceding sentence. But the pronominal adjectives suffixed to ቅጽር and መርገብ in the same (or in the following) sentence refer to Kädiḥ. I find it difficult to understand the details of this part of the paragraph.

66. The grammatical function of this word is not clear.

67. For ወርቀ

68. Probably ወታሕጕሎ ዕሴተክሙ or ወተሐጕል ዕሴትክሙ

69. For ይልእኮ

70. Probably ወለቡሎ ፍትወት . The ወ in ፍትወት has been slightly erased.

71. For ምድረ

72. The form ግቦብ (pl. of ግብ) is used in this text in the singular as well as the plural.

73. For ማኅደሪሆሙ. The ኅ is not clear in the text.

74. As ዝቦቱ and ውስቴቱ indicate, the form እጋንእት (pl. of ገነአ) is treated here as singular.

75. For ፬ወፎ

76. For ቀሡታት (?)

77. Perhaps the subject of the verb ሀለወ is missing, unless it refers to መዓዕጠንታት, in which case the form should be in the plural(ሀለው or ሀለዋ).

78. The phrase ending with this verb (ሀሎ) is obscure, the subject of the verb ሀሎ is not obvious.

79. Not clear ጸዳሳት (?)

NOTES TO THE TRANSLATION

1. The numbers 20 and 90 occur twice, in the margin and in the text. Names and numbers that are to be rubricated are usually noted first in the margins to remind the copyist(s) that the spaces left blank are to be filled with them in red ink. The number here could be 24, ". . . and [on] the 24th [of the same month] , they arrived at the River Kädiḥ".

2. I.e.. they were of the same thought concerning good deeds.

3. "He said to them" might have been more appropriate.

4. The original reporter who addresses the Righteous of Kädiḥ in the third person appears again.

5. A'əmär (A'əmärä, with the adverb marker) might not be a place name but the verb a'əmärä "to know". But such a verb would not make sense in this place.

6. The text has 24(th). 29(th) is the number noted in the margin.

7. The verb täbahalä expresses most probably disagreement in a discussion "to discuss differing views"; cf. Amharic täbabalä, Getatchew Haile, "Old Amharic Features in a Manuscript from Wollo", *Ethiopian Studies Dedicated to Wolf Leslau*, Wiesbaden, 1983, p.161.

8. The paragraph is probably dealing with groups of people from different villages who decided to go to Kädiḥ and establish a monastery at the site where the first Saints of Kädiḥ were "martyred". It may be worthy of note that the list does not include bishops.

9. The word is unknown to me; "children", "elderly" or "widow(er)s could fit in this place.

10. It is not clear who the 392 (people) are, the victims or the murderers. Since their number does not add up to 392, they cannot be the groups from the different villages who took "the road of monasticism", unless some groups have been left out by mistake in copying. Furthermore, "392" is not the object of the sentence in which it occurs, as it lacks the object marker *lä.*

11. Note the change of the person of the reporter.

12. The suffix pronoun meaning "me" has been erased from the text; perhaps, "The people of Kädiḥ came, and said to us . . .".

13. An important phrase is probably missing here. It could be the report on the manner in which the Saints were "silenced", e.g. "The people of Kädiḥ came and said to us, 'The villagers ambushed and massacred them' ". Another possible interpretation is, "The people of Kädiḥ came to us, and the people of the town spoke to us . . .".

14. This sentence probably expresses the miracle that the people were unable to remove the dead bodies.

15. This sentence can be understood perhaps only with the help of the sentences that follow. Another possible translation is, ". . . with the wise. They said, 'How (can) we remove them?' and 'We cannot'. The elders said to each other, 'Let us remove them and bury them, but how . . .?' ".

16. This number, which appears again below, is strikingly high, and does not represent the people in the groups that left for Kädiḥ, coming from the different towns. One should also note that this is the number of the bodies of only those whom the living removed. See also note 20 below.

17. The sentences which preserve the words of Abba Afrasəs are difficult. It is not even clear where his words end. The text is most probably corrupt.

18. The difficult nature of the texts continues. The subject of "entered" is not indicated.

19. It is not clear whether the words of Məlu'a Səbḥat are meant to rebuke those who suggested going back to normal life. Did he notice that the people (or those who were standing before them?) were not impressed with the whole episode?

20. This number of people is too small to remove 2003 dead bodies in one day. It seems that reports of incidents of different times are conflated in this section.

21. There is no significant semantic difference between *fəqr* and *täfaqəro*, which are translated here "love" and "mutual affection", respectively, only to show that we are dealing here with two words.

22. This casual remark on the life of the priests suggests that clerics might have lived together in a monastery, *monasterium canonicorum*, as opposed to monks who lived in a monastic center or *coenobium* or dwelling of monks.

23. It is interesting to note that Abunä Täklä Haymanot, too, looked for a cave in which to found his monastery; Getatchew Haile, "The Monastic Genealogy of the Line of Takla Haymanot of Shoa", *Rassegna di Studi Etiopici*, vol.29 (1982-83), p.11.

24. This is another part of the text which has elements that are difficult to understand. Sections seem to be marked sometimes with phrases concerning miracles. The second section deals with a cross of gold. This (third) section deals apparently with two crosses, one of silver found at the tomb of the righteous men and another of bronze — although "their" in the second "their tomb" is masculine — at the tomb of their women or wives. If my understanding of the text is right, the Righteous of Kädiḥ were families who rejected this world to lead a monastic life in a *coenobium*. The text could, of course, mean "Keep this account so that you may be the (spiritual) children of light and their (spiritual) wives crowned with righteousness". This section praises, not only the first Righteous of Kädiḥ, but also the settlers of Kädiḥ whom the author of the text considers part and parcel of the Righteous of Kädiḥ, that is, the monks and nuns of Kädiḥ, the "*Kädiḥočč*" or the "Kadiḥians".

25. The original sentence may have ended as follows, ". . . the needy, the hungry and the thirsty." Here "the deaf" is most probably out of place; *ṣəmmuman* "deaf (pl.)" could be a corruption of *ṣəmu'an* "the thirsty (pl.)".

26. The word *qənṣa't* for which I suggest "grain", is not known to me as a Gə'əz word. Morphologically and phonologically, there is little doubt that it is related to the Amharic *qənṭat* "grain".

27. The text has *śər'at,* "rule, order, regulation, ordinance", which does not seem to fit here. Could it be a corruption of *śərnay* "wheat"?

28. The number 7 ("seven fold") appears in the margin and not in the text (see n.1 above). The text is not clear; one notes even a tampering with the space where the number 7 ought to have been copied. There seems to be an allusion to Maccabees, cf., Dillmann, *Lexicon*, col.356, *säbl.* The entire sentence is unintelligible for me. It is not even clear if Abba Yəmraḥ Šännay, the *'aqqabe sä'at,* and the author of the text were contemporary or not.

29. This is probably the most difficult section of the entire text. Though faithful to the text as much as possible, the translation is uncertain.

30. I.e. stimulates the eye(s) to see.

31. I.e. seeing brings thoughts; here "heart" should be understood as "mind".

32. An allusion to Ps. 2, 11.

33. It is not clear what these numbers are. Both 28 and 23 are followed by *aganə't,* suggesting similar structures for the two sentences and, hence, similar translations, "28 amphoras" and "23 amphoras". But such a translation requires an explanation of the relationship between the 28 amphoras and the 32 amphoras containing gold.

34. An allusion to the price paid to Judas for delivering Jesus to his enemies; cf. Mt. 27, 9.

TOWARD AN ANALYSIS OF PRAGMATIC CONNECTIVES IN SILT'I

Ernst-August Gutt

1. INTRODUCTION

In 1977 van Dijk wrote that ". . . the semantics of natural connectives has hitherto resisted adequate treatment in the framework of current transformational generative grammars" (p.11). Van Dijk's own analysis of the meaning of the English conjunctions *and, also, too,* and *moreover* is an attempt to overcome the problem, but it results in a very complex account in terms of model-theoretic semantics and relevance logic.[1]

Rather than attempt to give a detailed critique of van Dijk's approach, I will show that the relevance theory of communication proposed by Sperber and Wilson (1982 and forthcoming) offers a framework that allows an explicit and yet comparatively simple account of the meaning of natural language connectives. I have chosen the connective *-m* found in Silt'i, an Ethio-Semitic language, for this purpose.[2]

2. THE PROBLEM

In the space given, it is not possible to deal with all the usages of Silt'i *-m*, and so I have selected a number of occurrences of this suffix that are common and that at the same time pose a challenge for an explicit analysis.[3] To start with, consider data set (1).

(1)　a.　*wut'at ayaam laam liyookb ulbaarag heeda.*
　　　　　Monday day cow he-to-buy Ulbarag he-went
　　　　　'On Monday he went to Ulbarag to buy a cow.'

　　　b.　*wut'atim ayaam laam liyookb ulbaarag heeda.*
　　　　　Monday-m day cow he to buy Ulbarag he-went
　　　　　'Also on Monday he went to U. to buy a cow.'

　　　c.　*wut'at ayaam laamim liyookb ulbaarag heeda.*
　　　　　Monday day cow-m he-to-buy Ulbarag he-went
　　　　　'On Monday he went to U. to buy also a cow.'

　　　d.　*wut'at ayaam laam liyookbim ulbaarag heeda.*
　　　　　Monday day cow he-to-buy-m Ulbarag he-went
　　　　　'On Monday he went to U. also to buy a cow.'

　　　e.　*wut'at ayaam laam liyookb ulbaaragim heeda.*
　　　　　Monday day cow he-to-buy Ulbarag-m he-went
　　　　　'On Monday he went also to U. to buy a cow.'

Looking at the Silt'i utterances in (1), it will be seen that while (1a) is without any occurrence of *-m*, (1b)-(1e) all have this suffix, but affixed to different constituents. Concerning the free translation, it will be noted a) that all occurrences of *-m* here are translated by English 'also', and b) that the position of 'also' in the translation correlates to some extent with the position of *-m* in the Silt'i sentences.[4] More interesting than the English translation of these utterances, however, are the interpretations given of them by three native Silt'i speakers.

(1)　a.　(No interpretation given beyond the information expressed in (1a).

　　　b.　He seems to have gone previously.

c. He wanted to buy something else besides a cow or he had gone previously and now went again to also buy a cow.

d. He has also other business.
(The K'ibbat dialect speaker inadvertently used (c) when referring to (d), and one other speaker said that he preferred (c) instead of (d).)

e. The K'ibbat speaker rejected (e).
The other informants interpreted it as suggesting that he had gone elsewhere before.

These interpretations raise the following questions. Why is it that for some of the utterances, i.e. for (1b)-(1e), the speakers felt that there was meaning conveyed to them that was not actually expressed in the utterances?[5] Why did they not suggest any such meaning for (1a)? How was it possible that they *agreed* on the non-expressed meaning in some cases, but not in others, considering that they were not given any contextual information? Since the only formal variation found between the utterances is the presence versus absence or the position of *-m*, the answers to these questions must throw light on the meaning and function of this suffix.

Similarly, consider example (2).

(2) a. *ulbaaragim laam liyookb heeda.*
Ulbarag-*m* cow he-to-buy he-went

a^1. He had gone before somewhere else for other business.

a^2. He went to U. to buy a cow — nothing else is suggested.

(2) looks very similar to (1e) — except that (2a^2) seems somewhat unexpected in view of all we have observed so far: here no specific meaning is perceived beyond what is explicitly expressed. It should be noted that (2a^1) and (2a^2) were volunteered by the same speaker, not elicited from different individuals. For the *-m* in (2a^2) the translation 'also' would seem inappropriate, and one wonders why the same utterance with *-m* can lead to two different interpretations.

Next let us consider some examples where the presence versus absence of *-m* seems to make a difference to the whole thrust of the utterance.

(3) a. *bitmač' haddam giz ilawoobaha.*
if-you-come any thing I-will-not-give-you
'If you come, I won't give you anything.'

b. *bitmač'im haddam giz ilawoobaha.*
if-you-come-*m* any thing I-will-not-give-you
'Even if you come, I won't give you anything.'

The informants interpreted (3) as follows:

(3) a. The main thrust of (3) is: 'Don't come!' It seems to be implied that 'if you don't come, I'll give you something'.

b. It communicates: 'I won't give you anything anyway'.

So the thrust of (3a) versus that of (3b) is quite different.

(4) a. A: *bašawa zilaam zalamaan.*
in-Addis-Ababa rain it-has-rained
'It has rained in Addis Ababa.'

666

b. B: *basilt'e zalamaan.*
in-Silt'i it-has-rained
'It has rained in Silt'i.'

c. B: *basilt'eem zalamaan.*
in-Silt'i-*m* it-has-rained
'It has rained also in Silt'i.'

This example is to be understood such that (4b) and (4c) are alternative comments speaker B might make on utterance (4a). According to the informants, (4b) conveys that B disagrees with the statement A: B seems to be implying that it did not rain in Silt'i. (4c), however, implies that B agrees with A and that he simply asserts that it rained also in Addis Ababa. Here again, the presence or absence of -*m* seems to affect the thrust of the utterance in important ways.[6]

Finally let us consider cases where the presence of -*m* makes an utterance infelicitous in certain contexts.

(5) a. *safiiy "saalo araašin; irasoot išlaan" baat.*
Safiya Salo he-is-farmer to-plough he-can she-said
'Safiya said, "Salo is a farmer: he can plough."'

b. *safiiya "sallo araašin; irasootam išlaan." baat.*
Safiya Salo he-is-farmer to-plough-*m* he-can she-said
'Safiya said, "Salo is a farmer; he can also plough." '

(6) a. *maymuna "wašooygoofaan; may eelabii." baat.*
Maymuna the-jug it-is-empty water there-is-not-in-it she-said
'Maymuna said, "The jug is empty; there is no water in it." '

b. *safiiya "wašooygoofaan; mayim eelabii" baat.*
Safiya the-jug it-is-empty water-*m* there-is-not-in-it she-said
'Safiya said, "The jug is empty; there is also no water in it." '

For example (5), all three informants judged the (a) utterance as acceptable, but rejected the (b) utterance. In the case of example (6), two informants found (a) fine, and objected to (b); one informant, however, made the reverse judgment, rejecting (a) and approving of (b). The question here is: Why does the presence of -*m* make an utterance infelicitous in some contexts? Also, why do the informants differ in their acceptability judgments?

As pointed out above, this selection of examples is not meant to be exhaustive, but to illustrate a number of important and interesting properties of -*m*. The next task will be to account for these properties in a coherent way.

3. THE THEORETICAL FRAMEWORK

The theoretical notions needed to account for the properties of -*m* illustrated above are the following: relevance and the principle of relevance: focus and background, and pragmatic connective.

3.1. Relevance and the principle of relevance

The communication theory of Sperber and Wilson (1982 and forthcoming) crucially involves the notion of relevance. There is no room here to outline the whole theory, and for present purposes an understanding of its central idea will be enough. This idea is that people can interpret utterances successfully because both the speaker and the hearer (unconsciously) observe the 'principle of relevance'. This principle says that the hearer expects the speaker to have done his best to express himself as relevantly as possible to the hearer under the prevailing circumstances. In this theory, an utterance increases in relevance the more it modifies the hearer's 'context' and the less effort it requires to process the utterance. 'Context' is here a technical term denoting a psychological concept; it can be roughly interpreted as referring to the sum total of information a person has available at the time of processing an utterance. But, of course, there is also a price to pay: to interpret that utterance, the hearer has to find the context in which the speaker wants his utterance to be understood. The context or knowledge of a person is highly structured in terms of the accessibility of any item in it at any given time. The less accessible an item of information is in the memory, the more processing effort will be required to use it in utterance interpretation; this will make the interpretation process 'more costly' and thus reduce the overall relevance of the utterance in question. Consequently, for successful communication, it will generally be important for the speaker to express himself in such a way that the hearer will need to access in his memory only information that is readily available to him at that time. To give a simple example, let us consider (7).

(7)   A to B: 'John said, he would do it.'

Here A can expect his utterance to convey the intended meaning to B only if B readily knows which 'John' A is talking about, who is meant by 'he' (whether John or another individual), what 'it' refers to, etc. If any of these conditions are not met, relevance theory would predict that the relevance of the utterance in that context will be reduced, and hence also its communicative success.

The view of context as a psychological notion has important consequences. In other pragmatic theories, it has often been suggested that there are different kinds of contexts: linguistic context, situational context, social context, etc., and that it is the task of pragmatics to explain the relation between utterances and these various context types. The relevance-theoretical view of context, on the other hand, while recognizing that contextual information can be derived from different sources, such as preceding utterances, environment, cultural tradition, etc., holds that the accessibility and logical properties of such information is more important than its source. Thus any information which the speaker believes to be highly accessible to the hearer at the time of making his utterance qualifies as a potential context for that utterance. This has important consequences concerning the kind of data that should form the basis of pragmatic research. In particular, it is not valid to assume *a priori* that the utterances U1 . . . Un-1 (or any subset of it) preceding the utterance Un in a coherent text are the speaker-intended context for the interpretation of Un. The reason for this is that the speaker is free to expect the hearer to supply as contextual information any information that is highly accessible at that point in time – regardless of its original source.

So, rather than treating the context of Un as *given* in terms of U1 . . . Un-1, the task of pragmatics is *to find out* what the speaker-intended context for Un is; while there is no doubt that the contents of U1 . . . Un-1 will play an important part in this process, the investigator must be aware that the correct interpretation of Un may require information *not* expressed in U1 . . . Un-1, i.e. that it may involve so-called 'implied information'.[7] Consequently, the best data for pragmatic research are those that reveal most directly what information the speaker or hearer actually uses in constructing or interpreting an utterance, and retrieving this information will require a careful questioning of the informant about his intuitions when interpreting that utterance.

3.2. Focus and Background

As explained above, for an utterance to satisfy the principle of relevance, two things are crucial: 1) the utterance must lead to some modification of the hearer's context, and 2) the hearer must be able to supply the right context (i.e. the one intended by the speaker) without great processing effort. As is not surprising, natural languages seem to have structural means to help with these tasks. One of these means is the 'focus' versus 'background' distinction. A number of different accounts have been offered for this. I shall use the one proposed by Wilson and Sperber (1979) (sketched also in Smith and Wilson (1979)), though reference will also be made to Culicover and Rochemont (1983).

According to Wilson and Sperber (1979), a sentence has a number of 'grammatically specified entailments', which are order relative to each other according to their entailment relationships. A grammatically specified entailment is obtained by substituting a semantic variable for a constituent, conveniently represented by such indefinite expressions as 'someone', 'something', etc. Thus, the English sentence (8) has the grammatically specified entailment set (9).

(8) Cynthia bought a bunch of flowers.

(9) a. Someone bought a bunch of flowers.
     b. Cynthia bought a bunch of something.
     c. Cynthia bought something.
     d. Cynthia did something.
     e. Something happened.[8]

Turning now to the focus-background distinction, it is claimed that a sentence with a constituent W marked as focus has, as its 'background', that entailment that has W substituted by a variable. Suppose that the bracketed constituent in (10) is the sentence focus.

(10) [Cynthia] bought a bunch of flowers.

Then the background of (10) would roughly be (10^1):

(10^1) Someone bought a bunch of flowers.

In terms of utterance interpretation, Wilson and Sperber suggest that, "The general point of the utterance will be seen as lying in the *increment of information* which has to be *added to the background* to obtain the proposition as a whole" (1979, 316, emphasis my own, EAG).

Conversely, the claim about the background is that ". . . the background entailment, and all entailments below it in the ordering must be irrelevant . . ." (Smith and Wilson, 1979, 182). According to relevance theory, a proposition is 'irrelevant' in the technical sense if it does not modify the hearer's context, and this is trivially true of propositions which the hearer already has in his context, i.e. which he already knows. Thus the claim that the background entailment must be irrelevant corresponds to our intuition that the background of a focused utterance is somehow shared knowledge between speaker and hearer. This point can be illustrated from (10) and (10^1); (10) would only be appropriate if (10^1) was already known to the hearer; if the hearer had not, in fact, known that somebody had bought some flowers, then (10) would seem infelicitous to him. Thus the background should normally be part of the context: the focused part will be expected to be responsible for the context modification leading to relevance. Thus, by marking a constituent as 'focused', linguistic structure helps to simplify the task of utterance interpretation.

3.3. Pragmatic Connectives

Other linguistic means for simplifying utterance interpretation are so-called 'pragmatic connectives', a notion developed by Brockway (1981, 1983). A pragmatic connective is a lexical item ". . . which links utterances and contexts" (Brockway 1981, 75). More specifically, pragmatic connectives often impose constraints on the kind of context that the hearer is expected to supply for interpreting that utterance. Brockway gives the following example:

(11) A: Fred's got the flu.
      B: So he won't be coming to the conference (1983, 6)

She comments: ". . . by prefacing his utterance by *so* the speaker not only enables the hearer to identify the conclusion which he is expected to derive from the preceding utterance, but also leads him to access the contextual assumption required for deriving that conclusion." (*op. cit.*, 8). In this case, for B's utterance to be a conclusion, A will need to supply some such contextual assumption as (12):

(12) If Fred's got the flu, then he won't be coming to the conference (*ibid.*).

The presence of *so* in B's remark in (11) induces A to make this particular contextual assumption; note that if the *so* in (11) is left out, there is no reason for A to assume that B sees a causal connection to A's remark. B might just be stating another fact concerning Fred, and his staying away from the conference might have a reason completely unrelated to his illness. In this manner, then, pragmatic connectives can constrain the kind of context that the hearer is to look for, and in doing so they reduce the processing cost for interpreting the utterance. Their ultimate contribution is thus to increase the relevance of an utterance.

4. THE AFFIX *-m* AS A PRAGMATIC CONNECTIVE

Returning to the question raised in section 2, it seems natural to suggest that the interpretations given beyond the meaning expressed reflect contextual knowledge. Furthermore, since the kind of contextual information accessed appeared to be related to the presence and specific position of *-m*, this suffix seems to be a kind of pragmatic connective. The question now is what lexical properties must one assume *-m* to have in order to account for the range of contextual phenomena discussed above. One might suspect that the answer would lie in an array of different semantic properties, different senses of *-m* perhaps, since it seems to cause meaning differences of various sorts. A look at Leslau's glosses for the meaning of *-m* in Silt'i might seem to support such an approach, since he lists three English words: "and, also, too" (1979, vol.I, 999). However, I shall start from the minimal assumption that *-m*, as a connective, has, in fact, only one lexically specified meaning or sense, and that the complexities which it seems to cause in utterance interpretation arise from the interaction of this connective with various components of our language faculty, such as syntax, semantics and pragmatics. For the present analysis of *-m*, then, I postulate the following properties:

A.   Syntactic properties: *-m* is suffixed to the leftmost subconstituent of the focused constituent of a sentence or to the sentence as a whole.[9]

B.   Semantic properties: The meaning of *-m* corresponds to the inferential properties of the conjunction "&" in propositional logic.

In the remainder of this section I will show how the range of examples given above can be accounted for under this analysis.

Let us begin by looking at example set (1). Here it is not difficult to see that there is a relationship of substitution between the utterance expressed and the additional meaning perceived by the informants and represented in (1b¹)-(1e¹). Thus, in (1b) *-m* marked the time phrase *wut'at ayaam*, 'on Monday' and in (1b¹) we find this replaced by another time phrase: 'previously'. In (1c) *-m* marked the direct object *laam*, 'cow', and in (1c¹) we find the substitution 'something else besides a cow'. In (1e¹) the locality phrase *ulbaarag*, 'Ulbarag', which is marked by *-m* in the original utterance (1e) has been replaced by 'elsewhere'. (In the second

670

half of ($1c^1$) and in ($1d^1$) the replacement relationship is not as obvious and we shall return to these cases later on.) The substitution of a constituent and the fact that part of the meaning is somehow assumed, suggest that here we are dealing with matters of focus and background, as presented above (section 3.2), and that is, of course, what we have assumed in A above. Consequently, example (1b) could have the following underlying structure:

(13) *[wut'at-m ayaam] laam liyookb ulbaarag heeda.*

Here the focused constituent would be the time phrase *wut'at ayaam*, 'on Monday', with the *-m* suffixed to its leftmost subconstituent *wut'at*, 'Monday'.[10] Variable substitution at the focus yields (14) as background entailment.

(14) *[X] laam liyookb ulbaarag heeda.*

The X is meant to indicate an appropriate semantic variable, ranging in this case over time expressions.

Now, by using the focused sentence (1b), the speaker induces the hearer to look for a contextual proposition corresponding closely to (14), but with some value of X substituted at the focus. This seems to be borne out by the fact that in our example the informants suggested that the person had gone 'previously'.[11]

Up to this point, our discussion suggests nothing more than that *-m* is some kind of a focus marker in Silt'i: what is still missing is an account of how the meaning roughly corresponding to English 'also' results. As stated in postulate B above, the semantic meaning of *-m* is simply equivalent to that of the logical conjunction '&'. Now, as is well-known, one of the inferential properties of '&' is that it is subject to the rule of &-exploitation, which states that: "From a proposition &A1, A2, . . . An any of the conjuncts Ai may be inferred" (McCawley 1981, 24). In a parallel manner, the semantic property of *-m* expresses the fact that *-m* conjoins the proposition expressed and the speaker-intended contextual proposition in such a way that both of the conjuncts may be inferred as valid. Thus, in example (1b), the use of *-m* first of all instructs the hearer to look for a contextual assumption in the way described above, and secondly tells him that this assumption is to be considered true.

Let us now turn to example (4) to see this more clearly. In that example, the natural reaction of Silt'i speakers was that (4b) conveys a sense of disagreement with (4a), but that (4c) conveys a sense of agreement with (4a). Since there seems to be no other overt difference than the absence vs. presence of *-m*, the meaning difference must be attributable to this suffix, and on the analysis assumed here, the reason is quite obvious: if *-m* indicates that both the context and the utterance are to be considered as true, and if (4a) is the context for B's response, then clearly B is expressing agreement with (4a) when replying with (4c).

Perhaps at this point a comment is in order as to why (4b) is interpreted as disagreement with (a), although there is no overt marker to signal this. Within the framework of relevance theory there seems to be a plausible explanation for this phenomenon. As indicated in section 3, the principle of relevance gives the hearer the expectation that the speaker has tried to be as relevant as possible in the circumstances, and this he would do by striving for maximal context modification at minimal processing cost. When speaker B utters (4b), if he is in agreement with context (4a), that context, i.e. the belief held by speaker A, will simply be increased by a new proposition. Under the disagreement interpretation, however, A is not only to add new information to his knowledge, but also to change the belief (4a) he originally held. Thus, other things being equal, the disagreement interpretation is predicted by the principle of relevance to be preferred as the more relevant one. The presence of the overt connective *-m*, indicating the truth of both context and utterance, would of course alter the interpretation.

In summary, this 'focal use' of *-m* can be characterized in its pragmatic effects as follows. Firstly, by its association with focus it helps the hearer to separate the main point of the utterance from its contextually assumed part; secondly, it clarifies the logical relationship that the hearer is to assume as holding between the utterance and the context. Both these functions reduce the processing effort for the hearer, and hence contribute to the relevance of the utterance. The other examples in (1) illustrate how different constituents of the sentence can be focused and marked by -*m*. (1c) is, however, of special interest in that it illustrates a property of -*m* which has not been discussed here yet, but which is, in fact, already predicted by our analysis. As will have been noted, the intuition of the native speakers suggested two somewhat different interpretations:

(1c¹) i. He wanted to buy something else besides a cow, or
     ii. He had gone previously and now went again to buy a cow also.

On interpretation i), the focused constituent clearly seems to be *laam*, 'cow', suggesting the following underlying representation:

(15) *wut'at ayaam [laam-m] liyookb ulbaarag heeda.*

The background could then be:

(16) *wut'at ayaam [X] liyookb ulbaarag heeda.*[1,2]

For interpretation ii), the focus-background division does not seem as obvious. What does seem clearly belong to the background is that he had gone to Ulbarag previously, because ii) asserts specifically that he "goes again" – and that is, in fact, expressly stated in the interpretation: "he had gone previously". This would leave as focused information "to also buy a cow"; on this analysis, the underlying representation of (1c) would be (17), with -*m* attached to the leftmost subconstituent in the verb phrase:

(17) *wut'at ayaam [laam-m liyookb] ulbaarag heeda.*

The background would then be:

(18) *wut'at ayaam [X] ulbaarag heeda.*

Thus, formally, the two interpretations differ in the size of the focused constituent, with a corresponding meaning difference in the context to be accessed: in i) the context specifies that he had gone with the purpose of buying something else besides a cow; in ii), the context specifies that he had gone to Ulbarag before with a purpose other than buying a cow. Further discussion with the informants confirmed this view; they suggested e.g. that the context could be that in ii) the main purpose of his going was, for example, to visit his father and that he then, as the utterance itself asserts, also wanted to buy a cow. Another piece of evidence for this is that (1d) was apparently felt by the informants to correspond closely to (1c) in meaning: note that one of them, whose dialect does require the -*m* to be on the first subconstituent of the focused constituent, did, in fact, use (1c) instead of (1d) without noticing it. Ambiguity of the kind just observed with (1c) is predicted by our analysis; it follows from the fact that -*m* is suffixed to only one subconstituent of the focused constituent. This implies that where the constituent marked by -*m* is part of a larger phrase, ambiguity about the scope of the focus can easily arise. Since such scope ambiguity with focus has been observed in other languages as well (cf. Wilson and Sperber 1979, Culicover and Rochemont 1983), this seems to again confirm that a solution that associates -*m* with focus is on the right track.

One question that needs further comments, is why (1e) was rejected by the K'ibbat speaker but found acceptable by the other two informants. While I cannot claim at this point to fully understand all the factors involved, there are indications that this may have to do with the preferred position of focused constituents in a sentence. Thus I have observed on other occasions that speakers of the K'ibbat dialect prefer to have focused constituents early in the sentence, where speakers from other dialects do not express such a preference. Further study is needed to clarify this issue. As it stands, the analysis adopted here allows for -*m* to be associated with a whole sentence as well as with the focus. This provision is motivated by examples like (2a^2), which illustrate what is probably the most common use of -*m* in running texts.[13] (2a^2) differs from all the examples considered so far in that the informant said that no meaning beyond that expressed in the utterance itself was conveyed to him. This is precisely what one would expect on our account: if an utterance is not seen as having a focus, then neither will it have a background that would automatically be suggested by it. Yet, pragmatically, the -*m* would still have relevance value: even though in these instances it does not help to constrain the *kind* of context to be supplied by the hearer, it still helps him to establish the *right logical relationship* between the utterance and the context to be supplied — i.e. to view them both as true. This indication again reduces processing effort.[14] If translated into English, this use of -*m* would probably normally be rendered by 'and'. Note that here again our analysis predicts potential ambiguity: where -*m* is suffixed to the first word of a sentence, it can be interpreted either as focal, with the first constituent in focus, or it can be seen as non-focal, i.e. as attaching to the whole sentence. This is, of course, precisely the ambiguity found in (2).

Lastly, let us turn to what are probably the most challenging cases, i.e. examples (3), (5) and (6). In example (3) the main concern is (3b), in a focal interpretation.[15] On this interpretation, (3b) would have the underlying structure (19) and the background (20).

(19) *[bitmač'-m] haddam giz ilawoobaha.*

(20) *[X] haddam giz ilawoobaha.*

Thus (3b) would access a context where the speaker assumes that the hearer already knows that under a certain condition X the speaker would not give anything to the hearer. The question is, how this could lead to the meaning (3b^1):

(3b^1) The implication is: I won't give you anything anyway!

Perhaps this will become easier to see when we look at another kind of paraphrase informants tend to give for -*m* plus a conditional verb form, as shown in (21^1) and (22^1) below:

(21) *[biyook'eet-m] faranka toobayaat.*
    if-he-beats-her-*m* money she-gives-him

(21^1) 'If he beats her, if he doesn't beat her, she gives him money.'

(22) *[zilaam biizalm-m] bagaar ilak'eer.*
    rain if-it-rains-*m* at-home he-does-not-stay

(22^1) 'If it rains or does not rain, he doesn't stay at home.'

From these two examples one can see how the meaning for cases like (4b) is arrived at: the informants apparently treat these cases as 'abbreviated' forms for claiming that both when the condition obtains and also when it does not obtain, the consequent will be true. Thus, the speaker in a sense exhausts the logical possibilities of the condition expressed, considering the case where it obtains and also the case where it does not obtain, asserting that the consequent will be true in either case. This means, in fact, that the consequent is claimed to be logically independent of the truth value of the condition — and that seems to be very similar in meaning to what the English expression 'anyway' in (3b^1) suggests. This observation, however, still does not explain why -*m* in a conditional clause should communicate the consideration of both the case where the condition is fulfilled and where it is not fulfilled. In terms of our analysis, for this to be true, we would have to assume that the value substituted for the variable in the assumed context is the negative of the value actually expressed. Since there is nothing in our analysis of the semantics of -*m* itself that could account for this, we shall have to look to relevance factors for a solution. First of all, assuming the symbolic representation p-*m*→q for the utterance expressed, the focus-association of -*m* leads us to concentrate on p as the relevance-establishing part of the utterance. Secondly, the principle of relevance calls for a highly accessible context, as well as a significant context modification. Considering context accessibility first, it seems that, given a proposition p, forming its negative -p is one of the simplest operations that will yield a new proposition related to p. If this is correct, then it would not be surprising to find that the hearer will consider the negative of the condition expressed when looking for an easily accessible context. Thus if p-*m*→q symbolizes the logical structure of the utterance, the hearer could easily construct as context the proposition -p→q.[16] This interpretation provides not only a highly accessible context for the utterance — it also entails that the utterance will lead to a substantial modification of this context. If the belief -p→q is contextually assumed, i.e. if this is what the speaker thinks the hearer originally believed, and if this assumption is correct, then the speaker's expressed claim that p→q will be novel to the hearer. Note, however, that the speaker is not simply asking the hearer to change his belief from one conditional, i.e. from -p→q, to another conditional, i.e. to p→q; rather, and here again the meaning '&' of -*m* seems well-motivated, he suggests to the reader to hold *both* conditionals as true, i.e. to believe (-p→q) & (p→q) — in other words, he suggests to the hearer that q is logically independent of p.[17] Applied to example (3b) this yields the interpretation (23):

(23) 'If you come, I won't give you anything, and if you don't come I won't give you any-thing.'

As is easily seen, (23) corresponds well to (3b[1]).

Finally, let us consider examples (5) and (6). Here it seems significant that in the utterances rejected by the informants the -*m*-marked part was entailed by the preceding part. Does the present analysis support this intuition? For our discussion, let us concentrate on example (5b). The significant part of (5b) is represented in (24).

(24) *irasootam išlaan.*
      to-plough-*m* he-can

Interpreting -*m* as focally-used, we obtain the underlying representation (25) and the background (26).

(25) *[irasoota-m] išlaan.*

(26) *[X] išlaan.*

According to focus theory and relevance theory, the increment of information that one needs to add to (26) in order to obtain (24) must be the main point, i.e. the context-modifying element, of the utterance. However, as the example has been construed, (24) is immediately preceded by (27):

(27) *saalo araašin.*
      Sale he-is-farmer

As was mentioned above, in Silt'i culture this would normally entail quite obviously that Salo is able to plough. Furthermore, according to relevance theory, the content of the immediately preceding utterance is a highly accessible context. For our example, this means that there is a highly accessible context for (24) that has as one of its obvious entailments what is supposed to be the main point of (24). In other words, the focused part of (24), which should establish its relevance, is, in fact, already contextually given in (27). Thus, under the present analysis, the unacceptability of (5b) can be explained as a violation of the principle of relevance. Note that an important assumption here is that -*m* is, in fact, used focally here. If the -*m* is viewed as non-focal, this argument will not hold. This is interesting in view of the fact that one of the informants had no problem accepting (6b), though it is closely parallel to (5b). If this informant happened to interpret -*m* here as non-focal, this apparent exception is taken care of, because then there would be no commitment on the speaker's part that the noun *may* is the crucial, context-modifying element, and so no clash with the principle of relevance would arise on this point.[18]

4. CONCLUSION

This analysis of -*m* in Silt'i is of significance in the following respects. Firstly, I hope that it will be a stimulus for the application of pragmatic theory to phenomena in Ethiopian languages — an area of study that seems to have found little interest so far. Secondly, noting that a number of other Ethiopian languages have morphemes that seem to be quite similar in function to that of Silt'i -*m* (for Amharic cf. Kapeliuk 1978; on Gurage varieties see Leslau 1979, vol.II, 17), some of the insights gained from Silt'i may prove relevant to some of these other languages as well. Thirdly, this study has shown that relevance theory can handle well issues of utterance interpretation in a language of the Afro-asiatic phylum, thus providing some concrete support for its claim to universal validity.

NOTES

1. Van Dijk's (1977) account of 'intensional conjunctions' in natural language (English *also, to, moreover*) runs as follows:

    $V(A.B,a.i) = 1$ iff
    (i) $(\exists b)(\exists j)(V(A,b,j) = 1)$
    (ii) $(\exists c)(\exists k)(V(B,c,k) = 1)$
    (iii) bCc, where $b=c$ or $b<c$
    (iv) $<b,c>Pa$
    (v) $jU\{A\}ck$
    (vi) $i = kU\{B\}$
    (vii) $a,b,c\exists\phi$
    (viii) $(\exists d)(dca)$
             or $(\exists C)((C\epsilon i)\&((C.A)\&(C.B)))$
             — for conjunctions where connection is indirect

    (ix) $(\exists C)((C\epsilon i)\&(C=A))$
             — when A is presupposed, e.g. in subordinates

             $V(A.B,a,i) = 0$ otherwise (p.43)

2. At this point I would like to thank my Silt'i informants, Ashagre Kebede, Hussein Redi and Mengistu Mulat, who patiently endured intensive questioning on their intuitions about Silt'i utterances. I thank the Institute of Ethiopian Studies, Addis Ababa University, for sponsoring my research, and I thank my colleagues at the Institute of Language Studies, Addis Ababa University, as well as Dr. L. Bliese, Miss U. Claudi and R. Sim for the comments they have given on this paper. The choice of this topic was determined not by the belief that this connective has particularly exotic properties not found in other Ethiopian languages (cf. e.g. Kapeliuk (1978) on Amharic), but by the challenge of trying this approach out on an Afro-Asiatic language, which, to my knowledge, has not been done before.

3. In particular, I will limit myself to connective usages of -*m*; there are other occurrences of

-m, e.g. with numerals and other quantifiers such as *hull*, 'all', that do not seem to be connective in nature. (Cf. also Kapeliuk's list in footnote 8 on p.273 of her article (1978)). There is, however, an important difference in her use of the term 'connective' and my own, in that her's refers to a connection between sentences in a text, rather than to a connection between utterances and contexts. For a discussion of the significance of this difference see section 3.1 below. Unless stated otherwise, my analysis deals with the dialect of Silt'i spoken around K'ibbat town.

4. Leslau (1979) lists three English glosses for Silt'i *-m*: "and, also, too" (vol.I, p.999).

5. The obvious answer here seems to be to appeal to presuppositions. However, as is well-known, this concept is in itself quite problematic (cf. e.g. Levinson 1983, McCawley 1981), and it will be seen that an adequate account of *-m* can be given without reference to presuppositional theories of meaning.

6. There were no significant differences in stress or intonation between (4b) and (4c). In fact, some preliminary investigations into the use of suprasegmentals seem to suggest that neither stress nor intonation are ordinarily used to mark sentence constituents as emphatic or focal. The normal means used for these purposes are syntactic (e.g. clefting) or morphological (suffixes).

7. The following example taken from running text illustrates the point. In one fable the following utterance is made by one of the participants, the mouse:

    yareer ašim yawaalšinni wulata iknablinšaaw.
    later you-*m* which-you-did-for-me favour I-will-return-to-you
    'Later I will return to you the favour you also did for me.'

    Here the informant's interpretation of *-m* was clearly focal: he said that it seemed to him that the speaker had said this before to someone else who had done her a favour, although this is simply not mentioned anywhere in the story, as the informant himself realized.

8. These are by no means all the entailments of (8), but only the grammatically specified ones. The following would also be an entailment of (8), but not one that is grammatically specified:

    Cynthia bought some plants.

9. This disjunction is reducible if we assume that the whole sentence can be in focus; Culicover and Rochemont briefly raise this issue in a footnote, but leave the matter undecided (1983, 150, fn.31). As far as I can determine, this issue has no direct bearing on the claims made here.

10. In other dialects of Silt'i, the requirement that *-m* be suffixed to the leftmost subconstituent does not seem to hold. Thus, in the dialect spoken around Elos, I have recorded instances of e.g. *wut'at ayaamin*.

11. The assumption that the context should have some definite value of X in focus at F seems reasonable, though it may not be a necessary one.

12. Whether or not *wut'at ayaam* here belongs to the background is debatable. When questioned, the informants' reactions indicate that this is possible, but not necessary.

13. Though I have not done extensive counts to check this impression, a quick count in three narrative texts seems to confirm it; the ratio of non-focal to other uses of *-m* in these texts were as follows: 28 to 12, 9 to 2, and 6 to 2.

14. Wilson and Sperber (forthcoming) have suggested that a necessary part of utterance interpretation for an individual is to decide what attitude to adopt toward the proposition expressed — whether e.g. to believe it or not. For further comments on this view cf. Gutt (1984).

15. I shall not deal with the possible, but uninteresting reading of (3b), where *-m* would be interpreted as non-focal.

16. This argument seems to find support from the following observation. When temporal clauses are marked by *-m* they do not convey the sense of 'anyway' to the hearers. This could easily be explained in terms of the present analysis: if conditional constructions represent thought sequences with the logical structure p→q, then the negative counterparts of the propositions are highly accessible because they follow from the simple logical operation of negation. It is the high accessibility of the negative counterparts that leads to the sense 'anyway'. For temporal clauses there is no such obvious operation that would generate a specific, highly accessible proposition closely related to the propositions expressed. Hence the sense 'anyway' does not naturally arise in temporal clauses with *-m*.

17. Standard logic shows that the conjunction (-p→q) & (p→q) is true only if q has the value 'true' — the truth value of p does not matter.

18. What seems less obvious is why he rejected (6a), which the other informants accepted. If he took the *-m* in the (b) example as non-focal, it is possible that he did not like (6a) in view of the fact that the two sentences were just juxtaposed, with no connective indicating their relation to each other. This, however, needs further investigation.

REFERENCES

Brockway, D., 1981 — "Semantic constraints on relevance" in H. Parret, M. Sbisa and J. Verschueren (eds.), *Possibilities and limitations of pragmatics*, Amsterdam, John Benjamins, pp.57-78.

——————— 1983 — "Pragmatic connectives", Paper read at the Spring 1983 meeting of the Linguistic Association of Great Britain, mim.

Culicover, P. W. and M. Rochemont, 1983 — "Stress and focus in English", *Language*, 59.1, pp.123-165.

Gutt, E. -A., 1984 — "Relevance theory and propositional attitudes", ms.

Jackendoff, R. S., 1972 — *Semantic interpretation in generative grammar*, MIT Press, Cambridge MA.

Kapeliuk, Olga, 1978 — "Particles of concatenation and reference in Amharic", *Bulletin of the School of Oriental and African Studies*, v.41, part 2, pp.274-282.

Leslau, W., 1979 — *Etymological Dictionary of Gurage (Ethiopic)*, Vol.I-III, Harrassowitz, Wiesbaden.

Levinson, S., 1983   *Pragmatics*, CUP, Cambridge.

McCawley, J. D., 1981   *Everything that linguists have always wanted to know about logic (but were ashamed to ask)*, Blackwell, Oxford.

Smith, N. V. and D. Wilson, 1979   *Modern Linguistics. The results of Chomsky's revolution*, Penguin, Harmondsworth.

Sperber, D. and D. Wilson, 1982   "Mutual knowledge and relevance in theories of comprehension" in N. V. Smith (ed.), *Mutual knowledge*, Academic Press.

——————   (forthcoming) "On defining relevance" (to appear in R. Grandy (ed.), *Festschrift for Paul Grice*).

Van Dijk, T. A., 1977   "Connectives in text grammar and text logic" in van Dijk and J. S. Petofi (eds.), *Grammars and Description*, de Gruyter, Berlin, 1977.

Wilson, D. and D. Sperber, 1979   "Ordered entailments: an alternative to presuppositional theories" in *Syntax and Semantics, Vol.II Presupposition*, Academic Press.

——————   (forthcoming) "Inference and implicature in utterance interpretation" (to appear in T. Myers (ed.), *Reasoning and discourse processes*, Academic Press.

IS THERE A LANGUAGE WITH AN INDEFINITE NOMINATIVE

– BURJI?

Dick Hayward

In his recent book *Language Universals and Linguistic Typology* (1981), Bernard Comrie proposes a functional explanation for the origin of systems of differential case marking, which predicts that there should exist languages in which the marked case (i.e. the nominative in an ergative/absolute system and the accusative in a nominative/accusative system) will only exhibit overt distinctiveness in NPs which *vis à vis* their clause functions are atypical or unnatural in the degree to which they are associated with animacy and/or definiteness. Thus, if case marking is partial only, it might be expected to appear either in 'Object' NPs high in animacy and/or definiteness or in 'Subject' NPs low in animacy and/or definiteness. Comrie notes (1981: 122ff) that while three of the predicted types are witnessed among various of the World's languages, the fourth, namely the case where overt nominative marking occurs only in a NP which is low in definiteness, has not yet been attested. In the present paper it is suggested that the predicted, though hitherto missing, type may well be represented by the Ethiopian language Burji.[1]

I

Before concentrating on the major theme of this paper, which, in accordance with its title and the preceding paragraph, will concern itself with clarifying the term 'indefinite nominative' and with the question of whether Burji does or does not exhibit such a phenomenon, I should like to draw attention to something of more general typological interest concerning the type of case system found not only in Burji but in many other languages of the Horn of Africa, for it seems to be the case that in this part of the World there is an uncomfortably large number of counterexamples to an alleged language universal. The universal in question claims that:

> "Where there is a case system, the only case which ever has only zero allomorphs is the one which includes among its meanings that of the subject of the intransitive verb." (Greenberg 1963: Universal No.38)

Expressed in somewhat easier language the claim made here is that given a system of case marking for subjects and objects, the most generally unmarked category will be the subject of an intransitive verb.

The functional explanation proposed for this universal by Comrie (1981: 118ff) invokes what we might call the 'odd-man-out' principle. To talk about this principle, as well as to facilitate discussion in the next part of the paper, I shall follow Comrie (1981: 104ff) and, yet earlier, Dixon (1972: 59ff) in making the following terminological distinctions: (i) S will represent the single argument of the predicate in an intransitive construction; (ii) A will represent the agent argument of the predicate in a transitive construction; (iii) P will represent the patient argument of the predicate in a transitive construction. Where the syntax of a language employs case marking to distinguish just one of these three arguments, it does so on the basis of an identification of the other two arguments. This principle of marking the 'odd-man-out' clearly accounts for the two major case systems encountered among languages. As shown in the following diagram:

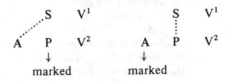

679

languages with a so-called nominative/accusative system (Latin, German and Amharic, for example) identify A and S, and so mark P; languages with a so-called ergative/absolutive system (Basque and Eskimo, for example) identify P and S, and so mark A.

The Yuman languages of California are cited by Comrie (1981:119[2]) as being exceptions to the Greenbergian universal quote earlier, but, as I observed above, there are a number of Northeast African languages which also violate Universal No.38. Like the Yuman languages, the way in which they do this involves identification of A and S, as in nominative/accusative languages, though, unlike those languages, they do not operate with the 'odd-man-out' principle with regard to case marking, for, rather than marking P, it is A and S that are marked, viz:

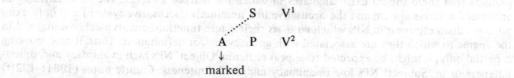

It should be noted that languages which do this are by no means members of a close-knit genetic group, for the following examples are taken from Qafar (an East-Cushitic language[3]), Zayse (a member of the Ometo cluster of the North Omotic languages[4]), and Turkana (an Eastern-Nilotic language[5]).

Qafar:

         S   V[1]
yí toobokoyti amaatéle
my brother-nom he-will-come
my brother will come

         A   P   V[2]
yí toobokoyti kabqíyta yiggife
my brother-nom leopard he-killed
my brother killed a leopard

         A   P   V[2]
kabqiytí yítoobokoyta yiggife
leopard-nom my brother he-killed
a leopard killed my brother

citation forms: *toobokóyta, kabqíyta*

Zayse:

         S   V[1]
ʔe gármáy hangi
the lion-nom went-away
the lion went away

         A   P   V[2]
ʔe tolkóy gárma dengi
the hyaena-nom lion he-saw
the hyaena saw a lion

         A   P   V[2]
ʔe gármáy tolkó dengi
the lion-nom hyaena he-saw
the lion saw a hyaena

Turkana:[6]

V^1 S
àŋìcìt ayɔ̀ŋ
be angry 1sg-nom
I am angry

V^2 A   P
àɲami ayɔ̀ŋ akiriŋ
eat 1sg-nom meat
I eat meat

V^2 A   P
kàmina ŋèsì ayɔ̀ŋ`
loves she-nom me
she loves me

citation forms: *ayɔ̀ŋ`, akiriŋ, ŋèsì`*

In the Qafar examples the nominative case marker replaces any word-final vowel. That this is not simply a mutual substitution of inflectional suffixes, and that the replaced vowel is a lexical element rather than an inflection is evident from the fact that the form found as a P is identical to the citation form.[7] The same argument needs to be applied in the Turkana examples, where the case distinction is signalled tonally, and where the unmarked case form is claimed to be that found as P on the basis of the fact that it is identical to the citation form.

In this aspect of their grammars Qafar, Zayse and Turkana are by no means unique among their respective language groups; indeed, it would not be surprising to find that such languages constitute a majority type in the Horn. It would be of some interest to test out this speculation empirically, though it would be of considerably more interest to compare languages of this type among themselves, as well as with the Yuman languages, to see whether some further common property (or properties) emerged such as might suggest an explanation for their case marking behaviour.[8] For the limited scope of the present paper I would like to underscore the fact that such languages naturally provide an additional source of data for any search for languages marking an indefinite nominative, for without them investigation would be confined in the main to languages with an ergative/absolutive case system. For discussion purposes it will be convenient to provide a label for the sort of case system seen in languages such as Burji, Qafar, Zayse, Turkana, Yuman, etc. If we refer to this type as 'nominative', equally simple labels can be adopted for case systems of the ergative/absolutive and nominative/accusative types, for which I propose the labels 'ergative' and 'accusative' respectively.

To account for the fact that there are languages in which in transitive clauses only some subject NPs actually undergo case marking the explanation advanced by Comrie takes into account the flow of information in discourse. Since subjects typically represent an intersection of the semantic argument of **agent** and the pragmatic role of **topic**, we most commonly encounter situations where subject NPs are **definite** and their head nouns are **animate**. With objects the reverse commonly holds true, for these typically present a **patient (goal)** argument as the **comment**, with the concomitant expectations that the NP concerned will be **indefinite**, and its head will be **inanimate**. The high probability that subjects will be animate and definite and objects will be inanimate and indefinite makes for a good deal of redundancy in information flow. Some of this redundancy would be obviated if subjects or objects were to receive overt case marking only when expectations **were not** fulfilled. Such an increased economy in case marking would be evident if, for example, objects in accusative languages were to be overtly indicated only when they were animate and/or definite[9], or if subjects in ergative or nominative languages were to be marked only when they were inanimate and/or indefinite. The situations predicted may be diagrammed, viz:

1. Accusative case system:

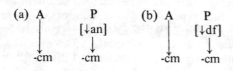

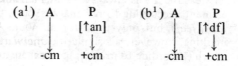

2. Ergative and Nominative case systems:

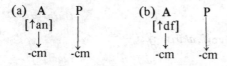

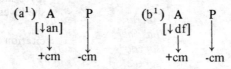

In the diagram **+cm** and **-cm** are abbreviations for '+ case marker' and '- case marker' respectively. The feature abbreviations **an** (animate) and **df** (definite) are preceded by upward or downward pointing arrows, which represents the fact that both animacy and definiteness are regarded as properties present to a relatively higher (upward arrow) or lower (downward arrow) degree. It should be made clear that for Comrie animate and inanimate are not seen as a binary or polar opposition, so much as scalar values in a hierarchy of animacy (1981: 178ff). Similarly, definiteness is in this framework seen as relative rather than absolute (1981: 127ff; see also the later discussion in the present paper).

Of the four types of situation *vis à vis* differential case marking which are predicted by the hypothesis outlined above (i.e. 1(a¹), 1(b¹), 2(a¹) and 2(b¹) in the above diagrams) empirical substantiation is available for all but one. Concerning this Comrie remarks:

> "Somewhat embarrassing is the absence of clear attestations of the fourth
> expected type, i.e. marking of an indefinite A . . ." (1981: 123)

In the next section we shall turn our attention to Burji, since there are at least some grounds for thinking that this language exhibits the fourth type of situation.

II

The outline analysis of the noun morphology of Burji and of certain aspects of the phonology of the language which are represented here represent some of the conclusions argued for in a fuller way in Hayward (forthcoming b).

At least at the underlying level all noun forms are vowel-final, though through the operation of certain automatic phonological rules a good many forms are actually pronounced either without a final vowel or with an extremely reduced one (see below). The lexical form of a noun is unmarked for case and is referred to as the absolutive form (AF). It is this form which is found as the P in transitive clauses; it is also the citation form. For expository convenience the final vowels found in AFs will be referred to as 'terminal vowels' (TVs). TVs are not predictable as to their qualities, and hence are lexical, though the fact that some of them can be replaced in certain word forms leads us to treat them as distinct formatives. Burji has grammatical gender, and whether a noun is masculine (m.) or feminine (f.) will determine its morphological behaviour when case marking occurs. In terms of the TVs which they have in the AF m. and f.

nouns show a lot of overlap; thus both genders contain nouns in which the underlying TVs are apparently /a/, /aa/ and /oo/. Where the TV is /i/, however, the noun can only be masculine, and where it is /ee/, the noun can only be feminine. Nevertheless, their behaviour under nominative case marking shows that any approach which starts by identifying TVs across genders is misguided. Indeed, according to my analysis, in two large groups of m. nouns the noun is regarded as ending in a sequence of two vowels of which only the second is the TV. Moreover, whereas the TV is always present in f. nouns, in m. nouns it has to be regarded as a detachable element. According to my analysis then, there are four types of TV for f. nouns (i.e. /a/, /aa/, /oo/, /ee/), but only three for m. nouns (i.e. /a/, /i/, /oo/). (When we come to consider case marking, however, all similarities between the two genders will disappear.) The nine nouns, which (according to my data) are exhaustively representative, are illustrated in Table 1.

Table 1

feminine		masculine	
[1] /sun+a/	(sún[ə])	[2] /min+a/	(mín[ə])
[3] /baš+aa/	(baš[á])	[4] /moona+a/	(moon[á])
[5] /sor+oo/	(sor[ó])	[6] /bidd+oo/	(bidd[ó])
[7] /gar+ee/	(gar[é])	[8] /gaaʄ+i/	(gaáʄ[ʲ])
		[9] /galda+i/	(gald[áj])

(Glosses: [1] nose; [2] house; [3] grass; [4] kraal; [5] knife; [6] centre-pole of a house; [7] calf; [8] rope; [9] baboon.)

To account for the surface forms shown for the above words, and in particular for the final segments in those words, three phonological processes need to be mentioned.

1. Accent Assignment: Assignment of the accent to the penultimate vowel mora of a word.[10]

2. Glide Epenthesis: Insertion of a palatal glide (/j/) after the low vowel (/a/) when it is followed by /i/.

3. Desyllabicization: Desyllabicization of any unaccented vowel in absolute word-final position.

The Desyllabicization process has the following effects:

(i) The rightmost of a sequence of two identical vowels is deleted.

(ii) A final single vowel is reduced to a 'shadow vowel'[11], and in the case where what precedes is a glide or a voiceless fricative, the vowel is usually lost altogether.

It is important to mention Glide Epenthesis and Desyllabicization at this point, for since they are absolutely general, they will be seen to apply also in the nominative forms, to which we now turn.

There are two sets of nominative forms, and, assuming for the moment the relevance of the terms, I shall refer to them as the definite nominative (DN) and indefinite nominative (IN) respectively. Table 2 sets out the details of these for the nine nouns shown in Table 1.

Examination of the phonological forms of the DN suggests that their formation involves:

(a) The truncation of the final mora in any TV having a double vowel in f. nouns.[12] In nouns such as /sun+a/ the TV is single, and in such cases the DN will be identical to the AF.

683

(b) The replacement of the TV by /i/ in m. nouns. This is, of course, a vacuous process in the case of nouns in which the TV is itself /i/.

All other relevant details of the pronunciation of DN forms result from the three phonological rules described earlier.

Table 2

absolute	definite nominative		indefinite nominative	
feminine:				
/sun+a/	/sun+a/	(sún[ə̥])	/sun+a+t+i/	(sun[áʃʸ])
/baš+aa/	/baš+a/	(báš[ə̥])	/baš+aa+t+i/	(baš[aːʃʸ])
/sor+oo/	/sor+o/	(sór[ʋ̥])	/sor+oo+t+i/	(sor[oːʃʸ])
/gar+ee/	/gar+e/	(gár[ɪ̥])	/gar+ee+t+i/	(gar[eːʃʸ])
masculine:				
/min+a/	/min+i/	(mín[ɪ̥])	/min+i+k+u/	(min[ʋ́h])
/moona+a/	/moona+i/	(moon[áj])	/moona+i+k+u/	(moon[ajʋ́h])
/gaaɟ+i/	/gaaɟ+i/	(gaaɟ[ɪ̥])	/gaaɟ+i+k+u/	(gaaɟ[ʋ́h])
/galda+i/	/galda+i/	(gald[áj])	/galda+i+k+u/	(gald[ajʋ́h])
/bidd+oo/	/bidd+i/	(bídd[ɪ̥])	/bidd+i+k+u/	(bidd[ʋ́h])

According to the analysis shown in the above table, the formation of the IN involves:

(c) The suffixation of /t+i/ to the AF of f. nouns.
(d) The suffixation of /k+u/ to the DN of m. nouns.

The analysis proposed in (c) raises an additional question, namely, how it is that an underlying /t+i/ is posited for surface [ʃʸ]. As some later examples will demonstrate (see Table 3), the element we are concerned with here consists of two distinct formatives: a f. gender marker /t/, and a nominative suffix /i/. When this phonological sequence arises in the morphology, palatalization occurs.[13] Palatalization only occurs, however, when the /t/ is preceded by some segment, i.e. it does not happen word-initially. If the preceding segment is underlyingly a non-continuant (an oral or nasal stop or /l/) /t/ is palatalized and affricated.[14] If the preceding segment is underlyingly continuant (vowel, glide, fricative or /r/), /t/ is palatalized and spirantized, and, unless further assimilatory processes apply to it, the resultant phonetic segment will be [ʃ].[15] Desyllabicization accounts for the virtual or even total loss of the final /i/ suffix.

The analysis in (d) is even less transparent, and requires some explanation with respect to the following matters: (i) how it is that underlying /k+u/ surfaces as [ʋh]; (ii) why it is that the DN suffix /i/, which is posited underlyingly for all m. nouns in both nominative forms, fails to appear in the IN of nouns such as *mina*, *gaaɟi* and *biddoo*.

Table 3

	absolute		nominative	
	masculine	feminine	masculine	feminine
1p 'our'	nin[k]a	nin[t]a	nin[k]u	nin[ʧ]i
2p 'your'	šin[k]a	šin[t]a	šin[k]u	šin[ʧ]i

Quite a lot of evidence could be adduced for the claim that the phonological form marking the m. nominative is /k+u/, but space is limited here.[16] Nevertheless, possessive determiners such as those shown in Table 3 point strongly to this conclusion. (Note, that the f. forms with underlying /t+i/, which were assumed in earlier discussion, also receive some of their justification from such possessive determiner forms.)

The distribution of phonetic /k/ in Burji shows one interesting gap: it does not occur post-vocalically.[17] In intervocalic positions where there is a preceding double low vowel one hears a segment fluctuating between a weak velar spirant /x/ and /h/. In other intervocalic contexts one hears only /h/. The most revealing analysis is, I believe, to say that these intervocalic weak fricatives arise from the lenition of an underlying /k/. As a result of this process the m. gender suffix /k/ exhibits an alternation such as that seen in comparing the predicative forms of consonant-final and vowel-final adjectivals, e.g.:

masculine:

haʃʃin[k]a 'strong', cf. f. form *haʃʃin[t]a*
hoyt'anee[h]a 'short', cf. f. form *hoyt'anee[t]a*
t'udaa[x ~ h]a 'white', cf. f. form *t'udaa[t]a*

If we assume the underlying representations for the INs of m. nouns to be like those shown in Table 2, we have a straightforward explanation for the /h/ in the surface forms.

The absence of any obvious reflex of the underlying /i/ in the IN forms *min[úh]*, *gaaʃ[úh]* and *bidd[úh]* is, I believe, the result of quite low level phenomena involving a leftwards 'trans-laryngeal' spreading of the lip rounding feature to any preceding high vowel, and the automatic Desyllabicization process, which in this case results rather naturally in the total loss of any distinct vocalic segment finally.[18]

Attention is directed to two things that motivate the proposal that there is an underlying /i/ in all m. INs. Firstly, unless we posit the presence of **some** vowel preceding the gender element /k/ in the INs *min[úh] et al.*, we have no way of explaining why /k/ should weaken to /h/, i.e. why the form is not **min[k]u* (cf. *nin[k]u* in Table 3). Secondly, to suggest that the vowel which precedes the gender element /k/ is simply the TV (a hypothesis which, admittedly, would imply a greater degree of generalisation in the formation of the IN for m. and f. nouns) would fail to explain the presence of a palatal glide in IN forms like *moon[ajúh]* (rather than **moonaa[x ~ h]u*). In the view presented here the /j/ is a direct consequence of the underlying /a+i/ sequence and Glide Epenthesis.

It is now appropriate to consider under what syntactic conditions DN and IN forms occur, since to this point it has simply been assumed that such a distinction is necessary for something other than morphological reasons.

DN forms are characteristic of subject NP heads which are accompanied by some type of 'expansion'. With respect to such 'expansions' no distinction needs to be made between specifiers and complements of heads, e.g.:

(a) *ičči harr[ɥ] laafaa*
my donkey is weak
AF: /harr+ee/ f. (cf. /gar+ee/ in Tables 1 and 2)

(b) *iyyu t'ung[ɥ] č'ind'akka*
my finger is small
AF: /t'ung+a/ m. (cf. /min+a/ in Tables 1 and 2)

(c) *ond'i manda[j] dansaa*
the girl is beautiful
AF: /manda+i/ m. (cf. /galda+i/ in Tables 1 and 2)

(d) *laafaa lamm[ʊ̆] d'ukkubanni*
the weak man fell sick
AF: /lamm+i/ m. (cf. /gaaʄ+i/n Tables 1 and 2)

(e) *reennoo[h] meen[ʊ̆] ninta gossa*
the people who died (were) our kinsfolk
AF: /meen+a/ m. (cf. /min+a/ in Tables 1 and 2)

(f) *kaači woččatta d'ag[ə̆] inaa beenni*[19]
that dog's ear is missing
AF: /d'ag+a/ f. (cf. /sun+a/ in Tables 1 and 2)

The IN is encountered in the heads of subject NPs where there is no 'expansion', e.g.:

(g) *č'iid'd'aa[ʃʊ̆] mina gaa tayd'aččeetta*
a bird is roosting on the house
AF: /č'iid'd'+aa/ f. (cf. /baš+aa/ in Tables 1 and 2)

(h) *wayr[ʋh] boolladdi gud'a*
a rat is hiding in the hole
AF: /wayr+a/ m. (cf. /min+a/ in Tables 1 and 2)

(i) *hoora[ʃʊ̥] urranka gabalaa d'ak'k'ad'a*
a forest stretches as far as the mountain
AF: /hoor+a/ f. (cf. /sun+a/ in Tables 1 and 2)

(j) *homas[ʋh] hak'k'aa gabi godaddi yed'a*
a snake is coming down from the tree
AF: /homas+i/ m. (cf. /gaaʄ+i/ in Tables 1 and 2)

(k) *roop'il[ajʋh] hil'ʔaalayči hala*
an aeroplane is falling from the sky
AF: /roop'ila+i/ m. (cf. /galda+i/ in Tables 1 and 2)

The distinction between IN and DN forms might appear to be simply related to gender marking. It might be argued that a m. or f. gender sensitive element has to appear on the head if, in the absence of any NP expansion to the left of the head, such an element cannot occur elsewhere in the phrase. But the force of this argument is considerably weakened by the fact that there is no parallelism of behaviour in NPs in non-subject functions. Thus, as a nominal predicate or as an object of a verb or postposition a head of an unexpanded NP does not appear with gender sensitive marking. This suggests that what is important is not so much gender as case.

It is, however, also necessary to question whether the IN : DN distinction is just syntactic or whether it has a pragmatic basis, i.e. whether 'definiteness' is really what is involved. It might be argued that the issue concerned is specificity; the DN and IN forms occurring with specified and non-specified NP heads respectively. But this would not explain the asymmetrical distribution of the distinction. Why should non-specificity matter only in **subject** NPs?

One piece of evidence that the DN : IN distinction is not simply a morphosyntactic response to the presence of some element(s) to the left of the NP head is seen in the behaviour of personal names and pronouns, which in Burji have DN forms. Regardless of the sex of the referents personal name nouns (at least as far as my data indicates) may behave like f. common nouns with respect to nominative marking[20], as Table 4 shows:

Table 4

name (AF)	sex	Nominative (one form only)
/goon+a/ (Goón[ə̢])	m.	goón[ə̢]
/waač̣'č̣'+ee/ (Waač̣'č̣'[é])	m.	waač̣'č̣'[ʮ]
/boor+oo/ (Boor[ó])	m.	boór[ʮ̣]
/t'umm+aa/ (T'umm[á])	f.	t'úmm[ə̢]
/god+ee/ (God[é])	m./f.	gód[ʮ]

The personal pronouns are less straightforward to assess, since comparison of the absolutive and nominative forms shows that morphologically determined allomorphy affects all non-3rd person stems, and in the 1s forms suppletion is involved, viz:

Table 5

	absolutive	nominative (one form only)
1s	/ee/	/an+i/ (án[ʮ])
2s	/š+ee/	/aš+i/ (áš[ʮ])
3ms	/is+i/	/is+i/ (ís[ʮ])
3fs	/iš+ee/	/iš+e/ (íš[ʮ])
1p	/ninsin+oo/	/naan+o/ (naán[ʮ̣])
2p	/šinsin+oo/	/ašin+o/ (ašín[ʮ̣])
3p	/isin+oo/	/isin+o/ (isín[ʮ̣])

It is certainly true to say that in the nominative there is no trace of the /k+u/ or /t+i/ termin-ations of the IN, even though their occurrence in 3ms and 3fs subject pronouns might have seemed *a priori* to be not unlikely. Furthermore, if we assume that in their morphological be-haviour all the personal pronouns, except that for 3ms[21], have f. gender (cf. personal names), then their nominative endings are exactly what we expect as DNs.

Definiteness in the highest degree presupposes that the hearer can uniquely identify the en-tity spoken about (Comrie 1981: 121). It might be thought, therefore, that the issue of whether the DN : IN distinction related to definiteness could be resolved by an examination of texts.[22] Unfortunately, such an examination has not proved to be entirely convincing. Cer-tainly there are cases where the DN occurs with subject NP heads where no expansion is present, though where the the occurrence of the DN would be explicable in terms of discourse identifiability. But there are also apparent counterexamples in which the IN appears in dis-course contexts in which the entity concerned has been introduced previously, and so would normally be thought of as definite — and would certainly require a definite article in English translation.

I believe we may interpret the situation in the following way. Failure to mark the IN can always be taken to mean that the subject entity is identifiable **to some degree**; but marking the IN cannot always be taken to mean that an entity is unidentifiable. The problem is simply that Burji does not show an exact 1 : 1 correlation between syntactic marking and the encoding of cues for pragmatic interpretation.[23] If we juggle with the definition of definiteness given at the beginning of the preceding paragraph, we might say that the highest degree of indefiniteness would mean that the hearer was incapable of identifying the entity spoken about at all. Here Burji would use the IN. A lower degree of indefiniteness would mean something less than a total inability to identify an entity. Here too Burji could still use the IN. However, the overt presence of some linguistic item(s) that places restriction on the scope of reference of the head will imply some degree of definiteness, and this will categorically require the DN form. I think that in all fairness one may claim that the morphological distinction between IN and DN forms is where the pragmatic difference between the polar extremes of unique identifiability and complete lack of identifiability happens to be grammaticalized as far as Burji is concerned.

Finally, it is necessary to address one very obvious objection to the claim that the IN forms of Burji represent the missing type of case marking system as described in section I. The objection is quite simply that Burji marks not only the heads of indefinite subject NPs but also those of definite subject NPs, whereas the description of the unattested type given in I assumed a situation where nominative marking was partial only. Here I think we need to have recourse to the notion of markedness, for if we compare the IN and DN forms of Burji, there can be little doubt that the former is the more strongly marked one. Table 2 shows that in three of the noun types DN forms surface as non-distinct from the absolutive. Moreover, perception of the DN always involves close attention to short final vowels, which due to the operation of Desyllabicization, makes these forms very much harder to hear than the IN forms.[24] But the strongest argument in support of saying that the mainthrust of nominative marking is carried by IN forms is a fact demonstrated earlier for masculine nouns, namely, that IN marking is **superimposed on** DN marking. Consideration of the highly marked status of IN forms compared to DN forms suggests that the latter are being superceded.

I believe that before one could establish the suggestion made tentatively here that Burji has a case system of the missing type, a number of matters would need further research. Of primary importance here would be a thorough examination of textual material, ideally carried out with the intuitions of a linguistically trained native speaker. But I think it may be pertinent to conclude this paper by recalling a general point made earlier, namely that case systems of the type I have referred to in this paper as 'nominative' have received too little attention. The hope is expressed, therefore, that by drawing attention to some aspects of the rich potential of Ethiopian languages for general theories about case, other linguists, especially Ethiopian linguists, may recognise the importance of this area for future research.

REFERENCES

Andrzejewski, B. W. 1957   'Some Preliminary Observations on the Booran Dialect of Galla', *Bulletin of the School of Oriental & African Studies*, 19: 354-74.

Bliese, L. F. 1981   *A Generative Grammar of Afar*. The University of Texas at Arlington: Summer Institute of Linguistics.

Comrie, B. 1981   *Language Universals and Linguistic Typology*. Oxford: Blackwell.

Dimmendaal, G. J. 1983   *The Turkana Language*. Dordrecht: Foris.

Dixon, R. M. W. 1972   *The Dyirbal Language of North Queensland*. Cambridge Studies in Linguistics 9. Cambridge: CUP.

Greenberg, J. H. 1963   'Some Universals of Grammer with Particular Reference to the Order of Meaningful Elements', pp.73-113 in Joseph H. Greenburg (ed.) *Universals of Language*. Cambridge, Massachusetts: M.I.T. Press.

Hayward, D. Forthcoming   a) 'Notes on the Zayse Language', to appear in Dick Hayward (ed.) *Omotic Language Studies*.

b) *Aspects of the Phonology of Burji*.

Hudson, G. 1976   'Highland East Cushitic', pp.232-277 in M. Lionel Bender (ed.) *The Non-Semitic Languages of Ethiopia*. Monograph No.5. Occasual Papers Series. African Studies Center. East Lansing: Michigan State University.

Moreno, M. M. 1938	'Note di lingua Burji', *Rivista degli studi orientali*, 17: 350-398.
Munro, P. 1974	*Topics in Mohave Syntax.* Unpublished Ph.D. dissertation, San Diego, University of California.
Sasse, H. J. 1982	*An Etymological Dictionary of Burji*, Kuschitische Sprachstudien Vol.1. Hamburg: Buske.
Sasse, H. J. and H. Straube 1977pp.	'Kultur und Sprache der Burji in Süd-Äthiopien: Ein Abriss', pp.239-266 in Möhlig, W. J. G. *et al.* (eds.), *Zur Sprachgeschichte und Ethnohistorie in Afrika.* Berlin: Reimer.
Vine, B. 1981	'Remarks on African "Shadow Vowels" ', pp.388-427 in George N. Clements (ed.), *Harvard Studies in Phonology Vol.II.* Bloomington, Indiana: reproduced by Indiana University Linguistics Club.
Wedekind, K. 1980	'Sidamo, Gedeo (Derasa), Burji: Phonological Differences and Likenesses', *Journal of Ethiopian Studies*, 14: 131-176.

NOTES

1. 'Burji' is the name which has traditionally been used in referring both to the D'aaši people and their language (*D'aašinkaa afai*). The majority of the D'aaši live in Ethiopia, mostly to the east of Lake Chammo. However, since the time of Menelik IInd a large colony of D'aasi have been living in the Northern Province of Kenya, especially around the township of Marsabit. My own research on the language was conducted at Marsabit in 1979. My main informant there was Ibrahim Woč'č'ee, a young man who had left his homeland near Soyyaama in Sidamo Province only six months previously. It is generally agreed by linguists that the language of the D'aaši belongs within the Highland group of East Cushitic. For further information on the language see Hudson 1976, Moreno 1938, Sasse 1982, Sasse and Straube 1977, Wedekind 1980.

2. See also Munro 1974.

3. For further information on Qafar see Bliese 1981.

4. For further information on Zayse see Hayward forthcoming a.

5. For further information on Turkana see Dimmendaal 1983.

6. The Turkana examples are taken from Dimmendaal 1983.

7. This same form also functions as head of a nominal predicate NP, and as direct object of a verb and of a postposition in Qafar.

8. For example, in my work on East Cushitic and Omotic languages it has often seemed to me that there is another very important syntactic function of NPs which may have a bearing on the matter of case systems. The function concerned is that of nominal predicate, i.e. a NP complement to verbs translating into English as 'be', become', etc. Here we have what is

syntactically a 'two place' verb. In all the languages which have a case system of the 'nominative' type that I am familiar with, nominal predicates appear in the absolutive. Furthermore, for pragmatic purposes, these same languages all seem to utilize cleft and pseudo-cleft constructions (i.e. equative clause structures) to a very marked degree. Perhaps we should include the nominal predicate function in the discussion, labelling it 'C(omplement)', say, and its subject 'S^1'. Then one might argue that nominative languages identify P, but not S, with C. Such an identification would be based on the syntactic similarity of the two 'two place' constructions. S (the 'odd-man-out' so far) might logically be classified with either C and P or A and S^1. Nominative languages select the latter grouping. This line of thought might be worth further investigation.

9. Amharic is a good example of a language which marks the accusative only in object NPs high in definiteness.

10. Some verb forms behave idiosyncratically, but apart from these, accent assignment is as stated here.

11. For an interesting discussion of 'shadow vowels', see Vine 1981. For discussion of this phenomenon in another Ethiopian language, Oromo, see Andrzejewski 1957.

12. It would seem probable that the vowel shortening process in Burji reflects what was an accent shift process at an earlier stage. The fact that Burji is now virtually a fixed accent language implies a reanalysis of the secondary effect (or by-product) of accent shift as the primary marker of grammatical distinction between the AF and DN forms.

13. This particular process of palatalisation appears to be quite general, and is the source of a number of morphological alternations in the converb (a non-final participle-like form, which in Burji is based on the old East Cushitic perfect).

14. Further assimilatory processes may interact with this, so that in addition to [tʃ], voiced [dʒ] and ejective [tʃ¹] may arise.

15. For example, if the preceding segment is /s/ total assimilation to it will occur.

16. For a more complete discussion, see Hayward (forthcoming b).

17. The statement does not include geminate /kk/, which, like other geminates in Burji, only occurs intervocalically. Preconsonantal /k/ undergoes assimilation.

18. Comparable pronunciation features are observed in Amharic, in, for example, በግሁ, እየሁ etc.

19. In some dialects the verb form here would be *inaa beenno*.

20. It should be noted that personal name nouns and certain kinship terms in Burji have an alternative (archaic-?) type of DN marking, e.g. *Goona+nkoo; Booroo+nkoo; Maree-+nkoo*; etc. (See also Hudson 1976: 253).

21. Explicably enough, the 3ms personal pronoun behaves like a masculine noun having a TV in *i*.

22. Unfortunately, examination of texts has been very restricted. Although there is no space in the present paper to exemplify the conclusions reached, the Burji texts available in Moreno (1938) illustrate the situation reasonably well.

23. In Burji certain items take the IN, even though they are definite, i.e. they behave grammatically as if they were indefinite. The reverse of this is seen in English, where items which are obviously definite (such as personal name nouns) never take a definite article, i.e. they behave within the grammar as if they were not definite.

24. Such case distinctions are signalled only by shadow vowels, and one relatively recent account of Burji (the linguistic analysis of which was based on tape-recorded material) describes the nominative solely in terms of the perceptually salient IN forms.

THE HIGHLAND CUSHITIC HYPOTHESIS

Grover Hudson
Michigan State University

In his important review of Cushitic characteristics and sub-grouping Robert Hetzron (1980) proposed three revisions in the generally accepted sub-groupings within Cushitic: the separation of Beja from the family, the inclusion of Southern Cushitic with the Lowland (Eastern) languages, and, only tentatively and cautiously, the joining of Agaw with Highland East Cushitic (HEC) as a new 'Highland Cushitic' group. This paper considers this third hypothesis on the basis of the evidence of the independent pronouns.

The 'Highland Cushitic' hypothesis deserves consideration because it is based on a careful review of the literature and is founded on stated principles and evidence, and also because it reminds us that, before Hetzron 1980, sub-classifications of Cushitic and the Cushitic hypothesis itself – the existence of a Cushitic proto-language branched from Afroasiatic – were rarely founded on the basis of evidence entirely acceptable today, but were largely geographical by-products of the pre-scientific Hamito-Semitic speculation, 'Cushitic' languages being in origin the non-Semitic but Semitic-looking languages of the Horn, more a geographical-typological than diachronic-linguistic establishment.

Evidence for the Highland Cushitic hypothesis is as follows: (1) a negative morpheme ti/di found in Agaw Awngi and Sidamo; (2) a velar element in the verb suffixes of the 2nd and 3rd plural of Awngi and Hadiyya; (3) the verb 'come' of the shape Vnt in Agaw and Burji, vs. mVt of the Lowland languages; (4) metathesis of n in HEC except Burji and with traces in Agaw 2nd pl. suffixes and the numeral 'five'; (5) case marking for definite accusative in Bilen, Kemant and Burji, and directive wa in Bilan, Kemant and Sidamo; (6) in various of the languages case agreement between adjective and noun; and (7) genitive markers attached to possessors but agreeing in gender with the possessed (Hetzron 1980: 54-61).

Hetzron was self-critical of this evidence for Highland Cushitic. He noted that explanations other than shared innovation were usually available, and that evidence sometimes concerned only one language of a group especially Awngi of Agaw and Burji of Highland East Cushitic, the most heterogeneous/archaic of their groups (see Hetzron 1976b for the correspondence of heterogeneity/archaicness, Hudson 1981 for the relative heterogeneity of Burji in HEC, and D. L. Appleyard's paper at this conference for the relative heterogeneity of Awngi in Agaw). Here I am extending his criticisms and pursuing his suggestion (p.61) that the Highland Cushitic hypothesis be at least seriously entertained.

As for the metathesis of n, this is a reasonable natural tendency where obstruent+n clusters arise, as they tended to in Cushitic verb and pronoun formation. There is, for example elsewhere than in HEC and Agaw, Elmolo 2nd pl. $iinse$ (Heine 1980:187) vs. e.g. Wellegga Oromo $isin(i)$. Likewise, the extension of case agreement to adjectives is a tendency reasonably found in miscellaneous languages of the world.

Regarding the verb 'come' Hetzron argued against a suggestion of H. J. Sasse that the Burji/Agaw form Vnt is a development from that of Lowland languages, mVt. His argument is plausible, nevertheless the latter is a completely natural source for the former via vowel loss and nearly universal nasal assimilation: $VmVt > Vmt > Vnt$. But in fact there appear to be separate roots with m and n, and HEC has them both. Burji has two imperatives of the verb 'come', regular $inte$ sg./$inteye$ pl., and $aamu/aame$, irregular. The latter root appears also in suppletive imperatives of 'come' in Gedeo (Darasa), Kambata, and Sidamo. In Kambata furthermore the imperatives are $ami/amecce$, the latter showing a stem with final t (cf. $iti/icce$ 'Eat!', stem it-), and in Alaba the regular stem for this verb is $ameet$-, though the final t is absent in imperatives $ami/amehe$.

Regarding the presence of a velar element in the 2nd and 3rd pl. of the verb, we seem to have this as well in the imperfect suffixes of Werizoid languages (Black 1976: 226), and we should note that k's also characterize the plural pronouns of various Cushitic languages (Wellegga Oromo: Gragg, p.178; Dasenech: Sasse, p.207), and particularly the 2nd and 3rd pl. pronouns of S. Cushitic Ma'a (Elderkin, p.289). That is, this feature could reasonably be an archaism or a development independent in Agaw and HEC.

As for the negative *di* of Sidamo, I can see this less as an archaism which Sidamo shares with Agaw (if as a product of proto-Highland Cushitic borrowing from Omotic), than as a Sidamo development of an HEC emphasis or focusing particle, also surviving in Burji questions as *da* (Hudson 1976: 266), in Kambata questions with *-n-do* (267), and in Hadiyya strong imperatives in *-du* (269). Of course Awngi *ti* could have a similar origin on the Highland Cushitic hypothesis, but this would be more speculative. By the way, a cognate morpheme may appear in Hadiyya's Ethiopian Semitic neighbor Ennemor, in which plural negative verbs have a non-Semitic extension *-da* (Leslau 1983: 14-17).

The Agaw-Burji definite accusative Hetzron admits is not a correspondence of form and meaning and, since the category appears elsewhere in Afroasiatic, "it may be an AA heritage" (p.58). Similarly, the seventh feature concerns not the arbitrary phonetic exponent of a would-be morphological innovation, but the peculiar use of the familiar Cushitic and Afroasiatic masc. *k* and fem. *t*. In fact I am not satisfied that Burji *-na* marks definite accusative. In my data it appears to have a broader function, perhaps marking focus.

Hetzron mentions that for two points, negative *ti/di* and directive *wa*, Omotic influence on both HEC and Agaw is a possibility. Regarding this, it should be noted that on recent evidence Omotic influence on both groups is more likely than the general present-day geographical position of the languages would support, with Omotic generally limited to areas west of HEC and well removed from Agaw. The northernmost Omotic language, Shinasha, is a near neighbour to Awngi, and the recently recognized divergent Omotic language, Mao (Fleming 1984, Bender 1984), appears in pockets of territory so far north of other Omotic as to suggest that it is a survival of Omotic languages once widespread in the area.

The possibility that Cushitic languages spread north at the expense of Omotic, already settled in central as well as western Ethiopia, emphasizes a characteristic of Afroasiatic language spread that just might have made Afroasiatic divergence significantly different from that of Indoeuropean. Afroasiatic almost certainly spread in populated regions, unlike most of Indoeuropean, which expanded later, in a time so soon after the last Ice Age in Europe, that this must largely have been in relatively unpopulated territory. I am not ignoring the evidence of the pre-Indoeuropean peoples of Europe, but the multiplicity and diversity of northcentral African languages (emphasized, for example, by Dalby 1970) suggests that the strength of substratum effects in the spread of Afroasiatic would have been great in comparison with that of Indoeuropean.

I mention this for two reasons. First, this probable difference between the circumstances of language divergence in the two families seems worth keeping in mind when substratum effects are being considered in Ethiopian linguistics. Second, the possibility of substratum influences might be suggested for some of the evidence from the pronouns of Agaw and HEC which I want to consider now in regard to the Highland Cushitic hypothesis.

When the independent pronoun sets of the five or six Agaw languages (Hetzron 1976a: 19-20) and the five HEC languages (Hudson 1976: 256) are abstracted and compared, four characteristics in particular are seen to typify the Agaw set in comparison to that of HEC: (1) 3rd sg. m. and f. based on *n* with the feminine augmented by *t* (vs. HEC *isi* m./*ise* f.); (2) in Awngi Bilen and Kemant 2nd sg. based on *an* (*ənt* vs. *ati* of HEC); (3) in Xamir and Xamta, 2nd sg. of the form *kVt*; (4) the Agaw 1st and 2nd person plural pronouns apparently derived from the singulars by suffixation of *Xn* (only the HEC 3rd pl. appears to have this source). Concerning each of these four characteristics it appears that Agaw is archaic, while HEC conforms to the Lowland Cushitic pattern.

(1) The 3rd m. sg. in *n* is seen elsewhere in Cushitic only in Oromo of Lowland, and in Iraqw of S. Cushitic (Elderkin, p.285). It appears in Afroasiatic in Egyptian, where all the pronouns have *n*-bases, in Berber where the 1st and 3rd have *n*-bases, and as one of the two Chadic 3 m. sg. forms. Something like HEC *isi* is common in the rest of Cushitic. Fem. 3 sg. *n* is seen in

Iraqw (Elderkin, 286), and this augmented by *t* is seen in Egyptian and Berber, as well as Agaw. Something comparable to HEC *ise* is typical of those Cushitic languages other than Agaw which distinguish the two 3rd person forms.

(2) The basis *an* (Agaw *ən-t*) of the 2nd sg. is known in Afroasiatic only in Agaw and Semitic. Egyptian forms the 2nd as well as other pronouns on the basis of *n*. The HEC form *ati* is perfectly Cushitic, except for Agaw.

(3) The Agaw 2nd sg. pronouns with *k-t*, in Xamir and Xamta, Hetzron (1976a: 19) suggested are replacements of *ənt*, and derivations involving the # prefixed possessive pronoun. But this appears to be basically k^w-, and there is no suggestion of the stem to which this was added to yield Xamir *kit* and Xamta *ketā/kit* (m./f.). On the other hand, 2nd sg. independent pronouns of shape *k*X are not uncommon in Afroasiatic: Dāsenech (Sasse, 207), Elmolo (Heine 1980, 187) and Iraqw (Elderkin, 285) of Cushitic, and Modern South Arabian (*h-t*), Berber, and Chadic.

(4) The seeming formation of plural pronouns of 1st and 2nd person by addition of X*n* to the singulars (this is far from obvious on internal and comparative reconstruction, but I think generally supported) is seen outside of Agaw in 'Sam' languages (Heine 1978: 52). The like formation of the 3rd plural, as well as 1st and 2nd, is suggested in Semitic, Egyptian, Berber and Chadic, though generally clearer for 2nd and 3rd than 1st. Again the HEC plural pronouns fit better the pattern of other Cushitic languages: a velar element in 2nd pl. in Werizoid (Black 1976: 226) and S. Cushitic (Elderkin, 285-93); and only the 3rd pl. seemingly formed on the 3rd sg. plus *n*: Konso (Black 1974: 131), Wellegga Oromo (Gragg, 178), Werizoid (Black 1976: 226), and S. Cushitic (Elderkin).

From the evidence of these independent pronoun features, the Highland Cushitic hypothesis is unsupported. Far from showing connection with HEC, Agaw shows connections miscellaneously within Cushitic, and maybe just as strongly with other Afroasiatic groups. The HEC forms, on the other hand, reinforce the typical association of this group with Lowland Cushitic.

Admittedly my survey is rather superficial, in the nature of mass comparison, and this makes possible the influence of chance associations, which are certain to arise, given the large number of languages and the small number of phonemes which typically figure in grammatical morphology (Jakobson 1965). But this combination of factors would throw up associations randomly, not in the pattern we have seen.

The modern Afroasiatic pronouns are probably not derivative of any Proto-Afroasiatic set, but rather the branches independently derived their own sets by use of proto-language deictic elements on different bases and in different patterns (Hodge 1969). Still, I believe the present survey supports the claim of Zaborski (1976: 77) that "Cushitic pronouns retain very archaic traits and they offer very promising material for comparative study." Besides evidence against the Highland Cushitic hypothesis, the independent pronouns suggest the early separation within Cushitic of Agaw, which shares features broadly in Cushitic and Afroasiatic. If Hetzron's other hypotheses (the exclusion of Beja from Cushitic and the grouping of Southern and Lowland languages, are borne out, as seems likely, Cushitic can be bifurcated into Agaw and the rest.

BIBLIOGRAPHY

Bender, M. L., (ed.) 1976   *The Non-Semitic Languages of Ethiopia*. E. Lansing, MI: African Studies Center, Michigan State University.

Bender, M. L., 1984   "Remnant languages of Ethiopia and Sudan", *Nilo-Saharan Language Studies*, M. L. Bender (ed.), E. Lansing, M.I.: African Studies Center, Michigan State University: pp.336-54.

Black, Paul 1974   "Lowland East Cushitic: subgrouping and reconstruction." Yale University, Ph.D. dissertation.

——————— 1976   "Werizoid", *in* M. L. Bender (ed.), 1976, 222-31.

Dalby, David 1970   "Reflections on the classification of African languages", *African Language Studies*, 2: 147-71.

Elderkin, E. Derek 1976   "Southern Cushitic", *in* M. L. Bender (ed.), 1976, 278-97.

Fleming, Harold 1984   "The importance of Mao", *Proceedings of the Seventh Conference of Ethiopian Studies*, S. Rubenson (ed.), 31-8, Lund.

Gragg, Gene 1976   "Wellegga Oromo" *in* M. L. Bender (ed.), 1976, 166-95.

Heine, Bernd. 1978   "The 'Sam' Languages: a history of Rendille, Boni, and Somali", *Afroasiatic Linguistics*, 6.2: 1-93.

——————— 1980   *The Non-Bantu Languages of Kenya* (*Language and Dialect Atlas of Kenya*, Vol.II), Berlin: Dietrich Reimer.

Hetzron, Robert 1976   a) "The Agaw Languages", *Afroasiatic Linguistics*, 3.3: 31-71.

———————   b) "Two principles of genetic classification", *Lingua*, 38: 89-108.

——————— 1980   "The Limits of Cushitic", *Sprache und Geschichte in Afrika*, 2: 7-126.

Hodge, Carleton 1969   "Afroasiatic Pronoun Problems", *International Journal of American Linguistics*, 35: 366-76.

Hudson, Grover 1976   "Highland East Cushitic", *in* M. L. Bender (ed.), 1976, 232-77.

——————— 1981   "The Highland East Cushitic Family Vine", *Sprache und Geschichte in Afrika*, 3, pp.87-121.

Jakobson, Roman 1965   "Quest for the essence of language", *Diogenes*, 51: 21-37 (Also in his *Selected Writings*, II, The Hague, 1971).

Leslau, Wolf 1983   *Ethiopians Speak*, Part V. Chaha-Ennemor, Wiesbaden: Franz Steiner.

Sasse, Hans-Jürgen 1976   "Dasenech", *in* M. L. Bender (ed.), 1976, 196-221.

Zaborski, Andrzej 1976   "Cushitic Overview", *in* M. L. Bender (ed.), 1976, 67-84.

SEMANTIC ANALYSIS OF SOME MORPHOLOGICAL PHENOMENA
IN AMHARIC

Olga Kapeliuk

In the Semitic languages it is not unusual that a bound morpheme, whether it is an affix or a nominal scheme, not only marks the word's grammatical category, but also places it within a specific semantic group. Thus, for instance, the nominal scheme *faʿāl* is used in Hebrew and in Arabic in the names of professions and trades: Hebrew *sabbāl* 'porter', *ṭabbāḫ* 'cook'; Arabic *naǧǧār* 'carpenter', *ṣarrāf* 'money changer'. In Arabic adjectives formed according to the scheme *ʾafʿal* denote colours and bodily or spiritual characteristics, mainly negative: *ʾaḥmar* 'red', *ʾaḥmaq* 'stupid', *ʾaḥwal* 'squinting'. In modern Hebrew the suffix *(ṭ)ron*, originally detached from the noun *teaṭron* 'theatre', is used in creating names of various bodies which perform on stage: *bubbaṭron* 'puppet show', *čizbaṭron* 'a satirical review' from *bubba* 'doll' and *čizbaṭ* 'joke' respectively.

In the modern Ethio-Semitic languages most of the morpho-semantic characteristics of the ancient languages were lost. Nevertheless we can mention several morphological formations, independent with respect to the ancient forms, in which morphological peculiarities are combined with a specific semantic content. In Amharic we can quote the following cases:

I

In the plural of names, beside the regular plural ending in *-očč* and beside the plural forms inherited from Geʿez, some names are found in which a suffix *-amočč* is attached to the singular. I have found this suffix, which is not listed in the grammars, with the following nouns:[1]

> ዘመድ 'relative' pl. ዘመዳሞች
> ጉዋደኛ 'companion' pl. ጉዋደኛሞች
> እጮኛ 'betrothed' pl. እጮኛሞች
> ወዳጅ 'friend' pl. ወዳጃሞች
> ባልንጀራ 'friend' pl. ባልንጀራሞች

These nouns can also be used with the regular plural suffix *-očč*. But their use with the special suffix *-amočč* is linked to their semantic content. All of them have this in common that they designate human beings related to each other by family ties, by betrothal or by friendship. Their relationship is reciprocal and symmetrical. When this aspect has to be stressed, *-amočč* is used, for example:

1. የቅርብ ፡ ባይሆን ፡ ዘመዳሞች ፡ ናቸው   "They are relatives, though not close"[2]

2. በኮሌጅ ፡ ጉዋደኛሞች ፡ ነበሩ   "They were friends in College"[3]

3. የመጨረሻ ፡ ወዳጃሞች፡መሆናቸውን ፡ ለማሪጋገጥ፡እጅ፡ለእጅ ፡ ተሳሳሙ   "They kissed one another's hand, to prove that they were the best friends in the world"[4]

When we analyse the use of the suffix *-amočč* we find that two other nouns — ወንድም 'brother' and እት / እነት / 'sister', which belong to the same semantic group as the nouns quoted above — have among their multiple and irregular plural forms also a form ending in *-amočč*. The plural 'brothers', as listed in the grammars and the dictionaries, is rendered by ወንድዎች (also 'brethren'), ወንዳማች, ወንድማማች and ወንድማሞች; 'sisters' are እትማማች , እትማ ማጆች and እትማሞች . The feminine form is obviously created after the analogy of the masculine. The plurals in which the consonant *m* is repeated denote brothers and sisters from the same father and mother. It is plausible that what was the repeated last consonant plus the plural suffix -*očč* in **ወንድማሞች** (and consequently in **እትማሞች**) came to be considered as the plural suffix of nouns designating persons with a reciprocal relationship between them. The analogy can be seen from the following example:

4. **ሁስቱ፡በመንገዱ ፡ ጕን ፡ ለጕን ፡ ሲሄዱ ፡ የቅርብ፡**
   ዘመዳሞች ፡ ወይንም እኅትማማቾች ይመስላሉ
   'When they both walk side by side in the street, they seem close relatives or sisters'[5]

II

The existence of another small group of irregular plurals can perhaps be also explained with the help of semantics. Let us consider the following two pairs of substantives and their plural forms as they are listed in the grammars and the dictionaries:

> **ጋዜጣወ** 'lady' pl. **ወይዛዝር** , **ወይዛዝርት**, **ወይዛዝርቶች**
> **ሹም** 'chief' pl. **ሹማምንት**, **ሹማምት**, **ሹማምንቶች**
> **ቄንጃ** 'young girl, beautiful' pl. **ቄነጃጅት**, **ቄነጃጅቶች**
> **ጕበዝ** 'young man, strong' pl. **ጕበዛዝት**

These unusual plural forms are derived from their singulars by a change in the nominal scheme, in the same way as the broken plurals are derived from their singulars in Arabic, Ge'ez or Tigrinya. In the Amharic plural forms the scheme is identical and it consists in the repetition of the third consonant (or of the second if there is no third one) and the insertion of the vowel *a* between the two identical consonants. Such a form has no parallel in Arabic or Ge'ez while Tigrinya has only the plural **ሹማሙ·ቲ**. The form, however, has some similarity to the Ge'ez plural which is used with singulars that have more than three consonants, like **መስፍን** pl. **መሳፍንት** or **መኩንን** pl. **መካዋንንት**. This brought Marcel Cohen to the following statement:

> "Sur le modèle, apparemment, des mots précédents (**መኩዋንንት, አጋንንት**)
> à deux radicales semblables, et peut-être avec d'autres influences acces-
> soires, il s'est formé une série de pluriels à répétitions ou additions de con-
> sonnes, designant des êtres humains, souvent des dignitaires: **ሹም** 'chef' a
> **ሹሞች, ሹማምንት, ሹማሞች, ሹማምንቶች** ; **ወይዘር** 'femme de qualité' connaît
> un pluriel **ወይዛዝር** ."[6]

This explanation could be adequate if only the plural of **ሹም** and **ወይዘር** existed, the more so since these two nouns are found quite often beside Ge'ez broken plurals which denote noble persons, connected with the royal court, for example:

5. **መከዋንንቱም ፡ ሹማምቱም** "The lords and the chiefs"[7]
6. **መከዋንንቱ ፡ መሳፍንቱ ፡ ወይዛዝሩ** "The lords, the princes and the ladies"[8]

Another possible explanation is that the plural forms of the four nouns in question be-longed to a larger group of broken plurals, perhaps at an early stage of Amharic or in some kind of proto-neo-Ethiopian, when this grammatical process was still active. F. Praetorius quotes the following plural forms, in addition to the four nouns mentioned before: **ሎሌ** 'servant' pl. **ሎላሌት** **ዶር** 'hen' pl. **ድራርት** , **ሚዜ** 'bridesman' pl. **ሚዛዙት** , **ሞነኮስ** 'monk' pl. **መነከዋከስት** and **ጣባል** 'young animal' pl. **ደብዋቡሎች** .[9] All these are lost today, with the exception of our four nouns. Perhaps they were preserved because they constitute one semantic group within which two pairs of human beings are opposed to each other by their sex on the one hand and by their age on the other hand, each pair carrying at the same time the most desirable attributes of its age and sex: respectability and office for the elders, beauty and strength for the young.

Another interesting nominal form is the abstract noun which ends in *-nnat*. This noun is derived from words which have an independent existence in the language, by adding to them the suffix *-nnat*. This abstract form is used extremely frequently in contemporary Amharic. But what is striking is not so much its frequent use, as its morphological potentiality and the semantic field it covers.

A quick comparison between Amharic and English, for instance, shows that in the former the potentiality of the abstract form is much greater, both in morphological and in semantic terms. In English most of the abstract nouns are derived either from adjectives, for example: justice, wisdom, bravery, height, truth, honesty, etc., or from nouns, but only such nouns which mark human beings or abstract notions, for example: manhood, heroism, friendship, relationship, etc. But otherwise no nouns serve as the base of abstract nouns, except if they first become adjectives, as in the following example:

> "I remember once going out to the whaling station at Durban . . . That was
> a smell to beat all smells: a real eighty-percent proof distillation of dis-
> gusting fishiness oiliness, oh, I don't know what."[10]

In Amharic, on the other hand, the derivational possibilities are much more diversified and, consequently, the semantic field covered by this form is much larger. If we examine the two following tables, which are arranged according to the grammatical, and in the case of the noun, also the semantic nature of the word from which the abstract noun is derived, we see that in Amharic nouns ending in *-nnat* are derived from adjectives, participles, pronouns, one adverb, one number and from nouns which designate human beings, names of instruments, abstract notions and concrete objects.

TABLE 1

Adjective	Participle	Pronoun	Adverb	Number
በጎነት	ፈሪነት	አንተነት	እኔ ብቻነት	አንድነት
መጥፎነት	ጎላፊነት	እኛነት		
ልዩነት	ጫኝነት	ማንነት		
ዓመለ ፡ ቢስነት	አጋቢነት	ምንነት		
ልብ ፡ ወለድነት	ከፋችነት			
ዓለም ፡ አቀፍነት	አቀባይነት			
ግድ ፡ የለሽነት	አነሣሽነት			
ጥፋተኛነት	አሽናፊነት			
ዘረኛነት	አስረጂነት			
ብሔረተኛነት	አማካይነት			
ሀሳባዊነት	ታማኝነት			
ሰብአዊነት	ተቀባይነት			
ቀኝናዊነት	ተነጣይነት			

TABLE 2

Name of Instrument	Human Being	Abstract Notion	Concrete Object
መጠባበቂያነት	ጌትነት	ሀልምነት	ጫማነት
ማነጋገሪያነት	ገባርነት	ኪራይነት	ገንዘብነት
መታሰቢያነት	ዓለቤትነት	ጤንነት	እስክዋድነት
መሳሪያነት	ሎሌነት	ምሳሌነት	ምርጥ ፡ ዘርነት
	ደጃዝማችነት	መስዋዕትነት	ምግብነት
	ወታደርነት	እውነትነት	ስፍራነት
	ጀግንነት	ነውርነት	
	ወጣትነት	ምስክርነት	
	እንግድነት	ምሽትነት	
	አባልነት		

Adjectives which occupy the first column in Table 1 are very frequently used as the base of the abstract noun. Many political and scientific neologisms are derived from Ge'ez roots with the help of adjectives with the Ge'ez suffix -āwi plus the abstract suffix -nnät. Generally speaking, the most common means to transform a noun into an abstract noun is to transform it first into an adjective, and then add the abstract suffix -nnät. In the second column are listed abstract nouns derived from participles. While translating into English abstract nouns, which are derived from participles which act as adjectives, is relatively easy, for example: ታማኝ 'loyal' — ታማኝነት 'loyalty'; there is some difficulty in translating those which are derived from participles acting as nouns, for example: ጫኝ 'porter' — ጫኝነት 'being a porter'. It seems that in English such words as *being, quality* or *essence* have to be added, for example:

7. ሀንሰሞ ፡ ለመኪና ፡ አጣቢነትና ፡ በር ፡ ከፋችነት ተቀጥሮ ፡ ገባ

"Hansämo entered [their house] having been hired for washing the car and opening the door (literally: having been hired for [the] being the car washer and the door opener)"[1 1]

The difficulty in the translation occurs also in the abstract nouns based on pronouns, on the adverb ብቻ and on all the nouns listed in Table 2, with the exception of certain abstract nouns based on names of human beings which denote the social position of a person or his military or social function, for example:

8. የወደድኩት ፡ እኮአንተንተህን፡ነው

"But it is your essence that I love"[1 2]

9. አሁን ደግሞ ፡ እቶ ፡ ማስረሻ ፡ ለዶክተር ... አንዱን ፡ ትንሽ ፡ ስጦታ ፡ ያበረከታሉ ። መታሰቢያነቱ ፡ ግን ለሆስፒታሉ ፡ ሠራተኞች ፡ በሙሉ ፡ ነው

"And now Mister Masräša will present to the doctor a small gift. But it will be a souvenir from all the hospital employees (lit.: its being a souvenir is for all the hospital employees)"[1 3]

10. ግዕዝ፡ወደ፡ድሮው፡ማነጋገሪያነቱ፡ቢመለስ

"If Ge'ez becomes spoken again, like in the past (lit.: if Ge'ez returns to its ancient being a means of conversation)"[14]

11. ይኽኔ፡ሚሌጎር፡ነበርኩ ። — የአንተን፡ሚሌጎርነትን፡ተወው

"At that time I was a millionaire" — "Leave your being a millionaire"[15]

12. ሐኪም፡ቤት፡ሲያስተኙት፡ከአንገቱ፡በላይ፡ስላበጠ፡መክበብነቱ፡አያሳታውቅም

"When they put him in the hospital, because he was swollen above his neck, his being Mäkbeb didn't let itself be known" (in this example a proper name acts as the base of the abstract noun)[16]

13. ቆይተው፡ቆይተው፡ግን፡ህልምነቱ፡ቀርቶ፡በውነት፡አባታቸው፡መሆኑን፡አወቁ

"But after some time its being a dream ceased and they knew he was their father"[17]

14. በቀኑ፡ምሽትነት፡ጉዞውን፡ለጊዜው፡አቋረጠ

"He interrupted temporarily his journey because the evening came (because of the day's becoming evening)"[18]

15. ለመሄጃ፡እንዲሆናት፡ጫማ፡ስትገዛ፡ከጫማነቱ፡በስተቀር፡ሞዱ፡ወይንም፡ዓይነቱ፡የመቼ፡ይሁን፡አይሁን፡በማለት፡ለማመራረጥ፡ጊዜዋን፡አታባክንም

"When she buys shoes for walking, except for their being shoes, she doesn't waste her time on choosing them for their fashion or style"[19]

16. ድምጿቸው ፡ ሕይወት ፡ የለሽ ፡ አሮጌ ፡ ሽክላነቱን ፡ አልቀየረም

"Her voice, with its quality of an old record, hasn't changed"[20]

We can conclude that in Amharic abstract nouns can be directly derived from almost all parts of speech, with the exception of verbs, prepositions and conjunctions. Now, all the parts of speech which can be used as bases of the abstract nouns, namely adjectives, participles, nouns, pronouns, the abverb *bečča* and numbers, have this in common that they can serve, contrary to verbs, prepositions or conjunctions, as part of the predicate in copula sentences. Consequently, the abstract noun can be considered as the transformation of a copula sentence. As O. Jespersen wrote about the abstract noun, in his *Philosophy of Grammar*: "the idea of 'being' is smuggled into the word".[21] Amharic makes a full use of the capacity of the copula sentence to be transformed into a noun.

IV

The negative form of the verb of possession in the feminine — *yälläš* — is used in Amharic in creating negative adjectives, for example ሕይወት ፡ የለሽ 'lifeless', ቅጥ ፡ የለሽ 'formless', etc. Because of the feminine gender these adjectives are not only negative, but they also have a pejorative connotation. Despite their feminine from they can qualify nouns in the masculine and in the plural, for example:

17. ስም ፡ የለሽ ፡ ተራው ፡ ሰው   "The ordinary, nameless man"[22]

18. መሬት ፡ የለሽ ፡ ምስኪኖች   "Poor landless [people]"[23]

Adjectives ending in *yallas* are often found among various neologisms, for example: መደብ ፡ የለሽ 'classless', መሰን ፡ የለሽ ፡ ኃይል 'omnipotence', etc. Nevertheless, another form seems to be preferred now: a form in which *yälläš* is replaced by its exact semantic equivalent in Ge'ez *'albā*. Although in Ge'ez *'albā* cannot create alone adjectives and has no pejorative meaning whatsoever, it was introduced into the Amharic political and literary language with all the characteristics inherent in *yälläš* for example መሬት ፡ አልባ 'landless', መደብ ፡ አልባ 'classless', etc.; like *yälläš* it can qualify a noun in the masculine and the plural, for example:

19. ልጆቻዋ ፡ አባት ፡ አልባ ፡ ቀርተዋል "Her children became fatherless"[24]

20. ሰው ፡ ከዎፍ ፡ እንሶ ፡ ጎጆ ፡ አልባ ፡ ይሁን "Should man be lesser than a bird and homeless?"[25]

V

Another construction which is currently gaining ground in the Amharic prose shows an interesting semantic and grammatical evolution. In this construction the word *biṭē* 'fellow creature, the like, poor creature' serves as a postpositional qualifier with a specific semantic content. The noun *biṭē* comes originally from Ge'ez *biṣ* 'fellow creature, the like, friend', with the addition of the Amharic possessive pronoun of the first person singular. The suffixed pronoun lost its meaning in the Amharic form[26], but it adds to the word a certain shade of commiseration. This is particularly clear in the reconstructed form of the possessive of the first person singular *yänē biṭē* which means 'poor fellow, beggar'.[27] Due to this meaning *biṭē* is often used as the qualifier of a preceding substantive to which it adds a shade of depreciation or smallness, for example:

21. ተዳፈርኩ ፡ ባትዶኝ ፡ ስጦታ ፡ ቢጤ ፡ አምጥቻለሁ
   "Only don't be offended, I brought you a small gift"[28]

22. አንድ ፡ ዶሴ ፡ ቢጤ ፡ ይዞ
   "Holding some kind of file"[29]

There seems to be some difficulty in defining the syntactical status of *biṭē* in this construction. It is true that it occupies the place of a postposition and could be considered as such if it weren't sometimes in the plural or accompanied by the possessive pronoun, like an ordinary noun, for example:

23. ትርኪ ፡ ምርኪ ፡ የሚሸጥባቸው ፡ ሱቅ ፡ ቢጤዎች
   "Some sort of poor shops where junk is sold"[30]

24. የመጀመሪያ ፡ ቁጣ ፡ ቢጤያቸው ፡ እየተለሳለሰ ፡ ሄደ
   "Her first anger eased progressively"[31]

Perhaps *biṭē* will evolve in the end into a postposition with a meaning close to the English 'sort of, kind of'. Thus it can be considered as one of the semantic phenomena which contribute to the enrichment of the Amharic morphology.

NOTES

1. I have mentioned this phenomenon and the next one in my review of J. Hartmann, *Amharische Grammatik*, in *Bibliotheca Orientalis*, vol.39 (May-July 1982), 475-476.

2. Berhanu Zäryehun, *Ma'bäl*, Addis Abäba, 1980-1983, part 3, 141/21.

3. *id.*, part 2, 256/12.

4. Mängestu Gädamu, *Kamsur*, Addis Abäba, 1956 E.C., 24/1.

5. Mängestu Gädamu, *Leğagärädïtwa*, Addis Abäba, 1960 E.C., 19/11-12.

6. Cohen, M., *Traité de langue amharique*, Paris, 1936, 72.

7. Gäbrä Sellasē, *Tarikä zämänä zä Dagmawi Menilek*, Addis Abäba, 1958 E.C., 158/8.

8. *id.*, 193/18-19.

9. Praetorius, F., *Die Amharische Sprache*, Halle, 1878, 187.

10. Gordimer, N., *A World of Strangers*, London, 1958, 48.

11. Taddälä Gäbrä Heywät, *Läqäyy abäba*, Addis Abäba, 1979, 15/1-2.

12. Berhanu Zäryehun, *Yäbädäl fessame*, Addis Abäba, 1956 E.C., 51/13.

13. *Ma'bäl*, part 2, 106/2-5.

14. Bäemnät Gäbrä Amlak, *Amareñña endätäsfaffa*, Addis Abäba, 1947 E.C., 36/3.

15. *Ma'bäl*, part 2, 14/19-21.

16. Taddälä Gäbrä Heywät, *op. cit.*, 64/13-14.

17. Afä Wärq Gäbrä Yäsus, *Lebb wälläd tarik*, Rome, 1908, 11/18-20.

18. *Kamsur*, 9/7.

19. *Leğagäräditwa*, 29/8-11.

20. *Ma'bäl*, part 1, 225/13-14.

21. Jespersen, O., *The Philosophy of Grammar*, London, 1924, 136.

22. Haddis Alämayyähu, *Feqer eskä mäqaber*[2], Addis Abäba, 1962 E.C., 443/21.

23. Taddälä Gäbrä Heywät, *op. cit.*, 30/20.

24. *Ma'bäl,* part 2, 211/17-18.

25. *id.*, part 2, 131/25.

26. Dässeta Täklä Wäld in his dictionary *Addis yamareñña mäzgäba qalat* (Addis Abäba, 1970, 163) still translates *balenğärayē*, *g^waddäññayē*.

27. Guidi, *Vocabolario amarico-italiano*, Rome, 1953, 352.

28. Bäalu Germa, *Yäqäyy kokäb terri*, Addis Abäba, 1980, 67/18-19.

29. Pawlos Noño, *Debleqleq*, Addis Abäba, 1957 E.C., 16/10.

30. *Ma'bäl,* part 3, 274/9.

31. *id.*, part 3, 71/22.

PHONETICS AND HISTORICAL RELATIONSHIPS IN SEMITIC

A Study of Ejective and Emphatic Consonants

Kiros Fre Woldu

METHOD AND OBJECTS OF STUDY

The main concern of my research has been to see if diachronic change from ejective to emphatic, or vice versa, is physiologically plausible, given the articulatory means of a normal speaker. The problem was approached with the belief that a good knowledge of how a speech sound is perceived and produced is a prerequisite for the ability to predict a plausible physio-logical/articulatory/phonetic change of that sound. The method used in my study is an in-depth experimental investigation and the objects of experimental inquiry are the ejective consonants found in Ethiopic-Semitic languages and emphatic consonants found in all variants of Arabic.

The speech production organs, due to their anatomical positioning, are not easily accessible to physical measurements. The observations of the various physiological adjustments made by the glottal and supraglottal articulators reported in this study have been studied indirectly by cineradiography and photoglottography. The movements of these articulators cause the modification of air volumes, which in turn cause air pressures. These pressure changes are measured directly by differential pressure transducers and flow meters. The movements of the articulators are caused by muscle contractions which reflect directly the motor commands carried by neural impulses. The electrical activity which accompanies muscle contraction is detected by means of electromyography (EMG). The air pressure is the source of sound or acoustic energy which is analyzed with the help of spectrographs and oscillographs.

After evaluating the results of the various production and perception experiments, a model will be proposed that could account for the plausible diachronic changes. Before the analysis of diachronic changes is presented, some experimental data concerning the production and perception of emphatic and ejective consonants will be briefly presented and discussed.

EMPHATIC CONSONANTS

At an early stage in our search for evidence, we discovered that our understanding of the production and perception of emphatic consonants was not complete. A study in the literature of laboratory phonetics showed the following findings.

Marcais (1948) made a lateral roentgenographic study and measured the distance between the root of the tongue and the posterior pharyngeal wall during emphatic and non-emphatic articulation. The results of his measurements showed that the distance in emphatic consonant production is much smaller or narrower than that of the non-emphatics. Al-Ani (1970) studied the spectral energy distribution of emphatic and non-emphatic consonants and assessed tongue movements and positions by means of X-ray tracings. He concluded that the so-called 'vela-rized' (emphatic) consonants are produced with a pharyngeal, rather than a velar constriction.

Ali and Daniloff (1972), using high-speed lateral cineradiography, traced and measured the movements of the dorsum, and the root of the tongue, the velum, the hyoid bone and the posterior pharyngeal wall. These measurements are contrasted with respect to emphatic and non-emphatic cognate pairs, as well as to vowel contexts. The results show that the tongue was the main active articulator involved in emphatic, as opposed to non-emphatics. During emphatic consonant production, the palatine dorsum moved towards the posterior pharyngeal wall.

Thus, what is so far known to us are the tongue movement activity and some spectral patterns associated with the production of emphatics and non-emphatics. In what follows, some attempts to shed further light on the production and perception process will be made.

In our (Fre Woldu 1981) report, we presented some new experimental findings concerning aerodynamic and acoustic events resulting from glottal and supraglottal manoeuvres in the production of emphatic consonants. More specifically, we have studied: 1. intraoral air pressure, 2. control of glottal opening, 3. fundamental frequency and 4. resonance properties of emphatics as opposed to non-emphatics. The results of these experiments could be summarized as follows:

1. There are no significant pressure differences between voiced emphatics and non-emphatics respectively.

2. The state of the glottis in voiceless and voiced emphatics was found to be predictable from aerodynamic requirements. The glottis is approximated for voicing in voiced emphatic and non-emphatic stops and fricatives, and is open during the hold and release of the voiceless emphatic and non-emphatic stops.

3. There are no F_0 differences in vowels following emphatic and non-emphatic consonants.

The results of the above experiments indicate that the production of emphatics and non-emphatics is basically the same, the only difference being the pharyngeal constriction or pharyngealization in the production of emphatic consonants. The results of the acoustic analysis show that the consequence of the tongue retracting gesture is the lowering of the high formants, especially F_2, and the slight rising of F_1, which tends to cause the approximation of F_1 and F_2. This acoustic pattern is the main feature that characterizes emphatic consonants in general. The initiation of the tongue movement, in emphatic consonant production, from basically a retracted position, creates a configuration of the vocal tract with a large front cavity and a small back cavity, as opposed to non-emphatic production. The perceived quality of such acoustic output is often judged as possessing a heavy, dull, fat or dark sound timbre.

Perceptually, there are two main cues that may signal the emphatic noise. In a stop CV . . . sequence, for instance, first there is a characteristic burst release which is of short duration, to be followed by rapid transitions into the vowel quality, all of which is audible. In words of the type . . VCV . . the 'colouring' of the vowel preceding the emphatic consonant, due to anticipatory coarticulation, is also a suffcent cue to the interpretation of the consonant as emphatic.

EJECTIVE CONSONANTS

The study of the perception, production and acoustical properties of Semitic-Ethiopic ejective consonants has been the object of the author's research for many years. In this section, some of the experiments which are relevant for the analysis of the historical reconstruction will be presented and discussed.

Frontal Cineradiographic Examination of the Larynx and the Aerodynamic Consequences of the Vertical Movements of the Larynx During the Production of Ejective Stops.

Fig.1 shows data from a frontal cineradiographic examination of the larynx during the production of ejective stops. From the film sequences, we can see the rising of the whole larynx and tightly closed glottis during the early period of occlusion, a gesture that reaches its maximal height slightly before, or just at the moment of release. After this moment the larynx sinks down again and returns back to its normal height. But the glottis remains closed and does not open until 20-60 msec. after the release.

From the aerodynamic point of view, it is obvious that the rising of the tightly closed larynx must produce intraoral excess pressure during the oral occlusion. This pressure is quickly released into the open air, immediately after the moment of the oral release. In other words, the tight closing of the glottis during occlusion totally isolates the air volume in the supraglottal cavities from the air in the lungs. The rising of the larynx with the constricted glottis functions like a piston, which is pushed into the anteriorly closed cavity. The effect of such a piston action is to increase the pressure of the air volume trapped between the two closures. In a separate experiment, we measured the peak pressure amplitudes from four native Tigrinya speakers as they uttered words containing ejective consonants contrasted with the voiced and voiceless cognates. Table 1 shows the results of these measurements and the statistical analysis of the measured values.

As can be seen from the table, the air pressure accumulated in the supraglottal cavities during the closure period of ejective stops is comparatively very high. When the lip or the tongue closure is removed, a short, sharp friction sound is produced. Since the glottis is totally constricted or tightly closed during this phase, it is *only* the air volume contained in the mouth cavity and the glottis that leaks out. Because of this, a brief and sharp friction sound is heard, whereupon a period of silence follows. This silence continues until the opening of the glottis has progressed far enough so that vocal fold vibrations can start.

Having thus summarized the vertical movements of the constricted larynx and the aerodynamic consequences brought about by these movements, the product of which is a characteristic explosion at the moment of release, I would now like to point out certain relationships that must be upheld in the timing of the three independent gestures performed by the tongue, the glottis and the larynx box; that is, these relationships seem to be necessary, if the typical auditory pattern just described is to materialize. The larynx box may be compared with a plug that can slide up or down a tube within certain limits set by the maximum and minimum height of the physiological larynx (Fig.2).

The sliding of the plug is mechanically independent of the opening or closing of the glottis in the plug. The aerodynamic consequences of varying conditions of larynx movement and glottis closure differ markedly, however. Suppose, for instance, that during the stop closure the larynx is raised with the glottis open. This will not cause an increased intraoral pressure beyond the pressure due to that of the air in the lungs. In fact, one could move one's larynx up or down between the maximum and minimum limits, without influencing the intraoral pressure appreciably. Conversely, if one makes an oral closure keeping the glottis open, with the larynx in its normal position, a subsequent closing of the glottis will not by itself influence the intraoral pressure. Hence, the rising of the larynx and the closing of the glottis must be coordinated in *a certain way* in order for the effect to obtain more particularly. Some understanding of these coordinations can be gained from electromyographic study (EMG). In Fig.3 the results of an EMG experiment are presented. It can be seen from the EMG curves that the activity of the vocalis muscle in ejective stop production reaches its maximum during the occlusion phase. The activity begins to decline approximately 30-40 msec. before the burst release, and at the moment of release it has reached a minimum. What can be gathered from these curves is that there is a direct innervation to the vocalis muscle at the closure onset. This innervation is responsible for the tight closure of the glottis. When the glottis is tightly closed, a mechanical pressure arises between the vocal folds. This transglottal mechanical pressure continues even when the innervation that has caused it has ceased. Another implication of these results is that the gesture of vocalis is independent of the strap muscles which are responsible in raising the larynx. The coordination in time of these two muscles is critical, however, if the required aerodynamic results are to be achieved.

The tight closure of the glottis has a double function. First, to act as an air-tight piston and to raise the pressure in the anteriorly closed air tube and, secondly, to assure that the high pressure accumulated in the cavity escapes *only* through the oral release. Since the pressure build-up in the mouth is higher than that of the subglottal and atmospheric pressures, opening the glottal closure *prior* to the articulatory release would result in the air rushing back to the lungs. Conversely, a *simultaneous* opening of the glottis and articulatory stricture would result in the flow of air in both directions and the sharp friction release would be less prominent, since the intraoral excess pressure caused by the piston push would then be considerably smaller.

Our conclusion is, therefore, that the exact relative timing of the three independent gestures, i.e. the lips or the tongue, the glottis and the larynx box, which join to make an ejective consonant is utterly important. In particular, the coordination that takes place at the moment of closure is highly critical. This fact is the more interesting, since these coordinations are made in preparation for the acoustic event which is to happen at the end of the closure interval.

AUDITORY SIMILARITY BETWEEN EJECTIVE AND EMPHATIC CONSONANTS

In enumerating all the possible hypotheses that may lead to a possible diachronic change *outside* the domain of articulatory movements and their acoustic product analysis, one question arises immediately, and that concerns the auditory similarity between ejective and emphatic consonants.

The various scholars who have studied the historical relationships between ejective and emphatic consonants have treated the two consonant types as two different, perceptually unrelated sounds. Earlier attempts at describing the difference between Ethiopic-Semitic ejectives and Arabic emphatics were restricted to the question of whether the consonant types exert influence on the following vowel or not. Emphatic consonants are described as changing the vowel quality from front vowels to back vowels, Brockelman (1950), and ejective consonants "n'ont aucune influence spéciale sur les voyelles voisines par le fait de leur articulation glottale", M. Chen, p.39 (1936).

To study the auditory similarity between emphatic and ejective consonants, we used native Tigrinya speakers, who have learned to speak Arabic (Fre Woldu 1984). The main question examined was whether Tigrinya speakers substitute "their own" consonants in place of emphatics, or if they do their best to imitate the native Arabic speakers. The data was collected as follows. In each recording session the informant sat comfortably on a chair and the experimenter on a nearby chair. A microphone connected to a tape recorder was held by the informant at a constant distance from his or her mouth. The experimenter then said a Tigrinya word from a selected list of speech material and the informant responded by translating the word to Arabic. Since the aim was to record the speaker's spontaneous Arabic speech habits, this method offered a reasonable way of doing just that. This method is certainly superior to that of just reading a list of words, because if the Arabic words were written in Arabic or Tigrinya the informants would either be misled, or at least influenced, by the graphic representation of the consonant in question. The speech material collected was analyzed by broadband spectograms. For control and matching purposes, recordings and spectograms were also made of the Arabic words read by native Arabic speakers. In addition, the whole recorded material was analyzed auditorily by two Arabic speakers, who had been instructed to detect minute deviation from their own speech. The result of this experiment was that most of the informants persistently substituted the ejective /ṭ/ in place of emphatic /t̠/, and the native Arabic speakers accepted the ejective /ṭ/ as being as good as an emphatic /t̠/. This leads to one conclusion, that there is a strong auditory similarity between Ethiopic-Semitic /ṭ/ and Arabic /t̠/. At this point, the interesting question is why listeners treat these two consonant types as a similar auditory phenomenon. From the descriptions that we have presented, it can be seen that the biomechanical and aerodynamic processes involved in the production of ejective /ṭ/ are totally different than those of emphatic /t̠/. The treatment by native Tigrinya and Arabic speakers of emphatic /t̠/ and ejective /ṭ/ as the same, simply suggests that it is the acoustic aspect that is decisive in shaping the auditory impression of speech perception. Furthermore, taking into account the acoustic structure of ejective and emphatic consonants, one would expect the perceptual patterns of these two sounds to differ markedly. The main perceptual cues of emphatic stops are the release burst and the formant transitions. These two cues function reciprocally, even when they are quite far removed from each other in time. The results of this study have demonstrated that native Tigrinya speakers are perceptually led by the quality of the release, rather than by the perceptually evident formant transitions. In a series of experiments made in our laboratory, we have demonstrated that the perceptual cues of an ejective stop are the burst release followed by a period of silence. Medially in consonant cluster and in final positions the burst release alone was found to be sufficient cue for the identification of place of articulation.

PLAUSIBLE DIACHRONIC CHANGES

From the studies that we have summarized, so far one can see a number of different ways in which an Ethiopic-Semitic ejective stop of the Tigrinya type could be expected to change diachronically. In general, each way in which a speaker may naturally *fail* to produce the optimal acoustic pattern points to a possible line of development. Also, each *alternative* method of naturally producing essentially the same effect suggests a possible direction for further developments. Hence, it should be possible for an ejective stop to develop into an injective one, if the speaker fails to constrict the glottis until slightly before the end of the closure, since retracting the constricted larynx at the release could suck air *into* the mouth. Conversely, closing the glottis too early (i.e. before the moment of oral closure) would bring about a preglottalized stop. Other variants are easily imaginable.

In particular, the piston effect, mentioned earlier (see Fig.2), could be replaced by an alternative type of adjustment, consisting in a simultaneous glottis and *pharynx constriction*. Such a constriction would reduce the volume of the air confined between the oral closure and the glottal constriction, and hence, according to Boyle's law, increase its pressure. An ejective burst release followed by a brief silence (while the glottis is still constricted) would then ensue. The burst release in this case would, of course, have a slight different (pharyngealized) auditory quality than the non-pharyngealized release of the Ethiopic-Semitic version.

Are pharyngealization and glottal constriction as independent a pair of parameters as larynx-raising and glottal constriction? As yet I cannot say, but I would not be surprised if they turn out to be more difficult to combine than the glottalization parameters.

It seems plausible that pharyngealization would tend to drop the glottal constriction. This presupposes a gradual redefinition of the auditory norm. The theory would be that the natives gradually gave up the hope of ever hearing a properly pronounced /ṭ/ (with pharyngealization *plus* glottal constriction) and started to accept the mere pharyngealized /ṭ/ as adequate. Conversely, a pharyngealized and glottal constricted stop could of course develop into a glottalized stop. The following alternatives are possible:

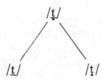

Whether /ṭ/ is the protosemitic precursor of Semitic-Ethiopic /ṭ/ on the one hand and Arabic /ṭ/ on the other, is a question I cannot answer at present.

ACKNOWLEDGEMENT

I have benefited a great deal from the generous help I have received from Professor Sven Öhman in developing the ideas presented in this study.

BIBLIOGRAPHY

Al-Ani, H. 1970
Arabic phonology: An acoustic and physiological investigation, The Hague: Mouton.

Ali, L. H. and R. G. Daniloff 1972
"A contrastive cinefluorographic investigation of the articulation of emphatic-non-emphatic cognate consonants", *Studia Ling.*, 26/11: 81-105.

Brockelmann, C. 1950
Abessinische Studien, Berlin.

Cohen, M. 1936
Traité de langue Amharique, Paris.

Fre Woldu, K. 1981
"Facts regarding Arabic emphatic consonant production",

| | (RUUL) Reports from Uppsala University, Department of Linguistics, No.7. |

Fre Woldu, K. 1984   "Evidence of auditory similarity between Tigrinya ejective /t̬/ and Arabic emphatic /t̤/", *Orientalia Swecana*, No.32.

Marcais, Ph. 1948   "Articulation de l'emphase dans un parler arabe maghrébin", *Annales de l'Institut d'Etudes Orientales*, Faculté des lettres de l'Université d'Alger, No.7.

TABLE I

N = 360

SUBJECTS		B	M	A	R	Analysis of Variance			
						P.Av.	P.Sd.	F*	t
b	X̄	41.5	44	35	65	46.5		62	
	s	2.42	3.16	6.24	7.62		5.31		3.36
p	X̄	69.5	82	70.5	116	84.5		94.9	
	s	4.97	5.37	5.5	10.75		7.06		7.37
p.	X̄	221	124	160	170	167.5		52.14	
	s	17.3	8.8	28	17.8		17.5		
d	X̄	38	42.5	42	78	50		140	
	s	2.58	4.86	7.15	4.22		4.98		2.58
t	X̄	63.5	76.5	72	123	83.75		193.9	
	s	2.42	7.09	8.23	4.83		6.07		10.5
t.	X	228.5	181	189	288	221.6		53.45	
	s	19.7	21.3	7.7	29.7		21.1		
g	X̄	39.5	52	37	64	48		168.9	
	s	4.38	4.22	4.83	5.16		5.97		6.7
k	X̄	70	87.5	72	123	88		71.34	
	s	6.24	4.25	6.32	6.75		18.8		18.8
k.	X̄	256	171.5	169	264	215		76.31	
	s	20.1	12	2.74	10.7		5.97		

Average peak intraoral pressure measurement values of voiced , voiceless asp. and ejective stops of the labial, dental and velar place of articulation. The table shows the average of each speaker's measured values (X̄), its standard deviation (s) the pooled average of the four speakers (P.AV), its standard deviation (P.Sd.), the estimated significant variance based on F - distribution (F*), the rejection level (R.L), level of significant differences between means (t) and probability (P).

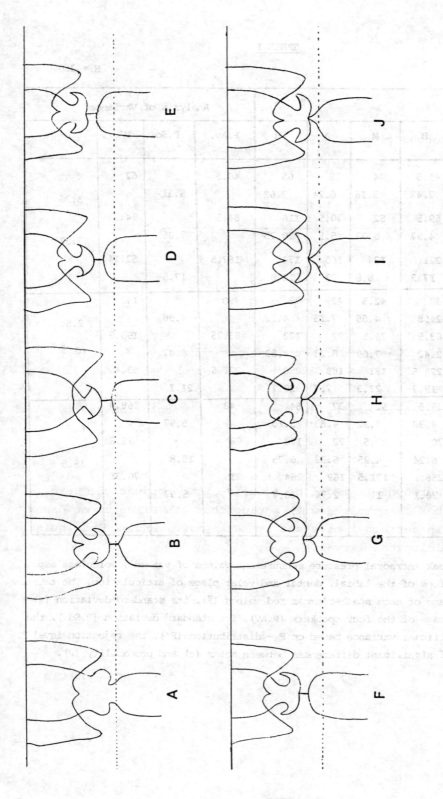

Fig. 1. Frame by frame tracings of a frontal cineradiographic examination of the utterance ta. The sequences show the behaviour of the vertical movements of the larynx during the production of Tigrinya ejective stops. (A) Vocal folds make adduction movements. (B) The vocal folds touch each other in entire surface. (C) and (D) The whole larynx rises. (E) Maximum height. (F), (G) and (H) Sinking and the vocal folds relaxing from the lower edge. (I) and (J) Configuration for the vibration of the followin vowel.

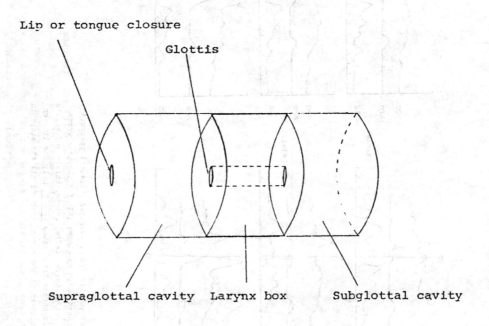

Fig. 2. An aerodynamic model of ejective stop production. Here, the larynx box is compared with a plug that can slide up or dawn a tube within certain limits set by the maximum and minimum height of the physiological larynx.

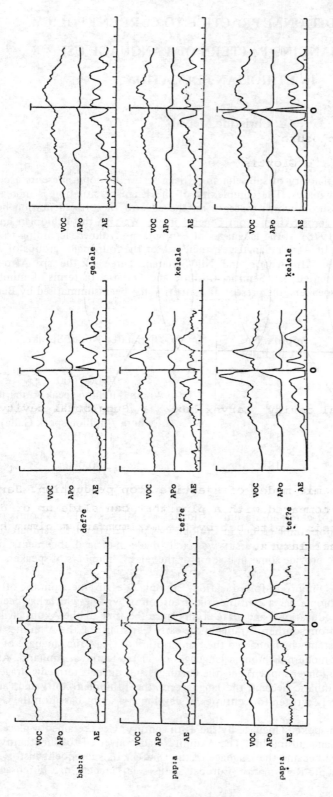

Fig.3. Averaged EMG curves of vocalis (VOC), averaged intraoral pressure traces (APo) and averaged audio envelopes (AE) for the test words babːa, papːa, papːa, defʔe, tefʔe, tefʔe, gelele, kelele and ḳelele embeded in the carrier phrase ʔatːa hawey __ bel. The line-up for averaging (0) was taken at the burst onset for all the stops in the test words.

FROM TRADITIONAL PRACTICE TO CURRENT POLICY:

THE CHANGING PATTERN OF LANGUAGE USE

IN ETHIOPIAN EDUCATION

Christine McNab

INTRODUCTION

In common with the majority of sub-saharan African states, Ethiopia presents a complex pattern of cultures and languages. The complexity of the language situation is increased by Ethiopia's geographical position, which places it on the edge of the "fragmentation belt" of languages which stretches across Africa from Senegal in the West to the Ethiopian and East African Highlands (Dalby 1978). If the languages of Ethiopia are grouped according to Greenberg's (1963) classification of African languages, then two of the four major groups of African languages are found there: Afro-Asiatic and Nilo-Saharan. Three of the six Afro-Asiatic language families are represented, i.e. Semitic, Cushitic and Omotic. In terms of numbers of languages and numbers of speakers, the present day situation has been summarised by Bender *et al.* (1976) as follows:

Language Group	Approx. No. of Languages	Estimated No. of Speakers
Semitic	12	12 000 000 (of whom 8 million speak Amharic)
Cushitic	22	11 000 000 (of whom 7 million speak Galla)
Omotic	18	1 500 000
Nilo-Saharan	18	500 000 (or fewer)

These figures are now out of date and are only estimates. As Markakis (1974) points out, the relative strength of the major ethnic groups in Ethiopia has been difficult to estimate as reference to ethnic, religious and linguistic diversity was rarely made in official documents, plans or statistics. However, they do provide some indication of the relative numbers of speakers in each language group.

In one respect which is important for education, Ethiopia does diverge from the other sub-saharan African states. Ethiopia has a centuries old tradition of writing which has been made use of in church, cultural, educational and state affairs since the time of the Axum civilisation. Invaded by Semitic tribes from southern Arabia in the early Christian era, the Axumites became endowed with a writing system which enabled the transcription of Geez, the language of Axum. From Geez developed the modern Ethiopian languages of Tigre, Tigrinya, Amharic, Argobba, Harari, Gafat (probably no longer spoken) and the languages and dialects termed Gurage (Hetzron and Bender 1976). Amharic became the language of the Ethiopian court and, although remaining unwritten or rarely written for centuries, it developed a script based on the Geez syllabary.

Although it was a non-spoken language by the 13th century, Geez retained a place of central importance in Ethiopian cultural life. The Axumites had converted to Christianity in the 4th century A.D. and Geez became the language of the Church. Its subsequent history largely paralleled that of Latin in pre-Reformation Europe: as the sole language of Church and literature, knowledge of Geez became the mark of the educated man. In the Muslim areas of Ethiopia, Arabic took on similar functions.

Meanwhile, despite its predominantly oral nature, Amharic increased in importance in Ethiopia. Levine (1974: 46) comments:

"As early as the 1620s it was observed that in spite of the enormous linguistic complexity of the land, anyone who knew Amharic could find in all parts of the country people with whom he could converse intelligibly. Gallinya subsequently came to play a similar role for those not reached by Amharic, particularly for traders in the southern part of the country."

Amharic was gradually established as a written language without being given a place in formal education. Skills in reading and writing in Amharic were developed indirectly through an education in Geez. Ultimately, Amharic was to replace Geez as the language of secular education, but this process took many centuries. Even by the end of the 19th century, it was not self-evident that Amharic should be used as a medium of instruction in Ethiopian schools, despite its widespread use in administrative affairs. In the first government schools, European languages, pre-eminently French, were the media of instruction. However, at the first government school to open, École Imperiale Menelik II, a pre-condition for entry was the ability to read and write in Amharic. This remained a condition of entry in all government schools. It was only in mission schools that use was made of local Ethiopian languages.

TRADITIONAL FORMAL EDUCATION IN ETHIOPIA

In this paper, the term formal education is used according to the definition of Coombs and Ahmed (1974), developed as part of a threefold taxonomy: formal, non-formal and informal education. Formal education is defined as:

"the institutionalized, chronologically graded and hierarchically structured education system, spanning lower primary school and the upper reaches of the university."

Both traditional Church and traditional Koranic schools fall within the limits of this definition, even if only a small minority of participants progressed to the higher levels of the system. Until very recently, the Church was the main provider of education in the Christian areas of Ethiopia. Geez was the sole language of instruction, and liturgy and holy scriptures the sole subject of study at the basic level of education, beyond which few pupils proceeded. Descriptions of traditional church schools in Ethiopia can be found in Pankhurst (1974, 1976), Haile G. Dagne (1976) and Alaka Embakom Kalewold (1970). The basic schools, *Nebab Bet*, were one-teacher schools attached to church or monastery. Learning was heavily dependent on memorisation of the Geez fidel and the aim was ability to read religious texts, particularly the Psalm of David. Writing was not taught until recently, when church schools took on the additional function of preparing students for entry to government schools. Until very recently there was no alternative to church school education in rural areas. When the first National Literacy Campaign was established in 1962, with the Emperor as patron, it was estimated that 520 000 pupils were attending the church schools. Only a minority were following the curriculum of the Ministry of Education, some 7600 pupils, of whom 4900 were in Grade One. For the others, Geez was still both the means and the end of education.

Haile G. Dagne, (*op. cit.*), Levine (*op. cit.*) and Pankhurst (*op. cit.*) also provide descriptions of the Koranic schools. In the Muslim areas the Koranic schools, *Tehaji*, had a similar style and function to the church schools in the Christian areas. The children learnt the Arabic letters and learnt to read the Koran. The relationship between Koranic school education and everyday life varied according to the area of Ethiopia. In Badiya, where spoken Arabic was not commonplace, the school experience must have been somewhat similar to that of children learning through the medium of Geez. In Megala towns, where Arabic was used in commerce and in the coastal areas and towns such as Dire Dawa and Jimma, children were more exposed to Arabic in their daily lives than were children in rural areas (Haile, G. Dagne, *op. cit.*).

EARLY MODERN EDUCATION

The development of the modern formal education system in Ethiopia is well documented (see, for example, Pankhurst 1974 and 1976, Haile Woldemikael 1976, Teshome G. Wagaw 1979 and Tekeste Negash 1982).

Modern education, in the sense of an education orientated to contemporary life, was introduced into Ethiopia by Western missionaries. Their early attempts to establish themselves were resisted by the Ethiopian Church and in the 19th century political disorder made mission expansion an even more hazardous exercise. However, by the end of the century, with political power once more centralised under the Emperor, both Protestant and Catholic missions were allowed into Ethiopia. In the colony of Eritrea the missions operated under the Italian colonial government.

It was not until the first government schools opened at the beginning of the 20th century that Amharic, the language of government and administration, was given a recognised place in Ethiopian education. French was the language of instruction at École Menelik II (opened 1908); Amharic featured alongside English and Italian as a subject. However, as literacy in Amharic was the sole entry requirement, there was an incentive to make use of it in church schools and in the private schools, which quickly expanded in number.

Both the government and mission school sectors expanded steadily until the Second World War. The increase in the number of mission schools was partly due to the support of the Regent, later Emperor Haile Selassie. In the mission schools, the language of instruction varied. In some, international languages, particularly French, were used but at the Swedish mission schools, both Amharic and Gallinya were used and at the United Presbyterian Church of North America in Sayo, instruction was exclusively in Galla (Pankhurst 1974). By 1935, there were about 100 mission stations in operation. If each had a school, it is likely that total enrolment was around 5000. The Italian invasion brought missionary work to a halt.

Until the Italian Occupation of 1935-41, the language of instruction was hardly a subject of debate. Usually it was French, but sometimes English; French and English were also taught as subjects, as were Amharic, Italian and Arabic. In any case, only a fraction of Ethiopian children entered government schools as the system, although in theory open to all, was in practice elitist and urban based. The Italian invasion totally disrupted the government education system. The schools were closed down or used for Italian children. Language policy was changed radically in those elementary schools provided for Ethiopian children. The Emperor had emphasised the use of Amharic as a vehicle for the unification of Ethiopia. The Italians came with diametrically opposed policies based on the enshrined colonial principle of "divide and rule" and on a fascist contempt for "the native" (Pankhurst 1974: 95). Accordingly, "the natives" were to be provided with only as much (very elementary) education as made them useful to the conquerors. Furthermore, local languages were to be used as the medium of instruction, not as a pedagogically sound first step in education, but as a means of repression. An edict of 1936 divided Ethiopia into six administrative units of the East African Empire, with the languages of education as follows: Tigrinya in Eritrea; Amharic in Amhara; Amharic and Gallinya in Addis Ababa; Harari and Gallinya in Harar; Gallinya and Kafficho in Galla Sidama and Somali in Somalia (Italy, Ministero delle Colonie 1936, cited in Pankhurst 1974: 75).

With the restoration of Haile Selassie to the throne of Ethiopia in 1941, work could begin on the reconstruction and then expansion of the formal education system. Until this post-war period there had been no written curriculum or formal objectives for the teaching of Amharic in government schools. In 1947 the Ministry of Education and Fine Arts produced the first elementary school curriculum to include Amharic as a subject. In this same period of post-war reconstruction, English became the medium of instruction; Amharic was taught from Grade Two. Only ten years later, 1958-9, Amharic was instituted as the medium of instruction for elementary education, i.e. Grades One to Six. English continued as the medium of instruction at secondary level.

This period was also characterised by a resurgence of mission activity that was supported by the Emperor, but this time also more firmly regulated. Missionary work was confined to Addis Ababa and to so-called Open Areas, i.e. areas outside the sphere of influence of the Ethiopian Church. Article 13 of the government directive controlling foreign missions decreed that:

> "The general language of instruction throughout Ethiopia shall be the Amharic language, which all Missionaries will be expected to learn."

But a concession regarding language use in mission schools was also made:

> "In Open Areas Missionaries may use orally local languages in the early stages of missionary work until such time as pupils and missionaries in Open Areas shall have a working knowledge of the Amharic language. The local languages may be used in the course of ordinary contacts with the local population."
> (Article 14, *Negarit Gazeta* 1944).

By 1968 there were 52 mission societies operating in Ethiopia with 289 schools (of which 238 were primary level) and 47 351 students. The mission schools were obliged to follow the curriculum of the Ministry of Education and Fine Arts (MEFA).

A new elementary school curriculum had appeared in 1963-4, recommending that English be taught as a subject "as early as possible" (MEFA 1964) and also recommending that teaching in the first two years be specially adapted to the needs of non-Amhara students. However, it was not easy to put the new Amharic policy into practice. The difficulties are well described in Tesfaye Shewaye and Taylor (1976). They were the difficulties usually encountered when a policy prescribing the use of African languages in education is first put into practice. There was a shortage of textbooks and a shortage of teachers trained in teaching Amharic as either a first or second language. Descriptions of Amharic were incomplete, as was the language mapping of the communities of Ethiopia. Those Amharic textbooks that were available were uneven in quality and often totally unrelated to the life experiences of the children using them.

Despite the problems, the policy was not abandoned, it being an important expression of the declaration in the Revised Constitution of Ethiopia that:

> "The Official Language of Ethiopia is Amharic"
> (*Negarit Gazeta* 1955).

Work on the development of Amharic as a language of formal education and on English textbooks and courses specially adapted to the needs of Ethiopia continued side by side. The textbooks and their use in Ethiopian schools are described by Asfaw Melaku and Murison-Bowie (1976). Tesfaye and Taylor concluded that "Ethiopia has a well worked-out curriculum for English language teaching, firmly grounded on the specialised needs of the country" (p.239) with, however, reservations about the gap between curriculum theory and classroom practice. As regards Amharic, they were rather less optimistic, particularly concerning the use of Amharic as a medium of instruction beyond elementary level.

EDUCATION IN TRANSITION

Despite steady expansion of the government education system, at the 1961 Addis Ababa Conference on Education in Africa, Ethiopia was clearly shown to be lagging behind in educational provision. Illiteracy in the rural areas had hardly been touched by government programmes and per capita spending on education (US Dollars 0.52) was one of the lowest for the continent. Over the next decade there was little improvement in either educational provision or quality. Although perhaps the biggest problem was that of finance (see Haile Woldemikael 1976 and Markakis 1974 for a discussion of this problem), the language of instruction was making educational progress difficult in non-Amhara speaking areas of Ethiopia. The problem is well described by Solomon Inquai (1969: 57):

> "Amharic, the national language, is fast becoming the language of the educated and the urbanised. However, it is totally unknown to a great many of the rural people who speak either their ethnic language or who use a language of trade which is predominant in the area they live . . . Recently a study conducted by the Central Statistical Office in the Wälamo Soddo area with a view to determining the extent of the Amharic spoken in that area revealed that of the entire population of 597 371 (which excludes the population of the regional capital) in the area, only 1.5% could speak Amharic and only 0.6% were literate in Amharic."
>
> (Ethiopian Central Statistical Office, *A Population Count in Wollamo Awraja*. Addis Ababa 1965).

The national literacy rate was a meagre 6.1% and there was a severe imbalance between town and country, men and women. In a Central Statistical Office survey (undated) cited by Solomon Inquai, (*op. cit.*, pp.58-9) less than 1% of women in the provinces were literate, whilst literacy rates for men ranged from 4.3% in Gamu Gofa to 12.1% in Tigre. However, in urban areas (which accounted for 10% of the total population) up to 50% of the men were literate.

Although such evidence existed for the failure of government education to reach the rural majority, little was done to reform the system. Commenting on the state of the government education system at this time, Hoerr (1974) remarked:

> "the country now finds that the internationally mixed educational model which it imported is (a) of questionable socioeconomic relevance to a largely rural-agricultural population and (b) highly inequitable in terms of educational opportunity."

An extensive Education Sector Review was carried out in 1971-2. The main recommendation of the review was a fundamental restructuring, so as to provide a massive expansion of primary and non-formal education. There was, however, no questioning of the use of Amharic as the means of instruction in all areas of the country. In June 1972, the National Academy of the Amharic Language was established with the aims:

> "(1) to foster the growth of the Amharic language and (2) encourage the development of Amharic literature."
>
> (*Negarit Gazeta* 1972)

Even in Eritrea, with its very different history of modern education, Amharic had been imposed as the language of education. In its period as an autonomous state federated to Ethiopia, Tigrinya and Arabic had been the official languages (1950-62). Furthermore, despite the emphasis given to mass primary education in the sector review report, another of the proposed reforms was that at the end of the fourth grade, pupils should go through a selection process based heavily on an examination in Amharic. Lefort (1981) cites this proposal as one of the causes of student unrest immediately prior to the revolution.

As Ethiopia came to the brink of revolution, the short-lived government of Endelkatchew Makonnen (28th February – 22 July 1974) produced a policy statement which indicated that Amharic language domination in all forms of government education might be open to question. In the general policy statement, reference is made to:

> "the strengthening of the country's diverse traditions as pillars of national

culture; the further consolidation of Ethiopian nationalism and cultural heritage without regard to ethnic affiliation, religion or sex."

As regards education:

"to the extent the resources of the government allow, full effort will be made to extend to our people academic, professional and vocational education on an equitable basis."
(Ethiopian Government 1974)

This government did not last long enough to implement any reforms. Haile Selassie was deposed on the 12th September 1974 and the Provisional Military Administrative Council became the Government of Ethiopia.

EDUCATION LANGUAGE POLICIES IN SOCIALIST ETHIOPIA

The guidelines for the educational policies pursued in Ethiopia since the Revolution are to be found in the *Programme of the National Democratic Revolution of Ethiopia*, published in April 1976 (see, for example, in Ethiopian Government 1977). Descriptions of education in Ethiopia since the revolution can be found in Gumbel *et al.* (1983), Ministry of Education Ethiopia (1984) and Teshome G. Wagaw (1979).

High on the list of priorities for the new government were a mass literacy campaign, the expansion of primary education in rural areas, renewal of the curriculum and production of relevant textbooks. One of the established education policies to become open to question was the exclusion of all Ethiopian languages except Amharic from government education.

The ideological foundation for the introduction of a number of Ethiopian languages into the education system is also to be found in the *Programme* of the Revolutionary Government. In section 4a of this document it is stated that:

"All the necessary effort will be made to free the diversified cultures of Ethiopia from Imperialist cultural domination and from their own reactionary characteristics. Opportunities will be provided to allow them to develop, advance and grow with the aid of modern means and resources."

This is spelled out even more clearly in Section 5, which deals with the nationality question:

"The right to self-determination of all nationalities will be recognised and fully respected. No nationality will dominate another one since the history, culture, language and religion of each nationality will have equal recognition in accordance with the spirit of socialism . . . "

Furthermore:

"within its environs, it (each nationality) has the right to determine the contents of its political, economic and social life, use its own language and elect its own leaders and administrators to head its internal organs."

As this policy is evidently influenced by the nationalities policy of the Soviet Union, it is interesting to consider how this policy is reflected in the education system of the Soviet Union. The implementation of this policy in the education system of the Soviet Union can be found described in Lewis (1980) and Grant (1979). In the All-Union Population Census of 1970 (cited in Grant), 130 nationalities are listed. In principle, all citizens have the right to use their mother tongue if they wish to do so, including its use in the education of their children. In practice, of course, language choice is much more difficult, being based on a complex of often emotionally

720

charged cultural and social values. Also, within this pluralist framework, Russian is the majority language and as the national language is taught in all non-Russian schools. It is even used as the medium of instruction in non-Russian areas if the parents request this. There are also practical problems, such as limited numbers of speakers, for the educational development of some of the minority languages.

The language policy of the Ethiopian government is, of course, not only derived from Soviet experience or Marxist ideology. Ethiopia can also draw on its own long experience of formal education and on the Pan-African discussions on education, which started with the 1961 Conference of African States on the Development of Education in Africa (UNESCO 1961), held in Addis Ababa. Since then, Ethiopia has been an active participant in the Conferences of African Ministers of Education organised by UNESCO. At these conferences and at other Pan-African discussions and meetings on language, culture and education, an ideological commitment to the use of African languages in education has been established. The principle of using mother tongue languages as the medium of instruction, as set out in the UNESCO monograph "The Use of Vernacular Languages in Education" (1953), was still being reiterated nearly 30 years later at the Harare Conference (UNESCO 1982a). In a paper on the use of African languages in education prepared for this conference, it was reported that 40 of the 50 African member states of UNESCO have institutions engaged in university level basic research into African languages and 38 also have institutions working on the development and preparation of curriculum materials (UNESCO 1982b). Ethiopia is included in both figures.

So far, the use of nationality languages (local languages) has been confined to non-formal education, especially the mass literacy campaign. Non-formal education is understood to mean:

> "any organised, systematic, educational activity carried on outside the framework of the formal system to provide selected types of learning to particular subgroups in the population, adults as well as children."
> (Coombs & Ahmed, *op. cit.*)

In pre-revolutionary Ethiopia, literacy education was conducted through the medium of Amharic (see Solomon Inquai, *op. cit.*, and Sjöström & Sjöström 1977, 1983). The programmes were very limited in both extent and success. Inquai is very critical of the use of Amharic regardless of participants' mother tongues, but the Sjöströms found some support for its use when they made a survey of both participants and non-participants in the area covered by the Yemissrach Dimts Campaign (*op. cit.*, 1983). Language policy for the mass literacy campaign of the socialist government is radically different.

For the mass literacy campaign, 15 Ethiopian languages have been selected which together cover about 90% of the population. These languages are listed in Appendix 1, together with indications of numbers of speakers and the stages at which they have been introduced into the campaign. Apart from Tigrinya, which also inherited its script from Geez, these languages have been largely unwritten before 1974. Some had been transcribed by missionaries using Roman script (e.g. Kunama), and others have previously been recorded in Arabic script (e.g. Harari and Tigre). Now they are all to be transcribed using Amharic script:

> "so that multiformity has been combined with an element of uniformity which may facilitate the movement towards a universal bi-lingual society which preserves the cultures of the distinct nationalities and at the same time promotes the objective of intercommunication, mutual understanding and national unity."
> (Last 1984)

Details of the organisation and achievements of the mass literacy campaign can be found in Sjöström (1984), NLCCC (1981) and Ministry of Education, Ethiopia (1984). The campaign and other non-formal education programmes are supported by the Educational Mass Media Service, which broadcasts in 4 of the campaign languages and has one of its objectives:

LITERACY CAMPAIGN LANGUAGES IN ETHIOPIA

Language[1]	Language Group[2]	Est. Mother-Tongue Speakers[3]	% of Pop. 1970[3]	Introduction in Literacy Campaign[4]		
				Rounds 1-4	Round 5	In Preparation
Amharic	E-S	7 800 400	31 (40)	X	X	
Oroma (Galla)	C	6 810 200	27	X	X	
Tigrinya	E-S	3 559 300	14		X	
Wolaito	O	908 000	3.5	X	X	
Somali	C	888 000	3.5	X	X	
Hadiya	C	700 000			X	
Kembatta	C	294 500			X	
Gedeo	C				X	
Tigre	E-S	117 000		X	X	
Kunama	N-S	40 000			X	
Sidama	C	857 000				X
Silti	E-S					X
Afar	C	363 000				X
Kefa-Mocha	O	170 000				X
Saho	C	120 000				X

(1) Language names as used by Ministry of Education 1984.
(2) Bender *et al.* 1976. E-S: Ethio-Semitic; C: Cushitic; O: Omotic; N-S: Nilo-Saharan.
(3) Bender *et al.*, 1976. Based on 1970 figure.
(4) NLCCC 1981. According to Min. Ed. 1984 all languages now in use.

> "to teach the official language as well as to utilise and develop the languages of the different nationalities in the education system making all the necessary cooperation with the concerned Ministries and agencies."
> (EMPDA 1981: 2)

So far, the use of national languages has been confined to the non-formal education system. Amharic continues to be the language of primary education, and English that of secondary and higher education. It is difficult to judge from the available literature to what extent languages other than Amharic and English are used in the classroom. The authors of a Swedish International Development Authority review of Ethiopian education (Gumbel *et al* 1983) remark that:

> "to make the transition to Amharic smoother and to ease the working situation of the teachers in areas where the majority speak other languages, the team supports the efforts to introduce vernaculars in the first three grades."

Given the present level of commitment to using local languages in non-formal education, it is perhaps not unrealistic to expect their eventual incorporation into the school classroom.

CONCLUSIONS

With its system of traditional church and Koranic schools, Ethiopia has had for many centuries a system of formal education unique in sub-saharan Africa. This system, however, hardly developed after the 16th century and thus had little to offer to the modernisation of the country in the 20th century. In many areas of Africa, it was Western missionaries who laid the foundations for modern, formal education systems: in Ethiopia, their contribution was severely limited by the politics of religion.

Ethiopia has undergone a traumatic transition from stagnant empire to socialist-oriented state. In the process, there has been a major rethinking and reorganisation of the education system. Traditional and mission schools have not been abolished but, with the massive expansion of the government education system, their relative importance has diminished. Government policy of expanding education into the rural areas and giving priority to adult literacy has necessitated a serious rethinking of the place of local (national) languages in education. So far, their use has been confined to non-formal education, but the ideological basis of the education policy should lead to their eventual incorporation in the schools as languages of instruction and/or subjects of study.

This review of the use of Ethiopian languages in education leaves many unanswered questions and gives only an incomplete picture. However, there are two striking features regarding language use and, as these are somewhat contradictory, they are worth commenting upon. Firstly, Ethiopia has a long tradition of using an indigenous language, Geez, in formal education. This tradition is unique in sub-saharan Africa. Even though Geez was to suffer the same fate as Latin in Europe, becoming totally remote from daily life, its traditional use in formal education opened the school door for an Ethiopian replacement, Amharic. In retrospect, the use of first French and then English as media of instruction in elementary schools can be seen as a temporary aberration. As soon as modern education expanded beyond narrow elitism, Amharic was established as the language of elementary/primary education. Interestingly, this move took place in the same decade that other sub-saharan African states were debating, and usually rejecting, the use of African languages as media of instruction. The contradictory second feature in Ethiopian formal education has been the very limited extent to which other Ethiopian languages have been made use of.

Ethiopia had to wait until the 1974 Revolution before serious consideration was given to the use of local languages in education. Their introduction into non-formal education was carried out with impressive speed and work still continues on their development as languages of education. In the meantime, curriculum development has among its aims the more effective teaching of Amharic and of English as the second language of education.

BIBLIOGRAPHY

Alaka M. Kalewold, 1970   *Traditional Ethiopian Church Education*, College Press, Columbia University.

Asfaw Melaku and S. Murison-Bowie, 1976   "Language Teaching Materials" in Bender, M. L. *et al.*, *Language in Ethiopia*, Oxford University Press, London.

Bender, M. L. *et al.*, 1976   *Language in Ethiopia*, Oxford University Press, London.

Coombs, P. H. and M. Ahmed, 1974   *Attacking Rural Poverty*, The John Hopkins University Press, Baltimore.

Dalby, D., 1978   *Language Map of Africa and the Adjacent Islands*, (Provisional Edition), International Africa Institute, London.

Ethiopian Government, 1974   *Policy Statement of the New Cabinet of the Ethiopian Government*, 8th April 1974, Addis Ababa.

——————, 1977   *Basic Documents of the Ethiopian Government*, Provisional Office for Mass Organisational Affairs: Agitation, Propaganda and Education Committee, Addis Ababa.

EMPDA, 1981   *Educational Mass Media Service: From . . . . To . . . ?*, EMPDA, Addis Ababa.

Grant, N., 1979   "The Education of Minorities in the USSR" in *World Year Book of Education: Education of Minorities*, Megarry, M., Nisbet, S., and E. Hoyle (eds.), Nicholas Publishing Co., New York and The Anchor Press, England.

Greenberg, J. H., 1963   *The Languages of Africa*, Indiana University Press, Bloomington.

Gumbel, P., Nyström, K. and R. Samuelsson, 1983   "Education in Ethiopia 1974-1982", *Education Division Documents*, No.11, SIDA, Stockholm.

Haile G. Dagne, 1976   "Non-Government Schools in Ethiopia" in M. L. Bender *et al.*, 1976.

Haile Woldemikael, 1976   "Government Schools in Ethiopia" in M. L. Bender *et al.*, 1976.

Hetzron, R. and M. L. Bender, 1976   "The Ethio-Semitic Languages" in M. L. Bender *et al.*, 1976.

Hoerr, O. D., 1974   "Educational Returns and Educational Reform in Ethiopia" in *Eastern Africa Economic Review*, Vol.6, No.2, Dec. 1974, pp.18-34, OUP Nairobi.

Italy, Ministero delle Colonie, 1936   *Bolletino Ufficiale*, cited in R. Pankhurst, 1974, 1976.

| Last, G. C., 1984 | "Letter to the Editor", *Development Forum*, Vol.XII, No.3, April 1984. |

Lefort, R., 1981 — *Ethiopia, An Heretical Revolution?*, English translation, 1983, Zed Press, London.

Levine, D. N., 1974 — *Greater Ethiopia: The Evolution of a Multi-ethnic Society*, The University of Chicago Press, Chicago and London.

Lewis, E. Glyn, 1980 — *Bilingualism and Bilingual Education*, University of New Mexico Press, Albuquerque.

Markakis, J., 1974 — *Ethiopia: Anatomy of a Traditional Polity*, Oxford University Press, Oxford and Addis Ababa.

MEFA, Ministry of Education and Fine Arts, Ethiopia, 1964 — *Elementary School Curriculum*, Addis Ababa.

Ministry of Education, 1984 — *Education in Socialist Ethiopia*, Addis Ababa.

NLCCC, 1981 — *Every Ethiopian will be Literate and will remain Literate*, National Literacy Campaign Coordinating Committee, May 1981, Addis Ababa (Reprinted 1983).

Negarit Gazeta, 1944 — "Regulations on the Establishment of Missions", Decree No.3 of 1944, Addis Ababa.

——————, 1955 — "Revised Constitution of Ethiopia", Proclamation 149 of 1955; 15.2.1955, Addis Ababa.

——————, 1972 — As cited in R. Richter, 1982.

Pankhurst, R., 1974 — "Education, Language and History: An Historical Background to Post-War Ethiopia" in *The Ethiopian Journal of Education*, June 1974, Vol.VII, No.1 (Reprinted in M. L. Bender *et al.*, 1976).

Richter, R., 1982 — "On Language Problems in Ethiopia (Language Policy in the interest of Social Progress)" in Brauner and Ochotina (eds.), *Studien zur Nationalsprächlichen Entwicklung in Afrika*, Akademie Verlag, Berlin.

Sjöström, M. and R., 1977 — "Literacy Schools in a Rural Society", *Educational Reports*, Umeå, No.13, 1977.

——————, 1983 — *How do you spell Development*, Scandinavian Institute of African Studies, Uppsala.

Sjöström, R., 1984 — "Education and Popular Mobilisation: The National Literacy Campaign in Ethiopia", (Mimeo), Paper presented at the 1984 Symposium of the Nordic Association for the Study of Education in Developing Countries, Stockholm.

Solomon Inquai, 1969 — "Adult Literacy in Ethiopia — A Profile", *Journal of Ethiopian Studies*, Vol.VII, No.1, January.

Tesfaye Shewaye and C. V. Taylor, 1976 — "Language Curricula" in M. L. Bender *et al.*, 1976.

Tekeste Negash, 1982 — "Etiopien" in *Från Förskola till Hog-Skola i Olika Länder*, S. Lindblad and E. Wallin (eds.), Student Litteratur, Lund.

Teshome G. Wagaw, 1979 — *Education in Ethiopia — Prospects — and Retrospect*, University of Michigan Press, Ann Arbor.

UNESCO, 1953 — "The Use of Vernacular Languages in Education", Monographs on Fundamental Education 8, UNESCO, Paris.

——————, 1961 — *Conference of African States on the Development of Education in Africa, Addis Ababa 1961: Final Report*, UNESCO, Paris.

——————, 1982 — a) *Conference of the Ministers of Education of African Member States, Harare, 28 June — 3 July 1982*, ED-82/MINEDAF, UNESCO, Paris.

b) *The Use of African Languages as Languages of Education*, ED-82/MINEDAF/REF5, UNESCO, Paris.

Languages in Use in the Literacy Campaign

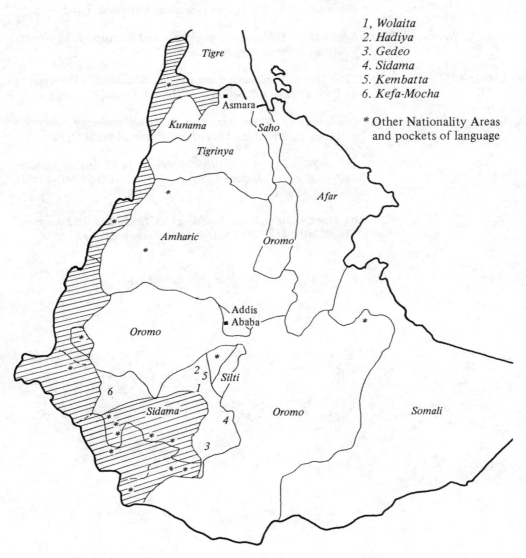

1, *Wolaita*
2. *Hadiya*
3. *Gedeo*
4. *Sidama*
5. *Kembatta*
6. *Kefa-Mocha*

* Other Nationality Areas
  and pockets of language

Source: Adapted from "Education in Socialist Ethiopia" 1984: 43
Ministry of Education, Addis Ababa.

A POSSIBLE ROLE FOR GEEZ QENE
IN ETHIOPIAN VERNACULAR POETRY

Mengistu Lemma

In the development of vernacular poetry, two sources of enrichment and rejuvenation are available: oral literature, and the classical heritage. The present contribution concerns itself with the second.

The question posed is whether the progressive principle of socialist cultural transformation, namely "the creation of a new culture on the basis of a critical assimilation of the cultural heritage of the past"[1], can be applied with regard to Geeze qene[2] in its relation to vernacular poetry.

More concretely, the same question can be posed as to whether the essential facets of Geez qene can be assimilated into a vernacular medium in such a way as to create forms in the vernacular incorporating the artistic achievements embodied in the qene tradition.

The basic assumption is that qene represents a veritable cultural heritage. However, the problem is how to make the artistic conventions of qene poetry serve secular and progressive ends, in contrast to the almost exclusively religious purposes to which it was dedicated in centuries past.

In the light of the above assumption, the age old question whether or not one can separate the qene form from its religious content will naturally arise.

Not all qene is, however, solely and purely religious. Kifle-Yohannes, a contemporary of Emperor Bekkaffa, in his famous Meweddis poem[3], says:

እምከዊነ ካህን ይኔይስ ከዊነ ኖላዊ
ወኅለ እንሰሳ ትትበደር እምቤተ መቅደስ ዓባይ ።
እስመ ቤተ መቅደስ ካነት ቤተ ፈያታይ

(Better by far to be a shepherd
       than a clergyman
And the barn is more elect than the
       temple august,
Because the temple is become
       the house of the robber)

A poem in Kebr-Yeiti form from an unknown author ends with these lines:

ባዕልስ ይትፈሳሕ ሶበ ዜና ረኃብ ሰምዐ
ወመቃብረ ይከሪ ለወርቁ እንዘ በድነ ቢጹ በአፍአ

(But the wealthy man is happy
       when news of famine he hears
And he digs a grave for his gold,
       while the dead body of his fellow
       lay prostrate at his gate).

One can quote many more examples of this kind of qene. It must nevertheless be admitted that the content of qene is overwhelmingly religious in both the devotional and theological aspects.

Our problem is how to take over the forms, conventions, and technical subtleties of qene and adapt these to modern secular needs. But this exercise should by no means be equated with an attempt to put the poetic clock back to a medieval state of affairs.

We note some efforts in the past and in more recent times aimed at turning vernacular verse into qene channels. For example, a Meweddis in Amharic opens with the line:

እግዚአብሔር አንተን በመብደል ጊዜ
የሚያሀለኝ የለም እኔን ከፈጠርከው ሁሉ ፍጡር

A Selassie in Oromo begins:

አርካ ኬቲ ሁንዱማ ጨብሴ
ሌንጫ ጐፍታቶ ኢጀሌ ሌንጫ የቢያ

and ends:

ማሎ ማሎ ጐፍታ ኪያ
መና ፈርዳ ፉደቴ አህያ

Other Meweddis opening lines go like this:

ካህን ቀላዋጭ ኢትናቅ ምጥዋ ነጋዴ
ወኢ.ትሰድብ ካዕብ ገበራርተ አራሽ በበሬ ።

ግማሽዋ ታጸግብ የጐንደር እንጀራ
አምጣነ ወፍራም ይእቲ ወክንድ ተሰንዝር ቄመታ

መኑ አብዓኪ ውስተ ቁም ነገር
ለቤተ ምናምን ኪያኪ እንዚ ከመ ኑግ ትቅለጥለጢ.

Further attempts have been made in the more recent past to acclimatize the qene form to secular and topical subject matter as exemplified in Yoftahe Negusse's Wazema poem beginning with:

ቆም የስኳር ጠጅ
ውስተ ደብረ ማሕው ልብን ሐገረ ሥቃይ ወተድላ

and concluding with:

እሳተ አራዳ ኩኖክ እሳው ተቃጥላ
አውአያታ ለባቢሎን ገላ ።

There is no doubt that there are many more qene poems of this type which need to be collected, even though they are characterized as "freckled" (*guramayle*) because of their mixed nature.

However, most attempts of this kind aimed at rendering qene in the vernacular are rarely successful, as the poet had to incorporate some Geez words or phrases when the vernacular refuses to scan to the Geez rhythm.

A comparatively recent and more sustained effort in this field is represented by Abbe Gubegna's Meskot. This volume of poems merits a more detailed consideration because it contains the fruits of a conscious systematic attempt by a well-known writer of the younger generation.

In Meskot, some fifty Amharic poems in qene form are included in the latter part of his volume, and the examples given cover the whole range of qene forms from the Guba'qana couplet to the eleven-line Etanemoger.

As far as Amharic meter is concerned, we know that the basis for its scanning is the number of syllables per metrical foot, and that every syllable counts equally in the line of verse.

It is the metrical and accentual patterns of qene versification that do merit a fresh look in depth. For the result of such an examination may give us a clue to the possibility, if possibility there is, of effecting a real integration of qene forms into Amharic poetry. Most attempts hitherto undertaken ignore the question of the natural rhythm, and try instead to impose Geez patterns on Amharic.

Geez qene meter primarily depends on accent or stress. It is an accentual meter for, as is well known, in the language itself stresses are heavily marked. In our qene schools the traditional pronunciation of Geez is taught on the assumption that there are rules of accent governing it, and that these rules are, in the words of Afewerq Gebreyesus, quoted by Edward Ullendorff, "perfettamente determinate".

In the qene school or even lower down in the Nebab Bet (house of reading) three modes of reciting Geez are recognized. These are the Wedaqi (falling) and the Tenesh (rising) accents, and the Tenababi (or liaison) chaining words to be read together in one breath.

We could indicate the three modes by three items of the Zema (musical) notation, as recently suggested by a well-known qene master: the Difat, a down-turned crescent, for the falling accents; the same in upright position, Qenat, for the rising accents; and for the liaison, the Hidet, which is roughly the same as the English hyphen.

If we take as an example the well-known Guba'e qana couplet, attributed to Kifle-Yohannes and addressed jestingly to Emperor Bekkaffa:

በካፉ / ኢትርሳዕ / ዘተዋነይነ / ክሌኤነ
እንዘ—አበ—አብርሃም / ኣንተ/ወብእሲተ—አብርሃም / ኣነ ።

we can see the three modes of the traditional pronunciation. The poem is composed predominantly of rising accents, we can see the essential difference between Geez and Amharic metrical feet. Amharic is syllable-counting: Geez counts the accents and is relatively indifferent to the number of syllables per line.

Furthermore, in Geez qene verse, both rising and falling accents have equal value and count equally in the line.

Qene masters teach the beginner, who has already passed through the school of zema music, how to sing some well-known poem in the Guba'e qana form to the tune traditionally set and fixed for the form. The next step for the student is to compose his own Guba'e qana poem "to that tune". He thus eventually learns to compose in any qene form "by ear", but takes great care that his poem does not violate its particular zema tune. Though the underlying factor is the number of accented feet per line, of this fact the beginner is hardly aware.

The insistence in qene schools on the strictest conformity of a poem to its zema or tune is quite understandable, since the qene poem is primarily intended for a singing recitation in church. There, its choral treatment with the use of the Mequamia crutch, the sistrum and the drum, is based on and must be consonant with the original tune to which a particular qene poem is composed in a particular form. Thus, a qene poet's departure from the tune, or his "breaking the zema" to be literal, is bound to entail a chain of consequences affecting, in the last analysis part of the religious rite itself. For qene is an original type of poetry that, upon recitation, partakes of the nature of a dramatized musical performance. In the performance, we have two actors, the whispering poet and the singing reciter; plus a chorus of debteras who take the poem sung through its different musical stages in a growing crescendo culminating in a climax.

However, we must not lose sight of the original question: how can our vernacular versifiers profit from the refinement, sense of form, and economy embodied in qene poetry? How can we transpose qene forms into vernacular poetry in an organic synthesis?

Such a synthesis cannot begin by simply pouring the new wine into the old vessel, as has been tried in the past. In the new approach, the Geez qene molds, which were made to measure for the classical language, must be made to accommodate the vernacular occupant. In other words, we can adopt the existing qene forms as suggested and seriously attempted by Abbe Gubegna, but at the same time find for them a syllabic equivalence in the vernacular. This approach can eliminate the main stumbling block that faced previous qene devotees who wished to see their favourite Geez qene form composed in Amharic, and yet failed to take account of the rhythmical difference between the two related languages.

Let us now look at a happy accident, author unknown, which approximates to the ideal synthesis of a Geez qene form in Amharic meter and rhythm. This is a well-known couplet in standard 12 syllable lines, composed of two disyllabic hexameter verses:

$$ ዕጻ—በሰስ/በልፉ/አዳም/ከንፈርሽ $$
$$ መድኃኔ—ዓለም / ልቢ ተሰቀለሽ ። $$

The couplet can be scanned in the Geez qene manner as a tetrameter line followed by a trimeter line. A semenna-worq (wax-and-gold) relation is clearly present in the last two words of the first line, and in the first three words of the second line.

Here we have a Guba'e qana line of 4 accents in the first line; but the second line of only 3 accents falls a little short of it. The accent throughout is a falling one.

The same couplet rendered in Geez qene form would result in a regular Guba'e qana of two tetrameter lines:

$$ በሊዕ በዕስ ከንፈረ—ዚኧኪ / አዳም $$
$$ ተሰቀለ / ኧኪ / ልበ — ዚኧየ / መድኃን ። $$

It has four accents in each line, but in varying combinations of rising and falling ones. In terms of syllables, it is not symmetrical like the Amharic model; it has 14 in the first line and only 12 in the second.

The virtue of the Amharic couplet considered above lies in its assimilation of the Geez qene convention of Semenna-worq in an approximate Guba'e qana form, without imposing Geez accentual patterns on the vernacular. In this it gives us a significant clue to the successful utilization of qene forms in vernacular versification; but only a clue. It cannot stand for a general solution to our problem because not all qene forms are built on the principle of plain tetrameter symmetry like the Guba'e qana, to be amenable to simple transposition like the one above. In fact it is the syllabic variety in the foot and of the feet in the line of verse, together with the strictly limited number of rhyming lines for each form, that is the charm of qene poems.

It is this aspect of qene which we could with profit import into Amharic verse, which at present is suffering from unrestrained length and metronomic regularity of rhythm, in the hands of a mass of new devotees.

To accomplish the main task, we must adopt a systematic approach. We should analyze the forms of Geez qene not in terms of their differing zema tunes, but of the frequency-pattern of the accents for every rhyming line in each form.

A preliminary survey on this line of a random selection of some 200 qene poems, mostly from Herou's collection, reveals some basic trends in the metrical structure of qene poetry.

Qene lines rhyme together. Regarding the number of feet per metrical line they range from the dimeter to the decameter, i.e. from two to ten feet per verse. Qene metrical feet have a wide range of variation in terms of syllable content extending from the monosyllabic to the hexasyllabic, i.e. from one to six syllables per foot. The combination of syllables in the foot also varies within the line of verse, because the metrical foot is tied to the musical phrase, and thus to the overall zema tune of a given form.

A further distinction is that qene stanzaic forms are not simple stanzas, or verse paragraphs as is commonly understood, and they do not form part of a sequence. They are complete, self-contained poems. The sonnet is the stanzaic form in English that can somewhat parallel the qene form in this respect. But an even better analogy would be the Japanese Haiku: short, concentrated, complete unto itself.

Qene forms having the same number of lines of verse (e.g. the Wazema, Sellassie, Zeye'ize quintains) differ in other respects. The first is their Zema tune, which need not concern us here.

A more significant aspect of variation for our purpose is the number and frequency of accents (or accented feet) per line of verse, which constitutes the basic yardstick for qene. From the accent point of view, qene forms can be tabulated as follows, from the two-line Guba'e qana to the eleven-line Etanermoger, with numbers indicating the amount of accents in each of the consecutive lines of a form:

Qene form	Accents per line
Guba'e qana	4–4
Kullikkimu	4–4
Hintseha	4–3
Zeamlakiye	4–4–4–
Mibezhu	6–4–6
Sahlike	3–4–6
Kibr Ye'iti	5–4–4–5
Wazema	6–4–4–3–3–
Sellassie	9–4–5–3–3–
Zeye'ize	7(3,4,6)–4–3–4
Etanemoger, geez	7–4–4–4–5–5–3
Meweddis (9 line)	7–4–(3,4,5,6)–2–4–4–4–4–4
Etanemoger, izi	4–3–4–2–5–4–5–5–2–4–3

(Some representative qene poems illustrating this by well-known poets of the past are found in the appendix to this paper).

A word is in place here about the process by which the table above is arrived at.

The random sample of 200 qene poems examined represents thirteen of the seventeen forms. The accent-pattern for each line of each form is a product of simple statistical frequency. (The Guba'e qana and the Hintseha couplets, for example, have the pattern of 4–4 and 4–3 respectively.) It is, therefore, the most frequent pattern of accents per line that is the basis of the above classification. One should note in this connection that the term "most frequent" is not synonymous with "majority", though in many instances it can be.

Concerning regularity of accent-patterns in a qene form, our preliminary examination has revealed that some forms exhibit more of it than others. The Guba'e qana and the Kullikkimu couplets, the Mibezhu triplet, and the seven-line Etanemoger, geez, are examples of such regularity. This fact indicates that not all qene forms are riddled with irregularity as some observers imagine.

Other forms are relatively irregular in this respect. The reason for this is that though any qene poem is composed to a Zema tune, the actual singing of the tune can vary to some extent within a prescribed limit. The variation is naturally reflected in the qene phrase and line. The latitude of variation is nonetheless generally limited to one accent more or one accent less per line in most cases. In fewer cases this latitude can vary between two or three accents plus or minus per line of verse.

In spite of such irregularities, however, most verses in a qene form do manifest reasonable consistency of accent-pattern, and irregular lines are usually limited and predictable. The third foot of the third line of the nine-line Meweddis can have anything from 3 to 7 accents, but most frequently 4 to 6 accents. Similarly, the second foot of the second line of the Zeye'ize most frequently can have 3, 4 or 6 accents.

To have a still closer glimpse of the metrical structure of qene forms, we must also consider the syllabic pattern of the qene metrical foot.

The qene foot can range from the monosyllabic to the hexasyllabic. Correspondingly, the qene line of verse shows a wide variety in the types of feet, though there are limits to this too.

If, for instance, we consider the first part of the opening line of the Meweddis form invariably consisting of three accented feet and compare its syllabic configuration in some randomly chosen poems, we get the result that:

— the three-foot opening line can contain a total of 8 to 15 syllables,
— the first foot extends from the monosyllabic to the hexasyllabic (i.e., 1-6),
— the second foot ranges from the monosyllabic to the trisyllabic (i.e. 1-3),
— the third foot can only be pentasyllabic or hexasyllabic (i.e. 5 or 6).

Such a range of latitude is made possible by the great flexibility of the qene poem based on a musical tune.

If we look more closely, we do discover an underlying order. The first foot has a range of 1 to 6 syllables but not of seven. In other words, it has an upper limit. Similarly, the second foot can have 1 to 3 syllables, but not four. It also has an upper limit. The third foot of 5- or 6 syllables however, has an upper and lower limit, it cannot have 7 or 4 syllables.

If a qene metrical foot exceeds or falls short of the range of syllables dictated by its position in the line composed to a particular zema tune, then the phrase containing the said foot is declared delinquent because it, literally speaking, "breaks the zema", *Zema yisebrall.*

The opening lines of the following Meweddis illustrate the general point:

ዘውገ — አንተ — አኮ / ዘኤለ / — አንተ—አኮ   (Herouy: p.353)

The above line is correct and does not break the zema, because all three feet are within the range of syllables allowed for their position in the line.

But this opening line:

እምኃየሴኒ / ሊተ / ሰበ—ኢተወለድኩ   (Herouy: p.77)

breaks the zema because in the third foot it oversteps the upper limit of 6 syllables and has seven instead.

Further examples:

ለፋሲለደስ / ናንብር / ምስለ — ሕጻናት   (Herouy: p.45)

Of the three feet in this line, the first and the third can change places to read:

ምስለ ሕጻናት / ናንብር / ለፋሲለደስ

without breaking the zema, because both are within the range of syllables allotted to their position in the line.

But if we apply the same test to the opening line:

ምኂልክ / እብ / ርእሰ—አእምሮ   (Herouy: p.56)

to make it read:

ርእሰ—አእምሮ / እብ / ምኂልክ

the rearrangement breaks the zema, because the third foot falls short of the lower limit set for it, which is five syllables.

If we modify the same trimeter line without changing the words or the word order and make a dimeter of it:

ርእሰ—አእምሮ—እብ / ምኂልክ

the first and second feet will each be within the bounds of the permitted range of syllables, namely 6 and 3; but we no longer have the third foot necessary for the opening line of a Meweddis. (In fact the meaning of the line has also changed, due to the addition of one more liaison between the second and third words.) We must therefore add one more, to make it read:

ርእሰ—አእምሮ—እብ / ምጌልክ / ለመንከራ-ቲክ

This is a correct opening for a Meweddis with a third foot of 6 syllables.

In the process we note that the total number of syllables is now 15 instead of 9. Yet the addition of 6 more syllables makes no difference to the metrical line, because the number of accents remains the same, namely three. This accords with the general proposition that in qene verse the accent is of paramount importance.

Here are some more examples to consider in the light of the foregoing:

—	ቦ / ሕይወት / በጥምቀተ — ባዕድ	(Herouy: p.355)
—	ንዒ ምግብ / መርዓተ—ኢያሱ	(Herouy: p.53)
—	ፊፋሁ ለሰብእ / ቀታሊ—ርእሱ	(Herouy: p.56)
—	ገጥራ / ወሰዶም / አሕጉረ—ፍዳ	(Herouy: p.57)
—	ረበናተ—ጽርዕ / ዕድቁ / በጽንፈ— ገጥራ	(Herouy: p.47)

The foregoing calculations and permutations are basic for the correct grasp of the underlying accentual and syllabic patterns of a qene form. It is such an analysis that reveals the full metrical intricacy of the qene poem.

For the frequency of accent-pattern per line and of syllabic range per metrical foot form are the basis for determining a representative model for each Geez qene form.

Once we reduce a given qene form to its accentual and syllabic skeleton long obscured by the overriding influence of the Zema tune, we will be able to construct the most frequent and therefore the most representative model of that particular form.

This model can then be transformed into an Amharic equivalent by retaining as much as possible the syllabic structure of its metrical feet, but ignoring the accent which is not paramount in Amharic. The successful achievement of such a transformation is the most important step to be taken by those interested in composing vernacular poetry in classical qene form.

How the shape of qene forms in Amharic will look in the end, and in any other vernacular, is beyond the range of the present paper to predict. Yet the possibility of reaching the goal is there, adumbrated by the couplet earlier quoted:

ዕጸበለስ በልቶ አዳም ከንፈርሽ
መድኃኔ ዓለም ልቢ ተሰቀለሽ ።

The pioneers need no longer be able to sing the zema tune of a form before attempting to compose Amharic poems in it because, like the Geez accent, the Geez zema can have no logical place in the new scheme. From the technical point of view, this represents a big gain.

Experimentation on the above lines will eventually reveal the shape of things to emerge from the novel venture into Geez qene territory.

Nevertheless, we can recapitulate broadly that the qene form in Amharic will have to shed its accent-counting properties and adapt itself to syllable-counting to take root in Amharic poetry. For the ideal should be nothing less than a synthesis in which one can compose Amharic poems in the Geez qene form without trying to impose the Geez rhythm on the vernacular.

But Geez qene is more than forms. It is a tradition in which the expression of content has been elevated to stylistic perfection and embellished by figurative language of great originality. Qene is replete with allusions to classical texts and popular wisdom; it is subtle and yet simple in most instances, though sometimes not easy to unravel without prolonged rumination. These aspects must be adopted as well by the vernacular medium and not the forms alone, though the adoption of the forms is the logical first step.

NOTES

1. See Boris Putrin's definition of cultural revolution in his *Political Terms*, Novosty Publishers, Moscow, 1982.

2. Herouy Wolde-Sellassie, p.279.

3. *Ibid.*

4. *Ibid.*, p.736.

5. *Ibid.*, p.116.

6. *Ibid.*, p.274.

7. *Ibid.*, pp.112, 179, 317.

8. Mersie-Hazen Wolde Qirqos, *Yamarigna Sewasiw*, Addis Ababa, 1935 Eth. C., p.219.

9. Abbe Gubegna, *Meskot*, Berhanenna Selam Printing Press, Addis Ababa, 1962 Eth. C., p.30.

10. See my "Technical Aspects of Amharic Versification", *Journal of Ethiopian Studies*, Vol.1, No.2, 1963.

11. Quoted in Edward Ullendorff, *The Semitic Languages of Ethiopia*, Taylor's (Foreign) Press, London, 1955, p.191.

12. Aleqa Afewerq Zewde, a contract employee at the Academy of Ethiopian Languages, Ministy of Culture.

APPENDIX

Some Representative Qene Poems
(Page numbers refer to Herouy, with two exceptions)

Mibezhu (6–4–6)
1. By Dinqe Zeraguel, Resise-debr. (P.211)

ገብረ—ዓመጼ / ልብየ ቅድመ — / እግዚአኩ / ወልድ / ዘዓለማተ / ይቆኒ

እስመ / ትእዛዙ / አድራዕክ / ጮንተ / ታመኩኒ ።

ለዘረቀ ጾስ / ጎብሩ / ሟ ሀብቶሙ ወንበረቶሙ / ይ � ኒ ።

2. By Lemma Hailu, Aleka. (Metsehafe-Tizzita, p.208)

ቃላተ—ነቢ ያት / እንዉ / እልህምተ—ዓብጸ / ይርዓዩ / ውስተ—ቤተ—ፈርያን / ሶኡ

ወውስተ—ምሳሌ / ገራህት / ሕጠታተ—ፈርያን / ዘሮ

ወዘዘቤተ—ፈርያን / ቃል / ወይነ—ምሳሌ / ሐዲስ / ጣዕመ—ዋሀድኝ / አይድኡ ።

Kibr Yeiti (5–4–4–5)
1. By Admasu, Nebure-id. (P.164)

ፆዕረ / ሥዓ / ርእሰ / ዘተአገሡ / ድእለት

ለኪፉ / ወሳውል / እንዘ — ይዔሔር / ሥርዓት ።

ስግዐተ—ልጻስ / ጌር / ከመ—ይትመካህ / ድገጼተ

ልቃሐ—ዋቱ / ፈዶየ / ለእግዚኡ ህየንተ—እሐፁ / ትርብእተ ።

Wazema (6–4–4–3–3)
1. By Samuel, Aleq. (Private Collection)

ፈድፈደ / በዕለ—ሥላሴ ፤

እንተ—ለሥላሴ / ተውገብ / ላሕመ—አብርሃም / አቡነ

ምስለ—ቱቃስ / ቢጹ / እስመ—ጽምደ / ኮነ ።

እንተ—ከመዝስ / ብዕል / ውስተ—ስግያት / ተውገነ ፣

እንዘ—ርስተ — ሰግይ / ንትካፈል / በበመጠኝነ

ስግያተ / ነሐርስ / ኩልነ ።

2. By Tecle-Sellassie, Aleqa. (P.252)

ግብርናተ / ዘካልዑ / መድጎኔ—ዓለም / አገዓኪ / ዲበ—ግእዛነ / ወስክ ፤

ወረገም / ርእሰ / ከመ—ያበቁል / ሥኮ ፤

እስመ—ፈነዎ / አቡሁ / እስከ—ነሴነ / ተልእከ

እንዘ—ይብል / ብላዕ / በሐፈ—ገጽከ

ተደፍዖተ / ዘድልው / ለከ ።

Meweddis, nine-line (7–4–3,4,5,6–2–4–4–4–4–4)
1. By Kebte, Aqqabe-saat. (P.117)

ፅንት / ውእቱ / ፍድፉዶ—ዚኦሂ ለምከሃ—ጠቢባን / ጥበብ ። / እስመ—በጥበብ / ወፆክር

ኢይዐዓዱ / ጸሊም / ወኢይኔውን / ሐጺር ፤

ወለእብድ / ዘይጽንሕም / ክልኤቱ / አጽራር

ፎት / ወመቃብር

ይጽንሕም / አኮኑ / ለጠቢብ ወማእምር ።

ከመስ / ኢያሰጥሙን / ዕመቀ—ብ ሂል—ባሕር

ታሳሥር / የዋሂት / ወጥበብ / ታከብር ፤

እንዘ—የዋሂት / ርግብ / በዓለ — አኮናፍ / ወእግር

የሐውር / በእንግጽዓ / ጠቢብ / አርዌ—ምድር ።

2. By Welde-Gabriel, Ras. (P.56)

ስነ—ጽጌረዳ / ዓለም / እንተ—ትተነጎሬ /

ወተሐልፈ / ቅጽበት / አርአያ—ጸላሎት / ወሕልም ፤

እምነ—አሐፁ / አፉኪ / እስመ—ይወጽአ / ዮም

ለፊ / ቡራኬ / ወለፊ ፤ መርገም /

ወፅንተ / ይኤድም

ዘመነኝኪ / ወሐረ / ፍናተ—አስቴዮስ / ገጻም ።

አነሰ / አረጋዊ / እንዘ — ክርስቲያናዊ / በስም ፤

ለለጽባሑ / በጋጢእት / እንዘ—ጸንዓ—ኃይል የ/አጀከም

ዘመንየ / ኩሉ / ፈጸምኩ / እንበለ—ጸሎት / ወጸም

መዓልተ / በመብልዕ / ወሌሊተ / በንዋም ።

737

RECHERCHES GEOGRAPHIQUES SUR LE MEÇÇA D'AMBO

Alain Gascon

Ambo, chef-lieu de l'*awraǧa* (province) de Čebat et Méçça, est situé dans la région du Choa, à 125 km à l'Ouest d'Addis Abäba, sur la route du Wällaga. C'est une station thermale dont l'eau minérale et la piscine sont fameuses en Ethiopie. Cette province est très vaste et je propose de réserver l'appellation Méçça à la région d'Ambo-Gudär, dépression double entre, au Nord, les plateaux de Gendäbärät qui bordent le Goǧǧam et le massif volcanique de Wonči-Dändi, front-ière au Sud avec l'*awraǧa* de Čäbo et Guragé.

Lors de mon premier séjour, entre 1969 et 1971, je comptais rédiger une monographie régionale. En Ethiopie, ce type d'étude ne pouvait convenir, faute de données immédiatement accessibles. En outre, toutes les questions abordées faisaient référence à des problèmes dont l'échelle était au minimum celle de l'Ethiopie ou de la Corne de L'Afrique, mais la plupart du temps, celle du continent africain dans son entier. En particulier, la situation du Méçça nécessite d'élargir le champ de la réflexion à tout l'ensemble éthiopien quand il s'agit de rendre compte des problèmes de contact entre milieux physiques et humains différents, ou quand il s'agit de comprendre les rapports entre le contrôle de la terre et l'identité culturelle.

Ce travail m'a demandé une longue familiarité avec le terrain et avec ses habitants, acquise malgré le manque de temps et de moyens, la recherche n'étant pas mon travail principal. Observations directes, contacts personnels, lectures bibliographiques se sont complétés, confortés, les uns me renvoyant aux autres.

Le Méçça préfigure le Sud-Ouest de l'Ethiopie, plus humide et plus chaud, avec les fossées et le faux bananier.

La plus grande partie du Méçça est occupée par le fossé dissymétrique de Gudär, bloqué au Nord-Est et au Nord-Ouest par des falaises aux facettes de failles très nettes. Au Sud, il s'élève en pente douce par de longues planèzes vers les deux 'caldeiras' du Dändi et du Wonči qui cul-minent à plus de 3000 m. Vers le sommet des volcans, les interfluves se rétrécissent jusqu'à devenir des 'barrancos' ravinés.

Dans les parties les plus basses du fossé, sous des coulées volcaniques fraîches, scoriacées, franchies en chutes d'eau par les rivières, il affleure une grande variété de faciès de roches sédi-mentaires, allant du secondaire au quaternaire. Cette variété lithologique contraste avec les vastes 'trapps' basaltiques des hauts plateaux du Nord.

La régularité des pentes du Wonči est parfois interrompue par des dômes et des cônes ad-ventices d'où s'échappent des coulées récentes qui se terminent dans le fond du fossé. La 'cal-deira' de Wonči est occupée par un lac aux versantes très raides, pénétré de presqu'îles aux formes tourmentées. A certains endroits, il y a des troncs fossiles ennoyés.

Que ce soit dans le domaine des roches sédimentaires ou dans celui des roches volcaniques, on est frappé par la jeunesse et la fraîcheur des formes du relief qui se manifestant par la vigeur des ravages de l'érosion.

Dans cette région, manquent les indications précises, non pas sur la nature des affleure-ments dans la mesure où différentes industries les utilisent, mais l'accord ne s'est pas encore fait sur les dates et sur leur étendue. Quant à l'activité volcanique récente, il y a de très fortes pré-somptions qu'il faudrait étayer par des études plus complètes.

Les mêmes lacunes se font sentir lorsque l'on veut établir des cartes climatiques à grande échelle. Il n'y a que deux stations dont les séries sont récentes et incomplètes, et on peut attendre beaucoup de travaux sur les bilans hydriques, sur les jours utiles pour l'agriculture, tout ceci étant complété par des observations d'hydrologie pour connaître l'activité réelle de l'érosion. Faute de tous ces renseignements, on est obligé de se retourner vers la végétation et les sols comme révélateurs des nuances climatiques à grande échelle.

Le grand intérêt du Méçça, c'est un gradient altitudinal qui va de 1600 m. à 3300 m., sur un versant où on peut observer toutes les transitions entre les grandes zones bioclimatiques qui, ailleurs, son bordées de versants très raides. L'inventaire des espèces naturelles a été fait, on constate des divergences de spécialistes sur l'identification de certaines plantes. Il manque une carte des formations végétales, d'autant plus difficile à réaliser que le Méçça est densément et anciennement humanisé.

J'ai parcouru ses versants; à l'aide de repères topographiques grossiers, j'ai tenté de reconstituer un étagement de la végétation naturelle et des espèces cultivées. Ce qui plaide pour une nuance climatique un peu plus chaude, c'est, à la fois, la présence d'espèces méridionales, la taille exceptionnelle atteinte par certains sujets et aussi le développement en altitude des céréales, de l'*ensät* et du café. Un autre indice en est la réussite de l'acclimatation de la vigne, des agrumes et des vrais bananiers.

Des observations personnelles de défrichement et d'écobuage, et la consultation de la bibliographie montrent une extension de la surface cultivée dans des sites très marginaux. Tous les observateurs abordent la question de la surcharge démographique du Méçça.

Les densités de population sont indépendantes de l'altitude

Dans tous mes déplacements, j'ai toujours rencontré des établissements humains, notamment le cratère du Wončì offre une impression de fourmillère humaine. La faune sauvage a totalement disparu et la flore naturelle a été largement entamée. Quand on se retourne vers les documents démographiques, on a la mauvaise surprise de constater qu'ils ne sont précis que pour Ambo et Gudär, et de ne trouver que des estimations à l'échelle de la province, échelle inadéquate. On doit se livrer à la tâche harassante de comptages en s'appuyant sur des travaux de pionniers accomplis par les étudiants éthiopiens.

Les résultats obtenus en recoupant un maximum de sources autorisent à avancer une remarquable uniformité des densités de population, quelle que soit l'altitude entre 2000 et 3000m. Si on convertit ces densités au km^2 en densités par ha cultivé, elles augmentent avec l'altitude. Paradoxalement, le bocage serré de plantations de faux bananiers des Galila et des Čäbo du Wončì a une densité supérieure à l''openfield' céréalier des basses terres peuplées d'Oromo Méçça.

Les exploitations des paysans Oromo sont constituées en majorité du regroupement de plusieurs petits champs, alors que les Galila du Wončì n'ont généralement qu'une seule parcelle de la taille d'un grand jardin. Les Oromo pratiquent une céréaliculture extensive avec des jachères, tandis que les planteurs d'*ensät* s'acharnent en une 'coltora promiscua' intensive.

Ces deux systèmes agraires ont en commun le parcellaire en mosaïque et l'habitat dispersé, singularisant ainsi le Méçça. En effet, dans la plus grande partie de l'Ethiopie, au Nord, l''openfield' céréalier est associé à un habitat groupé et à des champs en auréoles concentriques.

L'ensät, le Wončì, les Galila et les Méçça

Le Méçça est une marche au contact de deux civilisations agraires: au Nord, la céréaliculture à l'araire associée à l'habitat groupé et l''openfield', et au Sud, les plantations bocagères d'*ensät* travaillées à la 'fourche' dans une zone d'habitat dispersé.

On s'accorde sur l'idée qu'à une période plus ancienne, l'aire de l'*ensät* s'étendait au Nord et, pour le Méçça, plus bas que maintenant. Le Wončì et le Dändi sont dans cette analyse des témoins de cette avancée du faux bananier. Les plantations ont donc disparu, l''openfield' s'est installé, mais le parcellaire et l'habitat en ont gardé l'empreinte.

M. Tubiana m'a signalé un passage de Bruce qui rapporte que les Méçça " transplantés" au Sud du lac Țana cultivaient toujours l'*ensät* (XVIII° siècle). C'est d'ailleurs là que, le premier, il a identifié cette plante. Un siècle après Bruce, les d'Abbadie ont parcouru cette région; la publication en cours de leurs journaux devrait apporter plus amples informations.

La singularité des Galila ne tient pas seulement à leur système agraire, mais aussi à leur identité culturelle. Ils ne sont pas Oromo, contrairement aux Čäbo de la périphérie de la 'caldeira', eux aussi planteurs de faux bananiers. Bien avant l'incorporation du Méçça à l'Empire éthiopien, Antoine d'Abbadie a rencontré des prêtres du Wonǯi venus demander des secours pour une population chrétienne isolée au milieu des païens et des musulmans. Il les rapproche des Guragé, comme la plupart des éthiopisants. Nous serions en présence d'un isolat ethnique témoin d'une extension antérieure de ce peuple. Les Guragé sont les représentants les plus connus de l'"*ensete* culture', mais, eux, n'ont pas tous la même confession religieuse.

Cette question des populations relictes a une très grande importance pour l'histoire du Méǯǯa, surtout pour son histoire récente. Elle conduit à s'interroger sur le peuplement du Méǯǯa aux XVI° et XVII° siècles, avant les invasions Oromo. Le Méǯǯa où l'on a découvert des vestiges archéologiques de la présence des Abyssins était plutôt une marche frontière protectrice de cet Empire, comme le montrent les travaux des historiens. Les sémites chrétiens y étaient sans doute minoritaires et le Wonǯi est peut-être une trace d'un établissement remontant à cette période.

De tels îlots de populations relictes ont justifié la politique de 'Reconquista' de siècle dernier. Sous l'Ancien Régime, les habitants du Wonǯi ne subissaient pas la même oppression foncière que les Oromo. Même si l'*ensät* n'intéressait absolument pas les Choans, ils ont su utiliser les compétences des Guragé ou des Känbata. L'isolement et la petite taille du Wonǯi a dû jouer en faveur des Galila, mais peut-être est-ce l'Histoire?

Le système de tenure

Les Méǯǯa ayant été vaincus au siècle dernier, ils ont donc perdu tous leurs droits sur la terre. Ce point fondamental ne transparaissait pas dans le parcellaire d'utilisation, et la collecte de renseignements sur ce sujet était très difficile avant la Révolution.

Les paysans Méǯǯa étaient les *gäbbar*, tenanciers précaires de leurs vainqueurs, maintenus sur la terre comme instruments nécessaires à sa mise en valeur, une sorte de nouveau servage à la manière de Catherine II.

Les paysans étaient soumis à un double système de prélévements, payant un loyer aux concessionnaires qui, pour une grande part, avaient reçu une assignation d'impôts: ils prélevaient les impôts royaux moyennant le versement d'une somme fixe au Trésor.

La situation que je viens d'exposer était en réalité impossible à saisir sur place pour un observateur étranger. Le Méǯǯa n'était pas arpenté, et surtout les bénéficiaires du système étaient au-dessus des lois: haut-gradés, haut-fonctionnaires, familiers de la cour, famille royale, etc. Leur puissance et leur rapacité étaient tels que les intermédiaires autochtones (les *balabbat*) avaient un rôle effacé. (On attribue le succès rapide de la Révolution au Méǯǯa, entre autres raisons, à l'affaiblissement de ces cadres.)

L'occupation italienne a transformé le paysage agraire de la région de Gudär en y découpant de vastes plantations spéculatives qui ont bouleversé les rapports traditionnels entre les maîtres et les tenanciers. Les Italiens partis, les grands personnages se sont rués sur les exploitations modernes et ont entrepris de les agrandir en se débarassant de 'leurs' paysans, grâce à leurs prérogatives héritées de la Conquête. Une grave menace pesait sur les Méǯǯa, traqués par l'alliance objective de conquérants intérieurs et extérieurs. Il en résulta des évictions aux conséquences tragiques dont l'étendue fut révélée après la Révolution.

Ville étrangère

Lors des sorties dans la campagne, je fus frappé que la précarité de l'existence des paysans n'ait pas engendré un exode rural massif. Les deux villes principales, Ambo et Gudär, ne pouvaient guère leur offrir d'activités, étant tournées vers le commerce, l'artisanat, et, bien plus encore, vers le tertiaire administratif. La ville, la *kätäma*, est étrangère au paysan: les fonctionnaires, les policiers et les soldats, les prêtres parlent une langue que le Méǯǯa ne comprend pas. Les paysans ont des contacts brefs avec ce monde étranger, au marché, dans une boutique tenue par un yéménite, ou dans un tribunal. Les remparts qui entouraient les places fortes fondées par Ménélik ont été remplacés par un obstacle aussi efficace, le rempart de la langue qui ne peut être tourné que par l'Ecole.

Un tiers de la population d'Ambo fréquentait les écoles et les élèves venaient de tout l'Ouest de l'Ethiopie, jusqu'à la frontière avec le Soudan (années 1969-71).

Les Méčča étaient dans une situation d'exclus, d'exilés dans leur propre pays. Privés de toute représentation politique, ils ont privilégié, amplifié le domaine inexpugnable et secret des pratiques magiques. Beaucoup d'entre eux fréquentaient assidûment les rites des *qallu*, démiurges déviés du système politico-religieux des Oromo, le *gäda*. D'autre part, ils ont développé une très forte solidarité dans les associations d'entraide, et notamment les *edder*, précurseurs des associations de paysans de la Réforme Agraire.

Conclusion

Dans les dernières années de l'Ancien Régime, près d'un siècle après la perte de l'indépendance et de la terre, les Oromo Méčča étaient en passe de perdre leur mémoire collective et de n'être plus que des Galla. En même temps, ils étaient guettés par la perspective d'un départ définitif. Néanmoins, dans le plus amharisé des Galla, une petite flamme oromo brûlait qui était réveillée à chaque vexation que les fonctionnaires d'Haylä-Sellasé ne manquaient pas de leur faire subir.

Pendant l'été 1975, retrouvant le Méčča dans une véritable fièvre de labours, je fus étonné par la vivacité de la revendication oromo et par la facilité de communiquer avec les paysans. Ces Méčča avaient retrouvé et leurs terres et leur tradition culturelles.

Orientation bibliographique

Je ne puis donner qu'un extrait de la liste des nombreux ouvrages que j'ai dû dépouiller pour rédiger des travaux dont ce court article n'est qu'un résumé. Les lecteurs pourront se reporter pour une bibliographie plus complète:

Gascon, A. 1977   " Le dangʷara, pieu à labourer d'Ethiopie" in *J. A. T. B. A.*, vol XXIV, nos. 2-3, 111-126.

———————— 1983   *Identité culturelle et contrôle de la terre: le pays Méčča (Ethiopie du Centre-Ouest) de l'Ancien Régime à la Révolution.* L.A. 94 (E.H.E.S.S. — C.N.R.S.), 472pp. et fig. (thèse de doctorat de 3° cycle de géographie, Paris 1 publication en cours).

BIBLIOGRAPHIE SOMMAIRE

d'Abbadie, Antoine 1890   *Géographie de l'Ethiopie, ce que j'ai entendu faisant suite à ce que j'ai vu.* Paris, 475pp. et fig.

Asfaw Edessa 1970   *A micro geographical study of Mankata.* Addis-Abäba, 107 pp.

Berhanu Abäbä 1971   *Evolution de la propriété foncière au Choa (Ethiopie) du règne de Ménélik à la constitution de 1931.* Paris, Bibliothèque de l'Ecole des langues orientales vivantes, 270pp.

Borelli, J. 1890   *Ethiopie méridionale, journal de mon voyage aux pays amhara oromo et sidama, septembre 1885 à novembre 1888.* Paris, 521pp.

C. S. O. (Imperial Ethiopian Government) 1966   *Report on a survey of Shoa province.* Addis-Abäba, 37pp et fig.

Deherain, H. 1931 — *Figures coloniales françaises et étrangères.* Paris, Société d'éditions géographiques maritimes et coloniales, 267pp et fig.

Fantoli, A. 1965 — *Contributo alla climatologia dell'Etiopia.* Rome, O.P.I., 558pp.

Getačäw Asrat 1969 — *Regional study of lake Wonchi Area,* Addis-Abäba, 56 pp.

Giordano, G. 1948 — " Forêts et bois d'Ethiopie" in *Bois et forêts des tropiques*, nos. 5 et 6.

Knutsson, K. E. 1967 — " Authority and change. A study of the Kallu institution among the Macha Galla of Ethiopia" in *Etnologiska studies*, 29, 239pp et fig.

Kuls, W. 1957 — " Agrargeographische Beobachtungen in der Umgebung von Addis-Abeba" in V. E. B. Hermann Haack (éd.) *Petermans Geographische Mitteilungen*, pp.245-251.

Lemordant, D. 1959 — *Les plantes éthiopiennes.* Addis-Abäba, Central Printing Press, 105pp.

Lewis, H. S. 1966 — " Kud'Arfan: a multifunctional institution among the western Galla" in *IIId international conference of Ethiopian studies.* Addis-Abäba, 9pp.

Mahtämä-Sellase Wäldä-Mäsqäl 1960 — *Le régime foncier en Ethiopie.* (traduction) Addis-Abäba, 35pp.

Masfen Woldä-Maryam 1972 — *An introductory geography of Ethiopia.* Addis-Abäba, 215 pp et fig.

Ministero dell'Africa Italiana 1938-1943 — *Gli annali dell'Africa italiana.* Verone et Rome.

Mohr, P. A. 1962 — *The geology of Ethiopia.* Asmära, University College of Addis-Abäba Press, 268pp. et fig.

Şähaye Berhanä-Sellase 1975 — " The question of Damot and Wälamo" in *J. E. S.*, vol.XIII, no.1, pp.47-64.

Smeds, H. 1956 — " The population capacity of the Ethiopian highlands" in *XVIII° congrès international de géographie*, Rio, tome III, pp.465-473.

Stielher, W. 1948 — " Studien zur Landwirtschafts-u. Siedlungsgeographie Äthiopiens" in *Erdkunde*, vol.II, p.247.

Strelcyn, S. 1973 — *Médecine et plantes d'Ethiopie, II Enquête sur les noms et l'emploi des plantes en Ethiopie.* Naples, Istituto per l'Oriente, 280pp.

Tadässä Tamrat 1972 — *Church and state in Ethiopia, 1270-1527.* Oxford, O.U.P., 327pp. et fig.

Teka Gäbrä-Maryam 1969   *Kilinto-Senkelle. A study of socio-economic conditions in a rural area in Ethiopia.* Addis-Abäba, 94pp. et fig.

Troll, C. 1960   " Die Kultur-geographische Stellung und Eigenart des Hochlandes von Äthiopien zwischen dem Orient und Äquatorial-Afrika", in *Congrès des Etudes Ethiopiennes,* Rome, pp.29-45.

Verniere, M. 1974   " La photographie aérienne (pré-enquête et méthode de collecte de données à l'aide de la photographie aérienne)" in Manuel de collecte de démographie, *ORSTOM INSEE*, t.II, Ch.V.

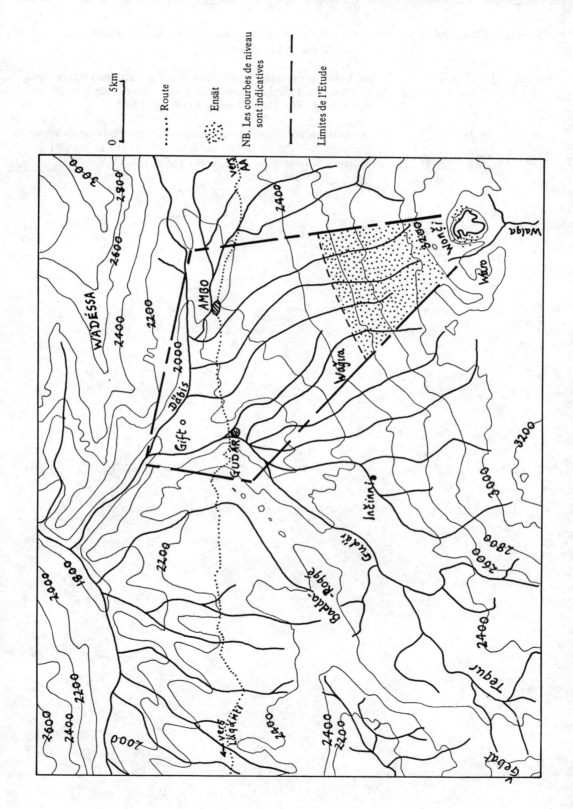

Route

Ensât

NB. Les courbes de niveau sont indicatives

Limites de l'Etude

0 5km

ANCESTOR VENERATION IN BLEAN* CULTURE

Adhana Mengeste-ab

BACKGROUND NOTE

The Blean people form one of the the several Agaw groups dispersed in isolated pockets throughout northern Ethiopia. The Agaw, once a powerful political force and a dominant population in their homeland in the northern highland plateau, are now scattered in several enclaves. The Blean are found in Keren District of Eritrea; the Qimant, Beta Israel and Kunfel in Gondar; those in Gojjam, Wollo and Tigrai speak Awngi, Xamir and Xamtanga respectively. They all speak dialects of Agaw, but are also bi-lingual in the surrounding language, e.g. Amharic, Tigrigna and Tigre. Many lost their mother-tongue and now are Amharic or Tigrigna speakers.

The Blean, who occupied a larger territory in former times, are today limited to Keren District. Like the ancestral Agaw, who have been cultivators and animal husbandmen, they are settled agriculturalists and cattle raisers. Most probably they migrated north around the second half of the tenth century. Surrounded by non-Agaws on all sides, in an isolated pocket, they still preserve their physionomy and language. Their spirit of independence, warlike stand and deep attachment to the ancestral culture made them able to preserve their own identity, withstanding many vicissitudes during trying times, especially the Era of the Princes and the Turco-Egyptian period. With the introduction of the railroad, motor road and a few vestiges of modernization by the Italian colonialists Blean society was weakened. Later, when schools, hospitals and other modern public institutions were set up in Eritrea, this area like other parts of the lowland was forgotten. Distribution of such services was unfair and unbalanced; affecting socio-economic development in these areas in comparison to the rest of the province.

It should be noted here, however, that the Blean, although individualistic, share many things in common with the surrounding peoples and the Ethiopian culture mosaic. To give one example, according to their own tradition, they borrowed the caste system of social structure from the Neptab of the Beja. The Bejas, who pushed south to the Barca Valley, Hamassen and parts of Tigray between the sixth and seventh centuries A.D., were well established in these areas up to the tenth century. The Blean and other Agaws resettled the Hamassien plateau, especially the land along and around the Ansaba river, most probably in the eleventh century A.D. The Zague dynasty, whose establishment date is not known, might have sent the Blean up north in military expeditions to reclaim lands lost to the Beja and free the trade and pilgrimage route via Suakin. Once warring neighbours – the Reja of the Barca, in particular the Beni-Amer, and the Blean share some common cultural traits. The Blean, despite centuries of isolation surrounded by Ethio-Semitic speakers and a struggle for survival as a cultural and linguistic entity, have succeeded in preserving their own identity. Ethiopicists have limited Agaw contribution to somatic, agricultural creativity and linguistic elements. A fresh look into the origins and character of Ethiopian civilization is overdue. The dominant myths and racialistic overtones must be cast out by genuine research and scholarship.

CONCEPT OF DEATH AND LIFE BEYOND AMONG THE BLEAN

God, who is called *Jar* by the Blean, is the author and possessor of everything. He can take away life or bring it into existence. The power and will of God has a fundamental position in their psyche and thinking. *Jar yini* (God permitting), *Jar areikhuw* (God knows) are common everyday phrases. Therefore, whenever death occurs it is the will of *Jar*. The term itself designated both the sky, which is the dwelling place of God, and God himself. To avoid the confusion *semay*, for heaven, has been adapted in Christian times. Even today the term is used in

---

*   The people call themselves by the term Blean, but Tigrigna and Tigre speaking neighbours call them Bilen.

its twofold sense, e.g. *Jardi bradi gawruncut* (may heaven and earth bless you), *Jardi bradi enterakhuw* (cursed by heaven and earth). In Blean religious belief the concept of polytheism was absent before Christianization, but as animists they worshipped intermediate spirits. High places, groves, streams and other bodies of water were revered as dwelling places of spirits. Despite centuries of Christianization, some of these beliefs can still be traced. Many pre-Christian ideas have been adapted to Christianity. Death is then the will of God and must be accepted with submission. That there is life in the netherworld is seen from the extremely careful manner in which the dead are buried and the services rendered to the deceased. The souls of the dead can be disturbed if certain services due to them are not rendered and they can haunt the living as a consequence; or they may have a benevolent influence on the devout and dutiful descendant. The souls of heroes and great ancestors might have been deified in pre-Christian eras. In recent history there is no evidence of this concept. The souls of the righteous enjoy everlasting bliss, while those of the wrongdoers are sent to a place of punishment, e.g. the souls of those who have committed suicide are condemned to wandering and loneliness, in fact they are buried in separate and isolated ground.

FUNERAL, BURIAL AND MOURNING

When a Blean dies, the body is prepared for burial. A fresh white cloth is bought for covering it and this, in turn, is covered with a mat of palm leaves. Messengers are sent out to relatives and surrounding villages to announce the sad news. The funeral might be postponed until the arrival of his far away son. The grave itself is painstakingly dug out to conform to the height and dimensions of the person to be buried. The bowl-like spade used in the process is later left on the tomb. Some personal effects might also be left on it, depending on the age of the deceased.

The two common forms of tombs are the *Arat* (bed) and the *Jakha* (heap). Both forms are enclosed in family cairns. The pyramidical tomb with great heaps of stones, marked at the top of the cone by quartz, is made for heroes or ancestors noted for their wisdom, authority and long life. Also, for men, the common rectangular forms are marked at the centre with quartz. No matter whether the terrain is difficult, or under any circumstances, the burial procedure does not change. The right distance must be dug and the right shape and form must be maintained. Hasty and superficial burial is considered a desecration and shame. The body must be buried in a respectable manner and be safe from scavengers, such as the hyenas. The funeral itself is a big event. All the adult members of the village, the surrounding villages, relatives and friends from far and near turn out for the occasion. Funerals of well known individuals, such as chiefs, notables, elders, etc., are exceptionally large. Crying and wailing women follow the corpse, carried and immediately followed by the menfolk. After the religious ceremony, Christian or Muslim, as the case may be, the body is interred amidst loud wailings and cries by all present. During the funeral close relatives slaughter cows in sign of grief and, probably, as a sacrifice for the deceased. The meat from these cows serves as food for the mourners, especially for those who have come from far away.

Both men and women mourn the dead from the evening of their passing away. But men, except those who were away on the day of the funeral, do not cry after the burial. If the deceased is a man, his wife mourns him for a whole year as a sign of sorrow. If she is a woman, her jewellery hangs from a visible corner of the house for the same purpose. On the seventh day of death a special commemorative service is held. The womenfolk weep and wail for the deceased and food is eaten. Again, on the twelfth day, a similar occasion is held. The heavy mourning period comes to an end after the *suk*. On this occasion a cow assigned for this purpose is slain by the eldest son. Relatives from far and near gather to mourn their beloved and the villagers also actively participate. Food is served for all present. The date of this occasion is set according to the season. If the harvest season is far away, it can be delayed until after it. If the family has economic possibilities it can be held after one month or, nowadays, even after one week.

COMMEMORATIONS

In addition to the commemorative services after the seventh and twelfth day, and the *suk*, the adult dead is remembered on the sixth month and on the anniversary. On the first anniversary, the mourning period is officially ended. From then on they are commemorated on each anniversary. For the male adult, home made beer is offered to his peers and all adult males who have passed through the rite of manhood initiation. For the woman, porridge is offered to married ladies, except brides. The sons of the deceased carry the full responsibility of caring for the dead. Each married son is bound by custom to perform all the duties for the dead. Above all, they must provide the cow for the *suk*. If a cow is not slaughtered on that occasion, the dead father will not rest in peace and the living descendants will always be haunted. Those who have committed suicide have no right to the ceremonies and services. Young men who have not passed through the initiation rite are not entitled to the *suk* or the commemorative anniversaries. However, if they were very close to the initiation age, a token ceremony of initiation could be performed on the corpse. Caring for the dead is simply a family affair. Through filial piety, the male offspring are bound to perform all the services established by custom or they will be considered a disgrace to the ancestors and the clan will face, thereby, the consequent social disfavour. Even if the family has only one cow, it is slaughtered for the *suk* of the father, which is a very harmful custom. Anniversaries of grandparents are also celebrated. If someone dies without offspring, their brothers or cousins carry the anniversary duty out of pity. Therefore, one's obligation is to one's parents and grandparents. Anniversaries for all of the ancestors are held at harvest time. Each loaf of bread baked for the celebration of St. Michael's feast at that season, is done so in memory of a particular deceased member of the family. Here, I have excluded Christian and Muslim religious ceremonies and services for obvious reasons.

THE INFLUENCE OF THE ANCESTORS ON THEIR DESCENDANTS

As stated a little earlier, the influence of ancestors on their descendants could be either benevolent or malevolent. If the descendant has carried out all his filial duties, he will get the blessing and protection of the dead. If, however, he is delinquent, he might earn their curse and ire. It is believed that such people meet misfortune and a bad end. On the whole, the ancestors are regarded as a benevolent force. The graveyard is looked at with great fear and respect. Not only the body of the dead and the burial grounds are kept with awe and reverence but, most importantly, also the values they left behind. The customary law, cultural values and norms are unchangeable. The laws left by the ancestors are rigidly observed. The classic example is the custom of not milking cows, as a sign of aristocracy. The Blean aristocracy borrowed the caste system from the Neptab, so tradition declares. Accordingly, they formed into a warrior class, leaving the cares of the farm and the cattle to minorities who sought refuge with them or were weak. The chore of milking cows gradually became unworthy of the noble class and was left to the serfs. This vestige of former aristocratic customs was so strong in Blean culture that it was abandoned only in the 1960s — and even then the older generation swore never to touch a cow's teat. Strangely enough, it was perfectly legitimate to milk goats and sheep. The stupid, tragi-comic consequence of this custom was a burning issue among the affected Blean group. It was so difficult to break that it only finally met its demise through religious intervention. Respect for ancestors preserves the social structure and enhances whatever is good in the system. But rigid adherence to ancestral norms and values can be negative. Social and technical innovations can not only be retarded, they can also be totally stifled. Collectively, ancestors in the netherworld could be a guiding spirit, an ideal, a heritage, or a cultural treasure. The elders, made wise by the rich experience of age, could be considered the trustees of the ancestors. Age, in particular primogeniture, has great value in such a system. Thus the veneration of the ancestors has a high place in Blean society. Although simple and brief in its execution, it is of deep consequence to the culture and structure of this society. Today, modern Blean women might be taken aback to see their mothers take off their slippers when passing by a graveyard, but the symbolism is clear. Although ancestor veneration is a family affair, it is the sacred duty of the whole of Blean society to guard and care for it.

BIBLIOGRAPHY

Abbadie, Antoine d'
Le droit bilen a propos du livre de Werner Munziger, Paris; E. Martinet, 1866.

Bel, L.
"Lettre de Mgr. Bel, vicaire apostelique d'Abyssinie, a MM. les etudiants et seminaristes de la Congregation de la Mission, a Paris: Massawa, 23 Avril, 1866". *Annales de la Congregation de la Mission*, Paris, tome 31, 1867, pp.591-626.

Conti Rossini, Carlo
Principii di diritto consuetudiaric dell'Eritrea, Rome, Unione Editrice, 1916.

Debrowski, Joanne Carol
"Excavations in Ethiopia: Lalibela and Matchabiet caves, Begemeder Province", Boston; Boston University, 1971. (Thesis).

Fattovich, Rodolfo
"Some data for the study of cultural history in ancient Northern Ethiopia". *Nyame Akuna*, no.10, 1977, pp.6-8.

Gamst, Frederick C.,
The Qemant: a pagan Hebraic peasantry of Ethiopia, New York: Holb, Rinehart and Winston: 1969.

Münzinger, Werner
Dei Costumi e del diritto dei Bogos, traduzione dal tedesco da A. Ostini, Rome; M. degli Affari Esteri, 1891.

Piva, Abele
Origine, fisionomia e storia delle antiche genti dell'Eritrea, Rome: Istituto Coloniale Italiano, 1907.

HISTORY OF EVENTS AND INTERNAL DEVELOPMENT

THE EXAMPLE OF THE BURJI-KONSO CLUSTER

Hermann Amborn

Recent historical research shows a tendency towards a "history from below", that is, towards a history which is no longer dominated by the exclusive viewpoint of a literate elite. The rediscovery of popular culture in European history is — among other things — a consequence of the crisis which befell optimistic progressivism. Moreover, within this trend a new place value is assigned to the study of anthropology, especially historically oriented ethnology.[1] I would like to the discrepancy existing between what is obviously bound to enter into a general history of events and a history as it affects the people involved. Thus, I would like to bring to light what lies beneath the kind of facts one might usually find written in the history books and, in so doing, shall analyze the dynamics of internal development and relate them to the relevant historical events. And here I am concerned with recent history, namely the period during and after the conquest of southern Ethiopia by the northerners, and up to the present day. Even though there was no direct relationship between these two domains — pressure was always one-sided — the affected people's reaction to the new reality was not merely passive. Rather, they gave their own collective feelings towards a continuous dialectical process which has now come to the surface in different socio-cultural patterns. While originally of a closely interlocked culture, the three South Ethiopian ethnic groups I shall present have each found their own way of solving the conflicts initiated by the same external event, namely the conquest.[2]

The first of the three groups referred to are the Konso. They are relatively well-documented in ethnographic literature.[3] I have also spent some months of fieldwork among them.

The second are a number of culturally and linguistically closely related peoples whom I shall refer to with the term Dullay (a term generally adopted by linguists). Concerning these people I rely exclusively on personal observations.[4]

Thirdly, the Burji; a people who have been studied by the late professor Helmut Straube of Munich.[5]

You may know these peoples as belonging to the so-called Burji-Konso Group, a term coined by Enrico and Ernesta Cerulli to designate an area of cultural homogeneity.[6] In order to avoid confusion I shall be using this term here — though it is not quite adequate.

The history of events in the area in question can be briefly outlined, for there is no great difference between what can be said about the above-mentioned groups and what is historically known about southern Ethiopia. We have our knowledge of historical events at the turn of the century through books and articles written by travellers, through the official Ethiopian chronicle of Gabre Selassie, and through the reports of certain British colonial officers, like Hodson.[7]

Early contact between the indigenous peoples and the northerners may be described as a "frontier situation". Following Thompson and Lamar, I understand "frontier not as a boundary or line, but as a territory or zone of interpenetration between two previously distinct societies. The frontier 'opens' in a given zone when the first representatives of the intrusive society arrive; it 'closes' when a single political authority has established hegemony over the zone."[8] The frontier situation in the south was quite relaxed, as a proper frontier ought to have been. But here, there are two phases which one should distinguish: the first one is from 1897 up to about 1906; and the second, from about 1906 to the time of World War I.

The initial stages of the frontier situation were marked by sporadic raids carried out by soldiers, mainly after cattle. On the part of the central government, there was a keen interest to show the flag on the shores of Lake Turkana. Thus, the Abyssinian presence documented its claim to that region and tried to stop the advance of British colonial expansion.[9]

Within the first phase only a few military outposts were established. The most important was located in Gardulla, above today's town of Gidole. The second phase was initiated by the

British pressuring the Abyssinian government to put its southern regions under tighter control in order to stop marauding soldiers and the so-called Tigre from crossing into their East African territories (what is now Kenya). For propaganda purposes the British contrasted their own well-organised and orderly colonial administration with the "chaotic control" of the Abyssinians.[10] For this and other reasons, military colonists from the north were settled in these southern regions and great landowners established themselves on the confiscated land. Hence, in the course of a few years, a dense network of katamas spread over the country upon which the administration could rely. This enabled the hegemony of the central government over the south to be firmly established. The native population was at the conquerors' disposal as a compulsory labor force.

At this point, the frontier situation has to be viewed as being more closed.[11] Further events, such as stronger centralization under Haile Selassie, the Italian occupation, and the subsequent re-establishment of the Ethiopian administration are well-known, so I shall go on to describe how these events affected the subdued population.

The events occurred as follows: At first, the Amhara plundered and ravaged large areas of Konso and Diraša; a few years later they returned to pillage, but this time they included the Burji country. They subjugated the people without any significant resistance. Only two Konso towns, which had dared to defend themselves, were completely destroyed. The conquered people soon came to feel the harsh demands of tribute. This experience led to an alliance of the not-yet-subdued tribes of the Dullay, who buried their internal animosities and so could face their all-too-powerful enemy who were armed with modern European weapons. It was only a short struggle. In a few days nearly the whole warrior age-set was wiped out. Town-like settlements, as they are still to be found in Konso, were sacked and destroyed and large parts of the country were depopulated due to famine and epidemics in the wake of war. The conquerors recruited the remaining population to compulsory labor, which is known in the south as *gabbar*. Together with the expropriation of the land, this *gabbar* system dissolved the autochthonous economic and social structure in the whole Burji-Konso cluster. For, after the conquest, all the land was confiscated and redistributed according to Amharic law and so the indigenous farmers were merely permitted to work on what had been their own land. They could almost have been turned away at any time, but this seldom happened since their labor was needed by the new landowners.[12] When the Italians invaded this region in 1936, they were welcomed as liberators by a large part of the population. The fact that the Italians did not abolish the compulsory labor for humanitarian reasons but for justification of their own imperialistic policy remained unknown to the population. The Burji even joined the Italians and engaged in the anti-guerrilla war, with heavy loss of life. In order to weaken the position of the Coptic Amhara, the Italians encouraged Islamic conversion. Due to this, combined with other influences, the Burji gave up their religion and turned to Islam.[13] In 1941 Haile Selassie took over the Italian taxation system, which was just being set up. Although the taxes were fixed by the provincial authorities, they were always too high and, for most people, this resulted in a debt which could only be redressed by a grant of land to the provincial officers. The land reform of 1974 was viewed by the farmers as the re-establishing of their traditional rights. For them, it was more an external than an internal revolutionary novelty, since great landowners had never existed in their society in any case. This positive impression gained by North Ethiopians for the land reform was, however, diminished by some young revolutionaries who, with well-meaning idealism but a lack of willingness to view local culture as important, managed to succeed in abolishing the rather democratic *gada* system and religious dignitaries.

So much for the historical framework. Let us now proceed to the economic situation.

* * *

The original intimate cultural ties of the peoples of the Burji-Konso cluster can especially be recognized in certain relationships which their traditional economy has with the social structure. Its characteristics can be reconstructed as they were in the 19th century before northern conquest. For some regions such a reconstruction is not necessary, since the cultural situation to be described continued more or less unbroken up to the present time. The economic basis of the entire cluster — and this is particularly typical for these people — consisted of a highly intensified, permanent field cultivation by means of terraces made of stone and irrigation operated through a complex system of canals, wooden pipes and reservoirs. They even take measures of soil conservation, to improve its texture, maintain and raise its degree of fertility. Fertilization is achieved with ash, dung and fecal manure and a mixed crop cultivation prevents soil exhaustion in the fields.

The fields are divided into several cultivation zones lying at different altitudes. Each of these was reserved for a certain crop, according to its needs for soil, climate and care. This again created an all-year-round working rhythm that increased productivity, for each crop in different zones had a different time of harvest. In an area with two annual rainy seasons, permitting two harvests in one year, the gathering of some ripe crops or fruit was possible nearly every month. Among the Burji, cultivation zones were laid out concentrically around the settlements, whereas in the Dullay area they consisted of different altitudinal zones on mountain sides. Here again, the crops were planted in adjustment to their needs of cultivative attention and environment. The spectrum of agricultural products ranged from *ensete* in the highlands to cotton in the lowlands. With this system of cultivation, the population could react to the fluctuating seasonal rainfall over a period of years. In years with little precipitation, agricultural activities were concentrated in the highlands and in times of heavy rains, the cultivation shifted to lower areas. With their intensified cultivation optimally adjusted to ecology and as long as their socio-economical system was still in balance, these people managed not only to secure their own subsistence, but also to supply their southern neighbouring pastoral tribes with agricultural products. The latter provided them with cattle, which (as suppliers of meat and dung) were highly esteemed by the mountain people.

The horticulture-like cultivation of fields is contextually linked with the pattern of settlement. This method of production necessitates much labor and a clear working system. All these requirements are reflected in the settlement pattern. In most cases it can be depicted as having stone walls or palisades, enclosing compact settlements of an urban character. These towns are divided into different wards, each having its own communal centres, such as threshing and meeting places. Its members perform economic, social and religious duties communally. Thus, the towns are not mere conglomerations incidentally formed by the terrain, but are made up of corporate units. Settlements of this type exist only sporadically in other parts of southern Ethiopia. Furthermore, these people are remarkable for the use of stone as a building material, which is an uncommon feature in traditional Africa. It is used for the construction of agricultural installations like terraces, reservoirs, canals, as well as paved lanes, stairways, meeting places, and town and house walls.[14]

Land tenure was handled in the following manner. Basically, it can be said that fields of zones nearby (inner zones) were for private use, whereas fields in the outer zones were communal property. Burji land tenure had already partly changed to private ownership. Among the Dullay, all land was nominally owned by a sacred chief as the religious head of the group. He had to sanction the distribution of land, by which act the recipient obtained a hereditary right of land use. Work on the fields, like clearing the undergrowth, preparing the soil and attending to the seeded land, was always done cooperatively so that, for any kind of work, regional groups of appropriate size were put together.

The fundamental social order is formed by the generation group system, by persons of a common generation passing through certain ranks at a given time. Apart from that, unilineal descendants as well as territorial groups were significant. The generation group system is very similar to the *gada* system of the Oromo and for this reason I shall use here the term *gada*.

Due to their social importance, two ranks have to be specified. Most authors refer to the one as being 'warriors', whereas the other can be described as including 'men of knowledge'. The latter, or rather their elected representatives, constituted the highest political body of the tribe. They were responsible for the warriors who, as an executive organ, had duties on the frontier, police functions and even economic responsibilities. They controlled the terraces and irrigation system. In case of need, they recruited working gangs for the maintenance and construction of new agricultural or irrigational installations. Thus, they were in charge of duties lying beyond domestic productivity, which, however, they made possible. As far as their demands for provisions were concerned, everyone had to comply. Hence, individually grown crops were distributed to a corporation which, by joint effort, created the conditions for their cultivation. A further redistribution of harvested goods took place during festivities that marked the transition of the various *gada* ranks.

Not directly integrated into this system, though linked with it, were certain lineage heads who exercised religious functions. Among the Dullay and, to a lesser degree, also among the Konso and Burji have appeared aspects of divine kingship, probably dating back to the 16th century, which connected up with beliefs concerning the lineage head. In the Dullay area, this development resulted in each of the different ethnic groups having one single lineage head succeeding as a sacred chief — moreover, it seems that having the sacred chief as a centre, a real micro-ethnogenesis has taken place. Their political influence, however, is limited by the *gada* system. Nevertheless, to a certain extent, they managed to transform their priestly function into political power.

Since I have elsewhere elaborated on the relationship of sacred chiefs to the *gada* system,[15] I would just like to point out that, with the *gada* system and a pronounced sacred chiefdom already existing in traditional society, two systems met whose intentions were diametrically opposed. For, the *gada* system embraces the whole society, whereas the sacred chiefdom is oriented towards a hierarchical social order. Even though these opposing factors at times formed a functional unit, there still remained a social conflict to be resolved.

In Burji lineage priests did not gain political power. Elected military leaders here tried to obtain permanent chiefly power. But they could only hold it in times of crisis. Yet one of them — obviously in the face of the menace from the north — managed to partially dissolve the *gada* system, before the invasion of the North Ethiopian troops. The influence of the sacred chiefs of Konso in the first decades of this century remained totally limited to the sphere of religion. They were, however, highly respected as mediators between hostile towns.[16]

Decisive changes were brought about by the conquest under Menelik. Among the Dullay almost an entire *gada* rank — the warriors — had been wiped out, throwing the system off-balance. The newly installed *gabbar* service reduced the cooperative *gada* system in the whole area to absurdity. Consequently, there followed an essential shift in the proportion of power between the *gada* system and the sacred chiefdom in favour of the latter. Nevertheless, the disintegration of the *gada* system should not be viewed as a process determined only by external factors and therefore appearing to us as an abrupt event. In fact, there existed among some tribes of the Dullay attempts to continue with the *gada* system. Some offices still existed until recent times which formerly were connected with the *gada* system. In many cases they became hereditary. By the way, this development led to an increased emphasis on lineage relationships among the Dullay. In Konso the *gada* system could continue to exist in spite of all these problems. On the one hand, economical preconditions were responsible for this — I shall give more detail about this later — on the other hand, it appears that some persons managed to evade the *gabbar* service, either by being covered by fellow tribesmen in the compactly built urban settlements where strangers can hardly find their way, or by escaping temporarily to the lowlands.[17]

In the sphere of agriculture there occurred an upheaval with grave consequences. Here, too, the area of the Dullay was the worst affected. After the eclipse of the warrior rank, there was no corporation left to take care of the terraces, lanes and irrigation system. The latter especially soon deteriorated. A necessary precondition for a secured permanent cultivation was thus destroyed. Services for the conquerors, which had to be performed by each individual at irregular intervals of time, prevented the formation of new working gangs.

In addition to these factors, which had already resulted in the decline of communal activities, the introduction of money economy and the imposition of a head tax, enforcing the cultivation of cash crops, had further destructive consequences. Crop surplus had been traded since early times, but only in order to get additional goods. The new cash crop to be planted was *teff*, a cereal most popular with North Ethiopians. The cultivation of *teff* not only led to an adaption to a new kind of grain, it also required a totally different method of production, which is contrary to the traditional hoe cultivation. The yield of *teff* per square unit is far lower than that of the original crop grown on terraced fields. It therefore became necessary to shift from intensive hoe cultivation — which enabled a large number of farmers to gain high yields on small fields by collaborating corporatively — to extensive plough cultivation, with few people working mostly individually on large fields in order to get the amount of yield needed to make ends meet. The subsequent transition to plough cultivation did not only mean the use of different working implements, but rather a complete change in the system of production! In the meantime, this change caused further negligence and hence a further deterioration of the terraces, a situation worsened by erosion during the rainy seasons, which in turn reduced available farm land. To make things even worse, the farmers no longer took much care of soil improvement, for their ambiguous legal situation as to their land rights made them uncertain whether they could harvest what they planted. The outcome of this, in the the period between 1900 and the land reform, was irreparable damage caused to their agriculture.

While the entire socio-economic complex degenerated, oriented as it was towards cooperation and connected with the *gada* system, the sacred chiefs among various peoples of the Burji-Konso cluster — especially the Dullay — succeeded in consolidating their political authority. A number of them gained a substantial increase in power by being appointed *balabats* by the administration. Markakis and other authors have already extensively analyzed the role of the *balabats* in southern Ethiopia.[18] It only remains to be said that the inherited and thus stable office of the sacred chiefs was integrated into the hierarchical order of the Ethiopian Empire with less complications than would have been the case with the temporarily elected *gada* leaders.

Considering the above-mentioned factors, it becomes clear that the decline of the *gada* system is not a result of a general cultural disintegration, but that those historically conditioned factors which were set off by the contradictions of the traditional society itself sparked off a vicious circle that brought it to an inevitable end. In Konso this process was less pronounced. How is this to be explained? Firstly, it has to be pointed out that the Konso warriors — as well as the Burji — did not suffer such a heavy loss as was the case among the Dullay. A further important factor was that at least some part of the land was of no great interest to the northerners. The steep terraced slopes of Konso were not suited for the cultivation of *teff*, and neither could the plough be used there. This and the relatively low altitude of many farms kept away the petty *naftaññas* and the great landowners as well, for the *naftaññas* feared the hot and already partially malaria-infested zones and the great landowners, who normally lived in the cities of the north, could not expect a worthwhile yield of cash crops from the small terraced fields. The situation differed on the plateau farms, where the common colonizing practices were used. Hence in 1974 nearly all the land suited for plough cultivation was in the possession of former government officials. On land left to the Konso they kept their traditional method of production, for in their experience it was the optimal way of farming. And along with this, the basic conditions of the *gada* system also continued to exist, that is to say, they were able to preserve their mode of production in a trunk area, with just a few alterations. Furthermore, a solution was also found to the demands of tribute and, later on, taxation without overstraining the traditional way of production: cultivation of cotton and weaving, already in existence since pre-Amharic times, were intensified. Like other peoples, the Konso had to submit to the *gabbar* service, but they built a wall of silence against the conquerors. Cultural adaptations to the northerners hardly occurred. There was an absolute separation between the indigenous population and the new arrivals. This situation prevailed, more or less, with all the other peoples of the Burji-Konso cluster. A more intensive change could only be seen in the Dullay area, but not before the Italian occupation. Since that time a far-reaching assimilation of the former conquerors has been taking place there.

How strictly observed is the line of separation between the *katama* population and the autochthonous people, I could personally witness as late as 1974, when I met a 10th grade student, born, grown up and living in the *katama* of Gidole (which is the administrative centre of an *awraja*) but whose ancestors came from the north, who had not once in his life been in the autochthonous area beginning just outside the *katama*. It was not that he abhorred travelling, he had already been in civilized Addis Ababa — and he was by no means the only case.

Let us return to Konso: there lineage priests, both in the past and up to very recent times, had only a few possibilities to gain political influence. Not only did the *gada* system keep them at bay, but it also engaged them in its service by assigning them to ceremonial duties during *gada* ceremonies. But there were more essential reasons to prevent the separate development of political power: the structure of this society is characterized by counteracting any tendency within any individual group to gain dominance. The kinship system, territorial groups ('city wards'), the *gada* system and, with it, all offices of political and religious affairs were linked to each other to such a degree that they kept themselves in due balance. This means that a person can belong to all these systems at the same time. Moreover, he can even hold office in different systems, though he is controlled by different groups with each member representing distinct interests. The same kind of structure is reflected in the relationships between the urban settlements. Konso society as a whole is not focused towards a centre, but is formed by various alliances and animosities between different autonomous towns. Hallpike has shown that, for example, the town A is an ally of town C, but is on bad terms with town B, whereas C and B enjoy friendly relations.[19] Though there is a certain fragmentation of these oppositions, preventing the dominance of one or the other town, they nevertheless constitute a community at the same time, since not one of them can exist in isolation.

Originally, there was also in Burji a stabilization through linked social institutions, which were probably less marked, however, at the time of conquest. A disengagement occurred during the above-mentioned changes in agriculture, additionally intensified by private farming and individual trade activities. For reasons of their geographical location, the Burji had already been involved with long-distance trade. More than the Konso and Dullay, the Burji formed a buttress of peasantry against the areas of their cattle-herding neighbours in the south, east and southwest. In order to avoid the *gabbar* service many Burji made use of their trade connections (which reached, among other places, far into the area of the Borana) by moving from one trade partner to the other. Though this was actually a flight, they made the best of the situation and expanded their trade connections even further, especially when more and more Burji followed this example, leading to the founding of outposts.[20]

Today, the majority of the Burji live in Kenya. Marsabit became their new centre, from which they play a major part in North Kenyan trade. Nevertheless, their traditional country is still their cultural and spiritual centre. Therefore, certain dignitaries are not supposed to leave the Burji homeland. The increase in trading activities since the turn of the century resulted in the accumulation of wealth by individuals. This wealth could not be invested in agriculture as, due to the limited size of their territory, further agricultural expansion was not possible. The relationship between individual and private property began to encroach upon the relationship between the individual and the community. The most advanced examples of this destabilization of cooperative communities were those traders who were very often away for months at a time. With the changing economic conditions the *gada* system also lost its importance. There was a brief period of revival during the time of the Italian occupation, but without the necessary economic base, and for reasons of increased individualism, as well as the loss of its ritual function after the conversion to Islam, the *gada* system was divested of its most important support and ceased to exist.

So far I have not shown a very bright picture of the societies discussed. We must keep in mind that the traditional culture was not only transformed under the pressure of political and economic necessities, but disappeared to a large extent. Yet these ethnic groups did not sink to a level of declassed and cultureless people, nor did they helplessly adapt to another culture. Against all adversities, they continued with their own creativity. The traditional culture was strong enough to react in a versatile way to new conditions. They were able to be selective about choosing new cultural elements by activating the latent components of their own cultures. And in spite of their political defeat, they were aware of their superior knowledge of the existing conditions of life as compared with that of the newcomers. They knew all about ecology, about working methods and the relationship they had with the cosmos, and from this self-confidence developed a more or less conscious attitude of opposition. Their self-confidence, however, was continually subjected to strain, owing to the incompatibilities between their culture and that of the conquerors — incompatibilities which had indeed the characteristics of class antagonism. But this tension, as experienced every day, was at the same time an essential condition for any new perspective to be derived from the learning processes out of which a new culture was to be shaped; they needed to weigh intellectually the contradictions between the old and the new culture.[21]

Acculturation seems to have gained most ground among the Dullay. They did not attempt to open new terrain by migration as did the Burji, but neither could they maintain their old structures. Yet, in fact, it is the Dullay who have been assimilating the northerners over the past forty years. In Konso I did not encounter any so-called Amhara capable of speaking the Konso language, whereas most northerners living in the Dullay area cannot be distinguished from the indigenous population of today, neither by language, nor by their way of life. The Dullay yielded to their oppressors with cunning and wit, thus always finding a loophole to maintain their position and identity. This kind of behaviour is mirrored in numerous fables which have a dispute between the small but sly and the powerful but clumsy animals as their theme.[22]

The Konso resisted any external influences more vigorously. They succeeded in doing so by closing their ranks. This seems to be due to the fact that, at the time of their subjugation by the northerners, the interweaving of socio-political institutions had already been well developed. In the heartland and in the marginal areas, where external influences were clearly more intensive, different ways of life could be observed. Being aware of this and drawn into a permanent struggle with the politically dominant culture, the Konso sharpened a collective confidence in their own values. Nonetheless, changes did occur and the balance of their values was shaken.[23]

The Burji reacted to the political events by migration, attempting thus to retain their individual, as well as their collective, identity. But under these conditions of exile came the beginning of an extreme transformation of their traditional culture. To view the situation from a different angle: due to their external sources of economic prosperity, a reconstruction of their society took place that now adequately meets the requirements of a modern African state. But they equally share the fate of so many other Africans: a feeling of not belonging, always in search of a lost identity.

These transformations of former cultures did not happen by accident; on the contrary, they prove the flexible ability of adaptation to a changing set of socio-economic conditions by the use of the manifold potentials inherent in traditional cultures. Furthermore, such transformations show the internal dynamics of traditional cultures; indeed, the various ethnic groups reacted differently, but in any case they reacted culture-adequately, responding to the kind of external pressures their respective culture had to endure, and by actualizing those cultural elements more to the fore at a time, they furnished the traditional structures with new contents. Hence there was no accidental animation. In the pool of existing cultural elements there is a large choice of which elements should be taken out, actualized and transformed. This choice very much depends upon the historical situation (for example, the emphasis on trade among the Burji at a given point in time). All three of the discussed societies followed a general logical path, but they show three distinct solutions to the ultimately similar problem.

However, these new cultures can in no way be described as harmonious and integrated; you may even wonder how they can function at all. But is it not the privilege of the elite to have a harmonic *Weltanschauung*? Is it not a necessity for the hegemonial culture to be harmonic, whereas the strength of the culture of the oppressed lies in its very openness?

History from below, joined with an anthropology from within, can show the complexity of the processes without stating them to be arbitrary. A history of events would merely establish a sequence of epochs, like frontier situation, *gabbar* system, Italian occupation, etc., and only notice in the social realm that a more or less intense acculturation to the higher (that is 'literate') culture had taken place. Such a point of view would make the Konso, cited here as the most stable people, seem the most backward. But that might well fit better to our own treasured way of looking at history.

NOTES

1. In the 18th century, Johann Gottfried HERDER already advocated an individualising historical approach to cultural philosophy, an approach which was also at the heart of his

anthropological thinking, in that he considered the monographic description of peoples in the course of their history as a precondition for the kind of universal history to which he aspired (see even his early *Journal meiner Reise im Jahr 1769*, in Herder's *Werke*. Hrsg.v. Heinrich Düntzer. 24 Theil, Berlin 1869-1879). For any people showing a specific character — what he was going to term *Nationalcharakter* — has the distinction of a specific culture: culture, however, according to HERDER is essentially a process, both in the development of the individual and of the whole people. From this imminent dynamic the denomination *Volk* (people) gains a new concrete significance; ethnic life, ethnic identity are being discovered as a historical force, the antitype of which HERDER comes to see in the state. Cultural productions and creations are, as defined by HERDER, concretes of a specific *Volksgeist* (ethnic spirit) in which the very essence or, in a modern term, the ethnicity of a people manifests itself (cf. *Ideen zur Philosophie der Geschichte der Menscheit. 1784-1791*, Darmstadt 1966).

It is true, the after-effect of HERDER's ideas is less to be found in a historical universalism or relativism, than with the seizing and mythication of his concept of ethnic spirit by the Romantic movement — *Volk* as an ideological vehicle — and with the contractions of nationalist thought which perverted HERDER's idea of nation ("one people") by means of political coercion. Also contrary in the end to HERDER's relativising approach, was the unlimited progressivism of the evolutionists, who transformed their universalistic claim into a kind of overall formula for the development of mankind, equally neglecting the value of single cultures and grown ethnicities. Not until recently, and initiated by historians, did the force and significance of ethnic popular culture also become the subject of reflection for ethnologists and folklorists of some European countries. Compare the inspiring article by N. SCHINDLER, "Spuren in die Geschichte der 'anderen' Zivilisation. Probleme und Perspektiven einer historischen Volkstumsforschung" in: R. VAN DÜLMEN & N. SCHINDLER (Hrsg.), *Volkskultur* (Frankfurt 1984).

In this respect, the work of social historian Edward P. THOMPSON has to be seen as substantial: in his eyes, customs and traditions are not mere survivals of the past, but gain their significance through their intrinsic cultural values. At least since his book *The Making of the English Working Class* (1963) he clearly espouses a history 'from below' and not 'of below'. To this effect, he is critically arguing the necessity of a connection between anthropology/ethnology and history, by showing its limitations (E. P. THOMPSON, "Folklore, Anthropology and Social History", *The Indian Historical Review* [1977] 3, pp.247-266). His cognitive approach, which makes the demand for the opening up of past layers of consciousness, is akin to that of the anthropologist Clifford GEERTZ, who discusses the possibilities and pitfalls of an actor-oriented view. For GEERTZ, "the aim (of ethnology) is to draw large conclusions from small, but very densely textured facts; to support broad assertions about the role of culture in the construction of collective life by engaging them exactly with complex specifics" (C. GEERTZ, "Thick Descriptions: Toward an Interpretive Theory of Culture" in: C. GEERTZ (ed.), *The Interpretation of Cultures* [New York 1973], p.28). I also want to refer to representatives of the French 'Nouvelle Histoire', among others, J. LE GOFF and E. LE ROY LADURIE.

2. As to the following comments on southern Ethiopia, let me here refer to — and this not only because of the geographical neighbourhood — BLACKHURST's research on the problem of ethnicity as exemplified by the antagonism of subdued Oromo (esp. Tulama and Arsi)/dominant Amhara. H. BLACKHURST, "Ethnicity in Southern Ethiopia: The General and the Particular", *Africa* (1980) 50, pp.55-65.

3. The Konso have been known since the turn-of-the-century travellers' accounts. The most detailed monograph was written by C. R. HALLPIKE, *The Konso of Ethiopia (Oxford 1972)*.

4. Fieldwork was carried out in 1973-74 (together with Gunter MINKER) and again in 1980-81. Cf. H. AMBORN, "Wandlungen im sozio-ökonomischen Gefüge der Bevölkerungsgruppen im Gardulla-Dobase-Horst in Südäthiopien", *Paideuma* (1976) 22, pp.151-161, and H. AMBORN, G. MINKER & H. J. SASSE, *Das Dullay* (Berlin 1980).

5. H. STRAUBE, *Die Burdji* (Ms compiled after his fieldwork in 1956).
H. STRAUBE, Feldjournal: Burji (unpublished field journal, 1973-74).
H. J. SASSE & H. STRAUBE, "Kultur und Sprache der Burji in Südäthiopien. Ein Abriß" in W. MÖHLIG *et al.* (eds.), *Zur Sprachgeschichte und Ethnohistorie in Afrika* (Berlin 1977), pp.239-266.
In Autumn 1981 I also stayed for a short period with the Burji in Marsabit, Kenya.

6. While for Enrico CERULLI, a linguistic typology besides a cultural one was primarily important, Ernesta CERULLI uses the denomination Burji-Konso Group for purposes of ethnographic classification. Enrico CERULLI, *Ethiopia Occidentale* (Roma 1933), p.181; Ernesta CERULLI, "Peoples of South-West Ethiopia and Its Borderland", *Ethnographic Survey of Africa*, North Eastern Africa, Part III (London 1956), pp.51.

7. A survey of early travellers is to be found in J. BUREAU, "Les voyageurs européens dans le Sud-Ouest Ethiopien (1890-1910)", *Revue française d'histoire d'outre-mer* (LXII, 1975), pp.594-618. Guèbrè Selassié, *Chronique du régime de Ménélik II. Roi des Rois d'Ethiopie*, Vol.II (Paris 1931); A. W. HODSON, *Seven Years in Southern Abyssinia* (London 1927); J. BARBER, *Imperial Frontier. A Study of Relations Between the British and the Pastoral Tribes of N. E. Uganda* (Nairobi 1968).

8. H. LAMAR and L. THOMPSON, *The Frontier in History* (New Haven and London 1981), p.7.

9. The years of 1897-98 saw particular efforts by the British, French and Abyssinians to assert their claims in the area of Lake Turkana. Special mention should be made of the Englishmen CAVENDISH and AUSTIN, the Frenchman MARCHAND and, among the Ethiopians, HAPTE GEORGIS and WOLDE GEORGIS. Accompanied by the Frenchman DARRAGON, HAPTE GEORGIS passed through Konso and the Dullay region in 1897.
G. MONTANDON, *Au pays Ghimirra* (Neuchâtel)1913), p. 267.
M. L. DARRAGON, "Le Sidama, l'Amara, le Konso, etc". *Comptes Rendus de Séances de la Société de Géographie . . .* (1898), pp.137-140.

10. H. S. H. CAVENDISH, "Through Somaliland and Around and South of Lake Rudolf", *Geographical Journal* (1898) 11, 4, p.373.
HODSON, *op. cit.*, esp. ch.10, 11, 16.
For a factual description and analysis of the conditions in colonial frontier situations see J. H. BODLEY who has compiled staggering cases in point. J. H. BODLEY, *Victims of Progress* (Menlo Park *et al.* 1975), pp.23-42.

11. I am inclined to speak of a *latent* frontier situation even for the two decades after World War I because, as will be shown below, the traditional culture including its political institutions still figured prominently, at least regionally.

12. Generally for South Ethiopia, cf. J. MARKAKIS, *Ethiopia: Anatomy of a Traditional Policy* (Oxford 1974), p. 108.

13. Archivio Storico del Ministero Africa Italiana: Posizone 181. Italian support of Islamization suited the Burji trend of rejecting assimilation into the dominant culture. KNUTSON, on making similar observations with the Arsi, defined this Islamization process as a

"boundary-maintaining mechanism", since they could not achieve their ethnic identity in the traditional way.

K. E. KNUTSON, "Dichotomization and Integration: Aspects of Inter-ethnic Relations in Southern Ethiopia" in F. BARTH (ed.), *Ethnic Groups and Boundaries* (Bergen 1969) p.93.

14. AMBORN *et al., op. cit.*, ch.1.3; C. R. HALLPIKE, "Konso Agriculture", *Journal of Ethiopian Studies* (1970) 8, pp.31-43; W. KULS, *Beiträge zur Kulturgeographie der süd-äthiopischen Seenregion* (Frankfurt 1958), pp.8-9; SASSE & STRAUBE, *op. cit.*, p.240; H. STRAUBE worked out the concept of the so-called *agrarischer Intensivierungs-komplex* (complex of intensified agriculture) in South Ethiopia, which he associated both functionally and historically with other East African examples. H. STRAUBE, "Der agrar-ische Intensivierungskomplex in Nordost-Afrika", *Paideuma* (1967) 8, pp.198-222.

In his recent article, John SUTTON commented on the frequently uncritical and infla-tionary use of the term 'intensive' in connection with specific modes of African agricul-ture (J. E. SUTTON, "Irrigation and Soil-Conservation in African Agricultural History . . . . .", *Journal of African History* [1984] 25, pp.25-41). Moreover, he could plausibly show that some of the exemplary sites hitherto known as typical of intensification are only local specializations of a more extensive agricultural practice. Konso terrace-use also gives the impression of a relatively extensive agricultural practice (Konso is not among SUT-TON's negative examples), since, for instance, not all of the Konso terraces are worked on permanently nowadays. But this cannot be seen (as it may be in Inyanga) as an extensive use over time. Firstly, Konso has not yet reached the former density of population it had prior to the Amharic annexation (as can be concluded from aerial photographs showing old settlement sites and from oral information I received) and secondly, the terraces have always been used in accordance with climatic conditions. In years of scarce rainfall rela-tively few cultivated terraces will be found, and these are near the towns and on valley-bottom plots. After a normal rainy season, however, nearly all the available terraces can be seen being tilled. With regard to Konso (and ultimately the whole Burji-Konso cluster) I consider the term 'intensive' to be adequate. The intensification here is based on a long-drawn historical process that affected the formation of a complex socio-political and socio-economic system whose important political institutions can be proved by genealo-gies to date back to the 16th century at least. According to oral tradition, the applied agricultural methods would be even older than the 16th century, but archaeological evi-dence for this has still to be obtained.

15. AMBORN (1976), *op. cit.*

16. HALLPIKE (1972), *op. cit.*, p.43; A. JENSEN, *Im Lande des Gada* (Stuttgart 1936), p.387.

17. The lowlands, shunned by the North Ethiopians until the fifties, were favoured as a refugee area. This applies less to the Burji who frequently feuded with the Guji down there.

18. MARKAKIS, *op. cit.*, p.155; U. BRAUKÄMPER, *Geschichte der Hadiya* (Wiesbaden 1980), p.316.

19. HALLPIKE (1972), *op. cit.*, p.52. What is supporting social complexity and allowing a flexible reaction to new events is the loose organization of a number of social institutions. Herbert S. LEWIS has pointed out the "capacity of voluntary associations", "the use and re-use in different combinations, of certain general principles, for organizing interaction". H. S. LEWIS, "Neighbors, Friends, and Kinsmen: Principles of Social Organization

Among the Cushitic-Speaking Peoples of Ethiopia" in *Proceedings of the First United States Conference on Ethiopian Studies 1973* (H. G. MARCUS, ed.), Chicago 1975, pp.193-207 (quotation p.204).

20. The problem of the Burji migration, it is true, has more levels to be reckoned with. One has to take into account that Burji lost its importance as a trading centre at least temporarily after the turn of the century (today the market of Burji is of scarcely more than local significance). The much evoked, so-called *Pax Amharica* certainly did nothing to encourage intertribal contact. On the contrary, the economic decline (as a consequence of conquest) was followed by an overall insecurity in the frontier area, resulting in the reduction of the old long-distance trade (via Lugh) with the Somali, at least for a time. This problem will be treated in detail in a forthcoming book of mine on the subject of artisans and merchants. One more problem waiting for a closer analysis: to what extent did merchants, who with lesser trading profits had to look for another economic activity, contribute to the scarcity of land which, in turn, would have favoured emigration?

21. Psychological effects of the military and political impotence deriving from colonisation must not be underestimated.
As with most ethnic groups of southern Ethiopia, there is a specific esteem of masculinity among the Burji-Konso peoples, linked to a distinct warrior ethic, which is marked by the so-called *Töterwesen* (the ritual slaying of enemies and big animals). The frustration over the fact that the Amhara proved to be superior warriors has not been digested until now. The high esteem of the hero in traditional culture led to a sometimes evident respect for the Amhara, even though Amharic culture as a whole was being rejected.

22. H. AMBORN, "Toritte alladi – Überlieferungen aus dem Dullay", *Trickster* (1982) 9/10, pp.30-36.

23. The psychological tensions the Konso have to endure come to the fore during drinking bouts, when aggressions are set free which often have a fatal outcome. Also cf. note 21.

ETHIOPIAN TRADITIONAL HERBAL DRUGS:

POTENTIALITY AND APPROPRIATE UTILIZATION

Belachew Desta

It is an often quoted and documented fact that Ethiopia lies in one of the six regions of the world in which up to 60% of the flora are indigenous to the locality. The lofty cloud-shrouded cool mountains, the temperate plateaus, the warm well-watered valleys and river gorges, along with the semi-arid and desert landscapes of the country, which are commonly described by the general name of *Degga, Woine-Degga, Kolla* and *Bereha* regions respectively, present a wide variety of plants whose potential medicinal value could be in a range and on a scale that is matched by only few countries in the World. The above statement may derive a fair degree of credibility from the fact that a wide variety of apparently effective traditional drugs is commonly used by about 80% of the Ethiopian population.

In Ethiopian rural society, the traditional health care delivery system may be depicted by the following scenario:

Somebody gets ill, and is lying in bed, at home. His family try the usual traditional household remedies that they think would be of help. Neighbours and friends come and visit the sick fellow, offer suggestions and their good wishes. Visitors give their diagnosis and tell the family that for such a disease (according to their diagnosis, that is) there is a *Medhanit Awaki*, meaning herbalist, medicine-man, witch-doctor, sorcerer, etc., that would offer the appropriate drug or therapy. And if consensus is reached about the disease, the *Medhanit Awaki* is entreated to dispense or administer the remedy. And hopefully the patient may get better and be able to be up and about. Or, as in some reported cases, the patient may have the benefits of modern medicine after having undergone and endured injurious and heroic treatment in the hands of traditional practitioners with the best of intentions.

In other words, in rural Ethiopia the line of defence against disease is put-up self-medication, traditional wisdom of family, neighbours and friends and, finally, by traditional practitioners, if the affliction persists. When the situation reaches a state of grave concern, attempts will be made, if materially possible, to seek the assistance of modern medicine, irrespective of whether or not it is too late.

Because of a lack of a better alternative or the inherent compulsion of traditional practices, or perhaps by and large due to its effectiveness, one must concede the basic premise that a "Traditional pharmacopoeia" plays a fundamental role in the health care of the Ethiopian people.

In consideration of the economic constraints of developing countries, The World Health Organization (WHO) and UNICEF have formulated a new strategy known as "Primary Health Care" at the Alma Ata Conference. This strategy is expected to address itself to a radically new framework based on prevention, the decontamination of the environment, the training of community health agents, the supply of drinking water, vaccines, essential drugs, etc. It is also expected by WHO that appropriately selected traditional herbal drugs will complement the provisions for essential drugs.

The development of useful and widely used drugs like Digoxin and Digitoxin, from *Digitalis* leaves; quinine from the cinchona bark; reserpine from *Rauwolfia Serpentina*; morphine from *Papaver Somniferum*; cocaine from *Erythroxzion coca* and the anti-cancer Vincristiner and Vinblastine from *Catharanthus Troseus* of Madagascar and again the anti-cancer compound, bruceantin, from the Ethiopian plant, *Brucea Antidysentrica*, just to name a few, are examples of the contributions of traditional pharmacopoeia. The Ethiopian flora has not yet been fully charted and investigations as to its medicinal value are scarcely even in their infancy. Given the wide diversity of the country's climatic conditions, it would not be presumptious to expect that the Ethiopian flora would be a source of drug products of considerable significance.

At the end of 1983, a meeting was organized in Budapest by the United Nations Industrial Development Organization (UNIDO), between the pharmaceutical industry and representatives of the Third World Countries. At this meeting, it was pointed out that even though in 1980 less than 30 percent of the Third World's inhabitants had access to modern drugs, at the cost of heavy indebtedness they spent a total of 5,500 million U.S. dollars. According to the UNIDO Executive Director, this amount is expected to reach 9,000 million by 1985. The magnitude of this burden and its direct effect on the national economies of Third World Countries cannot be over-emphasized.

In an attempt to alleviate this problem, the UNIDO meeting has suggested, among other steps, the development in the Third World of plant-derived drugs by equipping developing countries with factories for processing their own medicinal plants.

The feasibility of such a venture can be indicated by the variety and volume of vegetable raw material, mostly, imported from the Third World by the Developed Countries for purposes of drug production. In 1980 alone the European Economic Community and the United States respectively imported over 80,000 and 34,000 metric tons of plants for pharmaceutical production at a cost of 180 and 76 million U.S. dollars. This partial market involving 400 different medicinal plants totaled 258 million and was mostly supplied by China and India. The finished drug products formulated from such plants are sold by industry, even in the Third World Countries from which they originally came, at prices that are at least ten times that of the raw material.

Potentiality, by definition, is that which is not actually existing but which is expectable, latent. Therefore, for traditional herbal drugs (meaning all drugs of plant origin) to be of actual therapeutic and economic significance, one has to create a framework of appropriate utilization. Attempts towards an appropriate utilization of traditional herbal drugs should include the following:

1. An inventory of local plants which are claimed to have medicinal value. Particulars of the flora, as to common names, scientific name, habitat, part of plant used, etc., would have to be recorded.

2. Comprehensive documentation of traditional literature pertaining to medicinal plants, herbal drugs, disease entity, drug formulation and dosage regimens. This should include the whole range of exorcisms, rituals, exaltation techniques, amulets, religious practices, cults, etc., so that factors that may contribute to the psycho-social condition of the patient will not be left out.

3. Compilation of equivalent medical terminology for the nebulous vernacular descriptions of disease entities like *Megagna, Kuruba, Nekeresa, Miche, Buda, Wougat*, etc. This would be necessary for experimental and clinical validation of traditional therapeutic claims.

4. Development of selected herbal drugs on the basis of the priority needs of the country with the help of pharmaceutical technology. Such attempts at development will incorporate the following:

   a) Phytochemical screening — in order to separate, identify and characterize chemical ingredients that are responsible for the therapeutic effect.

   b) Pharmacological and toxicological studies for purposes of assessing therapeutic effect and possible toxicities.

   c) Formulation and standardization of crude extracts of herbal drugs for application in primary health care, subject to controlled clinical trial.

d) Development of appropriate dosage forms from pure crystalline compounds.

e) Preparation of formulations for pilot plant and scaled-up industrial production of crude extracts and purified compounds.

f) Establishment of drug gardens for purposes of botanical studies (cultivation requirements), chemical investigation (variation in drug content) and teaching (for students and the general public).

5. Identification and cultivation of medicinal plants that can be exported in crude form and/ or after processing.

6. Creation of an institutional and systematic approach that would facilitate the application of pharmaceutical technology towards an appropriate utilization of traditional herbal drugs. Such transfers of technology can best be mediated by the School of Pharmacy, where the establishment of a Drug Research Centre is, at present, in the process of being finalized.

Therefore in the light of what has previously been said, attempts for appropriate utilization of traditional herbal drugs can transform their potentiality into an actuality in terms of their resources that are therapeutic and economical.

THE ISLAMICIZATION OF THE ARSSI-OROMO

Ulrich Braukämper

Compared with Orthodox Christianity, Islam has been a neglected theme in Ethiopia. General studies which have been published, for example by E. Cerulli, J. S. Trimingham and J. Cuoq[1], explicitly call for further investigation in this field. The general response to this appeal has remained weak, although some valuable research has been conducted on the process and the socio-cultural effects of Islamicization in certain areas, such as the peripheries of southwestern Ethiopia.[2]

In the modern state of Ethiopia since the time of Menilek II onwards, Muslims have always occupied subordinate positions, a fact which obviously made them less attractive for research than the dominating Christian sector of the country. The dynamic expansion of Islam and its growing importance in world politics are now helping to focus more attention on the past and contemporary situation of Muslims in the Horn of Africa. Cases where the socio-religious transition from an indigenous folk religion to Islam can be traced back from the present to the end of the Middle Ages are not frequent in African history. The Arssi-Oromo of southeastern Ethiopia represent one such case. In this context only a limited number of factors and variables relevant to a theory of religious change in that area can be analysed.

The Arssi in the provinces of southern Shawa, Arssi and northern Bale occupy the largest territory among all Oromo subgroups and amount to about 2.5 million people.[3] Our state of knowledge about their history and culture is still fragmentary, although researchers such as E. Cerulli, E. Haberland and P. Baxter have provided a considerable amount of data.[4]

Notes on the genesis and ethnic differentiation of the Arssi

In written documents the name of a group called the Arssi — until recently the Amharic version Arussi was common in the literature — appears relatively late; it does in fact not seem to predate the 19th century. It remains unknown when Arssi, the name of an ancestor who is listed in the genealogies about 16 generations ago[5], was adopted as an ethnonym for an important fraction of the Oromo people. This general acceptance was obviously retarded by the fact that Arssi is to be found only in the genealogies of the "pure" Oromo, who do not constitute more than one third of the Arssi, whereas two thirds can be identified as assimilated elements from the Hadiya-Sidama cluster.[6] The division of the group into original Oromo called *borana* and assimilated people of alien origin, commonly labelled *mogāsa* ("adopted") or *garba* ("conquered"), is characteristic for most Oromo sections[7] and was of cultural and socio-political significance up to the middle of this century.

Before the great Oromo expansion at the beginning of the 16th century, the present-day dwelling-areas of the Arssi were occupied by the states of Bale, Hadiya, Ganz, Sharkha (Shirka) and Waj, whose inhabitants were predominantly Muslims of Hadiya-Sidama stock. By this time, according to the *History of the Galla* by the Christian priest Bahrey, the Oromo consisted of two major territorial factions — the Borana in the west and the Barentu in the east.[8] According to genealogical data which I collected in 1973, the ancestors of the Arssi, together with the Barentu proper of the Harar Plateau, the Ittu, and the Karayu of the middle Awash Valley, were part of the Barentu cluster. It can be assumed that the Borana, the forebears of the Macha- and Tulama-Oromo, passed the highlands east of the Lake Region in a quick advance to gain central Ethiopia. The *dāwē* or *jāwi* group which Emperor Sarsa Dengel fought in the 1570s — most probably in the region between Lake Zway and the mountain chain of Warra Lukko — were labelled "those who stay behind"[9], which implies that they represented a secondary wave of migration. The formation of the Arssi as a separate ethnic entity presumably started at this time. However, it seems anachronistic when Atmē Giyorgis, the late 19th century Amhara historian, explicitly linked events of the 16th and early 17th centuries with the Arssi. His text, which is obviously a compilation of written records and oral data, refers to them as follows:

"Aṣē Malak Sagad [Sarṣa Dengel] had found the Arusi which was called the Warantesa in the direction of Quara, and exterminated them, leaving none to tell the tale. There were, however, some that remained behind with luggage, and Aṣē Susenyos settled them later in Ačafar and Dambeya. That is, he made them *čawa*. The official appointed over Ačafar was called Arusi *Fitāwrāri*. The rest came and settled in the Adal land after the death of Aṣē Galāwdēwos."[10]

The occupation by the Arssi of their present dwelling-areas was a protracted process; and their expansion in the west was still continuing in the 1920s, whereas in the east, in the area of the Wabi Shebeli, they were continuously pushed back by the neighbouring Somali. During this whole period, from the 16th century to the 20th, the autochthonous Hadiya population was left with the alternative either to surrender to the Oromo and adopt the ethnic and cultural identity of their conquerors or to move to areas west of the Rift Valley.[11] This process of ethnic amalgamation proved to be of particular importance with respect to the religious situation of the Arssi. From the very beginning of their ethnogenesis, a dualism existed among the population: the majority were descendants of the autochthonous Muslims and the leading minority were representatives of a Cushitic folk religion inseparably connected with the *gada* order, an age-grade system, as their central socio-religious institution. Oral reports state that the "pagans" were called *awāma*, a term still common among the Guji- and Borana-Oromo, whereas those who preserved the Islamic tradition were labelled either *islāma* or *sagidda*. This latter term which is most probably derivated from the Arabic verb *sajada* (to bow down; to worship), refers to the ritual prayer of the Muslims.[12]

The Islamicization of the Arssi: a chronological outline

A competition between two antagonistic cultural tendencies was characteristic of Arssi society from its very genesis. The "pagan" Cushitic stratum is not of particular concern in this context, whereas the "Muslim sediment" will be carefully analysed in the next chapter. Before considering this phenomenon I wish to present a descriptive chronological account on how Islam expanded and became the dominant religion of the Arssi.

The period from the 17th century to the 19th is a dark age in the history of southeastern Ethiopia: literary and oral data are almost non-existent. However, gravestones with Arabic inscriptions indicate Islamic infiltration in the present-day northern Bale Province as early as the 13th century.[13] Since Arssiland was isolated by the Oromo expansion from the Muslim centres in the east and the north, a general decline of institutional Islam occurred. Yet, although the orthodox cadre of religion became weak, it never collapsed totally. Pockets where Muslim rules were observed more or less strictly persisted in the eastern part of Arssiland. The most important was Annajina in northern Bale, where the cult of Nūr Ḥusayn, a *shaykh* from Merca on the Somali coast whose lifetime can be dated to around 1200, had been established.[14] When the Oromo had penetrated Annajina (likewise called Dire Shaykh Ḥusayn) in the 16th century, they assimilated the cult and preserved the sanctuary.[15] A decisive event with respect to the cult of Nūr Ḥusayn, as far as can be reconstructed from the sources, took place at the end of the 18th century. 'Abd al-Shakūr, the *amīr* of Harar from 1783 to 1794, initiated the construction of a shrine in Annajina, which was dedicated to 'Abd al-Qādir al-Djīlānī, the founder of the Qādirīya order.[16] The establishment of this sanctuary was obviously intended to strengthen the Islamic mission among the "pagan" Arssi-Oromo. That is why 'Abd al-Shakūr also sent trained religious personnel to Bale, notably a Somali *shaykh* called *aw* Muḥammad, who originated from the region of Berbera and lived in Harar.[17] Oral traditions report that the whole of the present sanctuary in Annajina was constructed at about the middle of the last century.[18]

From this time onwards the impact of Islam on southeastern Ethiopia intensified. This is indicated by the number of shrines which were restored or where the cult of their saints was newly established. In Bale apart from Nūr Ḥusayn, Sof 'Umar is worshipped most. He is said to have been a *ṣūfī* (Arssi: *sof*), a member of a mystic brotherhood. According to the oral traditions, he originated from Tigray and died in Hamarra in the Gololcha district of Bale. People believe that he was Nūr Ḥusayn's favoured disciple, but it appears doubtful whether he was even his contemporary. In the genealogies of the Shakmarra clan of the Arssi, who claim descent from Sof 'Umar, a person Shakmarra (corruption of *shaykh* 'Umar) is to be found only 10-12 generations ago. Even if we take into account the possibility that the genealogies are considerably telescoped, it seems hardly reasonable to date him back as far as the 13th century. The oral data suggest that the veneration of Sof 'Umar, obviously as an appendix to the Nūr Ḥusayn cult, did not commence until the second half of the 19th century. A locality with natural caves created by the water of the Web River was named Sof 'Umar and became his most important place of worship.

Numerous sanctuaries can be identified with some certainty as derivations from the cult devoted to Nūr Ḥusayn. To mention just one notable example, a shrine for his son Muḥammad Tammām was built in the Gololcha district of Bale. Mount Abū'l-Qāsim in southern Arssi Province is named after one of Nūr Ḥusayn's alleged descendants whose shrine was erected there as a place of pilgrimage (*mūda*) for the Guri clan.[19]

Many of the saints whose cult is performed in Arssiland now, are reported by the oral traditions to have been contemporaries of Aḥmad b. Ibrāhīm, nicknamed Grāñ (the Left-handed), the famous leader of the Adalite "holy war" (1529-43) against the Christian Empire. If it can be verified that they were contemporaneous, we possess a solid chronological indication for their lifetimes. The genealogies of Arssi clans who claim descent from these saints generally support the possibility that they lived in the 16th century.[20] Moreover, in certain cases additional oral data confirm their presence during the time of the *jihād*. It is reported, for example, of Aṣḥāb Uthmān, whom the Arssi clans Wege and Doda (and also the Sidama clan Malge) regard as their ancestor, that he was a commander in Aḥmad Grāñ's army. He was killed in a quarrel by one of his own officers, the "Ogaden man" Aṭṭalībo (presumably of Somali origin), near Ticho in eastern Arssiland, where he was buried. The place of his cupola-shaped mausoleum, which was presumably erected in the 1880s, evolved as an important focus of Muslim diffusion in the region of Shirka north of the Wabi Shebeli. Centres of Islamic education had also been founded by this time in Robe/Dida'a and in Gobesa.

Although far from being accepted by the whole population, Islam had become the dominant religion in parts of eastern Arssi, particularly in Bale east of the Urgoma Massif and in Shirka, during the last decades of the 19th century. This is confirmed by the fact that missionaries from these areas moved westwards to propagate Islam in "pagan" regions. One person particularly remembered is Khana, a *shaykh* from Annajina, who — between c.1860 and 1890 — converted the Alaba on the western periphery of Arssiland. At the same time, Islamicization was on the advance among the Barentu-Oromo of the Harar Plateau[21], a historical development which also affected the religious situation of northeastern Arssiland. Mumina, an Arssi woman who established the famous centre of magic in Farakassa (*awrāĵā* of Arba-Gugu), had received her education at the Muslim sanctuary of *aw* 'Alī, an Ittu *shaykh*, near Galamso in the Chercher mountains.[22]

Members of the French expedition led by Bourg de Bozas, who passed through Bale in 1902, stated that the area of Goba had been islamicized about a dozen years ago, i.e. in about 1890.[23] It was commented, however, that Islam was not yet solidly established and a Roman-Catholic mission could therefore be envisaged. Genealogies, which I collected in Bale, confirm that in most cases conversion to Islam started in the lifetime of my informants' grandfathers, i.e. at the end of the last century. It can moreover be calculated by counting the *gada* periods that the Holbatmanna and other clans turned Muslim in 1917. The reason for this particular wave of Islamicization remains unknown to me. Shortly afterwards, in the 1920s, Islam achieved a decisive breakthrough in the Arba-Gugu region of northeastern Arssi Province. Clashes between the Muslim population and the Christian Amhara authorities on religious topics were hardly reported. Neumann, who travelled through Arssiland at the turn of the century, mentioned a case of a Muslim sanctuary near Sire which had been transformed into a Christian church.[24]

The range of data mentioned above is fully supported by Cerulli's observations during his established, from which missionary campaigns were initiated among the western Arssi. In Gadab, *shaykh* 'Abd al-Raḥmān converted many of the local people. All over the country the construction of mosques and koranic schools was generously supported by the colonial authorities.[29]

After the restoration of Ethiopian rule in the 1940s, the Christian Orthodox Church for the first time adopted an offensive missionary strategy to challenge Islam in the "pagan" areas. Arssi informants reported that *abuna* Baselyos travelled in the Lake Regions as far as Gadab in 1957 and baptized a considerable number of people. Two years later he is said to have conducted a second campaign between Goba and Kokossa in northern Bale, resulting in the Christianization of about 20,000 people. However, for reasons which will be discussed below, almost all Christian Arssi opted to turn Muslim shortly afterwards.[30]

By the beginning of the 1970s, Arssiland was almost completely Islamicized. In 1973 I met one of the last pockets of *awāma*, partisans of the traditional folk religion, in the area of Kokossa, near the Wabi Shebeli headwaters.[31] But it seemed to be only a matter of a few years until they would turn Muslim.

A map of the religious situation in the *Regional Atlas* of the Governorate General of Arssi, published in 1971, recorded 57 mosques, mostly concentrated in the eastern areas where Islamicization had begun earlier than in the west.[32] *Qāḍīs* had been appointed by the government for the provinces, as well as for the *awrājā* and *waradā* districts, to supervise cases where Islamic law was involved. However, although Ḥayla Sellāsē had proclaimed the legal equality of Islam and Christianity in 1944/45, blatant discrimination with respect to Muslims in political, socio-economic and cultural matters persisted. The secular-oriented military government after the revolution of 1974 introduced innovations in favour of Ethiopia's Muslim citizens, such as the official acknowledgement of their main feasts, but it has not yet achieved a solution to this historically deep-rooted problem.[33]

Analysis of factors favouring Islamicization

The reasons why Islam has become the religion of almost all the Arssi are manifold. First of all, as has already been indicated, a strong Muslim sediment had persisted in the Hadiya stratum of Arssi society. It is true that in the socio-political hierarchy of the Arssi the conquered Hadiya were initially considered inferior to the "pure" Oromo. However, the more intensive the impact of Islamic values on cultural patterns became, the more the prestige of representatives of the Muslim sediment rose. Consequently, for the Arssi-Hadiya, who constituted the majority of the population, Islamicization offered the means of vertical social mobility. By fostering the cult of the "saints" whom they claimed as their own ancestors, they manifested their "noble" origin. Corrupted Arabic names, such as Fakissa (Faqīh 'Isa), Shedamma (*shaykh* Adam), Aminya (Nūr Amīn), Alli ('Alī) or Djafarra (Dja'far), became a potential source of esteem for the respective clans.

The oral traditions of the Arssi-Hadiya claim that their ancestors were not *awāma* (as were those of the Oromo) but *sagidda*. They tend to equate *sagidda* with Islam, although they are aware that essential criteria of the Muslim religion were given up in favour of syncretistic elements from a local Cushitic background. However, many representatives of *sagidda* are said to have regularly performed prayers showing some similarity with the Islamic *ṣalāt*. to have observed a fasting period (*ṣōmu*) of 30 or 15 days, to have buried their dead so as to lie in the direction of Mecca, and at funerals to have performed a ritual sacrifice (*saḳadāda*) reminiscent of the Muslim equivalent.

Among the Hadiya clans of the Arssi those called Ḳalecha Shan or Awan Shan were famed as magicians and also retained important political functions alongside the *abba-gada*, or age-grade leaders. In Oromo *shan* means five; *ḳalecha* refers to a magician or priest; and *awan* is derived from the Harari/Somali title *aw*. The terms Ḳalecha Shan and Awan Shan, signifying "(the clans of) the five priests" can be used interchangeably. Opinions about the classification of these clans differ in Arssi. In the western areas, eight clans — Aminya, Adamonye, Allujanna, Say'manna, Funyamura, Madarsho, Abosara and Wege Haricho — were labelled *ḳalecha*. But expedition with Luigi di Savoia-Aosta in 1928. By this time the Chilalo-Warra Lukko-Urgoma mountain chains demarcated a borderline between a predominantly Muslim eastern and still largely "pagan" western part of Arssiland.[25] For the same decade Azaïs and Chambard state that Islam had not yet gained a noteworthy foothold among the western Arssi.[26] The genealogies and oral traditions confirm these reports: in most instances conversion to Islam occurred in the time of the informants' fathers.

One of the first Muslim sanctuaries in western Arssiland was established during the first decade of the 20th century in Hogisso, near the spring of the Wabi Shebeli. A member of the Adamonye clan, *ḥājji* Kādir Kajāwa, came to this desolate place from the region of Kofale and seems to have deliberately invented a legend about Nūr Ḥusayn in order to convert the locality to the cult of this saint. The story tells that Nūr Ḥusayn was once praying at Hogisso when an elephant attacked him. He cursed the animal in such a way that it sank down into the earth with only its tusks projecting above the ground. The place of this "miracle" was henceforth called Mume Ilka ("the peak of the tusk") in Oromo.[27] It then became a centre of pilgrimage guarded by members of the Adamonye clan.

All over Arssiland it is manifest that Islamicization occurred simultaneously with the establishment of shrines. In the 1930s the cult of *ḥājji* Nāṣir became popular in Hersha, between Meraro and Mount Ḳaḳa (Bekoji District). This man (who, I have suggested elsewhere, may have been the same person as 'Abd al-Nāṣir, one of Aḥmad Grān's most capable commanders[28]), is claimed by the Arssi clan Awlijanna (Allujanna) as their ancestor. (The same clan, but with the denomination Sha'amanna, is also to be found among the Alaba and Hadiya.)

Islamicization in the district of Gadab is particularly associated with the cult of *ḥājji* Shāle, who is considered to have been a war-leader of the Adalite *jihād* army and is regarded as the ancestor of the Bamudde clan. He is said to have reached Gadab via Bale with his wife Ḥalīma and to have died in Kankorro, where his mausoleum was built in the 1930s. I am by no means able to present a complete list of shrines which were established in Arssiland during the first decades of the 20th century — most of them of merely local importance. Instead, I wish to mention a few examples which are relevant for the cultural identity of certain clans (cf. map). A shrine of Nūranna Amīn, i.e. *amīr* Nūr b. Mujāhid of Harar (d.1568), Aḥmad Grān's successor in the command of the *jihād*, was built by his supposed descendants, the Aminya, in Agafra/ Bale. The Sinano of northern Bale devoted a sanctuary to their ancestor Dja'far in Gasara. For the region of Dida'a, north of the Wabi Shebeli, the shrine of the Say'manna for *shaykh* Mūdi near Kofale as well as sanctuaries of Abbās in the region of Seru and of Jabal Muri on the Chulul River (district of Gololcha/Arba-Gugu) may be mentioned.

The lowlands of the Rift Valley were the last area of Arssiland to which Islam expanded. Islamic conversion did not take place there prior to the time of the Italian occupation (1936-41), despite the fact that the neighbouring Alaba and East Gurage had already been islamicized during the second half of the 19th century. In the early 1940s a person called Kabīr Dāwa initiated the construction of a sanctuary dedicated to Nūr Ḥusayn's eldest son, Nūrullāh Aḥmad, in Ḳolito/Alaba, near the border of the Arssi dwelling-areas. Since Nūr Ḥusayn is considered the patron saint of the Arssi, the new cult was readily adopted by them. The fact that there is no historical testimony whatsoever that Nūrullāh Aḥmad ever set foot in this place does not matter to the worshippers. (In fact, most shrines in the area of our concern are undoubtedly fictitious ones.)

It was no coincidence that a considerable expansion of Islam occurred during the period of the Italian occupation. Aiming at strengthening the position of the southern peoples at the expense of the Christian Amhara, the major opponents of European colonial rule, the Italians more or less directly favoured Islam. At the same time Islamicization among the Arssi was welcomed by the new rulers as a means of pacification: when people turned Muslim, this automatically led them to abandon the *gada*-system, with its inherent obligation of killing members of neighbouring groups.

In Ticho, the provincial headquarters of Arssi, the Italians had appointed *ḥājji* Ussen as their representative. Assisted by *ḥājji* Aḥmad and *fitāwrāri* Mammīyo, he actively employed his powerful position for religious propaganda. In Robe/Dida'a a centre for religious training was only the five first-mentioned were generally regarded as their "pure" representatives.[34] In the eastern highlands, the Ataba, Abronye, Adamonye, Abdoiye and Awlijanna are commonly listed as Awan Shan. Their ritual power, notably in rain-making ceremonies, was believed to derive from their sharific origin, i.e. from their descent from the family of the Prophet Muḥammad. Although the genealogical data are insufficient to verify this claim, it can be assumed that the ancestors of the Ḳalecha clans constituted a religious (and political) elite in the pre-Oromo Muslim states of southeastern Ethiopia. Their main religious instrument, the big drum (dibbe), may be regarded as a contribution of the Islamic stratum to Arssi-Oromo culture.

Whereas the Sagidda and Ḳalecha sediment could not be accepted as being fully in line with Islamic orthodoxy, it seems likely that a few places preserved the continuity of a genuine Islam. As has already been indicated, this can be deduced with some certainty for Annajina and pockets in the Shirka area. Although there was a permanent state of hostility between the warlike Oromo, for whom the killing of alien people was an integral obligation of their gada-system, and those Muslim centres, the latter were principally respected as places of higher civilization and commercial activities. The Arssi — just like the Barentu with respect to the town of Harar — were therefore not interested in eliminating them. The more an economic symbiosis developed — for example, agricultural products were exchanged for tools made by local craftsmen — the greater the importance of the Muslim centres of religious diffusion became. It can thus be concluded that the Islamicization of the Arssi was first initiated within their area. It was then reinforced by an influx of foreign shaykhs, particularly Somali and members of the Warra Ḳalu ("priests") clans of the Barentu. The mission of aw Muḥammad from Harar to Annajina in about 1790 is an example documenting such enterprises.

In numerous cases, sacred places of the old folk religion were transformed into Muslim sanctuaries. This applies to the caves of Sof 'Umar, to Mume Ilka and many other distinguished localities and natural objects.

The Muslim centres had most probably maintained the tradition of religious orders, which have always acted as an important means of Islamic diffusion. Up to the present, the most widespread ṭuruq in Arssiland have been the Ḳādirīya and its offshoot, the Ḥusaynīya, which originated in Annajina. Other orders, such as the Rashadīya, the Sammānīya and the Tidjānīya, have been introduced only sporadically in the course of the 20th century.[35]

Apart from the fact that some Muslim centres had survived intact in the east, the westward diffusion of Islam in Arssiland can also be explained by the general geographical circumstances. After the decline of medieval Islam, eastern Arssi continued to be bordered along its eastern fringes by the Muslim Somali. The latter were actively engaged in expanding their territory from their arid lowland domiciles towards the more hospitable mountainous hinterland. Being the offensive ethnic element, the Somali imposed their cultural system on the Arssi by peaceful and warlike means where the two peoples came into contact.

Islamicization from the east was further favoured by the fact that the economic and commercial orientation of Arssiland was predominantly towards the east and the northeast, i.e. towards Harar and the seaports of the Indian Ocean, major focuses of Muslim diffusion for centuries. With these places the area was linked by much-frequented trade routes, whereas traffic to the west was far less important.[36]

Compared with its main rival, Orthodox Christianity, Islam was favoured by certain ecological and socio-economic conditions. To this day, the economy of the Arssi-Oromo has been based — besides the cultivation of barley — to a noteworthy extent on livestock raising. It would therefore be extremely difficult for them to observe the dietary obligations of Ethiopian Christianity, requiring believers to abstain from any kind of non-vegetarian food for more than 150 days a year. Those Arssi who were baptized following the missionary campaigns by abuna Baselyos in the 1950s (see above) are said to have turned Muslim just after the first period of Christian fasting they experienced. The Islamic Ramaḍān proves much easier to observe because it does not demand abstention from livestock products. Unlike Orthodox Christianity, Islam also permits its followers to eat the meat of camels, which is of economic importance to the Arssi on the eastern highland escarpment. On the other hand, the Muslim prohibition of consuming the blood of living animals — a custom widespread among northeast African herders — has apparently never been a significant obstacle to the spread of Islam.

Beside these basically rational factors, emotional attitudes appear to have favoured the Islamicization of Arssiland to a noteworthy extent. Following the occupation of their country by the Amhara in the late 19th century, many Oromo developed a deep-rooted antipathy towards the socio-religious system of their Christian conquerors. Although empirical data cannot be obtained in this field, it may be assumed that this attitude led many Arssi to give preference to Islam.

Effects and consequences of socio-religious change

For the Arssi, Islam did not merely become an institutionalized channel for expressing opposition to the system of Amhara rule: it also emerged as an important focus in the search for a new cultural identity. In pre-Islamic times, the *abba-mūda* (father of anointing), who resided in Horra Wolabo in the western part of today's Bale Province, was acknowledged as the spiritual leader of the Arssi. The religious complex associated with him declined considerably in the 1950s[37] and was replaced by the cult of *shaykh* Nūr Ḥusayn, the patron saint of Muslim Arssiland. Annajina increasingly acquired the reputation of a "northeast African Mecca". Minor saints played a similar role in the evolution of cultural consciousness at a territorial or clan level.

Although the institutional manifestation of religion — both higher education and material objects — remained relatively weak and obligations such as prayers were observed irregularly by the majority of the population, the changes Islamicization imposed on various spheres of life nevertheless proved to be significant. In a standardized manner the Arssi have allotted the days of the week to the worship of particular persons: Monday is remembered as the birthday of the Prophet Muḥammad; Tuesday is devoted to *shaykh* Nūr Ḥusayn; Wednesday to 'Abd al-Qādir al-Djīlānī; Thursday to *shaykh* Yicha and Saturday to *shaykh* al-Dīn (these two persons can alternatively be replaced by local saints). According to a popular belief, it was on a Friday, the Muslim holy day, that *nabī* Adām was created. Apart from the major feasts of the Muslim calendar — *'īd al-aḍḥā* ("sacrificial feast"), *'īd al-fiṭr* ("festival of breaking the fast") and *mawlūd al-nabī* (the Prophet's birthday) — pilgrimages and sacrifices are performed throughout the year on the memorial days of the local saints. The day when Muḥammad was conceived by his mother is called *galgalla gobana* in Oromo. Muslim hagiography had a modifying impact on indigenous oral literature and partly replaced it. The more Islamic values consolidated their position in the mind of people, the more traditional cultural patterns were despised. (This phenomenon is, of course, by no means limited to the Arssi.)

When observing public meetings and negotiations with government officials, I noticed that Arssi men who had accomplished the pilgrimage to Mecca laid claim to be addressed as *ḥājj(i)*. The outstanding esteem for honorary titles in Ethiopian societies thus found a particular Muslim expression.

Materially, Islam is manifested in a more or less stereotyped way by clothes such as turbans and caps (*kofīya*) for men and black head-scarves for women as well as by rosaries and decorated calabashes (*mashakulla*) for ritual washing.

However extensively Islam changed the original patterns of Arssi culture, local features and peculiarities persisted. The tradition of building graves with decorated stones not only survived, but in certain areas was even supplemented by the introduction of anthropomorphic reliefs and sculptures[38], although these are contrary to the rules of Islamic orthodoxy. Several times I observed first- or second-generation Muslims laying grass or butter on the trunk of a sacred tree from the pre-Islamic past and evoking the name of *wāqa*, the sky-god of the Cushitic folk religion, instead of Allāh.

One particular feature of Arssi popular Islam is the "Shaykh Ḥusayn pilgrims", generally called *garība* (pl. *garībatta*).[39] They are mostly people who roam around carrying Y-shaped sticks as a symbol of Nūr Ḥusayn. They are accustomed to live on the alms which are distributed on the occasion of religious festivals. The secular authorities and orthodox Muslims have always disliked this phenomenon, but since it is so well-established, they have been unable to abolish it.

Certain elements in the social structure obviously change much less readily than others. In the case of matrimony, for example, Islam advocates marriage between relatives and particularly favours connubial links between parallel cousins. The traditional Oromo rules, however, demanded exogamy at the lineage or clan level. Although this obligation is in principle being abandoned in Muslim society, the Arssi – with the exception of some *shaykhs* – continue to assert that the genealogies of the couple do not meet at a distance of less than four generations and they vehemently reject marriages between close relatives.[40] Also the Islamic law concerning the number of wives has frequently been transgressed. In the region of Kofale Baxter observed that several rich men, including *ḥājjis* had married more than four wives at a time.[41]

To sum up, Islam and pre-Muslim elements have to some extent achieved a compromise which has created a more or less homogeneous "national" culture of the Arssi. This seems to be a positive factor in the sense that it enhances their consciousness of a cultural identity and their group stability. On the other hand, this very emphasis on "national" characteristics potentially widens diversity within the Oromo ethnos – a diversity in which the four dominating religions, Islam, Orthodox Christianity, Protestantism and the old folk religion (each in itself representing a complex cultural system) play an important role but are not the only determinant factors. To establish solidarity by overcoming inherent socio-cultural barriers is a challenge to all Oromo. The same challenge faces all Ethiopians: religious tolerance and the preservation of cultural autonomy in all parts of the country are essential prerequisites for peaceful co-existence.

NOTES

1. E. Cerulli, "L'Islam nell'Africa Orientale", *Aspetti e problemi attuali del mondo musulmano*, Reale Accademia d'Italia (Roma, 1941), pp.5-21; J. S. Trimingham, *Islam in Ethiopia*, (London, 1952); L. Cuoq, *L'Islam en Ethiopie des origines au XVIe siècle* (Paris, 1981).

2. See for example A. Triulzi, "Trade, Islam and the Mahdia in Northwestern Wallagga, Ethiopia", *Journal of African History*, 16, 1 (1975), pp.35-71; cf. for eastern Ethiopia S. Waldron, *Social Organization and Social Control in the Walled City of Harar, Ethiopia* (Ann Arbor, 1975).

3. According to the new Ethiopian census of 1984 the population of the Governorate of Arssi amounted to 1.5 million. To this figure must be added the Arssi of Haykoch-Butajira (population 1.2 million) in southern Shawa and those of Bale (population 1 million). Since not all inhabitants of these areas are ethnically Arssi, an estimate of 2.5 million Arssi may be realistic.

4. E. Cerulli, "Le popolazioni del bacino superiore dello Uabi" in L. di Savoia-Aosta (ed.), *L'esplorazione dello Uabi – Uebi Scebeli* (Milano, 1932), pp.33-181; E. Haberland, *Galla Süd-Äthiopiens* (Stuttgart, 1963); P. Baxter, "Atete in a Highland Arssi Neighbourhood", *Northeast African Studies*, 1, 2 (1979), pp.1-22. My own investigations in the country of the Arssi-Oromo were carried out in the context of a study of the Hadiya-Sidama in 1973. The field research was sponsored by the German Research Association.

5. As a base of comparison I consulted c. 20 genealogies.

6. For a detailed analysis of this differentiation see Haberland, *op. cit.*, pp.442-46; U. Braukämper, *Geschichte der Hadiya Süd-Äthiopiens – Von den Anfängen bis zur Revolution 1974* (Wiesbaden, 1980), chapter 3, 4.

7. For the Macha see E. Cerulli, "The Folk-Literature of the Galla of Southern Abyssinia",

Harvard African Studies, 3 (1922), p.12; for the Barentu see Braukämper, *op. cit.*, pp.136-44.

8. See C. F. Beckingham and G. W. B. Huntingford (eds.), *Some Records of Ethiopia 1593-1646. Being Extracts from the History of High Ethiopia or Abassia by Manoel de Almeida together with Bahrey's History of the Galla* (London, 1954), p.112.

9. *Ibid.*, p.123; cf. C. Conti-Rossini, *Historia Regis Sarsa Dengel (Malak Sagad)*, (Louvain, 1955), p.144.

10. Aṭmē, G. M., *History of the Galla (Yagalla Tarik). I.* (Trans. Bairu Tafla), (Addis Ababa/Hamburg, n.d.), (Ms.), p.146. *Aṣē* is a traditional epithet bestowed on the Ethiopian kings; *chawā* refers to the military colonists of the Christian Empire in the Middle Ages.

11. The history of the Oromo-Hadiya relations has been extensively analysed in my *Geschichte der Hadiya*, chapters 3.4 and 3.5. Cf. Haberland, *op. cit.*, pp.410, 412, 415.

12. It does not only exist in the Arssi dialect of the Oromo language (Afan-Oromo). The version *sagaddu* for the Muslim prayer is also known among the Macha (oral communication).

13. See G. W. B. Huntingford, "Arabic Inscriptions in Southern Ethiopia", *Antiquity*, 29 (1955), p.231.

14. For the chronology and the cult of Nūr Ḥusayn see my paper "The Sanctuary of Shaykh Ḥusayn and the Oromo-Somali Connections in Bale", *Proceedings of the First International Congress of Somal Studies* (forthcoming).

15. Cerulli, "Le popolazioni . . .", pp.140, *passim*.

16. This was documented by E. Cerulli, *Studi Etiopici I: La lingua e la storia di Harar* (Roma, 1936), p.44. 'Abd al-Qādir al-Djīlānī died in Baghdad in A.D. 1166.

17. P. Paulitschke, *Ethnographie Nordost-Afrikas II: Die geistige Kultur der Danâkil, Galla und Somâl* (Berlin, 1896), p.71 and A. Donaldson-Smith, *Through Unknown African Countries. The First Expedition from Somaliland to Lake Lamu* (London/New York, 1897), p.106, confused this *aw* Muḥammad with Nūr Ḥusayn himself.

18. W. C. Harris, *The Highlands of Ethiopia* (London, 1844), vol. I, p.258, received information in the early 1840s that a "town" caled Nura Husayn existed in the Arssi country. In the language of the Arssi the whole compound of a shrine is called *fora*, the mausoleum *kubura* and the saint's grave *ater*.

19. Cf. O. Neumann, "From the Somali Coast through Southern Ethiopia", *Geographical Journal*, 20 (1902), pp.377 sq.

20. In the genealogies which I have examined for this purpose the names of the saints to whom the cult is devoted appear on average 14 generations ago.

21. A study of this area was presented in my paper "Notes on the Islamicization and the Muslim Shrines of the Harar Plateau", *Proceedings of the Second International Congress of Somali Studies* (Hamburg, 1984), II, pp.145-74.

22. Mumina who held the honorary title *gifti*, died in 1926. See H. Norden, *Durch Abessinien und Erythräa* (Berlin, n.d.), p.62.

23. R. du Bourg de Bozas, *Mission Scientifique de la Mer Rouge à l'Atlantique à travers l'Afrique Tropicale (octobre 1900 – mai 1903). Carnets de route* (Paris, 1906), p.170.

24. O. Neumann, "Von der Somali-Küste durch Süd-Äthiopien zum Sudan", *Zeitschrift der Gesellschaft für Erdkunde in Berlin*, 37 (1902), p.14.

25. Cerulli, "Le popolazioni . . . ", p.141.

26. R. P. Azaïs and R. Chambard, *Cinq années de recherches archéologiques en Ethiopie – Province de Harar et Ethiopie méridionale* (Paris, 1931), pp.208 sq.

27. Cerulli, "Le popolazioni . . . ", pp.50, 143, and Haberland, *op. cit.*, p.412. I also heard this story.

28. Braukämper, *Geschichte der Hadiya*, p.113.

29. Oral communications in 1973.

30. The individuals who remained Christians were in a hopelessly isolated position. In 1973 I interviewed a chief (*bālābbāt)* of the Haballosa clan south of Lake Zway, whose family were the only Christians in a completely Muslim environment.

31. According to a communication by P. Baxter, another small pocket of *awāma* existed in the region of Kofale in the early 1970s.

32. *Arusi. A Regional Atlas* (Addis Ababa, 1971), p.11. My own observations indicate that this figure is too low.

33. For critical comments see P. Baxter, "Ethiopia's Unacknowledged Problem, the Oromo", *African Affairs*, 77, 308 (1978), p.293; U. Braukämper, "Ethnic Identity and Social Change among Oromo Refugees in the Horn of Africa", *Northeast African Studies*, 3, 4 (1982/83), p.4.

34. Oral communications; cf. Haberland, *op. cit.*, p.444.

35. Informants in Robe/Dida'a told me that the Rashadīya was introduced there by a certain *shaykh* Ulḳāki from Wollo in the 1940s. This is one of the few examples suggesting Islamic influence in Arssiland from a northern direction.

36. Cf. M. Abir, "Caravan Trade and History in the Northern Parts of East Africa", *Paideuma*, 14 (1968), pp.103-120.

37. Oral communications; cf. Haberland, *op. cit.*, p.415.

38. I saw examples of this in Gadab and in the Bilate Valley.

39. Haberland, *op. cit.*, p.414, recorded that the western Arssi also called them *shekōta*, which is derived from the Arabic word *shaykh*.

40. This can be observed for many Islamic societies in Northeast Africa, including the Somali, among whom Islamicization started almost a millenium ago. See I. M. Lewis, *A Pastoral Democracy: A Study of Pastoralism and Politics among the Northern Somali of the Horn of Africa* (London, etc., 1967), pp.127 sq.

41. This was observed by P. Baxter. Personal communication.

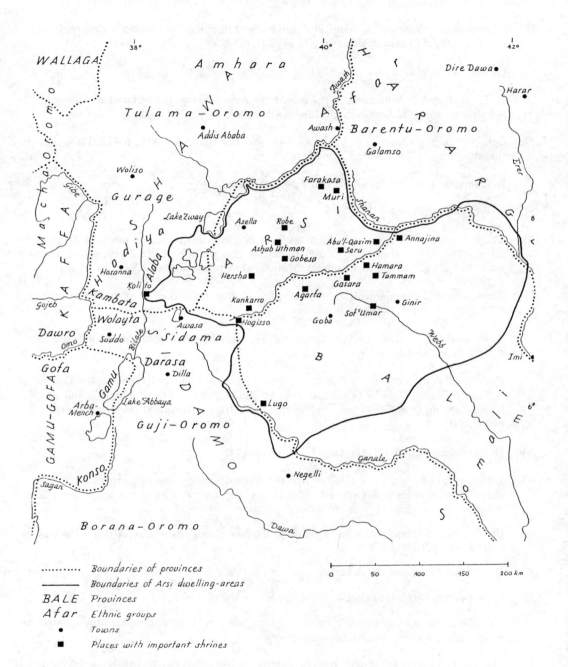

WALLAGA

38°

Amhara

40°

42°

Dire Dawa

Harar

Maccha-Oromo

Gibe

Tulama – Oromo

Addis Ababa

Woliso

Gurage

Lake Zway

HADIYA

Hosanna

Alaba

Koli sso

Kambata

Wolayta

Gojeb

Awash

Awash

Barentu – Oromo

Galamso

Farakasa

Muri

Asella

Robe

Ashab Uthman

Gobesa

Hersha

Abu'l-Qasim

Seru

Hamara

Tammam

Gasara

Agarfa

Annajina

Ginir

Goba

Sof 'Umar

Shanan

Erer

8

AFAR

HARAR

ARSI

S

R

A

Kankarro

Hogisso

Lugo

Awasa

Sidama

Soddo

Darasa

Dilla

Lake Abbaya

Arba-Mench

Guji – Oromo

Konso

Sagan

Borana – Oromo

Dawa

Ganale

Negelli

Webb

B

A

L

E

Imi

6°

SOMALI

Gamu

Bilate

Omo

DAMOS

Gofa

Dawro

GAMU-GOFA

KAFFA

Maccha-Oromo

Gamu

.... Boundaries of provinces

——— Boundaries of Arsi dwelling-areas

BALE Provinces

Afar Ethnic groups

• Towns

■ Places with important shrines

0   50   100   150   200 km

MUSLIM SHRINES IN ARSILAND

"LE MEURTRE DU SERPENT":

UNE NOUVELLE VERSION D'ETHIOPIE MERIDIONALE

J. Bureau

Le texte que nous présentons ici appartient à un ensemble de 190 récits que nous avons collectés, entre 1973 et 1984, chez les Gamo d'Ethiopie; leur transcription a été déposée à l'Institut d'Etudes Ethiopiennes.[1] Ce travail devrait aboutir à l'édition critique de ces textes, transcrits, traduits et analysés dans leur relation à l'ensemble de la littérature orale éthiopienne déjà répertoriée; beaucoup d'entre eux constituent en effet des versions nouvelles de récits connus ailleurs en Ethiopie, et celui que nous lirons aujourd'hui nous est à tout familier.

Il s'agit d'un récit complexe, riche et coloré, où s'insère l'épisode classique du "meurtre du serpent", ce prologue nécessaire à l'histoire légendaire des Princes Salomonides. Il nous a été conté en août 1973 par la mère du *Grazmach* Duré, notre principal informateur d'alors; elle s'exprimait dans la langue de Bonké. Une version différente, amputée de plusieurs séquences, avait été précédemment notée par Luc Desmarquest, dans le village d'Otchollo, à deux jours de marche de Bonké; mais elle n'a pas été publiée.[2]

La copie est de notre main, mais la transcription originale est d'Eshetu Wonbera, de Dorzé, et nous l'avons reprise ensemble, à l'écoute du texte, afin de corriger les emplois confus des 1° et 4° ordres amhariques, — ex: *bä* et *ba* — et des 3° et 6° ordres — ex: *ni* et *nə* — si fréquents chez les Gamo.

La transcription des langues éthiopiennes en caractères amhariques, adoptée par le gouvernement d'Addis Abeba, est maintenant largement répandue pour l'alphabétisation des sociétés non Amhara[3]; ce sont maintenant plus de dix langues qui sont ainsi transcrites, mais c'est au dépens des dialectes mineurs. La transcription des langues Ométo, et plus précisément du Wollaita, a été mise au point et des manuels d'enseignement élémentaire ont été publiés; transcription et manuels sont non seulement imposés aux Wollaita — ce qui va de soi puisqu'ils en sont les auteurs — mais aussi à tous les autres locuteurs Ométos. Or ceux-ci possèdent des variantes dialectales auxquelles ils tiennent beaucoup, de même qu'ils n'aiment pas être confondus avec leur plus puissant voisin du Wollaita.[4] Ne citons qu'un exemple: le *t* emphatique des Wollaita dans *keṭa*, la maison; *uṭa*, l'ensete; et *ṭosa*, Dieu, est un *ts* en Gamo: *ketsa, utsa, tsosa*, etc. . . Comme il est fort peu probable que des manuels puissent être jamais écrits dans chacun des dialectes Ométo, on peut craindre que le Wollaita s'impose à leur dépens, en tant que langue écrite. Si nous précisons ces faits c'est que notre transcription du Gamo est tenue pour irrégulière par les Wollaita et par le Ministère Ethiopien de l'Education qui tient le Wollaita pour représentatif de toutes les langues Ométo.[5] Suivant l'opinion des Gamo nous ne nous sommes pas préoccupés de la transcription Wollaita; nous avons simplement laissé les Gamo écrire leur propre langue, en caractères amhariques, tout en nous assurant que les principes suivants étaient respectés: ne pas altérer la valeur phonétique du syllabaire national, et limiter la création de nouveau signe à deux, pour *ɖ* et *ts*.[6]

Le texte Gamo est la transcription fidèle du récit enregistré; par contre, au moment de la traduction, une très courte séquence a été replacée dans son ordre logique. Il s'agit de la séquence au cours de laquelle un domestique raconte au roi que son gendre est castré, de sorte que le roi organize une chasse et un bain pour s'assurer de la virilité du héros; la narratrice plaçait cette scène après que la chasse ait eu lieu. Ce passage est mis entre crochets dans la transcription et dans la traduction (Cf. note no.16).

TRADUCTION

Un homme s'était marié. Après qu'il se soit marié, sa femme mourut. Elle avait accouché d'un fils. "Aussi longtemps que mon fils ne sera pas adulte, je ne me remarierai pas" disait-il. Le garçon ayant grandi dit à son père: "marie-toi!". Son fils lui dit de se marier; "oui?"; et l'homme prit une épouse. Après son mariage, comme l'homme partait aux labours avec ses boeufs, sa femme appela son fils; elle lui demanda de faire l'amour et elle se saisit de lui. "Je ne prendrai pas la femme de mon père; n'est-ce pas tabou?[7] Après la mort de ma mère, c'est lui qui m'a élevé; je ne veux pas coucher avec sa femme."[8] Et il la repoussa. "Tu ne me veux pas pour femme!"; alors elle se griffa le visage, s'arracha les cheveux et alla se coucher. Quand l'homme revint des labours avec ses boeufs, il la trouva couchée: "Femme! Pourquoi es-tu allongée?" "N'est-ce pas là ton fils, celui que tu as nourri! Il a voulu coucher avec moi en ton absence et, comme j'ai refusé, il m'a battue", dit-elle à son maître. "C'est moi qui l'ai élevé, et il a voulu coucher avec ma femme!" Alors, prenant son couteau, il *coupa le sexe de son fils*.

"Je suis innocent, mais pour ce que ta femme t'a dit tu m'as émasculé"; et il s'en alla au désert.[9] Il partit au *motsa*[10] de son père, prit un esclave, un cheval, une lance et un bouclier, et s'en alla au désert. Jusqu'à ce que la nuit s'achève il marcha dans le désert. Le matin, alors qu'il marchait, il rencontra trois jeunes filles assises au pied d'un arbre. Il leur demanda: "Que faites-vous là?" "Nous sommes données en tribut[11] au serpent." "Qui vous a données?" "L'une est la fille du roi, c'est la fille du *balabbat*[12]; les deux autres sont les filles de ses servantes; chaque maison a donné une fille jusqu'à ce qu'arrive le tour de la maison du roi; trois filles, dont la fille même du roi ont été prises et sont là." "Alors! Le serpent s'en retournera sans s'être battu?" "Nous sauveras-tu?" "Oui, je vous sauverai!" "Comment vas-tu nous sauver?" "Dépêchez-vous d'aller ramasser du bois." Les trois jeunes filles ramenèrent le bois qu'elles avaient ramassé. "Combien y-a-t-il de serpents?" "Il y en trois." "Quand viennent-ils?" "A midi." "Quand vous verrez arriver le serpent, appelez-moi." Un des serpents arriva du désert; elles appelèrent, et il mit le feu au bois. Le serpent apparut sur un *wola*.[13] Comme il arrivait pour prendre les jeunes filles, le garçon mit le feu et coupa le serpent en morceaux; le serpent brûla. Il avait brûlé un serpent. "Combien on reste-t-il?" "Il en reste deux." Tous les deux arrivèrent comme le précédent. Monté sur le *wola* où il s'assit, le garçon *tua et brûla les trois serpents*.

Il avait sauvé les trois jeunes filles du serpent. Il cacha les trois filles. Les ayant cachées, il s'en alla où le peuple, tout entier réuni, pleurait; il s'assit sur la haut d'une colline et regarda les gens (qui se lamentaient en bas). Le roi arriva, avec son domestique conduisant le cheval et portant la lance et le bouclier; "Nous avons offert la fille du roi au serpent et nous pleurons; qui est celui-là, assis là-haut, et ne pleure pas?" "Allez lui demander qui il est." Ils allèrent là où il était assis et lui demandèrent: "Toi." "Oui." "D'où es tu?" "Je suis un voyageur."[14] "Que fais tu assis?" "Je suis simplement assis." "Pourquoi es tu assis au lieu de pleurer la fille du roi?" "Qu'est-il arrivé à la fille du roi?" "Nous l'avons donnée en tribut au serpent." "Croyez-vous en finir avec lui par un tribut? Pourquoi ne pas se battre?" "Toi, maintenant, tu peux nous libérer du tribut au serpent?" "Oui, je vous en libérerai." "Nous libéreras-tu?" "Oui, je vous libérerai." Alors ils allèrent raconter la chose au roi: "Voilà ce qu'il a dit: nous libéreras-tu? Oui, a-t-il dit." Ils l'appelèrent et l'amenèrent. Après qu'il ait été amené chez le roi, on lui demanda: "Pourras-tu nous libérer du tribut au serpent?" "Oui, je vous en libérerai; mais alors, que ferez-vous pour moi?" "Tu partageras mes biens et mon royaume; tu auras la moitié de mes biens." "Je vous en libérerai." "Bien." Le garçon rapporta les serpents qu'il avait tués; il les montra. Et il montra les jeunes filles. A leur retour, les jeunes filles se placèrent au côté de celui qui les avait sauvées, plutôt que de se placer aux cotés du roi. Comme elles étaient assises auprès du garçon, elles virent que son pénis avait été coupé. "Alors! Toi, la fille du roi!" lui dit-il. "Oui?" "Mon père m'a tué, je suis venu, je suis perdu."[15] Que feras-tu de moi dans ta maison, sans rien?" "Moi, c'est au serpent que mon père m'a offerte; aussi pourquoi ne vivrai-je pas avec toi?" "Ne dis rien à personne; je ne dirai rien non plus." "Oui, oui." Et ils vécurent ainsi ensemble. Un domestique vint dire au premier roi: "Ton gendre n'a pas de pénis." "C'est un mensonge." "Non! Ce n'est pas un mensonge; si je mens, que mes os servent à faire des crochets pour suspendre les bols, et que mon sang serve à frotter le sol de votre maison."[16] (Alors le roi) dit: "Je vais aller au désert; achète moi un cheval." Quand le cheval fut acheté, ils partirent au désert. Le cheval acheté et les gens partis au désert, ils chassèrent et le roi dit: "Personne n'ira sans avoir pris un bain dans la rivière; en mon nom je le dis, personne n'évitera le bain dans la rivière." Alors qu'ils arrivaient à la rivière, ils trouvèrent une antilope. Quand il l'eut trouvée, (le garçon) se lança à sa poursuite. Celui qui n'avait pas de pénis était à la poursuite de l'antilope quand il rencontra Godayo (la déesse) assise, cachée de tous; de ses mains elle jouait avec la boue. L'animal qu'il poursuivait alla se mettre sous la protection de Godayo.[17] Lui, à cheval, menaçait l'antilope de sa lance. "Toi, le roi qui est à cheval" dit Godayo, "ne me tue pas, l'animal qui est derrière moi, ne le tue pas." "Que ferez-vous pour moi?" "Dis moi ce que tu as." "Regarde!" Et baissant son pantalon il lui montra qu'il n'avait plus de sexe. Prenant de la boue dont elle jouait, Godayo *lui façonna un pénis et le lui jeta. Et il resta bien en place.* "Voilà ton problème résolu" lui dit-elle. Tirant sur son sexe il vit qu'il tenait bon. Comme il arrivait au bain le pénis était toujours là, bien réel. Il alla se baigner au milieu des autres hommes. Plus tard, comme le domestique revenait, le roi lui dit: "Tu m'as menti, tu m'as dit qu'il n'avait pas de pénis, alors qu'il en a un, mon gendre!" On frotta le sol de son sang, et de ses os on fit des crochets pour suspendre les bols. Quinze jours plus tard, on creusa un fossé de sept coudées de large. (Le roi dit): "Nourris ton cheval, je nourrirai le mien; comment peut-il y avoir deux *balabbat* dans un même pays? Comment peut-il y avoir deux rois, côte à côte?"[18] "Bien." Et ils allèrent nourrir leurs chevaux. L'ancien roi nourrit son cheval, chez lui; il lui donna de la bière de *gashé*.[19] Le second roi fit galoper son cheval, le soir. Le cheval du second roi était alors sec et maigre. Alors que celui du premier roi était gras. "Creusez le fossé de sept coudées de large; celui qui le franchira sera roi; celui qui y tombera, qu'on l'y laisse et qu'on le recouvre de terre." Quinze jours plus tard le fossé avait été creusé par les gens du pays. "Tu franchiras le fossé le premier" dit l'ancien roi. "Non, vous êtes le père, je passerai après vous." "Non, tu passeras le premier." Alors on jugea le différent et l'on décida que le jeune passerait le premier. "Comme le roi l'a ordonné, tu passeras le premier." Comme il avait été dit, le jeune sauta et franchit dix coudées. Ses partisans l'entourèrent et l'acclamèrent. Ensuite, le cheval de l'ancien roi tomba dans le trou, à mi-distance. *On le couvrit de terre.*

Ayant épousé la fille du roi, il eut sept fils et sept filles. Alors qu'il était roi, la femme qui avait voulu qu'il la prenne, et le père qui l'avait émasculé, devenus pauvres, arrivèrent à sa porte; ils étaient vêtus de peaux de mouton et portaient des meules. Lui, il était assis à sa porte, jouant au *lamé*[20] avec ses gens. Comme il les vit venir de loin, il les reconnut; "Allez vers eux, mais ne les amenez pas ici" dit-il. Il les fit confortablement installer dans une maison. Deux jours après, ils vinrent: "Que voulez-vous?" "Nous sommes venus vendre des meules." "Les meules ne sont ni à vendre ni à acheter" fit-il dire à ses hommes. "Prenez soin d'eux pour une semaine; donnez leur à manger et à boire." Pendant une semaine on les nourrit et on leur donna des vêtements; on les fit beaux et gras, puis le roi demanda qu'on les fit venir. Quand ils arrivèrent devant lui, ils ne le reconnurent pas; ils l'avaient oublié. "Savez-vous qui je suis? Me connaissez-vous?" "Nous ne savons pas." "Autrefois j'étais votre fils et vous m'avez tué." Alors son père et sa mère furent frappés de stupeur. Il garda son père dans une maison. Sa mère, il la fit enterrer sur le chemin, jusqu'au cou, et *sur la tête qui sortait de terre, il fit passer toutes les vaches, tous les ânes et toutes les mules.*

REMARQUES

La mère du *Grazmach* Duré nous raconte une histoire familière à l'éthiopisant. Il y est question de serpents monstrueux, auxquels des jeunes filles sont offertes en tribut; un héros tue les serpents, sauve les victimes, épouse une des jeunes filles et devient, plus tard, roi. Nous pourrions reconnaître ici le grand mythe éthiopien — la mort du serpent — qu'il est d'usage d'interpréter comme un récit étiologique, puisque dans ses versions les mieux connues — celles qui sont marquées du sceau de la tradition savante locale et en particulier celle du *kǝbrǝ-nägäst* — le meurtre du serpent, dieu et roi, fonde à la fois la victoire du christianisme et la légitimité dynastique des Salomonides.[21]

Mais ce qu'elle nous raconte encore c'est l'histoire d'un héros, castré par son propre père et qui se venge plus tard par un acte équivalent; il fait décapiter sa mère incestueuse. Entre temps il n'achève pas seulement le serpent, par le fer et par le feu; il retrouve un sexe, fait de terre; il provoque la mort de son beau-père, qu'on ensevelira vif, et il fait enterrer sa mère jusqu'au cou. Cette part de l'histoire n'accompagnant généralement pas les versions déjà connues de la "mort du serpent" nous pourrions soupçonner la narratrice d'avoir confondu deux récits. Le soupçon ne serait pas sans fondement, s'il est vrai que ce récit renvoit à d'autres mythes; mais il n'exclut pas la cohérence de ce texte, bien clos, dont tous les éléments se répondent parfaitement. Ce texte nous amène alors à remettre partiellement en question l'analyse historique qui prévaut dans l'interprétation des nombreuses "morts du serpent" en Ethiopie.

"La mort du serpent"; c'est un mythe classique d'Ethiopie septentrionale que nous résumerons en rappelant la récente schématisation qu'en ont donnée M. M. Denais et Perret.[22] Partant d'une version qu'ils ont collectée dans le Tigré en 1974, et la confrontant à neuf autres versions déjà éditées, M. Perret propose un essai d'analyse qui nous rappelle les séquences essentielles du mythe, tel qu'il était jusqu'ici connu: la naissance du serpent, le règne du serpent, la conspiration, le meurtre du serpent et le changement de dynastie (en fait, la première séquence n'apparaît que dans trois des dix versions analysées). Les versions les plus connues de ce mythe concernent le règne du serpent Arwe, qui peut être effectivement considéré, dans la tradition éthiopienne, comme la préhistoire de la dynastie salomonide.[23] Le nom de ce serpent apparaît souvent en tête des listes royales et il est d'usage qu'un auteur populaire éthiopien entame un ouvrage d'histoire par le récit du roi serpent.[24]

De ce fait nous avancerons que l'interprétation politique du mythe, considéré comme un moyen de légitimation dynastique, constitue moins une analyse qu'une simple réplique du discours historique éthiopien; cette interprétation fait elle-même partie du mythe et elle en occulte tous les autres sens possibles.

L'état de nos connaissances ne permet pas d'envisager une analyse de la mythologie éthiopienne, à moins que nous nous contentions de reprendre les interprétations qu'en a donnée, *a posteriori*, la tradition chrétienne d'Ethiopie. Mais ces interprétations là constituent en fait un développement nouveau de ces mythes, qu'il fallait ancrer dans un contexte culturel nouveau, avec la christianisation du pays; ce ne sont pas des analyses. Qu'un simple texte comme celui qui est présenté ici puisse modifier l'acquis d'une interprétation devenue classique, c'est que nous n'avons pas assez de données. Jusqu'ici les différentes versions du mythe du serpent venaient pratiquement toutes du nord de l'Ethiopie et ont été analysées dans le cadre étroit de l'histoire de l'Empire chrétien. Or, cette Ethiopie là, par sa tradition écrite, religieuse puis séculière, façonne depuis des siècles les mythes dont elle a hérités, avant d'être chrétienne, pour imposer de nouvelles interprétations, mais de si magistrale manière que ces interprétations passent aussi pour des analyses. De plus, ce mythe n'est pas propre à l'Ethiopie et, dans ce pays même, il peut apparaître sous des formes trop riches pour y voir un simple moyen de légitimation dynastique.

Pour la narratrice de Bonké, l'histoire en question n'est d'ailleurs pas un mythe de fondation dynastique, notre héros n'étant qu'un roi de légende, sans sujets ni terroirs connus des hommes; c'est au désert qu'il est roi. Le héros castré ne devient pas seulement roi — c'est somme toute secondaire au regard de la création — mais homme, époux et père; pour cela il franchit une série d'obstacles qui tous renvoient aux étapes élémentaires de la vie. Castré par son père, exclu du monde des hommes, il renaît des mains de la Déesse et s'impose à la société par une série d'épreuves qui l'opposent: au monstre naturel, (complice du père — n'est ce pas le roi, son père, que la fille accuse de l'avoir abandonnée au serpent), aux hommes (il se baignera nu parmi eux), à son beau-père (qu'il vaincra dans un tournoi) et à ses père et mère, réel ou classificatoire. Ajoutons que les Gamo, comme beaucoup de leurs voisins, possèdent des mythes de fondation dynastique sans aucun rapport avec la mort du serpent qui nous est racontée ici. Bon nombre de ces mythes ont été publiés par W. Lange[25] et nous en avons plusieurs versions semblables chez les Gamo et les Wollaita. Ceux-ci se ramènent à deux schémas: selon certains de ces textes les premiers rois ont surgi de la terre que leurs descendants théoriques dominent encore; selon les autres, les rois sont les lointains rejetons d'immigrants devenus usurpateurs.

Ce texte nous donne alors à penser que l'épisode du serpent, détaché du contexte historico-politique prévalant en Ethiopie septentrionale, pourrait être réinterprété plus librement dans sa relation aux autres motifs mythiques composant le récit: la castration du héros, le façonnage d'un sexe de terre, le meurtre de la mère et la descente au désert, *bazo*, ce lieu sauvage où tout est possible à l'imagination des hommes; motifs qui réapparaissent dans d'autres récits éthiopiens.

NOTES

1. Depuis les travaux de Moreno les études sur les langues Ométo restent encore rares, à l'exception de la thèse du père Adams de la S.I.M., sur le Wollaita. Surtout, il n'existe aucun corpus en langue Ométo et le texte que je présente constitue la première publication d'un récit Ométo de cette importance, en caractères amharique. Nous n'avions jusqu'ici que des traductions de la bible et des manuels.

2. L. Desmarquest: *Notes prises au cours d'un séjour de trois semaines à Ochollo*, septembre 1970. Manuscrit.

3. A propos de cette politique qui n'est pas sans rapport avec celle de l'Union-Soviétique, cf: O. Kapeliuk, "Language policy in Ethiopia since the revolution of 1974", in *Asian and African Studies*, 1980, 14-3, pp.269-278.

4. Les Wollaita, comme je le faisais remarquer dans mon article d'*Abbay* no.11, ont une forte tendance à vouloir dominer leurs voisins Ométo. Pour cela, le prosélytisme religieux (par l'ex-S.I.M) et l'alphabétisation dans leur propre dialecte sont des moyens sans doute mineurs, mais qui donnent d'autant plus de force à leur action politique.

5. De son côté, le Ministère de la Culture tente une autre politique; au lieu de ramener les dialectes Ométo à la langue du Wollaita, il a confié à l'un de ses chercheurs, Ato Taddesse Wolde, le soin de rédiger un dictionnaire Ométo qui tienne justement compte de toutes les variantes dialectales.

6. Nous n'avons surtout pas modifier la valeur des 1^0 et 4^0 ordres, ainsi que le recommandent les auteurs de la campagne d'alphabétisation pour lesquels le *bä* amharique devient un *ba*, et le *ba* amharique un *bā*.

7. Nous traduisons *gomé* par tabou. Sur ce concept Gamo je renvoie à la seule étude encore disponible: D. Sperber, "The management of misfortune among the Dorzé", *Proceedings of the 5th Conference of Ethiopian Studies*, Chicago, 1978.

8. "Prendre femme" est pris, selon les contextes, dans les deux sens d'épouser et d'entretenir des rapports sexuels.

9. *Bazo*, traduit ici par désert, équivaut à l'amharique *bärähа*, le pays sauvage, en général les basses terres.

10. *Motsa*: les terres secondaires que les paysans Gamo pouvaient posséder à la périphérie du pays et qui constituaient parfois la première exploitation de leur fils aîné.

11. *Gira*: le terme a les deux sens d'offrande et de tribut. Il désigne par exemple aujourd'hui aussi bien l'impôt que les offrandes aux génies de lieu.

12. Tendance courante chez les Gamo qui utilisent indifféremment les deux termes de *ka'o* — roi, et de *balabbat* — le chef dans la terminologie amhara utilisée au sud de l'Ethiopie.

13. *Wola*: un arbre de grande taille que je n'ai pas identifié.

14. "Un homme du chemin", très précisèment.

15. Le héros dit bien: "Mon père m'a tué", renvoyant au fait qu'il a été castré. De fait, chez les Gamo, un homme castré est considéré comme mort et doit s'exiler du pays.

16. Ce passage était originellement situé après le retour du bain.

17. La périphrase renvoit au concept de *magana*, substitution du protecteur à son protégé.

18. Cf. note 12.

19. *Gashé* ou *ṭef* en amharique.

20. Lamé ou *gäbäta* en amharique.

21. Wallis Budge: *The Queen of Sheba and her only son Menvelek*. Londres, 1922.

22. Denais et Perret: "La mort du serpent", in *Guirlande à Abba Jérome*. Paris, 1983, pp.117-153.

23. *Ibid.*

24. Même s'ils la tiennent pour légendaire les historiens Ethiopiens commencent très régulièrement leur récit par l'histoire du roi serpent.

25. W. Lange: *History of the southern Gonga*. Wiesbaden,1982.

THE RELIGIOUS AND KINSHIP IDEOLOGY

OF MILITARY EXPANSION AMONG THE BODI (MELA)

Katsuyoshi Fukui

The present paper[1] outlines the history of the Bodi, paying particular attention to the Mela population of the eastern plain of the Omo Valley. It also examines the relationship between the historical ideology and the aggression towards the hill farmers to the east.

Repeatedly, the Bodi have made violent attacks on the *Su* or hill farmers, especially their eastern neighbours, the Dime. There was a spate of such attacks on the latter in 1968-71, and more recently in 1975-76, coinciding with my stay in the field. How have such conflicts arisen? Or what kinds of elements correspond to such conflicts?

Two kinds of inter-tribal conflicts occur in the surrounding area. Firstly, mutual fighting between peoples dependent on similar subsistence economies — between the area's pastoralists. Secondly, one-sided attack on peoples with different subsistence economies — pastoral peoples raid sedentary farmers in the surrounding hills. These two types of conflict seem to alternate, so that, for instance, Bodi tend to avoid the second type of conflict while they are involved in the first, and *vice versa*. Thus, Bodi began to attack their eastern hill farmer neighbours in 1968, after the conflict around 1966 between the Hamar[2] and the Bodi with the Mursi[3], had come to an end, so that a time of general confusion had given way to a more settled period. However, when conflict between the Mursi and the Bodi revived in 1971, Bodi ceased attacking the Dime. These attacks on the hill farmers then recommenced in 1975-76, after peace was accepted by both Bodi and Mursi.

These conflicts must be viewed from various angles[4], taking into consideration, besides external relations, the internal organization of the groups involved. My argument in this paper concerns the connection between Bodi historical ideology and territorial expansion. They do not only look "back nostalgically to their glorious (if mythical) past"[5], but also forward towards the future through the process of their history, including perhaps some pseudo-history, whether or not they acknowledge it to be so.

"Conflict" referred to here, comprises four elements as follows[6]: (1) war, (2) feud, (3) raid and (4) killing. In the case of attacks by Bodi on hill farmers, for instance, we need specify no more than two of these, namely raiding (*gurin*) and killing (*lufa*)[7]. But seen from the viewpoint of the long-term trends of Bodi history, conflict is not confined to such elements, but may also imply territorial expansion on their part, at the expense of the hill farmers.

AROUND AND WITHIN THE BODI

The Bodi are found in the eastern plain of the Omo Valley of southwest Ethiopia. They depend economically on the cultivation of millet, besides animal products, although cattle are in many respects a central preoccupation of their society. The estimated human population is 2,500, living in the scattered wooded savanna extending over ca. 2,000 km^2.

The term "Bodi" is applied to the Me'en (Meken)[8] speaking peoples of the east bank of the Omo, by their eastern neighbours and by administrators. They, however, do not call themselves Bodi but *me'en* (*meken*) when referring to the whole of the population, *mela* or *chirim* when they specify either of these smaller units. The Mela live in the southern part of the plain, while the Chirim live mainly in the northern part. The clan composition of each reveals that the two groups have different histories, and they have recent experience of fighting between themselves. In their way of life, however, they are very similar, sharing a cultural as well as an economic commitment to cattle.

Me'en found in the western and northern areas of the Omo are collectively called Tishana, and consist of five groups: Baiti, Bokol, K'asha, Gabiyo and Nyomoni. They are said to be engaged mainly in agriculture.

The Bodi's southern neighbours are the Mursi, called by the Bodi *Mun* or *Dhaama*. The Mursi speak a language similar to the Bodi, about half of the basic vocabularies being common to both[9], and depend on almost the same subsistence economy. Also along the Omo are to be found the hunting-gathering Kwegu, called Idinit by the Bodi; these are in a relationship of submissive symbiosis with Bodi.

Two other groups that come into contact with Bodi are called by them *amar* and *su*. The Amar, or Hamar, living some distance to the east of Bodi-land, are an agro-pastoral people, sharing the Bodi's preoccupation with cattle. In contrast, *Su* is a collective term indicating "hill farmers". Such *Su* groups include the Dime, Malo, and Basketo to the east, the Dizi to the west, and other hill farmers nearby. Linguistically, both the Hamar and these various *Su* belong to the Omotic family.[10]

The traditional enemies (*baragara*) of the Bodi are the Mursi and the Hamar. The second in particular are dauntless foes of both Bodi and Mursi. There is also enmity between the Chrim and the Mela, in spite of the fact that they both speak the same language, Me'en. Moreover, the Hana-Mela are contemptuous of Gura-Mela in ordinary circumstances, while the Mela as a whole despise the Chirim. The Bodi, both Mela and Chirim, are also apt to despise the Tishana, the other Me'en speaking peoples to the west of the Omo. On the other hand, all Me'en-speakers despise Kwegu, Mursi and *Su*, but I have not heard contempt expressed for Hamar.

Mela-land is geographically divided into two areas: Hana and Gura. In Hana there is one *komorut* or chief, while at present Gura has two. It is said that there was another *komorut*-ship, now lapsed, in Gura, which no longer has any territory. The term *komorut* denotes not only a priest as mediator with God (*tumo*), but also a chief as owner of territory, and a decision-maker — though their political structure is basically of a gerontocratic order. I thus interpret *komorut* to mean a chief subsuming the role of priest. But in everyday life, Bodi uphold an "egalitarian spirit".

In pursuing the present topic, I henceforth concentrate on the Mela population, since it was in the Hana area that I stayed, and collected most of my information from the Mela.

HISTORICAL BACKGROUND OF THE MELA POPULATION

In this section I outline the historical background of the Mela. The data derive mainly from tracing the locations of tombs of various clan ancestors, referred to in their oral traditions. Elders of a clan are well informed about the location of the burial place of each of the clan's ancestors. Any tract of land — each ca. 4-5km^2 — is known by a name usually derived from some natural feature or cultural association. By matching movements referred to in their traditions against such place-names, it is not difficult to trace the course of their territorial expansion so far as these oral traditions permit. What I collected from them may be mixed with pseudo-historical statements, but it nevertheless constitutes the theoretical basis for Mela history, as Buxton (1963) pointed out in connection with the Mandari.

Present-day Mela-land (Hana and Gura) has three distinct elements of population, which have been assimilated over the years. The first is the earlier indigenous population, the second is the population of the Saigesi clan[11] and other clans, whose ancestors are believed to have conquered the present territory, and the third is made up of groups of gradual immigrants into the territory.

1. The indigenous population

The indigenous population is said to have consisted of the following three kinds of people: Idinit (Kwegu), Oimulit, and Proto-Mela. The Kwegu were engaged in a hunting-gathering economy, over a more extensive territory than today. Two of their clans, called Solgut (Kudhun) and Gali, have merged with the present Mela. The second people, the Oimulit, raised cattle and goats in the plain. However, they were driven away by the ancestors of Saigesi and their followers, going to Hamar country, and are therefore said to be ancestors to the Hamar. Only a few Mela are knowledgeable about the Oimulit.

On the other hand, concerning the Proto-Mela or "True Mela (*Mela chim*)" most Mela are much better informed. These consisted of three clans: Mineguwa, Ajit (Elma), and Kilingkabur. The Mela say that the present Mela-land belonged to them.[12]

The Mineguwa's seasonal movements were between a place called T'eba during the rainy season, and Mungu in the dry season; both of these places are situated between Gura and Mara. The Ajit (Elma) were moving to Kulu, between Gura and Mara, during the rainy season, and to Elma in the dry season. The Kilingkabur were moving between Wora near the Elma river during the rainy season, and Buchuwa at the junction of the Elma and Mago rivers in the dry season. When the ancestors of the Saigesi conquered these areas, the Kilingkabur[13] fled to Hamar or Karo territory, while the other two clans, Mineguwa and Ajit, merged with the present Mela.

2. Conquest by the Saigesi clan and their followers

a) Delkaro: the first invader

There was a chief (*komorut*) called Dobulkama in Sai near Maji. His son, Delkaro, and his followers moved into the Mara area at the present northern boundary of Mursi territory, looking for enough pasture for their cattle. At that time, the Mara area belonged to the Kwegu people, while the Mursi were in a place known as Lukui in the lower part of the Omo. The Kwegu were angered by the invasion of their territory by such immigrants, and attacked them at night, killing Delkaro. Delkaro's group consisted of four clans: Timbach, Gilgu, Limech and Golme. Delkaro's body was buried at a spot called Lechelugu, and a bull, with a *seroji* (mixed colour) hide, was slaughtered for him.

b) Jalugu: a woman chief

There was no chief for a year following the death of Delkaro. The next year, Dobulkama from Sai became chief, but was soon rejected by the group. Then Delkaro's younger sister, Jalugu, was installed as chief. During the Jalugu era, she and her group stayed at Lechelugu for three years, and at Kologa for four years. But there were constant disputes among them. Before long, Delkaro's half-brother, Tugoloni, came from Sai, and there was talk of making him chief, but he refused. Meanwhile, however, the group supporting him continued to grow in size. Then, although Jalugu had tried to move into Mara with her followers, she was drowned in the Omo during the rainy season.

c) Tulogoni: the first conqueror of Mela-land

Those who had stayed in Lechelugu were often attacked by the Kwegu, and asked Dobulkama of Sai to help them. After three days, he arrived with his son Tugoloni and his younger brother Gartaso. Dobulkama advised a return to Sai, which Tugoloni refused to do. In consequence, Tugoloni and Gartaso decided to settle in the Mara area, to which they brought their families and livestock. At the same time, the people of the Gula clan immigrated from Sai, and those of the Marka clan from a place called Dilga near Sai. The group who had remained in Lechelugu gathered together and moved into Mara, where Tugoloni and others were already staying.

On the fourth day after settling there, they slaughtered a head of cattle to install Tugoloni as a *komorut*. Seven days later, they attacked the Kwegu in Mara, Hana, and Sigidan in the northern part of the Omo Valley. They killed some and captured others for partial exchange for cattle with Gabiyo-Me'en to the west of the Omo. The descendants of the Kwegu who became servants (*gaima*) to Tugoloni, have remained in Sigidan to this day.

Gartaso died from sickness at Talba towards the lower part of Hana. Meanwhile, Tugoloni and his group attacked the Mursi, who ran away to the south, after he had moved into Zingei, on the lower part of the Mara river. Then he moved to Oso (Saala) in the middle section of the Mago river, and to Tutubach in Gura. Finally, Tugoloni died at Dhaama in the Hana area, and his tomb, constructed of large stones, is at a place called Chobur near Dhaama. The descendants of Saigesi (Ulkui) continue to pay visits there to make offerings of cow's milk and blood, tobacco and coffee at the tomb of Tugoloni, their ancestor.

d) Movements of succeeding komoruts

Gidankaro, Tugoloni's eldest son, was after his death installed in his place. After his installation, Gidankaro, who had been born in the Oso, moved to Tekawoch in Gura, then to Ch'ao near the Oso, and died from sickness at Chamowa in Gura. Gidankaro's eldest son, Tulka, was installed after him, but was killed by foreign armies in the Oso. His younger half-brother, Tunto, succeeded (*alichasedo*) to his office, and moved to Gorku in the Hana area. He died at Jomeli at the lower end of the Hana river. He had six wives, his period in office, though, was very short.

Tulka's eldest son, Moine, was then installed as *komorut*, and moved to Kanchuwa in the Hana area, then to Kelechuchu at the lower end of the same area. His place of death is not known, however. Dhalichbhagoloni, Moine's eldest son, was born at Moizu in the Hana area. He was installed after Moine's death, later moving to Jakuku and Delmagoloni and finally dying at a place called Selo; all these places are located in the Hana area. He is said to have been a great *komorut*, with five wives. Since this time, his descendants have come to be called Biolugu, after the name he bore as a young man.

After Dhalichbhagoloni's death, his younger brother Bulasera succeeded to his office, but his period in office was very short; he died at Bol (Gerfa), the southernmost village in Dimeland. He was succeeded by Galamogut, Dhalichbhagoloni's eldest son, who moved near Dildi to the west of Bol. His older half-brother, Gunaremo, fought with him and became *komorut* of the Gura area, splitting away from him; this Gura *komorut*-ship has passed in Gunaremo's agnatic line to the present day.

Finally, Galamogut died at a place named Lalanyu, between Hana and Gura. As his eldest son had previously died of sickness, his second son Kangadibhonga succeeded; he later moved to Alumu in the Chirim's territory, raiding cattle from them. Afterwards, he moved to a place called Suluchu near Sigidan, in the Kwegu area; eventually, he was killed by Esku, later a successor to the Gura *komorut*-ship.

RELIGIOUS AND KINSHIP STRATEGIES FOR THE MERGING OF POPULATIONS

The above oral tradition, perhaps bolstered by pseudo-historical elaboration, appears to form the basis for present-day Mela ideology. The office of *komorut* passes through the agnatic line, but only sons born to mothers from five particular clans qualify for installation: Timbach, Mineguwa, Ajit, Gali and Gerf. Girls belonging to these clans may decorate themselves with the same kind of red necklace, called *gala*, as *komoruts* wear. Among these five, only one — Timbach — originated in Sai, having immigrated with Delkaro, the first Saigesi invader. The others are clans whose ancestors belonged to peoples conquered by the Saigesi. Two, Mineguwa and Ajit, belong to the former indigenous population termed "*Mela chim*" (True Mela). A fourth, Gali, is one of the clans of the Kwegu, the hunter-gatherers found along the Omo Valley. The fifth, Gerf, is Dime, the hill farmers to the east. A son born to a mother from any other clan is ineligible to be installed. The ancestors of a clan called Irsach immigrated with the first Saigesi invader, Delkaro, whose mother belonged to this clan. However, he was killed by a Kwegu poisoned arrow while invading the eastern bank of the Omo, so that the son of a mother from the Irsach clan can no longer be a *komorut*, even if he is the eldest son of a *komorut* father.

Let us, as an example, examine the wives, and the positions of their respective sons, of a recent *komorut* in Hana. His first wife belonged to Ajit, one of the "qualifying" clans, but she died after giving birth to a daughter only. It is said that had she given birth to a son, he would have been a *komorut*. As his second wife belongs to the Dombuloch clan, ancestors of which immigrated from Sai, her son has been rejected as *komorut* by the Hana people. His third wife belongs to Ajit, like his first. The present *komorut*, named Oikabur, is her eldest son. His fourth wife belongs to Gulach, a clan from the Chirim, so her son cannot be a *komorut* despite his being older than Oikabur. His fifth wife belongs to Gali, from the Kwegu, another of the "qualifying" clans, but her son died soon after being nominated as *komorut*, before Oikabur was installed.

While the Mela, led mainly by the Saigesi clan, have absorbed the peripheral peoples as servants, through conquest, they try to demonstrate their history and identify themselves with their homeland, Sai, by way of a ritual. After the installation of a *komorut*, he and his followers go to Sai near Maji to hold this ritual jointly with the chief of their putative country of origin, he himself also claiming descent from the same remote ancestors as the *komoruts* of Mela-land. It is interesting to note here that, besides this chief, it is a head of the Kwegu who takes charge of the ritual. They slaughter a male calf and purify each other with the blood. Then they purify the Mela-land *komorut*, and place a piece of the peritoneum, and a special necklace made of six or eight stones dipped in the blood, around the *komorut*'s neck. Lastly the Sai chief gives a black cow to the Mela *komorut* — over which he has sprayed sour milk by blowing it from his mouth — and also two calabashes used during the ritual. The Kwegu head, called the *gaima* (servant) of the *komorut*, drives the cow, together with the calabashes, back to Mela-land.

When they reach the *komorut*'s compound, they slaughter a further male calf and purify the necklace stones brought back from Sai. It is also worth noting that it is the Kwegu head and the Hana *komorut* who take charge of this ritual. Such cows brought back from Sai are called *bheliyach*, and have a particularly important role: milk from a *bheliyach* cow (which title is inherited through the female line by her progeny) is used in rituals to confer fertility on plants and animals, and upon the human population. The *komorut* sprays sour milk over his cattle every morning and evening, and also over members of his following in certain rituals — for example, before leaving to fight, and after killing enemies, they are purified in this manner.

THE UNDERCURRENTS OF POPULATION MOVEMENT

Whether the conquest was a real historical event or merely a myth, it plays an important role in forming the basic ideology of the Mela. It explains why the putative descendants of those ancestors who are believed to have come from outside to conquer Mela-land, continue to return to their "home country" in a demonstration of their history. The special cows they bring back reaffirm their origins and their subsequent assimilations.

We should not assume here that a population consists of separate and impervious units, but as being in a state of flux with neighbouring peoples, merging one with another at one stage, separating at another. And yet, most instances can be seen to comply with their implicit rules, or historical ideologies, whether these are consciously known or not.

The object of conflict is not, of course, conflict for its own sake, but the results. For the Bodi, one of the principal results appears to be the effect on their territories.[14] At a glance, however, it is not possible to observe such movement at any juncture, unlike movements of livestock. Because any change in an external boundary is a matter of great concern for their very existence, it might well be impossible to expand a territory by means of no more than a few conflicts, unless there were a major military imbalance between the two populations. It may be comparatively straightforward to displace a few persons, much harder to displace an entire population from a territory when the two parties to conflict are almost equally well armed. The best solution is to compromise with their opponents from a position of advantage in the aftermath of a series of attacks.

This suggestion accords with Turton's hypothesis regarding Mursi-Bodi relations[15] and Tornay's on population movements in the lower Omo[16], though both suffer a certain lack of historical data. A similar movement seems to be taking place by the Mela at the expense of their hill farmer neighbours.[17] Characteristics of the Mela strategy is not just to expand territorially, but to absorb former opponents into their society in relations of submissive symbiosis, by means of affinal kinship links.[18]

Recent conflict between the Mela and Chirim provide an illustration of this process. They fought for two years nearly two generations ago, when Zoge, the present *komorut*'s grandfather's cross-cousin, succeeded as chief after the previous *komorut*'s death. After this, all the Chirim are alleged to have fled to Nyomonit-land beyond the Omo, remaining there for three years. One evening,a *komorut* of the Chirim came to the compound, in Hana of the succeeding Mela *komorut* (father of the present one). He said: "Now our conflict is over. I offer one of my daughters to you. I will be your servant (*gaima*)". After this, many Chirim came to cultivate the fields of the Hana *komorut*, and stayed there for about ten years. The daughter of the Chirim *komorut* was purified with cattle's blood so as to be wife to the Hana *komorut*. Her eldest son, slightly older than the present *komorut*, always moved his compound in concert with him, even though other members are constantly separating from or merging with the chief's compound.

However, the hill farmers had yet to offer any girls to the present *komorut* — at any rate up to my departure from the country — although they had provided beer and labour to cultivate his fields while I was there.

IN AN ETHNOSYSTEM

The internal organisation, including the ideology derived from the historical process, determines the external relations, and *vice versa*. From the broad historical perspective, violent attacks by the Mela against farmers to their east are not resumed merely to raid for livestock, and to carry out killings according to a code derived from their favourite oxen (see Fukui, 1979), but also to support a historical ideology of territorial expansion. We see, from this Mela example, that a population may be said to be in continuous process, during which it assumes various forms. As part of the process, their own historical ideology with regard to their external relations may determine through which transitional forms the society will pass. A society is an element, with its own internal organisation, of a larger system the parts of which are connected organically to each other, interrelating and developing together as a whole in an *ethnosystem*, a concept analogous to that of "ecosystem".

NOTES

1. Field data used here were collected between 1973 and 1976, and the work was financed by the Institute for the Study of Languages and Cultures of Asia and Africa, Tokyo University of Foreign Studies (1973-75), and by the Toyota Foundation (1975-76). Grateful acknowledgment is made to them. Sincere thanks are also owed to Professor Maurice Bloch, who has commented on this paper during his stay in Osaka.

2. See Lydall (1976).

3. See the concrete data on conflict between Mursi and the Hamar, and between Mursi and Bodi, in Turton (1979).

4. See Fukui and Turton (1979).

5. Beattie (1971: 58).

6. Fukui (1984).

7. Elsewhere (Fukui 1979), I describe the relationship between inter-tribal homicide and favourite oxen among the Bodi.

8. Me'en belongs linguistically to the Surma group of East Sudanic languages.

9. Fifty-three percent of basic vocabularies between the Bodi and Mursi languages are the same (Bender 1971).

10. Fleming (1976).

11. The Mela have several names for each clan (*kabchoch*), based on their oral tradition. For instance, another name for Saigesi is Ulkui.

12. The ancestors of another clan, Kirijach, should be among these Proto-Mela according to their oral tradition. I think that they tend to avoid mentioning this because the clan belongs to the *komo* moiety, which is the agnatic line of one of the Gura *komoruts*.

13. *Kilingkabur* is also the name of an imaginary monster, believed to be the ancestor of the Kilingkabur clan wiped out by the Saigesi and their followers, and this creature is much feared by present-day Mela.

14. On this subject, Tornay's suggestion that territorial conquest is characteristic of sedentary peoples, seems to be contradicted by his final remark regarding northward movements (Tornay 1979: 115-6).

15. See Turton (1979: 196-7): "Thus, holding a peace-making ceremony at a certain spot may be a way of making . . . a claim to *de jure* ownership of territory which was formerly owned only in a *de facto* sense . . . In other words, it is these movements which bring about periodic wars, and not the wars which make possible the movements."

16. Tornay's conclusion (1979:116) is also of great interest in this connection: "These conflicts are to be seen as a particular moment in a major process of tribal evolution; the movement northwards seems to affect not only the Nyangatom, but also their neighbours along the river, from the shores of Lake Turkana to the Ethiopian Plateau. This drift might ultimately be attributable to inescapable contradictions between lowland pastoralism and highland agriculture."

17. This suggestion receives tacit support from Todd, who has carried out fieldwork among the Dime, the Mela's hill farmer neighbours (Todd 1979). According to him, Dime herded their numerous cattle in the lowlands near the Bodi, but since the war, the Bodi have moved into Dime-land on a large scale. He summarises: "the war has led to increasing Bodi encroachment on Dime territory, as well as a diminution of the Dime population" (Todd 1979: 211).

18. Beattie suggests that such a conceptual unity, whereby matrilateral links are transformed into patrilateral ones, is to be found more universally in patrilineal societies (Beattie 1971: 60).

BIBLIOGRAPHY

Beattie, John 1971   *The Nyoro State*. Oxford: Clarendon Press.

Bender, M. Lionel 1971   "The Languages of Ethiopia: A New Lexico-statistics Classification and Some Problems of Diffusion", *Anthropological Linguistics*, 13 (5): 165-288.

Buxton, J. C. 1963   *Chiefs and Strangers: a Study of Political Assimilation among the Mandari*. Oxford: Clarendon Press.

Fleming, Harold C. 1976   "Omotic" in Bender, M. Lionel, Bowen, J. Donald, Cooper, Robert L., and Charles A. Ferguson (eds.), *Language in Ethiopia*. Oxford University Press.

Fukui, Katsuyoshi 1979 "Cattle Colour Symbolism and Inter-Tribal Homicide among the Bodi" in K. Fukui and D. Turton (eds.), *Warfare among East African Herders*. Senri Ethnological Studies (SES), 3: 147-177.

——————— 1984 "Intertribal Relation through Conflict: the Pastoral Meken (Bodi) in South-West Ethiopia". *The Japanese Journal of Ethnology*, 48(4): 471-480.

Fukui, Katsuyoshi and David Turton (eds.) 1979 *Warfare among East African Herders*. Senri Ethnological Studies (SES), 3, National Museum of Ethnology, Osaka.

Lydall, J. 1976 "Hamar" in M. L. Bender (ed.), *The Non-Semitic Languages of Ethiopia*, African Studies Center, Michigan State University, 393-438.

Todd, Dave 1979 "War and Peace between the Bodi and Dime of Southwestern Ethiopia" in K. Fukui and D. Turton (eds.), *Warfare among East African Herders*. SES, 3: 211-225.

Tornay, Serge 1979 "Armed Conflicts in the Lower Omo Valley, 1970-1976: An Analysis from within Nyangatom Society" in K. Fukui and D. Turton (eds.), *op. cit.*: 97-117.

Turton, David 1979 "War, Peace and Mursi Identity" in K. Fukui and D. Turton (eds.), *op. cit.*: 179-210.

THE QEMANT THEOCRATIC CHIEFDOM IN THE

ABYSSINIAN FEUDAL STATE

Frederick C. Gamst

INTRODUCTION

The politico-religious institutions of the Qemant, a pre-Christian people of central Ethiopia, are the subject of this paper.[1] Although the Qemant were subordinated for centuries as an emergent peasantry within the feudal Abyssinian state, their underlying political integration was still manifest: that of a *theocratic chiefdom*. (For detailed explanation of the superordination of the *feudal Abyssinian state* over the Qemant tribalist-peasants, see Gamst 1969, 1970, 1974: 3-19.) The conceptual framework of theocratic chiefdom used in this paper follows the model of Elman Service (1975) and is augmented with ideas of other theoretically related ethnologists.

Given the wide acceptance in social science of the Marxian theory of the state, grounded in repressive social force and functioning to maintain state organization while protecting the interests of a ruling elite, a question arises. What kind of polity stands antecedent to the agrarian state and its elite? Considered both in terms of cultural evolution and social structure, a chiefdom is a very common polity, existing between the primal familistic egalitarian society and the relatively recent coercive state. The chiefdom is a centralized political institution of a territory and is permanent, hierarchical, and generally hereditary. Unlike the state, it has no formal legal mechanisms of compelling physical sanctions for directing behavior to some public goal. Thus, the chiefdom is relatively uncoercive. The chiefdom's legitimization is sacrosanct, hence, theocratically legal, and grounded in religious ideology and related customs and etiquette. "In a chiefdom, we find one essential of true law, the authority structure that can act as a third party above the familistic level" (Service 1975: 86). A chiefdom, then, can adjudicate conflict between kin-based groups, such as lineages.

The multi-village chiefdom developed out of segmental autonomous communities of semi-nomadic bands and settled villages (cf. Carniero 1978: 205-207; Oberg 1955: 484).[2] The centralization of social power in the chiefdom was undoubtedly the most revolutionary event in sociocultural evolution. Thus, a more efficient social control and reorganization (than that which previously obtained in egalitarian kinship-based societies) took hold of human groups, and, concomitantly, of the geographic environment. A new cultural process was unleashed on this earth, the dynamics of the chiefdom. This ecologically highly adaptive social organization put humans on the path to destructively dominating all other species of organisms and to firmly adapting environment to themselves (instead of vice versa, as with other organisms).

We analyze the Qemant's underlying political institutions to depict their theocratic chiefdom and, thereby, add to understanding of this type of polity. These Qemant institutions are ethnographically the most extensive of the pre-state hierarchical polities of any of the Central Ethiopians (cf. Murdock 1959: 181-187) now extant. The Qemant chiefdom survives into the present because these people posed no military antagonism to the all-powerful Amhara, who, consequently, built their permanent state capital, Gonder, in the midst of this long-time vassal population (Gamst 1969: 16, 117).

THEOCRATIC POWER

Although militarily efficient, the essence of the chiefdom is theocratic power.[3] Chiefdom "organization seems universally to be theocratic, and the form of submission to authority that of a religious congregation to a priest chief" (Service 1975: 16). Accordingly, apart from the authority of the Abyssinian state superimposed in recent centuries, the Qemant are unified and controlled by the religious ideology of their chiefdom. For the Qemant, as in typical chiefdoms, the worship of a high god is codified and made part of a cult applicable to all (cf. Sahlins 1968:

110-111). Specifically, Qemant ideology centers around a sky-father god, Mezgana, and a pantheon of related other spirits and ancestral culture heroes. The religion justifies the rule of an elite, restricted to certain lineages, over the children of Mezgana, as Qemant call themselves. A mixture of religious frightening by, and divine inspiring of, this elite (cf. Service 1975: 296-297) provides their mechanisms of power. Accordingly, in the chiefdom, authority and sanctions need not be secular but can be supernatural (Service 1975: 91). Despite possessing only sacred authority, the Qemant chief is a true authority — his power is that of a power-acknowledging group rather than a power-usurping individual.

The Qemant chief, called *wambar*, regulates the everyday activities of Mezgana's children by proclaiming new or enforcing old religious days of fast or of rest from work. He gives permission for ceremonial marriage and divorce. For violators of both religious prescriptions and secular mores, the *wambar* invokes sanctions ranging from public ridicule, to corporal penance, to fines, to ostracism and banishment, to supernatural maledictions reaching beyond the grave. Such acts of a *wambar* are always couched in the lore and law of Mezgana's religion. A *wambar's* legitimization of power and Qemant religion are thus part of a seamless politicoreligious web. Powers of adjudication of a *wambar* mediate disputes both within and between kinship-organized groups, thereby maintaining public peace and security. And in the more distant past, he also protected against external threats, for example, against the Falasha. In all, the *wambar*, as wielder of sacral authority upheld and augmented the rules of conduct and equity, saw to their enforcement, and judged those who broke them or disputed their interpretation. (A central meaning of the Qemant word *wambar* is "judge".)

CHIEFDOMS AND CHIEFS

As with classic chiefdoms, among the Qemant large chiefdoms consist of smaller ones, replicas of the greater grouping (Service 1975: 95-96). The degree of dependence versus autonomy of the constituent minor Qemant chiefdoms within the greater chiefdoms waxed and waned with the power and circumstances of the superior chiefs. There were two superior chiefs, or *wambars*, that of Karkar for the territory east of the Guwang River of Gonder province and that of Chelga for the territory to its west. The Karkar *wambar* was *paramount* and he validated, and at time blocked, the confirmation in office of the Chelga *wambar*. A *superior wambar* had a number of subordinate *area wambars*, each controlled one or more of the Qemant's internally dispersed communities.

Subordinated to the various *wambars*, who had high rank, are a number of middle-ranked officers. These include a higher priest, or *kamazana*; a lower priest, or *abayegariya*; and a more secular spokesman, or *afaliq*, who enforces the directives or levies the fines of a *wambar*. (It appears that in the distant past the spokesman was a war-and-police subchief.) A number of low-ranked officers exist also. Chiefs, middle-ranked office holders (except for the lower priest), and some of the low-ranked offices belong to the socially superior Keber moiety, and the rest to the socially inferior Yetanti moiety of Qemant society.

The office of *wambar* is impersonal, corporate, and "generally" hereditary, that is, based on selection of and by elite from high status priestly families. Certain patrilineages supply the office holders of the chiefdom. Thus, Qemant society, as with other chiefdoms, is hierarchical. At the apex of the pyramid of five social strata are members of the Keber and, then, Yetanti chiefly elites who hold the politicoreligious positions of leadership. Below these elites are the commoners of the Keber moiety and then those of the Yetanti moiety. Before the 1920s, a still lower social stratum of hereditary non-Qemant slaves existed. Elite receive deference from commoners and slaves. Keber receive deference from Yetanti and both are offered it by slaves. However, in the Qemant chiefdom, with its sacred authority, there is no true class society, as there is in the state, with its rulers who monopolize legitimate violent force and control land, the means of production, thereby suppressing the commoners. But in the social inequality of the Qemant chiefdom, the chiefly families have greater access to resources.

Among classic chiefdoms: "The chiefly line is usually considered the direct descendants of the founder of the line and of the society as a whole, now exalted in status as a major deity"

(Service 1975: 78). Actually, among the Qemant the apical ancestors of the chiefly lines are semi-deified culture heroes. Deference to a *wambar* is shown in maintaining certain etiquette and taboo. All commoners keep a social distance from him. Choice, ceremonial portions of meat are reserved for him. Although his priests sacrifice animals in ceremonies and his spokesmen wield weapons in strife, a *wambar* can kill no animal and hold no weapon, even a common knife. When he eats, someone must cut his meat for him. A woman may not give birth in or near his houses, thereby polluting his hallowed grounds.

CHIEFLY WEALTH AND REDISTRIBUTION

The wealth of each *wambar* and middle-ranked officer is derived in large part from the three days of corvée (consisting of plowing, weeding, and harvesting) each receives as an obligation of all commoners. Such corvée goes to each community priest from his own community or subcommunity, to each area *wambar* from his area, and to each superior *wambar* from his half of Qemantland. Additionally, each superior *wambar* receives tribute from his area *wambars*, and the paramount *wambar* receives small symbolic payments from the other superior *wambar*. All Qemant leaders get monetary and in kind payments for performing ceremonies. Additionally, the superior *wambars* receive monetary payments for adjudication of litigation, and for confirmation of the leadership positions of the Qemant chiefdom and of the lowest ranked administrative positions of the feudal stated superimposed on Qemantland. Through his prestige and authority, a superior *wambar* could activate more claims to arable land and through the vast amounts of corvée obligated to him, could cultivate more acreage than the wealthiest commoner. However, all of the great wealth of a superior *wambar* and considerable wealth of an area *wambar* were not entirely at the disposal of his own family consumption.

All classic chiefdoms have a redistributive economic system. This still exists for the Qemant, although by the 19th century, the market mode of exchange had become as important, and then more important.[4] Ethiopian grains store well and other food resources can be stored in the form of livestock. These storable foodstuffs, salt-bar money and, especially, corvée were collected by area and superior *wambars*, largely for eventual redistribution to Qemant society. Some of the labor went into maintaining public trails, but most went into cultivation for the *wambars'* food stores. The wealth of the *wambars* was redistributed to or for all: at frequent public ceremonies in the form of feasts, in the entertainment of important visitors, for welfare to those in need and, in the distant past, for feeding Qemant warriors in the service of the superior *wambars*, or through them, the Abyssinian emperor. This wealth also supported the chiefly families and the institution of chieftainship and enhanced the religious rites. In the 18th century and earlier, the *wambars* through their redistributive network also facilitated interarea trade. For example, cotton, for cloth, was exchanged out of low-elevation econiches into high-elevation ones having an abundance of livestock. But because in the 19th century markets had come to dominate interarea exchange within Qemantland, this trade was then outside of a *wambar's* control.

The yielding of small amounts of labor and produce by the commoner to the chiefly elite was not an onerous imposition. The commoner benefited directly in the participation in areal and community ritual feasts and in the honor and the prestige of being a religious benefactor. And he or she benefited indirectly in community well-being, cohesion and defense.

CONCLUSION

In all, the Qemant political system, underlying the former Abyssinian feudal state superimposed upon it and existing in part into the present, displays the characteristics of the classic chiefdom, an evolutionary type antecedent to the state. The Qemant polity was a theocracy, unified by religious ideology legitimating the rule of a generally hereditary elite and further reinforced by related custom and etiquette. Without possessing the state's repressive legitimate monopoly on physical coercion, the Qemant theocratic chiefdom, in common with the state, had a legitimate central authority: generating rules of conduct, enforcing them, and adjudicating infractions of them.

NOTES

1. Generally, this paper is written from the perspective of a cultural materialistic evolutionism, which has provided one theoretical base in American ethnology (cf. Sahlins and Service 1960; White 1966; Harris 1968: 142-249, 643-687; Gamst and Norbeck 1976). This evolutionism has strong roots in the scholarship of Lewis Henry Morgan and as such is related to other philosophies of social materialism. Accordingly, not in any way at odds with American cultural materialism is a central tenet from *A Contribution to the Critique of Political Economy*: "The mode of production in material life determines the general character of the social, political and spiritual processes of life. It is not the consciousness of men that determines their existence, but, on the contrary, their social existence determines their consciousness" (Marx 1904 [1859] : 12) (cf. Harris 1968: 228-241).

2. Central-Cushitic-speaking Agaw, horticultural communities in first-hand contact with the Aksumite and, later, the Abyssinian (Solomonoid) states lost their political autonomy as they were subjugated and incorporated into an expanding agrarian polity. More distant Agaw communities attempted to control access to Aksumite and Abyssinian trade and to defend against their military threat by establishment, for political survival, of supracommunity groupings, that is chiefdoms. Stronger Agaw villages must have controlled weaker ones in the early stages of this collective reaction to the expanding agrarian state. The stimulus of military and commercial contact with a state results in genesis of chiefdoms in a manner similar to the development hypothesized by Robert Carniero. He shows population pressure on circumscribed land as a generator of chiefdoms (Carniero 1970, 1978: 207-208). But with either internal population pressure or external state contact, warfare and other conflict is the mechanism of political evolution from segmental egalitarian to hierarchical chiefdom societies. The pressures of warfare toward chiefdom collectivities were all the more effective in the Horn of Africa, a region traditionally marked by extensive armed conflict (Gamst In Press). The central authority of a chiefdom enables it to wage war and maintain peace more effectively than in an egalitarian society (Service 1975: 100). Simply put, communities organized into chiefdoms were more adaptive to the political reality of the Horn than autonomous ones.

3. In surveying the aboriginal chieftains of the South American-Caribbean area, Julian Steward and Louis Faron (1959: 176-178) note two subtypes, "theocratic" and "militaristic". Each subtype has one of the characteristics more and the other less manifest. Both are attributes of chieftainships. However, although militarism is well developed in the chiefdom the basis of political power is theocratic: "under it the power to rule and the power or religion are one" (Wolf 1959: 79). The state's coercive use of a legitimate authority of law has not yet developed. "Theocratic legitimization, though perhaps inferior to monopoly of coercive force as an integrating device, was sufficient to overcome the internal stresses produced by accretions of wealth and position" (Webster 1976: 826). In a chiefdom, sacral sanction is used to wield political power, which thus has sacrosanct legitimization.

4. Ethnologists generally recognize three principal modes of allocation of goods and services. One is *market exchange* according to the law of supply and demand. The other two are forms of *status exchange*, because they are intertwined with the social status of those who exchange, that is, they are part of the rights and duties of group membership. The first of these two is *reciprocal exchange*, the giving of goods or services for those received. The second is the hallmark of a chiefdom, *redistributive exchange*. Redistribution has two elements. The first is inflow, or collection of some goods and labor to an administrative center, such as the community of a chief. The second is outflow, or distribution, that is the

reallotment of some part of these goods and labor to the people within the redistributive organization, for example, all or part of a chiefdom. The chiefly accumulation of goods and services "was a device whereby the inequalities of the environment and the ecological process were corrected by a centralized power" (Adams 1975: 243). The larger and denser the population and the larger the redistributive network was, the more powerful the redistributer (Harris 1983: 145-146), hence, the powerful superior *wambars* of the Qemant.

Most discussions of chiefdom redistribution emphasize goods and scarcely mention labor/services. But as Service notes: "The leadership can as easily require a certain amount of man-days per community for a public project as it can a certain portion of a crop" (1975: 96). Such a collection/inflow of labor provides for public works, such as Qemant maintenance of ways, and agricultural labor, also as among the Qemant, and for military conscription for defense and offense. Such control of territorial labor is quite difficult in the politically weaker egalitarian societies employing voluntary contributions (cf. Service 1975: 97). Finally, in contrast to many classic chiefdoms, none of the *wambars'* corvée was used for erecting monuments, perhaps, in part, because of the Qemants' sacred worship and burial groves of trees, which are pronounced natural monuments in a tree-bare landscape.

REFERENCES CITED

Adams, Richard N., 1975	*Energy and Structure: A Theory of Social Power.* Austin: University of Texas Press.
Carniero, Robert L., 1970	A Theory of the Origin of the State, *Science* 169: 733-738.
––––––––––– 1978	Political Expansion as an Expression of the Principle of Competitive Exclusion in *Origins of the State: The Anthropology of Political Evolution*, R. Cohen and E. R. Service, eds.: pp.205-223. Philadelphia: ISHI.
Gamst, Frederick C., 1969	*The Qemant: A Pagan-Hebraic Peasantry of Ethiopia.* New York: Holt, Rinehart and Winston.
––––––––––– 1970	Peasantries and Elites without Urbanism: The Civilization of Ethiopia. *Comparative Studies in Society and History* 12: 373-392.
––––––––––– 1974	*Peasants in Complex Society.* New York: Holt, Rinehart and Winston.
In Press	Conflict in the Horn of Africa in *Peace and War: Cross-Cultural Perspectives*. R. A. Rubinstein and M. L. Foster, eds. New York: Transaction Books.
Gamst, Frederick C. and Edward Norbeck, eds. 1976	*Ideas of Culture: Sources and Uses.* New York: Holt, Rinehart and Winston.
Harris, Marvin. 1968	*The Rise of Anthropological Theory: A History of Theories of Culture.* New York: Crowell.
––––––––––– 1983	*Cultural Anthropology.* New York: Harper and Row.
Marx, Karl. 1904 [1859]	*A contribution to the Critique of Political Economy.* [I. N. Stone, translator]. Chicago: International Library.

Murdock, George P. 1959   *Africa: Its Peoples and their Culture History*. New York: McGraw-Hill.

Oberg, Kalervo. 1955   Types of Social Structure among the Lowland Tribes of South and Central America. *American Anthropologist* 57: 472-487.

Service, Elman R. 1975   *Origins of the State and Civilization: The Process of Cultural Evolution*. New York: W. W. Norton.

Sahlins, Marshall D. 1968   *Tribesmen*. Englewood Cliffs, New Jersey: Prentice-Hall.

Sahlins, Marshall D. and   *Evolution and Culture*. Ann Arbor: The University of Michigan
Elman Service, eds. 1960   Press.

Steward, Julian H. and   *Native Peoples of South America*. New York: McGraw-Hill.
Louis C. Faron 1959

Webster, David L. 1976   On Theocracies. *American Anthropologist* 78: 812-828.

White, Leslie A. 1966   The Social Organization of Ethnological Theory. *Rice University Studies* 54 (4): 1-66.

Wolf, Eric R. 1959   *Sons of the Shaking Earth*. Chicago: University of Chicago Press.

THE POSITION OF WOMEN IN GUJI OROMO SOCIETY

John Hinnant

INTRODUCTION

The recent anthropological emphasis on the study of gender, which is due in part to factors outside the discipline, has led to a rethinking of the naturalness of gender differences. The general conclusion is that, beyond certain basic physiology, gender is a symbolic concept rather than a biological given.[1] In some parts of the world gender differences are minimized, whereas in others they not only are greatly emphasized but also form a major element in the metaphoric construction of cosmology.

The Guji Oromo of central Sidamo Governor Generalate, Ethiopia, fall into the latter category. When I first began fieldwork among them (in 1968), I was struck by the extreme status differences between the sexes. When walking down a path, all adult men precede all women. In some parts of Guji, women are relegated to the left side of the house, and their association with left is a negative one. Guji myths portray women as both stupid and the cause of disruption in the male-created order of things. In most ritual, men are the active agents while women are either passive recipients of male blessings or are merely preparers of the feast.

It was not until I had been in the field for a considerable period that I began to discover areas in which women, at least briefly, are dominant. These include some economic activities, arranging to elope rather than be 'properly' married to an undesirable suitor, the pitched battle of the marriage night, certain ritual activities, and the *garayu* (mistress-lover) relationship.

This paper explores the major realms of Guji life in which the statuses occupied by women are particularly important. It begins with a discussion of the portrayal of women in myth and cosmological concepts, then examines the effects of these ideas on the actual life cycle, and concludes with a discussion of ritual and social settings of female dominance.

MYTH AND COSMOLOGY

The central creation myth in Guji explains the origins of humans and of their travail:

> The first woman, Hawan, and the first man, Adani, fell to the earth from the sky (sky and god are both called *waka*). They landed at a spot called *elala* (he sees). God told them to enjoy the milk and honey of the earth, but forbade them to eat the fruit, *hidi*. One day the snake, *bofa*, came to Hawan and persuaded her that god was merely joking when he said not to eat the fruit. It was good to eat. Hawan later fed the *hidi* to Adani by disguising it. As he was swallowing the fruit god appeared and saw what had happened. He angrily asked Hawan, "Did I not tell you that this fruit was not to be eaten?" She replied, "*Bofa* told me that you did not mean it". God told her that he would punish her for disobeying. "In the future your blood will fall on the ground once every three months." "What, every month?" "No, every three months." "Every month?" "Yes, every month."
>
> God punished the snake like this. In the future when the snake gives birth the young will immediately disperse to the ends of the earth leaving their parents. The *hidi* will lose its sweetness and become bitter. Adani, who had been deceived, received no special punishment except that in the future all humans would be forced to struggle to live through dry seasons and wet seasons.

The second major myth relating to the nature of woman and man, as well as explaining the order of the contemporary world, concerns a mythic time when a queen ruled the land.

> Long ago there was a woman who was queen of all the people of the earth — the

Guji Darassa, Sidamo, Arussi, Borana. She was known as a very mean woman. People had to obey her because she was the queen and they must do what she told them. She was such a great queen that her husband had to carry their child on his back all the time. He had to draw water from the river and collect wood for the fire.

She gave the people a list of impossible jobs. First, they had to cut the strap used to tie loads on mules in half without using a knife — with their hands. After doing this, ruining the strap, they had to leave the area. But without the strap they could not leave, because they could not tie their belongings to the mule. She also told them to burn their houses.

There was a poor man who had no cattle and who lived by digging up nuts from the ground.

There was a meeting place. The men all had to carry the children on their backs when going to this place. The men went to the poor man and asked him for advice about how to do these impossible tasks they had been set. He could not tell them how to avoid cutting the leather and burning their houses, but he told them to consult him in the future.

The queen called the people to the meeting place and told them to find, and cut down, a pole that reaches to the sky. As the men were returning they came to the poor man who asked what the queen had said. They told him. He advised them the next day to go to her and ask for something with which to measure the pole.

Next, the queen asked the men to gather a sack of fleas. They went to the poor man. He asked what the queen had said. They told him. He advised them to fill a sack with cow dung and hang it over the fire that night. It filled with tiny dung flies, which look like fleas. They took the sack to the queen and fooled her with the fleas.

The queen and her husband were sitting side by side in the house. He had to hold the baby who was crying from hunger. Finally, the queen took the child to nurse. Then she gave it back. The husband then said that he was too tired to carry himself, much less the child. He offered to carry only his half of the child and drew his knife to cut it in half. She stopped him and from then onward women carried the child themselves.

Now the poor man told the men to each slaughter a white cow. The next day while the women were busy stretching the hides the men were to go to the meeting place, dig a deep hole and cover it with grass. And so, the next day the queen came to the meeting place. The men told her to come sit on the grass covering the hole. She fell into the pit and was buried.

Her final words were: "Now I am going to die. But first I say, women cheat your husbands. Pretend to respect them even though you do things against their rules."

In the first, the Guji creation myth, woman not only causes the world to become a place of travail but also foolishly causes menstruation to be more frequent than god originally intended. The association between woman, affinity, and snakes is a continual theme in Guji cosmology and ritual. It is also involved in a concept called *woyyu*. *Woyyu* is generally seen as a dangerous potency, associated with affinity, poisonous snakes, certain descent groups which have the powers to curse others, and the realm of nature outside the ordered world of (male-controlled) human society. *Woyyu* is also represented in the great *Kallu* of Guji, a man who represents the dimly perceived (and dangerous) creative forces of the universe. The *Kallu* lives in his own territory outside the eight phratries which constitute Guji society.[2]

The male-controlled realm of society, with reconciliation between people (*arrarsa*) and abundance through procreativity as its ideal state, is conceptualized by the contrasting concept *kayyo*. If *woyyu* presents the idea of a cosmos filled with dangerous but potentially useful powers and relationships (and of woman and affinity as problematic but essential), *kayyo* portrays a world of ordered society, properly run ritual, and general abundance (with woman, and the earth, a passive source of abundance).

The intent of the second story is clearly to justify male dominance and the division of labor. In this upside-down world, all work roles are reversed, with women controlling the political system. The behavior of the queen is arbitrary, malicious and inimicable to maintaining the social order. The poor man who outsmarts the queen is a marginal figure, a gatherer of wild plant food in a society of herdsmen, a liminal figure in van Gennep's and Turner's sense. He, being outside the social order, is able to transform it. The final message of the queen to the women is understood by men, in this often told story, to be an explanation for the origin of women's perceived deceitfulness.

GADA AND GENDER

The understanding of gender is further developed in the social and ritual institution of *gada*, which is or has been a central institution in many of the societies of southern Ethiopia. Since this paper is not directly concerned with the Guji *gada* system[3], for present purposes it need only be said that this 'generation grading' system is somewhat reminiscent of the 'age grade' systems found throughout much of Africa. It consists of a series of stages separated by rites of passage representing an ideal male life cycle. *Gada* is usually seen as an egalitarian system of organization, but even its most devoted adherents are unable to present it as egalitarian for both sexes. Women play largely passive roles in *gada* rituals (and in the conception of the life cycle contained in *gada*). Ultimately, *gada* is a male world of warriors, political leaders, and priests. Men achieve positions as the sacrificers in major rituals designed to maintain the well-being (*kayyo*) of society, while women play minor roles in a few ceremonies as wives and mothers. Women passively receive the benefits of sacrifice.

THE LIFE CYCLE

The life cycle observed during my fieldwork (1968-1971) is presented below. The position of women as the property of men — first fathers, then husbands — will become clear. It should also become apparent that women have ways of circumventing this male-controlled order.

Birth and Childhood

When a woman believes she is pregnant, "when the child is like water in the stomach," she calls in a midwife to confirm her self-diagnosis. Once the pregnancy is verified, the woman begins a period of seclusion during which she avoids her normal work[4] and is encouraged to eat a variety of foods (rather than being subjected to dietary prohibitions). When other people are present they avoid making any loud noise since it is believed that if the woman is startled she will abort. None of her kinsfolk or affines may discuss abortion or abnormal childbirth.

Later, when labor begins, the husband and wife squat facing on opposite sides of the main house pole (*otuba waka*)[5] while grasping each other's hands. Husbands report that they feel stomach pains while their wives are in labor. When the baby's head and shoulders appear, the husband must leave the house, and the rest of the delivery is assisted by the midwife. Once the baby is freed, she touches its head to the earth and says *"har'da lafa"* (mother is earth); then lifting its head heavenward she says *"abba waka"* (father is god or sky).

The father is called in to cut the umbilicus and then must leave again. The afterbirth and umbilicus are buried in the back of the house near the shrine (*boro*). Later, when the remaining umbilicus has dried and is removed from the baby, it is put in a container of coffee or barley. At this time the hair of the baby is cut and added to the mixture, which is either stored permanently in the household shrine or fed to cattle.

For the first few days after giving birth, the mother remains indoors, attended only by women. Those who enter her house bring barley and *insete* which are mixed with milk or butter and fed to her. After three days for a girl, four in the case of a boy[6], a ceremony for the initial naming of the child is held. The mother goes to the doorway with the baby in her arms. The father, who has not been allowed in the house since the baby's birth, approaches. The mother asks: "What cow will you give my child if I allow you to name it?" The husband indicates a cow and then names the child. Thus the personal herd begins almost with birth.

Guji babies receive constant attention. The mother carries the infant with her everywhere, allowing it to nurse whenever it cries. This is easily accomplished during the first two to six months when the mother is freed of all responsibility. As she becomes increasingly involved in her normal activities the baby may occasionally be tended by co-wives (who may also suckle the child), neighbors, kinsfolk, or other children of the mother.

Children soon learn that fathers and other males respond to them quite differently from women, who are always accessible and show them much affection. Men are more serious, preferring to teach and advise rather than be physically demonstrative. When men are busy, children must not interrupt.

After the age of five or six, boys and girls begin to tend small livestock (goats or calves) and to sit on perches in the fields to scare off birds and baboons. Also at this stage the gradual training in differential sex behavior begins. Girls spend increasing time assisting their mothers in the house. Boys, who have no proper work indoors other than tending the fire, spend most of their time in outdoor activities.

Boys and girls playing together base their games on adult gender roles. A favorite game involves drawing on the ground a homestead complete with house kraal and fields. Cattle are represented by the round *hidi* fruit. Both boys and girls play at cattle tending, while only the girls imitate household tasks.

Gender-specific activities continue to increase until puberty. There is also a gradual tendency for adults to treat maturing children as adults — advising them, teaching them customs and law, and even occasionally bringing chronic miscreants before the elders' court (*jarsa biyya*) to be admonished.

When a girl first menstruates, a circle of hair is shaved off the crown of her head (*banti*). Over this area is placed a square beaded ornament (*ficha*) from which a number of leather strips descend over the back of the head. This ornament indicates the girl is marriageable and a virgin. From this time until marriage she should not go out alone lest she lose her virginity. However, the need for her to tend cattle and to fetch water results in her being frequently alone.

Postpubescent boys increasingly devote themselves to men's activities. Much of their time is spent herding full-grown cattle, working in the fields, and helping their fathers with other chores. There is also increasing involvement in peer group activities. During what leisure they have, boys in groups practice spear throwing by rolling a hoop made from vines (*korbo*) along the ground and attempting to throw their small *abo* spears through the moving target. There are also contests of strength involving a type of wrestling resembling judo.

Boys, unlike girls, are free to participate in limited forms of sexual experimentation. A teenage boy occasionally may acquire a mistress. When approached by a boy, some women say: "No, you are like my son". Others say: *Asi koy* (come here).[7] A certain amount of sexual experimentation occurs between boys and girls, but this is dangerous for the boys as well as the girls. If a girl is made pregnant, or even if the hymen is broken, the boy is punished by the girl's parents and may have to marry her long before he has enough cattle for her support.

The activities of teenage boys have changed significantly during this century. In the past, they would take a few cattle to the forested lowlands of Guji (particularly to the eastern area bordering the Ganale Gudda River) and remain there for long periods, hunting and fending off wild animals. They would perhaps engage in some cattle raiding against neighbouring peoples across the nearby territorial boundary. Today, there are few game animals in Guji. The lowland pastures and mineral springs to which boys once drove their cattle are now private property, and one must pay for the right to use them.

Marriage

At marriage the bride leaves her natal home, alone and with almost no material resources, to enter the homestead of people who are frequently strangers. In the case of a man's first marriage, he takes his bride to live in his parents' homestead, but in her own new house, for a number of years. Thus the bride passes from a relatively secure existence to one in which she must obey a range of her husband's relatives.

Bridewealth payments in Guji are small, consisting of three cattle (plus one bull if the bride is a virgin), and these need not be paid at once. The prospective bridegroom also works for his future father-in-law as much as several years before the marriage. In addition to 'proper' marriage, which is arranged by the couple's kin, there is elopement. In this case, the bride has much say in the choice of a spouse but the bridewealth payment is considerably higher. In Guji, elopements are fairly frequent, especially when the bride has a strong aversion to the proposed husband and is secretly emotionally attached to another man.

I have described the marriage ceremony elsewhere[8] and will only mention the nature of the marriage night. Ideally, the consummation is a pitched battle during which the groom overcomes the resistance of the virgin bride. Women hope to prevent the consummation and put up a physical and verbal fight (the groom's friends stand outside the house shouting encouragement to the bride). Should the groom fail to consummate, his failure (and his bride's triumph) become the subject of gossip and amusement.

Adulthood

Following marriage, the new wife must remain in her husband's home in virtual seclusion for between one and twelve months. She is not to visit her kinsfolk or even the market and she is not to have lovers. During this 'training period' she is very much subservient to and dependent upon her husband and his kin. The seclusion can also be viewed as a liminal period[9] between childhood (all females who have never been married are referred to as *dura*, girl or virgin) and full adult status as a married woman in charge of her own domestic affairs. While in seclusion the woman has neither autonomy nor status. It is a time of humility and subservience to a degree not present at any other stage of life.

If this view of the seclusion period is valid, then the marriage ceremony is both a rite of passage in itself and a rite of separation from childhood. This view is further substantiated by the presence of another multifunctional rite at the end of seclusion, which serves to reintegrate the wife into full adult status. The husband buys new clothes and bead necklaces for his wife, takes her to visit her parents, and also takes a cow. Arriving at the parent's home, his wife is presented to them in her new status, and the cow is given to her mother to seal their relationship. From this time onward, the husband may never look at his wife's mother "lest he go blind", and should physically avoid her whenever possible. If the bridewealth cattle have been paid, this cow also marks the final cementing of all the affinal relations of reciprocity. At the end of the visit the wife's father blesses the couple after giving them milk to drink.

The wife returns home to begin the full range of adult responsibility. She also starts to form the *garayu* (mistress-lover) relations with men of the area and is free to select anyone outside the husband's lineage (and her own clan segment). Her husband, who has mistresses of his own, is aware of his wife's lovers and, in fact, profits from them. After four years a woman's lover must give her at least a milk cow if not a mule (and she may sue if it is not volunteered). If she is on good term with her husband, the gift is added to his domestic stock or else she hides the animal with her brother. Of course, the husband is providing the food given to his wife's lover each time he visits. A woman is only supposed to have one lover at a time, but some have more (particularly young women and older women of importance, such as spirit group leaders). Men tend to have as many mistresses as they can manage.

The *garayu* relationship should not be viewed simply as a sexual liaison. Men well beyond the age of sexual potency have mistresses. People discussing the relationship, and songs concerning *garayu*, speak more of food and animal exchange than of sex. Admittedly, this is partly euphemistic good manners, but the relationship is ideally a stable, affectionate one in which both partners have freely chosen a companion they personally like, an emotionally satisfying outlet in a society of arranged marriages. In addition to economic exchange, a great deal of subtle influence is exerted through this covert relationship. Indeed, it is difficult fully to understand interaction within neighborhoods and spirit possession groups without taking *garayu* into account.

Neighborhood and Economy

The basic residential unit in Guji is the neighborhood (*ola*), composed of a small number of round straw houses. In the fertile highlands (above 1800 metres elevation) these houses may completely encircle hilltops, while in the drier lowlands elevations an *ola* may consist of only four or five houses. Near the towns, neighborhoods are closer together than in the remote countryside. The length of time an *ola* is maintained in a particular locale varies from only two or three years in the arid lowlands, to a decade or longer in the highlands. At the end of this period the neighbors may move together to another location or go their separate ways.

Ideally, an *ola* consists of the houses of a man's wives, his sons, and eventually their wives and children. However, the desire for independence of the sons and the possibility of chronic disputes among wives and affines usually result in the break up of the family *ola*. Also, a father may send his sons with part of the family herd to distant areas for grazing. These factors operate frequently enough to create a pattern of homestead growth and dispersal each generation. The most frequent neighborhood pattern results from the desire to locate wives near the husband's patrilineal kin, or at least clansmen. A man with more than one wife often locates his spouses far apart in order to disperse the herd (and prevent fighting among co-wives) and then visits each periodically. If the wives live near his kin, there are people always available who are obligated to engage in mutual help (mainly of labor and food) in his absence. Men with only one wife may occasionally live with non-kin, since monogamous men generally are at home and do not need others to look after their wives. Due to the dispersed nature of Guji clans, the neighborhood may consist of members of virtually any of these. It is only in areas remote from towns that men from only two or three clans of one phratry may be found. What is significant for women in a polygynous family is that the husband will be away with other wives part of the time. Each wife periodically will have control of the house and its resources, while at the same time having the support of neighbors.

From the time a man first marries until the end of life, he devotes most of his time to the management of his herds and to agriculture. When he marries, a man will own cattle which he obtained from several sources, including the offspring of the cow he received at birth, possibly the offspring of the cow received at the *gada* name=giving ceremony of *makabasa*, any additional animals his father may have bestowed on him (or possibly those inherited after his father's death), and those loaned him by his wife's father (if he approved of the marriage).

If, in time, the herd becomes large, the man will lend some cattle to poor kin and affines. This is not entirely altruistic, but rather is part of a larger adaptive strategy. A man with sufficient milch cows, parcels out his herd in a way that takes advantage of the varied topography of Gujiland. To keep the entire herd in one area is seen as an invitation to the predations of drought and disease. A man will, therefore, first locate his wives, if he has more than one, so that they are distributed to the high, middle and low altitudes of Guji.

Parallel to cattle distribution is another allocation system involving crops, different ones of which are grown at the various altitudes. A man with wives (and homesteads) located in each is able to realize the crop potential and keep each household supplied with what is produced by the others. This, of course, involves transporting foodstuffs on donkeys and mules. Alternatively, those who have borrowed cattle may be expected to allow the lender to use some of their land for planting. The borrower, in this case, is also expected to tend and harvest the crops.

An important consequence of this system of cattle and crop distribution is the creation and reinforcement of social networks. Kin are 'automatically' available, but affines are also of great importance because they provide many additional possibilities. In actual practice, affinal networks figure extensively in both cattle distribution and crop spreading.

Within this economic system the basic division of labor between men and women is as follows. Men properly spend their days herding cattle, attending debates and rituals, and generally supervising their affairs. Women milk cows, tend the household and its children, cook and carry

804

out an endless number of domestic tasks. The daytime world of men is outside the house; that of women is largely within it.

The Status of Senior Women

As the life cycle develops and people begin to move into high status roles, it becomes apparent that the position of women in Guji society is sharply different from that of men. Women are generally restricted to the domestic realm. It is inconceivable that a woman could become an elder. In fact, women should keep silent during the frequent sessions at which affairs of the area are discussed or adjudicated and ritual reconciliation of people (*arrarsa*) is brought about. The few times I saw women speak (while suing lovers who had not given them gifts of cattle at the appropriate time) they were forced to remain on the periphery of the male group, treated with condescension and subjected to ridicule.

Women are likewise barred from the highly prestigious activities of warrior and hunter. Men with major achievements in these areas are shown great respect and are sung about during *gada* rituals long after their death. By contrast, there is a story concerning the eight women who went out one day to hunt. They dressed in their usual costume, with their leather aprons (*bonko*) banging loudly against their legs, and of course the game was frightened away. The women thought they saw animals hiding in the bushes and spent their time spearing the underbrush ("killing wood"). Finally, their female leader decided to count them before heading home to make certain no one was lost. She counted the other seven but not herself and concluded that someone was missing. There was much wailing until a man came to help, and he correctly counted eight. Such is the male view of woman the hunter.

A few women do gain prestige by becoming midwives and general curers (*cedetti*) for women. Also, women become *kallitti* (possessed female who serves as the main 'vessel' for all the spirits of a group to occupy) and possessed members (*tamari*) of spirit cults.[10] In this context women are still prevented from directly achieving high status since they are 'unconscious' while in trance and serve merely as 'hollow vessels' for their spirit hosts. It is not the *kallitti* who has the power and knowledge, but the spirit who uses her body. Nevertheless, people are very careful not to offend a woman known to have a spirit. Those possessed, male or female, are thought to be protected by the spirit, which it is said will attack anyone who insults or harms the human host. *Kallitti* are given special deference for this reason but within spirit cults in general, it is still the men who are seen to have direct authority, and it is men who maintain order in cult meetings.

In the economic arena local markets are an area in which women have some independence. Men sell cattle (and all other major animals), honey and large quantities of grain. Women offer a great array of smaller scale commerce, varying from eggs to small quantities of grain and other agricultural products. They use the profits to purchase household supplies and some clothing. It is my surmise that the profits are largely kept apart from men.

In the home the subservient position of women is maintained. Men do not believe women should control the household and the domestic economy; they are somewhat simpleminded servants (and, of course, childbearers). For women to assert themselves and exert any measure of control requires a great amount of indirection. Men view such behavior as devious and threatening to the male-created order of society. If wives are assertive, they are beaten, which is quite common. Another strategy used by men with more than one wife is to ignore the assertive one(s) and provide fewer cattle for their households.

If a wife feels her husband is unusually abusive or does not give her sufficient resources to maintain her household, she can ask his kinsmen to intervene. They meet with the couple and attempt to restore harmony. Quite often, the kinsmen find the husband at fault and reprimand him, even beat him if he does not heed repeated warnings. If the problem continues the wife will run away to live with one of her kinsmen (father or eldest brother). Usually the husband and a group of his patrilineal kinsmen will visit the wife and negotiate for her return.

Such negotiations do not invariably succeed. Numerous informants stated that the *sara* (law) of Guji does not permit divorce, yet I witnessed several instances in which a wife did leave her husband and eventually married another man. Since this violated the law, there were no rules concerning the return of bridewealth or the control of children. The case resolutions followed no set pattern, but it was clear that marital conflict led to antagonism between the couple's kinsmen even when there was no divorce.

Household conflict generally tends to spread to the larger group. The wife's kin blame the husband's for failing to control him; the husband accuses the wife's people of encouraging her rebelliousness. When matters reach a critical point, attempts are made to reconcile the disputants. At such proceedings (*arrarsa*), the two groups of affines remain mute while elders discuss the case and seek a settlement. Finally, the affines are encouraged to accept the decision, and there is a blessing for peace with god.

Old Age and Death

When a man and his wives grow old, several changes occur in the composition of the homestead. Sons and their wives eventually leave the sons' parents, but the latter still need assistance with herding and agriculture. The necessary labor is obtained by adopting grandchildren. Both maternal and paternal grandparents have this right, and the parents cannot refuse (unless they have only one child). The adoptions are temporary and can be terminated by parents or grandparents if the arrangement is unsatisfactory.

Usually when a man is in his sixties, wives will be brought together in one neighborhood (in individual houses). This is the result of the man's increasing inability to travel great distances to the dispersed wives. If the man's herd is large, cattle are distributed to sons. The latter are expected to provide food and occasional labor to their parents when necessary.

The household is disbanded when the husband dies. If he outlives all his wives he will join the household of a son (usually his eldest); if the wives outlive him they may form a secondary marriage with one of the dead husband's brothers. Alternatively, they may move in with a son or return to their own kinsmen.

Burial practices are partially dependent on the male *gada* system, and women are assigned burial categories based on the position of their husbands in that system. Men who have not achieved the manhood ceremony (*makabasa*) should not be given proper burial, but simply be dumped on the ground. Those in the adulthood grades are buried outside the house door, men on the right and women on the left. People in the 'retirement' grades are buried in the cattle kraal.

The corpse is washed, dressed in clean clothes, and taken outside on a stretcher over which cloth is held. The body is placed in the burial hole in a flexed position (laid on the right side for men and on the left for women). A pile of acacia branches is placed over the grave to discourage animals. All this is done in silence by sons of the deceased (or by brothers if there are no sons). In the case of a woman's funeral I witnessed, her main cooking pot was broken over the grave, her eldest son shouted "my mother, my mother", and the kin who had remained in the house began wailing. An elder soon told them to stop until other kin and affines came. During the week following a death, as groups of relatives arrive, mourning is renewed. Throughout this period, neighbors and friends provide all food for the household.

CONCLUSIONS

The Guji concepts of gender differences are constructed in many domains varying from cosmology to the customary division of labor. Each area contributes to a consistent male-controlled society. Life begins with an assertion of the metaphoric associations between male and female when the midwife states than mother is earth (and domesticated nature) and father is sky/god. This act is meaningful on two other levels, for it orients the baby in the culturally defined cosmos and demonstrates the validity of the procreative relationships associated with *kayyo*, of which the baby is the proof.

The next event in the birth ritual concerns the proprietary rights of the maternal and paternal lineages. The child is born of the mother and is still attached to her. The father enters the house, cuts the umbilicus, and thereby claims the infant as a biological being. A few days later he must again claim the baby, this time as a social person, by giving it a name. He will claim it once more, if it is a male, during the manhood ceremony that gives the boy an adult grade name in the *gada* system. The male offspring becomes a social person, an adult, in a ritual that closely resembles the first naming ceremony. In all three instances, the mother has first claim on the offspring and must relinquish it to the patrilineal order of society.

Man is the upholder of order and the active agent (along with god) in procreation. By contrast, woman is either passive agent or the disruptive force which challenges (or withholds) procreativity. This view of gender opposition extends to the 'institutional' organization of society. Men alone are in a position to make decisions and uphold the social rules; women are to be submissive. Whenever women are assertive, they are seen as devious and as disruptors of order.

This view appears to be particularly focused on marriage and affinity. The latter has the positive attribute of exchange (or mutual assistance), but it also has negative aspects. Affines begin as unknown strangers who must become 'friends'. This inherently problematic relationship is required by the rule of exogamy and the need for children. Marital conflict spreads to the larger group and (less frequently) discord among affines affects the linking marriage.

The tie between the married couple is a similarly mixed relationship. On the one hand, it provides the children of the next generation and the domestic setting for their rearing; on the other, it is a relationship fraught with conflict. The realization that this is a hazardous enterprise is first apparent when a suitor makes his initial visit to the potential bride's family. Signs that might be predictive of the future are carefully observed (by both families) and are later analyzed with great care. The marriage night itself symbolizes conflict. The groom must consummate the marriage, and the bride is determined to foil him. The ultimate triumph of the husband over his new wife is an affirmation both of male dominance and of procreativity.

The elements of the system of gender inequality are mutually reinforcing. The cultural distinction of gender is affirmed in myth, the underlying cosmological concepts, and the symbolism of ritual. Gender distinctions are also reinforced by, and form the basis for, the behavior of spouses (and, ultimately, affines). In sum, if women do not always conform to the ideal male-controlled order, the result is both interpersonal conflict and the affirmation (for men) that if women are not passive, they will be disruptive.

In Guji, meaning is built largely through dichotomies and mediations. Based on the above discussion, I believe an explanation can be offered for gender as the most pervasive dichotomy. Biological differences between male and female serve to perpetuate society through the creation of new generations; and patrilineal groups must go outside themselves in order to perpetuate themselves. The two 'facts' are inescapable. Another set of relationships is essential for life to be perpetuated: the earth must produce grain and grass, for which it is dependent upon the sky for rain and sun (both in proper measure). Guji symbolism appears to center, understandably, on the perpetuation of life. *Kayyo*, the cosmological concept of abundance through procreativity in a well-ordered society, appears to express this life-sustaining set of relationships.

Just as the earth is not always productive, marriages sometimes produce conflict rather than children; affinity may create enemies rather than cooperative friends. And there is the other face of nature, the domain of wild animals and unknown dangers. It is this set of inescapable 'facts' that is associated with earth, woman and the cosmological concept of *woyyu*. It is the interaction of the relationships subsumed under these concepts that provides both the meaning and the drama of Guji life.

NOTES

1. See, for example, Sherry Ortner and Harriet Whitehead, *Sexual Meanings* (Cambridge, 1981).

2. The Guji see themselves as a confederation of eight *gosa*, or phratries, each composed of seven clans. My research was conducted in the three southern phratries of Mati, Hoku and Uraga.

3. See John Hinnant, *The Gada System of the Guji of Southern Ethiopia: a Dissertation for the Degree of Ph.D. presented to the Faculty of the Department of Anthropology, The University of Chicago (Chicago, 1977)*, and "The Guji: Gada as a Ritual System", in *Age, Generation and Time*, edited by P. T. W. Baxter and Uri Almagor (London, 1978), pp.207-243. See also Eike Haberland, *Galla Sud Athiopiens* (Stuttgart, 1963).

4. Her duties are performed by other women of the neighborhood and her own kinswomen. Co-wives may also help.

5. The *otuba waka*, pole of god, is the ritual center of the house, where the man who 'owns' ceremonies performed in the house sits. Birthing is the only occasion when a woman is associated with the pole.

6. In general women are associated with (inauspicious) odd numbers and men with (auspicious) even numbers.

7. Boys are not particularly desirable lovers because they lack the economic resources for compensating a mistress. After four years of the relationship she should be given a cow.

8. See John Hinnant, "Guji Affinity: The Case of a Bad Marriage", in *Oromo Kinship and Marriage* (tentative title) edited by P. T. W. Baxter (n.d.).

9. 'Liminal' in this case refers to the transition period between clearly defined social statuses. See Victor Turner, *The Ritual Process: Structure and Anti-Structure* (Chicago, 1969), pp.94-203, and Arnold van Gennep, *The Rites of Passage* (London, 1960), *passim*.

10. See Dan F. Bauer and John Hinnant "Revolutionary and Normal Divination", in *Explorations in African Systems of Thought*, edited by Ivan Karp and Charles S. Byrd (Bloomington, 1980), pp.183-212.

REFERENCES CITED

Gennep, Arnold van. 1960 *The Rites of Passage*. London: Routledge and Kegan Paul.

Haberland, Eike 1963 *Galla Sud-Äthiopiens*. Stuttgart, W. Kohlhammer.

Hinnant, John 1977 *The Gada System of the Guji of Southern Ethiopia*. A Dissertation for the Degree of Ph.D., presented to the Faculty of the Department of Anthropology, The University of Chicago.

——————— 1978 "The Guji: Gada as a Ritual System" in *Age, Generation and Time*, edited by P. T. W. Baxter and Uri Almagor. London: C. Hurst. pp.207-243.

——————— n.d. "Guji Affinity: The Case of a Bad Marriage" in *Oromo Kinship and Descent* (tentative title), edited by P. T. W. Baxter. In Preparation.

Ortner, Sherry and Harriet Whitehead 1981 *Sexual Meanings*. Cambridge: Cambridge University Press.

Turner, Victor 1969 *The Ritual Process: Structure and Anti-Structure*. Chicago: Aldine Publishing Company.

"SONS OF SLAVES" OR "SONS OF BOYS":

ON THE PREMISE OF RANK AMONG THE

MACHA OROMO

Jan Hultin

For centuries the southwestern highlands were one of the main supply areas for slaves. Here the slave trade brought far-reaching political change. In the 16th century, the repeated campaigns by Abyssinian kings and their incessant demand for slaves turned the regions to the east and the south of the Abay into a waste land. The predatory campaigns and the constant slave-raids led to the depopulation and the destruction of the Gafat and Gonga societies south the Abay, which opened the way for the advancing Oromo pastoralists. (M. Hassan 1983: 303-373)

Macha society was thus born among the scattered remnants of societies wrecked by a war-like and slave-hungry Christian kingdom. Although the Oromo soon established some form of dominion over what remained of the aboriginal population — which at any rate seems to have outnumbered the Macha — they did not develop any form of institutionalized slavery during the early period of expansion and conquest. It is true that the subdued people, who were called *gabaro*, were forced to pay tribute to the Oromo, but at the same time they were adopted by the Oromo — individually or *in corpore*, made allies in the wars with the Christians, made into marriageable partners and granted social and legal rights. Over time, however, there developed several other forms of domination and dependence, including slavery, as well as a variety of modes of integration by adoption and foster-parentage, giving rise to a proliferation of terms for social categorization and ranking. This paper will deal with the premise of this categorization and ranking.

During my field work among the Sibu Macha of northwestern Wollega, I met a bewildering variety of terms that referred to social categories or groups. There were *borana* and *ilma garba*, the two main categories of Sibu, which in most other parts of Macha land were referred to as *borana* and *gabaro*. There were groups of endogamous craftsmen such as blacksmiths and weavers, *tumtu*; tanners, *faqi*; and potters, *waata*. There were supposed to be small endogamous groups of Oromo speakers called *ganka*, who were regarded as descendants of the original inhabitants of the area. Although slavery had been outlawed for more than thirty years, the term *garba* was frequently used to refer to ex-slaves, especially if they were *shanqalla*, people of the lowlands: both terms having pejorative and racist connotations. In the many raids and wars of the past, the Macha tried to take captives, *boodjuu*, and keep them as clients and retainers: the term is still used sometimes to denote descendants of such people. Many captives were taken in raids against the Sinicho north of the Abay, and *sinicho* is sometimes used as a near-equivalent of *boodjuu*. The Macha have several forms of adoption and foster-relationship, e.g. *gudifacha*, *mogassa*, *qollu* and *qubsisa*, which has also given rise to categorization.

Most of these terms referred to social categories. To the extent that they denoted social groups, it was groups that had existed, or that were believed to have existed, in the past: the exception being the groups of endogamous craftsmen. Many of these terms had pejorative connotations and could only be used for talking about people who were not present: to use them in the presence of the person referred to would have been an insult — which of course made inquiries among people with low-status labels rather complicated. Typically, there was often uncertainty and disagreement about who belonged to what category of people.

I met these terms mainly in talks about marriage, inheritance and property, that is, in contexts where descent was regarded as essential. They were important elements in shared beliefs about history and society, about what had been in the past and about what ought to be in the present: they were notions for talking about the order of the world, and in particular for talking about social and ritual rank. As notions in an ideology of rank they were precise enough to necessitate a code of etiquette for how and when they could be used – e.g. in the presence or absence of the person referred to by the term – at the same time as they were vague enough to allow manipulation and variability in interpretation. Taken together this made them highly useful for justifying claims, for example in litigation about land.

I shall deal mainly with one of these categories here, the *ilma garba*. In common parlance the term means 'son of slave' or 'descendant of slave' and yet it was one of the few category terms I have mentioned that could be used indiscriminately. In this respect it differed strikingly from the term *garba*, slave. The latter term was used to refer to ex-slaves and descendants of slaves, i.e. to people of low status, but it would be most improper to use it in the presence of such a person. The term *ilma garba* on the other hand had, in spite of its meaning, neither any connotation of low status nor any pejorative meaning: most people readily recognized that they were 'sons of slaves' and, in fact, the major part of the population belonged to this category. However, at the same time as all people agreed about the literal sense of the term, they all (irrespective of whether they were *ilma garba* or not) denied that the 'descendants of slaves' were of slave descent. In other words, while the son of a 'slave' was regarded as the descendant of a 'slave', the 'son of slave' was not. The remainder of this paper will deal with how this notion of 'slave' came about.

The Macha are subdivided into a large number of named, territorial groups, which I shall call tribes. Sometimes there is the idea of a genealogical relationship between the different tribes and that they can be defined with regard to a common, eponymous ancestor, but equally often such a notion of a common ancestor is missing. In past centuries the tribes were ritual units in that each one, or a group of them, had its own *gada* organization. Originally, the *gada* system also served judicial and political functions (Knutsson 1967). From the very beginning, however, secular aspects of the authority of its officials were challenged by war-leaders and men of wealth and by the 19th century the *gada* system functioned in most regions only in a more or less eroded form: chiefdoms and even centralized kingdoms, the five so-called Gibe states, emerged. Although there was a variety of political forms, from 'tribes without rulers' to state formations, the tribes continued to exist as territorial and political entities well into this century; when, for example, the imperial regime imposed its rule, the new administrative divisions were based on the old tribal borders.

In Macha history, tribes were thus ritual and political units. Yet, each tribe was internally divided into a large number of patrilineal segments. The tribes still consist of patrilocal, exogamous lineages, *qomo*. Each lineage has a name, not after a local founding father who is traceable in any existing genealogies, but after an eponymous ancestor who lived in the mythological past in a country beyond a river in the East from where the Macha, according to their myths of origin, once came. Thus, several lineages share a common name, and groups with the same name are found in many different places not only within each tribal territory, but all over Macha land. The same names of what anthropologists have called 'tribes', 'clans' and 'lineages' tend to appear again and again everywhere in Oromo land from Tigre in the north to central Kenya in the south.

Among themselves, the Macha distinguish between two major categories of people and of clans and lineages: the *borana* and the *gabaro* (Cerulli 1933: 126 ff., 139ff., Haberland 1963: 775, Knutsson 1967: 39, 181, Bartels 1983: 133-165). Among the Sibu, the two categories are called *borana* and *ilma garba* (Hultin 1979). Most observers have asserted that the distinction is one between people of pure Oromo descent and descendants of other people who have been integrated among the Oromo. Those who were integrated were mainly people who lived in what is now Macha land before the arrival of the Oromo: the *gabaro* are thus supposed to be the descendants of the aboriginal population of the area.

This also seems to be the opinion of most Macha, but not of all of them. Among the Sibu, people emphatically denied that the difference between the *borana* and the *ilma garba* was a question of 'pure' versus 'mixed' origin: the *ilma garba* were as 'pure' Oromo as the *borana*, the former had always been true Oromo, etc. The only difference between them was that the *ilma garba* were not allowed to wear or possess a *kallecha*, a sacred and extremely powerful ritual object that had been devolved from fathers to their eldest sons in *borana* lineages since time immemorial. To the Sibu, the *borana* and *ilma garba* categories have no relevance for determining social and jural rights, but rather for defining *ritual* prerogatives and obligations.

The Sibu thus explicitly deny that the criterion of descent is relevant in the definition of the two categories. Yet, the descent criterion is implicit in their definition of *borana*-ship and of what they evidently regard as two *ritual categories*. I have suggested before (Hultin 1979) that the *ilma garba* may be 'drop-outs' from the *gada* system. As Asmarom Legesse (1973) has demonstrated in the case of the *gada* system of the Borana of southern Ethiopia, a strict application of the rules for participation in the system did, over time, have the effect that an ever-increasing number of men became barred from active participation in the system, and so were all their descendants: they were ascribed the permanent ritual status as retired elders, a category the Borana refer to as *ilma jarsa*, 'son of an elder'. This permutation, which Asmarom Legesse calls "the *gada* process", had, evidently, similar effects among other Oromo tribes, and I have suggested that it also worked among the Macha (Hultin 1979). It will take us too long to explain how the system worked in principle, be it enough here to say that the *gada* process channelled men, irrespective of their physical age, into the status of permanently retired elders with neither secular nor ritual roles within the framework of the *gada* system: hence the label 'sons of the aged'. When the Macha changed one of the prescriptive rules for participation in the system, the ban on raising sons before one had reached the fifth grade of the system, this too caused the effect that an increasing number of men were pushed out of the system, this time, however, as permanent juniors; whatever their physical age, they could never obtain the status of ritual majority and become holders of *gada* offices; in terms of the *gada* system their role was one of eternal youth, and so were the roles of their descendants — 'the sons of youths' or 'the sons of boys'. Whereas a strict application of the rules for participation in the *gada* system produced ritually retired elders, and equally retired 'sons of elders', *ilma jarsa*, the change of one of the basic rules produced permanent ritual statuses — and their corresponding roles — of boyhood and youth as well as descendants of such ritual minors, the 'sons of boys' (Hultin 1979).

In the present Macha dialect the term *garba* means slave (Gragg 1982), but in some other dialects it need not necessarily be translated so. Thus, the Borana of southern Ethiopia allow the 'sons of elders' a limited role as 'assistant councillors', *garba hayu*, to the men of the ruling *gada* set, the *hayu* (Legesse 1973: 161). These *garba hayu* are certainly not 'slaves' of the *gada* officials. They may rather be said to be additional members of the council who, however, have no formal right to make decisions or to join resolutions. They are, in terms of the *gada* system, regarded as incapacitated: a 'son of an elder' is a ritual minor and so is an 'assistant councillor'. 'Minority' is thus an important feature of meaning in the concept '*garba*'.

A slave is by definition a minor, and in this respect he is ranked equal with a youth. Gragg (1982), whose dictionary is based on the Macha dialect, reports that while the term '*garba*' means 'slave', its derivation *garbicha* may be translated as 'boy', and that it does not necessarily mean slave boy. Otherwise the common term for boy is the rather similar word *gurbaa* and its derivation *gurbicha*. The point I am trying to make, however, is not concerned with the similarity of terms, but rather with their difference of meaning. I have no evidence myself of the word *garbicha* being used to refer to a boy, but yet I find no reason to dispute Gragg's statement. If a man used the word *garbicha* to refer to a boy, this simply means, I suggest, that he is emphasizing a particular aspect of that boy's status, viz. his minority, and that the man is talking about e.g. a ward and his guardian or parent.

Today, *gurbaa* means boy: Gragg (1982) even translates it as 'small boy'. In the sixteenth century, however, it denoted not a small boy, but rather a young man who was old enough to go to war. Says Bahrey:

> "They call the small children *mučā*, and those who are older, *elman*, those
> who are older still are called *guarba*, and these are they who begin to take
> part in warfare" (Bahrey 1954: 127).

The word *muchaa* means 'child', *ilma* (pl. *ilmaan*) means 'son', and Beckingham and Huntingford (1954) translate *gurbaa* as 'youth'. The transcription *'guarba'* is ambiguous, but I shall not deal with it here. Instead, I wish to emphasize that Bahrey here enumerates conceptually distinguished stages of the life-cycle that also have their correspondence in the lower grades of the *gada*-cycle: the term *gurbaa* here refers to young and unmarried warriors, i.e. to men who are physically of age but yet are regarded as minors in ritual terms. According to the rules of the *gada* system, these men were not allowed to marry and, more importantly, not allowed to raise sons. To have sons was the privilege of those who, in ritual terms, had attained their majority. When the latter rule was abandoned, this meant that a *gada* minor became free to raise sons. The son of such a father was an *ilma garba*. He was of course not the son of a slave. What the term suggests is rather that he is the son of a man in the junior grades of the *gada*-cycle, a man who in *gada* terms is a boy or a youth and therefore a minor.

Now, what about the *borana, gabaro* and *ilma garba*? Are they all of 'true' Oromo descent, as the Sibu say they are? (And the Sibu do not know the term *gabaro*.) Or, are only the *borana* 'true' Oromo, while the *gabaro* are descendants of non-Oromo, as evidently most Macha and most independent observers assert? Or are both propositions equally right and wrong? I would suggest that they are both right, simply because they refer to two different domains: the term *ilma garba* refers to a ritual category, while the term *gabaro* refers to a secular category; the Sibu concept refers to a ritual status and role and the other one to a secular status and role. As I have suggested elsewhere (1979), the Macha Oromo probably ascribed the status of ritual minors to those who were integrated into Macha society as *gabaro* and gave them the ritual role as 'youths' and 'sons of youth'. The lord of the land and his *gabaro* were also godfather and adopted son and their relationship was represented as a father-son type of relationship. It would thus be logical if the social and ritual roles were designed to agree.

I shall now first consider the historical context in which the *borana-gabaro* relationship was established and then describe the mode of integrating outsiders into Macha society and, finally, some aspects of the *borana-gabaro* relationship. Although we have no details about the relationship between the Oromo and the aboriginal population during the period of Oromo expansion, some general features emerge from the sources. I have suggested (1982) that the initial advances of the Oromo in the 16th century seem to have been raids for looting, after which they withdrew to their own territory. It seems from Bahrey's account of the events that in the south — in Bale, Dawaro and Fatagar — they began to demand tribute from the people in the defeated areas (where the population was already weakened and decimated by the "Granj wars") during the *gada* period 1546-1554, i.e. some thirty years after the first mention of Oromo raids on Bale, but that they still returned to their homelands south of the Wabi Shebelle (Bahrey 1954: 116, Almeida 1954:138 ff.). It was during this *gada* period, during the *luba* Bifole, that the people of Dawaro and Fatagar were made *gabare*. Beckingham and Huntingford suggest that the meaning of the term is 'taxpayer':

> "The literal translation of this passage [in Bahrey's *History*] appears to be: 'He made of them *agbert* (slaves) which he (Bifole) called *gabare*.' In Ethiopic, *gabr* means 'slave', but in Galla the word *gabare* which is derived from it means 'servant, cultivator, taxpayer'. Almeida's paraphrase of this passage (. . . 'he made the farmers pay him taxes') suggests that the last of these meanings is the right one here." (Beckingham and Huntingford 1954: 116)

Dawaro and Fatagar were regions through which Granj's marauding armies had marched for more than fifteen years; and, as we know, Ethiopian armies carried no supplies, but lived on spoliation. Then these countries were raided by the Oromo for another ten or fifteen years. Then, after the death of Granj in 1543 and the collapse of his empire, the Oromo began to systematize their plundering expeditions and started to demand tribute or taxes, but they did not settle down among their taxpaying farmers. Finally, some ten years later, the territorial occupation of these regions took place (Hultin 1982).

The same pattern is discernable for the penetration into the present Macha land in the region south of the Abay. The first Oromo appeared in the eastern parts of the area in the 1570s, when they "devastated Shoa and began to make war in Gojam" (Bahrey 1954: 119). Throughout 1570s and 1580s the Oromo raided Gojam, evidently from base areas to the south and the east of Abay. During the *luba* Mulata, the *gada* period 1587-1594, that is about twenty years after their first appearance in the area, there is possibly an indication that the Oromo began to organize their raiding into some sort of tribute system: "The country submits to him, Mul'atā, and none remains without submission to him" (Bahrey 1954: 124 f.). When, another twenty years later, the Jesuit father Fernandez in 1613 travelled from Gojam to Enarea, we learn that somewhere immediately south of the Abay the original inhabitants, the Gongas, lived as "subjects of the Gallas" (Almeida 1954: 146).

Thanks to the pioneering research by Merid Wolde Aregay (1971) and Muhammed Hassan (1983), we are able to grasp some main features of this early and critical period of Macha history. Their research shows that throughout the 16th and 17th centuries it was the armies of the well organized Christian and Muslim states and *not*, as the prevalent historiography has reiterated, the bands of the loosely-organized Oromo tribes that were a "destructive and purposeless force" (M. W. Mariam 1970: 17). A factor of decisive importance for the development in the region between the Abay and the Gibe basin was the difference in destructive capacity demonstrated by the Oromo and Christian regimes.

When the Oromo penetrated into this region they found a country where the population was exhausted and decimated by war, famine and incessant slave-raids: for half a century this region had suffered constant ravages by the predatory armies of the Abyssinian kings and warlords. These armies, which were very huge indeed (Pankhurst 1961: 159-178, Hultin 1982), carried no supplies and, therefore, had to live from whatever they could take from the farming population of the areas through which they marched. Conversely, they were helpless and could not survive in an environment where there was no sedentary farming population to plunder (M. Hassan 1973: 321 ff. *et pas.*).

The Oromo insistence on migratory pastoralism even in areas where more stationary forms of livestock rearing was possible — as was the case in the well-watered regions east and south of the Abay — was an adaptation to a harsh *political* environment rather than to an ecological environment[1]; the latter was, incidentally, extremely favourable for settled forms of pastoral life as well as for agro-pastoralism.[2]

It seems that in the 16th century the Abyssinian rulers could afford the aboriginal peoples little else than rapine, slavery and death; the Christians even refused to allow their pagan neighbours to be converted, even when they begged for it, because then the latter could not according to Christian law be abducted and sold as slaves (M. W. Aregay 1971: 371, M. Hassan 1983: 307). In contrast, the Macha Oromo were able to transform the initial period of warfare into some form of peaceful coexistence with the aborigines and offer an alliance against their common enemy, the Christians. The basis of this alliance was the *gabaro* institution.

As we have seen, within one or two decades the Oromo made the sedentary farming population into some kind of tribute paying clients or vassals, designated as *gabaro* or *garba*. The former term is known in most parts of Oromo land, including northern Kenya where the tribal name Gabra and its equivalent *gabara* is derived from it: Haberland regards the Gabra as a "vassal tribe" of the Borana (Haberland 1963: 131-132, 141 ff.). In other regions the alternative designation *garba* was used. Thus, the Arsi used to designate the Hadiya to the west of the Bilate as *garba*. When the latter term today is used as an ethnonym for Hadiya, this use has no connotation of 'slave' (Braukämper 1980: 5).

It seems that among the Macha the *gabaro* status was assigned on a collective basis, but it could probably also be granted to individuals. Mohammed Hassan (1983: 315, 350) states that in the decades around 1600 the aboriginal population was "adopted en masse", but he also states that "*gada* leaders adopted many of the vanquished people as members of their own clan or tribe" (1983: 347). Further, individuals or groups could be adopted by a clan or lineage whose members *in corpore* became "fathers of the new member or members, who were called 'son of the lineage', *ilma gossa*. Beside this corporate adoption by the lineage, there was also individual adoption by an individual foster father or couple of foster parents, *gudifacha*.

There are many forms of adoption among the Macha, but a common trait is that they usually confer full kinship status upon the adopted person who even takes on his adoptive father's genealogy. These forms must be distinguished from those forms of foster relations where the kinship status of the parties involved is not changed and where we may rather speak of godparentage than fosterparentage. But it must be emphasized that the modes of integration and the modes for establishing godparentage and adoption always seem to have been characterized by variability and change; the term *gabaro* has been given many different meanings and been applied to a variety of groups and individuals. Says d'Abbadie in the 1840s:

> "The *gabaro* is a stranger who is established among the Gallas. He is well received and if he sucks the little finer of a Galla he may marry even the daughter of a Borana. But on the day of the initiation of *gada*, he is obliged to hide himself because otherwise he will be killed." (d'Abbadie NAF 21300: 722. My translation)

Here, the *gabaro* is simply a non-Oromo who lives among the Oromo and who has probably, from one authority or another, negotiated the right to settle (like he would have to do in most other societies). He may intermarry with the *borana* provided he establishes a form of foster relation with an Oromo ("sucks his little finger"). The form of foster relation d'Abbadie refers to is called *qubaqabii*; *qubaqaba*, literally 'have a finger', is one of many Macha notions for standing in foster- or godparent relation. The Sibu used to talk about *qubaiisa*, 'making finger', which denoted those westward migrants who came to the new land in the West at such a late time that they found all land occupied by others who came before them, and therefore had to settle as clients on the land of a pioneer. In the beginning, the *qubsiisa* made some form of *corvée* labour for his godfather, but it seems that his service decreased gradually as the years went by and eventually his tenancy was unconditional.

Marriage did not affect the *borana/gabaro* status of the parties involved. D'Abbadie gives the example of a Gafat man who emigrated to Challia and there married a *borana* woman: "she regards herself as *borana* because she refuses to eat grains of flax and the meat of *irre*" (d'Abbadie NAF 21300: 722. My translation)

From around 1600 the Macha established a special relation with other groups who were adopted either *in corpore* or on an individual basis and given the status of *gabaro*. As such they formed part of Macha society: they were recognized as partners in marriage and they had recognized legal rights and obligations. In contrast, those non-Oromo who were not made *gabaro* were by definition *diina*, 'enemies': they stood outside society.

For a long time, perhaps from the very beginning, the *gabaro* have outnumbered the *borana*, which is reflected in Macha sayings like "nine are the *borana*, ninety are the *gabaro*".[3] The two categories of people have lived together in peace, they have been united by ties of marriage and of kinship and quasi-kinship, and they have been embraced by the same law.

While they are thus united by ties of kinship and alliance, they are at the same time separated and distinguished by the criterion of agnatic descent. In Oromo culture, descent is an ideology for representing property relations (Hultin 1984), although of course not *only* that. Purity of descent, that is of *borana*-ship, is also essential in all ritual contexts: the *borana* are the channels through which God acts as the source of all life (Bartels 1983: 136); they are *nama ebba*, people of blessings, which means that they are people blessed by God, *Waqa*, and transmitting this blessing to others (Bartels 1983: 151). Prayers and blessings are central features of Oromo culture. They are not only reserved for ritual occasions but are a prominent part of daily life. Baxter's observation from northern Kenya that "Boran society sometimes appears to float on a river of prayers and blessings" (Baxter 1978: 155) is, I think, true for most parts of Oromo land; it is a pan-Oromo feature.

The purity and exclusiveness of the *borana* is also maintained through the observation of certain food taboos: the *borana* must not eat the meat of sheep or meat from an animal's foreleg, *irre* (cf. the quotation from d'Abbadie above). Everywhere the Oromo of *borana* descent are distinguished from those of 'mixed' descent by the taboo on *irre*. These food taboos are explained by one of Bartel's informants in the following way:

"You know that we call a man's forearm and an animal's forelegs *'irre'*. But *'irre'* also means strength, power. While speaking of a man's strength, our people think first of all of his arms. We say of such a man: *'Irre qaba —* he has *irre'*. We say the same of Waqa: *'Irren Waqa si hadhau —* May Waqa's *irre* strike you' . . . the *borana* did not eat the foreleg of an animal [because] : *'Irren irre hinnyatu — irre* does not eat *irre*, power does not eat power'. This means: the borana are people of power; they have power to bless and to curse. The forelegs of animals have also power. Therefore the borana do not eat them.

It is the same with sheep. The sheep is an animal of peace and the borana, too, are people of peace. Therefore they do not eat sheep. It is like eating oneself. Man does not eat man." (Bartels 1983: 156)

Forelegs and sheep may not be "good to eat", but they are certainly "good to think".[4]

The essence of *borana*-ship is ritual efficacy. The privileged position of the *borana* is based upon the belief in the power of their blessings. Their efficacy derives from the purity of the *borana*: from their purity of descent which makes them "close to Waqa", and from their purity of life, i.e. of a life in accordance with ritual taboos and prescriptions, a life in accord with *saffu*[5], the cosmic order. Thus, the segregation of the *borana* and the *gabaro* is ultimately derived from ideas of ritual purity and pollution. Accordingly, the *gabaro* have always been segregated from the *borana* during the performance of the *gada* rituals as well as during the performance of certain other rituals (cf. the quotation from d'Abbadie above). Thus Cerulli (1933: 126 ff.) reports that the *gabaro* performed their own parallel *gada* rituals at the same time as the *borana*. These were copied on the 'real' rituals of the *borana*, but showed some symbolically significant differences. In the same way, the *gada* system and the *gada* rituals of the Boran of northern Kenya–southern Ethiopia differ from those of their 'vassals', the Gabra or *gabaro* (Baxter 1978, Torry 1978), and I would suggest that they do so for the same reason as they differ among the *borana* and the *gabaro* of the Macha.

The establishment of these parallel rituals can, in the case of the Macha, be dated to around 1620, when Macha society underwent a period of severe strife (Mohammed Hassan 1983: 350 ff., 357). Between 1616 and 1618 the two main segments of the *borana*, the Afre (the four) and the Sadacha (the three), were at war with each other, a conflict which led to the break-up of their common *gada* center at Oda Bisil (M. Hassan 1983: 348). In 1618 the *gabaro* rebelled against the *borana* (M. Hassan 1983: 350 ff.), and by the end of the year they allied with the emperor Sela Christos, who from Gojam crossed the Abay with a big army (M. Hassan 1983: 354). He inflicted some serious blows on the Oromo who, as usual, fled with their families and with their livestock and dispersed into the wilderness where the Christian army could not pursue them (cf. *supra* and footnote 1). Sela Christos, not wishing his army to plunder his new allies among the *gabaro* farmers, soon returned to Gojam. Many of the *gabaro*, who feared the revenge of the Oromo, followed him and were settled on the northern side of the Abay, where they were intended to constitute a bulwark against Oromo raids. In the wake of the rebellion the *gabaro* were granted the right to perform separate and ancillary *gada* rituals.

The reason for the *gabaro* uprising seems to have been that a section of the *borana* had abused their authority and overtaxed the *gabaro*. It seems that already from an early date the Macha pioneers became divided into two different sets of people characterized by their different modes of subsistence and orientation in life. One segment of the population evidently had a pastoral orientation, led a relatively mobile life and played a prominent part in the *gada* system. The other was oriented towards the accumulation of landed estate and wealth, led a sedentary life and was not an active participant in the *gada* rituals and assemblies; rather, they constituted a constant challenge to the authority of the *gada* officials. Perhaps they were people that had been marginalized by the *gada* process (cf. above p.3), perhaps they were people who just did not care much about it. While the pastoralists seem to have developed a paternalistic attitude *vis-à-vis* their adopted allies among the farmers, the 'men of wealth' seem to have been more inclined to dominate and exploit their subjects. It was against this landlord class that the *gabaro* uprising was directed (M. Hassan 1983: 345-348, 351).

We may thus conclude that the notion of *gabaro* was given widely variant interpretations and that these interpretations were related to the differing interests of two major groups of Oromo. On the one extreme, the *gabaro* was an adopted son or daughter and a social equal, on the other he was a serf and a social inferior, the difference being approximately the one between freedom and servitude.

I would suggest that these two interpretations provided a model for the integration of foreigners and outsiders in the following centuries. In one case the outsiders were made bondsmen of Oromo masters. They were given neither jural nor political rights; they could not be legally married, nor could they have ties of kinship. They were social and jural minors, they were just 'boys'.

In the other case they were adopted and regarded as the sons and equals of the 'true Oromo' in the social and jural, but not in the ritual respect. Being regarded as ritual juniors, they were ascribed the same status as that ascribed to drop-outs from the *gada* system: they were placed in the category "eternal youth", referred to as *ilma garba*, 'son of a minor'. This category was made up of ritually de-graded Oromo and ritually 'up-graded' outsiders. The Sibu are perfectly right, therefore, when they assert that the *ilma garba* are not 'sons of slaves' and that they are as 'true Oromo' as are the *borana*: they are just 'sons of boys'.

ACKNOWLEDGEMENTS

The fieldwork constituting the basis for this study was made possible by grants from the Swedish Humanities Research Council, the Swedish Council for Social Science Research, the Scandinavian Institute of African Studies, The Vega Foundation and the University of Gothenburg. My participation in this conference was made possible by travel grants from the Knut and Alice Wallenburg Foundation and SAREC.

NOTES

1. Says Almeida (1954: 136): "They never cultivate land and sow nothing at all. They live on the cattle which they pasture on wide expanses of country; they drink their milk and eat their flesh. This is all they live on, though when they invade the Abyssinians' territory, they also eat what food they find. The fact that they do not sow is of great importance to them in that the Abyssinians cannot penetrate far into their country; when the Gallas know that they are invading with a strong army, they retire with their cattle many days' journey into the interior. The Abyssinians therefore never seize, or can seize supplies, and are thus compelled to withdraw to their own territories, often with heavy losses of men from sheer hunger."

2. Haberland (1963: 5) has suggested that cultivation of cereals and especially of barley, played a vital part in the mode of subsistence of the Oromo homelands in southern Ethiopia prior to the 16th century; barley is still of great ritual significance. In all parts of Oromo land where, today, agriculture is at all possible, the Oromo are agro-pastoralists.

3. This familiar quotation is found among many Oromo tribes. The Arsi, who use the term *garba* to refer to the Hadiya proper as well as to assimilated people of Hadiya descent, say: "Nine are the *Borana* and ninety are the *Garba*" (Braukämper 1980: 7). He has found that among the Arsi more than half of the clans are of Hadiya descent.

4. Cf. Lévi-Strauss 1963: 89.

5. The notion of *saffu* is of such complexity that it defies every attempt at a short definition. It contains the idea of a divine, ordering principle: "the mutual relationship (rights and duties) between individual creatures or groups of creatures according to their place in the cosmic and social order" (Bartels 1983: 373). For an extensive explanation of the concept cf. Bartels 1983: 330-356.

REFERENCES CITED

d'Abbadie, Antoine (n.d.)   *Les Gallas.* Manuscript. Bibliothèque Nationale, Paris, fonds Nouvelles Acquisitions Françaises, NAF 21300, ff. 709-800.

Almeida, M. de (1954)   "The History of High Ethiopia or Abassia", *Some Records of Ethiopia, 1593-1646*, translated and edited by C. F. Beckingham and G. W. B. Huntingford. London: Hakluyt Society.

Merid Wolde Aregay (1971)   *Southern Ethiopia and the Christian kingdom 1508-1708, with special reference to the Galla migrations and their consequences.* Ph.D. thesis, London University.

Bahrey (1954)   "History of the Galla", *Some Records of Ethiopia, 1593-1646, op. cit.*

Bartels, Lambert (1983)   *Oromo Religion. Myths and Rites of the Western Oromo of Ethiopia — An Attempt to Understand.* Collectanea Instituti Anthropos, Vol.8. Berlin: Reimer.

Baxter, P. T. W. (1978)   "Boran Age-Sets and Generation-Sets: *Gada*, a puzzle or a maze?" In *Age, Generation and Time. Some Features of East African Age Organisations*, edited by P. T. W. Baxter and Uri Almagor. London: Hurst: 151-182.

Beckingham, C. F. and Huntingford, G.W.B. (1954)   *Some Records of Ethiopia, 1593-1646.* London: Hakluyt Society.

Braukämper, Ulrich (1980)   *Geschichte der Hadiya Süd-Äthiopiens.* Wiesbaden. Steiner.

Cerulli, E. (1933)   *Etiopia Occidentale.* Roma: Sindicato italiano artè grafiche.

Gragg, Gene B. (1982)   *Oromo dictionary.* Monograph No.12, Committee on North East African Studies. East Lansing: African Studies Center, Michigan State University.

Haberland, E. (1963)   "Galla Sud-Äthiopiens", *Volker Sud-Äthiopiens, Ergebnisse der Frobenius Expeditionen 1950-52 und 1954-56*, Band 2. Stuttgart: Kohlhammer.

Mohammed Hassan (1983)   *The Oromo of Ethiopia, 1500-1850: With Special Emphasis on the Gibe Region.* Ph.D. thesis, University of London, School of Oriental and African Studies.

Hultin, Jan (1979)   "Political Structure and the Development of Inequality among the Macha Oromo". *Pastoral Production and Society*, edited by Equipe écologie et anthropologie des sociétées pastorales. Cambridge: Maison des Sciences de l'Homme and Cambridge University Press: 283-293.

———————— (1982)   "The Oromo Expansion Reconsidered". *N. E. A. Journal of Research on North East Africa*. Vol.1, No.3: 188-203.

———————— (1984)   "Kinship and Property in Oromo Culture". *Proceedings of the Seventh International Conference of Ethiopian Studies*. Edited by Sven Rubenson. Addis Ababa, Uppsala, East Lansing: IES, SIAS, MSU: 451-457.

Knutsson, Karl Eric (1967)   *Authority and Change. A Study of the Kallu Institution among the Macha Galla of Ethiopia*. Etnologiska Studier 29. Göteborg: Etnografiska Muséet.

Asmarom Legesse (1973)   *Gada. Three Approaches to the Study of African Society*. New York: The Free Press/ London: Collier MacMillan.

Lévi-Strauss, Claude (1963)   *Totemism*. Boston: Beacon Press.

Mesfin Wolde Mariam (1972)   *An Introductory Geography of Ethiopia*. Addis Ababa: Berhanena Selam.

Pankhurst, Richard (1961)   *An Introduction to the Economic History of Ethiopia*. London.

Torry, William (1978)   "Gabra Age Organization and Ecology". In *Age, Generation and Time. Some Features of East African Age Organization. Op. cit.* 183-206.

GABBRA RITUAL AND SEASONAL CALENDARS

Anita Kassam

I. THE GABBRA

Culturally, socially, linguistically and historically, the Gabbra are related to the Galla peoples of Ethiopia and Northern Kenya. They speak a dialect belonging to the central Oromo cluster, in the eastern-Cushitic branch of the Afro-asiatic family of languages as classified by Greenberg (1966). Gabbra is most closely related to the Boran dialect and can be said to be virtually the same tongue, with only a few minor linguistic differences. The Gabbra live on both sides of the Kenya/Ethiopia border and, according to the 1979 Kenya National Census, there were estimated to be 30,553 Gabbra living in Kenya. Unfortunately, I do not have any precise figures for the number of Gabbra living on the Ethiopian side of the frontier. Gabbra territory in Ethiopia extends to Arbalee in the province of Sidamo, and in Kenya they occupy the semi-arid region on the edge of the Chalbi Desert to the east of Lake Turkana in Marsabit District. Although this region has probably been part of Gabbra grazing territory since the C17th, they did not occupy it on a semi-permanent basis until the end of the last century. The question of the historical origins and of the formation processes which led to the crystalization of the Gabbra into a distinct ethnic group are too complex to be treated here, but the origins of most of the Gabbra phratries can probably be traced to southern Ethiopia, where Gabbra ritual sites are still located today. The Gabbra practise a mixed livestock economy of camels, sheep and goats and sometimes cattle, and share a deep affinity with other eastern-Cushitic camel pastoralists, like the Somali and Rendille.

Before I embark upon the main topic of my paper, which is the Gabbra ritual and seasonal calendars, I will first examine the different temporal units which structure Gabbra perception of time, and I will briefly describe the annual feast of Almado, a rite which marks the beginning and the end of the Gabbra year, and which plays a central role in the computation of the latter.

II. GABBRA CONCEPTS OF TIME AND HISTORY

Like the Boran, whose concepts of time and history have been described by Legesse (1973) in his study of the *Gada* generation-set system, the Gabbra have a complex notion of time which determines the manner in which they record historical events and in which they perceive the environment. Despite the close cultural connections between the Gabbra and the Boran, and despite a certain number of structural similarities in their generic models of time and history, both of which can be said to be unique in Africa, there are a number of differences which are specific to both groups and which probably stem from divergencies in their socio-economic and political structures and in ritual practice. I will discuss the Gabbra model here, opposing it, where possible, to the Boran one, as it is described by Legesse. My own data is based on field-work conducted amongst the Gabbra between 1980 and 1983.[1]

1. Time units

For the Gabbra, all time is cyclical and the basic temporal unit for measuring these cycles is the week.

a) The week (*torbaan*, literally 'seven', instrumental case)[2]

Although the Gabbra perceive the week as being composed of seven days, in some instances, when they count the days of the week, for example, from one Monday to the next, they say that these days form a total of eight, as in French. Each of these days is named. Most of the Gabbra names are derived from Arabic. The Gabbra days of the week are the following:

alsinin[a]	Monday
talassa	Tuesday
arbaa	Wednesday
kamis[a]	Thursday
gumaat[a]	Friday
sabdi	Saturday
ahad[a]	Sunday

The Boran do not have the conceptual category of the week which, as we shall see, is extremely important in Gabbra historical time-reckoning. In the Boran system, there are twenty-seven names, and each day of the month is named in a circular fashion, so that there is no one-to-one association between the day and its name. When the twenty-seven days are exhausted, Boran merely revert back to the beginning of the list to finish the twenty-nine or thirty day count of the lunar month (Legesse, 1973: 181). The Boran days are:

> lumasa, gidada, ruda, areri dura, areri ballo, adula dura, adula ballo, garba dura, garba balla, garba dullacha, bita balla, sorsa, algajima, arba, walla, basa dura, basa balla, carra, maganatti jarra, maganatti briti, salban dura, salban balla, salban dullacha, garaduma, sonsa, rurruma.

The most important day of the week for the Gabbra is Friday, probably due to the Islamic influence, which marks many aspects of their cultural life. As Tablino (1974) has pointed out, data confirmed by my own fieldwork, the day (ayyaan[a] 'day', 'luck', kind of spirit) begins at sunset and each evening therefore marks the beginning of a new day. The time of day is described in relation to the position of the sun and to the particular herding activity associated with this time, for example, 'time when the camels begin to return to camp' (gise oraati gaala, literally "time when the camels face the sun"), 'time when the camels are nearing their enclosures' (derlam[a]), 'night' (halkan[a]), 'midnight' (halkan ya citan[i], literally, "night has been cut") and so forth. However, the Swahili clock is rapidly replacing these more traditional expressions for the time of day. Each of the days of the week is associated with a domestic or wild animal, for instance, arbaa is the word for 'elephant' and the Gabbra tell a myth to explain how the day was given this name, the only non-Arabic one. Friday is associated with the dabella, a religious dignatory and Tuesday with quarrels. Accordingly, some days are propitious, like Monday, ayyaan ree 'day of goats', Thursday, Friday and Sunday, ayyaan gaala, 'day of camels'. Unfortunately, I cannot treat all these points in detail in the present paper. The remaining days of the week are unpropitious, and the Gabbra therefore avoid performing certain activities, like marriage or moving, on these days, whilst they may be appropriate for other activities like burials, etc.

b) The month (jii[a], 'month', 'moon')

The Gabbra month, like the Boran, is a lunar one and is made up of 29 or 30 days. Once again, Gabbra and Boran adopt a different terminology in the naming of these months, which are:

Gabbra months:
yak'a, ragar kara, ragar eegee, faite, jii bor kara, jii bor eegee, somder kara, somder eegee, soom, furam, didiyaal, arafa

Boran months:
cikawa, sadasa, abrasa, ammaji, gurrandala, biottottessa, camsa, bufa, wacabajji, obora gudda, obora dikka, birra

(Legesse, 1973: 180)

The Gabbra month begins when the new moon (*baati*) is first sighted and is divided into two halves, fifteen days of 'light' (*addeess^a*, from *adii* 'white') and fifteen days of 'darkness' (*dukkan^a*), according to the waxing and waning phases of the moon. Each of these phases is carefully counted, as they play an important role in ritual (cf. *infra*). In Northern Kenya, where the skies are clear and sharp, it is quite easy to follow the course of the moon across the night sky as it sets later and later each evening, until it finally disappears, and so to count the two halves of the month. If the new moon is obscured by cloud, the Gabbra wait one day before starting the new count and a month can be twenty-nine or thirty days long, but the rites associated with the new moon are only performed when it is visible. Gabbra maintain that the new moon does not stay 'hidden' for more than one day.

Days and months form the basis of the ritual calendar and are regulated by the lunar count.

As far as I know, stars or constellations (*urjii*) do not play a very important role in time-reckoning for the Gabbra, whereas in the Boran system, experts (*ayyaantu*) use this astronomical information in their time-computations (Legesse, 1973: 181). In the Gabbra universe, these stars or constellations, some of which are associated with myths, may be used to indicate the state of fecundity (*finn^a*) of the environment, a complex cultural concept. However, I did not examine the role of stars in any detail, and it is likely that further field investigation will reveal new facts.

c) The year (*gann^a*)

The year is made up of twelve lunar months, but is calculated independently of these months, and consists, the Gabbra say, of 365 days. These days are counted in a very complex manner and form the basis of the seasonal calendar. The computation of these days is linked to the annual feast of Almado. This rite and the two calendars will be examined in the next section of the paper.

For the Gabbra, years also form larger units of time. The basic unit is the eight-year cycle, modelled on the 'eight'-day week. Thus every year in this cycle is given a week-day name. For instance, 1984 in the Gregorian calendar was the Wednesday year for the Gabbra and 1985, which started if my calculations are right, on Thursday 22 November 1984, is their Thursday year. Every year is also named according to the most important event which marked it, be it social, economic, political or ecological. And so 1984 will probably be called, amongst other things, the 'Wednesday Year of Drought'. Experts will remember the ecological disaster and, in the Gabbra conception of history, a similar disaster can be expected to happen again in the Wednesday year, sixty-four years hence, i.e. in our year 2048. For the Gabbra believe that when the cycle of eight years repeats itself eight times, there is an accumulation of evil which will erupt in the sixty-fourth year. If this is correct, then the present crisis is the repetition of an event which took place in 1920 (Tablino, 1974: 9 gives 1921 as the Wednesday year).[4] This repetition is called *dac'c'i*. Here my findings differ from Tablino's, who says that there is no "cyclical record of historic events" and that the Gabbra have only "a vague cyclical ideal of history" (p.5). P. Robinson (1980:11) confirms that such a cyclical pattern does indeed exist, but says that "the length of cycles depends on events themselves". However, I feel that Robinson is confusing this last kind of repetition, which the Gabbra call *idaa* and *dac'c'i*, the sixty-four year cycle.

It is this eight-year cycle which regulates the generation-set system (*luub^a*). Sets change ideally every eight years and it is at this time that the secular officials (*hayyu*) are invested with political power and religious dignitaries (*dabella*) tie the white turban (*hitu*) which is a symbol of their ritual authority.

The figure nine is full of ill-omen for both the Gabbra and the Boran, as the ninth repetition of a cycle of eight is linked with eschatological ideas and signifies the end of the world (*adaal^a*). And so the ninth transition ceremony, which was scheduled to take place on Thursday 1985 and the next year (Friday 1986) were particularly dangerous for the *dabella*.

Gabbra and Boran versions of *dac'c'i* are not quite similar, as in the Boran system it is linked to their *gaada* institution which is different from the Gabbra *luub^a* model, and for the

Boran, a whole cycle (*gogessa*) repeats itself. But the principle of *dac'c'i* as being a "mystical influence of history on the present course of events" is the same (Legesse, 1973: 194). Similarly, both peoples believe that the only way of averting the repetition of evil is by making proper sacrifice at the proper time on a community level. The Gabbra, therefore, see the present crisis as a punishment for their neglect of *aada* 'tradition' and they accept moral responsibility for their own plight.

It is through this ingenious method of remembering the past that the Gabbra record historical, socio-political and ecological events through their oral traditions. However, only a few reputed elders have a specialized knowledge of these cycles and the manner in which they repeat themselves (*marar*[a]). The oral historians are called *abooti marara*, literally "fathers of repetition", in other words, historical experts. It is these historians who also have the most profound knowledge of the seasonal calendar and how to calculate it.

d) The seasons

These are four major seasons recognized by the Gabbra, two wet seasons and two dry seasons. The long rains (*gann*[a] also the word for 'year') fall approximately between April and June and are brought by the south-east monsoons originating over the Indian Ocean. The short rains (*hagayya*) fall between October and December and are brought by the north-east monsoons originating in the Arabian region (Stiles & Kassam). The long rains are preceded by a hot, dry season between January and March, called *bon hagayya*, because it may be puctuated with non-seasonal showers, as may *adooless*[a], a cool, dry season which extends from July to September. *Furmaat*[a] is the name given to a rain in *bon hagayya*, whilst there are a number of words for showers in *adooless*[a], such as *sorar*[a], *buk'aa* and *alad*[a]. For a people of the desert, the Gabbra certainly have a rich 'rain' vocabulary.

2. Almado

Almado is the culmination, so to speak, of the ceremonial or ritual calendar. However, although this is so, the manner in which Almado is calculated, which I call the Almado count, does not influence the calendar of feast days, etc., as these are regulated, as I have already said, by the lunar count. On the other hand, the Almado count is an integral element of the seasonal calendar. All these complex parallel methods of time computation are rather confusing, as they are conceptually linked by Almado. It may help to visualize the Gabbra year in the form of the following diagram:

THE GABBRA YEAR

Seasonal Calendar

Almado

ritual calendar

12 lunar months

Almado

365 Solar Days

1. The Origin of Almado

According to two versions of a myth recounting the origin of Almado, which I collected in the field, it is a rite of expiation performed by all the Gabbra for an incestuous event which took place in the past in which an Odhol[a] man inadvertently married his own daughter.[5]

I will briefly summarize the two versions of this myth, which belongs, in the Gabbra classification, to the category of *aada duri duri*, or tales about traditional matters.

a) Version I

A man's family was almost annihilated when his camp was attacked by the Gelabba (Shankilla, Dassenetch). He himself managed to escape, but one of his daughters was captured by the enemy. The man's name was Halmado. Vowing vengeance, Halmado retaliated many years later by attacking a group of Gelabba. Amongst the group was a young woman, whom he spared and took back to his own people. He later married this young woman and, although he did not know it at the time, she was his own daughter. The couple prospered. Their herds grew and they were blessed with many children.

One day, however, Halmado discovered the truth. He sat down beneath a tree with an elder and told him that if anything were to happen to him and his family, he should see to it that all the people built a large fire and stoked it with firewood brought from each individual household. He instructed the old man to see to it that an offering of milk was also made by every household.

That evening, Halmado sacrificed and when all his family was asleep, he covered the whole house and all the family's belongings with fat and set fire to the house. The whole family perished in the fire.

b) Version II

During the terrible drought known as *Chin Tite Gurraac'a* ("time of the black flies"), a man's family was dispersed by the disaster. After the drought, the man met his own daughter but did not recognize her and they became man and wife. The girl's name was Almad.

When the man discovered what he had done, he lit a large fire and threw Almad into it, praying for forgiveness.

All the members of his phratry also lit fires to atone for this deed. At the time, however, the sons of Mamo were away at a dry-stock satellite camp (*fora*) and so Mamo's family only lit their expiatory fire one week after the rest had already done so.

2. Celebration of Almado

Almado is celebrated by all the Gabbra in the last month of their lunar year. The rites are performed for three consecutive weeks. In the first and second week these rites take place on the day after which the current year is named (for example, Wednesday). In the third week the rite is performed on the day after which the new year will be named, (for example, Thursday 1985). Nine weeks before the event, members of the Odhol[a] phratry signal the beginning of the expiation period by lighting fires for three weeks, on the day of the current year, on the day of the new year and once again on the day of the current year. In the last week, all the Gabbra women collect *gaalle*, a creeper (*Kedrostis gijef J.F. gmel., C. Jeffrey*), associated with camels, exorcism and keeping the enemy at bay, to adorn the entrance of their homes and of the stock enclosures. This week is known as *gaalle afaat[a]* "the spreading (?) of *gaalle*". *Gaalle* is also collected during the three weeks of Almado. In the tenth week, all the Gabbra phratries celebrate Almado together, by lighting a fire once a week, for three weeks running, praying and sharing milk together. Different milk containers are used: a container called *c'ic'oo* in the first week, and a container called *gorfa* in the last two weeks. On the third week, the fire is extinguished with water poured with the left hand, the hand of death. The following week, the last week of the lunar month, is known as Almado Ilman Mamo, "the Almado of the sons of Mamo" to commemorate historically the delayed celebration of this event by Mamo's family (cf. version II of Almado myth above). It is at the end of this week that the Gabbra begin to count the new year. To herald in the new year, in the last week of Almado, the branch (*bitume*) which serves as a gate to the stock enclosures, is changed and a fresh one cut.

3. The Ritual Calendar

Almado is the most important ceremonial event of the year in the Gabbra ritual calendar. During the four weeks of Almado and Almado Ilman Mamo, none of the members of the Odhol[a] phratry are allowed to cut their nails or their hair, and no blood must be spilt and so warfare, hunting and circumcision are activities which are avoided. These avoidances are those normally associated with mourning. As in the case of other Gabbra rituals, all the members of the family must be reunited in the base camp so as to be able to celebrate the event together and offer prayer and libations of milk for the welfare of the whole family and all the Gabbra nation. Stock is not taken out to graze on the morning of the celebration. Base camps should not move during this period, unless forced to do so by circumstances beyond their control.

In 1983 and 1984, Almado took place in the month of *yak'a*. *Yak'a, somder kara* and *somder eegee* are the most propitious months of the year. There are six propitious months and six unpropitious months. *Faite, arafa* and *furam* are also propitious months, but to a lesser degree. 'Propitiousness' is measured in terms of *finn[a]* 'fertility', 'prosperity', etc. The other months of the lunar year are considered unpropitious, with *ragar kara* and *ragar eegee* being the worst months. Almost all socio-cultural and economic activity, such as the rite of transition, livestock exchange or purchase, etc., are avoided in these 'bad' months.

The month of *yak'a* is, therefore, generally associated with festivity. For *sorio*, a sacrifice made for peace, rain and plenty is celebrated in this month, when small-stock is slaughtered so that blood may literally and symbolically flow into the ground to purify the members of the family for all wrong committed. *Sorio* is also celebrated in the two other propitious months, the two *somder*, on even 'light' or 'dark' 'good' days like a Monday, Thursday, Friday or Sunday. The two Gabbra moieties, Jiblo and Losa, celebrate *sorio* on different days and if, for any reason, *sorio* could not be done on the day designated for the moiety, both Jiblo and Losa can sacrifice together on a third day, called *oider*. After *sorio*, a period of mourning can be brought to a close by purification ceremonies; widowers can remarry; and a ceremony in which a newly-wed's wife's black veil (*agogo*) is 'lifted' by her husband is performed. Being months of *finn[a]*, all enterprises which are undertaken in these months are bound to succeed: warfare, hunting, circumcision, marriage, naming ceremonies, livestock transactions, plant and wood collecting expeditions for house materials and domestic items and marriage, herding and spear-handle sticks. According to Tablino (1974: 2), marriage is celebrated on odd days of the increasing moon ("light days"). Hair-cutting ceremonies, when married men shave their heads completely and trim their beards and put the trimmings under the conjugal bed, are performed on a propitious day during these months. *Jilla*, the transition ceremony rites, take place in the *somder* months.

In the month preceding *yak'a, arafa*, the ceremony of *saddett[a]* literally 'eight' is performed. I have not yet discovered the significance of this rite, but it may be linked to the 'name' of the month, *jii nama*, "month of man" when, according to oral tradition, man was first created by God. The number eight may have symbolic meaning, for it would appear to be an important one in the Gabbra numeric system. The ceremony takes place on the eighth day of 'light'. On this day, no-one must venture out of camp and livestock is not taken out to graze. A heavy silence reigns. Women collect a sufficient amount of firewood for domestic use on the evening before, which is consumed on the day of the ceremony.

Soom, the ninth lunar month, is not a propitious one, as during this month all Gabbra Muslims fast for forty days in accordance with Islamic law. No Muslim is allowed to cut his hair or his nails or spill any blood, as this would bring sure death. This is also true of other unpropitious months.

The Gabbra consider themselves to be highly religious people. They adhere closely to their traditions and this calendar is consulted for all their activities. At the beginning of every month, the rites of the new moon are observed, when the head of the household applies fat and small balls of gum resin, *kumbi* (sap of *Commiphora corriaceae Engl.* or myrrh) to the foreheads of all male members of the family, and when a special 'moon' song is sung and *dibayyu*, a libation of milk is offered in remembrance of the ancestors of the clan and family.

4. Seasonal Calendar

It is important to note that the seasonal calendar is not an actual, but an anticipatory one, based on a mythical model, a pattern of seasons which the Gabbra associate with events in oral tradition. However, this ideal pattern is used by the Gabbra histuro-climatologists as a framework of reference to make weather forecasts and to advise on grazing strategies based on their knowledge of the historical cycles (*marar^a*).

The Almado count, when the Almado-cycle of events are being enumerated, forms part of the seasonal count. Specialist start counting the 365 days of the year on the morrow of Almado Ilman Mamo and make weather predictions according to the calendar in their heads.

The seasonal calendar is calculated in the following manner:

a.   The first one hundred days are counted in decimal fashion, in 'batches' of ten and then "put aside". According to Tablino (1974: 3), these one hundred days, which the Gabbra say roughly represent three months or one season, are called D'ibb Abba Gura, the "one hundred days of Abba Gura" when Abba Gura committed suicide because he lost his herd of one hundred cattle in a drought. The one hundred days correspond to the season of *bon hagayya*, of hot, dry weather. *Furmaat^a* may fall in the first thirty day count.

This count of one hundred is further divided up, so that the last ten days can be counted in two sets of five, so that we have 90 + 5 + 5. This is done because the long rainy season of *gann^a* should begin on the ninety-fifth day, but often five days go by without any sign of rain. This five-day period is called *shaanaata*, or *shaambul*, from *shaani* 'five' and in the latter term we have the verb *bul-* 'to sleep' or 'to spend the night'. If there is no rain within this period, the Gabbra say that there will be heavy rain on the sixth day.

There is a folktale attached to this special five-day count which goes as follows:

"Once upon a time, Dik-Dik was shivering and trembling with cold. Giraffe asked her what the matter was. She replied that five days had gone by without rain and she could feel the cold rain coming, and that was why she was shivering."

These last ten days are counted in the following way:

1.   *tokkibulle*: derived from *tokk* 'one' and *bul-* 'to sleep' i.e. 'to spend the night'.

2.   *lamale*: derived from *lam* 'two' and an ordinal number suffix, *-ale*, giving the meaning 'second (day)'.

3.   *d'imale*: derived from *d'imu* 'flood' and *-ale*. The Gabbra have a version of the Biblical story of the Flood, and this third day refers to this myth.

4.   *bololito*: an archaic word meaning 'small drops of rain', signifying that rainfall was imminent.

5.   *jaarsibalete*: derived from *jaars^a* 'old man', 'elder' and ? referring to the time when an old man lost his bearings and could not find his way home. The people of his camp

went out to look for him, as is traditional in Gabbra society. On this day it rained heavily.

6. *agaga*: refers to the sound made by camels when it pours with rain.

7-10: are counted with the usual number words.

The first five days of this count, which form a unit called *shaanaata* or *shaambul*, are called *shaanale* 'five times'.

b.   The second set of one hundred days is the period which corresponds to the rainy season of *ganna*. Tablino (1974: 3), calls them D'ibb Safara because, according to the legend he collected, "the Somali were called in to pray so that the excessively heavy rains would stop".
The last one hundred and sixty-five days are calculated thus:

1-60 days: *adooless*, a period of dry cool weather.

21 days: *ibid Odhola*, the three weeks during which the Odhol phratry light fires preceding Almado. In the last week, *hagayya*, the short rains should begin to fall.

63 days: *ena afaat Almado* or *torbaan sagal*, the nine weeks preceding Almado.

21 days: the three weeks of Almado.

During *adooless*, non-seasonal showers may be expected to fall.

The Gabbra say that this seasonal calendar and the Almado count is specific to them and is unknown to the Boran, who do not celebrate Almado.
This Almado count, which I painstakingly obtained from my informants, differs from Tablino's (1974: 3). It is possible that there are as many versions of the count as there are myths. My version is no more 'logical' than Tablino's. In fact, there are inconsistencies which I have unfortunately been unable to check in the field after analyzing my data: firstly, the Gabbra say that the Odhol start lighting their fires nine weeks before Almado, whereas the above count shows that this is in fact more accurately twelve weeks; secondly, the new year count should start in the week following Almado, after Almado Ilman Mamo, which the count above does not take into consideration. I suggest, therefore, that neither version is completely correct, or that one of the versions (or both) is 'logical' in the Gabbra time conception.
To understand the system more fully, it will be necessary to grasp first how Gabbra conceptualize numbers and why they count in this fashion. It will also be necessary to understand number symbolism and discover why certain numbers, like eight (seven + one), are important and to discover the meaning of the so-called "mystical" numbers which Haberland (1963) discusses, and which Legesse (1973) vehemently criticizes. More comparative work needs to be done with other Galla peoples to trace the origins of this time-computation system and to measure the Arab influence on Gabbra time-reckoning.
To conclude on a positive note, however, I will say that with precise dates for Almado, a ceremony which I was unable to witness at first hand for two consecutive years, I did come up with a total of 365 days and I was able to calculate when the new Gabbra year would start, down to the day of the week to which it is associated.

NOTES

1. My fieldwork was supported by the Dean's Committee of the University of Nairobi (1980-1981) and the Ford Foundation (1982-1983). My data for this paper is based on a prelim-

inary investigation of the Gabbra concept of time, and was part of a much larger study of Gabbra oral traditions, so it was not done in depth. My results must therefore be considered as tentative ones subject to further revision pending more fieldwork.

2. All symbols used in transcribing the Gabbra dialect in this paper are those of the International Phonetic Alphabet, except that IPA /dʒ/ is written j, /tʃ/ is written c, /tʃʼ/ is written sh, and /ɲ/ is written ny. Raised letters signify that the vowel is devoiced. Vowel and consonant length are noted by doubling the letter. When quoting Legesse, his transcription has been respected.

3. The Gabbra make no allowances for leap years. When aligned to the Gregorian calendar, the Gabbra year begins one day earlier every fourth year. Tablino (1974: 9) sets the beginning of the Gabbra year at the second week of Almado, which Tablino (1974: 9) calls Almado *c'ic'oo*. I witnessed Almado in 1982 and 1983 and made a note of the following dates for 1983:

1st week of Almado (*c'ic'oo*)   Tuesday 1 November, 1983
2nd ” ” ” (*gorfa*)   ” 8 ” ”
3rd ” ” ” ”   Wednesday 16 November, 1983
4th ” ” ” (*Ilman Mamo*)   Tuesday 22 ” ”
Beginning of Gabbra year (1984): Wednesday, 23 November, 1983.

4. A record of these years has been made by Tablino (1974: 9-15) and Robinson (1980: annex). Tablino's record goes from 1897-1974, and Robinson's continues up to 1978. However, there does not seem to be any consistent method of naming years adopted by the Gabbra. Tablino calls 1921 Arba Hoften Mirga Dufte "the Wednesday year in which Hofte came from the North. The Hofte are the Borana who came from Ethiopia in that year and settled for the first time in Marsabit." My informants called this year Arbaa Sadetama or Arbaa Finnoo, the Wednesday year when it rained heavily for eighty days or the Wednesday year when it rained heavily for eighty days or the Wednesday year of small-pox. As Legesse (1973: 200) points out, the repetition of cycle can sometimes produce its complete opposite.

5. There are five Gabbra phratries: the Algana, Gaara, Sharbana, Galbo and Odhol[a].

REFERENCES

Greenberg, J. H. 1966   *The languages of Africa*, Bloomington: Mouton & Co.

Haberland, E. 1963   *Galla Süd-Äthiopiens*, Stuttgart: W. Kolhammer Verlag.

Legesse, A. 1973   *Gada. Three approaches to the study of African society*, New York: The Free Press.

Robinson, P. W. 1980   'Disaster and response among the Gabbra of Northern Kenya. An historical perspective.' Paper presented at the Conference on ecological stress in Eastern Africa, 15-17 June, 1980, Nairobi.

Stiles, D. N. & Kassam, A.   'An ethno-botanical study of Gabbra plant use, Marsabit District, Kenya', *Journal of the E. A. Natural History Society*.

Tablino, Fr. P. 1974   'Calculation of time among the Gabbra of Northern Kenya', Unpublished ms., Africana Section, University of Nairobi Library, Nairobi.

DIFFICULTÉS DE CORRESPONDANCE ENTRE

NOMS VERNACULAIRES ET NOMS SCIENTIFIQUES

Exemples de plantes d'Éthiopie

D. Lemordant

RÉSUMÉ

Dans le cadre d'une étude de l'histoire des plantes d'Éthiopie importantes pour leur intérêt alimentaire, médicinal, technique, etc . . . nous nous sommes attaché à analyser les causes des fréquentes difficultés à établir une correspondance entre nom vernaculaire et nom scientifique. Hormis les différences d'appellation, de nature bien évidente, suivant les régions, les raisons de confusion sont d'ordre botanique ou utilitaire mais peuvent participer de ces deux étiologies. Des erreurs initiales sont reconduites sans contrôle dans les écrits pendant longtemps.

Le but de notre étude est non seulement de rechercher les causes de ces erreurs ce qui permet d'expliquer et d'excuser certaines d'entre elles, mais aussi de fournir quelques informations permettant d'éviter les écueils et les pièges de la phytonymie populaire.

Des exemples ont été choisis chez les plantes alimentaires, les plantes médicinales ou simplement chez des plantes remarquables par une morphologie particulière ou une présence fréquente.

A l'occasion d'une étude de l'histoire de plantes éthiopiennes importantes pour l'intérêt utilitaire qu'elles présentent (plantes alimentaires, médicinales, d'usages divers), il nous a été donné de constater le cheminement souvent long et laborieux pour faire coïncider un nom populaire avec une identification botanique certaine. Ce parcours est couramment entaché d'erreurs longtemps perpétuées à travers les écrits. Ce sont justement les causes de ces erreurs qui ont retenu notre attention. Certaines dont nous ne parlerons pas, sont dues simplement à la reconduction d'une information antérieure non contrôlée mais qui, par la force de l'usage, risque de prendre valeur d'authenticité.

Une plante dont l'aire est bien localisée, appartient, si elle a un rôle à jouer, à une civilisation particulière.

Elle commence à être connue ailleurs sous le nom du pays d'où elle vient.

C'est à ce moment que commencent les difficultés pour connaître sa vraie nature, son identité botanique.

En effet, on sait de longue date que les appellations populaires font appel à deux types de critères:

— la morphologie; nous dirons plus largement les caractères organoleptiques car souvent sont pris en cause des critères comme l'odeur, la couleur, le goût; la morphologie d'une plante, immédiatement perceptible, est bien le premier élément qui sert à donner un nom et à établir une classification populaire ou scientifique;

— l'utilisation.

Les deux critères peuvent souvent se combiner.

Donner le même nom à des plantes de morphologies voisines ou d'utilisation identique est une simple association d'idées.

C'est à peine si quelquefois un deuxième terme qualificatif vient préciser entre deux espèces voisines une différence de couleur, d'habitat, de taille et l'on sait les sens particuliers que peuvent prendre par exemple dans le cas de la taille, les termes "mâle" et "femelle" qui sont sans rapport avec la sexualité; dans le cas de la couleur les termes "blanc" et "noir" signifiant "clair" et "sombre".

Malheureusement, ces appellations vulgaires sont très souvent malencontreuses car elles font référence à une plante connue pour désigner la nouvelle venue sans liens botaniques entre elles la plupart du temps.

De plus, ce dénominations sont souvent les seules connues du plus grand nombre de personnes et débouchent sur des rapprochements, des assimilations qui conduisent à des interprétations regrettables.

Le commerce, en diffusant la matière première végétale, répand par la même occasion son nom impropre, ce qui entretient la confusion dans l'espace et dans le temps. D'autant plus que souvent ce n'est qu'une partie de la plante qui est utilisée.

Les exemples classiques communs à plusieurs langues — (ce qui traduit bien un cheminement de pensée identique) — ne manquent pas. Toutes les "noix" sont là pour en témoigner alors qu'une seule est le fruit du noyer, *Juglans regia*. Deux, parmi tant d'autres, en français Noix muscade et Noix de coco, se retrouvent en arabe et en amharique.

Des appellations impropres continuent cependant à être largement employées dans le commerce mondial et même dans des secteurs aussi spécialisés que celui de la droguerie pharmaceutique qui réclamerait une précision scientifique plus rigoureuse.

On trouvera, ci-dessous, quelques exemples de noms de plantes en Éthiopie, illustrant les deux grands groupes des causes des difficultés d'identification que nous avons précédemment mentionnées.

MORPHOLOGIES VOISINES

1. Espèces d'une même famille

Les termes englobant plusieurs espèces voisines mais différentes se rencontrent à propos de familles très homogènes comme le sont chez les Monocotylédones: les Liliacées, les Amaryllidacées, les Graminées (Poacées)*, les Cypéracées, et chez le Dicotylédones: les Crucifères (Brassicacées)*, les Ombellifères (Apiacées)*, les Apocynacées, les Asclépiadacées, les Labiées (Lamiacées)*, les Verbénacées.

C'est naturellement plus souvent des espèces du même genre botanique qui sont confondues; c'est bien compréhensible pour un genre comme *Solanum*, dont les quelque 900 espèces posent bien des problèmes d'identification.

Plusieurs genres chez les Astéracées posent les mêmes problèmes (*Vernonia, Artemisia*). On notera au passage que les dénominations de beaucoup de ces familles ont dû être mises récemment en conformité avec les règles de la nomenclature taxinomique moderne; la disparité des premières désignations est la marque de l'ancienneté de leur connaissance; elles ont été en effet les premières décrites car les premières remarquées pour un aspect caractéristique, à une époque à laquelle les règles de nomenclature n'étaient pas établies. On trouvera ici quelques exemples à propos de familles importantes (par ordre alphabétique).

Asclépiadacées

tefrina BAETEMAN parle d'une plante à sève laiteuse des bords de cours d'eau. C'est vague mais déjà intéressant. Le mot sève est impropre, mais sève laiteuse pour latex est une indication précieuse qui restreint le champ d'investigation à un petit nombre de familles à latex dont les Asclépiadacées.

Le *tefrina* est membre de cette famille même si différents auteurs désignent sous ce nom plusieurs espèces botaniques: *Asclepias flavida* N.E. Br. chez MASINO et CHIOVENDA qui la donne en équivalence d'*A. abyssinica* N.E. Br. CUFODONTIS nous fournit *Taccazea apiculata* Oliv., *Gomphocarpus fruticosus* R. Br. et *Kanahia laniflora* R. Br.

Cette dernière espèce est également dénommée, d'après CHIOVENDA, *yä baher teferina*, ce qui voudrait dire qu'elle n'est pas indigène.

---

* Le nom entre parenthèses est celui de la nomenclature actuelle. Par commodité, nous avons conservé le nom habituellement plus connu de la majorité des lecteurs.

Encore faut-il remarquer du point de vue botanique que les équivalences entre ces différents genres sont nombreuses.

Célastracées

atat   Divers *Celastrus* pour RICHARD: *C. Schimperi* Hochst., *C. obscurus* Rich., *C. edulis* Hochst. Divers *Gymnosporia* (= *Maytenus*): *G. gracilipes* Loes. = *G. senegalensis* et *G. montana* Benth. pour MOONEY.

Composées

tcheqquñ   Chez les Composées, nous avons l'exemple de *tcheqquñ*. On trouve sous ce nom *Artemisia abyssinica* C. H. Schultz, *A. afra* Jacq. et Willd., *A. rehan* Chiov.

Le nom spécifique de cette dernière espèce est d'ailleurs un autre nom vernaculaire, *reyan = eryan = nätch shettu* (" parfum blanc").

CHIOVENDA donne aussi sous ce nom *A. arborescens* L.

Tous les botanistes connaissent les difficultés d'identification des espèces d'*Artemisia* au sein des Composées et ne s'étonnent jamais de relever un même nom vernaculaire pour des espèces différentes.

Dans cet exemple, l'odeur prend place au côté de la morphologie.

Un facteur chimique intervient donc, celui des constituants d'une essence, identiques pour un certain nombre d'espèces bien qu'en proportions relatives différentes, ce qui en fait un critère de distinction. Nous avons là un point de rencontre de plusieurs disciplines: botanique, chimiotaxinomie, génétique, écologie.

gujo   Diverses espèces de *Vernonia* dont *V. auriculifera* Hiern. (= *V. uniflora* Hutch. et Dalz.) et *V. regi* Logan.

käskässo = käskässe   *Conyza gnaphaloïdes* C. H. Schultz

Blumea tomentosa A. Rich., à odeur forte comme *Helichrysum odoratissimum* L. donné par CUFODONTIS.

Existe aussi sous ce nom *Laggera tomentosa* Sch. Bip. CHIOVENDA donne également *Vernonia inulaefolia* Steud.

Crucifères

féto   *Capsella bursa pastoris* Moench

Lepidium sativaum L., espèce très polymorphe en Éthiopie appartenant à une famille déjà remarquable pour son homogénéité.

Graminées

akerma   Graminée servant en vannerie (GUIDI) et comme ornement de parure (GRIAULE).

Cynodon dactylon L. et *C. plectosachyum* pour CHIOVENDA. CUFODONTIS donne *Eleusine floccifolia* Forsk., STRELCYN *E. jaegeri* Pilg.

asäandabo   GUIDI: jonc

RICHARD: *Panicum quadrifarium* Hochst.

CHIOVENDA: *Echinochloa stagnina* P. B.

sämbälet   Diverses espèces sont rassemblées sous ce nom, toutes données par MOONEY.

Andropogon laniger Desf. = *Cymbopogon commutatus* Stapf. *Themeda* sp.

Hyparrhenia rufa Stapf., *H. variabilis* Stapf., *H. hirta* L.

särdo   *Panicum dactylon* L.
        Cynodon dactylon Rich.
        Agrostis semi-verticillata Forsk.

Rosacées

endjori Diverses espèces de *Rubus*, si difficiles, on le sait, à déterminer:
        Rubus steudneri Schw.
        R. aethiopicus R. A. Grah.
        R. rosaefolius Sm. = *R. pinnatus* Willd.
        R. exsuccus Steud., endémique
        R. apetalus Rich.

2. Familles différentes

La deuxième possibilité de confusion porte sur des familles de morphologies très voisines au moins pour le vulgaire et parfois même pour le spécialiste : Liliacées et Amaryllidacées, Graminées et Cypéracées, Apocynacées et Asclépiadacées, Lamiacées et Verbénacées.

gadjdja = gajja   RICHARD: *Andropogon (= Cymbopogon) squamulatus* Hochst., Graminées.
            STRELCYN: *Andropogon gayanus* Kunth, Graminées.
            CHIOVENDA: *Cyperus fischerianus* Schimper, Cypéracées.

mäqa = shämbaqo *Arundo donax* L., *Phragmites communis* L., *P. isiacus* Kunth, *P. mauritanica* Kunth, Graminées.
            Cyperus papyrus L., Cypéracées.

märénz = merénz = mälänz. BAETEMAN: arbuste aux fruits vénéneux.
            MERAB: *Strychnos abyssinica* Del., Loganiacées = *Strychnos innocua* Del. donné par MOONEY.
    GANORA et CUFODONTIS en font un représentant de la famille des Apocynacées, *Acocanthera schimperi* Benth. et Hook. (= *A. ouabaîo* Poisson = *Carissa schimperi* D. C.).
    Le caractère toxique semble être ici le point commun à ces espèces. Les linguistes pourront dire si *märénz* est parent de *märz*, poison. Par ailleurs, *Strychnos innocua* possède un fruit non toxique mais est-ce connu ou bien est-ce par assimilation à des espèces de morphologie voisine connues comme toxiques que le même nom est attribué?

gätätenna = yä hayya djoro = yä färäs zang

    BAETEMAN: espèce de plante aux larges feuilles et à fleurs jaunes.
    Cette description sommaire peut correspondre à un *Verbascum* ou un *Celsia* (Scrofulariacées).
    D'ailleurs MOONEY nous donne *Verbascum sinaïticum* Benth., comme CUFODONTIS qui indique aussi *Celsia floccosa* Benth., mais de plus cet auteur mentionne *Pentas Schimperiana* Vatke (Rubiacées).
    GANORA: *Leonotis raineriana* De Vis, Lamiacées.
    RICHARD: *Leonotis rugosa* Benth.
    On trouve les *Leonotis* sous l'autre nom de *ras kämmer*, "multitude de têtes", qui correspond bien à la disposition étagée des glomérules floraux comme chez le *Phlomis* dont parle MERAB. Par ailleurs, les feuilles opposées ont conduit BAETEMAN à parler de plante rappelant l'ortie.
    PICHI-SERMOLLI signale une autre Labiée sous ce nom, *Otostegia minucii* et également une Composée, *Vernonia adoensis* Sch.-Bip.

täländj   Arbuste pour BAETEMAN.

        Diverses Amaranthacées du genre *Achyranthes: A. aspera* L., *A. argentea*   Lam., *A. aquatica* R. Br.

        AVETTA indique *Barleria ventricosa* Hochst. sous les noms de *nätch täländj* (*täländj* blanc) et *Hypoestes triflora* Roem. et Schultz sous celui de *tequr täländj* (*täländj* noir), deux Acanthacées.

tchegogwät   D'après GRIAULE c'est une plante couverte de poils et à fleurs bleu-violet.

        On pense déjà à une Borraginacée.

        GUIDI précise . . . "à aiguillons" ce qui répond mieux aux poils tecteurs rudes de cette famille que le mot épine.

        BAETEMAN indique *Myosotis*, une Borraginacée.

        CUFODONTIS désigne le *Cynoglossum montanum* Hoejer, de la même famille mais également une Amaranthacée, *Cyathula globulifera* Moq.-Tand. et une Astéracée, *Bidens pilosa* L.

embway   Un cas particulier est celui de l'*embway*.

        Sous ce nom on trouve des Solanacées et des Cucurbitacées. Les Éthiopiens distinguent: le grand, *gäbär embway*, à feuilles épineuses (BAETEMAN) *Solanum marginatum* L., à fleurs blanches, *Solanum campylacanthum* Hochst., à fleurs violettes, *Solanum indicum* L., *Solanum unguiculatum* Rich.

    — le petit, *zärtch embway*, *Solanum adoense* Hochst.

    — le moyen, *yä meder embway*, *Cucumis ficifolius* pour MASINO; *Cucumis prophetarum* L. pour MOONEY auxquels CUFODONTIS ajoute *Cucumis postulatus* Hook f., *Cucumis laevigatus* Chiov. *Citrullus colocynthis* porte aussi ce nom.

        Que penser d'un même vocable, pour des plantes d'apparences si différentes? Il est normal que les différents *Solanum* puissent être confondus entre eux. Ce genre comprend plusieurs centaines d'espèces très voisines avec un type de fleur remarquablement constant. Par ailleurs, les différents *Cucumis* se ressemblent beaucoup. Mais un *Cucumis* ne peut être pris pour un *Solanum* ni par son appareil végétatif, ni par sa fleur. Seul le fruit semble être le point commun. Dans les deux familles il s'agit d'une baie dont le péricarpe est très souvent marbré de jaune et de vert avant maturité. Et c'est finalement l'élément le plus facile à remarquer qui a retenu l'attention populaire.

        On peut rattacher au groupe des confusions entre espèces de familles différentes, certains termes généraux.

aräg   Désigne les lianes en général, les "creepers" des Anglo-Saxons, mais peut aussi désigner plus particulièrement *Clematis simensis* Fres. Renonculacées, *Glycine micrantha* Hochst., Papilionacées, *Jasminum abyssinicum* Hochst., Jasminacées.

tequr aräg   Liane noire, est *Periploca linaerifolia* Dill. et Rich., Asclépiadacées.

aräg resa (amharique) = *haffafalu* (tigrigna) = *sabyeq* (guèze)

        Peut être *Melothria tomentosa* L. d'après GRIAULE, *Zehneria scrobiculata* Hochst, et *Z. velutina* Endl. pour SCHWEINFURTH. Victime de l'homogénéité de la famille des Cucurbitacées, MERAB en avait fait par erreur *Bryonia dioîca* L., absente d'Afrique.

dändärro   Premier sens: ronce, épine.

        C'est un terme générique du type "chardon" en français qui regroupe des plantes épineuses de familles botaniques différentes, Composées, Ombellifères, Dipsacacées, y compris *Argemone mexicana*, le pavot épineux, papavéracée d'origine américaine introduite.

koshäshella   A lui aussi un sens général de chardon pour les espèces de taille moyenne. A ce titre on le trouve appliqué à des Acanthacées: *Acanthus arboreus* Forsk., *A.*

pubescens Engl., *A. eminens* C. B. Clarke, *A. polystachyus* Del., *A. sennii* Chiov., Acanthacées.

Diverses Composées du genre *Echinops* portent aussi ce nom: *E. boranensis* Lanza, *E. giganteus* A. Rich., *E. ellenbeckii* O. Hoffm. d'après CUFODONTIS et CHIOVENDA et même *Rubus petitianus* A. Rich., Rosacées. Les *Echinops* se rangent aussi sous le nom de *qäbäretcho*.

USAGES COMMUNS

L'usage d'une plante fait intervenir la notion de drogue. Le mot drogue est pris ici à son sens premier, c'est-à-dire la partie employée de la plante échantillons de référence prennent place dans un *droguier* et qu'on trouve dans le commerce sous la mention *droguerie*. Le mot a pris pas la suite une connotation péjorative avec le sens de stupéfiant.

L'utilisation d'une drogue réduit le champ de la morphologie à une partie de la plante seulement. L'usage à des fins identiques — condiment — ténifuge — de drogues d'aspect similaire augmente les chances d'appellation commune.

a. — Les Ombellifères (Apiacées)

Sont une des plus spectaculaires illustrations de la confusion provenant d'une morphologie voisine et d'un usage commun.

C'est le fruit qui permet souvent la détermination d'une espèce. Incontestablement pourtant les fruits de beaucoup d'espèces de cette famille se ressemblent énormément, au premier coup d'oeil tout au moins.

Caractéristiques de la famille, ils sont bâtis sur un même type et seuls des points de détail souvent inapparents d'emblée du fait de leur petite taille, viennent les distinguer (côtes, vallécules, poils, aile, forme).

Quoi de plus naturel qu'on les retrouve souvent sous le même nom quand on sait par ailleurs le rôle de condiment de beaucoup d'entre eux?

A propos de ces fruits d'Ombellifères on trouve en amharigna les mêmes problèmes d'identification qu'en français ou dans d'autres langues.

L'enquêteur est victime soit de l'ignorance de l'interlocuteur, soit du langage vulgaire qui fait usage d'un terme plus ou moins générique.

azmud   *Ammi copticum* L.
       Daucus coptica Lam.
       Ptychotis ajowan D. C.
       Carum copticum Benth. et Hook.

tequr azmud, l'*azmud* noir ou *abäsuda* est la nigelle, *Nigella sativa* L., Renonculacées, condiment et abortif depuis l'Antiquité. *Abäsuda* vient de l'arabe *habba sawda*, "grain noir" et est encore appelé *tequr mätäfät*. On le trouve chez BAETEMAN pour menthe poivrée, cumin, anis, fenouil, toutes plantes aromatiques. C'est assez dire l'usage condimentaire qui en est fait.

dembelal   La Coriandre, *Coriandrum sativum* L., a un fruit sphérique qui devrait être celui qui
       prête le moins à confusion. Or BAETEMAN qui donne *dämbelal*(888) en fait le gingembre par erreur mais le sens général d'épice est transparent.

Par contre, il donne *dembelal* (946) pour coriandre!!!

Et pourtant chez MOONEY on trouve le fenouil sous ce nom, *Foeniculum vulgare* L.

enselal   Désigne le fenouil.
       Foeniculum vulgare D. C.
       F. capillaceum Gilg.

Mais il est donné aussi pour l'Aneth, *Anethum graveolens* L., dont le nom amharique est en réalité *shelan*.

Quant à BAETEMAN il nous fournit carrément: *shelan = enselal = anis*

kämun   Le cumin, *Cuminum cyminum* L., mérite une attention particulière.

Il est originaire du Moyen-Orient, de Perse et d'Egypte d'où il s'est répandu en Afrique.

Une espèce européenne voisine, le Carvi, *Carum carvi* L., utilisée aussi comme condiment mais de saveur et d'odeur différentes, porte en français le nom de cumin des prés et sert à fabriquer une liqueur alcoolique portant en Europe Centrale le nom de "Kümmel" ce qui concourt à la confusion.

ROVESTI avait indiqué la confusion en Éthiopie avec *azmud, Carum opticum* Benth. et Hook.

Kamun est le nom arabe qui par le commerce s'est répandu dans les langues européennes et en Éthiopie. Ce terme est devenu catégoriel pour des plantes aromatiques ombellifères ou non.

COURBON en avait fait une sorte de basilic, condiment qui est une Labiée mais plus vraisemblablement parce qu'une variété commerciale de Cumin (*kamun*), provenant de Kirman, considérée comme la meilleure, était appelée *bāsilikūn*, c'est-à-dire royale, par les droguistes.

Nous avons mentionné précédemment les effets dangereux des appellations commerciales.

Le cumin nous en donne un nouvel exemple pour l'Éthiopie, puisqu'on connaît dans le commerce le *kororima* sous le nom de Cumin d'Éthiopie.

Or c'est une Zingibéracée, *Aframomun Kororima* Pers. dont on utilise les graines comme condiment bien sûr; cet emploi, la taille, la forme, et peut-être aussi la couleur de ces graines leur ont valu cette appellation commerciale combien pernicieuse.

shelan   Désigne l'aneth, *Anethum graveolens* L. Nous avons vu précédemment la confusion avec le fenouil, *enselal*. Notons l'existence du même type de confusion en français puisque l'aneth porte aussi le nom vulgaire de "fenouil bâtard".

b. – Besanna et Musséna

Un bel exemple de confusion historique due à un usage identique et de la difficulté d'identification nous est donné par *besanna* et *musséna.*

Les deux plantes fournissent leur écorce comme drogue ténicide.

bessana   est le *Croton macrostachys* Hochst., Euphorbiacées.
musséna   est *Albizzia anthelminthica* R. Br., Mimosacées.

En l'absence de matériel végétal complet, RICHARD avait d'ailleurs initialement créé le genre *Bessena* pour cette dernière espèce dont il faisait bien une légumineuse.

En 1841, le docteur AUBERT, dans un mémoire à l'Académie Royale de Médecine sur les anthelminthiques d'Éthiopie fait curieusement du *bissena* une espèce de cèdre qui ressemble à celui de Virginie; il est du même genre (*Juniperus*)". Voilà une information surprenante mais comme par ailleurs dans le même article, l'auteur parle d'une gousse comme fruit du *kosso*, dont il fait pourtant bien une rosacée, elle a au moins le mérite d'inciter à la plus grande prudence quant à la foi à accorder au reste du texte.

Le rapport de DUMERIL et MERAT sur ce mémoire assimile le *bissena* du docteur AUBERT au *mussena* adressé à M. de BLAINVILLE par d'ABBADIE.

En 1848, à propos d'une lettre de W. SCHIMPER, gouverneur à Adoua, à son cousin Ph. W. SCHIMPER, la *Gazette médicale* de Strasbourg écrit au sujet du *mussenna*: "On le trouve dans les provinces méridionales et occidentales de l'Abyssinie. On n'a pas encore déterminé botaniquement cette espèce. M. SCHIMPER n'a pu en obtenir qu'une branche fleurie qu'il a envoyée à la Société botanique d'Esslingen. Il s'agit d'un arbre de la famille des Légumineuses".

En 1851, dans la *Gazette médicale* de Paris, le docteur PRUNER-BEY parle du *mussena* comme remède populaire dans l'Abyssinie contre le ténia" et en fait une Légumineuse, ce qui est exact.

En 1855, dans une lettre du docteur PERRON à M. JOMARD, nous retrouvons la confusion entre *moussena* et *bessena*.

"Le *moucennah* (*sic*) est l'écorce d'une légumineuse . . . c'est le *Besennah anthelminthica* d'Achille RICHARD." Nous avons vu que RICHARD avait créé ce genre nouveau pour une drogue qu'il reconnaissait bien pour une légumineuse mais dont il avait eu qu'un échantillon insuffisant.

PERRON ajoutait: "Le nom de *besennah* est fautif, on a voulu dire et il faut dire *moucennah*".

Mais plus loin nous trouvons qu'il s'agit d'un arbre à ". . . écorce très grasse qui, lorsqu'on la coupe, laisse couler un liquide abondant". Manifestement il s'agit bien là du *Croton macrostachys* et de son latex d'euphorbiacée (*bessena*). L'identité d'emploi et le voisinage des noms sont les deux facteurs de confusion. Cette même lettre nous fournit d'autres exemples de l'incertitude régnant sur la nature des espèces végétales en cause et des suppositions trop hâtives. Il y est, entre autre, question d'une écorce amère nommée Quinquina de Faz Oglou, rapprochée de Quinquina jaune (*Cinchona calisaya* Wed) sans doute pour son amertume. Or, le genre Cinchona est un genre américain. Quant à l'apparence, il est évident que rien n'est plus difficile à distinguer macroscopiquement que les écorces entre elles. Ici, nous avons vraisemblablement affaire à l'écorce de *Brucea antidysenterica* D. C., Simarubacées, dont le nom amharique est *woginos*. Et pourtant PERRON avait été professeur à l'École de Médecine du Caire avant d'en être le directeur. Voilà qui conduit à ne pas se laisser influencer, en présence d'un texte, par le nom ou les titres de son auteur, et qui permet une plus grande indulgence pour les erreurs de bien d'autres.

En 1860, A. BRONGNIART commente dans le *Bulletin de la Société botanique de France* les résultats du voyage de COURBON. Il dit notamment que le *mussena* doit entrer dans le genre *Albizzia* où il constituera une espèce distincte sous le nom d'*Albizzia anthelminthica*, et précise que *mussena* est le nom amharique et *bessena* le nom donné au Tigré. La distinction qui s'amorce est un point positif. Mais l'écorce décrite est bien celle du *mussena*.

M. MOQUIN-TANDON présente alors les observations suivantes: "Connue grâce à G. SCHIMPER (G. pour Guillaume équivalent français de Wilhelm), cette plante a été importée en Europe par d'ABBADIE et PRUNER. Un botaniste éminent (dont MOQUIN-TANDON tait prudemment le nom) en avait fait *Brucea antidysenterica* Mill., Simarubacées, qui est en fait, nous l'avons dit, le *waginos*.

A la séance suivante de la Société (25.1.1861), il présente l'écorce de l'*Albizzia* mais la confusion de nom *mussena-bessena* persiste. Elle aura la vie dure puisque BETIS, en 1894, déclare encore dans sa thèse: "Le *moussena*, généralement appelé *mussena* est nommé par A. RICHARD *bisenna*, mais son nom véritable est *mecanna* (*sic*!) en amhara et *besanna* en tigré".

COURBON, dans sa thèse faisant suite à son voyage en mer Rouge, écrit: "Le *mesenna* est bien une légumineuse; il appartient à la tribu des Mimosées et se range par tous ses caractères auprès de l'acacia de la haute Egypte, *Acacia lebbek* Del. Nous l'appelons par conséquent, pour conserver, autant que possible, la dénomination d'Ach. RICHARD, *Albizzia anthelminthica*.

Après toutes ces péripéties, on sait maintenant enfin à quoi s'en tenir. Le *mussena* est bien l'*Albizzia anthelminthica* dont l'écorce contient un saponoside, la moussenine, actif contre le ver solitaire. Le *bessena*, lui, *Croton macrostachys* Hochst., est une euphorbiacée active par son latex.

Un autre exemple d'espèces ténifuges se rencontre chez les Myrsinacées avec les fruits de:

enqoqqo *Myrsine africana* L.
     Maesa lanceolata Forsk. = *M. picta* Hochst.
     Embelia schimperi Hochst.

Pour les plantes utilisées pour leurs propriétés colorantes nous avons un exemple classique avec *ensosella* et *gershet*.

ensosélla à edj aqalla   "Qui fait le main rouge" est *Impatiens tinctoria* Rich., Balsaminacées,
              utilisée pour la teinture rouge qu'elle fournit et que les femmes passent

sur leurs mains et leurs pieds. Morphologie florale en accord avec la définition de BAETEMAN: plante qui rappelle la gueule de lion (de loup).

gershet ou *gurshet* ou *gushert* est *Conyza abyssinica* C. H. Schultz, Composées, plante ressemblant à la carotte d'après BAETEMAN, ce qui s'explique par la feuille dé-
coupée et la racine tubérisée. Le colorant qu'elle fournit est employé aux mêmes fins que celui
de l'*ensosélla*.

hulgäb = elgäb   Nous avons déjà mentionné l'intervention de l'odeur à propos de *tcheqquñ*
(*Artemisia* diverses).

On retrouve ce critère à propos de *hulgäb*, plante ressemblant à la menthe pour BAETE-
MAN ce qui est vrai puisqu'il s'agit de *Salvia nilotica* Vatke (Labiées). Mais une Astéracée aro-
matique servant de condiment porte aussi ce nom d'après RICHARD, *Dicrocephala latifolia* D.
C.

Chez les plantes alimentaires, on trouve:

adängware   Terme tendant à désigner toute plante ressemblant par sa graine au haricot et de
même usage alimentaire: *Vigna catiang* A. Rich., *Canavalia sativa* L. et *Phaseolus
vulgaris* L. Ce dernier est quelquefois plus précisément désigné par *yä baher adängware* qui indique bien qu'il n'est pas indigène.

dennetch   Divers tubercules alimentaires sont rangés sous ce nom: Des lamiacées africaines du
genre *Coleus, C. tuberosus* Rich., *C. latifolius* Hochst., *C. rotundifolius* A. Chev., *C.
edulis* Vatke, *C. spicatus* Benth.; mais aussi la pomme de terre, *Solanum tuberosum* L., Solan-
acées, on le sait, d'origine américaine.

sekwar dennetch est *Ipomoea batatas* Poir., Convolvulacées.

On précise souvent *galla dennetch* pour les *Coleus* et *arab dennetch* pour la pomme de
terre.

godär = godäré = godorré   Autre tubercule alimentaire amylacé.
Colocasia antiquorum Schott., Aracées.
MASSA donne aussi *Dioscorea bulbifera* L., Dioscoréacées.

suf   Deux plantes à graine fournissant une huile alimentaire sont réunies sous ce nom.
Il s'agit du carthame, *Carthamus tinctorius* L., Composées et du tournesol, *Helianthus
annuus* L. Ce dernier est introduit ce que souligne l'appellation *yä baher suf* quelquefois
employée.

Nous terminerons par une illustration de l'interpénétration de différents facteurs inter-
venant dans la dénomination de végétaux utilisés avec la trilogie: même famille, familles voisines, utilisation.

Chez les Verbénacées un problème courant est celui de la distinction entre les espèces des
genres *Lantana* et *Lippia**. Les fruits — quand il y en a! — donnent la réponse.

C'est un fruit charnu (drupe) à un noyau à deux loges ou deux noyaux à une loge pour
Lantana; c'est un fruit sec à deux noyaux, inclus dans le calice pour *Lippia*.

Rappelons que le fruit typique des Verbénacées est un tétrakène comme chez les Labiées.
Les deux familles sont si voisines que certains auteurs font des Verbénacées une simple tribu des
Labiées.

---

* Pour les botanistes, la difficulté s'accroît de l'existence chez les Composées d'un genre *Lan-
tanopsis* dont le nom dit assez la rassemblance avec *Lantana*, mais heureusement absent
d'Éthiopie.

Cette ressemblance nous amène tout naturellement en transition aux confusions entre familles différentes par des détails mineurs. En effet, elle explique le rapprochement établi à propos de *dämakäse* et *bäsobela*.

bäsobela = *mä̱tafä̱t* = *zäqa qebé* COURBON, sous le dernier terme, désignait une espèce de thym. CUFODONTIS indique plusieurs espèces d'*Ocimum*, *O. graveolens* A. Braun, *O. urticifolium* Roth (= *O. gratissimum* L.), *O. basilicum* L. CHIOVENDA nous donne *O. suave* Willd. et on trouve *Lippia javanica* Spr. Verbénacées chez STRELCYN.

Le *bäsobela* est souvent confondu avec la plante suivante:

dämakäsé à käsé Plante odoriférante ressemblant à la menthe pour BAETEMAN, au thym pour GRIAULE. RICHARD en avait pourtant bien fait *Ocimum menthae-folium* Hochst. (Labiées) presqu'un siècle auparavant. Ce même genre est retenu par PIOVANO qui donne *O. lamiifolium* Hochst. et CUFODONTIS, *O. urticifolium* Roth (= *O. gratissimum* L.), mais ce même auteur mentionne aussi *Lippia abyssinica* Cuf. et *L. javanica* Spr., Verbénacées, *Lantana kisi* Rich et *L. viburnoïdes* Forsk. de la même famille. On trouve une autre espèce du même genre chez KLOOS, *Lantana trifolia* L. CHIOVENDA donne *Lippia asperifolia* Rich. et AVETTA, *Lippia adoensis* Hochst.

CONCLUSION

Nous avons pris ces quelques exemples, non pour établir une anthologie des erreurs, mais pour souligner les difficultés d'identification des plantes à partir des textes et pour dégager quelques règles destinées à la faciliter en expliquant les raisons.

Les erreurs provenant de la reconduction sans contrôle d'une information trompeuse perpétuée dans la littérature ne valent, bien entendu, que d'être signalées et non commentées.

A propos de ces exemples de noms de plantes en amharigna, il n'est pas sans intérêt de remarquer qu'on peut dégager trois conclusions d'ordre général:

* Certain vocables désignent une espèce végétale bien précise, puis ils peuvent s'appliquer de façon erronée à d'autres espèces du fait des ressemblances morphologiques.
  Mais tout naturellement ils prennent un sens général, catégoriel.

* Les drogues, parties employées, sont par excellence le lieu de recouvrement des caractères organoleptiques et de l'identité d'emploi.
  Ces conditions favorisent au maximum l'utilisation d'un terme commun à plusieurs d'entre elles.

* Il était bon de rappeler que les exemples donnés à propos de l'amharigna sont significatifs d'un processus mental d'assimilation très général.

Nous voudrions en profiter pour rappeler que l'ethnobotanique est pluridisciplinaire. Plus qu'une vague teinture des disciplines qui la constituent est nécessaire pour gagner du temps dans les investigations et surtout éviter les écueils de conclusions hasardeuses ou intempestives. L'ethnobotanique n'est ni une botanique vaguement ethnologique, ni une ethnologie plus ou moins végétale.

Nous ne pouvons mieux faire que citer STRELCYN qui disait à ce propos: " L'aide des botanistes — et nous ajouterons des pharmacognostes — pour débrouiller le problème de la polyvalence de certains noms vernaculaires est indispensable car c'est seulement une analyse simultanée des plantes du point de vue botanique et ethnographique (ressemblance de deux plantes ou de leurs parties — surtout la partie employée, dirons-nous — similitude des effets médicinaux, même emploi technique, etc.) qui peut nous donner la solution".

C'est justement ce que nous avons voulu illustrer dans cet exposé. Relever des noms de plantes est bien. Savoir les identifier est mieux et nécessite des notions plus qu'élémentaires de botanique. Noter leur emploi est précieux. Etre à même de prévoir si cet emploi est justifié par la composition chimique connue ou supposée est du domaine de la pharmacognosie.

BIBLIOGRAPHIE

ABBADIE A. (d')   "Note sur un nouveau remède pour le ténia ou ver solitaire", *C. R. Séances Acad. Sc.*, 1852, t.XXXIV, pp.167-168.

AUBERT-ROCHE L.   "Mémoire sur les substances anthelminthiques usitées en Abyssinie", *Mém. Acad. Roy. Méd.*, 1841, t.IX, pp.689-701.

AVETTA C.   "Contribuzioni alla flora dello Scioa", *Bull. della Soc. bot. ital.*, 1889, vol. XXI, pp.303-311, 332-339, 344-351; 1890, vol.XXII, pp.234-239, 242-247.

BAETEMAN J.   *Dictionnaire Amarigna-Français*, Dire-Dawa, 1921. Imprimerie St. Lazare des R. R. P. P. Capucins.

BETIS L.   *Sur quelques ténifuges nouveaux ou peu connus*, Thèse Pharm., Montpelier, 1894.

BRONGNIART A.   "Notice sur les résultats relatifs à la botanique obtenus par Monsieur le Docteur Alfred COURBON pendant le cours d'une exploration de la Mer Rouge exécutée en 1859-60", *Bull. Soc. bot. France*, 1860, t.7, pp.898-904.

CHIOVENDA E.   "Osservazioni botaniche, agrarie ed industriali", *Rapporti coloniali*, Roma 1912.

COURBON A.   *Observations topographiques et médicales recueillies dans un voyage à l'isthme de Suez, sur le littoral de la Mer Rouge et en Abyssinie"*, Thèse Médecine, Paris, 1861.

CUFODONTIS G.   *Enumeratio plantarum aethiopiae Spermatophyta*, 2 vol., Meise, Jardin botanique national de Belgique, 1953-1972.

DUMERIL et MERAT   "Rapport sur le mémoire de M. le Docteur AUBERT", *Bull. Acad. Roy. Méd.*, 1840, t.VI, pp.492-500.

GUIDI I.   *Vocabolario Amarico-italiano*, Roma, 1935, Istituto per l'Oriente, Supplemento 1940 (avec GALLINA F. et CERULLI E.).

GRIAULE M.   "Mythes, croyances et coutumes du Begamder", *Journal asiatique*, 1928, CCXII, 65, pp.19-123.

―――――――――   "Le livre de recettes d'un dabtara abyssin", *Travaux et Mémoires de l'Institut d'Ethnologie*, t.XII, Paris, 1930.

―――――――――   *Jeux et divertissements abyssins*, Paris, 1935, Ernest Leroux.

LEMORDANT D.   "Les plantes éthiopiennes", Addis-Abeba, 1960. Central Printing Press. Supplément *Ann. Inst. Pasteur d'Éthiopie*, 1962, no.2, pp.52-60.

LEMORDANT D.   "Contribution à l'ethnobotanique éthiopienne", *J. A. T. B. A.*, 1971, XVIII, no.1-2-3, pp. 1-35; no.4-5-6, pp.142-179.

MASINO C.   "Sulle piante medicinali dell'Africa orientale italiana", *Il Farmacista italiano*, 1937, fasc. 9, Mai.

MASSA L.   "Piante alimentari speciali coltivate nel Gimma", *L'Agric. col.*, 1938, XXXII, p.114.

MERAB Dr.   *Médecine et médecins en Éthiopie*, Paris, 1912. Vigot frères.

MOONEY H.F.   *A glossary of Ethiopian Plants Names*, Dublin, 1963.

MOQUIN-TANDON   *Bull. Soc. bot. France*, 1861, t.VIII, pp.32-33.

PERRON   "Lettre à M. JOMARD", *Bull. Soc. Géog.*, 4e série, 1854, t.VIII, pp.408-410.

PRUNER-BEY Dr.   "De l'écorce de l'arbre Musenna", *Gaz. méd.*, Paris, 1851, t.XXI, pp.822-823.

RICHARD A.   *Tentamen florae Abyssinicae*, 2 vol.: tomes IV et V de Voyage en Abyssinie par LEFEBVRE T., PETIT A., QUARTIN-DILLON, Paris, Arthus Bertrand, 1845-1851.

SCHIMPER W.   "Des médicaments employés en Abyssinie contre le ver solitaire", *Gaz. méd.*, Strasbourg, 20 Avril 1848, pp.447-451.

STRELCYN S.   *Médecine et plantes d'Éthiopie. II. Enquête sur les noms et l'emploi des plantes en Éthiopie*, Istituto Universitario Orientale, Naples, 1973.

List of Contributions in This Volume by Author

Bibliography of Proceedings

International Conference of Ethiopian Studies, 1st: 1959: Rome

Atti del Convegno Internazionale di Studi Etiopici (Roma 2-4 aprile 1959). Roma: Accademia dei Lincei, 1960. 2 v. (Problemi attuali di scienza e di cultura no. 48)
v. 1 Atti del Convegno Internazionale di Studi Etiopici
v. 2 Indice dei nome.

International Conference of Ethiopian Studies, 2nd: 1963: Manchester

Ethiopian Studies. Papers read at the Second International Conference of Ethiopian Studies (Manchester University, [8-11] July, 1963) - edited by C.F. Beckingham and Edward Ullendorff. *Journal of Semitic Studies* 9:1 (Spring, 1964).

International Conference of Ethiopian Studies, 3rd: 1966: Addis Ababa

Proceedings of the Third International Conference of Ethiopian Studies, Addis Ababa (3-7 April) 1966. Addis Ababa: Institute of Ethiopian Studies, Haile Sellassie I University, (1969-1970)
v. 1: (mainly history)
v. 2: (mainly language, literature and the church)
v. 3: (mainly geography, sociology, anthropology and law).

International Conference of Ethiopian Studies, 4th: 1972: Rome

IV Congresso Internazionale di Studi Etiopici (Roma 10-15 aprile 1972) Roma: Accademia dei Lincei, 1974. 2 v. (Problemi attuali di scienza e di cultura no. 191)
v. 1: Sezione storica
v. 2: Sezione linguistica.

International Conference of Ethiopian Studies, 5th (A): 1977: Nice

Modern Ethiopia: from the accession of Menelik II to the present: proceedings of the Fifth International Conference of Ethiopian Studies, Nice, 19-22 December 1977 - edited by Joseph Tubiana. *L'Ethiopie moderne: de l'avènement de Ménélik II à nos jours: compte-rendus du cinquième Congrès International des Etudes Ethiopiennes, Nice: 19-22 decembre 1977* - publiès par Joseph Tubiana. Rotterdam: Balkema, 1980.

International Conference of Ethiopian Studies, 5th (B): 1978: Chicago

Proceedings of the Fifth International Conference of Ethiopian Studies, session B, April 13-16, 1978, Chicago, U.S.A. - edited by Robert L. Hess. Chicago: University of Illinois at Chicago Circle, 1979.

International Conference of Ethiopian Studies, 6th: 1980: Tel Aviv

Proceedings of the Sixth International Conference of Ethiopian Studies, Tel Aviv, 14-17 April 1980. Published by Balkema (Secretary of local committee: Baruch Podolsky, Faculty of Humanities, Tel Aviv University, Ramat Aviv, 69978 Tel Aviv, Israel).

International Conference of Ethiopian Studies, 7th: 1982: Lund

Proceedings of the Seventh International Conference of Ethiopian Studies, University of Lund, 26-29 April, 1982 - edited by Sven Rubenson. Scandinavian Institute of African Studies, Uppsala, 1984.